SIXTH EDITION

Writing and Reading Across the Curriculum

Laurence Behrens
University of California
Santa Barbara

Leonard J. Rosen
Harvard University

An imprint of Addison Wesley Longman, Inc.
New York • Reading, Massachusetts • Menlo Park, California • Harlow, England
Don Mills, Ontario • Sydney • Mexico City • Madrid • Amsterdam

Executive Editor: Anne Elizabeth Smith
Director of Development: Patricia Rossi
Developmental Editor: Randee Falk
Project Coordination and Text Design: Ruttle, Shaw & Wetherill, Inc.
Cover Design: Kay Petronio
Electronic Production Manager: Christine Pearson
Manufacturing Manager: Helene G. Landers
Electronic Page Makeup: Ruttle, Shaw & Wetherill, Inc.
Printer and Binder: R. R. Donnelley & Sons Company
Cover Printer: The Lehigh Press, Inc.

For permission to use copyrighted material, grateful acknowledgment is made to the copyright holders on pp. 844–850, which are hereby made part of this copyright page.

Library of Congress Cataloging-in-Publication Data
Behrens, Laurence.
Writing and reading across the curriculum/Laurence Behrens, Leonard J. Rosen.—6th ed.
p. cm.
Includes bibliographical references.
ISBN 0-673-52475-2
1. College readers. 2. Interdisciplinary approach in education. 3. English language—Rhetoric. 4. Academic writing. I. Rosen, Leonard J. II. Title
PE1417.B396 1996
808'.0427—dc20 95-50386
CIP

ISBN 0-673-52475-2

12345678910—DOC—99989796

To Bonnie and Michael—
and to L.C.R., Jonathan, and Matthew

Brief Contents

Detailed Contents

PART I
How to Write Summaries, Critiques, and Syntheses 1

1
SUMMARY AND PARAPHRASE 3

2
THESIS, QUOTATIONS, INTRODUCTIONS, AND CONCLUSIONS 32

▼

3
CRITICAL READING AND CRITIQUE 59

▼

5
RESEARCH 154

PART II

6

POLITICAL SCIENCE

7

LEFT, RIGHT, CENTER: THE AMERICAN POLITICAL SPECTRUM 242

FOLKLORE

10

FAIRY TALES: A CLOSER LOOK AT "CINDERELLA" 480

Fiction and film are very different art forms, but they share at least four essential attributes: theme, narrative, character, and point of view. In our introductory selection a film professor suggests questions about each of these attributes we can ask of a story or a film that get to the heart of its particular effect on us.

"Movies help get books out of college classrooms and into the streets where they can do some good," argues Charles Eidsvik. As for literature, it "gives filmmakers an inferiority complex."

To what extent is it possible to transpose fiction to film? A professor of film studies considers the complex problems involved in turning a verbal artifact into a visual one. How does a filmmaker handle first-person point of view? Let audiences know what a character is thinking? Summarize the character's past?—all with filmic finesse?

"The birds had been more restless than ever this fall of the year," observed farm worker Nat Hocken; and "there were many more than usual . . ." Daphine du Maurier's terrifying story of our feathered enemies, subsequently relocated from southern England to northern California, and made into a classic suspense film by Alfred Hitchcock.

Did Leonard Vole murder wealthy Emily French so that he could inherit her fortune? Vole's not worried: he has a witness for the defense who can provide him with an alibi. (Maybe.) Agatha Christie's fast-paced short story is transmitted first into a full-length play, then into a film directed by Billy Wilder.

BUSINESS

▼

A mining accident raises many of the difficult questions that give laypeople and philosophers alike reason to insist on ethical conduct in business.

A Note to the Instructor

Writing and Reading Across the Curriculum, Sixth Edition, is a combination rhetoric-reader designed to help bridge the gap between the writing course and courses in other disciplines. The rhetorical portion introduces key writing skills that will serve students well throughout their academic careers, whatever their majors, and in their professional lives beyond the academy. The readings are arranged in topical chapters focused on a variety of academic disciplines; individual selections represent the kinds of issues studied—and written about—in courses throughout the curriculum.

The close relationships among readings in a particular chapter allows students to view a given issue from a variety of perspectives. For instance, in Chapter 11, students will learn how a journalist, a novelist, a sociologist, a geneticist, a political scientist, a disability activitist, a physician, and an attorney present their particular assumptions and observations about the "Brave New World of Biotechnology." In every chapter of the reader, students can practice the essential college-level skills introduced in the rhetoric:

- students will read and summarize articles;
- students will read articles critically and write critiques of them, identifying and discussing the authors' (and their own) assumptions.
- students will read several articles on a particular topic and synthesize them in both explanatory and argumentative essays.

The Organization of This Book

Like its predecessors, the sixth edition of *Writing and Reading Across the Curriculum* is divided into two parts. The first part introduces the skills of summary, critique, and synthesis. Students move step by step through the process of writing papers based on source material. The text explains and demonstrates how summaries, critiques, and syntheses can be generated from the kinds of readings students will encounter later in the book—and throughout their college careers. The first part also offers a chapter on formulating thesis statements, quoting sources, and writing introductions and conclusions, as well as a chapter on research.

The second part of the text consists of eight chapters (leading off with a practice chapter on "The Wal-Mart Wars") on such topics as privacy and technology, business ethics, and the American political spectrum.

A Note on the Sixth Edition

In preparing the current edition, as in earlier editions, we have tried to retain the essential multidisciplinary character of the text while providing ample new material to keep the book fresh and timely. Both Part I and Part II have been extensively revised.

In Part I, substantial revisions have been made to Chapters 3 ("Critical Reading and Critique") and 4 ("Synthesis"). While readings on bilingual education remain in Chapter 1 on "Summary," new readings related to Chapter 9, "Privacy and Technology," appear in Chapter 3 to provide the basis for the student critique. In Chapter 4, readings on the welfare debate, related to Chapter 7, "Left, Right, Center: The American Political Spectrum," provide the basis for the student explanatory and argument syntheses; and readings on the purpose of government, by Bill Clinton and Newt Gingrich, provide the basis for the student comparison-and-contrast essays. In Chapter 5, "Research," we have provided expanded coverage of researching and documenting electronic sources.

Chapter 6, which leads off Part II, now includes a number of relatively brief selections on "The Wal-Mart Wars" that provide students opportunities to practice the summary, critique, and synthesis skills they have learned in Part I.

The rest of Part II includes three new chapters: Chapter 7, "Left, Right, Center: The American Political Spectrum"; Chapter 9, "Privacy and Technology"; and Chapter 12, "From Fiction to Film: Exploring the Film Adaptation." The remaining chapters have been revised to varying degrees. Both Chapter 11, "The Brave New World of Biotechnology," and Chapter 13, "Business Ethics," are almost entirely new, with only two or three selections in each chapter remaining from the fifth edition. In Chapter 8, "Obedience to Authority," an important new addition is Philip K. Zimbardo's account of his famous prison experiment conducted at Stanford University in the early 1970s. Two other selections in this chapter are new. In Chapter 10, "Fairy Tales: A Closer Look at Cinderella" (along with "Obedience to Authority," a fixture of *Writing and Reading Across the Curriculum* since the first edition), we have added an amusing new variant of the "Cinderella" story.

As in the fifth edition, most subject chapters include at least one work of imaginative literature; and we have increased the representation of women and minority writers.

While each chapter in Part II has been identified in the Contents by a specific academic discipline, readers should note that selections in each chapter are drawn from across the curriculum and are not meant to represent only the named discipline. In this way, each chapter gives students experience reading and interpreting topic-related literature.

We encourage all users—students and teachers—of *Writing and Reading Across the Curriculum* to continue to send to the publisher their suggestions for improving the book and their evaluations of its effectiveness. In particular, we invite teachers to submit copies of especially successful students essays based on material in this text for possible inclusion in the Instructor's Edition for the next edition.

Acknowledgments

We would like to thank the following reviewers for their help in preparation of the sixth edition of this text: Chris Anson, University of Minnesota; Anne Bailey, Southeastern Louisiana University; Joy Bashore, Central Virginia Community College; Nancy Blattner, Southeast Missouri State University; Mary Bly, University of California, Davis; Susan Callendar, Sinclair Community College; Jeff Carroll, University of Hawaii; Michael Colonnese, Methodist College; Cathy Dice, University of Memphis; Kathleen Dooley, Tidewater Community College; Judith Eastman, Orange Coast College; David Elias, Eastern Kentucky University; Deborah Gutschera, College of Du Page; Kip Harvigsen, Ricks College; Mark Jones, University of Florida; Jane Kaufman, University of Akron; Rodney Keller, Ricks College; Walt Klarner, Johnson County Community College; Dawn Leonard, Charleston Southern University; Krista May, Texas A&M; Stella Nesanovich, McNeese State University; Susie Paul, Auburn University at Montgomery; Nancy Redmond, Long Beach City College; Priscilla Riggle, Bowling Green State University; Joyce Smoot, Virginia Tech; Jackie Wheeler, Arizona State University; and Kristin Woolever, Northeastern University.

Thanks to the many students of our writing courses who field-tested much of the material here and let us know when we hadn't made things clear. Our special gratitude to Randee Falk, who solicited and painstakingly organized and analyzed reader response to the fifth edition and to the draft manuscript of this edition, and who provided us with enormously valuable guidance in the preparation of the final draft. Finally, our heartfelt thanks for the counsel of our steadfastly supportive and energetic Director of Development, Patricia Rossi.

Laurence Behrens
Leonard J. Rosen

A Note to the Student

Your psychology professor assigns you to write a critical report on a recently published book on human motivation. You are expected to consult additional sources, such as book reviews and related material on the subject.

Your professor is making a number of assumptions about your capabilities. Among them:

- that you can read and comprehend college-level material
- that you can synthesize separate pieces of related material
- that you can intelligently respond to such material.

In fact, these same assumptions underlie practically all college writing assignments. Your professors will expect you to demonstrate that you can read and understand not only textbooks but also critical articles and books, primary sources, and other material related to a subject of study. For instance: In researching a paper on the Great Depression, you might read the historical survey you find in your history text, a speech by President Franklin D. Roosevelt reprinted in the *New York Times,* and a firsthand account of the people's suffering by someone who toured the country during the 1930s and witnessed harrowing scenes of poverty and despair. In a political science paper, you might discuss the concept of "executive privilege" in light of James Madison's Federalistic Paper No. 51 on the proposed constitutional provision for division of powers among the three branches of government. In a sociology paper, you might undertake a critical analysis of your assigned text, which happens to be Marxist.

The subjects are different, of course, but the skills you need to work with them are the same. You must be able to read and comprehend. You must be able to perceive the relationships among several pieces of source material. And you must be able to apply your own critical judgments to these various materials.

Writing and Reading Across the Curriculum provides you with the opportunity to practice the three essential college-level skills we have just outlined and the forms of writing associated with them, namely:

- the *summary*
- the *critique*
- the *synthesis*

Each chapter of Part II of this text represents a subject from a particular area of the academic curriculum: psychology, political science, folklore, technology, film studies, biology, and business. These chapters, dealing with such topics as "Obedience to Authority," "Privacy and Technology," and "The American Political Spectrum," illustrate the types of material you will be asked to study in your other courses.

Various sets of questions following the readings will allow you to practice typical college writing assignments. Review Questions help you recall key points of content in factual essays. Discussion and Writing Suggestions ask you for personal, sometimes imaginative responses to the readings. Synthesis Activities at the end of each chapter allow you to practice assignments of the type that are covered in detail in the first four chapters of this book. For instance, you may be asked to *describe* the Milgram experiment, and the reactions to it, or to *compare* and *contrast* a controlled experiment to a real-life (or fictional) situation. Finally, Research Activities ask you to go beyond the readings in this text in order to conduct your own independent research on these subjects.

Our selection of passages includes articles written by economists, sociologists, psychologists, lawyers, folklorists, political scientists, journalists, and specialists from other fields. Our aim is that you become familiar with the various subjects and styles of academic writing and that you come to appreciate the interrelatedness of knowledge. Geneticists, sociologists, and novelists have different ways of contributing to our understanding of biotechnology. Fairy tales can be studied by literary critics, folklorists, psychologists, and feminists. Don't assume that the novel you read in your literature course has nothing to do with an assigned article from your economics course. Human activity and human behavior are classified into separate subjects only for convenience.

We hope, therefore, that your writing course will serve as a kind of bridge to your other courses, and that as a result of this work you can become more skillful at perceiving relationships among diverse topics. Because it involves such critical and widely applicable skills, your writing course may well turn out to be one of the most valuable—and one of the most interesting—of your academic career.

Laurence Behrens
Leonard J. Rosen

PART I

How to Write Summaries, Critiques, and Syntheses

1

Summary and Paraphrase

WHAT IS A SUMMARY?

The best way to demonstrate that you understand the information and the ideas in any piece of writing is to compose an accurate and clearly written summary of that piece. By a *summary* we mean *a brief restatement, in your own words, of the content of a passage* (a group of paragraphs, a chapter, an article, a book). This restatement should focus on the *central idea* of the passage. The briefest of all summaries (one or two sentences) will do no more than this. A longer, more complete summary will indicate, in condensed form, the main points in the passage that support or explain the central idea. It will reflect the order in which these points are presented and the emphasis given to them. It may even include some important examples from the passage. But it will not include minor details. It will not repeat points simply for the purpose of emphasis. And it will not contain any of your own opinions or conclusions. A good summary, therefore, has three central qualities: *brevity, completeness,* and *objectivity.*

CAN A SUMMARY BE OBJECTIVE?

Of course, this last quality of objectivity might be difficult to achieve in a summary. By definition, writing a summary requires you to select some aspects of the original and to leave out others. Since depending what to select and what to leave out calls for your own personal judgment, your summary is really a work of interpretation. And certainly your interpretation of a passage may differ from another person's. One factor affecting the nature and quality of your interpretation is your *prior knowledge* of the subject. If you're attempting to summarize an anthropological article, and you're a novice in the field, then your summary of the article might be quite different from that of your professor, who has spent twenty years studying this particular area and whose judgment about what is more significant and what is less significant is undoubtedly more reliable than your own. By the same token, your personal or professional *frame of reference* may also affect your interpretation. A union representative and a management representative attempting to summarize the latest management offer would probably come up with two very different accounts. Still, we believe that in most cases it's possible to produce a reasonably objective summary of a passage if you make a conscious, good-faith effort to be unbiased and not to allow your own feelings on the subject to distort your account of the text.

▼

USING THE SUMMARY

In some quarters, the summary has a bad reputation—and with reason. Summaries are often provided by writers as substitutes for analyses. As students, many of us have summarized books that we were supposed to *review* critically. All the same, the summary does have a place in respectable college work. First, writing a summary is an excellent way to understand what you read. This in itself is an important goal of academic study. If you don't understand your source material, chances are you won't be able to refer to it usefully in an essay or research paper. Summaries help you to understand what you read because they force you to put the text into your own words. Practice with writing summaries also develops your general writing habits, since a good summary, like any other piece of good writing, is clear, coherent, and accurate.

Second, summaries are useful to your readers. Let's say you're writing a paper about the McCarthy era in America, and in part of that paper you want to discuss Arthur Miller's *Crucible* as a dramatic treatment of the subject. A summary of the plot would be helpful to a reader who hasn't seen or read—or who doesn't remember—the play. (Of course, if the reader is your American literature professor, you can safely omit the plot summary.) Or perhaps you're writing a paper about nuclear arms control agreements. If your reader isn't familiar with the provisions of SALT I or SALT II, it would be a good idea to summarize these provisions at some early point in the paper. In many cases (a test, for instance), you can use a summary to demonstrate your knowledge of what your professor already knows; when writing a paper, you can use a summary to inform your professor about some relatively unfamiliar source.

Third, summaries are frequently required in college-level writing. For example, on a psychology midterm, you may be asked to explain Carl Jung's theory of the collective unconscious and to show how it differs from Freud's theory of the personal unconscious. The first part of this question requires you to *summarize* Jung's theory. You may have read about this theory in your textbook or in a supplementary article, or your instructor may have outlined it in his or her lecture. You can best demonstrate your understanding of Jung's theory by summarizing it. Then you'll proceed to contrast it with Freud's theory—which, of course, you must also summarize.

It may seem to you that being able to tell (or to retell) exactly what a passage says is a skill that ought to be taken for granted in anyone who can read at high school level. Unfortunately, this is not so: For all kinds of reasons, people don't always read carefully. In fact, it's probably safe to say that they usually don't. Either they read so inattentively that they skip over words, phrases, or even whole sentences or, if they do see the words in front of them, they see them without registering their significance.

When a reader fails to pick up the meaning and the implications of a sentence or two, there's usually no real harm done. (An exception: You could lose credit on an exam or paper because you failed to read or to realize the significance of a crucial direction by your instructor.) But over longer stretches—the paragraph, the section, the article, or the chapter—inattentive or haphazard reading creates problems, for you must try to perceive the shape of the argument, to grasp the central idea, to determine the main points that compose it, to relate the parts of the whole, and to note key examples. This kind of reading takes a lot more energy and determination than casual reading. But, in the long run, it's an energy-saving method because it enables you to retain the content of the material and to use that content as a basis for your own responses. In other words, it allows you to develop an accurate and coherent written discussion that goes beyond summary.

▼

HOW TO WRITE SUMMARIES

Every article you read will present a different challenge as you work to summarize it. As you'll discover, saying in a few words what has taken someone else a great many can be difficult. But like any other skill, the ability to summarize improves with practice. Here are a few pointers to get you started. They represent possible stages, or steps, in the process of writing a summary. These pointers are not meant to be ironclad rules; rather, they are designed to encourage habits of thinking that will allow you to vary your technique as the situation demands.

HOW TO WRITE SUMMARIES

- *Read* the passage carefully. Determine its structure. Identify the author's purpose in writing. (This will help you distinguish between more important and less important information.)
- *Reread.* This time divide the passage into sections or stages of thought. The author's use of paragraphing will often be a useful guide. *Label,* on the passage itself, each section or stage of thought. *Underline* key ideas and terms.
- *Write one-sentence summaries,* on a separate sheet of paper, of each stage of thought.
- *Write a thesis: a one- or two-sentence summary of the entire passage.* The thesis should express the central idea of the passage, as you have determined it from the preceding steps. You may find it useful to keep in mind the information contained in the lead sentence or paragraph of most newspaper stories—the *what, who, why, where, when,* and *how* of the matter. For persuasive passages, summarize in a sentence the author's conclusion. For descriptive passages, indicate the subject of the description and its key feature(s). *Note:* In some cases, *a suitable thesis may already be in the original passage.* If so, you may want to quote it directly in your summary.
- *Write the first draft of your summary* by (1) combining the thesis with your list of one-sentence summaries or (2) combining the thesis with one-sentence summaries *plus* significant details from the passage. In either case, eliminate repetition and less important information. Disregard minor details or generalize them (e.g., Reagan and Bush might be generalized as "recent presidents"). Use as few words as possible to convey the main ideas.
- *Check your summary against the original passage* and make whatever adjustments are necessary for accuracy and completeness.
- *Revise your summary,* inserting transitional words and phrases where necessary to ensure coherence. Check for style. *Avoid a series of short, choppy sentences.* Combine sentences for a smooth, logical flow of ideas. Check for grammatical correctness, punctuation, and spelling.

▼

DEMONSTRATION: SUMMARY

To demonstrate these points at work, let's go through the process of summarizing a passage of expository material. Read the following passage carefully Try to identify its parts (there are four) and to understand how these parts work together to create a single, compelling idea.

Bilingual Education: A War of Words

RICHARD BERNSTEIN

In a well-worn classroom at the San Fernando Elementary School, 30 miles north of Los Angeles, Aracelis Tester, a second-grade teacher, is reading "Cuidado, un Dinosaurio!"—"Watch Out, a Dinosaur!"—with her diminutive pupils. This could just as well be Mexico City or San Salvador, Grenada or Seville: a roomful of Hispanic children and a Hispanic teacher speaking Spanish. 1

In downtown Los Angeles, at a school called the Wilton Place Elementary, Chan Hee Hong, a first-grade teacher, is talking in Korean with the children of recent immigrants about the wonderful world of frogs. There are public schools in Oklahoma where Cherokee is the language of instruction. In Astoria, Queens, Greek is taught in Public School 122; Haitian Creole is a language of instruction in some 20 public schools in Brooklyn and Queens; New York, in addition, offers schooling in Chinese, Korean, French, Italian, Russian, Vietnamese and Khmer. 2

In the San Fernando Elementary School, the teaching of non-English-speaking children in their native language enjoys a virtually religious status: it is seen as a kind of panacea for the generally poor performance of Hispanic children in public schools. But at the Glenwood Elementary School in the San Fernando Valley, a neighborhood of neatly kept stucco homes festooned with bougainvillea, bilingual education is anathema. The Glenwood teachers often conduct classes in Spanish, since they are given no choice by the Los Angeles School District. The school, a political model for some, is notorious for others. Hispanic demonstrators shouting "racist" and carrying signs printed "KKK" have picketed outside the school, where teachers have been outspoken in their view that teaching children in Spanish is a fraud, a trick played by tendentious adult theoreticians on innocent children. They say that bilingual education is a failure, a tactic that in the end will harm the chances of generally poor, non-English-speaking children ever having an equal share in the promise of American life. 3

The San Fernando school and the Glenwood school represent the two poles of a debate, already 20 years old, that has lately become more acrimonious than ever. This is a nation that has successfully absorbed millions of immigrants without creating a huge bureaucracy or spending tens of millions of dollars to teach them in the languages of their ancestors. But in the last few years, teaching children "Watch Out, a Dinosaur!" in Spanish and talking to them about frogs in Korean has become a matter of deep importance to an ever-growing minority. 4

Part of the reason for this is that in America today more people speak foreign languages than ever before. Neighborhoods like those in the San Fernando Valley, whose residents were largely white and English-speaking 10 to 20 years ago, today have a Hispanic population of at least 90 percent. In Los Angeles, school-district officials say that there are, besides Spanish 5 and English, seven other major languages being spoken in their district—Korean, Cantonese, Armenian, Vietnamese, Filipino, Farsi and Cambodian.

Why aren't these students being taught only in the language of their newly adopted land? One reason is that organized minority groups are demanding they be educated in their native language, and they have won allies within the local education establishments of quite a few cities. For many of these minorities, the subject evokes deep emotions. Advocates of bilingual education believe that it represents the best chance for non-English-speaking children—who, not so coincidentally, often come from the lower-income groups—to enjoy the richness and opportunities of American life. "We have found a way to achieve educational parity and, by the way, to have people who are competent in two languages," said Raul Yzaguirre, the director of the National Council of La Raza in Washington, an umbrella group of several hundred Hispanic organizations. . . . 6

The forces in favor of bilingual education . . . gained an ally in the [Bush] White House,[1] [but] there are still plenty of people on the other side of the issue, people who are convinced that teaching children in their native languages is bad, both for them and the country. Bilingual education, they argue, is more likely to prepare minority children for careers in the local Taco Bell than for medical school or nuclear physics. "It doesn't work," said Sally Peterson, a teacher at the Glenwood School and the founder of Learning English Advocates Drive, or LEAD, a group of teachers and citizens that has quickly gathered adherents across the country. "It seemed to make a lot of sense and I bought it at the beginning, but after a year or so I saw that children were languishing in the program." 7

The other, more subterranean part of the argument is political. Ethnic pride is involved here on one side, a sense that what is sometimes called "white, Anglo" education is demeaning, psychologically harmful to minority groups. On the other side, there is a deep-seated worry that more is involved than an educational program to help minority students. The country is becoming far more ethnically diverse. Immigration is no longer the European affair it was during the first half of this century. Hundreds of thousands of people each year come from the Caribbean Islands, from the Middle East and from a dozen countries in Asia. In other words, just at a time when a more powerful glue is needed to hold the various parts of the society together, some critics see an ethnic and cultural assertiveness pushing it apart. 8

Bilingual education is only one element in this picture, its opponents believe, a reflection of intensifying demands within the schools for courses that represent the interests of particular ethnic constituencies. It's no longer 9

[1]The reference is to Rita Equivel, a proponent of bilingual education who headed federal programs in the Department of Education during the Bush administration.

enough for children to learn who George Washington was. They have to learn to feel good about their own heritage. The much-discussed "Curriculum of Inclusion," produced by a special minority task force in New York State last year, argued that "African-Americans, Asian-Americans, Puerto Ricans/Latinos and Native Americans have all been the victims of an intellectual and educational oppression that has characterized the culture and institutions of the United States and the European-American world for centuries."

The solution, the task force concluded, was a new curriculum that, by concentrating on contributions by members of minority groups to the culture, would insure that minority children "have higher self-esteem and self-respect, while children from European cultures will have a less arrogant perspective of being part of the group that has 'done it all.' " 10

What's at stake, then, is nothing less than the cultural identity of the country. Those who argue that bilingual education is a right make up a kind of informal coalition with those who are pressing for changes in the way the United States is perceived—no longer as a primarily European entity to which all others have to adapt, but as a diverse collection of ethnic groups, each of which deserves more or less equal status and respect. 11

"Rather than see the United States as a melting pot, we like to think of it as a salad bowl, with equal recognition of everyone, and I think bilingual education is part of that," said Suzanne Ramos, a lawyer for the Mexican-American Legal Defense and Educational Fund, a group that has sued local school boards to force them to adopt native-language instruction for Hispanic youngsters. The fund's goal, she said, is to have Spanish-language instruction in conjunction with the teaching of English for Hispanic students through the 12th grade—in the fund's view, the best means of insuring that Hispanic culture is nurtured as part of the basic public-school routine. 12

"The disagreement is whether a child has a right to have his native language developed—not just maintained but developed," said James J. Lyons, the executive director of the National Association for Bilingual Education, a professional organization that drafted much of the Federal legislation on bilingual programs. "There is a racist xenophobia about Spanish in particular." 13

Those on the other side insist that diversity is all well and good; but they argue that bilingual education could lead to an erosion of the national unity, a fragmentation of the nation into mutually hostile groups. Leading the fight is a group called U.S. English, whose major objectives are to promote opportunities for people to learn English and to get a constitutional amendment adopted that would make English the official language of Government. Founded by former Senator S. I. Hayakawa and including such eminent figures as Saul Bellow, Barry Goldwater and Eugene McCarthy on its board of advisers, U.S. English has seen its membership swell to 400,000 in just seven years of existence. "Language is so much a 14 part of our lives that it can be a great tool either for unity or disunity," said Kathryn S. Bricker, the group's former executive director. "And we are getting close to the point where we have a challenge to the common language that we share. Just look at what's going on in Miami, where a candidate to be school superintendent wanted everybody to have to learn Spanish.

"We are basically at a crossroads," she added. "We can reaffirm our 15
need for a common language or we can slowly go down the road of division along language lines." . . .

In his autobiography, "A Margin of Hope," the critic Irving Howe, 16
speaking about the "ethnic" generation of the 1920's and 1930's, recalls his hunger for school as a child of Jewish immigrants growing up in the Bronx; for Howe, mastering the English language was a badge of Americanness. "The educational institutions of the city were still under the sway of a unified culture, that dominant 'Americanism' which some ethnic subcultures may have challenged a little, but which prudence and ambition persuaded them to submit to," he writes.

The question now is: What is the "dominant Americanism"? Can there 17
even be such a thing in a country committed to a kind of ethnic self-realization that did not exist when Howe was growing up? The answers will be hammered out in the years ahead in classrooms like Aracelis Tester's and Sally Peterson's, and they have to do with more than pedagogical philosophy. In the end, the way language is taught in this country will reflect where the country is going, its very identity.

▲ ▲ ▲

Reread, Underline, Divide into Stages of Thought

Let's consider our recommended pointers for writing a summary.

As you reread the passage, consider its significance as a whole and its stages of thought. What does it say? How is it organized? How does each part of the passage fit into the whole?

Many of the selections you read for your courses will have their main sections identified for you by subheadings. When a passage has no subheadings, as is the case with "Bilingual Education: A War of Words," you must read carefully enough that you can identify the author's main stages of thought.

How do you determine where one stage of thought ends and the next one begins? Assuming that what you have read is coherent and unified, this should not be difficult. (When a selection is unified, all of its parts pertain to the main subject; when a selection is coherent, the parts follow one another in logical order.) Look, particularly, for transitional sentences at the beginning of paragraphs. Such sentences generally work in one or both of the following ways: (1) they summarize what has come before; (2) they set the stage for what is to follow.

For example, look at the sentence that opens paragraph 4: "The San Fernando school and the Glenwood school represent the two poles of a debate, already 20 years old, that has lately become more acrimonious than ever." Notice how the first part of this sentence asks the reader to recall information from the previous three paragraphs. Holding in mind the two opposing views just presented, the reader is then cast forward into the coming paragraph with its discussion about the national debate on bilingual education. For a different transition, see paragraph 6, which begins with a question: "Why aren't these students being taught only in the language of their newly adopted land?" This question first requires the reader to recall the previous paragraph. Then the question helps the reader to anticipate what will immediately follow: an accounting of why bilingual education has gained support around the country.

Each section of an article will take several paragraphs to develop. Usually between paragraphs, and almost certainly between sections of an article, you will find transitions to help you understand. For articles that have no subheadings, try writing your own section headings in the margins as you take notes. Then proceed with your summary.

The sections of Bernstein's article are as follows:

Section 1: Introduction—the national debate on how non-English-speaking students should be taught (paragraphs 1–5).
Section 2: Debate on the merits of bilingual education (paragraphs 6–7).
Section 3: Debate on the larger political and cultural issues related to bilingual education (paragraphs 8–10).
Section 4: Significance of the overall debate—key issue of how America will perceive itself (paragraphs 11–17).

Here is how the first of these sections might look after you had marked the main ideas, by underlining and by marginal notation:

Intro

Teachers teaching in native language

In a well-worn classroom at the San Fernando Elementary School, 30 miles north of Los Angeles, Aracelis Tester, a second-grade teacher, is reading "Cuidado, un Dinosaurio!"—"Watch Out, a Dinosaur!"—with her diminutive pupils. This could just as well be Mexico City or San Salvador, Grenada or Seville: a roomful of Hispanic children and a Hispanic teacher speaking Spanish. 1

In downtown Los Angeles, at a school called the Wilton Place Elementary, Chan Hee Hong, a first-grade teacher, is talking in Korean with the children of recent immigrants about the wonderful world of frogs. There are public schools in Oklahoma where Cherokee is the language of instruction. In Astoria, Queens, Greek is taught in Public School 122; Haitian Creole is a language of instruction in some 20 public schools in Brooklyn and Queens; New York, in addition, offers schooling in Chinese, Korean, French, Italian, Russian, Vietnamese and Khmer. 2

Key example of debate in S. California

In the San Fernando Elementary School, the teaching of non-English-speaking children in their native language enjoys a virtually religious status; it 3 is seen as a kind of panacea for the generally poor performance of Hispanic children in public schools. But at the Glenwood Elementary School in the San Fernando Valley, a neighborhood of neatly kept stucco homes festooned with bougainvillea, bilingual education is anathema. The Glenwood teachers often conduct classes in Spanish, since they are given no choice by the Los Angeles School District. The school, a political model for some, is notorious for others. Hispanic demonstrators shouting "racist" and carrying signs printed "KKK" have picketed outside the school, where teachers have been outspoken in their view that teaching children in Spanish is a fraud, a trick played by tendentious adult theoreticians on innocent children. They say that bilingual education is a failure, a tactic that in the end will harm the chances of generally poor, non-English-speaking children ever having an equal share in the promise of American life.

Key example of debate in S. California

Debate is 20 yrs. old & heated

The San Fernando school and the Glenwood school represent the two poles of a debate, already 20 years old, that has lately become more acrimonious than ever. This is a nation that has successfully absorbed millions of immigrants without creating a huge bureaucracy or spending tens of millions of dollars to teach them in the languages of their ancestors. But in the last few years, teaching children "Watch Out, a Dinosaur!" in Spanish and talking to them about frogs in Korean has become a matter of deep importance to an ever-growing minority. 4

Debate: important to growing minority

More than ever, America is multilingual

Part of the reason for this is that in America today more people speak foreign languages than ever before. Neighborhoods like those in the San Fernando Valley, whose residents were largely white and English-speaking 10 to 20 years ago, today have a Hispanic population of at least 90 percent. In Los Angeles, school-district officials say that there are, besides Spanish and English, seven other major languages being spoken in their district—Korean, Cantonese, Armenian, Vietnamese, Filipino, Farsi and Cambodian. 5

Write a One-Sentence Summary of Each Stage of Thought

The purpose of this step is to wean you from the language of the original passage, so that you are not tied to it when writing the summary. Student Brian Smith has written one-sentence summaries for each of these sections as follows:

Section 1: Introduction—the national debate on how non-English-speaking students should be taught.

Over the past twenty years, there has been a bitter debate over the merits of bilingual education.

Section 2: Debate on the merits of bilingual education.

Proponents and opponents of bilingual education strongly disagree over how much benefit students receive from such programs.

Section 3: Debate on the larger political and cultural issues related to bilingual education.

Underlying the educational arguments are powerful political arguments arising from the increasing diversity of America.

Section 4: Significance of the overall debate—key issue of how America will perceive itself.

The debate over bilingual education is a debate over the cultural identity of America.

Write a Thesis: A One- or Two-Sentence Summary of the Entire Passage

The thesis is the most general statement of a summary (or any other type of academic writing—see Chapter 2). It is the statement that announces the paper's subject and the claim that you or—in the case of a summary—another author will be making about that subject. Every paragraph of a paper illuminates the thesis by providing supporting detail or explanation. The relationship of these paragraphs to the thesis is analogous to the relationship of the sentences within a paragraph to the topic sentence. Both the thesis and the topic sentences are general statements (the thesis being the more general) that are followed by systematically arranged details.

To ensure clarity for the reader, *the first sentence of your summary should begin with the author's thesis, regardless of where it appears in the article itself.* Authors may locate their thesis at the beginning of their work, in which case the thesis operates as a general principle from which details of the presentation follow. This is called a *deductive* organization: thesis first, supporting details second. Alternately, authors may locate their thesis at the end of their work, in which case they begin with specific details and build toward a more general conclusion, or thesis. This is called an *inductive* organization, an example of which you see in "Bilingual Education: A War of

Words," where the thesis is stated last and is part of the conclusion. (By contrast, a conclusion in a deductively organized piece *re*states the thesis, which has already been presented at the beginning of the selection.)

A thesis consists of a subject and an assertion about that subject. How can we go about fashioning an adequate thesis for "Bilingual Education: A War of Words"? Probably no two proposed thesis statements for this article would be worded exactly the same. But it is fair to say that any reasonable thesis will indicate that the subject is the debate over bilingual education and that the author asserts that this debate has large political and cultural significance. What issues, specifically, does Bernstein believe are raised by bilingual education? For a clue, look to his final sentence (his conclusion *and* his thesis, since this is an inductively organized piece): "The way language is taught in this country will reflect where the country is going, its very identity." Bernstein sees bilingual education as part of a larger debate about the role minorities will play in America's future identity. Mindful of Bernstein's subject and the assertion that he makes about it, we can write a single statement *in our own words* and arrive at the following:

> The longstanding and increasingly bitter debate over bilingual education is part of a larger national debate over the role minorities will play in shaping America's identity.

To clarify for our reader the fact that this idea is Bernstein's, rather than ours, we'll qualify the thesis as follows:

> In "Bilingual Education: A War of Words," Richard Bernstein claims that the longstanding and increasingly bitter debate over bilingual education is part of a larger national debate over the role minorities will play in shaping America's identity.

The first sentence of a summary is crucially important, for it orients your readers by letting them know what to expect in the coming paragraph(s). The preceding example sentence provides the reader with both a citation and thesis for the passage. The author and title reference also could be indicated in the summary's title, in which case it could be dropped from the thesis. And realize, lest you become too quickly frustrated, that writing an acceptable thesis for a summary takes time—in this case three drafts, roughly seven minutes of effort spent on one sentence and another few minutes of fine-tuning after a draft of the entire summary was completed. The first draft of the thesis was too cumbersome; the second draft was too vague; and the third draft needed minor refinements.

Draft 1: The debate over bilingual education is part of a larger national debate ~~about the extent to which the identity of ethnic minorities will become a visible part of the larger American identity.~~

too long

Draft 2: The debate over bilingual education is part of a larger national debate ~~about the direction in which America's cultural identity will develop.~~

too vague

and increasingly bitter

Draft 3: The longstanding ^ debate over bilingual education is part of a larger national debate over the role minorities will play in shaping America's ~~future~~ identity.

Final: The longstanding and increasingly bitter debate over bilingual education is part of a larger national debate over the role minorities will play in shaping America's identity.

Write the First Draft of the Summary

Let's consider two possible summaries of the example passage: (1) a short summary, combining a thesis with one-sentence section summaries, and (2) a longer summary, combining thesis, one-sentence section summaries, and some carefully chosen details. Again, realize that you are reading final versions; each of the following summaries is the result of at least two full drafts.

Summary 1: Combine Thesis with One-Sentence Section Summaries

In "Bilingual Education: A War of Words," Richard Bernstein claims that the longstanding and increasingly bitter debate over bilingual education is part of a larger national debate over the role minorities will play in shaping America's identity. Proponents and opponents of bilingual education strongly disagree over how much benefit students receive from such programs. But underlying the educational arguments in the debate over bilingual education are powerful political arguments arising from the increasing diversity of America. For Bernstein, then, the bilingual education debate is a debate over the cultural identity of America.

Discussion

This passage consists essentially of Brian Smith's restatement of the author's thesis plus the four section summaries, altered or expanded a little for stylistic purposes. Notice that Brian has folded his summary of the article's first section into his thesis:

Summary of section 1:

Over the past twenty years, there has been an acrimonious debate over the merits of bilingual education.

Thesis:

```
In "Bilingual Education: A War of Words," Richard
Bernstein claims that the longstanding and increasingly
bitter debate over bilingual education is part of a
larger national debate over the role minorities will
play in shaping America's identity.
```

In contrast to the section 1 summary, the thesis includes Bernstein's interpretation of the debate's significance. The first sentence also includes the article's author and title, information to help orient the reader. And for reasons of both content and style, Brian has condensed the section summary's "over the past twenty years" to the one-word adjective "longstanding." His original "acrimonious," revised to read "increasingly bitter," similarly becomes an adjective modifying "debate" and shows that the character of the debate has been changing.

Brian spent most of his energy folding the first section summary into the thesis. This accomplished, he followed with the other section summaries and made minor stylistic adjustments.

Summary 2: Combine Thesis Sentence, Section Summaries, and Carefully Chosen Details

The thesis and the one-sentence section summaries also can be used as the outline for a more detailed summary. Most of the details in the passage, however, won't be necessary in a summary. It isn't necessary even in a longer summary of this passage to discuss *particular* classrooms—for example, classes in which students are reading about dinosaurs in Spanish or frogs in Korean (paragraphs 1–4); it's sufficient to note that in schools where bilingual education is practiced students are taught in their native language. Nor is it necessary to quote extensively the various proponents and opponents of bilingual education that Bernstein cites—perhaps one or two *brief* quotations would do for your summary. Concentrate on a few carefully selected details that might be desirable for clarity. For example, you could mention New York State's "Curriculum of Inclusion" and its underlying principles (paragraphs 9–10); and you could mention the group U.S. English (paragraph 14), whose very existence and distinguished membership suggests the depth of the opposition's commitment to retaining English as the national language.

How do you know which details may be safely ignored and which ones may be advisable to include? The answer is that you won't always know. Developing good judgment in comprehending and summarizing texts is largely a matter of reading skill and prior knowledge (see page 3). Consider the analogy of the seasoned mechanic who can pinpoint an engine problem by simply listening to a characteristic sound that to a less experienced person is just noise. Or consider the chess player who can plot three separate winning strategies from a board position that to a novice looks like a hopeless jumble. In the same way, the more practiced a reader you are, the more knowledgeable you become about the subject, the better able you will be to make critical distinctions between elements of greater and lesser importance. In the meantime, read as carefully as you can and use your own best judgment as to how to present your material.

Here's one version of a completed summary, with carefully chosen details. Transitional words and phrases are circled:

Thesis

Section 1

In "Bilingual Education: A War of Words," Richard Bernstein claims that the longstanding and increasingly bitter debate over bilingual education is part of a larger national debate over the role minorities will play in shaping America's identity.

Summary of ¶s 1–5

Bilingual education programs have flourished because of the increasingly diverse ethnic makeup of American schools. (But) bilingual education is intensely controversial. At one southern California high school, Hispanics picketed teachers who denounced bilingual education programs as "a fraud." (These teachers) had argued that such programs end up harming the very minority groups they are intended to help.

Section 2

Summary of ¶6

(Those favoring) bilingual education believe that teaching students in their native languages offers young people their best chance for success in American life.

Summary of ¶7

(Those opposed) insist that bilingual education fails to prepare students for today's competitive and advanced job markets.

Section 3

Transition & topic sentence

(But) underlying the educational arguments in the debate over bilingual education are powerful political arguments arising from the increasing diversity of America.

Summary of ¶8

Most immigrants to this country are no longer from Europe, but from the Caribbean, from the Middle East, and from Asia. (Opponents) of bilingual education argue that now, more than ever, America needs the common bond of language to hold its increasingly diverse population together. (But advocates) see bilingual education as a means of moving away from the kind of "white Anglo" education that has belittled the ethnic identities of nonwhite minorities.

Summary of ¶s 9–10

(Moreover,) advocates of ethnic identity want to go beyond bilingual education programs to

Section 4 Transition & summary of ¶11

courses for all children emphasizing the role of America's ethnic minorities. For example, New York's "Curriculum of Inclusion" is designed to stress minority involvement in important historical developments.

Summary of ¶s 12–13

Summary of ¶s 14–15

For Bernstein, then, the bilingual education debate is a debate over the cultural identity of America. Those in favor of bilingual education and ethnic identity see America as a "salad bowl," rather than a "melting pot." They want each ethnic group to retain its own distinctive qualities. In contrast, opponents of bilingual education believe that while diversity is valuable, an overemphasis on ethnic identity could lead to hostility between ethnic groups and a breakdown of national unity. Indeed, one group, U.S. English, is lobbying for a constitutional amendment "that would make English the official language of Government."

Summary of ¶s 16–17

In the end, Bernstein believes, schools will encourage their students either to develop their "ethnic self-realization" or to be part of a "unified culture." These very different choices will determine America's future identity.

Discussion

The final two of our suggested steps for writing summaries are (1) to check your summary against the original passage, making sure that you have included all the important ideas, and (2) to revise so that the summary reads smoothly and coherently.

The structure of Brian Smith's summary reflects what he understood was the four-part structure of the original passage. He devoted one paragraph of summary to each of Bernstein's four sections:

1. Paragraphs 1–5, the introduction
2. Paragraphs 6–7, the debate on the merits of bilingual education
3. Paragraphs 8–10, the political underpinnings of that debate
4. Paragraphs 11–17, the relationship between the debate and America's cultural identity

Within individual paragraphs of the summary, the structure generally reflects the sequence of ideas in the original. For example, paragraph 2 of the summary is two sentences; section two of Bernstein's article is two paragraphs. Brian wrote one sentence of summary for each paragraph.

The expanded summary communicates many more details than does the first summary. The two summaries begin with the same thesis. In the expanded summary, Brian Smith adds four sentences (in paragraph 1) to provide more background information on the bilingual debate. Recall that in the brief summary he collapsed that same background into a single sentence—the thesis. The first summary reduces the debate over bilingual education—paragraphs 6 and 7 of the article—to a single sentence ("Proponents and opponents of bilingual education strongly disagree over how much benefit students receive from such programs"). The expanded summary, however, offers two detailed sentences (paragraph 2), one devoted to the proponents in the debate and another to the opponents. In the expanded summary, Brian devotes a full paragraph (paragraph 3), not a single sentence, to the political underpinnings of the argument over bilingual education. In this instance, Brian retains the sentence from his original summary and adds details on the origin of America's recent immigrants, on U.S. English, and on New York's "Curriculum of Inclusion." He similarly devotes a whole paragraph (paragraph 4), as opposed to a single sentence, to Bernstein's final point about the relation between the bilingual debate and America's identity. Once again, Brian begins with a sentence from his original summary and then adds details.

How long should a summary be? This depends on the length of the original passage. A good rule of thumb is that a summary should be no longer than one-fourth of the original passage. Of course, if you were summarizing an entire chapter or even an entire book, it would have to be much shorter than that. The summary above is about one-fifth the length of the original passage. Although it shouldn't be very much longer, you have seen (page 15) that it could be quite a bit shorter.

The length of a summary, as well as the content of the summary, also depends on its *purpose.* Let's suppose that you decided to use Bernstein's piece in a paper that dealt, primarily, with the evolution of America's cultural identity. You would likely be interested in summarizing the final section of the article, in which Bernstein introduces the "melting pot" and "salad bowl" as metaphors that can explain contrasting views of that identity. If, instead, you were writing a paper focused on the bilingual debate itself, you would likely be interested in summarizing the first three sections of Bernstein's article, which focus on the debate and its political underpinnings. Thus, depending on your purpose, you will summarize either *selected* portions of a source or an entire source, as we will see more fully in the chapter on synthesis.

▼

SUMMARIZING A NARRATIVE

A narrative is a story, a retelling of a person's experiences. That person and those experiences may be imaginary, as is the case with fiction, or they may be real, as in biography. Summarizing a narrative presents special challenges. You have seen that an author of an expository piece (such as Bernstein's "Bilingual Education: A War of Words") follows assertions with examples and statements of support. Narrative presentations are usually less direct. The author relates a story—event follows event—the point of which may never be stated directly. The charm, the force, and the very point of the narrative lies in the telling; and, generally, narratives do not exhibit the same logical development of expository writing. They do not, therefore, lend themselves to summary in quite the same way. Narratives do have a logic, but that logic may be emotional, imaginative, or plot-bound. The writer who summarizes a narrative is obliged to give an overview—a synopsis—of the story's events and an account of how these events affect the central character(s).

The following narrative appears in Rosalie Pedalino Porter's *Forked Tongue: The Politics of Bilingual Education,* which opposes bilingual education. In Porter's account of growing up as a member of an ethnic minority, you will find the seeds of her present-day opposition to bilingual education.

Perils in the Demand for Biculturalism

ROSALIE PEDALINO PORTER

My family was poor, so the first necessity was for us to gain the economic means to survive. We children did not enjoy the middle-class luxury of a choice of schooling or careers. The thought of taking time to "get in touch with myself" did not exist. I was fortunate that my mother convinced my father to let me finish high school and not leave school at sixteen to work in his grocery store. Because I was the oldest of five children and a girl, I did not think to question my fate: I should help my mother after school every day, and when I reached the age of sixteen, I should leave high school and help in the store. In fact, my father would have preferred that we stay closely attached to the family and neither attend school nor learn English. Mandatory attendance at school saved us! For me, convention dictated that family bondage would not end until I married—and married within the ethnic group and preferably in the neighborhood, when I would then no longer be my father's but my husband's responsibility. 1

School, however, opened up my horizons, and the English language gave me the entry not only to the excitement of academic advancement but to friendships with children from very different families, other ethnic groups, and other religions. I began to want to learn, with a desire for a range of experiences, and, yes, a desire for material things and an interesting job. 2

Of course, my experience was not unusual. I wanted to be free from what seemed the restrictive customs and language of my family and community, free from the burden of being "different." The desire is common to young people of various ethnic groups, and it is not surprising, therefore, that this liberation is the enduring subject of a large body of literature and drama, in novels such as *The Fortunate Pilgrim, Call It Sleep,* and *Goodbye, Columbus* and films such as *West Side Story, Hester Street,* and *Crossing Delancey.* 3

It is daunting for anyone to cross the ethnic divide, but for women the 4 voyage has been and continues to be even more difficult. To move out of poverty and beyond ethnicity requires individual motivation and strength of purpose *and* the reinforcement of outside help from the schools, job opportunities, and the presence of achievable role models.

I saw with renewed immediacy the clash of cultures and the hardship 5 it imposes on the young in the case of three refugee women from Afghanistan who were in the Newton North High School ESL program for two years. They had learned English fairly well and completed a good part of their high school graduation requirements. They longed to enroll in a local community college, but the families arranged marriages for all three, finding them Afghan husbands instead. The teacher who knew the students and their families and had been an advisor to the young women was deeply disappointed. It is often just not possible to effect such change in the first years of residence in a new country.

The language and culture shift in my own immigrant family took an 6 unusual twist. Oldest of the children in a family of three sons and two daughters, I have moved the farthest from my family geographically and in terms of assimilation into American middle-class life. My brothers and sister, who have all completed college degrees and achieved economic success, live near my mother and have, unlike me, married within the ethnic group and the religion of our upbringing. Yet I am the only one of us who has maintained and expanded her knowledge of Italian, which I speak and write fluently. None of the others is the least bit interested in the language, but they are still very close to the customs. Paradoxically, I am closer to our "roots," to our country of origin, because I travel to Italy frequently and have a husband and three sons who are all Italophiles. My sister and brothers, however, are more closely involved in Italian-American culture. We have each chosen the degree of ethnicity we wish to maintain. I am not convinced of the inevitability of guilt over some loss of ethnicity, the sort that Mario Puzo depicted in *The Fortunate Pilgrim,* when he wrote, "They spoke with guilty loyalty of customs they themselves had trampled into dust." It is not that I am without sentimental feelings, but I cannot honestly wish that I or my family had remained immersed in our original language and ethnicity. We are immeasurably richer for having that background and for having added to it some of the achievements that American life offers.

▲ ▲ ▲

Certainly, Porter's experiences bear on her present-day opposition to bilingual and bicultural education. Porter believes that emphasizing a non-English-speaking student's native culture and native language "disables" the student, denying him or her "the knowledge and skills [necessary] to attain social and economic equality." If you were discussing her views on the subject in a paper,

HOW TO SUMMARIZE NARRATIVES

- Your summary will *not* be a narrative, but rather the synopsis of a narrative. Your summary will likely be a paragraph at most.
- You will want to name and describe the principal character(s) of the narrative and describe the narrative's main actions or events.
- You should seek to connect the narrative's characters and events: describe the significance of events for (or the impact of events on) the character.

you might want to refer to her narrative. How would you do so? When you summarize a narrative, bear in mind a few additional principles, listed in the box.

To summarize events, reread the narrative and make a marginal note each time you see that an action advances the story from one moment to the next. The key here is to recall that narratives take place *in time*. In your summary, be sure to re-create for your reader a sense of time flowing. Name and describe the characters as well. (For our purposes, *character* refers to the person, real or fictional, about whom the narrative is written.) The trickiest part of the summary will be describing the connection between events and characters. Earlier (page 3) we made the point that summarizing any selection involves a degree of interpretation, and this is especially true of summarizing narratives. What, in the case of Porter, is the impact of the events described? An answer belongs in a summary of this piece, yet developing an answer is tricky. Five readers would interpret the narrative's significance in five distinct ways, would they not? Yes and no: yes, in the sense that these readers, given their separate experiences, will read from different points of view; no, in the sense that readers should be able to distinguish between the impact of events as seen from a main character's (i.e., Porter's) point of view and the impact of these same events as seen from their (the readers') points of view. We should be able to agree that Porter was grateful for mandatory high school attendance. She felt liberated.

At times, you will have to infer from clues in a narrative the significance of events for a character; at other times, the writer will be more direct. In either case, remember that it is the narrative's main character, real or imaginary, whose perspective should be represented in the summary. Here is a one-paragraph summary of Porter's narrative. (The draft is the result of two prior drafts.)

> In an excerpt from her book Forked Tongue: The Politics of Bilingual Education, Rosalie Pedalino Porter relates how attending school and learning English allowed her to see beyond the confines of her Italian-American com-

munity. Mandatory schooling moved Porter from a culturally closed environment to an open, heterogeneous one that motivated her to succeed, both intellectually and materially. Her transition into American culture had its difficulties, though: Porter and women like her were expected to marry young, within the ethnic group, and remain close to home. Her desire, therefore, to move "beyond ethnicity" into America's middle class resulted in a painful clash of cultures. But Porter was able to forge a distinct and satisfying identity by developing those parts of her Italian heritage that she cherished and by adding "some of the achievements that American life offers."

▼

SUMMARIZING FIGURES AND TABLES

In your reading in the sciences and social sciences, you will often find data and concepts presented in nontext forms—as figures and tables. Such visual devices offer a snapshot, a pictorial overview of material that is more quickly and clearly communicated in graphic form than as a series of (often complicated) sentences. The writer of a graph, which in an article or book is labeled as a numbered "figure," presents the quantitative results of research as points on a line or a bar, or as sections ("slices") of a pie. Pie charts show relative proportions, or percentages. Graphs, especially effective in showing patterns, relate one variable to another: for instance, income to years of education or a college student's grade point average to hours of studying.

In the following example, a graph relates enrollment in a bilingual program to test scores in mathematics for third-grade students with limited English proficiency (LEP). Over a five-year period, beginning in 1982–1983, a bilingual program was introduced in the Eastman Avenue School in Los Angeles. Study this graph (Figure 1.1) to distinguish the progress of students enrolled in the bilingual classes from those not enrolled.

Here is a summary of the information presented in this graph:

When taught in bilingual classrooms, third graders with limited English proficiency (LEP) at the Eastman Avenue School showed steady progress on a statewide mathematics test. In the 1980-1982 school years, before the beginning of bilingual instruction, third-grade Eastman students performed below the district average in mathematics. After two years of bilingual instruction (in

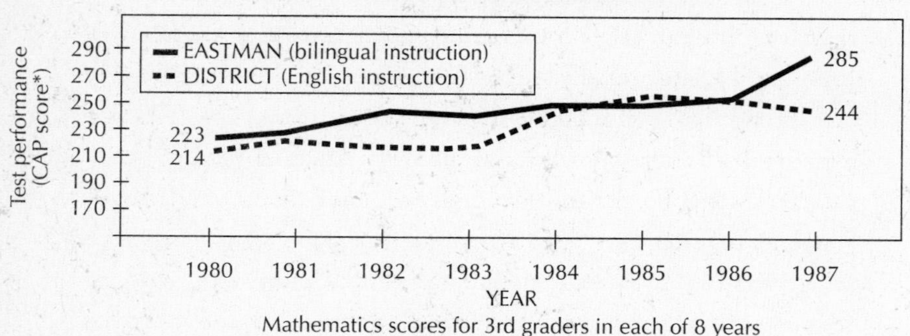

*California Assessment Program

FIGURE 1.1 Eastman Bilingual Project

Source: *"Eastman School Outcomes: Math"* by James Crawford from *Bilingual Education: History, Politics, Theory, and Practice,* 2nd Edition. (Los Angeles: Bilingual Education Services, 1991.) Reprinted by permission.

> the 1984-1985 academic year), LEP third graders taking the math test performed equally with their peers throughout the school district. After four years of bilingual instruction (kindergarten and grades 1-3), LEP third graders equaled or surpassed other district third graders in math.

In a second type of figure (see Figure 1.2), the writer presents a *conceptual overview.* Again the assumption is that a figure gives readers information more quickly and clearly than the same material in sentence form. In this next example, the author uses words, not numbers. Still, one variable is related to another: in this case, time (a three-year span) to the degree of instruction in a student's native language.

Here is a two-sentence summary of the "Transitional Bilingual Education Model":

> The "Transitional Bilingual Education Model" for non-English-speaking students seeks a gradual transition from native-language instruction to English-based instruction. In this model, non-native speakers of English initially learn academic subjects in their native language but within three years receive significant English-language instruction.

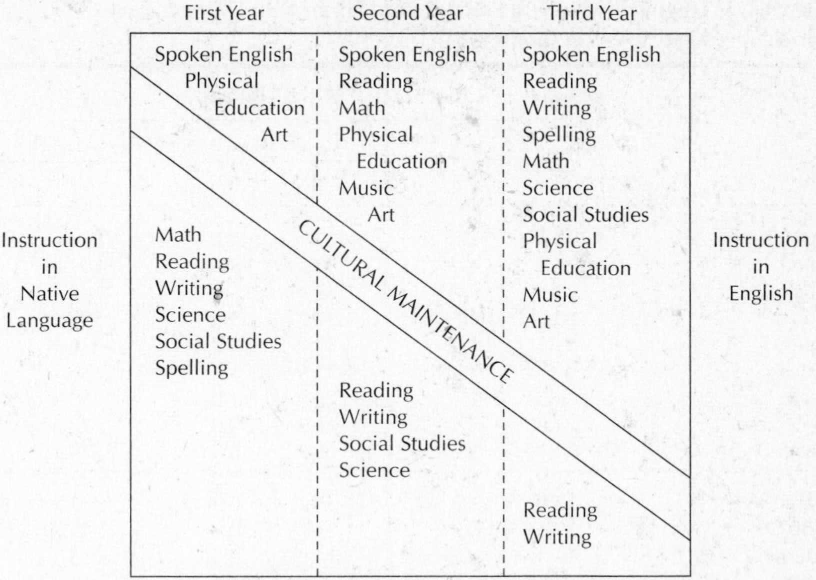

FIGURE 1.2 Transitional Bilingual Education Model: Instruction in Native Language and in English.

Source: From *Forked Tongue: The Politics of Bilingual Education* by Rosalie Pedalino Porter. Copyright © 1990 by Basic Books, Inc. Reprinted by permission of Basic Books, a division of HarperCollins Publishers, Inc.

A *table* presents numerical data in rows and columns for quick reference. Tabular information can be incorporated into graphs, if the writer chooses. Graphs are preferable when the writer wants to emphasize a pattern or relationship; tables are used when the writer wants to emphasize numbers. The following example shows projections, through the year 2000, for numbers of minority students (the "N" column) with limited skills in English. The percentage ("%") column shows the percentage a particular language group represents of the total student population being studied.

Here is a summary of the table "Linguistic Minority Student Population with Limited English Proficiency, Aged 5–14."

> By the year 2000, the number of five- to fourteen-year-old students in America with limited English proficiency (LEP) is projected to be 3.4 million, an increase of more than one million from 1980. Among these students, native speakers of Spanish constitute the overwhelming majority. In 1980, they were a projected 1,727,600

TABLE 1.1 Linguistic Minority Student Population with Limited English Proficiency, Aged 5–14 (in thousands)

	PROJECTIONS					
	1980		1990		2000	
LANGUAGE	N	%	N	%	N	%
Spanish	1727.6	72.2	2092.7	74.8	2630.0	77.4
Italian	94.9	4.0	100.1	3.6	109.6	3.2
French	89.0	3.7	93.9	3.4	102.9	3.0
German	88.8	3.7	93.7	3.4	102.6	3.0
Filipino	33.2	1.4	35.0	1.2	38.3	1.1
Chinese	31.3	1.3	33.0	1.2	36.2	1.0
Greek	26.5	1.1	27.9	1.0	30.6	0.9
Vietnamese	24.9	1.0	26.2	0.9	28.7	0.8
Navajo	24.3	1.0	25.6	0.9	28.1	0.8
Polish	24.0	1.0	25.3	0.9	27.5	0.8
Portuguese	23.8	1.0	25.1	0.9	27.5	0.8
Yiddish	22.5	0.9	23.7	0.8	26.0	0.7
Japanese	13.3	0.6	14.0	0.5	15.3	0.4
Korean	12.2	0.5	12.8	0.4	14.1	0.4
Not accounted for and other	158.5	6.6	167.5	6.0	192.9	5.4
Total	2394.2		2795.9		3400.0	

Source: "Linguistic Minority Student Population with Limited English Proficiency" by Henry Treuba from *Raising Silent Voices*. Copyright © 1989 by Heinle & Heinle/Newbury House Publishers, Boston, MA. Reprinted by permission.

(72.2 percent of all LEPS); in 1990 they were a projected 2,092,700 (74.8 percent); and in 2000 they were projected to number 2,630,000 (77.4 percent). Other LEP students (e.g., Korean, Navajo, and German) show a projected increase in numbers of the same period; yet these other students constitute a decreasing percentage of total LEP students, as compared to native speakers of Spanish.

▼

PARAPHRASE

In certain cases, you may want to *paraphrase* rather than to summarize material. Writing a paraphrase is similar to writing a summary: it involves recasting a passage into your own words, and so it requires your complete understanding of the material. The difference is that while a summary is a shortened version of the original, the paraphrase is approximately the same length as the original.

Why write a paraphrase when you can quote the original? You may decide to offer a paraphrase of material written in language that is dense, abstract, archaic, or possibly confusing. For example, suppose you were writing a paper on some aspect of human progress and you came across the following passage by the Marquis de Condorcet, a French economist and politician, written in the late eighteenth century:

> If man can, with almost complete assurance, predict phenomena when he knows their laws, and if, even when he does not, he can still, with great expectation of success, forecast the future on the basis of his experience of the past, why, then, should it be regarded as a fantastic undertaking to sketch, with some pretense to truth, the future destiny of man on the basis of his history? The sole foundation for belief in the natural science is this idea, that the general laws directing the phenomena of the universe, known or unknown, are necessary and constant. Why should this principle be any less true for the development of the intellectual and moral faculties of man than for the other operations of nature?

You would like to introduce Condorcet's idea on predicting the future course of human history, but you don't want to slow down your narrative with this somewhat abstract quotation. You may decide to attempt a paraphrase, as follows:

> The Marquis de Condorcet believed that if we can predict such physical events as eclipses and tides, and if we can use past events as a guide to future ones, we should be able to forecast human destiny on the basis of history. Physical events, he maintained, are determined by natural laws that are knowable and predictable. Since humans are part of nature, why should their intellectual and moral development be any less predictable than other natural events?

Each sentence in the paraphrase corresponds to a sentence in the original. The paraphrase is somewhat shorter, owing to the differences of style between eighteenth- and twentieth-century prose (we tend to be more brisk and efficient, although not more eloquent). But the main difference is that we have replaced the language of the original with our own language. For example, we have paraphrased Condorcet's "The general laws directing the phenomena of the universe, known or unknown, are necessary and constant" with "Physical events, he maintained, are determined by natural laws that are knowable and predictable." To contemporary readers, "knowable and predictable" might be clearer than "necessary and constant" as a description of natural (i.e., physical) laws. Note that we added the specific examples of eclipses and tides to clarify what might have been a somewhat abstract idea. Note also that we included two attributions to Condorcet within the paraphrase to credit our source properly.

When you come across a passage that you don't understand, the temptation is strong to skip over it. Resist this temptation! Use paraphrase as a tool for explaining to yourself the main ideas of a difficult passage. By translating another writer's language into your own, you can clarify what you understand and what you don't. Thus, the paraphrase becomes a tool for learning the subject.

The following pointers will help you write paraphrases.

HOW TO WRITE PARAPHRASES

- Make sure that you understand the source passage.
- Substitute your own words for those of the source passage; look for synonyms that carry the same meaning as the original words.
- Rearrange your own sentences so that they read smoothly. Sentence structure, even sentence order, in the paraphrase need not be based on that of the original. A good paraphrase, like a good summary, should stand by itself.

Let's consider some other examples. If you were investigating the debate on bilingual education, you would eventually want to examine the law mandating that students who are not proficient in English be taught in their native languages. Here is an excerpt from that law:

PUBLIC LAW 93–380, AUG. 21, 1974

BILINGUAL EDUCATIONAL PROGRAMS

Sec. 105. (a) (1) Title VII of the Elementary and Secondary Education Act of 1965 is amended to read as follows:

"TITLE VII—BILINGUAL EDUCATION

"SHORT TITLE

Sec. 701. This title may be cited as the "Bilingual Education Act".

"POLICY; APPROPRIATIONS

"Sec. 702. (a) Recognizing—

"(1) that there are large numbers of children of limited English-speaking ability;

"(2) that many of such children have a cultural heritage which differs from that of English-speaking persons;

"(3) that a primary means by which a child learns is through the use of such child's language and cultural heritage;

"(4) that, therefore, large numbers of children of limited English-speaking ability have educational needs which can be met by the use of bilingual educational methods and techniques; and

"(5) that, in addition, children of limited English-speaking ability benefit through the fullest utilization of multiple language and cultural resources, the Congress declares it to be the policy of the United States, in order to establish equal educational opportunity for all children (A) to encourage the establishment and operation, where appropriate, of educational programs using bilingual educational practices, techniques, and methods, and (B) for that purpose, to provide financial assistance to local educational agencies, and to State educational agencies for certain purposes, in order to enable such local educational agencies to develop and carry out such programs in elementary and secondary schools, in-

> cluding activities at the preschool level, which are designed to meet the educational needs of such children; and to demonstrate effective ways of providing, for children of limited English-speaking ability, instruction designed to enable them, while using their native language, to achieve competence in the English language.

Like most legal passages, this is somewhat forbidding to laypeople: it consists of one sentence more than two hundred words long, with typically impenetrable legal phrasing. You decide, for clarity's sake, to paraphrase the law for your lay audience. First, of course, you must understand the meaning of the passage, perhaps no small task. But having read the material carefully, you might eventually draft a paraphrase like this one:

> The federal guidelines for bilingual education are presented in Public Law 93-380 (Aug. 21, 1974), an amendment to Title VII of the Elementary and Secondary Education Act of 1965. The "Bilingual Education Act" (the short title) is premised on three assumptions: (1) that many children have limited ability to speak English; (2) that many come from ethnically diverse, non-English-speaking backgrounds; and (3) that native language and culture powerfully influence a child's learning. Based on these assumptions, Congress concluded that many children in the United States should be educated through programs in bilingual education. This approach makes full use of a student's native linguistic and cultural resources.
>
> Accordingly, Congress declared that in the interests of establishing equal educational opportunities for all children, the government would encourage the creation of bilingual programs in preschools and in elementary and secondary schools. Congress would fund such programs at the state and local levels with the understanding that these programs would enable students, "while using their native language, to achieve competence in the English language."

In our paraphrase of Congress's one long sentence, we have written six sentences arranged in two paragraphs. Our paragraphs follow the logic and structure of the original, which is presented in two parts. The first part consists of the five "recognizing that" clauses. We have taken these clauses and paraphrased them in two sentences: one dealing with the assumptions underlying the law and the other addressing the conclusions Congress reached based on these assumptions. The second part of the original—and of the paraphrase—presents Congress's two declarations. Notice that we ended the paraphrase with a quotation. From earlier reading on the debate over bilingual education, we knew that a student's eventual proficiency in English (or lack thereof) has become a contentious issue. We therefore wanted to preserve in our paraphrase the exact language of the original. Although our paraphrase is somewhat briefer than the original, it follows the original's logic and structure. The paraphrase may not stand up in court, but it accurately conveys the sense of the law to the lay reader.

Finally, let's consider a passage written by a fine writer that may, nonetheless, best be conveyed in paraphrase. In "Identify All Carriers," an article on AIDS, editor and columnist William F. Buckley makes the following statement:

> I have read and listened, and I think now that I can convincingly crystallize the thoughts chasing about in the minds of, first, those whose concern with AIDS victims is based primarily on a concern for them, and for the maintenance of the most rigid standards of civil liberties and personal privacy, and, second, those whose anxiety to protect the public impels them to give subordinate attention to the civil amenities of those who suffer from AIDS and primary attention to the safety of those who do not.

In style, Buckley's passage is more like Condorcet's than the legal extract: it is eloquent, balanced, and literate. Still, it is challenging. Here is another lengthy sentence, perhaps a bit too eloquent for some readers to grasp. For your paper on AIDS, you decide to paraphrase Buckley. You might draft something like this:

> Buckley finds two opposing sides in the AIDS debate: those concerned primarily with the civil liberties and the privacy of AIDS victims, and those concerned primarily with the safety of the public.

Our paraphrases have been somewhat shorter than the original, but this is not always the case. For example, suppose you wanted to paraphrase this statement by Sigmund Freud:

> We have found out that the distortion in dreams which hinders our understanding of them is due to the activities of a censorship, directed against the unacceptable, unconscious wish-impulses.

If you were to paraphrase this statement (the first sentence in the Tenth Lecture of his *General Introduction to Psychoanalysis*), you might come up with something like this:

> It is difficult to understand dreams because they contain distortions. Freud believed that these distortions arise from our internal censor, which attempts to suppress unconscious and forbidden desires.

Essentially, this paraphrase does little more than break up one sentence into two and somewhat rearrange the sentence structure for clarity.

Like summaries, then, *paraphrases* are useful devices, both in helping you to understand source material and in enabling you to convey the essence of this source material to your readers. When would you choose to write a summary instead of a paraphrase (or vice versa)? The answer to this question depends on your purpose in presenting your source material. As we've said, summaries are generally based on articles (or sections of articles) or books. Paraphrases are generally based on particularly difficult (or important) paragraphs or sentences. You would seldom paraphrase a long passage, or summarize a short one, unless there were particularly good reasons for doing so. (For example, a lawyer might want to paraphrase several pages of legal language so that his or her client, who is not a lawyer, could understand it.) The purpose of a summary is generally to save your reader time by presenting him or her with a brief and quickly readable version of a lengthy source. The purpose of a paraphrase is generally to clarify a short passage that might otherwise be unclear. Whether you summarize or paraphrase may also depend on the importance of your source. A particularly important source—if it is not too long—may rate a paraphrase. If it is less important, or peripheral to your central argument, you may choose to write a summary instead. And, of course, you may choose to summarize only part of your source—the part that is most relevant to the point you are making. In conclusion:

WHEN TO SUMMARIZE AND PARAPHRASE

Summarize:
- To present main points of a lengthy passage (article or book)
- To condense peripheral points necessary to discussion

Paraphrase:
- To clarify a short passage
- To emphasize main points

At times, you will want to *quote* a source, instead of summarizing or paraphrasing it. You'll find a full discussion on quoting sources starting on page 39. In brief, though, you should quote sources when:

- Another writer's language is particularly memorable and will add interest and liveliness to your paper.
- Another writer's language is so clearly and economically stated that to make the same points in your own words would, by comparison, be ineffective.
- You want the solid reputation of a source to lend authority and credibility to your own writing.

2
Thesis, Quotations, Introductions, and Conclusions

WRITING A THESIS

A thesis statement is a one-sentence summary of a paper's content. It is similar, actually, to a paper's conclusion but lacks the conclusion's concern for broad implications and significance. For a writer in the drafting stages, the thesis establishes a focus, a basis on which to include or exclude information. For the reader of a finished product, the thesis anticipates the author's discussion. *A thesis statement, therefore, is an essential tool for both writers and readers of academic material.*

This last sentence is our thesis for this section. Based on this thesis, we, as the authors, have limited the content of the section; and you, as the reader, will be able to form certain expectations about the discussion that follows. You can expect a definition of a thesis statement; an enumeration of the uses of a thesis statement; and a discussion focused on academic material. As writers, we will have met our obligations to you only if in subsequent paragraphs we satisfy these expectations.

The Components of a Thesis

Like any other sentence, a thesis includes a subject and a predicate, which consists of an assertion about the subject. In the sentence "Lee and Grant were different kinds of generals," "Lee and Grant" is the subject and "were different kinds of generals" is the predicate. What distinguishes a thesis statement from any other sentence with a subject and predicate is *that the thesis statement presents the controlling idea of the paper.* The subject of a thesis must present the right balance between the general and the specific to allow for a thorough discussion within the allotted length of the paper. The discussion might include definitions, details, comparisons, contrasts—whatever is needed to illuminate a subject and carry on an intelligent conversation. (If the sentence about Lee and Grant were a thesis, the reader would assume that the rest of the paper contained comparisons and contrasts between the two generals.)

Bear in mind when writing thesis statements that the more general your subject and the more complex your assertion, the longer your paper will be. For instance, you could not write an effective ten-page paper based on the following:

> Democracy is the best system of government.

Consider the subject of this sentence ("democracy") and the assertion of its predicate ("is the best system of government"). The subject is enormous in scope; it is a general category composed of hundreds of more specific subcategories, each of which would be appropriate for a paper ten pages in length. The predicate of our example is also a problem, for the claim that democracy is the best system of government would be simplistic unless accompanied by a thorough, systematic, critical evaluation of *every* form of government yet devised. A ten-page paper governed by such a thesis simply could not achieve the level of detail and sophistication expected of college students.

Limiting the Scope of the Thesis

To write an effective thesis and thus a controlled, effective paper, you need to limit your subject and your claims about it. Two strategies for achieving a thesis statement of manageable proportions are (1) to begin with a working thesis (this strategy assumes that you are familiar with your topic) and (2) to begin with a broad area of interest and narrow it (this strategy assumes that you are unfamiliar with your topic).

BEGIN WITH A WORKING THESIS

Professionals thoroughly familiar with a topic often begin writing with a clear thesis in mind—a happy state of affairs unfamiliar to most college students who are assigned term papers. But professionals usually have an important advantage over students: experience. Because professionals know their material, are familiar with the ways of approaching it, are aware of the questions important to practitioners, and have devoted considerable time to study of the topic, they are naturally in a strong position to begin writing a paper. Not only do professionals have experience in their fields, but they also have a clear purpose in writing; they know their audience and are comfortable with the format of their papers.

Experience counts—there's no way around it. As a student, you are not yet an expert and therefore don't generally have the luxury of beginning your writing tasks with a definite thesis in mind. Once you choose and devote time to a major field of study, however, you will gain experience. In the meantime, you'll have to do more work than the professional to prepare yourself for writing a paper.

But let's assume that you *do* have an area of expertise, that you are in your own right a professional (albeit not in academic matters). We'll assume that you understand your nonacademic subject—say, backpacking—and have been given a clear purpose for writing: to discuss the relative merits of backpack designs. Your job is to write a recommendation for the owner of a sporting-goods chain, suggesting which line of backpacks the chain should carry. The owner lives in another city, so your remarks have to be written. Since you already know a good deal about backpacks, you may already have some well-developed ideas on the topic before you start doing additional research.

Yet even as an expert in your field, you will find that beginning the writing task is a challenge, for at this point it is unlikely that you will be able to conceive a thesis perfectly suited to the contents of your paper. After all, a thesis statement is a summary, and it is difficult to summarize a presentation yet to be written—especially if you plan to discover what you want to say during the process of writing. Even if you know your material well, the best you can do at the early stages is to formulate a *working thesis*—a hypothesis of sorts, a well-informed hunch about your topic and the claim to be made about it. Once you have completed a draft, you can evaluate the degree to which your working thesis accurately summarizes the content of your paper.[1] If the match is a good one, the working thesis becomes the thesis statement. If, however, sections of the paper drift from the focus set out in the working thesis, you'll need to revise the thesis and the paper itself to ensure that the presentation is unified. (You'll know that the match between the content and thesis is a good one when every paragraph directly refers to and develops some element of the thesis.)

BEGIN WITH A SUBJECT AND NARROW IT

Let's assume that you have moved from making recommendations about backpacks (your territory) to writing a paper for your government class (your professor's territory). Whereas you were once the professional who knew enough about your subject to begin writing with a working thesis, you are now the student, inexperienced and in need of a great deal of information before you can begin to think of thesis statements. It may be a comfort to know that your government professor would likely be in the same predicament if asked to recommend backpack designs. He would need to spend several weeks, at least, backpacking to become as experienced as you; and it is fair to say that you will need to spend several hours in the library before you are in a position to choose a topic suitable for an undergraduate paper.

---

[1]Some writers work with an idea, committing it to paper only after it has been fully formed. Others begin with a vague notion and begin writing a first draft, trusting that as they write they'll discover what they wish to say. Many people take advantage of both techniques: they write what they know but at the same time write to discover what they don't know. As you'll see, we used both techniques in writing this section of the book.

Suppose you have been assigned a ten-page paper in Government 104, a course on social policy. Not only do you not have a thesis—you don't have a subject! Where will you begin? First, you need to select a broad area of interest and make yourself knowledgeable about its general features. What if no broad area of interest occurs to you? Don't despair—there's usually a way to make use of discussions you've read in a text or heard in a lecture. The trick is to find a topic that can become personally important, for whatever reason. (For a paper in your biology class, you might write on the digestive system because a relative has stomach troubles. For an economics seminar, you might explore the factors that threaten banks with collapse because your great-grandparents lost their life savings during the Great Depression.) Whatever the academic discipline, try to discover a topic that you'll enjoy exploring; that way, you'll be writing for yourself as much as for your professor. Some specific strategies to try if no topics occur to you: Review material covered during the semester, class by class if need be; review the semester's readings, actually skimming each assignment. Choose any subject that has held your interest, if even for a moment, and use that as your point of departure.

Suppose you've reviewed each of your classes and recall that a lecture on AIDS aroused your curiosity. Your broad subject of interest, then, will be AIDS. At this point, the goal of your research is to limit this subject to a manageable scope. Although your initial, broad subject will often be more specific than our example, "AIDS," we'll assume for the purposes of discussion the most general case (the subject in greatest need of limiting).

A subject can be limited in at least two ways. First, a general article like an encyclopedia entry may do the work for you by presenting the subject in the form of an outline, with each item in the outline representing a separate topic (which, for your purposes, may need further limiting). Second, you can limit a subject by asking several questions about it:

Who?
What aspects?
Where?
When?
How?

These questions will occur to you as you conduct your research and see the ways in which various authors have focused their discussions. Having read several sources and having decided that you'd like to use them, you might limit the subject "AIDS" by asking *who*—AIDS patients; and *which aspect*—civil rights of AIDS patients.

Certainly, "the civil rights of AIDS patients" offers a more specific focus than does "AIDS"; still, the revised focus is too broad for a ten-page paper in that a comprehensive discussion would obligate you to review numerous particular rights. So again you must try to limit your subject by posing a question. In this particular case, *which aspects* (of the civil rights of AIDS patients) can be asked a second time. Six aspects may come to mind:

- Rights in the workplace
- Rights to hospital care
- Rights to insurance benefits
- Rights to privacy
- Rights to fair housing
- Rights to education

Any *one* of these aspects could provide the focus of a ten-page paper, and you do yourself an important service by choosing one, perhaps two, of the aspects; to choose more would obligate you to too broad a discussion and you would frustrate yourself: Either the paper would have to be longer than ten pages or, assuming you kept to the page limit, the paper would be superficial in its treatment. In both instances, the paper would fail, given the constraints of the assignment. So it is far better that you limit your subject ahead of time, before you attempt to write about it. Let's assume that you settle on the following as an appropriately defined subject for a ten-page paper:

the rights of AIDS patients in the workplace

The process of narrowing an initial subject depends heavily on the reading you do. The more you read, the deeper your understanding of a topic. The deeper your understanding, the likelier it will be that you can divide a broad and complex topic into manageable—that is, researchable—categories. In the AIDS example, your reading in the literature suggested that the civil rights of AIDS patients was an issue at the center of recent national debate. So reading allowed you to narrow the subject "AIDS" by answering the initial questions—the *who* and *which aspects.* Once you narrowed your focus to "the civil rights of AIDS patients," you read further and quickly realized that civil rights in itself was a broad concern that also should be limited. In this way, reading provided an important stimulus as you worked to identify an appropriate subject for your paper.

MAKE AN ASSERTION

Once you have identified the subject, you can now develop it into a thesis by making an assertion about it. If you have spent enough time reading and gathering information, you will be knowledgeable enough to have something to say about the subject, based on a combination of your own thinking and the thinking of your sources. If you have trouble making an assertion, try writing your topic at the top of a page and then listing everything you now know and feel about it. Often from such a list you will discover an assertion that you then can use to fashion a working thesis. A good way to gauge the reasonableness of your claim is to see what other authors have asserted about the same topic. In fact, keep good notes on the views of others; the notes will prove a useful counterpoint to your own views as you write, and you may want to use them in your paper.

Next, make three assertions about your topic, in order of increasing complexity.

1. During the past few years, the rights of AIDS patients in the workplace have been debated by national columnists.
2. Several columnists have offered convincing reasons for protecting the rights of AIDS patients in the workplace.
3. The most sensible plan for protecting the rights of AIDS patients in the workplace has been offered by columnist Anthony Jones.

Keep in mind that these are *working thesis statements.* Because you haven't written a paper based on any of them, they remain *hypotheses* to be tested. After completing a first draft, you would compare the contents of the paper to the thesis and make adjustments as necessary for unity. The working theses is an excellent tool for planning broad sections of the paper, but—again—don't let it prevent you from pursuing related discussions as they occur to you.

Notice how these three statements differ from one another in the forcefulness of their assertions. The third thesis is *strongly argumentative.* "Most sensible" implies that the writer will explain several plans for protecting the rights of AIDS patients in the workplace. Following the explanation would come a comparison of plans and then a judgment in favor of Anthony Jones. Like any working thesis, this one helps the writer plan the paper. Assuming the paper follows the three-part structure we've inferred, the working thesis would become the final thesis, on the basis of which a reader could anticipate sections of the essay to come.

The first of the three thesis statements, by contrast, is *explanatory*:

> During the past few years, the rights of AIDS patients in the workplace have been debated by national columnists.

In developing a paper based on this thesis, the writer would assert only the existence of a debate, obligating himself merely to a summary of the various positions taken. Readers, then, would use this thesis as a tool for anticipating the contours of the paper to follow. Based on this particular thesis, a reader would *not* expect to find the author strongly endorsing the views of one or another columnist. The thesis does not require the author to defend a personal opinion.

The second thesis statement *does* entail a personal, intellectually assertive commitment to the material, although the assertion is not as forceful as the one found in statement 3:

> Several columnists have offered convincing reasons for protecting the rights of AIDS patients in the workplace.

Here we have an *explanatory, mildly argumentative* thesis that enables the writer to express an opinion. We infer from the use of the word *convincing* that the writer will judge the various reasons for protecting the rights of AIDS patients; and, we can reasonably assume, the writer himself believes in protecting these rights. Note the contrast between this second thesis and the first one, where the writer committed himself to no involvement in the debate whatsoever. Still, the present thesis is not as ambitious as the third one, whose writer implicitly accepted the general argument for safeguarding rights (an acceptance he would need to justify) and then took the additional step of evaluating the merits of those arguments in relation to each other.

As you can see, for any subject you might care to explore in a paper, you can make any number of assertions—some relatively simple, some complex. It is on the basis of these assertions that you set yourself an agenda in writing a paper—and readers set for themselves expectations for reading. The more ambitious the thesis, the more complex will be the paper and the greater will be the readers' expectations.

Using the Thesis

Different writing tasks require different thesis statements. The *explanatory thesis* is often developed in response to short-answer exam questions that call for information, not analysis (e.g., "List and explain proposed modifications to contemporary American democracy"). The *explanatory but mildly argumentative thesis* is appropriate for organizing reports (even lengthy ones), as well as essay questions that call for some analysis (e.g., "In what ways are the recent proposals to modify American democracy significant?"). The *strongly argumentative thesis* is used to organize papers and exam questions that call for information, analysis, *and* the writer's forcefully stated point of view (e.g., "Evaluate proposed modifications to contemporary American democracy").

The strongly argumentative thesis, of course, is the riskiest of the three, since you must unequivocally state your position and make it appear reasonable—which requires that you offer evidence and defend against logical objections. But such intellectual risks pay dividends, and if you become involved enough in your work to make challenging assertions, you will provoke challenging responses that enliven classroom discussions. One of the important objectives of a college education is to extend learning by stretching, or challenging, conventional beliefs. You breathe new life into this broad objective, and you enliven your own learning as well, every time you adopt a thesis that sets a challenging agenda both for you (as writer) and for your readers. Of course, once you set the challenge, you must be equal to the task. As a writer, you will need to discuss all the elements implied by your thesis.

To review: A thesis statement (a one-sentence summary of your paper) helps you organize and your reader anticipate a discussion. Thesis statements are distinguished by their carefully worded subjects and predicates, which should be just broad enough and complex enough to be developed within the length limitations of the assignment. Both novices and experts in a field typically begin the initial draft of a paper with a working thesis—a statement that provides writers with structure enough to get started but with latitude enough to discover what they want to say as they write. Once you have completed a first draft, you should test the "fit" of your thesis with the paper that follows. Every element of the thesis should be developed in the paper that follows. Discussions that drift from your thesis should be deleted, or the thesis changed to accommodate the new discussions.

▼

QUOTATIONS

A *quotation* records the exact language used by someone in speech or in writing. A *summary,* in contrast, is a brief restatement in your own words of what someone else has said or written. And a *paraphrase* is also a restatement, although one that is often as long as the original source. Any paper in which you draw upon sources will rely heavily on quotation, summary, and paraphrase. How do you choose among the three?

Remember that the papers you write should be your own—for the most part, your own language and certainly your own thesis, your own inferences, and your own conclusions. It follows that references to your source materials should be written primarily as summaries and paraphrases, both of which are built on restatement, not quotation. You will use summaries when you need a *brief* restatement, and paraphrases, which provide more explicit detail than summaries, when you need to follow the development of a source closely. When you quote too much, you risk losing ownership of your work: more easily than you might think, your voice can be drowned out by the voices of those you've quoted. So *use quotations sparingly,* as you would a pungent spice.

Nevertheless, *quoting just the right source at the right time can significantly improve your papers.* The trick is to know when and how to use quotations.

Choosing Quotations

You'll find that there are several situations in which using quotations can be particularly helpful.

WHEN TO QUOTE

- Use quotations when another writer's language is particularly memorable and will add interest and liveliness to your paper.
- Use quotations when another writer's language is so clear and economical that to make the same point in your own words would, by comparison, be ineffective.
- Use quotations when you want the solid reputation of a source to lend authority and credibility to your own writing.

QUOTING MEMORABLE LANGUAGE

Assume you're writing a paper on Napoleon Bonaparte's relationship with the celebrated Josephine. Through research you learn that two days after their marriage Napoleon, given command of an army, left his bride for what was to be a brilliant military campaign in Italy. How did the young general respond to leaving his wife so soon after their wedding? You come across the following, written from the field of battle by Napoleon on April 3, 1796:

> I have received all your letters, but none has such an impact on me as the last. Do you have any idea, darling, what you are doing, writing to me in those terms? Do you not think my situation cruel enough without intensifying my longing for you, overwhelming my soul? What a style! What emotions you evoke! Written in fire, they burn my poor heart![2]

A summary of this passage might read as follows:

> On April 3, 1796, Napoleon wrote to Josephine, expressing how sorely he missed her and how passionately he responded to her letters.

You might write the following as a paraphrase of the passage:

> On April 3, 1796, Napoleon wrote to Josephine that he had received her letters and that one among all others had had a special impact, overwhelming his soul with fiery emotions and longing.

How feeble this summary and paraphrase are when compared with the original! Use the vivid language that your sources give you. In this case, quote Napoleon in your paper to make your subject come alive with memorable detail:

> On April 3, 1796, a passionate, lovesick Napoleon responded to a letter from Josephine; she had written longingly to her husband, who, on a military campaign, acutely felt her absence. "Do you have any idea, darling, what you are doing, writing to me in those terms? . . . What emotions you evoke!" he said of her letters. "Written in fire, they burn my poor heart!"

Quotations can be direct or indirect. A *direct* quotation is one in which you record precisely the language of another, as we did with the sentences from Napoleon's letter. In an *indirect* quotation, you report what someone has said, although you are not obligated to repeat the words exactly as spoken (or written):

> *Direct quotation:* Franklin D. Roosevelt said: "The only thing we have to fear is fear itself."
>
> *Indirect quotation:* Franklin D. Roosevelt said that we have nothing to fear but fear itself.

The language in a direct quotation, which is indicated by a pair of quotation marks (" "), must be faithful to the language of the original passage. When us-

---

[2]Francis Mossiker, trans., *Napoleon and Josephine.* New York: Simon and Schuster, 1964.

ing an indirect quotation, you have the liberty of changing words (although not changing meaning). For both direct and indirect quotations, *you must credit your sources,* naming them either in (or close to) the sentence that includes the quotation or in a footnote.

QUOTING CLEAR AND CONCISE LANGUAGE

You should quote a source when its language is particularly clear and economical—when your language, by contrast, would be wordy. Read this passage from a text on biology:

> The honeybee colony, which usually has a population of 30,000 to 40,000 workers, differs from that of the bumblebee and many other social bees or wasps in that it survives the winter. This means that the bees must stay warm despite the cold. Like other bees, the isolated honeybee cannot fly if the temperature falls below 10°C (50°F) and cannot walk if the temperature is below 7°C (45°F). Within the wintering hive, bees maintain their temperature by clustering together in a dense ball; the lower the temperature, the denser the cluster. The clustered bees produce heat by constant muscular movements of their wings, legs, and abdomens. In very cold weather, the bees on the outside of the cluster keep moving toward the center, while those in the core of the cluster move to the colder outside periphery. The entire cluster moves slowly about on the combs, eating the stored honey from the combs as it moves.[3]

A summary of this paragraph might read as follows:

> Honeybees, unlike many other varieties of bee, are able to live through the winter by "clustering together in a dense ball" for body warmth.

A paraphrase of the same passage would be considerably more detailed:

> Honeybees, unlike many other varieties of bee (such as bumblebees), are able to live through the winter. The 30,000 to 40,000 bees within a honeybee hive could not, individually, move about in cold winter temperatures. But when "clustering together in a dense ball," the bees generate heat by constantly moving their body parts. The cluster also moves slowly about the hive, eating honey stored in the combs. This nutrition, in addition to the heat generated by the cluster, enables the honeybee to survive the cold winter months.

In both the summary and the paraphrase we've quoted Curtis's "clustering together in a dense ball," a phrase that lies at the heart of her description of wintering honeybees. For us to describe this clustering in any language other than Curtis's would be pointless since her description is admirably brief and precise.

---

[3]"Winter Organization" in Patricia Curtis, *Biology,* 2nd ed. New York: Worth, 1976, pp. 822–823.

QUOTING AUTHORITATIVE LANGUAGE

You will also want to use quotations that lend authority to your work. When quoting an expert or some prominent political, artistic, or historical figure, you elevate your own work by placing it in esteemed company. Quote respected figures to establish background information in a paper, and your readers will tend to perceive that information as reliable. Quote the opinions of respected figures to endorse some statement that you've made, and your statement becomes more credible to your readers. For example, in an essay that you might write on the importance of reading well, you could make use of a passage from Thoreau's *Walden:*

> Reading well is hard work and requires great skill and training. It "is a noble exercise," writes Henry David Thoreau in *Walden,* "and one that will task the reader more than any exercise which the customs of the day esteem. It requires a training such as the athletes underwent. . . . Books must be read as deliberately and reservedly as they were written."

By quoting a famous philosopher and essayist on the subject of reading, you add legitimacy to your discussion. Not only do *you* regard reading to be a skill that is both difficult and important; so too does Henry David Thoreau, one of our most influential thinkers. The quotation has elevated the level of your work.

You can also quote to advantage well-respected figures who've written or spoken about the subject of your paper. Here is a discussion of space flight. Author David Chandler refers to a physicist and a physicist–astronaut:

> A few scientists—notably James Van Allen, discoverer of the Earth's radiation belts—have decried the expense of the manned space program and called for an almost exclusive concentration on unmanned scientific exploration instead, saying this would be far more cost-effective.
>
> Other space scientists dispute that idea. Joseph Allen, physicist and former shuttle astronaut, says, "It seems to be argued that one takes away from the other. But before there was a manned space program, the funding on space science was zero. Now it's about $500 million a year."

Note that in the first paragraph Chandler has either summarized or used an indirect quotation to incorporate remarks made by James Van Allen into the discussion on space flight. In the second paragraph, Chandler directly quotes his next source, Joseph Allen. Both quotations, indirect and direct, lend authority and legitimacy to the article, for both James Van Allen and Joseph Allen are experts on the subject of space flight. Note also that Chandler has provided brief but effective biographies of his sources, identifying both so that their qualifications to speak on the subject are known to all:

> James Van Allen, *discoverer of the Earth's radiation belts . . .*
> Joseph Allen, *physicist and former shuttle astronaut . . .*

The phrases in italics are called *appositives.* Their function is to rename the nouns they follow by providing explicit, identifying detail. Any information about a person that can be expressed in the following sentence pattern can be made into an appositive phrase:

> James Van Allen is *the discoverer of the Earth's radiation belts.*
> He has decried the expense of the manned space program.
>
> ↓
>
> James Van Allen, *discoverer of the Earth's radiation belts,* has decried the expense of the manned space program.

Use appositives to identify authors whom you quote.

Incorporating Quotations into Your Sentences

QUOTING ONLY THE PART OF A SENTENCE OR PARAGRAPH THAT YOU NEED

We've said that a writer selects passages for quotation that are especially *vivid and memorable, concise, or authoritative.* Now put these principles into practice. Suppose that while conducting research on college sports you've come across the following, written by Robert Hutchins, former president of the University of Chicago:

> If athleticism is bad for students, players, alumni and the public, it is even worse for the colleges and universities themselves. They want to be educational institutions, but they can't. The story of the famous halfback whose only regret, when he bade his coach farewell, was that he hadn't learned to read and write is probably exaggerated. But we must admit that pressure from trustees, graduates, "friends," presidents and even professors has tended to relax academic standards. These gentry often overlook the fact that a college should not be interested in a fullback who is a half-wit. Recruiting, subsidizing and the double educational standard cannot exist without the knowledge and the tacit approval, at least, of the colleges and universities themselves. Certain institutions encourage susceptible professors to be nice to athletes now admitted by paying them for serving as "faculty representatives" on the college athletic board.[4]

Suppose that in this entire paragraph you find a gem, a sentence with quotable words that will enliven your discussion. You may want to quote part of the following sentence:

> These gentry often overlook the fact that a college should not be interested in a fullback who is a half-wit.

INCORPORATING THE QUOTATION INTO THE FLOW OF YOUR OWN SENTENCE

Once you've selected the passage you want to quote, work the material into your paper in as natural and fluid a manner as possible. Here's how we would quote Hutchins:

---

[4]Robert Hutchins, "Gate Receipts and Glory," *The Saturday Evening Post.* December 3, 1983.

> Robert Hutchins, a former president of the University of Chicago, asserts that "a college should not be interested in a fullback who is a half-wit."

Note that we've used an appositive to identify Hutchins. And we've used only the part of the paragraph—a single clause—that we thought memorable enough to quote directly.

AVOIDING FREESTANDING QUOTATIONS

A quoted sentence should never stand by itself—as in the following example:

> Various people associated with the university admit that the pressures of athleticism have caused a relaxation of standards. "These gentry often overlook the fact that a college should not be interested in a fullback who is a half-wit." But this kind of thinking is bad for the university and even worse for the athletes.

Even if it includes a parenthetical citation, a freestanding quotation would have the problem of being jarring to the reader. Introduce the quotation by attributing the source not in a parenthetical citation, but in some other part of the sentence—beginning, middle, or end. Thus, you could write:

> According to Robert Hutchins, "These gentry often overlook the fact that a college should not be interested in a fullback who is a half-wit."

A variation:

> "These gentry," asserts Robert Hutchins, "often overlook the fact that a college should not be interested in a fullback who is a half-wit."

Another alternative is to introduce a sentence-long quotation with a colon:

> But Robert Hutchins disagrees: "These gentry often overlook the fact that a college should not be interested in a fullback who is a half-wit."

Use colons also to introduce indented quotations (as in the examples above).

When attributing sources, try to vary the standard "states," "writes," "says," and so on. Other, stronger verbs you might consider: "asserts," "argues," "maintains," "insists," "asks," and even "wonders."

USING ELLIPSIS MARKS

Using quotations is made somewhat complicated when you want to quote the beginning and end of a passage but not its middle—as was the case when we quoted Henry David Thoreau. Here's part of the paragraph in *Walden* from which we quoted a few sentences:

> To read well, that is, to read true books in a true spirit, is a noble exercise, and one that will task the reader more than any exercise which the customs of the day esteem. It requires a training such as the athletes underwent, the steady in-

> tention almost of the whole life to this object. Books must be read as deliberately and reservedly as they were written.[5]

And here was how we used this material:

> Reading well is hard work and requires great skill and training. It "is a noble exercise," writes Henry David Thoreau in *Walden,* "and one that will task the reader more than any exercise which the customs of the day esteem. It requires a training such as the athletes underwent. . . . Books must be read as deliberately and reservedly as they were written."

Whenever you quote a sentence but delete words from it, as we have done, indicate this deletion to the reader by placing an ellipsis mark, three spaced periods, in the sentence at the point of deletion. The rationale for using an ellipsis mark is that a direct quotation must be reproduced *exactly* as it was written or spoken. When writers delete or change any part of the quoted material, readers must be alerted so they don't think the changes were part of the original. Ellipsis marks and brackets serve this purpose.

If you are deleting the middle of a single sentence, use an ellipsis in place of the deleted words:

> "To read well . . . is a noble exercise, and one that will task the reader more than any exercise which the customs of the day esteem."

If you are deleting the end of a quoted sentence, or if you are deleting entire sentences of a paragraph before continuing a quotation, add a period before the ellipsis:

> "It requires a training such as the athletes underwent. . . . Books must be read as deliberately and reservedly as they were written."

If you begin your quotation of an author in the middle of a sentence, you need not indicate deleted words with an ellipsis. Be sure, however, that the syntax of the quotation fits smoothly with the syntax of your sentence:

> Reading "is a noble exercise," writes Henry David Thoreau.

USING BRACKETS

Use square brackets whenever you need to add or substitute words in a quoted sentence. The brackets indicate to the reader a word or phrase that does not appear in the original passage but that you have inserted to avoid confusion. For example, when a pronoun's antecedent would be unclear to readers, delete the pronoun from the sentence and substitute an identifying word or phrase in brackets. When you make such a substitution, no ellipsis marks are needed. Assume that you wish to quote the underlined sentence in the following passage:

> Golden Press's *Walt Disney's Cinderella* set the new pattern for America's Cinderella. This book's text is coy and condescending. (Sample: "And her best

---

[5]Henry David Thoreau, "Reading" in *Walden.* New York: Signet Classic, 1960, p. 72.

> friends of all were—guess who—the mice!") The illustrations are poor cartoons. And Cinderella herself is a disaster. She cowers as her sisters rip her homemade ball gown to shreds. (Not even homemade by Cinderella, but by the mice and birds.) She answers her stepmother with whines and pleadings. She is a sorry excuse for a heroine, pitiable and useless. She cannot perform even a simple action to save herself, though she is warned by her friends, the mice. She does not hear them because she is "off in a world of dreams." Cinderella begs, she whimpers, and at last has to be rescued by—guess who—the mice![6]

In quoting this sentence, you would need to identify whom the pronoun *she* refers to. You can do this inside the quotation by using brackets:

> Jane Yolen believes that "[Cinderella] is a sorry excuse for a heroine, pitiable and useless."

If the pronoun begins the sentence to be quoted, as it does in this example, you can identify the pronoun outside of the quotation and simply begin quoting your source one word later:

> Jane Yolen believes that Cinderella "is a sorry excuse for a heroine, pitiable and useless."

If the pronoun you want to identify occurs in the middle of the sentence to be quoted, then you'll need to use brackets. Newspaper reporters do this frequently when quoting sources, who in interviews might say something like the following:

> After the fire they did not return to the station house for three hours.

If the reporter wants to use this sentence in an article, he or she needs to identify the pronoun:

> An official from City Hall, speaking on the condition that he not be identified, said, "After the fire [the officers] did not return to the station house for three hours."

You also will need to add bracketed information to a quoted sentence when a reference essential to the sentence's meaning is implied but not stated directly. Read the following paragraphs from Robert Jastrow's "Toward an Intelligence Beyond Man's":

> These are amiable qualities for the computer; it imitates life like an electronic monkey. As computers get more complex, the imitation gets better. Finally, the line between the original and the copy becomes blurred. In another 15 years or so—two more generations of computer evolution, in the jargon of the technologists—we will see the computer as an emergent form of life.
>
> The proposition seems ridiculous because, for one thing, computers lack the drives and emotions of living creatures. But when drives are useful, they can be programmed into the computer's brain, just as nature programmed them into our ancestors' brains as a part of the equipment for survival. For example, computers,

[6]Jane Yolen, "America's 'Cinderella,'" APS Publications, Inc. in *Children's Literature in Education* 8, 1977, pp. 21–29.

> like people, work better and learn faster when they are motivated. Arthur Samuel made this discovery when he taught two IBM computers how to play checkers. They polished their game by playing each other, but they learned slowly. Finally, Dr. Samuel programmed in the will to win by forcing the computers to try harder—and to think out more moves in advance—when they were losing. Then the computers learned very quickly. One of them beat Samuel and went on to defeat a champion player who had not lost a game to a human opponent in eight years.[7]

If you wanted to quote only the underlined sentence, you would need to provide readers with a bracketed explanation; otherwise, the words "the proposition" would be unclear. Here is how you would manage the quotation:

> According to Robert Jastrow, a physicist and former official at NASA's Goddard Institute, "The proposition [that computers will emerge as a form of life] seems ridiculous because, for one thing, computers lack the drives and emotions of living creatures."

Remember that when you quote the work of another, you are obligated to credit—or cite—the author's work properly; otherwise, you may be guilty of plagiarism. See pages 182–98 for guidance on citing sources.

▼

WRITING INTRODUCTIONS

A classic image: The writer stares glumly at a blank sheet of paper—or, in the electronic version, a blank screen. Usually, however, this is an image of a writer who hasn't yet begun to write. Once the piece has been started, momentum often helps to carry it forward, even over the rough spots, which can always be fixed later. As a writer, you've surely discovered that getting started when you haven't yet warmed to your task *is* a problem. What's the best way to approach your subject? With high seriousness, a light touch, an anecdote? How best to engage your reader?

Many writers avoid such agonizing choices by putting them off—productively. Bypassing the introduction, they start by writing the body of the piece; only after they're finished the body do they go back to write the introduction. There's a lot to be said for this approach. Because you have presumably spent more time thinking about the topic itself than about how you're going to introduce it, you are in a better position to begin directly with your presentation. And often, it's not until you've actually seen the piece on paper and read it over once or twice that a "natural" way of introducing it becomes apparent. Even if there is no natural way to begin, you are generally in better psychological shape to write the introduction after the major task of writing is behind you and you know exactly what you're leading up to.

---

[7]Excerpt from "Toward an Intelligence Beyond Man's" from *Time,* February 20, 1978.

Perhaps, however, you can't operate this way. After all, you have to start writing *somewhere,* and if you have evaded the problem by skipping the introduction, that blank page may loom just as large whenever you do choose to begin. If this is the case, then go ahead and write an introduction, knowing full well that it's probably going to be flat and awful. Set down any kind of pump-priming or throat-clearing verbiage that comes to mind, as long as you have a working thesis. Assure yourself that whatever you put down at this point (except for the thesis) "won't count" and that when the time is right, you'll go back and replace it with something that's fit for eyes other than yours. But in the meantime, you'll have gotten started.

The *purpose* of an introduction is to prepare the reader to enter the world of your essay. The introduction makes the connection between the more familiar world inhabited by the reader and the less familiar world of the writer's particular subject; it places a discussion in a context that the reader can understand.

There are many ways to provide such a context. We'll consider just a few of the most common.

Quotation

Here is an introduction to a paper on democracy:

> "Two cheers for democracy" was E. M. Forster's not-quite-wholehearted judgment. Most Americans would not agree. To them, our democracy is one of the glories of civilization. To one American in particular, E. B. White, democracy is "the hole in the stuffed shirt through which the sawdust slowly trickles . . . the dent in the high hat . . . the recurrent suspicion that more than half of the people are right more than half of the time" (915). American democracy is based on the oldest continuously operating written constitution in the world—a most impressive fact and a testament to the farsightedness of the founding fathers. But just how farsighted can mere humans be? In *Future Shock,* Alvin Toffler quotes economist Kenneth Boulding on the incredible acceleration of social change in our time: "The world of today . . . is as different from the world in which I was born as that world was from Julius Caesar's" (13). As we move toward the twenty-first century, it seems legitimate to question the continued effectiveness of a governmental system that was devised in the eighteenth century; and it seems equally legitimate to consider alternatives.

The quotations by Forster and White help set the stage for the discussion of democracy by presenting the reader with some provocative and well-phrased remarks. Later in the paragraph, the quotation by Boulding more specifically prepares us for the theme of change that will be central to the essay as a whole.

Historical Review

In many cases, the reader will be unprepared to follow the issue you discuss unless you provide some historical background. Consider the following introduction to an essay on the film-rating system:

> Sex and violence on the screen are not new issues. In the Roaring Twenties there was increasing pressure from civic and religious groups to ban depictions of "immorality" from the screen. Faced with the threat of federal censorship, the film producers decided to clean their own house. In 1930, the Motion Picture Producers and Distributors of America established the Production Code. At first, adherence to the Code was voluntary; but in 1934 Joseph Breen, newly appointed head of the MPPDA, gave the Code teeth. Henceforth all newly produced films had to be submitted for approval to the Production Code Administration, which had the power to award or withhold the Code seal. Without a Code seal, it was virtually impossible for a film to be shown anywhere in the United States, since exhibitors would not accept it. At about the same time, the Catholic Legion of Decency was formed to advise the faithful which films were and were not objectionable. For several decades the Production Code Administration exercised powerful control over what was portrayed in American theatrical films. By the 1960s, however, changing standards of morality had considerably weakened the Code's grip. In 1968, the Production Code was replaced with a rating system designed to keep younger audiences away from films with high levels of sex or violence. Despite its imperfections, this rating system has proved more beneficial to American films than did the old censorship system.

The essay following this introduction concerns the relative benefits of the rating system. By providing some historical background on the rating system, the writer helps readers to understand his arguments. Notice the chronological development of details.

Review of a Controversy

A particular type of historical review is the review of a controversy or debate. Consider the following introduction:

> The *American Heritage Dictionary*'s definition of civil disobedience is rather simple: "the refusal to obey civil laws that are regarded as unjust, usually by employing methods of passive resistance." However, despite such famous (and beloved) examples of civil disobedience as the movements of Mahatma Gandhi in India and the Reverend Martin Luther King, Jr., in the United States, the question of whether or not civil disobedience should be considered an asset to society is hardly clear cut. For instance, Hannah Arendt, in her article "Civil Disobedience," holds that "to think of disobedient minorities as rebels and truants is against the letter and spirit of a constitution whose framers were especially sensitive to the dangers of unbridled majority rule." On the other hand, a noted lawyer, Lewis Van Dusen, Jr., in his article "Civil Disobedience: Destroyer of Democracy," states that "civil disobedience, whatever the ethical rationalization, is still an assault on our democratic society, an affront to our legal order and an attack on our constitutional government." These two views are clearly incompatible. I believe, though, that Van Dusen's is the more convincing. On balance, civil disobedience is dangerous to society.[8]

---

[8]Michele Jacques, "Civil Disobedience: Van Dusen vs. Arendt." [Unpublished paper. Used by permission.]

The negative aspects of civil disobedience, rather than Van Dusen's essay, are the topic of this essay. But to introduce this topic, the writer has provided quotations that represent opposing sides of the controversy over civil disobedience, as well as brief references to two controversial practitioners. By focusing at the outset on the particular rather than the abstract aspects of the subject, the writer hoped to secure the attention of her readers and to involve them in the controversy that forms the subject of her essay.

From the General to the Specific

Another way of providing a transition from the reader's world to the less familiar world of the essay is to work from a general subject to a specific one. The following introduction to a discussion of the 1968 massacre at My Lai, Vietnam, begins with general statements and leads to the particular subject at hand:

> Though we prefer to think of man as basically good and reluctant to do evil, such is not the case. Many of the crimes inflicted on humankind can be dismissed as being committed by the degenerates of society at the prompting of the abnormal mind. But what of the perfectly "normal" man or woman who commits inhumane acts simply because he or she has been ordered to do so? It cannot be denied that such acts have occurred, either in everyday life or in war-time situations. Unfortunately, even normal, well-adjusted people can become cruel, inhumane, and destructive if placed in the hands of unscrupulous authority. Such was the case in the village of My Lai, Vietnam, on March 16, 1968, when a platoon of American soldiers commanded by Lt. William Calley massacred more than 100 civilians, including women and children.

From the Specific to the General: Anecdote, Illustration

Consider the following paragraph:

> In late 1971 astronomer Carl Sagan and his colleagues were studying data transmitted from the planet Mars to the earth by the Mariner 9 spacecraft. Struck by the effects of the Martian dust storms on the temperature and on the amount of light reaching the surface, the scientists wondered about the effects on earth of the dust storms that would be created by nuclear explosions. Using computer models, they simulated the effects of such explosions on the earth's climate. The results astounded them. Apart from the known effects of nuclear blasts (fires and radiation), the earth, they discovered, would become enshrouded in a "nuclear winter." Following a nuclear exchange, plummeting temperatures and pervading darkness would destroy most of the Northern Hemisphere's crops and farm animals and would eventually render much of the planet's surface uninhabitable. The effects of nuclear war, apparently, would be more catastrophic than had previously been imagined. It has therefore become more urgent than ever for the nations of the world to take dramatic steps to reduce the threat of nuclear war.

The previous introduction went from the general (the question of whether or not man is basically good) to the specific (the massacre at My Lai); this one goes from the specific (scientists studying data) to the general (the urgency of reducing the nuclear threat). The anecdote is one of the most effective means at your disposal of capturing and holding your reader's attention. For decades, speakers have begun their general remarks with a funny, touching, or otherwise appropriate story; in fact, there are plenty of books that are nothing but collections of such stories, arranged by subject.

Question

Frequently, you can provoke the reader's attention by posing a question or a series of questions:

> Are gender roles learned or inherited? Scientific research has established the existence of biological differences between the sexes, but the effect of biology's influence on gender roles cannot be distinguished from society's influence. According to Michael Lewis of the Institute for the Study of Exceptional Children, "As early as you can show me a sex difference, I can show you the culture at work." Social processes, as well as biological differences, are responsible for the separate roles of men and women.[9]

Opening your essay with a question can be provocative, since it places the reader in an active role: He or she begins by considering answers. *Are* gender roles learned? *Are* they inherited? In this active role, the reader is likely to continue reading with interest.

Statement of Thesis

Perhaps the most direct method of introduction is to begin immediately with the thesis:

> Computers are a mixed blessing. The lives of Americans are becoming increasingly involved with machines that think for them. "We are at the dawn of the era of the smart machine," say the authors of a cover story on the subject in *Newsweek,* "that will change forever the way an entire nation works," beginning a revolution that will be to the brain what the industrial revolution was to the hand. Tiny silicon chips already process enough information to direct air travel, to instruct machines how to cut fabric—even to play chess with (and defeat) the masters. One can argue that development of computers for the household, as well as industry, will change for the better the quality of our lives: computers help us save energy, reduce the amount of drudgery that most of us endure around tax season, make access to libraries easier. Yet there is a certain danger involved with this proliferation of technology.

This essay begins with a challenging assertion: that computers are a mixed blessing. It is one that many readers are perhaps unprepared to consider, since they may have taken it for granted that computers are an unmixed blessing. The advantage of beginning with a provocative (thesis) statement is that it forces the reader to sit up and take notice—perhaps even to begin protesting.

---

[9]Tammy Smith, "Are Sex Roles Learned or Inherited?" [Unpublished paper. Used by permission.]

The paragraph goes on to concede some of the "blessings" of computerization but then concludes with the warning that there is "a certain danger" associated with the new technology—a danger, the curious or indignant reader has a right to conclude, that will be more fully explained in the paragraphs to follow.

One final note about our model introductions: They may be longer than introductions you have been accustomed to writing. Many writers (and readers) prefer shorter, snappier introductions. This is largely a matter of personal or corporate style: there is no rule concerning the correct length of an introduction. If you feel that a short introduction is appropriate, use one. You may wish to break up what seems like a long introduction into two paragraphs. (Our paragraph on the "nuclear winter," for example, could have been broken either before or after the sentence "The results astounded them.")

WRITING CONCLUSIONS

One way to view the conclusion of your paper is as an introduction worked in reverse, a bridge from the world of your essay back to the world of your reader. A conclusion is the part of your paper in which you restate and (if necessary) expand on your thesis. Essential to any conclusion is the summary, which is not merely a repetition of the thesis but a restatement that takes advantage of the material you've presented. *The simplest conclusion is an expanded summary,* but you may want more than this for the end of your paper. Depending on your needs, you might offer a summary and then build onto it a discussion of the paper's significance or its implications for future study, for choices that individuals might make, for policy, and so on. You might also want to urge the reader to change an attitude or to modify behavior. Certainly, you are under no obligation to discuss the broader significance of your work (and a summary, alone, will satisfy the formal requirement that your paper have an ending); but the conclusions of better papers often reveal authors who are "thinking large" and want to connect the particular concerns of their papers with the broader concerns of society.

Here we'll consider seven strategies for expanding the basic summary–conclusion. But two words of advice are in order. First, no matter how clever or beautifully executed, a conclusion cannot salvage a poorly written paper. Second, by virtue of its placement, the conclusion carries rhetorical weight. It is the last statement a reader will encounter before turning from your work. Realizing this, writers who expand on the basic summary–conclusion often wish to give their final words a dramatic flourish, a heightened level of diction. Soaring rhetoric and drama in a conclusion are fine as long as they do not unbalance the paper and call attention to themselves. Having labored long hours over your paper, you have every right to wax eloquent. But keep a sense of proportion and timing. Make your points quickly and end crisply.

Statement of the Subject's Significance

One of the more effective ways to conclude a paper is to discuss the larger significance of what you have written, providing readers with one more reason to regard your work as a serious effort. When using this strategy, you move from the specific concern of your paper to the broader concerns of the reader's world. Often, you will need to choose among a range of significances: A paper on the Wright brothers might end with a discussion of air travel as it affects economies, politics, or families; a paper on contraception might end with a discussion of its effect on sexual mores, population, or the church. But don't overwhelm your reader with the importance of your remarks. Keep your discussion well focused.

The following paragraphs conclude a paper on George H. Shull, a pioneer in the inbreeding and crossbreeding of corn:

> . . . Thus, the hybrids developed and described by Shull 75 years ago have finally dominated U.S. corn production.
>
> The adoption of hybrid corn was steady and dramatic in the Corn Belt. From 1930 through 1979 the average yields of corn in the U.S. increased from 21.9 to 95.1 bushels per acre, and the additional value to the farmer is now several billion dollars per year.
>
> The success of hybrid corn has also stimulated the breeding of other crops, such as sorghum hybrids, a major feed grain crop in arid parts of the world. Sorghum yields have increased 300 percent since 1930. Approximately 20 percent of the land devoted to rice production in China is planted with hydrid seed, which is reported to yield 20 percent more than the best varieties. And many superior varieties of tomatoes, cucumbers, spinach, and other vegetables are hybrids. Today virtually all corn produced in the developed countries is from hybrid seed. From those blue bloods of the plant kingdom has come a model for feeding the world.[10]

The first sentence of this conclusion is a summary, and from it the reader can infer that the paper included a discussion of Shull's techniques for the hybrid breeding of corn. The summary is followed by a two-paragraph discussion on the significance of Shull's research for feeding the world.

Call for Further Research

In the scientific and social scientific communities, papers often end with a review of what has been presented (as, for instance, in an experiment) and the ways in which the subject under consideration needs to be further explored. If you raise questions that you call on others to answer, however, make sure you know that the research you are calling for hasn't already been conducted.

---

[10]From "Hybrid Vim and Vigor" by William L. Brown from pp. 77–78 in *Science 80–85*. November 1984. Copyright 1984 by the AAAS. Reprinted by permission.

This next conclusion comes from a sociological report on the placement of elderly men and women in nursing homes.

> Thus, our study shows a correlation between the placement of elderly citizens in nursing facilities and the significant decline of their motor and intellectual skills over the ten months following placement. What the research has not made clear is the extent to which this marked decline is due to physical as opposed to emotional causes. The elderly are referred to homes at that point in their lives when they grow less able to care for themselves—which suggests that the drop-off in skills may be due to physical causes. But the emotional stress of being placed in a home, away from family and in an environment that confirms the patient's view of himself as decrepit, may exacerbate—if not itself be a primary cause of—the patient's rapid loss of abilities. Further research is needed to clarify the relationship between depression and particular physical ailments as these affect the skills of the elderly in nursing facilities. There is little doubt that information yielded by such studies can enable health care professionals to deliver more effective services.

Notice how this call for further study locates the author in a large community of researchers on whom she depends for assistance in answering the questions that have come out of her own work. The author summarizes her findings (in the first sentence of the paragraph), states what her work has not shown, and then extends her invitation.

Solution/Recommendation

The purpose of your paper might be to review a problem or controversy and to discuss contributing factors. In such a case, it would be appropriate, after summarizing your discussion, to offer a solution based on the knowledge you've gained while conducting research. If your solution is to be taken seriously, your knowledge must be amply demonstrated in the body of the paper.

> . . . The major problem in college sports today is not commercialism—it is the exploitation of athletes and the proliferation of illicit practices which dilute educational standards.
>
> Many universities are currently deriving substantial benefits from sports programs that depend on the labor of athletes drawn from the poorest sections of America's population. It is the responsibility of educators, civil rights leaders, and concerned citizens to see that these young people get a fair return for their labor both in terms of direct remuneration and in terms of career preparation for a life outside sports.
>
> Minimally, scholarships in revenue-producing sports should be designed to extend until graduation, rather than covering only four years of athletic eligibility, and should include guarantees of tutoring, counseling, and proper medical care. At institutions where the profits are particularly large (such as Texas A & M, which can afford to pay its football coach $280,000 a year), scholarships should also provide salaries that extend beyond room, board, and tuition. The important thing is that the athlete be remunerated fairly and have the opportunity to gain skills from a university environment without undue competition from a physically and psychologically demanding full-time job. This may well require that scholarships be extended over five or six years, including summers.

> Such a proposal, I suspect, will not be easy to implement. The current amateur system, despite its moral and educational flaws, enables universities to hire their athletic labor at minimal cost. But solving the fiscal crisis of the universities on the backs of America's poor and minorities is not, in the long run, a tenable solution. With the support of concerned educators, parents, and civil rights leaders, and with the help from organized labor, the college athlete, truly a sleeping giant, will someday speak out and demand what is rightly his—and hers—a fair share of the revenue created by their hard work.[11]

In this conclusion, the author summarizes his article in one sentence: "The major problem in college sports today is not commercialism—it is the exploitation of athletes and the proliferation of illicit practices which dilute educational standards." In paragraph 2, he continues with an analysis of the problem just stated and follows with a general recommendation—that "concerned educators, parents, and civil rights leaders" be responsible for the welfare of college athletes. In paragraph 3, he makes a specific proposal, and in the final paragraph, he anticipates resistance to the proposal. He concludes by discounting this resistance and returning to the general point, that college athletes should receive a fair deal.

Anecdote

An anecdote is a briefly told story or joke, the point of which in a conclusion is to shed light on your subject. The anecdote is more direct than an allusion. With an allusion, you merely refer to a story ("Too many people today live in Plato's cave . . ."); with the anecdote, you actually retell the story. The anecdote allows readers to discover for themselves the significance of a reference to another source—an effort most readers enjoy because they get to exercise their creativity.

The following anecdote concludes an article on homicide. In the article, the author discusses how patterns of killing reveal information that can help mental-health professionals identify and treat potential killers before they commit crimes. The author emphasizes both the difficulty and the desirability of approaching homicide as a threat to public health that, like disease, can be treated with preventive care.

> In his book, *The Exploits of the Incomparable Mulla Nasrudin,* Sufi writer Idries Shah, in a parable about fate, writes about the many culprits of murder:
>
> "What is Fate?" Nasrudin was asked by a scholar.
>
> "An endless succession of intertwined events, each influencing the other."
>
> "That is hardly a satisfactory answer. I believe in cause and effect."
>
> "Very well," said the Mulla, "Look at that." He pointed to a procession passing in the street.

---

[11]From Mark Naison, "Scenario for Scandal," *Commonweal* 109 *(16),* September 24, 1982. Reprinted by permission.

> "That man is being taken to be hanged. Is that because someone gave him a silver piece and enabled him to buy the knife with which he committed the murder; or because someone saw him do it; or because nobody stopped him?"[12]

The writer chose to conclude the article with this anecdote. She could have developed an interpretation, but this would have spoiled the dramatic value for the reader. The purpose of using an anecdote is to make your point with subtlety, so resist the temptation to interpret. Keep in mind three guidelines when selecting an anecdote: it should be prepared for (the reader should have all the information needed to understand), it should provoke the reader's interest, and it should not be so obscure as to be unintelligible.

Quotation

A favorite concluding device is the quotation—the words of a famous person or an authority in the field on which you are writing. The purpose of quoting another is to link your work to theirs, thereby gaining for your work authority and credibility. The first criterion for selecting a quotation is its suitability to your thesis. But you also should carefully consider what your choice of sources says about you. Suppose you are writing a paper on the American work ethic. If you could use a line by comedian David Letterman or one by the current secretary of labor to make the final point of your conclusion, which would you choose and why? One source may not be inherently more effective than the other, but the choice certainly sets a tone for the paper. Here's an example of a conclusion that employs quotation:

> There is no doubt that machines will get smarter and smarter, even designing their own software and making new and better chips for new generations of computers. . . . More and more of their power will be devoted to making them easier to use—"friendly," in industry parlance—even for those not trained in computer science. And computer scientists expect that public ingenuity will come up with applications the most visionary researchers have not even considered. One day, a global network of smart machines will be exchanging rapid-fire burst of information at unimaginable speeds. If they are used wisely, they could help mankind to educate its masses and crack new scientific frontiers. "For all of us, it will be fearful, terrifying, disruptive," says SRI's Peter Schwartz. "In the end there will be those whose lives will be diminished. But for the vast majority, their lives will be greatly enhanced." In any event, there is no turning back: if the smart machines have not taken over, they are fast making themselves indispensable—and in the end, that may amount to very much the same thing.[13]

Notice how the quotation is used to position the writer to make one final remark.

Particularly effective quotations may themselves be used to end an essay, as in the following example. Make sure you identify the person you've

---

[12]From "The Murder Epidemic" by Nikki Meredith from pp. 42–48 in *Science 80–85*. December 1984. Copyright by AAAS. Reprinted by permission of the author.

[13]From "And Man Created the Chip," *Newsweek*, June 30, 1980. Copyright © 1980 by Newsweek, Inc. All rights reserved. Reprinted by permission.

quoted, although the identification does not need to be made in the conclusion itself. For example, earlier in the paper from which the following conclusion was taken, Maureen Henderson was identified as an epidemiologist exploring the ways in which a change in diet can prevent the onset of certain cancers.

> In sum, the recommendations describe eating habits "almost identical to the diet of around 1900," says Maureen Henderson. "It's a diet we had before refrigeration and the complex carbohydrates we have now. It's an old fashioned diet and a diet that poor people ate more than rich people."
>
> Some cancer researchers wonder whether people will be willing to change their diets or take pills on the chance of preventing cancer, when one-third of the people in the country won't even stop smoking. Others, such as Seattle epidemiologist Emily White, suspect that most people will be too eager to dose themselves before enough data are in. "We're not here to convince the public to take anything," she says. "The public is too eager already. What we're saying is, 'Let us see if some of these things work.' We want to convince ourselves before we convince the public."[14]

There is a potential problem with using quotations: If you end with the words of another, you may leave the impression that someone else can make your case more eloquently than you can. The language of the quotation will put your own prose into relief. If your own prose suffers by comparison—if the quotations are the best part of your paper—you'd be wise to spend some time revising. The way to avoid this kind of problem is to make your own presentation strong.

Question

Questions are useful for opening essays, and they are just as useful for closing them. Opening and closing questions function in different ways, however. The introductory question promises to be addressed in the paper that follows. But the concluding question leaves issues unresolved, calling on the readers to assume an active role by offering their own solutions:

> How do we surmount the reaction that threatens to destroy the very gains we thought we had already won in the first stage of the women's movement? How do we surmount our own reaction, which shadows our feminism and our femininity (we blush even to use that word now)? How do we transcend the polarization between women and women and between women and men to achieve the new human wholeness that is the promise of feminism, and get on with solving the concrete, practical, everyday problems of living, working and loving as equal persons? This is the personal and political business of the second stage.[15]

Perhaps you will choose to raise a question in your conclusion and then answer it, based on the material you've provided in the paper. The answered

---

[14]Reprinted by permission. From the September issue of *Science '84*. Copyright © 1984 by the American Association for the Advancement of Science.

[15]Betty Friedan, "Feminism's Next Step" in *The Second Stage*. New York: Summit Books, 1981.

question challenges a reader to agree or disagree with your response and thus also places the reader in an active role. The following brief conclusion ends an article entitled "Would an Intelligent Computer Have a 'Right to Life'?"

> So the answer to the question "Would an intelligent computer have the right to life?" is probably that it would, but only if it could discover reasons and conditions under which it would give up its life if called upon to do so—which would make computer intelligence as precious a thing as human intelligence.[16]

Speculation

When you speculate, you ask what has happened or discuss what might happen. This kind of question stimulates the reader because its subject is the unknown.

The following paragraph concludes "The New Generation Gap" by Neil Howe and William Strauss. In this essay, Howe and Strauss discuss the differences among Americans of various ages, including the "GI Generation" (born between 1901 and 1924), the "Boomers" (born 1943–1961), the "Thirteeners" (born 1961–1981), and the "Millennials" (born 1981–2000):

> If, slowly but surely, Millennials receive the kind of family protection and public generosity that GIs enjoyed as children, then they could come of age early in the next century as a group much like the GIs of the 1920s and 1930s—as a stellar (if bland) generation of rationalists, team players, and can-do civic builders. Two decades from now Boomers entering old age may well see in their grown Millennial children an effective instrument for saving the world, while Thirteeners entering midlife will shower kindness on a younger generation that is getting a better deal out of life (though maybe a bit less fun) than they ever got at a like age. Study after story after column will laud these "best damn kids in the world" as heralding a resurgent American greatness. And, for a while at least, no one will talk about a generation gap.[17]

Thus, Howe and Strauss conclude an essay concerned largely with the apparently unbridgable gaps of understanding between parents and childen with a hopeful speculation that generational relationships will improve considerably in the next two decades.

---

[16]Robert E. Mueller and Eric T. Mueller, "Would an Intelligent Computer Have a 'Right to Life'?" *Creative Computing*. August 1983.

[17]Excerpt from "The New Generation Gap" by Neil Howe and William Strauss. Originally appeared in *Atlantic*, Dcember 1992. Reprinted by permission of Raphael Sagalyn, Inc.

3
Critical Reading and Critique

CRITICAL READING

When writing papers in college, you are often called on to respond critically to source materials. Critical reading requires the abilities to both summarize and evaluate a presentation. As you have seen, a *summary* is a brief restatement in your own words of the content of a passage. An *evaluation* is a more difficult matter. In your college work, you read to gain and *use* new information; but as sources are not equally valid or equally useful, you must learn to distinguish critically among sources by evaluating them.

There is no ready-made formula for determining validity. Critical reading and its written analogue—the *critique*—require discernment, sensitivity, imagination, and, above all, a willingness to become involved in what you read. These skills cannot be taken for granted and must be developed through repeated practice. You must begin somewhere, though, and we recommend that you start by posing two broad categories of questions about passages, articles, and books that you read: (1) What is the author's purpose in writing? Does he or she succeed in this purpose? (2) To what extent do you agree with the author?

Question Category 1: What Is the Author's Purpose in Writing? Does He or She Succeed in This Purpose?

All critical reading *begins with an accurate summary.* Before attempting an evaluation, you must be able to locate an author's thesis and identify the selection's content and structure. You must understand the author's *purpose.* Authors write to inform, to persuade, and to entertain. A given piece may be *primarily informative* (a summary of the reasons for the rapid spread of AIDS), *primarily persuasive* (an argument on why the government must do something about poverty), or *primarily entertaining* (a play about the frustrations of young lovers), or it may be all three (as in John Steinbeck's novel *The*

Grapes of Wrath, about migrant workers during the Great Depression). Sometimes authors are not fully conscious of their purposes. Sometimes their purposes change as they write. But if the finished piece is coherent, it will have a primary reason for having been written, and it should be apparent that the author is attempting primarily to inform, persuade, or entertain you. To identify this primary reason, this purpose, is your first job as a critical reader. Your next job is to determine how successful the author has been. As a critical reader, you bring different criteria, or standards of judgment, to bear when you read pieces intended to inform or persuade.

Informative Writing

A piece intended to inform will provide definitions, describe or report on a process, recount a story, give historical background, and/or provide facts and figures. An informational piece responds to questions like the following:

> What (or who) is___________?
> How does ___________ work?
> What is the controversy or problem about?
> What happened?
> How and why did it happen?
> What were the results?
> What are the arguments for and against ___________?

To the extent that an author answers these and related questions and the answers are a matter of verifiable record (you could check for accuracy if you had the time and inclination), the selection is intended to inform. Having determined this, you can organize your response by considering three other criteria: accuracy, significance, and fair interpretation of information.

ACCURACY OF INFORMATION. If you are going to use any of the information presented, you must be satisfied that it is trustworthy. One of your responsibilities as a critical reader is to find out if it is.

SIGNIFICANCE OF INFORMATION. One useful question that you can put to a reading is, "So what?" In the case of selections that attempt to inform, you may reasonably wonder whether the information makes a difference. What can the person who is reading gain from this information? How is knowledge advanced by the publication of this material? Is the information of importance to you or to others? Why or why not?

FAIR INTERPRETATION OF INFORMATION. At times you will read reports, the sole function of which is to relate raw data or information. In these cases, you will build your response on the two questions in question category 1. More frequently, once an author has presented information, he or she will attempt to evaluate or interpret it—which is only reasonable, since information that has not been evaluated or interpreted is of little use. One of your tasks as a critical reader is to make a distinction between the author's presentation of facts and figures and his or her attempts to evaluate them. You may find that the information is valuable but the interpretation is not. Perhaps the author's conclusions are not justified. Could you offer a contrary explanation for the same facts? Does more information need to be gathered before conclusions can be drawn? Why?

Persuasive Writing

Writing is frequently intended to persuade—that is, to influence the reader's thinking. To make a persuasive case, the writer must begin with an assertion that is arguable, some statement about which reasonable people could disagree. Such an assertion, when it serves as the essential organizing principle of the article or book, is called a *thesis.* Examples:

> Because they do not speak English, many children in this affluent land are being denied their fundamental right to equal educational opportunity.

> Bilingual education, which has been stridently promoted by a small group of activists with their own agenda, is detrimental to the very students it is supposed to serve.

Thesis statements like this—and the subsidiary assertions used to help support them—represent conclusions that authors have drawn as a result of researching and thinking about the issue. You go through the same process yourself when you write persuasive papers or critiques. And just as you are entitled to critically evaluate the assertions of authors you read, so your professors—and other students—are entitled to evaluate *your* assertions, whether they are encountered as written arguments or as comments made in class discussion.

Keep in mind that writers organize arguments by arranging evidence to support one conclusion and oppose (or dismiss) another. You can assess the validity of the argument and the conclusion by determining whether the author has (1) clearly defined key terms, (2) used information fairly, (3) argued logically, and not fallaciously.

CLEARLY DEFINED TERMS. The validity of an argument depends to some degree on how carefully key terms have been defined. Take the assertion, for example—made in the 1930s by the official motion-picture production code—that no film should be made that will "lower the moral standards of those who see it." What do the authors of this code mean by "lower the moral standards"? The validity of their argument depends on whether or not they and their readers agree on a definition of moral standards and on a definition of lowered moral standards. If an author writes, "The public safety demands that reasonable precautions be taken to protect the public against infection from HIV-positive persons," readers need to know what, exactly, is meant by "reasonable" before they can assess the validity of the argument. An author who writes, "Some cultures are better than others" must be careful to define just what she means by "better." (We may not agree with her definition, but at least it is now on the table, a subject for discussion.) In such cases, the success of the argument—its ability to persuade—hinges on the definition of a term. So, in responding to an argument, be sure you (and the author) are clear on what exactly is being argued. Only then can you respond to the logic of the argument, to the author's use of evidence, and to the author's conclusions.

FAIR USE OF INFORMATION. Information is used as evidence in support of arguments. When presented with such evidence, ask yourself two questions: The *first:* "Is the information accurate and up-to-date?" At least a portion of an argument is rendered invalid if the information used to support it is inaccurate or out-of-date. The *second*: "Has the author cited *representative* information?" The evidence used in an argument must be presented in a spirit of fair play. An author is less than ethical who presents only evidence favoring his views when he is well aware that contrary evidence exists. For instance, it would be dishonest to argue that an economic recession is imminent and to cite as evidence only those indicators of economic well-being that have taken a decided turn for the worse while ignoring and failing to cite contrary (positive) evidence.

LOGICAL ARGUMENTATION; AVOIDING LOGICAL FALLACIES. At some point, you will need to respond to the logic of the argument itself. To be convincing, an argument should be governed by principles of logic—clear and orderly thinking. This does *not* mean that an argument should not be biased. A biased argument—that is, an argument weighted toward one point of view and against others—may be valid as long as it is logically sound.

Here are several examples of faulty thinking and logical fallacies to watch for:

Emotionally Loaded Terms. Writers sometimes will attempt to sway readers by using emotionally charged words: words with positive connotations to sway readers to their own point of view; words with negative connotations to sway readers away from the opposing point of view. For example, look again at the two assertions about bilingual education on page 61. In the first assertion (by Jeffrey W. Kobrick), the terms "fundamental right" and "equal . . . opportunity" carry positive connotations intended to sway the reader to the author's pro-bilingual education view. In the second assertion, the terms "stridently" and "small group of activists" carry negative connotations intended to influence the reader to reject the anti-bilingual arguments with which the author associates them. The fact that an author uses such emotionally loaded terms does not necessarily invalidate the argument. Emotional appeals are perfectly legitimate and time-honored modes of persuasion. But in academic writing, which is grounded in logical argumentation, they should not be the *only* means of persuasion. You should be sensitive to *how* emotionally loaded terms are being used. In particular, are they being used deceptively or to hide the essential facts?

Ad Hominem Argument. In an *ad hominem* argument, the writer rejects opposing views by attacking the person who holds them. By calling opponents names, an author avoids the issue:

> I could more easily accept my opponent's plan to increase revenues by collecting on delinquent tax bills if he had paid more than a hundred dollars in state taxes in each of the past three years. But the fact is, he's a millionaire with a millionaire's tax shelters. This man hasn't paid a wooden nickel for the state services he and his family depend on. So I ask you: Is *he* the one to be talking about taxes to *us?*

It could well be that the opponent has paid virtually no state taxes for three years; but this fact has nothing to do with, and is a ploy to divert attention from, the merits of a specific proposal for increasing revenues. The proposal is lost in the attack against the man himself, an attack that violates the principles of logic. Writers (and speakers) must make their points by citing evidence in support of their views and by challenging contrary evidence.

Faulty Cause and Effect. The fact that one event precedes another in time does not mean that the first event has caused the second. An example: Fish begin dying by the thousands in a lake near your hometown. An environmental group immediately cites chemical dumping by several manufacturing plants as the cause. But other causes are possible: A disease might have affected the fish; the growth of algae might have contributed to the deaths; or acid rain might be a factor. The origins of an event are usually complex and are not always traceable to a single cause. So you must carefully examine cause-and-effect reasoning when you find a writer using it. This fallacy is also known as *post hoc, ergo propter hoc* ("after this, therefore because of this").

Either/Or Reasoning. Either/or reasoning also results from an unwillingness to recognize complexity. If an author analyzes a problem and offers only two explanations, one of which he or she refutes, then you are entitled to object that the other is not thereby true. For usually, several other explanations (at the very least) are possible. For whatever reason, the author has chosen to overlook them. As an example, suppose you are reading a selection on genetic engineering and the author builds an argument on the basis of the following:

> Research in gene splicing is at a crossroads: Either scientists will be carefully monitored by civil authorities and their efforts limited to acceptable applications, such as disease control; or, lacking regulatory guidelines, scientists will set their own ethical standards and begin programs in embryonic manipulation that, however well intended, exceed the proper limits of human knowledge.

Certainly, other possibilities for genetic engineering exist beyond the two mentioned here. But the author limits debate by establishing an either/or choice. Such limitation is artificial and does not allow for complexity. As a critical reader, be on the alert for either/or reasoning.

Hasty Generalization. Writers are guilty of hasty generalization when they draw their conclusions from too little evidence or from unrepresentative evidence. To argue that scientists should not proceed with the human genome project because a recent editorial urged that the project be abandoned is to make a hasty generalization. This lone editorial may be unrepresentative of the views of most people—both scientists and laypeople—who have studied and written about the matter. To argue that one should never obey authority because the Milgram experiment shows the dangers of obeying authority is to ignore the fact that Milgram's experiment was concerned primarily with obedience to *immoral* authority. Thus, the experimental situation was unrepresentative of most routine demands for obedience—for example, to obey a parental rule or to comply with a summons for jury duty—and a conclusion about the malevolence of all authority would be a hasty generalization.

False Analogy. Comparing one person, event, or issue to another may be illuminating, but it also may be confusing or misleading. The differences between the two may be more significant than the similarities, and the conclusions drawn from the one may not necessarily apply to the other. A writer who argues that it is reasonable to quarantine people with AIDS because quarantine has been effective in preventing the spread of smallpox is assuming an analogy between AIDS and smallpox that (because of the differences between the two diseases) is not valid.

Begging the Question. To beg the question is to assume as a proven fact the very thesis being argued. To assert, for example, that America is not in decline because it is as strong and prosperous as ever is not to prove anything: it is merely to repeat the claim in different words. This fallacy is also known as circular reasoning.

Non Sequitur. "Non sequitur" is Latin for "it does not follow"; the term is used to describe a conclusion that does not logically follow from a premise. "Since minorities have made such great strides in the last few decades," a writer may argue, "we no longer need affirmative action programs." Aside from the fact that the premise itself is arguable (*have* minorities made such great strides?), it does not follow that because minorities *may* have made great strides, there is no further need for affirmative action programs.

Oversimplification. Be alert for writers who offer easy solutions to complicated problems. "America's economy will be strong again if we all 'buy American,'" a politician may argue. But the problems of America's economy are complex and cannot be solved by a slogan or a simple change in buying habits. Likewise, a writer who argues that we should ban genetic engineering assumes that simple solutions ("just say 'no'") will be sufficient to deal with the complex moral dilemmas raised by this new technology.

Writing That Entertains

Authors write not only to inform and persuade but also to entertain. One response to entertainment is a hearty laugh; but it is possible to entertain without laughter: A good book or play or poem may prompt you to ruminate, grow wistful, elated, angry. Laughter is only one of many possible reactions. You read a piece (or view a work) and react with sadness, surprise, exhilaration, disbelief, horror, boredom, whatever. As with a response to an informative piece or an argument, your response to an essay, poem, story, play, novel, or film should be precisely stated and carefully developed. Ask yourself some of the following questions (you won't have space to explore all of them, but try to consider some of the most important): Did I care for the portrayal of a certain character? Did that character seem too sentimentalized, for example, or heroic? Did his adversaries seem too villainous or stupid? Were the situations believable? Was the action interesting or merely formulaic? Was the theme developed subtly, powerfully, or did the work come across as preachy or shrill? Did the action at the end of the work follow plausibly from what had come before? Was the language fresh and incisive or stale and predictable? Explain as specifically as possible what elements of the work seemed effective or ineffective and why. Offer an overall assessment, elaborating on your views.

Question Category 2: To What Extent Do You Agree with the Author?

When formulating a critical response to a source, try to distinguish your evaluation of the author's purpose and success at achieving that purpose from your agreement or disagreement with the author's views. The distinction allows you to respond to a piece of writing on its merits. As an unbiased, evenhanded critic, you evaluate an author's clarity of presentation, use of evidence, and adherence to principles of logic. To what extent has the author succeeded in achieving his or her purpose? Still withholding judgment, offer your assessment and give the author (in effect) a grade. Significantly, your assessment of the presentation may not coincide with your views of the author's conclusions: You may agree with an author entirely but feel that the presentation is superficial; you may find the author's logic and use of evidence to be rock solid but may resist certain conclusions. A critical evaluation works well when it is conducted in two parts. After evaluating the author's purpose and design for achieving that purpose, respond to the author's main assertions. In doing so, you'll want to keep two considerations in mind.

IDENTIFY POINTS OF AGREEMENT AND DISAGREEMENT

Be precise in identifying points of agreement and disagreement with an author. You should state as clearly as possible what *you* believe, and an effective way of doing this is to define your position in relation to that presented in the piece. Whether you agree enthusiastically, disagree, or agree with reservations, you can organize your reactions in two parts: first, summarize the author's position; second, state your own position and elaborate on your reasons for holding it. The elaboration, in effect, becomes an argument itself, and this is true regardless of the position you take. An opinion is effective when you support it by supplying evidence. Without such evidence, opinions cannot be authoritative. "I thought the article on inflation was lousy." Why? "I just thought so, that's all." This opinion is valueless because the criticism is imprecise: The critic has taken neither the time to read the article carefully nor the time to explore his own reactions carefully.

EXPLORE THE REASONS FOR AGREEMENT AND DISAGREEMENT: EVALUATE ASSUMPTIONS

One way of elaborating your reactions to a reading is to explore the underlying *reasons* for agreement and disagreement. Your reactions are based largely on assumptions that you hold and how these assumptions compare with the author's. An *assumption* is a fundamental statement about the world and its operations that you take to be true. A writer's assumptions may be explicitly stated; but just as often assumptions are implicit and you will have to "ferret them out," that is, to infer them. Consider an example:

> *In vitro* fertilization and embryo transfer are brought about outside the bodies of the couple through actions of third parties whose competence and technical activity determine the success of the procedure. Such fertilization entrusts the life and identity of the embryo into the power of doctors and biologists and establishes the domination of technology over the origin and destiny of the human person. Such a relationship of domination is in itself contrary to the dignity and equality that must be common to parents and children.[1]

This paragraph is quoted from the February 1987 Vatican document on artificial procreation. Cardinal Joseph Ratzinger, principal author of the document, makes an implicit assumption in this paragraph: that no good can come of the domination of technology over conception. The use of technology to bring about conception is morally wrong. Yet there are thousands of childless couples, Roman Catholics included, who reject this assumption in favor of its opposite: that conception technology is an aid to the barren couple; far from creating a relationship of unequals, the technology brings children into the world who will be welcomed with joy and love.

Assumptions provide the foundation on which entire presentations are built. If you find an author's assumptions invalid, you may well disagree with conclusions that follow from these assumptions. The author of a book on developing nations may include a section outlining the resources and time that will be required to industrialize a particular country and so upgrade its general welfare. His assumption—that industrialization in that particular country will ensure or even affect the general welfare—may or may not be valid. If you do not share the assumption, in your eyes the rationale for the entire book may be undermined.

---

[1]From the Vatican document *Instruction on Respect for Human Life in Its Origin and on the Dignity of Procreation,* given at Rome, from the Congregation for the Doctrine of the Faith, February 22, 1987, as presented in *Origins: N.C. Documentary Service* 16*(40),* March 19, 1987, p. 707.

How do you determine the validity of assumptions once you have identified them? In the absence of more scientific criteria, validity may mean how well the author's assumptions stack up against your own experience, observations, and reading. A caution, however: The overall value of an article or book may depend only to a small degree on the validity of the author's assumptions. For instance, a sociologist may do a fine job of gathering statistical data about the incidence of crime in urban areas along the eastern seaboard. The sociologist also might be a Marxist, and you may disagree with her subsequent analysis of the data. Yet you may find the data extremely valuable for your own work.

▼

CRITIQUE

A *critique* is a *formalized, critical reading of a passage.* It is also a personal response; but writing a critique is considerably more rigorous than saying that a movie is "great," or a book is "fascinating," or "I didn't like it." These are all responses, and, as such, they're a valid, even essential, part of your understanding of what you see and read. But such responses don't help illuminate the subject for anyone—even you—if you haven't explained how you arrived at your conclusions.

Your task in writing a critique is to turn your critical reading of a passage into a systematic evaluation in order to deepen your reader's (and your own) understanding of that passage. Among other things, you're interested in determining what an author says, how well the points are made, what assumptions underlie the argument, what issues are overlooked, and what implications can be drawn from such an analysis. Critiques, positive or negative, should include a fair and accurate summary of the passage; they also should include a statement of your own assumptions. It is important to remember that you bring to bear an entire set of assumptions about the world. Stated or not, these assumptions underlie every evaluative comment you make; therefore, you have an obligation, both to the reader and to yourself, to clarify your standards. Not only do your readers stand to gain by your forthrightness, but you do as well: In the process of writing a critical assessment, you are forced to examine your own knowledge, beliefs, and assumptions. Ultimately, the critique is a way of learning about yourself.

How to Write Critiques

You may find it useful to organize your critiques in five sections: introduction, summary, analysis of the presentation, your response to the presentation, and conclusion.

The box (page 68) contains some guidelines for writing critiques. Note that they are guidelines, not a rigid formula. Thousands of authors write critiques that do not follow the structure outlined here. Until you are more confident and practiced in writing critiques, however, we suggest you follow the guidelines. They are meant not to restrict you, but to provide you with a

HOW TO WRITE CRITIQUES

- *Introduction.* Introduce both the passage under analysis and the author.

  State the author's main argument and the point(s) you intend to make about it.

  Provide background material to help your readers understand the relevance or appeal of the passage. This background material might include one or more of the following: an explanation of why the subject is of current interest; a reference to a possible controversy surrounding the subject of the passage or the passage itself; biographical information about the author; an account of the circumstances under which the passage was written; or a reference to the intended audience of the passage.
- *Summary.* Summarize the author's main points, making sure to state the author's purpose for writing.
- *Analysis of the presentation.* Evaluate the validity of the author's presentation, as distinct from your points of agreement or disagreement. Comment on the author's success in achieving his or her purpose by reviewing three or four specific points. You might base your review on one (or more) of the following criteria:

  Is the information accurate?
  Is the information significant?
  Has the author defined terms clearly?
  Has the author used and interpreted information fairly?
  Has the author argued logically?
- *Your response to the presentation.* Now it is your turn to respond to the author's views. With which views do you agree? With which do you disagree? Discuss your reasons for agreement and disagreement, when possible tying these reasons to assumptions—both the author's and your own.
- *Conclusion.* State your conclusions about the overall validity of the piece—your assessment of the author's success at achieving his or her aims and your reactions to the author's views. Remind the reader of the weaknesses and strengths of the passage.

workable method of writing critical analyses that incorporates a logical sequence of development.

When you write a critique based on an essay in this text, you'll find it helpful to first read the Discussion and Writing Suggestions following that essay. These suggestions will lead you to some of the more fruitful areas of inquiry. Beware of simply responding mechanically to them, however, or your essay could degenerate into a series of short, disjointed responses. You need to organize your reactions into a coherent whole: the critique should be informed by a consistent point of view.

▼

DEMONSTRATION: CRITIQUE

Read the following selection, "Total Surveillance" by Charles Ostman, which will be the subject of an example critique; and read also Irving Sloan's "Privacy and Technology," an excerpt from a book on privacy law that provides a larger context for Ostman's discussion. These discussions on the ways in which new technologies might be used to violate the privacy rights of individual citizens serve two purposes: first, they provide an occasion for the example critique on pages 81–86; second, they are meant to whet your appetite for Chapter 9, "Privacy and Technology," in Part II of this text.

Charles Ostman's thesis that we are quickly sliding into a "total surveillance" society is certainly arguable. It is based on points of logic, emotional appeals, and assumptions that you should read carefully and challenge. Draw on the preceding discussion to stimulate your responses to Ostman. Make notes in the margins: these will help you write a summary (be sure to underline the author's thesis, topic sentences, transitions, and important examples); notes in the form of questions and reactions can also help you to organize a critical response.

After you have read Ostman's article, read Sloan's for a much different perspective on the same issues. Then gather your notes and order them according to the five steps for writing critiques outlined above.

Total Surveillance

CHARLES OSTMAN

This article on surveillance technology first appeared in Mondo 2000 *(Issue 13, 1995), a glossy magazine on cyber-culture. Charles Ostman is a former research engineer.*

Imagine a world in which every aspect of your life, past and present, is encrypted on a personal ID card and stored on a nationwide database. Where virtually all communications media—soon to be 100 percent digital—are automatically monitored by computerized phone taps and satellites from control centers thousands of miles away. Where self-training neural net and artificial intelligence data search systems scan for undesirable lifestyles and target *you* for automatic monitoring. 1

Personal privacy was once considered the most sacred of our constitutional rights; agencies were severely limited by law. All that's about to 2 change drastically thanks to a deadly combination of extremely sophisticated surveillance technology, ubiquitous digital information collection, and centralized interagency data exchange.

Until recently the "supersecret" National Reconnaissance Organization did not exist—even though it has the largest budget of any intelligence agency. They are responsible for the design, development and procurement of all U.S. reconnaissance satellites and their continued management once in orbit. Recently photos have surfaced in the press of its huge new complex being completed in Chantilly, Virginia. (Senator John Warner—Liz Taylor's ex—has described the one million square foot complex as a "Taj Mahal.") The NRO is eagerly implementing such technologies as ultra-high storage capacity holographic films (allowing huge amounts of personal information to be present on your ID card) and self-training artificial intelligence software that tracks your personal data without human intervention. A new era of ubiquitous surveillance is dawning. 3

A struggling military-industrial complex searching for new markets for their technologies has merged forces with a government obsessed with ever tighter control over the activities of the general public. Congresswoman Barbara Jordan has proposed a "National Employment Verification Card" that will be required for all employment in the U.S. The card will, of course, have a magnetic data strip, and altering or counterfeiting the card will be a federal felony offense. 4

There is a dedicated and aggressive effort underway to chart various genetic features as part of one's personal information set. The fed's goal is to have the ability to screen individuals for everything from behavioral characteristics to sexual orientation, based on genetic information embedded in your personal (and required) national ID card. 5

Biometric signature technologies have been developing apace. There is even a technique available to translate human DNA into bar codes for efficient digital transmission between agencies. 6

Are these science fiction story lines or the ravings of a paranoid lunatic? I wish they were. As a former research engineer at Lawrence Livermore Labs and other government labs, I watched some of these mad schemes being hatched. This technology is on the street today or about to leave the labs and believe me, it goes way beyond Orwell's worst nightmares. Listen up and hunker down. 7

A fundamental shift in the legal definition of personal privacy is occurring right now. A court-issued warrant used to be a universal requirement for personal surveillance, such as phone tapping, observing physical papers, and probing financial or medical records. Now, in this new age of AI-driven monitoring and data tracking systems, there are no pesky people in the loop. 8

A computer doesn't need to seek a court warrant to monitor every aspect of your private life. A self-training automated surveillance system doesn't need permission to observe your movements or communications. 9

Total data tracking is already commonplace for financial institutions and private security operations. Tomorrow, it will be commonplace for all 10 of us. The technical elements of a massive surveillance engine are in place. It's just a matter of turning the key to fire it up. Let's examine these elements and why you should be concerned.

UNIVERSAL ENCRYPTION CHIP

It sounds logical. The feds want to preserve privacy, so their story goes, so 11
they've announced that an encryption chip will go into all phones and computers that they buy. But what do they *really* want in the long run?

How about a government-issue encryption chip in all personal comput- 12
ers and communication devices? That way, the feds can deal with drug smugglers, terrorists, kiddie porn merchants, and other miscreants who use encoded messages.

Of course, they'd have to prevent tampering with the chip. In fact, the 13
technology to do just that has already been developed at Sandia National Laboratory. Scientists there have developed an optical sensor that uses a powdered silicon optical absorption layer in an optical waveguide embedded in a chip. A micro photodetector detects even the slightest intrusion into the chip package by measuring a slight change in the photonic conduction through the waveguide. It can then send an alert via modem to a central monitoring system to notify an interested party that the device has been tampered with. Sandia is also developing a microchemical intrusion detector that would be sensitive to the chemical signature of human fingertips.

Is this all part of some master plan, or what? 14

In fact, in the near future, all encryption hardware and software will be 15
subject to federal registration/authorization. Possession of unauthorized encryption/decryption capability will be punishable as a federal felony. In other words, if it doesn't have a handy back door for NSA snoops, it ain't legal.

We can further speculate that the feds will embed chips in all equip- 16
ment sold for use in data transmission, digital phone calls and all other frequencies. Note: all new phone systems wired and wireless will be digital in the next three years.

INTELLIGENT VIDEO

Nor would you know *what's* watching you. Security cameras are becoming 17
standard in corporate and government facilities. They may soon even be required. Why? Ostensibly because they want to recover losses in cases of theft, keep insurance premiums down, monitor peculant employees and keep intruders out.

But the new genre of video cameras now coming out of the labs do a 18
lot more than that. They're intelligent. They can recognize faces, motion, and other interesting characteristics. In fact, they behave a lot like a human eye, with intelligent preprocessor abilities.

Intelligent cameras are needed because a security guard or cop can't monitor the dozens or hundreds of video cameras in a large facility (or dozens of satellite video surveillance channels). Intelligent cameras use artificial intelligence-based object and motion recognition. They scan for what a trained security guard looks for: certain motions, clothing, faces; the presence of people in off-limits places. Instead of watching 100 cameras, only a few at any time send pictures. A single guard or computer can deal with that. 19

In fact, a steady data stream from multiple intelligent cameras can be uploaded to computerized monitoring facilities anywhere, coupled with other automated observation systems. 20

The next big thing in intelligent cameras will be "content-addressable" imagery. That means they'll automatically detect the content of sophisticated patterns, like a specific person's face, by matching it against a digital "wanted" poster, say. New software that can even run on cheap personal computers makes that possible. MatchMaker from Iterated Systems (Norcross, GA), for example, uses a fractal algorithm that converts image data into mathematical form, automatically recognizing and categorizing real-time "targets"—untouched by human hands and tied into a centralized monitoring facility! 21

A related technology called focal plane array sensors (FPA) discriminates objects at just about any distance. FPA makes it possible to use neuromorphic sensors, modeled biologically on the human eye, which are built into a camera to recognize a person or object by "associative cognition." 22

Carver Mead at Cal Tech has designed a broad-spectrum "human-eye" sensor using FPAs and 3D artificial neural network processors. To prove the viability of such concepts, Raytheon, under contract with the Guided Interceptor Branch of the Air Force at Elgin AFB, has developed "smart eyes" using FPAs for recognizing objects in flight, thus relieving the pilot of visual target recognition tasks while in a high-pressure combat situation. 23

This technology is inexpensive, easily reproducible, and will be part of standard equipment for fully automated, on-site visual and infrared surveillance in the near future. 24

Langley Research Center (Hampton, VA) in conjunction with Telerobotics International (Knoxville, TN) is taking a step further. They're developing an advanced surveillance camera system that's even more intelligent: it uses self-aiming and analyzes motion or other parameters. A fisheye spherical lens views a very wide field of vision while a self-contained image processing subsystem tracks several moving targets at once in real time. Video for suspect targets can be transmitted in real time to a security center. 25

These smart cameras are also getting incredibly tiny and low cost. The Imputer from VLSI Vision Ltd. (Edinburgh, Scotland) is a credit card-sized device that fits in the palm of your hand. It consists of a complete CCD video camera mounted on a circuit board plus an on-board DSP (digital signal processing) coprocessor for realtime image enhancement, feature detection, correlation and convolution (for fast analysis on the fly), and 26 even an optional library of pre-stored feature data so that the camera can independently recognize a specific face or other security-oriented data. It can also download its captured visual data via telephone line to a data collection and processing facility.

With everything on a few chips, intelligent cameras can now be mass-manufactured like pocket radios. No need for security personnel—they can be linked to a computer surveillance monitoring and data base system. 27

That is where it gets really insidious. When the technology becomes so cheap, tiny, and powerful, and no guards are needed, they can sprinkle these things around like corn chips . . . secretly putting them on every street corner, in every waiting room, office, wherever. 28

Keep smiling, because you'll never know when you're on candid camera. And hey, relax, they've just captured your surfaces. 29

BIOMETRICS

Where it really starts to get hairy is when we enter the brave new world of Biometrics. Biometrics is the process of gathering biological information and converting it into data that can be uploaded into automated systems for identifying you. 30

They can use your fingerprint (via automated fingerprint identification systems), retinal scan, voice or other personal signatures. Miros of Wellesley, MA, has recently introduced a system called Face-to-Face, using neural nets, that is particularly insidious. Unlike fingerprint or palm recognition, it identifies your face "non-intrusively" (that's technospeak for surreptitiously) with 99 percent recognition. It can even identify your face when you add glasses or change your hairstyle. 31

There are biometric service bureaus like TRW that provide immediate access to personal dossier information to prisons, banks, military bases, research facilities, pharmaceutical companies, etc. The client simply installs a retinal scanner or other device and transmits your image to a service bureau, which sends back your complete dossier. This is big business for these service bureaus. We're talking *billions* in government and corporate contracts. 32

What's next? We can expect intelligent scanning systems will be installed in supermarket checkout lines, lobbies, airports, stores, ATM sites, and so on in the near future. Known shoplifters will be tracked from the time they walk into the store. There'll be a *cordon sanitaire* around playgrounds and day care centers. 33

What happens when the FBI ties its fingerprint verification system at its National Criminal Information Center, with its library of over 250,000 fingerprints, into the national health care system, employment ID card, IRS, and just about everything else? 34

If the FBI has *you* listed as a radical or some other species of undesirable, will they be automatically notified whenever you appear at a doctor's office? Every time you use an ATM? What about when you buy a naughty 35 magazine or subscribe to a "politically incorrect" publication? Where does this stuff stop?

SATELLITE SURVEILLANCE

It doesn't. Your image may be up for sale right now. Ten-meter-resolution satellite images of those strange weeds in your back yard are available to any buyer from the French company SPOT Image of Reston, Virginia. 36

Even sharper images are available. Spy satellite images at two meters resolution are now available from World Map. About 30 other countries—particularly Germany, Israel, and China—are planning to launch satellite surveillance systems. 37

Producers of satellite and surveillance equipment and large database processing services like TRW have huge financial stakes in this $8 billion market. They've put massive pressure on the CIA and DoD to loosen up control of satellite surveillance technology. Three of them—Lockheed, Orbital Sciences (which is launching Eyeglass), and World View—are launching satellites with resolutions from one to three meters by 1997. 38

Another recently formed U.S. company, Teledesic, is planning a vast $9 billion global communication system using 840 geosynchronous orbit satellites, scheduled for 2001. There would be no single area on the planet that could not be "seen" on demand, and more importantly, virtually all digital communications could be linked through this universal transponder system. 39

Suddenly we're just one step from a universal monitoring system. The satellites could conceivably serve as platforms for multi-spectral, on-demand, visual and IR surveillance of any coordinate on the planetary surface. Note: both founders of Teledesic, Bill Gates and Craig McCaw, declined to be interviewed by MONDO on this topic. 40

ROBOT SPIES

Unmanned robotic devices (airborne and land-based) are now here that can observe an individual or dwelling day or night from a distance. They can also monitor communications (using RF signatures) over a broad spectrum of frequencies. They can be activated from a distant control center thousands of miles away from the target; and surveillance data can be collected and examined in real time via satellite link. 41

For example, there's the SR2 Security Robot System from Cybermotion Inc. of Roanoke, Virginia. Designed to "replace human security personnel," the SR2 patrols a region of up to 15 square miles for 12 hour shifts (between charges), using ultrasonic, optical, and infrared sensors plus onboard "fuzzy logic" to navigate around complex obstacles and interpret data. An operator at a remote site controls and interacts with a group of these robots via bidirectional RF data link. 42

There's also NASA's High Altitude Long Endurance (HALE) unmanned aircraft. HALE can stay airborne for days at a time, carrying CCD 43 optical and infrared camera systems. These light-weight stealth aircraft are flown by remote control, using a satellite data link to an operational command center that can be thousands of miles away. Perfect for kamikaze-style strikes.

And the U.S. Navy is soliciting proposals to develop a robotic, flyable 44
platform for optical and infrared surveillance, designed for "riot control, border surveillance, and personnel detection."

A fuzzy logic based RF communications signal/signature analysis sys- 45
tem has been solicited by the U.S. Navy. It will be able to recognize the content of any transmitted signal from anywhere, regardless of spread spectrum, encryption, or other electronic signal countermeasures. Commercial applications cited in the solicitation are "law enforcement, surveillance, drug interdiction, illegal immigrant control, etc."

Realtime monitoring by these robotic devices can be remotely acti- 46
vated from anywhere. No search warrants, no court authorizations.

MASSIVELY PARALLEL COMPUTERS AND OPTICAL STORAGE

All these surveillance systems generate *massive* amounts of information. 47
Until recently this would have been impractical for millions of people.

Currently, massive optical data storage technologies coupled with ex- 48
tremely powerful, massively parallel processing computers are capable of very high-volume data storage and very high-speed data analysis.

The Department of Commerce is financing a joint project with Tama- 49
rack Storage Devices to develop a photo-refractive holographic data storage system capable of handling hundreds of terabytes (that's 10^{12} bytes) of data for extremely large database processing operations. This is *exactly* the type of information storage/processing capability required for a nationwide population monitoring system.

Thinking Machines Inc., of Cambridge, MA has recently announced a 50
massively parallel processing supercomputer, the CM-5, specifically designed for extremely huge database processing applications. It can access an astonishing 3.2 terabytes of data with a bandwidth of up to 4.2 gigabytes per second, distributed over a network of 16,000 processing nodes that can be located anywhere.

A handful of these systems can maintain an up-to-date population 51
monitoring/data processing system for the entire country.

What do you think is going to be in that secret $350 million National 52
Reconnaissance Organization (NRO) building in Chantilly, VA? Hint: they're not watching Russia any more.

NEURAL NETS AND AI

Of course, all these operations normally require huge staffs of trained ex- 53
perts. That's where neural nets and artificial intelligence come in.

Neural net processing systems can search for "behavioral tendencies" 54
within a database and automatically flag certain individuals for surveillance

and "attention" from interested enforcement agencies, employers, political researchers, etc. This is a rung up from knowbots and gobots.

A good example is the ominous Origin system (the U.S. base is Tampa, FL), a worldwide realtime, intelligent vision processing and networking database system designed for "intelligent security data base monitoring and observation" for law enforcement and government agencies. It uses Iterated Systems' Matchmaker software running on a global computer network. A surveillance camera or biometric sensor anywhere can feed signals into the network and get back a name of the person in seconds. 55

HNC's (San Diego, CA) DataBase Mining Workstation is a dedicated neural network processing engine designed to look for "interesting" data sets on its own. The user "trains" the system for topics or features of interest. Once effectively trained, the system automatically tracks anything (or anyone) that gets its attention and draws its own conclusions. 56

HNC also sells the Falcon neural net credit card "fraud and abuse" detection system. It automatically "learns" about unusual spending habits and related behavioral feature sets. Clients for this system include AT&T, Colonial National Bank, Eurocard Netherland, First USA Bank, Household Credit Services, and Wells Fargo Bank. HNC is also working on credit risk evaluation, bankruptcy potential, and other forms of financial activity pattern recognition. 57

Again, no need for pesky humans who can be held accountable for violation of privacy. "The machine did it!" Once this becomes routine, current legally defined barriers to privacy disappear totally. 58

AUTOMATED VOICE RECOGNITION

In the good old days, they had to attach electronic clips to your phone and get court authorization. Not so today. 59

Let's say you're on a list somewhere based on your politics, reading, or drug or sexual habits. Zap: you're suddenly on a priority list for surveillance. You make a call and your voice matches the profile. The system starts to listen in to your vocal communications in real time. The voice data can then be digitized, stored, and added to your surveillance dossier by the computer. 60

If you've seen the movie *Clear and Present Danger,* you know how easily intelligence agencies monitor cellular phone calls, satellite phone calls, and anything else that's broadcast. (It's actually easy for anyone to monitor cellular calls with a scanner covering 870 to 896 MHz or a UHF TV receiver tuned to channels 80 to 83 and a good UHF antenna.) Then they digitize speech signals and convert them into text data, which can then be processed to search for specific words or phrases. 61

All this will be a lot easier when the telephone companies introduce Asynchronous Transfer Mode (ATM) communications in a few years. Virtually all communications, including data transmission and business and personal phone calls, will be routed through the same universal communication channel, making the job of listening in much easier. 62

Dialogic Corp. (Parsippany, NJ) is developing "second generation" 63
modular telephone call-processing and automated speech recognition system hardware and software. Uses include online automatic keyword and phrase recognition. That is, any word or word communication that may be "interesting" to an automated listening system can cue automated storage of an entire conversation for further analysis.

The Sprint voice-activated phone card is already in use. But several 64
corporations including TRW have already taken it a step further. They can analyze and store voice signatures for every telephone caller in the country for a much larger market: voice recognition for phone credit card verification and voice-triggered ID security systems. Essentially, you'll be forced to use voice ID or no credit or access. It's a simple matter to adapt this kind of technology for a national tracking system.

The U.S. Navy wants to take it a step further. As evidenced by its re- 65
cent FY 94 "Global Surveillance and Communications" technology solicitations (as per the SBIR development funding program), they are developing a "robust signal processing of speech" capability with "voice communications countermeasures and counter-countermeasures" as part of a comprehensive, speech recognition and processing system.

Sun Microsystems workstations include a microphone and speech 66
recognition chip. A recent security alert from the Computer Emergency Response Team at Carnegie Mellon University disclosed that the workstations had been pre-programmed with a "world readable" status feature. That means any of these networked workstations could in fact serve as a remotely monitored microphone. A back door has already been built into this workstation. That means anyone can activate the microphone to listen in remotely from anywhere in the world.

DESKTOP NSA

But all this massive power is not limited to giant computer centers. Even 67
desktop computers are now becoming powerful enough to handle massive amounts of intelligence information.

Adaptive Solutions Inc. (Beaverton, OR) sells a $7000 CNAPS/PC 68
board that converts a 486 or Pentium computer into a massively parallel processing engine. The boards, each of which contains 128 processors, perform 2.56 billion multiply/accumulate operations per second. This means a 1000 times performance improvement in pattern recognition.

Companies are turning these powerful new surveillance tools on their 69
own people too. For example, Microsoft has a secret project to monitor all keystrokes of its personnel to "improve efficiency" using neural net and artificial intelligence software. And Edify Corp. (Santa Clara, CA) is supplying "intelligent agent" software to BellSouth Communications Systems (Roanoke, VA). It will be built into BellSouth's Electronic Workforce software. Its customers will use it for interactive voice response and recognition, personnel and client workforce screening, efficiency monitoring, and workflow automation.

PROBATION NATION

This is *not* another paranoid "1984" scenario based on some futuristic fantasy. For the first time in history, the technology is available to design and implement such a ubiquitous surveillance/monitoring system. The crisis climate created by the media—particularly television "news magazines"—is being used to *mandate* this horror. 70

The political will to do this is here and it is being touted as an accepted solution to such problems as crime and illegal immigrants. The general public is not even remotely familiar with the technical details of how such a repressive system could be implemented and won't wake up until they're virtual prisoners in a totally automated Surveillance Society. 71

Privacy and Technology

IRVING J. SLOAN

The following selection is excerpted from a book that Sloan edited, Law of Privacy Rights in a Technological Society. *Sloan's legal background brings him to the same issues that worry Ostman, but from a far different point of view. This selection will help to create a larger context for your reading of Ostman.*

When the Federal Constitution and the Bill of Rights were written . . . government left the individual largely unrestrained, arbitrating between individuals only at extreme limits of conduct. Yet in the century and a half that followed, government's role gradually shifted to promotion of the community welfare, even at the cost of individual property rights. 1

As technology advances, the problem shifts from the exertion of governmental authority over property rights to the potential for governmental intrusion on individual privacy rights. In the words of Justice [William O.] Douglas, "the central problem of the age is the scientific revolution and all the wonders and the damage it brings." The machine, which Orwell once called "the genie that man has thoughtlessly let out of its bottle and cannot put back again," has allowed new concentrations of power, particularly in government, which utterly dwarf the individual and threaten individuality as never before. "Where in this tightly knit regime," asked Justice Douglas, "is man to find liberty?" 2

On the vital subject of privacy and its place in the society of the future, Justice Douglas remarked, "We are rapidly entering the age of no privacy, where everyone is open to surveillance at all times; where there are no secrets from government. The aggressive breaches of privacy by the government increase by geometric proportions." 3

Justice [Louis D.] Brandeis, one of the fathers of the legal right of privacy, observed a similar development in his famous dissent in *Olmstead v.* 4

United States. When the Fourth Amendment was written, declared Brandeis, force and violence were the essential means by which privacy could be invaded. It was against such relatively simple evils that the constitutional guaranty was directed. With time, Brandeis noted, subtler and more far-reaching means of invading privacy have become available to the government. "Discovery and invention have made it possible for the government, by means far more effective than stretching upon the rack, to obtain disclosure in court of what is 'whispered in the closet.'"

But it is in the area of non-wiretap electronic eavesdropping that the 5
greatest scientific advances have occurred. The impact of these advances has been summarized by Justice [William J.] Brennan: "Electronic eavesdropping by means of concealed microphones and recording devices of various kinds has become as large a problem as wiretapping and is pervasively employed by private detectives, police, labor spies, employers and others for a variety of purposes; some downright disreputable. . . . These devices go far beyond simple 'bugging,' and permit a degree of invasion of privacy that can only be described as frightening."

The potential for invasion is greatly expanded by recent developments 6
in electronic surveillance such as parabolic microphones, which can pick up conversations at considerable distances, ultra-miniature wireless microphones no larger than a pencil eraser; recorders so small they can be built into cigarette lighters; and microwave-beam devices with a range of 1,000 feet or more, which can penetrate walls and other obstacles.

In his *Olmstead* dissent, Justice Brandeis foresaw the technological 7
revolution that so transformed the field of communications and magnified the potential for electronic eavesdropping: "The progress of science in furnishing the government with means of espionage is not likely to stop with wiretapping. Ways may someday be developed by which the government without removing papers from secret drawers, can reproduce them in court, and by which it will be enabled to expose to a jury the most intimate occurrences of the home."

The technological changes wrought by scientific progress have out- 8
stripped the law and legal commentary. Much of the [Earl] Warren Court's protective jurisprudence may become completely outmoded by the seven-league strides being made in long-distance eavesdropping techniques. As Justice Brennan put it in his dissent in *Lopez v. United States* in 1963: "To be secure against police officers' breaking and entering to search for physical objects is worth very little if there is no security against the officers' using secret recording devices to purloin words spoken in confidence within the four walls of home or office. . . . If electronic surveillance by government becomes sufficiently widespread, and there is little in prospect for checking it, the hazard that as a people we may become hagridden and furtive is not fantasy." One may now question how much of the concept of privacy itself will remain if, through the advances in applied science, the area of privacy remaining physically immune from official scrutiny were to all but disappear.

A major source of privacy invasion is the increasing use over the last several years by the federal government of "computer-matching" investigations to detect fraud, abuse, and waste in the administration of federal programs. These computerized general searches of personal data have been conducted in the files of welfare and medicaid recipients, draft-aged taxpayers, veterans, federal employees, persons entitled to supplemental security income, and thousands of other government files. The computer-matching technique is an effective way of combining personal data from a wide variety of separate record systems and using it to keep track of individuals. 9

Finally, for several years Congress has been considering a proposal to require all persons in the United States to carry a fraud-proof work authorization card in order to obtain and hold employment. The card, backed by a national databank of personal information concerning all persons lawfully in the United States, would constitute a secure national identification system that could block the employment of illegal aliens. The proposal has sparked controversy because the identification system could become a vehicle for the violation of civil rights if used by the police to conduct wide-ranging searches and investigations or by other government agencies to keep track of private, law-abiding citizens. 10

These examples demonstrate that the technological capability to collect, maintain, cross-index, and disclose vast quantities of information about private lives has far out-paced the legal protection of privacy in the United States. Many information systems containing sensitive data are being constructed to facilitate important social objectives, such as better law enforcement, faster delivery of public services, more efficient management of credit and insurance programs, improvement of telecommunications, and streamlining of financial activities. Nonetheless, these high technology systems are also being used at an increasing rate by large and public agencies to enhance their control of the lives of individuals. 11

Until this point, we have been talking about protection from government intrusion. In fact, however, the private sector has also rapidly increased its use of technology such as we have been describing here. For example, interactive cable television systems are capable of gathering vast amounts of personal data, not only on the viewing habits of consumers, but also on their buying and banking habits, as more services are added to the cable system. Cable companies, for example, offer burglar alarm systems which tell the company when a consumer is at home. This sensitive personal information is a valuable commodity which cable companies can sell to credit reporting companies and other interested buyers in order to finance their corporate growth. 12

Private companies as well as the federal government often require employees to submit to lie detector tests. Employees have no clear understanding of what rights, if any, they have to refuse to take a test, or to control the verification, storage, and dissemination of records generated by a test if they submit to it. 13

The technology for information collection, storage, and retrieval has outpaced the technology for safeguarding databanks of personal information. It is therefore increasingly compelling that the law and legislation reflect the citizen's rights and needs to protect his privacy from both governmental and private intrusions. 14

This growth of data banks and vast computerized pools of information about people in every aspect of their lives is probably the single most important element in the contemporary range of concerns about the right of privacy. 15

▲ ▲ ▲

Consider the following questions as you contemplate the ways in which one might critique Charles Ostman's "Total Surveillance":

- Ostman believes that a total surveillance state is inevitable. Why?
- Ostman makes frequent references to "they." To whom is Ostman referring, and what is the effect of these references?
- What are the positive uses of the technologies reviewed in this article?
- Given your reading of the excerpt from Irving Sloan's *Law of Privacy Rights in a Technological Society,* how do your views of Ostman's article change, if they change at all?
- What are some similarities and differences between Ostman's work and Sloan's?
- How does Sloan help to establish a larger context for Ostman's article?

In the following critique, one writer presents his responses to these questions. Thesis and transitional/topic sentences are highlighted.

They're After Us!

A Critique of Charles Ostman's "Total Surveillance"

What would life be like knowing that you were watched constantly: knowing that hidden monitors recorded private conversations; that supervisors at work read every keystroke from your computer; that for a service fee of $150 anyone who took an interest could access your credit, health, educational, military, and legal histories? What would life be like? In a piece written for Mondo 2000, former research engineer Charles Ostman claims 1 that we'll soon know first hand, because we're barrelling headlong into an Orwellian nightmare of "Total Surveillance."

Ostman devotes considerable attention to reviewing the technologies he says will be cobbled together to form a national, even international, surveillance net. From intelligent video cameras to biological probes ("biometrics") to satellites that can spot swimsuits on a clothesline to neural nets and more, the individual technologies of surveillance now being deployed are astonishing in their power to gather data. Combined, they present an unprecedented threat to individual privacy, according to Ostman. "For the first time in history," he writes, "the technology is available to design and implement . . . a ubiquitous surveillance/monitoring system." But exactly <u>who</u> would be spying on us and <u>why</u> Ostman never explains; nor does he question a core assumption: that the fact we have the technological know-how to build a super-spy system means, inevitably, that we <u>will</u> build and use it. Still, Ostman is both entertaining and informative. In the tradition of true paranoids, he surveys current trends and projects the bleakest of futures. The possibility that he may be right about surveillance technologies makes his article worth taking seriously--even if the threat he sees, for the moment, exists largely in his own head. 2

Many Americans have worried over privacy rights. In his dissenting view in the famous wiretapping case <u>Olmstead v. United States</u> (1928), Supreme Court Justice Louis Brandeis wrote: "Discovery and invention have made it possible for the government, by means far more effective than stretching upon the rack, to obtain disclosure in court of what is 'whispered in the closet'" (qtd. in Sloan 79). Thirty-five years later, Justice Brennan argued that "if electronic surveillance by government becomes sufficiently widespread, and there is little in prospect for checking it, the 3 hazard that as a people we may become hagridden and furtive is not fantasy" (qtd. in Sloan 79). Brennan and Brandeis provide an authoritative cover for Ostman, the tone of whose Mondo 2000 piece could certainly be described as "hagridden"--or tormented. Surveillance systems already in place give reason enough for at least a modest amount of anxiety. According to recent media accounts, insurance companies are requesting the results of genetic screenings so that they can set premium rates more accurately; employers want to know our psychological profiles; credit agencies like TRW regularly update their dossiers on our financial dealings. Charles Ostman's fears have some basis in fact.

Ostman wants "Total Surveillance" to be an alarm bell that alerts readers to a "fundamental shift in the legal definition of personal privacy" in the United States. His main concern is with the ways in which hi-tech surveillance systems are circumventing our privacy rights. Until now, privacy law in this country has protected individuals (outside their places of employment) from being monitored without a law enforcement official's first obtaining a warrant. What worries Ostman is the development of sophisticated, inexpensive, and (therefore) soon-to-be-ubiquitous recording devices that activate themselves when, for instance, the on-board computer "recognizes" a certain voice, a phrase in conversation, or a certain face. The surveillance systems thus triggered require no human agent, no warrant, and no judge to determine the legality of the surveillance. Download the data generated on individuals to globally linked computers and we have an invitation to abuse. 4

Is Charles Ostman paranoid? A paranoid sees threats that have little basis in fact and then frets about them endlessly. Ostman, a former research engineer at Lawrence Livermore Laboratories, is at the very least a borderline paranoid. 5

He fears a threat to his and our privacy but cannot tell us with any precision *who* will be watching us--and why. Still, the threat's out there, lurking, and we had better "Listen up and hunker down." Early in the article, he names the enemy: the "feds," in cahoots with the "struggling military-industrial complex searching for new markets." Ostman subsequently refers to the government as a monolithic "they," a tactic that places all federal employees and elected officials under suspicion. This tactic is unfair. We've seen two examples of Supreme Court justices who would never agree to the government's sprinkling surveillance technologies "around like corn chips." Brandeis and Brennan have found the prospect of total surveillance repugnant. Others in government agree, as can be seen with Ostman's own example of the proposed national identity card. True enough, Congress recently debated issuing the cards--which, with their encoded data about our health, financial, and legal histories, would have Orwellian potential. But Congress defeated the proposal. Apparently, Ostman is so set on the idea that "they" are out to get us that he can't imagine elected officials joining forces to defeat a proposal that would threaten the privacy rights of Americans.

Nor does Ostman acknowledge that each technology he fears has a specific, legitimate use unrelated to domestic spying. The encryption chip, intelligent video, biometrics, automated voice recognition, and massively parallel desktop computing all have primary uses that do *not* involve the surveillance of law-abiding citizens. For instance, several of these technologies have been put to use fighting drug smugglers and terrorists. Obviously, hi-tech tools can be misused, just as low-tech ones can. Imagine the good and the harm a hammer can do. Given all the legitimate uses of the technologies he has noted, Ostman's obsession about the coming surveillance society is like fo- 6 cusing on crimes that will be committed with hammers in the coming year. Yes, burglars and psychopaths will use hammers to break windows and break heads; but in overwhelmingly greater numbers, carpenters will use hammers to build homes and offices where people will live and work. The failure to mention these primary, productive uses in an article on hammers would be absurd--and this is precisely Ostman's error. Only in passing, and with irony, does he acknowledge that the hardware he has surveyed does have legitimate, legal uses.

Notwithstanding these problems, "Total Surveil- 7
lance" demands our attention because it is built on an assumption about technology that many people share: the view that when we have the technical capability to build something, we build it; and once we do, we use it--whatever the consequences. Those who endorse this view of technological inevitability sometimes explain themselves by pointing to the Manhattan project. In the 1940s, the government invested millions to build an atomic bomb; once that bomb was built, the chances were slim that the government would fail to use its new technology since, after all, the bomb was sitting in New Mexico waiting to be used. Even though some military strategists close to the President questioned the necessity of dropping the bomb, Truman gave the order. And, thus, Ostman's case for technological inevitability: if we can build a total surveillance society, we will build it; and if we build it, we'll use it.

Is Ostman's nightmare state inevitable? He cer- 8
tainly thinks so; but technological capability need not mandate the future. The difference between the construction of the atomic bomb and its use and the construction of a total surveillance system involves a question of motive. In the early 1940s, the military needed a weapon to end the war and invested heavily. Today, we don't find agreement in the federal government on the issue of

closely monitoring citizens (as the defeated ID card attests). True, we can point to shameful examples of domestic spying. In the 1950s, suspected Communists were the targeted subversives; in the 1960s and 1970s, the FBI put anti-war protesters and civil rights activists under surveillance for nothing more than exercising their right to free speech. That the government spied on its citizens is an ugly fact. Would the government spy on its citizens today with ubiquitous surveillance technologies? We can't rule out the possibility; but neither can we assume that we'll inevitably slip into an Orwellian nightmare. The burden of proof is on Ostman to show that the threat is real. Instead of proof, he invites us into his paranoia with questions like "Is this all part of some master plan, or what?"

We may well be becoming a total surveillance society, and Ostman has done a service by alerting us to potential harm. But he provides no evidence that the federal government, today, has Orwellian intentions. Nonetheless, we would be wise to be vigilant. Supreme Court justices guard against intrusions on personal privacy, and so should we. 9

Works Cited[1]

Ostman, Charles. "Total Surveillance." Mondo 2000 13 (1995):16-19.

Sloan, Irving J., ed. Law of Privacy Rights in a Technological Society. Legal Almanac Series 54. Dobbs Ferry, NY: Oceana, 1986.

▲ ▲ ▲

[1]These "Works Cited" entries refer to pagination of articles in their original sources. In-text citations in the example critique refer to pages in *Writing and Reading Across the Curriculum.*

Discussion

- In the first two paragraphs of this critique, the writer introduces his subject and describes Ostman's purpose in writing the article. The writer concludes paragraph 2 with his thesis: the article is worth our attention, despite problems in Ostman's argument.
- In paragraph 3, the writer sets a larger context for Ostman's argument by drawing on the concerns others have had about privacy rights. This paragraph establishes that Ostman's topic is one worth taking seriously. With a brief reference to current surveillance technologies, the paragraph further supports Ostman's claim that we have reasons to be concerned about our privacy rights.
- In paragraph 4, the writer summarizes Ostman's argument.
- The critical evaluation of the article begins in paragraph 5, with the question, "Is Ostman paranoid?" The writer addresses a first weakness in the article: Ostman's broad use of "they" to refer to the entire government, which he sees as the source of the surveillance threat.
- In paragraph 6, the writer challenges Ostman on a second point: his failure to acknowledge that the surveillance technologies in question have other, legitimate uses.
- The main part of the critique is reserved for paragraphs 7 and 8, where the writer of the critique identifies and then examines Ostman's core assumption about technological inevitability. Ostman believes that since massive surveillance is technically possible, it is inevitable; the writer of the critique questions this inevitability.
- In the final paragraph, the writer summarizes his position: that Ostman has done well to alert readers to potential danger, but that he has failed to establish that the danger is a real one.

4
Synthesis

WHAT IS A SYNTHESIS?

A *synthesis* is a written discussion that draws on two or more sources. It follows that your ability to write syntheses depends on your ability to infer relationships among sources—essays, articles, fiction, and also nonwritten sources, such as lectures, interviews, observations. This process is nothing new for you, since you infer relationships all the time—say, between something you've read in the newspaper and something you've seen for yourself, or between the teaching styles of your favorite and least favorite instructors. In fact, if you've written research papers, you've already written syntheses. In an *academic* synthesis, you make explicit the relationships that you have inferred among separate sources.

The skills you've already learned and practiced from the previous three chapters will be vital in writing syntheses. Clearly, before you're in a position to draw relationships between two or more sources, you must understand what those sources say; in other words, you must be able to *summarize* these sources. It will frequently be helpful for your readers if you provide at least partial summaries of sources in your synthesis essays. At the same time, you must go beyond summary to make judgments—judgments based, of course, on your *critical reading* of your sources. You should already have drawn some conclusions about the quality and validity of these sources; and you should know how much you agree or disagree with the points made in your sources and the reasons for your agreement or disagreement.

Further, you must go beyond the critique of individual sources to determine the relationship among them. Is the information in source B, for example, an extended illustration of the generalizations in source A? Would it be useful to compare and contrast source C with source B? Having read and considered sources A, B, and C, can you infer something else—D (not a source, but your own idea)?

Because a synthesis is based on two or more sources, you will need to be selective when choosing information from each. It would be neither possible nor desirable, for instance, to discuss in a ten-page paper on the battle of Wounded Knee every point that the authors of two books make about their subject. What you as a writer must do is select from each source the ideas and information that best allow you to achieve your purpose.

PURPOSE

Your purpose in reading source materials and then in drawing on them to write your own material is often reflected in the wording of an assignment. For instance, consider the following assignments on the Civil War:

American History: Evaluate your text author's treatment of the origins of the Civil War.

Economics: Argue the following proposition, in light of your readings: "The Civil War was fought not for reasons of moral principle but for reasons of economic necessity."

Government: Prepare a report on the effects of the Civil War on Southern politics at the state level between 1870 and 1917.

Mass Communications: Discuss how the use of photography during the Civil War may have affected the perceptions of the war by Northerners living in industrial cities.

Literature: Select two twentieth-century Southern writers whose work you believe was influenced by the divisive effects of the Civil War. Discuss the ways this influence is apparent in a novel or a group of short stories written by each author. The works should not be *about* the Civil War.

Applied Technology: Compare and contrast the technology of warfare available in the 1860s with the technology available a century earlier.

Each of these assignments creates for you a particular purpose for writing. Having located sources relevant to your topic, you would select, for possible use in a paper, only those parts that helped you in fulfilling this purpose. And how you used those parts, how you related them to other material from other sources, would also depend on your purpose. For instance, if you were working on the government assignment, you might possibly draw on the same source as another student working on the literature assignment by referring to Robert Penn Warren's novel *All the King's Men,* about Louisiana politics in the early part of the twentieth century. But because the purposes of these assignments are different, you and the other student would make different uses of this source. Those same parts or aspects of the novel that you find worthy of detailed analysis might be just mentioned in passing by the other student.

▼

USING YOUR SOURCES

Your purpose determines not only what parts of your sources you will use but also how you will relate them to one another. Since the very essence of synthesis is the combining of information and ideas, you must have some basis on which to combine them. *Some relationships among the material in your sources must make them worth synthesizing.* It follows that the better able you are to discover such relationships, the better able you will be to use your sources in writing syntheses. Notice that the mass communications assignment requires you to draw a *cause-and-effect* relationship between photographs of the war and Northerners' perceptions of the war. The applied technology assignment requires you to *compare and contrast* state-of-the-art weapons technology in the eighteenth and nineteenth centuries. The economics assignment requires you to *argue* a proposition. In each case, *your purpose will determine how you relate your source materials to one another.*

Consider some other examples. You may be asked on an exam question or in instructions for a paper to *describe* two or three approaches to prison reform during the past decade. You may be asked to *compare and contrast* one country's approach to imprisonment with another's. You may be asked to develop an *argument* of your own on this subject, based on your reading. Sometimes (when you are not given a specific assignment) you determine your own purpose: You are interested in exploring a particular subject; you are interested in making a case for one approach or another. In any event, your purpose shapes your essay. Your purpose determines which sources you research, which ones you use, which parts of them you use, at which points in your essay you use them, and in what manner you relate them to one another.

▼

HOW TO WRITE SYNTHESES

Although writing syntheses can't be reduced to a lockstep method, it should help you to follow the guidelines listed in the box on pages 91–92.

For clarity's sake, we'll consider two broad categories of essay (or synthesis) in the remainder of this chapter: the *explanatory* synthesis and the *argument* synthesis. We'll also consider techniques of developing your essays, including the techniques of *comparison-contrast.*

▼

THE EXPLANATORY SYNTHESIS

Many of the papers you write in college will be more or less explanatory in nature. An explanation helps readers to understand a topic. Writers explain when they divide a subject into its component parts and present them to the reader in a clear and orderly fashion. Explanations may entail descriptions that re-create in words some object, place, emotion, event, sequence of events, or state of affairs. As a student reporter, you may need to explain an event—to relate when, where, and how it took place. In a science lab, you would observe the conditions and results of an experiment and record them for review by others. In a political science course, you might review research

HOW TO WRITE SYNTHESES

- **Consider your purpose in writing.** What are you trying to accomplish in your essay? How will this purpose shape the way you approach your sources?
- **Select and carefully read your sources,** according to your purpose. Then reread the passages, mentally summarizing each. Identify those aspects or parts of your sources that will help you in fulfilling your purpose. When rereading, *label* or *underline* the sources for main ideas, key terms, and any details you want to use in the synthesis.
- **Formulate a thesis**. Your thesis is the main idea that you want to present in your synthesis. It should be expressed as a complete sentence. Sometimes the thesis is the first sentence, but more often it is *the final sentence of the first paragraph.* If you are writing an *inductively arranged* synthesis (see page 125), the thesis sentence may not appear until the final paragraphs. (See Chapter 2 for more information on writing an effective thesis.)
- **Decide how you will use your source material.** How will the information and the ideas in the passages help you to fulfill your purpose?
- **Develop an organizational plan,** according to your thesis. How will you arrange your material? It is not necessary to prepare a formal outline. But you should have some plan that will indicate the order in which you will present your material and that will indicate the relationships among your sources.
- **Draft the topic sentences for the main sections.** This is an optional step, but you may find it a helpful transition from organizational plan to first draft.
- **Write the first draft** of your synthesis, following your organizational plan. Be flexible with your plan, however. Frequently, you will use an outline to get started. As you write, you may discover new ideas and make room for them by adjusting the outline. When this happens, reread your work frequently, making sure that your thesis still accounts for what follows and that what follows still logically supports your thesis.
- **Document your sources.** You may do this by crediting them within the body of the synthesis or by footnoting them. (See Chapter 5 for more information on documenting sources.)
- **Revise your synthesis,** inserting transitional words and phrases where necessary. Make sure that the synthesis reads smoothly, logically, and clearly from beginning to end. Check for grammatical correctness, punctuation, spelling.

(*continued*)

Note: The writing of syntheses is a recursive process, and you should accept a certain amount of backtracking and reformulating as inevitable. For instance, in developing an organizational plan (step 5 of the procedure) you may discover a gap in your presentation, which will send you scrambling for another source—back to step 2. You may find that formulating a thesis and making inferences among sources occur simultaneously; indeed, inferences often are made before a thesis is formulated. Our recommendations for writing syntheses will give you a structure; they will get you started. But be flexible in your approach: expect discontinuity and, if possible, be comforted that through backtracking and reformulating you will eventually produce a coherent, well-crafted essay.

on a particular subject—say, the complexities underlying the debate over welfare—and then present the results of your research to your professor and the members of your class.

Your job in writing an explanatory paper—or in writing the explanatory portion of an argumentative paper—is not to argue a particular point, but rather *to present the facts in a reasonably objective manner.* Of course, explanatory papers, like other academic papers, should be based on a thesis. But the purpose of a thesis in an explanatory paper is less to advance a particular opinion than to provide a focus for the various facts contained in the paper.

Suppose you were writing a paper on the debate over welfare. (The welfare debate is, in fact, one of the subjects in Chapter 7, "Left, Right, Center: The American Political Spectrum.") Below are eight sources you might have gathered on the subject. As you read them, try to formulate a conclusion based on your sense of *what the main issues in the debate are and how the opinions expressed in the various sources relate to one another.*

We have arranged the selections in chronological order of publication, just as you might review them as you prepare to write, in order to get some sense of the historical development of the issue. (In this case, the time period is relatively narrow, from 1993 to 1995, but you should still get a sense of which arguments have influenced others.) Note also that the positions represented in these sources range the length of the political spectrum. As explained in Chapter 7, people on the *right* of the political spectrum—known as *conservatives*—tend to believe that governmental authority (and taxes) should be reduced and that individuals should assume personal responsibility for their own lives. People on the *left* of the political spectrum—known as *liberals*—tend to believe that government should work actively to promote equality, fairness, and social justice. As you read for content, you might also want to try placing the writers along the political spectrum, according to the positions they argue.

Ending Welfare as We Know It

BILL CLINTON

Bill Clinton, former governor of Arkansas, was elected President of the United States in 1992. The following speech was made before the National Governors' Association on February 2, 1993. Like all major presidential pronouncements, it was reprinted in the Weekly Compilation of Presidential Documents.

I'd like to spend just a few moments today talking about something that many of us have been working on since the middle 1980s, the issue of welfare reform. 1

I've often spoken with many of you about the need to end welfare as we know it, to make it a program that supports people who have fallen on hard times or who have difficulties that can be overcome, but eventually and ultimately, a program that helps people to get on their feet through health care, child care, job training, and ultimately a productive job. 2

No one likes the welfare system as it currently exists, least of all the people who are on it. The taxpayers, the social service employees themselves don't think much of it either. Most people on welfare are yearning for another alternative, aching for the chance to move from dependence to dignity. And we owe it to them to give them that chance. 3

In the middle 1980s, when I was a Governor here, I worked with Governor Castle . . . to try to work with the Congress to develop a national welfare reform program. With the support of people in the House and the Senate . . . and with the support of the White House, the Governors had an unprecedented role in writing the Family Support Act of 1988, which President Reagan signed into law shortly before he left office, and which Senator Moynihan said was the most significant piece of social reform in this area in the last generation. 4

The Family Support Act embodies a principle which I believe is the basis of an emerging consensus among people without regard to party or without regard to their traditional political philosophies. We must provide people on welfare with more opportunities for job training, with the assurance that they will receive the health care and child care they need when they go to work, and with all the opportunities they need to become self-sufficient. But then we have to ask them to make the most of these opportunities and to take a job. . . . 5

I want to tell you today that within the next 10 days I will announce a welfare reform group to work with you. I will ask top officials from the 6

White House, the Health and Human Services, and other agencies involved to sit down with Governors and congressional leaders and develop a welfare reform plan that will work. I have asked the best people in the Nation on this subject to come and help me do this.

The day I took office I promised the American people I would fight for 7
more opportunity for all and demand more responsibility from all. And that is a commitment I am determined to keep, with your help, by putting an end to welfare as we know it.

Our working group will learn from and work with State officials, busi- 8
ness and labor folks, and leaders from every walk of life who care about this issue. On welfare reform, as on health care reform, there are no top-down, made-in-Washington solutions that will work for everyone. The problems and the progress are to be found in the communities of this country.

But I do want to tell you the principles this morning that will guide my 9
administration as we work with you to reform welfare. First, welfare, should be a second chance, not a way of life. I want to give people on welfare the education and training and the opportunities they need to become self-sufficient. To make sure they can do it after they go to work, they must still have access to health care and to child care. So many people stay on welfare not because of the checks. The benefit levels, as many of you know, in real dollar terms, are lower than they were 20 years ago. They do it solely because they do not want to put their children at risk of losing health care or because they do not have the money to pay for child care out of the meager wages they can earn coming from a low education base. We have got to deal with that.

I believe 2 years after a training program is completed, you have to ask 10
people to take a job ultimately, either in the private sector or in public service. There must be, in addition to the full implementation of the welfare reform act of 1988, in my opinion, a time-certain beyond which people don't draw a check for doing nothing when they can do something. And there is a lot of work out there to be done.

Senator Boren and Senator Wofford have offered a bill to try to re-cre- 11
ate on a very limited basis a pilot project that would take the best of what was done with the work programs of the thirties and try to throw them into the context of the nineties. We must begin now to plan for a time when people will ultimately be able to work for the check they get, whether the check comes from a private employer or from the United States taxpayers.

Today, about half the people on welfare are just the people welfare was 12
meant to help. They fall on hard times, and they have to have public assistance. They're eager to move on with their lives. And after 5 or 6 months or 8 months they're right back at work again, struggling to make their way in the American way. About half the people on welfare stay on for over 2 years. But one in four persons, the people that we really need to try to help to break the cycle that is gripping their children and grandchildren, about one in four stays a recipient for 8 years or longer. Those are the folks that

Governor Wilder I know is now working on, that many of you have tried to address the problems of, and I want to help you with that.

Second, we need to make work pay. We have to make sure that every American who works full-time, with a child in the home, does not live in poverty. If there is dignity in all work, there must be dignity for every worker. Therefore, I will propose an expansion in the earned-income tax credit which supplements the income of the working poor. 13

We can do that. We ought to be able to lift people who work 40 hours a week, with kids in their home, out of poverty. And we will remove the incentive for staying in poverty. It will be much less expensive than to have Government direct supplements to pay people to remain idle. And it will reinforce the work ethic. If we can do that and at the same time do what we discussed yesterday, control health care costs and expand coverage so that no one has to stay on welfare just to take care of their children's medical needs, I think you will see a dramatic breakthrough in our efforts to liberate people from their dependency. 14

Third, we need tougher child support enforcement. An estimated 15 million children have parents who could pay child support but don't. We need to make sure that they do. Parents owe billions of dollars in child support that is unpaid, money that could go a long way toward cutting the welfare rolls and lifting single parents out of poverty and money that could go a long way toward helping us control Government expenditures and reducing that debt. We're going to toughen child support enforcement by creating a national databank to track down deadbeat parents, by having the States go as far as they possibly can to establish paternity at the hospital when children are born, and if I can prevail up here, by using the IRS to collect unpaid support in seriously delinquent cases. I've said it before because it's the simple truth: Governments don't raise children, people do. And even people who aren't around ought to do their part to raise the children they bring into this world. 15

Fourth, we need to encourage experimentation in the States. I will say again what you know so well: There are many promising initiatives right now at the State and local level, and we will work with you to encourage that kind of experimentation. I do not want the Federal Government, in pushing welfare reforms based on these general principles, to rob you of the ability to do more, to do different things. And I want to try to flesh out a little bit of the idea we discussed yesterday about the waivers. My view is that we ought to give you more elbow room to experiment. . . . 16

So I will encourage all of us to work together to try things that are different. And the only thing I want to ask you in return is, let us measure these experiments and let us measure them honestly, so that if they work, we can make them the rule, we can all adopt things that work. And if they don't, we can stop and try something else. That's the only thing I ask of you. . . . 17

I think all of us want what most people on welfare want, a country that gives you a hand up, not a handout. We don't have a person to waste. We 18 need the talent, the energy, the skills of every man and woman, every boy and girl in this country.

Of all the problems we have with competitiveness, whether it is the deficit or the level of investment or anything else, I think all of us know in our heart of hearts America's biggest problem today is that too many of our people never get a shot at the American dream and that if all of our people were living up to the fullest of their potential, we would surely have a much easier path in solving all the issues that we constantly debate about at these meetings. 19

Of all my moments as Governor, one I remember with the most pride occurred here at a National Governors' Association meeting during that 2-year period when we were working on welfare reform. Governor Castle and I sponsored a panel, and I think 40 Governors attended. And we had welfare recipients from all over the country come in and talk to the Governors about what it was like to be on welfare. 20

A woman from Arkansas who was there, whom I knew but had not vetted for this conversation, started talking about her program and how she'd gone into a training program and she had gotten a job, all of that. And I did something lawyers are told never to do: I asked a question without knowing the answer. I said, "Do you think this program ought to be mandatory? Should everybody have to participate in this?" She said, "I sure do." And I said, "Why?" And she said, "Well, because if it wasn't, there would be a lot of people like me home watching the soaps because we don't believe we can make anything of ourselves anymore. So you've got to make it mandatory." And I said, "What's the best thing about having a job?" She said, "When my boy goes to school, and they say, 'What does your mama do for a living?' he can give an answer." 21

I think that moment says more than I will ever be able to say about why this is important, not just important for the poor but important for the rest of us. We must end poverty for Americans who want to work. And we must do it on terms that dignify all of the rest of us, as well as help our country to work better. I need your help, and I think we can do it. 22

The Coming White Underclass

CHARLES MURRAY

Charles Murray, a fellow at the American Enterprise Institute, is the author of Losing Ground *and co-author (with Richard Herrnstein) of the controversial* Bell Curve *(1994). This widely quoted article originally appeared in the* Wall Street Journal *on October 29, 1993.*

Every once in a while the sky really is falling and this seems to be the case with the latest national figures on illegitimacy. The unadorned statistic is that, in 1991, 1.2 million children were born to unmarried mothers, within a hair of 30 percent of all live births. How high is 30 percent? About four 1 percentage points higher than the black illegitimacy rate in the early 1960s that motivated Daniel Patrick Moynihan to write his famous memorandum on the breakdown of the black family.

The 1991 story for blacks is that illegitimacy has now reached 68 percent of births to black women. In inner cities, the figure is typically in excess of 80 percent. Many of us have heard these numbers so often that we are inured. It is time to think about them as if we were back in the mid-1960s with the young Moynihan and asked to predict what would happen if the black illegitimacy rate were 68 percent. 2

Impossible, we would have said. But if the proportion of fatherless boys in a given community were to reach such levels, surely the culture must be "Lord of the Flies" writ large, the values of unsocialized male adolescents made norms—physical violence, immediate gratification and predatory sex. That is the culture now taking over the black inner city. 3

But the black story, however dismaying, is old news. The new trend that threatens the U.S. is white illegitimacy. Matters have not yet quite gotten out of hand, but they are on the brink. If we want to act, now is the time. 4

In 1991, 707,502 babies were born to single white women, representing 22 percent of white births. The elite wisdom holds that this phenomenon cuts across social classes, as if the increase in Murphy Browns were pushing the trendline. . . . 5

In raw numbers, European-American whites are the ethnic group with the most people in poverty, most illegitimate children, most women on welfare, most unemployed men, and most arrests for serious crimes. And yet whites have not had an "underclass" as such, because the whites who might qualify have been scattered among the working class. Instead, whites have had "white trash" concentrated in a few streets on the outskirts of town, sometimes a Skid Row of unattached white men in the large cities. But these scatterings have seldom been large enough to make up a neighborhood. An underclass needs a critical mass, and white America has not had one. 6

But now the overall white illegitimacy rate is 22 percent. The figure in low-income, working-class communities may be twice that. How much illegitimacy can a community tolerate? Nobody knows, but the historical fact is that the trendlines on black crime, dropout from the labor force, and illegitimacy all shifted sharply upward as the overall black illegitimacy rate passed 25 percent. 7

The causal connection is murky—I blame the revolution in social policy during that period, while others blame the sexual revolution, broad shifts in cultural norms, or structural changes in the economy. But the white illegitimacy rate is approaching that same problematic 25 percent region at a time when social policy is more comprehensively wrongheaded than it was in the mid-1960s, and the cultural and sexual norms are still more degraded. 8

The white underclass will begin to show its face in isolated ways. Look for certain schools in white neighborhoods to get a reputation as being unteachable, with large numbers of disruptive students and indifferent parents. Talk to the police; listen for stories about white neighborhoods where the incidence of domestic disputes and casual violence has been 9 shooting up. Look for white neighborhoods with high concentrations of dry activity and large numbers of men who have dropped out of the labor force.

As the spatial concentration of illegitimacy reaches critical mass, we 10
should expect the deterioration to be as fast among low-income whites in the 1990s as it was among low-income blacks in the 1960s. My proposition is that illegitimacy is the single most important social problem of our time—more important than crime, drugs, poverty, illiteracy, welfare or homelessness because it drives everything else. Doing something about it is not just one more item on the American policy agenda, but should be at the top. Here is what to do: . . . Human societies have historically channeled the elemental forces of human behavior via thick walls of rewards and penalties that constrained the overwhelming majority of births to take place within marriage. The past 30 years have seen those walls cave in. It is time to rebuild them.

The ethical underpinning for the policies I am about to describe it this: 11
Bringing a child into the world is the most important thing that most human beings ever do. Bringing a child into the world when one is not emotionally or financially prepared to be a parent is wrong. The child deserves society's support. The parent does not.

The social justification is this: A society with broad legal freedoms de- 12
pends crucially on strong nongovernmental institutions to temper and restrain behavior. Of these, marriage is paramount. Either we reverse the current trends in illegitimacy—especially white illegitimacy—or America must, willy-nilly, become an unrecognizably authoritarian, socially segregated, centralized state.

To restore the rewards and penalties of marriages does not require so- 13
cial engineering. Rather, it requires that the state stop interfering with the natural forces that have done the job quite effectively for millennia. Some of the changes I will describe can occur at the federal level; others would involve state laws. For now, the important thing is to agree on what should be done.

I begin with the penalties, of which the most obvious are economic. 14
Throughout human history, a single woman with a small child has not been a viable economic unit. Not being a viable economic unit, neither have the single woman and child been a legitimate social unit. In small numbers, they must be a net drain on the community's resources. In large numbers, they must destroy the community's capacity to sustain itself. *Mirabile dictu,* communities everywhere have augmented the economic penalties of single parenthood with severe social stigma.

Restoring economic penalties translates into the first and central policy 15
prescription: to end all economic support for single mothers. The AFDC (Aid to Families With Dependent Children) payment goes to zero. Single mothers are not eligible for subsidized housing or for food stamps. An assortment of other subsidies and in-kind benefits disappear. Since universal medical coverage appears to be an idea whose time has come, I will stipulate that all children have medical coverage. But with that exception, the signal is loud and unmistakable: From society's perspective, to have a baby

that you cannot care for yourself is profoundly irresponsible, and the government will no longer subsidize it.

How does a poor young mother survive without government support? The same way she has since time immemorial. If she wants to keep a child, she must enlist support from her parents, boyfriend, siblings, neighbors, church or philanthropies. She must get support from somewhere, anywhere, other than the government. The objectives are threefold. **16**

First, enlisting the support of others raises the probability that other mature adults are going to be involved with the upbringing of the child, and this is a great good in itself. **17**

Second, the need to find support forces a self-selection process. One of the most short-sighted excuses made for current behavior is that an adolescent who is utterly unprepared to be a mother "needs someone to love." Childish yearning isn't a good enough selection device. We need to raise the probability that a young single woman who keeps her child is doing so volitionally and thoughtfully. Forcing her to find a way of supporting the child does this. It will lead many young women who shouldn't be mothers to place their babies for adoption. This is good. It will lead others, watching what happens to their sisters, to take steps not to get pregnant. This is also good. Many others will get abortions. Whether this is good depends on what one thinks of abortion. **18**

Third, stigma will regenerate. The pressure on relatives and communities to pay for the folly of their children will make an illegitimate birth the socially horrific act it used to be, and getting a girl pregnant something boys do at the risk of facing a shotgun. Stigma and shotgun marriages may or may not be good for those on the receiving end, but their deterrent effect on others is wonderful—and indispensable. **19**

What about women who can find no support but keep the baby anyway? There are laws already on the books about the right of the state to take a child from a neglectful parent. We have some 360,000 children in foster care because of them. Those laws would still apply. Society's main response, however, should be to make it as easy as possible for those mothers to place their children for adoption at infancy. To that end, state governments must strip adoption of the nonsense that has encumbered it in recent decades. **20**

The first step is to make adoption easy for any married couple who can show reasonable evidence of having the resources and stability to raise a child. Lift all restrictions on interracial adoption. Ease age limitations for adoptive parents. **21**

The second step is to restore the traditional legal principle that placing a child for adoption means irrevocably relinquishing all legal rights to the child. The adoptive parents are parents without qualification. Records are sealed until the child reaches adulthood, at which time they may be unsealed only with the consent of biological child and parent. **22**

Given these straightforward changes—going back to the old way, which worked—there is reason to believe that some extremely large proportion of infants given up by their mothers will be adopted into good **23** homes. This is true not just for flawless blue-eyed blond infants but for babies of all colors and conditions. The demand for infants to adopt is huge.

Some small proportion of infants and larger proportion of older children will not be adopted. For them, the government should spend lavishly on orphanages. I am not recommending Dickensian barracks. In 1993, we know a lot about how to provide a warm, nurturing environment for children, and getting rid of the welfare system frees up lots of money to do it. Those who find the word "orphanages" objectionable may think of them as 24-hour-a-day preschools. Those who prattle about the importance of keeping children with their biological mothers may wish to spend some time in a patrol car or with a social worker seeing what the reality of life with welfare-dependent biological mothers can be like. 24

Finally, there is the matter of restoring the rewards of marriage. Here, I am pessimistic about how much government can do and optimistic about how little it needs to do. The rewards of raising children within marriages are real and deep. The main task is to shepherd children through adolescence so that they can reach adulthood—when they are likely to recognize the value of those rewards—free to take on marriage and family. The main purpose of the penalties for single parenthood is to make that task easier. 25

One of the few concrete things that the government can do to increase the rewards of marriage is make the tax code favor marriage and children. Those of us who are nervous about using the tax code for social purposes can advocate making the tax code at least neutral. 26

A more abstract but ultimately crucial step in raising the rewards of marriage is to make marriage once again the sole legal institution through which parental rights and responsibilities are defined and exercised. 27

Little boys should grow up knowing from their earliest memories that if they want to have any rights whatsoever regarding a child that they sire—more vividly, if they want to grow up to be a daddy—they must marry. Little girls should grow up knowing from their earliest memories that if they want to have any legal claims whatsoever on the father of their children, they must marry. A marriage certificate should establish that a man and a woman have entered into a unique legal relationship. The changes in recent years that have blurred the distinctiveness of marriage are subtly but importantly destructive. 28

Together, these measures add up to a set of signals, some with immediate and tangible consequences, others with long-term consequences, still others symbolic. They should be supplemented by others based on re-examination of divorce law and its consequences. 29

VIRTUE AND TEMPERANCE

That these policy changes seem drastic and unrealistic is a peculiarity of our age, not of the policies themselves. With embellishments, I have endorsed the policies that were the uncontroversial law of the land as recently as John Kennedy's presidency. Then, America's elites accepted as a matter of course that a free society such as America's can sustain itself only 30 through virtue and temperance in the people, that virtue and temperance depend centrally on the socialization of each new generation, and that the socialization of each generation depends on the matrix of care and resources fostered by marriage.

Three decades after that consensus disappeared, we face an emerging crisis. The long, steep climb in black illegitimacy has been calamitous for black communities and painful for the nation. The reforms I have described will work for blacks as for whites, and have been needed for years. But the brutal truth is that American society as a whole could survive when illegitimacy became epidemic within a comparatively small ethnic minority. It cannot survive the same epidemic among whites. 31

Subsidized Illegitimacy

CHARLES KRAUTHAMMER

Charles Krauthammer, formerly an editor at The New Republic, *writes for numerous publications. This op-ed (opposite–the–editorial page) piece originally appeared in the* Washington Post *on November 19, 1993.*

"Sex Codes Among Inner-City Youth" is the title of a remarkable paper presented this week by University of Pennsylvania Professor Elijah Anderson to a seminar at the American Enterprise Institute. Its 40 pages describe in excruciating detail the sex and abandonment "game" played by boys and girls in an inner-city Philadelphia community, one of the poorest and most blighted in the country. 1

Anderson is a scrupulous and sympathetic student of inner-city life. *Streetwise*, his book on life in a ghetto community, is a classic of urban ethnography. Five years of intensive observation and interviews have gone into the sex code study. It is the story, as told by the participants, of family breakdown on an unprecedented scale. 2

It is the story of a place where "casual sex with as many women as possible, impregnating one or more, and getting them to 'have your baby' brings a boy the ultimate in esteem from his peers and makes him a man." As for the girl, "her dream [is] of a family and a home." But in a subculture where for the boy "to own up to a pregnancy is to go against the peer-group ethic of 'hit and run,' " abandonment is the norm. 3

The results we know. Illegitimacy rates of 70, 80 percent. Intergenerational poverty. Social breakdown. 4

Toward the end of the seminar, I suggested that the only realistic way to attack this cycle of illegitimacy and its associated pathologies is by cutting off the oxygen that sustains the system. Stop the welfare checks. The check, generated by the first illegitimate birth, says that government will play the role of father and provider. It sustains a deranged social structure of children having children and raising them alone and abandoned by their men. To quote Anderson: "In cold economic terms, a baby can be an asset, 5 which is without doubt an important factor behind exploitative sex and out-of-wedlock babies."

It is a mark of how far the debate on welfare policy has come that my proposal drew respectful disagreement from only about half of the panel—including, I should stress, Prof. Anderson himself, who argued that the better answer is giving the young men jobs and hope through training and education for a changing economy. 6

In fact, the idea I proposed is not at all original. I was merely echoing Charles Murray, who in his book, *Losing Ground*, offered the cold turkey approach as a "thought experiment." That was a decade ago. Two weeks ago in the *Wall Street Journal*, the national illegitimacy numbers having become dramatically worse, Murray dropped the "experiment" part and proposed it as policy. 7

Nor is this idea coming only from conservatives. Neo-liberalist journalist Mickey Kaus proposed a similar idea in his book, *The End of Equality*, though in a less Draconian variant: He would replace AFDC and all other cash-like welfare programs with an offer of a neo-WPA jobs program. 8

And last year, candidate and "New Democrat" Bill Clinton gingerly approached the idea with his two-years-and-out welfare reform plan. But "two years and out," however well intentioned, misses the point. The point is to root out at its origin the most perverse government incentive program of all: the subsidy for illegitimacy. 9

Why? Because illegitimacy is the royal road to poverty and all its attendant pathologies. As the 1991 Rockefeller Commission on Children acknowledged, the one-parent family is six times more likely to be poor than the two-parent family. 10

The numbers simply translate common sense. In a competitive economy and corrupting culture, it is hard enough to raise a child with two parents. To succeed with only one requires heroism on the part of the young mother. Heroism is not impossible. But no society can expect it as the norm. And any society that does is inviting social catastrophe of the kind now on view in the inner cities of America. 11

The defenders of welfare will tell you that young women do not have babies just to get the check. Yes, there are other reasons: a desire for someone to love, a wish to declare one's independence, a way to secure the love of these elusive young males and a variety of other illusions. 12

But whether or not the welfare check is the conscious reason, it plays a far more critical role. As Kaus indicated at the seminar, the check is the *condition* that allows people to act on all the other reasons. Take it away, and the society built on babies having babies cannot sustain itself. 13

Taking it away is the single most immediate and direct measure that government can take to break the cycle of illegitimacy and dependency. Moreover, society will not long sustain such a system. Americans feel a civic obligation to help the unfortunate. There is no great protest when their tax dollars go for hurricane relief or for widows and orphans. But by what moral logic should a taxpayer be asked to give a part of his earnings to sus- 14 tain a child fathered by a young man who disappears, leaving mother and child a ward of the state? Underwriting tragedy is one thing. Underwriting wantonness is quite another.

On October 19, Sen. Daniel Patrick Moynihan held a Finance Commit- 15
tee hearing on "social behavior and health care costs." What he really meant by social behavior was illegitimacy. In his opening statement, he drew attention to the explosion of illegitimacy in the general population. It has now reached about 30 percent of all births, 5.5 times what it was 30 years ago. It is a tragedy for the people involved, a calamity for society at large. "Now then," asked Moynihan, "what are we going to do?"

Try this. Don't reform welfare. Don't reinvent it. When it comes to il- 16
legitimacy, abolish it.

Getting Off the Welfare Carousel

TERESA McCRARY

Teresa McCrary is a student at the University of Montana. This article originally appeared as a "My Turn" column in Newsweek, *December 6, 1993.*

I am a welfare mom, and I have one thing to say: stop picking on us! There 1
are 5 million families on welfare in the United States, most of them single women with kids. Is this really such a major financial burden? I believe we're targeted because we're an easy mark. Because we have no money, there are no lobbyists working on our behalf either in Washington, D.C., or in local legislatures. I want to tell you who we are and why we stay home with our children.

The stereotypical welfare mom has 10 kids, including a pregnant 2
teenage daughter, all taking advantage of the dole. I have never personally known such a woman. Most of the mothers I know are women who forgo the usual round of job searches and day care so they can mind their homes and children in a loving and responsible way. We may not have paying jobs, but any mother, married or single, working or retired, will tell you that motherhood is a career in itself.

Yet we are constantly told we should go out and get real jobs. Yes, 3
most of us are unemployed; do we really have a choice? Last time I looked, the unemployment rate was more than 6 percent. If the unemployed can't find work, where are we moms supposed to look? The only jobs open to us are maid work, fast-food service and other low-paying drudgery with no benefits. How are we expected to support our children? Minimum wage will not pay for housing costs, health care, child care, transportation and work clothes that an untrained, uneducated woman needs to support even one child.

Many of us take money under the table for odd jobs, and cash from 4
generous friends and relatives to help support our families. We don't report this money to the Aid to Families with Dependent Children, because we

can't afford to. Any cash we get, even birthday money from grandparents, is deducted from the already minuscule benefits. We're allowed between $1,000 and $3,000 in assets including savings and property, automobiles, and home furnishings. We are told that if we have more than that amount, we should be able to sell some things and live for a year from the proceeds. Can *you* imagine living on $3,000 for a year?

5 As for child support, unless the money sent to the state by the father is greater than AFDC benefits, the family receives only $50 monthly. This bonus decreases food-stamp benefits. We are told that the state intends to prosecute "deadbeat dads" for back support. Seldom do news stories mention that, in the case of welfare families, the state keeps collected back support. Although this reduces the tax burden, none of the money goes to the children. Outsiders are led to believe that the children will benefit, and they do not. No wonder some welfare moms—and their children's fathers—believe it's not worth the effort to try to get the dads to pay up. If we could have depended on these men in the first place, we would not be on welfare.

6 So what about family values? Those of us who do not have a man in our lives do the emotional job of both mother and father. My daughter says she should give me a Father's Day card, because I am just as much a father to her as a mother. On top of these two careers, we are told we should work.

7 We could hold down a minimum-wage job, unarguably the hardest work for the least amount of money, if we could find an employer willing to hire us full time (most low-wage jobs are part time). Unable to afford child care, we'd have latchkey children whose only good meal of the day would be school lunch. The whole paycheck would go to housing and job expenses. When we got home exhausted, we'd clean house, help with homework, listen to how the kids' day went—feeling relieved if none of them had been teased for their garage-sale clothes. We'd pray that nobody got sick, because we couldn't afford a day off work or doctor fees (welfare pays very little, but it has the important benefit of health care). We'd worry about getting laid off at any moment—in tough times, minimum-wage jobs are the first to go.

8 These fears cause stress that may result in child abuse. Many times we feel, no matter how hard we try, that in some way our children are being neglected if we are holding down a job. So we stay home. We've learned that we can depend only on ourselves. We don't enjoy living at the poverty level, but we can't see a minimum-wage job as the answer.

9 I believe that we single mothers must become self-sufficient through education and training. And that means both money and patience on the taxpayers' part. I'm in my fourth year at college. I, and the other welfare moms I know at school, maintain a 3.0 grade average or better. Are we exceptions to the rule? Maybe not; perhaps people in my circumstances are more motivated to make better lives for themselves. Fighting the low self-esteem brought on by divorce and poverty, we have taken the difficult step, usually without a support system, of going back to school. By carefully scheduling classes and studying late at night, I have been able to care for my kids while learning TV and radio production.

College may be out of reach for many. By raising tuition and entrance requirements, most colleges and universities are barring us from their campuses. Even President Clinton's proposed two-year training program may not help much. Vocational or technical schools mean training for low-paying jobs. Still, we'll be told to find work or lose our benefits. 10

If the government keeps decreasing or eliminating the programs we and the children depend upon for survival, here's what will happen: in a few years, instead of 5 million single women and their children on welfare, there will be 5 million single women and their children on the streets. I don't know how many starving millions the United Nations is trying to help in Somalia. But if people keep picking on us, the United Nations will have to help the United States feed *us*. 11

The Character Issue

VIRGINIA I. POSTREL

Virginia Postrel is editor of the libertarian magazine Reason, *where this article originally appeared in June 1994. Libertarians want to drastically reduce government power and authority and, according to their party platform, "oppose all interference by government in the areas of voluntary and contractual relations among individuals." See the material on libertarianism in the "Voter's Manual" and in Burns* et al. *in Chapter 7.*

Mrs. G. Harris Robertson is one of the most influential women in American history, though almost no one has heard of her and I couldn't tell you her given name. She is the mother of the welfare state, the progenitor of the nanny state and its resentful children. 1

A proper turn-of-the-century lady, Mrs. Robertson believed in full-time motherhood as both the greatest expression of feminine virtue and the strongest support for a healthy society; she campaigned for family values in a maternalist state. "Our government should be maternal, some may prefer to call it paternal, there is no difference," she said. "The state is a parent, and, as a wise and gentle and kind and loving parent, should beam down on each child alike." 2

With thousands of other clubwomen, Mrs. Robertson campaigned for "mothers' pensions," state subsidies to families without fathers. In a rousing 1911 speech that launched the National Congress of Mothers' successful crusade, she declared that such subsidies should even "include the deserted wife, and the mother who has never been a wife. . . . Today let us honor the *mother* wherever found—if she has given a citizen to the nation, then the nation owes something to her." (The campaign for a maternal state is sympathetically recounted by Harvard sociologist Theda Skocpol in her recent book *Protecting Soldiers and Mothers.*) 3

Mrs. Robertson and her organized mothers couldn't vote, but they influenced those who could. Mothers' pensions swept the states, though they 4 were never as generous, and rarely as inclusive, as Mrs. Robertson had wished. When FDR came along, these mother-honoring state programs were rolled into the Social Security Act. They became Aid to Families with Dependent Children, a.k.a. Welfare As We Know It.

In her day, Mrs. Robertson faced the same objections to her favorite 5
social program that Mrs. Clinton faces to hers, and she replied with a quainter version of the same rhetoric: "Do not rise up in indignation to call this Socialism—it is the sanest of statesmanship. If our public mind is maternal, loving and generous, wanting to save and develop all, our Government will express this sentiment. . . . [E]very step we make toward establishing government along these lines means an advance toward the Kingdom of Peace."

Eighty-two years later, we are a long way from the Kingdom of Peace, 6
and the public mind is anything but maternal, loving, and generous. We no longer believe that government policy can usher in a messianic age. Nor do we deem government aid an "honorable" payment for the service of raising a child.

To the contrary, Americans deeply resent both the welfare system and 7
its beneficiaries—resentment that has shattered the empathy that led Mrs. Robertson and her allies to identify with poor mothers, resentment that feeds ethnic stereotypes and racial hatreds, resentment that is turning a culture of self-reliance and individualism into a culture of victimhood and nosy animosity.

The welfare state has expanded beyond widows and orphans (and the 8
farm programs that inspired the mothers' movement) to include almost everyone in one way or another—through student loans, retirement money, ever-growing health-care benefits that the Clintons would expand even more. One in every 100 Americans works for a government social-service agency or hospital. Millions more depend indirectly on government transfers.

So your own business is now the public's: Cigarette smoking isn't a 9
private vice but a public-health issue; after all, says anti-smoking activist Ahron Leichtman, "Who pays for these people when they're ill and they're indigent and they go in the hospital?" The same goes for riding motorcycles without helmets, for drugs and drink, for driving without seat belts, for crossing the border to have an American-born baby.

We have become like the workers in Ayn Rand's story of the Twentieth 10
Century Motor Company, a factory in which work and wages were based on "from each according to his ability, to each according to his need." A fable drawn in broad strokes, it is nonetheless prophetic: "In the old days, we used to celebrate if somebody had a baby, we used to chip in and help him out with the hospital bills, if he happened to be hard-pressed for the moment. Now, if a baby is born, we didn't speak to the parents for weeks. Babies, to us, had become what locusts were to farmers."

Locusts to farmers. 11

You cannot go a block in Los Angeles without seeing immigrants 12
working; they bus tables and run shops, drill teeth and tend gardens, give

manicures and clean houses. They were noticeably absent from the hundreds of people lined up for post-earthquake food stamps at the welfare office I pass on my way to work. A few blocks away you could find Latin Americans by the side of the road: soliciting day work on construction sites, selling strawberries or roses. Farmers, not locusts.

But Mrs. Robertson's legacy makes us see mouths to feed, not hands to work, in every new American—every child, every immigrant. "At least in the short run, the large number of illegals in California, and the high birthrate they represent, also contribute disproportionately to the mushrooming cost of maintaining the state's public services: welfare, schools, prisons, health care," opines the *Sacramento Bee.* 13

Republican Assemblyman William Knight produced a less polite version of the same message, circulating a constituent's doggerel that read in part, "Sent for family, they just trash! But they all draw more welfare cash. . . . We have a hobby, it's called breeding, welfare pay for baby feeding." He was denounced as a racist, but his message is conventional wisdom: Immigrants are locusts. A lot of Americans, mostly off the record, believe the same of blacks. The welfare state feeds their prejudices. 14

And locusts are popular in some quarters. Welfare's defenders often disparage work—especially low-paid and manual work—and the people who value it. They imply that anyone who does such work is a victim or a sucker. 15

A lawsuit filed to block New Jersey's welfare reform, which stopped the practice of giving welfare mothers additional money if they have more kids, complains, "It is designed to compel adult AFDC recipients to work." *Newsday* columnist Robert Reno blasts "the Giuliani approach to welfare reform: Draft the poor to clean up New York and fill its potholes. Too bad there aren't some salt mines handy to the city. . . . [I]f New York has sunk to that level, what's the point of cleaning it up?" 16

We might ask the same question about our welfare state, about tinkering with reforms rather than scrapping a failed experiment. The fundamental issue behind welfare reform isn't whether the government should make welfare mothers work or whether it should deter them from having kids out of wedlock. It is what the welfare state, in all its manifestations, has done to all of us, how it has corrupted our character. Mrs. Robertson's legacy has proved to be a triumph of statecraft as soulcraft, and its results are not exactly the motherly love, lower crime rates, and humane citizens we were promised. 17

Eugenics Nuts Would Have Loved Norplant

ALEXANDER COCKBURN

Alexander Cockburn is a reporter and commentator who has written for The Village Voice, The Nation, The Wall Street Journal, *and for the alternative press, as syndicated through the* L.A. Weekly. *Some of his columns were collected into* Corruptions of Empire: Life Studies and the Reagan Era *(1988). This op-ed piece appeared in the* Los Angeles Times *on June 30, 1994.*

"With bated breath, the entire civilized world is watching the bold experiment in mass sterilization recently launched by Germany. It is estimated that some 400,000 of the population will come within the scope of this law, the larger portion of whom fall into that group classed as inborn feeblemindedness. . . . It is estimated that, after several decades, hundreds of millions of marks will be saved each year as a result of the diminution of expenditures for patients with hereditary diseases." 1

Thus in 1935 spake Dr. J. N. Baker, state health officer, as he addressed the Alabama Legislature on prospective laws for compulsory sterilization of a category vaguely sketched as the "feebleminded," but also including "any sexual pervert . . . or any prisoner who has been twice convicted of rape" or imprisoned three times for any offense. Similarly scheduled for sterilization were those "habitually and constantly dependent on public relief or support by charity." 2

Before Hitler and his fellow Nazis (who said they learned much from U.S. sterilization laws) made the discipline unfashionable, eugenics and the prevention of socially unworthy babies were hot topics among American social engineers. The keenest engineers were not Southern crackers but Northern liberals. Eugenic sterilization was most energetically pushed by progressive politicians, medical experts, and genteel women's groups. States pioneering sterilization laws early in the century included Robert M. LaFollette's Wisconsin and Woodrow Wilson's New Jersey. 3

It is conservatively estimated that between 1907 and 1960, 60,000 people were involuntarily sterilized. The science was bogus but its enthusiasts chanted that, within a few generations, society would be purged of imbeciles, criminals, the congenitally idle and other burdens on public patience and the public purse. 4

Today we are seeing a renewal of the same vile eugenic passions. Just as, at the turn of the century, vasectomy allowed eugenicists to abandon advocacy of crude castration, so today Norplant—capsules inserted in a woman's upper arm, preventing pregnancy for up to five years and approved by the FDA in 1990—substitutes for grosser attacks on women's fertility. 5

The argument of the social cleansers is that welfare mothers have babies to accrue more benefits. A few years down the road, they say, these babies ultimately repeat the cycle of dependency and insensate, benefit-related reproduction. Response: Curtail the babies by cutting the welfare benefits, end the cycle by ending welfare. 6

We are at a critical stage on the evolution of these policies. On April 25, Arizona and Nebraska both prohibited Aid to Families With Dependent Children benefit increases for recipients having further babies while on the dole, though in Arizona, the Legislature finally dropped an outright prohibition on welfare assistance for mothers with more than two children. 7

In Connecticut, a bill providing subsidies for AFDC recipients accepting Norplant ($700 when it's implanted, plus $200 annually) recently died. New Jersey, a pioneer in the old sterilization crusade, is eliminating its tiny increases for mothers having children while on welfare. Georgia has done the same, and similar proposals are being considered in at least 21 other states. Wisconsin, another sterilization pioneer, is also experimenting with exclusions of children born on welfare. 8

Vicious myths about greedy overbreeders fuel this legislative craze, which ignores the truth: Welfare recipients average fewer than two children per family and fertility rates of AFDC recipients are lower than among the general population. The prospect of additional benefits is statistically insignificant as a factor in the choice of a mother on welfare to have a baby. . . . 9

Beyond these, there is the profoundest myth of all, which blames young, poor, unmarried mothers for drug abuse, slums, poverty, a stagnant economy, and the falling rate of profit; as with the vasectomist's knife, Norplant will turn society around. These are gas-chamber economics and social prescriptions. 10

At this fraught moment, strong leadership from the White House would surely help in putting the social cleansers to flight. But under the most recent draft of President Clinton's welfare proposals, states will no longer have to seek a waiver from the federal government when embarking on a "child disincentive" program. 11

The door is swinging open and all the old filth seeping through. Wait for the social engineers to start insisting that poor black female teen-agers accept Norplant as a condition for probation or any form of social benefit, or for living in public housing, or for existing. 12

Newt's Welfare: Think of It as a Homeless Drill

ROBERT SCHEER

Robert Scheer, a former national correspondent for the Los Angeles Times, *now writes op-ed pieces. This piece originally appeared in the* Times *on February 12, 1995. "Newt" refers to the conservative Speaker of the House, Newt Gingrich; "Bill" refers to President Clinton.*

Looking over the Republican welfare plan, I finally understood where I went wrong. It was back when I was a tiny fetus swimming around somewhere in the first trimester. I should have kicked real hard and put it to my mother straight: "Get a job or have an abortion; either way, show some personal responsibility." 1

I didn't do that, and as a result, I spent the first years of my childhood in the Bronx being deformed by welfare. My mother never understood what a burden this welfare put on us. She thought it was a good thing the 2 heat stayed on and we ate regular until she could get a job sewing sweaters again.

My mother was a registered alien, so under Newt's welfare plan she wouldn't have been eligible for aid. Mom came through, though, and after a couple of years on the dole she put in 25 more years in a sweatshop and always paid her taxes, as a good alien should. 3

Like Newt's and Bill's backgrounds, mine was not exactly Ozzie and Harriet. My father was a great guy but he had another family and divorces were difficult and expensive in Catholic New York. He also got laid off the day I was born. When he got his job back four years later, he went 15 years without missing a day of work until he suffered a stroke at his machine, and then the New York Knitting Mills gave him a posthumous award. My father provided as best he could for two families and yet helped raise me better than any orphanage could. 4

I know the Republicans wouldn't have wanted my mother to get an abortion, because they would have believed that her fetus was sacred, even though she was unwed. Sure, they liked me as a fetus, but the second I popped out they labeled me illegitimate. 5

I was still in diapers and already made to feel like I'd committed a crime. The fact that I've never been indicted and have paid taxes ever since I was 12 and joined the private sector delivering orders for Mairowitz's grocery store doesn't mean a thing, because the Republican Heritage Foundation has studies proving that we illegitimates cause all the crime. 6

Of course I was different. I was white. I knew how to use welfare as a springboard to a job. When I was 16, I hitched down to Camden, N.J., in the summer and got a union job making real money. I was in Camden a few years ago—it has the highest welfare rate in the country and you don't see those black kids there making real money getting union jobs at the Campbell Soup factory, or at GE or the shipyards; all you hear is the lame excuse that these places are all closed down. 7

Tough love, baby, you picked the wrong time to be a fetus and you can't expect the federal government to bail you out. 8

Like Newt says, the Federalist papers make clear this is a republic, not a democracy, and it's every fetus for itself. That's why the Republicans plan to eliminate aid for severely disabled kids. Sink or swim. 9

Another group of ex-fetuses that better watch out are the ones who pick teen-age mothers. After the Republican revolution, they get *nada.* Certainly not birth control or abortion counseling. Like Republican welfare guru Rep. E. Clay Shaw Jr. of Florida told the National Chamber of Commerce, "It is time for society to send a signal to our teen-agers: Do not sleep with someone and expect the taxpayers to bail you out if you have a child." And that goes for your baby, too. 10

It all gets back to my point about knowing where to be born. The right mother is important. But neighborhood, class, race and wealth ought not to be overlooked. 11

It's also going to be very important to be born poor only in upward swings of the business cycle. Entitlement is out, so if you get a recession 12 and the unemployment and welfare rolls go up, it's every poor kid for himself. Also, the soup pot is going to be a lot smaller. The Republicans are planning to cut welfare by $40 billion over the next five years by sending block grants to the states, which they can use for other purposes. The states will no longer be required to provide a 50 percent match.

Maybe I'm being overly pessimistic. Perhaps the Republicans will create jobs by lowering the minimum wage. But jobs or no jobs, the Republican plan kicks the poor off welfare after two years. Where will they go? Don't get hung up on second-wave questions. 13

Think of the new welfare system as a two-year training camp for the future homeless. Yes, even the kids; they'll love it. Newt Inc. will package it as "Virtual Poverty—the Arcade Game." And if they don't like it? Tough love—they should have kicked harder in the womb. They had their chance. 14

The True End of Welfare Reform

SUMNER M. ROSEN

Sumner M. Rosen retired in 1993 as professor of social welfare at Columbia University School of Social Work. He is a founding member of the Jobs for All Coalition and Jews for Racial and Economic Justice. This article originally appeared in the Nation *on April 3, 1995.*

The advocates for women and children are right; the Gingrich juggernaut's proposed changes in Aid to Families with Dependent Children will inflict serious harm. Welfare advocates argue correctly that reform should at a minimum include affordable daycare and medical coverage if welfare mothers are required to seek work or enroll in training programs. But the central question is jobs, not only for women but for the fathers of their children. 1

Race is the unacknowledged obsession of the welfare reformers. They fear, and hope to extirpate if they cannot change, what they see as black patterns of illegitimacy and disrespect for traditional standards of sexual behavior, lifestyle and work ethic. This is a classic case of blaming the victim, an effort to punish those who have lost the most in the economic changes of past decades. In New York, Chicago, Detroit and other cities with large concentrations of (mostly black) AFDC clients, earlier generations of black men married the mothers of their children because the men had steady jobs. No more. In New York City, for example, the recovery that began in November 1992 restored only one in five of the jobs lost in the 1989–1992 decline, and this modest improvement ground to a halt in the second half of 1994. Job prospects for those with little or no experience and limited skills and education are dismal. Manufacturing jobs rose modestly in the United States but continued to decline in New York. 2

The 1994 unemployment rate for young people age 16–19 in New York was 32.3 percent, but this vastly understates the real level of joblessness. The number of young black men either not in the labor force at all or 3 unemployed and seeking work in New York City came to more than nine in ten in 1988, a "prosperity" year, and there has been no movement in the other direction since.

The real purpose of the GOP's attack on welfare is not to improve an admittedly flawed program but to advance a broader conservative agenda. Welfare is a natural early target because it lacks a powerful lobby, and because the Clinton Administration offers only token resistance—indeed, it was Clinton who first let the genie out of the bottle when he started talking welfare reform during the 1992 presidential campaign. 4

An immediate goal of the right is to insure a continuing supply of employees for the low-wage service industries and factory sweatshops, which depend on a nonunionized, disproportionately female work force. These women will be even more vulnerable to exploitation under the proposed legislation. This pressure will be applied by a welfare bureaucracy, whose job will be to require welfare mothers to accept the unappetizing employment choices they are given, at the risk of losing support for themselves and their children. We already have a flourishing system of coercive treatment of young black men, who are in prison or on parole in record numbers; welfare reform will complete the circle. 5

The GOP has proposed spending a limited amount of money on welfare each year, which would end its status as an entitlement automatically guaranteeing benefits to anyone who meets the minimum requirements. This opens the door to an attack on other entitlement programs, like Social Security, Medicaid, and Medicare. Conservative advocates have long had these programs in their sights; the cutbacks in welfare are a major step toward gutting others. 6

One of the weapons in the welfare assault involves turning AFDC over to the states, which opens the door to the ultimate elimination of the role the federal government has played since the New Deal: establishing and enforcing minimum standards that apply everywhere and to everyone. States already enjoy wide discretion in determining eligibility and establishing the level of AFDC benefit payments; the abandonment of all federal rule-making will expose women and children to the racism, indifference, and budget-cutting of conservative state governments. 7

Once federal standards are undermined in the area of welfare, those buttressing a whole range of other programs will become more vulnerable—occupational health and safety, affirmative action, union-management relations, provision of public housing, environmental protection and many others that have been enacted to meet basic human needs since the New Deal era. This New Deal heritage of an activist and caring government, armed with the tools to enforce the public will as expressed in federal legislation, is the real target of the welfare reformers. 8

But as the stakes go up and more programs come under attack, the prospects for resistance increase. Public opinion supports more jobs for the parents of AFDC children, a higher minimum wage, guaranteed health care, and quality daycare. As people come to understand the broader implications and effects of the attack on welfare, the base of opposition to it can 9 be expanded to include a wide spectrum of groups that share a stake in protecting the gains that Democratic administrations have made during the past half-century.

▲ ▲ ▲

Consider Your Purpose

Here, then, are eight sources on the debate over welfare in the United States. On what basis can you synthesize the material in these sources? Before you can even begin to answer this question, you must consider your *purpose.* Consider that three researchers, working with three different purposes, could read these same sources and write very different papers, each of which would satisfy their reasons for writing. What *you* write depends largely on *your* purpose in writing.

One purpose might simply be to survey, in some kind of order, the positions in the welfare debate. An exam question might require that you do just that. In such a case, your purpose can be satisfied by simple summaries of as many sources as you have space or time for, with an opening and a closing that say, in effect, here are some of the various positions on both left and right. Another purpose might be even more limited: to seek out specific proposals for dealing with welfare—from eliminating it, to reforming it, to leaving it pretty much as it is. In such a case, you would be looking only for those sections of the sources that had to do with specific proposals and passing over other sections that deal with, for example, the underlying reasons for what some (but not all) consider a social crisis.

Yet another purpose might be to take an informed position of your own on welfare. With such a purpose, you could lay out your own position, whether on the left, the right, or the center, using arguments from the sources to buttress this position and attempting to show the deficiencies of arguments with which you disagreed.

But let us suppose—since we are presently concerned with *explanatory* synthesis—that your purpose is to present an overview of the welfare debate, not simply as a series of summaries, but rather as a coherent analysis. This would require that you resist the temptation to organize your synthesis by source, to devote, for instance, one paragraph of your paper to each of several sources. You do not want to write a paper that says, in effect: *"I've read eight sources. Here's a summary of each."* A much stronger approach is to organize your synthesis according to *ideas.* An acceptable explanatory synthesis requires that you see in your sources an interplay of ideas. Based on the interplay you see, choose from your sources selectively, in a manner that promotes your readers' understanding.

Let's return, then, to the questions we posed before presenting the sources: *What are the main issues in the debate,* and *how do the opinions expressed in the various sources relate to one another?* We've already suggested that one useful way to relate the sources to one another is to arrange them along the political spectrum, from right (conservative) to left (liberal). If you view the sources in this light, you will soon conclude that Postrel, Murray, and Krauthammer are conservatives (of various kinds). They want to either drastically reform the welfare system or eliminate it altogether, in accordance with their underlying assumption that government should get out of the business of what they consider charity, and charity, moreover, that reinforces socially irresponsible behavior like having babies out of wedlock and staying on the dole rather than working. Rosen, Scheer, and Cockburn, on the other hand, would be classified as liberals. (Cockburn, in fact, would be classified as a radical.) While not explicitly defending the current welfare system, they attack those who call for its reform or elimination, accusing them of "blaming the victim," of wanting to perpetuate a sweatshop economy, and even of outright racism. McCrary, the only writer who is actually on welfare, attempts to counter the negative stereotype of welfare mothers with her own personal experience and observations. President Clinton, a moderate, calls for welfare reform, but of a much milder type than conservatives would find acceptable.

Formulate a Thesis

The difference between your purpose and your thesis is a difference primarily of sharpness of focus. Your purpose provides direction to your research and focus to your paper. Your thesis sharpens this focus by narrowing it and formulating it in the words of a single declarative statement. (Refer to Chapter 2 for additional discussion on formulating thesis statements.)

Since your purpose in this case is simply to present source material with little or no comment, your thesis would be the most obvious statement you can make about the relationship among these passages. By "obvious" statement we mean a statement that is clearly supported in all the passages.

Your first attempt at a thesis might yield something like this:

```
Many people are engaged in a debate over welfare.
```

While this thesis does identify the subject, it does not identify even in a general way the participants in this debate. The fact that the welfare controversy tends to split along liberal-conservative lines is significant. The first revision might therefore acknowledge this fact as follows:

```
Liberals and conservatives are engaged in a debate over
welfare.
```

This thesis is a little better, more sharply focused, but it fails to indicate the nature of the debate. Even the most casual analysis of the above sources would reveal at least two major points of contention in this debate: Who or what is responsible for the current welfare crisis, and what to do about it? A further revision of the thesis along these lines might yield the following:

```
Liberals and conservatives cannot agree on where to lay
the blame for the current welfare crisis or on how to
fix it.
```

This is a considerable improvement over the first thesis. One further pass might refine it yet further through an acknowledgment that both liberals and conservatives agree that the current system does not work:

```
Liberals and conservatives in the welfare debate agree
that the system is in need of reform, but they cannot
agree on where to lay the blame for the current welfare
situation, or on what the government should do about
it.
```

Decide How You Will Use Your Source Material

The easiest way to deal with sources is to summarize them. But because you are synthesizing ideas rather than sources, you will have to be more selective than if you were writing a simple summary. You don't have to treat *all* the ideas in your sources, just the ones related to your thesis. Some sources might be summarized in their entirety; others, only in part. Using the techniques of summary, determine section by section the main topics of each source, focusing on those topics related to your thesis. Write brief phrases in the margin, underline key phrases or sentences, or take notes on a separate sheet of paper. Decide how your sources can help you achieve your purpose and support your thesis.

Develop an Organizational Plan

An organizational plan is your plan for presenting material to the reader. What material will you present? To find out, examine your thesis. Does the content and structure of the thesis (that is, the number and order of assertions) suggest an organizational plan for the paper? Expect to devote at least one paragraph of your paper to developing each section of this plan. Having identified likely sections, think through the possibilities of arrangement. Ask yourself: What information does the reader need to understand first? How do I build on this first section—what block of information will follow? Think of each section in relation to others until you have placed them all and have worked your way through to a plan for the whole paper.

Study your thesis, and let it help suggest an organization. Bear in mind that any one paper can be written—successfully—according to a variety of plans. Your job before beginning your first draft is to explore possibilities. Sketch a series of rough outlines: arrange and rearrange your paper's likely sections until you sketch a plan that both facilitates the reader's understanding and achieves your objectives as writer. Your final paper may well deviate from your final sketch, since in the act of writing you may discover the need to explore new material, to omit planned material, or to refocus your entire presentation. Just the same, a well-conceived organizational plan will encourage you to begin writing a draft.

Based on the thesis he developed above, student Casey Cole developed a six-part paper, including introduction and conclusion:

A. Introduction: the two contending points of view in the welfare debate
B. The origin of the welfare system in this country; its current status
C. The conservative point of view
D. The moderate point of view
E. The liberal point of view
F. Conclusion: reiteration of the contending viewpoints

Write the Topic Sentences

This is an optional step; but writing draft versions of topic sentences will get you started on each main section of your synthesis and will help give you the sense of direction you need to proceed. Here are some examples of topic sentences for selections based on Casey Cole's thesis and organizational plan. Note also that when read in sequence following the thesis, these sentences give a very clear idea of the logical progression of the whole essay. (Note also that the first topic sentence contains information found in one or more background sources not reprinted here.)

At its inception during the Great Depression, welfare had a clearly defined goal: to temporarily provide financial aid to needy mothers whose husbands had died or become unable to work, so that they could support their families.

Conservatives think that the government should either drastically cut back these welfare programs or get out of the welfare business altogether.

Moderates, seeing a continuing role for the federal government, also believe that welfare programs should be reformed, but less drastically than conservatives would like.

Liberals, insisting that the federal government has a continuing obligation to provide assistance to the needy, applaud the President's reluctance to end welfare outright, but object to any provision for term limits on benefits.

Those who debate welfare disagree so vehemently that it becomes clear that deep-seated political viewpoints underlie the opposing positions.

Write Your Synthesis

Here is Casey Cole's completed synthesis, the product of two preliminary drafts. In the following example, thesis and topic sentences are highlighted. Modern Language Association (MLA) documentation style, explained in Chapter 5, is used throughout. Note that for the sake of clarity parenthetical references are to pages in *Writing and Reading Across the Curriculum.* (Two background sources referenced in this essay, Sancton and Rector, have not been reprinted here.)

Welfare and the American Dream

In an economy where a full-time minimum-wage job can't support a single parent with one child, does government have an obligation to provide welfare benefits to families who have no other means of survival? Or should government abandon welfare, since those on the dole often use it as a crutch to support themselves and their illegitimate children while avoiding getting a job and taking responsibility for their own lives? Liberals and conservatives in the welfare debate agree that the system is in need of reform, but they cannot agree on where to lay the blame for the current welfare situation, or on what the government should do about it. 1

At its inception during the Great Depression of the 1930s, welfare had a clearly defined goal: to temporarily provide financial aid to single mothers whose husbands had died or become unable to work, so that they could support their families. Mrs. G. Harris Robertson, driving force behind the original welfare program, declared in 1911: "Let us honor the <u>mother</u> wherever found--if she has given a citizen to the nation, then the nation owes something to her" (qtd. in Postrel 2

105). One program stood out above all others and became the government's primary means of welfare: Aid to Families With Dependent Children. In recent years, however, welfare rolls have exploded (there were 4.7 million welfare households in 1992), and AFDC's price tag has grown to $25 billion. And AFDC is only the tip of the iceberg. One estimate has the cost of AFDC and food stamps, also a welfare program, at more than $40 billion (Sancton 45). Another estimate, by the conservative Robert Rector, shows about 80 major welfare programs at the federal, state, and local levels costing a total of $324 billion in fiscal year 1993--a lot of money for a program that many believe doesn't work and that has created a permanent culture of dependency (B13). Add to the enormous costs of welfare the resentment felt by many at having to subsidize what they consider irresponsible behavior by those who have made welfare a way of life and one begins to get an idea of why welfare is considered a national crisis, crying out for reform. Addressing the National Governors' Convention in 1993, President Bill Clinton declared, "No one likes the welfare system as it currently exists, least of all the people who are on it" (93).

3 Conservatives think that the government should either drastically cut back these welfare programs or get out of the welfare business altogether. They blame welfare recipients for the crisis, asserting that they lack the personal responsibility needed to get off the dole. These critics believe that as long as lower-class single mothers receive money from the government, they have no incentive either to work or to raise their children within the context of marriage in two-parent families. Charles Krauthammer, writing in the *Washington Post*, believes that this "Subsidized Illegitimacy" lies at the heart of the welfare problem. For Krauthammer, "illegitimacy is the royal road to poverty and all its attendant pathologies" (102). The solution, he ar-

gues, is to abolish the AFDC. "Take [welfare] away," he maintains, "and the society built on babies having babies cannot sustain itself" (102). Welfare recipients would be forced, in effect, to sink or swim. And how would they prevent themselves from sinking? First, of course, they would do this by not having illegitimate children. But if they did, they would have two options, according to Charles Murray, a fellow at the conservative American Enterprise Institute. Either a mother would put her baby up for adoption, or the burden of supporting mother and child would fall upon the women's relatives or upon private charities--thus making "an illegitimate birth the socially horrific act it used to be" (99). The social stigma attached to unwed motherhood, Murray claims, would deter young women from having children they can't support.

Other conservatives focus on the corrupting effects of the welfare state. In her article "The Character Issue," Virginia Postrel, editor of the libertarian magazine Reason, claims that welfare debases both the givers and the recipients and leads to a devaluation of work and to increased prejudice. She compares the current welfare crisis to the situation in the Ayn Rand story in which babies are a pestilence, not a blessing. Later, she extends the metaphor, stating that many people believe that immigrants (who, they believe, comprise a large percentage of welfare recipients) are like locusts (106). Like Krauthammer and Murray, Postrel wants to abolish AFDC. Like them, she believes that the government should not be in the business of providing aid that should be provided--as it was provided in times past--by private charities and by relatives of the needy. Why, they ask, should the taxpayers be required to subsidize illegitimacy and personal immorality? 4

Moderates, seeing a continuing role for the federal government, also believe that welfare programs should 5 be reformed, but less drastically than conservatives would like. They try to mix compassion with practicality. While agreeing with conservatives that single mothers should support themselves, they oppose an immediate cutoff of funds, believing that the federal government should gradually wean AFDC recipients off the dole. The expanding welfare rolls, they believe, should be blamed not on the irresponsibility of the recipients, but rather on a shrinking job market and a reduced economy combined with poor educational opportunities for the people living in poverty. President Clinton sympathizes with welfare recipients:

> So many people stay on welfare not because of the checks. . . . They do it solely because they do not want to put their children at risk of losing health care or because they do not have the money to pay for child care out of the meager wages they can earn coming from a low education base. (94)

Welfare recipient Teresa McCrary, who is also a 6
student at the University of Minnesota, echoes the President's words in defense of welfare mothers. If the unemployed are unable to find work, she asks, how can welfare mothers like herself with inadequate education or training be expected to find more than minimum wage jobs? And who is to take care of her children while she works? McCrary asks for both "money and patience on the taxpayers' part" while she completes the education that will enable her to get a decent job (104). Clinton's welfare principles would provide this breathing space. It would continue the federal government's support of child and health care for working mothers who enroll in federally sponsored job skills programs. But welfare benefits would end two years after completion of this program. Thus, for both the President and the welfare mother, America should remain the land of opportunity where people can, through their own efforts--and with some help--lift themselves up to a better position in life.

Liberals, insisting that the federal government has a continuing obligation to provide assistance to the needy, applaud the President's reluctance to end welfare outright, but object to any provision for term limits on benefits. For them, social justice and compassion are paramount: all should have a fair shot at fulfilling the American dream. Liberals see conservative accusations that AFDC recipients lack responsibility as racial attacks and as examples of "blaming the victim." Sumner Rosen, retired professor of social welfare at the Columbia University School of Social Work, maintains that "[r]ace is the unacknowledged obsession of the welfare reformers. They fear . . . what they see as black patterns of illegitimacy and disrespect for traditional standards of sexual behavior, lifestyle and work ethic" (111). Other liberals point out that regardless of who is to blame for the welfare crisis (and they do not always admit that there is a crisis), it is the children of AFDC families who suffer when aid is cut off. These critics charge that conservative plans to abolish the AFDC are punitive to innocent victims--the children of welfare mothers. 7

Los Angeles Times columnist Robert Scheer recalls his own childhood in a family whose income was supplemented by welfare: "[My mother] thought it was a good thing the heat stayed on and we ate regular until she could get a job sewing sweaters again" (109-10). Scheer sees hypocrisy in conservative opposition to both AFDC *and* abortion: "[Republicans] liked me as a fetus, but the second I popped out they labeled me illegitimate" (110). Radical columnist Alexander Cockburn sees conservative attacks on AFDC as a direct attack on the fertility of poor women reminiscent of the sterilization programs in Nazi Germany (108). He describes a Connecticut bill that would have pressured AFDC recipients to accept subdermal Norplant (which prevents pregnancy for five years) as a condition of continuing to 8 receive welfare benefits. The conservative solution, Cockburn charges, is to "socially cleanse" poor women by keeping them from reproducing--just as the Nazis dealt with their undesirables in the 1930s. For the liberals, then, plans to cut back or eliminate welfare are cruel, racist, and sexist.

Those who debate welfare disagree so vehemently that 9
it becomes clear that deep-seated political attitudes underlie the opposing positions. In conflict are two versions of our nation: one, with an activist and compassionate government in the spirit of the New Deal; another, in which every person is free to excel by his or her own efforts, unhindered--and unhelped--by big government. The former is the ideal America of liberals like Rosen, Scheer, and Cockburn, who feel that the government has a responsibility to provide assistance to citizens who have been left behind through no fault of their own. The latter is the ideal America of conservatives like Krauthammer, Murray, and Postrel, who believe that perseverance and strength of character are all one needs to be successful.

What is the role of the government in providing for 10
the well-being of its citizens? That is the crucial question at the heart of the welfare debate.

Works Cited

Clinton, Bill. "Remarks to the National Governors' Association," 2 Feb. 1993. Weekly Compilation of Presidential Documents 5 Feb. 1993: 125-28.

Cockburn, Alexander. "Eugenics Nuts Would Have Loved Norplant." Los Angeles Times 30 June 1994: B7.

Krauthammer, Charles. "Subsidized Illegitimacy." Washington Post 19 Nov. 1993: A29.

McCrary, Teresa. "Getting Off the Welfare Carousel." Newsweek 6 Dec. 1993: 11.

Murray, Charles. "The Coming White Underclass." Wall Street Journal 29 Oct. 1993: A14(E).

Postrel, Virginia I. "The Character Issue." Reason June 1994: 4-5.

Rector, Robert. "Welfare Is the 800-Pound Gorilla." Los Angeles Times 11 July 1995: B13.

Rosen, Sumner M. "The True End of Welfare Reform." Nation 3 Apr. 1995: 456.

Sancton, Thomas. "How to Get America Off the Dole." Time 25 May 1992: 44-47.

Scheer, Robert. "Newt's Welfare: Think of It as a Homeless Drill." Los Angeles Times 12 Feb. 1995: M5.

Discussion

- Casey Cole devotes his first paragraph to introducing the two contending viewpoints on the welfare debate. He presents each viewpoint as a question and ends the paragraph with his *thesis.*
- In paragraph 2 Cole offers a brief account of the origin of the welfare system in this country and of its present scope and costs, and he quotes President Clinton on the need for welfare reform.
- In paragraphs 3 and 4 Cole presents the conservative viewpoint on the welfare debate—that the government must stop providing welfare benefits as a first step toward ending a culture of dependency—by considering the ideas of Charles Krauthammer, Charles Murray, and Virginia Postrel.
- Paragraphs 5 and 6 deals with the moderate viewpoint on welfare, covering the ideas of President Clinton, who promised to reform the welfare system, but in a less drastic manner than the conservatives advocate. Cole also quotes Teresa McCrary, who defends welfare mothers like herself from conservative critics.
- Paragraphs 7 and 8 consider the liberal viewpoint on welfare—that government has an obligation to continue welfare programs. Cole begins with the views of Sumner Rosen, who considers conservative attacks on welfare mothers as "blaming the victim." He also quotes Robert Scheer and Alexander Cockburn, who have nothing but scorn for conservatives who attack welfare families.
- In the final two paragraphs, 9 and 10, Cole returns to the philosophical differences—and visions of America—that underlie the contending viewpoints on welfare. The short final paragraph puts the essential issue in a nutshell.

Note that since this is an *explanatory* synthesis, Cole does not take a position on the welfare debate or even suggest which side (if any) he favors. His purpose in this essay is simply to explain as accurately as possible how people involved in the welfare debate cannot agree on the causes of the current crisis, or on the appropriate role of government in dealing with it.

▼

THE ARGUMENT SYNTHESIS

The explanatory synthesis, as we have seen, is fairly modest in purpose. It emphasizes the materials in the sources themselves, not the student writer's interpretation. Since your reader is not always in a position to read your sources, this kind of synthesis, if well done, can be very informative. But the main characteristic of the explanatory synthesis is that it is designed more to *inform* than to *persuade.* As we have said, the thesis in the explanatory synthesis is less a device for arguing a particular point than a device for providing focus and direction to an objective presentation of facts or opinions. As the writer of an explanatory synthesis, you remain, for the most part, a detached observer.

You might disagree with this, contending that the thesis we developed for the explanatory synthesis does represent a particular point of view: "Liberals and conservatives in the welfare debate agree that the system is in need of reform, but they can't agree on where to lay the blame for the current welfare situation or on what the government should do about it." To an extent, this does represent a point of view, but note that based on the sources we provided, no contrary point of view would be possible. Having read these sources, no one could disagree that liberals and conservatives argue over who or what is to blame for the welfare crisis and over what the government should do about it.

An argumentative thesis, in contrast to an explanatory one, *is debatable.* Writers working with the same source materials could conceive of and support other, opposite theses. So the theses for argument syntheses are propositions about which reasonable people could disagree. They are propositions about which (given the right arguments, as you formulate them) people might be persuaded to change their minds. Thus, the general purpose of the *argument* synthesis is to present your point of view—in a logical manner and supported by relevant facts.

Consider Your Purpose

As with the explanatory synthesis, your specific purpose in writing an argument synthesis is crucial. What exactly you want to do will affect your thesis, the evidence you select to support your thesis, and the way you organize the evidence. Your purpose may be clear to you before you begin research, may emerge during the course of research, or may not emerge until after you have completed your research. (Of course, the sooner your purpose is clear to you, the fewer wasted motions you will make. On the other hand, the more you approach research as an exploratory process, the likelier that your conclusions will emerge from the sources themselves, rather than from preconceived ideas. For a discussion on the process of research, see Chapter 5.)

Let's say that while reading your sources, what impresses you even more than the arguments themselves (on one side or the other) is the vehemence with which the debate is conducted. The writers are often angry, bitter, scornful of those they consider their ideological opponents. Welfare is one of those issues, like abortion or capital punishment, in which many people have a great moral investment because it goes to the heart of their own personal values. Should the government help out those in need? Should those in need help themselves? And why do they need help in the first place? Which is the better virtue—compassion or self-reliance? Of course, such questions oversimplify the issue, but the point is that questions like these seem to underlie many of the arguments in the welfare debate.

You decide to further pursue this matter. What do the sources show about the kind of arguments that are made over welfare? You are less interested in taking a side on the issue than in focusing on the manner in which the debate has been conducted—a manner that you have come to feel is ultimately irresponsible and self-defeating.

Formulate a Thesis

Your discussion is organized and held together by your own thesis, which may have nothing to do with the thesis of any of your sources. For example, one of your sources concludes that welfare needs to be eliminated because it perpetuates a culture of illegitimacy. This conclusion will not be your thesis. But you may use that source to help demonstrate your point that inflammatory language is common among arguments on both sides of the debate. You may use a source as a strawman, a weak argument that you set up only to knock down again. Or the author of one of your sources may be so convincing that you adopt his or her thesis—or adopt it to some extent but not entirely. The point is that *the thesis is in your hands:* you must devise it yourself and must use your sources in some way that will support that thesis.

You may not want to divulge your thesis until the very end of the paper, to draw the reader along toward your conclusion, allowing the thesis to flow naturally out of the argument and the evidence on which it is based. If you do this, you are working *inductively.* Or you may wish to be more direct and *begin* with your thesis, following the thesis statement with evidence to support it. If you do this, you are working *deductively.* In academic papers, deductive arguments are far more common than inductive arguments.

Based on your reactions to reading the sources, you decide to focus upon what you consider the irresponsible and self-defeating manner in which arguments on both sides of the welfare debate have been conducted. After a few tries, you arrive at the following tentative thesis:

> Those who are carrying on the welfare debate seem less interested in fostering a broad agreement on dealing with the situation than in giving way to emotionalism and irrationality and in making moral judgments about those they consider responsible for the problems.

Decide How You Will Use Your Source Material

Your tentative thesis commits you (1) to explain the emotional manner in which the welfare debate has been conducted, (2) to demonstrate that differences in moral values underlie the different positions in the debate, and (3) to explain how the manner in which the debate has been conducted is not conducive to the formation of a broad consensus. The sources provide plenty of examples that will allow you to fulfill these commitments. The more extreme writers on both sides—Postrel and Krauthammer on the right, Scheer and Cockburn on the left—will provide ample examples of emotional arguments. And assumptions about values are readily apparent in all of the selections.

It may become apparent, as you prepare to write, that you need to consult additional sources to flesh out your paper. For example, you may need to locate statistics and other factual information about welfare for the introductory paragraph. You may also need to consult a source to pin down the differences in philosophy between liberal and conservative viewpoints. (The model essay that follows incorporates and references such sources, though they are not included here.)

Develop an Organizational Plan

Having established your overall purpose, having developed a tentative thesis, and having decided how to use your source materials, how do you logically organize your essay? In many cases, including this one, a well-written thesis will suggest an overall organization. Thus, one part of the synthesis will be devoted to demonstrating the emotional nature of the arguments over welfare, another to showing how these arguments reflect differences in values. Upon further consideration, you may decide that the values issue is so fundamental that it precedes everything else (except for the introductory section). Your next task would be—through outlining perhaps—to subdivide the various sections of the paper. Such an outline does not have to be very complex—simply a series of topics. For example:

A. Introduction. Origin and present status of the welfare system. *Thesis.*
B. Opposing values of conservatives and liberals.
C. Value judgments made by various commentators.
   1. Conservatives
   2. Liberals
D. Emotional language of welfare debate.
E. "Bamboozling"—irrational rhetorical ploys
   1. *Argument ad hominem*
   2. Guilt by association
   3. Slippery slope
F. Conclusion—polarization of the welfare issue prevents the formation of a broad consensus.

Write Your Synthesis

The second draft of a completed synthesis, based on the above outline, follows. Thesis, transitional, and topic sentences are highlighted; Modern Language Association (MLA) documentation style, explained in Chapter 5, is used throughout. Note that for the sake of clarity, page references in the following essay (with the exception of the reference to Sancton) are to pages in *Writing and Reading Across the Curriculum,* including the selections by Burns et al. and Cross in Chapter 7.

The Angry Welfare Debate

Welfare in the United States began in 1935 as a means of providing cash payments to families in which the father had died or was unable to work. It continues to the present through such programs as AFDC (Aid to Families With Dependent Children), Medicaid, and food stamps. Many believe that welfare has reached crisis proportions, with more than $40 billion a year being paid to 4.7 million households. Although this sum is considerably less (in adjusted dollars) than what welfare cost twenty years ago, it is still large enough that what to do about welfare--continue it, reform it, eliminate it--has become the subject of intense debate in this country in the halls of Congress, on radio talk shows, in editorials and magazine articles, and over millions of dinner tables (Sancton 45). But anyone seeking reasonable, logical discussions of the welfare issue will have to look long and hard. What is most striking about many of the pieces written about welfare is not so much the positions taken or the kinds of evidence used to support these positions, but how angry the authors are and how much scorn they display toward those with opposing views (and, for anti-welfare pieces, against many of the people on welfare). In fact, those who are carrying on the welfare debate seem less interested in fostering a broad agreement on dealing with the situation than in giving way to emotionalism and irrationality and in making moral judgments about those they consider responsible for the problems. 1

At the heart of the conflict are fundamental difference of values. These differences are based on the opposing ways that liberals and conservatives view the role of government. Liberals believe in "the positive uses of government to bring about justice and equality of opportunity . . . [and] stress the need for a compassionate and affirmative government" (Burns et al. 263). Conservatives, on the other hand, "prefer private giving and individual voluntary efforts targeted at social and economic problems rather than government programs" (Burns et al. 267). From these assumptions, grounded largely on moral values, it follows that liberals tend to favor welfare programs and that conservatives tend to oppose them. Liberals see welfare as a means of providing a financial safety net for mothers who have no other means of providing for themselves and their children. They consider conservative views on welfare as callous and cruel. Conservatives, on the other hand, see welfare as a means of creating a society of dependents who are able, at the taxpayers' expense, to avoid personal responsibility for their actions. They consider liberal views on welfare as irresponsible and expensive. 2

These moral attitudes are often hidden beneath arguments on what to do about welfare, but sometimes they come to the surface. Conservatives, for example, sometimes link welfare policies to broader cultural trends. Charles Murray believes that the welfare crisis is a result of debased cultural and sexual standards. He blames the rising illegitimacy rate on a wrongheaded social policy that financially rewards single motherhood. Making welfare assistance contingent upon the mother's being married would help restore a society based on "virtue and temperance" (101). Another conservative, Charles Krauthammer, also objects to welfare payments to welfare mothers: "Underwriting tragedy is one thing," he says. "Underwriting wantonness is quite another" (103). Even President Clinton, considered a 3 liberal-to-moderate on welfare, argues that welfare mothers should be required to work, apparently implying that they prefer the dole to gainful employment (95). The most extreme value judgments of all the conservatives come from the libertarian editor Virginia Postrel, who cites Ayn Rand's comparison of immigrants on welfare to locusts, adding, "A lot of Americans, mostly off the record, believe the same of blacks" (107).

Liberal arguments on welfare are also filled with 4
value judgments, though they tend to be value judgments about conservatives. In his own way as extreme as Postrel, Nation writer Alexander Cockburn compares opponents of welfare to Nazis. Cockburn is writing about proposals to require AFDC mothers to accept Norplant, a contraceptive technique. He compares such proposals, and the attitudes that devise them, to the sterilization programs of Hitler's Germany, as well as to similar programs in this country in the first half of the century. Cockburn maintains that those who advocate such programs are also racists: "Wait for the social engineers to start insisting that poor black female teen-agers accept Norplant as a condition for probation or any form of social benefit" (109). Somewhat less inflammatory is former social welfare Professor Sumner M. Rosen, who believes that in advocating welfare reform, conservatives want "to insure a continuing supply of employees for the low-wage service industries and factory sweatshops, which depend on a nonunionized, disproportionately female work force" (112). Rosen sees the real target of the welfare reformers as the entire heritage of New Deal programs that were enacted "to meet basic human needs" (112). Los Angeles Times columnist Robert Scheer adopts a bitterly ironic attack on conservative advocates of welfare reform. He accuses conservatives--who oppose abortion, but advocate cutting off funds to welfare mothers--of cruel hypocrisy. They vigorously support fetuses but have no qualms

about cutting them loose once they're actually born: "it's every fetus for itself. That's why the Republicans plan to eliminate aid for severely disabled kids. Sink or swim" (110).

When people are either promoting their own values or 5
attacking someone else's values, their language often becomes emotional and even inflammatory. This is certainly the case with those debating welfare reform. Making his analogy of certain welfare reformers to Nazis, Alexander Cockburn writes of "vile eugenic passions" and "gas-chamber economics" (108, 109). He concludes his assessment of welfare reformers by asserting, "The door is swinging open and all the old filth seeping through" (109). Another liberal, Robert Scheer, writes that we should think of the proposed two-year limit on welfare payments as "a two-year training camp for the future homeless" (111). Sumner Rosen refers to the conservatives' plan as "the Gingrich juggernaut" (111). On the other end of the political spectrum, for Charles Krauthammer, to reform welfare is "to root out at its origin the most perverse government incentive program of all: the subsidy for illegitimacy" (102). Concluding his article with a final reference to black illegitimacy, Charles Murray turns to a disease metaphor in declaring that American society "cannot survive the same epidemic among whites" (101). Virginia Postrel refers to "Aid to Families with Dependent Children, a.k.a. Welfare As We Know It" (106). The term "a.k.a." (also known as), of course, is often used to identify aliases used by criminals. Thus, Postrel associates welfare with criminality.

Finally, it is clear that people on both sides of 6
the welfare debate often abandon rational arguments in favor of some of the common rhetorical ploys that Donna Cross labels "bamboozling" (300). One of the most common such devices is the argument ad hominem, the attempt to discredit a position on an issue by attacking

the person who supports it. Thus, Sumner Rosen seems to consider those who call for welfare reform as racists: "Race is the unacknowledged obsession of the welfare reformers. They fear, and hope to extirpate if they cannot change, what they see as black patterns of illegitimacy and disrespect for traditional standards of sexual behavior, lifestyle and work ethic" (111). On the other hand, Charles Krauthammer seems to attack welfare mothers when he approvingly quotes ethnographer Elijah Anderson to the effect that welfare mothers look upon babies as economic assets, a means of getting additional welfare money (101-102).

Another favorite irrational argument of those writing on welfare is "guilt by association," the attempt to discredit an idea by linking it with another idea that has already been discredited. We have seen that liberal Alexander Cockburn tries to discredit welfare reform, or at least the Norplant proposals, by associating them with the despised Nazis. On the other hand, conservative Virginia Postrel writes that the welfare state has made our society resemble the one described in an Ayn Rand novel, in which wages were based on a philosophy of "'from each according to his ability, to each according to his need'" (106). Since this quotation is one of the central tenets of Marxism, Postrel is clearly suggesting that the welfare state is like a Marxist state. 7

Yet another form of bamboozling is the "slippery slope" argument, the argument that once we make a single step (downhill) in a certain direction, we won't be able to stop until we slide all the way down. Thus, for Sumner Rosen, once we start the process of welfare reform, the conservatives won't be satisfied until we have totally dismantled the enlightened social legacy of the New Deal (112). For Charles Murray, unless we reform the welfare system, the country won't survive (101). Even Teresa McCrary, a welfare mother, concludes her 8 article (following a reference to United Nations aid to the starving people of Somalia) with an ironic slippery slope argument: "if people keep picking on us, the United Nations will have to help the United States feed <u>us</u>" (105).

Welfare <u>is</u> an emotional and value-laden issue, and it is unrealistic to hope that it can be treated in a completely rational and dispassionate manner. After all, trying to reform welfare is not like trying to debug a software program, a largely intellectual operation. Created originally out of a sense of compassion and good will, welfare involves attitudes and convictions that go to the heart of how human beings act toward and evaluate one another. Nevertheless, reading through a series of arguments on welfare leaves one with a feeling of frustration. Can't these people tone down their language? Can't they at least <u>try</u> to argue in a more rational manner? Above all, can't they see how counterproductive it is to polarize the issue into what is morally right and what is morally wrong? By attacking their perceived enemies so vigorously, by refusing to concede the good faith of those who disagree with them, they cut off the possibility of compromise. They prevent the formation of a broad consensus that could forge a new policy acceptable to the population at large. Unfortunately, that doesn't seem likely to happen. It's difficult to form a consensus with people who think of you as locusts, racists, or Nazis. 9

Works Cited

Burns, James MacGregor, J. W. Peltason, Thomas E. Cronin, and David B. Magleby. <u>Government By the People</u>. Basic Version. 16th ed. Englewood Cliffs, NJ: Prentice-Hall, 1995.

Clinton, Bill. "Remarks to the National Governors' Association," 2 Feb. 1993. <u>Weekly Compilation of Presidential Documents</u> 5 Feb. 1993: 125-28.

Cross, Donna. "Politics: The Art of Bamboozling." Word Abuse. New York: Coward, McCann, 1979.

Cockburn, Alexander. "Eugenics Nuts Would Have Loved Norplant." Los Angeles Times 30 June 1994: B7.

Krauthammer, Charles. "Subsidized Illegitimacy." Washington Post 19 Nov. 1993: A29.

McCrary, Teresa. "Getting Off the Welfare Carousel." Newsweek 6 Dec. 1993: 11.

Murray, Charles. "The Coming White Underclass." Wall Street Journal 29 Oct. 1993: A14(E).

Postrel, Virginia I. "The Character Issue." Reason June 1994: 4-5.

Rosen, Sumner M. "The True End of Welfare Reform." Nation 3 Apr. 1995: 456.

Sancton, Thomas. "How to Get America Off the Dole." Time 25 May 1992: 44-47.

Scheer, Robert. "Newt's Welfare: Think of It as a Homeless Drill." Los Angeles Times 12 Feb. 1995: M5.

Discussion

- In the introductory paragraph, the writer explains the origin and present status of the welfare system (drawing partially upon an article, not included here, by Thomas Sancton), introduces the intense debate over the issue, and concludes with the essay's *thesis*: "In fact, those who are carrying on the welfare debate seem less interested in fostering a broad agreement on dealing with the situation than in giving way to emotionalism and irrationality and in making moral judgments about those they consider responsible for the problems."
- The body of the essay (beginning with paragraph 2) consists of seven paragraphs. The second paragraph sets up the opposing assumptions of liberals and conservatives. (This section is based partially on material from the Burns passage that appear on pp. 264–81, later in this book.) Paragraph 3 quotes and summarizes some explicit value judgments on welfare and welfare recipients made by conservatives (Murray, Krauthammer, Postrel). Paragraph 4 does the same for liberal arguments on welfare by liberals (Cockburn, Rosen, Scheer).
- Paragraph 5 cites examples of inflammatory and emotional language made by people on both sides of the debate (Cockburn, Scheer, Rosen, Murray, Postrel).
- Paragraphs 6–8 deal with various kinds of rhetorical ploys, classified by Donna Cross as "bamboozling." (Cross's article appears on pp.

300–314 later in this book.) Paragraph 6 deals with examples of the *argument ad hominem,* as practiced by Rosen and Krauthammer. Paragraph 7 deals with *guilt by association,* as practiced by Cockburn and Postrel. Paragraph 8 deals with the *slippery slope* argument, as practiced by Rosen, Murray, and McCrary.

- The writer concludes by conceding that welfare is an inherently emotional and value-laden issue, but asserting that the polarizing manner in which the debate has been conducted prevents the formation of a broad consensus for dealing with the problems.

Of course, many other approaches to an argument synthesis would be possible based on the sources provided here. One, obviously, would be to make the opposite argument: the parties to the debate are *not* being overly emotional and that they are saying just exactly what needs to be said, in the *way* it needs to be said. Another would choose to take a position of one's own on the issue of welfare and to use the sources to buttress or shape one's own arguments and to attack other positions. Yet another might be to assess the quality of the various statements according, for example, to the nature of the evidence provided or the type of logic employed. Whatever your approach to the subject, in first *analyzing* the various sources and then *synthesizing* them to support your own argument, you are engaging in the kind of critical thinking that is essential to success in a good deal of academic and professional work.

▼

TECHNIQUES FOR DEVELOPING YOUR PAPERS

Experienced writers seem to have an intuitive sense of how to present their ideas. Less experienced writers wonder what to say first, and, when they've decided on that, wonder what to say next. There is no single method of presentation. But the techniques of even the most experienced writers often boil down to a few tried and tested arrangements.

Summary

The simplest—and least sophisticated—way of organizing an explanatory or an argument synthesis is to *summarize your most relevant sources, one after the other, but generally with the most important source(s) last.* The problem with this approach is that it reveals little or no independent thought on your part. Its main virtue is that it at least grounds your paper in relevant and specific evidence.

Summary can be useful—and effective—if handled judiciously, selectively, and in combination with other techniques. At some point, you may need to summarize a crucial source in some detail. At another point, you may wish to summarize a key section or paragraph of a source in a single sentence. Try to anticipate what your reader needs to know at any given point of your paper in order to comprehend or appreciate fully the point you happen to be making. (See Chapter 1 for a discussion of summary.)

Example or Illustration

At one or more points in your paper, you may wish to *refer to a particularly illuminating example or illustration from your source material.* You might paraphrase this example (i.e., recount it, in some detail, in your own words), summarize it, or quote it directly from your source. In all these cases, of course, you would properly credit your source. (See Chapter 5 on citation form.)

Two (or More) Reasons

In his book *A Short Course in Writing,* Kenneth Bruffee presents some of the most effective ways of developing arguments. The first one is simply called *two reasons,* but it could just as well be called *three reasons* or whatever number of reasons the writer has. Here is this method in outline form:

A. Introduction and thesis
B. Two reasons the thesis is true
   1. First reason
   2. Second reason (the more important one)

You can advance as many reasons for the truth of the thesis as you think necessary; but save the most important reason(s) for the end, because the end of the paper—its climax—is what will remain most clearly in the reader's mind.

Strawman

The next way of presenting an argument is called *strawman.* When you use the strawman technique, you present an argument *against* your thesis, but immediately afterward you show that this argument is weak or flawed. The advantage of this technique is that you demonstrate that you are aware of the other side of the argument and that you are prepared to answer it.

Here is how the strawman argument is organized:

A. Introduction and thesis
B. Main opposing argument
C. Refutation of opposing argument
D. Main positive argument

Concession

Finally, one can use *concession* in an argument. Like strawman, you present the opposing viewpoint, but you do not proceed to demolish the opposition. Instead, you concede that the opposition does have a valid point but that even so the positive argument is the stronger one. Here is an outline for a concession argument:

A. Introduction and thesis
B. Important opposing argument
C. Concession that this argument has some validity
D. Positive argument(s)

Sometimes, when you are developing a *strawman* or *concession* argument, you may become convinced of the validity of the opposing point of view and change your own views. Don't be afraid of this happening. *Writing is a tool for learning.* To change your mind because of new evidence is a sign of flexibility and maturity, and your writing can only be the better for it.

Comparison and Contrast

Comparison-and-contrast techniques enable you to examine two subjects (or sources) in terms of one another. When you compare, you consider *similarities.* When you contrast, you consider *differences.* By comparing and contrasting, you perform a multifaceted analysis that often suggests subtleties that otherwise might not have come to your attention.

To organize a comparison-and-contrast analysis, you must carefully read sources in order to discover *significant criteria for analysis.* A *criterion* is a specific point to which both of your authors refer and about which they may agree or disagree. (For example, in a comparative report on compact cars, criteria for *comparison* and *contrast* might be road handling, fuel economy, and comfort of ride.) The best criteria are those that allow you not only to account for obvious similarities and differences between sources but also to plumb deeper, to more subtle and significant similarities and differences.

There are two basic approaches to organizing a comparison-and-contrast analysis: organization by *source* and organization by *criteria.*

1. *Organizing by source.* You can organize a comparative analysis as two summaries of your sources, followed by a discussion in which you point out significant similarities and differences between passages. Having read the summaries and become familiar with the distinguishing features of each passage, your readers will most likely be able to appreciate the more obvious similarities and differences. Follow up on these summaries by discussing both the obvious and subtle comparisons and contrasts, focusing on the most significant.

   Organization by source is best saved for passages that are briefly summarized. If the summary of your source becomes too long, your audience might forget the remarks you made in the first summary while they read the second. A comparison-and-contrast synthesis organized by source might proceed like this:

   I. Introduce the essay; lead to thesis.
   II. Summarize passage A by discussing its significant features.
   III. Summarize passage B by discussing its significant features.

IV. Write a paragraph (or two) in which you discuss the significant points of comparison and contrast between passages A and B.

End with a conclusion in which you summarize your points and, perhaps, raise and respond to pertinent questions.

2. *Organizing by criteria.* Instead of summarizing entire passages one at a time with the intention of comparing them later, you could discuss two passages simultaneously, examining the views of each author point by point (criterion by criterion), comparing and contrasting these views in the process. The criterion approach is best used when you have a number of points to discuss or when passages are long and/or complex. A synthesis organized by criteria might look like this:

    I. Introduce the essay; lead to thesis.
    II. Criterion 1
        A. Discuss what author A says about this point.
        B. Discuss what author B says about this point.
    III. Criterion 2
        A. Discuss what author A says about this point.
        B. Discuss what author B says about this point.

And so on. Proceed criterion by criterion until you have completed your discussion. Be sure to arrange criteria with a clear method; knowing how the discussion of one criterion leads to the next will ensure smooth transitions throughout your paper. End with a conclusion in which you summarize your points and, perhaps, raise and respond to pertinent questions.

▼

A CASE FOR COMPARISON AND CONTRAST: WHAT GOOD IS GOVERNMENT?

We'll see how these principles can be applied to the following articles by President Bill Clinton and Speaker of the House of Representatives Newt Gingrich on what government does well and what it does badly. These statements appeared in *Newsweek,* on facing pages, on April 10, 1995.

What Good Is Government . . . ?

BILL CLINTON

One of my earliest political memories is from 1957, when I was 11 years old. Arkansas's governor, Orval Faubus, had used the National Guard to stop the racial integration of the Little Rock public schools. President Eisenhower then federalized the Guard to make sure integration happened. I was in a distinct minority among my friends in school because I thought Eisenhower had done the right thing. At the time, the Southern states were 1 using the doctrine of "states rights" to keep some people from having real opportunity.

Even earlier, I saw this discrimination all the time at my grandfather's grocery store in Hope. Most of his customers were black, and many of them lived either behind the store or behind the cemetery on roads that were not paved. I was aware as a little boy that the government treated some people differently from others. My grandfather thought his customers were entitled to paved roads since they paid taxes just like the white people did. That unfairness really didn't change until the 1960s when the federal government stepped in with the Voting Rights Act, which enabled blacks to vote in large numbers. That forced elected officials to treat them with more respect. 2

My grandfather also taught me about Franklin Roosevelt and the New Deal. He believed Roosevelt gave the American people a chance to work and then protected them when they were in trouble or retired. Conditions in Arkansas during the Great Depression were just miserable. In this case, the lesson was that sometimes the free market did not work by itself. 3

So I grew up with a sense that the absence of a strong federal government did not necessarily mean that people had more freedom and opportunity. In fact, the national government had to affirmatively step in to make sure everybody had a fair chance. 4

But I started to develop a slightly different view about government when I returned to Arkansas to serve in public office. There were many times when I thought the national government was doing things that didn't make sense. When I was attorney general, for instance, I saw that because of federal law, the appeals process in death penalty cases took, on average, eight years. That was crazy, cost a lot of money and didn't serve the ends of justice. 5

It became clear to me that we had to constantly reform and "reinvent" government. A professor of mine at Georgetown University, Carroll Quigley, used to say that you had to build institutions to make a civilization work—but that institutions tended to become "institutionalized." In other words, they would abandon the original purpose for which they were established, and, instead, become more concerned about preserving themselves, their prerogatives, their position, their power. 6

At its worst, government can act just as a powerful monopoly does in the private sector—unaccountable, abusive of power and immune to change. Examples include the welfare system, a lot of public housing, and some of our public schools. The schools that don't work, for instance, have guaranteed revenues, guaranteed customers, and the shots are being called in the central office bureaucracy. That's why some of the more promising school reforms involve giving parents a choice of public schools or letting groups of teachers set up new "charter schools." These reforms instill a sense of competition, while preserving our historic commitment to public education. 7

Sometimes the government starts out fine but doesn't adapt to changing conditions. The Environmental Protection Agency was set up under 8

President Nixon. I believe if the government had not said there was a national interest in protecting the environment, we would not have made the great progress we have in cleaning up our air and water. But we don't need to approach these issues today the same way we did in the 1970s. Why? Because now businesses have figured out that environmental protection is good economics. Entire industries have developed to design products and techniques to make factories cleaner and more efficient at the same time. Now, we have to look at more market-oriented solutions. My EPA is cutting the paperwork burdens of compliance by 25 percent next year, and giving businesses that ask for help six months to fix their problems without being fined.

There are some things the government does quite well. One, of course, 9
is national security. We have the finest military in the world. And with the FBI, the Drug Enforcement Administration and the crime bill that we passed last year, the government can help make people feel safer in our streets and schools.

The government is also good at what is known in the policy world as 10
"income transfers." In other words, it's good at taking in tax money from the population as a whole and redistributing it to people with special needs. The Social Security system has worked quite well, with a very low overhead. Some argue that people could get a better rate of return if they invested the money themselves, but Social Security has basically been stable, always made its payments, and the administrative costs are low. Medicare has problems due to the general inflation in health care costs, but its overhead is low too and compares favorably with any system in the world.

Government has successfully set up institutions that protect economic 11
markets from their own worst excesses. The Federal Reserve System, which regulates banks, and the Securities and Exchange Commission, which oversees the stock markets, have been crucial in fostering economic growth in this country. Some of the countries in the former Soviet Union have asked for advice on how to get their markets to thrive, and one of the things they've looked at is how to set up these institutions so their markets can flourish as ours have.

Carefully targeted government action can also work in other areas. Our 12
family leave law, the Brady bill, the school lunch program, and the proposed minimum wage increase are good examples.

Finally, the government has done well when it set out to provide edu- 13
cation to a broad base of Americans. Perhaps the single most important thing the government did to improve opportunity during my childhood was the GI Bill, which helped millions of young men go to college. Since then, other college loan programs, including our new direct loan program, have helped so many more students. And the Head Start program has helped disadvantaged kids become more prepared for school.

I've understood for nearly 20 years that big government is not the solu- 14
tion to every big problem. We have already eliminated or reduced 300 programs, and in my new budget I've asked Congress to eliminate or consolidate 400 more. The federal government now has 100,000 fewer people

than when I became president. But it is equally wrong to say that government is the source of all our problems. The difference between the Republicans and me is that I still believe that the federal government has an affirmative responsibility to help people to make the most of their own lives.

15 Today, government's job is to enable people to adjust to the changing economy. Technology and worldwide competition have depressed wages in the low-skilled jobs. Middle-class pay is stagnating and people must work harder just to stay in place. I don't mean to reduce everything to economics; we have deep problems of culture and of the spirit in this country. Still, many problems we face—the breakdown of family and community, the rise of crime and violence, anxiety about the future—are a direct result of economic changes. Parents have had longer work weeks, less sleep, less time for their children. We also have growing inequality of incomes based primarily on differences in education. We have to change that if we want to grow the middle class and shrink the underclass.

16 The most important thing government can do to achieve that goal is to help people raise their education and skill levels. We have to say to people, "We can't solve your problems for you—you have to go out and make your way in the private sector—but we're going to make sure you are empowered to make the most of your own lives." That's what I mean when I talk about the New Covenant: creating more opportunity but demanding more responsibility in return. You can see this in our efforts to reform a welfare system that has worked very poorly for people who are not self-motivated. Roughly half the people who get on welfare do so because they hit a bump in the road of life, and they get off quickly. But for those in the permanently dependent class, government has not done a good job because it has not demanded much from the recipients. That's why we want to require work and responsible parenting as we give people the help they need to get education and jobs. You can see it in our other efforts to give people the tools to make good lives for themselves: for example, making college loans available on good repayment terms or letting people earn college money by serving their communities in AmeriCorps.

17 I would love to go even further. We should collapse all the government job-training programs into one and increase the funding. That way people would know that they could always go back to school and get new skills and have a chance to raise their incomes. I would expand this direct college-loan program that we've started so that everyone would be able to benefit.

18 The role of government is not as simple and obvious as it was during the New Deal. At that time, the government helped working people directly by giving them jobs. The sorts of things we have to do now to create opportunity have major payoffs but you don't see them until later. Sometimes, because the connection of the policy to the job payoff is indirect, you don't see it all. For example, I believe with all my heart that our economic plan was in the best interests of America, bringing the deficit down, investing more in education and giving working families with incomes under

$25,000 a tax break, to encourage work over welfare. But it's hard for people to see the connection between these policies and economic growth. The same is true on trade. NAFTA opened up markets in Mexico and Canada, and the GATT treaty increased trade throughout the world. They contributed to the creation of 6.1 million new jobs and the lowest combined rate of unemployment and inflation in 25 years.

I think the American people are torn about what role government ought to play. They say they can't stand big government and they want less of it—but they have huge aspirations for it. After so many years of stagnant income and rising social problems, they want immediate results. But the best solutions can take a long time to work because the problems developed over a long time, and because making progress on them depends not only on government but also on people taking more personal responsibility. 19

This debate about the role of government could be very important. The American people have to decide what they have a right to expect and, indeed, demand of us in public office—and what they still have to do on their own. 20

Political leaders in turn must state more clearly what government can and cannot do, what results the American people can expect, and when they can expect them. In this new era, a lot of people are angry and frustrated because prosperity and stability do not cover all who work hard and play by the rules, and because they feel that government is helping special interests and not holding everyone equally accountable. Instead of exploiting the public's anger, we should seek to unify our people in a common mission to keep the American dream alive for ourselves and our children. In this effort, I believe the role of government is to help create good jobs; to increase our security at home and abroad; to reform government, making it smaller and less bureaucratic; to demand more personal responsibility from all our citizens; and most important, to expand education and training so that all our citizens have the chance to make the most of their own lives. 21

If we do these things our best days are still ahead. 22

. . . *And Can We Make It Better?*

NEWT GINGRICH

I was born into a post-World War II world that was orderly, structured, and seemed to make sense. It was a time of the New Deal and the Marshall Plan; there was a great faith in systems, a belief in the grand designs of social planners. But then, when I was a young man, came the chaos of the 1960s, beginning with the Bay of Pigs and culminating in Watergate. The orderly system of FDR and Eisenhower began to disintegrate. David Halberstam's 1972 book, *The Best and the Brightest,* profoundly describes how the American elite led us into Vietnam. It shows how the rational and linear projections of bureaucracy are inherently due to fail in a world that is too complex and too human to be linear and rational. There's a vivid scene 1 in which Lyndon Johnson comes to see Speaker Sam Rayburn after his first cabinet meeting. LBJ is impressed by all the brilliant people from Harvard, but he says he'd feel more secure if any one of them had run for local sheriff in Texas.

As a political science major at Emory University in the early 1960s, I had read all these studies that had graphs and charts and analyses. But then I dropped out of college and ran a congressional campaign in North Georgia in 1964 and encountered real human beings. They didn't resemble my political science graphs at all. They were too complicated, too different, too idiosyncratic. I went back to college and began to read history, to learn how real people lived. 2

Because I am a conservative, people get the mistaken idea that I hate government. But one can't grow up on U.S. Army bases, attend graduate school on a National Defense Education Act Fellowship, and then go on to teach at a state college and have a hatred of government. My stepfather served in the Army for 27 years, and my dad served in the Navy and worked for the Air Force, fixing B-52s. I revere the United States government as the greatest institution of freedom in the history of the human race. 3

Government does some things very well. It defends the nation. It keeps the peace. It freed the slaves. It builds useful things, like the Panama Canal, and enables valuable research, like discovering the cure for polio. It can shape market forces creating the right incentives for saving or investing. Those are things government can do. 4

But government, as a general rule, does a very poor job at fine-grained, detailed decisions. It's too slow, too political, it just doesn't have the capacity. The idea of the government in Washington trying to decide where to put a bridge in a Georgia county is just crazy. It's insane. Government can run very small, very elite bureaucracies very well. But the longer government stays in charge of something, the more bureaucratic, the slower, the more cumbersome, the more inefficient in becomes. 5

Federal agencies that stay in touch with reality every day—the FBI and the military, the Treasury and the Federal Reserve—have a different rhythm, a different flavor, a different style. They have to be responsive to real-world problems in real time. They're worth keeping. But in the case of the ones that don't touch reality every day, we ought to consider whether they have served their purpose. In the Department of Labor, the Department of Commerce, the Department of Education, people sit around in large rooms reading paper reports from people they've never met on topics they've never seen involving towns they've never visited. Why would you think such a system could possibly work? 6

Our modern leaders have forgotten that government cannot substitute for private initiative, personal responsibility, or faith. The role of a national leader is, first, to nurture the culture, second to encourage civic duty, and third, to strengthen the private sector. Managing the bureaucracy comes last. Thomas Jefferson understood this; so did FDR. Where Lyndon Johnson went wrong was that he thought government could do it all. In the 7

1960s, government crowded out private sector voluntarism. Secular bureaucracy crowded out spiritual commitment.

What was the result? The welfare state, a vast structure which leads to 12-year-olds getting pregnant, 14-year-olds getting killed, 17-year-olds dying of AIDS and 18-year-olds getting diplomas they can't read. We have public schools in some inner-city areas that are basically union-controlled monopolies which largely fail to educate. We have a tax system for poor people that punishes them if they get married. We have a Medicaid system that punishes you if you try to acquire wealth. We have a welfare system that punishes you if you try to save. We have a public housing system in which a bureaucrat treats you like dirt because you're not a customer that he could lose, but rather a dependent client. 8

Yes, there was poverty and squalor before the welfare state. The transition from a rural to an urban state in the 19th and early 20th centuries was harsh. But a tremendous effort was made to rise above that squalor, and most people did it. Huge numbers of immigrants arrived not speaking English and without any money, and a generation later they were full citizens earning a good living and moving to the suburbs. Now, under the current system, they get trapped in poverty for three generations. They get more desperate, more hopeless. They feel they have no future. That is the fruit of the 1960s when the Great Society began to destroy the spirit of America. 9

Let's be clear here: The years 1965 to 1995 were not a complete wasteland in which nothing good happened. It was absolutely essential to eliminate racial discrimination, and I don't think that would have happened without a strong shove from the federal government. Predictably, government went too far and began discriminating in reverse; we should remember that Martin Luther King's goal was a colorblind society, not one in which racial preferences divide us. 10

As another example, the impetus behind environmental and safety laws in the 1970s was right. I taught environmental studies and participated in Earth Day in 1971. I believe we need to figure out how to manage the planet, since we're the dominant species. But we let environmental protection become a maze of mindless rules. How can you possibly support a process that takes the most expensive way to get clean air instead of the least expensive way? 11

I would replace this degenerative system. Let's restore our church- and synagogue-based system of volunteer help for the poor. Where government is still necessary to provide a safety net, I would return the responsibility to states and local government. There ought to be some safeguards. We ought to have federal oversight, and if we find that a state is a disaster, then we should change the law. But I'm like FDR. I believe we have nothing to fear but fear itself. Our current goal should be to experiment, and if it fails, to experiment again, and if that fails, to experiment anew. 12

With the proper leadership and incentives, we can turn around our culture. Gertrude Himmelfarb, in her book, *The De-Moralization of Society,* reminds us that in Victorian England they reduced the number of children 13 born out of wedlock by almost 50 percent. They didn't do this through a new bureaucracy. They did it by re-establishing values, by moral leadership, and by being willing to look people in the face and say. "You should be ashamed of yourself when you get drunk in public. You should be ashamed if you're a drug addict." Marvin Olasky reminds us in *The Tragedy of American Compassion* that in the 19th century, there was a volunteer for every two poor people. They actually knew the person they were trying to help. An automatic reaction to a homeless person was to demand, "Are you willing to work?" If they were not, you had a moral obligation not to support them. If all you were doing was subsidizing their alcoholism or drug addiction, that itself was immoral.

Of course, it's not the 19th century anymore. But the principles of the past that worked are worthy of being re-examined. At the same time, we've also got to look forward. We are entering a new age in which we can harness technological forces to help us spread the idea of freedom and raise our standard of living—if we can just free these new forces from the coils of bureaucracy and excessive government regulation. The information revolution will speed and free commerce. It also allows leaders to reach the people instantly and directly. 14

Government redistribution of wealth has never worked in the past and will not in the future. It sets up a standard of grievance. It says, "You're successful, can I steal from you?" What you want is a standard of achievement. "How do I get to be successful" Fifty black Bill Gateses would change the entire equation of American life. You either have a system where you say, "Would you like to learn how to be rich, would you like to learn how to be successful?" Or you have a system where you say, "Well, you really ought to feel envy and resentment, so let's see if we can mug them." 15

Instead, the new Republican majority will approach this differently: Instead of a huge, intrusive, unproductive government, we'll create a massive level of entrepreneurial incentives. We'll cut the bureaucracy and reduce the burden of taxation. I would eliminate the red tape that makes it impossible for the candy lady in public housing to open up a candy store. We'll make it easy and natural to follow an entrepreneurial instinct to go out, make money and become successful. Indeed, that was basically our system—until we began to lose our way. 16

I don't believe President Clinton and I are really that far apart on what needs to be done. I don't know any politician in America who has a better intuitive sense of reengineering government and society, of the world market, and of information technologies. When you talk to President Clinton, he gets it. I think if the president were a Republican, we could work together easily. But I think he is surrounded by Democratic allies in Democratic institutions. He thinks in parallel to us, but he acts differently. He talks like us, but the decisions of his administration could have come from Mondale or Dukakis. When you get to the bureaucracy and the cabinet and the Democrats in the House and the Senate, somehow it all seems to just veer 17 to the left. The words are terrific, but when you get down to decisions, it's the same old Big Government nonsense.

The President now has an excellent opportunity. He can work with us to redefine government on a grand scale. If he joins with us, instructs his aides to balance the budget and eliminate unnecessary federal agencies, we'll know he's serious. If, unfortunately, he flinches and decides he can't make his allies mad, we'll know he's not serious. The balanced-budget discussion this spring is very serious business. It's about more than just economics; it speaks to where we've been as a society, where we are and where we need to go as we approach the 21st century. Developing a balanced budget is the first essential step we need to restore an American civil society. **18**

With or without President Clinton and the Democrats, the revolution will go on. We have accomplished a lot in 100 days. It may take a decade to accomplish the rest. But it will happen. **19**

▲ ▲ ▲

Comparison-Contrast (Organized by Source)

Here is a comparison-and-contrast analysis of the Clinton and Gingrich statements by *source.* (Thesis and topic sentences are highlighted.) The thesis is as follows:

> These two politicians represent not only opposing parties, but also diametrically opposed viewpoints about the roles of government in American society.

What's the Good of Government?

Is government the solution, or is it the problem? Many Americans believe that government plays an essential role in making our lives safer and our society more productive and more fair. But many others believe that government is too powerful and intrusive, and that it stifles personal initiative. Within the government itself, there are deep divisions, as evidenced in two recent articles by President Bill Clinton and Speaker of the House of Representatives Newt Gingrich that appeared on facing pages in the April 10, 1995 issue of <u>Newsweek</u>. These two politicians represent not only opposing parties, but also diametrically opposed viewpoints about the role of government in American society. **1**

For President Clinton government is a positive force in fostering social justice and national productivity. He begins his article by describing the federal government's role in enacting civil rights legislation in the 1960s and in putting people back to work during the Great Depression in the 1930s. Federal government intervention was necessary to combat racial discrimination because state officials like Governor Faubus of Arkansas were actively preventing African-Americans from exercising their rights as American citizens. And federal intervention was necessary in the Great Depression because the free market was obviously not working. For such reasons Clinton "grew up with a sense that the absence of a strong federal government did not necessarily mean that people had more freedom and opportunity." The President's next major argument goes to the heart of the controversy over the role of federal government: he asserts that the government is good at "income transfers. In other words, it's good at taking in tax money from the population as a whole and redistributing it to people with special needs." As examples, Clinton cites Social Security and Medicare. Clinton also believes that government has a role in regulating the "excesses" of the economic markets. Finally, Clinton believes that one of the government's most important roles is in fostering education and training, not only to prepare young people for the occupational requirements of a changing economy, but also to help people on welfare to live productive lives. 2

While Speaker Gingrich denies that he hates government, his view is certainly more negative than President Clinton's. Gingrich's main argument against government is that many of the bureaucrats who run it are detached from the needs and concerns of ordinary Americans. "The idea of the government in Washington trying to decide where to put a bridge in a Georgia county is just crazy," he asserts. "It's insane." By its nature, 3

Gingrich charges, government bureaucracies are slow, inefficient, and out of touch with reality. He cites as one example the "maze of mindless rules" that underlie the federal government's environmental protection programs. The speaker's second major charge against government is that it stifles "private initiative [and] personal responsibility." He would replace the government's welfare state with a network of "church- and synagogue-based system of voluntary help for the poor," pointing out that such private sector voluntarism was common in the 19th century. While the President believes that the government is good at "income transfers," the speaker asserts that "[g]overnment redistribution of wealth has never worked in the past and will not in the future." Gingrich promises to help cut the red tape that stifles entrepreneurs and restore the American system that worked so well "until we began to lose our way."

Clinton and Gingrich do agree on some important points. Both men revere our form of government and agree on the power of government to promote personal freedom. More specifically, both men believe that government has a vital role in national defense and in fighting crime through agencies such as the Federal Bureau of Investigation and the Drug Enforcement Administration. Gingrich believes that the government should be involved in medical research, and he even believes that the government "can shape market forces creating the right incentives for saving or investing." Pointing to the benefits he himself has received from government, the speaker emphasizes that he "revere[s] the United States government as the greatest institution of freedom in the history of the human race." For his part, President Clinton concedes that the government needs some major reforms--including welfare reforms. Like Gingrich, he worries that government sometimes becomes so "institutionalized" and encumbered with regulations that it becomes unresponsive to citizens' needs and to new realities. (Clinton cites his own "reinventing government" program to deal with such problems.) And he agrees with Gingrich that the government needs to do more to "demand more personal responsibility from all our citizens."

Despite these agreements, it is clear that Bill 5
Clinton's and Newt Gingrich's views of government are fundamentally different. In fact, these kinds of differences often lead to gridlock in government. Contentious issues can block up the legislative process so that government becomes incapable of action. Either Congress and the President are at odds, or Congress itself is divided. Recently, Congress and the President worked for more than a year to reform health care, and finally came up with--nothing. The same may happen with welfare reform. However, as Winston Churchill observed, democracy is the worst form of government, except for all of the others. The alternative to democracy is one-party rule or dictatorship. Our form of government does invite fierce debate. It encourages citizens and legislators to argue their differences, rather than to suppress them. Often enough, these debates do result in compromises that opposing parties can live with. At the very least, they allow citizens to feel that their views are being heard, even when they are frustrated that they do not prevail. So let Clinton and Gingrich--and their followers--debate the role of government. The fact that they can do so, on more or less equal terms, is an indication of the fundamental health of our democracy.

Discussion

- The writer uses the first paragraph to introduce the subject, the proper role of government in society, and the opposing views of President Clinton and Speaker Gingrich.
- In paragraph 2, the writer summarizes President Clinton's position.

- In paragraph 3, the writer summarizes Speaker Gingrich's position. Notice the transition from Clinton to Gingrich in the first sentence of this paragraph.
- In the fourth paragraph the writer points out that the two politicians do agree on some of the strong points and the weak points of government.
- In the fifth paragraph, the writer reiterates the fundamental differences between the two men, differences of the kind that sometimes lead to governmental paralysis. But the writer concludes that these kinds of debates are the essence of democracy and ultimately a sign of strength rather than weakness.

Comparison-Contrast (Organized by Criteria)

Here is a plan for a comparison-and-contrast synthesis, organized by *criteria*. The thesis is as follows:

These stories, which lead off the President's and the speaker's debate, set the tone for the disagreements over the role of government that follow.

A. Introduction: Personal anecdotes recounted by Clinton and Gingrich illustrative of their philosophical differences on government.
B. The effects of government in helping or hindering citizens
   1. Clinton's position
   2. Gingrich's position
C. The effects of government in redistributing income
   1. Clinton's position
   2. Gingrich's position
D. Clinton's and Gingrich's few agreements; reiteration of essential differences; weaknesses and strengths of a democratic system that encourages vigorous debate.

Following is a comparison-contrast synthesis by *criteria,* written according to the preceding plan: (Thesis and topic sentences are highlighted.)

More Government or Less?

Politicians love to tell stories that have morals, so we should not be surprised that when President Bill Clinton and House Speaker Newt Gingrich reach back into their pasts (as they do in a pair of articles in the April 10, 1995 issue of Newsweek), they recall anecdotes that illustrate their current philosophies on the role of government in American life. Clinton remembers 1 the time he was a boy in Arkansas when the federal government had to step in to compel his own state government to integrate the Little Rock public schools. For Clinton, this is an example of the federal government's "responsibility to help people to make the most of their own lives." Newt Gingrich remembers when he was a young man living in the "chaos of the 1960s"--the Bay of Pigs, Vietnam, Watergate. For him the breakdown of the rational orderly world of the past was a direct result of a bureaucratic big government elite, remote from the common sense of ordinary citizens, gone out of control. In one story we find a federal government that actively promotes social justice; in the other we find an out-of-touch federal bureaucracy that generally messes things up. These stories, which lead off the president's and the speaker's debate, set the tone for the disagreements over the role of government that follow.

While the liberal Clinton believes that government 2
should play an activist role, the conservative Gingrich believes that a bureaucratic government often does more harm than good. For the President, the most significant effect of government is the promotion of social justice and economic productivity. Clinton cites the federal government's role in putting people back to work in the Great Depression as well as its role in furthering civil rights in the 1960s. Today, Clinton believes, "government's job is to enable people to adjust to the changing economy." By promoting education (and educational loans) and training programs, the government helps prepare citizens for the jobs of the future and helps less fortunate citizens to lift themselves out of poverty and dependency. But to Gingrich such government programs have the effect of creating a massive, inefficient bureaucracy that stifles entrepreneurial initiative and that is detached from the needs and concerns of ordinary Americans. He asserts, "In the Department of Labor, the Department of Commerce, the Department of Education,

people sit around in large rooms reading paper reports from people they've never met on topics they've never seen involving towns they've never visited." Gingrich agrees that the federal government's efforts in promoting civil rights in the 1960s were needed; but he maintains that such efforts have gone too far and that the government is now "discriminating in reverse." Similarly, some environmental and safety laws are essential, Gingrich believes, but what we now have is "a maze of mindless rules." In sum, the speaker argues, we need a government that is less actively and less bureaucratically involved in the business of America.

The President's and the speaker's disagreements over 3
how active a role the federal government should play extend, naturally enough, to the hotly contested topic of federal programs that redistribute the nation's wealth. Clinton argues that the government is good at "income transfers"; that is, "it's good at taking in tax money from the population as a whole and redistributing it to people with special needs." The President cites the examples of Social Security and Medicare, about which few people disagree. But it is significant that he chooses not to discuss welfare as an example of an "income transfer," since this is the kind of government program about which liberals and conservatives clash most sharply. An advocate of tax cuts, Gingrich asserts that "[g]overnment redistribution of wealth has never worked in the past and will not in the future." Gingrich believes that far from promoting social justice, income transfers and attempts to redistribute wealth have resulted in a massive welfare state, "a vast structure which leads to 12-year-olds getting pregnant, 14-year-olds getting killed, 17-year-olds dying of AIDS and 18-year-olds getting diplomas they can't read." Instead of government welfare, Gingrich proposes a return to voluntarism and private charity, and a shift of responsibility for social programs from

the federal government to the states and localities, along with a renewed focus on moral values and personal responsibility.

Clinton and Gingrich do agree on some important points. . . . [*Remainder of essay is the same as that of the first comparison-contrast essay.*] 4

Discussion

- In the first paragraph, the writer summarizes the opening personal anecdotes of the two politicians and explains how they illustrate their essential differences over the benefits and drawbacks of a powerful federal government.
- In the second paragraph, the writer focuses on the first major difference between Clinton and Gingrich: their conclusions *about the overall effects of an activist federal government.* For Clinton, the federal government at its best can put people back to work, guarantee their civil rights, and prepare them for a changing economy. But for Gingrich, a powerful federal government means an inefficient bureaucracy, remote from the average citizen, that mainly serves to stifle individual initiative.
- In the third paragraph, the writer focuses on the second major difference between the two politicians: *the role of government in redistributing income.* For Clinton, such "income transfers" are essential for helping people with special needs and lifting people out of poverty. For Gingrich, such government redistribution of wealth never works and has resulted in the creation of the welfare state. He believes government's role here should be handled by the private sector and by volunteers.
- In the fourth paragraph (identical to the fourth paragraph of the comparison-contrast by source essay), the writer points out that the two politicians do agree on some of the strong points and the weak points of government.
- In the fifth paragraph (identical to the fifth paragraph of the comparison-contrast by source essay), the writer reiterates the fundamental differences between the two men, differences of the kind that sometimes lead to governmental paralysis. But the writer concludes that these kind of debates are the essence of democracy and ultimately a sign of strength rather than weakness.

Within any one essay, you are likely to adopt several techniques of development. We have reviewed here a few of the common techniques: summary, example, two (or more) reasons, strawman, concession, and comparison and contrast. Certainly, *critique* (see Chapter 3) would be another method of development. A critical evaluation does not need to exist in and of itself; often, a critique forms one part of a larger paper. The important point is that you be in control of your paper. Understand the main points you wish to make, understand the general sections, or stages, in which you intend to make them, and then use the various methods of development available to you.

▼

THE RESEARCH PAPER

The process of preparing and writing research papers is discussed in Chapter 5. Many of the principles of research-based writing, however, have already been treated in this chapter on synthesis. (In fact, the example syntheses in this chapter are short research papers.) Once you have researched your subject, your tasks in writing a research paper parallel those outlined on page 90–91 on writing a synthesis: considering your purpose; reviewing your sources; formulating a thesis; deciding how you will use your source material; developing an organizational plan; writing your first draft; documenting your sources; and revising your paper. And like explanatory and argument syntheses, research papers involve not only multiple sources but also elements of summary, paraphrase, quotation, and critique.

5
Research

GOING BEYOND THIS TEXT

In this chapter we'll discuss how you can use the skills you've learned in writing summaries, critiques, and syntheses to compose research papers and reports. A research paper is generally considered a major academic endeavor, and frequently it is. But even a paper based on only one or two sources outside the scope of assigned reading has been researched. Research requires you (1) to locate and take notes on relevant sources and organize your findings; (2) to summarize or paraphrase these sources; (3) to critically analyze them for their value and relevance to your subject; and (4) to synthesize information and ideas from several sources that best support your own critical viewpoint.

As you'll see, each chapter in Part II of *Writing and Reading Across the Curriculum* consists of a group of related readings on a particular subject—obedience to authority, privacy and technology, business ethics, and so on. The readings in a chapter will give you a basic understanding of the key issues associated with the subject. For a deeper understanding, however, you'll need to go beyond the relatively few readings included here. A paper based on even two or three additional sources will have a breadth missing from a paper that relies exclusively on the text readings.

Of course, you may be asked to prepare a research paper of some length. Each chapter in Part II concludes with a number of research activities on the subject just covered. In some cases, we suggest particular sources; in others, we provide only general directions. Your instructor may ask you to work on at least one of these assignments during the term. But whether you are preparing an in-depth research paper or just locating a few additional sources on your subject (or something in between), it's essential to know your way around a college library, to be able to locate quickly and efficiently the information you need. In this chapter, we'll give you some important research tips. For more comprehensive information (e.g., annotated lists of specialized reference tools), consult a text on research papers or the research section of a handbook.

▼

RESEARCH PAPERS IN THE ACADEMIC DISCIPLINES

Though most of your previous experience with research papers may have been in English classes, you should be prepared for instructors in other academic disciplines to assign papers with significant research components. Here, for example, is a sampling of research topics that have recently been assigned in a broad range of undergraduate courses:

ANTHROPOLOGY: Identify, observe, and gather data pertaining to a particular subculture within the campus community; describe the internal dynamics of this group, and account for these dynamics in terms of theories of relevant anthropologists and sociologists.

ART HISTORY: Discuss the main differences between Romanesque and Gothic sculpture, using the sculptures of Jeremiah (St. Pierre Cathedral) and St. Theodore (Chartres Cathedral) as major examples.

ASIAN-AMERICAN STUDIES: Address an important socio-psychological issue for Asian-American communities and/or individuals—for example, the effects of stereotypes, mental health problems, sex role relations, academic achievement, assertiveness, or interracial marriage. Review both the theoretical and research literature on the issue, conduct personal interviews, and draw conclusions from your data.

ENVIRONMENTAL STUDIES: Choose a problem or issue of the physical environment at any level from local to global. Use both field and library work to explore the situation. Include coverage of the following: (1) the history of the issue or problem; (2) the various interest groups involved, taking note of conflicts among them; (3) critical facts and theories from environmental science necessary to understand and evaluate the issue or problem; (4) impact and significance of management measures already taken or proposed; (5) your recommendations for management of the solution.

FILM STUDIES: Pick a particular period of British film and discuss major film trends or production problems within that period.

HISTORY: Write a paper analyzing the history of a public policy (example: the U.S. Suprerne Court's role in undermining the civil rights of African-Americans between 1870 and 1896), drawing your sources from the best, most current scholarly histories available.

PHYSICS: Research and write a paper on solar cell technology, covering the following areas: basic physical theory, history and development, structure and materials, types and characteristics, practical uses, state of the art, and future prospects.

POLITICAL SCIENCE: Explain the contours of California's water policy in the last few decades and then, by focusing on one specific controversy, explain and analyze the way in which policy was adapted and why. Consider such questions as where the water comes from, how much, what quantity, who uses the water, who pays and how much, and should we develop more water resources?

PSYCHOLOGY: Explore some issue related to the testing of mental ability; for example, the effects of time limits upon test reliability.

RELIGIOUS STUDIES: Select a particular religious group or movement present in the nation for at least twenty years and show how its belief or practice has changed since members of the group have been in America or, if the group began in America, since its first generation.

SOCIOLOGY: Write on one of the following topics: (1) a critical comparison of two (or more) theories of deviance; (2) field or library research study of a specific deviant career: thieves, drug addicts, prostitutes, corrupt politicians, university administrators; (3) portrayals of deviance in popular culture—e.g., television "accounts" of terrorism, incest, spouse abuse; (4) old age as a form of deviance; (5) the relationship between homelessness and mental illness.

Some of these research papers allow students a considerable range of choice (within the general subject); others are highly specific in requiring students to address a particular issue. Most of these papers call for some library research; a few call for a combination of library and field research; others may be based entirely on field research.

▼

FINDING A SUBJECT

In your present writing course, finding a general subject shouldn't be a problem, since your research likely will concern one of the subjects covered in this text. And, as we've suggested, your instructor may assign you one of the research activities at the end of each chapter, for which some focus will be provided in our directions. Or your instructor may specify his or her own particular directions for your research activity. In other cases, you'll be asked simply to write a paper on some aspect of the subject.

Which aspect? Review the readings, the questions following the readings, and your responses to these questions. Something may immediately (or eventually) spring to mind. Perhaps while reading the chapter from Aldous Huxley's enormously influential *Brave New World* you wonder how the book was received by critics and general readers when it first appeared in 1932. Maybe while reading the selections on the Milgram experiment in the chapter on obedience to authority, you become curious about later experiments that also tested obedience to authority, or about a recent event that demonstrated the malign effects of obedience to unlawful or immoral authority. Consider the readings on welfare. What has been written on this subject

WRITING THE RESEARCH PAPER

Here is an overview of the main steps involved in writing research papers. Keep in mind that as with other synthesis projects, writing research papers is a recursive process: You may not necessarily follow these steps in the order below, and you will find yourself backtracking and looping. This is not only normal, it is essential to carefully developed research.

- **Find a subject.** Decide what subject you are going to research and write about.
- **Develop a research question.** Formulate an important question that you would like to answer through your research.
- **Conduct preliminary research.** Consult knowledgeable people, general and specialized encyclopedias, overviews and bibliographies in recent books, the *Bibliographic Index*, and subject heading guides.
- **Conduct focused research.** Consult books, electronic databases, general and specialized periodicals, biographical indexes, general and specialized dictionaries, government publications, and other appropriate sources. Conduct interviews and surveys, as necessary.
- **Develop a working thesis.** Based on your initial research, formulate a working thesis that attempts to respond to your research question.
- **Develop a working bibliography.** Keep a working bibliography (either paper or electronic) of your sources. Make this bibliography easy to sort and rearrange.
- **Evaluate Sources.** Attempt to determine the veracity and reliability of your sources; use your critical reading skills; check *Book Review Digest;* look up biographies of authors.
- **Take notes from sources.** Paraphrase and summarize important information and ideas from your sources. Copy down important quotations. Note page numbers from sources of this quoted and summarized material.
- **Arrange your notes according to your outline.** Develop a working outline of topics to be covered in your paper. Arrange your notes according to this outline.
- **Write your draft.** Write the preliminary draft of your paper, working from your notes, according to your outline.
- **Avoid plagiarism.** Take care to cite all quoted, paraphrased, and summarized source material, making sure that your own wording and sentence structure differ from those of your sources.

(continued)

- **Cite sources.** Use in-text citations and a "Works Cited" or "References" list, according to the conventions of the discipline (e.g., MLA, APA, CBE).
- **Revise your draft.** Use transitional words and phrases to ensure coherence. Check for style. Make sure that the research paper reads smoothly, logically, and clearly from beginning to end. Check for grammatical correctness, punctuation, and spelling.

since these selections appeared? To what extent have the terms of the debate changed? What programs on the federal, state, or local level have been instituted to change the way welfare is administered?

▼

THE RESEARCH QUESTION

Research handbooks generally advise students to narrow their subjects as much as possible. A ten-page paper on the modern feminist movement would be unmanageable. You would have to do an enormous quantity of research (a preliminary computer search of this subject would yield several thousand items), and you couldn't hope to produce anything other than a superficial treatment of such a large subject. But a paper on the contemporary reception of *Brave New World* or on its relationship to other twentieth-century dystopias should be quite manageable. It's difficult to say, however, how narrow is narrow enough. (A literary critic once produced a twenty-page article analyzing the first paragraph of Henry James's *The Ambassadors.*)

Perhaps more helpful as a guideline on focusing your research is to seek to answer a particular question, a *research question.* For example, how did the Bush administration respond to the demand for bilingual education? To what extent is America perceived by social critics to be in decline? Did Exxon behave responsibly in handling the *Valdez* oil spill? How has the debate over genetic engineering evolved during the past decade? To what extent do contemporary cigarette ads perpetuate sexist attitudes? Or how do contemporary cigarette ads differ in message and tone from cigarette ads in the 1950s? Focusing on questions like these and approaching your research as a way of answering such questions is probably the best way to narrow your subject and ensure focus in your paper. The essential answer to this research question eventually becomes your *thesis,* and in the paper you present evidence that systematically supports your thesis.

▼

PRELIMINARY RESEARCH

Once you have a research question, you want to see what references are available. You want to familiarize yourself quickly with the basic issues and to generate a preliminary list of sources. There are many ways to go about

HOW TO FIND PRELIMINARY SOURCES AND NARROW THE SUBJECT

- Ask your professor for recommended sources on the subject.
- Ask your college librarian for useful reference tools in your subject area.
- If you're working on a subject from this text, use some of the sources we've mentioned in the research activities section.
- Read an encyclopedia article on the subject and use the bibliography following the article.
- Read the introduction to a recent book on the subject and review that book's bibliography.
- Consult the annual *Bibliographic Index* (see below for details).
- If you need help in narrowing a broad subject, consult one or more of the following:

  the subject heading in a computerized card catalog (the subject will be broken down into its components);

  the subject heading in an electronic periodical catalog, such as *InfoTrac,* or in a print catalog, such as the *Readers' Guide to Periodical Literature*;

  the *Library of Congress Subject Headings* catalog.

doing this; some of the more effective ones are listed in the box above. We'll consider a few of these suggestions in more detail.

Consulting Knowledgeable People

When you think of research, you may immediately think of libraries and print material. But don't neglect a key reference source—other people. Your *professor* can probably suggest fruitful areas of research and some useful sources. Try to see your professor during office hours, however, rather than immediately before or after class, so that you'll have enough time for a productive discussion.

Once you get to the library, ask a *reference librarian* which reference sources (e.g., bibliographies, specialized encyclopedias, periodical indexes, statistical almanacs) you need for your particular area of research. Librarians won't do your research for you, but they'll be glad to show you how to research efficiently and systematically.

You can also obtain vital information from people when you interview them, ask them to fill out questionnaires or surveys, or have them participate in experiments. We'll cover this aspect of research in more detail below.

Encyclopedias

Reading an encyclopedia entry about your subject will give you a basic understanding of the most significant facts and issues. Whether the subject is American politics or the mechanics of genetic engineering, the encyclopedia article—written by a specialist in the field—offers a broad overview that may serve as a launching point to more specialized research in a particular area. The article may illuminate areas or raise questions that you feel motivated to pursue further. Equally important, the encyclopedia article frequently concludes with an *annotated bibliography* describing important books and articles on the subject.

Encyclopedias have certain limitations. First, most professors don't accept encyclopedia articles as legitimate sources for academic papers. You should use encyclopedias primarily to familiarize yourself with (and to select a particular aspect of) the subject area and as a springboard for further research. Also, because new editions appear only once every five or ten years, the information they contain—including bibliographies—may not be current. The current editions of the *Encyclopaedia Britannica* and the *Encyclopedia Americana,* for instance, may not include information about the most recent developments in biotechnology.

Some of the most useful general encyclopedias include the following:

American Academic Encyclopedia
Encyclopedia Americana
New Encyclopaedia Britannica

Keep in mind that the library also contains a variety of more *specialized encyclopedias.* These encyclopedias restrict themselves to a particular disciplinary area, such as chemistry, law, or film, and are considerably more detailed in their treatment of a subject than general encyclopedias. Here are examples of specialized encyclopedias:

SOCIAL SCIENCES
Encyclopedia of Education
Encyclopedia of Psychology
Guide to American Law
International Encyclopedia of the Social Sciences

HUMANITIES
Encyclopedia of American History
Encyclopedia of Art
Encyclopedia of Religion and Ethics
International Encyclopedia of Film
The New College Encyclopedia of Music

SCIENCE AND TECHNOLOGY
Encyclopedia of Biological Sciences
Encyclopedia of Computer Science and Engineering
Encyclopedia of Physics

McGraw-Hill Encyclopedia of Environmental Science
Van Nostrand's Scientific Encyclopedia

BUSINESS
Encyclopedia of Banking and Finance
Encyclopedia of Economics

Overviews and Bibliographies in Recent Books

If your professor or one of your bibliographic sources directs you to an important recent book on the subject, skim the introductory (and possibly the concluding) material to the book, along with the table of contents, for an overview of the key issues. Look also for a bibliography. For example, Zvi Dor-Ner's 1991 book *Columbus and the Age of Discovery* includes a four-page annotated bibliography of important reference sources on Columbus and the age of exploration.

Keep in mind that authors are not necessarily objective about their subject, and some have particularly biased viewpoints that you may unwittingly carry over into your paper, treating them as objective truth.[1] However, you may still be able to get some useful information out of such sources. Alert yourself to authorial biases by looking up the reviews of your book in the *Book Review Digest* (described on page 163). Additionally, look up biographical information on the author (see Biographical Indexes, pages 167–168), whose previous writings or professional associations may suggest a predictable set of attitudes on the subject of your book.

Bibliographic Index

The *Bibliographic Index* is a series of annual volumes that enables you to locate bibliographies on a particular subject. The bibliographies it refers to generally appear at the end of book chapters or periodical articles, or they may themselves be book or pamphlet length. Browsing through the *Bibliographic Index* in a general subject area may give you ideas for further research in particular aspects of the subject, along, of course, with particular references.

---

[1]Bias is not necessarily bad. Authors, like all other people, have certain preferences and predilections that influence the way they view the world and the kinds of arguments they make. As long as they inform you of their biases, or as long as you are aware of them and take them into account, you can still use these sources judiciously. (You might gather valuable information from a book about the Watergate scandal, even if it were written by former President Richard Nixon or one of his top aides, as long as you make proper allowance for their understandable biases.) Bias becomes a potential problem only when it masquerades as objective truth or is accepted as such by the reader. For suggestions on identifying and assessing authorial bias, see the material on persuasive writing (pages 61–64) and evaluating assumptions (pages 66–67) in Chapter 3.

Subject-Heading Guides

Seeing how a general subject (e.g., education) is broken down in other sources also could stimulate research in a particular area (e.g., bilingual primary education in California). As in the table of contents of a book, the general subject (the book title) is analyzed into its secondary subject headings (the chapter titles). To locate such sets of secondary subject headings, consult:

- an electronic card catalog
- an electronic or print periodical catalog (e.g., *InfoTrac, Readers' Guide, Social Science Index*)
- *The Library of Congress Subject Headings* catalog.
- The *Propaedia* volume of the *New Encyclopaedia Britannica* (1995)

▼

FOCUSED RESEARCH

Once you've narrowed your scope to a particular subject and a particular research question (or set of research questions), you're ready to undertake more focused research. Your objective now is to learn as much as you can about your particular subject. Only in this way will you be qualified to make an informed response to your research question. This means you'll have to become something of an expert on the subject—or, if that's not possible, given time constraints, you can at least become someone whose critical viewpoint is based solidly on the available evidence. In the following pages we'll suggest how to find sources for this kind of focused research. In most cases, your research will be based on (1) *books;* (2) *articles;* (3) *electronic databases;* and (4) specialized *reference* sources. In certain cases, your research may be based partially or even primarily on (5) *interviews* and *surveys.*

Books

Books are often useful in providing both breadth and depth of coverage of a subject. Because they generally are published at least a year or two after the events treated, they also tend to provide the critical distance that is sometimes missing from articles. (Of course, books also may be shallow, inaccurate, outdated, or hopelessly biased; for help in making such determinations, see *Book Review Digest,* below.) You can locate relevant books through the electronic or card catalog. When using this catalog, you may search in three ways: (1) by *author,* (2) by *title,* and (3) by *subject.* Entries include the call number, the publication information, and, frequently, a summary of the book's contents. Larger libraries use the Library of Congress cataloging system for call numbers (example: E111/C6); smaller ones use the Dewey Decimal System (example: 970.015/C726).

BOOK REVIEW DIGEST

Perhaps the best way to determine the reliability and credibility of a book you may want to use is to look it up in the annual *Book Review Digest.* These volumes list (alphabetically by author) the most significant books published during the year, supply a brief description of each, and, most important, provide excerpts from (and references to) reviews. If a book receives bad reviews, you don't necessarily have to avoid it (the book still may have something useful to offer, and the review itself may be unreliable). But you should take any negative reaction into account when using that book as a source.

Electronic Databases

Much of the information that is available in print—and a good deal that is not—is available in electronic form. Almost certainly, your library card catalog has been computerized, allowing you to conduct searches much faster and more easily than in the past. Increasingly, researchers are accessing magazine, newspaper, and journal articles and reports, abstracts, and other forms of information through *online* databases (many of them on the Internet) and through databases on *CD-ROMs.* One great advantage of using databases (as opposed to print indexes) is that you search several years' worth of different periodicals at the same time.

Online databases—that is, those that originate outside your computer—are available through international, national, or local (e.g., campus) networks. The largest such database is DIALOG, which provides access to over 300 million records in over 400 databases, ranging from sociology to business to chemical engineering. In addition to being efficient and comprehensive, online databases are generally far more up-to-date than print sources. If your own computer has a modem, you can access many of these databases—including those available through commercial online services such as Prodigy, CompuServe, and America Online—without leaving your room.

Access to online databases often requires an account and a password, which you may be able to obtain by virtue of your student status. In some cases, you will have to pay a fee to the local provider of the database, based on how long you are online. But many databases will be available to you free of charge. For example, your library may offer access through its computer terminals to magazine and newspaper databases, such as MAGS and NEWS, as well as to the Internet itself.

Various sites and files on the Internet may be accessed through their *gopher* or *ftp* (file transfer protocol) addresses. (Once you locate a file, you may have to "download" it to your disk or to your e-mail address.) More user-friendly is the *World Wide Web,* which offers graphics, multimedia, and "hyperlinks" to related material in numerous sources. To access these sources, you can either browse (i.e., follow your choice of paths or links wherever they lead) or type in a site's address.

For example, to get information on recent Supreme Court rulings, you could go to the gopher site *info.umd.edu* at the University of Maryland. From there, you would follow the directory path first by selecting *Academic Resources by Topic,* then *United States and World Politics, Culture, and History,* then *United States,* and finally *Supreme Court Documents.* The relevant ftp site would be *ftp.cwru.edu* (at Case Western Reserve University), from which you would choose the path */hermes/*,* for Hermes Project. (The * is a symbol for a group of files, from which you would select according to your interest.) For corresponding information on the World Wide Web, go to *http://www.law.cornell.edu/supct/.* In many cases, you can narrow your searches through electronic databases by typing in *key words* or *descriptors*—the equivalent of subject headings.

CD-ROMs (compact disk-read only memory) used for research look just like sound CDs; but unlike sound CDs, they can display graphics. Many newspapers, magazines, and journals are available on CD-ROM: for example, *The Readers' Guide to Periodical Literature, The New York Times, Film Index International, PAIS International,* and *America: History and Life,* as are other standard reference sources, such as *Statistical Abstract of the U.S., Compton's Encyclopedia, Bibliography of Native North Americans, Environment Reporter,* and *National Criminal Justice Reference Service.* Of particular interest is *InfoTrac,* which provides access to over 1000 general interest, business, government, and technological periodicals.

Keep in mind, however, that while electronic sources make it far easier to access information than their print counterparts, they often do not go back more than a decade. For earlier information, therefore (e.g., contemporary reactions to the Milgram experiments of the 1960s), you would have to rely on print indexes.

Periodicals: General

MAGAZINES

Because many more periodical articles than books are published every year, you are likely (depending on the subject) to find more information in periodicals than in books. By their nature, periodical articles tend to be more current than books (the best way, for example, to find out about the federal government's current policy on AIDS is to look for articles in periodicals and newspapers). However, periodical articles may have less critical distance than books, and they also may date more rapidly—to be superseded by more recent articles.

General periodicals (such as *Time, The New Republic,* and *The Nation*) are intended for nonspecialists. Their articles, which tend to be highly readable, may be written by staff writers, free-lancers, or specialists. But they usually do not provide citations or other indications of sources and so are of limited usefulness for scholarly research.

The most well known general index is the *Readers' Guide to Periodical Literature,* an index of articles in several hundred general-interest magazines and a few more specialized magazines (such as *Business Week* and *Science Digest*). Articles in the *Readers' Guide* are indexed by author, title, and subject.

Another general reference for articles is the *Essay and General Literature Index,* which indexes articles contained in anthologies.

NEWSPAPERS

News stories, feature stories, and editorials (even letters to the editor) may be important sources of information. Your library certainly will have the *New York Times* index, and it may have indexes to other important newspapers, such as the *Washington Post,* the *Los Angeles Times,* the *Chicago Tribune,* the *Wall Street Journal,* and the *Christian Science Monitor.* Newspaper holdings will be on microfilm (your library may have the *New York Times* on CD-ROM), and you will need a microprinter/viewer to get hard copies.

Note: Because of its method of cross-referencing, the *New York Times* index may at first be confusing to use. Suppose that you want to find *Times* stories on bilingual education during 1994. When you locate the "Bilingual education" entry, you won't find citations, but rather a "*See also* Education" reference that directs you to seven dates (August 14, 15, and 17; September 11; October 20, 29, and 30) under the heading of "Education." Under this major heading, references to 1994 stories on education are arranged in chronological order from January to December. When you look up the dates you were directed to, you'll see brief descriptions of the stories on bilingual education.

Periodicals: Specialized

ARTICLES

Many professors will expect at least some of your research to be based on articles in specialized periodicals. So instead of (or in addition to) relying on an article from *Psychology Today* for an account of the effects of crack cocaine on mental functioning, you might (also) rely on an article from the *Journal of Abnormal Psychology.* If you are writing a paper on the satirist Jonathan Swift, you may need to locate a relevant article in *Eighteenth-Century Studies.* Articles in such journals normally are written by specialists and professionals in the field, rather than by staff writers or free-lancers, and the authors will assume that their readers already understand the basic facts and issues concerning the subject.

To find articles in specialized periodicals, you'll use specialized indexes—that is, indexes for particular disciplines. You also may find it helpful to refer to *abstracts.* Like specialized indexes, abstracts list articles published in a particular discipline over a given period, but they also provide summaries of the articles listed. Abstracts tend to be more selective than indexes, since they consume more space (and involve considerably more work to compile); but, because they also describe the contents of the articles covered, they can save you a lot of time in determining which articles you should read and which ones you can safely skip.

Here are some of the more commonly used specialized periodical indexes and abstracts in the various disciplines.

Note: Lists of electronic databases follow the print indexes, but some listed print indexes (e.g., PAIS) are also available in electronic form, such as CD-ROM.

SOCIAL SCIENCE
Abstracts in Anthropology
Education Index
Index to Legal Periodicals
Psychological Abstracts
Public Affairs Information Service (PAIS)
Social Science Index
Sociological Abstracts
Women's Studies Abstracts

Social Science Databases:
- ERIC (Educational Resources Information Center)
- PAIS (Public Affairs Information Service)
- PSYCHINFO (psychology)
- Psychological Abstracts
- Social SciSearch
- Sociological Abstracts

HUMANITIES
Abstracts of English Studies
America: History and Life
Art Index
Cambridge Bibliography of English Literature
Essay and General Literature Index
Film/Literature Index
Historical Abstracts
Humanities Index
International Index of Film Periodicals
MLA International Bibliography of Books and Articles on Modern Languages and Literatures
Music Index
Religion Index
Year's Work in English Studies

Humanities Databases:
- Arts and Humanities Citation Index
- MLA Bibliography
- Philosopher's Index
- Historical Abstracts

SCIENCE AND TECHNOLOGY
Applied Science and Technology Index
Biological Abstracts

Engineering Index
General Science Index
Index to Scientific and Technical Proceedings

Science and Technology Databases:
- Aerospace Database
- Agricola (agriculture)
- Biosis Previews (biology, botany)
- Chemical Abstracts search (chemistry)
- Compendex (engineering)
- Environment Abstracts
- MathSci
- MEDLINE (medical)
- ScienceCitation Index
- SciSearch
- WSPEC (physics, electronics, computer science)

BUSINESS
Business Index
Business Periodicals Index
Economic Titles/Abstracts
Wall Street Journal Index

Business Databases:
- ABI/INFORM
- Econ Abstracts International
- Labor Statistics
- Standard and Poor's News

Biographical Indexes

To look up information on particular people, you can use not only encyclopedias but an array of biographical sources. (You can also use biographical sources to alert yourself to potential biases on the part of your source authors.) A brief selection follows:

LIVING PERSONS
Contemporary Authors: A Biographical Guide to Current Authors and Their Works
Current Biography
International Who's Who
Who's Who in America

PERSONS NO LONGER LIVING
Dictionary of American Biography
Dictionary of National Biography (Great Britain)
Dictionary of Scientific Biography
Who Was Who

PERSONS LIVING OR DEAD
Biography Almanac
McGraw-Hill Encyclopedia of World Biography
Webster's Biographical Dictionary

Dictionaries

Use dictionaries to look up the meaning of general or specialized terms. Here are some of the most useful dictionaries:

GENERAL
Oxford English Dictionary
Webster's New Collegiate Dictionary
Webster's Third New International Dictionary of the English Language

SOCIAL SCIENCES
Black's Law Dictionary
Dictionary of the Social Sciences
McGraw-Hill Dictionary of Modern Economics

HUMANITIES
Dictionary of American History
Dictionary of Films
Dictionary of Philosophy
Harvard Dictionary of Music
McGraw-Hill Dictionary of Art

SCIENCE AND TECHNOLOGY
Computer Dictionary and Handbook
Condensed Chemical Dictionary
Dictionary of Biology
Dorland's Medical Dictionary

BUSINESS
Dictionary of Advertising Terms
Dictionary of Business and Economics
Mathematical Dictionary for Economics and Business Administration
McGraw-Hill Dictionary of Modern Economics: A Handbook of Terms and Organizations

Other Sources/Government Publications

You also may find useful information in other sources. For statistical and other basic reference information on a subject, consult a *handbook* (example: *Statistical Abstracts of the United States*). For current information on a subject as of a given year, consult an *almanac* (example: *World Almanac*). For annual updates of information, consult a *yearbook* (example: *The Statesman's Yearbook*). For maps and other geographic information, consult an *atlas* (example:

New York Times Atlas of the World). (Often, simply browsing through the reference shelves for data on your general subject—such as biography, public affairs, or psychology—will reveal valuable sources of information.)

Many libraries keep pamphlets in a *vertical file* (i.e., a file cabinet). For example, a pamphlet on AIDS might be found in the vertical file, rather than in the library stacks. Such material is accessible through the *Vertical File Index* (a monthly subject and title index to pamphlet material).

Finally, note that the U.S. government regularly publishes large quantities of useful information. Some indexes to government publications:

American Statistics Index
Congressional Information Service
The Congressional Record
Information U.S.A.

Interviews and Surveys

Depending on the subject of your paper, some or all of your research may be conducted outside the library. You may pursue research in science labs, in courthouses, in city government files, in shopping malls (if you are observing, say, patterns of consumer behavior), in the quad in front of the humanities building, or in front of TV screens (if you are analyzing, say, situation comedies or commercials, or if you are drawing on documentaries or interviews—in which cases you should try to obtain transcripts or tape the programs).

You may want to *interview* your professors, your fellow students, or other individuals knowledgeable about your subject. Before interviewing your subject(s), become knowledgeable enough about the topic that you can ask intelligent questions. You also should prepare most of your questions beforehand. Ask "open-ended" questions designed to elicit meaningful responses, rather than "forced choice" questions that can be answered with a word or two, or "leading questions" that presume a particular answer. (Example: Instead of asking, "Do you think that men should be more sensitive to women's concerns for equality in the workplace?" ask, "To what extent do you see evidence that men are insufficiently sensitive to women's concerns for equality in the workplace?") Ask follow-up questions to elicit additional insights or details. If you record the interview (in addition to, or instead of, taking notes), get your subject's permission, preferably in writing.

Surveys or *questionnaires,* when well prepared, can produce valuable information about the ideas or preferences of a group of people. Before preparing your questions, determine your purpose in conducting the survey, exactly what kind of information you want to obtain, and whom you are going to ask for the information. Decide also whether you want to collect the questionnaires as soon as people have filled them out or whether you want the responses mailed back to you. (Obviously, in the latter case, you have to provide stamped, self-addressed envelopes and specify a deadline for return.) Keep in mind that the larger and the more representative your sample of people, the more reliable the survey. As with interviews, it's important to devise and word questions carefully, so that they (1) are understandable and (2) don't reflect your own biases. If you're surveying attitudes on capital punishment, for example, and you ask, "Do you believe that the state should endorse legalized murder?" you've loaded the question to influence people to answer in the negative, and thus you've destroyed the reliability of your survey.

Unlike interview questions, survey questions should be short answer or multiple choice; open-ended questions encourage responses that are difficult to quantify. (You may want to leave space, however, for "additional comments.") Conversely, "yes" or "no" responses or rankings on a 5-point scale are easy to quantify. For example, you might ask a random sample of students in your residence hall the extent to which they are concerned that genetic information about themselves might be made available to their insurance companies—on a scale of 1 (unconcerned) to 5 (extremely concerned). For surveys on certain subjects (and depending on the number of respondents), it may be useful to break out the responses by as many meaningful categories as possible—for example, gender, age, ethnicity, religion, education, geographic locality, profession, and income. Obtaining these kinds of statistical breakdowns, of course, means more work on the part of your respondents in filling out the surveys and more work for you in compiling the responses. If the survey is too long and involved, some subjects won't participate or won't return the questionnaires.

▼

FROM RESEARCH TO WORKING THESIS

The search strategy we've just described isn't necessarily a straight-line process. In other words, you won't always proceed from the kinds of things you do in "preliminary research" to the kinds of things you do in "focused research." You may not formulate a research question until you've done a good deal of focused research. And the fact that we've treated, say, biographical sources before, say, specialized periodical articles does not mean that you should read biographical material before you read articles. We've described the process as we have for convenience; and, *in general,* it is a good idea to proceed from more general sources to more particular ones. In practice, however, the research procedure often is considerably less systematic. You might begin, for example, by reading a few articles on the subject, continue by looking up an encyclopedia article or two. Along the way, you might consult specialized dictionaries, book review indexes, and a guide to reference books in the area. Or, instead of proceeding in a straight line through the process, you might find yourself moving in circular patterns—backtracking to previous steps and following up leads you missed or ignored earlier. There's nothing wrong with such variations of the basic search strategy, as long as you keep in mind the kinds of resources that are available to you, and as long as you plan to look up as many of these resources as you can—given the constraints on your time.

One other thing you'll discover as you proceed: research is to some extent a self-generating process. That is, one source will lead you—through references in the text, citations, and bibliographic entries—to others. Your authors will refer to other studies on the subject; and, frequently, they'll indicate which ones they believe are the most important, and why. At some point, if your research has been systematic, you'll realize that you've already looked at most of the key work on the subject. This is the point at which you can be reasonably assured that the research stage of your paper is nearing its end.

As your work progresses, you may find that your preliminary research question undergoes a change. Suppose you are researching bilingual education. At first, you may have been primarily interested in the question of whether or not bilingual education is a good idea. During your research, you come across S. I. Hayakawa's controversial proposal that English be made the official language of the United States, and you decide to shift the direction of your research toward this particular debate. Or, having made an initial assessment that bilingual education is a good idea, you conclude the opposite. Be prepared for such shifts: they're a natural—and desirable—part of the research (and learning) process. They indicate that you haven't made up your mind in advance, that you're open to new evidence and ideas.

You're now ready to respond to your modified research question with a *working thesis*—a statement that controls and focuses your entire paper, points toward you conclusion, and is supported by your evidence. See our earlier discussion, in Chapter 2 (pages 32–39), on the process of devising and narrowing a thesis.

▼

THE WORKING BIBLIOGRAPHY

As you conduct your research, keep a working bibliography—that is, a set of bibliographic information on all the sources you're likely to use in preparing the paper. Compile full bibliographic information as you consider each source. It's better to spend time during the research process noting information on a source you don't eventually use than to go back to retrieve information—such as the publisher or the date—just as you're typing your final draft.

The most efficient way to compile bibliographic information is on 3″ x 5″ cards. (Note, however, that some software programs allow you to create sortable electronic cards.) You can easily add, delete, and rearrange cards as your research progresses. On each card record:

a. the author or editor (last name first)
b. the title (and subtitle) of the book or article
c. the publisher and place of publication (if a book) or the title of the periodical
d. the date of publication; if periodical, volume and issue number
e. the inclusive page numbers (if article)

You also may want to include on the bibliography card:

f. a brief description of the source (to help you recall it later in the research process)
g. the library call number (to help you relocate the source if you haven't checked it out)
h. a code number, which you can use as a shorthand reference to the source in your notecards

Your final bibliography, known as "Works Cited" in Modern Language Association (MLA) format and "References" in American Psychological Association (APA) format, consists of the sources you have actually summarized, paraphrased, or quoted in your paper. When you compile the bibliography, arrange the cards in alphabetical order and type the references one after another.

Here is an example of a working bibliography card for a book:

Sale, Kirkpatrick. The Conquest of Paradise: Christopher Columbus and the Columbian Legacy. New York: Knopf, 1990.

Attacks Columbian legacy for genocide and ecocide. Good treatment of Columbus's voyages (Chaps. 6–8).

Here is an example of a working bibliography card for an article:

Axtell, James. "Europeans, Indians and the Age of Discovery in American History Textbooks." American Historical Review 92.3 (1987): 621–32.

Finds treatments of subjects in title of article inadequate in most college-level American history texts. Specifies "errors," "half-truths" and "misleading assertions." Recommends changes in nine areas.

Some instructors may ask you to prepare—either in addition to or instead of a research paper—an *annotated bibliography.* This is a list of relevant works on a subject, with the contents of each briefly described or assessed. The bibliography cards shown provide examples of two entries in an annotated bibliography on the Columbian legacy. Annotations are different from *abstracts* in that they do not claim to be comprehensive summaries; they indicate, rather, how the items may be useful to the prospective researcher.

▼

EVALUATING SOURCES

As you sift through what seems a formidable mountain of material, you'll need to work quickly and efficiently; you'll also need to do some selecting. This means, primarily, distinguishing the more important from the less important (and the unimportant) material. The hints in the box below can simplify the task.

▼

NOTE-TAKING

People have their favorite ways of note-taking. Some use cards; others use legal pads or spiral notebooks; yet others type notes into a laptop computer, perhaps using a database program. We prefer 4″ x 6″ cards for note-taking. Such cards have some of the same advantages as 3″ x 5″ cards for working bibliographies: they can easily be added to, subtracted from, and rearranged to accommodate changing organizational plans. Also, discrete pieces of information from the same source can easily be arranged (and rearranged) into subtopics—a difficult task if you have three pages of notes on an entire article.

HOW TO EVALUATE SOURCES

- **Skim** the source: With a book, look over the table of contents, the introduction and conclusion, and the index; zero in on passages that your initial survey suggests are important. With an article, skim the introduction and the headings.
- Be on the alert for **references** in your sources to other important sources, particularly to sources that several authors treat as important.
- Other things being equal, the more **recent** the source, the better. Recent work often incorporates or refers to important earlier work.
- If you're considering making multiple references to a book, look up the **reviews** in the *Book Review Digest* or the *Book Review Index.* Also, check the author's credentials in a source like *Contemporary Authors* or *Current Biography.*
- Draw on your **critical reading** skills to help you determine the reliability and value of a source (see Chapter 3).

Whatever your preferred approach, we recommend including, along with the note itself,

a. a page reference
b. a topic or subtopic label, corresponding to your outline (see below)
c. a code number, corresponding to the number assigned the source in the working bibliography

Here is a sample notecard for an article by Charles Krauthammer entitled "Hail Columbus, Dead White Male" (*Time,* May 27, 1991):

Defenses of Columbus (III B)

Defends Columbus against revisionist attacks. Our civilization "turned out better" than that of the Incas. "And mankind is the better for it. Infinitely better. Reason enough to honor Columbus and 1492" (74).

Here is a notecard for the specialized periodical article by Axtell (see bibliography card on page 172):

Problems with Textbooks (II A)

American history textbooks do not give adequate coverage to the Age of Discovery. An average of only 4% of the textbook pages covering first-semester topics is devoted to the century that accounts for 30% of the time between Columbus and Reconstruction. "The challenge of explaining some of the most complex, important, and interesting events in human history—the discovery of a new continent, the religious upheavals of the sixteenth century, the forging of the Spanish empire, the Columbian biological exchange, the African diaspora—all in twenty or twenty-five pages is one that few, if any, textbook authors have met or are likely to meet" (623).

The notecard is headed by a topic label followed by the tentative location in the paper outline where the information will be used. The number in the upper right corner is coded to the corresponding bibliography card. The note itself in the first card uses *summary* ("Defends Columbus against revisionist attacks") and *quotation*. The note in the second card uses *summary* (sentence 1), *paraphrase* (sentence 2), and *quotation* (sentence 3). Summary was used to condense important ideas treated in several paragraphs in the sources; paraphrase, for the important detail on textbook coverage; quotation, for particularly incisive language by the source authors. For general hints on when to use each of these three forms, see page 31.

▼

ARRANGING YOUR NOTES: THE OUTLINE

Recall that your research originally was stimulated by one or more *research questions,* to which you may have made a tentative response in your *working thesis* (see page 33). As you proceed with your research, patterns should begin to emerge that either substantiate, refute, or otherwise affect your working thesis. These patterns represent the relationships you discern among the various ideas and pieces of evidence that you investigate. They may be patterns of cause and effect, of chronology, of logical relationships, of comparison and contrast, of pro and con, of correspondence (or lack of correspondence) between theory and reality. Once these patterns begin to emerge, write them down as the components of a preliminary outline. This outline indicates the order in which you plan to support your original working thesis or a new thesis that you have developed during the course of research.

For example, on deciding to investigate new genetic technologies, you devise a working thesis focused on the intensity of the debate over the applications of such technologies. Much of the debate, you discover, focuses on arguments about the morality of (1) testing for genetic abnormalities in the fetus, (2) using genetic information to screen prospective employees, and (3) disrupting the ecosystem by creating new organisms. Based on this discovery, you might create a brief outline, numbering each of these three main categories (as examples of the pro–con debates) and using these numbers on your notecards to indicate how you have (at least provisionally) categorized each note. As you continue your research, you'll be able to expand or reduce the scope of your paper, modifying your outline as necessary. Your developing outline becomes a guide to continuing research.

Some people prefer not to develop an outline until they have more or less completed their research. At that point they will look over their notecards, consider the relationships among the various pieces of evidence, possibly arrange their cards into separate piles, and then develop an outline based on their perceptions and insights about the material. They will then rearrange (and code) the notecards to conform to their newly created outline.

In the past, instructors commonly required students to develop multileveled formal outlines (complete with Roman and Arabic numerals) before writing their first drafts. But many writers find it difficult to generate papers from such elaborate outlines, which sometimes restrict, rather than stimulate, thought. Now, many instructors recommend only that students prepare an *informal outline,* indicating just the main sections of the paper, and possibly one level below that. Thus, a paper on how the significance of Columbus's legacy has changed over the years may be informally outlined as follows:

```
Intro: Different views of Columbus, past and present;
    —thesis: view of Columbus varies with temper of times
Pre-20th-century assessments of Columbus and legacy
The debate over the quincentennial
    —positive views
    —negative views
Conclusion: How to assess Columbian heritage
```

Such an outline will help you organize your research and should not be unduly restrictive as a guide to writing.

The *formal outline* (a multileveled plan with Roman and Arabic numerals, capital and small lettered subheadings) may still be useful, not so much as an exact blueprint for composition—although some writers do find it useful for this purpose—but rather as a guide to revision. That is, after you have written your draft, outlining it may help you discern structural problems: illogical sequences of material; confusing relationships between ideas; poor unity or coherence; sections that are too abstract or underdeveloped. Many instructors also require that formal outlines accompany the finished research paper.

The formal outline should indicate the logical relationships in the evidence relating to your particular subject (see example below). But it also may reflect the general conventions of presenting academic ideas. Thus, after an *introduction,* papers in the social sciences often proceed with a description of the *methods* of collecting information, continue with a description of the *results* of the investigation, and end with a *conclusion.* Papers in the sciences often follow a similar pattern. Papers in the humanities generally are less standardized in form. In devising a logical organization for your paper, ask yourself how your reader might best be introduced to the subject, be guided through a discussion of the main issues, and be persuaded that your viewpoint is a sound one.

Formal outlines are generally of two types: *topic* and *sentence outlines.* In the topic outline, headings and subheadings are indicated by words or phrases—as in the informal outline above. In the sentence outline, each heading and subheading is indicated in a complete sentence. Both topic and sentence outlines generally are preceded by the topic sentence.

Here is an example of a sentence outline:

Thesis: How Columbus, his voyages, and his legacy are assessed varies, depending on the values of the times.

I. Early 19th-century and late 20th-century assessments of Columbus are 180 degrees apart.
   A. 19th-century commentators idolize him.
   B. 20th-century commentators often demonize him.
   C. Shifting assessments are based less on hard facts about Columbus than on the values of the culture that assesses him.

II. In the 16th and 17th centuries, Columbus was not yet being used for political purposes.
   A. In the early 16th century, his fame was eclipsed by that of others.
      1. Amerigo Vespucci and Vasco da Gama were considered more successful mariners.
      2. Cortés and Pizarro were more successful in bringing back wealth from the New World.
   B. In the next century, historians and artists began writing of the achievements of Columbus, but without an overt political purpose.
      1. The first biography of Columbus was written by his son Fernando.
      2. Plays about Columbus were written by Lope de Vega and others.
   C. An important exception was that in 1542 the monk Bartolomé de Las Casas attacked the Spanish legacy in the Americas—although he did not attack Columbus personally.

III. In the 18th and 19th centuries, Columbus and his legacy began to be used for political purposes.
   A. During the late 18th century, Columbus's stature in America increased as part of the attempt to stir up anti-British sentiment.
      1. Columbus was opposed by kings, since he "discovered" a land free of royal authority.

2. Columbus, the bold visionary who charted unknown territories, became symbolic of the American spirit.

B. During the 19th century, Columbus's reputation reached its peak.

1. For some, Columbus represented geographical and industrial expansion, optimism, and faith in progress.
2. For others, Columbus's success was the archetypal rags-to-riches story at the heart of the American Dream.
3. After the Civil War, Catholics celebrated Columbus as an ethnic hero.
4. The 400th anniversary of Columbus's landfall both celebrated the past and expressed confidence in the future. Columbus became the symbol of American industrial success.

IV. By the quincentennial of Columbus's landfall, the negative assessments of Columbus were far more evident than positive assessments.

A. Historians and commentators charged that the consequences of Columbus's "discoveries" were imperialism, slavery, genocide, and ecocide.
B. The National Council of Churches published a resolution blasting the Columbian legacy.
C. Kirkpatrick Sale's *The Conquest of Paradise* also attacked Columbus.
D. Native Americans and others protested the quincentennial and planned counter-demonstrations.

V. Conclusion: How should we judge Columbus?

A. In many ways, Columbus was a man of his time and did not rise above his time.
B. In his imagination and boldness and in the impact of his discoveries, Columbus stands above others of his time.

C. When we assess Columbus and his legacy, we also assess our own self-confidence, our optimism, and our faith in progress.

WRITING THE DRAFT

Your goal in drafting your paper is to support your thesis by clearly and logically presenting your evidence—evidence that you summarize, critique, and synthesize. (For a review of the techniques of summary, critique, and synthesis, see Chapters 1, 3, and 4.) In effect, you are creating and moderating a conversation among your sources that supports the conclusions you have drawn from your exploration and analysis of the material. The finished paper, however, should not merely represent an amalgam of your sources; it should present your own particular critical perspective on the subject. Your job is to select and arrange your material in such a way that your conclusions seem inevitable (or at least reasonable). You also must select and arrange your material in a way that is fair and logical; remember that your paper will be evaluated to some degree on whether it meets the standards of logical argumentation discussed on pages 61–64. Try not to be guilty of such logical fallacies as hasty generalization, false analogy, and either/or reasoning.

As we suggested in the section on introductions (pages 47–52), when writing the first draft it's sometimes best to skip the introduction (you'll come back to it later when you have a better idea of just what's being introduced) and to start with the main body of your discussion. What do you have to tell your audience about your subject? It may help to imagine yourself sitting opposite your audience in an informal setting like the student center, telling them what you've discovered in the course of your research, and why you think it's interesting and significant. The fact that you've accumulated a considerable body of evidence (in your notecards) to support your thesis should give you confidence in presenting your argument. Keep in mind, too, that there's no one right way to organize this argument; any number of ways will work, provided each makes logical sense. And if you're working on a computer, it is particularly easy to move whole paragraphs and sections from one place to another.

Begin the drafting process by looking at your notecards. Arrange the cards to correspond to your outline. Summarize, paraphrase, and quote from your notecards as you draft. (One timesaving technique for the first draft is to tape photocopied quotations in the appropriate places in your draft.) If necessary, review the material on explanatory and argument syntheses (pages 88–134). In particular, note the table "How to Write Syntheses" (pages 91–92 and inside back cover) and "Techniques for Developing Your Papers" (pages 134–137). When presenting your argument, consider such rhetorical strategies as strawman, concession, and comparison and contrast. The sample student papers in the synthesis chapter may serve as models for your own research paper.

As you work through your notecards, be selective. Don't provide more evidence or discussion than you need to prove your point. Resist the urge to use *all* of your material just to show how much research you've done. (One experienced teacher, Susan M. Hubbuch, scornfully refers to papers with too much information as "memory dumps"—consisting of nothing but "mindless regurgitation of everything you have read about a subject.") Also avoid going into extended discussions of what are essentially tangential issues. Keep focused on your research questions and on providing support for your thesis.

At the same time, remember that you *are* working on a rough draft—one that will probably have all kinds of problems, from illogical organization to awkward sentence structure to a banal conclusion. Don't worry about it; you can deal with all such problems in subsequent drafts. The important thing now is get the words on paper (or on your disk).

AVOIDING PLAGIARISM

Plagiarism generally is defined as the attempt to pass off the work of another as one's own. Whether born out of calculation or desperation, plagiarism is the least tolerated offense in the academic world. The fact that most plagiarism is unintentional—arising from ignorance of conventions rather than deceitfulness—makes no difference to many professors.

You can avoid plagiarism and charges of plagiarism by following the basic rules below:

RULES TO AVOID PLAGIARISM

- Cite (a) *all* quoted material and (b) *all* summarized and paraphrased material, unless the information is common knowledge (e.g., the Civil War was fought from 1861 to 1865).
- Make sure that both the *wording* and the *sentence structure* of your summaries and paraphrases are substantially your own.

Following is a passage of text, along with several student versions of the ideas represented. (The passage is from Richard Rovere's April 30, 1967, *New York Times Magazine* article, "The Most Gifted and Successful Demagogue This Country Has Ever Known.")

> McCarthy never seemed to believe in himself or in anything he had said. He knew that Communists were not in charge of American foreign policy. He knew that they weren't running the United States Army. He knew that he had spent five years looking for Communists in the government and that—although some must

> certainly have been there, since Communists had turned up in practically every other major government in the world—he hadn't come up with even one.

One student version of this passage reads as follows:

> McCarthy never believed in himself or in anything he had said. He knew that Communists were not in charge of American foreign policy and weren't running the United States Army. He knew that he had spent five years looking for Communists in the government, and although there must certainly have been some there, since Communists were in practically every other major government in the world, he hadn't come up with even one.

Clearly, this is intentional plagiarism. The student has copied the original passage almost word for word.

Here is another version of the same passage:

> McCarthy knew that Communists were not running foreign policy or the Army. He also knew that although there must have been some Communists in the government, he hadn't found a single one, even though he had spent five years looking.

This student has attempted to put the ideas into her own words, but both the wording and the sentence structure are still so heavily dependent on the original passage that even if it *were* cited, most professors would consider it plagiarism.

In the following version, the student has sufficiently changed the wording and sentence structure, and she properly credits the information to Rovere, so that there is no question of plagiarism:

> According to Richard Rovere, McCarthy was cynical enough to know that Communists were running neither the government nor the Army. He also knew that he hadn't found a single Communist in government, even though he had been looking for five years (192).

Apart from questions of plagiarism, it's essential to quote accurately. You are not permitted to change any part of a question or to omit any part of it without using brackets or ellipses (see pages 44–47).

▼

CITING SOURCES

When you refer to or quote the work of another, you are obligated to credit or cite your source properly. There are two types of citations, and they work in tandem.

If you are writing a paper in the humanities, you probably will be expected to use the Modern Language Association (MLA) format for citation. This format is fully described in the *MLA Handbook for Writers of Research Papers,* 4th ed. (New York: Modern Language Association of America, 1995). A paper in the social sciences will probably use the American Psychological Association (APA) format. This format is fully described in the *Publication Manual of the American Psychological Association,* 4th ed. (Washington, D.C.: American Psychological Association, 1994).

In the following section, we will focus on MLA and APA styles, the ones you are most likely to use in your academic work. Keep in mind, however, that instructors often have their own preferences. Some require the documentation style specified in the *Chicago Manual of Style,* 14th ed. (Chicago: University of Chicago Press, 1993). This style is similar to the APA style, except that publication dates are not placed within parentheses. Instructors in the sciences often follow the Council of Biology Editors (CBE) format. Or they may prefer a number format: each source listed on the bibliography page is assigned a number, and all text references to the source are followed by the appropriate number within parentheses. Some instructors like the old MLA style, which calls for footnotes and endnotes. Check with your instructor for the preferred documentation format if this is not specified in the assignment itself.

In-Text Citation

The general rule for in-text citation is to include only enough information to alert the reader to the source of the reference and to the location within that source. Normally, this information includes the author's last name and page number (and, if you are using the APA system, the date). But if you have al-

TYPES OF CITATIONS

- Citations that indicate the source of quotations, paraphrases, and summarized information and ideas—these citations appear *in text,* within parentheses.
- Citations that appear in an alphabetical list of "Works Cited" or "References" following the paper.

ready named the author in the preceding text, just the page number is sufficient.

Here are sample in-text citations using the MLA and APA systems:

MLA

> From the beginning, the AIDS antibody test has been "mired in controversy" (Bayer 101).

APA

> From the beginning, the AIDS antibody test has been "mired in controversy" (Bayer, 1989, p. 101).

If you have already mentioned the author's name in the text, it is not necessary to repeat it in the citation:

MLA

> According to Bayer, from the beginning, the AIDS antibody test has been "mired in controversy" (101).

APA

> According to Bayer (1989), from the beginning, the AIDS antibody test has been "mired in controversy" (p. 101).

or:

> According to Bayer, from the beginning, the AIDS antibody test has been "mired in controversy" (1989, p. 101).

When using the APA system, provide page numbers only for direct quotations, not for summaries or paraphrases. If you do not refer to a specific page, simply indicate the date:

> Bayer (1989) reported that there are many precedents for the reporting of AIDS cases that do not unduly violate privacy.

In MLA format, you must supply page numbers for summaries and paraphrases, as well as for quotations:

> According to Bayer, the AIDS antibody test has been controversial from the outset (101).

Notice that in the MLA system there is no punctuation between the author's name and the page number. In the APA system, there is a comma between the author's name and the page number, and the number itself is preceded by "p." or "pp." Notice also that in both systems the parenthetical reference is placed *before* the final punctuation of the sentence.

For block (indented) quotations, however, place the parenthetical citation *after* the period:

MLA

Robert Flaherty's refusal to portray primitive people's contact with civilization arose from an inner conflict:

> He had originally plunged with all his heart into the role of explorer and prospector; before Nanook, his own father was his hero. Yet as he entered the Eskimo world, he knew he did so as the advance guard of industrial civilization, the world of United States Steel and Sir William Mackenzie and railroad and mining empires. The mixed feeling this gave him left his mark on all his films. (Barnouw 45)

APA

Robert Flaherty's refusal to portray primitive people's contact with civilization arose from an inner conflict:

> He had originally plunged with all his heart into the role of explorer and prospector; before Nanook, his own father was his hero. Yet as he entered the Eskimo world, he knew he did so as the advance guard of industrial civilization, the world of United States Steel and Sir William Mackenzie and railroad and mining empires. The mixed feeling this gave him left his mark on all his films. (Barnouw, 1974, p. 45)

Again, were Barnouw's name mentioned in the sentence leading into the quotation, the parenthetical reference would be simply (45) for MLA style and (1974, p. 45) for APA style.

If the reference applies only to the first part of the sentence, the parenthetical reference is inserted at the appropriate points *within* the sentence:

MLA

While Baumrind argues that "the laboratory is not the place to study degree of obedience" (421), Milgram asserts that such arguments are groundless.

APA

While Baumrind (1963) argued that "the laboratory is not the place to study degree of obedience" (p. 421), Milgram asserted that such arguments are groundless.

There are times when you must modify the basic author/page number reference. Depending on the nature of your source(s), you may need to use one of the following citation formats:

QUOTED MATERIAL APPEARING IN ANOTHER SOURCE

MLA: (qtd. in Milgram 211)
APA: (cited in Milgram, 1974, p. 211)

AN ANONYMOUS WORK

MLA: ("Obedience" 32)
APA: ("Obedience," 1974, p. 32)

TWO AUTHORS

MLA: (Woodward and Bernstein 208)
APA: (Woodward & Bernstein, 1974, p. 208)

A PARTICULAR WORK BY AN AUTHOR, WHEN YOU LIST TWO OR MORE WORKS BY THAT AUTHOR IN THE "WORKS CITED"

MLA: (Toffler, *Wave* 96–97)
APA: (Toffler, 1973, pp. 96–97)

TWO OR MORE SOURCES AS THE BASIS OF YOUR STATEMENT (ARRANGE ENTRIES IN ALPHABETIC ORDER OF SURNAME)

MLA: (Giannetti 189; Sklar 194)
APA: (Giannetti, 1972, p. 189; Sklar, 1974, p. 194)

A MULTIVOLUME WORK

MLA: (2: 88)
APA: (Vol. 2, p. 88)

THE LOCATION OF A PASSAGE IN A LITERARY TEXT

MLA: for example, Hardy's *The Return of the Native:* (224; ch. 7) [page 224 in the edition used by the writer; the chapter number, 7, is provided for the convenience of those referring to another edition]

THE LOCATION OF A PASSAGE IN A PLAY

MLA: (1.2.308–22) [act.scene.line number(s)]

THE BIBLE

MLA: (1 Chron. 21.8)

Content Notes

Occasionally, you may want to provide a footnote or an endnote as a *content* note—one that provides additional information bearing on or illuminating, but not directly related to, the discussion at hand. For example:

[1] Equally well known is Forster's distinction between story and plot: in the former, the emphasis is on sequence ("the king died and then the queen died"); in the latter, the emphasis is on causality ("the king died and then the queen died of grief").

Notice the format: Indent five spaces or one-half inch and type the note number, raised one-half line. Then space once more and begin the note. Subsequent lines of the note are flush with the left margin. If the note is at the bottom of the page (a footnote), quadruple-space between the text and the footnote, single-spacing the note itself. Content notes are numbered consecutively throughout the paper; do not begin renumbering on each page.

Reference Page

In MLA format, your list of sources is called "Works Cited." In APA format, it is called "References." Entries in this listing should be double-spaced, with the second and subsequent lines of each entry indented—five spaces or one-half inch. In both styles, a single space follows the period.

The main difference between MLA and APA styles is that in MLA style the date of the publication follows the name of the publisher; in APA style, the date is placed within parentheses following the author's name. Other differences: In APA style, only the initial of the author's first name is indicated, and only the first word (and any proper noun) of the book or article title and subtitle is capitalized. However, all main words of journal/magazine titles are capitalized, just as in MLA style. For APA style, do *not* place quotation marks around journal/magazine article titles. However, do use "p." and "pp." to indicate page numbers of newspaper articles. In APA format, extend underlining under title to include punctuation immediately following. In both MLA and APA styles, publishers' names should be abbreviated; thus, "Random House" becomes "Random"; "William Morrow" becomes "Morrow."

Note: While the hanging indent (second and subsequent lines indented) is the recommended format for APA-style references in student papers, manuscripts intended for publication follow paragraph-indent format in which the first line of each reference is indented.

Provided below are some of the most commonly used citations in both MLA and APA formats. For a more complete listing, consult the MLA *Handbook,* the APA *Manual,* or whichever style guide your instructor has specified.

Books

ONE AUTHOR

MLA

Rose, Mike. Lives on the Boundary. New York: Penguin, 1989.

APA

Rose, M. (1989). Lives on the boundary. New York: Penguin.

TWO OR MORE BOOKS BY THE SAME AUTHOR

MLA

Toffler, Alvin. Future Shock. New York: Random, 1970.

---. The Third Wave. New York: Morrow, 1982.

Note: For MLA style, references are listed in alphabetical order of title.

APA

Toffler, A. (1970). Future shock. New York: Random.

Toffler, A. (1982). The third wave. New York: Morrow.

Note: For APA style, references are listed in chronological order of publication.

TWO AUTHORS

MLA

Brockway, Wallace, and Herbert Weinstock. Men of Music: Their Lives, Times, and Achievements. New York: Simon, 1939.

APA

Brockway, W., & Weinstock, H. (1939). Men of music: Their lives, times, and achievements. New York: Simon.

THREE AUTHORS

MLA

Young, Richard E., Alton L. Becker, and Kenneth L. Pike. Rhetoric: Discovery and Change. New York: Harcourt, 1970.

APA

Young, R. E., Becker, A. L., & Pike, K. L. (1970). Rhetoric: Discovery and change. New York: Harcourt.

MORE THAN THREE AUTHORS

MLA

Maimon, Elaine, et al. Writing in the Arts and Sciences. Boston: Little, 1982.

APA

Maimon, E., Belcher, G. L., Hearn, G. W., Nodine, B. N., & O'Connor, F. W. (1982). Writing in the arts and sciences. Boston: Little.

BOOK WITH AN EDITOR

MLA

Weeks, Robert P., ed. Hemingway: A Collection of Critical Essays. Englewood Cliffs, NJ: Prentice, 1962.

APA

Weeks, R. P. (Ed.). (1962). Hemingway: A collection of critical essays. Englewood Cliffs, NJ: Prentice.

LATER EDITION

MLA

Houp, Kenneth W., and Thomas E. Pearsall. Reporting Technical Information. 3rd ed. Beverly Hills: Glencoe, 1977.

APA

Houp, K. W., & Pearsall, T. E. (1977). Reporting technical information (3rd ed.). Beverly Hills: Glencoe.

REPUBLISHED BOOK

MLA

Lawrence, D. H. Sons and Lovers. 1913. New York: Signet, 1960..

APA

Lawrence, D. H. (1960). Sons and lovers. New York: Signet. (Original work published 1913)

ONE VOLUME OF A MULTIVOLUME WORK

MLA

Bailey, Thomas A. The American Spirit: United States History as Seen by Contemporaries. 4th ed. 2 vols. Lexington, MA: Heath, 1978. Vol. 2.

APA

Bailey, T. A. (1978). The American spirit: United States history as seen by contemporaries (4th ed., Vol. 2). Lexington, MA: Heath.

SEPARATELY TITLED VOLUME OF A MULTIVOLUME WORK

MLA

Churchill, Winston. The Age of Revolution. Vol. 3 of A History of the English Speaking Peoples. New York: Dodd, 1957.

APA

Churchill, W. (1957). A history of the English speaking peoples: Vol. 3. The Age of revolution. New York: Dodd.

TRANSLATION

MLA

Chekhov, Anton. Chekhov: The Major Plays. Trans. Ann Dunnigan. New York: NAL, 1974.

APA

Chekhov, A. (1974). Chekhov: The major plays (A. Dunnigan, Trans.). New York: New American Library.

SELECTION FROM AN ANTHOLOGY

MLA

Russell, Bertrand. "Civil Disobedience and the Threat of Nuclear Warfare." Civil Disobedience: Theory and Practice. Ed. Hugo Adam Bedau. Indianapolis: Pegasus, 1969. 153–59.

APA

Russell, B. (1969). Civil disobedience and the threat of nuclear warfare. In H. Bedau (Ed.), Civil disobedience: Theory and practice (pp. 153–159). Indianapolis: Pegasus.

REPRINTED MATERIAL IN AN EDITED COLLECTION

MLA

McGinnis, Wayne D. "The Arbitrary Cycle of Slaughterhouse-Five: A Relation of Form to Theme." Critique: Studies in Modern Fiction 17. 1 (1975): 55–68. Rpt. in

<u>Contemporary Literary Criticism</u>. Ed. Dedria Bryfonski and Phyllis Carmel Mendelson. Vol. 8. Detroit: Gale, 1978. 530-31.

APA

McGinnis, W. D. (1975). The arbitrary cycle of <u>Slaughterhouse-five</u>: A relation of form to theme. In D. Bryfonski and P. C. Mendelson (Eds.), <u>Contemporary literary criticism</u> (Vol. 8, pp. 530-531). Detroit: Gale. Reprinted from <u>Critique: Studies in modern fiction,</u> 1975 (Vol. 17, No. 1), pp. 55-68.

GOVERNMENT PUBLICATION

MLA

United States. Cong. House. Committee on the Post Office and Civil Service, Subcommittee on Postal Operations. <u>Self-Policing of the Movie and Publishing Industry</u>. 86th Cong., 2nd sess. Washington: GPO, 1961.

United States. Dept. of Health, Education and Welfare. <u>The Health Consequences of Smoking</u>. Washington: GPO, 1974.

APA

U.S. Congress. House Committee on the Post Office and Civil Service, Subcommittee on Postal Operations. (1961). <u>Self-policing of the movie and publishing industry.</u> 86th Congress, 2nd session. Washington, DC: U.S. Government Printing Office.

U.S. Department of Health, Education and Welfare. (1974). <u>The health consequences of smoking.</u> Washington, DC: U.S. Government Printing Office.

THE BIBLE

MLA

<u>The New English Bible</u>. New York: Oxford UP, 1972.

SIGNED ENCYCLOPEDIA ARTICLE

MLA

Lack, David L. "Population." <u>Encyclopaedia Britannica: Macropaedia</u>. 1974 ed.

APA

Lack, D. L. (1974). Population. Encyclopaedia Britannica: Macropaedia.

UNSIGNED ENCYCLOPEDIA ARTICLE

MLA

"Tidal Wave." Encyclopedia Americana. 1982 ed.

APA

Tidal wave. (1982). Encyclopedia Americana.

Periodicals

CONTINUOUS PAGINATION THROUGHOUT ANNUAL CYCLE

MLA

Davis, Robert Gorham. "Literature's Gratifying Dead End." Hudson Review 21 (1969): 774-78.

APA

Davis, R. G. (1969). Literature's gratifying dead end. Hudson Review, 21, 774-778.

SEPARATE PAGINATION EACH ISSUE

MLA

Palmer, James W., and Michael M. Riley. "The Lone Rider in Vienna: Myth and Meaning in The Third Man." Literature/Film Quarterly 8.1 (1980): 14-21.

APA

Palmer, J. W., & Riley, M. M. (1980). The lone rider in Vienna: Myth and meaning in The third man. Literature/Film Quarterly, 8(1), 14-21.

MONTHLY PERIODICAL

MLA

Spinrad, Norman. "Home Computer Technology in the 21st Century." Popular Computing Sept. 1984: 77-82.

APA

Spinrad, N. (1984, September). Home computer technology in the 21st century. Popular Computing, 77-82.

SIGNED ARTICLE IN WEEKLY PERIODICAL

MLA

Hulbert, Ann. "Children as Parents." New Republic 10 Sept. 1984: 15-23.

APA

Hulbert, A. (1984, September 10). Children as parents. The New Republic, 15-23.

UNSIGNED ARTICLE IN WEEKLY PERIODICAL

MLA

"Notes and Comment." New Yorker 20 Feb. 1978: 29-32.

APA

Notes and comment. (1978, February 20). The New Yorker, 29-32.

SIGNED ARTICLE IN DAILY NEWSPAPER

MLA

Surplee, Curt. "The Bard of Albany." Washington Post 28 Dec. 1983: B1+.

APA

Surplee, C. (1983, December 28). The bard of Albany. Washington Post, pp. B1, B9.

UNSIGNED ARTICLE IN DAILY NEWSPAPER

MLA

"Report Says Crisis in Teaching Looms." Philadelphia Inquirer 20 Aug. 1984: A3.

APA

Report says crisis in teaching looms. (1984, August 20). Philadelphia Inquirer, p. A3.

REVIEW

MLA

Maddocks, Melvin. "A Most Famous Anthropologist." Rev. of Margaret Mead: A Life, by Jane Howard. Time 27 Aug. 1984: 57.

APA

Maddocks, M. (1984, August 27). A most famous anthropologist [Review of the book Margaret Mead: A life]. Time, 57.

Other Sources

INTERVIEW

MLA

Emerson, Robert. Personal interview. 10 Oct. 1989.

APA

Emerson, R. (1989, 10 October). [Personal interview].

DISSERTATION (ABSTRACTED IN DISSERTATION ABSTRACTS INTERNATIONAL)

MLA

Gans, Eric L. "The Discovery of Illusion: Flaubert's Early Works, 1835-1837." DA 27 (1967): 3046A. Johns Hopkins U.

APA

Pendar, J. E. (1982). Undergraduate psychology majors: Factors influencing decisions about college, curriculum and career. Dissertation Abstracts International, 42, 4370A-4371A.

Note: If the dissertation is available on microfilm, give University Microfilms order number in parentheses at the conclusion of the reference. Example, in MLA format: "Ann Arbor: UMI, 1993. 9316566." In APA format, enclose the order number in parentheses: "(University Microfilms No. AAD93-15947)."

LECTURE

MLA

Osborne, Michael. "The Great Man Theory: Caesar." Lecture. History 4A. University of California, Santa Barbara, 5 Nov. 1992.

APA

Baldwin, J. (1993, January). The self in social interactions. Sociology 2 lecture, University of California, Santa Barbara.

PAPER DELIVERED AT A CONFERENCE

MLA

Worley, Joan. "Texture: The Feel of Writing." Conference on College Composition and Communication. Cincinnati, 21 Mar. 1992.

APA

Worley, J. (1992, March). Texture: The feel of writing. Paper presented at the Conference on College Composition and Communication, Cincinnati, OH.

FILM

MLA

<u>Howard's End</u>. Dir. James Ivory. Perf. Emma Thompson and Anthony Hopkins. Merchant/Ivory and Film Four International, 1992.

APA

Thomas, J. (Producer), & Cronenberg, D. (Director). (1991). <u>Naked lunch</u> [Film]. 20th Century Fox.

TV PROGRAM

MLA

<u>Legacy of the Hollywood Blacklist</u>. Videocassette. Dir. Judy Chaikin. Written and prod. Eve Goldberg and Judy Chaikin, One Step Productions. Public Affairs TV. KCET, Los Angeles. 1987.

APA

Chaikin, J. (Co-producer, director, & co-writer), & Goldberg, E. (Co-producer & co-writer), One Step Productions. (1987). <u>Legacy of the Hollywood blacklist</u> [videocassette]. Los Angeles, Public Affairs TV, KCET.

RECORDING

MLA

Beatles. "Eleanor Rigby." <u>The Beatles 1962-1966</u>. Capitol, 1973.

Schumann, Robert. Symphonies Nos. 1 & 4. Cond. George Szell, Cleveland Orchestra. Columbia, 1978.

APA

Beatles. (Singers) (1973). Eleanor Rigby. The Beatles 1962–1966. (Cassette Recording No. 4X2K 3403). New York: Capitol.

Schumann, R. (Composer). (1978). Symphonies nos. 1 & 4. (Cassette Recording No. YT35502). New York: Columbia.

Electronic Sources

Electronic sources can be divided into two categories: portable sources (on CD-ROMs, diskettes, or magnetic tape) and online sources (accessed through a computer service or network). In either case, material in electronic sources may or may not be based on previously published printed sources or printed analogues.

According to MLA guidelines (see below for differences between MLA and APA guidelines), in citing material from an electronic source, you must provide the information for the printed source or analogue (if any) and the information for the electronic source—including the publication medium (e.g., CD-ROM, diskette, magnetic tape, or online); the vendor's name (e.g., if a database has been created by a publisher or other provider and then leased to a vendor for publication in electronic form); and the electronic publication date (for portable sources) or the date of your access. In MLA format, the electronic address you used to access the source (for online sources) is optional. In APA format it is required.

For nonperiodical portable electronic sources (e.g., CD-ROMs that, like books, are published a single time without plans to update or revise the work regularly), the publisher and vendor are usually the same, in which case you must provide the city of publication along with the publisher's name.

GENERAL MLA ORDER OF ITEMS FOR ELECTRONIC SOURCES

The general MLA order of items for electronic sources is as follows:

1. Name of the author (if given)
2. Other publication information for the printed source of analogue (if relevant)
3. Title of the electronic source
4. Edition, release, or version (if relevant)
5. Publication medium (CD-ROM, diskette, magnetic tape, or online)
6. *For portable sources:* City of publication and name of the publisher (e.g., Redmond: Microsoft), or name of the vendor (e.g., SilverPlatter), and electronic publication date

For online sources: Name of the computer service or network (e.g., America Online or Internet), date of your access, and electronic address preceded by "Available." (Do not put a period or other punctuation mark at the end of the electronic address; such marks may make it impossible to access the source.)

GENERAL APA ORDER OF ITEMS FOR ELECTRONIC SOURCES

The general APA order of items for electronic sources is the same as that for MLA except as follows:

If the citation includes a previously published printed source or analogue for which you have given the date, do not include the date of electronic publication; also do not include the page numbers of the printed source or analogue (instead, include the number of paragraphs). For online sources, do not include the date of your access.

PORTABLE SOURCES (CD-ROMs, DISKETTES, OR MAGNETIC TAPE)

MLA

Rich, Alan. "Sonata Form." Microsoft Multimedia Schubert: The Trout Quintet. CD-ROM. Redmond, WA: Microsoft, 1994.

APA

Rich, A. (1994). Sonata form. Microsoft Multimedia Schubert: The Trout Quintet [CD-ROM]. Redmond, WA: Microsoft.

MLA

Elmer-Dewitt, Philip. "The Genetic Revolution." Time 17 Jan. 1994: 40-52. Time Almanac 1990s. CD-ROM. Softkey, Jan. 1994.

APA

Elmer-Dewitt, P. (1994, January 17). The genetic revolution. Time [CD-ROM]. Time Almanac 1990s. Softkey.

ONLINE SOURCES

General MLA format for online periodical sources:

Author, First name. "Title of Article." Name of Periodical Date: page nos or number of paragraphs. Title of Electronic Source. Online. Name of Online Service or Network. Date of your access. Available: electronic address.

General APA format for online periodical sources:

Author, I. (Date). Title of article [number of paragraphs]. <u>Name of Periodical</u> [Online], volume no. Name of On-line Service or Network. Available: electronic address.

NEWSPAPER ARTICLE

MLA

Altman, Robert K. "Gene-Implant Experiments with Humans Are Put Off to Resolve Questions." <u>New York Times</u> 20 Oct. 1988: A7. <u>New York Times Online</u>. Online. Nexis. 30 Aug. 1995.

APA

Altman, R. K. (1977, October 20). Gene-implant experiments with humans are put off to resolve questions. <u>New York Times,</u> p. A7. <u>New York Times Online</u> [Online]. Nexis.

MAGAZINE ARTICLE

MLA

Gutin, Jo Ann C. "End of the Rainbow." <u>Discover</u> Nov. 1994: 70-75. <u>Magazine Index</u>. Online. Dialog. 27 May 1995.

APA

Gutin, J. C. (1994, November). End of the rainbow. <u>Discover,</u> 70-75. [Online]. Dialog.

ELECTRONIC JOURNAL

MLA

Zolo, Mary Beth. "The President's Health Care Plan: Implications for Institutional Ethics Committees." <u>Bioethics Bulletin Online</u> (Winter 1994). Online. Internet. 31 Aug. 1995.

APA

Zolo, M. B. (1994, Winter). The president's health care plan: Implications for institutional ethics committees. Bioethics Bulletin Online [On-line]. Internet.

GOPHER

MLA

"House Chamber Action for the Last Three Legislative Days." 4 Aug. 1995. Online. Internet. 31 Aug. 1995. Available: gopher//gopher.house.gov/ 0F-1%3A947%3AHouse%20Actions

APA

House chamber action for the last three legislative days. (1995, August 4). [On-line]. Available: gopher// gopher.house.gov/0F-1%3A947%3AHouse%20Actions

WORLD WIDE WEB

MLA

"The U.S. House of Representatives and the Legislative Process." Aug. 1995. Online. America Online. 31 Aug. 1995. Available http://www.house.gov/Legproc.html

APA

The U.S. House of Representatives and the legislative process. (1995, August). [On-line]. America Online. Available http://www.house.gov/Legproc.html

▼

SAMPLE RESEARCH PAPER

For an example of research paper format and documentation, see the student argument synthesis on pages 127–133. Although many research papers will be longer and draw on more sources than this example, the discussion and the text of "The Angry Welfare Debate" accurately represent both the finished product and the process by which a student goes from the research question to a systematic argument that supports a thesis.

PART II
An Anthology of Readings

6

The Wal-Mart Wars: A Practice Chapter

INTRODUCTION

This chapter gives you the opportunity to practice the skills of summary, critique, and synthesis that you learned in Part I of Writing and Reading Across the Curriculum. *The selections in Chapter 6 are generally shorter than those in the rest of the book, and the writing instructions are considerably more detailed. Once you have successfully completed several of the assignments at the end of this chapter, you should be able to handle confidently the critical reading and writing tasks in the chapters that follow.*

Your strategy with Chapter 6 should be to read the seven articles that follow this introduction and then to work on the writing assignments specified by your instructor. You will find these assignments at the end of the chapter: three for summary; two for critique; and three for synthesis (explanatory, comparison and contrast, and argument). Note that the assignments in each category increase in complexity.

In succeeding chapters, each reading selection is followed by "Review Questions" and "Discussion and Writing Suggestions," and each chapter concludes with "Synthesis Activities" and "Research Activities." Such assignments are not included in this chapter because we want to focus your attention on practicing your skills in summary, critique, and synthesis.

In 1950, Sam Walton opened the Walton five-and-dime in Bentonville, Arkansas. Twelve years later, he and his brother launched the first Wal-Mart discount store. Other stores followed, each built according to an invariable formula for success: locate the store outside of a town with a population of roughly 5,000; offer a dizzyingly wide range of goods, from lawnmowers to T-shirts to paprika, so that customers could do most of their shopping in a single outing; pass on to customers the steep discounts achieved through bulk buying; and advertise. Each new Wal-Mart store became a retail magnet, a local phenomenon drawing customers from up to twenty miles away. From a purely business point of view, Wal-Mart managed its expansion magnificently, creating 32 stores by

1970; 551 by 1983; and over 2400 by 1994, producing $80 billion in annual sales. For many years, the giant retailer's announced intention to build yet another store in small-town America was like a force of nature: unalterable.

Or nearly so. Not everyone welcomed Wal-Mart into their back yards. Town by town, an increasingly vocal opposition challenged the retailer on two grounds: economic and cultural. First, opponents accused Wal-Mart of undermining local economies. When residents take their business to the Arkansas-based superstore, they doom "mom and pop" stores on Main Street. Local money flows out of town (to corporate headquarters), and all too soon the Main Street retail district dies—and with it, a much-valued, local-merchant culture. Protecting small-town life against extinction constitutes the second rallying cry of anti–Wal-Mart forces. A much-quoted line from opponent and grass-roots organizer Albert Norman captures the mood: "You can't buy rural life style on any Wal-Mart shelf. Once you lose it, Wal-Mart can't sell it back to you."

Critics who make this "preserve our culture" argument find in Wal-Mart a conspicuous symbol of American consumerism, a pernicious source of corruption that must be run out of their communities. Indeed, many of the most vocal opponents left big cities to escape rampant consumerism. Inflamed by their resolve to prevent the cultural strip-mining of small-town America and determined to keep local stores from becoming cookie-cutter duplicates of Wal-Mart stores everywhere, opponents pass out leaflets to shoppers, call neighbors, and lobby town meeting members until the vote comes and Wal-Mart loses—in which case the store's agents merely go over the next hill to the next, more hospitable town and try again. Ironically, the towns that send Wal-Mart packing stand to lose doubly: They lose whatever tax revenue a superstore would have brought; and they lose their own retail base as local customers drive over the hill to that new store in Lakesboro.

Economists note that the decline of Main Street did not begin with the arrival of Wal-Mart. The automobile, the development of strip malls, and the new economies of business all have had roles to play. The fact is, the economic problems of small-town business were decades in the making. But this broader view does little to mollify critics, who continue to see in Wal-Mart the incarnation of much that is wrong with America: mammoth parking lots, fragmented communities, de-personalized commerce, and a depressing uniformity of culture. And so Wal-Mart has become a lightning rod for action among people who want their small towns to retain a small-town feel. Noisy opponents, of course, garner a great deal of press. The fact remains that Wal-Mart is a hugely successful, hugely popular enterprise that meets the daily consumer needs of tens of thousands. Sam Walton and his family shrewdly anticipated new retail trends in America, even if not everyone is lining up to congratulate them.

Many questions underlie the Wal-Mart wars, questions that prompt us to examine core beliefs about community, modern culture, and American myth. Here are several:

- To what extent do critics of Wal-Mart oppose a particular entity—a specific retailer—and to what extent is the fight about economic and cultural conditions over which individuals and even whole communities have little control?

- What, exactly, does Wal-Mart threaten? What *is* a small-town way of life? What are its values, its rhythms? Can a single store realistically threaten these intangible qualities?
- Why (at the very least) do we find of interest, and perhaps even take comfort in, the fact that many of our Presidents were born in places like Hope, Arkansas, and Independence, Missouri? What role in American myth do small towns play? Is there substance to the myth? How does this myth complicate the ways in which we perceive the changes brought on by mega-retailers like Wal-Mart?
- If Wal-Mart is defeated in a particular town, won't other mega-retailers come knocking on the door in a relentless, wearying procession?
- Is the small town "feel," the rural life style, that opponents are so fond of defending an anachronism? If, in changing economic times, small-town character is preserved through special zoning laws and grass-roots organizing, what are the risks that self-conscious, protective measures will produce an artificial quaintness? Might the small town thus "preserved" become more a simulation of small-town life than the real item?

When a Greenfield, Massachusetts, or a Warrenton, Virginia, debates the building of a Wal-Mart, it debates something quite tangible: a five-acre parking lot and a 150,000-square-foot building. But the town debates several intangibles as well: changing times, changing values, changing economies, and the ability of a community to define its own culture. The seven articles gathered here ask that you puzzle over these intangibles and make of them an occasion to think and write, testing your own assumptions about what communities are, how they are preserved, and how they change.

Ban the Bargains

BOB ORTEGA

Bob Ortega, reporter for the Wall Street Journal, *introduces the Wal-Mart debate with a particular slant: the involvement of aging activists from the 1960s and 1970s. This article appeared in the* Wall Street Journal *on October 11, 1994.*

First, it was the Vietnam War. Then came nuclear proliferation, destruction of the environment, the covert war against Nicaragua. Now, many of those who marched over such issues are taking on the establishment again. 1

Only this time, the establishment is Wal-Mart Stores Inc. 2

Across the country, self-described aging hippies such as Paul Glover are fighting to keep their communities free of Wal-Mart. A quarter-century ago, Mr. Glover was a conscientious objector and full-time anti-war organizer. Capitalism? He abhorred it. 3

But in the ongoing battle to keep Wal-Mart out of Ithaca, N.Y., Mr. Glover, who runs a community newspaper, has allied himself with a group often hailed as the bedrock of capitalism—small-business owners. How does he reconcile that? "I've gone beyond opposing all business," he says, explaining that he now advocates "small, community-responsible businesses." 4

As causes go, battling Wal-Mart may not be as noble as world peace. In fact, some activists are a little embarrassed to find themselves protesting a big discount store. "It's not as death-threatening as nuclear power," concedes Carol Rettew, a former protester against the Vietnam War and Three Mile Island. Having waged those battles, she says, "You'd think you'd be fighting something more world-devastating than Wal-Mart." 5

But middle age has many activists trying to preserve their neighborhoods rather than save the world. The quintessential chronicler of the Woodstock Generation—Garry Trudeau—these days is devoting his "Doonesbury" comic strip not to topics as momentous as Watergate or Vietnam; recently, two weeks' worth of strips concerned community opposition to Wal-Mart [see pp. 231–34]. 6

'ULTIMATE PREDATOR'

To denizens of the countercuture, Wal-Mart stands for everything they dislike about American society—mindless consumerism, paved landscapes and homogenization of community identity. 7

"We've lost a sense of taste, of refinement—we're destroying our culture and replacing it with . . . Wal-Mart," says Allan B. Wolf, a Kent State University alumnus now trying to keep Wal-Mart out of Cleveland Heights, Ohio, where he is a high-school teacher. 8

"We'd never have fought another business as hard as we've fought Wal-Mart," says Alice Doyle, of Cottage Grove, Ore., who calls the giant discounter "the ultimate predator." 9

At Wal-Mart headquarters in Bentonville, Ark., company officials characterize all opponents, ex-hippie and otherwise, as "a vocal minority." They deny that their store has become, for some activists, a kind of successor to Vietnam. 10

Don Shinkle, a Wal-Mart vice president, says "there are maybe eight to 10 sites where there is opposition." However, there are at least 40 organized groups actively opposing proposed or anticipated Wal-Mart stores in communities such as Oceanside, Calif.; Gaithersburg, Md.; Quincy, Mass.; East Lampeter, Penn.; Lake Placid, N.Y.; and Gallatin, Tenn. 11

Local opposition has delayed some stores and led the company to drop its plans in Greenfield, Mass., and two other towns in that state; as well as in Bath, Maine; Simi Valley, Calif.; and Ross and West Hempfield, Pa. 12

PROTEST MARCH

The residents of Cleveland Heights hope to join that list. On a recent Monday there, a large crowd, including some people who had been tear-gassed at Kent State 24 years ago for protesting the war, led a march on city hall 13 and chanted, "One, two, three, four—we don't want your Wal-Mart store." Says Jordan Yin, a leader of the anti–Wal-Mart coalition, "Old hippies describes the whole town."

In Fort Collins, Colo., Shelby Robinson, a former Vietnam War protester and member of the George McGovern campaign, has little success these days persuading her old companions to join her lobbying for solar power, animal rights or vegetarianism. But when Wal-Mart proposed coming to town, the activist impulses of her old friends came alive, and many joined her in fighting the store. 14

"I really hate Wal-Mart," says Ms. Robinson, a self-employed clothing designer. "Everything's starting to look the same, everybody buys all the same things—a lot of small-town character is being lost. They disrupt local communities, they hurt small businesses, they add to our sprawl and pollution because everybody drives farther, they don't pay a living wage—and visually, they're atrocious." 15

In Boulder, Colo., Wal-Mart real-estate manager Steven P. Lane tried appeasing the city's ex-hippies by proposing a "green store" that he said would be environmentally friendly, right up to the solar-powered sign out front. But when city council member Spencer Havlick, who helped organize the first Earth Day in 1970, suggested that the whole store be solar-powered, Mr. Lane fell silent. Dr. Havlick, professor of environmental design at the University of Colorado, says, "Their proposal wasn't as green as they thought it was." 16

These activists have hardly slowed Wal-Mart's overall expansion—it expects to add 125 stores next year to its existing 2,504. But even so, some Wal-Mart sympathizers find them irritating. William W. Whyte, who bid good riddance to hippies when he graduated from Kent State in 1970, now finds himself annoyed by them again, as an analyst following Wal-Mart for Stephens Inc. 17

"The same types of people demonstrating then are demonstrating now," grumbles Mr. Whyte. "If they had to worry about putting food on the table, they'd probably be working for Wal-Mart instead of protesting them." 18

Some Wal-Mart supporters call the protesters elitists for opposing a purveyor of low-priced goods. But Tim Allen, who at age 26 has been active in the development of a "green" housing co-op and an organizer of the Wal-Mart protest movement in Ithaca, replies that "people aren't poor because they're paying 15 cents more for a pair of underwear." 19

EXPERIENCED ORGANIZERS

Wal-Mart's traditional opponents—small-town merchants—initially didn't think much of former flower children, either. "I thought they were going to be a bunch of . . . hippies up there whining, 'We don't want a Wal-Mart, we don't want a Wal-Mart,'" says Stephanie Marx, a Wal-Mart opponent and co-owner of a bookstore in Ithaca. 20

But now, these business folks are finding that the old activists aren't slouches. Ms. Marx says the five-inch-thick environmental-impact state- 21 ment, or EIS, for the proposed Wal-Mart made her eyes glaze over. But "these people had read the entire EIS, which was huge, and they had one cogent argument after another. They are also very adept at getting people excited and keeping them enthusiastic about stopping the project," she says.

Ms. Rettew, the former Vietnam protester, says "we learned in the 1960s and 1970s how to organize, how to use the media." Recently, she persuaded three television newscasts and a daily paper to cover an anti-Wal-Mart vigil in Lititz, Pa. And even though few demonstrators showed up, the resulting publicity led to dozens of calls and new members for her anti–Wal-Mart coalition. 22

Unlike small-town merchants, the aging activists have no financial stake, which they say elevates the debate to a higher plane. Whereas merchants might complain about their inability to compete against Wal-Mart, James Howard Kunstler, a former Rolling Stone writer and current Wal-Mart opponent, says that Wal-Mart is "the exemplar of a form of corporate colonialism, which is to say, organizations from one place going into distant places and strip-mining them culturally and economically." 23

But some activist groups have happily accepted support from unions or competing developers; and some activists have put their expertise up for hire. In 1970, Al Norman organized lunch-hour protests on Manhattan's Madison Avenue during which he and others read aloud the names of the lastest casualties in Vietnam. Now he is a lobbyist and administrator for senior citizens' nonprofit consumer-rights groups in Massachusetts. As a consultant, he has helped coordinate anti–Wal-Mart campaigns across the U.S., Canada and Puerto Rico. 24

Hired last year to help a Greenfield, Mass., group block a proposed Wal-Mart, Mr. Norman sat in on a meeting at which local business owners tried concocting financial arguments against the store. He interrupted them. "The reason you haven't been doing well is that you're trying to appeal to people's brains," he said. "We want to appeal to their hearts. I want to make it clear Wal-Mart is the enemy here, and I don't want to appeal to the intellect to do that." 25

His campaign ads characterized Wal-Mart as a Pandora's box of urban blight, increased traffic and crime. "You can't buy small-town life at a Wal-Mart. You can only lose it there," read one ad. The campaign, since repeated in other towns, led to a referendum that kept the giant retailer out. 26

"In a way, Wal-Mart is a metaphor for the American dream run amok," says Peter Calthorpe, an urban designer from San Francisco who sees broader implications in this struggle. He thinks community-minded activists are at the forefront of a groundswell that will object to "an auto-based culture in which everywhere you go, the end destination is a parking lot." 27

CULTURE CLASH

In part, Wal-Mart's problem may be cultural. After all, this is a company whose managers sometimes bicker over whose necktie or haircut was cheapest; one whose executives intentionally adopt the mannerisms and 28 colloquialisms of backwoods Arkansas. Wal-Mart officials and people close to the company say there aren't any ex-hippies in the executive ranks—at least none eager to own up to it.

Retail analyst Janet Mangano admires the company's financial performance. But as for the stores, which tend to be identical, windowless blue boxes surrounded by seas of asphalt, "what can you say about Wal-Mart's sense of aesthetics?" she asks. "It doesn't have any." 29

Mr. Shinkle, Wal-Mart's spokesman, responds, "I think Wal-Mart stores are handsome buildings—they're beautiful." 30

Some say a culture clash was inevitable once the Arkansas retailer moved into urban or rural areas inhabited by former flower children. Its opponents in Ithaca, for instance, include such people as Clare Grady, who 10 years ago was jailed as a member of the antinuclear Plowshares group for pounding dents on the bomb-bay doors of a B-52 bomber with a hammer. And then there is Mr. Glover, the former conscientious objector, who says he changed his name and went underground for a few years in the early 1970s after he was charged with resisting the draft. Since then, he has run for public office as an anarchist. 31

When told that Wal-Mart dismisses its opponents as "a vocal minority," Mr. Glover grins. "Every large social change has begun with a small minority, from women's suffrage to stopping the Vietnam War," he says. "It's the cycle of history." 32

Eight Ways to Stop the Store

ALBERT NORMAN

Albert Norman, mentioned in the preceding article, is a well-known opponent of Wal-Mart and a former anti-Vietnam activist. In this article, which appeared in The Nation *(Mar. 28, 1994), Norman outlines his strategies for blocking Wal-Mart. Norman's bias is clear—and will be balanced by other selections in the chapter.*

Last week I received another red-white-and-blue invitation to a Wal-Mart grand opening in Rindge, New Hampshire. I say "another" because Wal-Mart has already invited me to its new store in Hinsdale, New Hampshire, just twenty miles away. With over $67 billion in annual sales, and more than 2,000 stores, Wal-Mart holds a grand opening somewhere in America almost every other day. But it will never invite me to its new store in Greenfield, Massachusetts, my home town, because Greenfield voters recently rejected Wal-Mart at the ballot box. 1

The Arkansas mega-retailer has emerged as the main threat to Main Street, U.S.A. Economic impact studies in Iowa, Massachusetts, and elsewhere suggest that Wal-Mart's gains are largely captured from other merchants. Within two years of a grand opening, Wal-Mart stores in an average-size Iowa town generated $10 million in annual sales—by "stealing" $8.3 million from other businesses. 2

Since our victory in Greenfield, we have received dozens of letters 3
from "Stop the WAL" activists in towns like East Aurora, New York; Palatine, Illinois; Mountville, Pennsylvania; Williston, Vermont; Branford, Connecticut—small communities fighting the battle of Jericho. If these towns follow a few simple rules of engagement, they will find that the WAL *will* come tumbling down:

Quote scripture: Wal-Mart founder Sam Walton said it best in his auto- 4
biography: "If some community, for whatever reason, doesn't want us in there, we aren't interested in going in and creating a fuss." Or, as one company V.P. stated, "We have so many opportunities for building in communities that want Wal-Marts, it would be foolish of us to pursue construction in communities that don't want us." The greater the fuss raised by local citizens, the more foolish Wal-Mart becomes.

Learn Wal-Math: Wal-Mathematicians only know how to add. They 5
never talk about the jobs they destroy, the vacant retail space they create or their impact on commercial property values. In our town, the company agreed to pay for an impact study that gave enough data to kill three Wal-Marts. Dollars merely shifted from cash registers on one side of town to Wal-Mart registers on the other side of town. Except for one high school scholarship per year, Wal-Mart gives very little back to the community.

Exploit their errors: Wal-Mart always makes plenty of mistakes. In our 6
community, the company tried to push its way onto industrially zoned land. It needed a variance not only to rezone land to commercial use but also to permit buildings larger than 40,000 square feet. This was the "hook" we needed to trip the company up. Rezoning required a Town Council vote (which it won), but our town charter allowed voters to seek reconsideration of the vote, and ultimately, a referendum. All we needed was the opportunity to bring this to the general public—and we won. Wal-Mart also violated state law by mailing an anonymous flier to voters.

Fight capital with capital: In our town (pop. 20,000) Wal-Mart spent 7
more than $30,000 trying to influence the outcome of a general referendum. It even created a citizen group as a front. But Greenfield residents raised $17,000 to stop the store—roughly half of which came from local businesses. A media campaign and grass-roots organizing costs money. If Wal-Mart is willing to spend liberally to get into your town, its competitors should be willing to come forward with cash also.

Beat them at the grass roots: Wal-Mart can buy public relations firms 8
and telemarketers but it can't find bodies willing to leaflet at supermarkets, write dozens of letters to the editor, organize a press conference or make calls in the precincts. Local coalitions can draw opinion-makers from the business community (department, hardware and grocery stores, pharmacies, sporting goods stores), environmentalists, political activists and homeowners. Treat this effort like a political campaign: The Citizens versus the WAL.

Get out your vote: Our largest expenditure was on a local telemarket- 9
ing company that polled 4,000 voters to identify their leanings on Wal-Mart. Our volunteers then called those voters leaning against the WAL two

days before the election. On election day, we had poll-watchers at all nine precincts. If our voters weren't at the polls by 5 P.M., we reminded them to get up from the dinner table and stop the mega-store.

Appeal to the heart as well as the head: One theme the Wal-Mart culture has a hard time responding to is the loss of small-town quality of life. You can't buy rural life style on any Wal-Mart shelf—once you lose it, Wal-Mart can't sell it back to you. Wal-Mart's impact on small-town ethos is enormous. We had graphs and bar charts on job loss and retail growth—but we also communicated with people on an emotional level. Wal-Mart became the WAL—an unwanted shove into urbanization, with all the negatives that threaten small-town folks. **10**

Hire a professional: The greatest mistake most citizen groups make is trying to fight the world's largest retailer with a mimeo-machine mentality. Most communities have a political consultant nearby, someone who can develop a media campaign and understand how to get a floppy disk of town voters with phone numbers. Wal-Mart uses hired guns; so should anti–Wal-Mart forces. **11**

"Your real mission," a Wal-Mart executive recently wrote to a community activist, "is to be blindly obstructionist." On the contrary, we found it was Wal-Mart that would blindly say anything and do anything to bulldoze its way toward another grand opening in America. But if community coalitions organize early, bring their case directly to the public and trumpet the downside of mega-store development, the WALs will fall in Jericho. **12**

Competing with the Discount Mass Merchandisers

KENNETH E. STONE

Kenneth E. Stone, Professor of Economics at Iowa State University, has gathered and analyzed data on what happens to a town, economically, when a Wal-Mart or another discount mass merchandiser moves in. Unlike Norman (who indirectly cites Stone's work in paragraph 2), Stone takes the position of a neutral researcher. In this piece, written in 1995, he summarizes his research; and, operating on the premise that Wal-Mart or other retailers will *move into small towns, he has prepared recommendations for local merchants who wish to compete.*

The nature of retailing has changed dramatically in the last decade, compared to previous decades. In the last decade there has been a great proliferation of discount general merchandise stores such as Wal-Mart, Kmart, Target and several regional chains. In addition there has been a great expansion of membership warehouse clubs, such as Sam's, Pace, Costco and Price Club. There has also been a rapid expansion of "category killer" stores such as Home Depot, Circuit City, Best Buy, Toys "R" Us, Office Depot, SportsAuthority and others. These stores are called category killer **1** stores because they have a very large selection within a narrow category of merchandise, along with low prices, and they "kill" smaller local stores within the same "category." We have also seen the development of many new factory outlet malls and the spread of specialty mail order. The net result of this expansion is the saturation of many retail markets, or what is commonly referred to as the *overstoring* of America. Many retail markets have more retail stores than can possibly be supported, and it would appear that a major shakeout is coming in the not-too-distant future, and it may involve large chains as much or more than local merchants.

IMPACTS OF DISCOUNT GENERAL MERCHANDISERS (BASED ON AN IOWA STUDY)

When a discount general merchandise store opens in a small-to-medium size town with little population growth, there will be both positive and negative effects. The retail trade area size will expand because of the reduction of outshopping by local consumers and the capture of more consumers from the surrounding area. Businesses selling merchandise different from the discounter usually benefit from the increased traffic flow the first few years. Businesses selling the same merchandise as the discounter usually lose sales. Unfortunately, the discounters usually saturate the market with their stores, which causes some towns' trade areas to shrink to a smaller size than before. 2

Towns of a similar size without a large mass merchandiser have suffered sales losses in nearly all categories except food, as residents either outshop to the nearby discount store or travel to the cities to shop at category killer stores. 3

It appears that discount mass merchandise stores are holding customers in the local area to shop to a greater extent than before, thereby causing fewer shopping trips to the bigger cities. 4

The smallest towns, especially those within 20 miles of a discount store, suffer heavy losses in sales, ranging from 16 percent to over 46 percent over a 10 year period. 5

The shopping habits of consumers fundamentally change after the introduction of discount mass merchandisers. They purchase much more of their merchandise at the mass merchandisers and less at local merchants. The result is the loss of many stores across the state. 6

The impacts of category killer stores are also substantial. Many of the following strategies will also apply to merchants competing with such stores. 7

HOW LOCAL MERCHANTS CAN COMPETE

Attitudes and Actions

In general it is best to take a positive attitude toward the opening of a new mass merchandise store in your area. The following thoughts are offered in this regard. 8

- *In a free-enterprise economy, all firms are free to compete.* However, local officials should be careful not to offer unduly generous incentives to large firms that could place smaller firms at a disadvantage.
- *Recognize that a discount mass merchandise store will probably enlarge your town's retail trade area size.* Try to figure out ways to capitalize on the increased volume of traffic to town.
- *It is possible to co-exist and even thrive in this type of environment.*
- *You may need to change your methods of operation as described below.*

Merchandise Tips

The following suggestions are offered with regard to merchandise mix. 9

- *Try not to handle the exact merchandise.* For example, at least three of the largest mass merchandisers sell a particular brand of men's jeans for around $10. There are cases where smaller merchants sell the same brand jean for $15. Customers automatically detect that the smaller merchant is 50 percent higher priced and often assume that everything else in the store is 50 percent higher. A better strategy would be to sell another brand that is not directly comparable. Consider private label merchandise.
- *Sell singles instead of pre-packaged groups.* Mass merchandisers often sell prepackaged merchandise that contain multiple items. Customers often need only one item. Independent merchants can often meet these needs by unbundling packages and selling items as singles. For example, a crafts store may gain new customers and make more profit by selling singles of various supplies such as templates, paint brushes, etc.
- *Try to handle complementary merchandise.* In many departments such as hardware, electrical, plumbing, lawn and garden, and others, the mass merchandisers handle only fast moving merchandise. Astute competing merchants should expand their lines to be more complete than their giant competitors. Customers will soon learn to go directly to the more complete store if their needs are out of the ordinary. For example, a customer building a back-yard storage shed requiring 15 pounds of nails and 100 bolts will be sadly disappointed if he or she shops at a discount general merchandiser and finds only small prepackaged assortments. Their needs will be much better met by a hardware store that has a wide assortment of these items in bulk quantities.
- *Look for voids in the mass merchandiser's inventory.* For example, most discount general merchandisers do not handle the higher priced name brand athletic shoes desired by so many people today. A smart competing sporting goods dealer would handle a full line of better athletic shoes.

- *Consider upscale merchandise.* Not all customers desire or demand lower priced merchandise. For example, there are cases of smaller children's wear stores that prosper in the shadow of a discount general merchandiser by catering to the tastes and preferences of middle-to-upper income clientele and to the "grandparent trade" where money is often not as much of a factor as it was when they were young parents.
- *Get rid of the "dogs."* Nearly all businesses end up with merchandise that does not sell and ends up cluttering the shelves. This is bad for at least two reasons: (1) merchandise must turn to generate a profit, and (2) old merchandise tarnishes the image of your store. Merchants should identify the "dogs" and clear them out by whatever means possible.
- *Buy well.* From time to time, nearly all merchants have an opportunity to purchase merchandise at exceptional prices. If the merchandise is something they know they can sell, they should take advantage of the good buys. They can enhance their pricing image while making better profit margins. Store owners should also be on the lookout for opportunities to purchase cooperatively with other local merchants or through a larger buying cooperative.
- *Find a niche that you can fill.* Smaller merchants can often succeed by merely finding the various voids in the mass merchandisers' inventory and filling them as described above.

Marketing Tips

There is always room for improving marketing practices. The following **10**
tips are offered to merchants regardless of their competition.

- *Know your customers.* It is important to know the demographics of your trade area in order to have the optimal merchandise mix. The breakdown of the population by income and age is available from census data kept on file at libraries and governmental agencies. However, computer marketing firms can quickly generate a detailed report, tailored to your specific trade area for a nominal fee. One such company is CACI Marketing Systems at (800) 292-CACI. In addition you may want to conduct customer focus groups where diverse groups of customers under the direction of a third party discuss what they like and dislike about your business. These can be done by community colleges, other colleges and universities, and private consultants.
- *Extended opening hours are a necessity!* Lifestyles have changed dramatically in the last generation. Now it is quite common for a household to have multiple wage earners working outside the household. Most of these people simply cannot get to local stores to shop if they stay open only from 8:00 A.M. to 5:00 P.M. and by necessity they shop at mass merchandisers and shopping malls where

the opening hours are more in tune with today's societal needs. Downtown merchants and other independent merchants cannot seriously compete in this environment unless they cooperate and offer similar convenient opening hours.

- *Look for ways to improve your returns policies.* Most mass merchandisers have very liberal returns policies. Unfortunately, many smaller independent merchants cannot offer comparable policies because of their lack of leverage with major suppliers. In the long run they need to work through trade associations and buying groups to achieve comparable leverage with suppliers. In the short run and at all other times, they need to use common sense with regard to returns policies. For example, if a customer purchases a piece of lawn equipment in May and brings it back shortly thereafter complaining of a malfunction that required factory repair, the dealer would be well advised to give the customer a new replacement immediately or at least offer a loaner until the repaired item is returned. I know of a case such as this where the customer was left empty handed until August when the repaired item finally came back from the factory. Needless to say, he was not happy.
- *Sharpen your pricing skills.* (E.g., lower prices on items that people purchase frequently.) It is my contention that many consumers do not know the "going price" of much of what they buy. They tend to know the price of the things they purchase frequently, or the things they have seen advertised recently. Discount mass merchandisers recognize this and tend to focus their lowest prices on these items. The average consumer then assumes that prices on all other items must also be less. Conversely, many local merchants have gotten a "bad rap" on price image when they have not been careful in pricing some of the "hot items" and consequently consumers then infer that everything else in the store is also high priced. Independent merchants need to carefully consider what items customers tend to know the price of and make special efforts to keep these prices competitive both through prominent displays and advertising.
- *Focus your advertising.* Stress your competitive advantage. Every business must have one or more competitive advantages in the eyes of the customer in order to succeed. For example, Sears established a huge competitive advantage when it adopted "Satisfaction Guaranteed" many years ago. With Wal-Mart, "Everyday Low Prices" is a strong competitive advantage. Large firms incorporate these competitive advantages into nearly every advertisement. Unfortunately, many smaller merchants do not get their full money's worth from their ads because they often fail to promote their competitive advantages. For example, a drug store with 24-hour prescription service and free delivery ought to incorporate those facts into every ad. Likewise, an apparel store that features special orders and in-store credit should stress those features in its ads. The point is that

after a while, customers will automatically know your competitive advantages and may patronize your store when the need arises.

Service Tips

Superior service can become an important competitive advantage for many smaller businesses. Large chain stores usually don't have the flexibility to offer many of these services. 11

- *Emphasize expert technical advice.* It is difficult to find workers in discount mass merchandise stores who know the merchandise. There are many examples of smaller merchants who build a loyal clientele because they are able to help customers analyze their problems and help them find the tools, supplies and equipment needed to meet their needs.
- *Offer deliveries where appropriate.* A certain segment of our population has a need for the delivery of certain items such as prescription drugs and heavy or bulky items. Typically, mass merchandisers cannot respond to these needs. Some smaller merchants can carve out a certain market share by offering delivery service.
- *Offer on-site repair or service of certain items.* Nearly everyone has a need to have some item repaired or serviced occasionally. Larger discount stores usually cannot readily provide this service. Independent merchants can draw a substantial volume of trade to their stores by providing repairs and service of merchandise.
- *Develop special order capability.* It is not possible for merchants to carry every conceivable item in inventory. However, they can make arrangements with certain suppliers or cooperating partner stores to priority ship needed items. Fax machines and express delivery services are making this feasible today. So rather than let a customer walk out the door when an item is not in inventory, it is better to say, "I'm sorry I do not have it in stock, but I can get it for you in two days."
- *Offer other services as appropriate.* Independent merchants can develop many loyal customers by offering "how to do it" classes, gift wrapping, rentals of certain items that will boost sales of collateral merchandise, etc.

Customer Relations Tips

In past years, small businesses had the reputation of excellent customer relations. However, nowadays many consumers perceive that they are treated no better in small firms than in larger ones. Research has shown that poor customer relations is the primary reason that customers quit doing business with a store. The following suggestions are offered for all businesses. 12

- *Make sure customers are "greeted."* According to surveys in Iowa, the primary thing that offends customers is the failure to be greeted or acknowledged when entering a store. This is particularly acute when the customer is in a buying mood. All store personnel should be trained to "greet" customers when they enter a store, determine their needs, and assist them.

- *Offer customers a smile instead of a frown.* All customers prefer to do business where they are treated in a friendly manner.
- *Make employees "associates."* Firms like Wal-Mart and J.C. Penney call their employees associates and treat them as part of the team. Independent merchants can emulate this. In particular, regular store meetings should be held where everyone is apprised of the latest happenings and plans and where all problems can be aired.
- *Solicit complaints.* Many times customers have a bad experience in a store, but they are reluctant to complain to store personnel for various reasons. Instead, they go around complaining to other people. Good merchants would rather hear of the complaint first so they can find a remedy. They can provide an environment where customers feel comfortable in complaining by soliciting complaints through ads, through signs at the checkout counters, by signs on shopping bags, etc.
- *Learn how to handle irate customers.* Dealing with irate customers is something few people enjoy, but it is crucial to the success of the business. The worst thing store representatives can do is to argue with or be rude to an irate customer. The following process with the acronym of LEAR is recommended. (L) Listen. It is easy to become defensive and to turn off the customer while you are thinking of your response, but it pays to set everything aside and listen intently. (E) Empathize; put yourself in the shoes of the customer and think how you would like the situation resolved. (A) Ask questions to get all the facts on the table. (R) Resolve the situation to the satisfaction of the customer. Most merchants have found that by merely asking "What do you see as a reasonable solution?" they can achieve a win-win solution.
- *Train employees (often).* In the eyes of the customer, the employee *is* the business. Training employees can have one of the highest payoffs of any investment in the business. Training is available through Small Business Development Centers, university extension services, community colleges, parent companies, franchisors, and others. Also, there is a wide array of video tapes available today [that allow training to] be conducted in the store.

Continually Improve the Efficiency of Your Business

Businesses may be doing all the right things as mentioned above, but unless they are efficiently operated, they are probably doomed to failure. Some of the top mass merchandisers such as Wal-Mart and Home Depot continually strive to improve their operating efficiency. 13

- *Adopt modern technology.* Mass merchandisers have improved their efficiency dramatically by adopting new technology. Much of that technology is now available and affordable to the smaller merchant. For example, powerful computers are available at ever decreasing prices. Software packages to handle nearly all store functions are also available. Computers reduce the need for people, improve accuracy, and provide quick analyses of the business' performance. In addition, point of sale (POS) scanner equipment is also now available and affordable to all but the smallest businesses. In addition to scanning prices and speeding customers through the checkout line, they can revolutionize inventory control when tied in with the store computer and ultimately with supplier's computers.
- *Become familiar with your financial statements.* Many merchants do not like to deal with the finances of the business. If they can "farm" this operation out to a bookkeeper or accountant, they feel "out of sight, out of mind." Good merchants must become intimately familiar with the finances and operations of their businesses. They should constantly monitor gross profit margins, operating expenses, net profits, and the various ratios important to the business.
- *Relentlessly find ways to reduce operating costs.* One of the reasons that the mass merchandisers can lower prices and still make a profit is that they continually reduce their operating costs. In addition to adopting technology, they find ways to save on utilities, transportation, etc. They are also always finding ways to reduce "shrinkage" by reducing shoplifting, pilferage and damage to merchandise. Smaller merchants can do the same thing.

Wal-Mart's War on Main Street

SARAH ANDERSON

Sarah Anderson is an economic analyst for a think tank in Washington, D.C. The daughter of a local retailer in Litchfield, Minnesota—a prime candidate for a Wal-Mart takeover—Anderson takes an anti–Wal-Mart stance grounded in a clear awareness that Main Street has been having its troubles for some time. If small-town life is to survive, it will have to change. Anderson's sisters become a part of that change. This essay originally appeared in The Progressive (Nov. 1994).

The basement of Boyd's for Boys and Girls in downtown Litchfield, Minnesota, looks like a history museum of the worst in children's fashions. All the real duds from the past forty years have accumulated down there: wool pedal-pushers, polyester bell-bottoms, wide clip-on neckties. There's a big box of 1960s faux fur hats, the kind with the fur pompon ties that dangle under a girl's chin. My father, Boyd Anderson, drags all the old stuff up the stairs and onto the sidewalk once a year on Krazy Daze. At the end of the 1 day, he lugs most of it back down. Folks around here don't go in much for the retro look.

At least for now, the museum is only in the basement. Upstairs, Dad continues to run one of the few remaining independent children's clothing stores on Main Street, USA. But this is the age of Wal-Mart, not Main Street. In 1994, the nation's top retailer plans to add 110 new U.S. stores to its current total of 1,967. For every Wal-Mart opening, there is more than one store like Boyd's that closes its doors. 2

Litchfield, a town of 6,200 people sixty miles west of Minneapolis, started losing Main Street businesses at the onset of the farm crisis and the shopping-mall boom of the early 1980s. As a high-school student during this time, I remember dinner-table conversation drifting time and again toward rumors of store closings. In those days, Mom frequently cut the conversation off short. "Let's talk about something less depressing, okay?" 3

Now my family can no longer avoid the issue of Main Street Litchfield's precarious future. Dad, at sixty-eight, stands at a crossroads. Should he retain his faith in Main Street and pass Boyd's down to his children? Or should he listen to the pessimists and close up the forty-one-year-old family business before it becomes obsolete? 4

For several years, Dad has been reluctant to choose either path. The transition to retirement is difficult for most people who have worked hard all their lives. For him, it could signify not only the end of a working career, but also the end of small-town life as he knows it. When pressed, Dad admits that business on Main Street has been going downhill for the past fifteen years. "I just can't visualize what the future for downtown Litchfield will be," he says. "I've laid awake nights worrying about it because I really don't want my kids to be stuck with a business that will fail." 5

I am not the aspiring heir to Boyd's. I left Litchfield at eighteen for the big city and would have a rough time readjusting to small-town life. My sister Laurie, a nurse, and my sister-in-law Colleen, who runs a farm with my brother Scott, are the ones eager to enter the ring and fight the retail Goliaths. Both women are well suited to the challenge. Between them, they have seven children who will give them excellent tips on kids' fashions. They are deeply rooted in the community and idealistic enough to believe that Main Street can survive. 6

My sisters are not alone. Across the country, thousands of rural people are battling to save their local downtowns. Many of these fights have taken the form of anti–Wal-Mart campaigns. In Vermont, citizens' groups allowed Wal-Mart to enter the state only after the company agreed to a long list of demands regarding the size and operation of the stores. Three Massachusetts towns and another in Maine have defeated bids by Wal-Mart to build in their communities. In Arkansas, three independent drugstore owners won a suit charging that Wal-Mart had used "predatory pricing," or selling below cost, to drive out competitors. Canadian citizens are asking Wal-Mart to sign a "Pledge of Corporate Responsibility" before opening in their towns. In at least a dozen other U.S. communities, groups have fought to keep Wal-Mart out or to restrict the firm's activities. 7

By attacking Wal-Mart, these campaigns have helped raise awareness of the value of locally owned independent stores on Main Street. Their concerns generally fall in five areas: 8

- *Sprawl Mart*—Wal-Mart nearly always builds along a highway outside town to take advantage of cheap, often unzoned land. This usually attracts additional commercial development, forcing the community to extend services (telephone and power lines, water and sewage services, and so forth) to that area, despite sufficient existing infrastructure downtown. 9
- *Wal-Mart channels resources out of a community*—studies have shown that a dollar spent on a local business has four or five times the economic spin-off of a dollar spent at a Wal-Mart, since a large share of Wal-Mart's profit returns to its Arkansas headquarters or is pumped into national advertising campaigns. 10
- *Wal-Mart destroys jobs in locally owned stores*—a Wal-Mart–funded community impact study debunked the retailer's claim that it would create a lot of jobs in Greenfield, Massachusetts. Although Wal-Mart planned to hire 274 people at its Greenfield store, the community could expect to gain only eight net jobs, because of projected losses at other businesses that would have to compete with Wal-Mart. 11
- *Citizen Wal-Mart?*—in at least one town—Hearne, Texas—Wal-Mart destroyed its Main Street competitors and then deserted the town in search of higher returns elsewhere. Unable to attract new businesses to the devastated Main Street, local residents have no choice but to drive long distances to buy basic goods. 12
- *One-stop shopping culture*—in Greenfield, where citizens voted to keep Wal-Mart out, anti–Wal-Mart campaign manager Al Norman said he saw a resurgence of appreciation for Main Street. "People realized there's one thing you can't buy at Wal-Mart, and that's small-town quality of life," Norman explains. "This community decided it was not ready to die for a cheap pair of underwear." 13

So far Litchfield hasn't been forced to make that decision. Nevertheless, the town is already losing at least some business to four nearby Wal-Marts, each less than forty miles from town. To find out how formidable this enemy is, Mom and I went on a spying mission to the closest Wal-Mart, twenty miles away in Hutchinson. 14

Just inside the door, we were met by a so-called Wal-Mart "greeter" (actually the greeters just say hello as they take your bags to prevent you from shoplifting). We realized we knew her. Before becoming a greeter, she had been a cashier at a downtown Litchfield supermarket until it closed early this year. I tried to be casual when I asked if she greets many people from Litchfield. "Oh, a-a-a-ll the time!" she replied. Sure enough, Mom immediately spotted one in the checkout line. 15

Not wanting to look too suspicious, we moved on toward the children's department, where we discreetly examined price tags and labels. Not 16 all, but many items were cheaper than at Boyd's. It was the brainwashing campaign that we found most intimidating, though. Throughout the store were huge red, white, and blue banners declaring BRING IT HOME TO AMERICA. Confusingly, the labels on the children's clothing indicated that they had been imported from sixteen countries, including Haiti, where an embargo on exports was supposed to be in place.

Of course, Wal-Mart is not Main Street's only foe. Over coffee at the Main Street Cafe, some of Litchfield's long-time merchants gave me a litany of additional complaints. Like my dad, many of these men remember when three-block-long Main Street was a bustling social and commercial hub, with two movie theaters, six restaurants, a department store, and a grand old hotel. 17

Present-day Litchfield is not a ghost town, but there are four empty storefronts, and several former commercial buildings now house offices for government service agencies. In recent years, the downtown has lost its last two drugstores and two supermarkets. As a result, elderly people who live downtown and are unable to drive can no longer do their own shopping. 18

My dad and the other merchants place as much blame for this decline on cut-throat suppliers as on Wal-Mart. The big brand names, especially, have no time anymore for small clients. Don Brock, who ran a furniture store for thirty-three years before retiring in 1991, remembers getting an honorary plaque from a manufacturer whose products he carried for many years. "Six months later I got a letter saying they were no longer going to fill my orders." 19

At the moment, Litchfield's most pressing threat is a transportation department plan to reroute the state highway that now runs down Main Street to the outskirts of town. Local merchants fear the bypass would kill the considerable business they now get from travelers. Bypasses are also magnets for Wal-Mart and other discounters attracted to the large, cheap, and often unzoned sites along the bypass. 20

When I asked the merchants how they felt about the bypass, the table grew quiet. Greg Heath, a florist and antique dealer, sighed and said, "The bypass will come—it might be ten years from now, but it will come. By then, we'll either be out of business or the bypass will drive us out." 21

The struggles of Main Street merchants have naturally created a growth industry in consultants ready to provide tips on marketing and customer relations. Community-development experts caution, though, that individual merchants acting on their own cannot keep Main Street strong. "Given the enormous forces of change, the only way these businesses can survive is with active public and government support," says Dawn Nakano, of the National Center for Economic Alternatives in Washington, D.C. 22

Some of the most effective efforts at revitalization, Nakano says, are community development corporations—private, nonprofit corporations governed by a community-based board and usually funded in part by foundation and government money. In Pittsburgh, for example, the city government and about thirty nonprofit groups formed a community development corporation to save an impoverished neighborhood where all but three 23 businesses were boarded up. Today, thanks to such financing and technical assistance, the area has a lively shopping district.

Although most community development corporations have been created to serve low-income urban neighborhoods, Nakano feels that they could be equally effective in saving Main Streets. "There's no reason why church, civic, and other groups in a small town couldn't form a community development corporation to fill boarded-up stores with new businesses. Besides revitalizing Main Street, this could go a long way toward cultivating a 'buy local' culture among residents." 24

The National Main Street Center, a Washington, D.C.–based nonprofit, provides some of the most comprehensive Main Street revitalization services. The Center has helped more than 850 towns build cooperative links among merchants, government, and citizens. However, the Center's efforts focus on improving marketing techniques and the physical appearance of stores, which can only do so much to counter the powerful forces of change. 25

No matter how well designed, any Main Street revitalization project will fail without local public support. Unfortunately, it is difficult for many rural people to consider the long-term, overall effects of their purchases, given the high levels of rural unemployment, job insecurity, and poverty. If you're worried about paying your rent, you're not going to pay more for a toaster at your local hardware store, no matter how much you like your hometown. 26

Another problem is political. Like those in decaying urban neighborhoods, many rural people have seen the signs of decline around them and concluded that they lack the clout necessary to harness the forces of change for their own benefit. If you've seen your neighbors lose their farms through foreclosure, your school close down, and local manufacturing move to Mexico, how empowered will you feel? 27

Litchfield Mayor Ron Ebnet has done his best to bolster community confidence and loyalty to Main Street. "Every year at the Christmas lighting ceremony, I tell people to buy their gifts in town. I know everyone is sick of hearing it, but I don't care." Ebnet has whipped up opposition to the proposed bypass, with strong support from the city council, chamber of commerce, the newspaper editor, and the state senator. He also orchestrated a downtown beautification project and helped the town win a state redevelopment grant to upgrade downtown businesses and residences. 28

Ebnet has failed to win over everyone, though. Retired merchant Don Larson told me about a local resident who drove forty miles to get something seventeen cents cheaper than he could buy it at the Litchfield lumberyard. "I pointed out that he had spent more on gas than he'd saved, but he told me that 'it was a matter of principle.' I thought, what about the principle of supporting your community? People just don't think about that, though." 29

Mayor Ebnet agrees, "Many people still have a 1950s mentality," he says. "They can't see the tremendous changes that are affecting these small businesses. People tell me they want the bypass because there's too much 30 traffic downtown and they have a hard time crossing the street. And I ask them, but what will you be crossing to? If we get the bypass, there will be nothing left!"

Last summer, with the threat of the bypass hanging over his head, Dad became increasingly stubborn about making a decision about the store. His antique Underwood typewriter was never more productive, as it banged out angry letters to the state transportation department. 31

My sisters decided to try a new tactic. While my parents were on vacation, they assaulted the store with paintbrushes and wallpaper, transforming what had been a rather rustic restroom and doing an unprecedented amount of redecorating and rearranging. 32

The strategy worked. "At first, Dad was a bit shocked," Laurie said. "He commented that in his opinion, the old toilet-paper dispenser had been perfectly fine. But overall he was pleased with the changes, and two days later he called for a meeting with us and our spouses." 33

"Your dad started out by making a little speech," Colleen said. "The first thing he said was, 'Well, things aren't how they used to be.' Then he pulled out some papers he'd prepared and told us exactly how much sales and profits have been over the years and what we could expect to make. He told us what he thinks are the negative and the positive aspects of the job and then said if we were still interested, we could begin talking about a starting date for us to take over." 34

Dad later told me, "The only way I could feel comfortable about Laurie and Colleen running the store is if it was at no financial risk to them. So I'm setting up an account for them to draw from—enough for a one-year trial. But if they can't make a good profit, then that's it—I'll try to sell the business to someone else. I still worry that they don't know what they're getting themselves into. Especially if the bypass goes through, things are going to be rough." 35

My sisters are optimistic. They plan to form a buying cooperative with Main Street children's clothing stores in other towns and have already drafted a customer survey to help them better understand local needs. "I think we're going to see a big increase in appreciation of the small-town atmosphere," Colleen says. "There are more and more people moving to Litchfield from the Twin Cities to take advantage of the small-town way of life. I think they might even be more inclined to support the local businesses than people who've lived here their whole lives and now take the town for granted." 36

Small towns cannot return to the past, when families did all their shopping and socializing in their hometown. Rural life is changing and there's no use denying it. The most important question is, who will define the future? Will it be Wal-Mart, whose narrow corporate interests have little to do with building healthy communities? Will it be the department of transportation, whose purpose is to move cars faster? Will it be the banks and suppliers primarily interested in doing business with the big guys? Or will it be the people who live in small towns, whose hard work and support are essential to any effort to revitalize Main Street? 37

In my hometown, there are at least two new reasons for optimism. First, shortly before my deadline for this article, the Minnesota transportation department announced that it was dropping the Litchfield highway bypass project because of local opposition. (My dad's Underwood will finally get a rest.) The second reason is that a new teal green awning will soon be hanging over the front door of Boyd's—a symbol of one family's belief that Main Street, while weary, is not yet a relic of the past. 38

Who's Really the Villain?

JO-ANN JOHNSTON

A freelance writer based in Greenfield, Massachusetts—a town that successfully fought off the construction of a Wal-Mart superstore—Jo-Ann Johnston challenges the logic of anti–Wal-Mart forces and argues that the store would have helped to address fundamental problems with the local economy. This selection originally appeared in the journal Business Ethics *(May–June 1995).*

Cheap underwear. That's all Wal-Mart Corp. contributes as it squeezes the life out of a community's downtown, according to Albert Norman, an outspoken Wal-Mart critic. His sentiment—and talent for rousing support—led folks in rural Greenfield, Massachusetts, to block the company's plans to build a store there. It also established the political consultant as one of the best known opponents to "Sprawl-mart" in the country. But fighting off Wal-Mart hasn't done much for the 18,845 residents of Greenfield. 1

As in numerous other communities during the past ten years, Wal-Mart simply found a site just a short distance away from its original target. In this case, it's in Orange, a smaller town located up the road about twenty-five minutes from downtown Greenfield. Meanwhile, this area ranks as the state's second poorest in per capita income. And in January, it posted an unemployment rate of 6.1 percent—attributable partly to the recent closings of a paper plant, a container factory, and a large store that sold liquidated merchandise. Wal-Mart would have brought to Greenfield 240 tax-paying jobs and increased retail traffic. 2

Set to open later this year, the store in Orange will be yet another example of how saying "go away" to the likes of Wal-Mart overlooks a much deeper problem facing small-town America: the need to change a way of doing business while maintaining, or improving, a deeply valued way of life. An increasing number of people are beginning to realize that small-town merchants need to adapt to changes in their communities, the economy, and their industries instead of chastising an outside company. That means accepting the fact that a Wal-Mart, or a similar retailer, may become a neighbor. 3

Such thinking is hogwash as far as anti–Wal-Marters are concerned. Consumerism has run amok if a town figures it needs a Wal-Mart, says Norman [see pp. 207–209], who today works with people in Illinois, Ohio, 4

New England, and other regions to stop Wal-Marts and other large discount retailers from setting up shop. His list of reasons to fight such chain stores is lengthy, with perhaps one of the most popular being the potential loss of small-town quality of life. People move to small towns from urban or suburban America in part to escape from mall and shopping strip development, he says, not to see it duplicated.

That emotional argument carries weight, especially in New England, 5
where twelve cities and one state, Vermont, have fought Wal-Mart. A current battle is taking place in Sturbridge, a historic town in eastern Massachusetts where community activists are fighting to keep Wal-Mart out. The town draws 60 percent of its general business from tourism-related trade, says local Wal-Mart opponent Carol Goodwin. "We market history," she says. The town and its re-creation of an early American village are the state's second largest tourist attraction. A big cookie-cutter mart off the freeway could obscure this town of eight thousand's special appeal, she says.

Sturbridge may want to take a lesson from its neighbor to the north- 6
west, however. Merchants in Greenfield face the possible loss of business due to the fact Wal-Mart found a location "just over the hill" from where it was first looking to build. Kenneth Stone, an economist at Iowa State University and the country's leading researcher on the economic impacts of Wal-Marts [see pp. 209–216], found that towns in the Midwest and East suffered a "retail leakage" of shoppers who instead drove to the closest regional shopping center with a discount store.

Does that mean Greenfield shoppers will now drive to Orange? Well, 7
several of the town's shoppers complained during the Wal-Mart battle that area merchants could use competition because of their poor selection, high prices, limited hours, and lackluster service. Meanwhile, Wal-Mart has a good reputation for service. A *Consumer Reports* reader poll in late 1994 found that fifty thousand people rated Wal-Mart the highest in customer satisfaction of "value-oriented chains."

In many ways, what is happening to small-town retail corridors is sim- 8
ilar to how mom-and-pop corporations were caught off guard during the takeover frenzy of the 1980s. Survivors became more efficient to avoid being picked off by raiders looking to maximize shareholder profits. With Wal-Mart, it's a matter of maximizing retailing opportunities for consumers.

By the time a community knows the demographically astute Wal-Mart 9
has its eye on an area, it's virtually too late to stop *somebody* from coming into town, says Bill Sakelarios, president of the Concord-based Retail Merchants Association of New Hampshire. In Greenfield, for instance, the threat of competition to that town's small retailers didn't disappear with the Wal-Mart vote. BJ's Wholesale club is considering the town for a store.

Wal-Mart is viewed as a threat, though, because it uses bulk buying, 10
discount pricing, and tight inventory and distribution management that smaller retailers can't keep up with. It also has the competitive advantage of size: The company's sales surged 22 percent to more than $82 billion,

while net income climbed 15 percent to more than $2.6 billion in the year ended January 31, 1995, compared with year-earlier results.

Because it's so huge, the best defense against Wal-Mart for small-town retailers is to adapt, evolve, and create some stronghold that will make them viable and worth keeping, even in the face of new competition, says Robert Kahn, a Lafayette, California, management consultant who has worked with the chain and publishes a newsletter called *Retailing Today.* All kinds of stores have found ways to survive in the shadow of Wal-Mart, he says. Grocery stores have maintained check cashing, hardware stores and nurseries have offered classes, women's clothing retailers have filled in the gaps in the Wal-Mart line. Others point to pharmacies that have been able to compete with Wal-Marts. Stone met one druggist who kept a loyal clientele of shut-ins who spent $200 to $300 a month individually on prescriptions by offering home delivery, something Wal-Mart didn't do in his market. 11

The argument that self-improvement and change for small retailers may be the answer is definitely scorned in some circles. But stores that balk at such notions may not get much sympathy from customers who have had to change jobs or learn new skills—all because of shifts in the structure of the economies in the fields in which they work. 12

"You read stories about how towns don't want Wal-Mart, but in many cases that's a very few people getting a lot of publicity. And I may have on my desk a petition signed by fifteen thousand people saying, 'Please come, ignore the one hundred people who are trying to block the store,'" Wal-Mart President and CEO David Glass told a press gathering in December. "In retailing, you have a very simple answer to all that. Any community that didn't want a Wal-Mart store—all they've got to do is not shop there. And I guarantee a store, even if it's [just] built, won't be there long." 13

Another thing to consider is what happens if Wal-Mart, or a store like it, comes into town, stays for ten years, and then leaves. Where that's happened, retailers who found ways to adapt to Wal-Mart's presence still believe they're much better as a result. In Nowata, Oklahoma, Wal-Mart pulled up stakes last year and deserted a town of 3,900 people who had come to depend on it as their second largest tax payer, as well as their major retailing center. But several local merchants survived Wal-Mart's stay of fourteen years because they learned to adjust their business practices. Wayne Clark, whose father opened Clark's Sentry Hardware in 1938, says he survived Wal-Mart's presence by providing better service and a more specialized inventory. 14

Nowata also brings up another interesting question on the Wal-Mart controversy: Could it be that old-time downtowns simply are obsolete and an impediment to efficient retailing? Many retailers have probably been in a precarious position for a long time, for a number of reasons, and then placed the blame for problems or eventual demise on the highly visible Wal-Mart, says Sakelarios. "Wal-Mart is being singled out. Small-town business districts brought a lot of this on themselves," agrees Iowa State's Stone. 15

As cars have drawn shopping to other locales, downtown districts haven't worked hard enough to remain competitive and efficient, data suggest. "Small retailers often believe that the community *owes them* rather than *they owe* the community," Kahn wrote in his December newsletter. 16

He cites as evidence a recent survey of more than 1,500 Illinois retailers conducted by the state's merchant association. Kahn found it stunning that 54 percent reorder inventory for their stores only when they're already out of stock. That translates into poor selection and service, Kahn says, because small retailers often can't get priority shipments from vendors and most often wait for five to fifteen days to get fresh stock in, leaving customers without that selection in the interim. "That's not providing any service. If it's not in stock, eventually the customer is going to go somewhere else," Kahn points out. 17

Kahn also criticized the 63 percent of the retailers surveyed who claimed to know what their customers want, even though they didn't track customer purchases. 18

Apart from self-inflicted injuries, retailers are also pressured on other fronts, says John Donnellan, a member of the Consumer Studies faculty at the University of Massachusetts in Ames. The growth of the mail-order catalogs, cable TV shopping networks, specialized category stores such as Toys 'R' Us, and now, possibly, shopping via on-line computer services, all present more competition for small merchants that draw from local markets. 19

The only difference with Wal-Mart is that it's the biggest, most identifiable source of that new and increasing competition. As a result, it has become a lightning rod for all the angst and anxiety of struggling shop keepers—deserved or not. 20

Savvy Expansion and Leadership

JAMES F. MOORE

James F. Moore, president of a management consulting group in Cambridge, Massachusetts, finds in Wal-Mart an illustration of how companies can succeed "by creating a complete ecosystem." Moore uses the metaphor of an ecosystem to describe the four-part evolution of a business in its market. In Stage 1, entrepreneurs define customer needs. In Stage 2, businesses expand into new territories in an effort to establish themselves as visionary industry leaders in Stage 3. In Stage 4, business leaders are challenged by newly emerging ecosystems and must evolve by developing new ideas. Throughout the discussion, Moore uses the language of interspecies competition—the language of "Predators and Prey" (the selection's original title)—to describe dynamics of the business world and, particularly, of Wal-Mart's success. This piece first appeared in the Harvard Business Review *(May–June 1993). The selection here begins with Moore's extended discussion of Wal-Mart and continues with excerpts from his explanation of business ecosystems.*

1 An ecological analysis of Wal-Mart reveals how a relatively small company, starting in a rural area of the United States, could turn its original isolation to advantage by creating a complete business ecosystem. Wal-Mart developed and continues to refine an offer that customers find nearly irresistible: low prices on a variety of brands as diverse as Gitano jeans and Yardman lawn mowers. Moreover, CEO Sam Walton managed the company's expansion superbly and increased bargaining power during the leadership stage.

2 *The Birth of Discounting.* In the early 1960s, Kmart, Wal-Mart, and other discounters recognized that the Main Street five-and-dime was giving way to the variety store. And variety stores, in turn, were threatened by the large discount store. In order to buy a wide range of goods at low prices in one location, customers were increasingly willing to get into cars and drive to malls or other non-Main Street locations.

3 Kmart and Wal-Mart appeared on the discount scene at about the same time. The Kmart stores were actually owned by old-style S.S. Kresge, which reinvented itself as a suburb-oriented discount retailer, with big stores located near existing malls and towns of more than 50,000 people. Kmart stores carried items aimed at the lower end of suburban tastes.

4 By the late 1960s, Wal-Mart had worked out the basic structure of its own business ecosystem: Wal-Mart stores, which supplied a variety of well-known brands, were located in relatively sparsely populated areas. The company went into towns of 5,000 people, particularly where several of these towns might be served by one store. Wal-Mart products were up to 15% cheaper than those available in "mom-and-pop" stores.

5 While the original Wal-Mart locations could support one store, the customer population wasn't large enough to maintain two rival discounters. Thus once Wal-Mart established a store in a particular area and had beaten back weak local retailers, it was seldom threatened with future local competition from other discounters, including Kmart.

6 *Expansion: Planning for a Chokehold.* Once its business strategy was up and running in a number of discount stores in the American South and Mid-West, Wal-Mart's top executives concentrated on developing organizational capabilities that would let it scale up successfully. They were obsessed with three things:

- Building a set of incentives that would ensure employee commitment to local stores, which led to a complex system of training, oversight, bonuses, and stock-purchase plans for workers.
- Managing communication and control of a network of remotely located stores, which required close monitoring of a carefully drawn set of measures that were transmitted daily to Wal-Mart headquarters in Bentonville, Arkansas.
- Setting up an efficient distribution system that allowed for joint purchasing, shared facilities, systematic ordering, and store-level distribution of a large number of different goods. This third obsession ul-

> timately became Wal-Mart's trademark hub-and-spoke distribution system: warehouses served constellations of stores located no more than a day's drive from the center.

In 1970, Wal-Mart went public to raise funds for its expansion. That 7
same year, the company built its first hub-and-spoke distribution center—embarking on a strategy of targeting a large geographic area, setting up a distribution center, and then populating the area with as many stores as the territory would support. Wal-Mart not only filled the needs of customers in small towns but also saturated entire regions, making it uneconomical for competitors to enter as either distributors or local store owners.

The number of Wal-Mart stores grew rapidly, from 32 in 1970 to 195 8
in 1978—when the first fully automated distribution center opened—to 551 in 1983—when Wal-Mart launched its own satellite, creating a communication network to keep in daily touch with its now far-flung empire.

Leadership: Building Bargaining Power. By 1984, Wal-Mart's man- 9
agerial agenda changed. What was in the birth and expansion stages a race to develop systems and conquer territory now became a concerted effort to build bargaining power. As the leaders of a highly successful and visible business ecosystem, Wal-Mart managers worked on continuing to assert the company's vision over other community members, including suppliers like Procter & Gamble, Rubbermaid, and Helene Curtis Industries.

First, Wal-Mart resisted the temptation to charge higher prices in the 10
markets and regions it dominated. Instead, top managers still viewed each market as "contestable"—as a potential opening for rivals if Wal-Mart ceased to give the maximum possible value to customers. Continued customer leadership, in turn, enhanced the Wal-Mart brand and further cemented the company's place in the minds and buying habits of consumers. Wal-Mart's system of "everyday low prices," in which there's no need for weekly sales or special promotions, has now become a standard in discount retailing.

Second, Wal-Mart—now a very large and powerful channel to cus- 11
tomers—started putting heavy pressure on suppliers to keep their prices down. Moreover, Wal-Mart compelled its suppliers to set up cross-company distribution systems to attain maximum manufacturing efficiency. For example, in 1987, Wal-Mart and Procter & Gamble reached an unprecedented accord to work together through extensive electronic ordering and information sharing between the companies. In return, Wal-Mart gives better payment terms than the rest of the retailing industry: on average, Wal-Mart pays its suppliers within 29 days, compared with 45 days at Kmart.

Third, Wal-Mart continued to invest in and enhance its own fundamen- 12
tal economies of scale and scope in distribution. By the leadership stage, distribution had become the crucial ecological component of the Wal-Mart ecosystem. In fact, Wal-Mart's distribution chokehold has allowed the ecosystem as a whole to triumph over others like Kmart's. While suppliers, big and small, may chafe under Wal-Mart's heavy hand, it's also clear that

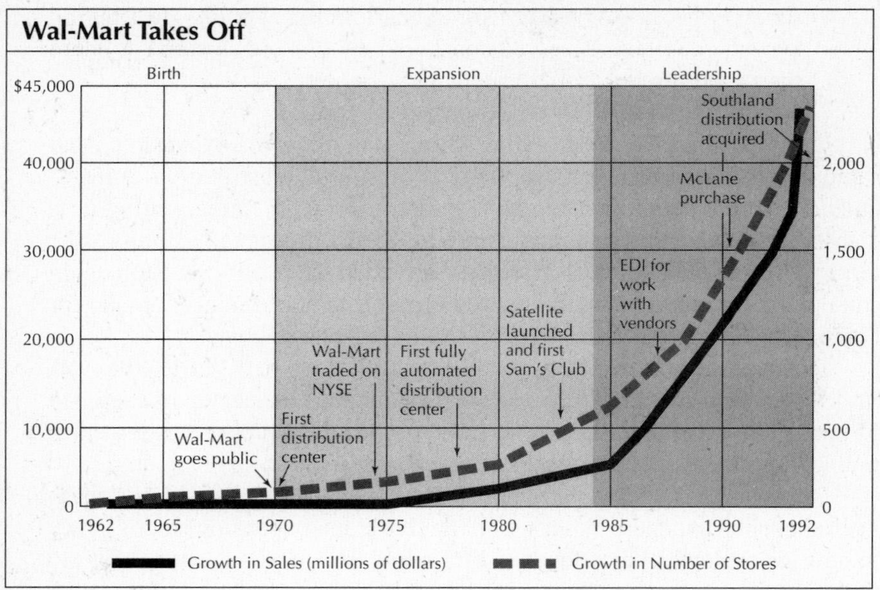

most of them need this particular leader to survive. The graph "Wal-Mart Takes Off" is a testament to the company's dominance and bargaining power in the leadership stage.

Finally, Wal-Mart has extended its reach into adjacent territories and ecosystems. In 1983, Wal-Mart entered the membership discount market with its Sam's Club, which by 1992 included 208 clubs that contributed over $9.4 billion in revenues. In 1990, Wal-Mart incorporated another ecosystem by acquiring McLane Company, the nation's largest distributor to the convenience store industry. McLane, under Wal-Mart's control, now serves about 30,000 retail stores, including 18,000 convenience stores. And in 1992, Wal-Mart also acquired the distribution and food processing divisions of Southland Corporation. Southland operates a large chain of 7-Eleven convenience stores, and this acquisition added as many as 5,000 more 7-Eleven stores to the McLane/Wal-Mart customer base. 13

[The following excerpts from Moore's "Predators and Prey," in the same edition of the *Harvard Business Review,* define key elements of "business ecosystems."—Ed.]

Successful businesses are those that evolve rapidly and effectively. Yet innovative businesses can't evolve in a vacuum. They must attract resources of all sorts, drawing in capital, partners, suppliers, and customers to create cooperative networks. 14

Much has been written about such networks, under the rubric of strategic alliances, virtual organizations, and the like. But these frameworks provide little systematic assistance for managers who seek to understand the 15 underlying strategic logic of change. Even fewer of these theories help executives anticipate the managerial challenges of nurturing the complex business communities that bring innovations to market.

How is it that a company can create an entirely new business community—like IBM in personal computers—and then lose control and profitability in that same business? Is there a stable structure of community leadership that matches fast-changing conditions? And how can companies develop leadership that successfully adapts to continual waves of innovation and change? These questions remain unanswered because most managers still frame the problem in the old way: companies go head-to-head in an industry, battling for market share. But events of the last decade, particularly in high-technology businesses, amply illustrate the limits of that understanding. 16

In essence, executives must develop new ideas and tools for strategizing, tools for making tough choices when it comes to innovations, business alliances, and leadership of customers and suppliers. Anthropologist Gregory Bateson's definition of *co-evolution* in both natural and social systems provides a useful starting place. In his book *Mind and Nature,* Bateson describes co-evolution as a process in which interdependent species evolve in an endless reciprocal cycle—in which "changes in species A set the stage for the natural selection of changes in species B"—and vice versa. Consider predators and their prey, for instance, or flowering plants and their pollinators. 17

Another insight comes from biologist Stephen Jay Gould, who has observed that natural ecosystems sometimes collapse when environmental conditions change too radically. Dominant combinations of species may lose their leadership. New ecosystems then establish themselves, often with previously marginal plants and animals at the center. For current businesses dealing with the challenges of innovation, there are clear parallels and profound implications. 18

To extend a systematic approach to strategy, I suggest that a company be viewed not as a member of a single industry but as part of a *business ecosystem* that crosses a variety of industries. In a business ecosystem, companies co-evolve capabilities around a new innovation: they work cooperatively and competitively to support new products, satisfy customer needs, and eventually incorporate the next round of innovations. 19

• • •

A business ecosystem, like its biological counterpart, gradually moves from a random collection of elements to a more structured community. Think of a prairie grassland that is succeeded by stands of conifers, which in turn evolve into a more complex forest dominated by hardwoods. Business ecosystems condense out of the original swirl of capital, customer interest, and talent generated by a new innovation, just as successful species spring from the natural resources of sunlight, water, and soil nutrients. 20

Every business ecosystem develops in four distinct stages: birth, expansion, leadership, and self-renewal—or, if not self-renewal, death. In reality, of course, the evolutionary stages blur, and the managerial challenges 21 of one stage often crop up in another. Yet I've observed the four stages in many companies over time, across businesses as diverse as retailing, entertainment, and pharmaceuticals. What remains the same from business to business is the process of co-evolution: the complex interplay between competitive and cooperative business strategies (see the table, "The Evolutionary Stages of a Business Ecosystem").

• • •

I anticipate that as an ecological approach to management becomes more common—as an increasing number of executives become conscious of co-evolution and its consequences—the pace of business change itself will accelerate. Executives whose horizons are bounded by traditional industry perspectives will find themselves missing the real challenges and opportunities that face their companies. Shareholders and directors, sensing the new reality, will eventually remove them. Or, in light of the latest management shifts, they may have already done so. 22

Unfortunately for employees and investors, this often occurs only after the companies involved have been deeply damaged. Companies that once dominated their industries, as traditionally defined, have been blindsided by new competition. Whether such companies can find the appropriate leadership to renew the ecosystems on which their future depends remains an open question. If they cannot, they'll be supplanted by other 23

THE EVOLUTIONARY STAGES OF A BUSINESS ECOSYSTEM

	COOPERATIVE CHALLENGES	COMPETITIVE CHALLENGES
Birth	Work with customers and suppliers to define the new value proposition around a seed innovation.	Protect your ideas from others who might be working toward defining similar offers. Tie up critical lead customers, key suppliers, and important channels.
Expansion	Bring the new offer to a large market by working with suppliers and partners to scale up supply and to achieve maximum market coverage.	Defeat alternative implementations of similar ideas. Ensure that your approach is the market standard in its class through dominating key market segments.
Leadership	Provide a compelling vision for the future that encourages suppliers and customers to work together to continue improving the complete offer.	Maintain strong bargaining power in relation to other players in the ecosystem, including key customers and valued suppliers.
Self-Renewal	Work with innovators to bring new ideas to the existing ecosystem.	Maintain high barriers to entry to prevent innovators from building alternative ecosystems. Maintain high customer switching costs in order to buy time to incorporate new ideas into your own products and services.

companies, in other business ecosystems, that will expand and lead over the next few years.

For the individuals caught up in these ecosystem struggles, the stakes 24
are high. As a society, we must find ways of helping members of dying ecosystems get into more vital ones while avoiding the temptation of propping up the failed ecosystems themselves. From an ecological perspective, it matters not which particular ecosystems stay alive; rather, it's only essential that competition among them is fierce and fair—and that the fittest survive.

Doonesbury on Wal-Mart

GARRY TRUDEAU

In the opening selection of this chapter, Wall Street Journal *reporter Bob Ortega referred to Garry Trudeau as the "quintessential chronicler of the Woodstock generation." Often a topic of conversation because of its pointed political barbs, Trudeau's comic strip "Doonesbury" appears in hundreds of newspapers nationwide. The cartoonist devoted twelve strips to the Wal-Mart debate in September 1994. As you will see, this is a comic strip with an attitude.*

Doonesbury BY GARRY TRUDEAU

1

Doonesbury BY GARRY TRUDEAU

2

THE WIDOW COULD NO LONGER CONTAIN HER CURIOSITY.
WHAT AM I "UP TO," MA'AM?
YES.

WELL, MA'AM, I'M PART OF A CREATIVE TEAM. WE'RE BUILDING SOMETHING MAGICAL HERE— A SPECIAL PLACE OF DREAMS!
UH-OH... HE'S FROM DISNEY!

I'LL BE EXPLAINING IT ALL AT A TOWN MEETING TONIGHT. WON'T YOU COME?
AND DON'T WORRY—I'M NOT FROM DISNEY.

THAT EVENING...
I STILL SMELL MOUSE.

3

AT THAT NIGHT'S TOWN MEETING, THE STRANGER ROSE TO HIS FEET...
GOOD PEOPLE, MY NAME IS DANNY DOYLE...

AS SOME OF YOU MAY KNOW, I'VE SPENT THE WEEK SURVEYING OUT AT THE MANION PLACE. THE FOLKS I WORK FOR ARE HOPING TO DEVELOP IT INTO SOMETHING QUITE SPECIAL...

WE PROPOSE TO BUILD A FIELD OF DREAMS, ACTUALLY, A WHOLE WORLD OF DREAMS! 120,000 SQ. FT. OF SHOPPERS' PARADISE!

HOLD IT! I OWN A SMALL FAMILY STORE...
BUT YOUR SELECTION STINKS, ED! LET THE MAN SPEAK!

4

AT THE TOWN MEETING, RUBY KILGORE WAS SKEPTICAL...
MR. DOYLE, YOU SAY YOU'RE BUILDING A "SHOPPERS' PARADISE"...

WELL, WHAT KIND OF VALUE ARE YOU TALKING ABOUT? LIKE, HOW MUCH WOULD A 24-COUNT PACKAGE OF EXTRA-LARGE PAMPERS COST ME?

ONE LOW PRICE—$5.99! YES, $5.99! BUY THREE, YOUR COST IS ONLY $14.99!
GASP!

BOY'S TURTLENECKS, FROM $2.49! RADIAL TIRES, ONLY $29.50!
DON'T LISTEN TO HIM! THOSE ARE THE DEVIL'S PRICES!
OOH...
AHH...

5

THE STRANGER COMES CLEAN...
SO WHAT DO WE CALL OUR 120,000 SQ. FT. OF EXCITEMENT?

WELL, WE CALL IT THE PEOPLE'S EMPORIUM, BUT YOU KNOW IT BY THE NAME WAL-MART!

WAL-MART?

...INSTANTLY DIVIDING THE TOWN.
MY BUSINESS IS RUINED!
FINALLY! ONE-STOP SHOPPING!
A WAY OF LIFE GONE!
GOOD RIDDANCE!

6

THE ASSEMBLED CITIZENRY COULD SCARCELY BELIEVE THEIR EARS...
WAL-MART?
YES, WAL-MART!
9-26

NOW, WE KNOW YOUR CONCERNS, BUT BELIEVE ME, THE OUTLET WE ENVISION HERE WILL BE THE **PRIDE** OF THE REGION!

FIRST OF ALL, IN THE DESIGN OF THE STRUCTURE, WE'LL RESPECT THE UNIQUE AGRARIAN CHARACTER OF THE SURROUNDING COUNTRYSIDE – TO THE POINT OF PLANTING **SOYBEANS** ON THE ROOF!

THE DREAM TAKES SHAPE
MOOO!
WAL-MART
WAL-MART
ENTRANCE

7

HERB BAUSER, OF HERB'S SUNDRIES, TAKES ON THE MAN FROM WAL-MART...
HOW'S THE LOCAL MERCHANT SUPPOSE TO SURVIVE IN YOUR SHADOW?
TELL HIM, HERB!
9-27

YOU'LL **KILL OFF** OUR DOWNTOWN!
THAT'S JUST A MYTH, HERB! ONCE THEY ADJUST, LOCAL BUSINESSES WILL FLOURISH AS **NEVER** BEFORE!

YOU SEE, BECAUSE OF OUR OBVIOUS ADVANTAGES, WE'LL FORCE YOU TO RUN A SHARPER OPERATION – MUCH MORE FOCUSED AND RESPONSIVE TO YOUR CUSTOMERS!

WELL, GOSH! YOU'D DO THAT FOR ME?
HECK, YES! IT'S ALL PART OF OUR TOUGH LOVE PROGRAM FOR LOCAL RETAILERS!

8

LOCAL PHARMACIST GILBERT WAX HAD HEARD ENOUGH.
IT'S NOT **FAIR**! I'M A THIRD-GENERATION DRUGGIST! YOU'LL **RUIN** ME!
9-28

NOW, GIL, YOU HAVE NOTHING TO WORRY ABOUT. WAL-MART WILL SERVE AS A MAGNET, CREATING A BOON FOR **ALL** LOCAL STORES!
OH, RIGHT...

YOUR 20,000 SQ. FT. SUPER-PHARMACY IS GOING TO ACT AS A DRAW FOR MY 600 SQ. FT. DRUG STORE? I DON'T THINK SO!

THEN SELL SOMETHING ELSE. LOCAL CRAFTS! CORNCOB PIPES.
CORNCOB PIPES?
I COULD SOURCE THOSE FOR YOU, GIL.

9

IT WAS GINNY MAYHEW'S TURN.
MR. DOYLE, WE OWN AN APPLIANCE STORE. IF YOU COME IN HERE, WE'RE DEAD MEAT.

WELL, AGAIN, IT MAY BE THAT YOU JUST NEED A CHANGE! YOU COULD CARRY KNICKKNACKS, FOR INSTANCE.
KNICKKNACKS?

HEAR THAT, MOM? WE DON'T HAVE TO SELL DISHWASHERS ANYMORE! WE CAN SWITCH TO **KNICKKNACKS**!
KNICKKNACKS! IT'S LIKE A DREAM COME TRUE! IF **ONLY** YOUR FATHER WERE ALIVE!
9-29

YOU KNOW, FOR RUSTICS, YOU FOLKS SURE ARE GIVEN TO SARCASM.
SO WE WATCH LETTERMAN. SUE US.

10

THE MAN FROM WAL-MART TRIED A DIFFERENT TACK...
YOU KNOW, FOLKS, YOU ALL HAVE BEEN FOCUSING ON THE DOWNSIDE OF WAL-MART...
9-30

BUT THERE'S A LOT OF GOOD NEWS ABOUT WAL-MART AS WELL! FOR STARTERS, NO MORE LONG TRIPS TO TULSA FOR BASIC NECESSITIES!

THEN THERE'S ECONOMIC DEVELOPMENT! PEOPLE WILL BE COMING INTO THIS AREA TO SPEND MONEY FROM AS FAR AWAY AS DENISON AND WICHITA FALLS!
GB Trudeau

HOLD IT! YOU'RE BRINGING TEXAS TRASH IN HERE?
OH, GOSH! WHAT IS THIS, SOME SORT OF FRIENDLY RIVALRY?

11

WELL, FOLKS, I WANT TO THANK YOU FOR ALL YOUR FEEDBACK! I'LL BE PRESENTING OUR PROPOSAL TO YOUR PLANNING BOARD SOON...
LOOKS LIKE WE'RE ALL HERE...!
10-1

UH... REALLY? WELL, I KNOW YOU'LL WANT TO DEBATE THIS! THE TOWN IS CLEARLY DIVIDED!
THINK SO? LET'S VOTE NOW. ALL IN FAVOR, SAY AYE!

WAIT A MINUTE! YOU CAN'T JUST...
ALL OPPOSED, SAY NAY!
NAY!!

THE MAN FROM WAL-MART NEVER KNEW WHAT HIT HIM.
'NIGHT!
'NIGHT!
'NIGHT!
MY GOD... WHAT'LL I TELL MY CORPORATE MASTERS?
GB Trudeau

12

▼ WRITING A SUMMARY:

Assignment 1— *"Wal-Mart's War on Main Street," by Sarah Anderson*

Write a summary of "Wal-Mart's War on Main Street." In this selection, Anderson examines the difficult decisions that Main Street business owners face when superstores like Wal-Mart enter their rural communities. As you begin to make notes toward writing a summary of Anderson's—or anyone's—article, think of some phrase that captures the gist of the author's work. You will extend this phrase into a thesis later, but for the moment get yourself started with a few orienting words.

Next, identify sections of the article. You may have begun this task when you read it the first time. Preparing your summary requires that you read the article at least once more. This time, you have the advantage of having read both the introduction and the conclusion. Use these to help you identify sets of related paragraphs, or sections, for which you will eventually write one- or two-sentence summaries. In Anderson's article, you might identify six sections: paragraphs 1–6, the problem defined; paragraphs 7–13, community complaints against Wal-Mart; paragraphs 14–16, spying on Wal-Mart; paragraphs 17–30, other (non–Wal-Mart) challenges to Main Street—and responses; paragraphs 31–36, family makes plans to pass the store on to a new generation; and paragraphs 37–38, the conclusion.

Following the boxed guidelines on page 6, write a one- or two-sentence summary of each section that you have identified. (In longer sections, especially in paragraphs 17–30, you might identify subsections and choose to write a one-sentence summary of each.) Next, recall the phrase with which you began thinking about Anderson's article. Review the section summaries you have just written and then extend your initial phrase into a thesis, which should function as a one-sentence summary of the entire article. Finally, place the thesis and sentence summaries together in a single paragraph. You will likely need to revise this rough summary for clarity and style.

▼ WRITING A SUMMARY:

Assignment 2— *"Ban the Bargains," by Bob Ortega*

Bob Ortega's piece for the *Wall Street Journal* takes a particular slant on the Wal-Mart debate by reporting on a vocal subgroup of Wal-Mart protesters: "aging activists." Ortega salts his article with many lively quotations and he presents distinct sections for his readers. As you write your summary, consider how many of these quotations you will use. Consider also whether or not you want to let Ortega's section heads (*Ultimate Predator, Protest March, Experienced Organizers, Culture Clash*) organize your note-taking and the structure of your summary. A newspaper article such as Ortega's exists to report information more than it does to make an argument. As such, it presents an opportunity for you to write an especially brief, though still effective, summary if you can distill that information. To achieve brevity, you may need to rearrange the information and ideas in Ortega's article, and you will certainly need to exercise restraint in your use of quotations.

▼ WRITING A SUMMARY:

Assignment 3— "Doonesbury on Wal-Mart," by Garry Trudeau

Garry Trudeau's "Doonesbury" is a comic strip, not an article. But this is not to say it has no content to summarize. To the contrary, Trudeau is well known for the highly politicized content of his strip—and you will have an opportunity to critique his work in a later assignment. For now, take on the challenge of summarizing the sequence on Wal-Mart. Essentially, Trudeau's twelve strips are a narrative: they tell a story—with a definite commentary, to be sure; but that commentary is carried on the back of a narrative, which you can relate to readers.

In Chapter 1, you saw that summarizing a narrative poses special challenges. First, your summary will not itself be a narrative but a paragraph-length synopsis. Second, describe the main actions or events of the narrative and the principal characters—in this case the Wal-Mart advance man and the Widow Doonesbury. (You might generalize the other characters as "local residents.")

How will you apply these guidelines to a summary of Trudeau's comic strip? Begin by rereading the piece and making "character" notes. Who is the stranger surveying land? Who is the Widow Doonesbury? How would you describe their personalities and those of the town residents? Make notes, as well, concerning the events in the twelve-strip sequence. Trudeau gives us a story, with a beginning, middle, and end, and you will be able to summarize that story. Remember that your summary should present events in such a way that your readers are aware of time flowing.

Your greatest challenge in summarizing the narrative will be to explain why this particular story has been told. Often, authors of a narrative will leave it to readers to infer meaning. Trudeau is fairly explicit, but still you will need to do some interpreting, and in this respect your summary will be subjective and may differ from others. Still, you can keep interpretation to a minimum in the summary if you can avoid agreeing or disagreeing with Trudeau (this will come later, in critique). You will be able to use this summary in your later critique of the comic strip.

▼ WRITING A CRITIQUE:

Assignment 1— "Eight Ways to Stop the Store," by Albert Norman

"Eight Ways to Stop the Store" provides an excellent opportunity to practice critique. As you read and reread the piece, especially in light of the other selections on Wal-Mart that you've read in this chapter, consider the extent to which you agree with Albert Norman's opposition to Wal-Mart. Any critique of Norman's argument would need to set a larger context: Who is Norman?

What is his history as an activist? What does he stand to gain from his opposition to Wal-Mart? What is the larger pattern of Wal-Mart entries into markets around the country? To answer these questions and set a context for your critique, see three other articles in this chapter: "Who's Really the Villain?" by Jo-Ann Johnston; "Wal-Mart's War on Main Street," by Sarah Anderson; and "Ban the Bargains," by Bob Ortega. Albert Norman is mentioned directly in each article.

Devote one part of your critique to summarizing Norman's argument. Norman's piece has a straightforward structure: a three-paragraph opening, an eight-paragraph body (strategies to use against Wal-Mart), and a one-paragraph conclusion. (See Chapter 1 for advice on writing summaries.) Use your summary both to introduce the selection to readers and to set the stage for the first part of your critical assessment: a neutral evaluation of the piece on its own terms. What is Norman's purpose, and does he succeed at it? Recall, from Chapter 3, this advice:

> As an unbiased, evenhanded critic, you evaluate an author's clarity of presentation, use of evidence, and adherence to principles of logic. To what extent has the author succeeded in achieving his or her purpose? Still withholding judgment, you offer your assessment and give the author (in effect) a grade. Significantly, your assessment of the presentation may not coincide with your views of the author's conclusion.

Your initial, objective assessment helps to establish your credibility as a critic, whether you ultimately agree or disagree with the author. *After* you have evaluated the success of a piece in terms of its clarity, logic, and use of evidence, you can weigh in with your own views.

Now for your reaction to Norman: Do you agree with his tactics as an organizer? This question rests on a more fundamental one: your view of Wal-Mart's retail expansion into small-town America. You may want to consider the following points in a critique:

- What has caused Main Street's economic troubles? Norman's position that Wal-Mart poses the main threat to small-town life has been challenged. To learn of other reasons for the decline of small-town economies, see the articles by Johnston and Anderson.
- What is your response to Norman's military and biblical metaphors? See paragraph 2: "main threat to Main Street"; and paragraph 3: "victory"; "small communities fighting the battle of Jericho"; "rules of engagement."
- What is your response to Norman's much-quoted position that "You can't buy rural life style on any Wal-Mart shelf—once you lose it, Wal-Mart can't sell it back to you"? (paragraph 10).
- Read Jo-Ann Johnston's "Who's Really the Villain?" for a negative response to Norman's anti–Wal-Mart campaigns. Johnston attacks Norman's arguments on a number of grounds, several of which (with attribution) you may want to incorporate into your critique.
- Norman is a paid political consultant.

One or more of these points, along with others that you define, will provide ample opportunities to launch a critique. Remember: it is possible to be anti–Wal-Mart and disagree with Norman and/or his tactics; it is possible to be pro–Wal-Mart and agree with Norman to some extent. The critique is yours. What's essential to an effective critique is that you have a definite opinion on Wal-Mart, generally, and on Albert Norman's stand against Wal-Mart.

▼ WRITING A CRITIQUE:

Assignment 2— "Doonesbury on Wal-Mart," by Garry Trudeau

Every bit as much as a formal argument written for a national magazine, comic strips have a point of view and content that can be debated, especially when that view and content are as overtly political as Garry Trudeau's in his nationally syndicated strip, "Doonesbury." Your goal in this critique is to read and evaluate the argument embedded in a series of twelve daily strips on Wal-Mart's attempted entry into the Widow Doonesbury's home town. As with any critique, you will want to create for your readers a larger context into which the piece you are examining fits. Context-setting is especially important for a comic strip like Trudeau's, which is known for its often biting commentaries on issues of the day. Without context, we are not likely to understand many of the strip's allusions. Look to other selections in the chapter to set a context for the Wal-Mart debate. (Note that Trudeau is mentioned directly in Bob Ortega's article for the *Wall Street Journal*.) Your reading should allow you to answer this question: At the time Trudeau was running these strips in September 1994, what was the state of the Wal-Mart wars?

Both to orient your readers and to set the stage for your assessment of Trudeau's strip, you'll need to summarize the Wal-Mart series. (See Writing a Summary, Assignment 3.) As part of your summary, you will need to infer the argument regarding Wal-Mart that Trudeau is embedding into the strip. Be sure to discuss with *specific* references to the strip how Trudeau establishes his argument. You'll of course want to respond to the argument. Do you agree with Trudeau? Account for your agreement or disagreement. In sum, your critique will need to address several questions:

- What is the Wal-Mart debate? (Your understanding of this debate is essential. The other selections in the chapter will provide the necessary background.)
- How effectively does Trudeau capture all sides of the debate?
- What is Trudeau's position in the Wal-Mart debate? What *argument* is he making? (Note: Given that comic strip artists work visually, you are entitled to make observations about both the written *and* the visual elements of Trudeau's argument.)
- What is your view of Trudeau's characterization of the Wal-Mart debate and his position in the debate?

Concerning this final question, which is the heart of the critique, remember that you're the one who decides which elements of the strip merit a response. A critique need not raise all possible responses, but certainly it should raise the ones you think are most important to a fair and thorough evaluation. For general advice on structuring your critique, see page 68.[1]

▼ WRITING A SYNTHESIS:

Assignment 1— An Explanatory Essay

The writers of this chapter create an occasion for you to examine the debates ignited when Wal-Mart attempts to build a superstore in yet another of America's small towns. Expressed a number of times explicitly, and very often implicitly, in these articles is an image of small-town America that is worth examining in the open. In a synthesis of four pages, draw on at least four sources to *explain* the small-town America that is being debated in the Wal-Mart wars. Your synthesis should answer these questions:

- What elements constitute "small-town life" that opponents of Wal-Mart are fighting to protect?
- Who are the various opponents of Wal-Mart? The proponents? How deep do their roots run in small-town life?
- What are the changing circumstances of small-town life?
- What role does small-town life play in American mythology?
- How does Wal-Mart, a retail store, threaten the quality of small-town life?

In responding to this assignment, and in preparing to write a synthesis, be sure of your purpose. As you reread the assignment, understand that it calls for an *explanation.* Nowhere does the assignment ask you to take a stand on the Wal-Mart debate. There is no room here for you to argue your views on where and whether Wal-Mart should build new stores. In your essay, try to remain neutral on this contentious issue, focusing instead on clarifying for yourself and for your readers what, exactly, is at stake in the Wal-Mart wars. Your ultimate goal is to explain what, both in American myth and American reality, small-town life *is.* Use your sources in this chapter to help clarify your thinking.

While the assignment poses several questions for you to address, avoid organizing your essay around these questions. Opt, instead, for your own organization. Develop a thesis and use *that* as a basis for organization. In the process of developing your ideas, you will respond to the questions.

▼ WRITING A SYNTHESIS:

Assignment 2— Comparison-and-Contrast Essay

In a four-page essay, compare and contrast the approaches to Wal-Mart taken by Albert Norman, political consultant to anti–Wal-Mart forces, and Kenneth Stone,

---

[1]As you discuss particular frames of the strip, you might for the sake of convenience adopt the following convention: Refer to an entire strip by its number in the series, 1–12; identify panels within a particular strip with a letter, *a–d.* Thus, you'd refer to the second panel in the fourth strip in the series as *4b.*

economist at Iowa State University. Though you should feel free to draw on any of the materials in this chapter to clarify the distinctions between the two, your primary sources for the assignment will be Norman's "Eight Ways to Stop the Store" and Stone's "Competing with the Discount Mass Merchandisers." Ultimately, your essay of comparison and contrast should serve as development for a thesis of your own design. Avoid writing an essay that merely lists, in effect, comparisons in one column and contrasts in another. You should be making a point in this essay. What will it be? How will your comparison and contrast serve to develop this point?

In a comparison-contrast essay, your purpose is to make careful observations of two or more related people, places, events, or ideas and to discuss (1) how they differ and how they are the same and (2) how these similarities and differences are significant. Albert Norman's "Eight Ways to Stop the Store" and Kenneth Stone's "Competing with the Discount Mass Merchandisers" provide you with ample opportunity to develop a comparison-contrast essay. It is worth observing that this comparison and contrast will *not* break down along the lines of pro– and anti–Wal-Mart or pro– and anti–small-town life. Your analysis will have to do more with *responses* to Wal-Mart's presence (or announced presence) in a community.

In an essay of comparison and contrast, you work with *criteria,* categories by which you examine the objects under study. (See pages 136–53 for a discussion of conducting a comparative analysis and on organizing comparison-and-contrast essays.) For your analysis of Norman and Stone, you might consider using as criteria the authors' assumptions concerning economic change, the proper role of business, the definition of small-town life, or the value of small-town life. You will likely discover other criteria. Choose *which* criteria to develop in the essay based on the overall point you wish to make. Remember that your comparative analysis needs to add up to something, needs to exist in service of a larger idea—your thesis—that you alone can provide. Do not submit an essay to your professor that is a laundry list, in effect, of similarities and differences.

A final note: In paragraph 2 of his article, Norman refers to Stone's economic analysis of Wal-Mart's impact on Iowa towns. Both Stone and Norman are mentioned in other selections in this chapter.

▼ WRITING A SYNTHESIS:

Assignment 3— An Argumentative Essay

Use several articles in this chapter to help you argue for or against the proposition that residents of rural communities should welcome Wal-Mart. (You may wish to couch your argument in the form of an editorial for a local newspaper.)

In the source materials collected here, you have many perspectives from which to draw: in Bob Ortega, a neutral reporting of the debate, with a particular slant on aging activists; in Kenneth Stone, a neutral economist's perspective; in Albert Norman, a staunchly anti–Wal-Mart perspective (from one who is relatively recent to small-town life); in Jo-Ann Johnston, a pro–Wal-Mart perspective (written by Norman's fellow citizen of Greenfield, Massachusetts); in Sarah Anderson, an anti–Wal-Mart perspective from one who has long-time roots in a small mid-western town; in James Moore, a staunchly pro–Wal-Mart, pro–big-business perspective; and in Garry Trudeau, a satirical look at the whole debate.

Albert Norman asks his clients to appeal to emotional attachments to small-town life when plotting a fight against Wal-Mart. Perhaps this would be a good place to begin your own reflections on this assignment. If the community in which you grew up never faced the opening of a Wal-Mart and the attending debate, play the imagining game: Picture yourself in one such rural community, with all that community's charms and problems. Wal-Mart makes a pitch to build a store. How do *you* respond?

To take a position for or against the proposition—that residents of rural communities should welcome Wal-Mart—represents a first step in your development of an argumentative synthesis. Both the logic by which you develop your position and your use of source materials to help you support your position will largely determine the success of your argument. Therefore, know your sources well. Know who makes which arguments; who provides which data. Very likely, you and some of your classmates will disagree (perhaps strongly) on the Wal-Mart debate. Disagreement may well turn on the values embedded in small-town life. You will want to understand and clearly define what these values are, the extent to which they are real (not myth), the extent to which they will change if Wal-Mart arrives, and the extent to which they are already changing (without the help of Wal-Mart).

You have a special challenge ahead of you: to argue in such a way that will penetrate the heated emotions of others so that they can, perhaps, remain open to your position.

7
Left, Right, Center: The American Political Spectrum

I often think it's comical—Fal, lal, la!
How Nature always does contrive—Fal, lal, la!
That every boy and every gal
That's born into the world alive
Is either a little Liberal
Or else a little Conservative!

—Gilbert and Sullivan, *Iolanthe*

Senator A thunders that President B's welfare proposal is a return to the failed liberal policies of the past. Columnist C worries about the growth of right wing fundamentalism. Editorialist D charges that group E is undermining the country's moral fiber, even as group F is working furiously to preserve it. Rush Limbaugh is hopping mad and so are his listeners. Jesse Jackson fumes and threatens to form a third party. Ross Perot has already done so. Just what are these people arguing about? Are they debating real issues or is it all meaningless political posturing? Is a third party candidate right to insist that there's "not a dime's worth of difference" between the Democrats and the Republicans?

If you're confused by the current political debate—and particularly by the difference between "liberal" and "conservative," or "left" and "right"—you're not alone. These terms have notoriously slippery meanings, and no one is quite sure what they mean anymore. One may be a liberal on one issue (like affirmative action) and a conservative on another (like abortion). American liberals are on the left; European liberals are often on the right. The original American liberals, like Thomas Jefferson, distrusted government ("That government governs best which governs least"), just the opposite of most of today's liberals. The original conservatives, like Alexander Hamilton and John Adams, on the other hand, favored a strong central government—again, the opposite of conservatives today. Among liberals one can find FDR New Deal Liberals, 1960s Progressive or "New Left" liberals, "neoliberals," even "paleoliberals." Among conservatives one can find traditional conservatives, neoconservatives, and New Rightists. (Interestingly, the most fervent conservatives today—just like the most fervent liberals in the 1960s—tend to be young.)

In recent years, politicians and social commentators have used "liberal" and "conservative" as sticks to beat their opponents. In particular, Democratic candidates are fearful of being tarred with the dreaded "L" word, lest they appear soft on crime or in favor of raising taxes. Many would like to give up on these terms altogether, believing not only that they have lost all meaning, but also that they encourage political mudslinging and oversimplification of complex issues. While this may be true to some extent, it is also true that "liberalism" and "conservativism" are likely to remain central to the political vocabulary for the foreseeable future, and that they are, in fact, indicators of real philosophical differences in the way that people view the role of government in dealing with a wide range of social, cultural, and economic issues. It is therefore worthwhile for us to examine these and other political ideas—such as "socialism" and "libertarianism"—so that we may join in the political dialogue with some measure of historical and social perspective.

The purpose of this chapter, then, is to provide some basis for understanding many of the key political debates of the day—for understanding both the differences between political positions on particular issues and the differences in ideological assumptions underlying positions on these issues. It is sometimes said, for example, that liberals tend to have an optimistic view of human nature, and conservatives a pessimistic view; from these diametrically opposed assumptions follow frequently diametrically opposed programs and policies on everything from welfare mothers to funding for public TV to the number of jails in the country. In addition to reading several selections focusing on the differences between left and right and on opposing positions on particular issues (such as welfare and school prayer), you will also read selections that provide tools for the analysis of the political scene and of political rhetoric.

One interesting question, on why "left" means liberal and "right" means conservative, is easily settled: the terms were first used in the aftermath of the French Revolution of 1789. The Revolution had quickly degenerated into factions, primarily *radicals* favoring the Revolution and its principles, as embodied in the Declaration of the Rights of Man ("The aim of all political association is the preservation of the natural . . . rights of man . . . liberty, property, security, and resistance to oppression"), *conservatives* favoring the continuation of the monarchy, with other factions somewhere in-between. At the first Legislative Assembly elected under the new constitution, the radical parties sat on the *left* of the presiding officer as he faced the assembly; the conservative parties sat on the *right,* and the parties in-between sat in the *center.* The words stuck and came into general use, even for legislative bodies, such as the U.S. Congress, that don't follow this kind of seating arrangement. Other terms we use today in political discussion date from about the same era: "liberalism" first appeared in 1819, "conservatism" in 1835, and "socialism" in 1832.

The chapter begins with a political quiz (by Victor Kamber and Bradley O'Leary) that enables you at the outset to determine whether you are a liberal or a conservative. Next, Jeff Smith's "The L.A. Riots: A Case Study of Debate Across the Political Spectrum" will introduce you to some of the fundamentally different attitudes underlying political debates on a variety of issues. Smith's passage is followed by an extended discussion of the contemporary political spectrum, "Liberalism, Conservatism, Socialism, Libertarianism," by historians James MacGregor Burns, J. W. Peltason, Thomas E. Cronin, and David B. Magleby, from their widely used textbook *Government By the People.* This selection will be an invaluable reference point for helping you define political positions in the debates in the latter half of the chapter as well as in your own independent research. Following, Donald Lazere's "Guides to the Political Conflicts" provides a variety of reference points to help you locate arguments along the political spectrum. "A Voter's Manual" provides capsule political platforms of six American political parties, along with a set of voter appeals from would-be officeholders ranging from the Libertarian candidate for senator to the Peace and Freedom candidate for governor. Next appears Donna Woolfolk Cross's "Politics: The Art of Bamboozling," which offers a useful set of tools for identifying such common types of political rhetoric and political language strategies as "glittering generalities," "red herrings," and the "two-extremes dilemma."

The latter part of the chapter deals with three current debates across the political spectrum. The first focuses on the touchstone issue that seems to divide liberals from conservatives: welfare. (Note that several selections on welfare are also included in Chapter 4; although these selections are employed to demonstrate the principles of synthesis, they are also intended to supplement the debate on welfare included here.) Also included are debates on federal funding of the arts and school prayer. All three debates were articulated in the halls of Congress, so you will have a good opportunity to closely examine political rhetoric, as practiced by actual politicians.

▼

INTRODUCTION: A NOTE ON THE THREE APPEALS OF POLITICAL RHETORIC: *LOGOS, ETHOS, PATHOS*

Two selections in this chapter—those by Lazere and Cross—focus on ways of "reading" political rhetoric. That is, they offer tools to help you recognize certain patterns of argumentation and of language intended by political writers to persuade audiences that their ideas are right and that their opponents' ideas are wrong or misguided. To this end, you should also find helpful the material on "Critical Reading" in Chapter 3, in particular the sections on logical argumentation (pages 62–64) and evaluating assumptions (pages 66–67).

In terms of reading political rhetoric, an even more basic tool was first offered by Aristotle, over 2000 years ago. Aristotle believed that speakers attempting to persuade others to their point of view achieved their purpose primarily by relying on one or more *appeals,* which he called *logos, ethos,* and *pathos.*

Logos

Logos is the rational appeal, the appeal to reason. If they expect to persuade their audiences, speakers must argue logically and must supply appropriate evidence to support their case. Logical arguments are commonly of two types (often combined). The *deductive* argument begins with a generalization, then cites a specific case related to that generalization, from which follows a conclusion. A familiar example of deductive reasoning, used by Aristotle himself, is the following:

All men are mortal. (*generalization*)
Socrates was a man. (*specific case*)
Socrates is mortal. (*conclusion about the specific case*)

An example of a more contemporary deductive argument may be seen in President John F. Kennedy's address to the nation in June 1963 on the need for sweeping civil rights legislation. Kennedy begins with the generalizations that it "ought to be possible . . . for American students of any color to attend any public institution they select without having to be backed up by troops . . ." and that "it ought to be possible for American citizens of any color to register and vote in a free election without interference or fear of reprisal." Kennedy then provides several specific examples (primarily recent events in Birmingham, Alabama) and statistics to show that this was not the case. He concludes:

> We face, therefore a moral crisis as a country and a people. It cannot be met by repressive police action. It cannot be left to increased demonstrations in the streets. It cannot be quieted by token moves or talk. It is time to act in the Congress, in your state and local legislative body, and, above all, in all of our daily lives.

Underlying Kennedy's argument is the following reasoning:

All Americans should enjoy certain rights.
Some Americans do not enjoy these rights.
Action must be taken to ensure that all Americans enjoy these rights.

Another form of logical argumentation is *inductive* reasoning. A speaker or writer who argues inductively begins not with a generalization, but with several pieces of specific evidence. The speaker then draws a conclusion from this evidence. For example, in a recent debate on gun control, Senator Robert C. Byrd (Democrat, Virginia) cites specific examples of rampant crime: "I read of young men being viciously murdered for a pair of sneakers, a leather jacket, or $20." He also offers statistical evidence of the increasing crime rate: "in 1951, there were 3.2 policemen for every felony committed in the United States; this year [1990] nearly 3.2 felonies will be committed per every police officer. . . ." He concludes, "something has to change. We have to stop the crimes that are distorting and disrupting the way of life for so many innocent, law-respecting Americans. The bill that we are debating today attempts to do just that."

Statistical evidence was also used by Senator Edward M. Kennedy (Democrat, Massachusetts) in arguing for passage of the Racial Justice Act of 1990, designed to ensure that minorities were not disproportionately singled out for the death penalty. Kennedy points out that 17 defendants in Fulton County, Georgia, between 1973 and 1980, were charged with killing police officers, but the only defendant who received the death sentence was a black man. Kennedy also cites statistics to show that "those who killed whites were 4.3 times more likely to receive the death penalty than were killers of blacks," and that "in Georgia, blacks who killed whites received the death penalty 16.7 percent of the time, while whites who killed whites received the death penalty only 4.2 percent of the time."

Of course, the mere piling up of evidence does not in itself make the speaker's case. As Donna Cross explains in her article "Politics: The Art of Bamboozling," politicians are very adept at "card-stacking." And statistics can be selected and manipulated to prove anything, as demonstrated in Darrell Huff's landmark book *How to Lie With Statistics* (1954). And what appears to be a logical argument may, in fact, be fundamentally flawed. (See Chapter 3 and Cross's article for a discussion of logical fallacies and faulty reasoning strategies.) On the other hand, the fact that evidence can be distorted, statistics misused, and logic fractured does not mean that these tools of reason can be dispensed with or should be dismissed. It means only that audiences have to listen and read critically—perceptively, knowledgeably, and skeptically (though not necessarily cynically).

Sometimes, politicians can turn their opponents' false logic against them. Major R. Owens, a Democratic Representative from New York, attempted to counter what he took to be the reasoning on welfare adopted by his opponents:

> Welfare programs create dependency and so should be reformed or abolished.
> Aid to Families with Dependent Children (AFDC) is a welfare program.
> ADFC should be reformed or abolished.

In his speech opposing the Republican welfare reform measure of 1995 Owens simply changes the specific (middle) term, pointing out that federal subsidies for electric power in the West and Midwest and farmers' low-rate home loan mortgages are, in effect, welfare programs ("We are spoiling America's farmers by smothering them with socialism . . ."). The logical conclusion—that we should reform or eliminate farmers' home loan mortgages—would clearly be unacceptable to many of those pushing for reform of AFDC. Owens thus suggests that opposition to AFDC is based less on reason than on lack of sympathy for its recipients.

Ethos

Ethos, or the ethical appeal, is an appeal based not on the ethical rationale for the subject under discussion, but rather on the ethical nature of the person making the appeal. A person making an argument must have a certain degree of credibility: That person must be of good character, be of sound sense, and be qualified to hold the office or recommend policy. For example, Elizabeth Cervantes Barrón, running for Senator as the Peace and Freedom candidate, begins her statement, "I was born and raised in Central Los Angeles. I grew up in a multi-ethnic, multi-cultural environment where I learned to respect those who were different from me. . . . I am a teacher and am aware of how cut-backs in education have affected our children and our communities." On the other end of the political spectrum, American Independent gubernatorial candidate Jerry McCready also begins with an ethical appeal: "As a self-employed businessman, I have learned firsthand what it is like to try to make ends meet in an unstable economy being manipulated by out of touch politicians." Both candidates are making an appeal to *ethos,* based on the strength of their personal qualities for the office they seek. L. A. Kauffman is not running for office but rather writing an article arguing against socialism as a viable ideology for the future ("Socialism: No." *Progressive,* April 1993). To defuse objections that he is simply a tool of capitalism, Kauffman begins with an appeal to *ethos*: "Until recently, I was executive editor of the journal *Socialist Review.* Before that I worked for the Marxist magazine, *Monthly Review.* My bookshelves are filled with books of Marxist theory, and I even have a picture of Karl Marx up on my wall." Thus, Kauffman establishes his credentials to argue knowledgeably about Marxist ideology.

Conservative commentator Rush Limbaugh frequently makes use of the ethical appeal by linking himself with the kind of Americans he assumes his audiences to be (what Cross calls "glory by association"):

> In their attacks [on me], my critics misjudge and insult the American people. If I were really what liberals claim—racist, hatemonger, blowhard—I would years ago have deservedly gone into oblivion. The truth is, I provide information and analysis the media refuses to disseminate, information and analysis the public craves. People listen to me for one reason: I am effective. And my credibility is judged in the marketplace every day. . . . I represent America's rejection of liberal elites. . . . I validate the convictions of ordinary people. ("Why I Am a Threat to the Left," *Los Angeles Times,* 9 Oct. 1994)

Pathos

Finally, speakers appeal to their audiences by the use of *pathos,* the appeal to the emotions. There is nothing inherently wrong with using an emotional appeal. Indeed, since emotions often move people far more powerfully than reason alone, speakers and writers would be foolish *not* to use emotion. And as *Star Trek*'s Spock demonstrates, it would be a drab, humorless world if human beings were not subject to the sway of feeling, as well as reason. The emotional appeal becomes problematic only if it is the *sole* or *primary* basis of the argument. This is the kind of situation that led, for example, to the internment of Japanese Americans during World War II or that leads to periodic political spasms to enact anti–flag-burning legislation.

President Reagan was a master of emotional appeal. He closed his first inaugural address with a reference to the view from the Capitol of Arlington National Cemetery, where lie thousands of markers of "heroes":

> Under one such marker likes a young man, Martin Treptow, who left his job in a small town barbershop in 1917 to go to France with the famed Rainbow Division. There, on the western front, he was killed trying to carry a message between battalions under heavy artillery fire. We're told that on his body was found a diary. On the flyleaf under the heading, "My Pledge," he had written these words: "America must win this war. Therefore, I will work, I will save, I will sacrifice, I will endure, I will fight cheerfully and do my utmost, as if the issue of the whole struggle depended on me alone." The crisis we are facing today does not require of us the kind of sacrifice that Martin Treptow and so many thousands of others were called upon to make. It does require, however, our best effort and our willingness to believe in ourselves and to believe in our capacity to perform great deeds, to believe that together with God's help we can and will resolve the problems which now confront us.

Surely, Reagan implies, if Martin Treptow can act so courageously and so selflessly, we can do the same. The logic is somewhat unclear, since the connection between Martin Treptow and ordinary Americans of 1981 is rather tenuous (as Reagan concedes); but the emotional power of Martin Treptow—whom reporters were sent scurrying to research—carries the argument.

A more contemporary president, Bill Clinton, is himself not above using *pathos*. Addressing an audience of the nation's governors on his welfare plan, Clinton closed his remarks by referring to a conversation he had held with a welfare mother who had gone through the kind of training program Clinton was advocating. Asked by Clinton whether she thought that such training programs should be mandatory, the mother said, "I sure do." When Clinton asked her why, she said:

> "Well, because if it wasn't, there would be a lot of people like me home watching the soaps because we don't believe we can make anything of ourselves any more. So you've got to make it mandatory." And I said, "What's the best thing about having a job?" She said, "When my boy goes to school, and they say, 'What does your mama do for a living?' he can give an answer."

Clinton uses the emotional power he counts in that anecdote to set up his conclusion: "We must end poverty for Americans who want to work. And we must do it on terms that dignify all of the rest of us, as well as help our country to work better. I need your help, and I think we can do it."

Political Quiz: Are You a Liberal or a Conservative?

VICTOR KAMBER AND BRADLEY S. O'LEARY

We begin this chapter on political attitudes with a selection designed to ferret out your own attitudes: a quiz designed to locate your views on the political spectrum and to suggest which of several current and recent political figures you most closely resemble in these views. The questions focus on your beliefs about government and about particular political and social issues. After you take and score the quiz, you'll be able to more confidently identify yourself as a liberal, conservative, or moderate. (The scoring guide appears at the end of this chapter on pages 346–348.) You must answer all the questions for the scoring to be valid.

This quiz originally appeared under the title "The Political Quiz Show" in the October 28–30, 1994 issue of USA Weekend, *a Sunday newspaper magazine supplement. Victor Kamber is a veteran Democratic consultant, president of the Kamber group, a political consulting firm in Washington, D.C., and author of* Giving Up on Democracy: Why Term Limits Are Bad for America *(1995); Bradley S. O'Leary is a Republican consultant. Together they write the* Kamber/O'Leary Report, *a political newsletter.*

1. Generally, do you tend to trust or distrust government's ability to solve problems?
   - Trust
   - Distrust
2. Which do you trust more?
   - The Pentagon or
   - The U.S. Postal Service?

   - The executive branch or
   - The legislative branch?

   - The IRS or
   - the FBI?

   - The CIA or
   - The Peace Corps?

   - The Joint Chiefs or
   - The United Nations?
3. What about private institutions and people? Which do you trust more?
   - Trial lawyers or
   - Doctors
   - Union leaders or
   - Business executives
   - Professional athletes or
   - Team owners

4. The federal government should do more to solve the nation's problems even if it means higher taxes on (pick as many as you want):
   - You
   - Big corporations
   - The wealthy
   - The middle class
   - Small businesses
   - None
5. Where should government be cut? (Pick as many as you want):
   - Eliminate farm subsidies
   - Eliminate subsidies to the arts
   - Abolish public broadcasting
   - Cut entitlement programs (Social Security, Medicaid, etc.)
   - Cut defense spending
   - Reduce welfare spending
   - Keep illegal immigrants from receiving public education
   - Reduce environmental regulation
   - Cut taxes
   - Don't cut at all
6. Which would do more to guarantee competitive elections?
   - Term limits
   - Public financing
7. Who was a better president?
   - Ronald Reagan
   - Franklin D. Roosevelt
8. Do you see the ideal America as an ethnic "melting pot" in which religious, cultural, and ethnic distributions are blurred, or as a nation in which ethnically diverse groups ought to coexist while retaining their cultural identity?
   - Melting pot
   - Multicultural identity
9. Whose political views do you consider more extreme, those of Rush Limbaugh or the Rev. Jesse Jackson?
   - Limbaugh
   - Jackson
   - Neither
10. Which would curb violent crime most?
    - Stricter controls on the sale of guns
    - Mandatory sentences for those who use guns in the commission of a crime
    - Both
11. In the long run, do you think we can reduce crime more by building more prisons or providing more financial assistance to rebuilding our inner cities?
    - Build prisons
    - Rebuild cities
    - Both

Please indicate whether you agree or disagree with each of the following statements:

12. Even if it means cutting programs, spending must be cut to reduce the federal deficit.
    - Agree
    - Disagree
13. The federal government is too big.
    - Agree
    - Disagree
14. U.S. interests were more seriously at stake in Haiti where we used armed force to restore democratically elected President Aristide to power than in Korea where we insisted that Communist North Korea cease nuclear weapons production.
    - Agree
    - Disagree
15. Gays and lesbians should be able to marry or at least be treated as married under law if they so desire.
    - Agree
    - Disagree
16. The news media is dominated by liberals.
    - Agree
    - Disagree
17. The religious right is a threat to our political system.
    - Agree
    - Disagree
18. The federal government should include funds to make abortion services part of any standard benefits package in health care reform.
    - Agree
    - Disagree
19. Deceptive political campaign commercials should be banned.
    - Agree
    - Disagree
20. Graphic pornography should be banned.
    - Agree
    - Disagree
21. As a society, we should spend more money trying to find a cure for AIDS than for cancer and heart disease because AIDS threatens younger people.
    - Agree
    - Disagree
22. Talk radio shows should be regulated to ensure both sides of a debate are represented, because talk radio has an unhealthy impact on the political process.
    - Agree
    - Disagree
23. The breakdown of the traditional American family is the most serious domestic crisis facing our society.

- Agree
- Disagree

24. Women and racial minorities should be given preferences until we achieve true gender and racial equality in America.
    - Agree
    - Disagree
25. Certain environmental problems call for government action, even if it means new programs or increased taxes.
    - Agree
    - Disagree

▲ ▲ ▲

Discussion and Writing Suggestions

1. Do you think that your score on this quiz accurately reflects your own political inclinations? If not, explain which questions and which responses may have tended to misrepresent your views.
2. Select two issues represented in questions to this quiz; for each write a fully developed paragraph expanding your views. Begin with a topic sentence (based on your initial response to the question); develop the paragraph with examples and details based on your own experience, observation, or reading.
3. Role play: imagine you are a political analyst evaluating your responses to this quiz. Based on the pattern of responses that are apparent (that is, the types of programs, activities, etc. the responder favors and those she or he doesn't; the types of assertions the responder tends to agree or disagree with), develop a political profile of the responder. This question requires that you *categorize* related responses and that you *analyze* their significance.
4. Those experienced in developing questionnaires like this one know that the type of response a question receives often depends as much on the way the question is worded as on the responder's opinions on the subject. Select two or three questions in this quiz and rephrase them so that they might have evoked from you different responses from the ones you originally gave. Then, in a few sentences, explain why the different language evokes different responses.

The L.A. Riots: A Case Study of Debate Across the Political Spectrum

JEFF SMITH

Who or what was responsible for the Los Angeles riots of 1992, following the verdict in the Rodney King case? The following selection illustrates how differing opinions on a single issue can represent deep and often irreconcilable ideological divisions among both elected officials and ordinary citizens.

On April 29, 1992, an all-white jury acquitted four white police officers of savagely beating an African-American, Rodney King, after they had stopped him for speeding. Immediately following the verdict, the streets of South-Central Los Angeles erupted in riots that lasted several days. In the burning, looting, and general destruction that followed, 51 people died, 2,100 were injured, and the neighborhoods in the area sustained over $1 billion worth of property damage. (After retrial on federal civil rights charges, two of the four officers were convicted and sentenced to prison terms.)

This selection is an adaptation by Smith of his article "Against Illegeracy" which appeared in the May 1994 issue of College Composition and Communication, *a journal for writing professionals. Smith defines "illegeracy"—a word he has coined—as a kind of political and cultural illiteracy.*

Jeff Smith, who has been a newspaper commentator and a television news consultant, teaches in the UCLA Writing Programs. Another version of this article appears as the first chapter of his book Why Americans Disagree, *currently in preparation.*

1 What are the real issues on which Americans disagree? How are these issues concealed within the many issues on which we *think* we disagree? How might we learn to recognize our real disagreements and begin to carry them on more productively? To begin to answer these questions, let's look more closely at the public debate that followed the Los Angeles riots. That debate was a classic example of what, I believe, happens again and again in American public discussion: one set of more or less explicit disagreements obscures our view of another, underlying set. This hidden nexus of issues never really gets discussed. Because they're not discussed, the issues don't get resolved, and because they're not resolved, they go on and on indefinitely generating ever new disagreements. The post-riot debate is an excellent case study in how public issues in America are simultaneously engaged and avoided.

A CONTEST OF OUTLOOKS

2 As it happened, the riots occurred in the middle of a presidential campaign—that is, just when the opportunity was greatest actually to *vote* one's response to them. Yet the ensuing public debate was something less than many had hoped. One of the more common complaints heard in the aftermath was that there was no serious discussion, only a lot of political posturing and "finger-pointing," particularly on the part of the presidential contenders still campaigning at that point (Pat Buchanan, George Bush, Bill Clinton, and Jerry Brown). For instance, President Bush's press secretary was attacked for suggesting that America's urban problems were the result of the failed policies of the 1960s "Great Society." While to those of a like mind this was a statement of the obvious, to many others it was either a sign of the Bush camp's complacency and lack of social concern or an example of the kind of blame-shifting and political point-scoring one has come to expect from politicians these days.

Yet if we take the candidates' statements and put them side-by-side, what emerges is something considerably more complex. It's true, none of the candidates' responses to the riots—as voiced in speeches, interviews, and off-the-cuff answers to reporters' questions—was especially surprising. As usually happens, candidates took the riots as a chance not so much to formulate whole new policies as to restate and re-emphasize whatever they'd been saying all along. It's also true that they did this with an eye to their own interests, in hopes of rallying core constituencies and appealing to as many "swing" voters as they could. But it is too cynical and it tells us nothing anyway if everything the candidates said is chalked up to political calculation. Nor should we be disappointed that they *didn't* stop themselves in their tracks and start rethinking their whole positions. To the contrary, the very fact that what the candidates said about the riots was of a piece with what they'd been saying all along helps confirm that their responses *weren't* pure calculation, but a real contest of outlooks, a clash of sincerely held beliefs. 3

Here is the essence of the major candidates' differing "takes" on the riots. I've grouped them along a spectrum from (roughly) right to left: 4

- *The Buchanan approach* saw the unrest as a law-and-order issue requiring simply a more effective use of force. The riots were "a police problem, pure and simple," in Republican Patrick J. Buchanan's words. In California, Republican Senate candidate Bruce Herschensohn put this view even more bluntly: The only "underlying cause" of the riots, he said, "is that some people are rotten."
- *The Bush approach* acknowledged broader social causes than this, but stressed general economic development, driven by the free market, as the best answer to them. By way of addressing areas of acute need, President Bush argued for tax and other incentives to lure businesses to depressed areas and to encourage home ownership—thus giving people "a stake in the community," as Bush's spokesman put it. In part, this approach was based on the view that earlier efforts involving massive federal intervention, efforts like the 1960s "Great Society," had not only failed but had worsened some problems by, in effect, institutionalizing them.
- *The Clinton approach,* like Bush's, also envisioned strengthened communities and families. This was to be achieved partly through government's targeting of existing laws and partly through ethnic self-help and "personal responsibility." But Democrat Bill Clinton vowed to be more pro-active than Bush, moving the government toward formal partnerships with nonprofit organizations and helping in the creation of new private institutions, such as inner-city development banks.
- *The Brown approach,* echoing that of many big-city mayors, called for tens of billions of dollars in direct federal spending on cities, much of it in jobs programs. Former California Gov. Jerry Brown

> thus came the closest of the candidates to re-invoking [President Johnson's] Great Society principles and, indeed, the New Deal approach to unemployment and poverty in the 1930s.

Although not formally a candidate at that point, Ross Perot was a force to be reckoned with, and his comments on the disorder were showcased in the same way as other candidates'. So let's include here a comparable synthesis of what he had to say (though I won't try to fit it on the right-left spectrum):

- *The Perot approach* emphasized procedural reforms. Without specifying exactly what to do about cities, Perot focused on how this and other decisions ought to be made: by reviewing existing proposals, trying out the most promising as pilot programs, putting alternative policies before the public through "electronic town meetings," and exerting presidential leadership both to thwart the watering-down influence of private interests and to see that other agencies of government fall in line with whatever consensus emerges. Perot also stressed the need for reducing public debt, both to promote economic well-being and to avoid choking off the private resources needed to help solve urban and other problems.

Of course, many people besides politicians had reactions to the riots too, often more deeply felt than any of the above. (At various points Bush, Clinton and Perot, the three candidates still running in the fall, each indicated that the problems of inner cities were not first on his political agenda.) But for the moment we don't need to consider all those, nor worry about how personally committed each candidate was to the views I've outlined. The crucial thing is that the candidates' analyses and proposals, despite some overlap, do differ significantly, particularly as we move from one end of the spectrum to the other. And they are distinct enough to suggest that as a society, we can't simultaneously pursue them all. We are offered—or perhaps confronted with—a genuine choice. 5

ANALYZING THE ANALYSES

To understand this choice we need to look at the candidates' statements again, this time at a deeper level of generality—analyze the analyses, as it were. Politicians are sometimes said, loosely, to have "political philosophies," and we can begin by considering this concept and its implications. "Philosophy" is the key: The reason the candidates' positions differ is that they reflect different answers to the kinds of questions we usually call "philosophical." Indeed, as a group they show a surprisingly broad range of clashing assumptions on such basic philosophical issues as human nature, society, government, justice. 6

The problem is that those deeper assumptions are never talked through *in and of themselves.* Yet without seeing them it's hard to grasp what the 7 candidates were really disagreeing about—hence what the rest of us really disagree about. Our next task, therefore, is to make the deeper issues explicit. On the surface, each candidate's position was an answer to the question, "What caused the riots and what should we do about them?" But implicitly they were answers to quite different questions, most of them having nothing to do with riots per se. These questions resemble the surface question in one sense: Different answers to them will give us different political outcomes or views. That is, they are questions which, if answered one way, will give us a view like Buchanan's, if another way a view like Bush's, and if in still other ways, views like Clinton's, Brown's and Perot's. But they are also much larger questions, invoking issues raised so often in history and in connection with so many different situations and events that they have rightly come to be called "perennial."

Here are some questions of the kind I'm referring to, questions which 8
in my view underlay and motivated the candidates' explicit disagreements:

1. *Human nature and responsibility.* Under what circumstances are people responsible for their own actions? When is it legitimate to think of people in the aggregate—to assume that if X number of people do something normally thought wrong, there must be a justification? At what point does bad behavior cease to be understandable (and punishable) as individual actions—"crimes"—and become a "social problem" (or even "epidemic") for which the individuals involved ought not be held to account?
2. *Community.* What is a "community"? The new police chief Los Angeles hired after the riots declared that "people [who] are robbing and stealing and looting . . . are not our community." Should the term "community" thus be confined to the law-abiding? Or does the bad behavior we saw in the riots express genuine, buried urges of a "community" in extreme crisis?

   More generally, who owes what to whom? Is it fair to tax suburbanites to support inner-city programs? To tax people in rural Nebraska to solve problems in Los Angeles (as federal programs do)? Or do people who have "escaped" the cities, or chosen never to live in them, have a right to be free of the cities' problems?
3. *Justice.* "No justice, no peace." That was a slogan of many who blamed "the system" for provoking the riots. Is this the right view of cause and effect—can real social peace be founded only on justice? Or, as conservative philosophers from Edmund Burke to Sidney Hook have argued, is it the other way around: Is the quest for justice impossible unless some measure of peace is guaranteed first?

   And just what do we mean by "justice"? Is it basically a matter of prosecuting troublemakers (as in "bringing someone to justice"), or does it involve seeing to the fair distribution of society's goods?

4. *Wealth.* What distribution *would* be "fair"? Must actual wealth be spread with a certain evenness, or is fairness achieved by ensuring equality of *opportunity* to acquire wealth? And where does wealth come from anyway? Is it the product of some individuals' special vision and energy, and is society best served if those individuals have maximum freedom—including the freedom to decide for themselves how to invest what they make? Would expropriating that wealth for society's use also take away the "incentive" for people to keep generating more wealth? Or should we assume that the wealthy got what they have not by "generating" wealth (to everyone's ultimate benefit), but by expropriating it from others—so that society's re-appropriation of it is merely a righting of the balance?
5. *Government.* What is the role of government? Is it mainly policing—establishing justice in the formal, law-and-order sense? Or is part of government's job to ensure substantive justice by ironing out inequalities in wealth? Indeed, when should government make *any* substantive choice? Should government promote certain "values" or simply keep a free market functioning so that each individual can pursue his or her own vision of the good? What makes a society stronger—diversity and individual freedom, or the shared values and cohesion of a "common culture"?

   And whatever government does, how energetically should it do it? Which is best—a government empowered to take bold action even at the risk of failing or doing something unfair, or a government always checked and restrained, forced to seek a broad consensus before acting . . . even if that means its actions are forever slowed and watered down?
6. *America.* As a matter of fact, what positions on each of the above issues is the United States—through its various governments and other social institutions—actually taking? And what social conditions have thus already been achieved? For instance, is there, on balance, equality of opportunity (Issue 4) such that we can assume that current distributions of wealth are more or less fair? Or are those distributions based on longstanding practices that have given some people greater opportunity than others, perhaps even allowed them to benefit by *denying* opportunity to others?
7. *History.* For that matter, how much in history is necessary (or "determined" or "preordained"), and how much is open to deliberate human choice? Is the world simply a tragic place, and is our energy better spent getting used to that fact? Or are we obliged always to seek better policies and fairer social arrangements, even at the risk of making things worse—of running afoul of the so-called "Law of Unintended Consequences"?

If there is any question above on which all candidates agree, it might 9
be only the last one. Simply by running for president, one implicitly asserts that things can be made to happen by human choice, that people can make a

difference in history. But even here, agreement is only partial. And the first six questions appear totally up for grabs—even in the context of a party/political system often criticized for its ideological homogeneity and narrowness. Let's try next to group different sets of answers into unified, internally consistent philosophical statements, each one defined as clearly as possible by its points of difference from the others. Here are five such statements:

A. American society already provides people opportunities. It doesn't need to change, just to protect what's already been achieved. This it does by restraining those evil or irrational souls who would disrupt things. We can't "solve" evil; it's not a "social problem." It's a fact of human nature. It's not just pointless but positively arrogant to imagine that we have it in our power to reform something that's part of nature. All we can, and must, do is mount a never-ending effort to punish evil and rein it in. That, indeed, is government's core function—policing—and it coincides with a larger obligation of government to preserve society's values. In fact, government must enforce a certain exclusiveness; it must be aggressive not only in locking some people away but in keeping other people out, people who wouldn't "fit in" culturally. In the interests of internal cohesion, it must sometimes build walls—figuratively or (in the case of territorial borders) literally. When government fails to do this, problems take hold and spread, affecting the "body politic" like poisons.

B. America already provides most needed opportunities, though not all. In those isolated pockets where it doesn't, government may need to stimulate the free market, but it should avoid applying public resources directly. That's not what government naturally does best, and it just keeps problems from getting solved in the long run. Government's job, rather, is to clear the way for private initiative, and part of our problem up to now is that well-intended but failed efforts by government to solve problems—"social engineering"—have undercut and crowded out private efforts that would have worked better.

   And just as they should be sought privately, solutions should also be sought, whenever possible, locally—since remaining problems are largely isolated—and gradually, since we ought to be duly humble about our ability to engineer large-scale solutions. Abrupt, overly ambitious efforts are as likely as not to make things worse.

C. The areas where opportunity is lacking aren't isolated pockets. Problems can be and are spreading—but less like poisons (from outside) than *cancers*: the "body politic" eating away at itself. Against this threat, direct public action is called for and should take two forms. First, it should goad and guide the market and continually monitor it to make sure its products are distributed fairly. Second, government should take aim at disruptive individuals, but less to punish or restrain them than to re-integrate them into the body politic. Just as doctors must be careful how they treat cancer for fear of harming the body itself, we must be extremely sparing of those we judge, slow to dismiss as irremediably "evil" those impulses that may be simply misguided and self-destructive but still open to reform. Our efforts must seek to ensure that "we" includes everyone. This isn't a matter just of fairness but of self-interest, since a society functions best (and is wealthiest) to the extent that it makes the best use of the abilities of all.

D. The private market has proven a failure at providing fair opportunity. Direct public intervention to correct this—government action—must be both immediate and massive. In some cases, those who cause problems are reacting understandably, if regrettably, to conditions not of their own making. Far from simply threatening society, these individuals are important "leading indicators" of where the rest of us may be going. Rather than judge them, society should judge itself by what it's done for them. Present conditions are not inherent in the nature of things. But likewise, there are good reasons for believing that concerted, large-scale efforts at social improvement can succeed again, as they have in the past.

E. Basically, recent events reflect technical malfunctions in our mechanisms for solving problems and putting society in order. Government is a major one of these malfunctioning mechanisms. Its job would normally be to sort through disagreements like the one we've got going here. But it can't currently do this, partly because of certain flaws in its structure and even more because it happens at the moment to be in the hands of weak individuals. A leadership that was more technically adept, more oriented toward fixing things, could once again give us a government whose capabilities matched the size of our problems. Then we could get on to deciding specifically what to do here.

Each of these statements approximates the views of one of the five candidates: *A* aligns with Buchanan's calls to restrict immigration, *C* echoes Clinton's "We don't have a single person to waste," *E* recalls Perot's metaphor of "getting under the hood" to fix what's wrong with the system. But I haven't attached names to them because the statements are no longer *just* political candidates' views, nor just responses to the L.A. riots. They are translations of those responses into more general philosophical terms. We are beyond candidates, campaigns, urban issues, riots. The debate can now be viewed as occurring at the level of basic political philosophy. 10

Such a broadly philosophical debate, I'm arguing, was implicit in the post-riot political debate and the 1992 presidential campaign. It and other disagreements like it are implicit in a great many issues all the time. *But they're never posed in those terms.* The real issues are never made clear, 11 hence we as citizens never really get to discuss them. Certainly the media don't initiate such discussions. Maybe the candidates would, if they were stranded on a desert island or all locked together for a while in the same room. But under the pressures of campaigning and even more of governing, with nearly everything they say prompted by narrow, policy-specific questions or spoken with an eye to the filtering the media will do, this never seems to happen. Nor does the movement toward direct, unmediated contact with voters—the increasing use of celebrity-interview shows, MTV and the like, a development widely seen as the wave of the future—yet look likely to prompt such discussions. Neither Larry King nor the private citizens assembled to question candidates in "town meetings" are likely to ask them to discuss their general philosophical views, whether on energy in government, justice versus peace or the best way to define "community." In fact, the questions ordinary voters ask in the much-touted new formats sound remarkably like efforts to imitate the way they remember journalists questioning candidates. And when they don't, it's because the questioner has veered into personal experience—that is, even further away from the level of generality required for a discussion like the above.

"EVERYBODY'S GOT A VIEW"

Now it's probably not possible or even desirable to have political cam- 12
paigns turned into seminars on the great questions of the Western philosophical tradition. But if it's the case that our disagreements aren't currently moving us forward, part of the reason would have to be our failure to make *some* explicit use of questions like these. As the above analysis makes clear, we can't avoid them. Such questions are already there. Like propellers, they lie beneath the surface, driving candidates' efforts—and like torpedoes, they can also be used to sink them.

Actually, some political leaders in some cases probably would be capa- 13
ble of discussing these questions in straightforward philosophical terms. I'm thinking here not only of the fact that Bill Clinton studied at Oxford and George Bush at Yale, but of an even more interesting, little-noted coincidence: Both Pat Buchanan and Jerry Brown are Catholics educated in part by Jesuits. That's considerable intellectual common ground (they even both know some Latin!) on which to base a philosophical debate—a debate one would be all the more curious to hear given their obvious and sharp divergence of views.

But let's assume debates like that will never be central to political cam- 14
paigns. What use, then, is this kind of analysis? Is there any reason even to look for this hidden layer of disagreement? And if there is, how can we get people to look for it who aren't currently bothering to?

Consider a radio program called *Which Way LA?* Begun in the wake of 15
the riots as a series of special reports for KCRW, National Public Radio's leading L.A.-area affiliate, the program continues to air each weekday. It

has already furnished several hundred hours of detailed discussion, ranging well beyond the riots themselves, of Los Angeles's problems and those of the nation and world.

16 But *Which Way LA?* straitjackets itself in a format depressingly like that of too many public-affairs shows (*Nightline, Crossfire,* PBS's *Newshour*), not to mention most media coverage of political campaigns. First, issues are treated in isolation. One day the topic is gangs, the next it's illegal immigration, the next it's the closing of public libraries. The host opens the microphone to guests A, B, and C in turn, each of whom says something at cross-purposes to the others—then replies to the others by restating his or her views unchanged. Moreover, the guests are usually chosen by virtue of some self-interested stake they have in their views. Thus the police spokesman says the cops are handling gangs exactly right; the harassed business owner says they're too lax; the social worker or ex-gang leader says the cops are too harsh. No, replies the police spokesman, we've got it just right. Whoops, says the host: Our time is up.

17 It shouldn't take too many such go-rounds for people to catch on that all we're really doing here is *reproducing* disputes. While it might help fill in details of what the contending views are, at bottom *Which Way LA?* amounts to a daily announcement simply that disagreement exists. Sometimes the host will even take despairing note of this: "Well," he'll say, as the decibel level rises, "this is an issue we obviously won't be able to settle today"—as if shows like this weren't all but designed to keep things unsettled.

18 When I consider that I'm keenly interested in political and social issues and even *I'm* usually bored by this program, I can only imagine what it would sound like, for instance, to most of the young, politically disengaged college students I've taught over the years. Students already tend to see public affairs as a cacophony of largely pointless disagreement. They already assume that most of that disagreement is motivated by self-interest, not by principled (if differing) visions of the good. It's tempting just to tune out. Everybody's got a view; what's right for me ain't right for you. What do we accomplish, students and other citizens must wonder, when we drag these differences into the open—other than just angering each other more?

TOWARD DELIBERATION

19 Instead of equating public discussion with emphasizing people's differences, the people who most help shape that discussion—especially those in the media—should be looking to frame issues in such a way as to make real debate possible. They should be helping us move from disagreement to deliberation. Let's consider what this might involve amid the debates we've been considering here.

20 Most simply, it would require that each participant—whether politician, activist or panel-show guest—be asked to restate his or her view *in*

something other than its own terms. Terms, as we've seen, are crucial. As long as each speaker in a debate gets to say not only what the point ought to be but in what terms the whole issue should be discussed—what the question is—it's too easy for everyone to keep talking at cross-purposes. That's when we hear charges of "finger-pointing" and "ducking the issue." When people find they don't share terms, it becomes easy for them to suppose that their opponents don't just have different views but have no coherent views at all—that they're simply trying to rationalize inaction or evade responsibility.

But since people don't share terms any more naturally than they share 21
views, it usually falls to someone else to provide the common terms. That's the job of a *moderator* in the true sense. In a debate like the one we've examined here, common terms can be found by reanalyzing issues into their philosophical components and by asking the contenders to respond, not just to each other's stated positions, but to the philosophical assumptions that lead to them. Thus, Candidate C above might be challenged not simply to charge Candidate B with doing nothing about inner cities, but speak to C's underlying fear of the Law of Unintended Consequences. Isn't C right to see this law as having frequently dogged some of government's best efforts? Similarly, Candidate A could be challenged to say how he squares his belief that America basically does provide opportunity with the fact that poverty and misery aren't randomly distributed, but instead concentrated in certain locales like inner cities. If people's success or failure in America is owed to their own qualities of character, wouldn't there be a roughly equal number of successful people in every neighborhood, even in every large family, instead of the vast pockets of generationally perpetuated poverty we have now? And so on, through many permutations as the various candidates' (or experts', or panel-show guests') views were rephrased in terms that allowed them to be seriously compared.

These aren't necessarily "killer" questions. Astute panelists and politi- 22
cians would likely have answers for them. Nor would questions framed in this way *force* agreement where we lack it now. But they could force something like a real dialogue, a real encounter among different outlooks. Even if discussants themselves didn't benefit from that, citizens at large surely would. It would give us a better sense of what the disagreements are, and would enhance our ability to decide which views are most plausible. Indeed, precisely to the extent that moderators don't currently ask questions like these—that they don't really moderate—it's all the more important that we as citizens be able to, if only in the privacy of our own living rooms.

And once we do that, it becomes a whole lot harder to be cynical. Of 23
course human beings form their views partly as defenses of self-interest. But once we recognize them as *views,* we can't help but give the people espousing them a little more credit. We can't help but begin thinking of those individuals less as people who want to get something at our expense or—in the case of politicians—gain power so they can lord it over us, and more as *fellow citizens* with whom we share some important things: anxieties about where we're all headed (even if their anxieties aren't precisely ours), a con-

sequent common stake in public decisions, and a willingness to deliberate rather than achieve things by corruption or force.

Best of all, perhaps, the approach I'm suggesting would make it harder for citizens to claim they were just *bored.* True, the broad questions I've cited here are the kind that college students joke about having to study in Philosophy 101. By themselves they sound awfully abstract, and the overly abstract strikes few people as interesting. But they're not being offered by themselves. What we've seen here is precisely the intimate link between these questions and urgent decisions—decisions that bear on how we all live, on where our money comes from and goes, on what our society will be like in the future. That link is what gives the philosophical issues concreteness, even as it gives the political disputes clarity. It's hard to imagine that too many citizens would fail to pay attention to a discussion that was clear, concrete, urgent and directly relevant to their lives—and wallets. 24

▲ ▲ ▲

Review Questions

1. What views of government do the Buchanan approach, the Bush approach, the Clinton approach, and the Brown approach represent for the purpose of Smith's article?
2. In terms of how such riots as occurred in L.A. may be prevented, what is the chief difference among these approaches?

Discussion and Writing Suggestions

1. Which of the approaches described by Smith (Buchanan, Bush, Clinton, Brown) make most sense to you? Explain, drawing upon specific examples from your own experience, observation, or reading.
2. In a brief essay, respond to one or two of the seven sets of questions concerning the L.A. riots posed by Smith. If you would rather not deal with this particular subject, focus on another subject for which these questions (perhaps somewhat adapted) might be appropriate (e.g., drug crimes).
3. Locate several editorials and op-ed pieces on a particular issue (e.g., abortion, gun control, affirmative action, health care). Then adapt the kind of analysis used by Smith to categorize the various ideological perspectives represented in the different articles. *First,* summarize the key idea of each editorial. *Second,* categorize the types of questions and assumptions underlying each perspective. *Third,* "recast in more broadly philosophic terms" each of the approaches you have identified. *Finally,* discuss *your own* position on the issue by responding to some of the questions you developed for the second part of the assignment.

Liberalism, Conservatism, Socialism, Libertarianism

JAMES MACGREGOR BURNS, J. W. PELTASON, THOMAS E. CRONIN, AND DAVID B. MAGLEBY

As we suggested in the chapter introduction, "liberal" and "conservative" are notoriously slippery terms. This does not mean, however, that they lack all meaning or that they don't signify real and significant differences in political philosophy. In the following selection, James MacGregor Burns, J. W. Peltason, Thomas E. Cronin, and David B. Magleby offer extended definitions of these and other important terms, explain how the ideologies they represent have evolved over time, and offer much interesting statistical information about the political attitudes of the American public. You should find this selection extremely useful in helping you to analyze particular political statements on a variety of issues, some covered in this book, others that you may discover in the course of your own research.

James MacGregor Burns is Distinguished Scholar in Leadership at the University of Maryland and Professor Emeritus of Government at Williams College. He has authored numerous books, including Roosevelt: Soldier of Freedom *(1970) and* A People's Charter: The Pursuit of Rights in America *(1991). A past president of the American Political Science Association, he has won numerous awards, including the Pulitzer Prize. J. W. Peltason has been a Professor of Political Science at the University of California, Irvine, president of the University of California system, and past president of the American Council on Education. His books include* Federal Courts in the Political Process *(1955),* Fifty-Eight Lonely Men: Southern Federal Judges and School Desegregation *(1961), and* Understanding the Constitution *(1993). Thomas E. Cronin teaches and serves as president of Whitman College. He has been a White House fellow and president of the Western Political Science Association. His books include* The State of the Presidency *(1980) and* Direct Democracy: The Politics of Initiative, Referendum, and Recall *(1989). David B. Magleby is a professor of political science and department chair at Brigham Young University. He has taught at the University of California at Santa Cruz and the University of Virginia. His books include* Direct Legislation *(1984) and* The Myth of the Independent Voter *(1992).*

The following selection is reprinted from the authors' widely used political science textbook, Government by the People *(16th ed., 1995).*

IDEOLOGY AND PUBLIC POLICY

Ideology refers to the structure of a person's ideas or beliefs about political values and the role of government. It includes the views people develop as they mature about how government should work and how it actually works. 1

Ideology links our basic values to the day-to-day operations or policies of government.

Two major, yet rather broad, schools of political thinking dominate American politics today: *liberalism* and *conservatism.* Two lesser, but more defined, schools of thought, *socialism* and *libertarianism,* also help define the spectrum of ideology in the United States. We turn now to a more detailed description of these approaches. 2

Liberalism

In the seventeenth and eighteenth centuries, classical liberals fought to minimize the role of government. They stressed individual rights and perceived of governments as the primary threat to these rights and liberties. Thus they favored a limited government and sought ample guarantees of protection from governmental harassment. Over time the emphasis on individualism has remained constant, but the perception of the need for government has changed. Nowadays, liberals view government as protecting individuals from being abused by a variety of governmental and non-governmental forces such as market vagaries, business decisions, and discriminatory practices. 3

In its modern American usage, *liberalism* refers to a belief in the positive uses of government to bring about justice and equality of opportunity. Modern-day liberals wish to preserve the rights of the individual and the right to own private property, yet they are also willing to have the government intervene in the economy to remedy the defects of capitalism and a market economy. Contemporary American liberalism has its roots in Franklin Roosevelt's New Deal programs, designed to aid the poor and to protect people against unemployment and bank failures. Today, liberals also seek protection against inadequate or deficient medical assistance and inadequate or deficient housing and education. They generally believe in affirmative action programs, regulations that protect workers' health and safety, tax rates that rise with income, and the right of unions to organize as well as to strike. 4

On a more philosophical level, liberals generally believe in the possibility of progress. They believe things can be made to work, that the future will be better, that obstacles can be overcome. This positive set of beliefs may explain some of their willingness to believe in the potential benefits of governmental action, a willingness to alter or even negate the old Jeffersonian notion that "government governs best when it governs least." Liberals contend that the character of modern technology and the side effects of industrialization cry out for at least limited governmental programs to offset the loss of liberties suffered by the less well-to-do and the weak. Liberals frequently stress the need for a compassionate and affirmative government. 5

Liberals contend that conservatives will usually rule in their own interest and are motivated by the maxim, "Let the government take care of the rich, and the rich in turn will take care of the poor." Liberals, on the other 6 hand, prefer that government take care of the weak, for the strong can nearly always take care of themselves. "We have rejected the discredited theory that the fortunes of the nation should be in the hands of a privileged few," said President Harry Truman. "Instead, we believe that our economic system should rest on a democratic foundation and that wealth should be created for the benefit of all. . . . Every segment of our population and every individual has a right to expect from his government a fair deal."[1]

In the liberal view, all people are equal. Equality of opportunity is essential, and, toward that end, discriminatory practices must be eliminated. Some liberals favor the reduction of great inequalities of wealth that make equality of opportunity impossible. Most favor a certain minimum level of income. Rather than placing a cap on wealth, they want a floor placed beneath the poor. In short, liberals have sought "to lessen the harsh impact of oligarchical rule in economic life, to introduce a measure of democracy within or democratic controls over the industrial-technological process, to assure freedom from arbitrary command within the economic no less than within the political sphere."[2] They ask: How can citizens be equal and free if they are dependent on and necessarily servile to the powers that be? 7

TYPES OF LIBERALS Liberals, it should be emphasized, come in many varieties. Some stress civil rights or women's rights or high-quality public education. Others urge government to adopt a more progressive tax system and do more to help the homeless, the handicapped, and society's "have-nots." Still others decry militarism and crusade for treaties and alliances that might bring about a world without terrorism and war. And yet other liberals are preoccupied with environmental or consumer issues. Some liberals embrace all these issues, placing them on an equal plane. 8

In a sense, liberals who emphasize economic issues may be called *New Deal liberals;* others are *social liberals* or *peace liberals.* If this is not confusing enough, there are those who call themselves *neoliberals.* Neoliberals believe in liberty, justice, and a fair chance for everyone, and they argue that the truly down-and-out must have government assistance. Yet they do not automatically favor unions and big government, nor do they automatically criticize big business or the military. Neoliberals are best characterized as liberals who have lost faith in many welfare programs and are skeptical about the efficiency and responsiveness of large, Washington-based bureaucracies. They are better at diagnosing some of the deficiencies of old liberalism than they are at pointing out what should be done. A sample of neoliberal thinking regularly appears in *The Washington Monthly.*[3] 9

CRITICISMS OF LIBERALISM Not everyone, by a long shot, is convinced that liberals in whatever form have the answers for the problems of the 1990s. Critics of liberalism, old and new, say they place too much reliance on governmental solutions, higher taxes, and bureaucrats. Opponents of liberalism say that somewhere along the line liberals forgot that government, to serve our best interests, has to be limited. Power tends to corrupt, 10 they add, and too much reliance or dependence on government can corrupt the spirit, can undermine self-reliance, and can make us forget about those cherished personal freedoms and property rights our Republic was founded to secure and protect. When we get too much government, it tends to start dictating to us, and then our rights and liberties are at risk. Further, too many governmental controls or regulations and too much taxation undermine the self-help ethic that has "made America great." In short, critics of liberalism contend that the welfare and regulatory state pushed by liberals will ultimately destroy individual initiative, the entrepreneurial spirit, and the very engine of economic growth that might lead to true equality of economic opportunities.

Some liberals admit that Ronald Reagan and George Bush redefined the issues in the 1980s and 1990s in such a way that liberalism sounded unnecessary and dated, if not wholly harmful. Wrapping themselves in the symbols of nationalism and patriotism, conservatives took a strong stand in favor of business, the death penalty, and prayer in schools—issues popular with most voters. Liberals, on the other hand, wrapped themselves in the symbols of compassion, fairness, equality, and social justice, also popular issues, but perhaps more relevant in races for Congress than for the White House. 11

The 1992 election contest between Bill Clinton and George Bush centered on the economy. Hanging in Clinton's campaign headquarters was a poster that read, "It's the economy, stupid!" reminding the Clinton campaign that it would be stupid to let the campaign stray from that issue. George Bush, on the other hand, wanted to stress his experience in defense and foreign policy, his success in the war against Iraq, and his more conservative position on issues like abortion and school prayer. In the end, the economic concerns were too great for Bush to counter, and Clinton won the election. 12

Kevin Phillips believes that economic divisions will be the major theme of politics in the 1990s: 13

> One could reasonably assume that the 1990s would be a time in which to correct the excesses of the 1980s, for the dangers posed by excessive individualism, greed and insufficient concern for America as a community went beyond the issue of fairness and, by threatening the ability of the United States to maintain its economic position in the world, created an unusual meeting ground for national self-interest and reform.[4]

But Michael Barone, a well-regarded political observer, disputes the view that economics is the most important dimension of American politics. Rather, he says, cultural divisions matter most: "Civil rights, the Vietnam War, drugs, abortion, policy toward the Soviets and the Third World tended to divide Americans more often on cultural than on economic lines."[5] 14

Is it possible to reconcile these two positions? Politics in the United States has several focal points. As those change, so do the electoral fortunes of liberals and conservatives. Still, elections often turn on how the 15 economy is doing, with voters blaming the party of the president if it is doing poorly or responding positively if it is doing well. This tendency is true both in presidential elections and mid-term elections.

Liberals were defeated in presidential elections in 1972, 1984, and 1988, yet they won in many state and congressional elections. On a long list of issues—the environment, Social Security, women's rights, unemployment assistance, military spending, arms control, and new programs for the homeless—liberal positions helped elect state and local politicians. Perhaps even more important, the winning candidates often were incumbents running with the advantages of incumbency, and they had maintained close relations with their constituents. Still, a number of allegedly liberal positions are out of favor. National surveys indicate what Americans want from government is lower taxes, less government regulation, less reliance on bureaucracies, a strong defense, stronger anticrime measures, less permissiveness, and a return to prayer in the schools. These are conservative positions. 16

As the agenda of American politics changes, so does the popularity of liberal or conservative positions. With the collapse of communism many Americans are now less concerned about defense spending and more inclined to focus on solving problems at home. Yet the fiscal constraints imposed by the tax cuts of 1981 and the crushing budget deficit changed the debate about government solutions because few are willing to raise taxes to fund new programs or new ideas. Moreover as the North American Free Trade Agreement (NAFTA) demonstrates, we live in a global economy, and our jobs and economic progress are linked to our neighbors and other countries around the world. The net effect of these changes is [that] our national government, while focusing on domestic issues like health care, crime, and welfare, does so in a context much more aware of the constraints of the budget deficit and the unpopularity of tax increases. 17

Conservatism

American *conservatism* has its roots in the political thinking of John Adams, Alexander Hamilton, and many of their contemporaries. They believed in limited government and encouraged individual excellence and personal achievement. Private property rights and belief in free enterprise are cardinal attributes of contemporary conservatism. In contrast to liberals, conservatives want to keep government small, except in the area of national defense. However, because conservatives take a more pessimistic view of human nature than liberals do, they maintain that most people need strong leadership institutions, firm laws, and strict moral codes to keep their appetites under control. Government, they think, needs to ensure order. Conservatives are also inclined to believe that those who fail in life are in some way the architects of their own misfortune and thus must bear the main responsibility for solving their own problems. Conservatives have a preference for the status quo and desire change only in moderation. A sam- 18 ple of conservative thinking can be found in *The National Review,* a weekly magazine.

Most conservatives opposed the New Deal programs of the 1930s and the War on Poverty in the 1960s, and they have seldom favored aggressive civil rights and affirmative action programs. Human needs, they say, can and should be taken care of by families and charities. Equal treatment can be achieved by encouraging citizens to be more tolerant. Conservatives place substantial faith in the private sector, and they consider social justice to be essentially an economic question. They dislike the tendency to turn to government, especially the national government, for solutions to societal problems. Government social activism, they say, has been highly inflationary and counterproductive. Conservatives also prize stability—stability of the dollar, stability in international affairs, and stability in political and economic affairs. They prefer private giving and individual voluntary efforts targeted at social and economic problems rather than government programs. 19

TRADITIONAL CONSERVATIVES Traditional conservatives recognize that government must exist, yet insist it should be limited in what it does, and that within its proper sphere of action, it should be strong and resolute. "The purpose of government is to maintain the framework of order within which other private institutions can operate effectively."[6] The traditional conservative applauds the heartfelt compassion implicit in Franklin Roosevelt's Second Bill of Rights but believes that to turn to the federal government to solve those problems is to guarantee a too powerful, intrusive, and expensive government. 20

Liberals favor national action and a stronger central government. Conservatives, however, contend that centralization means higher taxes, that the freedom of the majority would greatly diminish, and that the initiative and risk-taking entrepreneurial impulses of inventors, capital investors, and ingenious business leaders would be irreversibly discouraged.[7] 21

Former U.S. Senator Barry Goldwater, the Republican candidate for president in 1964 and an outspoken conservative, condemned "government welfarism" as one of the greatest evils of the twentieth century: 22

> Let welfare be a private concern. Let it be promoted by individuals and families, by churches, private hospitals, religious service organizations, community charities and other institutions that have been established for this purpose. If the objection is raised that private institutions lack sufficient funds, let us remember that every penny the federal government does not appropriate for welfare is potentially available for private use—and without the overhead charge for processing the money through the federal bureaucracy.[8]

In addition to fighting the welfare state, traditional conservatives, in the name of freedom, have been emphatically pro-business. Thus, they oppose higher taxes and resist all but the most necessary antitrust, trade, and environmental regulations on corporations. The functions of government should be, say conservatives, to encourage family values, protect us against 23 foreign enemies and criminals, preserve law and order, enforce private contracts, foster competitive markets, and encourage free and fair trade.

Traditional conservatives have customarily favored dispersing power 24
broadly throughout the political and social systems, precisely to avoid concentration of power at the national level. They favor having the market, rather than the government, distribute goods. Traditional conservatives subordinate economic and social equality to liberty and freedom. To allow the worst-off to take advantage of the best-off is to hurt both groups in the end.

THE NEW RIGHT Another brand of conservatism—sometimes called the 25
New Right, ultraconservatism, or even the Radical Right—emerged in the past generation. The New Right shares the love of freedom shown by the traditional conservatives and, during the 1980s, backed an aggressive effort to combat international communism, especially in Central America. It has also developed an activist public policy agenda that it would like implemented by conservatives in Congress and in the White House. The New Right favors the return of organized prayer in the public schools and renewal of covert operations by the Central Intelligence Agency. It wants strict limits on abortion; it opposes policies like job quotas, busing, and any tolerance of pornography. In short, a defining characteristic of the New Right is a strong desire to impose various social controls.

One driving force in the New Right is the Religious Right. Leaders of 26
this group include Pat Robertson, a candidate for the presidency in 1988, and Jerry Falwell, who founded and promoted the Moral Majority in the 1980s. Much of the Religious Right's agenda overlaps that of the New Right—a concern with moral issues like abortion, homosexuality, and prayer in public school and public meetings. Adherents of the Religious Right have been especially active at the state and local levels, in political parties and initiative campaigns and on school boards. The 1992 initiative in Colorado to overturn ordinances protecting gays and lesbians from discrimination was placed on the ballot largely through their efforts.[9] The Colorado law was later declared unconstitutional by the state supreme court.*

Senator Jesse Helms (R.–N.C.) is one of the most influential leaders of 27
the New Right. Helms built an impressive coalition in the South and elsewhere by uniting various groups: fundamentalist Christians worried about "secular humanism" and in favor of official school prayer; conservative Catholics opposed to abortion; white parents opposed to drugs, pornography, and forced busing; small business owners resentful of government intrusion; and manufacturers in favor of less governmental regulation and more defense spending. Patrick Buchanan tried to rally the New Right in

---

*In May 1996, the U.S. Supreme Court, by a vote of 6 to 3, overturned the Colorado law.

his 1992 presidential campaign, but rarely got above 30 percent of the Republican primary vote, and those votes appeared to be based more on opposition to George Bush than on ideology.[10] The New Right remains an important but not dominant part of conservatism in the United States.

Some conservatives question the moralistic tone of the New Right. For **28**
example, Barry Goldwater worries that too much prominence and influence have been granted to the New Right, especially the Moral Majority and those he calls the "checkbook clergy." Our Constitution, Goldwater says, seeks to allow freedom for everyone, not merely those professing certain moral or religious views of ultimate right. Goldwater points to the bloody divisions in Northern Ireland, the holy wars in Lebanon, and the pernicious religious righteousness in Iran as examples of the politicalization of churches. "The Moral Majority has no more right to dictate its moral and political beliefs to the country than does any other group, political or religious," says Goldwater. "The same is true of pro-choice, abortion, or other groups. They are free to persuade us because this land is blessed with liberty, but not assign religious or political absolutes—complete right or wrong."[11] Goldwater fears that the great danger of the New Right is that instead of broadening its base, it will tear his beloved Republican party apart. He also, one gathers, opposes moral absolutes—the kind the Moral Majority thrives on.

NEOCONSERVATIVES The past generation has also witnessed the emer- **29**
gence of people who call themselves *neoconservatives.* Many are former Democrats who admired FDR and Harry Truman but left the Democratic party over Vietnam, busing, and the decisions of the liberal (overly liberal in their view) Earl Warren Supreme Court. They want to continue programs that work and are truly necessary, but reject the rest. An example of a successful program they would be inclined to keep is Head Start, the federally funded program for disadvantaged preschool children. Neoconservatives believe that too many government programs will lead to a paternalistic state. Though willing to interfere with the market for overriding social purposes, neoconservatives prefer finding market solutions to social problems. An example of neoconservative writing can be found in *Commentary,* a monthly magazine.

Neoconservatives favor larger military expenditures than do liberals. **30**
They remain skeptical of the intentions of some of the republics of the Commonwealth of Independent States as well as other nations. Conservatives also favor sufficient military spending to permit the United States to play a role in mediating conflicts around the world, especially in settings where U.S. interests are involved. But conservatives are not always united in their support for the use of military force, as indicated by the opposition of some conservatives to the use of American troops in Somalia, Bosnia, and Haiti in the 1990s. They also favor the death penalty and are more worried about crime than about the homeless. They say the courts have gone

too far in protecting the rights of the criminal and are too little concerned about the rights of the victims of crime.

Neoconservatives are credited with various original writings on social 31
policy, supply-side economics, education, and the role of "national interest" in foreign affairs. *Supply-side economics* (which during the 1980s was often called "Reaganomics") is the belief that lower taxes will encourage economic growth, new jobs, and ultimately new tax revenues. The United States, in the neoconservative view, should use its power to shape events; it cannot retreat into isolationism. Thus neoconservatives heartily approved Reagan's invasion of Grenada, his bombing of Libya, and U.S. assertiveness in Central America.[12] More recently they strongly supported the use of military force in Panama and Kuwait.

CRITICISMS OF CONSERVATISM Not everyone agreed with Ronald Reagan's 32
statement that "government is the problem."[13] Indeed, critics of conservatism before and during the Reagan-Bush era saw hostility to government as counterproductive and inconsistent. Conservatives, they argued, have a selective opposition to government. They want more government when it serves their needs—by regulating pornography and abortion, for example—but are opposed to it when it serves somebody else's. Critics point out that government spending, especially for defense, grew during the 1980s when the conservatives were in control. Conservatives are often criticized for insensitivity to the social needs for the homeless and mentally ill.

Conservatives place great faith in our market economy—critics would 33
say too much faith. This posture often puts them at odds with labor unions and consumer activists and in close alliance with business people, particularly large corporations. Hostility to regulation and a belief in competition are some of the reasons conservatives pushed deregulation in the 1980s. These changes did not always have the intended positive effects, as the collapse of many savings and loans revealed.[14] During the same decade, according to some critics, the Reagan administration's decision not to pursue antitrust actions encouraged a flurry of mergers and acquisitions that diverted our economy from more productive economic activity.[15] Conservatives counter that relying on "market solutions" and encouraging the free market are still the best course of action in most policy areas.[16]

Consistent with the conservative hostility to government was the pol- 34
icy of the Reagan years of lowering taxes. In his 1981 address to the nation on the state of the economy, Reagan likened government to children who spend more than their parents can afford. He mentioned that such extravagance could be cured by "simply reducing their allowance."[17] Implied was the idea that government could be controlled by reducing the amount government was allowed to spend. Many conservatives embraced the idea that if we lower taxes on the rich, their economic activity will "trickle down" to the poor. This view was criticized by many Democrats in the 1992 election campaign, who pointed out that the growth in income and wealth in the 1980s was largely concentrated among the well-to-do.[18]

Conservatives are also criticized for their failure to acknowledge and 35
endorse policies that deal with racism and sexism in the United States. Their opposition to the civil rights laws in the 1960s and their opposition to affirmative action in the 1990s are examples of this perspective. Not only have conservatives opposed new laws in these areas, they have hampered the activity of the executive branch when in power, and have sought to limit the activity of the courts in these matters as well.

Socialism and Libertarianism

Our review of American political ideology would not be complete without 36
a brief comment on socialism and libertarianism.

SOCIALISM *Socialism* is an economic and governmental system based on 37
public ownership of the means of production and exchange. Karl Marx once described socialism as a transitional stage of society between capitalism and communism. In a capitalist system, the means of production and most of the property are privately owned, whereas in a communist or socialist system, property is "owned" by the state in common for all the people. In the ultimate socialist country, justice is achieved by having participants determine their own needs and take what is appropriate from the common product of society. Marx's dictum was, "From each according to his ability, to each according to his needs."[19]

In one of the most dramatic transformations in recent times, Russia, its 38
sister republics, and its former European satellites abandoned their version of socialism—communism—and are now attempting to establish free markets. These countries had previously rejected capitalism, preferring state ownership and centralized government planning of the economy. But by the 1990s the disparities in economic well-being between capitalist and communist nations produced a tide of political and economic reform that left communism intact in only a few countries, such as Cuba.

American socialists—of whom there are very few outspoken or promi- 39
nent examples—favor a greatly expanded role for the government. They would nationalize certain industries, institute a public jobs program so that all who want work would be put to work, and place a much steeper tax burden on the wealthy. In short, American socialists favor policies to help the underdog by means of income redistribution programs. They also favor stepped-up efforts toward greater equality in property rights. American socialists would drastically cut defense spending as well.[20] Most of the democracies of Western Europe are far more influenced by socialist ideas than we are in the United States, but they remain, like the United States, largely market economies.

LIBERTARIANISM *Libertarianism* is an ideology that cherishes individual 40
liberty and insists on a sharply limited government. It carries some overtones of anarchism, of the classical English liberalism of the past, and of a

1930s-style conservatism. The Libertarian party has gained a modest following among people who believe that both liberals and conservatives lack consistency in their attitude toward the power of the national government. Libertarians preach opposition to government and just about all its programs. They favor massive cuts in government spending, an end to the Federal Bureau of Investigation and the Central Intelligence Agency and most regulatory commissions, and a minimal defense establishment (one that would defend the United States only if directly attacked). They oppose *all* government regulation, including, for example mandatory seat-belt and helmet laws. A poster at one of their recent national conventions read "U.S. out of Latin America; U.S. out of North America!" Libertarians favor eliminating not only welfare programs but also programs that subsidize business, farmers, and the rich. They opposed government-backed guaranteed loans for Chrysler and other businesses and would turn the functions of the Postal Service over to private companies. Unlike most conservatives, libertarians would repeal laws that regulate personal morality, including abortion, pornography, prostitution, and recreational drugs.

A Libertarian party candidate for president has been on the ballot in all 41
50 states in recent presidential elections, although never obtaining more than 1 percent of the vote. The Libertarian candidate for president in 1992, André Marrou, ran on a platform that emphasized elimination of corporate subsidies, social welfare, and foreign military welfare; decriminalization of drugs; abolition of the Federal Reserve Board and return of the gold standard; withdrawal of the overseas military from Japan, Korea, the Philippines, Germany, and elsewhere; and abolition of the Internal Revenue Service and the income tax. Libertarian positions are rarely timid; at the very least, they prompt intriguing political debates.

A Word of Caution

. . . Debates about communist expansionism are increasingly dated and ir- 42
relevant in American politics. In the 1990s there is little fear that the United States will become communist, and the communist threat around the world is greatly diminished. But people of varying ideologies do indeed worry about whether the United States is becoming too soft and losing ground in the global economy. Today we are more likely to debate what will make us beat, or at least compete with, "those capitalists from Japan" and other Pacific Rim nations. Ideological controversy centers on how we can improve our schools, encourage a stronger work ethic, and stop the flow of drugs into the country; whether to permit openly gay people into the military or sanction gay marriages; and the best ways to instill religious values, build character, and encourage cohesive and lasting families.

Do social programs and job-training programs make things better or 43
worse? Is reliance on the marketplace or on government planners a better way to make long-term policy decisions for the nation? What is the best way to balance the budget and curb inflation? Are foreign investors and in-

WE THE PEOPLE

Differences in Political Ideology: Conservative, Moderate, Liberal

	SELF-CLASSIFICATION		
	CONSERVATIVE	MODERATE	LIBERAL
SEX			
Male	36%	44%	20%
Female	25	55	20
RACE			
Black	14	63	23
White	32	47	20
American Indian	40	44	16
Asian	44	44	12
Hispanic	22	64	14
AGE			
18–24	21	55	23
25–34	29	48	24
35–44	33	40	27
45–54	37	44	19
55–64	29	58	13
65+	28	60	12
EDUCATION			
Less than high school	19	70	12
High school graduate	26	59	15
Some college	32	45	23
Bachelor's degree	46	25	30
Advanced degree	36	23	40
RELIGION			
Protestant	33	50	17
Catholic	30	51	19
Jewish	16	32	52
PARTY IDENTIFICATION			
Republican	55	39	6
Independent	20	54	26
Democrat	17	52	31

SOURCE: 1992 American National Election Studies, Center for Political Studies, University of Michigan.

Note: We have combined with the moderates persons who do not know their ideology or had not thought much about it. For the party identification, we have combined Independent leaners with their respective parties. Rows may not add up to 100% due to rounding.

ternational conglomerates shaping our lives as well as our economic policy decisions? Ideological debate and differences are always with us, but the nature of the issues changes. There are likely to be even more changes as we approach the end of the century.

A CLOSER LOOK
HOW AMERICANS DEFINE THEIR IDEOLOGY

Most Americans are not deeply "ideological." They lack an internally consistent and coherent set of beliefs about politics and public issues. The average citizen does not spend a lot of time thinking about government and public policies. Still, many Americans have ideological moorings, and some hold them fiercely. Politically, Americans are often said to be moderate and pragmatic rather than ideological. The most common measure of ideology is simply to ask people where they would place themselves on a liberal/conservative scale.

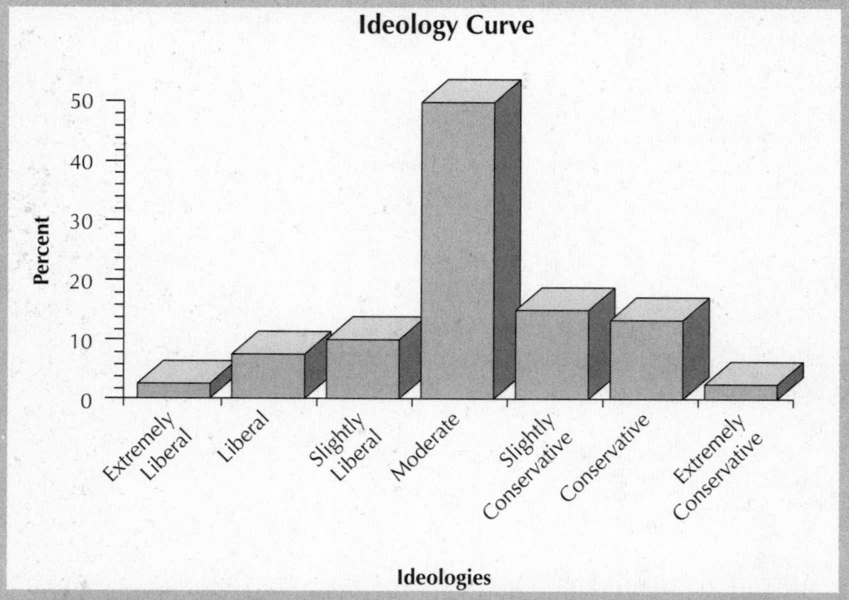

SOURCE: 1992 National Election Study, Center for Political Studies, University of Michigan.

IDEOLOGY AND THE AMERICAN PEOPLE

Despite the twists and turns of American politics, the distribution of ideol- **44**
ogy in our nation has been remarkably consistent in the past 20 years (see box). There are more conservatives than liberals, but the proportion of conservatives did not increase substantially with the decisive Republican presidential victories of the 1980s. Survey questions used to ascertain ideology permit respondents not only to answer "moderate" but also to indicate that they "don't know" their ideology or "have not thought much about it." The combined "moderate" and "don't know" categories are consistently much

What the Public Thinks It Means to Be a Liberal or a Conservative

Q: What sort of things do you have in mind when you say someone's political views are Liberal? (top five responses)

Accept change	38%
Favor social programs	20
Favor government spending/spend freely	17
Favor abortion	14
Favor freedom to do as one chooses/ not interested in setting moral standards	11

Q: What sort of things do you have in mind when you say someone's political views are Conservative? (top five responses)

Resist change or new ideas	44%
Spend less freely/tight economic policy	18
Are slow or cautious in response to problems/do nothing	14
Support free enterprise/capitalism	13
Oppose abortion.	11

SOURCE: 1992 National Election Study, Center for Political Studies, University of Michigan.

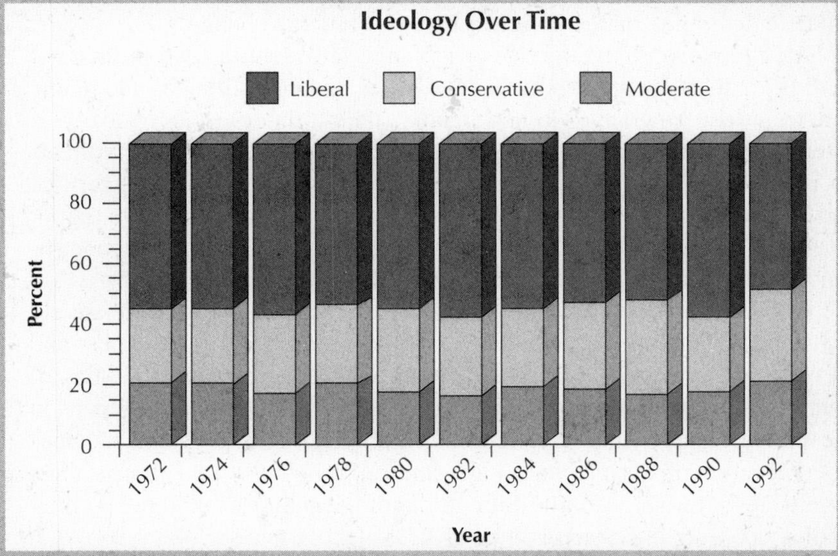

SOURCES: National Election Study, 1952–88, Cumulative Data File; 1990 National Election Study and 1992 National Election Study, Center for Political Studies, University of Michigan.

larger than either the conservative or liberal group and constitute a cluster more interested in pragmatism than ideology. These people vote for liberals in some races and conservatives in others because they simply prefer one candidate over another. Indeed there are more who indicate no ideology than indicate liberal and conservative combined. In sum, most Americans are unconstrained by a consistent ideology.[21]

One other important fact about ideology in the United States is that 45
very few people see themselves as extreme conservatives or extreme liberals. In 1992, only 3 percent of the population saw themselves as extreme conservatives, and an even smaller percentage, 2 percent, saw themselves as extreme liberals. These percentages also have changed very little over time. When given the option to describe themselves as "conservative" or "slightly conservative," 15 percent say "slightly conservative" and only 13 percent say "conservative."[22] The same tendency is true of liberals.

For those who have a liberal or conservative preference, ideology pro- 46
vides a lens through which to view politics. It helps simplify the complexities of politics, policies, personalities, and programs. An ideology may be an accurate or an inaccurate description of reality, yet it is still the way a person thinks about people, power, and society. For these reasons, it is important to understand how people view candidates, issues, and public policy. Among legislators, lobbyists, and party activists, ideology is even more important. Their ideologies shape our social and political institutions and help determine public policies and constitutional change.

An alternative to the liberal/conservative self-identification measure of 47
ideology is to ask people about their attitudes toward politicians and public policies. Most Americans do not organize their attitudes systematically. A voter may want increased spending for defense but vote for the party that is for reducing defense spending because he or she has always voted for that party or prefers its stand on the environment. Or a person may favor adoption of the North American Free Trade Agreement and government-financed health care for all and still support Ross Perot.

Consistency among various attitudes and opinions is often relatively 48
low. Much of the time people view political issues as isolated matters and do not apply a general standard of performance in evaluating parties or candidates. Indeed, many citizens find it difficult to relate what happens in one policy situation to what happens in another. This problem becomes worse as government gets into more and more policy areas. Hence, most people, not surprisingly, have difficulty finding candidates who reflect their ideological preferences across a range of issues.

The absence of widespread and solidified liberal and conservative po- 49
sitions in the United States makes for politics and policy-making processes that are markedly different from those in many European and other nations. Our policy making is characterized more by coalitions of the moment than by fixed alignments that pit one set of ideologies against another. And our politics is marked more by moderation, pragmatism, and accommodation than a prolonged and strained battle between two, three, or more competing philosophies of government. Elsewhere, especially in countries where a strong Socialist or Christian Democratic party exists, things are different.

By no means, however, does this mean that policies or ideas are not 50
elements in our politics. Such issues as affirmative action, NAFTA, the

Supreme Court's abortion rulings, and options for health care reform, gun control, and environmental protection have aroused people who previously were passive about politics and political ideas.

IDEOLOGY AND TOLERANCE

Is there a connection between support for civil liberties and tolerance for 51
racial minorities and the ideologies of liberalism and conservatism? Some political scientists assert that conservatives are generally less tolerant than liberals. This view is stoutly contested by conservatives, who have charged liberals with trying to impose a "politically correct" position on universities and the media. "Conservatives," observe Herbert McClosky and Alida Brill, "have repeatedly shown their fear of political and social instability. With rare exceptions, the conservatives have been the party of tradition, stability, duty, respect for authority, and the primacy of 'law and order' over all competing values."[23]

Liberals share many of these views but place a different emphasis on 52
the interpretation. They have more faith in government and readily turn to government to help achieve greater equality of opportunity. Liberals are usually more tolerant of dissent and the expression of unorthodox opinions. However, liberals, too, can be intolerant—of antiabortion forces, for example, or the National Rifle Association, or the views of Rush Limbaugh.

Most liberals are strongly opposed to crime and lawbreaking, yet they 53
are as concerned about the roots or causes of crime as they are about the punishment of criminals. Perhaps for this reason, liberals exhibit somewhat greater concern than conservatives for the rights of the accused and are more willing to expand the rights of due process. Conservatives usually take a harder line and, in recent years, have won widespread popular support for their greater concern for the victims of crime than for the rights of the accused.

Such differences are most evident in the responses of liberals and con- 54
servatives to questions of civil rights and civil liberties. Research in the early 1980s found that, despite our common political culture and despite our widespread allegiance to constitutionalism and the Bill of Rights, many Americans sharply disagree on some basic political matters. Liberals are ordinarily more willing than conservatives to defend the rights of those who are in the minority, who may be wrong, or who take unorthodox or unpleasing stands.

In the area of free speech, conservatives were once seen as less willing 55
to permit speech that was out of the political or cultural mainstream. Perhaps conservatives were less tolerant because those who claimed to be exercising the right of free speech often attacked established values. Now the argument that liberalism is correlated with tolerance is more complicated and the evidence less persuasive.

Conservatives believe that the United States has become too permis- 56
sive. Many conservatives, especially in the New or Religious Right, are

highly critical of homosexuals, drug users, prostitutes, unwed mothers, and pornography. They worry about what they claim has been a decline in moral standards and, interestingly, call on government to help reverse these trends. Liberals, on the other hand, generally accept nonconformity in conduct and opinion as an inescapable by-product of freedom:

> Like John Stuart Mill, contemporary liberals tend to perceive the free exchange of divergent views and attempts at social experimentation as potential harbingers of social improvement and progress. They regard the dangers to society from unorthodox beliefs and behavior as minimal compared with their potential benefits—a small price to be paid for social advancement."[24]

In this regard, liberals are like libertarians.

It is these sharp cleavages in political thinking that stir opposing inter- 57
est groups into formation and action. Groups such as the Moral Majority, the American Civil Liberties Union, Amnesty International, Mothers Against Drunk Driving, Queer Nation, and countless others promote their views of what is politically desirable. It is also these differences in ideological perspectives that reinforce party loyalties and that divide us at election time. Policy fights in Congress, between Congress and the White House, and during judicial confirmation hearings also have their roots in our uneasily coexisting ideological values.

Ideologies have consequences. Although Americans share many ideas 58
in common, we as a people also hold many contradictory ideas. Our hard-earned rights and liberties are never entirely safeguarded; they are fragile and are shaped by the political, economic, and social climate of the day.

REFERENCES

1. Harry S. Truman, State of the Union Address, 1949, *The Public Papers of the President of the United States, 1949* (Government Printing Office, 1964), pp. 1–7.
2. David Spitz, "A Liberal Perspective on Liberalism and Conservatism," in *Left, Right and Center,* ed. Robert Goldwin (Rand McNally, 1965), p. 31.
3. See also Charles Peters and Philip Keisling, eds., *A New Road for America: The Neoliberal Movement* (University Press of America, 1984); Randall Rothenberg. *The Neoliberals: Creating the New American Politics* (Simon & Schuster, 1984).
4. Kevin Phillips, *The Politics of Rich and Poor: Wealth and the American Electorate in the Reagan Aftermath* (New York: Random House, 1990), pp. 220–21.
5. Michael Barone, *Our Country: The Shaping of America from Roosevelt to Reagan* (Free Press, 1990), p. xii.
6. Kenneth R. Hoover, *Ideology and Political Life* (Brooks/Cole, 1987), p. 34.
7. See the writings of Milton Friedman, *Capitalism and Freedom* (University of Chicago, 1962). See also Friedrich A. Hayek, *The Road to Serfdom* (University of Chicago Press, 1944).
8. Barry Goldwater, *The Conscience of a Conservative* (Victor, 1960), p. 76.
9. Paula Poundstone, "He Didn't Even Like Girls," *Mother Jones* (May 1993), p. 37.
10. Walter H. Capps, *The New Religious Right: Piety, Patriotism, and Politics* (University of South Carolina Press, 1990).
11. Barry Goldwater with Jack Casserly, *Goldwater* (Doubleday, 1988), p. 387.
12. For a general discussion of this ideology, see Peter Steinfels, *The Neoconservatives* (Simon & Schuster, 1979). For a general text from this perspective, see Richard T. Saeger, *American Government and Politics: A Neoconservative Approach* (Scott, Foresman, 1982).

13. Ronald Reagan, Inaugural Address, 1981, *The Public Papers of the President of the United States: Ronald Reagan, 1981* (Government Printing Office, 1982), p. 1.
14. Kathleen Day, *S & L Hell: The People and the Politics Behind the $1 Trillion Savings and Loan Scandal* (W.W. Norton & Co., 1993).
15. See Edward A. Snyder, "The Effects of Higher Criminal Penalties on Antitrust Enforcement," *Journal of Law and Economics 33* (October 1990), pp. 439–62; also Brian Burrough and John Helyar, *Barbarians at the Gate: The Fall of RJR Nabisco* (Harper, 1990).
16. Dan Goodman, "Bleeding-Heart Conservatives," *Time,* May 18, 1992, p. 37.
17. Ronald Reagan, Address to the Nation on the Economy, February 5, 1981, *Public Papers of the Presidents: Ronald Reagan, 1981* (Government Printing Office, 1982), p. 81.
18. Sylvia Nassar, "Even among the Well-Off, the Rich Get Richer," *The New York Times,* March 5, 1992, p. A1.
19. Karl Marx, "Critique of the Gotha Program," in *Marx Selections,* ed. Allen W. Wood (Macmillan Publishing, 1988), p. 190.
20. Irving Howe, *Socialism and America* (Harcourt, 1985); Michael Harrington, *Socialism: Past and Future* (Arcade, 1989).
21. Eric R. A. N. Smith, *The Unchanging American Voter* (University of California Press, 1989), pp. 171–72.
22. Center for Political Studies, University of Michigan, *American National Election Study, 1990: Post Election Survey* (April 1991).
23. Herbert McClosky and Alida Brill, *Dimensions of Tolerance: What Americans Believe about Civil Liberties* (Russell Sage Foundation, 1983), pp. 274–75.
24. Dinesh D'Sousa, *Illiberal Education: The Politics of Race and Sex on Campus* (Free Press, 1991), p. 313.

▲ ▲ ▲

Review Questions

1. Define some of the key political beliefs of liberals.
2. Describe some of the different varieties of liberalism.
3. Define some of the key political beliefs of conservatives.
4. Define *New Right* and *neoconservative.*
5. Define some of the key political beliefs of socialists.
6. Define some of the key political beliefs of libertarians.

Discussion and Writing Suggestions

1. Where do you locate your own ideas on the political spectrum described by Burns, Peltason, Cronin, and Magleby? What particular issues are important to you, and what kinds of events, observations, and experiences have contributed to the forming of your own political attitudes?
2. Locate a recent editorial or op-ed piece in the newspaper and analyze its ideas and assertions according to the ideologies described by the authors. The editorial should be one that identifies a problem and recommends a means of dealing with the problem (or that attacks one solution to the problem as wrong-headed or ineffectual).
3. In a short essay, respond to Barry Goldwater's comments on welfare in paragraph 22. To what extent do you agree with the ideas he expresses? Why?

4. Can you detect a bias, on the part of the authors, toward (or against) one or more of the ideological viewpoints they are describing? If so, explain how what they say and the way they say it appear to indicate a leaning toward or an aversion to a particular set of political attitudes.
5. Write an editorial on one of the following issues from *either* the liberal, conservative (or if appropriate), socialist, or libertarian viewpoint: *affirmative action, immigration policy, abortion, education, drug policy, school prayer, federal aid to the arts.* For a more ambitious version of this assignment, write two editorials on the same issue, representing opposing viewpoints.
6. Write two or three paragraphs based on the material in the tables "We the People" and "How Americans Define Their Ideology." Do not merely repeat in sentence form the information contained in the tables; rather, draw on this information to support a *thesis* or *topic sentences* of your own.
7. Write two paragraph-length definitions of either "tolerance" or "intolerance"—one from the viewpoint of a staunch conservative, the other from the viewpoint of an equally staunch liberal. Use specific illustrations of your own to support the two general definitions. Then, in a third paragraph, explain what you think would be necessary for the liberal to accept the conservative's definition and vice versa.

Guides to the Political Conflicts

DONALD LAZERE

Is an article by Barbara Ehrenreich likely to be liberal or conservative? How about an unsigned editorial in The Nation*?* Reason*?* Mother Jones*? What kind of books does Praeger Press publish? Is* Newsweek *more liberal than* Time*? Before assessing a particular political statement, it's important to know where that statement is coming from. What is the background and affiliation of the author or authors? What are the political inclinations of the periodical in which the writer's work appears or of the publisher or organization that presents his or her work to the public? Anyone noddingly familiar with George Will expects to get the conservative slant on any subject he takes up. One who reads the* Progressive, *on the other hand, wants to get the liberal view of the subject.*

Some useful roadmaps to this complex political terrain are provided in the following selection by Donald Lazere. This piece originally appeared as a set of appendices to Lazere's "Teaching the Political Conflicts" in the May 1992 issue of College Composition and Communication, *a journal for writing professionals. (The appendices have been somewhat re-arranged in this version.) In addition to providing information on a wide variety of authors, periodicals, institutes, and publishers, Lazere includes a couple of rhetorical appendices (Sections Five and Six, as reprinted here) to help readers locate clues to political inclinations by noticing patterns of argument and language by which left and right may be distinguished. This selection, along with the one that follows by Cross, will provide a valuable set of tools by which you may analyze almost any political statement. Keep in mind, however, that Lazere's classifications are not absolute and that others might view things differently.*

Donald Lazere is a professor of English at California Polytechnic State University at San Luis Obispo. A member of the NCTE Committee on Public Doublespeak, his articles on literacy and culture have appeared in The Chronical of Higher Education, New Literary History, *and the* New York Times *and* Los Angeles Times *book review sections.*

[*Note:* In the listings below, column placements and indentations to the left or right indicate positioning along the political spectrum.]

SECTION ONE: AMERICAN MEDIA AND COMMENTATORS FROM LEFT TO RIGHT

Left			*Center*		*Right*
			Media		
People's World	*The Nation*	*Village Voice*	*NY Times*	*Time*	*New American*
The Guardian	*In These Times*	*LA Times*	*Wash. Post*	*US News &*	*Plain Truth*
	Mother Jones	*NY Review*	*Newsweek*	*World Report*	*Wash. Times*
	The Progressive	*Atlantic*	*New*	*Readers Digest*	*(Insight)*
	Z Magazine	*New Yorker*	*Republic*	*Wall St. Journal*	
	Tikkun	PBS	*Harper's*	*Commentary*	
	Pacifica Radio	documentaries	*Reason*	*American*	
	"60 Minutes"	NPR	CBS news	*Spectator*	
	McNeil-Lehrer [now		NBC,	Most newspapers,	
	"The News Hour		ABC news	local TV and radio	
	with Jim Lehrer"]			*National Review*	
				McLaughlin Group	

Commentators

Alexander Cockburn				
Edward Said	Gore Vidal	Michael Kinsley	George Will	Pat Buchanan
Noam Chomsky	Barbara Ehrenreich	Anthony Lewis	Chas. Krauthammer	Phyllis Schlafly
Edward Herman	Jesse Jackson	Tom Wicker	William Safire	Pat Robertson
	Todd Gitlin	Richard Reeves	Evans and Novak	Paul Harvey
	Robert Scheer	Bill Moyers	Henry Kissinger	Jerry Falwell
	Betty Friedan	Gloria Steinem	Irving Kristol	
	Stanley Aronowitz	Seymour Hersh	Norman Podhoretz	
	Molly Ivins	David Halberstam	Midge Decter	
	Irwin Knoll	Bob Woodward and	Jeane Kirkpatrick	
	James Weinstein	Carl Bernstein	William Buckley	
	Ralph Nader	Ted Koppel	Michael Novak	
	Victor Navasky	John K. Galbraith	Milton Friedman	
	Roger Wilkins		Thomas Sowell	
	Cornel West	Murray Rothbard (libertarian)		
		Douglas Bandow (libertarian)		

SECTION TWO: POLITICAL ORIENTATIONS OF PUBLISHERS AND FOUNDATIONS

Book Publishers

LIBERAL OR SOCIALIST
Pantheon
Monthly Review Press
South End Press
Praeger
Beacon Press
Seabury/Continuum Books
International Publishers
Pathfinder Press
Routledge
Methuen
Schocken
Bergin & Garvey

CONSERVATIVE OR LIBERTARIAN
Arlington House
Freedom House
Brandon Books
Reader's Digest Books
Greenhill Publishers
Laissez-Faire Books (Libertarian)
Paragon House

Research Institutes and Foundations

LIBERAL OR SOCIALIST
Institute for Policy Studies
Center for Responsive Law (Journal: *Public Citizen*)
Public Interest Research Groups
Common Cause (Journal: *Common Cause*)
Brookings Institute
Institute for Democratic Socialism (Journals: *Democratic Left, Socialist Forum*)
Center for the Study of Democratic Institutions (Journal: *New Perspectives Quarterly*)

CONSERVATIVE OR LIBERTARIAN
American Enterprise Institute (Journal: *Public Opinion*—not *Public Opinion Quarterly*)
Center for Strategic and International Studies
Hoover Institution (Stanford)
The Media Institute
Hudson Institute
Heritage Foundation (Journal: *Policy Review*)
Olin Foundation
Scaife Foundation
Cato Foundation (Libertarian: *Cato Journal*)

SECTION THREE: CURRENT GENERAL PERIODICALS

This is a partial list intended to supplement, not replace, the more accessible, mass circulation newspapers and magazines, most of which have a center-conservative to center-liberal orientation.

American Scholar	Quarterly	Left-conservative
American Spectator	Monthly	Center-to-left conservative
Atlantic Monthly	Monthly	Center-liberal
The Black Scholar	Quarterly	Socialist
Chronicles of Culture	Monthly	Left-conservative
Commentary	Monthly	Center-conservative
Commonweal	Biweekly	Left-liberal Catholic
Conservative Digest	Monthly	Center-to-right conservative
Dissent	Bimonthly	Socialist to center-liberal
Foreign Affairs	Quarterly	Center-conservative to right-liberal
The Guardian	Weekly	Socialist
Harper's	Monthly	Center-liberal to left-conservative
Human Events	Weekly	Center-to-right conservative
Insight (Washington Times)	Weekly	Center-to-right conservative

In These Times	Weekly	Socialist
Modern Age	Quarterly	Center-conservative
Mother Jones	Monthly	Socialist to left-liberal
Ms.	Monthly	Center to left-liberal
The Nation	Weekly	Socialist to left-liberal
National Review	Biweekly	Center-conservative
New American	Biweekly	Right-conservative (formerly *American Opinion*)
New Guard	Quarterly	Center-conservative
New Politics	Quarterly	Socialist
New Republic	Weekly	Right-liberal to left-conservative
New York Review of Books	Biweekly	Center-liberal
New York Sunday Times	Weekly	Center-liberal to left-conservative
New Yorker	Weekly	Left-to-center-liberal
People's World	Daily	Community Party USA
Progressive	Monthly	Socialist to left-liberal
Public Interest	Quarterly	Left-to-center-conservative
Public Opinion	Monthly	Center-conservative
Reason	Monthly	Conservative libertarian
Rolling Stone	Biweekly	Center-liberal
Social Policy	Bimonthly	Left-liberal
Socialist Review	Quarterly	Socialist
Tikkun	Bimonthly	Left-liberal
Utne Reader	Bimonthly	Digest of liberal journals
Village Voice	Weekly	Left-liberal
Washington Monthly	Monthly	Center-liberal to left-conservative
World Press Review	Monthly	Digest of diverse foreign viewpoints
Z Magazine	Monthly	Socialist

SECTION FOUR: A GLOSSARY OF POLITICAL TERMS AND POSITIONS

Left wing and right wing

"The left wing" (adjective: "left-wing" or "leftist") is a broad term that includes a diversity of parties and ideologies (which often disagree among themselves but usually agree in their opposition to the right wing) including liberals, nearest the center of the spectrum, and—progressively toward the left—socialists and communists (the latter two are also sometimes called "radical").

"The right wing" (adjective: "right-wing" or "rightest") is a broad term that includes a diversity of parties and ideologies (which often disagree among themselves but usually agree in their opposition to the left wing) including libertarians, nearest the center of the spectrum, and—progressively toward the right—conservatives, ultraconservatives, plutocrats, and fascists.

LEFTISTS TEND TO SUPPORT:	**RIGHTISTS TEND TO SUPPORT:**
The poor and working class	Middle and upper class
Labor, consumers, environmental and other controls over business	Business, management, unregulated enterprise
Equality (economic, racial, sexual)	Inequality (economic, racial, sexual)
Civil and personal liberties	Economic liberty; controls on personal liberties (e.g., sexual conduct, abortion, obscenity, drugs)

Cooperation	Competition
Internationalism	Nationalism (primary loyalty to one's own country)
Pacifism (exception: Communists)	Strong military and willingness to go to war
Questioning of authority—skepticism (exception: Communism is authoritarian)	Acceptance of authority, especially in military, police, and strong "law and order" policies
Government spending for public services like education, welfare, health care, unemployment insurance	Government spending for military, subsidies to business as incentive for profit and growth
Progressive taxes, i.e., greatest burden on wealthy individuals and corporations	Low taxes for wealthy individuals and corporations as incentive for investment ("supply-side economics" or "trickle-down theory")
Religious pluralism, skepticism, or atheism	Religious orthodoxy

Capitalism

An economic system based on private investment for profit. Jobs and public services are provided, and public needs met, to the extent that investment in them will predictably result in a return of capital outlay. In its principles capitalism does not provide any restrictions on extremes of wealth and poverty or of social power, but its advocates (especially pure, libertarian capitalists) believe that the workings of a free-market economy, unrestricted by government controls or regulation, will minimize social inequity.

Capitalism is not a political system; in principle, a capitalist economy can operate under either a democratic government or a dictatorship, as in plutocracy or fascism.

Socialism

An economic system based on public investment to meet public needs, provide full employment, and reduce socioeconomic inequality. In various models of socialism, investment and industrial management are controlled either by the federal government, local governments, workers' and consumers' cooperatives, a variety of community groups, etc.

Socialism is not a political system; in principle, a socialist economy can operate under either a democratic government or a dictatorship, as in Communism.

Communism

With lower-case "c": Marx's ideal of the ultimate, future form of pure democratic socialism, with virtually no need for centralized government.

With upper-case "C" as in present-day Communist Parties: A socialist economy under undemocratic government. Historically, Communists have manipulated appeals to left-wing values like socioeconomic equality and worldwide cooperation in order to impose police-state dictatorship and military aggression.

Plutocracy

Rule by the rich. A capitalist economy under undemocratic government.

Fascism

A combination of capitalist and socialist economies under an undemocratic government. Historically, fascists have manipulated appeals to conservative values like patriotism, religion, competitiveness, anti-communism, respect for authority and law and order, traditional morality and the family, in order to impose police-state dictatorship.

Fascism typically is aggressively militaristic and imperialistic, and promotes racial hatred based on theories of white (or "Pure Aryan") supremacy and religious persecution of non-Christians. It glorifies strong authority figures with absolute power.

Conservatives, Liberals, and Socialists in America

In the American context, conservatives are pro-capitalist. They believe the interests of business also serve the interests of labor, consumers, the environment, and the public in general—"What's good for General Motors is good for America." They believe that abuses by businesses can and should be best policed or regulated by business itself, and when conservatives control government, they usually appoint businesspeople to cabinet positions and regulatory agencies without perceiving any conflict of interest therein.

American liberals believe that the interests of business are frequently contrary to those of labor, consumers, the environment, and the public in general. So although they basically support capitalism, liberals think business abuses need to be policed by government regulatory agencies that are free from conflicts of interests, and that wealth should be limited.

American socialists, or radicals, believe even more strongly than liberals that the interests of business are contrary to the public interests; they believe that capitalism is basically an irrational and corrupt system where wealthy business interests inevitably gain control over government, foreign and military policy, the media, education, etc., and use the power of employment to keep the workforce and electorate under their control. They think liberal government reforms and attempts to regulate business are usually thwarted by the power of business lobbies, and that even sincere liberal reformers in government offices usually come from and represent the ethnocentric viewpoint of the upper classes. The socialist solution is to socialize at least the biggest national and international corporations, as well as the defense industry, and operate them on a nonprofit basis, and to place much higher taxes on the rich, so as to reduce the power of wealthy corporations and individuals.

SECTION FIVE: A SEMANTIC CALCULATOR FOR BIAS IN RHETORIC[1]

1. What is the author's vantagepoint, in terms of social class, wealth, occupation, ethnic group, political ideology, educational level, age, gender, etc.? Is that vantagepoint apt to color her/his attitudes on the issue under discussion? Does she/he have anything personally to gain from the position she/he is arguing for, any conflicts of interest or other reasons for special pleading?
2. What organized financial, political, ethnic, or other interests are backing the advocated position? Who stands to profit financially, politically, or otherwise from it?
3. Once you have determined the author's vantagepoint and/or the special interests being favored, look for signs of ethnocentrism, rationalization or wishful thinking, sentimentality, and other blocks to clear thinking, as well as the rhetorical fallacies of onesidedness, selective vision, or a double standard.
4. Look for the following semantic patterns reflecting the biases in No. 3:
   a. Playing up:
      (1) arguments favorable to his/her side,
      (2) arguments unfavorable to the other side.
   b. Playing down (or suppressing altogether):
      (1) arguments unfavorable to her/his side,
      (2) arguments favorable to the other side.
   c. Applying "clean" words (ones with positive connotations) to her/his side. Applying "dirty" words (ones with negative connotations) to the other.
   d. Assuming that the representatives of his/her side are trustworthy, truthful, and have no selfish motives, while assuming the opposite of the other side.
5. If you don't find strong signs of the above biases, that's a pretty good indication that the argument is a credible one.
6. If there *is* a large amount of one-sided rhetoric and semantic bias, that's a pretty good sign that the writer is not a very credible source. However, finding signs of the above biases does not in itself prove that the writer's arguments are fallacious. Don't fall into the *ad hominem* ("to the man") fallacy—evading the issue by attacking the character of the writer or speaker without refuting the substance of the argument itself. What the writer says may or may not be factual, regardless of the semantic biases. The point is not to let yourself be swayed by words alone, especially when

---

[1]This guide derives from Hugh Rank's ''Intensify-Downplay'' schema, various forms of which appear in Hugh Rank, *Persuasive Analysis: A Companion to Composition* (Park Forest: Counter-Propaganda Press, 1988) and *The Pitch* (Park Forest: Counterpropaganda Press, 1982) and Daniel Dietevich, ed. *Teaching About Doublespeak* (Reading, MA: Addison-Wesley, 1979).

you are inclined to wishful thinking on one side of the subject yourself. When you find these biases in other writers, *or in yourself,* that is a sign that you need to be extra careful to check the facts out with a variety of other sources and to find out what the arguments are on the other side of the issue.

SECTION SIX: PREDICTABLE PATTERNS OF POLITICAL RHETORIC

LEFTISTS WILL PLAY UP:	*RIGHTISTS WILL PLAY UP:*
Conservative ethnocentrism, wishful thinking, and sentimentality rationalizing the selfish interests of the middle and upper class and America abroad	Leftist "negative thinking," "sour grapes," anti-Americanism, and sentimentalizing of the lower classes and Third World rebellion
Right-wing bias in media and education	Left-wing bias in media and education
US military strengths, selfish interests of the military and defense industry; right-wing scare tactics about the Russians or other adversaries being ahead	Russians' or other adversaries' military strengths; manipulation of leftist "doves" by Communists et al.; left-wing scare tactics about nuclear war
Rip-offs of taxpayers' money by the rich; luxury and waste in private industry and the military	Rip-offs of taxpayers' money by the poor; luxury and waste by government bureaucrats; selfish interests and inefficiency of labor, teachers, students, etc.

▲ ▲ ▲

Discussion and Writing Suggestions

1. Locate an article on a subject of current political interest and analyze the rhetoric and language of the piece, using Lazere's last two appendices ("A Semantic Calculator for Bias in Rhetoric" and "Predictable Patterns of Political Rhetoric") as a guide. (You may also wish to refer to Burns, Peltason, Cronin, and Magleby's discussions of liberals, conservatives, etc., earlier in this chapter.) Discuss several different patterns of rhetoric and language that provide clear indications of the author's political ideology. Be alert for what Lazere calls "clean" and "dirty" words. Explain the extent to which you feel the author has been successful in composing a persuasive argument.
2. Using Lazere as a guide, locate two articles on a particular subject that represent opposite ends (or at least different points) of the political spectrum. *Compare and contrast* these essays. (For guidelines on comparison-contrast essays, see pages 136–37.)
3. Explain how some of the "Predictable Patterns of Political Rhetoric" in Section Six follow from the left- and right-wing ideas listed on pages 285–86 and from left- and right-wing ideas as discussed by Burns et al. in the previous selection. Based on the discussion of left and right in Burns et al. and Lazere, what else might the left and the right play up?

4. Compile an *annotated bibliography* of at least 10 items on a subject of current political interest, taking care to locate sources that may be arranged along the entire political spectrum, from right to left (or vice versa). Use Lazere's "Guides" to help you in your search. Check your handbook for annotated bibliography format. Document the source in MLA style.

   In the annotations, identify each author's political position, using clues from affiliation with a particular research institute, book publisher, journal of opinion, party, or organization, and—more importantly—from arguments she or he presents that exemplify Lazere's glossary terms and the particular patterns of political rhetoric in Sections Five and Six. Give enough quotations to support your identification. In cases where the author is not arguing from an identifiable position but only reporting facts, indicate which position the reported facts support, and explain how. (*Note:* some newspapers, magazines, etc., have an identifiable political viewpoint in general, in their news and op-ed orientation, but also attempt to present other views at least some of the time. For example, the *Los Angeles Times* is predominantly liberal, but often carries conservative op-ed columns, letters, etc. So you shouldn't assume that any article appearing in such a periodical will automatically have its predominant viewpoint; look for other identifying clues. [*Paragraph adapted from Lazere.*]

A Voter's Manual for the Political Parties and the Candidates

While the previous readings about ideological differences may be enlightening, they were written by (relatively polite) academics; and so they lack the spirit of partisanship and blood-lust that we're accustomed to getting from actual politicians who are either fighting to dislodge their opponents or struggling to hold on to the offices that they already have. The following selection is of the latter kind. It is excerpted from voter information pamphlets that were sent to registered California voters a few weeks in advance of two recent elections. While some of the issues are specific to California (e.g., the emphasis on illegal immigration), the majority have national significance.

The selection is divided into six parts, each part consisting of a statement of purpose for the political party in question and then two statements by candidates running for office in that party. The party and candidate statement have been arranged to form a political spectrum from left to right: Peace and Freedom, Green, Democratic, Republican, American Independent, Libertarian.

Peace and Freedom Party

The Peace and Freedom Party stands for democracy, ecology, feminism and socialism. We work for a world where cooperation replaces competition; where all people are well fed, clothed and housed; where all women and men have equal status; a world of freedom and peace where every community retains its cultural integrity and lives with others in harmony. Our vision includes:

- Self-determination for all nations and peoples.
- Conversion from a military to a peace economy.
- Social ownership and democratic management of industry and natural resources.
- Full employment with a shorter work week.
- End homelessness; abolish vagrancy laws; provide decent affordable housing for all.
- Quality health care, education and transportation.
- Free birth control; abortion on demand; no forced sterilization.
- Restore and protect clean air, water, land and ecosystems; develop renewable energy.
- End discrimination based on race, sex, sexual orientation, age or disability.
- Democratic elections through proportional representation.
- Defend and extend the Bill of Rights; oppose the phony drug war, legalize marijuana; decriminalize and treat drug use.
- Abolish the death penalty and laws against victimless acts.
- Tax the rich to meet human needs.

PEACE AND FREEDOM PARTY CANDIDATE FOR U.S. SENATOR
ELIZABETH CERVANTES BARRÓN

I was born and raised in Central Los Angeles. I grew up in a multi-ethnic, multi-cultural environment where I learned to respect those who were different from me. I joined the Peace and Freedom Party in 1968. I am a teacher and am aware of how cut-backs in education have affected our children and communities. Our children hold the key to our country's future. We must provide a safe environment and a decent education for our children. Money needs to be returned to schools so that all those who want an education can go as far as they want or are able. At this time the rich and powerful run the country. They are not interested in our needs. We must not let them divide us by race, class, religion, sex, sexual preference, citizenship, etc. We want an end to the scapegoating of immigrants. The fact is they pay more in taxes than they receive in services. The single payer health plan will give all of us medical service when we need it. Clean, non-contaminated air, water and food is something we are entitled to. Large corporations that have been polluting these resources need to be held accountable.

PEACE AND FREEDOM PARTY CANDIDATE FOR GOVERNOR
GLORIA ESTELE LA RIVA

Six million Californians have no healthcare, three million are unemployed. In the richest state, why are millions becoming poorer? Because the capitalist politicians, Republican and Democrat, run the state to enrich corporations and banks, at the expense of workers and poor people. The 1994–1995 state budget is a disaster: Assistance for the disabled, elderly, women and children will be cut; college fees will increase 10% while taxes for the rich are reduced. Workers create all the wealth, but the corporations reap huge profits. I say tax big business to provide jobs and services, and balance budget. Stop union-busting; we need unions. I oppose racist immigrant-bashing and Proposition 187. Immigrants must have equal rights, living wages. We must unite—all workers and poor people—to win jobs, housing, healthcare, childcare, education, environmental protections—not prisons. I oppose the death penalty and "Three Strikes" Proposition 184. I support proportional representation, and Health Care Proposition 186. No to racism, sexism, anti-gay bigotry. I oppose all U.S. interventions abroad. As a socialist, member of Peace and Freedom Party and Workers World Party, I am the only candidate who firmly defends the working class.

Green Party

- Social Justice
- Non Violence
- Decentralization
- Community-based Economics
- Personal and Global Responsibility
- Ecological Wisdom
- Respect for Diversity
- Sustainable Future Focus
- Post Patriarchal Values
- Grassroots Democracy

These are the ten key values of the GPCA, which is part of a global network of Green Parties existing in 73 countries and across the U.S.

We're a new party which has arisen in response to the need for a new political vision. We recognize that all life is interconnected, and dependent upon the natural systems of our world. Politics must reflect this reality, and political structures and processes must be based upon this concept if humanity is to survive.

We stand for policy development in the following areas:

- Social justice based on honoring diversity, self-determination and self-definition of all people
- Ecological stewardship of the Earth through personal responsibility and the teaching and practicing of sustainable methods of living

- Government reform to implement a multiparty, proportional representation system and serious campaign reform
- Development of a new political culture of participation with the goal of direct democracy
- Community-based economics to bring vitality to regional areas by decentralizing ownership and control of the economy

GREEN PARTY CANDIDATE FOR U.S. SENATOR
BARBARA BLONG

An educator and environmentalist, I am your candidate for hope, change and growth. The Green Party is founded on values of environmental and social justice, nonviolence, feminism and respect for diversity. These values frame our stand against the racist, hate-mongering Anti-Immigrant Initiative 187: *Greens Say No!* The Three-Strikes Initiative attacks the symptoms of crime, not its causes: *Greens Say No!* Instead of focusing resources on punitive measures, we must care for ourselves and our society by supporting the *Single Payer Health Plan,* restoring our education system to excellence, and respectfully nurturing the well-being of all. I'll introduce a Full Employment Bill, locally administered, making environmental, creative, healing jobs available to everyone. I'll advocate non-violent resolution of conflict and re-consideration of NAFTA/GATT—free trade should not cost American jobs or weaken environmental laws. Disgusted with outrageously expensive, negative campaigning? I'll introduce electoral reforms to promote issue-based campaigns. As we transform our relations with each other and with the earth from dominance and exploitation to partnership, we begin healing our society and our planet. Vote for me as you next U.S. Senator—a caring, feminist representative for *all* the people!

GREEN PARTY CANDIDATE FOR LIEUTENANT GOVERNOR
DANIEL MOSES

The Green Party calls for a new definition of "progress," one based on qualitative factors like healthy cities, environmental justice, sustainability, ecological restoration, and nonviolence. Help us change the current political agenda that mistakenly promotes corporate growth as the answer to all economic problems. Without ecology there's no economy. The following major duties of the Lt. Governor would benefit from a Green perspective: (1) Chairing the Economic Development Commission—increase emphasis on community-based economics (keeping money circulating within communities), including start-up help for nonprofit community-development corporations, profit-sharing or employee-owned businesses, cooperatives, protection of credit unions, farmers' markets; support for organic agriculture. (2) Serving on the State Lands Commission—shift toward preserving "ecosystem integrity" of our public lands; protect entire California coast from further gas and oil drilling (while pushing renewable energy and efficiency). (3) Serving on U.C. Board of Regents and C.S.U. Board of Trustees—stop fee hikes; trim administrative budget fat; democratize selection of regents; encourage curriculum changes to include ecoliteracy, critical thinking skills, respect for diversity, and nonviolence. Only truthfulness, love, and nonviolence can foster a better California.

Democratic Party

We believe in putting people first. We want your support.

After twelve years of Reagan-Bush-Quayle, the basic assumptions of America are under threat:

- The ability to support your family if you work hard;
- The access to medical help if your children get sick;
- The expectation that, when you send your children to school, they will be given the best education;
- The right to live in neighborhoods that are free of violence, crime and drugs;
- The confidence to know that our government respects our privacy, civil liberties, and individual lifestyle and choice; and
- The knowledge that the air we breathe, the water we drink, and the planet on which we live, are safe.

We believe that you deserve a government that will fight on your behalf to see that these basics of the American dream are restored.

We believe that politics is about making people's lives better, not about getting re-elected by smearing your opponents and by dividing us by race or by income.

The 1992 Democratic ticket—Bill Clinton and Al Gore, Dianne Feinstein, Barbara Boxer, and our local Democratic candidates—need your help to restore the American dream.

DEMOCRATIC PARTY CANDIDATE FOR U.S. SENATOR
DIANNE FEINSTEIN

Elected as California's senior Senator in 1992, I've been an independent voice working hard to break gridlock in Washington and make a difference on issues that affect all Californians. As a new member of the Senate Judiciary Committee, I fought for and the Senate passed the strongest crime bill in history, making more than 50 federal crimes death penalty offenses and putting 100,000 more police officers on our streets. I sponsored zero-tolerance legislation to rid our schools of guns. As a member of the Appropriations Committee, I fought for $8.6 billion in earthquake aid and funds to hire 1,300 new border patrol agents. We passed a deficit reduction plan, cutting the deficit three years in a row for the first time since Truman, that helped lower interest rates, gave tax incentives to 90% of small businesses and created 3 million jobs nationally. But more is needed. That's why I authored a program for small business to create 100,000 new jobs. I'm proud of what I've been able to accomplish for California in my first year, but much more needs to be done: to reduce violence, create jobs, stop illegal immigration and improve education—my top priorities as a Senator.

DEMOCRATIC PARTY CANDIDATE FOR GOVERNOR
KATHLEEN BROWN

For generations, families came to California for the promise of good jobs, affordable homes, quality schools, and safe neighborhoods. But today, California has broken its promise to middle-class families. Year after year, state government has mismanaged our budget and wasted our tax dollars—then forced California families to pay the price. Middle-class families were hit by a 7 billion dollar tax hike and massive takeaways of family services like sheriff and fire protection, libraries, parks and hospitals. All this while California families lost 550,000 jobs. As Governor, I'll be a tough money manager strengthening our economy by cutting bureaucracy, overhauling welfare, and eliminating our 3 billion dollar budget deficit. By investing in our schools and making colleges affordable, I'll halt the decline of our education system. With more cops on the street, an assault weapons ban, boot camps for juvenile lawbreakers, and enforcement of the death penalty, I'll help make our neighborhoods safe for families again. And my economic plan will create one million private sector jobs for middle-class families. Only tough management can rebuild our economy and restore the California promise for middle-class families.

Republican Party

As the nation enjoys a continued era of unprecedented prominence, it is clear the application of Republican policies and principles has reaped untold benefits for the nation and the world.

The Republican Party has dedicated itself to strengthening the nation's economy, and providing the social stability that comes with strong, decisive leadership.

The Republican Party supports freedom for the individual at home, while calling upon the world to reject tyranny and accept democracy. As freedom rings throughout the globe, there is no doubt that the Republican philosophy of "peace through strength" has resulted in the expansion of democracy to Eastern Europe, Central America and around the world.

The Republican Party is dedicated to equality and fairness for all Americans, and rejects the quotas and set-asides that discriminate against all individuals regardless of race or gender.

The Republican Party is also dedicated to a lawful society, and believes that leaders must have the courage to ensure public safety and maintain public order. And Republicans believe that both criminals *and* victims must be guaranteed rights under the law.

The Republican message of hope, opportunity and prosperity: a message that will successfully lead our nation into the 21st century.

REPUBLICAN PARTY CANDIDATE FOR U.S. SENATOR
MICHAEL HUFFINGTON

My career has been spent in business—not politics. I view public service as a way to help people, not as a profession. If you elect me, here's my Contract with you and the people of California. 1. I will not become a career politician. I will serve only two terms in office. 2. I will accept no campaign contributions from special interests. 3. I will vote to cut spending, taxes, and eliminate the budget deficit by working for a constitutional amendment to balance the budget. Above all, I'll be an independent voice for California—for tough laws on criminals, welfare reform, smaller government, lower taxes, good jobs, and those values which strengthen individuals and families, not government. Together, we'll finally restore common sense to government.

INCUMBENT, REPUBLICAN PARTY CANDIDATE FOR GOVERNOR
PETE WILSON

Together, we've survived tough times in California—fires, earthquakes, global recession and massive defense cuts. But despite tough times, we've made important, needed change to make California healthy again. I've signed America's toughest "Three Strikes, You're Out" law to remove career criminals from our streets and implemented California's death penalty for the first time in 25 years. I slashed red tape to rebuild earthquake-damaged freeways in record time and created thousands of new jobs for our workers. I've sued Washington to control illegal immigration and sent the National Guard to back up the Border Patrol. And I launched welfare reform, saving taxpayers $2.2 billion. The working people of California—who work hard, pay their taxes, and raise their children to obey the law—deserve a break. You deserve lower taxes and less government—with able-bodied adults off welfare, working, earning self-respect. You deserve to choose your child's school—safe from drugs, guns and gangs. You deserve an end to illegal immigration that's overwhelming our state. With strong leadership we can beat tough times. I ask your support to continue making the change California must make to be safe, prosperous and fair.

American Independent Party

The American Independent Party stands for government of the people, by the people and for the people. We reaffirm the principle of individual rights upon which our nation was founded; that all people have, inherent in their being, an inalienable right to life, liberty and the pursuit of their own interests.

A primary function of the government is the safeguarding of these rights. History reveals, however, that governments generally have failed in their obligations, becoming themselves the major violators of individual rights. Therefore, the American Independent Party is strongly committed to the principle that government's powers must be carefully divided and limited.

American Independent positions on the issues reflect the common sense thinking of the American people:

- Honest, representative Government!
- Tax relief for *all* Americans!
- Preservation of traditional values and respect for life!
- Safe streets and neighborhoods!
- A halt to illegal immigration!
- An end to Foreign aid—Let's take care of America first!
- Trade policies that are fair for American industry and American workers!
- Protection of rights and benefits for veterans and senior citizens!
- Preservation of rights guaranteed by the Second Amendment!

AMERICAN INDEPENDENT PARTY CANDIDATE FOR GOVERNOR
JEROME (JERRY) McCREADY

As a self-employed businessman, I have learned firsthand what it is like to try to make ends meet in an unstable economy being manipulated by out of touch politicians. I know it is impossible to create utopia here in our state overnight; however, when given the opportunity, I will show you how free citizens can take our state back with the most powerful weapon we have, our vote. I believe we all need to pay an equal amount of taxes and we have a right to expect an equal amount of services and total accountability from elected servants. I am pro-life, pro-second amendment, pro-death penalty, for tougher penalties for serious juvenile offenders, for boot camp and work farms for non-violent offenders, less spending on prisons, and less government involvement in education and our daily lives! I believe the Federal government should enforce immigration laws already in existence; if they can't or won't, then the state should step in and take whatever steps are needed to protect the lives, rights, and property of free legal citizens!

AMERICAN INDEPENDENT PARTY CANDIDATE FOR LIEUTENANT GOVERNOR
ROBERT LEWIS

Californians, when headlines read "Assembly OK's Sham Budget, Legislators Refuse $5 Billion Shortfall, State to Borrow from Foreign Banks and Lawmakers Granted 37 Percent Pay Raise," why keep voting the same way? My primary statement gave alarm about unbalanced budgets, uncontrolled debt and how government seeks to abdicate its voter "accountability." This Tuesday—November 8th, you can again vote for a Lieutenant

Governor pledged to "see no evil" in the Legislature, "hear no evil" about corruption and "speak no evil" about money, the "golden calf" that has purchased the "allegiance" of career hacks. Or you can vote a candidacy based on the petitions of Independents—American Independents throughout California, and not money. You can remake this Ceremonial Officer Lieutenant Governor into the "independent conscience" of the Executive Branch, not another hack beholden to the *"golden calf"*!

Libertarian Party

We, the members of the Libertarian Party, challenge the cult of the omnipotent state and defend the rights of the individual.

We hold that all individuals have the right to exercise sole dominion over their own lives, and have the right to live in whatever manner they choose, so long as they do not forcibly interfere with the equal right of others to live in whatever manner they choose.

Governments throughout history have regularly operated on the opposite principle, that the State has the right to dispose of the lives of individuals and the fruits of their labor. Even within the United States, all political parties other than our own grant to government the right to regulate the lives of individuals and seize the fruits of their labor without their consent.

We, on the contrary, deny the right of any government to do these things, and hold that where governments exist, they must not violate the rights of any individual: namely (1) the right to life—accordingly we support the prohibition of the initiation of physical force against others; (2) the right to liberty of speech and action—accordingly we oppose all attempts by government to abridge the freedom of speech and press, as well as government censorship in any form; and (3) the right to property—accordingly we oppose all government interference with private property, such as confiscation, nationalization, and eminent domain, and support the prohibition of robbery, trespass, fraud, and misrepresentation.

Since governments, when instituted, must not violate individual rights, we oppose all interference by government in the areas of voluntary and contractual relations among individuals. People should not be forced to sacrifice their lives and property for the benefit of others. They should be left free by government to deal with one another as free traders; and the resultant economic system, the only one compatible with the protection of individual rights, is the free market.

LIBERTARIAN PARTY CANDIDATE FOR U.S. SENATOR
RICHARD BENJAMIN BODDIE

Voting for Richard Boddie (say "body") and other Libertarians is not a wasted vote. You should vote for the candidate you agree with. Voting is not a horse race. Your vote sends a message to incumbents that you aren't happy with the way they're running things. I believe strongly in individual rights, the free market, very limited government, and tolerance. It's time to really clean house in Washington, and you must know by now that the establishment parties have no desire to do it. I'll work to repeal the federal income tax and abolish the IRS. We must end the destructive War on Drugs and re-legalize drugs like they were before 1914. I oppose U.S. military intervention abroad and will work to bring our troops home. I strongly oppose Clinton's health care plan, which will destroy our liberties and nationalize one-seventh of the nation's economy. I support the right of Americans to keep and bear arms for self-defense. The federal government must not be allowed to commit criminal acts against our people. I call for the prosecution of Janet Reno and other government officials for the mass murder of Branch Davidians at Waco.

LIBERTARIAN PARTY CANDIDATE FOR LIEUTENANT GOVERNOR
BOB NEW

I am a small business owner who has seen Democratic and Republican politicians alike wreck California's economy and crush our personal liberties. I will use the position of Lt. Governor as a forum to promote less government and more personal responsibility. I will work to: repeal the state income tax; deregulate the economy by eliminating all state agencies that stifle the free market; privatize public services (private companies provide more efficient and economic services than government agencies do); slash crime by ending the failed War on Drugs and re-legalizing drugs as they once were; provide tax credits to parents who home school or send their kinds to private schools; repeal paternalistic safety regulations like seat belt and motorcycle helmet laws; end welfare for everyone, not just illegal immigrants; and strongly defend our 2nd Amendment right to keep and bear arms for self-defense. The Libertarian Party platform calls for abolishing the office of Lt. Governor, an official who waits around for the Governor to die. Seven states (including Oregon and Arizona) don't have such an unnecessary position, and they are getting along just fine. Eliminating this office will save taxpayers $1.5 million per year.

▲ ▲ ▲

Review Questions

1. Summarize in one to two pages the main ideological positions of each of the party statements of purpose.
2. How have some of the political candidates made an appeal based on *ethos*—that is, an appeal based partly on their own credentials and characters?

Discussion and Writing Suggestions

1. How useful do these statements seem to you in providing information to voters?
2. To what extent do the range of the positions represented in these statements illustrate the ideological divisions discussed by Smith (see

especially, paragraphs 8 and 9), Burns et al., and Lazere in their passages? Provide illustrations to support your opinions.

3. Which candidate and which party most represent the direction that you think the nation ought to take? Which proposals do you find most appealing? Most objectionable? Explain your conclusions as specifically as possible.
4. How do the Democratic candidates for senator and governor line up with the traditional liberal positions, as described by Burns et al. and Lazere? How do they diverge from the traditional liberal positions? *Or,* respond to the same question about the Republican candidates.
5. On what issues do Democratic and Republican candidates appear to agree? How do you account for these agreements among the rival mainstream parties? On what issues do they disagree?
6. What are the main ways in which the non-mainstream parties (Green, Peace and Freedom, American Independent, Libertarian) differ from the mainstream (Democratic and Republican) parties? In what ways do the non-mainstream parties from left and right *resemble* one another? In what ways do they most *differ?*
7. Write an analysis of the ways in which the parties and the candidates make skillful use of *language* to persuade voters to their points of view. Focus particularly on emotionally charged (connotative) words and phrases (what Lazere calls "clean" and "dirty" words), as well as on what Donna Cross ("Politics: The Art of Bamboozling") calls *glittering generalities*—that is, phrases that are "seductive and appealing" but that have "no specific, definable meaning."
8. Imagine a United States whose president and Congress were controlled by one of the non-mainstream parties. Write a short story or section of a screenplay dramatizing some national crisis in this new order. Perhaps a dissident group has decided to challenge the establishment, and the government must deal with the situation. The story or sequence could be written from the point of view of the government or of the rebels (or both).

Politics: The Art of Bamboozling

DONNA WOOLFOLK CROSS

In 1969, a book by Joe McGinnis called The Selling of the President, 1968 *garnered much attention through its detailed revelations of how Presidential candidates Richard Nixon and Hubert Humphrey were "packaged" and sold to the public like so much soap. Although it's true that the techniques of political salesmanship have become increasingly sophisticated in the age of mass media, it's also true that politicians and would-be officeholders of all kinds (and their supporters) have been selling themselves to their constituents since time immemorial. Their main goal, of course, is to make themselves seem as appealing as possible and their opponents as unappealing as possible—or to make it sound as if the Republic will be saved if they are elected or irretrievably lost if their opponents are voted in. How do they do this (they ponder), especially since (as most of the public suspects) it seldom makes any difference* who *wins. Their usual technique is to practice bamboozling which, according to Donna Cross, is a set of propaganda techniques by which the truth may be stretched, if not actually broken.*

It is important to acknowledge that politicians and political writers are not necessarily liars: generally, they sincerely believe that their ideas and programs are better for their constituents than are those of their opponents. It is only natural that they would try to make their position sound as appealing as possible. But if politicians are salespeople and voters are customers, then the old adage of caveat emptor*—buyer beware—applies in both cases. And buyers can best beware by making themselves knowledgeable about the rhetorical techniques used to sway them. To this end, you will find Donna Cross's article invaluable; it provides a set of tools for the analysis of political rhetoric in this chapter (and in the selections on welfare in Chapter Four), as well as in your own research.*

Donna Cross, author of Word Abuse, *teaches at Onondaga Community College in Syracuse, New York.*

> Political language . . . is designed to make lie sound truthful and murder respectable, and to give an appearance of solidity to pure wind.
>
> *George Orwell*

Propaganda. How do we feel about it? If an opinion poll were taken tomorrow, nearly everyone would be against it. For one thing it *sounds* so bad. "Oh, that's just propaganda" means, to most people, "That's a pack of lies." 1

But propaganda doesn't have to be untrue—nor does it have to be the devil's tool. It can be used for good causes as well as for bad—to persuade people to give to charity, for example, or to love their neighbors, or to stop polluting the environment, or to treat the English language with more respect. 2

The real problem with propaganda is not the end it's used for, but the means it uses to achieve the end. Propaganda works by tricking us, by momentarily distracting the eye while the rabbit pops out from beneath the cloth. This is why propaganda always works best with an uncritical audience, one that will not stop to challenge or question. Most of us are bamboozled, at one time or another, because we simply don't recognize propaganda when we see it. 3

Here are some of the more common pitfalls for the unwary: 4

Name-calling is an obvious tactic but still amazingly effective. It's just what you would expect it to be—calling people names. The idea is to arouse our contempt so that we'll dismiss the "bad name" person or idea without examining the merits. 5

The old saw "Sticks and stones may break my bones but names will never hurt me" has always been nonsense. Names *do* hurt, and badly, as any child who has been called one can tell you. Name-calling can be devastating to a child's psychological development. 6

Bad names may wreak havoc with a child's ego, but they're even more dangerous when they're used against political opponents, policies, or belief. During the vice-presidential debates, when Senator Robert Dole denounced Senator Walter Mondale as "probably the most liberal Senator in the entire U.S. Senate," he wanted conservatives to react blindly, emotionally to the "liberal" label without stopping to consider Mondale's ideas. Name-calling is at work whenever a candidate for office is described as a "foolish idealist" or an incumbent's policies are denounced as "reckless," "reactionary," or just plain "stupid." Some of the most effective names a public figure may be called don't really mean anything at all: "Congresswoman Jane Doe is a *bleeding heart"* or "The Senator is a *tool of the military-industrial complex!"* 7

A variation of name-calling is **argumentum ad hominem,** which tries to discredit a particular issue or idea by attacking a person who supports it. For example, one of Phyllis Schlafly's supporters recently said that she was against the Equal Rights Amendment because "the women who support it are either fanatics or lesbians or frustrated old maids." Aside from the fact that the statistical probability of this being true is nil, it is also specious reasoning. The Equal Rights Amendment should be judged on its merits, not the alleged "personal problems" of its supporters. The fact that Alexander Hamilton was a bastard foreigner born to unmarried parents outside the continental limits of the United States does not reflect on the American Revolution nor on his policies as Secretary of the Treasury. And the fact that Thomas Jefferson had a black mistress who bore him several children does not diminish the eloquence of the Declaration of Independence. Issues are different from the people who support them, and deserve to be judged on their own merits. 8

Name-calling and *argumentum ad hominem* are sometimes done with style. In the nineteenth-century when Lord John Russell became leader of the House of Commons, Disraeli remarked, "Now man may well begin to comprehend how the Egyptians worshipped an insect." But the best practitioner of name-calling in recent times was Winston Churchill. He once described fellow statesman Clement Attlee as "a modest man with much to be modest about," and, on another occasion, as "a sheep in sheep's clothing." Of political rival Stanley Baldwin, Churchill remarked, "He occasionally stumbles over the truth, but he always hastily picks himself up and hurries on as if nothing had happened." He punctured an arrogant political rival by 9 murmuring as the man left the room, "There, but for the grace of God, goes God."

Where name-calling tries to get us to *reject* or *condemn* someone or something without examining the evidence, the **glittering generality** tries to get us to *accept* and *agree* without examining the evidence. The Institute for Propaganda Analysis calls glittering generalities "virtue words," and adds that every society has certain "virtue words" it feels deeply about. "Justice," "Motherhood," "The American Way," "Our Constitutional Rights," "Our Christian Heritage," are words many people in our society believe in, live by—and are willing to die for. "Let us fight to preserve our American Birthright!" cries the Congressman, and the crowd roars its approval. We might not be in favor of war, but who wants to go on record as being opposed to our "American Birthright"? 10

Glittering generalities have extraordinary power to move men. Condorcet, the great French leader, went to the guillotine for "Liberty, Equality, Fraternity!" He might not have gone so willingly had he known that the French Revolution was fought to establish the predominance of the bourgeoisie over the aristocracies, of the new-emerging capitalism over the surviving remnants of feudalism. Can anyone imagine Condorcet or any of the others like him giving up their lives for a cause stated in such terms? The struggle had to represent itself to men in glorious ringing terms to win their hearts and minds. 11

A glittering generality is very seductive and appealing, but when you open it up and look inside, it is usually empty. There is no specific, definable meaning. If you doubt that, try getting definitions from a dozen people and discover for yourself how widely the interpretations differ. Just what parts of the American society and culture does our "American Birthright" include? The Bill of Rights? The free enterprise system? The democratic process? The rights of citizens to bear arms? The rights of oil companies to fix prices? The rights of coal companies to strip the land? The rights of women to terminate their pregnancies? The rights of gays to equal employment? The rights of the government to limit these rights? All of the above? 12

These glittering generalities are slippery creatures, all right. They can slide into almost any meaning. "We demand justice," say the workers, who mean that they want more money and the right to join a union. "*We* want justice" say the owners, who mean that they want the right to fire any worker who demands more money or the right to join a union. 13

In his Inaugural Address, President Carter announced the beginning of a "New Spirit" in the land, and asked us to dedicate ourselves to that spirit. What exactly is this "New Spirit" that he proclaimed? Where can one go to find it—much less dedicate one's self to it? Earlier, Carter also said, "We can have an American President who does not govern with negativism and fear of the future, but with vigor and vision and aggressive leadership—a President who is not isolated from our people, but who feels your pain and shares your dreams, and takes his strength and wisdom and courage from you." Well, we're all in favor of that. Clearly, then-President Gerald Ford 14 would have heartily endorsed the very same sentiments. He was, after all, not running on a platform that promised he would be isolated from the people, ignore their pain and laugh at their dreams, or take from them only their weakness, ignorance, and cowardice.

In his satirical book, *Our Gang,* Philip Roth has President "Trick E. 15
Dixon" defend his decision to go to war with Denmark because of the eleventh-century "expansionist policies" of Eric the Red, which, President Dixon says, clearly are in "direct violation of the Monroe Doctrine." The speech is a perfect example of how glittering generalities can be used to support any course of action, no matter how inane:

> I am certain . . . that the great majority of Americans will agree that the actions I have taken in the confrontation between the United States of America and the sovereign state of Denmark are indispensable to our dignity, our honor, our moral and spiritual idealism, our credibility around the world, the soundness of the economy, our greatness, our dedication to the vision of our forefathers, the human spirit, the divinely inspired dignity of man, our treaty commitments, the principles of the United Nations, and progress and peace for all people.
>
> Now no one is more aware than I am of the political consequences of taking bold and forthright action in behalf of our dignity, idealism and honor, to choose just three. But I would rather be a one-term President and take these noble, heroic measures against the state of Denmark, than be a two-term President by accepting humiliation at the hand of a tenth-rate military power. I want to make that perfectly clear.[1]

There are times when fiction pales before reality. Trick E. Dixon's speech bears a startling resemblance to Richard M. Nixon's speech on August 23, 1972, the day he accepted the Republican nomination for president the second time. Here is how he defended his policy of continuing the war in Vietnam:

> Let us reject . . . the policies of those who whine and whimper about our frustrations and call on us to turn inward. Let us not turn away from greatness. . . . With faith in God and faith in ourselves and faith in our country, let us have the vision and the courage to seize the moment and meet the challenge before it slips away.
>
> On your television screens last night, you saw the cemetery in Leningrad I visited on my trip to the Soviet Union where 300,000 people died . . . during World War II. At the cemetery I saw the picture of a 12-year-old girl. She was a beautiful child. Her name was Tanya. I read her diary. It tells the terrible story of war. In the simple words of a child, she wrote of the deaths of the members of her family—Senya in December, Granny in January, then Yenka, then Uncle Basha, then Uncle Leosha, then Mama in May.
>
> And finally, these were the words in her diary: "All are dead, only Tanya is left."
>
> Let us think of Tanya and of the other Tanyas and their brothers and sisters everywhere in Russia and in China and in America as we proudly meet

[1]Philip Roth, *Our Gang* (New York: Random House, 1971).

our responsibilities for leadership in the world in a way worthy of a great people.

I ask you, my fellow Americans, to join . . . in achieving a hope that mankind has had since the beginning of civilization.

Let us build a peace that our children and all the children of the world can enjoy for generations to come.

Tanya, touching as she is, has absolutely no relationship whatever to our former policy in Vietnam. But that doesn't matter. When it comes to politics, all that glitters is just gabble.

Both name-calling and glittering generalities work by stirring emotions to befog thinking. Another approach is to create a distraction, a **red herring** that will divert people's attention from the real issues. There are several different kinds of red herrings that can be used effectively. Most effective is the *plain folks* appeal. This is the verbal stratagem by which a speaker tries to win confidence and support by appearing to be "just one of the plain folks." "Wal, now, y'know I've been a farm boy all my life," says the millionaire cattle rancher to the crowd in Dallas. The same man speaking to a luncheon of Wall Street bankers might be heard saying, "Now, you know, I'm a businessman just like yourselves." Plain folks is a favorite on the campaign trail, a proven vote-getter, which is why so many candidates go around pumping factory workers' hands, kissing babies in supermarkets, and sampling pasta with Italians, fried chicken with Southerners, bagels and blintzes with Jews. 16

Crowds love plain folks talk. When, during the Watergate hearings, Senator Sam Ervin remarked, "Well, I'm sorry Senator Gurney does not approve of my method of examining the witness. I'm an old country lawyer, and I don't know the finer ways to do it," the audience went wild and it took five minutes to restore order in the room. Obviously, the people must not have been aware of Lyndon Johnson's famous quip that "Whenever I hear someone say, 'I'm just an old country lawyer,' the first thing I reach for is my wallet to make sure it's still there." 17

In the 1978 South Carolina Senate race, Strom Thurmond's main campaign document was a leaflet of "Family Recipes." "Estill pumpkin bread" and "Orangeburg hand cookies" won an easy victory over Democratic opponent Charles Ravenel, whose family boasted no such "down-home" cooking. 18

Anybody can get into the plain folks act with no trouble at all: 19

I understand only too well that a world-wide distance separates Roosevelt's ideas and my ideas. Roosevelt comes from a rich family and belongs to the class whose path is smoothed. . . . I was only the child of a small, poor family and had to fight my way by work and industry. When the Great War came Roosevelt occupied a position where he got to know only its pleasant consequences, enjoyed by those who do business while others bleed. I was only one of those who carried out orders as an ordinary soldier, and naturally returned from the war just as poor as I was in the autumn of 1914. I shared the fate of millions, and Franklin Roosevelt only the fate of the so-called Upper

> Ten Thousand. . . . After the war, Roosevelt tried his hand at financial speculations. He made profits out of inflation, out of the misery of others, while I . . . lay in a hospital. . . .

That's Adolf Hitler speaking to the Reichstag after Germany declared war on America in 1941.

20 Another interesting red herring is *argumentum ad populum,* more popularly known as *stroking.* We all like to be liked, so it stands to reason that we will get nice, warm feelings about anybody who "strokes" or compliments us. It's nice to hear that we are "hardworking taxpayers" or "the most generous, free-spirited nation in the world." Farmers are told they are the "backbone of the American economy" and college students are hailed as the "leaders and policymakers of tomorrow." A truly gifted practitioner of *argumentum ad populum* can manage to stroke several different groups of people in the same breath. Here is how Philip Roth's Trick E. Dixon, in a speech that evokes memories of the famed "Checkers" television address, manages to cover as many bases as possible:

> When I was a young, struggling lawyer, and Pitter [his wife] and I were living on nine dollars a week out in Prissier, California . . . I would read through my lawbooks and study long into the night in order to help my clients, most of whom were wonderful young people. . . . At that time, by the way, I had the following debts outstanding:
>
> —$1,000 on our neat little house
> 200 to my dear parents
> 110 to my loyal and devoted brother
> 15 to our fine dentist, a warmhearted Jewish man for whom we had the greatest respect
> 4.35 to our kindly grocer, an old Italian who always had a good word for everybody. I still remember his name. Tony.
> 5 cents to our Chinese laundryman, a slightly-built fellow who nonetheless worked long into the night over his shirts, just as I did over my lawbooks, so that his children might one day attend the college of their choice. I am sure they have grown up to be fine and outstanding Chinese-Americans.
> 60 cents to the Polish man, or polack, as the Vice-President would affectionately call him, who delivered the ice for our oldfashioned icebox. He was a strong man, with great pride in his native Poland.
>
> We also owed monies amounting to $2.90 to a wonderful Irish plumber, a wonderful Japanese-American handyman and a wonderful couple from the deep South who happened to be of the same race as we were, and whose children played with ours in perfect harmony, despite the fact that they were from another region.[2]

[2]Philip Roth, *Our Gang* (New York: Random House, 1971).

A piquant variation of the stroking appeal is the "personal" letter which uses a computer to insert the recipient's name mechanically. The recipient is supposed to feel that the sender is saying all those nice things about him personally. Here's an interesting example: 21

> Dear Mr. Hudgins:
>
> The American Historical Society has created a flag in your honor. This flag commemorates the American Bicentennial and your Hudgins family name. Our research indicates that you are an affluent and achieving American family. You contribute to our society and pull your weight. . . . You are a winner. . . . You should see your Hudgins flag. We feel this flag finally gives your great name of Hudgins the recognition it so richly deserves. . . .

Presumably, the same compliments are being sent to people all over the United States. ("You should see your Kronkheit flag . . ." and "We feel this flag finally gives your great name of Ballsworth the recognition it so richly deserves.")

These advertise-by-mail manufacturers accurately pitch their sales to the political and emotional makeup of the consumer. They do it by studying the profiles of the kind of people who read *Ladies' Home Journal* or *Reader's Digest* or *Ms.* magazines or whatever subscription list they get the recipient's name from. Here's an example of a "stroking appeal" I recently received: 22

> Dear Mrs. Cross,
>
> Frankly, you're someone magazines such as *Harper's, The New Yorker* and *Time* want as a subscriber. Judging from your neighborhood, you're far above average in means, intellect, and influence among those in the Syracuse and nearby areas.
>
> . . . And when you think about it, Mrs. Cross, in just an hour or two a week, this is the most respected source for a busy intelligent person like yourself to keep informed on the events and ideas that affect our lives. . . .

There's something unsettling about having a computer say all those nice things about me. I'd invite him (it?) for dinner, but my stuffed cabbage might gum up his (its?) gears. Of course, all those flattering assumptions about my neighborhood, my income, my intellect, and my influence are machine-tooled and calculated to stroke me into a mood of warm acceptance. Not just me, obviously, but everyone else winnowed out from those all-knowing mailing lists as the kind who will be most susceptible to this particular sales pitch.

Another device that almost everyone is susceptible to is the transfer device, also known as *guilt or glory by association.* In glory by association, the propagandist tries to "transfer" the positive feeling of something we love and respect over to the idea he wants us to accept. "Abraham Lincoln and Thomas Jefferson would have been proud of the Supreme Court decision to support school busing" is glory by association. 23

The process works equally well in reverse, when guilt by association is used to transfer dislike or disapproval of one thing to an idea or group that the propagandist wants us to reject. "John Doe says we need to make some 24 changes in the way our government operates. That's exactly what the Symbionese Liberation Army wants!" There's no logical connection between John Doe and the Symbionese Liberation Army apart from the one the propagandist is trying to create in our minds.

In a recent issue of *American Opinion* magazine, columnist Gary Allen comes out in favor of censorship of school text-books, saying, 25

> Parents have been asked to pay and pay, but are told to leave the education of their children "to the experts. . . ." Adolf Hitler had his experts, often brilliant scholars with impressive degrees after their names, who prescribed curricula and textbooks designed to fashion the Nazi mind. In Moscow, there is a Ministry of Education composed of equally brilliant educational experts whose job it is to manipulate the minds of Soviet youth. . . .

The implication is that Nazi storm troopers and Russian secret agents are leagued in a dastardly plot to overthrow America by infiltrating our third-grade readers and spelling workbooks.

To illustrate the last of the red herring devices, consider the *lemmings.* 26
Lemmings are arctic rodents with a queer habit: periodically, for reasons no one entirely understands, they mass together in a large herd and commit group suicide by rushing into deep water and drowning themselves. They run in blindly, and not one has been observed to stop, scratch its little head, and ask. "*Why* am I doing this? This doesn't look like such a great idea," and thus save itself from destruction.

Obviously, lemmings are driven to perform this strange mass-suicide 27
rite by common instinct. People also choose to "Follow the herd," perhaps for more complex reasons, yet just as blindly. The **bandwagon** appeal capitalizes on people's urge to merge with the crowd.

Basically, the bandwagon appeal gets us to support an action or an 28
opinion merely because it is popular—because "everyone else is doing it." Advertising relies heavily on the bandwagon appeal ("join the Pepsi people") but so do politicians ("Thousands of people have already shown their support by sending in a donation in the enclosed envelope. Won't you become one of us and work together to build a great America?")

The great success of the bandwagon appeal is evident in the various 29
fashions and trends which capture the avid interest—and money—of thousands of people for a short time, then disappear utterly. "Oh, how I wish I could keep up with all the latest fashions as they go rushing by me into oblivion," English critic Max Beerbohm once wrote. Not so long ago, every child in North America wanted a coonskin cap so he could be like Davy Crockett. After that came the hula hoop and, more recently, the skateboard. Children are not the only group susceptible to bandwagon buying. Not so long ago, millions of adults rushed to the stores to buy their very own "pet rocks"—a concept silly enough to set even a lemming atwitter.

The fallacy of the bandwagon appeal is obvious. Just because every- 30
one's doing something doesn't mean that it's worth doing. Large numbers of people have supported actions we now condemn. Dictators have risen to power in sophisticated and cultured countries with the support of millions of

people who didn't want to be "left out" at the great historical moment. Once the bandwagon begins to move, momentum builds up dangerously fast.

If a propagandist can't reel you in by stirring your emotions or distracting your attention, he can always try a little faulty logic. This approach is more insidious than the other two because it gives the appearance of reasonable, fair argument. You have to look closely to see the holes in the logical fiber. The most common kind of faulty logic is the *false-cause-and-effect fallacy,* also known as **post hoc, ergo propter hoc** ("after this, therefore because of this"). 31

A good example of false-cause-and-effect reasoning is the story of the woman aboard the steamship *Andrea Doria,* who woke up from a nap and, feeling seasick, looked around for a call button to summon the steward to bring medication. She finally located a button on one of the walls of her cabin and pushed it. A split second later, the *Andrea Doria* collided with the *Stockholm* in the crash that was to send the ship to her destruction. "Oh God, what have I done?" the woman screamed. 32

Her reasoning was understandable enough: a clear example of *post hoc, ergo propter hoc.* False-cause-and-effect reasoning can be persuasive because it *seems* so logical, or is confirmed by our own experience. "I swallowed X product—and my headache went away," says one woman, "We elected Y official—and unemployment went down," says another. We conclude, "There *must* be a connection." Maybe it would be good to keep in mind Harry Reasoner's remark, that "to call that cause and effect is to say that sitting in the third row of burlesque theatres is what makes men bald." Cause and effect is an awfully complex phenomenon; you need a good deal of evidence to prove that one event following another in time is, in fact, "caused" by the first. 33

False cause and effect is used—and with great effect—by our ever-reliable politicians. During the final weeks of the 1976 campaign, Carter and Ford flooded the airwaves with their *post hoc, ergo propter hoc* messages. "Since I came to office," said Ford, "the inflation rate has dropped to 6%." "Since Gerald Ford took office," countered Carter, "the unemployment rate has risen 50% from 5.5% to 7.9%" Or how about this snip from a local political column for false-cause-and-effect reasoning: 34

> [Sex educators] loudly protest there is no relationship between their methods and promiscuity.
>
> Yet the facts are disheartening, to say the least.
>
> At a time when youngsters know more about sex than any preceding generation, we have more venereal disease, more teenage prostitution, more rape and generally, more sex-related problems than at any other time in history. If the advocates of sex education as now taught consider this an endorsement of their approach, then I think they're more in need of "instruction" than their childish charges.

Carry on with this reasoning and you can argue that the Boston Strangler, the Son of Sam, and the Zodiac Killer were all the monster creations of their ninth-grade hygiene classes. Of course, the writer blithely ignores all the multiple alternative possibilities for the phenomenon. It would be interesting to know whether the rate of venereal disease or of teenaged pregnancies increased following the publication of this column. Then, by the same reasoning, we could argue that the "disheartening" rise was hardly an endorsement of such "irresponsible" attacks upon the methods of the "sex educators."

Another tricky use of false logic is the fallacy known as the **two-** 35
extremes dilemma. Linguists have long noted that the English language tends to view reality in extreme or polar opposites. In English, things are either black or white, tall or short, up or down, front or back, left or right, good or bad, guilty or not guilty. "C'mon now, stop with all the talk—just give me a straightforward yes-or-no answer," we say, the understanding being that we will not accept anything in between. The problem is that there *are* things that can only be said in between; reality cannot always be dissected along strict lines. "Now, let's be fair," we say, "and listen to *both* sides of the argument." But who is to say that every argument has two sides? Can't there be a third—a fourth, fifth, or sixth—point of view? To say otherwise is to deny the nature of the world we live in, and accept the reality imposed by language.

In this statement by Lenin, the famed Marxist leader, we have a clear 36
example of the two-extremes fallacy:

> You cannot eliminate *one* basic assumption, one substantial part of this philosophy of Marxism [it is as if it were a block of steel] without abandoning truth, without falling into the arms of bourgeois-reactionary falsehood.

In other words, if you don't agree 100 percent with every premise of Marxism, you do not pass go, but move directly to jail for the ideological crime of "bourgeois-reactionary falsehood"—the other extreme of the political spectrum. There's no option to be 99 3/4 percent in favor of Marxism, with perhaps a few quibbles about how a Communist state should be administered. If you're not with it, you're agin it, and that's that.

"Bourgeois reactionaries" are also capable of this kind of faulty rea- 37
soning. Texas Senator John Tower, in his 1978 reelection campaign, stated, "I cast light on the issues; my opponent (conservative Democrat Robert Krueger) plunges them into darkness." A recent advertisement against gun control said, "If you're not helping to save hunting, you are helping to outlaw it." There is no place between these polar opposites for the millions of people in the world who might favor hunting, but oppose handguns or Saturday night specials, or even for those who might favor guns and yet oppose hunting, not to mention all the gradations of opinion in between.

A famous example of the two-extremes dilemma is the slogan "Amer- 38
ica: Love it or leave it." The implicit suggestion is that we must either accept *everything* in America today *just as it is*—or get out. Of course, there's a whole range of action and belief between those two extremes which the slogan entirely overlooks. The path of American history is littered with slogans that display the two-extremes dilemma—"Fifty-four forty or fight." "Better dead than Red," "Millions for defense but not one cent for tribute."

There's one more propaganda technique that's the most underhanded of them all. It's called **card stacking,** and means selecting only those facts—or falsehoods—which support the propagandist's point of view, ignoring all others. For example, a candidate could be made to look like a legislative dynamo if you say, "Representative McNerd introduced more new bills than any other member of the Congress," and neglect to mention that most of them were so preposterous that they never got out of committee. **39**

When we feel deeply about something, it's difficult to resist the temptation to stack the deck. Take this recent statement issued by an antiabortion group: **40**

> Why does this sin-sick society show leniency toward murderers, rapists, robbers, and other vicious criminals and then does an about-face by wanting to destroy these little bundles of innocence through abortive murder: Let's face the truth. The majority of those who want to get rid of what God has created in their wombs are the unmarried who had a fling in the back seat of a parked automobile or some dingy motel room. Now when the price for a night of adventure is beginning to manifest itself, they want to add to their wickedness by slaying this innocent little baby. . . .

The Second Amendment Foundation, a group opposing gun control and an affiliate of the national gun lobby, recently published a small pamphlet "warning Americans against the dangers of gun confiscation," which includes the following dire forecast: **41**

> Even though you may not own or have any direct interest in firearms, I believe you must be informed of the terribly serious consequences of what the liberal press refers to as "gun control."
>
> My friend, they are not talking about *control,* they want complete and total confiscation. This will mean the elimination and removal of *all police revolvers, all sporting rifles* and *target pistols* owned by law-abiding citizens. Throughout our country a crime of violence, like murder, assault or rape, occured once every 31 seconds in 1976. This means that over 1,026,280 men, women and children or elderly persons fell victims to thieves and hoodlums. . . .
>
> Tell me, how high would the crime rate be if the criminal knew our police were unarmed? . . . I don't believe we can sit back and allow the "gun confiscation" people in this country to pass laws that would set the stage for the most terrifying crime wave ever to occur in modern history. . . .

No mention here that England and Japan, where guns are banned, have a much lower crime rate than the United States, or that the rate of homicides is dramatically less. That wouldn't fit into this carefully stacked deck. Nor would a contrary argument citing only the English and Japanese experience pass any test. For there might be any number of other explanations (see the *post hoc* fallacy) for that phenomenon. But never mind these picky details—the big picture is clear enough in the gun lobby pamphlet: vote for gun control, and if the bill passes, the next day every pervert and gangster in the city will be scratching at your windows and jimmying your door, while the police stand by helplessly, swatting them with their hats.

Card stacking was used shamelessly throughout the 1976 election campaign. In the New York State [U.S. Senate] race, the "Democrats for Jim Buckley" came out with a campaign poster that announced: 42

> Two thirds of all Democrats who voted in the recent primary did not vote for Moynihan. He won with a one percent margin. That's not what we call a party mandate. . . . So, what is there about Moynihan that turns off so many members of his own party?

A cleverly loaded question. Since there were four strong candidates running in the Democratic primary, it was well-nigh impossible for *anyone* to get anything approaching a "mandate." And the fact that the vote was so widely split among the candidates did not necessarily mean that anyone was "turned off" to Moynihan, just that they were "turned on" to other people. In the last weeks of the presidential race, Carter's people took out an ad that stated, "Today's inflation rate of 6% is higher than it was at any time between the Korean War and the Inauguration of Richard Nixon." True enough. But they neglected to mention that the inflation rate actually *dropped* from 12 percent to 6 percent during Ford's Administration—not the kind of omission that's likely to be an unconscious oversight. For their part, the Ford people came up with the remark that "This administration doesn't believe the way to end unemployment is to go to war." Of course, no one is depraved enough to suggest that the way to end unemployment is to go to war, but somehow that remark suggests that this may be what Carter had in mind.

Card stacking isn't necessarily *untrue;* it just isn't the whole truth. It's a bit reminiscent of the story about the three blind men who encountered an elephant one day. The first blind man felt the elephant's trunk and concluded he was confronted with a snake; the second felt the elephant's leg and decided it must be a tree trunk; the third felt the tusk and was convinced it was the antler of a deer. A skillful card stacker can take *part* of the truth and use it to argue for a particular issue and take another part to argue against the very same issue he just argued for. When one of his constituents wrote to him complaining about federal spending, Arizona Congressman Morris Udall replied tongue in cheek with this tour de force of card stacking: 43

> If, when you say "federal spending," you mean the billions of dollars wasted on outmoded naval shipyards and surplus airbases in Georgia, Texas and New York; if you mean the billions of dollars lavished at Cape Kennedy and Houston on a "moondoggle" our nation cannot afford; if, sir, you mean the $2-billion wasted each year in wheat and corn price supports which rob midwestern farmers of their freedoms and saddle taxpayers with outrageous costs of storage in already bulging warehouses . . . if you mean the bloated federal aid to education schemes calculated to press federal educational controls down upon every student in this nation; if you mean the $2-billion misused annually by our Public Health Service and National Institutes of Health on activities designed to prostitute the medical profession and foist socialized medicine on every American; if, sir, you mean all these ill-advised, unnecessary federal activities which have destroyed state's rights, created a vast, ever-growing, empire-building bureaucracy regimenting a once free people by illusory bait of cradle-to-grave security, and which indeed have taken us

so far down the road to socialism that it may be, even at this hour, too late to retreat—then I am unyielding, bitter and foursquare in my opposition, regardless of the personal or political consequences.

But, on the other hand, if when you say "federal spending," you mean those funds which maintain Davis Monthan Air Force Base, Fort Huachuca and other Arizona defense installations so vital to our nation's security, and which every year pour hundreds of millions of dollars into our state's economy . . . if you mean those funds to send our brave astronauts voyaging, even as Columbus, into the unknown, in order to guarantee that no aggressor will ever threaten these great United States by nuclear blackmail from outer space; if you mean those sound farm programs which insure our hardy Arizona cotton farmers a fair price for their fiber, protect the sanctity of the family farm, ensure reasonable prices for consumers, and put to work for all the people of the world the miracle of American agricultural abundance . . . if you mean the federal education funds which built desperately needed college classrooms and dormitories for our local universities, provide little children in our Arizona schools with hot lunches (often their only decent meal of the day), furnish vocational training for our high school youth, and pay $10-million in impact funds to relieve the hard-pressed Arizona school property taxpapers from the impossible demands created by the presence of large federal installations; if you mean the federal medical and health programs which have eradicated the curse of malaria, small-pox, scarlet fever and polio from our country, and which even now enable dedicated teams of scientists to close in mercilessly on man's age-old enemies of cancer, heart disease, muscular dystrophy, multiple sclerosis, and mental retardation that afflict our little children, senior citizens and men and women in the prime years of life; if you mean all these federal activities by which a free people in the spirit of Jefferson, Lincoln, Teddy Roosevelt, Wilson and FDR, through a fair and progressive income tax, preserve domestic tranquility and promote the general welfare while preserving all our cherished freedoms and our self-reliant national character, then I shall support them with the all vigor at my command.[3]

Perhaps a good way to wind up is to show you how all these propaganda devices, from name-calling through card stacking, can be put to work together. Let's take a local candidate who doesn't have any very good reason why people should vote for him instead of his opponent, so he's going to have to rely on propaganda and not reasoned argument. Here, then, is State Senator Al Yakalot, running for reelection to the State Senate, addressing a crowd of his constituents on election day: **44**

SPEECH BY SENATOR YAKALOT TO HIS CONSTITUENTS

My dear friends and fellow countrymen in this great and beautiful town of Gulliville, I stand before you today as your candidate for State Senator. And before I say anything else, I want to thank you wonderful people, you hardworking, right-living citizens that make our country great, for coming here **45**

[3]Morris Udall, *Preface to Critical Reading,* ed. Richard Altick (New York: Holt, Rinehart and Winston, 1969).

today to hear me speak. Now, I'm at a disadvantage here because I don't have the gift of gab that a big-city fella like my opponent has—I'm just a small-town boy like you fine people—but I'm going to try, in my own simple way, to tell you why you should vote for me, Al Yakalot.

Now, my opponent may appear to you to be a pretty nice guy, but I'm here today to tell you that his reckless and radical policies represent a dire threat to all that we hold dear. He would tear down all that is great and good in America and substitute instead his own brand of creeping socialism. **46**

For that's just what his ridiculous scheme to set up a hot meal program for the elderly in this town amounts to—socialism. Sure, *he* says our local citizens have expressed their willingness to donate some of their time and money to a so-called senior citizens' kitchen. But this kind of supposed "volunteer" work only undermines our local restaurants—in effect, our private enterprise system. The way I see it, in this world a man's either for private enterprise or he's for socialism. Mr. Stu Pott, one of the leading strategists of the hot meal campaign (a man who, by the way, sports a Fidel Castro beard) has said the program would be called the "Community Food Service." Well, just remember that the words "Community" and "Communism" look an awful lot alike! **47**

After all, my friends, our forefathers who made this country great never had any free hot meal handouts. And look at what they did for our country! That's why I'm against the hot meal program. Hot meals will only make our senior citizens soft, useless, and dependent. **48**

And that's not all you should know about my opponent, my fellow citizens. My pinko opponent has also called for a "consumers crusade" against what he terms "junk food" in school lunches. By "junk food," he means things like potato chips and hot dogs. Potato chips and hot dogs! My friends, I say that we've raised generations of patriotic American children on potato chips and hot dogs and we're not about to stop now! Potato chips have been praised by great Americans as well as by leading experts on nutrition. **49**

What's more, potato chips are good for our children, too. A recent study shows that after children were given lunches that often included potato chips, their energy and attention spans improved by over ten percent. Obviously, potato chips have a beneficial effect on children's ability to learn. My opponent has tried to tell you that his attack on the venerable American custom of potato chip eating is just an attempt to improve our children's health and beauty. Yet this plan is supported by Congresswoman Doris Schlepp, who is no beauty herself! **50**

My fellow taxpayers, I'm here today to tell you that this heartless plot to deprive our little ones of the food that they need most and love best won't work, because it's just plain unworkable. Trying to discourage children from eating potato chips is like trying to prevent people from voting—and the American people just aren't going to stand for it! **51**

I'm mighty grateful to all of you wonderful folks for letting me speak what is in my heart. I know you for what you are—the decent, law-abiding citizens that are the great pulsing heart and the lifeblood of this, our beloved country. I stand for all that is good in America, for our American way and our American Birthright. More and more citizens are rallying to my cause every day. Won't you join them—and me—in our fight for America? **52**

Thank you and May God Bless You All.

▲ ▲ ▲

Review Questions

1. Cross implies, rather than provides, a definition of "propaganda" at the outset of her analysis. What is this implied definition?
2. Define the following terms: *argumentum ad hominem; glittering generality; red herring; stroking; bandwagon appeal; post hoc, ergo propter hoc; two extremes dilemma; card-stacking.*

Discussion and Writing Suggestions

1. Examine a speech by a recent President. (The *New York Times* routinely prints major Presidential speeches such as inaugural addresses and State of the Union messages; they may be located, under the name of the President, through the *Times Index,* either printed or electronic.) Locate several *glittering generalities* and other propaganda techniques discussed by Cross and explain how they are intended to move the audience. To provide equal time, you may also want to look at the opposing party response (generally reprinted in the same place). *Alternate assignment:* Analyze a speech by some other politician than a president. Check *The Congressional Digest* for excerpts from legislative speeches on important issues.
2. The rhetorical devices that Cross discusses are used, of course, in other areas than politics—notably advertising. Examine one or more advertisements and discuss the use of propaganda for the purpose of selling products or services, using advertising language for your examples. (Remember that a lot of advertising comes in the form of mail solicitations.) Don't ignore how images are used to enhance the message, but focus on *language.*
3. Analyze the speech by Senator Yakalot at the end of Cross's article. What kinds of propaganda does the senator use and for what purpose?
4. Compose a speech on some issue of concern on your campus, using as many of the propaganda techniques covered by Donna Cross (see Review Question 2 above) as you can manage. Try out the speech on one or more of your classmates and get their reactions. *Alternate assignment:* Compose a speech taking care not to use a single one of these propaganda techniques. Give the speech to one or more of your classmates and ask them whether or not they find it persuasive.

A Debate on Welfare

Welfare is perhaps the touchstone issue that serves to divide liberals from conservatives. Liberals, believing as they do in social justice and equality of opportunity, feel that the government has an important role in protecting society's less fortunate members from the often harsh consequences of market forces in a capitalist economy. Conservatives, believing as they do in individual responsibility and minimal interference of the government in the free enterprise system, see welfare programs as an intolerable government redistribution of wealth.

The conservative position on welfare was epitomized by Barry Goldwater, former Senator from Arizona, in his 1960 book The Conscience of a Conservative *(quoted by Burns, Peltason, Cronin, and Magleby in their selection earlier in this chapter):*

> *Let welfare be a private concern. Let it be promoted by individuals and families, by churches, private hospitals, religious service organizations, community charities and other institutions that have been established for this purpose. If the objection is raised that private institutions lack sufficient funds, let us remember that every penny the federal government does not appropriate for welfare is potentially available for private use—and without the overhead charge for processing the money through the federal bureacracy.*

For Goldwater, taxation to support welfare amounts to confiscation of property. He argues that welfare is bad both for those who receive it (because it creates a sense of entitlement) and because it enlarges the powers of the state and results in a loss of freedom and liberty.

Two years after Goldwater's book, a powerful opposing viewpoint was articulated by Michael Harrington in his influential book (which helped launch President Johnson's War on Poverty) The Other America: Poverty in the United States. *Harrington argued that the extent of poverty in the affluent United States was a national disgrace. He asserted that the so-called welfare state benefits the well-off (in the form of subsidies for corporations and for the middle class) far more than the poor. While these subsidies are true "socialism for the rich," the poor have been unjustly stigmatized as "merrily freeloading on the public dole." Asserting that only the federal government has the ability to abolish the debilitating culture of poverty, Harrington poses the classic liberal questions: "How long shall we ignore this underdeveloped nation in our midst? How long shall we look the other way while our fellow human beings suffer? How long?"*

Welfare is not a single government program, but a set of programs, the largest of which is Aid to Families With Dependent Children (AFDC), established in 1935 to provide temporary government aid (in the form of cash benefits) to families in which the father had died or become disabled. Other welfare programs include Medicaid (medical benefits) and food stamps. Critics charge that welfare encourages irresponsible behavior and creates dependency. Advocates of welfare, while acknowledging the need for reform, reply that cutting off welfare would punish innocent children and would force welfare families into poverty and crime.

In 1992, Democratic Presidential candidate Bill Clinton promised to "end welfare as we know it." As President, Clinton advanced the "Work and Responsibility Act," which called for the cutting off of welfare bene-

fits to able-bodied adult recipients after two years. But this bill was seen as too weak by Republicans, and after their sweep of both houses of Congress in 1994, they introduced their own bill, H.R. [House of Representatives] 4, the "Personal Responsibility Act" (part of their "Contract With America"). H.R. 4 essentially would turn over responsibility for welfare programs from the federal government to the states, which would be given "block grants" to spend as they saw fit. Such a measure effectively ends welfare as a federal entitlement. The Act requires recipients to find work within two years or have their benefits cut off; it restricts welfare benefits to five years, even for those who do work; it prohibits payments to unwed mothers under 18, prohibits additional payments to mothers that have additional children while on welfare, and prohibits payments to all non-citizens. H.R. 4 passed the Republican-dominated House on March 24, 1995, by a vote of 234 to 199. A Senate version was passed in December of that year, but the following month President Clinton vetoed the measure for cutting too deeply into benefits.

The following selection consists of exerpts from six speeches on the floor of the House of Representatives, all given on March 21, 1995. Speaking for H.R. 4 are its sponsor, Representative Bill Archer, Republican from Texas; Marge Roukema, Republican from New Jersey; and Michael Collins, Republican from Georgia. Speaking against the bill are Democratic Representatives William J. Coyne of Pennsylvania, George E. Brown, Jr., of California, and Maxine Waters, Democrat from California. All of these statements, except the one by Waters, appeared in the June–July 1995 issue of Congressional Digest. *Waters' statement appeared in the* Congressional Record *for March 22, 1995.*

You will find a set of additional statements on the welfare debate in Chapter 4, on "Synthesis." These statements range the political spectrum, from libertarian to moderate to radical. As you read the following arguments, examine not only the authors' varied positions, but also the rhetorical devices they employ to persuade readers that their views are valid and that opposing views should not be taken seriously. (Review Lazere and Cross on the use of these devices and techniques.) Suggestions for writing assignments based on these selections appear in the "Synthesis Activities" at the end of this chapter.

Welfare Reform: Pro

HONORABLE BILL ARCHER

UNITED STATES REPRESENTATIVE, TEXAS, REPUBLICAN

The Republican welfare revolution is at hand. Today begins the demise of the failed welfare state that has entrapped the Nation's needy for too long. Today we begin to replace that disaster in social engineering with a reform plan that brings hope to the poor of this Nation and relief to the Nation's taxpayers. Working Americans who carry the load will get relief. 1

Government has spent $5.3 trillion on welfare since the war on poverty began—the most expensive war in the history of this country—and the Census Bureau tells us we have lost the war. The bill we bring to the floor today constitutes the broadest overhaul of welfare ever proposed. 2

The status quo welfare state is unacceptable. 3

Today we have the chance to move beyond the rhetoric of previous years of endless campaign promises to end welfare as we know it. Today there must be no doubt. The rhetoric is stopping, the solution is beginning. 4

Our bill is constructed on three principles which strike at the very foundations of the Nation's failed welfare state. The three principles are: personal responsibility, work, and returning power over welfare to our States and communities where the needy can be helped in the most efficient way. 5

The first and most fundamental principle, captured by the title of our bill, is personal responsibility, the character trait that built this country. 6

The current welfare system destroys families and undermines the work ethic. It traps people in a hopeless cycle of dependency. Our bill replaces this destructive welfare system with a new system based on work and strong families. 7

Virtually every section of the bill requires more personal responsibility. Recipients are required to work for their benefits. Drug addicts and alcoholics are no longer rewarded with cash payments that are often spent on their habit. Aliens who were allowed into the country because they promised to be self-supporting are held to their promises; fathers who do not live with their children are expected to pay child support or suffer severe consequences; and welfare can no longer be a way of life. After five years, no more cash benefits will be provided. 8

This bill will reverse the decades-long Federal policy of rewarding unacceptable and self-destructive behavior. We will no longer reward for doing the wrong thing. 9

The second underlying principle of our bill flows naturally from the first. Able-bodied adults on welfare must work for their benefits. Here it appears that the Democrats have surrendered completely to Republican philosophy. On work we are all Republicans now, but it was not always so. 10

During the welfare debate of 1987 and 1988, Democrats perpetuated a system in which able-bodied adults could stay on welfare year after year without doing anything. Now the Clinton Administration and Democrats in the House are finally claiming they want mandatory work too, but the substitutes they will offer later do not require serious work. 11

If the Democrats were serious about welfare reform, they would have taken action last year when they had the chance. House Republicans signed a *Contract With America* that promised we would provide a vote on the House floor on true welfare reform, and we are now fulfilling that promise within less than 80 days. The third principle which forms the foundation of our bill is our commitment to shrink the Federal Government by returning power and flexibility to the States and communities where the needy can be helped the most. My own mayor in Houston, Texas, a Democrat, talked to me several weeks ago and said you can cut the amount of Federal money 12 coming to Houston by 25 percent, but give me the flexibility without the Federal regulations and I will do more with 25 percent less.

Some say, however, that only those in their ivory towers in Washington care enough to help the needy and aid the poor; the only caring people in all of government throughout the United States are here in Washington. That is what they say. They say you cannot trust the States. These people seem to think that the governors are still standing in the schoolhouse doors not letting people in. But rather, it is the Democrats in Washington who are standing in the doors of our Nation's ghettos and not letting people out. 13

The current regulatory morass is shown on the chart standing next to me. It shows that the welfare system Republicans inherited consists of at least 336 programs in eight domains of welfare policy. The Federal Government expects to be spending $125 billion on these programs this year. Here it is, proof of the ridiculous tangle of overlapping bureaucratic programs that have been thrust upon the Nation since the beginning of the war on poverty, and the worst part is that the American taxpayers, working Americans, are paying the bill. 14

But these 336 programs are only the tip of the iceberg. Imagine how many regulations had to be written to implement these 336 programs. Just let me show you. These are the regulations from just two of the 336 programs. They are standing right next to me here on the desk. They weigh 62.4 pounds. 15

I can think of no more fitting symbol of the failed welfare state than these pounds of Federal regulations. It is time to remove the Federal middleman from the welfare system. We can cut these unnecessary regulations, eliminate Federal bureaucrats, and give our States and communities the freedom they need to help their fellow citizens. Our bill will end 40 of the biggest and fastest growing programs and replace them with five block grants. By ending counterproductive, overlapping, and redundant programs, we will win half the battle. We are proud, though, that we have hit upon a much better approach to helping the poor than this top-heavy Federal system. 16

The laboratories of democracy are in the States, not Washington, D.C. Block grants will bring the decisions closer to the people affected by them. They will give governors more responsibility and resources to design and run their own programs. 17

And once we have given the States this flexibility and eliminated the need for them to beg Washington for permission to operate outside the stack of rules in that pile on the desk, the reforms they have implemented thus far will be dramatically expanded and spread to every State. 18

Welfare today has left a sad mark on the American success story. It has created a world in which children have no dreams for tomorrow and grownups have abandoned their hopes for today. 19

The time has come to replace this failed system with a new system that uplifts our Nation's poor, a new system that turns the social safety net from a trap into a trampoline, a new system that rewards work and personal responsibility in families, a new system that lifts a load off working, taxpaying Americans. It represents a historic shift, long overdue. 20

HONORABLE MARGE ROUKEMA
UNITED STATES REPRESENTATIVE, NEW JERSEY, REPUBLICAN

I rise in support of H.R. 4, the Personal Responsibility Act of 1995. 1

The American people are convinced that the welfare system is out of 2
control. As one prominent citizen of New Jersey, a Democrat at that, said to me last week: "No other civilized nation in the world pays young girls to have babies. But that's what our welfare system does."

He is not far from wrong. And that is the perception among many other 3
good, generous, caring people who are deeply concerned about this country.

They worry that we are wasting billions upon billions in hard-earned 4
taxpayer dollars to support a system that promotes unhealthy, unproductive, dysfunctional families that sentence children to a lifetime of economic, social, and emotional deprivation. In a system like this, it is the children who are the first victims. But the taxpayers are not far behind.

We must act now. We need welfare reform based on the notion of indi- 5
vidual responsibility. Reform must restore public assistance to its original purpose: a temporary safety net for those in need—not a permanent way of life for generations of families. H.R. 4 makes a number of important changes.

First, this plan requires that 50 percent of welfare recipients must be 6
working. There is no good reason why able-bodied welfare recipients cannot, and should not, be required to work for their benefits.

Second, this bill allows States the flexibility to terminate a family's 7
welfare benefits after two years, and it requires States to terminate a family's welfare benefits after five years. It is clear. Some people take advantage of the current welfare program's lax bureaucracy and simply live off welfare—generation after generation—by skillfully gaming the system.

Also, H.R. 4 clearly denies welfare benefits to illegal aliens and legal 8
immigrants, thereby limiting welfare eligibility to citizens of the United States.

While the exclusion for legal aliens has received quite a bit of criti- 9
cism, I want to make sure that everyone realizes an often overlooked, but essential, component of our immigration laws. For decades, our immigration laws have required immigrants to stipulate that they will be self-sufficient once they arrive in America as a condition of their being allowed to immigrate in the first place. Consequently, receiving welfare has been grounds for deportation for these very same immigrants for generations.

H.R. 4 only makes explicit what has been implicit for so long. The United 10
States of America welcomes immigrants of all kinds to our Nation. However, an important prerequisite has always been that immigrants will not become wards of the State, but rather self-supporting members of our society.

I want to conclude my statement with some remarks about the Child 11
Support Enforcement title of H.R. 4.

Let me make clear one unequivocal fact: Effective child support en- 12
forcement reforms must be an essential component of any true welfare re-

form plan. In fact, nonsupport of children by their parents is one of the primary reasons so many families end up on the welfare rolls to begin with.

Research has found that anywhere between 25 and 40 percent of mothers on public assistance would not be on welfare if they were receiving the child support they are legally and morally entitled to. It's a national disgrace that our child support enforcement system continues to allow so many parents who can afford to pay for their children's support to shirk these obligations. The so-called enforcement gap—the difference between how much child support could be collected and how much child support is collected—has been estimated at $34 billion. 13

Remember, we are addressing the problems of deadbeats who are willfully avoiding their legal obligations under the divorce edicts of their individual States. They are avoiding both their legal and moral obligations. Failure to pay court-ordered child support is not a victimless crime. The children going without these payments are the first victims. But the taxpayers who have to pick up the tab for the deadbeat parents evading their obligations are the ultimate victims. 14

Strong, effective child support enforcement is welfare prevention. The single best method to reduce welfare spending is to ensure that custodial parents with children get their child support payments on time, every month. 15

Perhaps the most salient fact we must keep in mind as we seek to improve our child support enforcement system is: Our interstate child support system is only as good as its weakest link. States that have made enforcing and collecting child support payments a priority are penalized by those that have failed to reciprocate. In other words, the deadbeat under the existing loopholes can slip over the State line or just across the Delaware River and escape his legal obligations to his kids. 16

That is precisely what we need—comprehensive Federal reform of our child support system—to ensure that all States come up to the highest common denominator, not sink to the lowest common denominator as has happened all too frequently in the past. 17

In conclusion, I believe that H.R. 4 contains the kind of reforms to our long-broken welfare system that the American people have been expecting. In general, this bill has earned my support, and I look forward to the amendment process where I believe that this important measure will only be improved upon. 18

HONORABLE MICHAEL COLLINS
UNITED STATES REPRESENTATIVE, GEORGIA, REPUBLICAN

The President, during his campaign, ran on the platform of changing welfare. In fact, he said. "We're going to end welfare as we know it today." 1

To end it does not mean you reform it. It means you change it. Because to reform it only changes the shape of it and leaves the same substance. Is change necessary? It is long overdue. The answer is yes. 2

Why? It is because 26 percent of the families in this country are in some way, shape, or fashion drawing some type of government benefit that comes under the entitlement of welfare. What is the real problem with welfare? It is called cash—the old saying, cash is the root of all evil. Cash has been the real problem, and is the real problem, in welfare. 3

What is the history of cash in welfare? It goes back to the mid-1930s. In fact, it was called Aid to Dependent Children, later called AFDC. It was actually created in 1935 as a cash grant to enable States to aid needy children, children who did not have fathers at home. 4

Was the AFDC program intended to be an indefinite program? No, it was not to last forever. The priority of it was to help children whose fathers were either deceased or disabled or unable to work. The program was supposed to sunset after the Social Security laws were changed. 5

When AFDC was created, no one ever imagined that a father's desertion and out-of-wedlock births would replace the father's death or disability as the most prevalent reason for triggering the need for assistance. No one ever dreamed that fathers would abandon children as they have. 6

In order to facilitate the sunset of the AFDC program, in 1939, the Federal Government expanded Social Security benefits by adding survivors benefits. This was to help wives and children of workers who died at any early age. 7

In 1956, the Federal Government added disability to Social Security to try to cover those children whose fathers were unable to work because of some severe disability. But rather than sunset AFDC, the program continued to grow and has ballooned in recent years, because the very nature of the program has encouraged illegitimacy and irresponsible behavior. 8

Let me give Members a few statistics. In 1940, for 41 percent of children on AFDC, their father had died. The fathers had abandoned 20 percent of the children. The fathers were disabled to work for 27 percent. 9

In 1992, 1.6 percent of the children's fathers have died; for 86 percent of children on AFDC, their fathers have abandoned them; and for only 4.1 percent, their fathers are disabled to work. 10

The AFDC system has created a real problem. It has encouraged irresponsible behavior by embracing a philosophy that says the government will take care of a child if a father won't. H.R. 4 stops this problem. It stops cash benefits in certain years, requires personal responsibility, and gives the States the flexibility, the very same thing that was supposed to happen in 1935, to handle the situation. 11

Welfare Reform: Con

HONORABLE WILLIAM J. COYNE

UNITED STATES REPRESENTATIVE, PENNSYLVANIA, DEMOCRAT

I rise in strong opposition to the welfare reform package brought to the floor today by the Republican Majority. This mean-spirited attack on children and poor families in America fails every test of true welfare reform. 1

The Republican bill is tough on children and weak on work. This plan 2
will punish children who happen to be born into poverty. At the same time, this plan cuts child care funding and other programs that are essential if an adult on welfare is to get a job and leave the welfare rolls.

Instead of fixing welfare and moving Americans from welfare to work, 3
the Republican bill is simply an exercise in cutting programs that serve children, the disabled, and families living in poverty.

What can possibly be the motive for launching such a cruel attack on 4
the children of America? The answer is the Republican Majority will cut programs for the poor to provide tax cuts for the wealthy. Cuts in child care, school lunches, and programs for the poor will be used to finance tax breaks like the capital gains tax cut. We are literally short-changing America's children to give tax breaks to individuals with incomes over $100,000 a year.

The Republican bill will punish over 15 million innocent American chil- 5
dren. It would punish children who are born out of wedlock to a mother under the age of 18. It punishes any child who happens to be born to a family already on welfare. This bill does not guarantee that a child will have safe child care when their parents work. It cuts SSI [Supplemental Security Insurance] benefits to over 680,000 disabled children. Under this bill, State accountability for the death of a child is limited simply to reporting the child's death. Finally, this bill adds to the injuries of abused and neglected children by cutting $2 billion from Federal programs to care for these children.

The Republican bill will increase the risk of a child in poverty suffer- 6
ing from abuse and neglect. And yes, the result will be that some mothers who want to give birth to a child will be pushed to consider ending their pregnancy.

The Republican bill is a cruel attack on America's children, but it also 7
fails to provide the essential tools needed by parents who want to move from welfare to work. A mother who takes a minimum wage job can only do so if she has access to safe child care. Unfortunately, this bill will cut Federal funds for child care by 25 percent in the year 2000. This means that over 400,000 fewer children will receive Federal child care assistance. Pennsylvania alone will lose $25.7 million in Federal child care assistance funding by the year 2000. That means that over 15,000 children in Pennsylvania will be denied Federal assistance for safe child care.

The legislation will result in America's poor children being left home 8
alone. Mothers who are required by the State to work will no longer be guaranteed child care. States that seek to provide child care assistance will have to make up for Federal child care cuts by raiding other State programs or increasing State taxes.

Again, the Republican bill is tough on children and weak on work. It 9
allows States to push a person off the welfare rolls and then count that person toward meeting the Republicans' so-called work requirement. There is no requirement for education, training, and support services for individuals who need help moving from welfare to a job. In fact, nearly $10 billion for job training programs have been cut from the first Republican welfare plan.

Apparently, these funds were needed more to pay for tax cuts for upper income Americans.

HONORABLE GEORGE E. BROWN, JR.
UNITED STATES REPRESENTATIVE, CALIFORNIA, DEMOCRAT

I have followed the debate over the withdrawal of Federal support of poverty programs, which has passed for a debate on welfare reform over the past few weeks, with considerable interest. It seems to me that we have been avoiding a broader discussion of the deep structural problems in our society which the growth of welfare expenditures represents. . . . 1

The real problem is unemployment, and the culture of despondency and poverty that it creates. We seem to be proceeding under the assumption that there are enough jobs in our economy to accommodate those who are now on the welfare rolls, and that those now receiving benefits will be equipped to accept the jobs that do exist. I doubt it. I would draw your attention to an example of the type of portrait that we have been presented with by the media. The people described are not the type of people that engender sympathy among our hard-working, taxpaying constituents. In fact, I suspect that these descriptions of unmotivated individuals who are irresponsible parents and frequent participants in criminal activities make it easy for us to vote to cut the system that subsidizes their antisocial behavior. But I would like us to think carefully about these portraits from the perspective of an employer. We are being led to believe that by cutting them off, these people will enter the labor force. But would you hire such a person? Would this person, who we are judging to be an unacceptable recipient of public assistance, be a desirable job candidate? Absolutely not. Serious intervention would be required to convert these people from destructive to productive members of this society. It is far more likely that without intervention these people will turn to criminal means of survival rather than to jobs in the legitimate economy. 2

These articles are also doing a serious injustice to the many poor in our country who continue to struggle to be productive, responsible citizens in the face of insurmountable odds. There are many on public assistance who work hard every day for wages that are simply too low to allow them to rise above the poverty level. We should not forget these people or lump them together with the unsympathetic persons described above. Even if the current welfare recipients were ready and qualified to work, are there enough jobs to accommodate them? Unfortunately, the Department of Labor does not collect data on the number of available jobs that exist. However, I decided to investigate the job availability in my region of California by examining as much data as are available. I believe that what I found for my region will mirror what exists throughout the country. In San Bernardino County, there are 64,000 AFDC [Aid to Families with Dependent Children] welfare families, which means that at least one adult in that family is unemployed or employed at such a low income level that they still receive 3 some AFDC benefits. Thus, if we want to fully employ at least one adult from each of these families, we need to have 64,000 vacant jobs.

That is a lot of jobs. Now, how many vacant jobs are there in San Bernardino County? The two daily newspapers in the county listed a combined total of 1,363 jobs in recent Sunday classified ads. Clearly, not all jobs openings are listed in newspapers, but the classified ads listed enough jobs to accommodate only two percent of our region's welfare recipients. A more precise figure comes from the State of California employment office, which currently has listings for 1,056 jobs in San Bernardino County. A rule of thumb is that State employment offices have listings for about 20 percent of available jobs. That means that there might actually be 5,280 public and private sector jobs available in the county right now. And yet, we have a need for 64,000 jobs if we are going to employ at least one adult from each welfare family. 4

Obviously, if we are going to tell adults in welfare families to just go and get jobs, which is what the Republican welfare proposal would do, then we are setting up these families—and ourselves as policy creators—for a real disappointment. The bottom line: Without some kind of public commitment to create large numbers of entry-level jobs, we cannot have a solution to the problem of welfare dependency which we seek to solve. 5

If we consider the bigger picture, the macroeconomic trends are even less comforting. The current trend in both the public and private sector is downsizing, and economists spend a good deal of time monitoring labor productivity, hoping to see it increase. What does this mean in human terms? Downsizing means fewer people doing more work (or the same amount of work). What is an increase in labor productivity? More units of product output for fewer units of labor input. This is fine if overall output rises, but if it does not, this simply means that fewer people are doing more work. Our population is not downsizing. It continues to upsize and probably will for the forseeable future. Therefore, we need more jobs, not fewer. 6

If there are not enough jobs in the private sector, then we should create them in the public sector. This is not as radical as many of my colleagues will suggest. We justify many Federal expenditures on the basis that they will create jobs. There is much work to be done in this society. 7

We must also stop pretending that the problem of illegitimate births is strictly a women's problem. 8

We are going to have to stop trying to legislate morality and acknowledge that there are many female-headed households with children, and child care and health care are necessary support services to enable these women to work. What will we have accomplished if the standard of living for families actually declines when parents leave welfare and go back to work? Ironically, obtaining employment and losing public child care assistance and health benefits often forces many working poor families back onto the welfare rolls. 9

We cannot have more people working without doing much more in the area of education. Many of these who have become permanent welfare recipients are illiterate and lack the basic skills necessary to qualify for a de- 10 cent paying job. Until they acquire these skills, they will remain permanently unemployed, especially since our economy has changed to require higher skill levels of workers. If we are to finally recognize child-rearing as the important and complex job that it is, then we can acknowledge its importance by paying women to do this job. However, many will require job training in this area as well, since many, as teenage mothers, have not acquired the necessary parenting skills that they need to raise children to be productive citizens.

If you want to end the Federal welfare program, and pass the national 11
problem and all of its related social ills on to the States, vote for this legislation. But if we want to end poverty, empower all of our citizens, and diminish the expenditure of funds on welfare programs and social damage control, we had better start over again.

MAXINE WATERS

UNITED STATES REPRESENTATIVE, CALIFORNIA, DEMOCRAT

Mr. Speaker, we are entering one of the most important debates of the 1
104th Congress. The lives of innocent children and families are at stake. Democrats want change, and we have responsible legislation for change. Democrats want reform.

However, the Republicans just go too far. The Republicans are taking 2
America to the edge. It is scary when well-fed Republican politicians take away children's lunches. It is scary when Republicans, who claim family values, advocate putting America's children in orphanages. It is scary when Republican policymakers refuse to formulate responsible welfare reform with child care for mothers to get training for work and a guarantee of jobs for families who desperately want to work.

I know there are a lot of unhappy folks in this country, unhappy about 3
the fact that there are too many families and too many children on welfare. I know that most people want change.

We must be fair in our representations about who wants change. Re- 4
publicans want change. Democrats want change. Workers want change, and recipients want change. I think it is one thing that we can agree on.

No one has the corner on wanting reform. We would all like to see re- 5
form in the system, and it is absolutely incorrect to say that the President or Democrats did not have a bill, did nothing about reform.

The President had a comprehensive piece of legislation that he at- 6
tempted to get into this Congress, the 103d Congress, and we got caught up in the health debate, and it turned into a nightmare, and there was not the opportunity to move on welfare reform as the President had planned. So it is not true that the President did not want welfare reform.

The difference between the Democrats and Republicans is the question 7
of implementation. How will we do welfare reform? Will it be a plan that will offer real opportunities for people to get off welfare or will it simply be a plan to punish folks because for whatever reasons they have found themselves on welfare?

I think it is time for us to try and speak about this in a language that the American public can understand. No, they don't really understand block grants and waivers. 8

Let's put a face on this discussion. We are talking about, for the most part, just plain old poor people and working people. We are talking about people, some of whom were born into situations through no choice of their own that keeps them locked into the cycle of poverty, and there have been no real guidelines, rules by which they can get out of the cycle of poverty. 9

We have some folks who work every day, and they are poor. They can't take care of their families. They need food stamps. They need some help with their health care needs. 10

And so these are real people. These are not pawns that should be used by politicians to gain favor with people who are very vulnerable at this time. This should not simply be a political issue where some politician stands up and says vote for me. I am going to save you money. I am going to get rid of all these bad people. 11

And we should not have politicians simply defining all of America's problems by talking about the welfare state. And we certainly should not have politicians who talk about taking America's children and putting them in institutions, in orphanages. 12

We need to talk about these problems in a real way. Yes, there are teenage pregnancies, too many of them, and most of us don't like the idea that babies have babies. But we live in a society where sex is glamorized, where it is promoted, where it is expected. In order for young women to be looked upon with favor, they must be sexual. Young women are sought after by young men and old men, some of them in their neighborhoods, some out of their neighborhoods, some of them who are poor young men who have not very much to offer, some of them politicians and others. We know what is going on in American society. 13

We need sex education. We need jobs. Jobs have been exported to Third World countries for cheap labor. We need jobs for educated people and not-so-educated people. We need a better education system. We need to deal with the root causes of this problem, and we need to build into welfare reform the real opportunity for people to become independent by offering real jobs, job training and child care. 14

▲ ▲ ▲

Review Questions

1. According to Archer, what are the three principles underlying the Personal Responsibility Act that aim to "strike at the very foundations of the nation's failed welfare state"?
2. Why has the original intent of the AFDC program been violated, according to Collins?
3. How does Roukema justify the exclusion of welfare benefits to *legal* immigrants?

4. What are Coyne's main objections to the Personal Responsibility Act?
5. For Brown, what are the underlying problems that would make it possible for the Personal Responsibility Act to work?
6. How does Waters respond to the charge that a Democratic president did nothing about welfare reform?

Discussion and Writing Suggestions

1. If you were a member of Congress would you vote to support or oppose this legislation? Explain why you think the arguments of one side are stronger than those of the other. (You may wish to couch your response in the form of a speech.) Take into account the views of those you disagree with. For example, if you support the bill, how would you answer the charges of critics like Coyne and Brown that the bill makes no provision for jobs, education, or child care programs? If you oppose the bill, address the charges of Archer and Collins that the existing welfare system encourages irresponsible behavior by mothers and absent fathers.
2. How does the debate over welfare play out along liberal/conservative lines? Using the definitions provided by Burns, Peltason, Cronin, and Magleby, explain in a multi-paragraph essay what makes Archer's and Collins's position *conservative?* What makes Coyne's and Brown's positions *liberal?* Consider not only this particular issue, but also how this issue relates to the broader agendas of conservatives and liberals. (See also Smith, paragraphs 8–9.)
3. How do Congresspersons on both sides of this debate make use of some of the "propaganda" devices discussed by Donna Cross and by Donald Lazere? Write a short essay in which you categorize and illustrate some of the chief ways in which the legislators attempt to persuade their audience of the validity of their views and the weakness of the other side.

A Debate on Federal Funding of the Arts

Since their creation in 1965 the National Endowment for the Arts (NEA) and the National Endowment for the Humanities (NEH) have provided federal funding for thousands of artists and educational projects. In fact, federal support for the arts goes back to 1817 when the 14th Congress commissioned artist John Trumbull to paint four murals depicting scenes of the Revolutionary War for the Capitol Rotunda. During the Depression of the 1930s, President Franklin D. Roosevelt created many programs, including the Federal Writers Project, for the support of artists. But the subject of federal funding for the arts is a controversial one, revealing a critical fault line between liberals and conservatives. Liberals believe that the government has an obligation to support culture, particularly in bringing art and educational programs to those who might otherwise not have access to it. Conservatives contend that the government has no legitimate role in funding art and that, particularly in times of budget deficits, taxpayers should not be required to support projects that benefit a cultural elite. The debate has been exacerbated in recent years by publicity that federal funds were used to support homoerotic photographer Robert Mapplethorpe and artist Andre Serrano, who produced works (e.g., "Piss Christ," a picture of a crucifix in a jar of urine) that many conservatives considered obscene and blasphemous.

The following selection consists of excerpts from four speeches delivered on the floor of the House of Representatives on October 11, 1990, during a debate to pass a bill (H.R. 4825, the Arts, Humanities and Museums Amendments of 1990), the purpose of which was to continue funding for the NEA. Major R. Owens, who co-founded the black "reform" faction of the Brooklyn Democratic Party, has been in the House of Representatives since 1982 (he is also a trained librarian). Claudine Schneider (defeated in the 1994 elections) was a Republican Representative from Rhode Island. Richard K. Armey, a Republican from Texas, is Majority Leader of the House of Representatives. Barbara Vucanovich is a Republican Representative from Nevada. The statements appear in the January 1991 issue of Congressional Digest.

Federal Funding of the Arts: Pro

HONORABLE MAJOR R. OWENS

UNITED STATES REPRESENTATIVE, NEW YORK, DEMOCRAT

Some 80,000 projects have been funded by NEA since its inception and only 25 of those 80,000 have aroused any controversy whatsoever. This is clearly a program that benefits America. This is clearly a program that we need more of and not less of. The problem is that a few people who are very skillful at fanning the flames and leading us into diversion have commanded the media and the press and generated a stampede. Unfortunately, we have a compromise here which I do not particularly like, but I am going to vote for it because the stampede has been so successful that it is going to be necessary to compromise in order to keep the program alive. 1

While I do not question the sincerity of any Member of Congress, in total this whole stampede has been a diversion from very serious matters. It serves to divert us from the real obscenities in the Nation. 2

Webster defines obscenity as anything that is morally repugnant. There is a whole list of morally repugnant national matters that we ought to be concerned with. 3

I am proud to speak this afternoon in strong support of reauthorizing the National Endowment for the Arts. One of our former Presidents once said: 4

"Artists stretch the limits of understanding. They express ideas that are sometimes unpopular. In an atmosphere of liberty, artists and patrons 5 are free to think the unthinkable and create the audacious . . . where there's liberty, art succeeds. In societies that are not free, art dies."

I stress that point because the debate over the relative merits of the NEA has been centering on the wrong issues. It has been centering on what a very few artists have been doing with their grants and whether or not the works of art they have created are appropriate or decent. We are not artists. Very few of us would claim to be experts on art. So how can this body sit in judgment over the content of art and even attempt to deem it appropriate or inappropriate or good or bad. 6

As thousands of people who are knowledgeable about art assert, artists create art to reflect society, to explore societal ideas and concepts. They do not choose only those ideas which are comfortable and acceptable to us. If they did, art would be universally boring. There would be nothing new, nothing daring, nothing to make us think about the art itself and about what it is reflecting. 7

A person who grew up in the savage ghettos of an inner city, who lived in run-down housing projects and went to school in a crumbling, rat-infested school is not going to paint pretty pictures of landscapes and fruit bowls and frolicking kittens. That artist's portrayals are more likely to reflect the experiences of his or her life and the anger of being shut out from the prosperity apparently being realized elsewhere in society. 8

This art reflects things that are happening in our society, and closing our eyes will not make those things go away. Such art can help us recognize other influences on our culture and even help us understand them. And if it does not help me or you specifically, you can be sure that it is helping someone, somewhere, who can relate to it. 9

Artistic freedom enables us to depict images and realities which may or may not be offensive but which help us explore influences in our culture that we would otherwise not experience. An image or a picture or a book can travel places and affect people all over the world. People who live in remote communities, even in the United States, may have access to a library program which contains books of stories or books of art or musical reproductions which can allow the people in that community to explore the arts and to witness the reflections of people from all corners of the world. 10

The NEA has financed many programs which promote access to the arts for people who otherwise would not be able to experience art. These programs may include bringing a dance troupe into rural areas on a tour, or it may include sponsoring a musical exploration program for poor students in the inner city. 11

In my district in central Brooklyn, the NEA has funded many small and worthwhile community programs. With such programs, restoration has become well known and attracts children and adults from throughout the city to participate in those and many other community minded programs. 12

Another cultural program funded by the NEA in my district is New Radio and Performing Arts, a pioneer in the fields of experimental documentaries, contemporary radio drama and sound experiments for the broadcast media. Endowment support over several years has helped this organi- 13 zation to explore new projects about women poets of color and identify new talents for underrepresented radio themes and contents.

Endowment support to another institution in my district has funded a variety of projects intended to showcase new art forms and smaller programs targeted to the local multiethnic community which seek to increase access to different art forms and encourage exploration of the arts by children. 14

These and many other worthwhile community programs in my district have been funded by the NEA and thousands more have been funded nationwide. Of more than 80,000 grants, only 20 to 25 have been considered controversial. For this, some Members of this body are advocating that we eliminate the entire program. 15

Members are rising up in arms because tax dollars have been spent on funding these controversial projects. Each taxpayer is responsible for only 62 cents of the total yearly budget for the NEA. Compare that with the cost per taxpayer for each $5 billion B-2 bomber that falls from the sky, or each $20 million rocket that blows up, or the astronomical cost of the $500 billion S&L bail-out. Where is the outrage over the cost to the taxpayers of these million and billion dollar black holes? 16

Members are rising up in arms over supposedly morally repugnant projects being sponsored by the Government. Where is the outrage over the equally morally repugnant problems being created by the Government? 17

The situation with the National Endowment of the Arts has been blown way out of proportion. There are no rational reasons for restricting this program and there are no reasons at all to eliminate it altogether. This Congress has been stampeded into making wrong and potentially disastrous decisions too frequently in the recent past. We must not bow to these illogical forces. We must fight to preserve this program based not on fear and intimidation, but based on the history and good experiences of this particular program. I urge my colleagues to have courage and to vote to defend the National Endowment for the Arts reauthorization. 18

HONORABLE CLAUDINE SCHNEIDER

UNITED STATES REPRESENTATIVE, RHODE ISLAND, REPUBLICAN

Over the summer, more than two dozen amendments to the NEA bill were introduced in the House. They range from prohibitions over funding art that contains human fetal tissue or that encourages defacing the American flag, to requirements that Federal arts grantees buy only American-made products, to the outright abolition of the NEA. 1

The problem with such proposals, constitutional issues aside, is that they suggest an agency run amok, an Endowment out of control. In fact, in the 25-year history of the NEA, fewer than 25 grants out of some 85,000 have even caused a stir. That is less than one-quarter of one-tenth of one percent. Had the Pentagon, HUD or agencies overseeing the savings and loan industry been as scrupulous with Federal moneys, we taxpayers would not be facing a bill of thousands of dollars each to fix the damage. 2

Instead, the NEA asks each of us for 68 cents, pocket change for the millions of students the agency reaches through its arts education programs; the cost of a cup of coffee for supporting the Nation's best orchestras, museums, theatres and public broadcasting; a handful of coins for bringing the arts into the rural parts of America; less than six bits for helping stimulate more than $6 billion in private giving to the arts. This is 68 cents from each American as compared to per capita spending for the arts in Canada ($32), France ($32) and West Germany ($27). 3

In all, NEA support for culture in Rhode Island totals more than $940,000 so far this year. With requirements that every dollar awarded to an organization be matched with a dollar of private support, Endowment grants to Rhode Island have helped pump millions more dollars into our State's culture and, consequently, our economy. 4

The NEA has helped bring about a cultural renaissance in this country over the last quarter century. Since 1965, we have seen the number of orchestras double, dance companies grow seven times, theatre companies expand eightfold and State arts agencies multiplied by 10. 5

Despite this unparalleled record, the very existence of this tiny agency which does so much with so little is being threatened. Because of two grants over the past three years that some have found objectionable—grants that indirectly funded the exhibition of some photographs which, incidentally, no NEA panel ever saw—some in Congress want to abolish the Endowment. While it does not appear that they have the votes to succeed, a more chilling threat centers on congressional efforts to restrict what the Endowment funds. 6

These so-called content restrictions have been the focus of much debate. Some believe that such funding standards are necessary and proper when doling out taxpayers' money. Others contend that artistic expression is a form of speech protected by the First Amendment, that to restrict such expression is akin to censorship. In fact, funding standards already exist—the toughest standards of all, artistic excellence. Individual artists and arts organizations selected from among the 18,000 applications for grants have passed a rigorous review process that recommends funding for only the best projects. In some categories, such as visual artists fellowships, less than four percent of the applicants are recommended for grants. 7

While some congressmen are calling for a ban against obscene art, the fact is: first, obscenity is already against the law; second, obscenity runs counter to artistic quality and would never knowingly be funded anyway; and third, questions of obscenity are traditionally decided in the courts, applying local community standards, and not by a Federal agency. 8

Returning the responsibility of determining obscenity to the courts is the basis by which the Senate committee overseeing the Endowment's reauthorization overwhelmingly forged a compromise. The legislation enables the Endowment to recoup funds from a grantee whose work has been found in the courts to be obscene. The most notable aspect of the bill is the broad bipartisan support it received, approved by the committee 15 to 1. In the 18 months since this controversy began, the senators seemed to have 9 unearthed the largest chunk of middle ground that we have seen. The question now is whether it is big enough to accommodate a majority in the House as well. I hope so.

It is time to resolve that the ideas and works of those with the courage and talent to create new art never be threatened. Congress should support free speech, not suppress it. 10

Federal Funding of the Arts: Con

HONORABLE RICHARD K. ARMEY
UNITED STATES REPRESENTATIVE, TEXAS, REPUBLICAN

It has been my observation that every dollar's worth of Government spending of the taxpayers' hard-earned money brings with it one million dollars' worth of audacity and presumptuousness. In this debate, the most audacious presumption of all is the presumption that without the National Endowment for the Arts there would not be a participation in and enjoyment of the arts in the United States. 1

That presumption is ludicrous. The American people enjoyed the arts, produced the arts and participated in the arts long, long before the existence of the National Endowment. So if in fact there is going to be Government spending on the arts, it is not a question then of how much art will we have and enjoy, but what will be the nature and the type of the art that we will enjoy. 2

I would suggest that nobody spends somebody else's money as wisely as they would spend their own, and that is certainly true in this case. 3

Last year alone, there were 18,000 people or organizations that made application to the National Endowment for the Arts. Five thousand of those were granted. Thirteen thousand were not. 4

Are we to believe that none of those 13,000 artistic endeavors that were denied funding by the U.S. Government's agency ever took place? Are we to believe that each of those 5,000 that were funded should have taken place instead? Are we to believe that none of the 5,000 would have taken place without the grants? I think not. I think it is time to end this intrusion into freedom of expression in the arts. 5

I appreciate this opportunity to pass along my thoughts regarding the future of the National Endowment for the Arts, and to discuss the volatile mix of taxpayer money and artistic freedom in a somewhat reasoned setting. Until now, the nature of the discussion has been anything but reasoned. 6

Those of us who question whether or not tax dollars should be used to fund individual artists or organizations in the self-described arts community, or whether such spending should be subject to limits that reflect the sensibilities of the American taxpayer, have been the focus of strident *ad hominem* attacks. I have had the distinction of being called in the media a "petty moralist," "public pinhead," "troglodyte," "philistine," "bozo," "fascist" and, of course, "censor" by advocates of no strings attached Federal 7 spending on art. And I know that some on the other side of this issue have been charged with willfully funding pornography, which never goes over big with the voters back home.

In reasonably addressing the future of the National Endowment for the Arts, we must ask ourselves three fundamental questions: 8

First, is it the proper role of the Federal Government to grant money to individual artists, arts organizations and the more traditional fine arts? 9

Second, if a majority of Members of Congress feel it is the proper role of the Federal Government to fund these individuals and groups, do we have the resources to do it in an era of $200 billion-plus deficits? 10

Third, if funding individual works of art and performance art is of such high priority, should the Congress have the right to impose standards on works of art which will be funded? 11

It is no coincidence that freedom of speech is protected by our Constitution's First Amendment, for it may be our most important right in America. Anyone who values freedom of expression as deeply as I do should find abhorrent the very existence of a Federal panel charged with determining what art is worthy of funding. 12

Let's look at this curious contention that withholding tax funds from certain artists is censorship. According to the budget director at the National Endowment for the Arts, the NEA received 17,879 grant applications in Fiscal Year 1989. They chose to fund 4,372 of these. In the language of the demagogues in the arts community, the NEA censored 13,507 artists last year. Doesn't that have a chilling effect on the arts community? 13

Throughout last summer's debate, many outside Congress who opposed content restrictions on NEA grants argued that Federal grants were important because they constitute a stamp of approval that enables an artist to receive greater funding in the private sector. Doesn't that scare any of you? Don't you find it frightening that a Government agency is putting its stamp of approval on what is acceptable art, art which is worthy of funding? 14

Unfortunately, those who cry out for Government funding of individual works of art in one breath and shout "censorship" in the next refuse to acknowledge the inherent contradiction in their actions. They don't want freedom of expression, they want the money. They care less about freedom of expression than they do about the greenback dollar. If, however, you accept the premise that a Federal agency should spend taxpayers' money to fund individual works of art, you must put it in the context of a Federal budget with competing demands on limited resources. Then the question becomes: "When we have a projected Federal deficit in excess of $200 billion, can we afford to spend $180 million on art?" 15

Some say that figure is a mere drop in the bucket, but how many homeless families could be housed with $180 million? How many scientists could continue researching a cure for AIDS? How many veterans could be given vouchers to allow them to purchase high-quality medical care closer to their homes? How many fledgling democracies might be assisted? How many new law enforcement personnel could be enlisted in our war on 16 drugs? Or how many taxpayers would appreciate some tax relief and deficit reduction?

Surely, funding for museums, individual artists, opera productions, city orchestras and plays would be high on Maslow's Pyramid of Human Needs, which may be why those who take advantage of their availability tend to be the more privileged members of American society. In other words, spending tax dollars to fund works of art amounts to an inequitable transfer of income from lower- and middle-class taxpayers to indulge the less urgent needs of society's more privileged class. 17

It is this Congress's job to prioritize spending, and I would strongly suggest that funding any artistic activity is at or near the bottom of most taxpayers' priorities. 18

But, if the majority in the House determine that their constituents deem funding for the arts community a national priority, then the question is: "Should the National Endowment for the Arts be held accountable for how it spends tax dollars?" 19

Boom! This is the explosive question at the center of so much heated debate and rhetoric. 20

One of my distinguished colleagues summed up the conflict earlier this year by saying: "The Federal Government should not diminish the artist's right to offend," but that on the other hand, "Taxpayers have a right to determine how their money should be used." 21

I cannot see that conflict here. The indisputable right for an artist to offend the public is different from a claimed right to offend the public at public expense. 22

So how do you protect the taxpayer? Obviously, the easiest way is to abolish the agency and rid ourselves of the heart of the problem. Barring that, the answer becomes less clear. 23

Many artists felt the NEA was being unfairly singled out for congressional oversight during last year's debate when, in fact, every agency in the Federal Government is subject to such oversight. What distinguishes the NEA and its grant recipients from all other Government agencies is its assertion that it be exempted from such congressional oversight. 24

Many advocates of no strings attached Federal arts funding assert that war is too important to be left to the warriors in the Pentagon. Then they assert that art is more important than war, but art should be left to the artists. And not all artists should determine spending priorities at the NEA, but a small clique on the fringe of the art world, sometimes known as the avant garde, but which I prefer to call the loony left. 25

I do not believe we should spend NEA money for the enjoyment of artists. I believe we should spend NEA money for the enjoyment of the public, if we spend it at all, and that NEA grants should reflect the public's sensibilities and values. 26

Obviously, defining what the public's sensibilities and values are is a tricky business. It is a business more easily conducted at local levels, where the sense of community standards is readily identifiable. In this regard, the best way to ensure that Americans are given the opportunity to enjoy works 27 of art, to ensure that rural communities across America can still have access to the fine arts, and to reduce the possibility that tax dollars will be used in a way that denigrates rather than lifts the human spirit may be to grant NEA funds to individual communities for them to spend. I am very disappointed that Congress has allowed this controversy to continue for much too long and hope that we will do right by the taxpayers today.

HONORABLE BARBARA F. VUCANOVICH
UNITED STATES REPRESENTATIVE, NEVADA, REPUBLICAN

I will vote in favor of the Crane amendment to H.R. 4825. This amendment would abolish the National Endowment for the Arts. 1

This was not an easy decision, yet it was an extremely important one. Our Nation's budget deficit has grown to an unacceptable level. During this time of fiscal crisis, it is essential that we, as lawmakers, prioritize what is important for our country's welfare. In doing so, I simply cannot put the authorization of the arts in the same category as providing Medicare for the elderly or ensuring our country's defense. 2

When speaking on this issue, other Members of Congress have shown their distaste for certain federally subsidized exhibits. While I may share their concern about the content of artwork, I do not believe that it is a question of censorship, but simply a question of appropriate use of the taxpayers' dollars. 3

Personally, I am a great supporter of the arts. I have supported many organizations within my district which provide us with the joy of music, heritage and culture, to name a few. Private donations and endorsements certainly are paramount to the existence of the arts and humanities; now and in the future. The $175 million lost in public funds could easily be recovered by the public sector; the private sector spends nearly $7 billion on arts advancement each year. 4

During this time of financial constraint, however, we must examine our programs and cut those which are not at the top of the list. Coming to this realization, I simply must support the Crane amendment. 5

I believe this is in the best interest of my constituents as well as all Americans so that they may receive the services they so desperately need during this time of fiscal despair. 6

▲ ▲ ▲

Review Questions

1. According to Owens, why is it partisan and irrational to oppose funding for the NEA because of the controversy over obscene art?
2. What kind of specific illustrations does Owens cite to demonstrate the value of NEA funding?
3. What kind of safeguards are presently in place to prevent "obscene" art from being funded, according to Schneider?

4. Why does Armey reject the assumption that eliminating federal funding of the arts would have a serious effect on the output of art?
5. How does Armey attempt to respond to charges that he is censoring art?

Discussion and Writing Suggestions

1. What is the essential nature of the debate between Owens and Armey? That is, how do they differ in the way they see the relationship between the government, artists, and communities? How do Owens and Schneider represent the *liberal* viewpoint and Armey and Vucanovich the *conservative* viewpoint, as defined by Smith and by Burns, Peltason, Cronin, and Magleby? Whose views make most sense to you? (For example, to what extent do you agree with Armey that taxpayers should not be forced to subsidize artists?) Whose reasoning and evidence are more persuasive? Explain, using examples from your own experience and observation.
2. How do Owens, Schneider, Armey, and Vucanovich make use of some of the "propaganda" devices discussed by Donna Cross and by Donald Lazere? Write a short essay in which you categorize and illustrate some of the chief ways in which these members of Congress attempt to persuade their audience of the validity of their views and the weakness of the other side.
3. Write a magazine article in which, while taking an objective stance on the subject, you give an organized account of the debate among these Congresspersons. Determine their main areas of disagreement, and in a comparison-contrast format, discuss their respective viewpoints.
4. Imagine you are an artist whose particular subject matter and style may not appeal to conservatives like Armey and Vucanovich, and may not even appeal to liberals like Owens and Schneider—a fact of which you are aware. Write a grant proposal to the National Endowment for the Arts, applying for funding, in which you describe your project and justify your request. Then write a response from the Director of the NEA either turning down the proposal or requesting modifications, and explaining your reasons.

A Debate on School Prayer

Should students in the nation's public schools have the option of beginning each day with a voluntary prayer—or at least with a moment of silence? Although school prayer has not been as central a subject of national debate in recent years as, say, affirmative action or abortion, it is one that is argued with equal passion. As with federal funding for the arts, one's position on school prayer depends on whether one is a liberal or a conservative. Liberals maintain that allowing prayer during school hours violates the separation of church and state, subverts religious liberty, and would be coercive on young children for whom the concept of "voluntary" prayer is made meaningless by peer pressure. Conservatives maintain with equal fervor that nothing in the Bill of Rights prohibits voluntary school prayer (as opposed to Government-established religion), that school prayer would act as a positive force in a society suffering from moral breakdown (drugs, teenage pregnancy, school drop-out rates, etc.), and they cite polls showing that most Americans favor school prayer.

In 1962, the Supreme Court, in Engel v. Vitale, *ruled that government sponsorship of prayer and Bible reading in public schools violated the First Amendment. Since then, legislation has been introduced in every Congress attempting to override or restrict this judicial ruling. Although these attempts were generally unsuccessful, in 1984 Congress enacted the Equal Access Act, which provided that schools allowing extracurricular groups to meet in school facilities outside school hours must also allow the same access to extracurricular groups meeting for religious purposes. In 1985 the Supreme Court (in* Wallace v. Jaffree*) overturned as unconstitutional an Alabama law providing for silent meditation as well as voluntary prayer. And in 1994, Congress barred state and local educational agencies from using funding under the "Educate America" act to institute policies that would prevent students from engaging in silent meditation or voluntary prayer. Clearly, the school prayer debate will continue to polarize the nation in years to come.*

The following statements on school prayer were made in conjunction with Congressional debate on H.R. [House of Representatives] 6 and S [Senate] 1513, the "Improving America's Schools Act." While much of this bill was uncontroversial, the attention of many legislators was focused on a proposed school prayer constitutional amendment (H.J. Res 242), officially introduced in November 1994, which states:

> Nothing in this Constitution shall be construed to prohibit individual or group prayer in public schools or other public institutions. No person shall be required by the United States or by any State to participate in prayer. Neither the United States nor any State shall compose the words of any prayer to be said in public schools.

Senator Jesse Helms, Republican from North Carolina (one of the most conservative members of the Senate), made his speech on the Senate floor on October 6, 1994. The statement by the American Center for Law and Justice (Jay Alan Sekulow, Chief Counsel; Joel Thornton, Associate Counsel) was prepared for Congressional Digest *on December 8, 1994. Senator Mark O. Hatfield, Republican (a moderate-liberal, who has been in the Senate since 1966) made his speech on the Senate floor on July 27, 1994. The passage by Americans United for Separation of Church and State (Barry W. Lynn, Executive Director) was prepared as a press statement in November 1994. All of these statements appear in the January 1995 issue of* Congressional Digest.

School Prayer: Pro

HONORABLE JESSE A. HELMS
UNITED STATES SENATOR, NORTH CAROLINA, REPUBLICAN

What is really taking place in this Nation today is a struggle for the soul of America. How it is finally resolved will determine whether America will move forward, or end up on the ash heap of history as so many nations have done before us. 1

The American people, I guarantee you, are more aware than ever before as to what is at stake. They are sick and tired of crime and pornography, mediocre schools, and politicians who cater to every fringe group that comes down the pike. 2

We are in the midst of an historic struggle for survival in terms of restoring traditional values, family values—whatever you want to call them—and then we vote down time after time every attempt to restore these values. 3

That is what we are struggling through right now. You can stand on the Capitol steps and almost throw a rock into neighborhoods where you cannot walk at night because of the violence that takes place nightly. As Members of Congress, we pass great big expensive crime bills—but they do no good. Then we go home and say, boy, we really took care of it this time. There is not going to be any more crime because we are going to kill it with money. We are going to appropriate enough money to solve this problem. 4

Mr. President, we have been passing crime bill after crime bill almost since I came here in 1973. And what has been the result? 5

There is more crime than ever before, and crimes are more heinous than ever before. There has been, in short, an absolute disintegration of morality. 6

Reader's Digest published an article a year or so ago which was titled "Let Us Pray." In that article, *Reader's Digest* reported the results of a poll which found that 75 percent of the American people strongly favor prayer in the public schools and want it restored. 7

The subtitle of that article was what caught my attention. The article said at the top, "Let Us Pray," and then right below that in smaller print it said, "Why can't the voice of the people be heard on prayer in schools?" Why indeed? 8

Reader's Digest pointed out that opinions in favor of school prayer "were expressed by Democrats, Republicans, blacks and whites, rich and poor, high school dropouts and college graduates—reflecting a profound disparity between the citizenry and the [Supreme] Court." 9

Yet, despite this massive outcry, the liberals in Congress and in the media claim that the Constitution somehow forbids governmental establishment of religion and, ipso facto, prayer in school cannot be permitted. 10

Of course, they never point out that the Constitution specifically forbids government restrictions on the free exercise of religion. You never hear that mentioned. But they talk incessantly about separation of church 11 and state even though it is not even in the Constitution. The First Amendment says, "Congress shall make no law respecting an establishment of religion, or prohibiting the free exercise thereof." It certainly does not say anything about the separation of church and state.

Something else the Constitution says that nobody mentions very often. 12
The Constitution protects students' rights to free speech, whether religious or not, and that student-initiated, voluntary prayer—expressed in an appropriate time, place, and manner—has never been outlawed by the Supreme Court. But try telling that to school principals and school superintendents—or the teachers' unions.

If we really care about cleaning up the streets and the classrooms, if we 13
really care about the long-term survival of our Nation, is there anything more important for the Senate to protect than the right of America's children to participate in voluntary, constitutionally protected prayer in school?

We already spend more money per pupil than any other industrialized 14
country in the world and what has it brought? We have the lowest math scores, the lowest English scores, and the highest crime rate of any of our major trading partners. And this has happened to education since Federal aid to education began. We should be number one, based on the hundreds of billions of dollars we have spent on education in this country at the Federal, State, and local levels.

The point being, we can spend all the money we dare tax out of people 15
and it is not going to improve our children's achievement, or happiness, or well-being one whit unless and until we take traditional morality out of government-imposed exile and bring it back—and put it back in the place of prominence and respect it once enjoyed in our lives and in our schools.

The American Center for Law and Justice

JAY ALAN SEKULOW, CHIEF COUNSEL
JOEL THORNTON, ASSOCIATE COUNSEL

For the past six years, we have dedicated a substantial amount of our re- 1
sources to defend students who desire to pray and have Bible and prayer clubs at the public schools. In 1990, when we argued the Bible club case, *Westside Community Schools v. Mergens* before the U.S. Supreme Court, we committed substantial resources in order for our organization to stand up for students whenever their rights are being denied because of their faith.*

The amount of requests for assistance for cases involving the public 2
schools are increasing at an unprecedented rate. Despite the passage of the Equal Access Act in 1984 and the Supreme Court's decision in *Mergens,*

*In the *Mergens* decision, the Court voted 8–1 that secondary schools may not bar religious student groups from using school facilities for meetings during noninstructional time if they also permit secular groups to do the same.

students across our land are being denied fundamental rights of freedom of speech, including the right to pray.

This fact hit home most recently when the U.S. Court of Appeals for the Ninth Circuit, on November 18, 1994, ruled that student prayer at a graduation ceremony was unconstitutional. The Ninth Circuit held that there was "no meaningful distinction between school authorities actually organizing the religious activities and officials merely permitting students to direct the exercises" (*Harris v. Joint School District No. 241*). 3

This decision of the Ninth Circuit runs contrary to the language written by the Supreme Court in the *Mergens* case, which noted that "there is a crucial difference between government speech endorsing religion which the Establishment Clause forbids, and private speech endorsing religion which the Free Speech and Free Exercise Clauses protect." 4

We have consistently taken the position that students have the right to share their faith at graduation ceremonies through testimony, or through prayer. This apparently is not the view of the U.S. Court of Appeals for the Ninth Circuit. This decision, left unchecked, could create a further zone of hostility for religious students on public school campuses. This is why we need some affirmative protection for religious liberty for students. 5

When the debate began on the constitutional amendment for prayer these past few weeks, we initially were hesitant to take a public position. After reviewing the proposed amendment to the Constitution, however, and then recommending to Congressman Istook and others significant changes to the language, we are convinced that if we work through the amendment process we can obtain justice for students in our Nation's public schools. 6

The language we have proposed is this: 7

> Nothing in this Constitution shall be construed to prohibit individual or group prayer by students in the public schools, or individual or group prayer in other public institutions. No person shall be required by the United States or by any State to participate in prayer. Neither the United States nor any State shall compose the words of any prayer to be said in public schools.

Our proposed language focuses on students not being denied the right to have prayer at their pubic schools. We have seen the abuses that students have been confronted with when they have been threatened with arrest, have been arrested for praying around their school flagpole, suspected for possession of Christian material on campus, or told that establishing a Bible club would violate the separation of church and state. By using the word "students," and possibly including the word student-initiated or student-led, we will be in a position to affirmatively protect students who desire to pray on public school campuses. 8

We need to see affirmative protection for students on the public school campus who want to exercise their faith. We have reached a point in our country where we have more of a freedom from religion than a freedom of religion. 9

When students are told that they cannot pray at graduation ceremonies, when the president of a Christian Bible club is told to remove the word 10

"God" or "Jesus" from a sign advertising the club meetings, and when students are told that they cannot do book reports on historical figures if those figures are referenced in the Bible, we have a serious misunderstanding of freedom and liberty.

Based on the surveys we have seen, and the phone calls and letters that pour into our offices, it's time for affirmative protection for students who want to engage in prayer in our Nation's public schools. Do we want to have a constitutional amendment? No. We certainly would have been more satisfied if the courts simply upheld the true understanding of freedom and liberty, but in many circumstances they have not. 11

For those students involved in the Ninth Circuit decision, their freedom was lost on November 18, 1994, when the Court held that students could not pray at graduation. Through this constitutional amendment process not only is the issue of school prayer placed before the Nation, but we have an opportunity to see a change in the right direction for freedom. 12

School Prayer: Con

HONORABLE MARK O. HATFIELD
UNITED STATES SENATOR, OREGON, REPUBLICAN

We are dealing with a very personal issue in the matter of prayer. We are dealing with the issue of protecting religion and religious convictions. 1

I must say very frankly that I oppose all prescriptive prayer of any kind in public schools. Does that mean I am against prayer? No. It does not mean that at all. I am very strong in my belief in the efficacy of prayer. But I must say that there is no way this body or the Constitution or the President or the courts could ever abolish prayer in the public schools. That is an impossibility. 2

I often use, somewhat facetiously, the example and experience of having prayed my way through every math course examination I ever took. I was not praying to my fellow students. I was engaged in silent prayer to God, who I thought was more powerful than I and all the students put together. 3

So I think we get ourselves into a great thicket of trying to prescribe parameters surrounding prayer in public schools. I have also sometimes said facetiously, I do not have the time to write the prayers for the schools and I do not trust anybody else to write them. That is my religious heritage, always questioning ecclesiastical authority as well as political authority. 4

All I am saying is that this can be very personal, and silent prayer is happening all the time. I am not sure that I know of anything in any of the great religions that requires audible prayer to validate the efficacy or the importance of prayer. I can pray silently, or I can pray verbally and audibly. 5

So I would like to say that prayer is being given every day in public schools through this country—silent prayer, personal prayer that in no way could we ever abolish even if we wanted to. 6

So I do not see any great crises about the right of prayer in public schools. 7

I also feel very strongly that when we begin to talk about personal prayer again, we should remember that it is a matter of free speech as well as freedom of religion. I happened to co-author here on the Senate side the Equal Access Act legislation, coming from the *Widmar case* [U.S. Supreme Court case *Widmar v. Vincent* (1981)] of the University of Missouri, where the university had provided access to facilities on the campus for students to voluntarily congregate in pursuing a common interest. But when they wanted to get together for Bible study, the university ruled against that. That was religion. 8

The Supreme Court very quickly handled that case by saying wherever the institution of learning gives a right to forum, they have no right to dictate the subject of the forum, and upheld the right of students to voluntarily gather themselves together for Bible study on that campus. 9

We took the same principle of the *Widmar* case, and we applied it to the secondary school system of this country under the Equal Access Act. If the school before or after hours provides an opportunity for students to voluntarily gather themselves using facilities of the school for a particular interest, for a camera club, music club, or whatever it might be, those students should have the same right to gather themselves together for prayer or Bible study. 10

Now that is a free speech issue, but like many of our freedoms it also correlates to the freedom of religion. I would like to see us move beyond and outside of this particular debate because I do not see the necessity for this Senate to take any action on the subject of school prayer. 11

If there are those schools that are unfriendly to religious practices or free speech, then let that be handled through the individual communities and through the legal authorities in each of those communities with injunctions or whatever remedy may be issued by the court. We do not have to cut off funds to enforce court actions. 12

So I believe that the simplest and best way to deal with this subject is to take no action relating to school prayer. Let students continue to pray as they do now, silently, as an undeniable personal right. 13

Americans United for Separation of Church and State

BARRY W. LYNN, EXECUTIVE DIRECTOR

In 1843, an ugly riot rocked the Philadelphia suburb of Kensington. For three days, mobs roamed the streets of the City of Brotherly Love as the police struggled to regain control. When it was all over, several buildings had been reduced to rubble, and 13 people were dead. 1

The Philadelphia riot was notable for its particularly violent character, but what's even more unusual is what sparked it. The country was restless with pre–Civil War tensions at the time, but it wasn't race relations, slav- 2 ery, or "preserving the union" that tore the community asunder. The people of Philadelphia rioted over prayer in public schools.

Tensions between Roman Catholics and Protestants were near the breaking point in mid–19th century America, and public schools had become the flash point. When local education officials in southeastern Pennsylvania assented to Catholic demands and ruled that Catholic children could be excused from mandatory daily—and generally Protestant—Bible reading and prayer, the Protestant majority generated a violent backlash. 3

The incident is worth remembering as the nationwide debate over religion in public schools resumes again, thanks to soon-to-be Speaker of the House Newt Gingrich's promise to hold a congressional vote on a school prayer amendment by July 4. 4

Prayer in schools is one of the most misunderstood social concerns Americans face today. Many people wonder why the issue is so emotional. What is the harm, they ask, in a little prayer. 5

What these people fail to understand is that religious passions run deep. Many Americans are offended by the idea that their children may be forced to participate in religious exercises in public school that clash with what the children are taught at home or at the family's house of worship. These parents rightly see school prayer as a usurpation of parental authority. 6

Other parents have no desire to have their children participate in the type of bland, watered-down prayers that are commonly offered for public consumption. They cite the words of Jesus from the sixth book of Matthew who, in cautioning against gaudy public displays of religion, said, "When you pray, enter your closet and shut the door. Pray to your Father, who is in secret, and your Father, who sees in secret, will reward you openly." 7

As the religious pluralism of the United States continues to expand, it is impossible that a "To-Whom-It-May-Concern" prayer could be fashioned that would please fundamentalist Protestants and Roman Catholics as well as Jews, Buddhists, Muslims, and the thousands of other religious groups. Even if this type of prayer could be written, who would care to recite such theological pablum? 8

Some school prayer advocates suggest letting each community decide what prayer is recited. If Southern Baptists predominate, for example, the Lord's Prayer would be recited. If Catholics hold sway, it will be the Our Father. 9

Such a "majority rules" set-up would violate the right of conscience of millions of American schoolchildren. Their choice would be to either participate in religious ceremonies alien to them or risk ostracism by getting up and leaving the room. 10

In a country that was founded on religious freedom, this is an unfair situation to put any child in, especially very young children, who may not even understand what is going on. 11

The great tragedy of the school prayer debate is that it is unnecessary. Nothing in the Constitution now prohibits children from engaging in truly 12 voluntary prayer. They may pray at the beginning of the day, over lunch, before tests, at any time they have a free moment.

Under the Federal Equal Access Act, high school students may even form prayer clubs and meet outside class hours for Bible study and worship. No court in the land has ever struck down personal religious devotions. 13

Despite the rhetoric, what Gingrich and some of his colleagues are offering is not voluntary prayer. The wording of the proposed amendment says that "group prayer" will be permitted in public schools. 14

In other words, the entire class, at the direction of a teacher or school official, can be ordered to recite a prayer. The only option for those who choose not to take part is to grin and bear it or get up and leave. There is nothing "voluntary" about this type of coercion. 15

Religion is best left as a private matter, as the Nation's founders intended. It should never be forced onto anyone, especially a child. Public schools are for educating children about the basics—reading, 'riting, and 'rithmetic. Let's leave the "fourth R," religion, where it rightly belongs—in the homes and houses of worship of our country. 16

▲ ▲ ▲

Review Questions

1. Why does Helms reject the argument that the American tradition of separation of church and state forbids prayer in public schools?
2. How do Sekulow and Thornton propose to overcome the objection to school-sanctioned prayer?
3. Why does Hatfield refuse to believe that there is a crisis over the right to pray in school?
4. For what main reasons does Lynn think that group prayer should not be permitted during school hours?

Discussion and Writing Suggestions

1. How does the debate over school prayer play out along liberal/conservative lines? Using the definitions provided by Burns, Peltason, Cronin, and Magleby, explain in a multi-paragraph essay what makes Jesse Helms's and the American Center for Law and Justice's position *conservative* (perhaps each in his own way) and Mark Hatfield's and the Americans United for Separation of Church and State's position *liberal*. Consider not only this particular issue, but also how this issue relates to the broader agendas of conservatives and liberals. (See also Smith, paragraphs 8 and 9.)
2. How do those who argue on both sides of the school prayer issue make use of some of the "propaganda" devices discussed by Donna

Cross and by Donald Lazere? Write a short essay, in which you categorize and illustrate some of the chief ways in which the speakers attempt to persuade their audience of the validity of their views and the weakness of the other side.

3. Taking into account these arguments for and against school prayer, does the Constitutional amendment proposed by the American Center for Law and Justice seem a reasonable compromise to you? Explain why or why not, perhaps casting your response in the form of a senatorial speech either in support of or in opposition to this proposal.
4. Write a short critique of one of the selections on school prayer. Take into account some of your responses to the questions above.

SCORING GUIDE FOR "POLITICAL QUIZ" (PAGES 249–252)

How to assign points:

1. "Trust"—0 points. "Distrust" gets 2 points. The major difference between liberals and conservatives is that liberals tend to trust government while conservatives do not.
2. Any of the following gets 1 point (for a maximum of 5 points):

   The Pentagon
   The executive branch
   The FBI
   The CIA
   The Joint Chiefs

   Any of these gets 0 points:

   The U.S. Postal Service
   The legislative branch
   The IRS
   The Peace Corps
   The United Nations

   Liberals would pick the U.S Postal Service, the IRS, the Peace Corps, the United Nations and the legislative branch because they tend to believe in these institutions.
3. Any of the following gets 1 point (for a maximum of 3 points):

   Doctors
   Business executives
   Team owners

   These answers score 0 points:

Trial lawyers
Union leaders
Professional athletes

Liberals favor trial lawyers over doctors, and workers over executives because they tend to distrust businessmen and favor workers and advocates.

4. Give yourself 1 point on this question ONLY if you answered "none." All other answers: 0.
5. You get 1 point for every answer (for a maximum of 9), EXCEPT "Cut defense spending" and "Don't cut at all," which score 0.
6. "Term limits"—1 point.
   "Public financing"—0.
7. "Ronald Reagan"—1 point.
   "Franklin D. Roosevelt"—0.
8. "Melting pot"—1 point.
   "Multicultural society"—0.
9. "Jackson"—1 point
   "Limbaugh"—0.
   "Neither"—0.
10. "Stricter controls"—0 points.
    "Mandatory sentences"—1.
    "Both"—0.
11. "Build prisons"—1 point.
    "Rebuild cities"—0.
    "Both"—0.
12. "Agree"—1. "Disagree"—0.
13. "Agree"—1. "Disagree"—0.
14. "Agree"—0. "Disagree"—1.
15. "Agree"—0. "Disagree"—1.
16. "Agree"—1. "Disagree"—0.
17. "Agree"—0. "Disagree"—1.
18. "Agree"—0. "Disagree"—1.
19. "Agree"—0. "Disagree"—1.
20. "Agree"—1. "Disagree"—0.
21. "Agree"—0. "Disagree"—1.
22. "Agree"—0. "Disagree"—1.
23. "Agree"—1. "Disagree"—0.
24. "Agree"—0. "Disagree"—1.
25. "Agree"—0. "Disagree"—1.

About Your Score:

Respondents with the most points (40) are 100 percent conservative; those with the least (0) are 100 percent liberal. See where you fall on the chart below. Take note: A higher number of points is not meant to imply a higher level of political consciousness! The system of accumulating points for conservative answers is simply a practical method for assigning politically left-to-right slots on the spectrum.

Left			**Center**					**Right**
Jesse Jackson	Ted Kennedy	Hillary Clinton	Bill Clinton	Colin Powell	George Bush	Jack Kemp	Bob Dole	Ronald Reagan
0	5	10	15	20	25	30	35	40

SYNTHESIS ACTIVITIES

1. Write an article for a newsmagazine about the current political landscape in the United States. Focus on the difference between liberals and conservatives, but include other political ideologies further to the left and to the right. Discuss the various viewpoints on key issues that divide politicians and political observers. Don't take sides, but do your best to give an objective account of some of the key political debates and the kind of arguments they have generated.

   Draw upon as many of the selections in this chapter as you can. You will need to use Smith, Burns et al., and Lazere to define the differences between the various political viewpoints; you will draw primarily from the three debates at the end of the chapter (on welfare, federal funding for the arts, and school prayer), as well as candidate statements from "A Voter's Manual for the Political Parties and the Candidates") to provide particular examples.
2. Write a newspaper feature article summarizing for voters the candidates and the issues discussed in the "Voter's Manual for the Political Parties and the Candidates." Using summary, paraphrase, and quotation, explain to voters the key issues in the upcoming election and discuss the candidates' positions on the key issues. Make the discussion as objective as possible. Keep in mind that mainstream newspapers are likely to give the lion's share of space to the Democratic and Republican parties. (Of course, you may choose to write for a non-mainstream newspaper.)
3. Examine the use of political rhetoric in ideological debates today. Focusing on the three particular "debates" in this chapter, as well as on the language in the "Voter's Manual," apply the rhetorical tools discussed in Lazere and Cross to the arguments in these other sources. Try not to be partisan in your treatment; that is, don't single out one particular ideological viewpoint for particular blame or praise, unless you find unmistakable evidence that one party or ideology is significantly more blatant than another.

   Keep in mind, also, that we have to grant a certain degree of "poetic license" to political rhetoric; we can't expect the same kind of objectivity in political speeches or articles in partisan magazines as we do, say, in *Consumer Reports,* or in an objective news summary. It is part of the game for politicians and political advocates to play up their own side and play down the other, and there's no point in venting moral indignation when they do this. What you do want to do is examine how skillfully—or how deceptively—they use the rhetorical tools at their disposal.

4. Write a speech, either for the President or a congressperson, advocating a position and a recommended course of action on welfare. Draw upon not only the "Debate on Welfare" in this chapter, but also upon the selections across the political spectrum on this issue in Chapter 4 ("Synthesis"). Using a "concession" format, acknowledge and then respond to opposing points of view.
5. You are a public relations consultant for one of the six parties described in the "Voter's Manual" (Libertarian, American Independent, Republican, Democratic, Green, or Peace and Freedom). Write a campaign or a fund-raising letter designed for mass mailing to prospective voters. Focus on one, two, or three of the issues in which this party has greatest interest and explain why it is essential to support your candidate or to pass (or defeat) a particular voter initiative or a referendum on the ballot. Refer to information and ideas in whatever selections in this chapter are appropriate to provide support for your arguments. (Even though such a letter would not ordinarily contain citations, you should provide citations in your work.) You can use such material both to show how your programs and proposals deserve voter backing and to show how competing proposals deserve rejection.
6. Although we are most accustomed to discussing liberal, conservative, and other ideological views as they apply to political life, such terms can also be applied to other areas of activity, such as popular culture. A recent issue of *National Review* included an article by Spencer Warren entitled "The 100 Best Conservative Movies." In the article, Warren surveyed movies in such categories as "Best Pictures Celebrating Religion and Faith" (*A Man for All Seasons, Chariots of Fire, The Ten Commandments),* "Best Pictures Indicating the Spiritual Barrenness of Hedonistic Yuppieism" (*Carnal Knowledge* and *Ten*), "Best Picture About Defending America" (*Sergeant York*), and "Best Picture Indicating the Sixties Counterculture" (*Forrest Gump*). Providing not quite equal time, Warren threw in a few good liberal movies, including "the most haunting anti-war film" (*All Quiet on the Western Front*) and "Best film on anti-Semitism" (*Crossfire*).

   TV shows can also be ideological. Producer Norman Lear was famous partly for creating shows like "All in the Family" that made fun of conservative attitudes. Vice President Dan Quayle made headlines for indicting "Murphy Brown" for its liberal take on single motherhood. And recently, the conservative Media Research Center published a list of top 10 shows that were "most guilty of pushing a liberal agenda." (among them: "Roseanne," "Dennis Miller Live," and "Sisters").

Imagine that you are a member of a watchdog group like the Media Research Center or a liberal counterpart. Consider some movies and TV shows that you have seen that seem to be pushing either a liberal or a conservative view of social issues. Draw upon the discussions in Burns, Peltason, Cronin, and Magleby, and in Lazere, as well as viewpoints stated or implied in other selections in this chapter, to analyze the movies and shows for liberal or conservative slant. Write a report praising or indicting your subjects for their political attitudes. Categorize your discussion either by issue or by movie or TV show. Include a set of recommendations at the end.

▼

RESEARCH ACTIVITIES

1. Write an article of five to seven pages for a newsmagazine on the ideological debate surrounding a particular domestic issue, representing views across the political spectrum. Possible issues: affirmative action, immigration policy, abortion, education, law and order, health care, gays in the military, school prayer, drug policy, federal aid to the arts. Try to be as objective as possible. Your job is to inform your readers of the nature of the debate, not to argue one side or another on any particular issue. Use information in Lazere to locate suitable sources from a variety of viewpoints.
2. Prepare an *annotated bibliography* of sources across the political spectrum on some issue. Write at least ten bibliographical entries, on five *leftist* and five *rightist* sources, including at least one magazine or newspaper article or editorial and one book or monograph report from the left-wing publishers and one article or editorial or book report from the right-wing publishers in Sections Two and Three in Lazere. Use *MLA format* for citations. Instead of arranging these citations alphabetically, however, arrange them into a political spectrum going from far right to far left—or vice versa. Thus, your bibliography will serve as a detailed plan—in terms of both content and organization—for an actual paper dealing with the range of political positions and political rhetoric. Each entry should be one-half page to one page long.

   - Identify each author's political position, using clues from affiliation with a particular research institute, book publisher, journal of opinion, party, or organization, and—more importantly—from arguments he or she presents that exemplify Lazere's glossary terms and the particular patterns of political rhetoric in Sections Five and Six, as well as the discussions of political ideology in Burns et al. Give enough quotations to support your identification. In cases for which the author is not arguing from an identifiable position

but only reporting facts, indicate which position the reported facts support, and explain how. (*Note:* some newspapers, magazines, etc., have an identifiable political viewpoint in general, in their news and op-ed orientation, but also attempt to present other views at least some of the time. For example, the *Los Angeles Times* is predominantly liberal, but often carries conservative op-ed columns, letters, etc. So you shouldn't assume that any article appearing in such a periodical will automatically have its predominant viewpoint; look for other identifying clues.
- Apply to each source Lazere's "Semantic Calculator for Bias in Rhetoric" (Section Five), along with the more general principles of "propaganda" analysis in Cross.

(*Assignment adapted from Lazere's "Section I" in "Teaching the Political Conflicts."*)

3. As a member of a group of three or four, select one of the following scenarios:

- You are a member of an election (or re-election) campaign staff for a political candidate—prospective senator, governor, president, etc.
- You are a member of a citizen's action group that is working for the passage of a voter referendum on the November ballot.
- Some other comparable scenario of your own choosing.

Focus your efforts on one particular controversial *domestic* issue, for example, affirmative action, immigration policy, abortion, education, law and order, health care, gays in the military, school prayer, drug policy. (If you are working for a political candidate, recognize that there may be other issues in the campaign, but imagine that this particular issue is the crucial one at this particular time.)
Produce *three reports* for the benefit of your candidate or your group:

- A background survey of the issue. What is the history of this issue, both in a social context, and as it has affected recent political events and campaigns? (4-5 pp.)
- A survey and analysis of the *pro* and *con* arguments on the issue, as they have been articulated by recent commentators and political figures. Organize your discussion of these arguments and positions *along a political spectrum,* ranging from *extreme left* (or *right*) to *moderate* to *extreme right* (or *left*). If you have already prepared the annotated bibliography called for in the previous assignment, you may wish to use it as a basis for this section. (6-8 pp.)
- A set of *recommendations for strategy* based on your assignment of the most effective way to proceed and for your side to prevail.

Suggest effective *rhetorical* ways of promoting your side and attacking the other side. Suggest ways of using *language* for maximum effect. At the same time, suggest ways to avoid coming across as extreme in your position, ways by which your position might be perceived as the most reasonable one. (4-5 pp.)

4. Select a major issue, case, or law in the past several decades, research positions across the political spectrum, and write a paper discussing what you have learned. For example, you might consider the debate over escalating the Vietnam War, the Bakke affirmative action case, the impeachment of President Nixon, debates about the Pledge of Allegiance or burning of the American flag (these latter most recently in 1988 and 1989), about violence or objectionable lyrics in the mass media, or—like Jeff Smith—you might select the 1992 Los Angeles riots. Notice how such debates concern not only the immediate issues, but also the larger ideological differences among left, right, and center. *Note:* For tracking Congressional debates, see *Congressional Digest* and the various *Congressional Quarterly (CQ)* sources, including *Congressional Quarterly, CQ Guide to the Congress of the United States, CQ Guide to United States Elections,* and *CQ Alert* (database). See also *CIS Congressional Information Service Bulletin, United States Political Science Documents,* and *Public Affairs Information Service Bulletin (PAIS),* print or CD-ROM.
5. Select one of the four non-mainstream political parties treated in the "Voter's Manual"—*Libertarian, American Independent, Green, Peace and Freedom*—and write a report on its philosophy and political activities in the past decade or so. Or research the American Socialist or Communist parties. Check major newspaper and magazine indexes; check government documents; write to the parties themselves, asking for information. Who have been some of their candidates? What were their programs? How well have they done at election time? Has their popularity been increasing or decreasing?
6. Examine two or three successive issues of *one* of the magazines or journals at the left or right ends of the political spectrum (see Lazere) and write an analysis of the kinds of positions authors of articles in these periodicals take on various issues, as well as the type of rhetorical devices they use to persuade their readers. (Draw on Burns, Peltason, Cronin, and Magleby for the former part of this assignment and on the guidelines in Lazere and Cross for the latter part.) For example, if you chose *Reason,* a libertarian journal, you would look at several articles and editorials over a three- or four-month period and analyze ideological patterns you discover that promote the libertarian (anti-government) viewpoint and reject others. By the same token, were you to examine several issues of *The Progressive,* you would find articles favoring the "socialist to left-liberal" viewpoint on a variety of issues.

Your general strategy in this assignment would be (1) to locate the authors' positions on the political spectrum, citing evidence from both the author and from other sources such as Smith, Burns et al., and Lazare, and (2) to classify the types of rhetorical devices used, drawing on examples from the words of authors themselves and relating these examples to general strategies discussed by Cross and discussed also in the chapter introduction on the "Three Types of Political Appeals."

7. Select an issue on which some recent American presidents have taken stands (see issues suggested in question 1). Using the indexes in *The Weekly Compilation of Presidential Documents,* write a comparison-contrast paper looking at what post–World War II Democratic presidents (Kennedy, Johnson, Carter, Clinton) have said about the issue versus what Republican presidents (Eisenhower, Nixon, Ford, Reagan, Bush) have said. How do the ideological assumptions of the Presidents compare and contrast? Their perceptions of the problem? Their recommended solutions? Keep in mind that the various presidents were speaking or writing in different eras, each with its own history and set of problems. Thus, Kennedy and Nixon governed (unlike Bush and Clinton) during the height of the Cold War, a fact that affected their domestic as well as their foreign policy agendas.

8
Obedience to Authority

Would you obey an order to inflict pain on another person? Most of us, if confronted with this question, would probably be quick to answer: "Never!" Yet if the conclusions of researchers are to be trusted, it is not psychopaths who kill noncombatant civilians in wartime and torture victims in prisons around the world but ordinary people following orders. People obey. This is a basic, necessary fact of human society. As an author in this chapter has put it, "Obedience is as basic an element in the structure of social life as one can point to. Some system of authority is a requirement of all communal living."

The question, then, is not, "Should we obey the orders of an authority figure?" but rather, "To what *extent* should we obey?" Each generation seems to give new meaning to these questions. During the Vietnam war, a number of American soldiers followed a commander's orders and murdered civilians in the hamlet of My Lai. More recently, and less grotesquely, former White House aide Oliver North pleaded innocent to illegally funding the Contra (resistance) fighters in Nicaragua. North's attorneys claimed that he was following the orders of his superiors. And, although North was found guilty,[1] the judge who sentenced him to perform community service (there was no prison sentence) largely agreed with this defense when he called North a pawn in a larger game played by senior officials in the Reagan administration.

In less dramatic ways, conflicts over the extent to which we obey orders surface in everyday life. At one point or another, you may face a moral dilemma at work. Perhaps it will take this form: The boss tells you to overlook File X in preparing a report for a certain client. But you're sure that File X pertains directly to the report and contains information that will alarm the client. What should you do? The dilemmas of obedience also emerge on some campuses with the rite of fraternity hazing. Psychologists Janice Gibson and Mika Haritos-Fatouros have recently made the startling observation that

[1]In July 1990, North's conviction was overturned on appeal.

whether the obedience in question involves a pledge's joining a fraternity or a torturer's joining an elite military corps, the *process* by which one acquiesces to a superior's order (and thereby becomes a member of the group) is remarkably the same:

> There are several ways to teach people to do the unthinkable, and we have developed a model to explain how they are used. We have also found that college fraternities, although they are far removed from the grim world of torture and violent combat, use similar methods for initiating new members, to ensure their faithfulness to the fraternity's rules and values. However, this unthinking loyalty can sometimes lead to dangerous actions: Over the past 10 years, there have been countless injuries during fraternity initiations and 39 deaths. These training techniques are designed to instill obedience in people, but they can easily be a guide for an intensive course in torture.
>
> 1. **Screening to find the best prospects***:* Normal, well-adjusted people with the physical, intellectual and, in some cases, political attributes necessary for the task.
> 2. **Techniques to increase binding among these prospects**: Initiation rites to isolate people from society and introduce them to a new social order, with different rules and values.
>
>   Elitist attitudes and "in-group" language, which highlight the differences between the group and the rest of society.
> 3. **Techniques to reduce the strain of obedience**: Blaming and dehumanizing the victims, so it is less disturbing to harm them.
>
>   Harassment, the constant physical and psychological intimidation that prevents logical thinking and promotes the instinctive responses needed for acts of inhuman cruelty.
>
>   Rewards for obedience and punishments for not cooperating.
>
>   Social modeling by watching other group members commit violent acts and then receive rewards.
>
>   Systematic desensitization to repugnant acts by gradual exposure to them, so they appear routine and normal despite conflicts with previous moral standards.[2]

In this chapter, you will explore the dilemmas inherent in obeying the orders of an authority. First, in a brief essay adapted from a lecture, British novelist Doris Lessing helps set a context for the discussion by questioning the manner in which we call ourselves individualists yet fail to understand how groups define and exert influence over us. Psychologist Stanley Milgram then reports on a landmark study in which he set out to determine the extent to which ordinary individuals would obey the clearly immoral orders of an authority figure. The results were shocking, not only to the psychiatrists who predicted that few people would follow such orders but also to many other social scientists and people—some of whom applauded Milgram for his

---

[2]"The Education of a Torturer" by Janice T. Gibson and Mika Haritos-Fatouros from *Psychology Today,* November 1986. Reprinted with permission from *Psychology Today Magazine.* Copyright © 1986 Sussex Publishers, Inc.

fiendishly ingenious design, some of whom bitterly attacked him for unethical procedures. The first of two reviews challenges the ethics of Milgram's experimental design; the second challenges Milgram's explanation for the unsettling observations he made. Next, psychologist Philip Zimbardo reports on his famous (and controversial) Stanford Prison Experiment, in which volunteers exhibited astonishingly convincing authoritarian and obedient attitudes as they play acted at being prisoners and guards. Two essays and a short story conclude the chapter. In "Disobedience as a Psychological and Moral Problem," Erich Fromm discusses the comforts of obedient behavior; then journalist Susan Walton laments an overly obedient life and vows to be bold in the future. The chapter concludes with "The Lottery," Shirley Jackson's story of a community that faithfully meets its yearly obligation.

Group Minds

DORIS LESSING

Doris Lessing sets a context for the discussion on obedience by illuminating a fundamental conflict: We in the Western world celebrate our individualism, but we're naive in understanding the ways that groups largely undercut our individuality. "We are group animals still," says Lessing, "and there is nothing wrong with that. But what is dangerous is . . . not understanding the social laws that govern groups and govern us." This chapter is largely devoted to an exploration of these tendencies. As you read selections by Milgram and the other authors here, bear in mind Lessing's troubling question: If we know that individuals will violate their own good common sense and moral codes in order to become accepted members of a group, why then can't we put this knowledge to use and teach people to be wary of group pressures?

Doris Lessing, the daughter of farmers, was born in Persia, now Iran, in 1919. She attended a Roman Catholic convent and a girls' high school in southern Rhodesia (now Zimbabwe). From 1959 through to the present, Lessing has written more than twenty works of fiction and has been called "the best woman novelist" of the postwar era. Her work has received a great deal of scholarly attention. She is, perhaps, best known for her Five Short Novels *(1954),* The Golden Notebook *(1962), and* Briefing for a Descent into Hell *(1971).*

People living in the West, in societies that we describe as Western, or as the free world, may be educated in many different ways, but they will all emerge with an idea about themselves that goes something like this: I am a citizen of a free society, and that means I am an individual, making individual choices. My mind is my own, my opinions are chosen by me, I am free to do as I will, and at the worst the pressures on me are economic, that is, I may be too poor to do as I want. 1

This set of ideas may sound something like a caricature, but it is not so far off how we see ourselves. It is a portrait that may not have been ac- 2 quired consciously, but is part of a general atmosphere or set of assumptions that influence our ideas about ourselves.

People in the West therefore may go through their entire lives never thinking to analyze this very flattering picture, and as a result are helpless against all kinds of pressures on them to conform in many kinds of ways. 3

The fact is that we all live our lives in groups—the family, work groups, social, religious and political groups. Very few people indeed are happy as solitaries, and they tend to be seen by their neighbors as peculiar or selfish or worse. Most people cannot stand being alone for long. They are always seeking groups to belong to, and if one group dissolves, they look for another. We are group animals still, and there is nothing wrong with that. But what is dangerous is not the belonging to a group, or groups, but not understanding the social laws that govern groups and govern us. 4

When we're in a group, we tend to think as that group does: we may even have joined the group to find 'like-minded' people. But we also find our thinking changing because we belong to a group. It is the hardest thing in the world to maintain an individual dissident opinion, as a member of a group. 5

It seems to me that this is something we have all experienced—something we take for granted, may never have thought about it. But a great deal of experiment has gone on among psychologists and sociologists on this very theme. If I describe an experiment or two, then anyone listening who may be a sociologist or psychologist will groan, oh God not *again*—for they will have heard of these classic experiments far too often. My guess is that the rest of the people will never have heard of these experiments, never have had these ideas presented to them. If my guess is true, then it aptly illustrates my general thesis, and the general idea behind these talks, that we (the human race) are now in possession of a great deal of hard information about ourselves, but we do not use it to improve our institutions and therefore our lives. 6

A typical test, or experiment, on this theme goes like this. A group of people are taken into the researcher's confidence. A minority of one or two are left in the dark. Some situation demanding measurement or assessment is chosen. For instance, comparing lengths of wood that differ only a little from each other, but enough to be perceptible, or shapes that are almost the same size. The majority in the group—according to instruction—will assert stubbornly that these two shapes or lengths are the same length, or size, while the solitary individual, or the couple, who have not been so instructed will assert that the pieces of wood or whatever are different. But the majority will continue to insist—speaking metaphorically—that black is white, and after a period of exasperation, irritation, even anger, certainly incomprehension, the minority will fall into line. Not always, but nearly always. There are indeed glorious individuals who stubbornly insist on telling the truth as they see it, but most give in to the majority opinion, obey the atmosphere. 7

When put as badly, as unflatteringly, as this, reactions tend to be in- 8
credulous: "I certainly wouldn't give in, I speak my mind. . . ." But would you?

People who have experienced a lot of groups, who perhaps have ob- 9
served their own behavior, may agree that the hardest thing in the world is to stand out against one's group, a group of one's peers. Many agree that among our most shameful memories is this, how often we said black was white because other people were saying it.

In other words, we know that this is true of human behavior, but how 10
do we know it? It is one thing to admit it, in a vague uncomfortable sort of way (which probably includes the hope that one will never again be in such a testing situation) but quite another to make that cool step into a kind of objectivity, where one may say, "Right, if that's what human beings are like, myself included, then let's admit it, examine and organize our attitudes accordingly."

This mechanism, of obedience to the group, does not only mean obedi- 11
ence or submission to a small group, or one that is sharply determined, like a religion or political party. It means, too, conforming to those large, vague, ill-defined collections of people who may never think of themselves as having a collective mind because they are aware of differences of opinion—but which, to people from outside, from another culture, seem very minor. The underlying assumptions and assertions that govern the group are never discussed, never challenged, probably never noticed, the main one being precisely this: that it *is* a group mind, intensely resistant to change, equipped with sacred assumptions about which there can be no discussion.

But suppose this kind of thing were taught in schools? 12

Let us just suppose it, for a moment. . . . But at once the nub of the 13
problem is laid bare.

Imagine us saying to children, "In the last fifty or so years, the human 14
race has become aware of a great deal of information about its mechanisms; how it behaves, how it must behave under certain circumstances. If this is to be useful, you must learn to contemplate these rules calmly, dispassionately, disinterestedly, without emotion. It is information that will set people free from blind loyalties, obedience to slogans, rhetoric, leaders, group emotions." Well, there it is.

▲ ▲ ▲

Review Questions

1. What is the flattering portrait Lessing paints of people living in the West?
2. Lessing believes that individuals in the West are "helpless against all kinds of pressures on them to conform in many kinds of ways." Why?
3. Lessing refers to a class of experiments on obedience. Summarize the "typical" experiment.

Discussion and Writing Suggestions

1. Lessing writes that "what is dangerous is not the belonging to a group, or groups, but not understanding the social laws that govern groups and govern us." What is the danger Lessing is speaking of here?
2. Lessing states that "we (the human race) are now in possession of a great deal of hard information about ourselves, but we do not use it to improve our institutions and therefore our lives." First, do you agree with Lessing? Can you cite other examples (aside from information on obedience to authority) in which we do not use knowledge to better humankind?
3. Explore some of the difficulties in applying this "hard information" about humankind that Lessing speaks of. Assume she's correct in claiming that we don't incorporate our knowledge of human nature into the running of our institutions. Why don't we? What are the difficulties of *acting* on information?
4. Lessing speaks of "people who remember how they acted in school" and of their guilt in recalling how they succumbed to group pressures. Can you recall such an event? What feelings do you have about it now?

The Perils of Obedience

STANLEY MILGRAM

In 1963, a Yale psychologist conducted one of the classic studies on obedience that Doris Lessing refers to in "Group Minds." Stanley Milgram designed an experiment that forced participants either to violate their conscience by obeying the immoral demands of an authority figure or to refuse those demands. Surprisingly, Milgram found that few participants could resist the authority's orders, even when the participants knew that following these orders would result in another person's pain. Were the participants in these experiments incipient mass murderers? No, said Milgram. They were "ordinary people, simply doing their jobs." The implications of Milgram's conclusions are immense.

Consider: Where does evil reside? What sort of people were responsible for the Holocaust, and for the long list of other atrocities that seem to blight the human record in every generation? Is it a lunatic fringe, a few sick but powerful people who are responsible for atrocities? If so, then we decent folk needn't ever look inside ourselves to understand evil since (by our definition) evil lurks out there, in "those sick ones." Milgram's study suggested otherwise: that under a special set of circumstances the obedience we naturally show authority figures can transform us into agents of terror.

The article that follows is one of the longest in this text, and it may help you to know in advance the author's organization. In paragraphs 1–11, Milgram discusses the larger significance and the history of dilemmas involving obedience to authority; he then summarizes his basic experimental design and follows with a report of one experiment. Milgram organizes the remainder of his article into sections, which he has subtitled "An Unexpected Outcome," "Peculiar Reactions," "The Etiquette of Submission," and "Duty without Conflict." He begins his conclusion in paragraph 108. If you find the article too long to complete in a single sitting, then plan to read sections at a time, taking notes on each until you're done. Anticipate the two articles immediately following Milgram's: they are reviews of his work and the first largely concerns the ethics of his experimental design. Consider these ethics as you read so that you, in turn, can respond to Milgram's critics.

Stanley Milgram (1933–1984) taught and conducted research at Yale and Harvard universities and at the Graduate Center, City University of New York. He was named Guggenheim Fellow in 1972–1973 and a year later was nominated for the National Book Award for Obedience to Authority. *His other books include* Television and Antisocial Behavior *(1973),* The City and the Self *(1974),* Human Aggression *(1976), and* The Individual in the Social World *(1977).*

Obedience is as basic an element in the structure of social life as one can point to. Some system of authority is a requirement of all communal living, and it is only the person dwelling in isolation who is not forced to respond, with defiance or submission, to the commands of others. For many people, obedience is a deeply ingrained behavior tendency, indeed a potent impulse overriding training in ethics, sympathy, and moral conduct. 1

The dilemma inherent in submission to authority is ancient, as old as the story of Abraham, and the question of whether one should obey when commands conflict with conscience has been argued by Plato, dramatized in *Antigone,* and treated to philosophic analysis in almost every historical epoch. Conservative philosophers argue that the very fabric of society is threatened by disobedience, while humanists stress the primacy of the individual conscience. 2

The legal and philosophic aspects of obedience are of enormous import, but they say very little about how most people behave in concrete situations. I set up a simple experiment at Yale University to test how much pain an ordinary citizen would inflict on another person simply because he was ordered to by an experimental scientist. Stark authority was pitted against the subjects' strongest moral imperatives against hurting others, and, with the subjects' ears ringing with the screams of the victims, authority won more often than not. The extreme willingness of adults to go to almost any lengths on the command of an authority constitutes the chief finding of the study and the fact most urgently demanding explanation. 3

In the basic experimental design, two people come to a psychology laboratory to take part in a study of memory and learning. One of them is 4 designated as a "teacher" and the other a "learner." The experimenter explains that the study is concerned with the effects of punishment on learning. The learner is conducted into a room, seated in a kind of miniature electric chair; his arms are strapped to prevent excessive movement, and an electrode is attached to his wrist. He is told that he will be read lists of simple word pairs, and that he will then be tested on his ability to remember the second word of a pair when he hears the first one again. Whenever he makes an error, he will receive electric shocks of increasing intensity.

The real focus of the experiment is the teacher. After watching the 5
learner being strapped into place, he is seated before an impressive shock generator. The instrument panel consists of thirty lever switches set in a horizontal line. Each switch is clearly labeled with a voltage designation ranging from 15 to 450 volts. The following designations are clearly indicated for groups of four switches, going from left to right: Slight Shock, Moderate Shock, Strong Shock, Very Strong Shock, Intense Shock, Extreme Intensity Shock, Danger: Severe Shock. (Two switches after this last designation are simply marked XXX.)

When a switch is depressed, a pilot light corresponding to each switch 6
is illuminated in bright red; an electric buzzing is heard; a blue light, labeled "voltage energizer," flashes; the dial on the voltage meter swings to the right; and various relay clicks sound off.

The upper left-hand corner of the generator is labeled SHOCK GENERA- 7
TOR, TYPE ZLB, DYSON INSTRUMENT COMPANY, WALTHAM, MASS. OUTPUT 15 VOLTS—450 VOLTS.

Each subject is given a sample 45-volt shock from the generator before 8
his run as teacher, and the jolt strengthens his belief in the authenticity of the machine.

The teacher is a genuinely naïve subject who has come to the labora- 9
tory for the experiment. The learner, or victim, is actually an actor who receives no shock at all. The point of the experiment is to see how far a person will proceed in a concrete and measurable situation in which he is ordered to inflict increasing pain on a protesting victim.

Conflict arises when the man receiving the shock begins to show that 10
he is experiencing discomfort. At 75 volts, he grunts; at 120 volts, he complains loudly; at 150, he demands to be released from the experiment. As the voltage increases, his protests become more vehement and emotional. At 285 volts, his response can be described only as an agonized scream. Soon thereafter, he makes no sound at all.

For the teacher, the situation quickly becomes one of gripping tension. 11
It is not a game for him; conflict is intense and obvious. The manifest suffering of the learner presses him to quit; but each time he hesitates to administer a shock, the experimenter orders him to continue. To extricate himself from this plight, the subject must make a clear break with authority.[1]

---

[1]The ethical problems of carrying out an experiment of this sort are too complex to be dealt with here, but they receive extended treatment in the book from which this article is adapted.

The subject, Gretchen Brandt,[2] is an attractive thirty-one-year-old medical technician who works at the Yale Medical School. She had emigrated from Germany five years before. 12

On several occasions when the learner complains, she turns to the experimenter coolly and inquires, "Shall I continue?" She promptly returns to her task when the experimenter asks her to do so. At the administration of 210 volts, she turns to the experimenter, remarking firmly, "Well, I'm sorry, I don't think we should continue." 13

EXPERIMENTER: The experiment requires that you go on until he has learned all the word pairs correctly. 14

BRANDT: He has a heart condition, I'm sorry. He told you that before. 15

EXPERIMENTER: The shocks may be painful but they are not dangerous. 16

BRANDT: Well, I'm sorry, I think when shocks continue like this, they *are* dangerous. You ask him if he wants to get out. It's his free will. 17

EXPERIMENTER: It is absolutely essential that we continue. . . . 18

BRANDT: I'd like you to ask him. We came here of our free will. If he wants to continue I'll go ahead. He told you he had a heart condition. I'm sorry. I don't want to be responsible for anything happening to him. I wouldn't like it for me either. 19

EXPERIMENTER: You have no other choice. 20

BRANDT: I think we are here on our own free will. I don't want to be responsible if anything happens to him. Please understand that. 21

She refuses to go further and the experiment is terminated. 22

The woman is firm and resolute throughout. She indicates in the interview that she was in no way tense or nervous, and this corresponds to her controlled appearance during the experiment. She feels that the last shock she administered to the learner was extremely painful and reiterates that she "did not want to be responsible for any harm to him." 23

The woman's straightforward, courteous behavior in the experiment, lack of tension, and total control of her own action seem to make disobedience a simple and rational deed. Her behavior is the very embodiment of what I envisioned would be true for almost all subjects. 24

AN UNEXPECTED OUTCOME

Before the experiments, I sought predictions about the outcome from various kinds of people—psychiatrists, college sophomores, middle-class adults, graduate students and faculty in the behavioral sciences. With remarkable similarity, they predicted that virtually all subjects would refuse to obey the experimenter. The psychiatrists, specifically, predicted that most subjects would not go beyond 150 volts, when the victim makes his first explicit demand to be freed. They expected that only 4 percent would 25

[2]Names of subjects described in this piece have been changed.

reach 300 volts, and that only a pathological fringe of about one in a thousand would administer the highest shock on the board.

These predictions were unequivocally wrong. Of the forty subjects in the first experiment, twenty-five obeyed the orders of the experimenter to the end, punishing the victim until they reached the most potent shock available on the generator. After 450 volts were administered three times, the experimenter called a halt to the session. Many obedient subjects then heaved sighs of relief, mopped their brows, rubbed their fingers over their eyes, or nervously fumbled cigarettes. Others displayed only minimal signs of tension from beginning to end. 26

When the very first experiments were carried out, Yale undergraduates were used as subjects, and about 60 percent of them were fully obedient. A colleague of mine immediately dismissed these findings as having no relevance to "ordinary" people, asserting that Yale undergraduates are a highly aggressive, competitive bunch who step on each other's necks on the slightest provocation. He assured me that when "ordinary" people were tested, the results would be quite different. As we moved from the pilot studies to the regular experimental series, people drawn from every stratum of New Haven life came to be employed in the experiment: professionals, white-collar workers, unemployed persons, and industrial workers. *The experiment's total outcome was the same as we had observed among the students.* 27

Moreover, when the experiments were repeated in Princeton, Munich, Rome, South Africa, and Australia, the level of obedience was invariably somewhat *higher* than found in the investigation reported in this article. Thus one scientist in Munich found 85 percent of his subjects to be obedient. 28

Fred Prozi's reactions, if more dramatic than most, illuminate the conflicts experienced by others in less visible form. About fifty years old and unemployed at the time of the experiment, he has a good-natured, if slightly dissolute, appearance, and he strikes people as a rather ordinary fellow. He begins the session calmly but becomes tense as it proceeds. After delivering the 180-volt shock, he pivots around in his chair and, shaking his head, addresses the experimenter in agitated tones: 29

PROZI: I can't stand it. I'm not going to kill that man in there. You hear him hollering? 30

EXPERIMENTER: As I told you before, the shocks may be painful, but . . . 31

PROZI: But he's hollering. He can't stand it. What's going to happen to him? 32

EXPERIMENTER *(his voice is patient, matter-of-fact)*: The experiment requires that you continue, Teacher. 33

PROZI: Aaah, but unh, I'm not going to get that man sick in there—know what I mean? 34

EXPERIMENTER: Whether the learner likes it or not, we must go on, through all the word pairs. 35

PROZI: I refuse to take the responsibility. He's in there hollering! 36

EXPERIMENTER: It's absolutely essential that you continue, Prozi. 37

PROZI *(indicating the unused questions)*: There's too many left here, I 38
mean, Jeez, if he gets them wrong, there's too many of them left. I mean,
who's going to take the responsibility if anything happens to that gentleman?

EXPERIMENTER: I'm responsible for anything that happens to him. Con- 39
tinue, please.

PROZI: All right. *(Consults list of words.)* The next one's "Slow—walk, 40
truck, dance, music." Answer, please. *(A buzzing sound indicates the
learner has signaled his answer.)* Wrong. A hundred and ninety-five
volts. "Dance." *(Zzumph!)*

LEARNER (*yelling*): Let me out of here! My heart's bothering me! *(Teacher* 41
looks at experimenter.)

EXPERIMENTER: Continue, please. 42

LEARNER *(screaming)*: Let me out of here! You have no right to keep me 43
here! Let me out of here, my heart's bothering me, let me out!

PROZI (*shakes head, pats the table nervously)*: You see, he's hollering. Hear 44
that? Gee, I don't know.

EXPERIMENTER: The experiment requires . . . 45

PROZI *(interrupting)*: I know it does, sir, but I mean—hunh! He don't know 46
what he's getting in for. He's up to 195 volts! *(Experiment continues,
through 210 volts, 225 volts, 240 volts, 255 volts, 270 volts, at which
point Prozi, with evident relief, runs out of word-pair questions.)*

EXPERIMENTER: You'll have to go back to the beginning of that page and go 47
through them again until he's learned them all correctly.

PROZI: Aw, no. I'm not going to kill that man. You mean I've got to keep 48
going up with the scale? No sir. He's hollering in there. I'm not going to
give him 450 volts.

EXPERIMENTER: The experiment requires that you go on. 49

LEARNER: Ohhh. I absolutely refuse to answer anymore. *(Shouting urgently* 50
now.) Let me out of here! You can't hold me here! Get me out. Get-me-
out-of-here!

EXPERIMENTER: Continue. The next word is "Green," please. 51

PROZI: "Green—grass, hat, ink, apple." *(Nothing happens. No answering* 52
buzz. Just gloomy silence.)

PROZI: I don't think he is going to answer. 53

EXPERIMENTER: If the learner doesn't answer in a reasonable time, about 54
four or five seconds, consider the answer wrong. And follow the same
procedures you have been doing for wrong answers. Say, "Wrong," tell
him the number of volts, give him the punishment, read him the correct
answer. Continue, please.

PROZI: "Green—grass, hat, ink, apple." Answer, please. *(More silence.* 55
Subject just sits there.)

EXPERIMENTER: Go on with the procedure, please. 56

PROZI: Three hundred and fifteen volts. The answer is "ink." *(Zzumph!)* 57

LEARNER: Ohh. Ooohh. 58

PROZI *(relieved to hear response)*: Next one . . . 59

LEARNER: I absolutely refuse to answer. 60

PROZI: You got to. You get a shock if you don't answer. *(Experiment con-* 61
tinues with learner refusing to answer, and, finally, failing even to grunt or groan. At 375 volts, the subject stands up.)

PROZI: I think something's happened to that fellow in there. I don't get no 62
answer. He was hollering at less voltage. Can't you check in and see if he's all right, please?

EXPERIMENTER *(with same detached calm)*: Not once we've started. Please 63
continue, Teacher.

PROZI *(sits down, sighs deeply)*: "Cool—day, shade, water, paint." Answer, 64
please. Are you all right in there? Are you all right?

EXPERIMENTER: Please continue, Teacher. Continue, please. *(Subject pushes* 65
lever. Zzumph!)

PROZI *(swiveling around in his chair)*: Something's happened to that man 66
in there. *(Swiveling back.)* Next one. "Low—dollar, necklace, moon, paint." *(Turning around again.)* Something's happened to that man in there. You better check in on him, sir. He won't answer or nothing.

EXPERIMENTER: Continue. Go on, please. 67

PROZI: You accept all responsibility? 68

EXPERIMENTER: The responsibility is mine. Correct. Please go on. *(Subject* 69
returns to his list, starts running through words as rapidly as he can read them, works through to 450 volts.)

PROZI: That's that. 70

EXPERIMENTER: Continue using the 450 switch for each wrong answer. 71
Continue, please.

PROZI: But I don't get anything! 72

EXPERIMENTER: Please continue. The next word is "white." 73

PROZI: Don't you think you should look in on him, please? 74

EXPERIMENTER: Not once we've started the experiment. 75

PROZI: What if he's dead in there? *(Gestures toward the room with the elec-* 76
tric chair.) I mean, he told me he can't stand the shock, sir. I don't mean to be rude, but I think you should look in on him. All you have to do is look in on him. All you have to do is look in the door. I don't get no answer, no noise. Something might have happened to the gentleman in there, sir.

EXPERIMENTER: We must continue. Go on, please. 77

PROZI: You mean keep giving him what? Four-hundred-fifty volts, what 78
he's got now?

EXPERIMENTER: That's correct. Continue. The next word is "white." 79

PROZI *(now at a furious pace)*: "White—cloud, horse, rock, house." An- 80
swer, please. The answer is "horse." Four hundred and fifty volts. *(Zzumph!)* Next word, "Bag—paint, music, clown, girl." The answer is "paint." Four hundred and fifty volts. *(Zzumph!)* Next word is "Short—sentence, movie . . ."

EXPERIMENTER: Excuse me, Teacher. We'll have to discontinue the experi- 81
ment.

PECULIAR REACTIONS

Morris Braverman, another subject, is a thirty-nine-year-old social worker. 82
He looks older than his years because of his bald head and serious demeanor. His brow is furrowed, as if all the world's burdens were carried on his face. He appears intelligent and concerned.

When the learner refuses to answer and the experimenter instructs 83
Braverman to treat the absence of an answer as equivalent to a wrong answer, he takes his instruction to heart. Before administering 300 volts he asserts officiously to the victim, "Mr. Wallace, your silence has to be considered as a wrong answer." Then he administers the shock. He offers halfheartedly to change places with the learner, then asks the experimenter, "Do I have to follow these instructions literally?" He is satisfied with the experimenter's answer that he does. His very refined and authoritative manner of speaking is increasingly broken up by wheezing laughter.

The experimenter's notes on Mr. Braverman at the last few shocks are: 84

> *Almost breaking up now each time gives shock. Rubbing face to hide laughter. Squinting, trying to hide face with hand, still laughing. Cannot control his laughter at this point no matter what he does. Clenching fist, pushing it onto table.*

In an interview after the session, Mr. Braverman summarizes the ex- 85
periment with impressive fluency and intelligence. He feels the experiment may have been designed also to "test the effects on the teacher of being in an essentially sadistic role, as well as the reactions of a student to a learning situation that was authoritative and punitive." When asked how painful the last few shocks administered to the learner were, he indicates that the most extreme category on the scale is not adequate (it read EXTREMELY PAINFUL) and places his mark at the edge of the scale with an arrow carrying it beyond the scale.

It is almost impossible to convey the greatly relaxed, sedate quality of 86
his conversation in the interview. In the most relaxed terms, he speaks about his severe inner tension.

EXPERIMENTER: At what point were you most tense or nervous? 87

MR. BRAVERMAN: Well, when he first began to cry out in pain, and I real- 88
ized this was hurting him. This got worse when he just blocked and refused to answer. There was I. I'm a nice person, I think, hurting somebody, and caught up in what seemed a mad situation . . . and in the interest of science, one goes through with it.

When the interviewer pursues the general question of tension, Mr. 89
Braverman spontaneously mentions his laughter.

"My reactions were awfully peculiar. I don't know if you were watching me, but my reactions were giggly, and trying to stifle laughter. This isn't the way I usually am. This was a sheer reaction to a totally impossible situation. And my reaction was to the situation of having to hurt somebody. And being totally helpless and caught up in a set of circumstances where I just couldn't deviate and I couldn't try to help. This is what got me." 90

Mr. Braverman, like all subjects, was told the actual nature and purpose of the experiment, and a year later he affirmed in a questionnaire that he had learned something of personal importance: "What appalled me was that I could possess this capacity for obedience and compliance to a central idea, i.e., the value of a memory experiment, even after it became clear that continued adherence to this value was at the expense of violation of another value, i.e., don't hurt someone who is helpless and not hurting you. As my wife said, 'You can call yourself Eichmann.'[3] I hope I deal more effectively with any future conflicts of values I encounter." 91

THE ETIQUETTE OF SUBMISSION

One theoretical interpretation of this behavior holds that all people harbor deeply aggressive instincts continually pressing for expression, and that the experiment provides institutional justification for the release of these impulses. According to this view, if a person is placed in a situation in which he has complete power over another individual, whom he may punish as much as he likes, all that is sadistic and bestial in man comes to the fore. The impulse to shock the victim is seen to flow from the potent aggressive tendencies, which are part of the motivational life of the individual, and the experiment, because it provides social legitimacy, simply opens the door to their expression. 92

It becomes vital, therefore, to compare the subject's performance when he is under orders and when he is allowed to choose the shock level. 93

The procedure was identical to our standard experiment, except that the teacher was told that he was free to select any shock level on any of the trials. (The experimenter took pains to point out that the teacher could use the highest levels on the generator, the lowest, any in between, or any combination of levels.) Each subject proceeded for thirty critical trials. The learner's protests were coordinated to standard shock levels, his first grunt coming at 75 volts, his first vehement protest at 150 volts. 94

The average shock used during the thirty critical trials was less than 60 volts—lower than the point at which the victim showed the first signs of 95

[3]*Adolf Eichmann* (1906–1962), the Nazi official responsible for implementing Hitler's "Final Solution" to exterminate the Jews, escaped to Argentina after World War II. In 1960, Israeli agents captured Eichmann and brought him to Israel, where he was tried as a war criminal and sentenced to death. At his trial, Eichmann maintained that he was merely following orders in arranging murders of his victims.

discomfort. Three of the forty subjects did not go beyond the very lowest level on the board, twenty-eight went no higher than 75 volts, and thirty-eight did not go beyond the first loud protest at 150 volts. Two subjects provided the exception, administering up to 325 and 450 volts, but the overall result was that the great majority of people delivered very low, usually painless, shocks when the choice was explicitly up to them.

This condition of the experiment undermines another commonly offered explanation of the subjects' behavior—that those who shocked the victim at the most severe levels came only from the sadistic fringe of society. If one considers that almost two-thirds of the participants fall into the category of "obedient" subjects, and that they represented ordinary people drawn from working, managerial, and professional classes, the argument becomes very shaky. Indeed, it is highly reminiscent of the issue that arose in connection with Hannah Arendt's 1963 book, *Eichmann in Jerusalem.* Arendt contended that the prosecution's effort to depict Eichmann as a sadistic monster was fundamentally wrong, that he came closer to being an uninspired bureaucrat who simply sat at his desk and did his job. For asserting her views, Arendt became the object of considerable scorn, even calumny. Somehow, it was felt that the monstrous deeds carried out by Eichmann required a brutal, twisted personality, evil incarnate. After witnessing hundreds of ordinary persons submit to the authority in our own experiments, I must conclude that Arendt's conception of the banality of evil comes closer to the truth than one might dare imagine. The ordinary person who shocked the victim did so out of a sense of obligation—an impression of his duties as a subject—and not from any peculiarly aggressive tendencies. 96

This is, perhaps, the most fundamental lesson of our study: ordinary people, simply doing their jobs, and without any particular hostility on their part, can become agents in a terrible destructive process. Moreover, even when the destructive effects of their work become patently clear, and they are asked to carry out actions incompatible with fundamental standards of morality, relatively few people have the resources needed to resist authority. 97

Many of the people were in some sense against what they did to the learner, and many protested even while they obeyed. Some were totally convinced of the wrongness of their actions but could not bring themselves to make an open break with authority. They often derived satisfaction from their thoughts and felt that—within themselves, at least—they had been on the side of the angels. They tried to reduce strain by obeying the experimenter but "only slightly," encouraging the learner, touching the generator switches gingerly. When interviewed, such a subject would stress that he had "asserted my humanity" by administering the briefest shock possible. Handling the conflict in this manner was easier than defiance. 98

The situation is constructed so that there is no way the subject can stop shocking the learner without violating the experimenter's definitions of his own competence. The subject fears that he will appear arrogant, untoward, 99 and rude if he breaks off. Although these inhibiting emotions appear small in scope alongside the violence being done to the learner, they suffuse the mind and feelings of the subject, who is miserable at the prospect of having to repudiate the authority to his face. (When the experiment was altered so that the experimenter gave his instructions by telephone instead of in person, only a third as many people were fully obedient through 450 volts.) It is a curious thing that a measure of compassion on the part of the subject—an unwillingness to "hurt" the experimenter's feelings—is part of those binding forces inhibiting his disobedience. The withdrawal of such deference may be as painful to the subject as to the authority he defies.

DUTY WITHOUT CONFLICT

The subjects do not derive satisfaction from inflicting pain, but they often **100** like the feeling they get from pleasing the experimenter. They are proud of doing a good job, obeying the experimenter under difficult circumstances. While the subjects administered only mild shocks on their own initiative, one experimental variation showed that, under orders, 30 percent of them were willing to deliver 450 volts even when they had to forcibly push the learner's hand down on the electrode.

Bruno Batta is a thirty-seven-year-old welder who took part in the **101** variation requiring the use of force. He was born in New Haven, his parents in Italy. He has a rough-hewn face that conveys a conspicuous lack of alertness. He has some difficulty in mastering the experimental procedure and needs to be corrected by the experimenter several times. He shows appreciation for the help and willingness to do what is required. After the 150-volt level, Batta has to force the learner's hand down on the shock plate, since the learner himself refuses to touch it.

When the learner first complains, Mr. Batta pays no attention to him. **102** His face remains impassive, as if to dissociate himself from the learner's disruptive behavior. When the experimenter instructs him to force the learner's hand down, he adopts a rigid, mechanical procedure. He tests the generator switch. When it fails to function, he immediately forces the learner's hand onto the shock plate. All the while he maintains the same rigid mask. The learner, seated alongside him, begs him to stop, but with robotic impassivity he continues the procedure.

What is extraordinary is his apparent total indifference to the learner; **103** he hardly takes cognizance of him as a human being. Meanwhile, he relates to the experimenter in a submissive and courteous fashion.

At the 330-volt level, the learner refuses not only to touch the shock **104** plate but also to provide any answers. Annoyed, Batta turns to him, and chastises him: "You better answer and get it over with. We can't stay here all night." These are the only words he directs to the learner in the course of an hour. Never again does he speak to him. The scene is brutal and depressing, his hard, impassive face showing total indifference as he subdues the screaming learner and gives him shocks. He seems to derive no pleasure from the act itself, only quiet satisfaction at doing his job properly.

When he administers 450 volts, he turns to the experimenter and asks, 105
"Where do we go from here, Professor?" His tone is deferential and expresses his willingness to be a cooperative subject, in contrast to the learner's obstinacy.

At the end of the session he tells the experimenter how honored he has 106
been to help him, and in a moment of contrition, remarks, "Sir, sorry it couldn't have been a full experiment."

He has done his honest best. It is only the deficient behavior of the 107
learner that has denied the experimenter full satisfaction.

The essence of obedience is that a person comes to view himself as the 108
instrument for carrying out another person's wishes, and he therefore no longer regards himself as responsible for his actions. Once this critical shift of viewpoint has occurred, all of the essential features of obedience follow. The most far-reaching consequence is that the person feels responsible *to* the authority directing him but feels no responsibility *for* the content of the actions that the authority prescribes. Morality does not disappear—it acquires a radically different focus: the subordinate person feels shame or pride depending on how adequately he has performed the actions called for by authority.

Language provides numerous terms to pinpoint this type of morality: 109
loyalty, duty, discipline all are terms heavily saturated with moral meaning and refer to the degree to which a person fulfills his obligations to authority. They refer not to the "goodness" of the person per se but to the adequacy with which a subordinate fulfills his socially defined role. The most frequent defense of the individual who has performed a heinous act under command of authority is that he has simply done his duty. In asserting this defense, the individual is not introducing an alibi concocted for the moment but is reporting honestly on the psychological attitude induced by submission to authority.

For a person to feel responsible for his actions, he must sense that the 110
behavior has flowed from "the self." In the situation we have studied, subjects have precisely the opposite view of their actions—namely, they see them as originating in the motives of some other person. Subjects in the experiment frequently said, "If it were up to me, I would not have administered shocks to the learner."

Once authority has been isolated as the cause of the subject's behavior, 111
it is legitimate to inquire into the necessary elements of authority and how it must be perceived in order to gain his compliance. We conducted some investigations into the kinds of changes that would cause the experimenter to lose his power and to be disobeyed by the subject. Some of the variations revealed that:

- *The experimenter's physical presence has a marked impact on his* 112
  authority. As cited earlier, obedience dropped off sharply when or-

ders were given by telephone. The experimenter could often induce a disobedient subject to go on by returning to the laboratory.

- *Conflicting authority severely paralyzes action.* When two experimenters of equal status, both seated at the command desk, gave incompatible orders, no shocks were delivered past the point of their disagreement. 113
- *The rebellious action of others severely undermines authority.* In one variation, three teachers (two actors and a real subject) administered a test and shocks. When the two actors disobeyed the experimenter and refused to go beyond a certain shock level, thirty-six of forty subjects joined their disobedient peers and refused as well. 114

Although the experimenter's authority was fragile in some respects, it is also true that he had almost none of the tools used in ordinary command structures. For example, the experimenter did not threaten the subjects with punishment—such as loss of income, community ostracism, or jail—for failure to obey. Neither could he offer incentives. Indeed, we should expect the experimenter's authority to be much less than that of someone like a general, since the experimenter has no power to enforce his imperatives, and since participation in a psychological experiment scarcely evokes the sense of urgency and dedication found in warfare. Despite these limitations, he still managed to command a dismaying degree of obedience. 115

I will cite one final variation of the experiment that depicts a dilemma that is more common in everyday life. The subject was not ordered to pull the lever that shocked the victim, but merely to perform a subsidiary task (administering the word-pair test) while another person administered the shock. In this situation, thirty-seven of forty adults continued to the highest level on the shock generator. Predictably, they excused their behavior by saying that the responsibility belonged to the man who actually pulled the switch. This may illustrate a dangerously typical arrangement in a complex society: it is easy to ignore responsibility when one is only an intermediate link in a chain of action. 116

The problem of obedience is not wholly psychological. The form and shape of society and the way it is developing have much to do with it. There was a time, perhaps, when people were able to give a fully human response to any situation because they were fully absorbed in it as human beings. But as soon as there was a division of labor things changed. Beyond a certain point, the breaking up of society into people carrying out narrow and very special jobs takes away from the human quality of work and life. A person does not get to see the whole situation but only a small part of it, and is thus unable to act without some kind of overall direction. He yields to authority but in doing so is alienated from his own actions. 117

Even Eichmann was sickened when he toured the concentration camps, but he had only to sit at a desk and shuffle papers. At the same time the man in the camp who actually dropped Cyclon-b into the gas chambers was able to justify *his* behavior on the ground that he was only following 118 orders from above. Thus there is a fragmentation of the total human act; no one is confronted with the consequences of his decision to carry out the evil act. The person who assumes responsibility has evaporated. Perhaps this is the most common characteristic of socially organized evil in modern society.

▲ ▲ ▲

Review Questions

1. Milgram states that obedience is a basic element in the structure of social life. How so?
2. What is the dilemma inherent in obedience to authority?
3. Summarize the obedience experiments.
4. What predictions did experts and laypeople make about the experiments before they were conducted? How did these predictions compare with the experimental results?
5. What are Milgram's views regarding the two assumptions bearing on his experiment that (1) people are naturally aggressive and (2) a lunatic, sadistic fringe is responsible for shocking learners to the maximum limit?
6. How do Milgram's findings corroborate Hannah Arendt's thesis about the "banality of evil"?
7. What, according to Milgram, is the "essence of obedience"?
8. How did being an intermediate link in a chain of action affect a subject's willingness to continue with the experiment?
9. In the article's final two paragraphs, Milgram speaks of a "fragmentation of the total human act." To what is he referring?

Discussion and Writing Suggestions

1. "Conservative philosophers argue that the very fabric of society is threatened by disobedience, while humanists stress the primacy of the individual conscience." Develop the arguments of both the conservative and the humanist regarding obedience to authority. Be prepared to debate the ethics of obedience by defending one position or the other.
2. Would you have been glad to have participated in the Milgram experiments? Why or why not?
3. The ethics of Milgram's experimental design came under sharp attack. Diana Baumrind's review of the experiment typifies the criticism; but before you read her work, try to anticipate the objections she raises.
4. Given the general outcome of the experiments, why do you suppose Milgram gives as his first example of a subject's response the German émigré's refusal to continue the electrical shocks?
5. Does the outcome of the experiment upset you in any way? Do you feel the experiment teaches us anything new about human nature?

6. Comment on Milgram's skill as a writer of description. How effectively does he portray his subjects when introducing them? When recreating their tension in the experiment?
7. Mrs. Braverman said to her husband: "You can call yourself Eichmann." Do you agree with Mrs. Braverman? Explain.
8. Reread paragraphs 29 through 81, the transcript of the experiment in which Mr. Prozi participated. Appreciating that Prozi was debriefed, that is, was assured that no harm came to the learner, imagine what Prozi might have been thinking as he drove home after the experiment. Develop your thoughts into a monologue, written in the first person, with Prozi at the wheel of his car.

▼

REVIEWS OF STANLEY MILGRAM'S *OBEDIENCE TO AUTHORITY*

Many of Milgram's colleague's saluted him for providing that "hard information" about human nature that Doris Lessing speaks of. Others attacked him for violating the rights of his subjects. Still others faulted his experimental design and claimed he could not, with any validity, speculate on life outside the laboratory based on the behavior of his subjects within.

We reproduce something of this debate in the pieces that follow. First, psychologist Diana Baumrind excoriates Milgram for "entrapping" his subjects and potentially harming their "self-image or ability to trust adult authorities in the future." In a footnote, we summarize Milgram's response to Baumrind's critique. In a second review, psychologist Moti Nissani questions the logic with which Milgram interpreted his data.

Review of Stanley Milgram's Experiments on Obedience

DIANA BAUMRIND

Diana Baumrind is a psychologist who, when writing this review, worked at the Institute of Human Development, University of California, Berkeley. The review appeared in American Psychologist *shortly after Milgram published the results of his first experiments in 1963.*

. . . The dependent, obedient attitude assumed by most subjects in the experimental setting is appropriate to that situation. The "game" is defined by the experimenter and he makes the rules. By volunteering, the subject 1 agrees implicitly to assume a posture of trust and obedience. While the experimental conditions leave him exposed, the subject has the right to assume that his security and self-esteem will be protected.

There are other professional situations in which one member—the patient or client—expects help and protection from the other—the physician or psychologist. But the interpersonal relationship between experimenter and subject additionally has unique features which are likely to provoke initial anxiety in the subject. The laboratory is unfamiliar as a setting and the rules of behavior ambiguous compared to a clinician's office. Because of the anxiety and passivity generated by the setting, the subject is more prone to behave in an obedient, suggestible manner in the laboratory than elsewhere. Therefore, the laboratory is not the place to study degree of obedience or suggestibility, as a function of a particular experimental condition, since the base line for these phenomena as found in the laboratory is probably much higher than in most other settings. Thus experiments in which the relationship to the experimenter as an authority is used as an independent condition are imperfectly designed for the same reason that they are prone to injure the subjects involved. They disregard the special quality of trust and obedience with which the subject appropriately regards the experimenter. 2

Other phenomena which present ethical decisions, unlike those mentioned above, *can* be reproduced successfully in the laboratory. Failure experience, conformity to peer judgment, and isolation are among such phenomena. In these cases we can expect the experimenter to take whatever measures are necessary to prevent the subject from leaving the laboratory more humiliated, insecure, alienated, or hostile than when he arrived. To guarantee that an especially sensitive subject leaves a stressful experimental experience in the proper state sometimes requires special clinical training. But usually an attitude of compassion, respect, gratitude, and common sense will suffice, and no amount of clinical training will substitute. The subject has the right to expect that the psychologist with whom he is interacting has some concern for his welfare, and the personal attributes and professional skill to express his good will effectively. 3

Unfortunately, the subject is not always treated with the respect he deserves. It has become more commonplace in sociopsychological laboratory studies to manipulate, embarrass, and discomfort subjects. At times the insult to the subject's sensibilities extends to the journal reader when the results are reported. Milgram's (1963) study is a case in point. The following is Milgram's abstract of his experiment: 4

> This article describes a procedure for the study of destructive obedience in the laboratory. It consists of ordering a naive S to administer increasingly more severe punishment to a victim in the context of a learning experiment.[1] Punishment is administered by means of a shock generator with 30 graded

[1]In psychological experiments, *S* is an abbreviation for *subject; E* is an abbreviation for *experimenter.*

> switches ranging from Slight Shock to Danger: Severe Shock. The victim is a confederate of E. The primary dependent variable is the maximum shock the S is willing to administer before he refuses to continue further.[2] 26 Ss obeyed the experimental commands fully, and administered the highest shock on the generator. 14 Ss broke off the experiment at some point after the victim protested and refused to provide further answers. The procedure created extreme levels of nervous tension in some Ss. Profuse sweating, trembling, and stuttering were typical expressions of this emotional disturbance. One unexpected sign of tension—yet to be explained—was the regular occurrence of nervous laughter, which in some Ss developed into uncontrollable seizures. The variety of interesting behavioral dynamics observed in the experiment, the reality of the situation for the S, and the possibility of parametric variation[3] within the framework of the procedure point to the fruitfulness of further study [p. 371].

The detached, objective manner in which Milgram reports the emo- 5
tional disturbance suffered by his subjects contrasts sharply with his graphic account of that disturbance. Following are two other quotes describing the effects on his subjects of the experimental conditions:

> I observed a mature and initially poised businessman enter the laboratory smiling and confident. Within 20 minutes he was reduced to a twitching, stuttering wreck, who was rapidly approaching a point of nervous collapse. He constantly pulled on his earlobe, and twisted his hands. At one point he pushed his fist into his forehead and muttered: "Oh God, let's stop it." And yet he continued to respond to every word of the experimenter, and obeyed to the end [p. 377].
>
> In a large number of cases the degree of tension reached extremes that are rarely seen in sociopsychological laboratory studies. Subjects were observed to sweat, tremble, stutter, bite their lips, groan, and dig their fingernails into their flesh. These were characteristic rather than exceptional responses to the experiment.
>
> One sign of tension was the regular occurrence of nervous laughing fits. Fourteen of the 40 subjects showed definite signs of nervous laughter and smiling. The laughter seemed entirely out of place, even bizarre. Full-blown, uncontrollable seizures were observed for 3 subjects. On one occasion we observed a seizure so violently convulsive that it was necessary to call a halt to the experiment . . . [p. 375].

Milgram does state that,

> After the interview, procedures were undertaken to assure that the subject would leave the laboratory in a state of well being. A friendly reconciliation was arranged between the subject and the victim, and an effort was made to reduce any tensions that arose as a result of the experiment [p. 374].

---

[2]In the context of a psychological experiment, a *dependent variable* is a behavior that is expected to change as a result of changes in the experimental procedure.

[3]*Parametric variation* is a statistical term that describes the degree to which information based on data for one experiment can be applied to data for a slightly different experiment.

It would be interesting to know what sort of procedures could dissipate the type of emotional disturbance just described. In view of the effects on subjects, traumatic to a degree which Milgram himself considers nearly unprecedented in sociopsychological experiments, his casual assurance that these tensions were dissipated before the subject left the laboratory is unconvincing.

What could be the rational basis for such a posture of indifference? 6
Perhaps Milgram supplies the answer himself when he partially explains the subject's destructive obedience as follows, "Thus they assume that the discomfort caused the victim is momentary, while the scientific gains resulting from the experiment are enduring [p. 378]." Indeed such a rationale might suffice to justify the means used to achieve his end if that end were of inestimable value to humanity or were not itself transformed by the means by which it was attained.

The behavioral psychologist is not in as good a position to objectify his 7
faith in the significance of his work as medical colleagues at points of breakthrough. His experimental situations are not sufficiently accurate models of real-life experience; his sampling techniques are seldom of a scope which would justify the meaning with which he would like to endow his results; and these results are hard to reproduce by colleagues with opposing theoretical views. Unlike the Sabin vaccine,[4] for example, the concrete benefit to humanity of his particular piece of work, no matter how competently handled, cannot justify the risk that real harm will be done to the subject. I am not speaking of physical discomfort, inconvenience, or experimental deception per se, but of permanent harm, however slight. I do regard the emotional disturbance described by Milgram as potentially harmful because it could easily effect an alteration in the subject's self-image or ability to trust adult authorities in the future. It is potentially harmful to a subject to commit, in the course of an experiment, acts which he himself considers unworthy, particularly when he has been entrapped into committing such acts by an individual he has reason to trust. The subject's personal responsibility for his actions is not erased because the experimenter reveals to him the means which he used to stimulate these actions. The subject realizes that he would have hurt the victim if the current were on. The realization that he also made a fool of himself by accepting the experimental set results in additional loss of self-esteem. Moreover, the subject finds it difficult to express his anger outwardly after the experimenter in a self-acceptant but friendly manner reveals the hoax.

A fairly intense corrective interpersonal experience is indicated 8
wherein the subject admits and accepts his responsibility for his own actions, and at the same time gives vent to his hurt and anger at being fooled. Perhaps an experience as distressing as the one described by Milgram can be integrated by the subject, provided that careful thought is given to the matter. The propriety of such experimentation is still in question even if

[4]The Sabin vaccine provides immunization against polio.

such a reparational experience were forthcoming. Without it I would expect a naive, sensitive subject to remain deeply hurt and anxious for some time, and a sophisticated, cynical subject to become even more alienated and distrustful.

In addition the experimental procedure used by Milgram does not ap- 9
pear suited to the objectives of the study because it does not take into account the special quality of the set which the subject has in the experimental situation. Milgram is concerned with a very important problem, namely, the social consequences of destructive obedience. He says,

> Gas chambers were built, death camps were guarded, daily quotas of corpses were produced with the same efficiency as the manufacture of appliances. These inhumane policies may have originated in the mind of a single person, but they could only be carried out on a massive scale if a very large number of persons obeyed orders [p. 371].

But the parallel between authority-subordinate relationships in Hitler's Germany and in Milgram's laboratory is unclear. In the former situation the SS man or member of the German Officer Corps, when obeying orders to slaughter, had no reason to think of his superior officer as benignly disposed towards himself or their victims. The victims were perceived as subhuman and not worthy of consideration. The subordinate officer was an agent in a great cause. He did not need to feel guilt or conflict because within his frame of reference he was acting rightly.

It is obvious from Milgram's own descriptions that most of his subjects 10
were concerned about their victims and did trust the experimenter, and that their distressful conflict was generated in part by the consequences of these two disparate but appropriate attitudes. Their distress may have resulted from shock at what the experimenter was doing to them as well as from what they thought they were doing to their victims. In any case there is not a convincing parallel between the phenomena studied by Milgrm and destructive obedience as that concept would apply to the subordinate-authority relationship demonstrated in Hitler's Germany. If the experiments were conducted "outside of New Haven and without any visible ties to the university," I would still question their validity on similar although not identical grounds. In addition, I would question the representativeness of a sample of subjects who would voluntarily participate within a noninstitutional setting.

In summary, the experimental objectives of the psychologist are sel- 11
dom incompatible with the subject's ongoing state of well being, provided that the experimenter is willing to take the subject's motives and interests into consideration when planning his methods and correctives. Section 4b in *Ethical Standards of Psychologists* (APA, undated) reads in part:

> Only when a problem is significant and can be investigated in no other way is the psychologist justified in exposing human subjects to emotional stress or other possible harm. In conducting such research, the psychologist must seriously consider the possibility of harmful aftereffects, and should be prepared to remove them as soon as permitted by the design of the experiment. Where

> the danger of serious aftereffects exists, research should be conducted only when the subjects or their responsible agents are fully informed of this possibility and volunteer nevertheless [p. 12].

From the subject's point of view procedures which involve loss of dignity, self-esteem, and trust in rational authority are probably most harmful in the long run and require the most thoughtfully planned reparations, if engaged in at all. The public image of psychology as a profession is highly related to our own actions, and some of these actions are changeworthy. It is important that as research psychologists we protect our ethical sensibilities rather than adapt our personal standards to include as appropriate the kind of indignities to which Milgram's subjects were exposed. I would not like to see experiments such as Milgram's proceed unless the subjects were fully informed of the dangers of serious aftereffects and his correctives were clearly shown to be effective in restoring their state of well being.[5]

---

[5]Stanley Milgram replied to Baumrind's critique in a lengthy critique of his own [From Stanley Milgram, "Issues in the Study of Obedience: A Reply to Baumrind," *American Psychologist* 19, 1964, pp. 848–851]. Following are his principal points:

- Milgram believed that the experimental findings were in large part responsible for Baumrind's criticism. He writes:

  Is not Baumrind's criticism based as much on the unanticipated findings as on the method? The findings were that some subjects performed in what appeared to be a shockingly immoral way. If, instead, every one of the subjects had broken off at "slight shock," or at the first sign of the learner's discomfort, the results would have been pleasant, and reassuring, and who would protest?

- Milgram objected to Baumrind's assertion that those who participated in the experiment would have trouble justifying their behavior. Milgram conducted follow-up questionnaires. The results, summarized in Table 1, indicate that 84 percent of the subjects claimed they were pleased to have been a part of the experiment.

Table 1

Excerpt from Questionnaire Used in a Follow-up Study of the Obedience Research

NOW THAT I HAVE READ THE REPORT, AND ALL THINGS CONSIDERED. . .	DEFIANT	OBEDIENT	ALL
1. I am very glad to have been in the experiment	40.0%	47.8%	43.5%
2. I am glad to have been in the experiment	43.8%	35.7%	40.2%
3. I am neither sorry nor glad to have been in the experiment	15.3%	14.8%	15.1%
4. I am sorry to have been in the experiment	0.8%	0.7%	0.8%
5. I am very sorry to have been in the experiment	0.0%	1.0%	0.5%

Note—Ninety-two percent of the subjects returned the questionnaire. The characteristics of the nonrespondents were checked against the respondents. They differed from the respondents only with regard to age; younger people were overrepresented in the nonresponding group.

- Baumrind objected that studies of obedience cannot meaningfully be carried out in a laboratory setting, since the obedience occured in a context where it was appropriate. Milgram's response: "I reject Baumrind's argument that the observed obedience does not count because it occurred where it is appropriate. That is precisely why it *does* count. A soldier's obedience is no less meaningful because it occurs in a pertinent military context."
- Milgram concludes his critique in this way: "If there is a moral to be learned from the obedience study, it is that every man must be responsible for his own actions. This author accepts full responsibility for the design and execution of the study. Some people may feel it should not have been done. I disagree and accept the burden of their judgment."

REFERENCES

American Psychological Association. Ethical standards of psychologists: A summary of ethical principles. Washington, D.C.: APA, undated.

Milgram, S. Behavioral study of obedience. *J. Abnorm. Soc. Psychol.* 67, 1963, pp. 371–378.

Review Questions

1. Why might a subject volunteer for an experiment? Why do subjects typically assume a dependent, obedient attitude?
2. Why is a laboratory not a suitable setting for a study of obedience?
3. For what reasons does Baumrind feel that the Milgram experiment was potentially harmful?
4. For what reasons does Baumrind question the relationship between Milgram's findings and the obedient behavior of subordinates in Nazi Germany?

Discussion and Writing Suggestions

1. Baumrind contends that the Milgram experiment is imperfectly designed for two reasons: (1) The laboratory is not the place to test obedience; (2) Milgram disregarded the trust that subjects usually show an experimenter. Do you agree with Baumrind's objections? Do you find them equally valid?
2. Baumrind states that the ethical procedures of the experiment keep it from having significant value. Do you agree?
3. Do you agree with Baumrind that the subjects were "entrapped" into committing unworthy acts?
4. Assume the identity of a participant in Milgram's experiment who obeyed the experimenter by shocking the learner with the maximum voltage. You have just returned from the lab, and your spouse asks you about your day. Compose the conversation that follows.

Review of Stanley Milgram's Experiments on Obedience

MOTI NISSANI

Diana Baumrind challenges Milgram's experiments primarily on ethical grounds; Moti Nissani, professor of interdisciplinary studies at Wayne State University, challenges the experimental validity of Milgram's conclusions. In this selection, then, the issue is not whether or not Milgram should have carried out his experiment but, rather, did he reason soundly based on the data collected? Nissani's view is that Milgram's key explanation of people's willingness to disobey malevolent authority "is either incorrect or only partially correct." This article first appeared in American Psychologist *(Dec. 1990).*

Stanley Milgram's (1974) observations on obedience to authority have exerted a great deal of influence on such diverse disciplines as social psychology, holocaust studies, and political science. In Milgram's basic paradigm, a subject walks into a laboratory believing that he or she is about to take part in a study of memory and learning. After being assigned the role of a teacher, the subject is asked to teach word associations to a fellow subject (who in reality is a collaborator of the experimenter). The teaching method, however, is unconventional—administering increasingly higher electric shocks to the learner. Once the presumed shock level reaches a certain point, the subject is thrown into a conflict. On the one hand, the strapped learner demands to be set free and appears to suffer pain, and continuing the experiment may pose a risk to his or her health. On the other hand, the experimenter, if asked, insists that the experiment is not as unhealthy as it appears to be, and that the teacher must go on. In sharp contrast to the expectations of professionals and laymen alike, some 65 percent of all subjects continue to administer shocks up to the very highest levels. 1

Milgram's classic experiments have come under severe attack. Some critics argue that their validity hinges on the acting ability of the learner and experimenter, and that most subjects were probably able to sense the unreality of the situation. Others question the relevance of these laboratory results to the larger world. Still others question the ethics of the basic experimental design. Milgram, for his part, insists that these and other misgivings are traceable to the unsavory nature of his results: "Underlying the criticism of the experiment is an alternative model of human nature, one holding that when confronted with a choice between hurting others and complying with authority, normal people reject authority" (Milgram, 1974, p. 169). 2

Although Milgram's observations attracted much criticism and praise and have somewhat altered our views of the human condition, the interpretation he provided for his results has received scant attention—the debate focuses for the most part on the reality and extent of obedience, not on its underlying causes. 3

According to Milgram (1974), 4

> The essence of obedience consists in the fact that a person comes to view himself as the instrument for carrying out another person's wishes, and he therefore no longer sees himself as responsible for his actions. Once this critical shift of viewpoint has occurred in the person, all of the essential features of obedience follow. [Thus] the major problem for the subject is to recapture control of his own regnant processes once he has committed them to the purposes of the experimenter. (pp. xii, xiii)

In addition to this presumed agentic state, Milgram explained, a variety of factors lock the subject into the situation. These include situational factors such as politeness and awkwardness of withdrawal, absorption in the technical aspects of the task, the tendency to attribute impersonal quality to forces that are essentially human, a belief that the experiment serves a desirable end, the sequential nature of the action, and anxiety. 5

6 It seems reasonable to suppose that something like the constellation of factors above accounts for the subjects' obedience. At the time Milgram made his fascinating observations, such an explanation appeared highly probable and fairly complete. However, unlike Milgram's observations, the evidence in favor of this explanation is fairly circumstantial. The best that can be said, for instance, about Milgram's key postulate of the agentic state is that it makes sense and that, if true, it may account for the data.

7 Certain developments in cognitive psychology that came to their own after 1974 suggested the presence of another key causative factor. Before making the connection between obedience and cognition, we need to familiarize ourselves with these developments. For the sake of brevity, I shall describe here only a few recent experiments that seem most directly applicable in this context (Nissani, 1989a, 1989b; Nissani & Hoefler, 1992; Nissani & Maier, 1990).

8 These experiments were patterned after, and provide striking confirmation of, earlier observations (Festinger, Riecken, & Schachter, 1964; Karmiloff-Smith & Inhelder, 1975; Kuhn, 1974; Milgram 1974, 1984; Ross & Anderson, 1982). In these more recent experiments, subjects were recruited to evaluate the efficacy of a self-contained instructional manual. Before they could provide the needed appraisal, they were told, they needed to acquire a first-hand experience of its content by studying it and following the instructions it provided for about four hours. At some point in the teaching process, the manual introduced a false volume formula for a sphere—a formula that led subjects to believe that spheres were 50 percent larger than they actually were. Subjects were then given an actual sphere and asked to determine its volume, first by using the formula and then by filling the sphere with water, transferring the water to a box, and directly measuring the volume of the water in the box. The key question was, Would subjects believe the evidence of their senses and abandon their prior beliefs in the formula, the competence of the experimenter, and the legitimacy of the entire setup? Preliminary observations (Nissani, 1989a, 1989b) suggested to the subjects that the task was far more difficult than expected: No subject decisively rejected the false formula or declined to use it in subsequent tasks. In later experiments, various attempts were made to ease the conceptual transition called for by this experiment. In one variation (Nissani & Hoefler, 1992), all subjects held a PhD in a natural science and were employed as research scientists and professors in two major research universities. A special section, involving measurements of a second ball, was introduced and constructed with the deliberate aim of helping these scientists break away from the false formula. In another variation (Nissani & Maier, 1990), the discrepancy concerned the circumference of an ellipse, thereby ruling out the possibility that earlier results were ascribable to the difficulty of dealing with three-dimensional concepts. But none of these variations substantially altered the initial results:

> The preliminary observations reported here suggest that the importance of conceptual conservatism has been underestimated in the psychological litera-

> ture and that the insistence that the phenomenon constitutes one of the major impediments to progress in the history of ideas could very well be correct. In particular, although conceptual conservatism has received the attention of experimentalists, although its importance in human affairs has been long recognized and although the results reported here are based on a small sample, the qualitative outcome of this study—all subjects clung in practice to an observationally absurd formula and none rejected it outright even on the verbal level—are surprising. Even when we deal with ideologically neutral conceptions of reality, when these conceptions have been recently acquired, when they came to us from unfamiliar sources, when they were assimilated for spurious reasons, when their abandonment entails little tangible risks or costs, and when they are sharply contradicted by subsequent events, we are, at least for a time, disinclined to doubt such conceptions on the verbal level and unlikely to let go of them in practice. (Nissani, 1989a, pp. 23–24)

These results poignantly suggest a rather counterintuitive conclusion **9**
that could not be fully appreciated by Milgram 16 years ago: Transitions from one belief to another are not as smooth as common sense or intuition would suggest. For instance, attempting to provide a retrospective explanation for his failure to reject the false formula of the sphere, one of the subject-scientists wrote "It is difficult to imagine that one could be deliberately deceived in an exercise like this" (Nissani & Hoefler, 1992).

Consider the typical subjects in Milgram's basic paradigm. They came **10**
to participate in a scientific investigation at an impressive, well-equipped laboratory at Yale University. They had every reason to *believe* that the experiment was conducted by responsible people. They had never before heard of tortures, killings, inhumanity, or immorality associated with modern scientific experiments. In fact, not only Milgram's subjects, but all of us, share this eminently reasonable belief. We know that university scientists are working under various legal and ethical constraints, and that barbarism of any kind is simply out of the question. Milgram's subjects walked into the experiment taking for granted the responsibility and basic morality of the entire setup. As in the case of subjects in a conceptual shift experiment, the experimental evidence contradicted this belief. Disobedience in such a setting presupposes a conceptual shift. Milgram's subjects had to discard their belief in the morality of the experimenter. "I knew you wouldn't let anything happen" to the learner, one of Milgram's subjects said in an effort to explain his obedience (Milgram, 1974, p. 83). In contrast, one disobedient subject treated the experimenter "as a dull technician who does not see the full implications of what he is doing" (Milgram, 1974, p. 48).

If this conclusion is correct, Milgram's opinion that "people can't be **11**
counted on to disobey malevolent authority" and that "they obey as long as the command comes from legitimate authority" (Milgram, 1974, p. 89) is either incorrect or only partially correct. Rather, what people cannot be counted on is to realize that a seemingly benevolent authority is in fact malevolent, even when they are faced with overwhelming evidence that suggests that this authority is indeed malevolent. Hence, the underlying

cause for the subjects' striking conduct could well be conceptual and not the alleged "capacity of man to abandon his humanity . . . as he merges his unique personality into larger institutional structures" (Milgram, 1974, p. 188).

Some of Milgram's own data support this interpretation: 12

1. Milgram's results are surprising. Laymen and social scientists alike 13
were unable to foretell the extent to which subjects would obey the experimenter. Likewise, laypersons and social scientists were unable to predict the behavior of subjects in conceptual shift experiments (Nissani & Hoefler, 1992). It is entirely possible that both inadequate forecasts are traceable to a single factor—underestimating the excruciating difficulty of abandoning a strongly held, eminently reasonable belief.

2. In one of Milgram's variations, subjects were led to believe that the 14
experiment was conducted by a private research firm. This single difference decreased obedience rate from 65 percent to 48 percent (Milgram, 1974, p. 69). This is consistent with the conceptual shift interpretation: Because private research firms are less prestigious than Ivy League schools, it is easier under these conditions to abandon the belief in the experimenter's essential decency.

3. In another experimental variation, a single element of betrayal and 15
patent injustice was introduced, leading obedience to drop from 50 percent to 40 percent (Milgram, 1974, p. 66). This result is again consistent with the conceptual shift interpretation proposed here.

A new experimental variation in Milgram's protocol could readily test 16
the purely moral conflict Milgram's observations have so far failed to capture. As in other variations, the authority figure must be portrayed as legitimate. But, by the time the teaching session begins, this figure must appear as highly callous and irresponsible. If successful, this variation would create a genuine conflict between willing obedience to malevolent authority and the voice of conscience. The data from Milgram's own experiments, the near-unanimous consent of Milgram's survey respondents, and the cognitive data underscoring the difficulty of discarding reasonable beliefs, strongly suggest that obedience in such situations would be substantially lower than it was in Milgram's basic paradigm.

I hope that this crucial experiment will be undertaken by one or more 17
readers of these lines.

REFERENCES

Festinger, L., Riecken, H. W., & Schachter, S. (1964). *When prophecy fails.* New York: Harper.

Karmiloff-Smith, A., & Inhelder, B. (1975). If you want to get ahead, get a theory. *Cognition, 3,* 195.

Kuhn, T. S. (1974). *The structure of scientific revolutions.* Chicago: University of Chicago Press.

Milgram, S. (1974). *Obedience to authority.* New York: Harper & Row.

Milgram, S. (1984, August). *Cyranoids.* Paper presented at the 92nd Annual Convention of the American Psychological Association, Toronto, Ontario, Canada.

Nissani, M. (1989a). An experimental paradigm for the study of conceptual conservatism and change. *Psychological Reports, 65,* 19–24.

Nissani, M. (1989b). A hands-on instructional approach to the conceptual shift aspect of scientific discovery. *Journal of College Science Teaching, 19,* 105–107.

Nissani, M., & Hoefler, D. M. (1992). Experimental studies of belief-dependence of observations and of resistance to conceptual change. *Cognition and Instruction 9,* 97–111.

Nissani, M., & Maier, C. (1990). *Further explorations of conceptual conservatism: Reconciling incompatible beliefs and observations concerning the circumference of the ellipse.* Unpublished manuscript.

Ross, L., & Anderson, C. A. (1982). *Shortcomings in the attribution process: On the origins and maintenance of erroneous social assessment.* In D. Kahneman, P. Slovic, & A. Tversky (Eds.), *Judgment under uncertainty: Heuristics and biases* (pp. 129–152). Cambridge, England: Cambridge University Press.

Review Questions

1. In paragraphs 1–4, Nissani summarizes the Milgram experiments and reactions to them. What were the principal critiques of the experiments? What was Milgram's response?
2. What, according to Milgram, was the important psychological shift that occurred in his subjects?
3. What is the distinction Nissani makes between Milgram's observations and explanations?
4. What is "conceptual conservatism"? What were the circumstances in which the term emerged?
5. According to Nissani, what is the "rather counterintuitive" conclusion of the more recent obedience experiments? And what are the implications of this new conclusion for Milgram's experiments?

Discussion and Writing Suggestions

1. How fundamentally different from Milgram's own interpretation of his work is Nissani's interpretation?
2. How persuaded are you by Nissani's re-assessment of Milgram's conclusions? Given Milgram's arguments and Nissani's, which do you find more compelling? Why?
3. Does Nissani's conclusion about "conceptual conservatism" make the behavior that Milgram observed (and the behavior of the Ph.D. subjects in Nissani's own obedience experiments) any less disturbing to you? Explain your response.
4. In what ways does Nissani's article suggest how knowledge is built in the social sciences?
5. Consult the reference list at the end of this article. Read other articles by Nissani, and write a summary report for your classmates.

The Stanford Prison Experiment

PHILIP K. ZIMBARDO

As well known—and as controversial—as the Milgram obedience experiments, the Stanford Prison Experiment (1973) raises troubling questions about the ability of individuals to resist authoritarian or obedient roles, if the social setting requires these roles. Philip K. Zimbardo, professor of psychology at Stanford University, set out to study the process by which prisoners and guards "learn" to become compliant and authoritarian, respectively. To find subjects for the experiment, Zimbardo placed an advertisement in a local newspaper:

> Male college students needed for psychological study of prison life. $15 per day for 1–2 weeks beginning Aug. 14. For further information & applications, come to Room 248, Jordan Hall, Stanford U.

The ad drew 75 responses. From these Zimbardo and his colleagues selected 21 college-age men, half of whom would become "prisoners" in the experiment, the other half "guards." The elaborate role-playing scenario, planned for two weeks, had to be cut short due to the intensity of subjects' responses. This article first appeared in the New York Times Magazine *(April 8, 1973).*

In prison, those things withheld from and denied to the prisoner become precisely what he wants most of all.

—Eldridge Cleaver, "Soul on Ice"

Our sense of power is more vivid when we break a man's spirit than when we win his heart.

—Eric Hoffer, "The Passionate State of Mind"

Every prison that men build is built with bricks of shame, / and bound with bars lest Christ should see how men their brothers maim.

—Oscar Wilde, "The Ballad of Reading Gaol"

Wherever anyone is against his will that is to him a prison.

—Epictetus, "Discourses"

The quiet of a summer morning in Palo Alto, Calif., was shattered by a 1
screeching squad car siren as police swept through the city picking up college students in a surprise mass arrest. Each suspect was charged with a felony, warned of his constitutional rights, spread-eagled against the car, searched, handcuffed and carted off in the back seat of the squad car to the police station for booking.

After fingerprinting and the preparation of identification forms for his 2
"jacket" (central information file), each prisoner was left isolated in a detention cell to wonder what he had done to get himself into this mess. After a while, he was blindfolded and transported to the "Stanford County

Prison." Here he began the process of becoming a prisoner—stripped naked, skin-searched, deloused and issued a uniform, bedding, soap and towel.

The warden offered an impromptu welcome: 3

"As you probably know, I'm your warden. All of you have shown that 4
you are unable to function outside in the real world for one reason or another—that somehow you lack the responsibility of good citizens of this great country. We of this prison, your correctional staff, are going to help you learn what your responsibilities as citizens of this country are. Here are the rules. Sometime in the near future there will be a copy of the rules posted in each of the cells. We expect you to know them and to be able to recite them by number. If you follow all of these rules and keep your hands clean, repent for your misdeeds and show a proper attitude of penitence, you and I will get along just fine."

There followed a reading of the 16 basic rules of prisoner conduct. 5
"Rule Number One: Prisoners must remain silent during rest periods, after lights are out, during meals and whenever they are outside the prison yard. Two: Prisoners must eat at mealtimes and only at mealtimes. Three: Prisoners must not move, tamper, deface or damage walls, ceilings, windows, doors, or other prison property. . . . Seven: Prisoners must address each other by their ID number only. Eight: Prisoners must address the guards as 'Mr. Correctional Officer.'. . . Sixteen: Failure to obey any of the above rules may result in punishment."

By late afternoon these youthful "first offenders" sat in dazed silence 6
on the cots in their barren cells trying to make sense of the events that had transformed their lives so dramatically.

If the police arrests and processing were executed with customary de- 7
tachment, however, there were some things that didn't fit. For these men were now part of a very unusual kind of prison, an experimental mock prison, created by social psychologists to study the effects of imprisonment upon volunteer research subjects. When we planned our two-week-long simulation of prison life, we sought to understand more about the process by which people called "prisoners" lose their liberty, civil rights, independence and privacy, while those called "guards" gain social power by accepting the responsibility for controlling and managing the lives of their dependent charges.

Why didn't we pursue this research in a real prison? First, prison sys- 8
tems are fortresses of secrecy, closed to impartial observation, and thereby immune to critical analysis from anyone not already part of the correctional authority. Second, in any real prison, it is impossible to separate what each individual brings into the prison from what the prison brings out in each person.

We populated our mock prison with a homogeneous group of people 9
who could be considered "normal-average" on the basis of clinical interviews and personality tests. Our participants (10 prisoners and 11 guards) were selected from more than 75 volunteers recruited through ads in the city and campus newspapers. The applicants were mostly college students

from all over the United States and Canada who happened to be in the Stanford area during the summer and were attracted by the lure of earning $15 a day for participating in a study of prison life. We selected only those judged to be emotionally stable, physically healthy, mature, law-abiding citizens.

This sample of average, middle-class, Caucasian, college-age males (plus one Oriental student) was arbitrarily divided by the flip of a coin. Half were randomly assigned to play the role of guards, the others of prisoners. There were no measurable differences between the guards and the prisoners at the start of the experiment. Although initially warned that as prisoners their privacy and other civil rights would be violated and that they might be subjected to harassment, every subject was completely confident of his ability to endure whatever the prison had to offer for the full two-week experimental period. Each subject unhesitatingly agreed to give his "informed consent" to participate. 10

The prison was constructed in the basement of Stanford University's psychology building, which was deserted after the end of the summer-school session. A long corridor was converted into the prison "yard" by partitioning off both ends. Three small laboratory rooms opening onto this corridor were made into cells by installing metal barred doors and replacing existing furniture with cots, three to a cell. Adjacent offices were refurnished as guards' quarters, interview-testing rooms and bedrooms for the "warden" (Jaffe) and the "superintendent" (Zimbardo). A concealed video camera and hidden microphones recorded much of the activity and conversation of guards and prisoners. The physical environment was one in which prisoners could always be observed by the staff, the only exception being when they were secluded in solitary confinement (a small, dark storage closet, labeled "The Hole"). 11

Our mock prison represented an attempt to simulate the psychological state of imprisonment in certain ways. We based our experiment on an in-depth analysis of the prison situation, developed after hundreds of hours of discussion with Carlo Prescott (our ex-con consultant), parole officers and correctional personnel, and after reviewing much of the existing literature on prisons and concentration camps. 12

"Real" prisoners typically report feeling powerless, arbitrarily controlled, dependent, frustrated, hopeless, anonymous, dehumanized and emasculated. It was not possible, pragmatically or ethically, to create such chronic states in volunteer subjects who realize that they are in an experiment for only a short time. Racism, physical brutality, indefinite confinement and enforced homosexuality were not features of our mock prison. But we did try to reproduce those elements of the prison experience that seemed most fundamental. 13

We promoted anonymity by seeking to minimize each prisoner's sense of uniqueness and prior identity. The prisoners wore smocks and nylon stocking caps; they had to use their ID numbers; their personal effects were removed and they were housed in barren cells. All of this made them appear similar to each other and indistinguishable to observers. Their smocks, 14 which were like dresses, were worn without undergarments, causing the prisoners to be restrained in their physical actions and to move in ways that were more feminine than masculine. The prisoners were forced to obtain permission from the guard for routine and simple activities such as writing letters, smoking a cigarette or even going to the toilet; this elicited from them a childlike dependency.

Their quarters, though clean and neat, were small, stark and without esthetic appeal. The lack of windows resulted in poor air circulation, and persistent odors arose from the unwashed bodies of the prisoners. After 10 P.M. lockup, toilet privileges were denied, so prisoners who had to relieve themselves would have to urinate and defecate in buckets provided by the guards. Sometimes the guards refused permission to have them cleaned out, and this made the prison smell. 15

Above all, "real" prisons are machines for playing tricks with the human conception of time. In our windowless prison, the prisoners often did not even know whether it was day or night. A few hours after falling asleep, they were roused by shrill whistles for their "count." The ostensible purpose of the count was to provide a public test of the prisoners' knowledge of the rules and of their ID numbers. But more important, the count, which occurred at least once on each of the three different guard shifts, provided a regular occasion for the guards to relate to the prisoners. Over the course of the study, the duration of the counts was spontaneously increased by the guards from their initial perfunctory 10 minutes to a seemingly interminable several hours. During these confrontations, guards who were bored could find ways to amuse themselves, ridiculing recalcitrant prisoners, enforcing arbitrary rules and openly exaggerating any dissension among the prisoners. 16

The guards were also "deindividualized": They wore identical khaki uniforms and silver reflector sunglasses that made eye contact with them impossible. Their symbols of power were billy clubs, whistles, handcuffs and the keys to the cells and the "main gate." Although our guards received no formal training from us in how to be guards, for the most part they moved with apparent ease into their roles. The media had already provided them with ample models of prison guards to emulate. 17

Because we were as interested in the guards' behavior as in the prisoners', they were given considerable latitude to improvise and to develop strategies and tactics of prisoner management. Our guards were told that they must maintain "law and order" in this prison, that they were responsible for handling any trouble that might break out, and they were cautioned about the seriousness and potential dangers of the situation they were about to enter. Surprisingly, in most prison systems, "real" guards are not given much more psychological preparation or adequate training than this for what is one of the most complex, demanding and dangerous jobs our society has to offer. They are expected to learn how to adjust to their new employment mostly from on-the-job experience, and from contacts with the "old bulls" during a survival-of-the-fittest orientation period. According to an orientation manual for correctional officers at San Quentin, "the only 18 way you really get to know San Quentin is through experience and time. Some of us take more time and must go through more experiences than others to accomplish this; some really never do get there."

You cannot be a prisoner if no one will be your guard, and you cannot be a prison guard if no one takes you or your prison seriously. Therefore, over time a perverted symbiotic relationship developed. As the guards became more aggressive, prisoners became more passive; assertion by the guards led to dependency in the prisoners; self-aggrandizement was met with self-deprecation, authority with helplessness, and the counterpart of the guards' sense of mastery and control was the depression and hopelessness witnessed in the prisoners. As these differences in behavior, mood and perception became more evident to all, the need for the now "righteously" powerful guards to rule the obviously inferior and powerless inmates became a sufficient reason to support almost any further indignity of man against man: 19

Guard K: "During the inspection, I went to cell 2 to mess up a bed which the prisoner had made and he grabbed me, screaming that he had just made it, and he wasn't going to let me mess it up. He grabbed my throat, and although he was laughing I was pretty scared. . . . I lashed out with my stick and hit him in the chin (although not very hard), and when I freed myself I became angry. I wanted to get back in the cell and have a go with him, since he attacked me when I was not ready." 20

Guard M: "I was surprised at myself . . . I made them call each other names and clean the toilets out with their bare hands. I practically considered the prisoners cattle, and I kept thinking: 'I have to watch out for them in case they try something.'" 21

Guard A: "I was tired of seeing the prisoners in their rags and smelling the strong odors of their bodies that filled the cells. I watched them tear at each other on orders given by us. They didn't see it as an experiment. It was real and they were fighting to keep their identity. But we were always there to show them who was boss." 22

Because the first day passed without incident, we were surprised and totally unprepared for the rebellion that broke out on the morning of the second day. The prisoners removed their stocking caps, ripped off their numbers and barricaded themselves inside the cells by putting their beds against the doors. What should we do? The guards were very much upset because the prisoners also began to taunt and curse them to their faces. When the morning shift of guards came on, they were upset at the night shift who, they felt, must have been too permissive and too lenient. The guards had to handle the rebellion themselves, and what they did was startling to behold. 23

At first they insisted that reinforcements be called in. The two guards who were waiting on stand-by call at home came in, and the night shift of guards voluntarily remained on duty (without extra pay) to bolster the morning shift. The guards met and decided to treat force with force. They got a fire extinguisher that shot a stream of skin-chilling carbon dioxide and forced the prisoners away from the doors; they broke into each cell, 24 stripped the prisoners naked, took the beds out, forced the prisoners who were the ringleaders into solitary confinement and generally began to harass and intimidate the prisoners.

After crushing the riot, the guards decided to head off further unrest by creating a privileged cell for those who were "good prisoners" and then, without explanation, switching some of the troublemakers into it and some of the good prisoners out into the other cells. The prisoner ringleaders could not trust these new cellmates because they had not joined in the riot and might even be "snitches." The prisoners never again acted in unity against the system. One of the leaders of the prisoner revolt later confided: 25

"If we had gotten together then, I think we could have taken over the place. But when I saw the revolt wasn't working, I decided to toe the line. Everyone settled into the same pattern. From then on, we were really controlled by the guards." 26

It was after this episode that the guards really began to demonstrate their inventiveness in the application of arbitrary power. They made the prisoners obey petty, meaningless and often inconsistent rules, forced them to engage in tedious, useless work, such as moving cartons back and forth between closets and picking thorns out of their blankets for hours on end. (The guards had previously dragged the blankets through thorny bushes to create this disagreeable task.) Not only did the prisoners have to sing songs or laugh or refrain from smiling on command; they were also encouraged to curse and vilify each other publicly during some of the counts. They sounded off their numbers endlessly and were repeatedly made to do pushups, on occasion with a guard stepping on them or a prisoner sitting on them. 27

Slowly the prisoners became resigned to their fate and even behaved in ways that actually helped to justify their dehumanizing treatment at the hands of the guards. Analysis of the tape-recorded private conversations between prisoners and of remarks made by them to interviewers revealed that fully half could be classified as nonsupportive of other prisoners. More dramatic, 85 percent of the evaluative statements by prisoners about their fellow prisoners were uncomplimentary and deprecating. 28

This should be taken in the context of an even more surprising result. What do you imagine the prisoners talked about when they were alone in their cells with each other, given a temporary respite from the continual harassment and surveillance by the guards? Girl friends, career plans, hobbies or politics? 29

No, their concerns were almost exclusively riveted to prison topics. Their monitored conversations revealed that only 10 percent of the time was devoted to "outside" topics, while 90 percent of the time they discussed escape plans, the awful food, grievances or ingratiating tactics to use with specific guards in order to get a cigarette, permission to go to the toilet or some other favor. Their obsession with these immediate survival concerns made talk about the past and future an idle luxury. 30

And this was not a minor point. So long as the prisoners did not get to know each other as people, they only extended the oppressiveness and real- 31 ity of their life as prisoners. For the most part, each prisoner observed his fellow prisoners allowing the guards to humiliate them, acting like compliant sheep, carrying out mindless orders with total obedience and even being cursed by fellow prisoners (at a guard's command). Under such circumstances, how could a prisoner have respect for his fellows, or any self-respect for what *he* obviously was becoming in the eyes of all those evaluating him?

The combination of realism and symbolism in this experiment had fused to create a vivid illusion of imprisonment. The illusion merged inextricably with reality for at least some of the time for every individual in the situation. It was remarkable how readily we all slipped into our roles, temporarily gave up our identities and allowed these assigned roles and the social forces in the situation to guide, shape and eventually to control our freedom of thought and action. 32

But precisely where does one's "identity" end and one's "role" begin? When the private self and the public role behavior clash, what direction will attempts to impose consistency take? Consider the reactions of the parents, relatives and friends of the prisoners who visited their forlorn sons, brothers and lovers during two scheduled visitors' hours. They were taught in short order that they were our guests, allowed the privilege of visiting only by complying with the regulations of the institution. They had to register, were made to wait half an hour, were told that only two visitors could see any one prisoner; the total visiting time was cut from an hour to only 10 minutes, they had to be under the surveillance of a guard, and before any parents could enter the visiting area, they had to discuss their son's case with the warden. Of course they complained about these arbitrary rules, but their conditioned, middle-class reaction was to work within the system to appeal privately to the superintendent to make conditions better for their prisoners. 33

In less than 36 hours, we were forced to release prisoner 8612 because of extreme depression, disorganized thinking, uncontrollable crying and fits of rage. We did so reluctantly because we believed he was trying to "con" us—it was unimaginable that a volunteer prisoner in a mock prison could legitimately be suffering and disturbed to that extent. But then on each of the next three days another prisoner reacted with similar anxiety symptoms, and we were forced to terminate them, too. In a fifth case, a prisoner was released after developing a psychosomatic rash over his entire body (triggered by rejection of his parole appeal by the mock parole board). These men were simply unable to make an adequate adjustment to prison life. Those who endured the prison experience to the end could be distinguished from those who broke down and were released early in only one dimension—authoritarianism. On a psychological test designed to reveal a person's authoritarianism, those prisoners who had the highest scores were best able to function in this authoritarian prison environment. 34

If the authoritarian situation became a serious matter for the prisoners, it became even more serious—and sinister—for the guards. Typically, the guards insulted the prisoners, threatened them, were physically aggressive, 35 used instruments (night sticks, fire extinguishers, etc.) to keep the prisoners in line and referred to them in impersonal, anonymous, deprecating ways: "Hey, you," or "You [obscenity], 5401, come here." From the first to the last day, there was a significant increase in the guards' use of most of these domineering, abusive tactics.

Everyone and everything in the prison was defined by power. To be a guard who did not take advantage of this institutionally sanctioned use of power was to appear "weak," "out of it," "wired up by the prisoners," or simply a deviant from the established norms of appropriate guard behavior. Using Erich Fromm's definition of sadism, as "the wish for absolute control over another living being," all of the mock guards at one time or another during this study behaved sadistically toward the prisoners. Many of them reported—in their diaries, on critical-incident report forms and during post-experimental interviews—being delighted in the new-found power and control they exercised and sorry to see it relinquished at the end of the study. 36

Some of the guards reacted to the situation in the extreme and behaved with great hostility and cruelty in the forms of degradation they invented for the prisoners. But others were kinder; they occasionally did little favors for the prisoners, were reluctant to punish them, and avoided situations where prisoners were being harassed. The torment experienced by one of these good guards is obvious in his perceptive analysis of what it felt like to be responded to as a "guard": 37

"What made the experience most depressing for me was the fact that we were continually called upon to act in a way that just was contrary to what I really feel inside. I don't feel like I'm the type of person that would be a guard, just constantly giving out . . . and forcing people to do things, and pushing and lying—it just didn't seem like me, and to continually keep up and put on a face like that is just really one of the most oppressive things you can do. It's almost like a prison that you create yourself—you get into it, and it becomes almost the definition you make of yourself, it almost becomes like walls, and you want to break out and you want just to be able to tell everyone that 'this isn't really me at all, and I'm not the person that's confined in there—I'm a person who wants to get out and show you that I am free, and I do have my own will, and I'm not the sadistic type of person that enjoys this kind of thing.' " 38

Still, the behavior of these good guards seemed more motivated by a desire to be liked by everyone in the system than by a concern for the inmates' welfare. No guard ever intervened in any direct way on behalf of the prisoners, ever interfered with the orders of the cruelest guards or ever openly complained about the subhuman quality of life that characterized this prison. 39

Perhaps the most devastating impact of the more hostile guards was their creation of a capricious, arbitrary environment. Over time the prisoners began to react passively. When our mock prisoners asked questions, they got answers about half the time, but the rest of the time they were insulted and punished—and it was not possible for them to predict which 40 would be the outcome. As they began to "toe the line," they stopped resisting, questioning and, indeed, almost ceased responding altogether. There was a general decrease in all categories of response as they learned the safest strategy to use in an unpredictable, threatening environment from which there is no physical escape—do nothing, except what is required. Act not, want not, feel not and you will not get into trouble in prisonlike situations.

Can it really be, you wonder, that intelligent, educated volunteers 41
could have lost sight of the reality that they were merely acting a part in an elaborate game that would eventually end? There are many indications not only that they did, but that, in addition, so did we and so did other apparently sensible, responsible adults.

Prisoner 819, who had gone into an uncontrollable crying fit, was 42
about to be prematurely released from the prison when a guard lined up the prisoners and had them chant in unison, "819 is a bad prisoner. Because of what 819 did to prison property we all must suffer. 819 is a bad prisoner." Over and over again. When we realized 819 might be overhearing this, we rushed into the room where 819 was supposed to be resting, only to find him in tears, prepared to go back into the prison because he could not leave as long as the others thought he was a "bad prisoner." Sick as he felt, he had to prove to them he was not a "bad" prisoner. He had to be persuaded that he was not a prisoner at all, that the others were also just students, that this was just an experiment and not a prison and the prison staff were only research psychologists. A report from the warden notes, "While I believe that it was necessary for *staff* [me] to enact the warden role, at least some of the time, I am startled by the ease with which I could turn off my sensitivity and concern for others for 'a good cause.'"

Consider our overreaction to the rumor of a mass escape plot that one 43
of the guards claimed to have overheard. It went as follows: Prisoner 8612, previously released for emotional disturbance, was only faking. He was going to round up a bunch of his friends, and they would storm the prison right after visiting hours. Instead of collecting data on the pattern of rumor transmission, we made plans to maintain the security of our institution. After putting a confederate informer into the cell 8612 had occupied to get specific information about the escape plans, the superintendent went back to the Palo Alto Police Department to request transfer of our prisoners to the old city jail. His impassioned plea was only turned down at the last minute when the problem of insurance and city liability for our prisoners was raised by a city official. Angered at this lack of cooperation, the staff formulated another plan. Our jail was dismantled, the prisoners, chained and blindfolded, were carted off to a remote storage room. When the conspirators arrived, they would be told the study was over, their friends had been sent home, there was nothing left to liberate. After they left, we would redouble the security features of our prison making any future escape attempts futile. We even planned to lure ex-prisoner 8612 back on some pretext and imprison him again, because he had been released on false pretenses! The rumor turned out to be just that—a full day had passed in

which we collected little or no data, worked incredibly hard to tear down and then rebuild our prison. Our reaction, however, was as much one of relief and joy as of exhaustion and frustration.

When a former prison chaplain was invited to talk with the prisoners 44
(the grievance committee had requested church services), he puzzled everyone by disparaging each inmate for not having taken any constructive action in order to get released. "Don't you know you must have a lawyer in order to get bail, or to appeal the charges against you?" Several of them accepted his invitation to contact their parents in order to secure the services of an attorney. The next night one of the parents stopped at the superintendent's office before visiting time and handed him the name and phone number of her cousin who was a public defender. She said that a priest had called her and suggested the need for a lawyer's services! We called the lawyer. He came, interviewed the prisoners, discussed sources of bail money and promised to return again after the weekend.

But perhaps the most telling account of the insidious development of 45
this new reality, of the gradual Kafkaesque metamorphosis of good into evil, appears in excerpts from the diary of one of the guards, Guard A:

Prior to start of experiment: "As I am a pacifist and nonaggressive in- 46
dividual I cannot see a time when I might guard and/or maltreat other living things."

After an orientation meeting: "Buying uniforms at the end of the meet- 47
ing confirms the gamelike atmosphere of this thing. I doubt whether many of us share the expectations of 'seriousness' that the experimenters seem to have."

First Day: "Feel sure that the prisoners will make fun of my appear- 48
ance and I evolve my first basic strategy—mainly not to smile at anything they say or do which would be admitting it's all only a game. . . . At cell 3 I stop and setting my voice hard and low say to 5486, 'What are you smiling at?' 'Nothing, Mr. Correctional Officer.' 'Well, see that you don't.' (As I walk off I feel stupid.)"

Second Day: "5704 asked for a cigarette and I ignored him—because I 49
am a non-smoker and could not empathize. . . . Meanwhile since I was feeling empathetic towards 1037, I determined not to talk with him . . . after we had count and lights out [Guard D] and I held a loud conversation about going home to our girl friends and what we were going to do to them."

Third Day (preparing for the first visitors' night): "After warning the 50
prisoners not to make any complaints unless they wanted the visit terminated fast, we finally brought in the first parents. I made sure I was one of the guards on the yard, because this was my first chance for the type of manipulative power that I really like—being a very noticed figure with almost complete control over what is said or not. While the parents and prisoners sat in chairs, I sat on the end of the table dangling my feet and contradicting anything I felt like. This was the first part of the experiment I was really enjoying. . . . 817 is being obnoxious and bears watching."

Fourth Day: ". . .The psychologist rebukes me for handcuffing and blindfolding a prisoner before leaving the [counseling] office, and I resentfully reply that it is both necessary security and my business anyway." 51

Fifth Day: "I harass 'Sarge' who continues to stubbornly overrespond to all commands. I have singled him out for special abuse both because he begs for it and because I simply don't like him. The real trouble starts at dinner. The new prisoner (416) refuses to eat his sausage . . . we throw him into the Hole ordering him to hold sausages in each hand. We have a crisis of authority; this rebellious conduct potentially undermines the complete control we have over the others. We decide to play upon prisoner solidarity and tell the new one that all the others will be deprived of visitors if he does not eat his dinner. . . . I walk by and slam my stick into the Hole door. . . . I am very angry at this prisoner for causing discomfort and trouble for the others. I decided to force-feed him, but he wouldn't eat. I let the food slide down his face. I didn't believe it was me doing it. I hated myself for making him eat but I hated him more for not eating." 52

Sixth Day: "The experiment is over. I feel elated but am shocked to find some other guards disappointed somewhat because of the loss of money and some because they are enjoying themselves." 53

We were no longer dealing with an intellectual exercise in which a hypothesis was being evaluated in the dispassionate manner dictated by the canons of the scientific method. We were caught up in the passion of the present, the suffering, the need to control people, not variables, the escalation of power and all of the unexpected things that were erupting around and within us. We had to end this experiment: So our planned two-week simulation was aborted after only six (was it only six?) days and nights. 54

Was it worth all the suffering just to prove what everybody knows—that some people are sadistic, others weak and prisons are not beds of roses? If that is all we demonstrated in this research, then it was certainly not worth the anguish. We believe there are many significant implications to be derived from this experience, only a few of which can be suggested here. 55

The potential social value of this study derives precisely from the fact that normal, healthy, educated young men could be so radically transformed under the institutional pressures of a "prison environment." If this could happen in so short a time, without the excesses that are possible in real prisons, and if it could happen to the "cream-of-the-crop of American youth," then one can only shudder to imagine what society is doing both to the actual guards and prisoners who are at this very moment participating in that unnatural "social experiment." 56

The pathology observed in this study cannot be reasonably attributed in pre-existing personality differences of the subjects, that option being eliminated by our selection procedures and random assignment. Rather, the subjects' abnormal social and personal reactions are best seen as a product of their transaction with an environment that supported the behavior that would be pathological in other settings, but was "appropriate" in this 57 prison. Had we observed comparable reactions in a real prison, the psychiatrist undoubtedly would have been able to attribute any prisoner's behavior to character defects or personality maladjustment, while critics of the prison system would have been quick to label the guards as "psychopathic." This tendency to locate the source of behavior disorders inside a particular person or group underestimates the power of situational forces.

Our colleague, David Rosenhan, has very convincingly shown that 58
once a sane person (pretending to be insane) gets labeled as insane and committed to a mental hospital, it is the label that is the reality which is treated and not the person. This dehumanizing tendency to respond to other people according to socially determined labels and often arbitrarily assigned roles is also apparent in a recent "mock hospital" study designed by Norma Jean Orlando to extend the ideas in our research.

Personnel from the staff of Elgin State Hospital in Illinois role-played 59
either mental patients or staff in a weekend simulation on a ward in the hospital. The mock mental patients soon displayed behavior indistinguishable from that we usually associate with the chronic pathological syndromes of acute mental patients: Incessant pacing, uncontrollable weeping, depression, hostility, fights, stealing from each other, complaining. Many of the "mock staff" took advantage of their power to act in ways comparable to our mock guards by dehumanizing their powerless victims.

During a series of encounter debriefing sessions immediately after our 60
experiment, we all had an opportunity to vent our strong feelings and to reflect upon the moral and ethical issues each of us faced, and we considered how we might react more morally in future "real-life" analogues to this situation. Year-long follow-ups with our subjects via questionnaires, personal interviews and group reunions indicate that their mental anguish was transient and situationally specific, but the self-knowledge gained has persisted.

For the most disturbing implication of our research comes from the 61
parallels between what occurred in that basement mock prison and daily experiences in our own lives—and we presume yours. The physical institution of prison is but a concrete and steel metaphor for the existence of more pervasive, albeit less obvious, prisons of the mind that all of us daily create, populate and perpetuate. We speak here of the prisons of racism, sexism, despair, shyness, "neurotic hang-ups" and the like. The social convention of marriage, as one example, becomes for many couples a state of imprisonment in which one partner agrees to be prisoner or guard, forcing or allowing the other to play the reciprocal role—invariably without making the contract explicit.

To what extent do we allow ourselves to become imprisoned by 62
docilely accepting the roles others assign us or, indeed, choose to remain prisoners because being passive and dependent frees us from the need to act and be responsible for our actions? The prison of fear constructed in the delusions of the paranoid is no less confining or less real than the cell that every shy person erects to limit his own freedom in anxious anticipation of

being ridiculed and rejected by his guards—often guards of his own making.

▲ ▲ ▲

Review Questions

1. What was Zimbardo's primary goal in undertaking the prison experiment?
2. What was the profile of subjects in the experiments? Why is this profile significant?
3. Zimbardo claims that there is a "process" (paragraphs 2, 7) of becoming a prisoner. What is this process?
4. What inverse psychological relationships developed between prisoners and guards?
5. What was the result of the prison "riot"?
6. Why did prisoners have no respect for each other or for themselves?
7. How does the journal of Guard A illustrate what Zimbardo calls the "gradual Kafkaesque metamorphosis of good into evil"? See paragraphs 45–54.
8. What are the reasons people would voluntarily become prisoners?
9. How can the mind keep people in jail?

Discussion and Writing Suggestions

1. Reread the four epigraphs to this article. Write a paragraph of response to any one of them, in light of Zimbardo's discussion of the prison experiment.
2. You may have thought, before reading this article, that being a prisoner is a physical fact, not a psychological state. What are the differences between these two views?
3. In paragraph 8, Zimbardo explains his reasons for not pursuing his research in a real prison. He writes that "it is impossible to separate what each individual brings into the prison from what the prison brings out in each person." What does he mean? And how does this distinction prove important later in the article (see paragraph 58)?
4. Zimbardo reports that at the beginning of the experiment each of the "prisoner" subjects "was completely confident of his ability to endure whatever the prison had to offer for the full two-week experimental period" (paragraph 10). Had you been a subject, would you have been so confident, prior to the experiment? Given what you've learned of the experiment, do you think you would have psychologically "become" a prisoner or guard if you had been selected for these roles? (And if not, what makes you so sure?)
5. Identify two passages in this article: one that surprised you relating to the prisoners; and one that surprised you relating to the guards. Write a paragraph explaining your response to each. Now read the

two passages in light of each other. Do you see any patterns underlying your responses?

6. Zimbardo claims that the implications of his research matter deeply—that the mock prison he created is a metaphor for prisons of the mind "that all of us daily create, populate and perpetuate" (paragraph 61). Zimbardo mentions the prisons of "racism, sexism, despair, [and] shyness." Choose any one of these and discuss how it is a mental prison.
7. Reread paragraphs 61 and 62. Zimbardo makes a metaphorical jump from his experiment to the psychological realities of your daily life. Prisons—the artificial one he created and actual prisons—stand for something: social systems in which there are those who give orders and those who obey. All metaphors break down at some point. Where does this one break down?
8. Zimbardo suggests that we might "choose to remain prisoners because being passive and dependent frees us from the need to act and be responsible for our actions" (paragraph 62). Do you agree? What are the burdens of being disobedient?

Disobedience as a Psychological and Moral Problem

ERICH FROMM

Erich Fromm (1900–1980) was one of this century's distinguished writers and thinkers. Psychoanalyst and philosopher, historian and sociologist, he ranged widely in his interests and defied easy characterization. Fromm studied the works of Freud and Marx closely, and published on them both, but he was not aligned strictly with either. In much of his voluminous writing, he struggled to articulate a view that could help bridge ideological and personal conflicts and bring dignity to those who struggled with isolation in the industrial world. Author of more than thirty books and contributor to numerous edited collections and journals, Fromm is best known for Escape from Freedom *(1941),* The Art of Loving *(1956), and* To Have or To Be? *(1976).*

In the essay that follows, first published in 1963, Fromm discusses the seductive comforts of obedience and he makes distinctions among varieties of obedience, some of which he believes are destructive, and others, life affirming. His thoughts on nuclear annihilation may seem dated in these days of post–cold war cooperation, but it is worth remembering that Fromm wrote his essay just after the Cuban missile crisis, when fears of a third world war ran high. (We might note that despite the welcomed reductions of nuclear stockpiles, the United States and Russia still possess, and retain battle plans for, thousands of warheads.) On the major points of his essay, concerning the psychological and moral problems of obedience, Fromm remains as pertinent today as when he wrote more than thirty years ago.

For centuries kings, priests, feudal lords, industrial bosses and parents have insisted that *obedience is a virtue* and that *disobedience is a vice.* In order to introduce another point of view, let us set against this position the following statement: *human history began with an act of disobedience, and it is not unlikely that it will be terminated by an act of obedience.* 1

Human history was ushered in by an act of disobedience according to the Hebrew and Greek myths. Adam and Eve, living in the Garden of Eden, were part of nature; they were in harmony with it, yet did not transcend it. They were in nature as the fetus is in the womb of the mother. They were human, and at the same time not yet human. All this changed when they disobeyed an order. By breaking the ties with earth and mother, by cutting the umbilical cord, man emerged from a prehuman harmony and was able to take the first step into independence and freedom. The act of disobedience set Adam and Eve free and opened their eyes. They recognized each other as strangers and the world outside them as strange and even hostile. Their act of disobedience broke the primary bond with nature and made them individuals. "Original sin," far from corrupting man, set him free; it was the beginning of history. Man had to leave the Garden of Eden in order to learn to rely on his own powers and to become fully human. 2

The prophets, in their messianic concept, confirmed the idea that man had been right in disobeying; that he had not been corrupted by his "sin," but freed from the fetters of pre-human harmony. For the prophets, *history* is the place where man becomes human; during its unfolding he develops his powers of reason and of love until he creates a new harmony between himself, his fellow man and nature. This new harmony is described as "the end of days," that period of history in which there is peace between man and man, between man and nature. It is a "new" paradise created by man himself, and one which he alone could create because he was forced to leave the "old" paradise as a result of his disobedience. 3

Just as the Hebrew myth of Adam and Eve, so the Greek myth of Prometheus sees all of human civilization based on an act of disobedience. Prometheus, in stealing the fire from the gods, lays the foundation for the evolution of man. There would be no human history were it not for Prometheus' "crime." He, like Adam and Eve, is punished for his disobedience. But he does not repent and ask for forgiveness. On the contrary, he proudly says: "I would rather be chained to this rock than be the obedient servant of the gods." 4

Man has continued to evolve by acts of disobedience. Not only was his spiritual development possible only because there were men who dared to say no to the powers that be in the name of their conscience or their faith, but also his intellectual development was dependent on the capacity for being disobedient—disobedient to authorities who tried to muzzle new thoughts and to the authority of long-established opinions which declared a change to be nonsense. 5

If the capacity for disobedience constituted the beginning of human history, obedience might very well, as I have said, cause the end of human 6 history. I am not speaking symbolically or poetically. There is the possibility, or even the probability, that the human race will destroy civilization and even all life upon earth within the next five to ten years. There is no rationality or sense in it. But the fact is that, while we are living technically in the Atomic Age, the majority of men—including most of those who are in power—still live emotionally in the Stone Age; that while our mathematics, astronomy, and the natural sciences are of the twentieth century, most of our ideas about politics, the state, and society lag far behind the age of science. If mankind commits suicide it will be because people will obey those who command them to push the deadly buttons; because they will obey the archaic passions of fear, hate, and greed; because they will obey obsolete clichés of State sovereignty and national honor. The Soviet leaders talk much about revolutions, and we in the "free world" talk much about freedom. Yet they and we discourage disobedience—in the Soviet Union explicitly and by force, in the free world implicitly and by the more subtle methods of persuasion.

But I do not mean to say that all disobedience is a virtue and all obedi- 7
ence a vice. Such a view would ignore the dialectical relationship between obedience and disobedience. Whenever the principles which are obeyed and those which are disobeyed are irreconcilable, an act of obedience to one principle is necessarily an act of disobedience to its counterpart and vice versa. Antigone is the classic example of this dichotomy. By obeying the inhuman laws of the State, Antigone necessarily would disobey the laws of humanity. By obeying the latter, she must disobey the former. All martyrs of religious faiths, of freedom and of science have had to disobey those who wanted to muzzle them in order to obey their own consciences, the laws of humanity and of reason. If a man can only obey and not disobey, he is a slave; if he can only disobey and not obey, he is a rebel (not a revolutionary); he acts out of anger, disappointment, resentment, yet not in the name of a conviction or a principle.

However, in order to prevent a confusion of terms an important qualifi- 8
cation must be made. Obedience to a person, institution or power (heteronomous obedience) is submission; it implies the abdication of my autonomy and the acceptance of a foreign will or judgment in place of my own. Obedience to my own reason or conviction (autonomous obedience) is not an act of submission but one of affirmation. My conviction and my judgment, if authentically mine, are part of me. If I follow them rather than the judgment of others, I am being myself; hence the word *obey* can be applied only in a metaphorical sense and with a meaning which is fundamentally different from the one in the case of "heteronomous obedience."

But this distinction still needs two further qualifications, one with re- 9
gard to the concept of conscience and the other with regard to the concept of authority.

The word *conscience* is used to express two phenomena which are 10
quite distinct from each other. One is the "authoritarian conscience" which is the internalized voice of an authority whom we are eager to please and afraid of displeasing. This authoritarian conscience is what most people ex-

perience when they obey their conscience. It is also the conscience which Freud speaks of, and which he called "Super-Ego." This Super-Ego represents the internalized commands and prohibitions of father, accepted by the son out of fear. Different from the authoritarian conscience is the "humanistic conscience"; this is the voice present in every human being and independent from external sanctions and rewards. Humanistic conscience is based on the fact that as human beings we have an intuitive knowledge of what is human and inhuman, what is conducive of life and what is destructive of life. This conscience serves our functioning as human beings. It is the voice which calls us back to ourselves, to our humanity.

Authoritarian conscience (Super-Ego) is still obedience to a power outside of myself, even though this power has been internalized. Consciously I believe that I am following *my* conscience; in effect, however, I have swallowed the principles of *power;* just because of the illusion that humanistic conscience and Super-Ego are identical, internalized authority is so much more effective than the authority which is clearly experienced as not being part of me. Obedience to the "authoritarian conscience," like all obedience to outside thoughts and power, tends to debilitate "humanistic conscience," the ability to be and to judge oneself. 11

The statement, on the other hand, that obedience to another person is *ipso facto* submission needs also to be qualified by distinguishing "irrational" from "rational" authority. An example of rational authority is to be found in the relationship between student and teacher; one of irrational authority in the relationship between slave and master. Both relationships are based on the fact that the authority of the person in command is accepted. Dynamically, however, they are of a different nature. The interests of the teacher and the student, in the ideal case, lie in the same direction. The teacher is satisfied if he succeeds in furthering the student; if he has failed to do so, the failure is his and the student's. The slave owner, on the other hand, wants to exploit the slave as much as possible. The more he gets out of him the more satisfied he is. At the same time, the slave tries to defend as best he can his claims for a minimum of happiness. The interests of slave and master are antagonistic, because what is advantageous to the one is detrimental to the other. The superiority of the one over the other has a different function in each case; in the first it is the condition for the furtherance of the person subjected to the authority, and in the second it is the condition for his exploitation. Another distinction runs parallel to this: rational authority is rational because the authority, whether it is held by a teacher or a captain of a ship giving orders in an emergency, acts in the name of reason which, being universal, I can accept without submitting. Irrational authority has to use force or suggestion, because no one would let himself be exploited if he were free to prevent it. 12

Why is man so prone to obey and why is it so difficult for him to disobey? As long as I am obedient to the power of the State, the Church, or public opinion, I feel safe and protected. In fact it makes little difference what power it is that I am obedient to. It is always an institution, or men, 13 who use force in one form or another and who fraudulently claim omniscience and omnipotence. My obedience makes me part of the power I worship, and hence I feel strong. I can make no error, since it decides for me; I cannot be alone, because it watches over me; I cannot commit a sin, because it does not let me do so, and even if I do sin, the punishment is only the way of returning to the almighty power.

In order to disobey, one must have the courage to be alone, to err and to sin. But courage is not enough. The capacity for courage depends on a person's state of development. Only if a person has emerged from mother's lap and father's commands, only if he has emerged as a fully developed individual and thus has acquired the capacity to think and feel for himself, only then can he have the courage to say "no" to power, to disobey. **14**

A person can become free through acts of disobedience by learning to say no to power. But not only is the capacity for disobedience the condition for freedom; freedom is also the condition for disobedience. If I am afraid of freedom, I cannot dare to say "no," I cannot have the courage to be disobedient. Indeed, freedom and the capacity for disobedience are inseparable; hence any social, political, and religious system which proclaims freedom, yet stamps out disobedience, cannot speak the truth. **15**

There is another reason why it is so difficult to dare to disobey, to say "no" to power. During most of human history obedience has been identified with virtue and disobedience with sin. The reason is simple: thus far throughout most of history a minority has ruled over the majority. This rule was made necessary by the fact that there was only enough of the good things of life for the few, and only the crumbs remained for the many. If the few wanted to enjoy the good things and, beyond that, to have the many serve them and work for them, one condition was necessary: the many had to learn obedience. To be sure, obedience can be established by sheer force. But this method has many disadvantages. It constitutes a constant threat that one day the many might have the means to overthrow the few by force; furthermore there are many kinds of work which cannot be done properly if nothing but fear is behind the obedience. Hence the obedience which is only rooted in the fear of force must be transformed into one rooted in man's heart. Man must want and even need to obey, instead of only fearing to disobey. If this is to be achieved, power must assume the qualities of the All Good, of the All Wise; it must become All Knowing. If this happens, power can proclaim that disobedience is sin and obedience virtue; and once this has been proclaimed, the many can accept obedience because it is good and detest disobedience because it is bad, rather than to detest themselves for being cowards. From Luther to the nineteenth century one was concerned with overt and explicit authorities. Luther, the pope, the princes, wanted to uphold it; the middle class, the workers, the philosophers, tried to uproot it. The fight against authority in the State as well as in the family was often the very basis for the development of an independent and daring person. The fight against authority was inseparable from the intellectual mood which characterized the philosophers of the enlightenment and the scientists. This "critical mood" was one of faith in reason, and at the same **16** time of doubt in everything which is said or thought, inasmuch as it is based on tradition, superstition, custom, power. The principles *sapere aude* and *de omnibus est dubitandum*—"dare to be wise" and "of all one must doubt"—were characteristic of the attitude which permitted and furthered the capacity to say "no."

The case of Adolf Eichmann is symbolic of our situation and has a significance far beyond the one in which his accusers in the courtroom in Jerusalem were concerned with. Eichmann is a symbol of the organization man, of the alienated bureaucrat for whom men, women and children have become numbers. He is a symbol of all of us. We can see ourselves in Eichmann. But the most frightening thing about him is that after the entire story was told in terms of his own admissions, he was able in perfect good faith to plead his innocence. It is clear that if he were once more in the same situation he would do it again. And so would we—and so do we. 17

The organization man has lost the capacity to disobey, he is not even aware of the fact that he obeys. At this point in history the capacity to doubt, to criticize and to disobey may be all that stands between a future for mankind and the end of civilization. 18

▲ ▲ ▲

Review Questions

1. What does Fromm mean when he writes that disobedience is "the first step into independence and freedom"?
2. Fromm writes that history began with an act of disobedience and will likely end with an act of obedience. What does he mean?
3. What is the difference between "heteronomous obedience" and "autonomous obedience"?
4. How does Fromm distinguish between "authoritarian conscience" and "humanistic conscience"?
5. When is obedience to another person *not* submission?
6. What are the psychological comforts of obedience, and why would authorities rather have people obey out of love than out of fear?

Discussion and Writing Suggestions

1. Fromm suggests that scientifically we live in the twentieth century but that politically and emotionally we live in the Stone Age. As you observe events in the world, both near and far, would you agree? Why?
2. Fromm writes: "If a man can only obey and not disobey, he is a slave; if he can only disobey and not obey, he is a rebel (not a revolutionary)." Explain Fromm's meaning here. Explain, as well, the implication that to be fully human one must have the freedom to both obey and disobey.
3. Fromm writes that "obedience makes me part of the power I worship, and hence I feel strong." Does this statement ring true for you?

Discuss, in writing, an occasion in which you felt powerful because you obeyed a group norm.

4. In paragraph 16, Fromm equates obedience with cowardice. Can you identify a situation in which you were obedient but, now that you reflect on it, also were cowardly? That is, can you recall a time when you caved in to a group but now wish you hadn't? Explain.
5. Fromm says that we can see ourselves in Adolf Eichmann—that as an organization man he "has lost the capacity to disobey, he is not even aware of the fact that he obeys." To what extent do you recognize yourself in this portrait?

The Obedient, Unlived Life

SUSAN WALTON

Journalist Susan Walton has waged a long battle to cultivate a willingness to disobey; still, she finds the habit of obedience difficult to break. She calls herself a "recovering coward"—and struggles on. As you read, you might reflect on the comforts—and the dangers—of a safe, obedient life. What is it about disobedience that is so attractive to Walton? Which forms of disobedience, particularly? This article first appeared in the New York Times *(April 4, 1987).*

Little herds of people mill around intersections in the morning, waiting for the lights to change. Washington is full of traffic circles, so sometimes you have to wait through several lights, standing on narrow islands of concrete while traffic comes at you from unexpected directions. 1

Not everyone waits. Some people dash, even when they see the No. 42 bus bearing down on them or some squirrel of a driver running every red light for blocks. The particularly daring ones make the cars stop for them. 2

I seldom walk until the light turns green. It is part of being obedient, a manifestation of the misbegotten belief that you must do what people tell you to do, and if you do, you will be rewarded. This syndrome of behavior is characterized by a dedication to form at the expense of spontaneity and substance. It is turning papers in on time and expecting to receive better grades than those who turn them in late, even if theirs are superior. It is believing your mother—who probably didn't believe it herself—when she says that boys prefer nice girls. This toe-the-line mentality is not confined to women; men, too, lie awake wondering how things ended up so wrong when they so carefully did everything right. Which is exactly the problem. 3

• • •

Some people are born to follow instructions. They are quiet children who always finish their homework, are never caught being bad, never sneak off and do undetected wicked things. They never figure out that it is possible to ignore what others want you to do and do whatever you like. The consequences of deviation are usually minimal. Nobody really expects 4 you to be that good. If you are born this way, you acquire a look of puzzlement. You are puzzled because you can't figure out how or why these other people are doing outrageous things when the rules have been so clearly stated. Nor do you understand why people are not impressed with your mastery of those rules.

Puzzlement may turn to smugness. At first, when people asked me whether I had completed an assignment, I was surprised: of course I had; didn't the teacher *tell* us to? After I realized that punctuality was not all that common, I became smug. Yes, of course I turned my paper in on time. I did not see that the people who got noticed were likely to be erratic and late, rushing in explaining that their thesis had not fallen into place until 4 A.M. of the third Monday after the paper was due. Us punctual types did not wait for theses to fall into place. Whatever could be knocked into shape in time was what got turned in. The thing was due, wasn't it? 5

The message did not sink in for years, during which I always showed up for work, double pneumonia and all. I wandered into a field—journalism—mined with deadlines and populated by more missed deadlines, per capita, than any other. I repeated the process—first the assumption that you had to make the deadline, or why did they call it a deadline? Then I realized that this behavior was not universal. By the time I began working for a weekly, I had deluded myself into thinking that reliability was the way to success. 6

And it was, sort of. At this job, however, I encountered one of those people apparently sent by life as an object lesson. For every deadline I made, he missed one. Stories that everyone was counting on failed to materialize for weeks, as he agonized, procrastinated and interviewed just one more person. Everyone was annoyed at the time, but when the work was completed, mass amnesia set in. Only the product mattered, and the product, however late it was, was generally acceptable. 7

We advanced together, but what I gained with promotion was the opportunity to meet more deadlines per week and to hang around waiting to edit the copy of those who were late. What he got was the opportunity to linger over ever more significant stories. In my case, virtue was its own punishment. The moral of this story is that you should stop to think whether being good is getting you anywhere you want to go. 8

The most common and forgivable reason for the cautious, obedient life is fear. It is true, something terrible could happen if you stray. Something terrible could also happen if you do not stray, which is that you might be bored to death. Some people are lucky; what they are supposed to do is also what they like to do: They do not need to muster their nerve. I do not consider myself a nervy person. Rather, I think of myself as a recovering coward. Cowardice, like alcoholism, is a lifelong condition. 9

• • •

The James boys, William and Henry, are instructive on the subject of following too narrow a path. William James wrote in a letter to Thomas Ward in 1868 that the great mistake of his past life was an "impatience of re- 10 sults," which, he thought, should not be "too voluntarily aimed at or too busily thought of." What you must do, he believed, is to go on "in your own interesting way." Then the results will float along under their own steam. Henry left the classic record of the unlived life in "The Beast in the Jungle." It is the story of a man convinced that fate has something momentous in store for him, and he sits around carefully waiting for it to arrive. Consequently, his fate turns out to be that of a man to whom nothing ever happens. Better for him had he not listened quite so earnestly to the inner voice murmuring about fate. Better had he been distracted from his mission.

Be bold, my graduate school adviser, Mr. Ragsdale, used to say—his only advice. I see now that he was right. Think again of your future self: the little old lady sitting on the porch of the old folks' home. When she thinks back on opportunities, will she regret the ones that passed unused? 11

Or find some other device. Myself, I keep a dumb postcard in my desk drawer. It is light purple, with a drawing of a cowering person standing on the edge of a diving board. Beneath the drawing it says, "If you don't do it, you won't know what would have happened if you had done it." Think about the possible headline: "Cautious Pedestrian Squashed by Bus While Waiting on Traffic Island—Should Have Jaywalked, Police Say." Then look both ways, and go. 12

▲ ▲ ▲

Discussion and Writing Suggestions

1. In your view, to what extent is walking when the light is green the sign of a "misbegotten belief that you must do what people tell you to do, and if you do, you will be rewarded" (paragraph 3)?
2. How do Walton's word choices help to convey her frustration with living a cautious, obedient life?
3. Walton suggests in paragraph 3 that obedience has much to do with "a dedication to form at the expense of spontaneity and substance." What does she mean? Do you agree?
4. "In my case, virtue was its own punishment. The moral of this story is that you should stop to think whether being good is getting you anywhere you want to go" (paragraph 8). Your response? To what extent does this "moral" apply to your own circumstances?
5. Walton is advocating that we "look both ways, and go": that we break some conventions in the interest of living an interesting life. How does one determine which conventions, if followed, lead to an "unlived" life? Which forms of disobedience will society permit? Which not? Why?
6. In your experience, is fear (as Walton suggests in paragraph 9) related to obedience?
7. What indication, if any, does Walton give that she has a plan for deciding which issues warrant her disobedience?
8. A teacher of Walton's advised her to be bold (paragraph 11). What is the relationship between boldness and disobedience?

9. Walton made a special effort to follow rules and meet deadlines—to no advantage. Have you noticed, like Walton, that obedience has a slim connection to success?

The Lottery

SHIRLEY JACKSON

On the morning of June 28, 1948, I walked down to the post office in our little Vermont town to pick up the mail. I was quite casual about it, as I recall—I opened the box, took out a couple of bills and a letter or two, talked to the postmaster for a few minutes, and left, never supposing that it was the last time for months that I was to pick up the mail without an active feeling of panic. By the next week I had to change my mailbox to the largest one in the post office, and casual conversation with the postmaster was out of the question, because he wasn't speaking to me. June 28, 1948, was the day *The New Yorker* came out with a story of mine in it. It was not my first published story, nor my last, but I have been assured over and over that if it had been the only story I ever wrote or published, there would be people who would not forget my name.[1]

So begins Shirley Jackson's "biography" of her short story "The Lottery." The New Yorker *published the story the summer of 1948 and some months later, having been besieged with letters, acknowledged that the piece had generated "more mail than any . . . fiction they had ever published"—the great majority of it negative. In 1960, Jackson wrote that "millions of people, and my mother, had taken a pronounced dislike to me" for having written the story—which, over the years, proved to be Jackson's most widely anthologized one. If you've read "The Lottery," you will have some idea of why it was so controversial. If you haven't, we don't want to spoil the effect by discussing what happens.*

Shirley Jackson, short-story writer and novelist, was born in San Francisco in 1919 and was raised in California and New York. She began her college education at the University of Rochester and completed it at Syracuse University. She married Stanley Edgar Hyman (writer and teacher) and with him had four children. In her brief career, Jackson wrote six novels and two works of nonfiction. She won the Edgar Allen Poe Award (1961) as well as a Syracuse University Arents Pioneer Medal for Outstanding Achievement (1965).

The morning of June 27th was clear and sunny, with the fresh warmth of a full-summer day; the flowers were blossoming profusely and the grass was richly green. The people of the village began to gather in the square, between the post office and the bank, around ten o'clock; in some towns there were so many people that the lottery took two days and had to be started on 1

[1]"Biography of a Story," from *Come Along With Me,* by Shirley Jackson. Copyright 1948, 1952, © 1960 by Shirley Jackson. Used by permission of Viking Penguin, a division of Penguin Books USA Inc. 1st paragraph, p. 211 + selected quotations, pp. 214–221.

June 26th, but in this village, where there were only about three hundred people, the whole lottery took less than two hours, so it could begin at ten o'clock in the morning and still be through in time to allow the villagers to get home for noon dinner.

The children assembled first, of course. School was recently over for the summer, and the feeling of liberty sat uneasily on most of them; they tended to gather together quietly for a while before they broke into boisterous play, and their talk was still of the classroom and the teacher, of books and reprimands. Bobby Martin had already stuffed his pockets full of stones, and the other boys soon followed his example, selecting the smoothest and roundest stones; Bobby and Harry Jones and Dickie Delacroix—the villagers pronounced this name "Dellacroy"—eventually made a great pile of stones in one corner of the square and guarded it against the raids of the other boys. The girls stood aside, talking among themselves, looking over their shoulders at the boys, and the very small children rolled in the dust or clung to the hands of their older brothers or sisters. 2

Soon the men began to gather, surveying their own children, speaking of planting and rain, tractors and taxes. They stood together, away from the pile of stones in the corner, and their jokes were quiet and they smiled rather than laughed. The women, wearing faded house dresses and sweaters, came shortly after their menfolk. They greeted one another and exchanged bits of gossip as they went to join their husbands. Soon the women, standing by their husbands, began to call to their children, and the children came reluctantly, having to be called four or five times. Bobby Martin ducked under his mother's grasping hand and ran, laughing, back to the pile of stones. His father spoke up sharply, and Bobby came quickly and took his place between his father and his oldest brother. 3

The lottery was conducted—as were the square dances, the teenage club, the Halloween program—by Mr. Summers, who had time and energy to devote to civic activities. He was a round-faced, jovial man and he ran the coal business, and people were sorry for him, because he had no children and his wife was a scold. When he arrived in the square, carrying the wooden black box, there was a murmur of conversation among the villagers, and he waved and called, "Little late today, folks." The postmaster, Mr. Graves, followed him, carrying a three-legged stool, and the stool was put in the center of the square and Mr. Summers set the black box down on it. The villagers kept their distance, leaving a space between themselves and the stool, and when Mr. Summers said, "Some of you fellows want to give me a hand?" there was a hesitation before two men, Mr. Martin and his oldest son, Baxter, came forward to hold the box steady on the stool while Mr. Summers stirred up the papers inside it. 4

The original paraphernalia for the lottery had been lost long ago, and the black box now resting on the stool had been put into use even before Old Man Warner, the oldest man in town, was born. Mr. Summers spoke frequently to the villagers about making a new box, but no one liked to upset even as much tradition as was represented by the black box. There was 5 a story that the present box had been made with some pieces of the box that had preceded it, the one that had been constructed when the first people settled down to make a village here. Every year, after the lottery, Mr. Summers began talking again about a new box, but every year the subject was allowed to fade off without anything's being done. The black box grew shabbier each year; by now it was no longer completely black but splintered badly along one side to show the original wood color, and in some places faded or stained.

Mr. Martin and his oldest son, Baxter, held the black box securely on 6
the stool until Mr. Summers had stirred the papers thoroughly with his hand. Because so much of the ritual had been forgotten or discarded, Mr. Summers had been successful in having slips of paper substituted for the chips of wood that had been used for generations. Chips of wood, Mr. Summers had argued, had been all very well when the village was tiny, but now that the population was more than three hundred and likely to keep on growing, it was necessary to use something that would fit more easily into the black box. The night before the lottery, Mr. Summers and Mr. Graves made up the slips of paper and put them in the box, and it was then taken to the safe of Mr. Summers' coal company and locked up until Mr. Summers was ready to take it to the square next morning. The rest of the year, the box was put away, sometimes one place, sometimes another; it had spent one year in Mr. Graves's barn and another year underfoot in the post office, and sometimes it was set on a shelf in the Martin grocery and left there.

There was a great deal of fussing to be done before Mr. Summers de- 7
clared the lottery open. There were the lists to make up—of heads of families, heads of households in each family, members of each household in each family. There was the proper swearing-in of Mr. Summers by the postmaster, as the official of the lottery; at one time, some people remembered, there had been a recital of some sort, performed by the official of the lottery, a perfunctory, tuneless chant that had been rattled off duly each year; some people believed that the official of the lottery used to stand just so when he said or sang it, others believed that he was supposed to walk among the people, but years and years ago this part of the ritual had been allowed to lapse. There had been, also, a ritual salute, which the official of the lottery had had to use in addressing each person who came up to draw from the box, but this also had changed with time, until now, it was felt necessary only for the official to speak to each person approaching. Mr. Summers was very good at all this; in his clean white shirt and blue jeans, with one hand resting carelessly on the black box, he seemed very proper and important as he talked interminably to Mr. Graves and the Martins.

Just as Mr. Summers finally left off talking and turned to the assembled 8
villagers, Mrs. Hutchinson came hurriedly along the path to the square, her sweater thrown over her shoulders, and slid into place in the back of the crowd. "Clean forgot what day it was," she said to Mrs. Delacroix, who stood next to her, and they both laughed softly. "Thought my old man was out back stacking wood," Mrs. Hutchinson went on, "and then I looked out the window and the kids was gone, and then I remembered it was the

twenty-seventh and came a-running." She dried her hands on her apron, and Mrs. Delacroix said, "You're in time, though. They're still talking away up there."

Mrs. Hutchinson craned her neck to see through the crowd and found 9
her husband and children standing near the front. She tapped Mrs. Delacroix on the arm as a farewell and began to make her way through the crowd. The people separated good-humoredly to let her through; two or three people said, in voices just loud enough to be heard across the crowd, "Here comes your Missus, Hutchinson," and "Bill, she made it after all." Mrs. Hutchinson reached her husband, and Mr. Summers, who had been waiting, said cheerfully, "Thought we were going to have to get on without you, Tessie." Mrs. Hutchinson said, grinning, "Wouldn't have me leave m'dishes in the sink, now, would you, Joe?," and soft laughter ran through the crowd as the people stirred back into position after Mrs. Hutchinson's arrival.

"Well, now," Mr. Summers said soberly, "guess we better get started, 10
get this over with, so's we can go back to work. Anybody ain't here?"

"Dunbar," several people said. "Dunbar, Dunbar." 11

Mr. Summers consulted his list. "Clyde Dunbar," he said. "That's 12
right. He's broke his leg, hasn't he? Who's drawing for him?"

"Me, I guess," a woman said, and Mr. Summers turned to look at her. 13
"Wife draws for her husband," Mr. Summers said. "Don't you have a grown boy to do it for you, Janey?" Although Mr. Summers and everyone else in the village knew the answer perfectly well, it was the business of the official of the lottery to ask such questions formally. Mr. Summers waited with an expression of polite interest while Mrs. Dunbar answered.

"Horace's not but sixteen yet," Mrs. Dunbar said regretfully. "Guess I 14
gotta fill in for the old man this year."

"Right," Mr. Summers said. He made a note on the list he was holding. 15
Then he asked, "Watson boy drawing this year?"

A tall boy in the crowd raised his hand. "Here," he said. "I'm drawing 16
for m'mother and me." He blinked his eyes nervously and ducked his head as several voices in the crowd said things like "Good fellow, Jack," and "Glad to see your mother's got a man to do it."

"Well," Mr. Summers said, "guess that's everyone. Old Man Warner 17
make it?"

"Here," a voice said, and Mr. Summers nodded. 18

A sudden hush fell on the crowd as Mr. Summers cleared his throat 19
and looked at the list. "All ready?" he called. "Now, I'll read the names—heads of families first—and the men come up and take a paper out of the box. Keep the paper folded in your hand without looking at it until everyone has had a turn. Everything clear?"

The people had done it so many times that they only half listened to the 20
directions; most of them were quiet, wetting their lips, not looking around. Then Mr. Summers raised one hand high and said, "Adams." A man disengaged himself from the crowd and came forward. "Hi, Steve," Mr. Sum-

mers said, and Mr. Adams said, "Hi, Joe." They grinned at one another humorously and nervously. Then Mr. Adams reached into the black box and took out a folded paper. He held it firmly by one corner as he turned and went hastily back to his place in the crowd, where he stood a little apart from his family, not looking down at his hand.

"Allen," Mr. Summers said. "Anderson. . . . Bentham." 21

"Seems like there's no time at all between lotteries any more," Mrs. 22
Delacroix said to Mrs. Graves in the back row. "Seems like we got through with the last one only last week."

"Time sure goes fast," Mrs. Graves said. 23

"Clark. . . . Delacroix." 24

"There goes my old man," Mrs. Delacroix said. She held her breath 25
while her husband went forward.

"Dunbar," Mr. Summers said, and Mrs. Dunbar went steadily to the 26
box while one of the women said, "Go on, Janey," and another said, "There she goes."

"We're next," Mrs. Graves said. She watched while Mr. Graves came 27
around from the side of the box, greeted Mr. Summers gravely, and selected a slip of paper from the box. By now, all through the crowd there were men holding the small folded papers in their large hands, turning them over and over nervously. Mrs. Dunbar and her two sons stood together, Mrs. Dunbar holding the slip of paper.

"Harburt. . . . Hutchinson." 28

"Get up there, Bill," Mrs. Hutchinson said, and the people near her 29
laughed.

"Jones." 30

"They do say," Mr. Adams said to Old Man Warner, who stood next to 31
him, "that over in the north village they're talking of giving up the lottery."

Old Man Warner snorted. "Pack of crazy fools," he said. "Listening to 32
the young folks, nothing's good enough for *them.* Next thing you know, they'll be wanting to go back to living in caves, nobody work any more, live *that* way for a while. Used to be a saying about 'Lottery in June, corn be heavy soon.' First thing you know, we'd all be eating stewed chickweed and acorns. There's *always* been a lottery," he added petulantly. "Bad enough to see young Joe Summers up there joking with everybody."

Some places have already quit lotteries," Mrs. Adams said. 33

"Nothing but trouble in *that,*" Old Man Warner said stoutly. "Pack of 34
young fools."

"Martin." And Bobby Martin watched his father go forward. 35
"Overdyke. . . . Percy."

"I wish they'd hurry," Mrs. Dunbar said to her older son. "I wish 36
they'd hurry."

"They're almost through," her son said. 37

"You get ready to run tell Dad," Mrs. Dunbar said. 38

Mr. Summers called his own name and then stepped forward precisely 39
and selected a slip from the box. Then he called, "Warner."

"Seventy-seventh year I been in the lottery," Old Man Warner said as 40
he went through the crowd. "Seventy-seventh time."

"Watson." The tall boy came awkwardly through the crowd. Someone 41
said, "Don't be nervous, Jack," and Mr. Summers said, "Take your time, son."

"Zanini." 42

After that, there was a long pause, a breathless pause, until Mr. Sum- 43
mers, holding his slip of paper in the air, said, "All right, fellows." For a minute, no one moved, and then all the slips of paper were opened. Suddenly, all the women began to speak at once, saying, "Who is it?," "Who's got it?," "Is it the Dunbars?," "Is it the Watsons?" Then the voices began to say, "It's Hutchinson. It's Bill," "Bill Hutchinson's got it."

"Go tell your father," Mrs. Dunbar said to her older son. 44

People began to look around to see the Hutchinsons. Bill Hutchinson 45
was standing quiet, staring down at the paper in his hand. Suddenly, Tessie Hutchinson shouted to Mr. Summers, "You didn't give him time enough to take any paper he wanted. I saw you. It wasn't fair!"

"Be a good sport, Tessie," Mrs. Delacroix called, and Mrs. Graves 46
said, "All of us took the same chance."

"Shut up, Tessie," Bill Hutchinson said. 47

"Well, everyone," Mr. Summers said, "that was done pretty fast, and 48
now we've got to be hurrying a little more to get done in time." He consulted his next list. "Bill," he said, "you draw for the Hutchinson family. You got any other households in the Hutchinsons?"

"There's Don and Eva," Mrs. Hutchinson yelled. "Make *them* take 49
their chance!"

"Daughters draw with their husbands' families, Tessie," Mr. Summers 50
said gently. "You know that as well as anyone else."

"It wasn't *fair,*" Tessie said. 51

"I guess not, Joe," Bill Hutchinson said regretfully. "My daughter 52
draws with her husband's family, that's only fair. And I've got no other family except the kids."

"Then, as far as drawing for families is concerned, it's you," Mr. Sum- 53
mers said in explanation, "and as far as drawing for households is concerned, that's you, too. Right?"

"Right," Bill Hutchinson said. 54

"How many kids, Bill?" Mr. Summers asked formally. 55

"Three," Bill Hutchinson said. "There's Bill, Jr., and Nancy, and little 56
Dave. And Tessie and me."

"All right, then," Mr. Summers said. "Harry, you got their tickets back?" 57

Mr. Graves nodded and held up the slips of paper. "Put them in the 58
box, then," Mr. Summers directed. "Take Bill's and put it in."

"I think we ought to start over," Mrs. Hutchinson said, as quietly as she 59
could. "I tell you it wasn't *fair.* You didn't give him enough time to choose. *Everybody* saw that."

Mr. Graves had selected the five slips and put them in the box, and he 60
dropped all the papers but those onto the ground, where the breeze caught
them and lifted them off.

"Listen, everybody," Mrs. Hutchinson was saying to the people around 61
her.

"Ready, Bill?" Mr. Summers asked, and Bill Hutchinson, with one 62
quick glance around at his wife and children, nodded.

"Remember," Mr. Summers said, "take the slips and keep them folded 63
until each person has taken one. Harry, you help little Dave." Mr. Graves
took the hand of the little boy, who came willingly with him up to the box.
"Take a paper out of the box, Davy," Mr. Summers said. Davy put his hand
into the box and laughed. "Take just *one* paper," Mr. Summers said. "Harry,
you hold it for him." Mr. Graves took the child's hand and removed the
folded paper from the tight fist and held it while little Dave stood next to
him and looked up at him wonderingly.

"Nancy next," Mr. Summers said. Nancy was twelve and her school 64
friends breathed heavily as she went forward, switching her skirt, and took
a slip daintily from the box. "Bill, Jr.," Mr. Summers said, and Billy, his
face red and his feet overlarge, nearly knocked the box over as he got a paper out. "Tessie," Mr. Summers said. She hesitated for a minute, looking
around defiantly, and then set her lips and went up to the box. She snatched
a paper out and held it behind her.

"Bill," Mr. Summers said, and Bill Hutchinson reached into the box 65
and felt around, bringing his hand out at last with the slip of paper in it.

The crowd was quiet. A girl whispered, "I hope it's not Nancy," and 66
the sound of the whisper reached the edges of the crowd.

"It's not the way it used to be," Old Man Warner said clearly. "People 67
ain't the way they used to be."

"All right," Mr. Summers said. "Open the papers. Harry, you open lit- 68
tle Dave's."

Mr. Graves opened the slip of paper and there was a general sigh 69
through the crowd as he held it up and everyone could see that it was blank.
Nancy and Bill, Jr., opened theirs at the same time, and both beamed and
laughed, turning around to the crowd and holding their slips of paper above
their heads.

"Tessie," Mr. Summers said. There was a pause, and then Mr. Sum- 70
mers looked at Bill Hutchinson, and Bill unfolded his paper and showed it.
It was blank.

"It's Tessie," Mr. Summers said, and his voice was hushed. "Show us 71
her paper, Bill."

Bill Hutchinson went over to his wife and forced the slip of paper out 72
of her hand. It had a black spot on it, the black spot Mr. Summers had made
the night before with the heavy pencil in the coal-company office. Bill
Hutchinson held it up, and there was a stir in the crowd.

"All right, folks," Mr. Summers said. "Let's finish quickly." 73

Although the villagers had forgotten the ritual and lost the original black box, they still remembered to use stones. The pile of stones the boys had made earlier was ready; there were stones on the ground with the blowing scraps of paper that had come out of the box. Mrs. Delacroix selected a stone so large she had to pick it up with both hands and turned to Mrs. Dunbar. "Come on," she said. "Hurry up." 74

Mrs. Dunbar had small stones in both hands, and she said, gasping for breath, "I can't run at all. You'll have to go ahead and I'll catch up with you." 75

The children had stones already, and someone gave little Davy Hutchinson a few pebbles. 76

Tessie Hutchinson was in the center of a cleared space by now, and she held her hands out desperately as the villagers moved in on her. "It isn't fair," she said. A stone hit her on the side of the head. 77

Old Man Warner was saying, "Come on, come on, everyone." Steve Adams was in front of the crowd of villagers, with Mrs. Graves beside him. 78

"It isn't fair, it isn't right," Mrs. Hutchinson screamed, and then they were upon her. 79

▲ ▲ ▲

Discussion and Writing Suggestions

1. Many readers believed that the events depicted in "The Lottery" actually happened. A sampling of the letters that Jackson received in response to the story:

    (Kansas) Will you please tell me the locale and the year of that custom?
    (Oregon) Where in heaven's name does there exist such barbarity as described in the story?
    (New York) Do such tribunal rituals still exist and if so where?
    (New York) To a reader who has only a fleeting knowledge of traditional rites in various parts of the country (I presume the plot was laid in the United States) I found the cruelty of the ceremony outrageous, if not unbelievable. It may be just a custom or ritual which I am not familiar with.
    (New York) Would you please explain whether such improbable rituals occur in our Middle Western states, and what their origin and purpose are?
    (Nevada) Although we recognize the story to be fiction is it possible that it is based on fact?

    What is your response to comments such as these that suggest surprise, certainly, but also acceptance of the violence committed in the story?
2. One reader of "The Lottery," from Missouri, wrote to the *New Yorker* and accused it of "publishing a story that reached a new low in human viciousness." Do you feel that Jackson has reached this "new low"? Explain your answer.
3. Several more letter writers attempted to get at the meaning of the story:

(Illinois) If it is simply a fictitious example of man's innate cruelty, it isn't a very good one. Man, stupid and cruel as he is, has always had sense enough to imagine or invent a charge against the objects of his persecution: the Christian martyrs, the New England witches, the Jews and Negroes. But nobody had anything against Mrs. Hutchinson, and they only wanted to get through quickly so they could go home for lunch.

(California) I missed something here. Perhaps there was some facet of the victim's character which made her unpopular with the other villagers. I expected the people to evince a feeling of dread and terror, or else sadistic pleasure, but perhaps they were laconic, unemotional New Englanders.

(Indiana) When I first read the story in my issue, I felt that there was no moral significance present, that the story was just terrifying, and that was all. However, there has to be a reason why it is so alarming to so many people. I feel that the only solution, the only reason it bothered so many people is that it shows the power of society over the individual. We saw the ease with which society can crush any single one of us. At the same time, we saw that society need have no rational reason for crushing the one, or the few, or sometimes the many.

Take any one of these readings of the story and respond to it by writing a brief essay or, perhaps, a letter.

4. What does the story suggest to you about authority and obedience to authority? Who—or what—holds authority in the village? Why do people continue with the annual killing, despite the fact that "some places have already quit lotteries"?

▼

SYNTHESIS ACTIVITIES

1. Assume for the moment you agree with Doris Lessing: Children need to be taught how to disobey so they can recognize and avoid situations that give rise to harmful obedience. If you were the curriculum coordinator for your local school system, how would you teach children to disobey? What would be your curriculum? What homework would you assign? What class projects? What field trips? One complicated part of your job would be to train children who understand the difference between *responsible* disobedience and anarchy. What is the difference?

   Take up these questions in an essay that draws on both your experiences as a student and your understanding of the selections in this chapter. Points that you might want to consider in developing the essay: defining overly obedient children; appropriate classroom behavior for responsibly disobedient children (as opposed to inappropriate behavior); reading lists (would "The Lottery" be included?); homework assignments; field trips; class projects.
2. A certain amount of obedience is a given in society, observe Stanley Milgram and others. Social order, civilization itself, would not be possible unless individuals were willing to surrender a portion of

their autonomy to the state. Allowing that we all are obedient (we must be), define the point at which obedience to a figure of authority becomes dangerous.

As you develop your definition, consider the ways you might use the work of authors in this chapter and their definitions of acceptable and unacceptable levels of obedience. Do you agree with the ways in which others have drawn the line between reasonable and dangerous obedience? What examples from current stories in the news or from your own experience can you draw on to test various definitions?

3. Describe a situation in which you were faced with a moral dilemma of whether or not to obey a figure of authority. After describing the situation and the action you took (or didn't take), discuss your behavior in light of any two readings in this chapter. You might consider a straightforward, four-part structure for your essay: (1) your description; (2) your discussion, in light of source A; (3) your discussion, in light of source B; and (4) your conclusion—an overall appraisal of your behavior.
4. At one point in his essay (paragraph 16), Erich Fromm equates obedience with cowardice. Earlier in the chapter, Doris Lessing (paragraph 9) observes that "among our most shameful memories is this, how often we said black was white because other people were saying it." Using the work of these authors as a point of departure, reconsider an act of obedience or disobedience in your own life. Describe pertinent circumstances for your reader. Based on what you have learned in this chapter, reassess your behavior. Would you behave similarly if given a second chance in the same situation?
5. Reread "The Lottery" and analyze the patterns of and reasons for obedience in the story. Base your analysis on two sources in this chapter: Erich Fromm's essay, especially paragraphs 13–16 on the psychological comforts of obedience; and Doris Lessing's speech on the dangers of "not understanding the social laws that govern groups."
6. In his response to Diana Baumrind, Stanley Milgram makes a point of insisting that follow-up interviews with subjects in his experiments show that a large majority were pleased, in the long run, to have participated. (See Table 1 in the footnote to Baumrind, page 378.) Writing on his own post-experiment surveys and interviews, Philip Zimbardo writes that his subjects believed their "mental anguish was transient and situationally specific, but the self-knowledge gained has persisted" (paragraph 60). Why might they *and* the experimenters nonetheless have been eager to accept a positive, final judgment of the experiments? Develop an essay in response to this question, drawing on the selections by Milgram, Zimbardo, and Baumrind.
7. Develop a synthesis in which you extend Baumrind's and Nissani's different critiques of Milgram to the Stanford prison experiment. This assignment requires that you understand the core elements of both

Baumrind's and Nissani's critiques; that you have a clear understanding of Zimbardo's experiment; and that you systematically apply elements of the critiques, as you see fit, to Zimbardo's work. In your conclusion, offer your overall assessment of the Stanford Prison Experiment. To do this, you might answer Zimbardo's own question in paragraph 55: "Was [the experiment] worth all the suffering?" Or you might respond to another question: Do you agree that Zimbardo is warranted in extending the conclusions of his experiment to the general population?

8. In response to the question "Why is man so prone to obey and why is it so difficult for him to disobey?" Erich Fromm suggests that obedience lets people identify with the powerful and invites feelings of safety. Disobedience is psychologically more difficult and requires an act of courage. (See paragraphs 13 and 14.) On the same question, Susan Walton writes that the "most common and forgivable reason for the cautious, obedient life is fear." And in his final paragraph, Philip Zimbardo writes that a "prison of fear" keeps people compliant and frees them of the need to take responsibility for their own actions. In a synthesis that draws on these three sources, explore the interplay of *fear* and its opposite, *courage,* in relation to obedience. To prevent the essay from becoming too abstract, direct your attention repeatedly to a single case, the details of which will help to keep your focus. "The Lottery" could serve nicely as this case, as could a particular event from your own life.
9. Use the reading selections in this chapter to provide a larger context on which to draw as you analyze "Peter Green's First Day," which is a case in Chapter 13, "Business Ethics," pages 768–843. After you read this brief case study, argue a course of action for Peter Green. Should he obey his manager and commit an unethical act or should he disobey—and possibly lose his job? Your essay should draw explicitly on the selections in the current chapter (Obedience).

▼

RESEARCH ACTIVITIES

1. When Milgram's results were first published in book form in 1974, they generated heated controversy. The two reactions reprinted here (by Baumrind and Nissani) represent only a very small portion of that controversy. Research other reactions to the Milgram experiments and discuss your findings. Begin with the reviews listed and excerpted in the *Book Review Digest;* also use the *Social Science Index,* the *Readers' Guide to Periodical Literature,* and newspaper indexes to locate articles, editorials, and letters to the editor on the experiments. (Note that editorials and letters are not always indexed. Letters appear within two to four weeks of the weekly magazine articles to which they refer, and within one to two weeks of newspaper

articles.) What were the chief types of reactions? To what extent were the reactions favorable?

2. Milgram begins his article "Obedience to Authority" with a reference to Nazi Germany. The purpose of his experiment, in fact, was to help throw light on how the Nazi atrocities could have happened. Research the Nuremberg war crimes tribunals following World War II. Drawing specifically on the statements of those who testified at Nuremberg, as well as those who have written about it, show how Milgram's experiments do help explain the Holocaust and other Nazi crimes. In addition to relevant articles, see Telford Taylor's *Nuremberg and Vietnam: An American Tragedy* (1970); Hannah Arendt's *Eichmann in Jerusalem: A Report on the Banality of Evil* (1963); Richard A. Falk, Gabriel Kolko, and Robert J. Lifton (eds), *Crimes of War* (1971).
3. Obtain a copy of the transcript of the trial of Adolf Eichmann—the Nazi official who carried out Hitler's "final solution" for the extermination of the Jews. Read also Hannah Arendt's *Eichmann in Jerusalem: A Report on the Banality of Evil,* along with the reviews of this book. Write a critique both of Arendt's book and of the reviews it received.
4. The My Lai massacre in Vietnam in 1969 was a particularly egregious case of overobedience to military authority in wartime. Show the connections between this event and Milgram's experiments. Note that Milgram himself treated the My Lai massacre in the epilogue to his *Obedience to Authority: An Experimental View* (1974).
5. Investigate the court-martial of Lt. William Calley, convicted for his role in the My Lai massacre. Discuss the question of whether or not President Nixon was justified in commuting his sentence. Examine in detail the dilemmas the jury must have faced when presented with Calley's defense that he was only following orders.
6. Research the Watergate break-in of 1972 and the subsequent coverup by Richard Nixon and members of his administration, as an example of overobedience to authority. Focus on one particular aspect of Watergate (e.g., the role of the counsel to the president, John Dean, or why the crisis was allowed to proceed to the point where it actually toppled a presidency). In addition to relevant articles, see Robert Woodward and Carl Bernstein, *All the President's Men* (1974); Leon Jaworski, *The Right and the Power: The Prosecution of Watergate* (1976); *RN: The Memoirs of Richard Nixon* (1978); John Dean, *Blind Ambition* (1976); John Sirica, *To Set the Record Straight: The Break-in, the Tapes, the Conspirators, the Pardon* (1979); Sam Ervin, *The Whole Truth: The Watergate Conspiracy* (1980); John Ehrlichman, *Witness to Power: The Nixon Years* (1982).
7. At the outset of his article, Stanley Milgram refers to imaginative works revolving around the issue of obedience to authority: the story of Abraham and Isaac, three of Plato's dialogues, "Apology," "Crito," and "Phaedo," and the story of Antigone (dramatized by both the

fifth-century B.C. Athenian Sophocles and the twentieth-century Frenchman Jean Anouilh). In this chapter, we have reprinted Shirley Jackson's "The Lottery," which also can be read as a story about obedience to authority. And many other fictional works deal with obedience to authority—for example, Herman Wouk's novel *The Caine Mutiny* (and his subsequent play *The Caine Mutiny Court Martial*). Check with your instructor, with a librarian, and with such sources as the *Short Story Index* to locate other imaginative works on this theme. Write a paper discussing the various ways in which the subject has been treated in fiction and drama. To ensure coherence, draw comparisons and contrasts among works showing the connections and the variations on the theme of obedience to authority.

9
Privacy and Technology

American workers walk off their jobs with roughly one-half billion dollars in scavenged computer parts each year. The most frequently sought item is the memory chip, which slips into a pocket, lacks traceable serial numbers, and can be sold to the gray market of computer discounters—or saved for use on the thief's home computer.

You're an employer who's lost $100,000 in computer parts during the past 6 months. What do you do? Surveillance cameras might catch the thief. You could install cameras. But suppose, on the other hand, that you're one of the forty-nine out of fifty employees who is *not* stealing. How do you react to being told that the boss will be watching—constantly?

Within 10 years, you will have the option of getting a DNA analysis of your blood as a routine part of physical examinations.[1] *Technicians will check for genetic markers that reveal the likelihood of your developing inherited diseases—like Huntington's disease, multiple sclerosis, and some forms of cancer.*

As an executive at Cliff Paperworks, your job is to reduce steeply rising health-care costs, which are beginning to affect the company's profitability so severely that layoffs will soon be likely. One way to achieve a savings is to motivate employees to adopt healthy lifestyles, so you offer discounted health club memberships, nutrition workshops, and a smoke-free workplace. A second strategy is to eliminate from the workforce people who are likely to develop debilitating, and expensive, medical conditions. To this end, you order DNA analyses as a standard part of company-sponsored physical examinations. The test results can tell you who is likely to develop which inherited disease. Painful though it may be, you will have to consider letting these employees go. Now assume you're an employee of Cliff Paperworks. You may have a keen personal interest in your genetic inclinations, especially if there's a history of disease in your family. But you definitely do not want

[1]The topic of DNA analysis is addressed at length in Chapter 11, ''The Brave New World of Biotechnology,'' pages 550–650.

your DNA profile released to company executives. This is your business, you feel—not theirs.

Governments and businesses have long collected "intelligence" on individuals, well before the advent of hi-tech surveillance systems. For instance, the Constitution mandates that the federal government take a national census every ten years, a massive enterprise and a direct intrusion into the private lives of ordinary citizens. But the greater good is served, goes the argument, when the government can track population trends. Most people agree that this particular intrusion into our private lives is warranted. But what of other intrusions? What of DNA scans and hidden cameras? The intrusive power of these new technologies makes more urgent than ever the fundamental question raised by surveillance: How are we to balance the individual's "right to be let alone," as Supreme Court Justice Louis Brandeis put the matter, with the legitimate needs of the state and of business to know what people are doing? The difficulties of this balancing act are well illustrated in the recent (and not yet completed) story of the "Clipper" chip.

Federal courts give police the authority to investigate the private lives of individuals if there is probable cause to think these individuals are committing crimes. Over the years the government has used whatever technologies were then available to gather intelligence. In the early years, investigation meant physical searches of people and property. Beginning a hundred years ago, with the rapid evolution of technology, techniques for surveillance grew more sophisticated and came to include wiretaps, concealed photographic cameras, movie cameras, miniature microphones, and parabolic eavesdroppers. In 1994, the government proposed the Clipper chip, a device that would scramble data transmissions and make them secure against tampering. No one could decode and understand the transmissions besides the interested parties—*and* (here's the rub) the federal government, which wanted access in the event of suspected criminal activities. The proposal to let the government listen-in to all traffic on the information superhighway met with furious opposition from those convinced that government could not be trusted with back-door keys, so to speak, to virtually every transfer of data in the information age. The potential for abuse and the consequences of abuse were simply too great. To back away even one step from a rigorous defense of the right to secure, *private* information exchange would be to invite an Orwellian nightmare.

In his dystopian novel *1984*, George Orwell tells the story of a (then) future totalitarian society that maintains a ruthlessly oppressive rule over its citizens. Electronic monitoring via ubiquitous "telescreens" provides the technology by which the government can spy on its citizens, some of whom, like the main character Winston Smith, disappear either to be killed or to be "rehabilitated"—that is, tortured into accepting the party line. Even if you haven't read the novel, perhaps you've heard the much-quoted line: "Big Brother Is Watching You." The sentence serves as a chilling, frequent reminder throughout the novel that totalitarian governments must keep citizens under constant surveillance in order to maintain control. In a world where all is known by the State, merely the hint of a private, independent thought becomes a punishable offense. *Orwellian,* then, denotes a species of oppression made easier by electronic surveillance. Given our current capabilities—the scenarios introducing this chapter are fact, not fiction; and given our knowledge that those in power are too easily tempted by the excesses of power (think of Watergate), the Orwellian state looms as a reminder of what can happen should we forget that the right to privacy is a precious, foundational principle of a free society.

When paranoids examine powerful monitoring technologies such as the Clipper chip and DNA scans, they see only the Orwellian potentials—and will not grant the government any legitimate rights to intrude upon the private lives of citizens. One needn't be a certified paranoid, however, to see problems near at hand. Observing the government's sophisticated techniques for intelligence gathering, Supreme Court Justice William O. Douglas wrote that "We are rapidly entering the age of no privacy, where everyone is open to surveillance at all times; where there are no secrets from government. The aggressive breaches of privacy by the government increase by geometric proportions." When a justice of the Supreme Court voices such concerns, we may all be forgiven a touch of paranoia.

Privacy rights of individuals in the workplace are also a matter for concern. Employees effectively surrender their rights to privacy the moment they begin a job. Management's position is clear: "If I own the machines on which you work," says the manager, "I am entitled to videotape you (to protect my machines), read your e-mail, monitor your phone calls, and monitor your every keystroke on my computers." Chilling, yes; Orwellian, maybe—but recall that computer theft in this country amounts to $500 million annually. Should companies stand by and watch their equipment walk out the door? Computer theft is a crime, and companies deserve to be protected. Managers have other legitimate needs to know: If an employee is taking too many breaks on company time, doesn't this constitute a form of theft? And if we agree that an employee's inefficiency costs a company money, isn't management entitled to know—entitled to monitor the situation and use in-house intelligence to remedy the problem? Many employers think so. In 1995, as many as 26 million Americans were monitored electronically at their places of work. The number is sure to increase, and the chances are good that you will one day be monitored on the job.

Thus the debate takes shape: the government has legitimate needs to know; businesses have legitimate needs; and individuals have legitimate, though opposing, needs. Modern surveillance technology did not create the phenomenon of intelligence gathering; but it has undoubtedly exacerbated the tensions inherent in that gathering, so much so that we have today an open, furious debate. This chapter asks you to take part in this debate because, like it or not, you live at a moment in history when technologies can be put to great advantage or disadvantage.

In the chapter's first selection, "The Nature and Meaning of Data," Bryan Glastonbury and Walter LaMendola explain the ways in which dossiers about *you* are created. After the Glastonbury's introduction, the reading selections focus more narrowly on data collection in the workplace. Writing for *Wired* magazine, John Whalen reports from a national convention of surveillance experts that the paranoids are right: we *are* being watched.[2] Next, you'll find several surveys on Americans' attitudes regarding privacy in our information age, including a *Macworld* survey of electronic monitoring in the workplace. Sharply conflicting testimony before a House Subcommittee on Labor-Management Relations follows, including one statement by a former airline reservations agent who developed stress-related illness after being monitored electronically, and a second statement by a representative for the Air Transport Association of America. You will then find three commentaries. The first, by legal and privacy expert Anne Wells Branscomb, argues that the law has not caught up with dilemmas forced on us by new surveillance technologies. Alan F. Westin, professor of law at Columbia University, sets current privacy issues in American employment in a larger, historical context. Writing for *The Futurist,* Kristen Bell DeTienne takes the optimistic view that computer monitors in the workplace will function more as "Friendly Coaches" than as a "Big Brother." The chapter ends with an excerpt from Jeremy Bentham's "Panopticon." This work was written in 1787 as a series of letters promoting a system of architecture that would allow near-complete surveillance of prisoners, workers, asylum inmates, students, hospital patients, and employees. At this point, you can decide whether we are approaching the electronic equivalent of Bentham's Panopticon.

The Nature and Meaning of Data

BRYAN GLASTONBURY AND WALTER LAMENDOLA

"Have you purchased a new home appliance lately?" From this innocuous question, about a seemingly inconsequential, commonplace act in our consumer culture, authors Glastonbury and LaMendola launch their explanation of the ways in which personal data is collected about an imaginary high-school student, just bound for college. That student, of course, could be you. If you have ever received an unsolicited advertisement in the mail or a solicitation by phone, a file about you exists in one or more computer databases that will be sold and resold to companies (and nonprofit institutions, such as colleges!) looking to expand their consumer base. With every credit card purchase you make, with every form you file, information in these databases grows. "The Nature and Meaning of Data" appears as Chapter 3 in The Integrity of Intelligence: A Bill of Rights for the Information Age *(1992). Bryan Glastonbury is Professor in the Department of Social Work Studies, University of Southampton [England]; Walter LaMendola is Vice President of the Colorado Trust.*

[2]See also the selections in Chapter 3: "Total Surveillance," by Charles Ostman, and "Privacy and Technology," by Irving Sloan. These selections complement the materials here.

COLLECTING DATA ABOUT YOU

Have you purchased a new home appliance lately? Let's pretend that what you really need is a new vacuum cleaner. You buy one. As you unpack your new appliance, you carefully put aside the enclosed product information and warranty registration. The machine works well the next morning, so you have extra time to fill out and return your product registration card. It asks for your name, address, and telephone number. It asks where you made the purchase—their name, address, and telephone number. It probably goes on to ask for your age, gender, income group, number of members in household, and whether or not you own your own home. How much a year do you spend on appliances? What prompted you to buy the cleaner? Where will it be used? Why did you purchase this brand? Was it purchased for a specific member of your family? Was the decision to buy this cleaner made by a man, woman, or jointly? Have you ever owned a similar product? What was it? What brand? Do you own another cleaner? What model? Such questions are always posed with courtesy, without any sense of compulsion, and with an explanation that your answers will help the company to a better understanding of its customers' needs. 1

When you fill out and return your card, perhaps wondering what it has to do with your purchase of the cleaner, you might be surprised to know that it usually goes to a company that has paid the manufacturer for the rights to the data. In due course the data will be computerized and resold to other companies, and you have unwittingly become a participant in a wide network, without your knowledge and outside your control. For example, your data may turn up being sold to a firm which markets carpets. As a result, you may start receiving any number of unwanted mailings and telephone calls. In one case reported in a national news service, a data company sold material obtained from a national weight loss association to a chocolate company, which reported a rise in sales as a consequence of using it. 2

Most of us probably consider the mailing label as the type of data that is commonly bought and sold in the marketplace. That is just the tip of the iceberg, but we can start there. A typical mailing label will contain a name and address. Some of the data companies (also called list brokers) may also want your telephone number. It may be that they can buy a list of names and telephone numbers already on computer, or they have to go through the directory. It is also possible to obtain lists of names linked to job, place of employment and business phone number. By using a computer program these separate sources of data can be merged to build up a comprehensive route for contacting families, at home and work. The computer can cross-reference and link in any other material that is available, like court records of debts or criminal convictions, or the age and income profile you provided with your vacuum cleaner registration. 3

This type of collection and work with data represents the fastest growing use of computerized data today, and list selling between businesses and industries has become a major activity. For example, credit bureau income 4 from selling data lists to marketing firms or list brokers, presently at about one third of total revenue, may exceed their income from providing credit references within the next few years. Data is a big business for everyone. But what type of data is collected? Is it just the basic factual background material that we have considered so far, or is more involved?

If we start with the example of a high school student, age 15, in USA, 5
we may be able to trace some of the major sources of data collection. As high school students enter their second year their names will start to find a place on computerized lists, especially if they have been selected for any specific recognition or honours. A student of high academic accomplishments will begin to receive mailings from colleges and universities, encouraging the student to consider them A little later the student may fill out an application for automobile insurance, and this data will be entered into a database and matched with criminal and credit files before the insurance application will be considered for approval. The student will not know the results of the application check or whether the data is bought and sold in the marketplace.

The student may now want a vacation job, and when applying may be 6
asked questions about medical history, brushes with the police, home life, what parents do, and performance in school. If the company is large, the job application will be stored on computer and another check of the applicant will occur. The check may include credit and criminal checks as well as checks of driving record and personal references. Again none of the outcomes will be known to the student. Our student passes the checks and is employed. On receiving the first pay cheque, he or she goes to the bank and opens an account. Here is another application form to fill in, and if the student wants an overdraft facility, some material about the parents' financial viability may be requested.

While the student is working, playing, studying, and becoming a pro- 7
ductive citizen, the marketing of personal data is leading to mailings about subscriptions to periodicals, cassette tape and compact disk buying clubs, and hosts of other consumers items aimed at teenagers. At the point of leaving school the mailings increase. Depending upon social and economic status, the contents of databases, and some further screening by a credit reporting bureau, the mail could bring an invitation to apply for a credit card. Our student still has not left the family home or gone to college, but look at the data already gathered. The computerized files have material on:

Insurance
Driving record
Criminal record
Employment
Medical history and condition
Educational record
Credit
Banking
Home life

Family relationships
Own and family finances
Lifestyle
Preferences and ideologies
Leisure activities
Shopping and consumption patterns
Travel and communications

So far we have shown how personal profiles are established as part of massive data systems. How else can we use the material? To return to vacuum cleaners, as well as using those questionnaires to assemble personal profiles, we can use them compositely to build a model of the way groups of people act to purchase such appliances. We might analyze the data statistically, and find that people with medium family incomes say they spend the most money on appliances, and that in those families the woman makes the buying decision for herself, usually at Acme Hardware Stores. The commercial value of this information is significant. 8

But what if we take it a step further. As a data company, I have product registration data for vacuum cleaners, but I have also bought hundreds of other such databases. By performing operations upon the data, such as matching, selecting, relating, and modelling, I am now able to offer a comprehensive marketing tool to others. One such tool, developed by Lotus and Equifax, is a piece of personal computer based marketing software called MarketPlace which, using a compact disc that contains data on about 120 million people in 80 million households in the US, allows the user to type in consumer profiles and print out mailing labels for the people who match the profile. The data about each person includes name, address, age, gender, estimated annual income, marital status, and shopping habits. 9

Such types of data collection, facilitated by computing and communication systems, are commonplace in a modern industrialized society, though the public presentation of MarketPlace led to opposition and its temporary withdrawal in 1990. It is certainly true that many of the valued services that we receive depend upon the systematic and orderly collection of data about us. What this example begins to outline is the pervasiveness of the data collection and the underlying ability to match and model pieces of data for the purpose of creating information which can be used to influence our decision making. Even more to the point, these data are the basis for others to make decisions about us and therefore control and manipulate our everyday life. And yet, as large and wide scale as these data systems are, they must be considered *personal* information systems because they hold data which relates to specific, identifiable individuals. 10

THE PERSONAL IN DATA SYSTEMS

Laws in different countries generally hold that storing data which relates to specific, identifiable individuals constitutes a personal database, but they often do not go a stage further, to distinguish between differing types of 11 data. While a computer system that collects your buying habits may be intrusive, for example, by sending you mail you do not want, a system which contains data about your mental health or political activities may be used in ways that can cause you serious harm, for example, by releasing your past history of depression to a potential employer. There is some data which people consider to be more personal than others, or that we consider to be intimate and do not want to be shared. Alternatively, there is data which we share, but only in confidence. In some situations, not limited to conversations with a lawyer or doctor, people expect that what is shared will be protected in some way by confidentiality. But how do we know that other people share our view of what is personal?

In a most interesting demonstration of defining personal data, Wacks 12
(1989, pp. 226–238) created an index. This is based upon the extent to which the exposure of data could potentially cause harm to a person. The data is rated by the degrees of sensitivity, low, medium or high. He defines *low sensitivity* as biographical data, and puts in this category basic facts about home, job and educational record. *Medium sensitivity* he describes as judgmental, including reports on us (school, employment) and matters involving a judgment or opinion of another person. Data which is *high sensitivity* is intimate, like our mental health record, where "there is a persuasive case for maintaining that at least some . . . should not be collected at all" (p. 229).[3]

Generally, people are highly sensitive to health, ideological, criminal 13
justice, and sexual data. It is true that sensitivity is difficult to define, and may change not only from culture to culture, but from time to time. However, the combination of the ability to identify a particular individual, the potential to cause that individual harm, and the sensitivity of the data being collected are personal considerations which surely need to be, in almost all cases, under the control of the individual.

It is true that many of the services we need, such as health or social se- 14
curity services, rely on us to furnish accurate and truthful data to them. One might also argue that much of this data could be seen as trivial, as opposed to private or sensitive. Indeed, in some countries (all of Scandinavia, for example), data has been categorized to account for differences in sensitivity. It is also possible to argue that some data is of such import to society, and perhaps being HIV positive presently fits this description, that it must not only be collected but also related to specific individuals. Despite these arguments, the ultimate concern needs to be framed within the context of protecting the individual in everyday life. We can do this by honouring the right of the individual to advise and consent. Not only should consent be the cornerstone of all approaches, but also people need to have the right to be informed when and where data about them is collected or stored. They need to give their specific consent to any activity which accesses, operates

---

[3]Wacks, R. (1989). *Personal Information.* Clarendon Press, Oxford.

upon and uses this data. They need to be able to access and correct data without risking vulnerability or expense.

The location and correction of data is not as simple as it may sound. It 15
is easiest to understand if we assume that the data is stored in one computer, but of course it is not. The fact that it is traded means that it has passed to many computers, possibly linked in a network, but just as possibly quite separate. Leaving aside the complex practicalities, what is the value of a right to view, correct and sanction the use of our personal data, without a parallel right to be informed of all computers on which it is held?

In order to illustrate these difficulties we can continue the example of 16
our student, who is now a high achieving university student nearing graduation, but needing support, advice, and counselling about moving into a career. Though a hard worker, the student has got involved in other activities, and is worried about a number of matters. Can a campus counsellor help? The counsellor, a psychologist, administers a number of tests which hint at a rather unbalanced character. Consequently, in their discussions, they cover the student's uncertainty about sexuality, disgust with war and government, experimentation with alcohol and drugs, and concerns about the future of the world. These discussions are very helpful to the student. They not only relieve anxiety, but they contribute to a number of healthy decisions to change living patterns. Things feel a lot more balanced, and, as the lifestyle changes, so uncertainties disappear.

The future our student desires is a good beginning position in a large 17
firm of stockbrokers. After interviews for a number of positions, none of the applications succeeds. The student's father has a close friend in one of the firms, so makes a discreet enquiry. The friend reveals the reasons why no job was offered. Apparently, there are some damaging psychological test results which come up in the employment check. In addition, there is a psychological report which describes the student as confused, possibly sexually maladjusted, with occasional depression, marginally psychotic, and a potential non-conformist who may be addicted to drugs and alcohol. After calming down, the student recalls talks with the university counsellor, and also remembers in the first job application agreeing to a recruitment firm seeking a report from that source.

The student is able to find out that the firm is a subsidiary of Greater 18
Data. They admit to having the files in their main computer in Taiwan and agree to a formal request to review them for errors and corrections. In talking to a supervisor at Greater Data, the student finds that they have sold the files to others, and probably those have sent them to others again. In addition, the supervisor explains that while the student has the right to correct erroneous or incorrect data, the correct data will not be removed.

The student has now encountered a number of the major problems we 19
can expect in data collection and retention. The counsellor may have professional values about confidentiality, but does not ensure that they are extended to the computer system. Old data has been retained, with subjective interpretations which, while useful at the time of counselling, were later

damaging to the interests of the student. No-one, least of all the student, had been given the opportunity to assess whether old test results and notes were relevant to the present search for employment. Most critically, the student had no knowledge that the data was being kept, no knowledge of the use to which the data would be put, and had not been asked to consent to the use of the data.

▲ ▲ ▲

Review Questions

1. What are the ways in which industries can collect personal data about private citizens?
2. What types of data are collected on individual citizens?
3. What is the "Wacks Index"?
4. Glastonbury and LaMendola both explain *and* argue in this chapter from their book, *The Integrity of Intelligence.* What is the main argument they are making?
5. In what ways would individuals find it difficult to locate and correct erroneous data about them?

Discussion and Writing Suggestions

1. Insurance companies claim that they need to know the likelihood of illness or credit trouble before agreeing to insure you; thus, companies will seek data about you: about your health, your financial dealings, your driving record, and more. To what extent are insurance companies entitled to have information about you? Does the (electronic) manner in which they collect information play any part in your response?
2. The marketing software "MarketPlace," developed by data vendor Equifax and software developer Lotus, contained "data on about 120 million people in 80 million households in the U.S., [allowing] the user to type in consumer profiles and print out mailing labels for the people who match the profile." On learning of the venture, consumers protested and "MarketPlace" was withdrawn. Why? On what grounds would people protest such a product? Explain your position on the product.
3. "It is true that many of the services we need, such as health or social security services, rely on us to furnish accurate and truthful data to them," writes Glastonbury. Identify one such service that is so dependent, and discuss the ways in which delivery of this service is improved because of modern techniques of data collection.
4. List as many forms as you can recall in which you willingly provided personal information. List, as well, any source (counselors, physicians, etc.) who, confidentially or not, may have collected information on you. If all of the information from these lists could be made

available in a single database, what, in general terms, would be known about you to someone willing to pay for a personal dossier?

5. Having responded to the previous question, consider this: To what extent would this dossier represent you? How accurately would the collected data describe the person you are? How comfortable would you be in having others make judgments about you based on this information?
6. As a student reader, you may be quite sympathetic to Glastonbury and LaMendola's hypothetical student who seeks employment at several companies and is turned away. Assume you are an executive at one of the stock brokerage firms to which the student has applied. (See paragraphs 16–19.) How easy or difficult would it be for you to disregard the computer dossier on the job applicant? That is, how would you reconcile the importance of what the dossier says with what you see, in person, of the applicant in direct job interviews?

You're Not Paranoid: They Really Are *Watching You*

JOHN WHALEN

This article appeared in Wired *magazine (March 1995) and represents what has become nearly a genre in popular magazines: the "Beware! Big Brother Is Watching!" piece. The possibility that Big Brother (whether as government or employer)* is *watching surprises no one familiar with twentieth-century American history, let alone with the history of totalitarian governments. Well before the advent of computers, both individuals and whole organizations in this country clearly documented that their privacy was being invaded. What has prompted the recent spate of articles has been the development of sophisticated, remote surveillance technologies that make the job of spying on citizens and employees considerably easier and less detectable. Notwithstanding the title of this piece, John Whalen captures the paranoid spirit of those on the lookout for spies. Unlike many paranoids, he has a sense of humor, history, and restraint. (To appreciate these qualities, compare "You're Not Paranoid" with another representative of the genre. "Total Surveillance," on pages 69–78.) Whalen is a freelance writer in San Jose, California.*

Turns out it's pretty easy to crash the lunch spread at the American Society for Industrial Security's annual convention. You just walk in, sit down, start munching on salad. I didn't set out to trespass—I only wanted to chat up some corporate dicks, ex G-men, and card-carrying government spooks when their guard was down, beef-tip gravy on their chins. The thing was, when I got busted (halfway through a stale roll), it wasn't by the so-called security specialists with the Efrem Zimbalist Jr. haircuts—it was by one of 1 those superannuated babes with a cotton-candy coif who police the floor of the Las Vegas Convention Center.

And what better locale, by the way, for a convocation of gumshoes, rent-a-cops, drug-sniffing dogs, and keystroke monitors than surveillance-friendly Vegas, the desert home of swivel-mount ceiling cameras and heat-packing casino muscle? If you didn't immediately get the idea that the American Society for Industrial Security is a heavyweight organization to be reckoned with, the Stonehenge-size block letters dominating the lobby of the convention center might have clued you in. Looking about as foreboding as Stanley Kubrick's 2001 obelisk, they spell authority in four giant letters: "A.S.I.S." As in "kick asses." 2

Based in Arlington, Virginia, just a brief Beltway jaunt from the Pentagon and CIA central, ASIS is the world's largest and oldest association for security professionals. It boasts more than 24,000 members worldwide who are dedicated to defending management and company assets from the teeming threats from within and without the modern corporation. ASIS members work for Fortune 500 companies and multinational conglomerates like Coca-Cola, Kodak, Bechtel, Ford, and Disney, and, of course, America's élite law-enforcement agencies and spook hives—from the FBI and Secret Service to the CIA and NSA. According to the latest ASIS figures, more than half of the group's members spend between US $100,000 and $5 million per year on security, much of it to set up access-control systems and TV surveillance. When the FBI needs advice on foreign moles in the workplace, it turns to ASIS "to expand our understanding of industrial espionage," as FBI Director Louis Freeh recently put it. Here in Vegas, over the course of three days, nearly 15,000 crime stoppers, tech shoppers, and amateur gawkers will fan out on the convention floor to swap war stories and hawk amazing gadgets—each more diminutive and diabolically inventive than the gizmos in the previous booth. 3

Oddly, it's the professionals who cover for me when my gate-crashing fails. My table neighbor, a security-fence salesman from New Jersey (razor wire, barbed wire, electrified wire—your complete line of perimeter defense products), has recovered a wayward ID badge from the floor, and it's stuffed with official meal tickets. Mr. Perimeter Defense peels a coupon off the wad and saves me the embarrassment of ejection from the ASIS gathering. "Even though our business is security," he cracks, "sometimes you gotta break the rules." 4

Pretty easygoing guys, these latter-day Praetorian guards. Now imagine what would have happened if I had bombed into the cherry-paneled boardroom of one of their Fortune 500 clients, or if I had been an employee hell-bent on sharing a non-reciprocal luncheon engagement with the security-conscious CEO. At best—at best—I might have been wrestled to the ground and "pacified" with pepper mace, taser guns, or hand-held lasers that can "flash blind" perpetrators ("perps") for up to two minutes. After all, business is business. (One of the door prizes in the exhibit hall? A Browning shotgun. Leave your business card in the fishbowl.) 5

I had come to the ASIS conference not to breach lunchtime security, but to feast on the latest technology guaranteed to repel vengeful employees—the nest-feathering, profit-skimming, paper-clip-pilfering, gold-bricking, shoplifting, ax-grinding, monkey-wrenching malcontents. That's not to say that ASIS is concerned exclusively with bad seeds in the workplace. Judging from seminars with titles like "Radical Fundamentalism: Terrorism of the Future?" and "Sue Yourself: Before Someone Else Does," security professionals are nothing if not diversified in their occupational apprehensions. 6

But hands down, the favorite statistic traded in the cavernous exhibit hall is this one: "Eighty to ninety percent of your business theft is internal." Among the numerous vendors who might sound this klaxon is Mike Bolte, an engineering whiz at Diamond Electronics Inc., which networks cash registers to a computer server that "looks for unusual key-punching activity" and —when it finds likely monkey business—activates surveillance videocams at many of your Wal-Mart, J.C. Penney, and Eddie Bauer outlets. 7

As those venerable shamuses at the Pinkerton private-eye agency warn, "$15 to 25 billion a year is lost to employee theft." And those numbers climb to $170 billion a year as soon as you stop ignoring "losses from time theft that include bogus sick days, late arrivals, early departures, and excessive socializing on the job." Richard Heffernan, a member and past chairman of the ASIS committee on safeguarding proprietary information, submits, "Fifty-eight percent of the problem of misappropriation of information involves insiders." 8

The second most popular factoid bandied about by the merchants of corporate defense is no less worrisome: computer-data trashing and other economic sabotage is on the rise because of employee resentment in the era of corporate "downsizing." 9

As one lecturer puts it, "The so-called American dream—I don't think we have that anymore in most companies." What we have instead are disgruntled ex-employees and soon-to-be-ex-employees who will "steal, vandalize, spread rumors, tamper with products, screw with your computers, and urinate in the coffee pot," he warns. 10

Kvetch about Big Brother in the workplace to these guys and they'll call your attention to the thin blue line protecting innocent employees like you from the thin yellow line, better known as the ol' Sanka chamber pot. "That has happened twice," our lecturer dutifully adds, "as far as I'm aware." At least twice, judging from the mileage coffee-pot crime is getting as a conversational icebreaker. That's hot factoid Number Three, in fact, and to be sure, it was a hidden surveillance camera that exposed one such culprit in the heinous act. This, in case you missed it, was broadcast to the world on *Hard Copy,* or so several conventioneers feel compelled to tell me. 11

What kind of person would stoop to such abomination? "There are 2 million schizophrenic people in this country," our vigilant lecturer states, 12 resuming his theme after digressing briefly into the realms of caffeine and purity of essence. "Not every one of them is extreme, but you've got to be prepared."

ROBOBOSS

Like most everything else, industrial security is feeling the tidal pull of the information age. Whereas wary employers formerly hired platoons of human watchdogs, today a whole panoply of surveillance technology can handle the business of workplace monitoring at a fraction of the cost. Thanks to high-speed modems, cell phones, and ISDN lines, the boss can now tune into surveillance video from the office on his home PC or in his car. Digital "smart-card" keys "remember" which gateways employees have swiped their cards through. Is Homer Simpson malingering with the doughnuts in the break room again? Doh! Yes, according to this handy computerized audit trail of his peregrinations throughout the building. 13

"You can track how long employees are in any given area," explains Sandra Wagner, a salesperson for Advantor Corp., manufacturer of one such system. You can monitor them even at their computer workstations if you have them log in with their card key. If you really want to get fancy, in a Tom Clancy kind of way, there are proximity readers that can vet your ID cards up to 8 feet away, and a whole line of "biometric" devices that can scan your retina or iris, the length of your fingers, and even your weight, to make sure an impostor doesn't suddenly take up residence in your cubicle. 14

Many modern factories now require workers to log in at their heavy equipment "to see how long they use it," offers Wagner's colleague, Kevin Brooks. But doesn't that fuel the kind of employee resentment that can lead to stealing, rumor spreading, screwing with computers, java tampering, the whole nine yards? I ask, "You gotta do a little PR to the employees," Brooks explains. "Tell them it's for their protection. Say you don't want outsiders hitting the vending machines in the employee lounge." Brooks is no slouch when it comes to PR. "A lot of managers don't want to install video monitors," he explains, "I tell them. 'Why don't you tell your employees it's for their protection?'" 15

Says Richard J. Heffernan, who runs a security consulting firm in Branford, Connecticut: "Competitive advantage—that's how you sell security to the *Roseanne* crowd. You tell them that if they want to have a job down the road, they'd better be prepared to accept workplace security measures, including monitoring." 16

But why don't you just hire trustworthy people in the first place, the kind who don't require management by high-tech stakeouts? Well, it turns out that the security professionals have got that angle covered, too. There are dozens of consultants eager to hit the infobahn and run down crucial data on a prospective employee's past record—workers' comp claims, health insurance status, criminal rap sheets, proclivity to pocket Post-it 17 notes, general bad attitudes, you name it. Applicants can submit computerized evaluations via phone.

Though most "reputable" security firms shun legally sticky psychological surveys like the classic Minnesota Multiphasic Personal Inventory (which asks privacy-invading true/false questions such as whether applicants are strongly attracted to members of their own sex), they nonetheless promise to weed out the kleptos, schizos, nutsos, "time thieves," and general chip-embedded-on-shoulder types. A series of rapid-fire questions about a candidate's work history gives the prospective prevaricator little time to trump up answers. 18

Talk about your high-octane paranoia. There's enough of it on the show floor to keep the adrenal glands of G. Gordon Liddy, H. Ross Perot, and Oliver Stone throbbing for weeks. You'd think that the proletarian rabble was about to face the guillotine first thing Monday morning—well, make that Monday afternoon, after late arrivals and excessive socializing on the job. 19

To be fair, though, not everyone here is obsessed with Joe Lunchbox as the crime wave of the future. There are plenty of legitimate security wares that any large employer would be smart to look into—for example, revolving door "mantraps" equipped with metal detectors, essentially a Roach Motel for gun-toting loners. (A squad of South American corporate-security jocks was especially intrigued by this technology.) Then there are the shredders and disintegrators "approved for top-secret destruction," which have a certain harmless utility. There are also sensible bulletproof plexiglass shields-cum-teleprompters just like the ones Bill Clinton uses, semiautomatic pistols small enough to holster inside a Slurpee cup, and the latest in motion-sensing alarms. 20

For those extra-sensitive security concerns, George Wackenhut is on hand. Wackenhut is the founder of The Wackenhut Corporation—not a fast-food franchise, as the name might imply, but the global-security concern that has been described as the CIA's favorite dirty tricks subcontractor. In 1992, a Department of Energy investigation into the illegal use of eavesdropping equipment at plants operated by Westinghouse and other nuclear energy contractors rooted up 147 electronic surveillance devices. One of the devices could listen in on 200 company phones simultaneously. The company responsible for planting many of the bugs? Wackenhut, of course, a firm with a reputation for leaning on employee whistle-blowers. (For more on Wackenhut exploits, see "The Inslaw Octopus." *Wired* 1.1, page 76.) 21

GRAND THEFT TEMPO

But we're back to employee monitoring again. All secured roads seem to lead there, even when the concern isn't grand larceny but those management bugaboos: "long breaks, lack of productivity . . . time theft." Which is why I'm surprised to find neither hide nor hair of electronic-mail letter 22 openers, keystroke-monitoring programs, or other spying paraphernalia that are becoming so commonplace in the discipline gingerly referred to as "personnel tracking." Apparently, these tech tools are not exotic enough for licensed gumshoes.

But that's just the point! The fact that these technologies have become so routine means that any manager who purchases network-operating software is probably getting built-in snoop features. In an office hardwired with a server-based local area network managed by software such as Microsoft LAN Manager, a technically inclined boss or network administrator can turn any employee workstation into a covert surveillance post. So there's no need to call in the big guns from Wackenhut. 23

A recent ad for Norton-Lambert's Close-Up/LAN software package tempted managers to "look in on Sue's computer screen. . . . Sue doesn't even know you're there!" Often, however, software makers don't even need to advertise these "remote monitoring" capabilities, which allow network administrators to peek at an employee's screen in real time, scan data files and e-mail at will, tabulate keystrokes speed and accuracy, overwrite passwords, and even seize control of a remote workstation, if they find it necessary. Products like Dynamics Corp.'s *Peak & Spy,* Microcom Inc.'s *LAN Word;* Novell Inc.'s *Net-Ware;* and Neon Software's *NetMinder* not only improve communications and productivity, they turn employees' cubicles into covert listening stations. Other software applications count the number of keystrokes per minute, the employee's error rate, the time it takes a worker to complete each task, and the time a person spends away from the computer. 24

Not surprisingly, the Orwellian potential of such technology has privacy advocates and working stiffs a bit paranoid. But are concerns about employee monitoring irrational? Remote monitoring certainly happens more frequently and routinely than we tend to think. In 1995, *Macworld* magazine conducted a study of CEOs and computer-systems directors and turned up some rather unsettling statistics. Twenty-two percent of the polled business leaders admitted to searching employee voicemail, computer files, and electronic mail. The larger the company, the more the snooping. Extrapolating to the workplace at large. *Macworld* estimated that as many as 20 million Americans "may be subjected to electronic monitoring through their computers (not including telephones) on the job." 25

POTHOLES ON THE SURVEILLANCE HIGHWAY

As is often the case, the patchwork of regulations and laws addressing such new sociotechnological wrinkles aren't exactly models of clarity. Although the US Constitution addresses privacy in the First, Third, Fourth, Fifth, and Fourteenth amendments, there's no amendment specifically guaranteeing it. While the courts have ruled that employers cannot monitor their workers' personal calls, the Electronic Communications Privacy Act of 1986 26 grants bosses a "business-use exception," which allows supervisory and quality-control monitoring. Practically speaking, that leaves a loophole big enough to fly a Stealth bomber through.

In 1993, the Computer Systems Laboratory of the National Institute of 27
Standards and Technology issued a bulletin titled "Guidance on the Legality of Keystroke Monitoring." The report stated that the US Justice Department "advises that if system administrators are conducting keystroke monitoring or anticipate the need for such monitoring—even for the purposes of detecting intruders—they should ensure that all system users, authorized and unauthorized, are notified that such monitoring may be undertaken."

Still, ambiguity reigns, for the courts have yet to set a clear precedent 28
on the legality of keystroke monitoring.

"It gets even trickier when you look at e-mail privacy," says Marc 29
Rotenberg of the Electronic Privacy Information Center in Washington, DC. I dialed Rotenberg up several days after the Las Vegas convention. "Employees often think that they should have privacy in their personal electronic-mail communications," he explains. "But in practice, there really is no legal safeguard within the organization."

Several years ago, e-mail privacy advocates lost an important test case 30
when a California judge ruled against Alana Shoars, a former e-mail administrator at Epson America Inc. Shoars alleged that her supervisor had printed out and read messages that employees had been assured were private. After she discovered the managerial snooping, Shoars was fired for insubordination, she said. The judge dismissed the case on the grounds that state privacy statutes make no mention of e-mail or the workplace.

The ruling has left civil libertarians glum about the future of e-mail 31
privacy at work. Says Lewis Maltby, who runs the ACLU's workplace rights project, "We have the perfect set of circumstances: we had a wonderful plaintiff, we were in California of all places, and we had a great attorney. We lost. I don't think you're going to see any more e-mail litigation. If we can't win that case in California, we can't win it anywhere."

Telephone communications and e-mail have some protections under 32
the Electronic Communications Privacy Act, but only insofar as they are carried out through a telco common carrier or commercial system such as CompuServe or MCI Mail. Internal electronic mail in the workplace is considered company property.

STRESS UNDER SURVEILLANCE

Assorted studies have found links between employee monitoring and 33
stress—both physical and psychological. A 1990 survey of telecommunications workers conducted by the University of Wisconsin and the Communications Workers of America found that 43 percent of monitored employees said they suffered a loss of feeling in their fingers or wrists, while only 27 percent of unmonitored workers had those symptoms. More than 83 percent of monitored employees complained about high tension as opposed to 67 percent of unmonitored workers. An earlier report by the Of-

fice of Technology Assessment also concluded that monitoring "contributes to stress and stress-related illness."

These studies are hardly news on Capitol Hill, where privacy advocates and employee unions have been pushing for fair-monitoring legislation since the mid-1980s. The latest attempt (1993's Privacy for Consumers and Workers Act) expired in Washington gridlock, a victim of the legislative coma brought on by the prospect of health-care reform (but also dinged by the manufacturing lobby). Privacy advocates say the bill will be back this session. It would require employers to tell new hires that they may be monitored via phone, computer, or e-mail. It would also force managers to notify workers when they are being surveyed—possibly by a beep tone or red light—and to explain how the data will be used. 34

"Employees have the right to dignity," submits Lawrence Fineran of the National Association of Manufacturers, the front-line foe of the bill. "But," he says, "the employer certainly has a right to any kind of data generated by an employee on an employer's time and on an employer's equipment." 35

"There need to be limits on how that kind of technology is used," counters Erica Foldy, former executive director of the Massachusetts Coalition on New Office Technology. 36

"We shouldn't re-create the company town," says Gary Marx, a sociologist at the University of Colorado who has written extensively on technologies "that can extract personal information" and threaten privacy. Marx argues that intrusive monitoring not only invites managerial abuse—providing cover for illegal attempts to thwart unionizing efforts, for example—it also elevates inequity in the workplace. 37

"This stuff often increases the gap between managers and workers," he says. "If managers really believe in monitoring, let's apply it in a more universal way and require *managers* to be monitored electronically." The economic "damage that can be done by a few corrupt or unprofessional executives is really far greater than somebody taking a little too long on a coffee break," he adds. 38

According to Marx, extractive technologies have upset another fundamental balance in the workplace. "Traditionally, on an assembly line, there would be a supervisor who would walk by," he explains, "and you knew who that person was. You also knew when he or she was there. That may have generated some anxiety, but in fact, you could gear your behavior accordingly. But now with the mediated and potentially unseen nature of this, it creates a sense of fear and stress, because employees really never know when they are being watched." 39

In other words, Big Bro could be tuning in any time. 40

PANOPTICON REDUX?

The prospect of total and constant surveillance may sound a bit like science fictional overkill, but the prototype of tomorrow's monitoring has the potential to do just that. You can find it—or more accurately, it can find you— 41 at Xerox PARC in Palo Alto, California. Security is tight at "the PARC," where, after all, the latest edgy tech is conceived and test driven. Yet the security here is rather primitive, and the visitor's badge I'm wearing is, well, positively antique. It's handwritten on paper—and this in the proving ground of the paperless office. As I'm pondering this anachronism, I'm greeted in the lobby by Roy Want, a pleasant chap of 33 years whose boyish features and arched eyebrows suggest a certain capacity for mischief.

It's more than slightly ironic that Want hails from England, the former 42
empire that gave the world Jeremy Bentham, philosopher of utilitarianism and author of *Panopticon, or The Inspection House.* (See this chapter, pp. 467–74.) Published in 1791, Bentham's treatise described a polygonal prison workhouse that placed the penal/industrial overseers in a central tower with glass-walled cells radiating outward. Mirrors placed around the central tower allowed the guards to peer into each cell while remaining invisible to the prisoners—a concept Bentham referred to as "universal transparency." Knowing that they were under surveillance—but not knowing for sure whether they were being watched at any given moment—prisoners would theoretically be on their best behavior at all times.

More than 200 years later, Want, a computer engineer, has essentially 43
reinvented the Panopticon. More accurately, his brainchild, known as the "Active Badge," would have made Bentham proud. Want's active badge, worn by some 50 researchers and staffers in Xerox PARC's Computer Science Lab, is about a quarter of an inch thick and 2 inches by 2 inches square. Clipped to a shirt pocket or belt and powered by a lithium battery, the black box emits an infrared signal—just like a TV remote—every 15 seconds. Throughout the computer lab at the PARC, infrared detectors are velcro-mounted to the ceiling and networked into a Sun workstation. Because each employee's badge emits a unique signal, the computer system "knows" where any given employee is at all times. Any other staffer can access that information on his or her personal computer.

Want explains to me that he developed the hardware while working at 44
the Olivetti Cambridge research laboratory in England. His initial idea was to build smart telephones that forwarded calls automatically to the phone extension nearest a staffer at any given moment. But since defecting to Xerox PARC and working with a team to develop the system's "Birddog" software, he's discovered sundry new uses for the technology, he says. While privacy tribunes see active badges as an ominous new development in the brave new workplace, Want and his colleagues see them as "a double-edged sword," with the potential for both benign and malignant uses. "If you can build the system correctly with the appropriate privacy, encryption, and access safeguards, then I think you've built an acceptable system." At the PARC, management and staff have an agreement that the technology will not be used as an authoritarian carrot and stick. The badges are intended as tools to help staffers locate their "friends," as one researcher puts it.

Want is eager to stress the technology's limitations and the ease with 45
which anyone can thwart its abuse. "At any point in time, you can take

your badge off and leave it on your desk and go shopping if you want. You can also put it in your desk drawer."

Potential misuse of the technology is more than an academic concern now, for Olivetti is going commercial with the badges, marketing the gizmos to insurance companies, hospitals, and other large institutions with an interest in the whereabouts of key personnel or patients. About 70 researchers at two of Digital Equipment Corporation's research labs have also given Want's badges a trial run. Dave Redell, a researcher who has been outspoken about the badges, has mixed thoughts. "There's a strong feeling around a place like this that we're all colleagues," he says, "as opposed to having a rigid management hierarchy. Use of the badge is completely voluntary. In other kinds of workplaces, though, the potential for oppression is far greater. Even in a situation where you have an official policy saying that this is completely voluntary, it would be much easier for there to be a lot of pressure to wear these things at all times." Others, including the ACLU's Maltby, see active badges in more monochrome tones. "Like rats in a maze," Maltby mutters when I call him for a comment. "They want a pager that you can't refuse to answer." 46

UBIQUITOUS COMPUTING ÜBER ALLES?

PARC researchers are understandably excited about some of the more benign applications. As a companion piece to the badges, Want has developed a personal digital assistant he calls the PARCTab. About half the size of an Apple Newton, Want's palm-held PDA sends and receives wireless data signals to another network of infrared detectors salted throughout the building. It's part of Xerox PARC's "ubiquitous computing" project, an attempt to banish paper from the workplace (see *Wired* 3.01, page 124). Want can program his personal assistant to trade e-mail and other files with his workstation, and he can access the Internet through his PDA anywhere in the building (except in the bathroom). 47

Want sees the tabs getting thinner and lighter. Each of us would have dozens scattered around the office, in the car, and at home. Detector "cells will start appearing in public places or the home," he says. "The device will tell you where you are, wherever you are." 48

Of course, it might also tell *them* where you are. Surely, that's a concept that's hardly foreign to wired world citizens. Cell phones made it possible for LA's finest to triangulate on O.J. Simpson during his slo-mo odyssey along the Disneyland freeway. And anytime you use a credit card or make a long-distance phone call, you're essentially leaving a trail of virtual bread crumbs for the telcos, Visa, and law enforcers. 49

"There are always these trade-offs, between what's useful and what could be done to us," says Want from the belly of the kinder, gentler Panopticon. "The benefits to be had are so great; we just have to be sure that the people who are in control respect our privacy." 50

I keep thinking of what the block-shouldered gumshoe from one of the major security firms told me in Vegas. Are there certain technologies and 51 techniques that you guys aren't showing me? I asked. "Some things," he said, shaking his head at the naïveté of my query, "we aren't gonna broadcast here in public."

▲ ▲ ▲

Review Questions

1. According to Whalen's sources, what percentage of business theft is internal to a company?
2. What is the variety of information that employers can gather on employees with current surveillance techniques.
3. Why is keystroke monitoring not displayed at the ASIS convention, according to Whalen? Why is this development significant?
4. What is the "business-use exception" to the Electronic Communications and Privacy Act of 1986—and why is it significant, according to Whalen?
5. Why was the Alana Shoars case important to privacy advocates?
6. What kinds of effects are observed in workers who are monitored electronically, according to studies?
7. What is the "Panopticon" and what is its relationship to research being conducted at the Palo Alto Research Center (PARC)?
8. What is the significance of "über alles" in the article's final subheading?

Discussion and Writing Suggestions

1. Comment on John Whalen's writing style, as compared to the style of Alan Westin (pages 454–60) or Bryan Glastonbury (pages 423–429). Illustrate your description of the style with references to specific sentences and paragraphs.
2. Having interviewed a salesperson from Adventor Corp., manufacturer of automated monitors, Whalen learns that when instituting an employee monitoring system in the workplace, "you gotta do a little PR to the employees. . . . Tell them it's for their own protection." Assuming that the ASIS statistics regarding employee theft are real, to what extent *do* you feel that monitoring protects employees?
3. In a Yankelovich survey conducted in 1991 (see page 444), 67 percent of respondents said that computerized credit checks of job applicants should not be allowed, while 31 percent said they should be. Credit checks, along with applicant histories of "workers' compensation claims, health insurance status, [and] criminal rap sheets" are available through security firms that belong to ASIS. What are an employer's legitimate needs in these areas? Given these needs, what, in your view, constitutes a fair and balanced background check?
4. Whalen reports on the prevalence of keystroke and e-mail monitoring, and he quotes a Justice Department advisory "that if system administrators are conducting keystroke monitoring . . . they should ensure

that all system users . . . are notified." The advisory is not law, however, and as Whalen points out, "ambiguity reigns." What is your view of keystroke monitoring? How would you react in a job where supervisors advised you that your keystrokes would be monitored?

5. What's your response to the employer who says: "I own the machine you work on; I pay your salary; I own the intellectual property—and the data—in your computer; and I reserve the right to access that property"?
6. Within the collegial atmosphere of a trusting workplace, the PARC badge has distinct advantages; for instance, phone calls can be routed to the phone nearest to where the recipient of the call happens to be; employee-to-employee questions can be quickly answered; efficiency can be improved. Given these and other advantages, how interested would you be in wearing a PARC badge at your workplace?
7. Reread the final two paragraphs of this selection. PARC researcher Want alludes to the "trade-offs" between a technology's advantages and its dangers. How confident is Whalen that these tradeoffs can be managed? How confident are you?

Privacy in the Workplace

CQ RESEARCHER

How closely and under what circumstances should employees be monitored? Congress debated this question in the summer of 1993, when the then-pending Privacy for Consumers and Workers Act was being studied in various subcommittees. The Act never reached a vote: in that session, Congress preoccupied itself with health-care reform and put off action. Still, committees took testimony, two examples of which appear here, following an overview of the debate prepared by the CQ [Congressional Quarterly] Researcher.

Of all the freedoms Americans enjoy, privacy often tops the list. Supreme Court Justice Louis D. Brandeis certainly thought so.[1] He called it the "right most valued by civilized men." 1

Lately, though, privacy has become an embattled right. Video cameras scan supermarket aisles and subway platforms. Names and addresses gleaned by telemarketers join millions of others in computerized data banks. Electronic snoops illegally eavesdrop on cordless phone calls. Employees of the Internal Revenue Service browse through tax returns of friends, relatives, neighbors and celebrities. 2

Distaste for such practices is growing, as a recent Louis Harris and Associates poll showed. Fifty-three percent of those questioned said they 3

[1]Brandeis served on the Supreme Court from 1916 to 1939.

were "very concerned" about threats to their privacy. This represented a significant jump from the 47 percent who gave the same response in an identically worded 1992 survey.

The most recent Harris poll was commissioned by *Privacy & American* 4
Business, a newly launched bimonthly newsletter. Alan F. Westin, its publisher and editor, is a Columbia University law professor who has written extensively on workplace privacy issues. [See pp. 454-60.] Next June, Westin and his colleagues hope to hold the first in an annual series of national conferences on American business and privacy in Washington.

The newsletter's focus on business is not surprising, since many pri- 5
vacy encroachments occur on the job. "From the moment an individual first walks through an employer's entrance, privacy rights are relinquished," attorney Kurt H. Decker wrote in his book on employee privacy. "As an employment condition, employees must disclose personal facts about their background and continually submit to employer scrutiny that may or may not be performance-related. The employee may confront a physical examination, polygraph examination, psychological evaluation or even an [AIDS] antibody test. . . . Physical intrusion may also occur through locker searches or frisking as employees leave the workplace, even though no reasonable suspicion of theft exists."

Control of employee behavior on the job—and sometimes off the 6
job—has long been a management prerogative. The rule of thumb is that employers can dismiss workers or reject job applicants for any reason that a contract or a law does not expressly prohibit. This power flows from the judicial concept of "at will" employment, which holds that workers can quit their jobs at any time, with or without cause, and that employers can fire workers just as freely.

Over the years, employees have gained a bit more breathing room. 7
Congress approved legislation in 1988 that restricted the use of lie detectors by most private businesses. And nearly three dozen states have enacted laws safeguarding the confidentiality of AIDS test results.

Still, employers continue to intrude on what many employees regard as 8
private matters. Concern centers at present on electronic workplace monitoring, typically without employees' knowledge. The aim might be to tally the number of calls handled by a telemarketer or the number of keystrokes per minute made by a computer-terminal operator. More controversial is video monitoring of restrooms and dressing areas to discourage drug trafficking or other criminal activity—a practice that many employers have forsworn as demeaning to all parties.

"Most people don't realize there are very few restrictions on employ- 9
ers when it comes to testing for drugs, monitoring computer-terminal output, using hidden cameras and so forth," says Jeff Miller, a spokesman for the Communications Workers of America (CWA), a union representing about 650,000 telecommunications workers. "Invasion of workplace privacy is definitely becoming a bigger issue. As technology grows more sophisticated, it's becoming easier to keep track of people."

Reliable statistics on electronic workplace surveillance are hard to 10
come by. Two years ago, Rep. Pat Williams, D-Mont., said "as many as 26 million workers may be under computer surveillance." *Macworld* magazine reported in its July 1993 issue that some 20 million U.S. workers are affected. The monthly magazine extrapolated that figure from information supplied by 301 companies nationwide.

FEAR OF SPYING: POLLS REFLECT PUBLIC'S CONCERNS

Recent public opinion polls indicate the public is concerned about the amount of computerized information being kept about them, resents privacy intrusions by their employers, but supports drug testing in the workplace.

Percentage of Americans who say they are "very concerned" about their privacy:

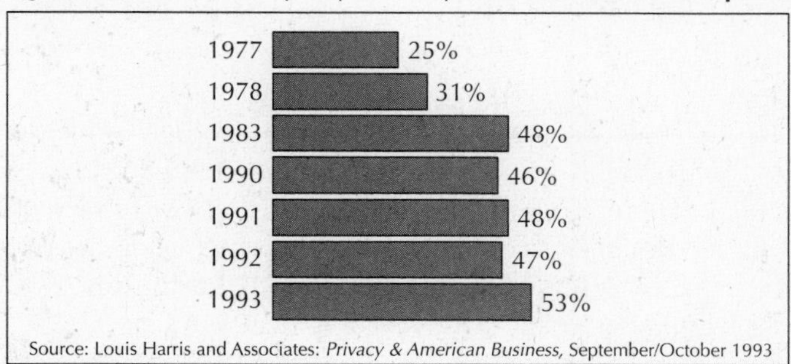

Source: Louis Harris and Associates: *Privacy & American Business,* September/October 1993

Percentage of Americans who say they are concerned about the amount of computerized information collected by:

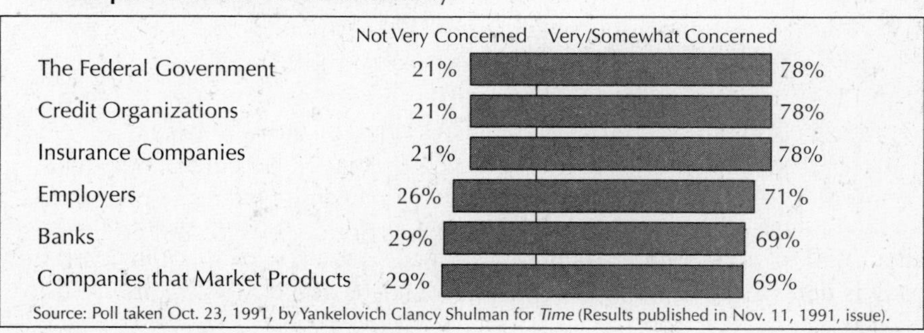

Source: Poll taken Oct. 23, 1991, by Yankelovich Clancy Shulman for *Time* (Results published in Nov. 11, 1991, issue).

Percentage of Americans who say employers should be allowed or not allowed to:

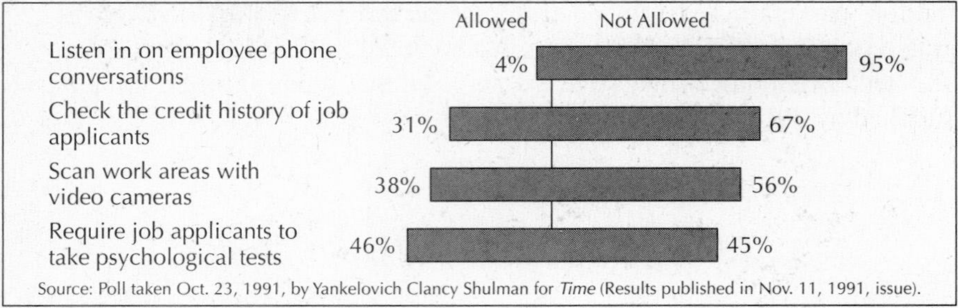

Source: Poll taken Oct. 23, 1991, by Yankelovich Clancy Shulman for *Time* (Results published in Nov. 11, 1991, issue).

Opinions on Drug Testing

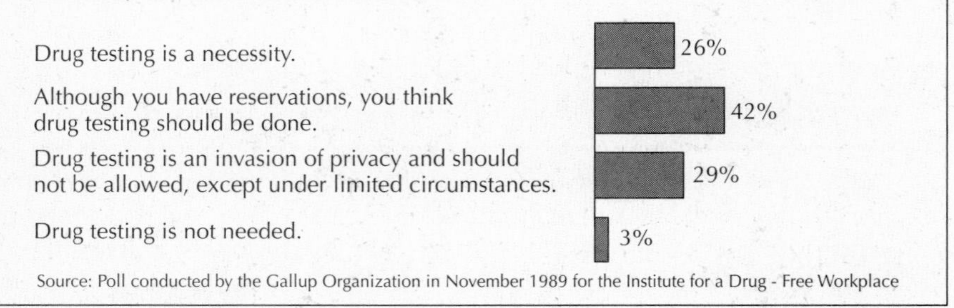

Source: Poll conducted by the Gallup Organization in November 1989 for the Institute for a Drug - Free Workplace

MacWorld Poll
ELECTRONIC EAVESDROPPING AT WORK

Workers are routinely monitored in some industries, but how pervasive is the practice? To find out, *Macworld* conducted the first national survey designed to find out how and why businesses monitor employees. Top corporate managers from 301 businesses of all sizes and in a wide range of industries participated.

More than 21 percent of respondents—30 percent in large companies—have "engaged in searches of employee computer files, voice mail, electronic mail, or other networking communications." Nearly 16 percent report having checked computerized employee work files, and 9 percent having searched employee E-mail.

These data suggest that some 20 million Americans are subject to electronic monitoring. Is your hard drive or office network searched? Better ask your boss directly. Only 18 percent of respondents' companies had a written policy regarding electronic privacy. And only 31 percent of companies that conduct electronic monitoring or searches of employee computers, voice mail, E-mail, or networking communications give employees advance warning.

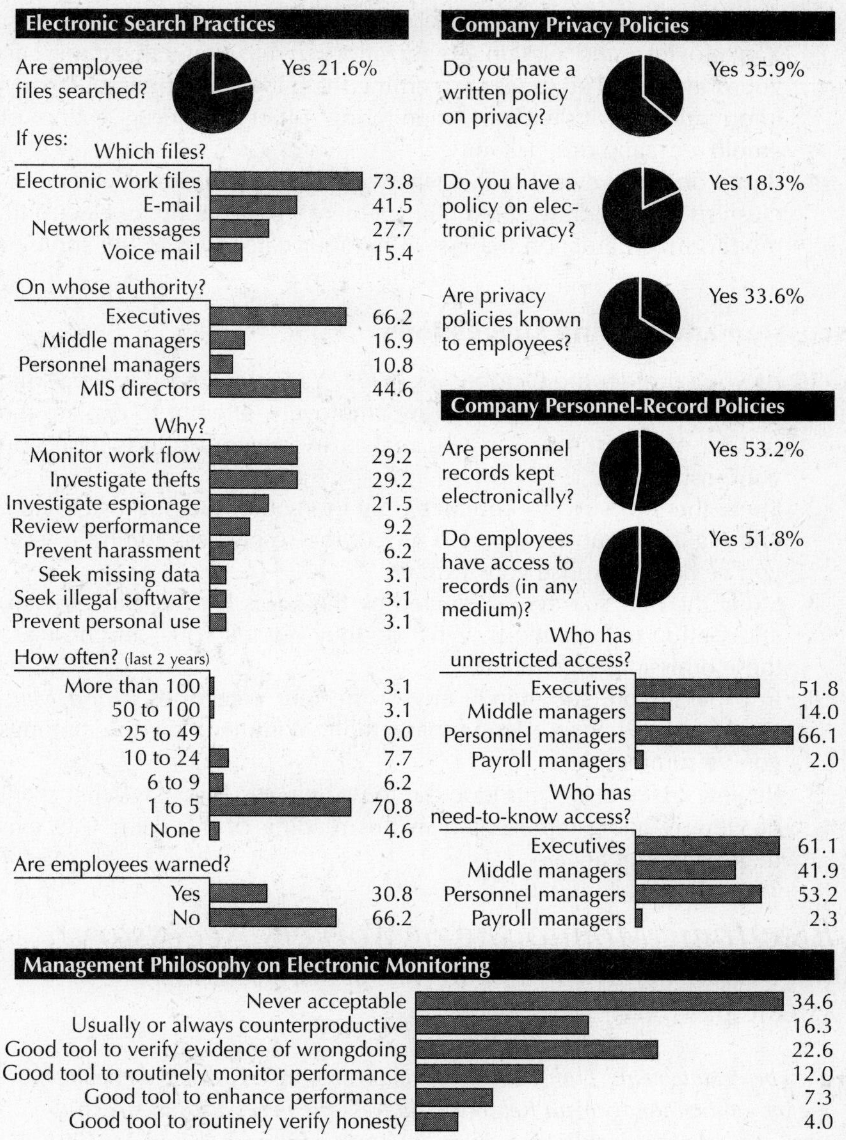

Reprinted by permission of *Macworld,* 501 2nd Street, San Francisco, Calif., 94107.

▲ ▲ ▲

Review Questions

1. What is the status of privacy rights for individuals in the workplace, as opposed to rights of individuals in their homes?
2. What is the judicial concept of "at will" employment, and what is its significance with regard to privacy law?

3. Based on the four surveys conducted by the Louis Harris, Yankelovich, and Gallup organizations, what generalizations can you draw about attitudes concerning the gathering of computerized information on individuals, monitoring (other than drug testing) of employees, and drug testing?
4. Based on your review of the *Macworld* survey responses, what conclusions do you draw about management's philosophy on electronic monitoring (that is, on the last of the four categories in the survey)?

Discussion and Writing Suggestions

1. As you consider the October 23, 1991, Yankelovich study on public attitudes regarding monitoring by employers, attempt to explain the pattern of responses. Can you make any generalizations based on your insights?
2. Study the four surveys conducted by the Louis Harris, Yankelovich, and Gallup organizations. Do any of the responses confirm a view you've held? Surprise you? Explain.
3. Study the four surveys conducted by the Louis Harris, Yankelovich, and Gallup organizations. What do they *not* tell you—and how are these omissions significant?
4. In a paragraph, summarize any of the four categories in the *Macworld* survey. In a second paragraph, comment on the findings you've summarized.
5. Review *Macworld's* introduction to its own survey data. What point of view is being represented in this reading of the data? Cite evidence for your answer.

Is Electronic Monitoring of Workers Necessary?

HARRIET TERNIPSEDE AND THE AIR TRANSPORT ASSOCIATION OF AMERICA

Two brief statements, both given as testimony before a House Subcommittee on Labor-Management Relations, address the necessity and stressfulness of workplace monitoring. First, in a transcript of her July 23, 1991 testimony, former TWA reservations agent Harriet Ternipsede argues against electronic surveillance in the workplace; then, a trade group representative for the Air Transport Association of America argues for surveillance.

HARRIET TERNIPSEDE

During my 30 years as a reservation agent, I have personally witnessed how my workplace has been turned into an electronic sweatshop by monitoring. . . . It was not always this way. Before 1970, manual procedures to 1 log reservations were used and employee monitoring by telephone was at a minimum. But in the early 1970s, as technology developed, companies discovered that they could monitor many workers at one time. Things rapidly changed and the nightmare of electronic monitoring emerged.

Today, through computer programs and communications systems, employers can electronically observe and review workers' every move—every word. . . . 2

The constant use of monitoring to measure employees' performance creates an enormous amount of pressure and stress on agents. The stress that is created by monitoring has caused serious physical effects. I refer you to an excellent study completed by the University of Wisconsin's Department of Industrial Engineering. . . . The study concluded that electronic monitoring was seen as a major cause of psychological and physical health complaints among workers. Unfortunately, my own personal experience verifies this study. . . . 3

After years of stress from constant monitoring, my work and health suffered: I lost patience with my passengers and I rarely smiled. I suffered nausea, severe sleep disturbance, weakened eyesight, mental confusion, headaches, muscle aches, exhaustion and lymph node pain. I went on sick leave and was diagnosed with Chronic Fatigue Immune Dysfunction Syndrome (CFIDS). . . . It has taken me four years to gain back a measure of health, but I may never again enjoy half of my prior health. I blame my poor health on the incredible stress that is caused by electronic monitoring. 4

Today's high-tech workplace has wrought erosion of dignity, invasion of privacy and caused stress-related illnesses. Monitoring makes us feel like prisoners hooked up to a computer, mistreated, guilty, paranoid, enslaved, violated, angry and driven at a relentless pace. Laws must be updated to protect the worker and private citizen against this abuse. Only when the laws are changed to protect the worker against this outrageous form of surveillance can businesses achieve their hope for increased productivity. 5

AIR TRANSPORT ASSOCIATION

Electronic monitoring in our industry is not intended to harm the employee. It is not a manipulative or coercive device. On the contrary, electronic monitoring is an indispensable means to enhance employee productivity and quality assurance. . . . The beneficiaries of monitoring are the employee, the employer and the customer. 1

Electronic monitoring enables an employer to evaluate the productivity of the processes it uses to produce goods or services. That evaluation may yield changes in the way work is accomplished or in the manner in which work is distributed. . . . 2

The monitoring of employees is not a new development. Employers have historically monitored the performance of their employees. It is a reasonable exercise of managerial oversight responsibilities. What has 3 changed in more recent times has been the method of supervision. Electronic monitoring, although it is newer in origin, is intrinsically no more invasive than traditional personal supervision. Indeed, for most employees electronic monitoring is less invasive than direct personal supervision.

Electronic monitoring offers a distinct advantage to the employee: it is objective. Whatever the form of the monitoring, the means used afford a uniform, accurate method of evaluating an employee. . . . 4

Furthermore, electronic monitoring benefits the consumer. It is through such monitoring that the airline assures that a customer receives prompt, polite and complete service. This is particularly important for airline reservations activities because of the numerous fare and itinerary changes that occur daily. Monitoring helps ensure that customer fare or schedule inquiries are responded to accurately. . . . 5

The efficiency enhancing results of monitoring are important for consumers, employees and airline management. Improvements in efficiency translate directly into more economical service for the consumer. Providing service more economically is essential for airlines today. Our industry is intensely competitive. An airline must vigilantly pursue opportunities to make its operations more efficient. If it does not, it will inevitably suffer serious, and ultimately fatal, competitive disadvantage. Electronic monitoring is an important resource in the pursuit of improved efficiency, and, therefore, competitiveness. Thus, from the perspective of the airline industry, electronic monitoring is an indispensable tool in the ongoing effort to make air transportation more productive. 6

▲ ▲ ▲

Discussion and Writing Suggestions

1. Given the two arguments on workplace monitoring, which do you find more compelling? Why?
2. What are the assumptions about the needs of workers underlying Harriet Ternipsede's position? The assumptions about the prerogatives of management, as expressed by the representative for the Air Transport Association?
3. In this debate over the electronic surveillance of reservation agents, pay close attention to the wide discrepancy between the positions of management and labor. If management's intent was to benefit employees, employers, and customers, where did it go wrong (if you believe it went wrong)?
4. Given the heated and emotionally charged arguments such as this one, in which the positions of antagonists appear to be separated by a gulf of mistrust, misunderstanding, and ill will, what are the prospects for successful negotiation? Assume you are a labor-management consultant called in to find some mutually acceptable position on surveillance in the workplace. What is your analysis of the opposing positions? What would be your strategy in negotiating a middle-ground position?

5. Management claims that employee monitoring has, historically, been a commonplace, reasonable, and necessary practice. To management, merely the *method* of surveillance has changed, not the fact that employees have and will continue to be monitored on the job. In your view, is this change in method significant?
6. These arguments were delivered as testimony to a House Subcommittee on Labor-Management Relations. The presentation of widely divergent views is commonplace in Congress, the work of which is to enact legislation that navigates between the competing interests of varied constituents. In three or four pages, design a piece of legislation that represents such a compromise. Your work-up should consist of two parts: (1) a list of the proposed law's salient features, which you could present as bullet points; and (2) a commentary on the proposed law, in which you explain how the law represents an acceptable middle ground between the competing needs of two vocal constituent groups.
7. As a consumer who makes airline reservations, you expect (and have a right to expect) efficiency, economy, and courtesy from reservation agents. Management claims that electronic monitoring of agents ensures these consumer benefits. Speaking *as a consumer,* do you except and endorse management's techniques for guaranteeing quality in its reservations systems?

The Changing Nature of Information

ANNE WELLS BRANSCOMB

This selection appears in the introduction to a book-length study, Who Owns Information? From Privacy to Public Access (1994), *in which Anne Wells Branscomb studies changing patterns of information use, along with the legal implications of these changes. Branscomb organizes her study around nine "Who Owns" questions: Who Owns Your Name and Address, Your Telephone Number, Your Medical History, Your Image, Your Electronic Messages, Video Entertainment, Religious Information, Computer Software, and Government Information? Each of these discussions will provide an excellent starting point, should you decide to pursue library research on the changing legal status of information in our society. Anne Wells Branscomb practices communications and computer law. She is also a scholar-in-residence at the Program on Information Resources Policy at Harvard University.*

Pick up any newspaper reporting on new government efforts to keep the nation competitive; open any book attempting a thoughtful analysis of what we as individuals and as a society must do to prepare for the twenty-first century; sit in on any discussion about the impact of new technologies on our industries, our educational systems, our ability to wage war and to 1 keep peace, and invariably there will be one point of consensus: as we embark upon a plan for the future, we must first come to terms with what it means to be in an information age.

It is only in the past two decades that we have come to realize that information has taken on a new character, that it has passed from being an instrument through which we acquire and manage other assets to being a primary asset itself. Until very recently, for instance, commentators referred to our society as a post-industrial, service-based economy, descriptions that accept the idea that information industries were becoming more and more important but that still failed to recognize the emergence of information as a commodity, now calling out for protection and definition of ownership rights. A natural consequence has been that our courts and our legislatures are now being asked to address information issues never before the subject of contention. What has changed between then and now to make information ownership and use the hot new legal issue? 2

One can assume that the very moment our earliest ancestors realized that speech is capable of communicating ideas—rather than just emotions—they began trading facts, judgments, condemnations, and insights. They did so in the planting fields and in the marketplace, in the privacy of their own homes and in public arenas, in small and in large groups—wherever two or more people came together. 3

Not surprisingly, in virtually all societies, control of and access to information became instruments of power, so much so that information came to be bought, sold, and bartered by those who recognized its value. Information experts—from those who could glean from the heavens information useful to the farmer planting his fields, to those who could fathom the medical value of different plants, to those community gurus who acted as repositories of tribal history—were guaranteed status if not wealth in every society in which they existed. Advisers to kings, elders of local societies, information vendors whose judgments were sought on a variety of issues, were all at the right hand of power. But they were not considered the society's property owners. Their cache of information, however valuable, was not of a class with a few ounces of gold. 4

Information acquired even greater value with the development of written language, and then the printing press. Both these developments greatly expanded the reach of this exchange, so that like-minded people could now communicate across miles and even across generations. In time, those who organized and analyzed information sought protection for their interpretations, and it soon became apparent that some sort of legal redress for unauthorized use was necessary. 5

The arrival of radio and then television made inter-community, international, and even intercontinental communication almost immediate, altering in important ways our sense of what constitutes a community, as well as introducing a new and much-expanded commercial value to the information being communicated. Yet despite the high value humankind has always placed on information, and the stresses placed on the law by changes in the commercial value of many kinds of information, until very re- 6 cently the law governing information exchange—for the most part, intellectual property law—has been evolving with the creep of a receding glacier.

• • •

What explains [the] sudden explosion of questions about the legal status of information? At one level the answer is obvious: information that formerly resided in encoded scribblings on sheets of paper in dispersed locations, difficult to find, laborious to collect, and virtually impossible to correlate, can now be collected easily, read by electronic laser beams, recorded in magnetic patterns invisible to the human eye, and quickly aggregated and correlated. Collections of data that had once been dispersed to cubbyholes and file drawers now wend their way as patterns of electronic impulses into vast databases where, by virtue of their comprehensive nature and instant cross-accessibility, they become commodities more valuable than the sum of their independent parts. Information whose value could once be protected by guarding against those who would try to copy from the paper on which it was recorded could now be compromised in ways invisible to the human eye and at speeds almost unintelligible to the human mind. 7

But the technological revolutions of the past decades have brought about changes more troubling than those revolving around the question of who owns what piece of information. The new speed and accuracy of collection and correlation methods have given value to previously worthless information (in terms of its value in the marketplace), creating new ownership interests and conflicts and a tension between the need to foster new technology-based information businesses and to determine what will be responsible social behavior in an information society. A great deal of information we consider to be highly personal, and of interest only to ourselves and the town gossip—our names, telephone numbers, marital status, educational accomplishments, job and credit histories, even medical, dental, and psychiatric records—is now being sold on the open market to anyone who believes he or she might be able to use such information to turn a profit. These transactions usually take place without our knowledge or consent. 8

In their most benign use, these transactions generate telemarketing calls that intrude upon our private hours or bring a deluge of mail into our homes, tempting us to purchase items we did not know we needed and forcing us to dispose of mountains of paper we did not request, eventually clogging up our communities' disposal and recycling efforts. Put to more dangerous use, this marketing of our personal information determines whether or not we will be offered professional opportunities or promotions, be subjected to surveillance by government agencies, or be accepted for medical, property, or life insurance. 9

Most of us are bewildered by the amazing new array of instruments for acquiring, organizing, and assessing information. Even the law has found itself in disarray in trying to apply the old rules to a new game. Some factors that have changed the world of information collection and retrieval include: 10

- An explosion of replication techniques that facilitate the wide distribution of information clones, often almost indistinguishable from the originals in terms of legibility and utility: computer disks, CD-ROMs, videocassette recorders, digital audio, audiotapes, and facsimile transmissions;
- The deployment of satellites in a geostationary earth orbit where information can be collected from and dispensed to all corners of the earth at almost the speed of light;
- The advent of powerful mainframe computers that can search vast quantities of data, identifying similarities and differences beyond the capability of human time and patience;
- The arrival of the bar code and electronic "smart cards," which record so many of our personal transactions: purchases, trips to the bank, the doctor, the drug store, the auto repair shop, the movies, schools, even the supermarket;
- The democratization of access to information has made many of us accessories after the fact. The proliferation of the personal computer and certain of its common accoutrements—such as the modem and the fax card—has rendered every one of us a potential user, publisher, or distributor of information products.

If annoyance to the general public were the only by-product of the new information society, enacting legislation to rectify abuses might be an easy task. But the information society has produced a rich marketplace of new information products, and the ease of entry into the new marketplace attracts a large number of small entrepreneurs who depend for their livelihood upon access to these new information resources. As a consequence, the information industries are among the fastest-growing sectors of our economy and a growing foundation for economic success in the global market. Past legislation told us little about how these new industries should be allowed to operate—in their dealings with each other or with the general public. 11

What was a more or less orderly information marketplace, based upon oral communication, the handwritten note, and the printed word, and enhanced by radio and telephone, has evolved into a multimedia melting pot of new information businesses that find this treasure trove of archived information a valuable resource for many utilitarian as well as charitable purposes. What the future portends, we are told, is an information distribution system that can transmit five hundred or more channels of information services (voice, video text, or a combination of all three) to our homes and places of businesses with the additional capability of interacting in innovative ways. 12

The law will lumber along like an unwieldy dinosaur wending its way to extinction if it cannot keep up with the pace of change in this new interactive, information-intense environment. But the law is by nature conservative, attempting to bring order out of chaos only as fast as consensus can be reached among social groups willing to conform to norms they believe are fair and workable. Human beings are by nature social animals, desirous 13 of interacting through whatever means are readily available. However, in order to interact without stepping on each other's toes or offending each other's sensibilities, we develop social conventions and norms and ethical behavior. As time goes by these behavioral norms are written into statutes and constitutions that then govern future human behavior. The law is—or should be—a sociopolitical process through which free citizens agree on the norms and rules of behavior. It is too important to be left to the lawyers. Everyone must contribute to the vision of how an information society should function.

The difficulty with today's information societies is that we have not **14**
had enough experience to agree upon acceptable behavior. We are like children trying out all the toys to see how they work. Until something goes awry and the injustice of it becomes immediately apparent, we sit back and wait to see what will happen next.

▲ ▲ ▲

Review Questions

1. What essential change has occurred with respect to information in the last two decades?
2. According to Branscomb, why is this change in the purpose of information gathering of concern?
3. Branscomb briefly reviews the status of information providers in the earliest societies. She claims that, historically, information providers were not "property owners" but now they are. What does she mean?
4. The laws protecting the privacy rights of individuals lag behind technological developments. Why? And why is this lag time significant?
5. What challenges do new information industries pose?

Discussion and Writing Suggestions

1. Branscomb asserts that hi-tech systems for information gathering have created a "tension between the need to foster new technology-based information businesses and to determine what will be responsible social behavior in an information society" (paragraph 8). What, precisely, *is* this tension? What are the legitimate interests that are in conflict?
2. To what extent must remedies to problems created by hi-tech gathering of personal information be *legislative* remedies? To what extent do you think we can and should count on good will in the technological community to avoid abuses? The larger question: Are laws necessary to ensure responsible behavior among individuals?
3. In her final paragraph, Branscomb offers an analogy: that in our use of hi-tech, we're "like children trying out all the toys to see how they work. Until something goes awry and the injustice of it becomes immediately apparent, we sit back and wait to see what will happen next." How apt do you find the comparison?

4. What are the difficulties in making plans for the orderly, socially responsible use of a technology *before* its appearance in the marketplace? That is, must we wait "until something goes awry" with a new technology before we respond with legal protections?
5. Branscomb writes that the law "is too important to be left to the lawyers" (paragraph 13). What does she mean? Do you agree?
6. How directly and personally do you take Branscomb's statement that "[e]veryone must contribute to the vision of how an information society should function" (paragraph 13)? To the extent that you can identify, do you have any personal stake in contributing to such a vision?

Computers in the Workplace: Elysium or Panopticon?

ALAN F. WESTIN

This selection reviews the issue of privacy in American employment history. Alan Westin defines two distinct eras in that history and then identifies the present moment as a "transformation" in American working life that will raise at least four serious challenges. Westin is a law professor at Columbia University. He writes—and is quoted—extensively on privacy issues in the American workplace. He is also publisher and editor of the bimonthly newsletter Privacy & American Business. *Westin delivered the selection that follows as a speech at the Second Conference on Computers, Freedom, and Privacy in 1992. Note: the "Panopticon" of Westin's title is an architectural design devised by Jeremy Bentham in 1787 for keeping people under surveillance. You'll find an excerpt from Bentham's work on pages 468–74. (John Whalen also refers to the Panopticon, in paragraphs 41–42 on page 438.)*

When information technology enters an area of social activity, the best fit is when the rules and the norms in that area are well-defined, publicly understood, and in which there are very crystallized values about standards and processes. When that happens, information technology can come in. It can be finely tuned to those prevailing values and norms, and there can be the most comfortable fit between technology and societal interests. On the other hand, when you have an area that is undergoing profound change, conflict of values, and tensions in terms of competing interests, it becomes a dangerous time for technological applications, because either the technological applications will be used to enforce the older standards that are in disarray and breaking up, or they may be used to prefer one or another of the competing interests before there has been a social consensus on just how that area ought to perform in American society. And I'd like to suggest to you that that's exactly the situation in which we find ourselves as we think about computers in the workplace in the next decade. 1

It helps to understand what I mean by the transformation of the workplace and how this is a very perilous setting for technological applications. Anyone familiar with American employment history and law knows that we have traversed at least two eras to get to the 1990s. First, from about the 1890s until the 1950s, we managed what could be called, the *era of employer prerogative in American law and practice.* Employers were free to hire, administer, and fire at will. 2

They could set any standards they wished in terms of selecting people for employment, employ any tests they wished to verify or to gauge people's ideas, orientations, lifestyles, or fitness for work as the employer defined it. On the job, there was no concept that there was any employer limitation when it came to watching, controlling, keeping records on employees. Obviously, this was before the era in which any kind of equality standards defined opportunities for equal treatment on the part of diverse groups in the population. Employment, the law said, was *at will,* because the employee was free to quit when the employee wanted to; therefore, the employer was free to fire whenever the employer wanted to. It was an axiom of American employment law that courts would not inquire into the reason why a person was discharged from private employment. The employer could do it for good reason, bad reason, or no reason *at all,* the famous court construction of employment at will put it. And this was the system that, by and large, prevailed with only minor modifications as far as government employment was concerned, throughout this long 60-year era of the 1890s into the 1950s. 3

The second era that we pass through is the shift into what I would call the *sociomediated concept of employment,* where, for a number of critical public policy vantage points, American society decided to limit the total employer prerogative concept. Equal employment opportunity standards were written, guaranteeing access to jobs on a non-discriminatory basis for a steadily enlarging set of protective categories: race, religion, sex, nationality, disability or handicap, etc. In addition, statutes were passed in this era of the 1960s into the early 1980s giving employees, in most states, the right to see what was in their personnel records and to have access to the recordkeeping function. The Fair Credit Reporting Act, enacted in 1969 and put into effect in 1970, provided some rights for individuals to know if a report had been drawn on them, to see what information had been used by an employer not to hire them, and to have various rights of challenge and contest. 4

We also began to define protection of whistle blowers if they reported what they thought was illegal behavior on the part of their employer—protection against being fired or disciplined for trying to adhere to government regulations or to laws governing the conduct of the employment relationship. As a result of these kinds of new public policies limiting the classic employer prerogative, most American employers went out of the business of being as intrusive and as discriminatory as they had been in the earlier first epoch of the employer prerogative period. If you looked at the practices of most large private corporations, and the practices, obviously, of government agencies, what you found was that in the period of the 1960s 5 until the mid-1980s, a lot of what had been the standard privacy-intrusive kind of activity was either discarded as not being necessary or functional to get employees to pursue productive work relationships, or not the kind of things that the public was comfortable with. So the great majority of employers in this period retreated or walked away from what had been the most intrusive or the most controlling practices in the earlier era.

Something happened in the late 1980s, and it's this transformation that 6
has to be seen as the dominant thrust of the 1990s. For a number of reasons, employers have been invited back—and many have been forced or have joyfully moved—into a new intervention in the private lives and into the activities of their employees. The first reason is the thread of legal liability. There are lawsuits now that hold an employer liable if there is negligent hiring. This means that the criminal history record of the person applying for the job has not been investigated and ascertained, especially where there is a criminal history or some kind of violent behavior or sex-related crimes that could affect the employee in relationships with the public, customers, or fellow employees.

The government made a major thrust on employers to get into the drug 7
testing business in the late 1980s. Public concern about drugs in the workplace, crime, and losses as a result of drug abuse in the workplace pushed large numbers of employers into adopting drug testing programs, which enjoyed very high public opinion support. Whenever the public is asked whether they approve, or do not approve, of drug testing at the workplace for people whose jobs affect public safety, public attitudes are overwhelmingly in favor of drug testing programs.

Health care costs have become so major at workplaces that there is 8
tremendous employer concern to control those kinds of costs, since in a global competitive world, astronomical health costs can put a tax on American competitiveness. This is of direct concern to the survival and viability of many enterprises. As a result, since we are not a society that seems to be willing to enact national health insurance, employers are being driven to try to select applicants and to administer their work forces in ways that will, in a major sense, control their expenditures on health utilization, disabilities, worker's compensation, and other health-related costs. These and other kinds of trends that I could mention are driving employers back into a desire to learn more about job applicants, to control behavior on and off the job once people are hired, and to seek sources of information about their employees in ways that, while not quite going back to the earlier era of employer prerogative, resemble it in terms of employer thrust in favor of the collection and utilization of very sensitive and personal information.

I think there are four areas in terms of technological application in this 9
changing workplace where we are going to be seeing enormous privacy conflicts played out in the 1990s. In mentioning these four, I think it's also important to note that they're unfolding at a time when we are reshaping the very nature of work and authority relationships in our society. It's clear that the traditional authoritarian structures of work in America have broken down. We are now, virtually as a whole society, committed to experimenta-

tion and decentralized work structures in new employer/employee relationships with cooperative participation and not rigid authoritarianism. We are also concerned about new relationships between work and family, and dealing with harmful stress at workplaces and its effect on the physical and mental health of employees in society, etc. The very structures and relationships of the workplace are undergoing dramatic change, wholly apart from these privacy issues, but it's in those settings in which the privacy issues unfold.

What are the kinds of issues that I think are central? . . . First is *applicant selection* itself. There is strong public support in all the surveys for verifying job-relevant information when applicants give their qualifications for jobs. There are now many, many database-oriented kinds of files which can be consulted to verify information. In the new amendments to the Fair Credit Reporting Act that are presently being developed in Congress, there will be important new rights for job applicants to be informed in advance that verification of their qualifications and of employment background will be done. If the Act is passed, they will be entitled to receive a copy of that report and respond to it before adverse action is taken by the employer. This is a very important addition to due process, if not privacy rights, on the part of applicants for employment long overdue. I think that it is something that industry and consumer advocates and privacy advocates see as an important addition to the employee rights dimension. 10

There is strong opposition in all the survey data to employers looking into personal lifestyles and off-the-job civic and political activities in making job selection decisions. For example, about 18 states in the last several years have passed statutes that forbid employers to make off-the-job smoking or the use of other legal substances such as alcohol a criterion for denying employment. I think that reflects a strong sense that the public is not ready to make public-health-oriented kinds of concerns a basis for employers excluding people from the workplace. That's very different from forbidding smoking at the workplace but it deals with whether off-the-job smoking and testing people for off-the-job smoking can be made a criterion for applicant selection. 11

Just one other point about applicant selection. The status that comes into effect July 26 of this year [1992]—the Americans with Disabilities Act—is probably the most sweeping privacy protection (but not called that) that we've had in workplaces in the past several decades. It will require all employers under that statute to define the essential functions of every job and to prove that they have selected people only on the basis of those essential functions. The ADA also forbids the giving of any medical test, unless it is provided for all applicants equally, and that has a very important effect on preventing selective application of medical, or mental tests, as an employer practice. 12

I think the most dramatic issue, looking into the future in terms of selecting applicants, is the potential for genetic screening of job applicants. Recent surveys done by Gallup show that about 75 to 90 percent of the American public oppose employers using genetic screening in order to find 13 out the potential health hazards that job applicants possess. That's a cheery note for me on which to begin the decade, but I think there will be many efforts to portray the use of genetic screening as something that is necessary for employers to control health costs and for employers to have the right information with which to place employees even if they do hire them. I'm not at all confident that that kind of concerted public opinion at the early end of the curve about genetic testing will hold. I think it's going to take a lot of vigilance to make sure that as the Human Genome Project develops,[1] and all the reasons why genetic screening is an important tool for employers, for productivity, etc. are stated, that we hold to that kind of limitation. My own feeling is that this could easily produce a two-class society of people who genetically seem to be mostly healthy and those who would be relegated to substandard employment because they would be seen as being health hazardous or in high-cost types of relationships. I think that we have one major cluster of issues that will deal with applicant selection.

Second is *administering work activity.* Here one of the central issues . . . 14
deals with the new work machine—the video display terminal and related office systems technology. This issue is what is and is not appropriate monitoring of work, especially by clerical workers in data entry, or customer service operators using terminal or telephone. It seems to me that we have a sharp collision of legitimate interests here. Employers need to be sure that their customer service operators are courteous, that they follow proper business rules in handling customers; that they comply with legal rules as to how they treat complaints; and that they provide services where there is regulation, as there are many, many types of telephone transactions. In the old days, where you counted widgets, employers could supervise people physically.

In addition, consumers want to be treated courteously. They do not 15
want to be rudely and improperly treated; therefore, any business that wants to survive in a service-oriented environment is going to have to be very concerned about the quality of service that is delivered through the telecommunications and database-oriented interface with the consumer.

On the other hand, there can be such an oppressive kind of electronic 16
sweatshop monitoring done on video display terminal systems that we have created a highly stressful and intrusive means of employer surveillance. Since we have in the United States an 85 percent nonunion set of workplaces, it's not typical to have a labor-management environment for resolution of this issue. So, it will either have to be a market-based decision on what employees will or will not select as jobs—a very slender reed in an era of heavy unemployment, to add a concern about job security—or we're going to have to have some kind of regulatory or rulemaking process that will deal with those employers who are abusing the capacity to monitor, and make sure those employers use that capacity in an intelligent way. I think we'll be working on that kind of balance throughout the 1990s.

[1]See Chapter 11, pages 589–597, for extended discussion of the Human Genome Project.

A third area that I see is developing is the whole area of *new voice and data communications at work.* E-mail systems pose a fascinating set of problems. This is the system paid for by the employer which is supposed to be used for work and not personal reasons. It is an instrument supplied for accomplishing the work of the employer. On the other hand, it is an instrument that people use for a variety of expressions, not always loyal to the employer, or deferential in the way that they converse about what is going on in the workplace. It's not entirely clear what kind of supervisory role the employer ought to have over E-mail systems. Clearly if crimes are being committed over the E-mail systems—such as distributing drugs—there is a probable cause type reason for the employer on a warrant/limited basis to monitor use of the E-mail system in order to deal with illegal activity. On the other hand, I think that any employer who monitors the content of E-mail in order to find out who is loyal to which faction in the employer management force, or to try to control people's freedom of expression, in the better sense, inside the work relationship is perverting a very important new means of communication. 17

Let me give a second example of the kind of problems that we will be wrestling with. Many of you are familiar with something called call detail accounting—the capacity of the carrier to give the employer a list of every telephone number that is called from an office telephone extension. As a means of controlling improper calls, etc., it is a tool, for example, that MCI has been touting with ads that show an employer looking very accounting-oriented. The big slug says, "We will tell you about every call—every single call made from your premises." Well, that's a very dangerous kind of tool for employers to have, if they can trace every call that every employee makes from the telephones on the premises. European data protection approaches have been, I think, very creative here. They have suggested that we ought to suppress the last four digits of that call detail accounting, so that all you get is the exchange notification, but you do not get the actual called telephone line. There are many ways we can attempt to set the rules by which a technology that provides for cost containment and for analysis of telephone telecommunication use can be properly monitored. 18

Fourth and finally, let me give an example of an emerging application of technology that I think poses some very powerful issues. About two or three dozen companies that I am aware of are building something called health surveillance data banks at the workplace. They put in exposure data as to where employees are working and what chemicals and substances they are exposed to: health utilization data on health benefit programs, worker's compensation, and disability claims by the employee, personnel information on performance appraisals and absenteeism, etc., and finally, epidemiological data about the effect of these substances in medical studies. By putting these components together, they have what is seen as a very important new tool to enhance the health and safety of employees at the workplace. It could be used in very positive ways, to reduce health risks at workplaces that have dangerous substances and processes. On the other hand, it can be a way of pushing out employees who exhibit adverse health 19 effects; it can intrude into many intimate aspects of life, as medical data is collected from medical practitioners, or from employees who are forced to produce the data for the company. And it provides a very attractive database, again, for third-party users in government and elsewhere who will at various times seek access to these medical records for a variety of civil and criminal purposes. So we have an example of a potentially important breakthrough in health protection in the workplace, but one that also poses, classically, many hazards to the balance between private and public.

Let me close this overview by suggesting that we have clearly passed 20
the era in which it is correct or right to say that there is no right to privacy for employees in the workplace. Courts, legislators, and social commentators agree that there must be reasonable expectations of privacy even on the employer's premises, even in the record systems that the employer generates, even when the employer has the responsibility to prevent crime and misconduct in the workplaces. I think that it will be the work of this decade to apply the definition of reasonable expectation of privacy in ways that will allow the new tools of technology to be picked up and enhanced, but without the kind of deep and powerful threats to these emerging employee privacy rights that I think are so central to the way in which we are all going to want to live our lives at work in this century.

▲ ▲ ▲

Review Questions

1. Write a summary of Westin's overview of computers in the workplace. You may find it useful to divide his presentation into its component parts and then to summarize each.
2. What was the "era of employer prerogative in American law and practice"? The "sociomediated concept of employment"?
3. What is a whistleblower, and why does the law protect whistleblowers?
4. What are the reasons employers are returning to practices that potentially threaten the privacy of employees?
5. Why would employers be interested in an employee's genetic information? How does the public view the gathering of genetic information?
6. What are the challenges facing employers and the larger society as we institute the practice of workplace monitoring?

Discussion and Writing Suggestions

1. Closely examine the structure of Westin's presentation. Where does he locate his main idea? How does he support this idea?
2. What does "sociomediated" mean in the context of American employment history? (See paragraph 4.) Demonstrate your understanding of this term by applying it to some other element of American life. That is, what—aside from a phase of American employment history—could be described as sociomediated?

3. The reference to "Panopticon" you will find explained later in this chapter. (See pages 466–74.) Familiarize yourself with Jeremy Bentham's *Panopticon,* as well as with the term "Elysium," and then explain the opposition implied by this selection's title.
4. Do employers have a legitimate right to inquire into the genetic information of their employees? Explain your position.
5. Westin locates current debates in labor-management relations in a larger historical context. Review jobs you have held or now hold. Describe your employer's view of labor-management relations in terms of Westin's two eras and the transformations he sees taking place. How do Westin's historical categories help you to understand your personal employment history?
6. In his first paragraph, Westin claims we live in a time "that is undergoing profound change, conflict of values, and tensions in terms of competing interests. . . ." In such times it is dangerous, says Westin, to implement new technologies. Drawing on personal experience with *any* technology, examine Westin's statement. Does his generalization hold up, given your experience?
7. Should employers have any rights to information about the private lives of employees when they are off the job?

Big Brother or Friendly Coach: Computer Monitoring in the 21st Century

KRISTEN BELL DETIENNE

The "Big Brother" of Kristen Bell DeTienne's title is a reference to Orwell's 1984, *in which a fascist government maintains vigilant surveillance of its citizens through ubiquitous "telescreens": hence, the novel's famous phrase, "Big Brother Is Watching You." DeTienne is clearly aware of the Orwellian potential of electronic monitoring, but she takes a decidedly optimistic stance on the issue and predicts that monitoring in the twenty-first century is likely to be used by employers as a coach. Kristen Bell DeTienne teaches in the Marriott School of Management at Brigham Young University. This article first appeared in* The Futurist *(September–October 1993).*

Picture this as the workplace of the future: A computer tells you if you are making too many typos and suggests that you take a break from typing. Or it tells your boss if you are talking to a customer. Or taking too long a break. Or what you are saying on the phone. Through a computer, your boss can see what you are doing every minute and every second while you are at work. 1

Does this description sound like a portrayal of the far-off future? It isn't. It's today. Currently, as many as 26 million workers in the United States are monitored in their jobs, and this number will increase as computers are used more and more within companies and as the cost of these monitoring systems goes down. By the end of the decade, as many as 30 million people may be constantly monitored in their jobs. But exactly how will these monitoring systems change in the next 20 years, and how will they affect workers? 2

Alan Westin, a professor at Columbia University, believes that monitoring can be done in a humane fashion if employees are guaranteed several rights, including access to all information gathered through monitoring. Furthermore, it can be motivational to give employees personal access to this information. As Michael J. Smith, a professor at the University of Wisconsin-Madison, asserts, "Information given to the supervisor often turns out to be a club, but when it goes directly to the worker, it can become a positive motivator." 3

EVASION-PROOF MONITORING

Computer monitoring in the future will have fewer of the loopholes that today's employees discover and use to circumvent company rules and regulations governing their actions. Systems will become increasingly more complex and be able to prevent much of the evasion and game playing that goes on now. 4

A look at the reservation offices at the major airlines helps to illustrate the meaning of computer loopholes. All of the major airlines have computerized reservation systems, and they use computers to monitor the reservation agents' work. The agents are assigned specific time periods for breaks, and except for these assigned times, the agents are not to leave their seats. 5

To enforce these rules, computers keep track of the agents' actions. However, the computer only keeps a record of the agents' average time between calls and their average time during calls. The agents are allowed a short time between calls to enter information from the call into the computer system The airlines examine the agents' records to make sure the elapsed time between calls is not too large (usually not over a minute). 6

However, some agents have discovered that, if they keep customers on the line while they enter information (thus keeping their time between calls to only one second), they can take an additional five-minute break every two hours. Agents can take this additional break because the computer only keeps track of the average time between calls. More-sophisticated future monitoring systems will keep records of actual times, not just the average time between calls. 7

There will be two main implications of this trend. First, the computers will be able to prevent certain employees from evading the system. As a result, employees who do not take advantage of the system will no longer re- 8 sent the unfair work habits of their co-workers. Second, employees who are accustomed to evading the monitoring system may no longer be able to tolerate it. Unable to use loopholes as a coping mechanism, some employees may suffer from higher levels of stress and fatigue.

SUGGESTIONS FOR IMPROVING PERFORMANCE

Advanced computer systems will be able to make suggestions based on information that the employee enters. Not only will these computers keep closer tabs on employees, but based on this added information, the computer will be able to help employees do their jobs more effectively. 9

Hotel reservation agents, for instance, are required to remember a great deal of information about current joint ventures and promotions. They are trained to know what types of service or package deals should be offered to which customers. Often agents are reminded at the start of each shift about the promotions currently being offered. However, sometimes the agents forget to tell the customers about these programs. 10

In the future, prompts will appear on the computer screen to remind agents of promotions. Let's say that Hotel A is involved in a joint venture with Car Rental Agency B to offer a discount on car rental for customers who stay in Hotel A in either Miami or Houston. If an agent uses the computer to answer a customer's inquiry about reserving a hotel room in Miami or Houston, the computer will remind the employee about the promotion and then provide the details. 11

Overall, the use of prompts will be positive, for employees will not have to worry as much about remembering countless details. Other implications will depend on a particular organization's use of this technology. For example, if the organization uses the prompts to inform employees every time they take too long on a transaction or fall below the group average, there may be more negative outcomes. 12

INFORMATION FOR SELF-EVALUATION

New technology will also give employees access to information about their own performance. Few monitoring systems that are currently operating can do this. In the future, employees will be able to check their own performance and to compare it with that of their co-workers. 13

This knowledge could increase employee performance and efficiency. For example, a study conducted by Christopher Earley in 1988 indicated that computer-based feedback has a greater impact on an employee's performance if he or she receives it directly from the computer system than if it is provided by a supervisor. The largest implication of this trend is positive. Employees will be given access to all information gathered in monitoring. 14

NEW FOCUS ON RESULTS

Monitoring will be seen as part of a more result-oriented focus in companies 15
of the future. Currently, most employees who are monitored are given specific instructions they must follow while doing their jobs. This often leads to a focus on the means rather than the ends. In the future, companies will allow employees more personal freedom in *how* they accomplish their objectives.

An examination of the telemarketing industry provides an illustration 16
of the results-oriented focus. Many telemarketers are given a script that they must follow when selling their product. These scripts have been developed based on the techniques that tend to be the most effective for most telemarketers on most customers. Instead of being required to use scripts and step-by-step instructions, future employees will be given tips on methods that tend to be most effective, trained to use these methods, and then allowed to choose the method that works best for them.

As long as the means are ethical and portray a positive image for the 17
company, performance will be measured by examining the ends. In the future, more organizations will concentrate on the desired results, rather than forcing every employee to use the exact same technique.

The major implication of the growing emphasis on results will be pos- 18
itive. The increased freedom regarding how they do their job will tend to motivate workers. However, a difficulty lies in the supervisor's qualitative evaluation of an employee's work. Most organizations that use computers to count the number of keystrokes or transactions also use "electronic spies" to randomly listen in on calls to make sure that both the quantity and the quality of the work are high. These electronic spies may have personal preferences about techniques that should or should not be used and may be subjective in their qualitative evaluations of employee performance.

COMPUTERS AS COACHES

Information gathered via computer monitoring will increasingly be used to 19
coach employees. Currently, many organizations use the information gathered as a basis for criticism. Companies will begin to realize that it is more motivating for employees to be coached rather than reproached.

Current monitoring systems fail as coaches. For instance, in one case 20
involving a major U.S. airline, reservation agents were monitored electronically to make sure they stayed within the allotted time for restroom breaks. They were permitted a total of 12 minutes for restroom breaks during a seven-and-a-half-hour period. If an agent spent over 12 minutes a day for breaks, it was grounds for a disciplinary warning.

One employee was threatened with firing because she spent 13 minutes 21
over her allotted time. This employee said that her supervisor "told me that while I was in the bathroom my co-workers were taking extra calls to make up for my 'abusive' work habits."

After this incident, the reservation agent suffered a nervous breakdown, which she blamed on "bathroom break harassment." A manager at the airline argued that the supervisors were "not spying on workers but trying to enhance their competitive position." 22

In the future, companies that use monitoring will recognize the need to be more sensitive to the messages they send to their employees. If companies are too harsh, they will lose in the long run due to increased turnover, absenteeism, medical costs, and worker's compensation claims. Supervisors will have to work as coaches rather than critics whenever possible, and employees should receive helpful feedback on their performance. 23

The implication of this trend is positive in that it overcomes two of the biggest complaints about the current use of monitoring: (1) that the results are used only for work speedups, and (2) that too much emphasis is placed on the quantity of work rather than the quality. If supervisors primarily use coaching information to motivate employees, both the company and the workers will benefit. 24

• • •

REGULATING COMPUTER MONITORING

There will be increased attempts to pass legislation that regulates employee monitoring via computers. As long as companies use technology to monitor human work, some humans will react negatively to the procedure and demand protection through legislation. The issues will focus on management's desire to know "who is doing what" in the office and an employee's right to privacy and human dignity. 25

Recently, several attempts have been made to pass legislation that limits the use of monitoring. If it is legal for companies to use insensitive or unfair monitoring practices, companies that do will be less profitable because of an increase in turnover, absenteeism, stress-related illnesses, and so on. On the other hand, if companies are legally restricted in their use of technological methods for evaluating performance, many will achieve the same ends through the use of regular human supervision. 26

Both positive and negative implications can arise from increased legislation. On the positive side, such regulation may ensure the humane treatment of all employees, regardless of the organization for which they work. Legislation may protect many employees' right to privacy, which may otherwise be neglected. On the negative side, some legislation could make it difficult for companies to compensate employees in a fair and equitable manner. Also, legislation could unfairly restrain some organizations that need information gathered by monitoring to remain competitive in the global market. 27

In the future, the most successful companies will be those that treat their employees equitably and respectfully. As John Sculley, the chairman 28 of Apple Computer, has noted, "Instead of emulating the autocratic, invincible models of the past, successful managers must lead by inspiring individuals." Although risks of abuse are real, computer monitoring can indeed inspire some employees to achieve excellence.

▲ ▲ ▲

Review Questions

1. How can computer monitoring free employees from cumbersome tasks?
2. How can computer monitoring help to shift the focus of employee evaluation from "means" to "ends," and why is this a hopeful development?
3. In what ways could computer monitors be used as coaches?
4. What are the advantages and disadvantages of legislation written to protect the privacy rights of employees?

Discussion and Writing Suggestions

1. For the most part, DeTienne writes in the future tense, appropriately enough for an article appearing in *The Futurist.* The operative auxiliary verb in this article is "will"—as in "Information gathered via computer monitoring will increasingly be used to coach employees." On the basis of what evidence, authority, and logic does DeTienne make predictions about the future of workplace monitoring? Do these predictions persuade you?
2. To what extent do you think DeTienne leans toward the interests of workers in this article? To what extent toward the interests of management? Cite passage from the article to support your answer.
3. As an example of goldbricking employees (those who circumvent company rules in order to avoid work), DeTienne cites airline ticketing agents who keep customers on the line while entering information into the computer—thereby earning an extra five-minute break every second hour. What is your response to this rule-breaking? What is your response to the prospect of ever-more savvy computers that will be able to identify such goldbrickers to management?
4. In paragraph 8, DeTienne writes that one consequence of more vigilant computers in the workplace will be that "employees who are accustomed to evading the monitoring system may no longer be able to tolerate it. Unable to use loopholes as a coping mechanism, some employees may suffer from higher levels of stress and fatigue." What assumptions does DeTienne make here concerning the reasons employees might find computer monitoring stressful? Can you think of a competing assumption? (To get an airline reservation agent's view of computer monitoring, see Harriet Ternipsede's testimony before a 1991 House Subcommittee on Labor-Management Relations, pages 446–48.)

5. Given the articles you've read in this chapter, to what extent do you share DeTienne's belief that electronic monitors of the future will be used as productive coaches, rather than as electronic taskmasters? Explain.
6. In paragraphs 23, 24, 26, and 28, DeTienne argues that companies will come to use electronic monitoring positively, to encourage employees, for to do otherwise would result in high levels of "turnover, absenteeism, [and] stress-related illnesses" (paragraph 26). In other words, since these problems would have a negative impact on business, businesses will use electronic monitoring responsibly. Write a one-paragraph critique of this logic.

Panopticon

JEREMY BENTHAM

Jeremy Bentham (1748–1832) was an English philosopher best known as the founder of Utilitarianism, an ethical doctrine by which individuals and institutions (e.g., legislatures and courts) can guide their actions in ways that maximize happiness for the greatest number of people. Trained as a lawyer (though he never practiced law), Bentham used utilitarian principles to bring order to chaotic systems of jurisprudence and social welfare. He and his followers sponsored initiatives for the relief of the poor, for insurance reform, and for health care; Bentham also wrote a series of Codes of Law that were adopted by countries in Europe and several states in the newly formed United States.

"Panopticon; or, The Inspection-House" was Bentham's attempt in 1787 to design an orderly system, literally a building, for keeping prisoners, workers, and others under surveillance. In the excerpt that follows, he describes a circular building that allows a centrally located inspector to observe prisoners without being observed. He focused on the design of a prison with the reasoning that if he could satisfy the extreme security demands of that structure, less demanding applications to "manufactories," schools, and hospitals could easily be designed as subsets of the more comprehensive plan. Bentham's system may strike you as severe, even inhumane; but realize that he was addressing a social necessity of his time and ours: institutions exist—prisons, workplaces, hospitals, schools—in which people must be watched or supervised. In "Panopticon," Bentham was suggesting a method of surveillance consistent with the utilitarian principle of the "greatest happiness of the greatest number." The Utilitarians, in fact, were responsible for initiating humane reforms of British prisons.

"Panopticon" originated as a series of letters from Bentham (then visiting Russia) to a correspondent in England. Bentham's brother was evidently responsible for early designs; Bentham related these to his correspondent, and then elaborated. We begin with the title page, which

clearly summarizes Bentham's intent. (A "lazaretto," by the way, is a hospital for the treatment of contagious diseases.) A final note on Bentham's language: his sentences are long, the vocabulary sometimes obscure. However, your patience in rereading sentences you may not initially understand (and your frequent use of a dictionary) will be rewarded. Bentham's plans for the surveillance of "subordinates" sets the debate of this chapter in a clear historical context. Well before the advent of computers, before the use of electricity, people in power had a security, economic, and educational interest in monitoring employees and others. Our world is recognizable in Bentham's: Though technologies have changed, the need for some form of surveillance persists—as do the debates sparked by this need.

PANOPTICON;

OR,

THE INSPECTION-HOUSE:

CONTAINING THE

IDEA OF A NEW PRINCIPLE OF CONSTRUCTION

APPLICABLE TO

ANY SORT OF ESTABLISHMENT, IN WHICH PERSONS OF ANY DESCRIPTION ARE TO BE KEPT UNDER INSPECTION;

AND IN PARTICULAR TO

PENITENTIARY-HOUSES,

PRISONS, HOUSES OF INDUSTRY, WORK-HOUSES, POOR-HOUSES, MANUFACTORIES, MAD-HOUSES, LAZARETTOS, HOSPITALS, AND SCHOOLS:

WITH

A PLAN OF MANAGEMENT

ADAPTED TO THE PRINCIPLE:

IN A SERIES OF LETTERS,

WRITTEN IN THE YEAR 1787, FROM CRECHEFF IN WHITE RUSSIA, TO A FRIEND IN ENGLAND.

BY JEREMY BENTHAM,

OF LINCOLN'S INN, ESQUIRE.

DUBLIN, PRINTED: LONDON, REPRINTED; AND SOLD BY T. PAYNE,
AT THE MEWS GATE, 1791.

LETTER I.

IDEA OF THE INSPECTION PRINCIPLE.

Crecheff in White Russia, 1787.

DEAR****,—I observed t'other day in one of your English papers, an advertisement relative to a HOUSE of CORRECTION therein spoken of, as intended for *******. It occurred to me, that the plan of a building, lately contrived by my brother, for purposes in some respects similar, and which, under the name of the *Inspection House,* or the *Elaboratory,* he is about erecting here, might afford some hints for the above establishment. I have accordingly obtained some drawings relative to it, which I here inclose. Indeed I look upon it as capable of applications of the most extensive nature; and that for reasons which you will soon perceive. 1

To say all in one word, it will be found applicable, I think, without exception, to all establishments whatsoever, in which, within a space not too large to be covered or commanded by buildings, a number of persons are meant to be kept under inspection. No matter how different, or even opposite the purpose: whether it be that of *punishing the incorrigible, guarding the insane, reforming the vicious, confining the suspected, employing the idle, maintaining the helpless, curing the sick, instructing the willing* in any branch of industry, or *training the rising race* in the path of *education:* in a word, whether it be applied to the purposes of *perpetual prisons* in the room of death, or *prisons for confinement* before trial, or *penitentiary-houses,* or *houses of correction,* or *work-houses,* or *manufactories,* or *mad-houses,* or *hospitals,* or *schools.* 2

It is obvious that, in all these instances, the more constantly the persons to be inspected are under the eyes of the persons who should inspect them, the more perfectly will the purpose of the establishment have been attained. Ideal perfection, if that were the object, would require that each person should actually be in that predicament, during every instant of time. This being impossible, the next thing to be wished for is, that, at every instant, seeing reason to believe as much, and not being able to satisfy himself to the contrary, he should *conceive* himself to be so. This point, you will immediately see, is most completely secured by my brother's plan; and, I think, it will appear equally manifest, that it cannot be compassed by any other, or to speak more properly, that if it be compassed by any other, it can only be in proportion as such other may approach to this. 3

To cut the matter as short as possible, I will consider it at once in its application to such purposes as, being most complicated, will serve to exemplify the greatest force and variety of precautionary contrivance. Such 4 are those which have suggested the idea of *penitentiary-houses:* in which the objects of *safe custody, confinement, solitude, forced labour,* and *instruction,* were all of them to be kept in view. If all these objects can be accomplished together, of course with at least equal certainty and facility may any lesser number of them.

LETTER II.

PLAN FOR A PENITENTIARY INSPECTION-HOUSE.

BEFORE you look at the plan, take in words the general idea of it. 5

The building is circular. 6

The apartments of the prisoners occupy the circumference. You may 7
call them, if you please, the *cells.*

These *cells* are divided from one another, and the prisoners by that 8
means secluded from all communication with each other, by *partitions* in
the form of *radii* issuing from the circumference towards the centre, and
extending as many feet as shall be thought necessary to form the largest dimension of the cell.

The apartment of the inspector occupies the centre; you may call it if 9
you please the *inspector's lodge.*

It will be convenient in most, if not in all cases, to have a vacant space 10
or *area* all round, between such centre and such circumference. You may
call it if you please the *intermediate* or *annular* area.

About the width of a cell may be sufficient for a *passage* from the out- 11
side of the building to the lodge.

Each cell has in the outward circumference, a *window,* large enough, 12
not only to light the cell, but, through the cell, to afford light enough to the
correspondent part of the lodge.

The inner circumference of the cell is formed by an iron *grating,* so 13
light as not to screen any part of the cell from the inspector's view.

Of this grating, a part sufficiently large opens, in form of a *door,* to ad- 14
mit the prisoner at his first entrance; and to give admission at any time to
the inspector or any of his attendants.

To cut off from each prisoner the view of every other, the partitions are 15
carried on a few feet beyond the grating into the intermediate area: such
projecting parts I call the *protracted partitions.*

It is conceived, that the light, coming in in this manner through the cells, 16
and so across the intermediate area, will be sufficient for the inspector's
lodge. But, for this purpose, both the windows in the cells, and those corresponding to them in the lodge, should be as large as the strength of the building, and what shall be deemed a necessary attention to economy, will permit.

To the windows of the lodge there are *blinds,* as high up as the eyes of 17
the prisoners in their cells can, by any means they can employ, be made to
reach.

To prevent *thorough light,* whereby, notwithstanding the blinds, the 18
prisoners would see from the cells whether or no any person was in the
lodge, that apartment is divided into quarters, by *partitions* formed by two

diameters to the circle, crossing each other at right angles. For these partitions the thinnest materials might serve; and they might be made removeable at pleasure; their height, sufficient to prevent the prisoners seeing over them from the cells. Doors to these partitions, if left open at any time, might produce the thorough light. To prevent this, divide each partition into two, at any part required, setting down the one-half at such distance from the other as shall be equal to the aperture of a door.

These windows of the inspector's lodge open into the intermediate 19
area, in the form of *doors,* in as many places as shall be deemed necessary to admit of his communicating readily with any of the cells.

Small *lamps,* in the outside of each window of the lodge, backed by a 20
reflector, to throw the light into the corresponding cells, would extend to the night the security of the day.

To save the troublesome exertion of voice that might otherwise be nec- 21
essary, and to prevent one prisoner from knowing that the inspector was occupied by another prisoner at a distance, a small *tin tube* might reach from each cell to the inspector's lodge, passing across the area, and so in at the side of the correspondent window of the lodge. By means of this implement, the slightest whisper of the one might be heard by the other, especially if he had proper notice to apply his ear to the tube.

With regard to *instruction,* in cases where it cannot be duly given with- 22
out the instructor's being close to the work, or without setting his hand to it by way of example before the learner's face, the instructor must indeed here as elsewhere, shift his station as often as there is occasion to visit different workmen; unless he calls the workmen to him, which in some of the instances to which this sort of building is applicable, such as that of imprisoned felons, could not so well be. But in all cases where directions, given verbally and at a distance, are sufficient, these tubes will be found of use. They will save, on the one hand, the exertion of voice it would require, on the part of the instructor, to communicate instruction to the workmen without quitting his central station in the lodge; and, on the other, the confusion which would ensue if different instructors or persons in the lodge were calling to the cells at the same time. And, in the case of hospitals, the quiet that may be insured by this little contrivance, trifling as it may seem at first sight, affords an additional advantage.

A *bell,* appropriated exclusively to the purposes of *alarm,* hangs in a 23
belfry with which the building is crowned, communicating by a rope with the inspector's lodge.

The most economical, and perhaps the most convenient, way of *warm-* 24
ing the cells and area, would be by flues surrounding it, upon the principle of those in hot-houses. A total want of every means of producing artificial heat might, in such weather as we sometimes have in England, be fatal to the lives of the prisoners; at any rate, it would often times be altogether incompatible with their working at any sedentary employment. The flues, however, and the fire-places belonging to them, instead of being on the outside, as in hot-houses, should be in the inside. By this means, there would be less waste of heat, and the current of air that would rush in on all sides

through the cells, to supply the draught made by the fires, would answer so far the purpose of ventilation. But of this more under the head of Hospitals.

• • •

[*In letters III and IV, Bentham details the construction of the Inspection House.*]

LETTER V.

ESSENTIAL POINTS OF THE PLAN.

IT may be of use, that among all the particulars you have seen, it should be 25
clearly understood what circumstances are, and what are not, essential to the plan. The essence of it consists, then, in the *centrality* of the inspector's situation, combined with the well-known and most effectual contrivances for *seeing without being seen.* As to the *general form* of the building, the most commodious for most purposes seems to be the circular: but this is not an absolutely essential circumstance. Of all figures, however, this, you will observe, is the only one that affords a perfect view, and the same view, of an indefinite number of apartments of the same dimensions: that affords a spot from which, without any change of situation, a man may survey, in the same perfection, the whole number, and without so much as a change of posture, the half of the whole number, at the same time: that, within a boundary of a given extent, contains the greatest quantity of room:—that places the centre at the least distance from the light:—that gives the cells most width, at the part where, on account of the light, most light may, for the purposes of work, be wanted:—and that reduces to the greatest possible shortness the path taken by the inspector, in passing from each part of the field of inspection to every other.

You will please to observe, that though perhaps it is the most important 26
point, that the persons to be inspected should always feel themselves as if under inspection, at least as standing a great chance of being so, yet it is not by any means the *only* one. If it were, the same advantage might be given to buildings of almost any form. What is also of importance is, that for the greatest proportion of time possible, each man should actually *be* under inspection. This is material in *all* cases, that the inspector may have the satisfaction of knowing, that the discipline actually has the effect which it is designed to have: and it is more particularly material in such cases where the inspector, besides seeing that they conform to such standing rules as are prescribed, has more or less frequent occasion to give them such transient and incidental directions as will require to be given and enforced, at the commencement at least of every course of industry. And I think, it needs not much argument to prove, that the business of inspection, like every other, will be performed to a greater degree of perfection, the less trouble the performance of it requires.

Not only so, but the greater chance there is, of a given person's being 27
at a given time actually under inspection, the more strong will be the persuasion—the more *intense,* if I may say so, the *feeling,* he has of his being

so. How little turn soever the greater number of persons so circumstanced may be supposed to have for calculation, some rough sort of calculation can scarcely, under such circumstances, avoid forcing itself upon the rudest mind. Experiment, venturing first upon slight trangressions, and so on, in proportion to success, upon more and more considerable ones, will not fail to teach him the difference between a loose inspection and a strict one.

It is for these reasons, that I cannot help looking upon every form as less and less eligible, in proportion as it deviates from the *circular.* 28

A very material point is, that room be alloted to the lodge, sufficient to adapt it to the purpose of a complete and constant habitation for the principal inspector or headkeeper, and his family. The more numerous also the family, the better; since, by this means, there will in fact be as many inspectors, as the family consists of persons, though only one be paid for it. Neither the orders of the inspector himself, nor any interest which they may feel, or not feel, in the regular performance of his duty, would be requisite to find them motives adequate to the purpose. Secluded oftentimes, by their situation, from every other object, they will naturally, and in a manner unavoidably, give their eyes a direction conformable to that purpose, in every momentary interval of their ordinary occupations. It will supply in their instance the place of that great and constant fund of entertainment to the sedentary and vacant in towns—the looking out of the window. The scene, though confined, would be a very various, and therefore, perhaps, not altogether an unamusing one. 29

LETTER VI.

ADVANTAGES OF THE PLAN.

I FLATTER myself there can now be little doubt of the plan's possessing the fundamental advantages I have been attributing to it: I mean, the *apparent omnipresence* of the inspector (if divines will allow me the expression) combined with the extreme facility of his *real presence.* 30

A collateral advantage it possesses, and on the score of frugality a very material one, is that which respects the *number* of the inspectors requisite. If this plan required more than another, the additional number would form an objection, which, were the difference to a certain degree considerable, might rise so high as to be conclusive: so far from it, that a greater multitude than ever were yet lodged in one house might be inspected by a single person; for the trouble of inspection is diminished in no less proportion than the strictness of inspection is increased. 31

Another very important advantage, whatever purposes the plan may be applied to, particularly where it is applied to the severest and most coercive purposes, is, that the *under* keepers or inspectors, the servants and subordinates of every kind, will be under the same irresistable controul with respect to the *head* keeper or inspector, as the prisoners or other persons to be governed are with respect to *them.* On the common plans, what means, what possibility, has the prisoner, of appealing to the humanity of the principal for redress against the neglect or oppression of subordinates in that 32 rigid sphere, but the *few* opportunities which, in a crowded prison, the most conscientious keeper *can* afford—but the none at all which many a keeper *thinks* fit to give them? How different would their lot be upon this plan!

In no instance could his subordinates either perform or depart from 33
their duty, but he must know the time and degree and manner of their doing so. It presents an answer, and that a satisfactory one, to one of the most puzzling of political questions—*quis custodiet ipsos custodes?*[1] And, as the fulfilling of his, as well as their, duty would be rendered so much easier, than it can ever have been hitherto, so might, and so should, any departure from it be punished with the more inflexible severity. It is this circumstance that renders the influence of this plan not less beneficial to what is called *liberty,* than to necessary coercion; not less powerful as a controul upon subordinate power, than as a curb to delinquency; as a shield to innocence, than as a scourge to guilt.

Discussion and Writing Suggestions

1. Bentham articulates the central aim of "Panopticon" in Letter I, paragraph 3:

   > Ideal perfection, if that were the object, would require that each person should actually be [under the eyes of the persons who should inspect them], during every instant of time. This being impossible, the next thing to be wished for is, that, at every instant, . . . he should *conceive* himself to be [under the eyes of the inspector].

   In Letter V, paragraph 25, Bentham presents the first "essential" point of the plan:

   > The essence of [the plan] consists . . . in the *centrality* of the inspector's situation, combined with the well-known and most effectual contrivances for *seeing without being seen.*

   Describe your responses to Bentham's plan for creating a more perfect system of surveillance. If possible, separate your responses into two categories: (1) responses to the plan *as a plan*—is it practical, thorough, efficient? and (2) personal, even visceral, responses to the plan.
2. In the title of the talk that he gave at the second conference on Computers, Freedom, and Privacy, Alan Westin opposes Paradise (or "Elysium") with Panopticon. The full title: "Computers in the Workplace: Elysium or Panopticon?" Now that you've read portions of Bentham's work, explain why Westin would want to use it to set an opposite pole to Elysium in the debate over workplace surveillance.
3. In the preface to "Panopticon," Bentham writes that had he a view of the whole while he worked on the project, he would have adver-

[1]Latin: "Who will guard the guards themselves?"

tised it as follows: "Morals reformed—health preserved—industry invigorated—instruction diffused—Economy seated, as it were, upon a rock . . . all by the simple idea of Architecture!" Having read portions of "Panopticon," would you say that these claims represent truth in advertising?

4. To what extent do the modern technologies of surveillance described in this chapter (and in Chapter 3, pages 69–78) reproduce the effects that Bentham is imagining for the Panopticon?
5. Bentham claims that one system of architecture will satisfy the surveillance needs of multiple institutions; including prisons, places of employment, poor houses, hospitals, insane asylums, and schools. Do you agree that each of these settings requires the same basic system of close surveillance or inspection? Does a change in institutional setting (say, from prison to hospital to school) warrant a change not only in the *type* but also in the degree of surveillance maintained?
6. Is surveillance appropriate in all institutional settings? For instance, would you want to claim that employees—or students!—should not be under the scrutinizing eye of a superior? Explain your position.
7. Why, in Bentham's words (from Letter VI, paragraph 30) is it so important to the plan that those being observed feel "the *apparent omnipresence* of the inspector"? What is the psychological importance of "apparent omnipresence"? How like, or unlike, is this feature of the Panopticon to methods of electronic surveillance in the modern workplace?
8. Letter VI ends with a laying out of balances between the necessary and appropriate use of power and the abuse of power. Bentham balances liberty with coercion; control of subordinate power with control of delinquency; protection of innocence with the condemnation of guilt. In what ways is Bentham articulating here the core debates over surveillance in the modern workplace?
9. In Bentham's system, the head inspector guards subordinate inspectors (middle management, as it were). See Letter VI. Who guards the head inspector?

▼

SYNTHESIS ACTIVITIES

1. One of the clear themes to emerge in the debates over electronic monitoring is the balance that must be struck between the privacy rights of individuals and the security rights of the state and of employers. Write an explanatory essay in which you draw on the selections in this chapter to explain the competing interests in the debates over electronic intrusions into people's lives. Such an essay would clearly distinguish between the legitimate interests of individuals and of governments (or employers).

2. In a more ambitious version of essay 1, explain the fundamental issues of the debate *and* argue for or against this proposition: in certain circumstances the state's or an employer's need to know information about an individual outweighs the individual's right to privacy. You define the circumstances. They might involve issues of health (AIDS, tuberculosis, ebola); sexual offenses; politics; or criminal investigations. Be specific. Ground your discussion in one or more cases—perhaps the Ternipsede case. A variant on this assignment: Assume you are a labor-management consultant called in to find some mutually acceptable position on surveillance in the workplace. Present a particular case (perhaps Ternipsede's) and develop an analysis of the opposing positions. Propose and defend a solution.
3. Neither government nor business has a successful record of correcting flawed data. Who should take the responsibility of correcting misinformation about you that exists in one or more electronic databases? (See Glastonbury, paragraphs 15–19.) In a synthesis drawing on several sources in this chapter, develop a clear policy that you would enforce, if you could, that would help individuals track down and correct flawed data. As part of your policy, you would want to address the ease with which individuals could identify all computers that hold files on them.
4. In Chapter 3, *"Critical Reading and Critique,"* pages 69–78, you will find Charles Ostman's article from *Mondo 2000,* "Total Surveillance." In that piece, Ostman writes: "Personal privacy was once considered the most sacred of our constitutional rights; agencies were severely limited by law. All that's about to change drastically, thanks to a deadly combination of extremely sophisticated surveillance technology, ubiquitous digital information collection, and centralized interagency data exchange" (paragraph 2). Ostman and others suggest that our technological ability to collect and merge information into dossiers on private citizens is tantamount to its happening—that technology, in effect, is destiny. In an essay drawing on the selections in this chapter, argue for or against the validity of the assumption that "since we *can* do it, we *will* do it." You will want to address these general questions: If we concede that total surveillance is, or will soon be, possible, must we also concede that it is inevitable: that the array of technologies described in Ostman's and Whalen's articles will be used to construct electronic dossiers on all Americans—or on a significant subset of Americans? What role does human decision-making play in a government's or corporation's use of modern technology?
5. As Anne Branscomb makes clear, our laws are created by people who exist in a social, political, and economic setting. The legal process is essentially conservative, and legislators usually make laws in *response to* (not in advance of) conflicts. In a synthesis that draws on the selections in this chapter (particularly on Branscomb and Westin), argue that we exist at a moment in the evolution of surveil-

lance and computer technology that demands a legislative response. A more ambitious essay will not only argue that new laws are necessary to govern increasingly abusive intrusions into personal privacy, but will suggest specific laws to safeguard specific privacy rights.

6. You have undoubtedly benefitted personally from the development of information technologies—for instance, if you have ever made an airline or hotel reservation; shopped by phone; used a credit card; used an automatic teller; or used a calling card to make a long-distance call. The same technology that makes your personal life more convenient and your business transactions more efficient is the technology that, according to several authors in this chapter, threatens your privacy. How threatened, in fact, do you feel? Given what you've read in this chapter, if you don't perceive a threat to your privacy, is that the same as believing that you are *not* threatened? In a synthesis that draws on selections in this chapter and on your personal experience, account for the gap between your welcomed acceptance of hi-tech's conveniences on the one hand and hi-tech's pervasive threats to privacy on the other.
7. In 1991, Harriet Ternipsede, an airline reservation agent at TWA, argued before a Congressional subcommittee that electronic monitoring had turned her workplace into a "sweatshop," which led to her stress-related illness and a loss of dignity. Are physical, emotional, and ethical problems the inevitable results of a Panopticon-like culture in which employees are monitored continually—or at least "always feel themselves as if under inspection" (Bentham, V, paragraph 26)? Answer this question in an argument synthesis that draws on Bentham's "Panopticon" and other selections in this chapter.
8. Consider the titles of two selections in this chapter: "Computers in the Workplace: Elysium or Panopticon?" and "Big Brother or Friendly Coach: Computer Monitoring in the 21st Century." Both titles create a debate, an opposition between two possible outcomes of increased surveillance in the workplace. Indeed, this opposition can be found in all the selections in this chapter. As the electronic monitoring of employees becomes commonplace, what is the likelihood that we'll see one or the other of these predicted outcomes in its pure form? Write a synthesis that makes a predictive argument about the ways in which electronic monitoring will be used—and to what effect—in the workplace of the year 2020, your mid-career working environment. The logic of your predictions must be clear. It will not do to claim that something will happen merely because you think it will. In the essay, provide a complete rationale for your predictions; use the sources in this chapter in ways that support your predictions. You can write the essay from the present moment, in which case you will rely heavily on the auxiliary verb "will"; you can also write assuming the perspective of a worker (or manager) in 2020.

9. Insurance companies claim that they need to know the risks you pose before agreeing to insure you; thus, companies will seek data about you: about your health, your financial dealings, your driving record, and more. In your view, are insurance companies entitled to information about you? Does the (electronic) manner in which they collect information play any part in your response? Answer these questions in an argument synthesis that draws on several selections in this chapter.
10. Bryan Glastonbury writes: "It is certainly true that many of the valued services that we receive depend upon the systematic and orderly collection of data about us." Write an explanatory synthesis in which you identify one such service that is so dependent, and discuss the ways in which delivery of this service is improved because of modern techniques of data collection.

▼

RESEARCH ACTIVITIES

1. In 1994 and 1995, some in Congress called for a National Identity or Employment card to combat the problem of illegal immigration. Research and report on the debate over this initiative, making sure to identify the key positions of proponents and opponents. Discuss the ways in which the issues you've read about in this chapter, concerning encroachments on individual privacy, are at issue in the debate over identity cards.
2. What is the "Clipper" Chip, and why did its introduction cause such a furor? More generally, research the security of data transmitted over phone lines. Who wants access to this data—for what reasons? Who wants to control access? Why? In investigating encryption problems, you might consult the work of encryption expert Dorothy Denning. With regard to the Clipper Chip, you should be able to locate a great deal of Congressional testimony, given during the summer of 1994.
3. Research the legal history of privacy rights in the United States. A good place to begin your search would be with the excellent overview in *CQ Researcher,* November 19, 1993. You will want to consult primary documents, especially the Warren and Brandeis paper in the *Harvard Law Review* (December 15, 1890) and Justice Brandeis's dissenting opinion in the *Olmstead v. United States* wiretapping case (1928). You'll want to familiarize yourself with more recent documents: the Omnibus Crime Bill (1968), which requires law enforcement agents to secure warrants before tapping phones; the Electronic Communications Privacy Act (1986); and the Employee Polygraph Protection Act (1988). Finally, you might benefit from a visit to a law school library, where you will find books devoted to the issue of privacy. Two especially good ones are *Law of Privacy Rights in a Technological Society* (1986), edited by Irving J. Sloan;

and *Private Rights, Public Wrongs: The Computer and Personal Privacy* (1988), by Michael Rogers Rubin.

4. Read several dystopian novels and view several dystopian movies in an effort to gain insight into the ways creators of dark, futuristic worlds imagine the interplay of technology and individual privacy. Possible novels: *Frankenstein; or The Modern Prometheus* (Mary Shelley, 1818), *Brave New World* (Aldous Huxley, 1932), *1984* (George Orwell, 1949), *Do Androids Dream of Electric Sheep?* (Philip K. Dick, 1968), and *Neuromancer* (William Gibson, 1984). Possible movies: *Metropolis* (Fritz Lang, 1926), *Frankenstein* (James Whale, 1931; Kenneth Branagh, 1995), *Fahrenheit 451* (François Truffaut, 1966); *Blade Runner* (Ridley Scott, 1982), *1984* (Michael Radford, 1984), and *Robocop* (Paul Verhoeven, 1987).
5. Locate a copy of the proceedings of the First (1991) or Second (1992) *Conference on Computers, Freedom and Privacy.* In these books you will find a wide range of "sessions"—transcripts of papers presented and follow-up discussions—on topics relating to privacy in the computer age. A sampling of session titles: "The Constitution in the Information Age"; "NetWork Environments of the Future"; "Security Capabilities, Privacy, and Integrity"; "Who's in Your Genes?"; "Free Speech and the Telephone Network." Each session consists of three or four papers, and so provides an excellent way to orient yourself to key issues in a particular debate. Use these sessions as jumping-off points in your research of a particular topic relating to privacy and technology.
6. Research the changing legal status of information in our society. Begin by consulting *Who Owns Information? From Privacy to Public Access* (1994), by Anne Wells Branscomb, author of one selection in this chapter. In her book, Branscomb studies changing patterns of information use, along with the legal implications of these changes. She organizes her study around nine questions: Who Owns Your Name and Address, Your Telephone Number, Your Medical History, Your Image, Your Electronic Messages, Video Entertainment, Religious Information, Computer Software, Government Information? Each of these discussions will provide an excellent starting point for your own research.

10
Fairy Tales: A Closer Look at "Cinderella"

"Once upon a time. . . ." Millions of children around the world have listened to these (or similar) words. And, once upon a time, such words were magic archways into a world of entertainment and fantasy for children and their parents. But in our own century, fairy tales have come under the scrutiny of anthropologists, linguists, educators, psychologists, and psychiatrists, as well as literary critics, who have come to see them as a kind of social genetic code—a means by which cultural values are transmitted from one generation to the next. Some people, of course, may scoff at the idea that charming tales like "Cinderella" or "Snow White" are anything other than charming tales, at the idea that fairy tales may really be ways of inculcating young and impressionable children with culturally approved values. But even if they are not aware of it, adults and children use fairy tales in complex and subtle ways. We can, perhaps, best illustrate this by examining variants of a single tale—"Cinderella."

"Cinderella" appears to be the best-known fairy tale in the world. In 1892, Marian Roalfe Cox published 345 variants of the story, the first systematic study of a single folktale. In her collection, Cox gathered stories from throughout Europe in which elements or motifs of "Cinderella" appeared, often mixed with motifs of other tales. All told, more than 700 variants exist throughout the world—in Europe, Africa, Asia, and North and South America. Scholars debate the extent to which such a wide distribution is explained by population migrations or by some universal quality of imagination that would allow people at different times and places to create essentially the same story. But for whatever reason, folklorists agree that "Cinderella" has appealed to storytellers and listeners everywhere.

The great body of folk literature, including fairy tales, comes to us from an oral tradition. Written literature, produced by a particular author, is preserved through the generations just as the author recorded it. By contrast, oral literature changes with every telling: The childhood game comes to mind in which one child whispers a sentence into the ear of another; by the time the second child repeats the sentence to a third, and the third to a fourth (and so on), the sentence has changed considerably. And so it is with oral literature, with the qualification that these stories are also changed quite consciously when a teller wishes to add or delete material.

The modern student of folk literature finds her- or himself in the position of *reading* as opposed to hearing a tale. The texts we read tend to be of two types, which are at times difficult to distinguish. We might read a faithful transcription of an oral tale or a tale of *literary* origin—a tale that was originally written (as a short story would be), not spoken, but that nonetheless may contain elements of an oral account. In this chapter, we include tales of both oral and literary origin. Jakob and Wilhelm Grimm published their transcription of "Cinderella" in 1812. The version by Charles Perrault (1697) is difficult to classify as the transcription of an oral source, since he may have heard the story originally but appears (according to Bruno Bettelheim) to have "freed it of all content he considered vulgar, and refined its other features to make the product suitable to be told at court." Of unquestionable literary origin are the Walt Disney version of the story, based on Perrault's text; Anne Sexton's poem; Tanith Lee's "When the Clock Strikes," a version in which the Cinderella figure is a witch bent on avenging the murder of her royal family; and James Finn Garner's "Politically Correct 'Cinderella.'" We include, as well, three transcriptions from oral sources: a Chinese version of the tale; an African version, originally told in the Hausa language; and an Algonquin (Native American) version.

Preceding these nine variants of "Cinderella," we present a general reading on fairy-tale literature by Stith Thompson. Following the variants are three selections that respond directly to the tale. We hear from Bruno Bettelheim, who, following psychoanalytic theory, finds in "Cinderella" a "Story of Sibling Rivalry and Oedipal Conflicts." Madonna Kolbenschlag then offers a feminist reading of the tale, followed by Jane Yolen's lament on the "gutting" of a story that once was richly magical and instructive.

A note on terminology: "Cinderella," "Jack and the Beanstalk," "Little Red Riding Hood," and the like are commonly referred to as fairy tales, although, strictly speaking, they are not. True fairy tales concern a "class of supernatural beings of diminutive size, who in popular belief are said to possess magical powers and to have great influence for good or evil over the affairs of humans" *(Oxford English Dictionary).* "Cinderella" and the others just mentioned concern no beings of diminutive size, although extraordinary, magical events do occur in the story. Folklorists would be more apt to call these stories "wonder tales." We retain the traditional "fairy tale," with the proviso that in popular usage the term is misapplied. You may notice that the authors in this chapter use the terms "folktale" and "fairy tale" interchangeably. The expression "folktale" refers to *any* story conceived orally and passed on in an oral tradition. Thus, "folktale" is a generic term that incorporates both fairy tales and wonder tales.

Universality of the Folktale

STITH THOMPSON

Folklorists travel around the world, to cities and rural areas alike, recording the facts, traditions, and beliefs that characterize ethnic groups. Some folklorists record and compile jokes; others do the same with insults or songs. Still others, like Stith Thompson, devote their professional careers to studying tales. And, as it turns out, there are many aspects of stories and storytelling worth examining. Among them: the art of narrative—how tellers captivate their audiences; the social and religious significance of tale telling; the many types of tales that are told; the many variants, worldwide, of single tales (like "Cinderella"). In a preface to one of his own books, Thompson raises the broad questions and the underlying assumptions that govern the folklorist's study of tales. We begin this chapter with Thompson's overview to set a context for the variants of "Cinderella" that you will read.

Note the ways that Thompson's approach to fairy tales differs from yours. Whether or not you're conscious of having an approach, you do have one: Perhaps you regard stories like "Cinderella" as entertainment. Fine—this is a legitimate point of view, but it's only one of several ways of regarding folktales. Stith Thompson claims that there's much to learn in studying tales. He assumes, as you might not, that tales should be objects of study as well as entertainment.

Stith Thompson (1885–1976) led a distinguished life as an American educator, folklorist, editor, and author. Between 1921 and 1955, he was a professor of folklore and English, and later dean of the Graduate School and Distinguished Service Professor at Indiana University, Bloomington. Five institutions have awarded Thompson honorary doctorates for his work in folklore studies. He has published numerous books on the subject, including European Tales Among North American Indians *(1919),* The Types of the Folktales *(1928), and* Tales of the North American Indian *(1929). He is best known for his six-volume* Motif Index of Folk Literature *(1932–1937; 1955–1958, 2nd ed.).*

The teller of stories has everywhere and always found eager listeners. 1 Whether his tale is the mere report of a recent happening, a legend of long ago, or an elaborately contrived fiction, men and women have hung upon his words and satisfied their yearnings for information or amusement, for incitement to heroic deeds, for religious edification, or for release from the overpowering monotony of their lives. In villages of central Africa, in outrigger boats on the Pacific, in the Australian bush, and within the shadow of Hawaiian volcanoes, tales of the present and of the mysterious past, of animals and gods and heroes, and of men and women like themselves, hold listeners in their spell or enrich the conversation of daily life. So it is also in Eskimo igloos under the light of seal-oil lamps, in the tropical jungles of Brazil, and by the totem poles of the British Columbian coast. In Japan too, and China and India, the priest and the scholar, the peasant and the artisan all join in their love of a good story and their honor for the man who tells it well.

When we confine our view to our own occidental world, we see that for at least three or four thousand years, and doubtless for ages before, the art of the story-teller has been cultivated in every rank of society. Odysseus entertains the court of Alcinous with the marvels of his adventures. Centuries later we find the long-haired page reading nightly from interminable chivalric romances to entertain his lady while her lord is absent on his crusade. Medieval priests illustrate sermons by anecdotes old and new, and only sometimes edifying. The old peasant, now as always, whiles away the winter evening with tales of wonder and adventure and the marvelous workings of fate. Nurses tell children of Goldilocks or the House that Jack Built. Poets write epics and novelists novels. Even now the cinemas and theaters bring their stories direct to the ear and eye through the voices and gestures of actors. And in the smoking-rooms of sleeping cars and steamships and at the banquet table the oral anecdote flourishes in a new age. 2

In the present work we are confining our interest to a relatively narrow scope, the traditional prose tale—the story which has been handed down from generation to generation either in writing or by word of mouth. Such tales are, of course, only one of the many kinds of story material, for, in addition to them, narrative comes to us in verse as ballads and epics, and in prose as histories, novels, dramas, and short stories. We shall have little to do with the songs of bards, with the ballads of the people, or with poetic narrative in general, though stories themselves refuse to be confined exclusively to either prose or verse forms. But even with verse and all other forms of prose narrative put aside, we shall find that in treating the traditional prose tale—the folktale—our quest will be ambitious enough and will take us to all parts of the earth and to the very beginnings of history. 3

Although the term "folktale" is often used in English to refer to the "household tale" or "fairy tale" (the German *Märchen*), such as "Cinderella" or "Snow White," it is also legitimately employed in a much broader sense to include all forms of prose narrative, written or oral, which have come to be handed down through the years. In this usage the important fact is the traditional nature of the material. In contrast to the modern story writer's striving after originality of plot and treatment, the teller of a folktale is proud of his ability to hand on that which he has received. He usually desires to impress his readers or hearers with the fact that he is bringing them something that has the stamp of good authority, that the tale was heard from some great story-teller or from some aged person who remembered it from old days. 4

So it was until at least the end of the Middle Ages with writers like Chaucer, who carefully quoted authorities for their plots—and sometimes even invented originals so as to dispel the suspicion that some new and unwarranted story was being foisted on the public. Though the individual genius of such writers appears clearly enough, they always depended on authority, not only for their basic theological opinions but also for the plots of 5 their stories. A study of the sources of Chaucer or Boccaccio takes one directly into the stream of traditional narrative.

The great written collections of stories characteristic of India, the Near East, the classical world, and Medieval Europe are almost entirely traditional. They copy and recopy. A tale which gains favor in one collection is taken over into others, sometimes intact and sometimes with changes of plot or characterization. The history of such a story, passing it may be from India to Persia and Arabia and Italy and France and finally to England, copied and changed from manuscript to manuscript, is often exceedingly complex. For it goes through the hands of both skilled and bungling narrators and improves or deteriorates at nearly every retelling. However well or poorly such a story may be written down, it always attempts to preserve a tradition, an old tale with the authority of antiquity to give it interest and importance. 6

If use of the term "folktale" to include such literary narratives seems somewhat broad, it can be justified on practical grounds if on no other, for it is impossible to make a complete separation of the written and the oral traditions. Often, indeed, their interrelation is so close and so inextricable as to present one of the most baffling problems the folklore scholar encounters. They differ somewhat in their behavior, it is true, but they are alike in their disregard of originality of plot and of pride of authorship. 7

Nor is complete separation of these two kinds of narrative tradition by any means necessary for their understanding. The study of the oral tale . . . will be valid so long as we realize that stories have frequently been taken down from the lips of unlettered taletellers and have entered the great literary collections. In contrary fashion, fables of Aesop, anecdotes from Homer, and saints' legends, not to speak of fairy tales read from Perrault or Grimm, have entered the oral stream and all their association with the written or printed page has been forgotten. Frequently a story is taken from the people, recorded in a literary document, carried across continents or preserved through centuries, and then retold to a humble entertainer who adds it to his repertory. 8

It is clear then that the oral story need not always have been oral. But when it once habituates itself to being passed on by word of mouth it undergoes the same treatment as all other tales at the command of the raconteur. It becomes something to tell to an audience, or at least to a listener, not something to read. Its effects are no longer produced indirectly by association with words written or printed on a page, but directly through facial expression and gesture and repetition and recurrent patterns that generations have tested and found effective. 9

This oral art of taletelling is far older than history, and it is not bounded by one continent or one civilization. Stories may differ in subject from place to place, the conditions and purposes of taletelling may change as we move from land to land or from century to century, and yet everywhere it ministers to the same basic social and individual needs. The call for entertainment to fill in the hours of leisure has found most peoples very limited in their resources, and except where modern urban civilization has penetrated deeply they have found the telling of stories one of the most satisfying of pastimes. Curiosity about the past has always brought eager listeners to tales of the 10 long ago which supply the simple man with all he knows of the history of his folk. Legends grow with the telling, and often a great heroic past evolves to gratify vanity and tribal pride. Religion also has played a mighty role everywhere in the encouragement of the narrative art, for the religious mind has tried to understand beginnings and for ages has told stories of ancient days and sacred beings. Often whole cosmologies have unfolded themselves in these legends, and hierarchies of gods and heroes.

World-wide also are many of the structural forms which oral narrative has assumed. The hero tale, the explanatory legend, the animal anecdote—certainly these at least are present everywhere. Other fictional patterns are limited to particular areas of culture and act by their presence or absence as an effective index of the limit of the area concerned. The study of such limitations has not proceeded far, but it constitutes an interesting problem for the student of these oral narrative forms. 11

Even more tangible evidence of the ubiquity and antiquity of the folktale is the great similarity in the content of stories of the most varied peoples. The same tale types and narrative motifs are found scattered over the world in most puzzling fashion. A recognition of these resemblances and an attempt to account for them brings the scholar closer to an understanding of the nature of human culture. He must continually ask himself, "Why do some peoples borrow tales and some lend? How does the tale serve the needs of the social group?" When he adds to his task an appreciation of the aesthetic and practical urge toward storytelling, and some knowledge of the forms and devices, stylistic and histrionic, that belong to this ancient and widely practiced art, he finds that he must bring to his work more talents than one man can easily possess. Literary critics, anthropologists, historians, psychologists, and aestheticians are all needed if we are to hope to know why folktales are made, how they are invented, what art is used in their telling, how they grow and change and occasionally die. 12

▲ ▲ ▲

Review Questions

1. According to Thompson, what are the reasons people consistently venerate a good storyteller?
2. What does Thompson state as features that distinguish a "folktale" from modern types of fiction?
3. How does religion help encourage the existence of folktale art?
4. What is a strong piece of evidence for the great antiquity and universality of folktales?

Discussion and Writing Suggestions

1. Based on Thompson's explanation of the qualities of oral folktales, what do you feel is gained by the increasing replacement of this form of art and entertainment by TV?

2. What do you suppose underlies the apparent human need to tell stories, given that storytelling is practiced in every culture known?
3. Interview older members of your family, asking them about stories they were told as children. As best you can, record a story. Then examine your work. How does it differ from the version you heard? Write an account of your impressions on the differences between an oral and written rendering of a story. Alternately, you might record a story and then speculate on what the story might mean in the experiences of the family member who told it to you.

Nine Variants of "Cinderella"

It comes as a surprise to many that there exist Chinese, French, German, African, and Native American versions of the popular "Cinderella," along with 700 other versions worldwide. Which is the real *"Cinderella"? The question is misleading in that each version is "real" for a particular group of people in a particular place and time. Certainly, you can judge among versions and select the most appealing. You can also draw comparisons. Indeed, the grouping of the stories that we present here invites comparisons. A few of the categories you might wish to consider as you read:*

- *Cinderella's innocence or guilt, concerning the treatment she receives at the hands of her stepsisters*
- *Cinderella's passive (or active) nature*
- *Sibling rivalry—the relationship of Cinderella to her sisters*
- *The father's role*
- *The rule that Cinderella must return from the ball by midnight*
- *Levels of violence*
- *Presence or absence of the fairy godmother*
- *Cinderella's relationship with the prince*
- *Characterization of the prince*
- *The presence of Cinderella's dead mother*
- *The function of magic*
- *The ending*

Cinderella

CHARLES PERRAULT

Charles Perrault (1628–1703) was born in Paris of a prosperous family. He practiced law for a short time and then devoted his attentions to a job in government, in which capacity he was instrumental in promoting the advancement of the arts and sciences and in securing pensions for writ-

ers, both French and foreign. Perrault is best known as a writer for his Contes de ma mère l'oie (Mother Goose Tales), *a collection of fairy tales taken from popular folklore. He is widely suspected of having changed these stories in an effort to make them more acceptable to his audience—members of the French court.*

Once there was a nobleman who took as his second wife the proudest and 1
haughtiest woman imaginable. She had two daughters of the same character, who took after their mother in everything. On his side, the husband had a daughter who was sweetness itself; she inherited this from her mother, who had been the most kindly of women.

No sooner was the wedding over than the stepmother showed her ill- 2
nature. She could not bear the good qualities of the young girl, for they made her own daughters seem even less likable. She gave her the roughest work of the house to do. It was she who washed the dishes and the stairs, who cleaned out Madam's room and the rooms of the two Misses. She slept right at the top of the house, in an attic, on a lumpy mattress, while her sisters slept in panelled rooms where they had the most modern beds and mirrors in which they could see themselves from top to toe. The poor girl bore everything in patience and did not dare to complain to her father. He would only have scolded her, for he was entirely under his wife's thumb.

When she had finished her work, she used to go into the chimney-cor- 3
ner and sit down among the cinders, for which reason she was usually known in the house as Cinderbottom. Her younger stepsister, who was not so rude as the other, called her Cinderella. However, Cinderella, in spite of her ragged clothes, was still fifty times as beautiful as her sisters, superbly dressed though they were.

One day the King's son gave a ball, to which everyone of good family 4
was invited. Our two young ladies received invitations, for they cut quite a figure in the country. So there they were, both feeling very pleased and very busy choosing the clothes and the hair-styles which would suit them best. More work for Cinderella, for it was she who ironed her sisters' underwear and goffered their linen cuffs. Their only talk was of what they would wear.

"I," said the elder, "shall wear my red velvet dress and my collar of 5
English lace."

"I," said the younger, "shall wear just my ordinary skirt; but, to make 6
up, I shall put on my gold-embroidered cape and my diamond clasp, which is quite out of the common."

The right hairdresser was sent for to supply double-frilled coifs, and 7
patches were bought from the right patch-maker. They called Cinderella to ask her opinion, for she had excellent taste. She made useful suggestions and even offered to do their hair for them. They accepted willingly.

While she was doing it, they said to her: 8

"Cinderella, how would you like to go to the ball?" 9

"Oh dear, you are making fun of me. It wouldn't do for me." 10

"You are quite right. It would be a joke. People would laugh if they 11
saw a Cinderbottom at the ball."

Anyone else would have done their hair in knots for them, but she had 12
a sweet nature, and she finished it perfectly. For two days they were so excited that they ate almost nothing. They broke a good dozen laces trying to tighten their stays to make their waists slimmer, and they were never away from their mirrors.

At last the great day arrived. They set off, and Cinderella watched 13
them until they were out of sight. When she could no longer see them, she began to cry. Her godmother, seeing her all in tears, asked what was the matter.

"If only I could . . . If only I could . . ." She was weeping so much that 14
she could not go on.

Her godmother, who was a fairy, said to her: "If only you could go to 15
the ball, is that it?"

"Alas, yes," said Cinderella with a sigh. 16

"Well," said the godmother, "be a good girl and I'll get you there." 17

She took her into her room and said: "Go into the garden and get me a 18
pumpkin."

Cinderella hurried out and cut the best she could find and took it to her 19
godmother, but she could not understand how this pumpkin would get her to the ball. Her godmother hollowed it out, leaving only the rind, and then tapped it with her wand and immediately it turned into a magnificent gilded coach.

Then she went to look in her mouse-trap and found six mice all alive in 20
it. She told Cinderella to raise the door of the trap a little, and as each mouse came out she gave it a tap with her wand and immediately it turned into a fine horse. That made a team of six horses, each of fine mouse-coloured grey.

While she was wondering how she would make a coachman, Cin- 21
derella said to her:

"I will go and see whether there is a rat in the rat-trap, we could make a 22
coachman of him."

"You are right," said the godmother. "Run and see." 23

Cinderella brought her the rat-trap, in which there were three big rats. 24
The fairy picked out one of them because of his splendid whiskers and, when she had touched him, he turned into a fat coachman, with the finest moustaches in the district.

Then she said: "Go into the garden and you will find six lizards behind 25
the watering-can. Bring them to me."

As soon as Cinderella had brought them, her godmother changed them 26
into six footmen, who got up behind the coach with their striped liveries, and stood in position there as though they had been doing it all their lives.

Then the fairy said to Cinderella: 27

"Well, that's to go to the ball in. Aren't you pleased?" 28

"Yes. But am I to go like this, with my ugly clothes?" 29

Her godmother simply touched her with her wand and her clothes were 30
changed in an instant into a dress of gold and silver cloth, all sparkling with

precious stones. Then she gave her a pair of glass slippers, most beautifully made.

So equipped, Cinderella got into the coach; but her godmother warned her above all not to be out after midnight, telling her that, if she stayed at the ball a moment later, her coach would turn back into a pumpkin, her horses into mice, her footmen into lizards, and her fine clothes would become rags again. 31

She promised her godmother that she would leave the ball before midnight without fail, and she set out, beside herself with joy. 32

The King's son, on being told that a great princess whom no one knew had arrived, ran out to welcome her. He handed her down from the coach and led her into the hall where his guests were. A sudden silence fell; the dancing stopped, the violins ceased to play, the whole company stood fascinated by the beauty of the unknown princess. Only a low murmur was heard: "Ah, how lovely she is!" The King himself, old as he was, could not take his eyes off her and kept whispering to the Queen that it was a long time since he had seen such a beautiful and charming person. All the ladies were absorbed in noting her clothes and the way her hair was dressed, so as to order the same things for themselves the next morning, provided that fine enough materials could be found, and skillful enough craftsmen. 33

The King's son placed her in the seat of honour, and later led her out to dance. She danced with such grace that she won still more admiration. An excellent supper was served, but the young Prince was too much occupied in gazing at her to eat anything. She went and sat next to her sisters and treated them with great courtesy, offering them oranges and lemons which the Prince had given her. They were astonished, for they did not recognize her. 34

While they were chatting together, Cinderella heard the clock strike a quarter to twelve. She curtsied low to the company and left as quickly as she could. 35

As soon as she reached home, she went to her godmother and, having thanked her, said that she would very much like to go again to the ball on the next night—for the Prince had begged her to come back. She was in the middle of telling her godmother about all the things that had happened, when the two sisters came knocking at the door. Cinderella went to open it. 36

"How late you are!" she said, rubbing her eyes and yawning and stretching as though she had just woken up (though since they had last seen each other she had felt very far from sleepy). 37

"If you had been at the ball," said one of the sisters, "you would not have felt like yawning. There was a beautiful princess there, really ravishingly beautiful. She was most attentive to us. She gave us oranges and lemons." 38

Cinderella could have hugged herself. She asked them the name of the princess, but they replied that no one knew her, that the King's son was much troubled about it, and that he would give anything in the world to know who she was. Cinderella smiled and said to them: 39

"So she was very beautiful? Well, well, how lucky you are! Couldn't I see her? Please, Miss Javotte, do lend me that yellow dress which you wear about the house." 40

"Really," said Miss Javotte, "what an idea! Lend one's dress like that to a filthy Cinderbottom! I should have to be out of my mind." 41

Cinderella was expecting this refusal and she was very glad when it came, for she would have been in an awkward position if her sister really had lent her her frock. 42

On the next day the two sisters went to the ball, and Cinderella too, but even more splendidly dressed than the first time. The King's son was constantly at her side and wooed her the whole evening. The young girl was enjoying herself so much that she forgot her godmother's warning. She heard the clock striking the first stroke of midnight when she thought that it was still hardly eleven. She rose and slipped away as lightly as a roe-deer. The Prince followed her, but he could not catch her up. One of her glass slippers fell off, and the Prince picked it up with great care. 43

Cinderella reached home quite out of breath, with no coach, no footmen, and wearing her old clothes. Nothing remained of all her finery, except one of her little slippers, the fellow to the one which she had dropped. The guards at the palace gate were asked if they had not seen a princess go out. They answered that they had seen no one go out except a very poorly dressed girl, who looked more like a peasant than a young lady. 44

When the two sisters returned from the ball, Cinderella asked them if they had enjoyed themselves again, and if the beautiful lady had been there. They said that she had, but that she had run away when it struck midnight, and so swiftly that she had lost one of her glass slippers, a lovely little thing. The Prince had picked it up and had done nothing but gaze at it for the rest of the ball, and undoubtedly he was very much in love with the beautiful person to whom it belonged. 45

They were right, for a few days later the King's son had it proclaimed to the sound of trumpets that he would marry the girl whose foot exactly fitted the slipper. They began by trying it on the various princesses, then on the duchesses and on all the ladies of the Court, but with no success. It was brought to the two sisters, who did everything possible to force their feet into the slipper, but they could not manage it. Cinderella, who was looking on, recognized her own slipper, and said laughing: 46

"Let me see if it would fit me!" 47

Her sisters began to laugh and mock at her. But the gentleman who was trying on the slipper looked closely at Cinderella and, seeing that she was very beautiful, said that her request was perfectly reasonable and that he had instructions to try it on every girl. He made Cinderella sit down and, raising the slipper to her foot, he found that it slid on without difficulty and fitted like a glove. 48

Great was the amazement of the two sisters, but it became greater still when Cinderella drew from her pocket the second little slipper and put it on her other foot. Thereupon the fairy godmother came in and, touching Cin- 49 derella's clothes with her wand, made them even more magnificent than on the previous days.

Then the two sisters recognized her as the lovely princess whom they 50
had met at the ball. They flung themselves at her feet and begged her forgiveness for all the unkind things which they had done to her. Cinderella raised them up and kissed them, saying that she forgave them with all her heart and asking them to love her always. She was taken to the young Prince in the fine clothes which she was wearing. He thought her more beautiful than ever and a few days later he married her. Cinderella, who was as kind as she was beautiful, invited her two sisters to live in the palace and married them, on the same day, to two great noblemen of the Court.

Ashputtle

JAKOB AND WILHELM GRIMM

Jakob Grimm (1785–1863) and Wilhelm Grimm (1786–1859) are best known today for the 200 folktales they collected from oral sources and reworked in Kinder- und Hausmärchen *(popularly known as* Grimm's Fairy Tales)*, which has been translated into seventy languages. The techniques Jakob and Wilhelm Grimm used to collect and comment on these tales became a model for other collectors, providing a basis for the science of folklore. Although the Grimm brothers argued for preserving the tales exactly as heard from oral sources, scholars have determined that they sought to "improve" the tales by making them more readable. The result, highly pleasing to lay audiences the world over, nonetheless represents a literary reworking of the original oral sources.*

A rich man's wife fell sick and, feeling that her end was near, she called her 1
only daughter to her bedside and said: "Dear child, be good and say your prayers; God will help you, and I shall look down on you from heaven and always be with you." With that she closed her eyes and died. Every day the little girl went out to her mother's grave and wept, and she went on being good and saying her prayers. When winter came, the snow spread a white cloth over the grave, and when spring took it off, the man remarried.

His new wife brought two daughters into the house. Their faces were 2
beautiful and lily-white, but their hearts were ugly and black. That was the beginning of a bad time for the poor stepchild. "Why should this silly goose sit in the parlor with us?" they said. "People who want to eat bread must earn it. Get into the kitchen where you belong!" They took away her fine clothes and gave her an old gray dress and wooden shoes to wear. "Look at the haughty princess in her finery!" they cried and, laughing, led her to the kitchen. From then on she had to do all the work, getting up before daybreak, carrying water, lighting fires, cooking and washing. In addition the sisters did everything they could to plague her. They jeered at her

and poured peas and lentils into the ashes, so that she had to sit there picking them out. At night, when she was tired out with work, she had no bed to sleep in but had to lie in the ashes by the hearth. And they took to calling her Ashputtle because she always looked dusty and dirty.

One day when her father was going to the fair, he asked his two step- 3
daughters what he should bring them. "Beautiful dresses," said one. "Diamonds and pearls," said the other. "And you, Ashputtle. What would you like?" "Father," she said, "break off the first branch that brushes against your hat on your way home, and bring it to me." So he brought beautiful dresses, diamonds and pearls for his two stepdaughters, and on the way home, as he was riding through a copse, a hazel branch brushed against him and knocked off his hat. So he broke off the branch and took it home with him. When he got home, he gave the stepdaughters what they had asked for, and gave Ashputtle the branch. After thanking him, she went to her mother's grave and planted the hazel sprig over it and cried so hard that her tears fell on the sprig and watered it. It grew and became a beautiful tree. Three times a day Ashputtle went and sat under it and wept and prayed. Each time a little white bird came and perched on the tree, and when Ashputtle made a wish the little bird threw down what she had wished for.

Now it so happened that the king arranged for a celebration. It was to 4
go on for three days and all the beautiful girls in the kingdom were invited, in order that his son might choose a bride. When the two stepsisters heard they had been asked, they were delighted. They called Ashputtle and said: "Comb our hair, brush our shoes, and fasten our buckles. We're going to the wedding at the king's palace." Ashputtle obeyed, but she wept, for she too would have liked to go dancing, and she begged her stepmother to let her go. "You little sloven!" said the stepmother. "How can you go to a wedding when you're all dusty and dirty? How can you go dancing when you have neither dress nor shoes?" But when Ashputtle begged and begged, the stepmother finally said: "Here, I've dumped a bowlful of lentils in the ashes. If you can pick them out in two hours, you may go." The girl went out the back door to the garden and cried out: "O tame little doves, O turtledoves, and all the birds under heaven, come and help me put

the good ones in the pot,
the bad ones in your crop."

Two little white doves came flying through the kitchen window, and then came the turtledoves, and finally all the birds under heaven came flapping and fluttering and settled down by the ashes. The doves nodded their little heads and started in, peck peck peck peck, and all the others started in, peck peck peck peck, and they sorted out all the good lentils and put them in the bowl. Hardly an hour had passed before they finished and flew away. Then the girl brought the bowl to her stepmother, and she was happy, for she thought she'd be allowed to go to the wedding. But the stepmother said: "No, Ashputtle. You have nothing to wear and you don't know how to dance; the people would only laugh at you." When Ashputtle began to cry, the stepmother said: "If you can pick two bowlfuls of lentils out of the ashes in an hour, you may come." And she thought: "She'll never be able to do it." When she had dumped the two bowlfuls of lentils in the ashes, Ashputtle went out the back door to the garden and cried out: "O tame little doves, O turtledoves, and all the birds under heaven, come and help me put

the good ones in the pot,
the bad ones in your crop."

Two little white doves came flying through the kitchen window, and then came the turtledoves, and finally all the birds under heaven came flapping and fluttering and settled down by the ashes. The doves nodded their little heads and started in, peck peck peck peck, and all the others started in, peck peck peck peck, and they sorted out all the good lentils and put them in the bowls. Before half an hour had passed, they had finished and they all flew away. Then the girl brought the bowls to her stepmother, and she was happy, for she thought she'd be allowed to go to the wedding. But her stepmother said: "It's no use. You can't come, because you have nothing to wear and you don't know how to dance. We'd only be ashamed of you." Then she turned her back and hurried away with her two proud daughters.

When they had all gone out, Ashputtle went to her mother's grave. She 5
stood under the hazel tree and cried:

"Shake your branches, little tree,
Throw gold and silver down on me."

Whereupon the bird tossed down a gold and silver dress and slippers embroidered with silk and silver. Ashputtle slipped into the dress as fast as she could and went to the wedding. Her sisters and stepmother didn't recognize her. She was so beautiful in her golden dress that they thought she must be the daughter of some foreign king. They never dreamed it could be Ashputtle, for they thought she was sitting at home in her filthy rags, picking lentils out of the ashes. The king's son came up to her, took her by the hand and danced with her. He wouldn't dance with anyone else and he never let go her hand. When someone else asked for a dance, he said: "She is my partner."

She danced until evening, and then she wanted to go home. The king's 6
son said: "I'll go with you, I'll see you home," for he wanted to find out whom the beautiful girl belonged to. But she got away from him and slipped into the dovecote. The king's son waited until her father arrived, and told him the strange girl had slipped into the dovecote. The old man thought: "Could it be Ashputtle?" and he sent for an ax and a pick and broke into the dovecote, but there was no one inside. When they went indoors, Ashputtle was lying in the ashes in her filthy clothes and a dim oil lamp was burning on the chimney piece, for Ashputtle had slipped out the back end of the dovecote and run to the hazel tree. There she had taken off her fine clothes and put them on the grave, and the bird had taken them away. Then she had put her gray dress on again, crept into the kitchen and lain down in the ashes.

Next day when the festivities started in again and her parents and stepsisters had gone, Ashputtle went to the hazel tree and said: 7

"Shake your branches, little tree,
Throw gold and silver down on me."

Whereupon the bird threw down a dress that was even more dazzling than the first one. And when she appeared at the wedding, everyone marveled at her beauty. The king's son was waiting for her. He took her by the hand and danced with no one but her. When others came and asked her for a dance, he said: "She is my partner." When evening came, she said she was going home. The king's son followed her, wishing to see which house she went into, but she ran away and disappeared into the garden behind the house, where there was a big beautiful tree with the most wonderful pears growing on it. She climbed among the branches as nimbly as a squirrel and the king's son didn't know what had become of her. He waited until her father arrived and said to him: "The strange girl has got away from me and I think she has climbed up in the pear tree." Her father thought: "Could it be Ashputtle?" He sent for an ax and chopped the tree down, but there was no one in it. When they went into the kitchen, Ashputtle was lying there in the ashes as usual, for she had jumped down on the other side of the tree, brought her fine clothes back to the bird in the hazel tree, and put on her filthy gray dress.

On the third day, after her parents and sisters had gone, Ashputtle went back to her mother's grave and said to the tree: 8

"Shake your branches, little tree,
Throw gold and silver down on me."

Whereupon the bird threw down a dress that was more radiant than either of the others, and the slippers were all gold. When she appeared at the wedding, the people were too amazed to speak. The king's son danced with no one but her, and when someone else asked her for a dance, he said: "She is my partner."

When evening came, Ashputtle wanted to go home, and the king's son said he'd go with her, but she slipped away so quickly that he couldn't follow. But he had thought up a trick. He had arranged to have the whole staircase brushed with pitch, and as she was running down it the pitch pulled her left slipper off. The king's son picked it up, and it was tiny and delicate and all gold. Next morning he went to the father and said: "No girl shall be my wife but the one this golden shoe fits." The sisters were overjoyed, for they had beautiful feet. The eldest took the shoe to her room to try it on and her mother went with her. But the shoe was too small and she couldn't get her big toe in. So her mother handed her a knife and said: "Cut your toe off. Once you're queen you won't have to walk any more." The girl cut her toe off, forced her foot into the shoe, gritted her teeth against the pain, and went out to the king's son. He accepted her as his bride-to-be, lifted her up 9 on his horse, and rode away with her. But they had to pass the grave. The two doves were sitting in the hazel tree and they cried out:

"Roocoo, roocoo,
There's blood in the shoe.
The foot's too long, the foot's too wide,
That's not the proper bride."

He looked down at her foot and saw the blood spurting. At that he turned his horse around and took the false bride home again. "No," he said, "this isn't the right girl; let her sister try the shoe on." The sister went to her room and managed to get her toes into the shoe, but her heel was too big. So her mother handed her a knife and said: "Cut off a chunk of your heel. Once you're queen you won't have to walk any more." The girl cut off a chunk of her heel, forced her foot into the shoe, gritted her teeth against the pain, and went out to the king's son. He accepted her as his bride-to-be, lifted her up on his horse, and rode away with her. As they passed the hazel tree, the two doves were sitting there, and they cried out:

"Roocoo, roocoo,
There's blood in the shoe.
The foot's too long, the foot's too wide,
That's not the proper bride."

He looked down at her foot and saw that blood was spurting from her shoe and staining her white stocking all red. He turned his horse around and took the false bride home again. "This isn't the right girl, either," he said. "Haven't you got another daughter?" "No," said the man, "there's only a puny little kitchen drudge that my dead wife left me. She couldn't possibly be the bride." "Send her up," said the king's son, but the mother said: "Oh, no, she's much too dirty to be seen." But he insisted and they had to call her. First she washed her face and hands, and when they were clean, she went upstairs and curtseyed to the king's son. He handed her the golden slipper and sat down on a footstool, took her foot out of her heavy wooden shoe, and put it into the slipper. It fitted perfectly. And when she stood up and the king's son looked into her face, he recognized the beautiful girl he had danced with and cried out: "This is my true bride!" The stepmother and the two sisters went pale with fear and rage. But he lifted Ashputtle up on his horse and rode away with her. As they passed the hazel tree, the two white doves called out:

"Roocoo, roocoo,
No blood in the shoe.
Her foot is neither long nor wide,
This one is the proper bride."

Then they flew down and alighted on Ashputtle's shoulders, one on the right and one on the left, and there they sat.

On the day of Ashputtle's wedding, the two stepsisters came and tried to ingratiate themselves and share in her happiness. On the way to church the elder was on the right side of the bridal couple and the younger on the left. The doves came along and pecked out one of the elder sister's eyes and one of the younger sister's eyes. Afterward, on the way out, the elder was on the left side and younger on the right, and the doves pecked out both the remaining eyes. So both sisters were punished with blindness to the end of their days for being so wicked and false. 10

When the Clock Strikes

TANITH LEE

Tanith Lee has written what might be called an inversion of "Cinderella" wherein the heroine is a witch. You will find all elements of the traditional tale here, and Lee's rendering is unmistakably "Cinderella." But with devious consistency, Lee turns both the magic and the unrighted wrong that lie at the heart of the tale to a dark purpose: revenge. Tanith Lee is a prolific writer of stories for young adults and of adult fantasy and science fiction. Born in 1947 in London, Lee had her first story published when she was twenty-four and has written more than two dozen stories and plays since.

Yes, the great ballroom is filled only with dust now. The slender columns of white marble and the slender columns of rose-red marble are woven together by cobwebs. The vivid frescoes, on which the Duke's treasury spent so much, are dimmed by the dust; the faces of the painted goddesses look grey. And the velvet curtains—touch them, they will crumble. Two hundred years now, since anyone danced in this place on the sea-green floor in the candle-gleam. Two hundred years since the wonderful clock struck for the very first time. 1

I though you might care to examine the clock. It was considered exceptional in its day. The pedestal is ebony and the face fine porcelain. And these figures, which are of silver, would pass slowly about the circlet of the face. Each figure represents, you understand, an hour. And as the appropriate hours came level with this golden bell, they would strike it the correct number of times. All the figures are unique, as you see. Beginning at the first hour, they are, in this order, a girl-child, a dwarf, a maiden, a youth, a lady and a knight. And here, notice, the figures grow older as the day declines: a queen and king for the seventh and eighth hours, and after these, an abbess and a magician and next to last, a hag. But the very last is strangest of all. The twelfth figure; do you recognize him? It is Death. Yes, a most curious clock. It was reckoned a marvelous thing then. But it has not struck for two hundred years. Possibly you have been told the story? No? Oh, but I am certain that you have heard it, in another form, perhaps. 2

However, as you have some while to wait for your carriage, I will re- 3
count the tale, if you wish.

I will start with what was said of the clock. In those years, this city was 4
prosperous, a stronghold—not as you see it today. Much was made in the city that was ornamental and unusual. But the clock, on which the twelfth hour was Death, caused something of a stir. It was thought unlucky, foolhardy, to have such a clock. It began to be murmured, jokingly by some, by others in earnest, that one night when the clock struck the twelfth hour, Death would truly strike with it.

Now life has always been a chancy business, and it was more so then. 5
The Great Plague had come but twenty years before and was not yet forgotten. Besides, in the Duke's court there was much intrigue, while enemies might be supposed to plot beyond the city walls, as happens even in our present age. But there was another thing.

It was rumored that the Duke had obtained both his title and the city 6
treacherously. Rumor declared that he had systematically destroyed those who had stood in line before him, the members of the princely house that formerly ruled here. He had accomplished the task slyly, hiring assassins talented with poisons and daggers. But rumor also declared that the Duke had not been sufficiently thorough. For though he had meant to rid himself of all that rival house, a single descendant remained, so obscure he had not traced her—for it was a woman.

Of course, such matters were not spoken of openly. Like the prophecy 7
of the clock, it was a subject for the dark.

Nevertheless, I will tell you at once, there was such a descendant he 8
had missed in his bloody work. And she was a woman. Royal and proud she was, and seething with bitter spite and a hunger for vengeance, and as bloody as the Duke, had he known it, in her own way.

For her safety and disguise, she had long ago wed a wealthy merchant 9
in the city, and presently bore the man a daughter. The merchant, a dealer in silks, was respected, a good fellow but not wise. He rejoiced in his handsome and aristocratic wife. He never dreamed what she might be about when he was not with her. In fact, she had sworn allegiance to Satanas. In the dead of night she would go up into an old tower adjoining the merchant's house, and there she would say portions of the Black Mass, offer sacrifice, and thereafter practise witchcraft against the Duke. This witchery took a common form, the creation of a wax image and the maiming of the image that, by sympathy, the injuries inflicted on the wax be passed on to the living body of the victim. The woman was capable in what she did. The Duke fell sick. He lost the use of his limbs and was racked by excruciating pains from which he could get no relief. Thinking himself on the brink of death, the Duke named his sixteen-year-old son his heir. This son was dear to the Duke, as everyone knew, and be sure the woman knew it too. She intended sorcerously to murder the young man in his turn, preferably in his father's sight. Thus, she let the Duke linger in his agony, and commenced planning the fate of the prince.

Now all this while she had not been toiling alone. She had one helper. It was her own daughter, a maid of fourteen, that she had recruited to her service nearly as soon as the infant could walk. At six or seven, the child had been lisping the satanic rite along with her mother. At fourteen, you may imagine, the girl was well versed in the Black Arts, though she did not have her mother's natural genius for them. 10

Perhaps you would like me to describe the daughter at this point. It has a bearing on the story, for the girl was astonishingly beautiful. Her hair was the rich dark red of antique burnished copper, her eyes were the hue of the reddish-golden amber that traders bring from the East. When she walked, you would say she was dancing. But when she danced, a gate seemed to open in the world, and bright fire spangled inside it, but she was the fire. 11

The girl and her mother were close as gloves in a box. Their games in the old tower bound them closer. No doubt the woman believed herself clever to have got such a helpmate, but it proved her undoing. 12

It was in this manner. The silk merchant, who had never suspected his wife for an instant of anything, began to mistrust the daughter. She was not like other girls. Despite her great beauty, she professed no interest in marriage, and none in clothes or jewels. She preferred to read in the garden at the foot of the tower. Her mother had taught the girl her letters, though the merchant himself could read but poorly. And often the father peered at the books his daughter read, unable to make head or tail of them, yet somehow not liking them. One night very late, the silk merchant came home from a guild dinner in the city, and he saw a slim pale shadow gliding up the steps of the old tower, and he knew it for his child. On impulse, he followed her, but quietly. He had not considered any evil so far, and did not want to alarm her. At an angle of the stair, the lighted room above, he paused to spy and listen. He had something of a shock when he heard his wife's voice rise up in glad welcome. But what came next drained the blood from his heart. He crept away and went to his cellar for wine to stay himself. After the third glass he ran for neighbours and for the watch. 13

The woman and her daughter heard the shouts below and saw the torches in the garden. It was no use dissembling. The tower was littered with evidence of vile deeds, besides what the woman kept in a chest beneath her unknowing husband's bed. She understood it was all up with her, and she understood too how witchcraft was punished hereabouts. She snatched a knife from the altar. 14

The girl shrieked when she realized what her mother was at. The woman caught the girl by her red hair and shook her. 15

"Listen to me, my daughter," she cried, "and listen carefully, for the minutes are short. If you do as I tell you, you can escape their wrath and only I need die. And if you live I am satisfied, for you can carry on my labor after me. My vengeance I shall leave you, and my witchcraft to exact it by. Indeed, I promise you stronger powers than mine. I will beg my lord Satanas for it and he will not deny me, for he is just, in his fashion, and I have served him well. Now, will you attend?" 16

"I will," said the girl. 17

So the woman advised her, and swore her to the fellowship of Hell. 18
And then the woman forced the knife into her own heart and dropped dead on the floor of the tower.

When the men burst in with their swords and staves and their torches 19
and their madness, the girl was ready for them.

She stood blank-faced, blank-eyed, with her arms hanging at her sides. 20
When one touched her, she dropped down at his feet.

"Surely she is innocent," this man said. She was lovely enough that it 21
was hard to accuse her. Then her father went to her and took her hand and lifted her. At that the girl opened her eyes and she said, as if terrified: "How did I come here? I was in my chamber and sleeping—"

"The woman has bewitched her," her father said. 22

He desired very much that this be so. And when the girl clung to his 23
hand and wept, he was certain of it. They showed her the body with the knife in it. The girl screamed and seemed to lose her senses totally.

She was put to bed. In the morning, a priest came and questioned her. 24
She answered steadfastly. She remembered nothing, not even of the great books she had been observed reading. When they told her what was in them, she screamed again and apparently would have thrown herself from the narrow window, only the priest stopped her.

Finally, they brought her the holy cross in order that she might kiss it 25
and prove herself blameless.

Then she knelt, and whispered softly, that nobody should hear but 26
one—"Lord Satanas, protect thy handmaid." And either that gentleman has more power than he is credited with or else the symbols of God are only as holy as the men who deal in them, for she embraced the cross and it left her unscathed.

At that, the whole household thanked God. The whole household sav- 27
ing, of course, the woman's daughter. She had another to thank.

The woman's body was burnt, and the ashes put into unconsecrated 28
ground beyond the city gates. Though they had discovered her to be a witch, they had not discovered the direction her witchcraft had selected. Nor did they find the wax image with its limbs all twisted and stuck through with needles. The girl had taken that up and concealed it. The Duke continued in his distress, but he did not die. Sometimes, in the dead of night, the girl would unearth the image from under a loose brick by the hearth, and gloat over it, but she did nothing else. Not yet. She was fourteen and the cloud of her mother's acts still hovered over her. She knew what she must do next.

The period of mourning ended. 29

"Daughter," said the silk merchant to her, "why do you not remove 30
your black? The woman was malign and led you into wickedness. How long will you mourn her, who deserves no mourning?"

"Oh my father," she said, "never think I regret my wretched mother. It 31
is my own unwitting sin I mourn." And she grasped his hand and spilled

her tears on it. "I would rather live in a convent," said she, "than mingle with proper folk. And I would seek a convent too, if it were not that I cannot bear to be parted from you."

Do you suppose she smiled secretly as she said this? One might suppose it. Presently she donned a robe of sackcloth and poured ashes over her red-copper hair. "It is my penance," she said, "I am glad to atone for my sins." 32

People forgot her beauty. She was at pains to obscure it. She slunk about like an aged woman, a rag pulled over her head, dirt smeared on her cheeks and brow. She elected to sleep in a cold cramped attic and sat all day by a smoky hearth in the kitchens. When someone came to her and begged her to wash her face and put on suitable clothes and sit in the rooms of the house, she smiled modestly, drawing the rag or a piece of hair over her face. "I swear," she said, "I am glad to be humble before God and men." 33

They reckoned her pious and they reckoned her simple. Two years passed. They mislaid her beauty altogether, and reckoned her ugly. They found it hard to call to mind who she was exactly, as she sat in the ashes, or shuffled unattended about the streets like a crone. 34

At the end of the second year, the silk merchant married again. It was inevitable, for he was not a man who liked to live alone. 35

On this occasion, his choice was a harmless widow. She already had two daughters, pretty in an unremarkable style. Perhaps the merchant hoped they would comfort him for what had gone before, this normal cheery wife and the two sweet, rather silly daughters, whose chief interests were clothes and weddings. Perhaps he hoped also that his deranged daughter might be drawn out by company. But that hope foundered. Not that the new mother did not try to be pleasant to the girl. And the new sisters, their hearts grieved by her condition, went to great lengths to enlist her friendship. They begged her to come from the kitchens or the attic. Failing in that, they sometimes ventured to join her, their fine silk dresses trailing on the greasy floor. They combed her hair, exclaiming, when some of the ash and dirt were removed, on its color. But no sooner had they turned away, than the girl gathered up handfuls of soot and ash and rubbed them into her hair again. Now and then, the sisters attempted to interest their bizarre relative in a bracelet or a gown or a current song. They spoke to her of the young men they had seen at the suppers or the balls which were then given regularly by the rich families of the city. The girl ignored it all. If she ever said anything it was to do with penance and humility. At last, as must happen, the sisters wearied of her, and left her alone. They had no cares and did not want to share in hers. They came to resent her moping greyness, as indeed the merchant's second wife had already done. 36

"Can you do nothing with the girl?" she demanded of her husband. "People will say that I and my daughters are responsible for her condition and that I ill-treat the maid from jealousy of her dead mother." 37

"Now how could anyone say that?" protested the merchant, "when you are famous as the epitome of generosity and kindness." 38

Another year passed, and saw no huge difference in the household. 39

A difference there was, but not visible. 40

The girl who slouched in the corner of the hearth was seventeen. Under the filth and grime she was, impossibly, more beautiful, although no one could see it. 41

And there was one other invisible item—her power (which all this time she had nurtured, saying her prayers to Satanas in the black of midnight), her power was rising like a dark moon in her soul. 42

Three days after her seventeenth birthday, the girl straggled about the streets as she frequently did. A few noted her and muttered it was the merchant's ugly simple daughter and paid no more attention. Most did not know her at all. She had made herself appear one with the scores of impoverished flotsam which constantly roamed the city, beggars and starvelings. Just outside the city gates, these persons congregated in large numbers, slumped around fires of burning refuse or else wandering to and fro in search of edible seeds, scraps, the miracle of a dropped coin. Here the girl now came, and began to wander about as they did. Dusk gathered and the shadows thickened. The girl sank to her knees in a patch of earth as if she had found something. Two or three of the beggars sneaked over to see if it were worth snatching from her—but the girl was only scrabbling in the empty soil. The beggars, making signs to each other that she was touched by God—mad—left her alone. But, very far from mad, the girl presently dug up a stoppered clay urn. In this urn were the ashes and charred bones of her mother. She had got a clue as to the location of the urn by devious questioning here and there. Her occult power had helped her to be sure of it. 43

In the twilight, padding along through the narrow streets and alleys of the city, the girl brought the urn homewards. In the garden at the foot of the old tower, gloom-wrapped, unwitnessed, she unstoppered the urn and buried the ashes freshly. She muttered certain unholy magics over the grave. Then she snapped off the sprig of a young hazel tree, and planted it in the newly turned ground. 44

I hazard you have begun to recognize the story by now. I see you suppose I tell it wrongly. Believe me, this is the truth of the matter. But if you would rather I left off the tale . . . No doubt your carriage will soon be here—No? Very well. I shall continue. 45

I think I should speak of the Duke's son at this juncture. The prince was nineteen, able, intelligent, and of noble bearing. He was of that rather swarthy type of looks one finds here in the north, but tall and slim and clear-eyed. There is an ancient square where you may see a statue of him, but much eroded by two centuries, and the elements. After the city was sacked, no care was lavished on it. 46

The Duke treasured his son. He had constant delight in the sight of the young man and what he said and did. It was the only happiness the invalid had. 47

Then, one night, the Duke screamed out in his bed. Servants came running with candles. The Duke moaned that a sword was transfixing his 48 heart, an inch at a time. The prince hurried into the chamber, but in that instant the Duke spasmed horribly and died. No mark was on his body. There had never been a mark to show what ailed him.

The prince wept. They were genuine tears. He had nothing to reproach his father with, everything to thank him for. Neverthelesss, they brought the young man the seal ring of the city, and he put it on. 49

It was winter, a cold blue-white weather with snow in the streets and countryside and a hard wizened sun that drove thin sharp blades of light through the sky, but gave no warmth. The Duke's funeral cortege passed slowly across the snow, the broad open chariots draped with black and silver, the black-plumed horses, the chanting priests with their glittering robes, their jeweled crucifixes and golden censers. Crowds lined the roadways to watch the spectacle. Among the beggar women stood a girl. No one noticed her. They did not glimpse the expression she veiled in her ragged scarf. She gazed at the bier pitilessly. As the young prince rode by in his sables, the seal ring on his hand, the eyes of the girl burned through her ashy hair, like a red fox through grasses. 50

The Duke was buried in the mausoleum you can visit to this day, on the east side of the city. Several months elapsed. The prince put his grief from him, and took up the business of the city competently. Wise and courteous he was, but he rarely smiled. At nineteen his spirit seemed worn. You might think he guessed the destiny that hung over him. 51

The winter was a hard one, too. The snow had come, and having come was loath to withdraw. When at last the spring returned, flushing the hills with color, it was no longer sensible to be sad. 52

The prince's name day fell about this time. A great banquet was planned, a ball. There had been neither in the palace for nigh on three years, not since the Duke's fatal illness first claimed him. Now the royal doors were to be thrown open to all men of influence and their families. The prince was liberal, charming and clever even in this. Aristocrat and rich trader were to mingle in the beautiful dining room, and in this very chamber, among the frescoes, the marbles and the candelabra. Even a merchant's daughter, if the merchant were notable in the city, would get to dance on the sea-green floor, under the white eye of the fearful clock. 53

The clock. There was some renewed controversy about the clock. They did not dare speak to the young prince. He was a skeptic, as his father had been. But had not a death already occurred? Was the clock not a flying in the jaws of fate? For those disturbed by it, there was a dim writing in their minds, in the dust of the street or the pattern of blossoms. *When the clock strikes*—But people do not positively heed these warnings. Man is afraid of his fears. He ignores the shadow of the wolf thrown on the paving before him, saying: It is only a shadow. 54

The silk merchant received his invitation to the palace, and to be sure, thought nothing of the clock. His house had been thrown into uproar. The most luscious silks of his workshop were carried into the house and laid before the wife and her two daughters, who chirruped and squealed with excitement. The merchant stood smugly by, above it all yet pleased at being 55 appreciated. "Oh, father!" cried the two sisters, "may I have this one with the gold piping?" "Oh, father, this one with the design of pineapples?" Later, a jeweler arrived and set out his trays. The merchant was generous. He wanted his women to look their best. It might be the night of their lives. Yet all the while, at the back of his mind, a little dark spot, itching, aching. He tried to ignore the spot, not scratch at it. His true daughter, the mad one. Nobody bothered to tell her about the invitation to the palace. They knew how she would react, mumbling in her hair about her sin and her penance, paddling her hands in the greasy ash to smear her face. Even the servants avoided her, as if she were just the cat seated by the fire. Less than the cat, for the cat saw to the mice—Just a block of stone. And yet, how fair she might have looked, decked in the pick of the merchant's wares, jewels at her throat. The prince himself could not have been unaware of her. And though marriage was impossible, other less holy, though equally honorable contracts, might have been arranged to the benefit of all concerned. The merchant sighed. He had scratched the darkness after all. He attempted to comfort himself by watching the two sisters exult over their apparel. He refused to admit that the finery would somehow make them seem but more ordinary than they were by contrast.

The evening of the banquet arrived. The family set off. Most of the ser- 56
vants sidled after. The prince had distributed largesse in the city; oxen roasted in the squares and the wine was free by royal order.

The house grew somber. In the deserted kitchen the fire went out. 57

By the heart, a segment of gloom rose up. 58

The girl glanced around her, and she laughed softly and shook out her 59
filthy hair. Of course, she knew as much as anyone, and more than most. This was to be her night, too.

A few minutes later she was in the garden beneath the old tower, stand- 60
ing over the young hazel tree which thrust up from the earth. It had become strong, the tree, despite the harsh winter. Now the girl nodded to it. She chanted under her breath. At length a pale light began to glow, far down near where the roots of the tree held to the ground. Out of the pale glow flew a thin black bird, which perched on the girl's shoulder. Together, the girl and the bird passed into the old tower. High up, a fire blazed that no one had lit. A tub steamed with scented water that no one had drawn. Shapes that were not real and barely seen flitted about. Rare perfumes, the rustle of garments, the glint of gems as yet invisible filled and did not fill the restless air.

Need I describe further? No. You will have seen paintings which de- 61
pict the attendance upon a witch of her familiar demons. Now one bathes her, another anoints her, another brings clothes and ornaments. Perhaps you do not credit such things in any case. Never mind that. I will tell you what happened in the courtyard before the palace.

Many carriages and chariots had driven through the square, avoiding 62
the roasting oxen, the barrels of wine, the cheering drunken citizens, and so through the gates into the courtyard. Just before ten o'clock (the hour, if you recall the clock, of the magician) a solitary carriage drove through the

square and into the court. The people in the square gawked at the carriage and pressed forward to see who would step out of it, this latecomer. It was a remarkable vehicle that looked to be fashioned of solid gold, all but the domed roof that was transparent flashing crystal. Six black horses drew it. The coachman and postillions were clad in crimson, and strangely masked as curious beasts and reptiles. One of these beast-men now hopped down and opened the door of the carriage. Out came a woman's figure in a cloak of white fur, and glided up the palace stair and in at the doors.

There was dancing in the ballroom. The whole chamber was bright and clamorous with music and the voices of men and women. There, between those two pillars, the prince sat in his chair, dark, courteous, seldom smiling. Here the musicians played, the deep-throated viol, the lively mandolin. And there the dancers moved up and down on the sea-green floor. But the music and the dancers had just paused. The figures on the clock were themselves in motion. The hour of the magician was about to strike. 63

As it struck, through the doorway came the figure in the fur cloak. And, as if they must, every eye turned to her. 64

For an instant she stood there, all white, as though she had brought the winter snow back with her. And then she loosed the cloak from her shoulders, it slipped away, and she was all fire. 65

She wore a gown of apricot brocade embroidered thickly with gold. Her sleeves and the bodice of her gown were slashed over ivory satin sewn with large rosy pearls. Pearls, too, were wound in her hair that was the shade of antique burnished copper. She was so beautiful that when the clock was still, nobody spoke. She was so beautiful it was hard to look at her for very long. 66

The prince got up from his chair. He did not know he had. Now he started out across the floor, between the dancers, who parted silently to let him through. He went toward the girl in the doorway as if she drew him by a chain. 67

The prince had hardly ever acted without considering first what he did. Now he did not consider. He bowed to the girl. 68

"Madam," he said. "You are welcome. Madam," he said. "Tell me who you are." 69

She smiled. 70

"My rank," she said. "Would you know that, my lord? It is similar to yours, or would be were I now mistress in my dead mother's palace. But, unfortunately, an unscrupulous man caused the downfall of our house." 71

"Misfortune indeed," said the prince. "Tell me your name. Let me right the wrong done you." 72

"You shall," said the girl. "Trust me, you shall. For my name, I would rather keep it secret for the present. But you may call me, if you will, a pet name I have given myself—Ashella." 73

"Ashella. . . . But I see no ash about you," said the prince, dazzled by her gleam, laughing a little, stiffly, for laughter was not his habit. 74

"Ash and cinders from a cold and bitter hearth," said she. But she smiled again. "Now everyone is staring at us, my lord, and the musicians 75 are impatient to begin again. Out of all these ladies, can it be you will lead me in the dance?"

"As long as you will dance," he said. "You shall dance with me." 76

And that is how it was. 77

There were many dances, slow and fast, whirling measures and gentle 78
ones. And here and there, the prince and the maiden were parted. Always then he looked eagerly after her, sparing no regard for the other girls whose hands lay in his. It was not like him, he was usually so careful. But the other young men who danced on that floor, who clasped her fingers or her narrow waist in the dance, also gazed after her when she was gone. She danced, as she appeared, like fire. Though if you had asked those young men whether they would rather tie her to themselves, as the prince did, they would have been at a loss. For it is not easy to keep pace with fire.

The hour of the hag struck on the clock. 79

The prince grew weary of dancing with the girl and losing her in the 80
dance to others and refinding her and losing her again.

Behind the curtains there is a tall window in the east wall that opens on 81
the terrace above the garden. He drew her out there, into the spring night. He gave an order, and small tables were brought with delicacies and sweets and wine. He sat by her, watching every gesture she made, as if he would paint her portrait afterward.

In the ballroom, here, under the clock, the people murmured. But it 82
was not quite the murmur you would expect, the scandalous murmur about a woman come from nowhere that the prince had made so much of. At the periphery of the ballroom, the silk merchant sat, pale as a ghost, thinking of a ghost, the living ghost of his true daughter. No one else recognized her. Only he. Some trick of the heart had enabled him to know her. He said nothing of it. As the step-sisters and wife gossiped with other wives and sisters, an awful foreboding weighed him down, sent him cold and dumb.

And now it is almost midnight, the moment when the page of the night 83
turns over into day. Almost midnight, the hour when the figure of Death strikes the golden bell of the clock. And what will happen when the clock strikes? Your face announces that you know. Be patient; let us see if you do.

"I am being foolish," said the prince to Ashella on the terrace. "But 84
perhaps I am entitled to foolish, just once in my life. What are you saying?" For the girl was speaking low beside him, and he could not catch her words.

"I am saying a spell to bind you to me," she said. 85

"But I am already bound." 86

"Be bound then. Never go free." 87

"I do not wish it," he said. He kissed her hands and he said, "I do not 88
know you, but I will wed you. Is that proof your spell has worked? I will wed you, and get back for you the rights you have lost."

"If it were only so simple," said Ashella, smiling, smiling. "But the 89
debt is too cruel. Justice requires a harsher payment."

And then, in the ballroom, Death struck the first note on the golden 90
bell.

The girl smiled and she said, 91

"I curse you in my mother's name." 92

The second stroke. 93

"I curse you in my own name." 94

The third stroke. 95

"And in the name of those that your father slew." 96

The fourth stroke. 97

"And in the name of my Master, who rules the world." 98

As the fifth, the sixth, the seventh strokes pealed out, the prince stood 99
nonplussed. At the eighth and the ninth strokes, the strength of the malediction seemed to curdle his blood. He shivered and his brain writhed. At the tenth stroke, he saw a change in the loveliness before him. She grew thinner, taller. At the eleventh stroke, he beheld a thing in a ragged black cowl and robe. It grinned at him. It was all grin below a triangle of sockets of nose and eyes. At the twelfth stroke, the prince saw Death and knew him.

In the ballroom, a hideous grinding noise, as the gears of the clock 100
failed. Followed by a hollow booming, as the mechanism stopped entirely.

The conjuration of Death vanished from the terrace. 101

Only one thing was left behind. A woman's shoe. A shoe no woman 102
could ever have danced in. It was made of glass.

Did you intend to protest about the shoe? Shall I finish the story, or 103
would you rather I did not? It is not the ending you are familiar with. Yes, I perceive you understand that, now.

I will go quickly, then, for your carriage must soon be here. And there 104
is not a great deal more to relate.

The prince lost his mind. Partly from what he had seen, partly from the 105
spells the young witch had netted him in. He could think of nothing but the girl who had named herself Ashella. He raved that Death had borne her away but he would recover her from Death. She had left the glass shoe as token of her love. He must discover her with the aid of the shoe. Whomsoever the shoe fitted would be Ashella. For there was this added complication, that Death might hide her actual appearance. None had seen the girl before. She had disappeared like smoke. The one infallible test was the shoe. That was why she had left it for him.

His ministers would have reasoned with the prince, but he was past 106
reason. His intellect had collapsed as totally as only a profound intellect can. A lunatic, he rode about the city. He struck out at those who argued with him. On a particular occasion, drawing a dagger, he killed, not apparently noticing what he did. His demand was explicit. Every woman, young or old, maid or married, must come forth from her home, must put her foot into the shoe of glass. They came. They had not choice. Some approached in terror, some weeping. Even the aged beggar women obliged, and they cackled, enjoying the sight of royalty gone mad. One alone did not come.

Now it is not illogical that out of the hundreds of women whose feet 107
were put into the shoe, a single woman might have been found that the shoe fitted. But this did not happen. Nor did the situation alter, despite a

lurid fable that some, tickled by the idea of wedding the prince, cut off their toes that the shoe might fit them. And if they did, it was to no avail, for still the shoe did not.

Is it really surprising? The shoe was sorcerous. It constantly changed 108
itself, its shape, its size, in order that no foot, save one, could ever be got into it.

Summer spread across the land. The city took on its golden summer 109
glaze, its fetid summer smell.

What had been a whisper of intrigue, swelled into a steady distant 110
thunder. Plots were being hatched.

One day, the silk merchant was brought, trembling and grey of face, to 111
the prince. The merchant's dumbness had broken. He had unburdened himself of his fear at confession, but the priest had not proved honest. In the dawn, men had knocked on the door of the merchant's house. Now he stumbled to the chair of the prince.

Both looked twice their years, but, if anything, the prince looked the 112
elder. He did not lift his eyes. Over and over in his hands he turned the glass shoe.

The merchant, stumbling too in his speech, told the tale of his first wife 113
and his daughter. He told everything, leaving out no detail. He did not even omit the end: that since the night of the banquet the girl had been absent from his house, taking nothing with her—save a young hazel from the garden beneath the tower.

The prince leapt from his chair. 114

His clothes were filthy and unkempt. His face was smeared with sweat 115
and dust . . . it resembled, momentarily, another face.

Without guard or attendant, the prince ran through the city toward the 116
merchant's house, and on the road, the intriguers waylaid and slew him. As he fell, the glass shoe dropped from his hands, and shattered in a thousand fragments.

There is little else worth mentioning. 117

Those who usurped the city were villains and not merely that, but 118
fools. Within a year, external enemies were at the gates. A year more, and the city had been sacked, half burnt out, ruined. The manner in which you find it now, is somewhat better than it was then. And it is not now anything for a man to be proud of. As you were quick to note, many here earn a miserable existence by conducting visitors about the streets, the palace, showing them the dregs of the city's past.

Which was not a request, in fact, for you to give me money. Throw 119
some from your carriage window if your conscience bothers you. My own wants are few.

No, I have no further news of the girl, Ashella, the witch. A devotee of 120
Satanas, she has doubtless worked plentiful woe in the world. And a witch is long-lived. Even so, she will die eventually. None escapes Death. Then you may pity her, if you like. Those who serve the gentleman below—who can guess what their final lot will be? But I am very sorry the story did not please you. It is not, maybe, a happy choice before a journey.

And there is your carriage at last. 121

What? Ah, no, I shall stay here in the ballroom where you came on me. 122
I have often paused here through the years. It is the clock. It has a certain—what shall I call it—power, to draw me back.

I am not trying to unnerve you. Why should you suppose that? Be- 123
cause of my knowledge of the city, of the story? You think that I am implying that I myself am Death? Now you laugh. Yes, it is absurd. Observe the twelfth figure on the clock. Is he not as you have always heard Death described? And am I in the least like that twelfth figure?

Although, of course, the story was not as you have heard it, either. 124

A Chinese "Cinderella"

TUAN CH'ÊNG-SHIH

"The earliest datable version of the Cinderella story anywhere in the world occurs in a Chinese book written about 850–860 A.D." Thus begins Arthur Waley's essay on the Chinese "Cinderella" in the March 1947 edition of Folk-Lore. *The recorder of the tale is a man named Tuan Ch'êng-shih, whose father was an important official in Szechwan and who himself held a high post in the office arranging the ceremonies associated with imperial ancestor worship.*

Among the people of the south there is a tradition that before the Ch'in and 1
Han dynasties there was a cave-master called Wu. The aborigines called the place the Wu cave. He married two wives. One wife died. She had a daughter called Yeh-hsien, who from childhood was intelligent and good at making pottery on the wheel. Her father loved her. After some years the father died, and she was ill-treated by her step-mother, who always made her collect firewood in dangerous places and draw water from deep pools. She once got a fish about two inches long, with red fins and golden eyes. She put it into a bowl of water. It grew bigger every day, and after she had changed the bowl several times she could find no bowl big enough for it, so she threw it into the back pond. Whatever food was left over from meals she put into the water to feed it. When she came to the pond, the fish always exposed its head and pillowed it on the bank; but when anyone else came, it did not come out. The step-mother knew about this, but when she watched for it, it did not once appear. So she tricked the girl, saying, "Haven't you worked hard! I am going to give you a new dress." She then made the girl change out of her tattered clothing. Afterwards she sent her to get water from another spring and reckoning that it was several hundred leagues, the step-mother at her leisure put on her daughter's clothes, hid a sharp blade up her sleeve, and went to the pond. She called to the fish. The fish at once put its head out, and she chopped it off and killed it. The fish was now more than ten feet long. She served it up and it tasted twice as good as an ordinary fish. She hid the bones under the dung-hill. Next day, when the girl came to the pond, no fish appeared. She howled with grief in

the open countryside, and suddenly there appeared a man with his hair loose over his shoulders and coarse clothes. He came down from the sky. He consoled her, saying, "Don't howl! Your step-mother has killed the fish and its bones are under the dung. You go back, take the fish's bones and hide them in your room. Whatever you want, you have only to pray to them for it. It is bound to be granted." The girl followed his advice, and was able to provide herself with gold, pearls, dresses and food whenever she wanted them.

When the time came for the cave-festival, the step-mother went, leaving the girl to keep watch over the fruit-trees in the garden. She waited till the step-mother was some way off, and then went herself, wearing a cloak of stuff spun from kingfisher feathers and shoes of gold. Her step-sister recognized her and said to the step-mother, "That's very like my sister." The step-mother suspected the same thing. The girl was aware of this and went away in such a hurry that she lost one shoe. It was picked up by one of the people of the cave. When the step-mother got home, she found the girl asleep, with her arms around one of the trees in the garden, and thought no more about it. 2

This cave was near to an island in the sea. On this island was a kingdom called T'o-han. Its soldiers had subdued twenty or thirty other islands and it had a coast-line of several thousand leagues. The cave-man sold the shoe in T'o-han, and the ruler of T'o-han got it. He told those about him to put it on; but it was an inch too small even for the one among them that had the smallest foot. He ordered all the women in his kingdom to try it on, but there was not one that it fitted. It was light as down and made no noise even when treading on stone. The king of T'o-han thought the cave-man had got it unlawfully. He put him in prison and tortured him, but did not end by finding out where it had come from. So he threw it down at the wayside. Then they went everywhere[1] through all the people's houses and arrested them. If there was a woman's shoe, they arrested them and told the king of T'o-han. He thought it strange, searched the inner-rooms and found Yeh-hsien. He made her put on the shoe, and it was true. 3

Yeh-hsien then came forward, wearing her cloak spun from halcyon feathers and her shoes. She was as beautiful as a heavenly being. She now began to render service to the king, and he took the fish-bones and Yeh-hsien, and brought them back to his country. 4

The step-mother and step-sister were shortly afterwards struck by flying stones, and died. The cave people were sorry for them and buried them in a stone-pit, which was called the Tomb of the Distressed Women. The men of the cave made mating-offerings there; any girl they prayed for there, they got. The king of T'o-han, when he got back to his kingdom, made Yeh-hsien his chief wife. The first year the king was very greedy and by his prayers to the fish-bones got treasures and jade without limit. Next year, there was no response, so the king buried the fish-bones on the seashore. He covered them with a hundred bushels of pearls and bordered 5

---

[1]Something here seems to have gone slightly wrong with the text. [Waley]

them with gold. Later there was a mutiny of some soldiers who had been conscripted and their general opened (the hiding-place) in order to make better provision for his army. One night they (the bones) were washed away by the tide.

This story was told me by Li Shih-yüan, who has been in the service of my family a long while. He was himself originally a man from the caves of Yung-chou and remembers many strange things of the South. 6

The Maiden, the Frog, and the Chief's Son (An African "Cinderella")

The version of the tale that follows was recorded in the (West African) Hausa language and published, originally, in 1911 by Frank Edgar. The tale remained unavailable to nonspeakers of Hausa until 1965, when Neil Skinner (of UCLA) completed an English translation.

There was once a man had two wives, and they each had a daughter. And the one wife, together with her daughter, he couldn't abide; but the other, with her daughter, he dearly loved. 1

Well, the day came when the wife that he disliked fell ill, and it so happened that her illness proved fatal, and she died. And her daughter was taken over by the other wife, the one he loved; and she moved into that wife's hut. And there she dwelt, having no mother of her own, just her father. And every day the woman would push her out, to go off to the bush to gather wood. When she returned, she had to pound up the *fura.* Then she had the *tuwo* to pound, and, after that, to stir. And then they wouldn't even let her eat the *tuwo.* All they gave her to eat were the burnt bits at the bottom of the pot. And day after day she continued thus. 2

Now she had an elder brother, and he invited her to come and eat regularly at his home—to which she agreed. But still when she had been to the bush, and returned home, and wanted a drink of water, they wouldn't let her have one. Nor would they give her proper food—only the coarsest of the grindings and the scrapings from the pot. These she would take, and going with them to a borrow-pit, throw them in. And the frogs would come out and start eating the scrapings. Then, having eaten them up, they would go back into the water; and she too would return home. 3

And so things went on day after day, until the day of the Festival arrived. And on this day, when she went along with the scrapings and coarse grindings, she found a frog squatting there; and realized that he was waiting for her! She got there and threw in the bits of food. Whereupon the frog said, "Maiden, you've always been very kind to us, and now we—but just you come along tomorrow morning. That's the morning of the Festival. Come along then, and we'll be kind to you, in our turn." "Fine" she said, and went off home. 4

Next morning was the Festival, and she was going off to the borrow-pit, just as the frog had told her. But as she was going, her half-sister's 5 mother said to her, "Hey—come here, you good-for-nothing girl! You haven't stirred the *tuwo,* or pounded the *fura,* or fetched the wood or the water." So the girl returned. And the frog spent the whole day waiting for her. But she, having returned to the compound, set off to fetch wood. Then she fetched water, and set about pounding the *tuwo,* and stirred it till it was done and then took it off the fire. And presently she was told to take the scrapings. She did so and went off to the borrow-pit, where she found the frog. "Tut tut, girl!" said he, "I've been waiting for you here since morning, and you never came." "Old fellow" she said, "You see, I'm a slave." "How come?" he asked. "Simple" she said, "My mother died—died leaving me her only daughter. I have an elder brother, but he is married and has a compound of his own. And my father put me in the care of his other wife. And indeed he had never loved my mother. So I was moved into the hut of his other wife. And, as I told you, slavery is my lot. Every morning I have to go off to the bush to get wood. When I get back from that I have to pound the *fura,* and then I pound the *tuwo,* and then start stirring it. And even when I have finished stirring the *tuwo,* I'm not given it to eat—just the scrapings." Says the frog, "Girl, give us your hand." And she held it out to him, and they both leaped into the water.

Then he went and picked her up and swallowed her. (And he vomited her up.) "Good people" said he, "Look and tell me, is she straight or crooked?" And they looked and answered, "She is bent to the left." So he picked her up and swallowed her again and then brought her up, and again asked them the same question. "She's quite straight now" they said. "Good" said he. 6

Next he vomited up cloths for her, and bangles, and rings, and a pair of shoes, one of silver, one of gold. "And now" said he, "Off you go to the dancing." So all these things were given to her, and he said to her, "When you get there, and when the dancing is nearly over and the dancers dispersing, you're to leave your golden shoe, the right one, there." And the girl replied to the frog, "Very well, old fellow, I understand," and off she went. 7

Meanwhile the chief's son had caused the young men and girls to dance for his pleasure, and when she reached the space where they were dancing he saw her. "Well!" said the chief's son, "*There's* a maiden for you, if you like. Don't you let her go and join in the dancing—I don't care whose home she comes from. Bring her here!" So the servants of the chief's son went over and came back with her to where he was. He told her to sit down on the couch, and she took her seat there accordingly. 8

They chatted together for some time, till the dancers began to disperse. Then she said to the chief's son, "I must be going home." "Oh, are you off?" said he. "Yes," said she and rose to her feet. "I'll accompany you on your way for a little" said the chief's son, and he did so. But she had left her right shoe behind. Presently she said, "Chief's son, you must go back now," and he did so. And afterwards she too turned and made her way back. 9

And there she found the frog by the edge of the water waiting for her. He took her hand and the two of them jumped into the water. Then he 10 picked her up and swallowed her, and again vomited her up; and there she was, just as she had been before, a sorry sight. And taking her ragged things she went off home.

When she got there, she said, "Fellow-wife of my mother, I'm not feeling very well." And the other said, "Rascally slut! You have been up to no good—refusing to come home, refusing to fetch water or wood, refusing to pound the *fura* or make the *tuwo*. Very well then! No food for you today!" And so the girl set off to her elder brother's compound, and there ate her food, and so returned home again. 11

But meanwhile, the chief's son had picked up the shoe and said to his father, "Dad, I have seen a girl who wears a pair of shoes, one of gold, one of silver. Look, here's the golden one—she forgot it and left it behind. She's the girl I want to marry. So let all the girls of this town, young and old, be gathered together, and let this shoe be given to them to put on." "Very well" said the chief. 12

And so it was proclaimed, and all the girls, young and old, were collected and gathered together. And the chief's son went and sat there beside the shoe. Each girl came, and each tried on the shoe, but it fitted none of them, none of the girls of the town; until only the girl who had left it was left. Then someone said "Just a minute! There's that girl in so-and-so's compound, whose mother died." "Yes, that's right," said another, "Someone go and fetch her." And someone went and fetched her. 13

But the minute she arrived to try it on, the shoe itself of its own accord, ran across and made her foot get into it. Then said the chief's son, "Right, here's my wife." 14

At this, the other woman—the girl's father's other wife—said, "But the shoe belongs to my daughter; it was she who forgot it at the place of the dancing, not this good-for-nothing slut." But the chief's son insisted that, since he had seen the shoe fit the other girl, as far as he was concerned, she was the one to be taken to his compound in marriage. And so they took her there, and there she spent one night. 15

Next morning she went out of her hut and round behind it, and there saw the frog. She knelt respectfully and said, "Welcome, old fellow, welcome" and greeted him. Says he, "Tonight we shall be along to bring some things for you." "Thank you" said she, and he departed. 16

Well, that night, the frog rallied all the other frogs, and all his friends, both great and small came along. And he, their leader, said to them, "See here—my daughter is being married. So I want every one of you to make a contribution." And each of them went and fetched what he could afford, whereupon their leader thanked them all, and then vomited up a silver bed, a brass bed, a copper bed, and an iron bed. And went on vomiting up things for her—such as woollen blankets, and rugs, and satins, and velvets. 17

"Now" said he to the girl, "If your heart is ever troubled, just lie down on this brass bed" and he went on, "And when the chief's son's other wives come to greet you, give them two calabashes of cola-nuts and ten thousand cowrie shells; then, when his concubines come to greet you, give them one calabash of cola-nuts and five thousand cowries." "Very well" said she. 18

Then he said, "And when the concubines come to receive corn for making *tuwo,* say to them, 'There's a hide-bag full, help yourselves.'" "Very well" she said. "And" he went on, "If your father's wife comes along with her daughter and asks you what it is like living in the chief's compound, say 'Living in the chief's compound is a wearisome business—for they measure out corn there with the shell of a Bambara groundnut.'"

So there she dwelt, until one day her father's favorite wife brought her 19
daughter along at night, took her into the chief's compound, and brought the other girl out and took her to her own compound. There she said. "Oh! I forgot to get you to tell her all about married life in the chief's compound." "Oh, its a wearisome business" answered our girl. "How so?" asked the older woman, surprised. "Well, they use the shell of a Bambara groundnut for measuring out corn. Then, if the chief's other wives come to greet you, you answer them with the 'Pf' of contempt. If the concubines come to greet you, you clear your throat, hawk, and spit. And if your husband comes into your hut, you yell at him." "I see" said the other—and her daughter stayed behind the chief's son's compound.

Next morning when it was light, the wives came to greet her—and she 20
said "Pf" to them. The concubines came to greet her, and she spat at them. Then when night fell, the chief's son made his way to her hut, and she yelled at him. And he was amazed and went aside, and for two days pondered the matter.

Then he had his wives and concubines collected and said to them, 21
"Look, now—I've called you to ask you. They haven't brought me the same girl. How did that one treat all of you?" "Hm—how indeed!" they all exclaimed. "Each morning, when we wives went to greet her, she would give us cola-nuts, two calabashes full, and cowries, ten thousand of them to buy tobacco flowers. And when the concubines went to greet her, she would give them a calabash of cola-nuts, and five thousand cowries to buy tobacco flowers with; and in the evening, for corn for *tuwo,* it would be a whole hide-bag full." "You see?" said he, "As for me, whenever I came to enter her hut, I found her respectfully kneeling. And she wouldn't get up from there, until I had entered and sat down on the bed."

"Hey," he called out, "Boys, come over here!" And when they came, 22
he went into her hut and took a sword, and chopped her up into little pieces, and had them collect them and wrap them up in clothing; and then taken back to her home.

And when they got there, they found his true wife lying in the fire- 23
place, and picking her up they took her back to her husband.

And next morning when it was light, she picked up a little gourd wa- 24
ter-bottle and going around behind her hut, there saw the frog. "Welcome, welcome, old fellow," said she, and went on. "Old fellow, what I should like is to have a well built; and then you, all of you, can come and live in it and be close to me." "All right" said the frog, "You tell your husband." And she did so.

And he had a well dug for her, close to her hut. And the frogs came and 25
entered the well and there they lived. That's all. *Kungurus kan kusu.*

Oochigeaskw—The Rough-Faced Girl (A Native American "Cinderella")

The following version of the tale was told, originally, in the Algonquin language. Native Americans who spoke Algonquian lived in the Eastern Woodlands of what is now the United States and in the northern, semiarctic areas of present-day Canada.

There was once a large village of the MicMac Indians of the Eastern Algonquins, built beside a lake. At the far end of the settlement stood a lodge, and in it lived a being who was always invisible. He had a sister who looked after him, and everyone knew that any girl who could see him might marry him. For that reason there were very few girls who did not try, but it was very long before anyone succeeded. 1

This is the way in which the test of sight was carried out: at evening-time, when the Invisible One was due to be returning home, his sister would walk with any girl who might come down to the lakeshore. She, of course, could see her brother, since he was always visible to her. As soon as she saw him, she would say to the girls: 2

"Do you see my brother?" 3

"Yes," they would generally reply—though some of them did say "No." 4

To those who said that they could indeed see him, the sister would say: 5

"Of what is his shoulder strap made?" Some people say that she would enquire: 6

"What is his moose-runner's haul?" or "With what does he draw his sled?" 7

And they would answer: 8

"A strip of rawhide" or "a green flexible branch," or something of that kind. 9

Then she, knowing that they had not told the truth, would say: 10

"Very well, let us return to the wigwam!" 11

When they had gone in, she would tell them not to sit in a certain place, because it belonged to the Invisible One. Then, after they had helped to cook the supper, they would wait with great curiosity, to see him eat. They could be sure he was a real person, for when he took off his moccasins they became visible, and his sister hung them up. But beyond this they saw nothing of him, not even when they stayed in the place all the night, as many of them did. 12

Now there lived in the village an old man who was a widower, and his three daughters. The youngest girl was very small, weak and often ill: and yet her sisters, especially the elder, treated her cruelly. The second daughter was kinder, and sometimes took her side: but the wicked sister would burn her hands and feet with hot cinders, and she was covered with scars from this treatment. She was so marked that people called her *Oochigeaskw,* the Rough-Faced-Girl. 13

14 When her father came home and asked why she had such burns, the bad sister would at once say that it was her own fault, for she had disobeyed orders and gone near the fire and fallen into it.

15 These two elder sisters decided one day to try their luck at seeing the Invisible One. So they dressed themselves in their finest clothes, and tried to look their prettiest. They found the Invisible One's sister and took the usual walk by the water.

16 When he came, and when they were asked if they could see him, they answered: "Of course." And when asked about the shoulder strap or sled cord, they answered: "A piece of rawhide."

17 But of course they were lying like the others, and they got nothing for their pains.

18 The next afternoon, when the father returned home, he brought with him many of the pretty little shells from which wampum was made, and they set to work to string them.

19 That day, poor Little Oochigeaskw, who had always gone barefoot, got a pair of her father's moccasins, old ones, and put them into water to soften them so that she could wear them. Then she begged her sisters for a few wampum shells. The elder called her a "little pest," but the younger one gave her some. Now, with no other clothes than her usual rags, the poor little thing went into the woods and got herself some sheets of birch bark, from which she made a dress, and put marks on it for decoration, in the style of long ago. She made a petticoat and a loose gown, a cap, leggings and a handkerchief. She put on her father's large old moccasins, which were far too big for her, and went forth to try her luck. She would try, she thought, to discover whether she could see the Invisible One.

20 She did not begin very well. As she set off, her sisters shouted and hooted, hissed and yelled, and tried to make her stay. And the loafers around the village, seeing the strange little creature, called out "Shame!"

21 The poor little girl in her strange clothes, with her face all scarred, was an awful sight, but she was kindly received by the sister of the Invisible One. And this was, of course, because this noble lady understood far more about things than simply the mere outside which all the rest of the world knows. As the brown of the evening sky turned to black, the lady took her down to the lake.

22 "Do you see him?" the Invisible One's sister asked.

23 "I do, indeed—and he is wonderful!" said Oochigeaskw.

24 The sister asked:

25 "And what is his sled-string?"

26 The little girl said:

27 "It is the Rainbow."

28 "And, my sister, what is his bow-string?"

29 "It is The Spirit's Road—the Milky Way."

30 "So you *have* seen him," said his sister. She took the girl home with her and bathed her. As she did so, all the scars disappeared from her body. Her hair grew again, as it was combed, long, like a blackbird's wing. Her

eyes were now like stars: in all the world there was no other such beauty. Then, from her treasurers, the lady gave her a wedding garment, and adorned her.

Then she told Oochigeaskw to take the *wife's* seat in the wigwam: the one next to where the Invisible One sat, beside the entrance. And when he came in, terrible and beautiful, he smiled and said: 31

"So we are found out!" 32

"Yes," said his sister. And so Oochigeaskw became his wife. 33

Walt Disney's "Cinderella"

ADAPTED BY CAMPBELL GRANT

Walter Elias Disney (1901–1966), winner of thirty-two Academy Awards, is world famous for his cartoon animations. After achieving recognition with cartoons shorts populated by such immortals as Mickey Mouse and Donald Duck, he produced the full-length animated film version of Snow White and the Seven Dwarfs *in 1937. He followed with other animations, including "Cinderella" (1950), which he adapted from Perrault's version of the tale. A Little Golden Book, the text of which appears here, was then adapted from the film by Campbell Grant.*

Once upon a time in a far-away land lived a sweet and pretty girl named Cinderella. She made her home with her mean old stepmother and her two stepsisters, and they made her do all the work in the house. 1

Cinderella cooked and baked. She cleaned and scrubbed. She had no time left for parties and fun. 2

But one day an invitation came from the palace of the king. 3

A great ball was to be given for the prince of the land. And every young girl in the kingdom was invited. 4

"How nice!" thought Cinderella. "I am invited, too." 5

But her mean stepsisters never thought of her. They thought only of themselves, of course. They had all sorts of jobs for Cinderella to do. 6

"Wash this slip. Press this dress. Curl my hair. Find my fan." 7

They both kept shouting, as fast as they could speak. 8

"But I must get ready myself. I'm going, too," said Cinderella. 9

"You!" they hooted. "The Prince's ball for you?" 10

And they kept her busy all day long. She worked in the morning, while her stepsisters slept. She worked all afternoon, while they bathed and dressed. And in the evening she had to help them put on the finishing touches for the ball. She had not one minute to think of herself. 11

Soon the coach was ready at the door. The ugly stepsisters were powdered, pressed, and curled. But there stood Cinderella in her workaday rags. 12

"Why, Cinderella!" said the stepsisters. "You're not dressed for the ball." 13

"No," said Cinderella. "I guess I cannot go." 14

Poor Cinderella sat weeping in the garden. 15

Suddenly a little old woman with a sweet, kind face stood before her. It 16
was her fairy godmother.

"Hurry, child!" she said. "You are going to the ball!" 17

Cinderella could hardly believe her eyes! The fairy godmother turned a 18
fat pumpkin into a splendid coach.

Next her pet mice became horses, and her dog a fine footman. The barn 19
horse was turned into a coachman.

"There, my dear," said the fairy godmother. "Now into the coach with 20
you, and off to the ball you go."

"But my dress—" said Cinderella. 21

"Lovely, my dear," the fairy godmother began. Then she really looked 22
at Cinderella's rags.

"Oh, good heavens," she said. "You can never go in that." She waved 23
her magic wand.

"Salaga dolla,
Menchicka boola,
Bibbidi bobbidi boo!" she said.

There stood Cinderella in the loveliest ball dress that ever was. And on 24
her feet were tiny glass slippers!

"Oh," cried Cinderella. "How can I ever thank you?" 25

"Just have a wonderful time at the ball, my dear," said her fairy god- 26
mother. "But remember, this magic lasts only until midnight. At the stroke of midnight, the spell will be broken. And everything will be as it was before."

"I will remember," said Cinderella. "It is more than I ever dreamed of." 27

Then into the magic coach she stepped, and was whirled away to the 28
ball.

And such a ball! The king's palace was ablaze with lights. There was 29
music and laughter. And every lady in the land was dressed in her beautiful best.

But Cinderella was the loveliest of them all. The prince never left her 30
side, all evening long. They danced every dance. They had supper side by side. And they happily smiled into each other's eyes.

But all at once the clock began to strike midnight, Bong Bong Bong— 31

"Oh!" cried Cinderella. "I almost forgot!" 32

And without a word, away she ran, out of the ballroom and down the 33
palace stairs. She lost one glass slipper. But she could not stop.

Into her magic coach she stepped, and away it rolled. But as the clock 34
stopped striking, the coach disappeared. And no one knew where she had gone.

Next morning all the kingdom was filled with the news. The Grand 35
Duke was going from house to house, with a small glass slipper in his hand. For the prince had said he would marry no one but the girl who could wear that tiny shoe.

Every girl in the land tried hard to put it on. The ugly stepsisters tried 36
hardest of all. But not a one could wear the glass shoe.

And where was Cinderella? Locked in her room. For the mean old 37
stepmother was taking no chances of letting her try on the slipper. Poor
Cinderella! It looked as if the Grand Duke would surely pass her by.

But her little friends the mice got the stepmother's key. And they 38
pushed it under Cinderella's door. So down the long stairs she came, as the
Duke was just about to leave.

"Please!" cried Cinderella. "Please let me try." 39

And of course the slipper fitted, since it was her very own. 40

That was all the Duke needed. Now his long search was done. And so 41
Cinderella became the prince's bride, and lived happily ever after—and the
little pet mice lived in the palace and were happy ever after, too.

Cinderella

ANNE SEXTON

Anne Sexton (1928–1974) has been acclaimed as one of America's outstanding contemporary poets. In 1967, she won the Pulitzer Prize for poetry for Live or Die. *She published four other collections of her work, including* Transformations, *in which she recast, with a modern twist, popular European fairy tales such as "Cinderella." Sexton's poetry has appeared in* The New Yorker, Harper's, *the* Atlantic, *and* Saturday Review. *She received a Robert Frost Fellowship (1959), a scholarship from Radcliffe College's New Institute for Independent Study (1961–1963), a grant from the Ford Foundation (1964), and a Guggenheim Award (1969). In her book* All My Pretty Ones, *Sexton quoted Franz Kafka: "The books we need are the kind that act upon us like a misfortune, that make us suffer like the death of someone we love more than ourselves. A book should serve as the axe for the frozen sea within us." Asked in an interview (by Patricia Marz) about this quotation, Sexton responded: "I think [poetry] should be a shock to the senses. It should almost hurt."*

You always read about it:
the plumber with twelve children
who wins the Irish Sweepstakes.
From toilets to riches.
That story.

Or the nursemaid,
some luscious sweet from Denmark
who captures the oldest son's heart.
From diapers to Dior.
That story.

Or a milkman who serves the wealthy,
eggs, cream, butter, yogurt, milk,
the white truck like an ambulance
who goes into real estate
and makes a pile.
From homogenized to martinis at lunch.

Or the charwoman
who is on the bus when it cracks up
and collects enough from the insurance.
From mops to Bonwit Teller.
That story.

Once
the wife of a rich man was on her deathbed
and she said to her daughter Cinderella:
Be devout. Be good, Then I will smile
down from heaven in the seam of a cloud.
The man took another wife who had
two daughters, pretty enough
but with hearts like blackjacks.
Cinderella was their maid.
She slept on the sooty hearth each night
and walked around looking like Al Jolson.
Her father brought presents home from town,
jewels and gowns for the other women
but the twig of a tree for Cinderella.
She planted that twig on her mother's grave
and it grew to a tree where a white dove sat.
Whenever she wished for anything the dove
would drop it like an egg upon the ground.
The bird is important, my dears, so heed him.

Next came the ball, as you all know.
It was a marriage market.
The prince was looking for a wife.
All but Cinderella were preparing
and gussying up for the big event.
Cinderella begged to go too.
Her stepmother threw a dish of lentils
into the cinders and said: Pick them
up in an hour and you shall go.
The white dove brought all his friends;
all the warm wings of the fatherland came,
and picked up the lentils in a jiffy.
No, Cinderella, said the stepmother,
you have no clothes and cannot dance.

That's the way with stepmothers.

Cinderella went to the tree at the grave
and cried forth like a gospel singer:
Mama! Mama! My turtledove,
send me to the prince's ball!
The bird dropped down a golden dress
and delicate little gold slippers.
Rather a large package for a simple bird.
So she went. Which is no surprise.

Her stepmother and sisters didn't
recognize her without her cinder face
and the prince took her hand on the spot
and danced with no other the whole day.

As nightfall came she thought she'd better
get home. The prince walked her home
and she disappeared into the pigeon house
and although the prince took an axe and broke
it open she was gone. Back to her cinders.
These events repeated themselves for three days.
However on the third day the prince
covered the palace steps with cobbler's wax
and Cinderella's gold shoe stuck upon it.
Now he would find whom the shoe fit
and find his strange dancing girl for keeps.
He went to their house and the two sisters
were delighted because they had lovely feet.
The eldest went into a room to try the slipper on
but her big toe got in the way so she simply
sliced it off and put on the slipper.
The prince rode away with her until the white dove
told him to look at the blood pouring forth.
That is the way with amputations.
They don't just heal up like a wish.
The other sister cut off her heel
but the blood told as blood will.
The prince was getting tired.
He began to feel like a shoe salesman.
But he gave it one last try.
This time Cinderella fit into the shoe
like a love letter into its envelope.

At the wedding ceremony
the two sisters came to curry favor
and the white dove pecked their eyes out.

Two hollow spots were left
like soup spoons.

Cinderella and the prince
lived, they say, happily ever after,
like two dolls in a museum case
never bothered by diapers or dust,
never arguing over the timing of an egg,
never telling the same story twice,
never getting a middle-aged spread,
their darling smiles pasted on for eternity.

Regular Bobbsey Twins.
That story.

The Politically Correct Cinderella

JAMES FINN GARNER

We end the variant readings of "Cinderella" on a light note, with James Finn Garner's "politically correct" version of the tale. There has been fierce debate on campuses nationwide, over the past several years, on the extent to which faculty and students feel themselves pressured to express left-leaning views on gender, race, culture, and politics. Some faculty have accused colleagues of acting as a "PC police" that patrols the intellectual content of the classroom. The PC police, in the context of this chapter, would be the critics who point out just how loaded with offensive assumptions about men, women, and culture a fairy tale can be. Garner is poking fun at such analyses. We begin the selection with the introduction to his book, Politically Correct Bedtime Stories *(Macmillan, 1994).*

INTRODUCTION

When they were first written, the stories on which the following tales are 1
based certainly served their purpose—to entrench the patriarchy, to estrange people from their own natural impulses, to demonize "evil" and to "reward" an "objective" "good." However much we might like to, we cannot blame the Brothers Grimm for their insensitivity to women's issues, minority cultures, and the environment. Likewise, in the self-righteous Copenhagen of Hans Christian Andersen, the inalienable rights of mermaids were hardly given a second thought.

Today, we have the opportunity—and the obligation—to rethink these 2
"classic" stories so they reflect more enlightened times. To that effort I submit this humble book. While its original title, *Fairy Stories For a Modern World,* was abandoned for obvious reasons (kudos to my editor for pointing out my heterosexualist bias), I think the collection stands on its own. This,

however, is just a start. Certain stories, such as "The Duckling That Was Judged on Its Personal Merits and Not on Its Physical Appearance," were deleted for space reasons. I expect I have volumes left in me, and I hope this book sparks the righteous imaginations of other writers and, of course, leaves an indelible mark on our children.

If, through omission or commission, I have inadvertently displayed any sexist, racist, culturalist, nationalist, regionalist, ageist, lookist, ableist, sizeist, speciesist, intellectualist, socioeconomicist, ethnocentrist, phallocentrist, heteropatriarchalist, or other type of bias as yet unnamed, I apologize and encourage your suggestions for rectification. In the quest to develop meaningful literature that is totally free from bias and purged from the influences of its flawed cultural past, I doubtless have made some mistakes. 3

Cinderella

There once lived a young woman named Cinderella, whose natural birthmother had died when Cinderella was but a child. A few years after, her father married a widow with two older daughters. Cinderella's mother-of-step treated her very cruelly, and her sisters-of-step made her work very hard, as if she were their own personal unpaid laborer. 4

One day an invitation arrived at their house. The prince was celebrating his exploitation of the dispossessed and marginalized peasantry by throwing a fancy dress ball. Cinderella's sisters-of-step were very excited to be invited to the palace. They began to plan the expensive clothes they would use to alter and enslave their natural body images to emulate an unrealistic standard of feminine beauty. (It was especially unrealistic in their case, as they were differently visaged enough to stop a clock.) Her mother-of-step also planned to go to the ball, so Cinderella was working harder than a dog (an appropriate if unfortunately speciesist metaphor). 5

When the day of the ball arrived, Cinderella helped her mother- and sisters-of-step into their ball gowns. A formidable task: It was like trying to force ten pounds of processed nonhuman animal carcasses into a five-pound skin. Next came immense cosmetic augmentation, which it would be best not to describe at all. As evening fell, her mother- and sisters-of-step left Cinderella at home to finish her housework. Cinderella was sad, but she contented herself with her Holly Near records. 6

Suddenly there was a flash of light, and in front of Cinderella stood a man dressed in loose-fitting, all-cotton clothes and wearing a wide-brimmed hat. At first Cinderella thought he was a Southern lawyer or a bandleader, but he soon put her straight. 7

"Hello, Cinderella, I am your fairy godperson, or individual deity proxy, if you prefer. So, you want to go to the ball, eh? And bind yourself into the male concept of beauty? Squeeze into some tight-fitting dress that will cut off your circulation? Jam your feet into high-heeled shoes that will ruin your bone structure? Paint your face with chemicals and makeup that have been tested on nonhuman animals?" 8

"Oh yes, definitely," she said in an instant. Her fairy godperson heaved a great sigh and decided to put off her political education till another day. With his magic, he enveloped her in a beautiful, bright light and whisked her away to the palace. 9

Many, many carriages were lined up outside the palace that night; apparently, no one had ever thought of carpooling. Soon, in a heavy, gilded carriage painfully pulled by a team of horse-slaves, Cinderella arrived. She was dressed in a clinging gown woven of silk stolen from unsuspecting silkworms. Her hair was festooned with pearls plundered from hard-working, defenseless oysters. And on her feet, dangerous though it may seem, she wore slippers made of finely cut crystal. 10

Every head in the ballroom turned as Cinderella entered. The men stared at and lusted after this wommon who had captured perfectly their Barbie-doll ideas of feminine desirability. The womyn, trained at an early age to despise their own bodies, looked at Cinderella with envy and spite. Cinderella's own mother- and sisters-of-step, consumed with jealousy, failed to recognize her. 11

Cinderella soon caught the roving eye of the prince, who was busy discussing jousting and bear-baiting with his cronies. Upon seeing her, the prince was struck with a fit of not being able to speak as well as the majority of the population. "Here," he thought, "is a wommon that I could make my princess and impregnate with the progeny of our perfect genes, and thus make myself the envy of every other prince for miles around. And she's blond, too!" 12

The prince began to cross the ballroom toward his intended prey. His cronies also began to walk toward Cinderella. So did every other male in the ballroom who was younger than 70 and not serving drinks. 13

Cinderella was proud of the commotion she was causing. She walked with head high and carried herself like a wommon of eminent social standing. But soon it became clear that the commotion was turning into something ugly, or at least socially dysfunctional. 14

The prince had made it clear to this friends that he was intent on "possessing" the young wommon. But the prince's resoluteness angered his pals, for they too lusted after her and wanted to own her. The men began to shout and push each other. The prince's best friend, who was a large if cerebrally constrained duke, stopped him halfway across the dance floor and insisted that *he* was going to have Cinderella. The prince's response was a swift kick to the groin, which left the duke temporarily inactive. But the prince was quickly seized by other sex-crazed males, and he disappeared into a pile of human animals. 15

The womyn were appalled by this vicious display of testosterone, but try as they might, they were unable to separate the combatants. To the other womyn, it seemed that Cinderella was the cause of all the trouble, so they encircled her and began to display very unsisterly hostility. She tried to escape, but her impractical glass slippers made it nearly impossible. Fortunately for her, none of the other womyn were shod any better. 16

The noise grew so loud that no one heard the clock in the tower chime midnight. When the bell rang the twelfth time, Cinderella's beautiful gown and slippers disappeared, and she was dressed once again in her peasant's rags. Her mother- and sisters-of-step recognized her now, but kept quiet to avoid embarrassment. 17

The womyn grew silent at this magical transformation. Freed from the confinements of her gown and slippers, Cinderella sighed and stretched and scratched her ribs. She smiled, closed her eyes and said, "Kill me now if you want, sisters, but at least I'll die in comfort." 18

The womyn around her again grew envious, but this time they took a different approach: Instead of exacting vengeance on her, they stripped off their bodices, corsets, shoes, and every other confining garment. They danced and jumped and screeched in sheer joy, comfortable at last in their shifts and bare feet. 19

Had the men looked up from their macho dance of destruction, they would have seen many desirable womyn dressed as if for the boudoir. But they never ceased pounding, punching, kicking, and clawing each other until, to the last man, they were dead. 20

The womyn clucked their tongues but felt no remorse. The palace and realm were theirs now. Their first official act was to dress the men in their discarded dresses and tell the media that the fight arose when someone threatened to expose the crossdressing tendencies of the prince and his cronies. Their second was to set up a clothing co-op that produced only comfortable, practical clothes for womyn. Then they hung a sign on the castle advertising CinderWear (for that was what the new clothing was called), and through self-determination and clever marketing, they all—even the mother- and sisters-of-step—lived happily ever after. 21

"Cinderella": A Story of Sibling Rivalry and Oedipal Conflicts

BRUNO BETTELHEIM

Having read several variants of "Cinderella," you may have wondered what it is about this story that's prompted people in different parts of the world, at different times, to show interest in a child who's been debased but then rises above her misfortune. Why are people so fascinated with "Cinderella"?

Depending on the people you ask and their perspectives, you'll find this question answered in various ways. As a Freudian psychologist, Bruno Bettelheim believes that the mind is a repository of both conscious and unconscious elements. By definition, we aren't aware of what goes on in our unconscious; nonetheless, what happens there exerts a powerful influence on what we believe and on how we act. This division of the mind into conscious and unconscious parts is true for children no less than for adults. Based on these beliefs about the mind, Bettelheim analyzes "Cinderella" first by pointing to what he calls the story's essential theme: sibling rivalry, or Cinderella's mistreatment at the hands of her stepsisters. Competition among brothers and sisters presents a profound and largely unconscious problem to children, says Bettelheim. By hearing "Cinderella," a story that speaks directly to their unconscious, children are given tools that can help them resolve conflicts. Cinderella resolves her difficulties; children hearing the story can resolve theirs as well: This is the unconscious message of the tale.

Do you accept this argument? To do so, you'd have to agree with the author's reading of "Cinderella's" hidden meanings; and you'd have to agree with his assumptions concerning the conscious and unconscious mind and the ways in which the unconscious will seize upon the content of a story in order to resolve conflicts. Even if you don't accept Bettelheim's analysis, his essay makes fascinating reading. First, it is internally consistent—that is, he begins with a set of principles and then builds logically upon them, as any good writer will. Second, his analysis demonstrates how a scholarly point of view—a coherent set of assumptions about the way the world (in this case, the mind) works—creates boundaries for a discussion. Change the assumptions (as Kolbenschlag and Yolen will in the articles that conclude the chapter) and you'll change the analyses that follow from them.

Bettelheim's essay is long and somewhat difficult. While he uses no subheadings, he has divided his work into four sections: paragraphs 2–10 are devoted to sibling rivalry; paragraphs 11–19, to an analysis of "Cinderella's" hidden meanings; paragraphs 20–24, to the psychological makeup of children at the end of their Oedipal period; and paragraphs 25–27, to the reasons why "Cinderella," in particular, appeals to children in the Oedipal period.

Bruno Bettelhiem, a distinguished psychologist and educator, was born in 1903 in Vienna. He was naturalized as an American citizen in 1939 and served as a professor of psychology at Rockford College and the University of Chicago. Awarded the honor of fellow by several prestigious professional associations, Bettelheim was a prolific writer and contributed articles to numerous popular and professional publications. His list of books includes Love Is Not Enough: The Treatment of Emotionally Disturbed Children *(1950),* The Informed Heart *(1960),* Surviving, *and* The Uses of Enchantment, *from which this selection has been excerpted. Bettelheim died in 1990.*

By all accounts, "Cinderella" is the best-known fairy tale, and probably also the best-liked. It is quite an old story; when first written down in China during the ninth century A.D., it already had a history. The unrivaled tiny foot size as a mark of extraordinary virtue, distinction, and beauty, and the 1 slipper made of precious material are facets which point to an Eastern, if not necessarily Chinese, origin.[1] The modern hearer does not connect sexual attractiveness and beauty in general with extreme smallness of the foot, as the ancient Chinese did, in accordance with their practice of binding women's feet.

"Cinderella," as we know it, is experienced as a story about the ago- 2
nies and hopes which form the essential content of sibling rivalry; and about the degraded heroine winning out over her siblings who abused her. Long before Perrault gave "Cinderella" the form in which it is now widely known, "having to live among the ashes" was a symbol of being debased in comparison to one's siblings, irrespective of sex. In Germany, for example, there were stories in which such an ash-boy later becomes king, which parallels Cinderella's fate. "Aschenputtel" is the title of the Brothers Grimm's version of the tale. The term originally designated a lowly, dirty kitchenmaid who must tend to the fireplace ashes.

There are many examples in the German language of how being forced 3
to dwell among the ashes was a symbol not just of degradation, but also of sibling rivalry, and of the sibling who finally surpasses the brother or brothers who have debased him. Martin Luther in his *Table Talks* speaks about Cain as the God-forsaken evildoer who is powerful, while pious Abel is forced to be his ash-brother *(Asche-brüdel),* a mere nothing, subject to Cain; in one of Luther's sermons he says that Esau was forced into the role of Jacob's ash-brother. Cain and Abel, Jacob and Esau are Biblical examples of one brother being suppressed or destroyed by the other.

The fairy tale replaces sibling relations with relations between step- 4
siblings—perhaps a device to explain and make acceptable an animosity which one wishes would not exist among true siblings. Although sibling rivalry is universal and "natural" in the sense that it is the negative consequence of being a sibling, this same relation also generates equally as much positive feeling between siblings, highlighted in fairy tales such as "Brother and Sister."

No other fairy tale renders so well as the "Cinderella" stories the inner 5
experiences of the young child in the throes of sibling rivalry, when he feels hopelessly outclassed by his brothers and sisters. Cinderella is pushed down and degraded by her stepsisters; her interests are sacrificed to theirs by her (step)mother; she is expected to do the dirtiest work and although she performs it well, she receives no credit for it; only more is demanded of her. This is how the child feels when devastated by the miseries of sibling rivalry. Exaggerated though Cinderella's tribulations and degradations may seem to the adult, the child carried away by sibling rivalry feels, "That's me; that's how they mistreat me, or would want to; that's how little they

[1]Artistically made slippers of precious material were reported in Egypt from the third century on. The Roman emperor Diocletian in a decree of A.D. 301 set maximum prices for different kinds of footwear, including slippers made of fine Babylonian leather, dyed purple or scarlet, and gilded slippers for women. [Bettelheim]

think of me." And there are moments—often long time periods—when for inner reasons a child feels this way even when his position among his siblings may seem to give him no cause for it.

When a story corresponds to how the child feels deep down—as no realistic narrative is likely to do—it attains an emotional quality of "truth" for the child. The events of "Cinderella" offer him vivid images that give body to his overwhelming but nevertheless often vague and nondescript emotions; so these episodes seem more convincing to him than his life experiences. 6

The term "sibling rivalry" refers to a most complex constellation of feelings and their causes. With extremely rare exceptions, the emotions aroused in the person subject to sibling rivalry are far out of proportion to what his real situation with his sisters and brothers would justify, seen objectively. While all children at times suffer greatly from sibling rivalry, parents seldom sacrifice one of their children to the others, nor do they condone the other children's persecuting one of them. Difficult as objective judgments are for the young child—nearly impossible when his emotions are aroused—even he in his more rational moments "knows" that he is not treated as badly as Cinderella. But the child often feels mistreated, despite all his "knowledge" to the contrary. That is why he believes in the inherent truth of "Cinderella," and then he also comes to believe in her eventual deliverance and victory. From her triumph he gains the exaggerated hopes for his future which he needs to counteract the extreme misery he experiences when ravaged by sibling rivalry. 7

Despite the name "sibling rivalry," this miserable passion has only incidentally to do with a child's actual brothers and sisters. The real source of it is the child's feelings about his parents. When a child's older brother or sister is more competent than he, this arouses only temporary feelings of jealousy. Another child being given special attention becomes an insult only if the child fears that, in contrast, he is thought little of by his parents, or feels rejected by them. It is because of such an anxiety that one or all of a child's sisters or brothers may become a thorn in his flesh. Fearing that in comparison to them he cannot win his parents' love and esteem is what inflames sibling rivalry. This is indicated in stories by the fact that it matters little whether the siblings actually possess greater competence. The Biblical story of Joseph tells that it is jealousy of parental affection lavished on him which accounts for the destructive behavior of his brothers. Unlike Cinderella's, Joseph's parent does not participate in degrading him, and, on the contrary, prefers him to his other children. But Joseph, like Cinderella, is turned into a slave, and, like her, he miraculously escapes and ends by surpassing his siblings. 8

Telling a child who is devastated by sibling rivalry that he will grow up to do as well as his brothers and sisters offers little relief from his present feelings of dejection. Much as he would like to trust our assurances, most of the time he cannot. A child can see things only with subjective eyes, and comparing himself on this basis to his siblings, he has no confidence that 9 he, on his own, will someday be able to fare as well as they. If he could believe more in himself, he would not feel destroyed by his siblings no matter what they might do to him, since then he could trust that time would bring about a desired reversal of fortune. But since the child cannot, on his own, look forward with confidence to some future day when things will turn out all right for him, he can gain relief only through fantasies of glory—a domination over his siblings—which he hopes will become reality through some fortunate event.

Whatever our position within the family, at certain times in our lives 10
we are beset by sibling rivalry in some form or other. Even an only child feels that other children have some great advantages over him, and this makes him intensely jealous. Further, he may suffer from the anxious thought that if he did have a sibling, his parents would prefer this other child to him. "Cinderella" is a fairy tale which makes nearly as strong an appeal to boys as to girls, since children of both sexes suffer equally from sibling rivalry, and have the same desire to be rescued from their lowly position and surpass those who seem superior to them.

On the surface, "Cinderella" is as deceptively simple as the story of 11
Little Red Riding Hood, with which it shares greatest popularity. "Cinderella" tells about the agonies of sibling rivalry, of wishes coming true, of the humble being elevated, of true merit being recognized even when hidden under rags, of virtue rewarded and evil punished—a straightforward story. But under this overt content is concealed a welter of complex and largely unconscious material, which details of the story allude to just enough to set our unconscious associations going. This makes a contrast between surface simplicity and underlying complexity which arouses deep interest in the story and explains its appeal to the millions over centuries. To begin gaining an understanding of these hidden meanings, we have to penetrate behind the obvious sources of sibling rivalry discussed so far.

As mentioned before, if the child could only believe that it is the infir- 12
mities of his age which account for his lowly position, he would not have to suffer so wretchedly from sibling rivalry, because he could trust the future to right matters. When he thinks that his degradation is deserved, he feels his plight is utterly hopeless. Djuna Barnes's perceptive statement about fairy tales—that the child knows something about them which he cannot tell (such as that he likes the idea of Little Red Riding Hood and the wolf being in bed together)—could be extended by dividing fairy tales into two groups: one group where the child responds only unconsciously to the inherent truth of the story and thus cannot tell about it; and another large number of tales where the child preconsciously or even consciously knows what the "truth" of the story consists of and thus could tell about it, but does not want to let on that he knows. Some aspects of "Cinderella" fall into the latter category. Many children believe that Cinderella probably deserves her fate at the beginning of the story, as they feel they would, too; but they don't want anyone to know it. Despite this, she is worthy at the end to be exalted, as the child hopes he will be too, irrespective of his earlier shortcomings.

Every child believes at some period of his life—and this is not only at rare moments—that because of his secret wishes, if not also his clandestine actions, he deserves to be degraded, banned from the presence of others, relegated to a netherworld of smut. He fears this may be so, irrespective of how fortunate his situation may be in reality. He hates and fears those others—such as his siblings—whom he believes to be entirely free of similar evilness, and he fears that they or his parents will discover what he is really like, and then demean him as Cinderella was by her family. Because he wants others—most of all, his parents—to believe in his innocence, he is delighted that "everybody" believes in Cinderella's. This is one of the great attractions of this fairy tale. Since people give credence to Cinderella's goodness, they will also believe in his, so the child hopes. And "Cinderella" nourishes this hope, which is one reason it is such a delightful story. 13

Another aspect which holds large appeal for the child is the vileness of the stepmother and stepsisters. Whatever the shortcomings of a child may be in his own eyes, these pale into insignificance when compared to the stepsisters' and stepmother's falsehood and nastiness. Further, what these stepsisters do to Cinderella justifies whatever nasty thoughts one may have about one's siblings: they are so vile that anything one may wish would happen to them is more than justified. Compared to their behavior, Cinderella is indeed innocent. So the child, on hearing her story, feels he need not feel guilty about his angry thoughts. 14

On a very different level—and reality considerations coexist easily with fantastic exaggerations in the child's mind—as badly as one's parents or siblings seem to treat one, and much as one thinks one suffers because of it, all this is nothing compared to Cinderella's fate. Her story reminds the child at the same time how lucky he is, and how much worse things could be. (Any anxiety about the latter possibility is relieved, as always in fairy tales, by the happy ending.) 15

The behavior of a five-and-a-half-year-old girl, as reported by her father, may illustrate how easily a child may feel that she is a "Cinderella." This little girl had a younger sister of whom she was very jealous. The girl was very fond of "Cinderella," since the story offered her material with which to act out her feelings, and because without the story's imagery she would have been hard pressed to comprehend and express them. This little girl had used to dress very neatly and liked pretty clothes, but she became unkempt and dirty. One day when she was asked to fetch some salt, she said as she was doing so, "Why do you treat me like Cinderella?" 16

Almost speechless, her mother asked her, "Why do you think I treat you like Cinderella?" 17

"Because you make me do all the hardest work in the house!" was the little girl's answer. Having thus drawn her parents into her fantasies, she acted them out more openly, pretending to sweep up all the dirt, etc. She went even further, playing that she prepared her little sister for the ball. But she went the "Cinderella" story one better, based on her unconscious understanding of the contradictory emotions fused into the "Cinderella" role, 18 because at another moment she told her mother and sister, "You shouldn't be jealous of me just because I am the most beautiful in the family."

This shows that behind the surface humility of Cinderella lies the conviction of her superiority to mother and sisters, as if she would think: "You can make me do all the dirty work, and I pretend that I am dirty, but within me I know that you treat me this way because you are jealous of me because I am so much better than you." This conviction is supported by the story's ending, which assures every "Cinderella" that eventually she will be discovered by her prince. 19

Why does the child believe deep within himself that Cinderella deserves her dejected state? This question takes us back to the child's state of mind at the end of the oedipal period.[2] Before he is caught in oedipal entanglements, the child is convinced that he is lovable, and loved, if all is well within his family relationships. Psychoanalysis describes this stage of complete satisfaction with oneself as "primary narcissism." During this period the child feels certain that he is the center of the universe, so there is no reason to be jealous of anybody. 20

The oedipal disappointments which come at the end of this developmental stage cast deep shadows of doubt on the child's sense of his worthiness. He feels that if he were really as deserving of love as he had thought, then his parents would never be critical of him or disappoint him. The only explanation for parental criticism the child can think of is that there must be some serious flaw in him which accounts for what he experiences as rejection. If his desires remain unsatisfied and his parents disappoint him, there must be something wrong with him or his desires, or both. He cannot yet accept that reasons other than those residing within him could have an impact on his fate. In this oedipal jealousy, wanting to get rid of the parent of the same sex had seemed the most natural thing in the world, but now the child realizes that he cannot have his own way, and that maybe this is so because the desire was wrong. He is no longer so sure that he is preferred to his siblings, and he begins to suspect that this may be due to the fact that *they* are free of any bad thoughts or wrongdoing such as his. 21

All this happens as the child is gradually subjected to ever more critical attitudes as he is being socialized. He is asked to behave in ways which run counter to his natural desires, and he resents this. Still he must obey, which makes him very angry. This anger is directed against those who make demands, most likely his parents; and this is another reason to wish to get rid of them, and still another reason to feel guilty about such wishes. This is why the child also feels that he deserves to be chastised for his feelings, a punishment he believes he can escape only if nobody learns what he is thinking when he is angry. The feeling of being unworthy to be loved by his parents at a time when his desire for their love is very strong leads to 22

[2]*Oedipal:* Freud's theory of the Oedipus complex held that at an early stage of development a child wishes to replace the parent of the same sex in order to achieve the exclusive love of the parent of the opposite sex.

the fear of rejection, even when in reality there is none. This rejection fear compounds the anxiety that others are preferred and also maybe preferable—the root of sibling rivalry.

Some of the child's pervasive feelings of worthlessness have their origin in his experiences during and around toilet training and all other aspects of his education to become clean, neat, and orderly. Much has been said about how children are made to feel dirty and bad because they are not as clean as their parents want or require them to be. As clean as a child may learn to be, he knows that he would much prefer to give free rein to his tendency to be messy, disorderly, and dirty. 23

At the end of the oedipal period, guilt about desires to be dirty and disorderly becomes compounded by oedipal guilt, because of the child's desire to replace the parent of the same sex in the love of the other parent. The wish to be the love, if not also the sexual partner, of the parent of the other sex, which at the beginning of the oedipal development seemed natural and "innocent," at the end of the period is repressed as bad. But while this wish as such is repressed, guilt about it and about sexual feelings in general is not, and this makes the child feel dirty and worthless. 24

Here again, lack of objective knowledge leads the child to think that he is the only bad one in all these respects—the only child who has such desires. It makes every child identify with Cinderella, who is relegated to sit among the cinders. Since the child has such "dirty" wishes, that is where he also belongs, and where he would end up if his parents knew of his desires. This is why every child needs to believe that even if he were thus degraded, eventually he would be rescued from such degradation and experience the most wonderful exaltation—as Cinderella does. 25

For the child to deal with his feelings of dejection and worthlessness aroused during this time, he desperately needs to gain some grasp on what these feelings of guilt and anxiety are all about. Further, he needs assurance on a conscious and an unconscious level that he will be able to extricate himself from these predicaments. One of the greatest merits of "Cinderella" is that, irrespective of the magic help Cinderella receives, the child understands that essentially it is through her own efforts, and because of the person she is, that Cinderella is able to transcend magnificently her degraded state, despite what appear as insurmountable obstacles. It gives the child confidence that the same will be true for him, because the story relates so well to what has caused both his conscious and his unconscious guilt. 26

Overtly "Cinderella" tells about sibling rivalry in its most extreme form: the jealousy and enmity of the stepsisters, and Cindrella's sufferings because of it. The many other psychological issues touched upon in the story are so covertly alluded to that the child does not become consciously aware of them. In his unconscious, however, the child responds to these significant details which refer to matters and experiences from which he consciously has separated himself, but which nevertheless continue to create vast problems for him. 27

Review Questions

1. What does living among ashes symbolize, according to Bettelheim?
2. What explanation does Bettelheim give for Cinderella's having stepsisters, not sisters?
3. In what ways are a child's emotions aroused by sibling rivalry?
4. To a child, what is the meaning of Cinderella's triumph?
5. Why is the fantasy solution to sibling rivalry offered by "Cinderella" appropriate for children?
6. Why is Cinderella's goodness important?
7. Why are the stepsisters and stepmother so vile, according to Bettelheim?
8. In paragraphs 20–26, Bettelheim offers a complex explanation of oedipal conflicts and their relation to sibling rivalry and the child's need to be debased, even while feeling superior. Summarize these seven paragraphs, and compare your summary with those of your classmates. Have you agreed on the essential information in this passage?

Discussion and Writing Suggestions

1. One identifying feature of psychoanalysis is the assumption of complex unconscious and subconscious mechanisms in human personality that explain behavior. In this essay, Bettelheim discusses the interior world of a child in ways that the child could never articulate. The features of this world include the following:

   All children experience sibling rivalry.

   The real source of sibling rivalry is the child's parents.

   Sibling rivalry is a miserable passion and a devastating experience.

   Children have a desire to be rescued from sibling rivalry (as opposed to rescuing themselves, perhaps).

   Children experience an Oedipal stage, in which they wish to do away with the parent of the same sex and be intimate with the parent of the opposite sex.

   "Every child believes at some point in his life . . . that because of his secret wishes, if not also his clandestine actions, he deserves to be degraded, banned from the presence of others, relegated to a netherworld of smut."

   To what extent do you agree with these statements? Take one of the statements and respond to it in a four- or five-paragraph essay.

2. A critic of Bettelheim's position, Jack Zipes argues that Bettelheim distorts fairy-tale literature by insisting that the tales have therapeutic value and speak to children almost as a psychoanalyst might. Ultimately, claims Zipes, Bettelheim's analysis corrupts the story of

"Cinderella" and closes down possibilities for interpretation. What is your view of Bettelheim's psychoanalytic approach to fairy tales?

A Feminist's View of "Cinderella"

MADONNA KOLBENSCHLAG

Madonna Kolbenschlag approaches "Cinderella" from a feminist's point of view. Feminist criticism, as it is applied across the curriculum, attempts to clarify the relations of women and men in a broad array of human activities: for instance, in literary works, the structure of family life, and economic and political affairs. The object of analysis in the case of "Cinderella" is a story, and Kolbenschlag brings a unique set of questions to bear: In the world of "Cinderella," what is the relationship between men and women? Among women themselves? How is power divided in this world? How is a woman's achievement defined as opposed to a man's? What would children reading this story learn about gender identity? Feminists themselves might disagree in answering these questions; but the fact that these and not Bettelheim's questions are guiding the analysis ensures that Kolbenschlag's treatment of "Cinderella" and what we can learn from it will differ significantly from Bettelheim's.

Note that the essay begins with epigraphs, or brief statements, from other writers meant to suggest something of the content of what follows. Authors place epigraphs to set a context for you, and the author who places two or more before a piece is implicitly suggesting that you make comparisons among them.

You'll encounter two particularly difficult sentences: the last sentence of the essay, in which the author equates the behavior of women in "Cinderella" to the behavior of women in our own society, where power is largely held by men. And there's another difficult sentence in paragraph 5: "The personality of the heroine is one that, above all, accepts abasement *as a prelude to and precondition of affiliation." Read these sentences in the context of the entire essay. Try getting the gist of Kolbenschlag's main point and then try seeing how these sentences fit in.*

Madonna Kolbenschlag is the author of Kiss Sleeping Beauty Good-Bye: Breaking the Spell of Feminine Myths and Models (1979), *in which the following selection appears.*

Overtly the story helps the child to accept sibling rivalry as a rather common fact of life and promises that he need not fear being destroyed by it; on the contrary, if these siblings were not so nasty to him, he could never triumph to the same degree at the end. . . . There are also obvious moral lessons: that surface appearances tell nothing about the inner worth of a person; that if one is true to oneself, one wins over those who pretend to be what they are not; and that virtue will be rewarded, evil punished.

Openly stated, but not as readily recognized, are the lessons that to develop one's personality to the fullest, one must be able to do hard work and be able to separate good from evil, as in the sorting of the lentils. Even out of lowly matter like ashes things of great value can be gained, if one knows how to do it.

—Bruno Bettelheim, *The Uses of Enchantment*

The literature on female socialization reminds one of the familiar image of Cinderella's stepsisters industriously lopping off their toes and heels so as to fit into the glass slipper (key to the somewhat enigmatic heart of the prince)—when of course it was never intended for them anyway.

—Judith Long Laws, "Woman as Object"

The important factor to us is Cinderella's conditioning. It is decidedly not to go on dutifully sweeping the floor and carrying the wood. She is conditioned to get the hell out of those chores. There is, the American legend tells her, a good-looking man with dough, who will put an end to the onerous tedium of making a living. If he doesn't come along (the consumer must consequently suppose), she isn't just lacking in good fortune, she is being cheated out of her true deserts. Better, says our story, go out and make the guy. In other words, we have turned the legend backwards and our Cinderella now operates as her sisters did. . . .

The goal of security, seen in terms of things alone and achieved in those terms during the least secure period in human history, has predictably ruined Cinderella; she has the prince, the coach, the horses—but her soul's a pumpkin and her mind's a rat-warren. She desperately needs help.

—Philip Wylie, *Generation of Vipers*

Cinderella, the best-known and probably best-liked fairy tale, is above all a success story. The rags-to-riches theme perhaps explains its equal popularity among boys as well as girls. It is a very old fairy tale, having at least 345 documented variants and numerous unrecorded versions. The iconic focus of the tale on the lost slipper and Cinderella's "perfect fit" suggests that the story may have originated in the Orient where the erotic significance of tiny feet has been a popular myth since ancient times. 1

The basic motifs of the story are well-known: an ill-treated heroine, who is forced to live by the hearth; the twig she plants on her mother's grave that blossoms into a magic tree; the tasks demanded of the heroine; the magic animals that help her perform the tasks and provide her costume for the ball; the meeting at the ball; the heroine's flight from the ball; the lost slipper; the shoe test; the sisters' mutilation of their feet; the discovery of the true bride and the happy marriage. The variants retain the basic motifs; while differing considerably in detail, they range more widely in their origins than any other fairy tale: Asiatic, Celtic, European, Middle-Eastern and American Indian versions numbered among them. 2

The Horatio Alger quality of the story helps to explain its special popularity in mercantile and capitalistic societies. As a parable of social mobility 3 it was seized upon by the writers of the new "literature of aspiration" in the seventeenth and eighteenth centuries as a basic plot for a new kind of private fantasy—the novel. Our literary world has not been the same since *Pamela* and all her orphaned, governess sisters.[1] Most Anglo-American novels, early and late, are written in the shadow of *Pamela* and the Cinderella myth. Even Franklin's *Autobiography,* the seminal work in the success genre, owes much to the myth. The primary "moral" of the fairy tale—that good fortune can be merited—is the very essence of the Protestant Ethic.

At the personal and psychological level, Cinderella evokes intense identification. It is a tale of sibling rivalry (and subliminally, of sex-role stereotyping)—a moral fable about socialization. Very few themes could be closer to the inner experience of the child, an emerging self enmeshed in a family network. As Bettelheim observes, it is deceptively simple in the associations it evokes: 4

> *Cinderella* tells about the agonies of sibling rivalry, of wishes coming true, of the humble being elevated, of true merit being recognized even when hidden under rags, of virtue rewarded and evil punished—a straightforward story. But under this overt content is concealed a welter of complex and largely unconscious material. . . .

The personality of the heroine is one that, above all, accepts *abasement* as a prelude to and precondition of *affiliation.* That abasement is characteristically expressed by Cinderella's servitude to menial tasks, work that diminishes her. This willing acceptance of a condition of worthlessness and her expectation of rescue (as a reward for her virtuous suffering) is a recognizable paradigm of traditional feminine socialization. Cinderella is deliberately and systematically excluded from meaningful achievements. Her stepmother assigns her to meaningless tasks; her father fails her as a helpful mentor. Her sisters, inferior in quality of soul, are preferred before her. 5

But Cinderella does not become a teenage runaway, nor does she wreak any kind of Gothic sabotage on the family. Like many of the Jews who went to the gas chambers in World War II, she has internalized the consciousness of the victim. She really believes she belongs where she is. The paradox of this acceptance of a condition of worthlessness in the self, along with a conviction of the ultimate worthiness and heroism of one's role, is part of the terrible appeal of the fairy tale. For women, especially, it is both mirror and model. Perrault's version of the tale ends with a pointed poetic moral: 6

> 'Tis that little gift called grace,
> Weaves a spell round form and face . . .
> And if you would learn the way
> How to get that gift today—

[1]*Pamela* by Samuel Richardson (1689–1761) is a sentimental romance set in early-eighteenth-century England in which a virtuous servant girl, Pamela Andrews, holds off the lascivious advances of her master until, struck by her goodness, he proposes marriage.

How to point the golden dart
That shall pierce the Prince's heart—
Ladies, you have but to be
Just as kind and sweet as she!

Cinderella's place by the hearth and her identification with ashes suggests several associations. At the most obvious level, her place by the chimney is an emblem of her degradation. But it is also symbolic of her affinity with the virtues of the hearth: innocence, purity, nurturance, empathy, docility. Cinderella has a vestal quality that relieves her of any obligation to struggle and strive to better her world. She must apprentice herself to this time of preparation for her "real" life with the expected One. 7

Like most fairy tales, *Cinderella* dramatizes the passage to maturity. Her sojourn among the ashes is a period of grieving, a transition to a new self. On the explicit level of the story, Cinderella is literally grieving for her dead mother. Grimm's version of the tale preserves the sense of process, of growth that is symbolized in the narrative. Instead of a fairy godmother—*deus ex machina*[2]—Cinderella receives a branch of a hazel bush from her father. She plants the twig over her mother's grave and cultivates it with her prayers and tears. This is her contact with her past, her roots, her essential self. Before one can be transformed one must grieve for the lost as well as the possible selves, as yet unfulfilled—Kierkegaard's existential anguish.[3] 8

The mother is also identified in several variants with helpful animals, a calf, a cow, or a goat—all milk-giving creatures. In Grimm's version the magic helpers are birds that live in the magic tree. The animals assist her in the performance of the cruel and meaningless tasks her stepmother assigns. The magic trees and helpful animals are emblems of the faith and trust that is demanded of Cinderella, the belief that something good can be gained from whatever one does. There is a subliminal value implied here, that work is seldom to be enjoyed for its own sake, but only to be endured for some greater end. It is essentially a "predestined" view of work as incapable of redemption. Service at the hearth is not intrinsically worthwhile, but acquires its value through the virtue it extracts from the heroine. Significantly, when the heroine is released from her servitude, the structure of belief—the myth—collapses. Cinderella's father destroys the pear tree and the pigeon house. 9

The Perrault version places great emphasis on the "Midnight" prohibition given to Cinderella. A traditional connotation would, of course, associate it with the paternal mandate of obedience, and a threat: if the heroine does not return to domesticity and docility at regular intervals she may lose her "virtue" and no longer merit her expected one. Like the old conduct manuals for ladies, the moral of the tale warns against feminine excursions 10

---

[2] *"deus ex machina":* literally, "God out of the machine"; a sudden and unexpected (and often unconvincing) solution to a major problem faced by a character or group of characters toward the end of a literary or dramatic work.

[3] [Soren] Kierkegaard: Danish existentialist philosopher (1813–1855).

as well as ambition. Too much time spent "abroad" may result in indiscreet sex or unseemly hubris, or both. "No excelling" and "no excess."

As a dynamic metaphor of the feminine condition, it illuminates the double life that many women experience: the attraction of work and achievement, perhaps "celebrity," outside the home, and the emotional pull of the relationships and security within the home. For most women diurnal life is not a seamless robe. There are sharp divisions between creative work and compulsive activity, between assertiveness and passivity, between social life and domestic drudgery, between public routines and private joys. Women are, in the contemporary world, acutely aware of the need for integration. "Midnight" strikes with a terrible insistence, a cruel regularity in their lives. 11

Cinderella's threefold escape from the ball (Perrault's version) is of course designed to make her more desirable to the Prince. Or is it a reflection of her own ambivalence? (In Grimm's version, she is under no prohibition, she leaves of her own accord.) Bettelheim offers two interesting interpretations: 12

1. She wants to be "chosen" for herself, in her natural state, rather than because of a splendid appearance wrought by magic.
2. Her withdrawals show that, in contrast to her sisters, she is not "aggressive" in her sexuality but waits patiently "to be chosen."

The latter interpretation is underscored by the "perfect fit" of Cinderella's foot in the slipper, and by the sisters' frantic efforts to mutilate their own feet in order to diminish their size (symbolic of their aggressive, masculine traits). Here we see the two sides of the "formula female." On the surface, perfectly conformed to the feminine stereotype; within, massive lacerations of the spirit. The slipper is indeed the ultimate symbol of "that which is most desirable in a woman," with all of its stereotypical seductiveness and destructiveness. 13

The slipper, the central icon in the story, is a symbol of sexual bondage and imprisonment in a stereotype. Historically, the virulence of its significance is born out in the twisted horrors of Chinese foot-binding practices. On another level, the slipper is a symbol of power—with all of its accompanying restrictions and demands for conformity. When the Prince offers Cinderella the lost slipper (originally a gift of the magic bird), he makes his kingdom hers. 14

We know little of Cinderella's subsequent role. In Grimm's version she is revenged by the birds which pluck out the eyes of the envious sisters. But Perrault's version celebrates Cinderella's kindness and forgiveness. Her sisters come to live in the palace and marry two worthy lords. In the Norse variant of the tale, Aslaug, the heroine, marries a Viking hero, bears several sons, and wields a good deal of power in Teutonic style. (She is the daughter of Sigurd and Brynhild.) But in most tales Cinderella disappears into the vague region known as the "happily ever after." She changes her name, no doubt, and—like so many women—is never heard of again. 15

There are moments when all of us can find ourselves in the Cinderella tale: as bitchy, envious, desperate sibling-peers; or victim-souls like Cinderella, passive, waiting patiently to be rescued; or nasty, domineering "stepmothers," fulfilling ourselves by means of manipulative affiliations—all of them addicted to needing approval. And then we know that for the Prince we should read "Patriarchy."[4] 16

At Madonna Kolbenschlag's request, neither Review Questions nor Discussion and Writing Suggestions are provided.

America's "Cinderella"

JANE YOLEN

As a writer of children's stories, Jane Yolen is used to making decisions about ways in which stories develop: who wins, who loses (if anyone), what's learned, what traits of character endure, how relations among characters resolve themselves—these are just a few of the decisions a writer makes in shaping a story. So it's no surprise to find Yolen interested in decisions that other writers have made regarding "Cinderella." The tale has changed in the telling—Yolen is well aware of the many variants and in her article traces the changes "Cinderella" has undergone in becoming an American tale.

As you read, note Yolen's analysis of the "Cinderella" texts. Like Bettelheim and Kolbenschlag, she weaves quotations from the story into her article. This is standard procedure when writing an essay—a procedure you yourself should adopt when pulling together sources in a paper. Regardless of what point you're making (and the points made by Bettelheim, Kolbenschlag, and Yolen are certainly diverse), you will want to allude to the work of other writers into your own work, to suit your own purposes.

A noted author of children's books, Jane Yolen (b. 1939) began her career in the editorial departments of Saturday Review, *Gold Medal Books, Ruttledge Books, and Alfred A. Knopf. Since 1965, she has been a full-time professional writer, publishing more than seventy books for children as well as books for adults (about writing for children). According to one reviewer, she "is uncommonly skilled at using elements from other storytellers and folklorists, transforming them into new and different tales."*

It is part of the American creed, recited subvocally along with the pledge of allegiance in each classroom, that even a poor boy can grow up to become president. The unliberated corollary is that even a poor girl can grow up 1

[4]"Patriarchy": A social system in which authority is vested in the male.

and become the president's wife. This rags-to-riches formula was immortalized in American children's fiction by the Horatio Alger stories of the 1860s and by the Pluck and Luck nickel novels of the 1920s.

It is little wonder, then, that Cinderella should be a perennial favorite in the American folktale pantheon. 2

Yet how ironic that this formula should be the terms on which "Cinderella" is acceptable to most Americans. "Cinderella" is *not* a story of rags to riches, but rather riches recovered; *not* poor girl into princess but rather rich girl (or princess) rescued from improper or wicked enslavement; *not* suffering Griselda[1] enduring but shrewd and practical girl persevering and winning a share of the power. It is really a story that is about "the stripping away of the disguise that conceals the soul from the eyes of others. . . ." 3

We Americans have it wrong. "Rumpelstiltskin," in which a miller tells a whopping lie and his docile daughter acquiesces in it to become queen, would be more to the point. 4

But we have been initially seduced by the Perrault cinder-girl, who was, after all, the transfigured folk creature of a French literary courtier. Perrault's "Cendrillon" demonstrated the well-bred seventeenth-century female traits of gentility, grace, and selflessness, even to the point of graciously forgiving her wicked stepsisters and finding them noble husbands. 5

The American "Cinderella" is partially Perrault's. The rest is a spun-sugar caricature of her hardier European and Oriental forbears, who made their own way in the world, tricking the stepsisters with double-talk, artfully disguising themselves, or figuring out a way to win the king's son. The final bit of icing on the American Cinderella was concocted by that master candy-maker, Walt Disney, in the 1950s. Since then, America's Cinderella has been a coy, helpless dreamer, a "nice" girl who awaits her rescue with patience and a song. This Cinderella of the mass market books finds her way into a majority of American homes while the classic heroines sit unread in old volumes on library shelves. 6

Poor Cinderella. She has been unjustly distorted by storytellers, misunderstood by educators, and wrongly accused by feminists. Even as late as 1975, in the well-received volume *Womenfolk and Fairy Tales,* Rosemary Minard writes that Cinderella "would still be scrubbing floors if it were not for her fairy godmother." And Ms. Minard includes her in a sweeping condemnation of folk heroines as "insipid beauties waiting passively for Prince Charming." 7

Like many dialecticians, Ms. Minard reads the fairy tales incorrectly. Believing—rightly—that the fairy tales, as all stories for children, acculturate young readers and listeners, she has nevertheless gotten her target wrong. Cinderella is not to blame. Not the real, the true Cinderella. She 8

---

[1]In Chaucer's "Clerk's Tale" (from *The Canterbury Tales*) Griselda endures a series of humiliating tests of her love for and fidelity to her husband. She has become a symbol of the patient and enduring wife.

does not recognize the old Ash-girl for the tough, resilient heroine. The wrong Cinderella has gone to the American ball.

The story of Cinderella has endured for over a thousand years, surfac- 9
ing in a literary source first in ninth-century China. It has been found from the Orient to the interior of South America and over five hundred variants have been located by folklorists in Europe alone. This best-beloved tale has been brought to life over and over and no one can say for sure where the oral tradition began. The European story was included by Charles Perrault in his 1697 collection *Histoires ou Contes du temps passé* as "Cendrillon." But even before that, the Italian Straparola had a similar story in a collection. Since there had been twelve editions of the Straparola book printed in French before 1694, the chances are strong that Perrault had read the tale *"Peau d'Ane"* (Donkey Skin).

Joseph Jacobs, the indefatigable Victorian collector, once said of a 10
Cinderella story he printed that it was "an English version of an Italian adaption of a Spanish translation of a Latin version of a Hebrew translation of an Arabic translation of an Indian original." Perhaps it was not a totally accurate statement of that particular variant, but Jacobs was making a point about the perils of folktale-telling: each teller brings to a tale something of his/her own cultural orientation. Thus in China, where the "lotus foot," or tiny foot, was such a sign of a woman's worth that the custom of foot-binding developed, the Cinderella tale lays emphasis on an impossibly small slipper as a clue to the heroine's identity. In seventeenth-century France, Perrault's creation sighs along with her stepsisters over the magnificent "gold flowered mantua" and the "diamond stomacher." In the Walt Disney American version, both movie and book form, Cinderella shares with the little animals a quality of "lovableness," thus changing the intent of the tale and denying the heroine her birthright of shrewdness, inventiveness, and grace under pressure.

Notice, though, that many innovations—the Chinese slipper, the Per- 11
rault godmother with her midnight injunction and her ability to change pumpkin into coach—become incorporated in later versions. Even a slip of the English translator's tongue (*de vair,* fur, into *de verre,* glass) becomes immortalized. Such cross fertilization of folklore is phenomenal. And the staying power, across countries and centuries, of some of these inventions is notable. Yet glass slipper and godmother and pumpkin coach are not the common incidents by which a "Cinderella" tale is recognized even though they have become basic ingredients in the American story. Rather, the common incidents recognized by folklorists are these: an ill-treated though rich and worthy heroine in Cinders-disguise; the aid of a magical gift or advice by a beast/bird/mother substitute; the dance/festival/church scene where the heroine comes in radiant display; recognition through a token. So "Cinderella" and her true sister tales, "Cap o'Rushes"[2] with its King Lear judg-

[2]*"Cap o'Rushes":* One of the 700 variants of "Cinderella" in which the heroine is debased by having to wear a cap (and in other variants, a coat) made of rushes.

ment[3] and "Catskin" wherein the father unnaturally desires his daughter, are counted.

Andrew Lang's judgment that "a naked shoeless race could not have invented Cinderella," then, proves false. Variants have been found among the fur-wearing folk of Alaska and the native tribes in South Africa where shoes were not commonly worn. 12

"Cinderella" speaks to all of us in whatever skin we inhabit: the child mistreated, a princess or highborn lady in disguise bearing her trials with patience and fortitude. She makes intelligent decisions for she knows that wishing solves nothing without the concomitant action. We have each of us been that child. It is the longing of any youngster sent supperless to bed or given less than a full share at Christmas. It is the adolescent dream. 13

To make Cinderella less than she is, then, is a heresy of the worst kind. It cheapens our most cherished dreams, and it makes a mockery of the true magic inside us all—the ability to change our own lives, the ability to control our own destinies. 14

Cinderella first came to America in the nursery tales the settlers remembered from their own homes and told their children. Versions of these tales can still be found. Folklorist Richard Chase, for example, discovered "Rush Cape," an exact parallel of "Cap o'Rushes" with an Appalachian dialect in Tennessee, Kentucky, and South Carolina among others. 15

But when the story reached print, developed, was made literary, things began to happen to the hardy Cinderella. She suffered a sea change, a sea change aggravated by social conditions. 16

In the 1870s, for example, in the prestigious magazine for children *St. Nicholas,* there are a number of retellings or adaptations of "Cinderella." The retellings which merely translate European variants contain the hardy heroine. But when a new version is presented, a helpless Cinderella is born. G. B. Bartlett's "Giant Picture-Book," which was considered "a curious novelty [that] can be produced . . . by children for the amusement of their friends . . ." presents a weepy, prostrate young blonde (the instructions here are quite specific) who must be "aroused from her sad revery" by a godmother. Yet in the truer Cinderella stories, the heroine is not this catatonic. For example, in the Grimm "Cinder-Maid," though she weeps, she continues to perform the proper rites and rituals at her mother's grave, instructing the birds who roost there to: 17

Make me a lady fair to see,
Dress me as splendid as can be.

---

[3]*"King Lear judgment":* The story of King Lear has been identified as a variant of "Cinderella." In this variant, the King's one faithful daughter is cast out of the home because she claims to love her father according to her bond (but certainly not more than she would love her husband). The King's other daughters, eager to receive a large inheritance, profess false love and then plot against their father to secure their interests. The evil sisters are defeated and the father and faithful daughter, reunited. Before his death, Lear acknowledges his error.

And in "The Dirty Shepherdess," a "Cap o'Rushes" variant from France, "... she dried her eyes, and made a bundle of her jewels and her best dresses and hurriedly left the castle where she was born." In the *St. Nicholas* "Giant Picture-Book" she has none of this strength of purpose. Rather, she is manipulated by the godmother until the moment she stands before the prince where she speaks "meekly" and "with downcast eyes and extended hand." 18

St. Nicholas was not meant for the mass market. It had, in Selma Lanes' words, "a patrician call to a highly literate readership." But nevertheless, Bartlett's play instructions indicate how even in the more literary reaches of children's books a change was taking place. 19

However, to truly mark this change in the American "Cinderella," one must turn specifically to the mass-market books, merchandised products that masquerade as literature but make as little lasting literary impression as a lollipop. They, after all, serve the majority the way the storytellers of the village used to serve. They find their way into millions of homes. 20

Mass-market books are almost as old as colonial America. The chapbooks of the eighteenth and nineteenth century, crudely printed tiny paperbacks, were the source of most children's reading in the early days of our country. Originally these were books imported from Europe. But slowly American publishing grew. In the latter part of the nineteenth century one firm stood out—McLoughlin Bros. They brought bright colors to the pages of children's books. In a series selling for twenty-five cents per book, *Aunt Kate's Series,* bowdlerized folk tales emerged. "Cinderella" was there, along with "Red Riding Hood," "Puss in Boots," and others. Endings were changed, innards cleaned up, and good triumphed with very loud huzzahs. Cinderella is the weepy, sentimentalized pretty girl incapable of helping herself. In contrast, one only has to look at the girl in "Cap o'Rushes" who comes to a great house and asks "Do you want a maid?" and when refused, goes on to say " . . . I ask no wages and do any sort of work." And she does. In the end, when the master's young son is dying of love for the mysterious lady, she uses her wits to work her way out of the kitchen. Even in Perrault's "Cinderella," when the fairy godmother runs out of ideas for enchantment and "was at a loss for a coachman, I'll go and see, says Cinderella, if there be never a rat in the rat-trap, we'll make a coachman of him. You are in the right, said her godmother, go and see." 21

Hardy, helpful, inventive, that was the Cinderella of the old tales but not of the mass market in the nineteenth century. Today's mass-market books are worse. These are the books sold in supermarket and candystore, even lining the shelves of many of the best bookstores. There are pop-up Cinderellas, coloring-book Cinderellas, scratch-and-sniff Cinderellas, all inexpensive and available. The point in these books is not the story but the *gimmick.* These are books which must "interest 300,000 children, selling their initial print order in one season and continuing strong for at least two years after that." Compare that with the usual trade publishing house print order of a juvenile book—10,000 copies which an editor hopes to sell out in a lifetime of that title. 22

All the folk tales have been gutted. But none so changed, I belie "Cinderella." For the sake of Happy Ever After, the mass-market boo have brought forward a good, malleable, forgiving little girl and put her in Cinderella's slippers. However, in most of the Cinderella tales there is no forgiveness in the heroine's heart. No mercy. Just justice. In "Rushen Coatie" and "The Cinder-Maid," the elder sisters hack off their toes and heels in order to fit the shoe. Cinderella never stops them, never implies that she has the matching slipper. In fact, her tattletale birds warn the prince in "Rushen Coatie":

Hacked Heels and Pinched Toes
Behind the young prince rides,
But Pretty Feet and Little Feet
Behind the cauldron bides.

Even more graphically, they call out in "Cinder-Maid":

Turn and peep, turn and peep,
There's blood within the shoe;
A bit is cut from off the heel
And a bit from off the toe.

Cinderella never says a word of comfort. And in the least bowdlerized of the German and Nordic tales, [when] the two sisters come to the wedding "the elder was at the right side and the younger at the left, and the pigeons pecked out one eye from each of them. Afterwards, as they came back, the elder was on the left, and the younger at the right, and then the pigeons pecked out the other eye from each. And thus, for their wickedness and falsehood, they were punished with blindness all their days." That's a far cry from Perrault's heroine who "gave her sisters lodgings in the palace, and married them the same day to two great lords of the court." And further still from Nola Langner's Scholastic paperback "Cinderella":

> [The sisters] began to cry. They begged Cinderella to forgive them for being so mean to her. Cinderella told them they were forgiven.
>
> "I am sure you will never be mean to me again," she said.
>
> "Oh, never," said the older sister.
>
> "Never, ever," said the younger sister.

Missing, too, from the mass-market books is the shrewd, even witty 24
Cinderella. In a Wonder Book entitled "Bedtime Stories," a 1940s adaptation from Perrault, we find a Cinderella who talks to her stepsisters, "in a shy little voice." Even Perrault's heroine bantered with her stepsisters, asking them leading questions about the ball while secretly and deliciously knowing the answers. In the Wonder Book, however, the true wonder is that Cinderella ever gets to be princess. Even face-to-face with the prince, she is unrecognized until she dons her magic ball gown. Only when her clothes are transformed does the Prince know his true love.

In 1949, Walt Disney's film *Cinderella* burst onto the American scene. The story in the mass market has not been the same since. 25

The film came out of the studio at a particularly trying time for Disney. He had been deserted by the intellectuals who had been champions of this art for some years. Because of World War II, the public was more interested in war films than cartoons. But when *Cinderella,* lighter than light, was released it brought back to Disney—and his studio—all of his lost fame and fortune. The film was one of the most profitable of all time for the studio, grossing $4.247 million dollars in the first release alone. The success of the movie opened the floodgates of "Disney Cinderella" books. 26

Golden Press's *Walt Disney's Cinderella* set the new pattern for America's Cinderella. This book's text is coy and condescending. (Sample: "And her best friends of all were—guess who—the mice!") The illustrations are poor cartoons. And Cinderella herself is a disaster. She cowers as her sisters rip her homemade ball gown to shreds. (Not even homemade by Cinderella, but by the mice and birds.) She answers her stepmother with whines and pleadings. She is a sorry excuse for a heroine, pitiable and useless. She cannot perform even a simple action to save herself, though she is warned by her friends, the mice. She does not hear them because she is "off in a world of dreams." Cinderella begs, she whimpers, and at last has to be rescued by—guess who—the mice! 27

There is also an easy-reading version published by Random House, *Walt Disney's Cinderella.* This Cinderella commits the further heresy of cursing her luck. "How I did wish to go to the ball," she says. "But it is no use. Wishes never come true." 28

But in the fairy tales wishes have a habit of happening—*wishes accompanied by the proper action,* bad wishes as well as good. That is the beauty of the old stories and their wisdom as well. 29

Take away the proper course of action, take away Cinderella's ability to think for herself and act for herself, and you are left with a tale of wishes-come-true-regardless. But that is not the way of the fairy tale. As P. L. Travers so wisely puts it, "If that were so, wouldn't we all be married to princes?" 30

The mass-market American "Cinderellas" have presented the majority of American children with the wrong dream. They offer the passive princess, the "insipid beauty waiting . . . for Prince Charming" that Rosemary Minard objects to, and thus acculturate millions of girls and boys. But it is the wrong Cinderella and the magic of the old tales has been falsified, the true meaning lost, perhaps forever. 31

▲ ▲ ▲

Review Questions

1. Why does Yolen find it ironic that Americans regard "Cinderella" as the classic rags-to-riches story?
2. According to Yolen, why have feminists misdirected their attack on "Cinderella"?

3. What does Yolen find objectionable in Walt Disney's *"Cinderella"?*
4. In what ways have we each been Cinderella, according to Yolen?

Discussion and Writing Suggestions

1. Yolen contends that "fairy tales, as all stories for children, acculturate young readers and listeners." How are children acculturated by tales like "Cinderella"?
2. Yolen believes that "Walt Disney's *Cinderella* is a "heresy of the worst kind." Respond to this comment in a brief essay. (Review Yolen's reasons for stating this view and then agree and/or disagree.)
3. "All the folk tales have been gutted," says Yolen. Having read the different versions of Cinderella, would you agree—at least with respect to this one tale? Explain your answer.

▼

SYNTHESIS ACTIVITIES

1. In 1910, Antti Aarne published one of the early classifications of folktale types as an aid to scholars who were collecting tales and needed an efficient means for telling where, and with what changes, similar tales had appeared. In 1927, folklorist Stith Thompson, translating and enlarging Aarne's study, produced a work that is now a standard reference for folklorists the world over. We present the authors' description of type 510 and its two forms 510A ("Cinderella") and 510B. Use this description as a basis on which to compare and contrast any three versions of "Cinderella."

510. *Cinderella and Cap o' Rushes.*

I. *The Persecuted Heroine.* (a) The heroine is abused by her stepmother and stepsisters, or (b) flees in disguise from her father who wants to marry her, or (c) is cast out by him because she has said that she loved him like salt, or (d) is to be killed by a servant.

II. *Magic Help.* While she is acting as servant (at home or among strangers) she is advised, provided for, and fed (a) by her dead mother, (b) by a tree on the mother's grave, or (c) a supernatural being, (d) by birds, or (e) by a goat, a sheep, or a cow. When the goat is killed, there springs up from her remains a magic tree.

III. *Meeting with Prince.* (a) She dances in beautiful clothing several times with a prince who seeks in vain to keep her, or she is seen by him in church. (b) She gives hints of the abuse she has endured, as servant girl, or (c) she is seen in her beautiful clothing in her room or in the church.

IV. *Proof of Identity.* (a) She is discovered through the slipper-test, or (b) through a ring which she throws into the prince's drink or bakes in his bread. (c) She alone is able to pluck the gold apple desired by the knight.

V. *Marriage with the Prince.*

VI. *Value of Salt.* Her father is served unsalted food and thus learns the meaning of her earlier answer.

Two forms of the type follow.

A. *Cinderella.* The two stepsisters. The stepdaughter at the grave of her own mother, who helps her (milks the cow, shakes the apple tree, helps the old man). Threefold visit to church (dance). Slipper test.

B. *The Dress of Gold, of Silver, and of Stars. (Cap o' Rushes).* Present of the father who wants to marry his own daughter. The maiden as servant of the prince, who throws various objects at her. The threefold visit to the church and the forgotten shoe. Marriage.

2. Speculate on the reasons folktales are made and told. As you develop a theory, rely first on your own hunches regarding the origins and functions of folktale literature. You might want to recall your experiences as a child listening to tales so that you can discuss their effects on you. Rely as well on the variants of "Cinderella," which you should regard as primary sources (just as scholars do). And make use of the critical pieces you've read—Thompson, Bettelheim, Kolbenschlag, and Yolen—selecting pertinent points from each that will help clarify your points. *Remember:* Your own speculation should dominate the paper. Use sources to help you make *your* points.
3. At the conclusion of his article, Stith Thompson writes:

> Literary critics, anthropologists, historians, psychologists, and aestheticians are all needed if we are to hope to know why folktales are made, how they are invented, what art is used in their telling, how they grow and change and occasionally die.

What is your opinion of the critical work you've read on "Cinderella"? Writing from various perspectives, authors in this chapter have analyzed the tale. To what extent have the analyses illuminated "Cinderella" for you? (Have the analyses in any way "ruined" your ability to enjoy "Cinderella"?) To what extent do you find the analyses off the mark? Are the attempts at analysis inappropriate for a children's story? In your view, what place do literary critics, anthropologists, historians, and psychologists have in discussing folktales?

In developing a response to these questions, you might begin with Thompson's quotation and then follow directly with a statement of your thesis. In one part of your paper, critique the work of Bettelheim, Kolbenschlag, and/or Yolen as a way of demonstrating which analyses of folktales (if any) seem worthwhile to you. In another section of the paper (or perhaps woven into the critiques), you'll refer directly to the variants of "Cinderella." For the sake of convenience, refer to a single variant. If so, state as much to the reader and explain your choice of variant.

4. Review the variants of "Cinderella" and select two you would read to your child. In an essay, justify your decision. Which of the older European variants do you prefer: Grimm? Perrault? How do the recent ver-

sions by Sexton, Lee, Disney, and Garner affect you? And what of the Chinese, African, and Algonquin versions—are they recognizably "Cinderella"?

You might justify the variants you've selected by defining your criteria for selection and then analyzing the stories separately. (Perhaps you will use Aarne and Thompson's classification—see Synthesis Activity 1.) You might justify your choices negatively—that is, by defining your criteria and then *eliminating* certain variants because they don't meet the criteria. In concluding the paper, you might explain how the variants you've selected work as a pair. How do they complement each other? (Or, perhaps, they *don't* complement each other and this is why you've selected them.)

5. Try writing a version of "Cinderella" and setting it on a college campus. For your version of the story to be an authentic variant, you'll need to retain certain defining features, or motifs. See Aarne and Thompson—Synthesis Activity 1. As you consider the possibilities for your story, recall Thompson's point that the teller of a folktale borrows heavily on earlier versions; the virtue of telling is not in rendering a new story but in retelling an old one and *adapting* it to local conditions and needs. Unless you plan to write a commentary "Cinderella," as Sexton's poem is, you should retain the basic motifs of the old story and add details that will appeal to your particular audience: your classmates.
6. In her 1981 book *The Cinderella Complex,* Colette Dowling wrote:

> It is the thesis of this book that personal, psychological dependency—the deep wish to be taken care of by others—is the chief force holding women down today. I call this "The Cinderella Complex"—a network of largely repressed attitudes and fears that keep women in a kind of half-light, retreating from the full use of their minds and creativity. Like Cinderella, women today are still waiting for something external to transform their lives.

In an essay, respond to Dowling's thesis. First, apply her thesis to a few of the variants of "Cinderella." Does the thesis hold in each case? Next, respond to her view that "the chief force holding women down today" is psychological dependency, or the need for "something external" (i.e., a Prince) to transform their lives. In your experience, have you observed a Cinderella complex at work? (You might want to discuss the views of Jane Yolen, who in her article—paragraphs 7, 8, and 31—responds directly to a feminist's criticisms of "Cinderella.")

7. Discuss the process by which Cinderella falls in love in these tales. The paper that you write will be an extended comparison and contrast in which you observe this process at work in the variants and then discuss similarities and differences. (In structuring your paper, you'll need to make some choices: Which variants will you discuss and in what order?) At the conclusion of your extended comparison and contrast, try to answer the "so what" question. That is, pull your observations together and make a statement about Cinderella's falling in love. What is the significance of what you've learned? Share this significance with your readers.

8. Write an essay in which you attempt to define a feminist perspective on "Cinderella," as this is expressed by Kolbenschlag, Sexton, and Garner. Once you have defined this perspective, compare and contrast it with other perspectives in the chapter. To what extent do the feminist items here differ significantly from the nonfeminist analyses or tales?

▼

RESEARCH ACTIVITIES

1. Research the fairy-tale literature of your ancestors, both the tales and any critical commentary that you can find on them. Once you have read the material, talk with older members of your family to hear any tales they have to tell. (Seek, especially, oral versions of stories you have already read.) In a paper, discuss the role that fairy-tale literature has played, and continues to play, in your family.
2. Locate the book *Morphology of the Folktale* (1958), by Russian folklorist Vladimir Propp. Use the information you find there to analyze the elements of any three fairy tales of your choosing. In a paper, report on your analysis and evaluate the usefulness of Propp's system of classifying the key elements of fairy-tale literature.
3. Bruno Bettelheim's *Uses of Enchantment* (1976) generated a great deal of reaction on its publication. Read Bettelheim and locate as many reviews of his work as possible. Based on your own reactions and on your reading of the reviews, write an evaluation in which you address Bettelheim's key assumption that fairy-tale literature provides important insights into the psychological life of children.
4. Locate and study multiple versions of any fairy tale other than "Cinderella." ("Little Red Riding Hood" would be a likely candidate.) Having read the versions, identify—and write your paper on—what you feel are the defining elements that make the tales variants of a single story. See if you can find the tale listed as a "type" in Aarne and Thompson, *The Types of Folk-Tales*. If you wish, argue that one version of the tale is preferable to others.
5. Various critics, such as Madonna Kolbenschlag (who has an essay in this chapter) and Jack Zipes, author of *Breaking the Magic Spell* (1979), have taken the approach that fairy tales are far from innocuous children's stories; rather, they inculcate the unsuspecting with the value systems of the dominant culture. Write a paper in which you evaluate an interpretation of fairy-tale literature. In your paper, explicitly address the assumption that fairy tales are not morally or politically neutral but, rather, imply a distinct set of values.
6. Write a children's story. Decide on the age group that you will address, and then go to a local public library and find several books directed to the same audience. (1) Analyze these books and write a brief paper in which you identify the story elements that seem especially important for your intended audience. (2) Then attempt your own story. (3) When you

have finished, answer this question: What values are implicit in your story? What will children who read or hear the story learn about themselves and their world? Plan to submit your brief analytical paper, your story, and your final comment.

7. Videotape, and then study, several hours of Saturday morning cartoons. Then locate and read a collection of Grimm's fairy tales. In a comparative analysis, examine the cartoons and the fairy tales along any four or five dimensions that you think are important. The point of your comparisons and contrasts will be to determine how well the two types of presentations stack up against each other. Which do you find more entertaining? Illuminating? Ambitious? Useful? (These criteria are suggestions only. You should generate your own criteria as part of your research.)
8. Arrange to read to your favorite young person a series of fairy tales. Based on your understanding of the selections in this chapter, develop a list of questions concerning the importance or usefulness of fairy-tale literature to children. Read to your young friend on several occasions and, if possible, talk about the stories after you read them (or while you are reading). Then write a paper on your experience, answering as many of your initial questions as possible. (Be sure in your paper to provide a profile of the child with whom you worked; to review your selection of stories; and to list the questions you wanted to explore.)

11
The Brave New World of Biotechnology

> Career competition in the 21st century will be tough. The prizes will go only to those with the right combination of high-level physical and mental attributes. Why take a chance? You can guarantee that your unborn child will have what it takes to succeed in this demanding environment. Our highly trained medical staff stands ready to assist you in designing and executing a genetic profile for your offspring. Call today for an appointment with one of our counselors.
>
> *GenePerfect, Inc.*

The above ad hasn't appeared anywhere yet; but many people are afraid that something like this could result if the revolution in biotechnology continues, unchecked by ethical considerations.

The moral dilemmas now enveloping biotechnology would not be so hotly debated if the technology itself were not so remarkable—and effective. Thanks to its successes so far—in making possible, for instance, the cheap and plentiful production of such disease-fighting agents as insulin and interferon—numerous people have been able to live longer and healthier lives. Its promise in improved agricultural production is exciting. And even without considering the practical consequences, we have the prospect of a new world of knowledge about life itself and the essential components of our own humanity, our own individuality, as revealed in our distinctive genetic codes.

What is biotechnology? Broadly speaking, biotechnology encompasses "all the studies and techniques that combine the ideas and needs of biology and medicine with engineering" (Grolier's *Academic American Encyclopedia*). In the public mind, however, biotechnology has mainly come to be associated with a range of controversial applications in the areas of genetic engineering, medicine, human genetics, and the forensic use of DNA. In this chapter, we will focus on these controversies—on the science behind them and on the ethical, social, political, and legal issues that make them important.

Genetics, the science of inherited characteristics, has figured in human history, in a rough and ready way, for thousands of years—in the breeding of domesticated plants and animals to obtain desired types. Formal scientific studies in genetics, however, date only from the experiments of the Austrian botanist Gregor Mendel (1822–1884). Mendel established some of the basic laws of inheritance by crossbreeding plants with certain characteristics and noting how those characteristics were distributed in subsequent generations. But the means for understanding the molecular basis of those laws was not developed until 1953, when James Watson, an American, and Francis Crick, a Briton, published a landmark article in the scientific journal *Nature* that first elucidated the molecular structure of DNA (deoxyribonucleic acid). It had been known for some time that DNA is the chemical compound forming the genetic material (chromosomes and genes) of all organisms, but understanding how DNA functions in the process of inheritance required knowledge of DNA's molecular structure. Watson and Crick showed that DNA has the structure of a double helix—that is, two interconnected helical strands.

Each of the two strands of the DNA molecule consists of a sugar-phosphate "backbone" and sequences of nucleotides, or bases, attached to the backbone. The bases pair up in specific ways to connect the two strands. In most organisms, DNA is present in all cells in the form of chromosomes gathered in the cell's nucleus. Genes are parts of chromosomes—that is, they are segments of DNA. Each gene is a sequence of bases that governs the production of a certain protein, so the sequence of bases that forms a gene can be viewed as a "code" for producing a protein; hence, the term *genetic code.* Acting separately and together, the proteins produced by the genes determine many of the organism's physical and behavioral characteristics, including the way in which the organism progresses through its life cycle. And because genes are passed along from one generation to the next, they are the basis for heredity.

Watson and Crick's discovery and the subsequent advances in genetics provided the foundation for genetic engineering, and the techniques developed for genetic engineering made possible the controversial applications in medicine, human genetics, and law that are the focus of this chapter.

Genetic engineering (a branch of biotechnology) is "the application of the knowledge obtained from genetic investigations to the solution of such problems as infertility, diseases, food production, waste disposal, and improvement of a species" (Grolier's *Academic American Encyclopedia*). Genetic engineering is also known as "gene splicing" and as "recombinant DNA technology" because it involves combining the DNA (that is, splicing together the genes) of different organisms. For example, a gene with a certain desired function (e.g., that of generating a particular antibody) could be taken from the cells of one person and inserted into the cells of a person lacking that gene, thus enabling the second person to produce the desired antibody.

In another kind of application, genes that generate desired products can be inserted into the DNA of bacteria or other types of cells that replicate

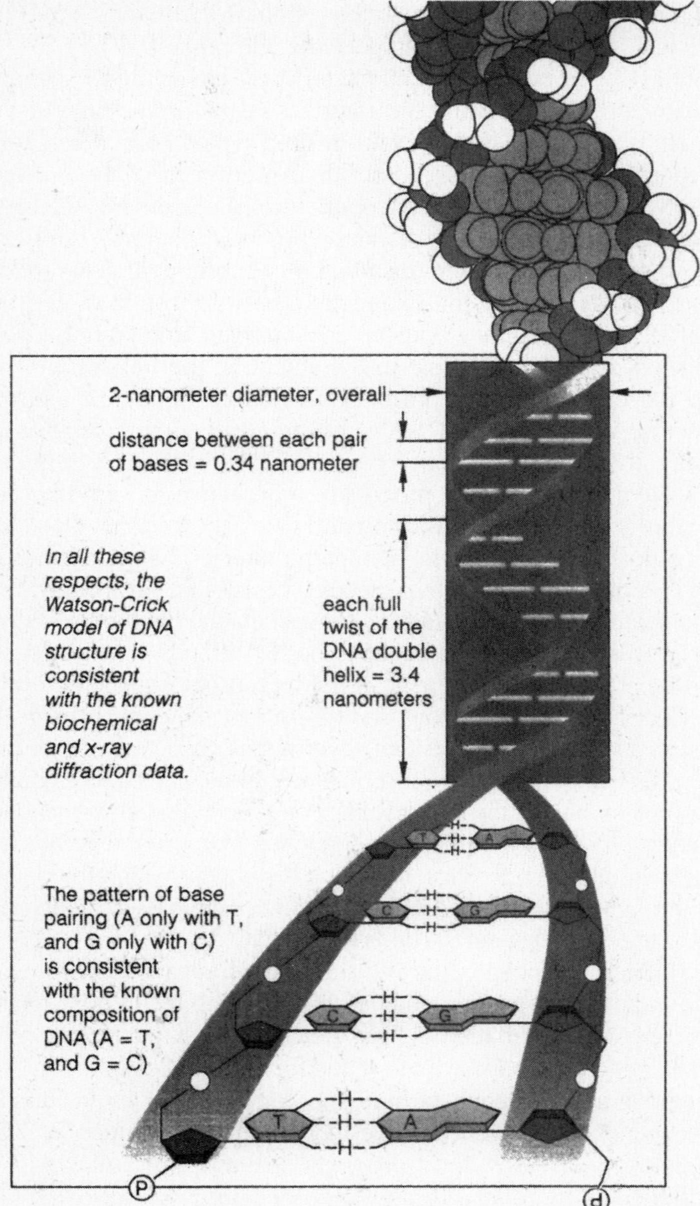

The double helix structure of DNA (deoxyribonucleic acid). The "backbone" of each strand is composed of sugar-phosphate molecules. Nucleotide bases are attached to the backbones, and the two strands are linked by pairs of these bases. There are four different bases in DNA—the nucleotides adenine (A), cytosine (C), guanine (G), and thymine (T)—and they pair up in a highly restricted way: A pairs only with T, and C pairs only with G. Each unit of three successive base pairs (i.e., a "triplet") governs the production of an amino acid. Proteins are composed of amino acids. Thus, a gene is a sequence of triplets governing the production of a protein that consists of the amino acids specified by those triplets.

Cecie Starr & Ralph Taggart, *Biology: The Unity and Diversity of Life,* used later in chapter.

rapidly. When the "engineered" cells replicate, they copy the foreign genes along with their own and generate the products specified by those genes. Populations of such cells can function as "factories" to produce large quantities of useful products.

Gene splicing can be done by means of special enzymes ("restriction enzymes") that can split DNA from one organism into fragments that will combine with similarly formed fragments from another organism, thus forming a new DNA molecule. Copies of this new molecule can be obtained by inserting it into a host cell that replicates the molecule every time it divides, as in the examples just described. In 1985, however, a more efficient method of gene splicing was developed, called *polymerase chain reaction (PCR),* done in a test tube rather than with living cells. PCR allows the double helix of the new DNA molecule to be split into its two complementary strands. When mixed with DNA polymerase from certain bacteria, the two strands function as templates for the generation of two copies of the new molecule. Thus PCR allows a repeated, rapid doubling in the number of desired molecules.

Gene splicing experiments began in the early 1970s, at first involving DNA exchanges between unicellular organisms, such as viruses and bacteria. But recipients of "foreign" DNA soon included more complex organisms, such as fruit flies and frogs (although no humans, at this stage). During this early period of experimentation, some began to worry about the possibility of a genetic disaster. What if some newly engineered microbes escaped from the lab and caused an epidemic of a new and unknown disease, for which there was no known cure? What if the delicate ecological balance of nature or the course of evolution were drastically affected? (Fears of DNA experimentation gone haywire were expertly—and thrillingly—exploited by Michael Crichton's book [and Steven Spielberg's movie] *Jurassic Park,* in which a new race of rampaging dinosaurs is cloned from ancient DNA, and spliced with frog DNA.) Some proposed an outright ban on genetic engineering experiments. At an international conference in Asilomar, California, in 1975, scientists agreed on a set of guidelines to govern future research.

In time, these early fears turned out to be groundless, and the restrictions were eased or lifted. Meantime, considerable strides were made in genetic engineering, with new applications discovered in agriculture, pollution control, and the fight against a host of diseases. Genetic engineering became big business, as many scientists abandoned the academy to found and work for firms with names like Genentech and Genex.

But reservations persist. Some are uncomfortable with the fact of genetic engineering itself, considering it an unwarranted intrusion by human beings into the fragile structure of Nature, with too little knowledge or care about the consequences. Others have no philosophical objections to genetic engineering but worry about its effects on the environment and on humans. Or they worry about the kind of ethical problems raised by the new field of *genetic therapy*—the kind of problems suggested by the imaginary ad at the beginning of our introduction. Of course, this is an extreme example. Most people would have no problem with using genetic therapy to cure life-threatening diseases or conditions. For example, in a pioneering experiment in 1992, genes were injected into the blood cells of three infants lacking an enzyme whose absence prevented their bodies from fighting off potentially deadly viral and bacterial infections. Three years later, the infants' cells appeared to be producing the enzyme that is crucial to their survival.

There is little controversy over such forms of genetic therapy. But should genetic therapy be conducted to "correct" left-handedness? Nearsightedness? Baldness? Or even to *detect* such potential conditions? A recent survey for *Redbook* magazine revealed that while only 18 percent of respondents disapproved of *genetic testing* and manipulation to discover whether a child would have a disease or disability, an overwhelming 86 percent disapproved of using such a tool to select the sex of a child; 91 percent, to increase the child's IQ; and 94 percent, to improve the child's athletic ability. (Of course, such figures could change dramatically when the possibilities become real instead of abstract.)

There are other troubling aspects of biotechnology. Genetic testing may be used as a *screening* device by employers and insurance companies—in other words, it may be used as a means of genetic discrimination. Employers may be disinclined to hire prospective employees for whom genetic screening has revealed a present or potential health problem, such as heart disease. Since many genetic traits are linked to race or sex, genetic discrimination could be another form of racial or gender discrimination. Another area of concern is the *Human Genome Project,* a massive scientific undertaking begun in the late 1980s (and initially directed by James Watson) to determine the complete genetic makeup of human chromosomes. Armed with the knowledge of what each gene does and where it is located, scientists (it is feared) would be able to manipulate human cells to create individuals with qualities considered desirable, while eliminating qualities considered undesirable. For many, such possibilities bring to mind the notorious Nazi eugenics programs aimed at creating an Aryan "master" race and exterminating "inferior" races. A somewhat related project, the Human Genome Diversity Project, has also become embroiled in controversy. Finally, as the O.J. Simpson trial has dramatically demonstrated, there is controversy over the *forensic* use of DNA—the use of DNA testing in legal proceedings to determine guilt. While many suspects—and some convicted persons—have been exonerated as a result of DNA testing, some defense attorneys have contested the validity and reliability of DNA evidence when it is used by the prosecution.

For most, then, the problem is not so much biotechnology itself as its possible abuses. As *Time* writer Philip Elmer-Dewitt notes, "To unlock the secrets hidden in the chromosomes of human cells is to open up a host of thorny legal, ethical, philosophical and religious issues, from invasion of privacy to the question of who should play God with [people's] genes." Some of these thorny issues are explored in the following pages. We begin with the opening chapter of Aldous Huxley's dystopian novel *Brave New World,* which for more than sixty years has served as an unforgettable warning of the dark side of scientific progress. Here we see human ova fertilized outside the womb, the embryos and fetuses conditioned and then decanted (born) from bottles, prepared to do specific jobs and to be contented and productive citizens in a stable society. Huxley's dark vision is followed by Cecie Starr and Ralph Taggart's "Recombinant DNA and Genetic Engineering," which explains the mechanics of genetic engineering as well as some of the ethical problems involved in its use. Next, in "Tinkering With Destiny," three *U.S. News & World Report* staffwriters discuss the complex issues of human gene therapy, as faced not only by the families most directly concerned, but also by scientists, doctors, genetic counselors, and entrepreneurs. In "The Grandiose Claims of Geneticists," sociology professor Dorothy Nelkin acknowledges the accomplishments of biotechnology, but cautions against an uncritical acceptance of what she considers the exaggerated self-promotions of the biotechnologists.

In "The Human Genome Project: A Personal View," James D. Watson, co-discoverer of DNA's helical structure, defends the Human Genome Project from adversaries and skeptics and asserts its potential role in helping us to understand and combat diseases. Three of the skeptics (if not outright adversaries), biologist Anne Fausto-Sterling, political scientist Diane Paul, and disability rights activist Marsha Saxton, address some of the scientific and ethical problems arising from the Genome Project in "The Politics of Genetics," an interview published in the *Women's Review of Books.* The following two pieces deal with the controversy of the Human Genome Diversity Project. First, in an open letter appearing in the journal *Genomics,* geneticist Luigi Luca Cavalli-Sforza and his colleagues propose the landmark project. In "End of the Rainbow" Jo Ann C. Gutin surveys the unexpected avalanche of criticism provoked by the Human Genome Diversity Project—or, as some call it, the "Vampire Project." The final pair of readings in the chapter address the controversy over the forensic use of DNA. In "When Science Takes the Witness Stand," attorney Peter J. Neufeld and physician Neville Colman advise readers of *Scientific American* that DNA evidence should be regarded with great skepticism. In "DNA in Court," William Tucker debunks such doubts.

Brave New World

ALDOUS HUXLEY

The title of Aldous Huxley's novel Brave New World *(1932) derives from a line in Shakespeare's final comedy,* The Tempest. *Miranda is a young woman who has grown up on an enchanted island; her father is the only other human she has known. When she suddenly encounters people from the outside world (including a handsome young prince), she remarks, "O brave [wondrous] new world that has such people in it!" Shakespeare used the line ironically (the world of* The Tempest *is filled with knaves and fools); and almost three hundred years later, Huxley employed not only the language but also the irony in labeling his nightmare society of* A.F. *632 (After [Henry] Ford).*

In comparison with other dystopias, like George Orwell's 1984, *Huxley's brave new world of creature comforts seems, at first glance, a paradise. People are given whatever they need to keep happy: unlimited sex, tranquilizers, and soothing experiences. No one goes hungry; no one suffers either physical or spiritual pain. But the cost of such comfort is an almost total loss of individuality, creativity, and freedom. Uniformity and stability are exalted above all other virtues. The population is divided into castes, determined from before birth, with the more intelligent Alphas and Betas governing and managing the society, while the less intelligent Deltas, Gammas, and Epsilons work at the menial tasks. Epsilons are not unhappy with their lot in life because they have been conditioned to be content; and, in fact, they are incapable of conceiving anything better. Love, art, and science are suppressed for all castes because they lead to instability, and instability threatens happiness. Idle reflection is discouraged for the same reason; and, to avoid the effects of any intense emotions, positive or negative, the inhabitants of this brave new world are given regular doses of the powerful tranquilizer "soma."*

Huxley's brave new world, then, is a projection into the future of tendencies he saw in his own world that he thought were disturbing or dangerous. In the context of our present chapter on biotechnology, we are most interested in Huxley's portrait of a "hatchery," where human ova are removed from the womb and fertilized, and the embryos and fetuses grown in bottles are programed before "birth" to produce an assortment of the kind of people who will be most desirable to society. In the following passage, the first chapter of Brave New World *(1932), we are taken on a tour through the Central London Hatchery and Conditioning Centre, where we follow an egg from fertilization through conditioning. To many people today, Huxley's dramatic portrait of the manipulation of human germ cells is uncomfortably close to what modern genetic engineers are beginning, with ever greater facility, to make possible: the substitution of "more desirable" for "less desirable" genes in order to create "better" people.*

Born in Surrey, England, Aldous Huxley (1894–1963), grandson of naturalist T. H. Huxley, intended to pursue a medical career; but after being stricken with a corneal disease that left him almost blind, he turned to literature. Among his works are Crome Yellow *(1921),* Antic Hay *(1923),* Point Counter Point *(1928), and* Eyeless in Gaza *(1936). Huxley moved to the United States in 1936, settling in California. In the latter part of his life, he tended toward the mystical and experimented with naturally occurring hallucinogenic drugs—the subject of his* Doors of Perception *(1954).*

A squat grey building of only thirty-four stories. Over the main entrance the words, CENTRAL LONDON HATCHERY and CONDITIONING CENTRE, and, in a shield, the World State's motto: COMMUNITY, IDENTITY, STABILITY. 1

The enormous room on the ground floor faced towards the north. Cold for all the summer beyond the panes, for all the tropical heat of the room itself, a harsh thin light glared through the windows, hungrily seeking some draped lay figure, some pallid shape of academic gooseflesh, but finding only the glass and nickel and bleakly shining procelain of a laboratory. 2

Wintriness responded to wintriness. The overalls of the workers were white, their hands gloved with a pale corpse-coloured rubber. The light was frozen, dead, a ghost. Only from the yellow barrels of the microscopes did it borrow a certain rich and living substance, lying along the polished tubes like butter, streak after luscious streak in long recession down the work tables.

"And this," said the Director opening the door, "is the Fertilizing Room." 3

Bent over their instruments, three hundred Fertilizers were plunged, as the Director of Hatcheries and Conditioning entered the room, in the scarcely breathing silence, the absent-minded, soliloquizing hum or whistle, of absorbed concentration. A troop of newly arrived students, very young, pink and callow, followed nervously, rather abjectly, at the Director's heels. Each of them carried a notebook, in which, whenever the great man spoke, he desperately scribbled. Straight from the horse's mouth. It was a rare privilege. The D.H.C. for Central London always made a point of personally conducting his new students round the various departments. 4

"Just to give you a general idea," he would explain to them. For of course some sort of general idea they must have, if they were to do their work intelligently—though as little of one, if they were to be good and happy members of society, as possible. For particulars, as every one knows, make for virtue and happiness; generalities are intellectually necessary evils. Not philosophers but fret-sawyers and stamp collectors compose the backbone of society. 5

"To-morrow," he would add, smiling at them with a slightly menacing geniality, "you'll be settling down to serious work. You won't have time for generalities. Meanwhile . . ." 6

Meanwhile, it was a privilege. Straight from the horse's mouth into the notebook. The boys scribbled like mad. 7

Tall and rather thin but upright, the Director advanced into the room. He had a long chin and big, rather prominent teeth, just covered, when he was not talking, by his full, floridly curved lips. Old, young? Thirty? Fifty? Fifty-five? It was hard to say. And anyhow the question didn't arise; in this year of stability, A.F. 632, it didn't occur to you to ask it. 8

"I shall begin at the beginning," said the D.H.C. and the more zealous students recorded his intention in their notebooks: *Begin at the beginning.* "These," he waved his hand, "are the incubators." And opening an insulated door he showed them racks upon racks of numbered test-tubes. "The week's supply of ova. Kept," he explained, "at blood heat; whereas the male gametes," and here he opened another door, "they have to be kept at thirty-five instead of thirty-seven. Full blood heat sterilizes." Rams wrapped in thermogene beget no lambs. 9

Still leaning against the incubators he gave them, while the pencils scurried illegibly across the pages, a brief description of the modern fertilizing process; spoke first, of course, of its surgical introduction—"the op- 10 eration undergone voluntarily for the good of Society, not to mention the fact that it carries a bonus amounting to six months' salary"; continued with some account of the technique for preserving the excised ovary alive and actively developing; passed on to a consideration of optimum temperature, salinity, viscosity; referred to the liquor in which the detached and ripened eggs were kept; and, leading his charges to the work tables, actually showed them how this liquor was drawn off from the test-tubes; how it was let out drop by drop onto the specially warmed slides of the microscopes; the eggs which it contained were inspected for abnormalities, counted and transferred to a porous receptacle; how (and he now took them to watch the operation) this receptacle was immersed in a warm bouillon containing free-swimming spermatozoa—at a minimum concentration of one hundred thousand per cubic centimetre, he insisted; and how, after ten minutes, the container was lifted out of the liquor and its contents re-examined; how, if any of the eggs remained unfertilized, it was again immersed, and, if necessary, yet again; how the fertilized ova went back to the incubators; where the Alphas and Betas remained until definitely bottled; while the Gammas, Deltas and Epsilons were brought out again, after only thirty-six hours, to undergo Bokanovsky's Process.

"Bokanovsky's Process," repeated the Director, and the students un- 11
derlined the words in their little notebooks.

One egg, one embryo, one adult—normality. But a bokanovskified egg 12
will bud, will proliferate, will divide. From eight to ninety-six buds, and every bud will grow into a perfectly formed embryo, and every embryo into a full-sized adult. Making ninety-six human beings grow where only one grew before. Progress.

"Essentially," the D.H.C. concluded, "bokanovskification consists of 13
a series of arrests of development. We check the normal growth and, paradoxically enough, the egg responds by budding."

Responds by budding. The pencils were busy. 14

He pointed. On a very slowly moving band a rack-full of test-tubes 15
was entering a large metal box, another rack-full was emerging. Machinery faintly purred. It took eight minutes for the tubes to go through, he told them. Eight minutes of hard X-rays being about as much as an egg can stand. A few died; of the rest, the least susceptible divided into two; most put out four buds; some eight; all were returned to the incubators, where the buds began to develop; then, after two days, were suddenly chilled, chilled and checked. Two, four, eight, the buds in their turn budded; and having budded were dosed almost to death with alcohol; consequently burgeoned again and having budded—bud out of bud out of bud—were thereafter—further arrest being generally fatal—left to develop in peace. By which time the original egg was in a fair way to becoming anything from eight to ninety-six embryos—a prodigious improvement, you will agree, on nature. Identical twins—but not in piddling twos and threes as in the old viviparous days, when an egg would sometimes accidentally divide; actually by dozens, by scores at a time.

"Scores," the Director repeated and flung out his arms, as though he were distributing largesse. "Scores." 16

But one of the students was fool enough to ask where the advantage lay. 17

"My good boy!" The Director wheeled sharply round on him. "Can't you see? Can't you *see?*" He raised a hand; his expression was solemn. "Bokanovsky's Process is one of the major instruments of social stability!" 18

Major instruments of social stability. 19

Standard men and women; in uniform batches. The whole of a small factory staffed with the products of a single bokanovskified egg. 20

"Ninety-six identical twins working ninety-six identical machines!" The voice was almost tremulous with enthusiasm. "You really know where you are. For the first time in history." He quoted the planetary motto. "Community, Identity, Stability." Grand words. "If we could bokanovskify indefinitely the whole problem would be solved." 21

Solved by standard Gammas, unvarying Deltas, uniform Epsilons. Millions of identical twins. The principle of mass production at last applied to biology. 22

"But, alas," the Director shook his head, "we *can't* bokanovskify indefinitely." 23

Ninety-six seemed to be the limit; seventy-two a good average. From the same ovary and with gametes of the same male to manufacture as many batches of identical twins as possible—that was the best (sadly a second best) that they could do. And even that was difficult. 24

"For in nature it takes thirty years for two hundred eggs to reach maturity. But our business is to stabilize the population at this moment, here and now. Dribbling out twins over a quarter of a century—what would be the use of that?" 25

Obviously, no use at all. But Podsnap's Technique had immensely accelerated the process of ripening. They could make sure of at least a hundred and fifty mature eggs within two years. Fertilize and bokanovskify—in other words, multiply by seventy-two—and you get an average of nearly eleven thousand brothers and sisters in a hundred and fifty batches of identical twins, all within two years of the same age. 26

"And in exceptional cases we can make one ovary yield us over fifteen thousand adult individuals." 27

Beckoning to a fair-haired, ruddy young man who happened to be passing at the moment, "Mr. Foster," he called. The ruddy young man approached. "Can you tell us the record for a single ovary, Mr. Foster?" 28

"Sixteen thousand and twelve in this Centre," Mr. Foster replied without hesitation. He spoke very quickly, had a vivacious blue eye, and took an evident pleasure in quoting figures. "Sixteen thousand and twelve; in one hundred and eighty-nine batches of identicals. But of course they've done much better," he rattled on, "in some of the tropical Centres. Singapore had often produced over sixteen thousand five hundred; and Mombasa has actually touched the seventeen thousand mark. But then they have un- 29 fair advantages. You should see the way a negro ovary responds to pituitary! It's quite astonishing, when you're used to working with European material. Still," he added, with a laugh (but the light of combat was in his eyes and the lift of his chin was challenging), "still, we mean to beat them if we can. I'm working on a wonderful Delta-Minus ovary at this moment. Only just eighteen months old. Over twelve thousand seven hundred children already, either decanted or in embryo. And still going strong. We'll beat them yet."

"That's the spirit I like!" cried the Director, and clapped Mr. Foster on 30
the shoulder. "Come along with us and give these boys the benefit of your expert knowledge."

Mr. Foster smiled modestly. "With pleasure." They went. 31

In the Bottling Room all was harmonious bustle and ordered activity. 32
Flaps of fresh sow's peritoneum ready cut to the proper size came shooting up in little lifts from the Organ Store in the sub–basement. Whizz and then, click! the lift-hatches flew open; the bottle-liner had only to reach out a hand, take the flap, insert, smooth-down, and before the lined bottle had had time to travel out of reach along with endless band, whizz, click! another flap of peritoneum had shot up from the depths, ready to be slipped into yet another bottle, the next of that slow interminable procession on the band.

Next to the Liners stood the Matriculators. The procession advanced; one 33
by one the eggs were transferred from their test-tubes to the larger containers; deftly the peritoneal lining was slit, the morula dropped into place, the saline solution poured in . . . and already the bottle had passed, and it was the turn of the labellers. Heredity, date of fertilization, membership of Bokanovsky Group—details were transferred from test-tube to bottle. No longer anonymous, but named, identified, the procession marched slowly on; on through an opening in the wall, slowly on into the Social Predestination Room.

"Eighty-eight cubic metres of card-index," said Mr. Foster with relish, 34
as they entered.

"Containing *all* the relevant information," added the Director. 35

"Brought up to date every morning." 36

"And co-ordinated every afternoon." 37

"On the basis of which they make their calculations." 38

"So many individuals, of such and such quality," said Mr. Foster. 39

"Distributed in such and such quantities." 40

"The optimum Decanting Rate at any given moment." 41

"Unforeseen wastages promptly made good." 42

"Promptly," repeated Mr. Foster. "If you knew the amount of over- 43
time I had to put in after the last Japanese earthquake!" He laughed good-humouredly and shook his head.

"The Predestinators send in their figures to the Fertilizers." 44

"Who give them the embroys they ask for." 45

"And the bottles come in here to be predestinated in detail." 46

"After which they are sent down to the Embryo Store." 47

"Where we now proceed ourselves." 48

And opening a door Mr. Foster led the way down a staircase into the basement. 49

The temperature was still tropical. They descended into a thickening twilight. Two doors and a passage with a double turn insured the cellar against any possible infiltration of the day. 50

"Embroys are like photograph film," said Mr. Foster waggishly, as he pushed open the second door. "They can only stand red light." 51

And in effect the sultry darkness into which the students now followed him was visible and crimson, like the darkness of closed eyes on a summer's afternoon. The bulging flanks of row on receding row and tier above tier of bottles glinted with innumerable rubies, and among the rubies moved the dim red spectres of men and women with purple eyes and all the symptoms of lupus. The hum and rattle of machinery faintly stirred the air. 52

"Give them a few figures, Mr. Foster," said the Director, who was tired of talking. 53

Mr. Foster was only too happy to give them a few figures. 54

Two hundred and twenty metres long, two hundred wide, ten high. He pointed upwards. Like chickens drinking, the students lifted their eyes towards the distant ceiling. 55

Three tiers of racks: ground floor level, first gallery, second gallery. 56

The spidery steel-work of gallery above gallery faded away in all directions into the dark. Near them three red ghosts were busily unloading demijohns from a moving staircase. 57

The escalator from the Social Predestination Room. 58

Each bottle could be placed on one of fifteen racks, each rack, though you couldn't see it, was a conveyor travelling at the rate of thirty-three and a third centimeters an hour. Two hundred and sixty-seven days at eight metres a day. Two thousand one hundred and thirty-six metres in all. One circuit of the cellar at ground level, one on the first gallery, half on the second, and on the two hundred and sixty-seventh morning, daylight in the Decanting Room. Independent existence—so called. 59

"But in the interval," Mr. Foster concluded, "we've managed to do a lot to them. Oh, a very great deal." His laugh was knowing and triumphant. 60

"That's the spirit I like," said the Director once more. "Let's walk round. You tell them everything, Mr. Foster." 61

Mr. Foster duly told them. 62

Told them of the growing embryo on its bed of peritoneum. Made them taste the rich blood surrogate on which it fed. Explained why it had to be stimulated with placentin and thyroxin. Told them of the *corpus luteum* extract. Showed them the jets through which at every twelfth metre from zero to 2040 it was automatically injected. Spoke of those gradually increasing doses of pituitary administered during the final ninety-six metres of their course. Described the artificial maternal circulation installed on every bottle at Metre 112; showed them the reservoir of blood-surrogate, the centrifugal pump that kept the liquid moving over the placenta and drove it through the synthetic lung and waste-product filter. Referred to the embryo's troublesome tendency to anæmia, to the massive doses of hog's 63 stomach extract and fetal foal's liver with which, in consequence, it had to be supplied.

Showed them the simple mechanism by means of which, during the last two metres out of every eight, all the embryos were simultaneously shaken into familiarity with movement. Hinted at the gravity of the so-called "trauma of decanting," and enumerated the precautions taken to minimize, by a suitable training of the bottled embryo, that dangerous shock. Told them of the tests for sex carried out in the neighbourhood of metre 200. Explained the system of labelling—a T for the males, a circle for the females and for those who were destined to become freemartins a question mark, black on a white ground. 64

"For of course," said Mr. Foster, "in the vast majority of cases, fertility is merely a nuisance. One fertile ovary in twelve hundred—that would really be quite sufficient for our purposes. But we want to have a good choice. And of course one must always leave an enormous margin of safety. So we allow as many as thirty per cent of the female embryos to develop normally. The others get a dose of male sex-hormone every twenty-four metres for the rest of the course. Result: they're decanted as fremartins—structurally quite normal ("except," he had to admit, "that they *do* have just the slightest tendency to grow beards), but sterile. Guaranteed sterile. Which brings us at last," continued Mr. Foster, "out of the realm of mere slavish imitation of nature into the much more interesting world of human invention." 65

He rubbed his hands. For of course, they didn't content themselves with merely hatching out embryos: any cow could do that. 66

"We also predestine and condition. We decant our babies as socialized human beings, as Alphas or Epsilons, as future sewage workers or future . . ." He was going to say "future World controllers," but correcting himself, said "future Directors of Hatcheries," instead. 67

The D.H.C. acknowledged the compliment with a smile. 68

They were passing Metre 320 on rack 11. A young Beta-Minus mechanic was busy with screwdriver and spanner on the blood-surrogate pump of a passing bottle. The hum of the electric motor deepened by fractions of a tone as he turned the nuts. Down, down . . . A final twist, a glance at the revolution counter, and he was done. He moved two paces down the line and began the same process on the next pump. 69

"Reducing the number of revolutions per minute," Mr. Foster explained. "The surrogate goes round slower; therefore passes through the lung at longer intervals; therefore gives the embryo less oxygen. Nothing like oxygen-shortage for keeping an embryo below par." Again he rubbed his hands. 70

"But why do you want to keep the embryo below par?" asked an ingenuous student. 71

"Ass!" said the Director, breaking a long silence. "Hasn't it occurred to you that an Epsilon embryo must have an Epsilon environment as well as an Epsilon heredity?" 72

It evidently hadn't occurred to him. He was covered with confusion. 73

"The lower the caste," said Mr. Foster, "the shorter the oxygen." The 74
first organ affected was the brain. After that the skeleton. At seventy per cent of normal oxygen you got dwarfs. At less than seventy eyeless monsters.

"Who are no use at all," concluded Mr. Foster. 75

Whereas (his voice became confidential and eager), if they could dis- 76
cover a technique for shortening the period of maturation what a triumph, what a benefaction to Society!

"Consider the horse." 77

They considered it. 78

Mature at six; the elephant at ten. While at thirteen a man is not yet 79
sexually mature; and is only full-grown at twenty. Hence, of course, that fruit of delayed development, the human intelligence.

"But in Epsilons," said Mr. Foster very justly, "we don't need human 80
intelligence."

Didn't need and didn't get it. But though the Epsilon mind was mature 81
at ten, the Epsilon body was not fit to work till eighteen. Long years of superfluous and wasted immaturity. If the physical development could be speeded up till it was as quick, say, as a cow's what an enormous saving to the Community!

"Enormous!" murmured the students. Mr. Foster's enthusiasm was in- 82
fectious.

He became rather technical; spoke of the abnormal endocrine coordi- 83
nation which made men grow so slowly; postulated a germinal mutation to account for it. Could the effects of this germinal mutation be undone? Could the individual Epsilon embryo be made a revert, by a suitable technique, to the normality of dogs and cows? That was the problem. And it was all but solved.

Pilkington, at Mombasa, had produced individuals who were sexually 84
mature at four and full-grown at six and a half. A scientific triumph. But socially useless. Six-year-old men and women were too stupid to do even Epsilon work. And the process was an all-or-nothing one; either you failed to modify at all, or else you modified the whole way. They were still trying to find the ideal compromise between adults of twenty and adults of six. So far without success. Mr. Foster sighed and shook his head.

Their wanderings through the crimson twilight had brought them to the 85
neighbourhood of Metre 170 on Rack 9. From this point onwards Rack 9 was enclosed and the bottles performed the remainder of their journey in a kind of tunnel, interrupted here and there by openings two or three metres wide.

"Heat conditioning," said Mr. Foster. 86

Hot tunnels alternated with cool tunnels. Coolness was wedded to dis- 87
comfort in the form of hard X-rays. By the time they were decanted the embryos had a horror of cold. They were predestined to emigrate to the tropics, to be miners and acetate silk spinners and steel workers. Later on their

minds would be made to endorse the judgment of their bodies. "We condition them to thrive on heat," concluded Mr. Foster. "Our colleagues upstairs will teach them to love it."

"And that," put in the Director sententiously, "that is the secret of 88
happiness and virtue—liking what you've *got* to do. All conditioning aims at that: making people like their unescapable social destiny."

In a gap between two tunnels, a nurse was delicately probing with a 89
long fine syringe into the gelatinous contents of a passing bottle. The students and their guides stood watching her for a few moments in silence.

"Well, Lenina," said Mr. Foster, when at last she withdrew the syringe 90
and straightened herself up.

The girl turned with a start. One could see that, for all the lupus and the 91
purple eyes, she was uncommonly pretty.

"Henry!" Her smile flashed redly at him—a row of coral teeth. 92

"Charming, charming," murmured the Director and, giving her two or 93
three little pats, received in exchange a rather deferential smile for himself.

"What are you giving them?" asked Mr. Foster, making his tone very 94
professional.

"Oh, the usual typhoid and sleeping sickness." 95

"Tropical workers start being inoculated at Metre 150," Mr. Foster ex- 96
plained to the students. "The embryos still have gills. We immunize the fish against the future man's diseases." Then, turning back to Lenina, "Ten to five on the roof this afternoon," he said, "as usual."

"Charming," said the Director once more, and with a final pat, moved 97
away after the others.

On Rack 10 rows of next generation's chemical workers were being 98
trained in the toleration of lead, caustic soda, tar, chlorine. The first of a batch of two hundred and fifty embryonic rocket-plane engineers was just passing the eleven hundred metre mark on Rack 3. A special mechanism kept their containers in constant rotation. "To improve their sense of balance," Mr. Foster explained. "Doing repairs on the outside of a rocket in mid-air is a ticklish job. We slacken off the circulation when they're right way up, so that they're half starved, and double the flow of surrogate when they're upside down. They learn to associate topsyturvydom with well-being; in fact, they're only truly happy when they're standing on their heads.

"And now," Mr. Foster went on, "I'd like to show you some very in- 99
teresting conditioning for Alpha Plus Intellectuals. We have a big batch of them on Rack 5. First Gallery level," he called to two boys who had started to go down to the ground floor.

"They're round about Metre 900," he explained. "You can't really do 100
any useful intellectual conditioning till the fetuses have lost their tails. Follow me."

But the Director had looked at his watch. "Ten to three," he said. "No 101
time for the intellectual embryos, I'm afraid. We must go up to the Nurseries before the children have finished their afternoon sleep."

Mr. Foster was disappointed. "At least one glance at the Decanting 102
Room," he pleaded.

"Very well then." The Director smiled indulgently. "Just one glance." 103

▲ ▲ ▲

Review Questions

1. What is the Bokanovsky Process? Why is it central to Huxley's "brave new world"?
2. How does Huxley comment sardonically on the racism of the Hatchery's personnel—and of Europeans in general?
3. What is the difference—and the social significance of the difference—among Alphas, Betas, Deltas, Gammas, and Epsilons?
4. What technological problems concerning the maturation process have the scientists of *Brave New World* still not solved?

Discussion and Writing Suggestions

1. How does the language of the first two paragraphs reveal Huxley's tone, that is, his attitude toward his subject? For example, what is the function of the word "only" in the opening sentence: "A squat grey building of only thirty-four stories"? Or the adjectives describing the building?
2. What does the narrator mean when he says (paragraph 5) that "particulars, as every one knows, make for virtue and happiness; generalities are intellectually necessary evils. Not philosophers but fret-sawyers [operators of fretsaws, long, narrow, fine-toothed hand saws used for ornamental detail work] and stamp collectors compose the backbone of society"? To what extent do you believe that such an ethic operates in our own society? Give examples of the relatively low value placed on "philosophers" and the relatively high value placed on "fret-sawyers."
3. Throughout this chapter, Huxley makes an implied contrast between the brisk, technological efficiency of the Hatchery and the ethical nature of what takes place within its walls. What aspects of our own civilization show similar contrasts? (Example: We are now able to build more technologically sophisticated weapons of destruction than ever before in history.) Explore this subject in an essay, devoting a paragraph or so to each aspect of our civilization that you consider.
4. In the Hatchery, bottled, fertilized eggs pass into the "Social Predestination Room." In that room, their future lives will be determined. Is there an equivalent of the Social Predestination Room in our own society? (In other words, are there times and places when and where our future lives are determined?) If so, describe its features, devoting a paragraph to each of these features.
5. Foster explains how the undecanted embryos are conditioned to adapt to certain environments—for instance, conditioned to like

heat so that, years later, they will feel comfortable working in the tropics or working as miners; or they may be conditioned to improve their sense of balance, so that they will be able to repair rockets in midair. What evidence do you see in our own society that people are or will be subject to conditioning to "like their unescapable social destiny"? Consider, for example, the influence of the conditioning exerted by parents, siblings, teachers, friends, or various social institutions. If you have lived or traveled abroad, what evidence do you see that conditioning in the United States is different from that in other countries? Explore this subject in a multiparagraph essay.

6. As we noted in the headnote, Huxley's *Brave New World* (like much science fiction) is a projection into the future of contemporary aspects of culture that the author finds disturbing or dangerous. Select some present aspect of our culture that *you* find disturbing or dangerous and—in the form of a short story, or chapter from a novel, or section from a screenplay—dramatize your vision of what *could* happen.

Recombinant DNA and Genetic Engineering

CECIE STARR
RALPH TAGGART

Many of the public policy dilemmas of our modern world—the use of nuclear weapons, for example, or the debate about when to "pull the plug" on persons near death, or the debate about privacy from electronic snooping—have arisen as a direct result of scientific breakthroughs. Much of this chapter will deal with various aspects of the public policy debate surrounding biotechnology. But we thought it would be illuminating to precede these discussions with a scientific description of just what is entailed in a key aspect of the new field—genetic engineering.

In the following selection, reprinted from a textbook widely used in introductory college-level biology courses, the authors survey the field of genetic engineering, describe some recent developments in the field, and conclude by discussing some of the social, legal, ecological, and ethical questions regarding its benefits and risks.

Cecie Starr is a science writer who lives in Belmont, California. Ralph Taggart teaches biology at Michigan State University. This passage is from their textbook Biology: The Unity and Diversity of Life *(7th ed. 1995).*

In 1990, when she was four years old, Ashanthi DeSilva received a historic genetic reprieve. Ashanthi was born without defenses against viruses, bacteria, and other agents of disease. She has no immune system. Of her forty- 1 six chromosomes, one bears a defective gene that normally would specify adenosine deaminase (ADA), an enzyme.

Without the enzyme, Ashanthi's cells cannot properly break down excess amounts of a nucleotide (AMP), and a reaction product accumulates that is toxic to lymphoblasts in the bone marrow. Lymphoblasts give rise to white blood cells—the immune system's army. With too few of those cells (or none at all), the outcome is a *severe combined immune deficiency* (SCID), and it leads to a devastating set of disorders. In this particular case, symptoms included dangerous infections of the ears and lungs, high fevers, severe diarrhea, and an inability to gain weight. Ashanthi was so vulnerable to germs, her parents would not let her attend school. 2

Bone marrow transplants help some individuals with SCID when the donated lymphoblasts go on to produce functional white blood cells. ADA injections help others. But these are not permanent cures. 3

Given the options, the girl's parents consented to the first federally approved gene therapy test for humans. Using recombinant DNA methods of the sort described in this chapter, medical researchers had already identified and isolated the ADA gene, and they were producing quantities of it in the laboratory. They also were able to splice those genes into the genetic material of a harmless type of virus that could serve roughly the same function as a hypodermic needle. That is, by infecting targeted cells, the harmless virus could deliver copies of the "good" gene to them. 4

The researchers harvested some of Ashanthi's white blood cells, cultured them in petri dishes, then exposed them to the modified virus. The ADA gene became incorporated in some cells—which started to synthesize ADA. Later, the researchers inserted about a billion copies of the genetically modified cells into the girl's bloodstream. 5

The gene therapy worked. At first Ashanthi received additional infusions of fortified cells every month. Now she receives them once a year. And she is attending school. Four more ADA-deficient patients also have started treatment—and they are doing well at this writing. 6

Some medical researchers are now employing lymphoblasts. They retrieved small amounts of lymphoblasts from blood in the umbilical cord (which is discarded following childbirth). They exposed these stem cells to viruses that could deliver copies of the ADA gene into them. Afterward, they exposed the cells to factors that stimulated growth and division, then reinserted the cells into the newborn patients. It is too soon to tell whether these patients have permanent stem cells that are producing functional copies of the ADA gene. If this turns out to be the case, gene therapy will have given them a continuous, lifelong supply of the crucial enzyme—and of functional disease fighters. 7

As this example suggests, recombinant DNA technology has staggering potential for medicine. It has equally staggering potential for agriculture and industry. It does not come without risks. [In what follows] we consider some basic aspects of the new technology, and we address ecological, social, and ethical questions related to its application. 8

RECOMBINATION IN NATURE—AND IN THE LABORATORY

For more than 3 billion years, nature has been conducting genetic experiments by way of mutation, then by crossing over between chromosomes and other events. Genetic messages have changed countless times, and this is the source of life's diversity. 9

For many thousands of years, we humans have been changing genetically based traits of species. Through artificial selection, we produced modern crop plants and new breeds of cattle, birds, dogs, and cats from wild ancestral stocks. We developed meatier turkeys, sweeter oranges, seedless watermelons, flamboyant ornamental roses, and other wonderfully useful or novel plants. We produced the tangelo (tangerine × grapefruit) and the mule (donkey × horse). 10

Currently, researchers employ *recombinant DNA technology* to analyze genetic changes. With this technology, they cut and splice together DNA from different species, then insert the modified molecules into bacteria or other types of cells that engage in rapid replications and cell divisions. The cells copy the foreign DNA right along with their own. In short order, huge bacterial populations can produce useful quantities of recombinant DNA molecules. The new technology also is the basis of *genetic engineering.* Genes are being isolated, modified, and inserted back into the same organism or into a different one. 11

Believe it or not, this astonishing technology had its origins in the innards of bacteria. Bacterial cells have a single chromosome, a circular DNA molecule with all the genes needed for growth and reproduction. Many bacteria also have *plasmids,* which are small, circular molecules of "extra" DNA having a few genes. Replication enzymes can copy plasmid DNA, just as they copy the chromosomal DNA. 12

Many bacteria can transfer plasmid genes to a bacterial neighbor. Transferred plasmids may even get integrated into a recipient's chromosome, forming a recombinant DNA molecule (Figure 1). Specific enzymes mediate the recombination events. A bacterial enzyme recognizes a short nucleotide[1] sequence present in both the plasmid and the chromosome. It cuts the molecules at that sequence, then another enzymes splices the cut ends together. In nature, viruses as well as bacteria dabble in gene transfers and recombinations. 13

GENETIC ENGINEERING OF BACTERIA

Many years have passed since the first transfer of foreign DNA into a bacterial plasmid, yet the transfer started a debate that is sure to continue into the next century. The point of contention is this: Do the benefits of gene modifications and transfers outweigh the potential dangers? Before coming 14

---

[1]*nucleotide:* "A small organic compound having a fire-carbon sugar (deoxyribose), nitrogen-containing base, and a phosphate group." (Starr and Taggart).

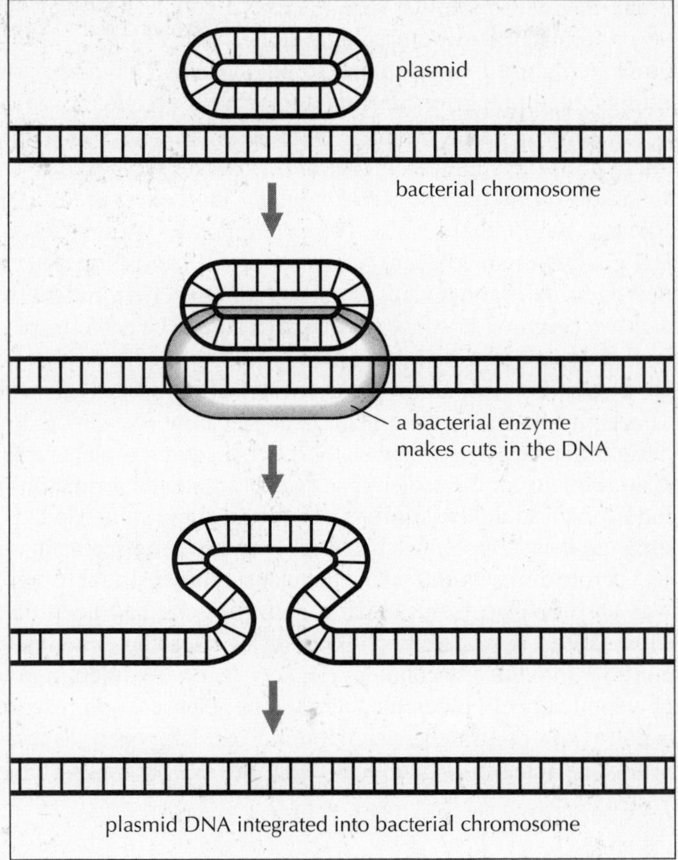

FIGURE 1

Plasmid integration into a bacterial chromosome.

to any conclusion about this, reflect on the following examples of work with bacteria, then with plants and animals.

Imagine a miniaturized factory that churns out insulin or another protein having medical value. This is an apt description for the huge stainless steel vats of genetically engineered, protein-producing bacteria. 15

Think of the diabetics who require insulin injections for as long as they live. Insulin is a protein hormone of the pancreas, and until the 1970s, medical supplies of it had to be obtained from cattle and pigs. Some diabetics developed allergic reactions to the foreign insulin. Also, the demand started outstripping the supplies. Then synthetic genes for human insulin were transferred into *E. coli* cells. . . . This was the start of bacterial factories for human insulin and, later, growth hormone, hemoglobin, serum albumin, interferon, and other proteins. 16

At this writing, several other lines of genetically engineered bacteria have been established or are being developed. Among them are bacterial 17 strains that can degrade oil spills, manufacture alcohol and other chemicals, process minerals, or leave crop plants alone.

The strains being used are harmless to begin with. They are grown in confined settings, behind barriers designed to prevent escape. As an added precaution, the foreign DNA usually includes "fail-safe" genes. Such genes are silent *until* the engineered bacterium becomes exposed to conditions characteristic of the outside environment. Upon exposure, the genes become activated, with lethal results. For example, the foreign DNA may include a *hok* gene with an adjacent promoter of the lactose operon. Thus, if the engineered bacterium manages to escape into the environment, where lactose sugars are common, the *hok* gene is activated. The protein specified by the gene destroys membrane function and so destroys the cell. 18

Even so, there is concern about possible risks of introducing genetically engineered bacteria into the environment. Consider how Steven Lindow altered a bacterium that can [in its new state] make many crop plants less vulnerable to frost. Proteins at the bacterial surface promote the formation of ice crystals. Lindow excised the ice-forming gene from some cells. He hypothesized that spraying these "ice-minus bacteria" on strawberry plants in an isolated field just before a frost would make the plants more resistant to freezing. 19

Here was an organism from which a harmful gene had been deleted, yet it triggered a bitter legal debate on the risks of releasing genetically engineered microbes into the environment. The courts finally ruled in favor of allowing the genetically engineered bacteria to be released, and researchers sprayed a small patch of strawberries. Nothing bad happened. Since then, rules governing the release of genetically engineered organisms have become less restrictive. 20

GENETIC ENGINEERING OF PLANTS

Years ago, Frederick Steward and his coworkers cultured cells of carrot plants and induced the cells to grow into small embryos. Some embryos actually grew into whole plants. Today many plant species, including major crop plants, are regenerated from cultured cells. The culturing methods increase mutation rates, so the cultures are a source of genetic modifications. 21

Researchers can pinpoint a useful mutation among millions of cells. Suppose a culture medium contains a toxin that is produced by a disease agent. If a few cells have a mutated gene that confers resistance to the toxin, they will end up being the only live cells in the culture. Now suppose plants are regenerated from the cells, then hybridized with other varieties. The hybrid plants may end up with the new gene that confers disease resistance. 22

Today, researchers are successfully inserting genes into cultured plant cells. For example, they have inserted DNA fragments into the "Ti" plasmid from *Agrobacterium tumefaciens,* a bacterium that infects many flowering plants. Some plasmid genes become integrated into the DNA of infected plants, and they induce the formation of crown gall tumors. Before the plasmid is introduced into a plant, the tumor-inducing genes are re- 23 moved from it and desired genes are inserted into it. Then the genetically modified bacterial cells are grown with cultured plant cells. Selected plants that are regenerated from infected cultures contain the foreign genes within their DNA. In some cases, the foreign genes are expressed in the plant tissues, with observable effects.

Vivid evidence of a successful gene transfer came from researchers 24
who used *A. tumefaciens* to deliver a firefly gene into cultured tobacco plant cells. The gene codes for luciferase, an enzyme required for bioluminescene. Plants regenerated from the infected culture cells have the peculiar ability to glow in the dark.

A. tumefaciens only infects the plants called dicots. Wheat, corn, rice, 25
oats, and other major food crop plants are monocots. In some cases, genetic engineers use chemicals or electric shocks to deliver DNA directly into protoplasts (plant cells stripped of their walls). For some species, however, regenerating whole plants from protoplast cultures is not yet possible.

Not long ago, someone came up with the idea to deliver genes into cul- 26
tured plant cells by shooting them with a pistol. Instead of bullets, blanks are used to drive DNA-coated, microscopic tungsten particles into the cells. Although this "gene gun" might seem analogous to using a battleship cannon to light a match, the shooters are reporting some success.

Despite the obstacles, many improved varieties of crop plants have 27
been developed or are on the horizon. For example, certain cotton plants have been genetically engineered for resistance to worm attacks. Such gene insertions are ecologically safer than pesticide applications. They kill only the targeted pest and do not interfere with beneficial insects, including the ladybird beetles that prey on aphids. Also on the horizon are genetically engineered plants that may serve as pharmaceutical factories. Two years ago, genetically engineered tobacco plants that produce human hemoglobin, melanin, and other proteins were planted in a field in North Carolina on a trial basis. A year after the trial was completed, ecologists found no trace of the foreign genes or proteins in the soil or in any plants or animals in the vicinity.

GENETIC ENGINEERING OF ANIMALS

Supermice and Biotech Barnyards

Mice were the first mammals subjected to genetic engineering experiments. 28
Consider how R. Hammer, R. Palmiter, and R. Brinster managed to correct a hormone deficiency that causes dwarfism in mice. Such mice have trouble producing somatotropin (also called growth hormone). The researchers used a microneedle to inject the gene for rat somatotropin into fertilized mouse eggs, then they implanted the eggs into an adult female. The gene was successfully integrated into the mouse DNA. The baby mice in which the foreign gene was expressed were 1-1/2 times larger than their dwarf littermates. In other experiments, the gene for human somatotropin was transferred into a mouse embryo, where it became integrated into the DNA. A "supermouse" resulted.

Today, as part of research into the genetic basis of Alzheimer disease 29
and other genetic disorders, several other human genes are being inserted into mouse embryos. Besides microneedles, microscopic laser beams are being used to open temporary holes in the membrane of cultured cells, although such methods have varying degrees of success. Retroviruses also are used to insert genes into cultured cells, virtually all of which incorporate the foreign genes into their DNA. However, the genetic material of retroviruses often undergoes rearrangments, deletions, and other alterations that render the introduced genes ineffective. There is also the possibility that viral particles can escape and infect other individuals.

Soon, "biotech barnyards" may be competing with bacterial factories 30
as genetically engineered sources of proteins. Farm animals produce the proteins in far greater quantities, at less cost. Consider Herman, a Holstein bull that received the human gene for lactoferrin, a milk protein, when he was just an embryo. His female offspring may mass-produce the protein, which can be used as a supplement for infant formulas. Similarly, goats are providing CFTR protein (used in the treatment of cystic fibrosis), and TPA (which lessens the severity of heart attacks). Sheep are producing alpha-1 antitrypsin, used in the treatment of emphysema. Cattle may soon be producing human collagen, a key component of skin, cartilage, and bone.

Applying the New Technology to Humans

Researchers in laboratories throughout the world are now working their 31
way through the 3.2 billion base pairs that are present in the twenty-three pairs of human chromosomes. This ambitious effort is called the *human genome project.* Some researchers are working on specific chromosomes, others on specific gene regions only. For example, rather than busying themselves with noncoding sequences (introns), J. Venter and Sidney Brenner are isolating mRNAs from brain cells and using them to make cDNA. By sequencing only the cDNAs, they already have identified hundreds of previously unknown genes.

About 99.9 percent of the nucleotide sequence is the same in every hu- 32
man on earth. Thus, once the sequencing project is completed, we will have the ultimate reference book on human biology and genetic disorders. (Or should we say reference *books*—the complete sequence will fill the equivalent of 200 Manhattan telephone directories.)

What will we do with the information? Certainly we will use it in the 33
search for effective treatments and cures for genetic disorders. Of 2,000 or so genes studied so far, 400 already have been linked to genetic disorders. The knowledge opens doors to *gene therapy,* the transfer of one or more normal or modified genes into body cells of an individual to correct a genetic defect or boost resistance to disease. But what about forms of human gene expression that are neither disabling nor life-threatening? Will we tinker with these, also?

Some Implications of Human Gene Therapy

Recombinant DNA technology and genetic engineering are advancing rapidly. We are only beginning to work our way through their social and ethical implications. 34

To most of us, human gene therapy to correct genetic abnormalities seems like a socially acceptable goal. Is it also socially acceptable to insert genes into a *normal* human individual (or sperm or egg) to alter or enhance traits? The idea of selecting desirable human traits is called *eugenic engineering*. Yet who decides which forms of a trait are most "desirable"? What if prospective parents could pick the sex of a child by way of genetic engineering? Three-fourths of one survey group said they would choose a boy. So what would be the long-term social implications of a drastic shortage of girls? 35

Would it be okay to engineer taller or blue-eyed or curlier-haired individuals? If so, would it be okay to engineer "superhuman" offspring with exceptional strength or breathtaking intelligence? 36

Some say that the DNA of any organism must never be altered. Put aside the fact that nature itself alters DNA much of the time. The concern is that we don't have the wisdom to bring about beneficial changes without causing harm to ourselves or to the environment. 37

When it comes to manipulating human genes, one is reminded of our human tendency to leap before we look. When it comes to restricting genetic modifications of any sort, one also is reminded of an old saying: "If God had wanted us to fly, he would have given us wings." And yet, something about the human experience gave us the *capacity* to imagine wings of our own making—and that capacity has carried us to the frontiers of space. 38

Where are we going from here with recombinant DNA technology, this new product of our imagination? To gain perspective on the question, spend some time reading the history of our species. It is a history of survival in the face of all manner of new challenges, threats, bumblings, and sometimes disasters on a grand scale. It is also a story of our connectedness with the environment and with one another. 39

The questions confronting you today are these: Should we be more cautious, believing that one day the risk takers may go too far? And what do we as a species stand to lose if the risks are *not* taken? 40

▲ ▲ ▲

Review Questions

1. What are restriction enzymes, and how do scientists use them in genetic engineering?
2. How did "ice-minus bacteria" highlight the controversy over the use of genetically engineered products outside the laboratory?
3. What is Starr and Taggart's definition of "human gene therapy"? To what extent do they express an opinion on the morality of human gene therapy?

Discussion and Writing Suggestions

1. Write a one-page summary of this selection.
2. This selection originally appeared in an introductory college biology text. To what extent did you find it difficult to comprehend? Locate those passages that gave you particular trouble. Does the problem lie in the terminology Starr and Taggart employ? The scientific concepts under discussion? The organization or writing style? See if your instructor or other, more scientifically inclined students can throw light on these troublesome sections.
3. Toward the end of this selection Starr and Taggart discuss genetic engineering at the bacterial, plant, animal, and human levels. To what extent do you see a different set of ethical standards operating from one level to another? Taking into account the kind of considerations discussed at the end of the passage, what kind of ethical standards do you believe should operate at the level of human gene therapy? To what extent do you believe that it will be possible or practical to maintain such standards? For example, who has an interest in imposing such standards? Who has an interest in resisting them?
4. Describe (if possible, in scientific report format) an experiment that you conducted in high school, or that you are conducting now in chemistry, physics, or biology. Write in language that your nonscientific readers will be able to follow.

Tinkering with Destiny

SHANNON BROWNLEE
GARETH G. COOK
VIVA HARDIGG

For both scientists and the general public, one of the most exciting aspects of biotechnology lies in the prospect of treating human disease. If, as many like DNA pioneer James Watson believe, most diseases have a genetic basis, then locating the genes responsible for diseases should be a major priority in genetic research. (As Watson points out, "Ignoring genes is like trying to solve a murder without finding the murderer.") But of course, locating the culpable genes is only the first step. The next major step is to find ways of repairing or replacing the defective genes. Another consideration—ethical and philosophical, rather than medical—is to decide upon the criteria for "defectiveness." Yet another is how or even whether to notify people that they, their children, or their fetuses, are carrying "defective" genes. As Rachel Nowak asks in a recent article on genetic testing for Science, *"If your mother had died of Huntington's disease, would you want to be tested to see whether you had inherited the flawed gene that causes this fatal condition? A negative result would give you tremendous peace of mind, allowing you to lead an ordinary life. A positive result, on the other hand, would cause you to live the rest of your life knowing your ultimate fate would be the intellectual deterioration and involuntary movements that characterize Huntington's disease."*

The following article, "Tinkering With Destiny," by U.S. News & World Report *staffwriters Shannon Brownlee, Gareth G. Cook, and Viva Hardigg, discusses how various types of people—family members, scientists, counselors, doctors, and entrepreneurs—are dealing with the complex issues raised by our new-found knowledge about the relationships between genes and disease. It originally appeared in* U.S. News *on August 22, 1994.*

The last thing Joey Paulowsky needs is another bout with cancer. Only 7 years old, the Dallas native has already fought off leukemia, and now his family worries that Joey could be hit again. The Paulowsky family carries a genetic burden, a rare form of inherited cancer of the thyroid. Deborah, his mother, found a lump in her neck six years ago, and since then one family member has died of the cancer and 10 others have had to have their thyroids removed. "Do I have cancer?" Joey asks his mother. "Will it hurt?" The Paulowskys will know the answer next month, when the results of a genetic test will show whether their son carries the family's fateful mutation. 1

Joey is too young to know that he is participating in a medical revolution, one that will change the practice of medicine as profoundly as the invention of the microscope or the discovery of antibiotics. The snippet of DNA that will determine his fate was identified barely a year ago. Now, this mutant gene, along with the more than 150 others that have been captured thus far, are making it possible for doctors to peer into their patients' medical futures. Today, at least 50 genetic tests for hereditary diseases are available; by the turn of the century, DNA tests are almost certain to be a standard part of medical exams. From a single sample of a patient's blood, doctors will be able to spot genetic mutations that signal the approach not only of rare hereditary diseases, such as the thyroid cancer that stalks the Paulowsky clan, but also the common killers, including breast cancer, heart disease and diabetes—and defeat them. 2

For all its promise, the ability to glimpse the future will not come without costs. Knowing a patient's genetic predispositions will be central to preventive medicine, a keystone of health care reform; a physician will one day be able to advise the young adult at risk for high blood pressure in middle age to cut down on salt long before the appearance of symptoms. But for many other inherited ailments, a genetic test offers a Faustian bargain. For example, women who are members of families at high risk for breast cancer will soon be able to undergo a genetic test for the breast cancer gene (known as BRCA1), which is responsible for as many as 1 in 10 of the 180,000 cases diagnosed in the United States each year. Those who are found to be free of the mutation will be spared the dread of the unknown. 3

But those who do carry the mutation can only hope that self-examinations and mammograms catch the tumor early enough. Some women opt to have their healthy breasts removed, though there is little evidence that even this will prevent the cancer.

The rate of change is unlike anything medicine has witnessed before, as researchers fish genes out of cells at a dizzying rate. Last year saw the discovery of more than a dozen mutations responsible for diseases ranging from Alzheimer's to hyperactivity to colon cancer. Almost as soon as a gene is discovered, commercial laboratories are ready to offer a genetic test—a pace that threatens to outstrip both physicians' and patients' abilities to make sense of the information. Couples forgo having children after misunderstanding the result of genetic tests, while patients who carry mutations can lose their insurance under the current health care system. Scientists, genetic counselors and ethicists are racing to develop guidelines for the new age of genetic medicine, while families ponder the dilemmas presented by an incomplete medical revolution. "If we screw this up," says Francis Collins, director of the National Center for Human Genome Research, "I don't think the public will conclude that this was a useful revolution." 4

THE FAMILY

With cancer in my genes, is it safe to marry and have children?

On the surface, the five daughters of the Kostakis family seem alike. They all have the same mass of curly hair, the same lively manner of speaking and the same propensity to start an argument in English and finish it in Greek. Yet an invisible and devastating distinction divides them: Two of the sisters inherited their mother's gene for a deadly form of colon cancer; the other three, like their brother, did not. 5

The family immigrated in 1977 from an impoverished village in Greece, intent on forging a new and better life in America and oblivious to the genetic cargo that menaced their dream. "If I had known I carried the disease, I never would have gotten married and had children," says their mother, Eleni, in Greek. It was only when she went for a tubal ligation at age 39 that clues to the family's legacy began to emerge. 6

Eleni told the doctor that her father had died at age 28, with a stomach tumor so large she could feel it with her hand, and that her older brother had undergone mysterious surgery he didn't like to talk about. The gynecologist immediately scheduled a colonoscopy—a jarring, uncomfortable procedure done under sedation. The eye of the colonoscope revealed the warning signs: benign polyps numbering in the hundreds or even thousands—harbingers of familial adenomatous polyposis colon cancer, a disease that can strike in some families as early as the teens. 7

Soon after Eleni had her colon removed, her younger brother was hit. He refused to see a doctor until a week before he died, at age 43, in a man- 8 ner hauntingly reminiscent of her father's death. "He died because he chose to," she says, shaking her head and balling her hands into tight fists in her lap. Eleni vowed that her children would know what they were up against. That meant yearly colonoscopies for the Kostakis siblings, each of whom had a 50–50 chance of inheriting the ancestral cancer gene. Two of the sisters had the telltale polyps and each had a portion of her colon removed at age 16.

Now, the family knows definitively who in the new generation has **9**
been spared. In 1991, researchers discovered the gene that when mutated is responsible for adenomatous polyposis, and like 90 percent of those offered the gene test at the Johns Hopkins School of Public Health, Eleni's other four children opted to take it as soon as it was offered. "Anything that might stop those colonoscopies was a great relief," says Maria, 26, the eldest. But when it came time to find out the results, everyone was on edge. Petros, 25, remembers his heart pounding in the doctor's office before the genetic counselor told him and his sisters the good news: all negative. "Finding out was the biggest relief of my entire life," Petros recalls. "It was better than making a million dollars, better than sex—almost." Two weeks ago, a 14-year-old cousin received the same happy tidings.

Maria felt a similar surge of freedom. "There are two struggles in a **10**
cancer family," she says. "One is the disease and one is not knowing. You have inside this *anchos,* we call it in Greek. It's like a bugging feeling, this worry." For known carriers of the gene, knowledge has its price, especially when it comes to the agonizing issue of parenthood. Katerina, the youngest of the family, has recovered well from her colectomy and has resumed the life of a typical high school senior. But the future haunts her. She clutches a small pillow against her stomach and fights back tears as she says, "The thing that scares me the most is if I found out my baby had it, I would abort it."

As devastating as their illness is, the Kostakises are among the lucky **11**
ones. Not only is there a gene test for their type of cancer but, for those who carry it, the telltale polyps show where and when to operate. By contrast, Huntington's disease, the devastating neurological degeneration that killed folk singer Woody Guthrie at 55, has a test but no cure. About 85 percent of people at risk for Huntington's have declined the test, preferring to live in blissless ignorance.

For families suffering from many other familial cancers, the *anchos* re- **12**
mains, and each year is a waiting game. Margaret Todd, 66, of Towson, Md., watched her parents die of colon cancer, and she herself has had malignant polyps removed. Her family's tumors arise from hereditary nonpolyposis colon cancer, which often fails to produce warning polyps and cannot yet be detected through genetics, even though the genes responsible were discovered last year. If there were a test, Todd's four children would know whether they had to endure the discomfort and expense of the annual colonoscopies, which cost about $1,000 apiece. She says, "We keep praying for a gene test and they keep saying it might come this year."

THE SCIENTISTS

Where are the seeds of cancer and other genetic diseases?

Ray White knows which members of the Smith family will get colon cancer, but most of the Smiths still do not. It is a position relished by neither the Smiths nor White, who heads the Huntsman Cancer Institute at the University of Utah. White's team of researchers discovered the gene responsible for the Smiths' colon cancer three years ago. Since then, he says, "they have been beating on our door for the information." But for a variety of reasons, all aimed at protecting the Smiths, the researchers were not ready until this June to share the news with the family. 13

White did not set out to be the keeper of such grave information when he arrived in Salt Lake City in 1980, armed only with a new genetic technique of his own invention and the desire to hunt disease-causing genes. This was the dawn of the genetic age, when White and other scientists would finally begin to make sense of more than 4,000 heritable diseases. In the previous two decades, scientists had unraveled the mystery of inheritance, showing that it is governed by DNA, the genetic material contained in the nucleus of each of the body's cells. In 1980, White and a colleague at the Massachusetts Institute of Technology devised a means for searching through DNA, infinitesimal section by infinitesimal section. By comparing the length of the same section from one family member to another, researchers now had a way to zero in on the approximate location of genes corresponding to inherited diseases. 14

In 1982, White aimed his sights at the mangled DNA responsible for adenomatous polyposis colon cancer, or APC. APC accounts for only 1 percent of all colon cancer cases, but it snakes through the family trees of half a dozen Mormon clans in Utah. Mormons proved perfect subjects for White's team: They keep meticulous genealogies, and many families bear as many as 10 to 12 children, giving an inherited disease a chance to show up in each generation. The researchers spent a decade flying around the state collecting blood samples, often at family reunions. "On holidays, I can figure I'm going to be drawing blood," says Utah geneticist Ken Ward. In 1991, White's team, along with a group led by Bert Vogelstein at Johns Hopkins Oncology Center in Baltimore, announced simultaneously that they had nailed the colon cancer gene. 15

Yet even in their euphoria the researchers knew they could not simply call the Smiths, a clan of some 2,000 to 3,000, and blurt out who was safe and who wasn't. First, they had to find the precise mutations in the gene that ran through their broad family tree—then estimate the odds that an individual carrying a mutation would actually be hit with cancer. The researchers also worried that family members could lose their insurance once it was discovered they harbored the defective gene. One man's insurance was canceled simply because he participated in the genetic study—though it turned out he did not have the gene. The researchers had to be certain of just what their scientific findings meant in practical terms to families at risk 16 for cancer. This June, the first letters arrived in Smith mailboxes, offering a chance to learn their genetic legacy.

Researchers around the world will find themselves in a similar fix with each new gene they uncover. A gene found in 1991 by Utah geneticist Jean Marc LaLouel now appears to bestow some of its owners with high blood pressure while leaving others vulnerable to certain complications of pregnancy. Earlier this year, researchers at Thomas Jefferson University in Philadelphia announced they are close to the long-sought gene responsible for manic-depression. This summer, a French lab fetched up a gene that leads to melanoma, a deadly form of skin cancer, while geneticists at the National Institutes of Health announced that p53, a gene notorious for its role in more than half of all cancers, may also make mischief in the cells lining the arteries, thus contributing to heart disease. But while these bits of DNA are already opening new avenues to combatting and perhaps even preventing illness, cures are probably years, if not decades, away. 17

Until then, researchers want to put their newfound genes to use, spotting diseases as early as possible. Johns Hopkins University's David Sidransky is confident that the ubiquitous p53 gene can serve as a red flag for tumors of the mouth and bladder. Sidransky analyzed a urine specimen saved from Hubert Humphrey in 1967 and found mutant copies of p53. If the gene had been known at the time, it might have alerted doctors to the bladder cancer that would kill the senator a decade later. Another cancer gene, called RAS, can warn of impending lung cancer; RAS and the APC gene in stool samples may one day alert doctors to as many as 80 percent of colon cancers—even among the 150,000 cases that arise each year in people with no familial history. For cancer, more than almost any other illness, such early-warning systems are desperately needed. We are going to figure out how to identify precancerous lesions and get rid of them," says White, "before they turn into full-blown cancer." 18

THE COUNSELOR

Are people capable of understanding genetic risk?

The day a cure for cancer is discovered will be the day Barbara Biesecker's job is made easier. Biesecker is a genetic counselor, one of the medical messengers who are trained in both psychology and human genetics—and who bear the responsibility for making sure that people like the Smiths and the Kostakises understand the implications of their genetics tests. The result of these tests is rarely a simple thumbs up or down. More often, the best a genetic test can offer is a degree of risk, and conveying the meaning of risk is no easy task. 19

Weighing the odds. Even when people comprehend the numbers (and many cannot), they find uncertainty psychologically troubling. When confronted with a 50 percent risk, many patients conclude their chances are either zero or 100 percent, says Biesecker, head of genetic counseling at the 20

DNA TESTS AVAILABLE NOW

DISEASE	DESCRIPTION	INCIDENCE	COST
Adult polycystic kidney disease	Multiple kidney growths	1 in 1,000	$350
Alpha–1-antitrypsin deficiency	Can cause hepatitis, cirrhosis of the liver, emphysema	1 in 2,000 to 1 in 4,000	$200
Charcot-Marie-Tooth disease	Progressive degeneration of muscles	1 in 2,500	$250–$350
Familial adenomatous polyposis	Colon polyps by age 35, often leading to cancer	1 in 5,000	$1,000
Cystic fibrosis	Lungs clog with mucus; usually fatal by age 40	1 in 2,500 Caucasians	$125–$150
Duchenne/Becker muscular dystrophy	Progressive degeneration of muscles	1 in 3,000 males	$300–$900
Hemophilia	Blood fails to clot properly	1 in 10,000	$250–$350
Fragile X syndrome	Most common cause of inherited mental retardation	1 in 1,250 males; 1 in 2,500 females	$250
Gaucher's disease	Mild to deadly enzyme deficiency	1 in 400 Ashkenazi Jews	$100–$150
Huntington's disease	Lethal neurological deterioration	1 in 10,000 Caucasians	$250–$300
"Lou Gehrig's disease" (ALS)	Fatal degeneration of the nervous system	1 in 50,000 10% familial	$150–$450
Myotonic dystrophy	Progressive degeneration of muscles	1 in 8,000	$250
Multiple endocrine neoplasia	Endocrine gland tumors	1 in 50,000	$900
Neurofibromatosis	*Café au lait* spots to large tumors	1 in 3,000	$900
Retinoblastoma	Blindness; potentially fatal eye tumors	1 in 20,000	$1,500
Spinal muscular atrophy	Progressive degeneration of muscles	7 in 100,000	$100–$900
Tay-Sachs disease	Lethal childhood neurological disorder	1 in 3,600 Ashkenazi Jews	$150
Thalassemia	Mild to fatal anemia	1 in 100,000	$300
TESTS OF THE FUTURE			
Alzheimer's	Most likely multiple genes involved	4 million cases	Not available
Breast cancer	Five to 10% of all cases are thought to be hereditary	2.6 million cases	Not available
Diabetes	Most likely multiple genes involved	13–14 million cases	Not available
Nonpolyposis colon cancer	Several genes cause up to 20% of all cases	150,000 cases per year	Not available
Manic-depression	Most likely multiple genes involved	2 million cases	Not available

Source: Helix: National Directory of DNA Diagnostic Laboratories, Children's Hospital and Medical Center, Seattle, Wash. For more information: Alliance of Genetic Support Groups, (800) 336–4363

National Center for Human Genome Research in Bethesda, Md. "It's either, 'I've got it' or 'I don't.'"

The flood of new gene discoveries has left genetic counselors unsure of how to proceed in the new age of medical genetics. The counselors' credo requires that they help clients come to their own decisions, but they are concerned about the increasing numbers of people—particularly expectant couples—who demand the newest genetic tests even when there is little evidence of medical risk. "We have this fantasy in this country that if we have enough information, we can control events," says Biesecker. 21

This desire for information is especially troubling when parents want their children tested for diseases whose symptoms will not appear for many years. "Parents think they want their children tested, but what they really want to hear is that their child does not have the disease," says Randall Burt, a gastroenterologist at the Veterans Hospital in Salt Lake City. They haven't thought through what a positive result will mean to them. 22

Few of the new genes have raised more nettlesome issues than BRCA1, the breast cancer gene. Geneticists estimate that 1 in 200 women may carry mutations in this gene; millions will no doubt want to be tested. There are only about 1,200 genetic counselors in the country, not nearly enough to handle the job of deciphering the results. For example, a positive test means a woman's daughters could also harbor the mangled gene. A negative test for BRCA1, on the other hand, does not mean a woman has entirely dodged the bullet; she still faces the possibility of getting other forms of breast cancer. And for women who have watched their mothers and sisters die of breast cancer, a negative test sometimes leads to "survivor guilt," feelings similar to those of victims who escaped the Holocaust. 23

With a shortage of genetic counselors, the task of sorting through such dilemmas will fall to doctors or even to commercial testing services. "What will happen when this is in the hands of primary care physicians scares me a lot," says Biesecker. "Are physicians prepared to draw the line between giving advice about treatment and advising a couple whether or not to have children?" 24

THE DOCTOR

Are doctors ready to practice medicine in the genetic age?

How physicians will use the fruits of the genetic revolution is a major concern of Gail Tomlinson, a pediatric oncologist at the University of Texas Southwestern Medical Center in Dallas. Tomlinson knows firsthand both the power and the peril of genetic tests: As 7-year-old Joey Paulowsky's physician, she will use the test results due next month to decide whether the child's thyroid should be removed. 25

But few of Tomlinson's colleagues are as well trained as she is in the complexities of medical genetics. Unlike genetic counselors, who learn the 26 tricky business of informing without recommending, most doctors are taught to tell patients what is best for them. That is not easy when all a test offers is a measure of risk. For example, among Tomlinson's patients are families afflicted with Li Fraumeni syndrome, a rare hereditary mutation in the p53 gene that can bring on a bewildering variety of cancers. But until there are better ways to detect the tumors early enough to stop them, the test for p53, says Tomlinson, "may not do patients a lot of good. You can't fix the defective gene, and you can't catch many of the cancers."

Eventually, genetic tests will belong in the hands of the doctors on the front lines of medicine, says Tomlinson. "But things are moving so fast. We know how to clone genes, but we don't know how to talk about it to patients. Just how to apply this predictive testing hasn't been worked out." 27

Until it is, some physicians will view genetic tests with a mixture of unease and distrust. Sandra Byes, an oncologist at the University of Utah Medical Center, is uncertain whether she will advise her patients to take a genetic test for the breast cancer gene once it is discovered: "It's a lot more comforting to say to a patient, 'You are from a high-risk family' than 'You have the gene, try not to let it ruin your life.' " 28

THE ENTREPRENEUR

Is American society on the verge of a genetic gold rush?

In 1989, business was so bad at the DNA lab at Integrated Genetics that the company was close to shutting it down. Now, the respected Framingham, Mass., lab boasts nearly one fifth of the $8 million market in DNA tests for inherited diseases, a fledgling industry poised to take off. Industry analysts foresee a $500 million market in genetic tests in the next decade. 29

The potential for profits is bringing entrepreneurs like IG President Elliott Hillback face to face with a marketplace filled with moral pitfalls. With the discovery of each disease-causing gene, a new and lucrative market opens, but it can take years before anyone understands the medical seriousness of any given genetic mutation (and some genes can have hundreds of mutations). Last year, for example, more than 30,000 tests were performed to detect one or more of some 350 mutations in the gene behind cystic fibrosis, a heritable and often fatal lung disease. Yet scientists are only now discovering that some mutations actually cause none of the classic symptoms. The danger is that some labs will make a test available before the results can be meaningfully interpreted. 30

Private codes. Critics also fear for the patient's right *not* to know the contents of his genes. Today, the final responsibility for explaining the untoward consequences of a test—such as losing health insurance—lies with the laboratory itself. But turning away patients means turning away profits. 31

The two government agencies charged with overseeing the burgeoning genetics market, the Food and Drug Administration and the Health Care Financing Administration, have been slow to step in. Most of the companies that manufacture the chemical tools of the genetics trade have not bothered 32 to submit their products to the FDA for approval as required by law. Labs serve a vital role in making tests cheaper and more accurate. But HCFA, charged with ensuring test accuracy, "has dragged its feet," according to Neil Holtzman, a member of a Human Genome Project working group investigating genetic testing. This is in part because the agency lacks inspectors with the necessary genetic training. For now, there is nothing—beyond the lab director's personal ethics—to keep a lab from introducing new tests, regardless of their potential for misuse.

A few companies are already pushing the boundaries. Genica Pharmaceuticals of Worcester, Mass., for example, is offering a test for a gene linked to Alzheimer's disease even though the Alzheimer's Association has said that too little is known about the gene and its mutations to interpret test results properly. Genica President Robert Flaherty admits that "it is not a definitive test," but believes that under the right circumstances "it can be very useful." 33

While Hillback worries that a few reckless labs might cause a public backlash against the entire enterprise, it is ultimately not the responsibility of commercial establishments to set boundaries. Americans must decide where to draw the ethical line. And wherever they finally choose to draw it, Hillback and his colleagues know that there will be no turning back. "It's much easier to say that society as a whole is not ready for a test," says James Amberson, a vice president at Dianon Systems, a testing company. "But it's awfully hard to look a mother in the eye and say no." 34

▲ ▲ ▲

Review Questions

1. What is a "genetic predisposition"?
2. In terms of what doctors are able to do, what is the difference between the form of colon cancer that struck the Kostakis family and Huntington's disease?
3. How are doctors making use of newly discovered genes like p53 and RAS?
4. In what ways has counseling of people who want to take or have taken genetic tests become a problem, according to the authors?
5. What kind of problems in genetic testing are introduced by the "entrepreneurs"—that is, the labs that provide genetic testing services?

Discussion and Writing Suggestions

1. According to the authors, genetic testing offers a "Faustian bargain"—a bargain in which the cost of knowledge may be too high. Eleni Kostakis, for example, asserts that had she known that she carried a gene for colon cancer, "I never would have gotten married and had children." Were you in her place, would you feel the same

way? Would you feel that the possibility of transmitting the deadly gene to your offspring was so great (50 percent) that the only morally responsible choice was to forego parenthood?

2. The case of Woodie Guthrie, the famous folk singer who died at age 55 of Huntington's disease, is frequently cited in discussions of genetic testing. Suppose such testing had been available to Woody Guthrie's mother and she discovered that her unborn child carried the gene. Might she not have aborted? Would it have been better had Guthrie never been born? A related question is whether people who are at genetic risk for this disease should undergo testing to determine if they are likely to develop it in later life. Would you be one of the 85 percent who prefer to live in "blissless ignorance" or one of the 15 percent who want to know? Respond to these questions in a two to three-page journal entry.
3. Use the information in the tables "DNA Tests Available Now" and "Tests of the Future," along with information provided in the article itself, to write a two or three paragraph summary of diseases for which genetic tests are currently available or are expected to be available in the future.
4. Barbara Biesecker, a genetic counselor, is quoted as saying, "We have this fantasy in this country that if we have enough information, we can control events." What do you think she means? To what extent do you think that what she says is true of people's attitudes in areas *other than* genetic testing? In other words, to what extent is information power? To what extent is it only the illusion of power?
5. To what extent do you see connections between the type of concern expressed by the authors and by some of the people they discuss about the downside of genetic testing and the kind of concerns by Aldous Huxley in *Brave New World?* To what extent, in other words, does the world of "Tinkering With Destiny" have the seeds of a Brave New World? Are some of the scientists, or some of the entrepreneurs, like the Director of Hatcheries?

The Grandiose Claims of Geneticists

DOROTHY NELKIN

The authors of many articles about genetic research and development in newspapers and popular magazines seem awestruck by the accomplishments of biotechnology and by the prospects for scientific advances and new medical tools. Sociology professor Dorothy Nelkin takes a more skeptical view of the claims of geneticists. While Nelkin does not advocate restrictions on genetic research, she does express serious reservations about the way that developments in biotechnology are being presented to the public. In particular, she argues that genetic research could be misappropriated by politicians and others to justify a conservative social agenda. Nelkin, author of Selling Science: How the Press Covers Science and Technology *(1988), teaches sociology at New York University. This article first appeared in the* Chronicle of Higher Education *on March 3, 1993.*

Until recently, scientists have paid little attention to communicating with the public, assuming that a record of accomplishment was sufficient to maintain public support for research. Concerned that public visibility could result in external control, they have disdained "visible scientists," ignored popularizers of science, and avoided journalists. But the stakes have changed in the face of growing mistrust of science, questions about the morality and honesty of research practices, and threats of outside regulation. 1

Now that the public is questioning the wisdom of the government's relatively unfettered support of science, scientists are worrying about their public image and trying harder to communicate the excitement and benefits of their research. They see gaining visibility through the media as crucial to securing support and assuring favorable public policies toward science. 2

Researchers mapping the human genome, the complete set of all human genes, are particularly concerned about their public image, both to assure the continuity of public financing for their long-term, costly project and to counter the negative images of genetics stemming from its historical association with eugenics. What can we learn from their efforts to shape the public image of the Human Genome Project? Do the images disseminated by geneticists inform the public accurately and fairly about this complex field? How are these images received? 3

The evidence suggests that geneticists may create new problems for themselves by using overblown rhetoric and misleading metaphors to convey the importance of their work. 4

As part of a project looking at how genes are understood and represented in American popular culture, I have been collecting the metaphors that geneticists repeatedly use to describe their work. I find three related themes: a definition of the gene as the essence of identity and the basis of human differences; a promise that genetic research will enhance prediction and allow control of behavior and disease; and an image of the genome, the exact chemical sequencing of genes, as a text that will define a natural order. 5

The idea that identity lies in the genes appears in images of the body as a set of "genetic instructions," a "program" transmitted from one generation to another. People are "readouts" of their genes. If scientists can decipher the text, classify the markers on the map, and read the instructions, they will reconstruct the essence of human beings. This, in turn, will unlock the key to human ailments and human nature and provide, as one scientist puts it, "the ultimate answers to the commandment 'Know thyself.'" The geneticist Walter Gilbert introduces his public lectures on gene sequencing by pulling a compact disk from his pocket and announcing to his audience: "This is you." And the Cold Spring Harbor Laboratory has published a children's book called *Cells Are Us*. 6

Scientists also emphasize the predictive powers of genetics by calling the gene a "Delphic Oracle," a "time machine," a "trip into the future," a "medical crystal ball." James Watson, co-discoverer of the structure of the DNA molecule and the first director of the Human Genome Project, announces that "our fate is in our genes." Futuristic scenarios promise that genetic prediction will enhance control of human behavior and disease. In the future, says one geneticist, "present methods of treating depression will seem as crude as former pneumonia treatments seem now." Describing acts of violence, a science editor claims: "When we can accurately predict future behavior, we may be able to prevent the damage." 7

Geneticists frequently refer to the genome as the Bible, the Holy Grail, or the Book of Man. Such religious images suggest that the genome—once mapped and sequenced—will be a powerful guide to human behavior, a sort of secular text that will define the natural and moral order. Other common images of the genome—as map, dictionary, library, or recipe—imply order, suggesting that genetic information will reduce the ambiguity of a complex environment and fix things in their proper place. 8

The rhetorical strategies of geneticists have clearly captured public interest. Genetics has become a coffee-table science and the gene, a ubiquitous popular image. We encounter the gene in supermarket tabloids and soap operas, in television sitcoms and talk shows, in comic books and advertising slogans, and even in biographies of Elvis. We read about genes in women's magazines and child-advice books as well as in science reports. 9

Stimulated by the grandiose claims of geneticists, the media have appropriated genetic images in ways that serve their goals—but not necessarily the goals of scientists. The power of genetic images for the public derives less from people's interest in science than its relationship to social concerns. 10

The biological sciences have long served to justify social arrangements as "natural," based on scientific reality. Darwin's theory of evolution by natural selection served to explain and legitimize the inequalities brought about by the industrial revolution: It is the fittest who survive. 11

Today, models of molecular biology are appropriated to support prevailing ideologies, traditional biases, and social stereotypes. Media interest in genetics partly rests on the possibility of finding therapies for devastating diseases, and the message in repeated headlines is one of awe and expectation. "Genetics: The War on Aging, the Medical Story of the Century." But the media's use of genetic images also suggests their resonance with sensitive social issues. 12

For example, picking up on scientists' metaphors locating identity in the genes, many stories discuss genes in the context of the stability of the family. The frequent use of phrases such as "biological connections" or "genetic rights" suggests the importance of genetic relationships. Genealogical services have proliferated, advertised as a way to define identity through knowing genetic ties. Adoption stories emphasize the urgent need to find "biological roots." These stories use genetics to reinforce traditional family values. 13

The language of biological determinism is pervasive in the media, where genes are held to be responsible for obesity, criminality, shyness, intelligence, political leanings, and even preferred styles of dressing—as if such complex attributes are transmitted like brown hair or blue eyes. The gene in popular culture is an anthropomorphized entity—given a wide range of behavior attributes. There are selfish genes, pleasure-seeking genes, criminal genes, celebrity genes, homosexuality genes, couch-potato genes, depression genes, genes for genius, genes for saving, and even genes for sinning. 14

These images convey a striking picture of DNA as the essence of the person. Appropriating the images used by scientists, the media interpret them in literal and concrete ways, often simplifying important subtleties. Thus, the gene in popular culture has become the agent of identity, the most powerful force in shaping behavior. But above all, the gene is seen as the source of human difference, a "natural" basis of social stereotypes, as seen in statements like: "Differences lie in the genes." Countless media stories focus on the biological differences between genders: Women are predisposed to their "natural" role of nurturance; boys are "genetically programmed" to be aggressive. Others stories say something like, "Why are women different? They are born that way." 15

Just as scientists have talked about genetic research as enabling the prediction of disease, so promises of prediction appear in the ubiquitous media preoccupation with "predispositions." Stories refer to "gene-impelled compulsions" or "natural bents." The gene has become the key to the human future; we are programmed to succeed or to fail. News articles and magazine stories explain deviant behavior in terms of genetic predisposition: "Is Crime in the Family Tree?" or "Addicted to the Bottle? It May Be in the Genes." Stories about "bad genes" offer hope that those predisposed to crime or addiction can be identified and controlled. As one writer puts it, crime could be reduced if we determined which persons were biologically predisposed and took "preemptive action" before they committed crime. And another remarks: "It seems pointless to wait until high-risk prospects actually commit crimes before trying to do something to control them." 16

To journalists looking for certainty, genetic explanations that can be mapped and catalogued or deciphered from nature's text seem more objective, and less ambiguous, than environmental or social explanations. They seem to provide hard ways to codify what is normal or deviant, to justify inequities on the basis of "natural" characteristics, and to differentiate "them" from "us." They appeal as a solid, apparently neutral guide to social policy. 17

Media interpretations are consequential, affecting both individual decisions and social policies. The idea of fate, for example, enters conflicts over responsibility. If behavior is genetically predetermined, families are not to blame for the problems of their children. And if certain people are defined as inherently and irretrievably problematic, society is absolved from responsibility. Why worry about rehabilitation, remedial education, or 18 social support? Those who fail could be defined as intrinsically flawed, while others are destined to succeed.

Defining people as "predisposed" to immutable traits could justify discriminatory social practices. If we believe that there are "criminal genes," for example, this could sanction the use of tests to predict dangerousness, overriding issues of justice or fairness. And if the concept of genetic determinism is extended to groups, this could compromise the rights or obligations of classes of people. 19

To locate complex human behavior in a molecular entity is to ignore that behavior's social context. There are no genes for behavior, only genes for proteins that influence physiological processes. Indeed, to explain human beings in biological terms, to jump from the molecular level of genetic systems to the behavior of human beings, requires a profound leap of faith. But this leap is encouraged by the scientists' metaphors of order and scenarios of prediction. 20

Scientists often dismiss the way in which their work is appropriated by the media, calling it oversimplified and distorted. But much of the popular rhetoric about genes draws support from the promises generated by scientists and the language they use to describe their research. In the interest of public understanding, then, scientists should restrain their tendencies to oversell their work and consider the biases and beliefs that will ultimately shape the uses of a powerful science—one that offers prospects for promising applications, but that also opens possibilities for pernicious abuse. 21

▲ ▲ ▲

Review Questions

1. What is the thesis of Nelkin's article? If possible, locate the thesis in the author's own words.
2. What three related themes does Nelkin find in the metaphors that geneticists use to describe their work?
3. Why does Nelkin object to the proposition that genes determine human identity?
4. According to Nelkin, what group of people share with scientists the responsibility for the overselling of genetic knowledge? Why?

Discussion and Writing Suggestions

1. Nelkin claims that "the biological sciences have long served to justify social arrangements as 'natural,' based on scientific reality." Thus, Darwin's "survival of the fittest" theory has been appropriated by social Darwinists who use Darwin's biological ideas to argue against welfare. How have some people appropriated genetic knowledge for social and political, rather than scientific ends? Do you share Nelkin's concern that such ideological use of scientific knowledge poses a significant threat in the future? Draw upon partic-

ular examples, both those advanced by Nelkin and others that occur to you, to support your argument.

2. You are an aspiring screenwriter who has seized upon genetic research as the basis for a science fiction film. Write a treatment (that is, a summary description of the action) of a proposed film involving the creation or manipulation of what Nelkin sarcastically calls "selfish genes, pleasure-seeking genes, criminal genes," etc.
3. Write a critique of Nelkin's article. Use the general guidelines provided in Chapter 3 in planning your critique, and draw also upon some of your responses to the Review Questions.

The Human Genome Project: A Personal View

JAMES D. WATSON

One of the most monumental scientific undertakings of our time is the Human Genome Project, launched in 1988. A genome is the complete set of genes in the chromosomes of organisms (humans have twenty-three pairs of chromosomes in the nucleas of each cell); and the purpose of the Human Genome Project is to identify, locate, and sequence all of the genes in human chromosomes. As a* Time *magazine article explained, "Encoded in the genome, the DNA in the . . . 46 chromosomes, are instructions that affect not only structure, size, coloring and other physical attributes, but also intelligence, susceptibility to disease, life-span and even some aspects of behavior. The ultimate goal of the Human Genome Project is to read and understand those instructions." Among the instructions that scientists are most eager to understand are those that determine human diseases, many of which are genetic in origin.*

In the following article, James D. Watson, the first director of the Human Genome Project, offers a "personal" perspective on this project and its meaning for him. One of the most influential scientists of modern times, Watson, together with Francis Crick, discovered the double-helix structure of the DNA molecule, a discovery that won them the 1962 Nobel Prize and that has been the basis of almost all subsequent genetic research. Born in 1928, Watson earned his doctorate in biology from Indiana University. In 1951, while conducting research at the Cavendish Laboratory at Cambridge University. Watson met Francis Crick, and the two began their epoch-making studies into the molecular basis of heredity. Watson and Crick's paper, announcing their discovery, was published in the journal Nature *in 1953.*

Watson taught at Harvard University from 1955 to 1976, and starting in 1968 served as director of the Cold Spring Harbor Biological Laboratories, working primarily on cancer research. In 1989 Watson was

---

*For its first five years the Genome Project was headed by DNA pioneer and Nobel laureate James D. Watson; since March 1993, it has been headed by Francis S. Collins, a physician and chemist who discovered the gene responsible for cystic fibrosis.

appointed director of the National Institutes of Health's (NIH) Human Genome Project. Watson's books include The Double Helix *(1968), an account of the discovery of DNA structure;* The Molecular Biology of the Gene *(1965); and* Recombinant DNA *(1985; with John Tooze and David T. Kurtz). This article first appeared in an anthology,* The Code of Codes: Scientific and Social Issues in the Human Genome Project *(1992), edited by Daniel J. Kevles and Leroy Hood.*

When I was going into science, people were concerned with questions of where we came from. Some people gave mystical answers—for example, "the truth came from revelation." But as a college kid I was influenced by Linus Pauling, who said, "We came from chemistry." I have spent my career trying to get a chemical explanation for life, the explanation of why we are human beings and not monkeys. The reason, of course, is our DNA. If you can study life from the level of DNA, you have a real explanation for its processes. So of course I think that the human genome project is a glorious goal. 1

People ask why *I* want to get the human genome. Some suggest that the reason is that it would be a wonderful end to my career—start out with the double helix and end up with the human genome. That *is* a good story. It seems almost a miracle to me that fifty years ago we could have been so ignorant of the nature of the genetic material and now can imagine that we will have the complete genetic blueprint of man. Just getting the complete description of a bacterium—say, the five million bases of *E. coli*—would make an extraordinary moment in history. There is a greater degree of urgency among older scientists than among younger ones to do the human genome now. The younger scientists can work on their grants until they are bored and still get the genome before they die. But to me it is crucial that we get the human genome now rather than twenty years from now, because I might be dead then and I don't want to miss out on learning how life works. 2

Still, I sometimes find myself moved to wonder, Is it ethical for me to do my job? A kind of backlash against the human genome project has cropped up from some scientists—good ones as well as not so good ones. What seems to have outraged many people was that, in 1990, against the proposed increase of 3.6 percent in the president's budget for all NIH funds, the human genome project was proposed for an increase of 86 percent—from roughly \$60 million to \$108 million. Feeling dispossessed, some scientific groups have begun to behave like postal workers' unions. The biological chemists, the molecular biologists, and the cell biologists have hired a lobbyist, a former congressman from Maine, to get the overall NIH appropriation increased. If such moves succeed, then maybe we won't have this terrible situation of really good scientists claiming that they are not getting funded because all the money is going to the human genome project. 3

In the meantime, hate letters have made the rounds, including the rounds of Congress, contending that the project is "bad science"—not 4 only bad, but sort of wicked. The letters say that the project is wasting money at a time when resources for research are getting threatened: If good people are failing to get grants, why go ahead with a program that is just going to spend billions of dollars sequencing junk? In 1990, someone in my office tried to get a distinguished biologist to help peer-review a big grant application. The biologist said, "No, not the human genome!" as though he were talking about syphilis.

The biologist sent me a fax asking me to explain why he should not oppose the human genome program. I called him up and said that, though I couldn't prove it, Congress actually seemed to *like* the human genome program because it promised to find out something about disease. Congress was excited that maybe we scientists were worried about disease instead of just about getting grants. The primary mission of the National Institutes of Health is to improve American health, to give us healthier lives, not to give jobs to scientists. I think that the scientific community, if it wants to be ethically responsible to society, has to ask whether we are spending research money in a way that offers the best go at diseases. 5

The fact is that understanding how DNA operates provides an enormous advantage over working only with proteins or fats or carbohydrates. The best illustration of this advantage has been tumor viruses. If we had not been able to study cancer at the level of the change in DNA that starts it, the disease would still be a hopeless field. Every time a new enzyme was discovered, hope would rise that it was the cause of cancer. Cancer used to be considered a graveyard for biochemists, even good ones, many of whom wanted to cap their careers by solving cancer but failed. Not until the genetic foundation for cancer was identified could you really begin to say what goes wrong to make this terrible human affliction. 6

A similar example is Alzheimer's disease. Are we going to find out what Alzheimer's is and why it causes brain failure without getting the genes that we know predispose certain people to the disease? Maybe we will, but I would not bet on it. But if we can get the gene or genes implicated in the disease, I am confident that we will save hundreds of millions of dollars, if not billions, that would have been spent on worthless research. 7

Every year, Congress passes a bill for even more money to study Alzheimer's. Congress is voting for good goals, but we do not really know how to use the money. It is not as if all the federal budget for health and all the basic research grants add up to good research. All the study sections in the National Institutes of Health do not receive applications of equal value; they often endorse research projects or programs because they address important problems. The programs themselves are not terrible, but they often have a low probability of paying off. I am sure that half the NIH budget is spent on good intentions rather than on a realistically high probability that a research program will have a direct impact on one of the major human diseases. 8

The pressure is enormous to do something about mental disease because it can be terrible, as anyone knows who has a friend or family mem- 9 ber suffering from it. We do spend a vast amount of money studying mental diseases, yet the effort yields very little. Manic-depressive disease leads to great moments of mania—perhaps the successful careers of a number of scientists can be attributed to it—but it also leads to depression, tragedy, and suicides. Lithium relieves some of the symptoms, but a drug is not the complete answer, as any psychiatrist will tell you. It is pretty clear that manic depression has a genetic cause. Several scientists thought they had located the gene on a chromosome. But then it got lost, and so long as it is lost, we are lost.

10 It is also pretty clear that alcoholism bears some relationship to genes. This view comes from studies on identical twins adopted and raised by different families. There *are* alcoholic families. It is not likely that their members are morally weak; they just cannot tolerate alcohol chemically. But no one has found the gene or genes for susceptibility to alcoholism, and the chance of finding the genetic sources are probably low until a much more sophisticated human genetic community exists—plus the money to get the pedigrees and all the genetic markers.

11 Some diseases are not going to be easy to crack. For a long time, people have been trying to discover the cause of schizophrenia by looking for chemical differences in the urine or the blood, a research strategy that has not been successful. It is not going to be easy to find the genes behind schizophrenia either, because reliable pedigree data[1] are difficult to compile and the condition is hard to diagnose. Thus both directions offer low probabilities, but it is still better to waste your money doing genetics because genetics lies at the heart of so much. Of course scientists should find out what the brain is. I believe in neurobiology and have tried to help raise money to support the field. But I do not believe that its current approaches will necessarily lead to the real, deep cause of manic-depressive disease.

12 In 1989 Congressman Joe Early said to me, "I'm tired of putting fingers in dikes!" In combating disease, genetics helps enormously if it is a bad gene that contributes to the cause. Ignoring genes is like trying to solve a murder without finding the murderer. All we have are victims. With time, if we find the genes for Alzheimer's disease and for manic depression, then less money will be wasted on research that goes nowhere. Congressmen can only feel good if they are spending money on good things, so we have to convince them that the best use for their money is DNA research.

13 The human genome project is really trying to push a little more money toward DNA-based research. Since we can now produce good genetic maps that allow us to locate culprit chromosomes and then actually find the genes for disease (as Francis Collins found the gene for cystic fibrosis), genetics should be a very high priority on the agenda of NIH research. We are extremely lucky that when James Wyngaarden was director of NIH, he saw to the establishment of what is now a permanent division within NIH called

[1]*pedigree data:* data that establish the genetic lineage of a particular trait or defect; the process involves gathering genetic information about the parents, grandparents, and so on.

the Center for Human Genome Research. I doubt that I convinced the biologist who sent me the fax, but I may eventually, since he is very bright. I want to convince as many people as I can of the merits of the human genome project, but not to cap my career and have something that sounds good in my obituary. I can make best use of my time by trying to mobilize the country to do something about diseases that have hit my family and many others. I am sort of a concerned parent for whom things have not gone completely right. So, I am trying to enlist a group of people who will help us get these genes, and do what I think Congress wants us to do.

The ultimate objective of the human genome program is to learn the nucleotide sequence of human DNA. We want the program completed in roughly fifteen years. By completed we do not mean every last nucleotide sequence. If we get 98 percent of the regions that are functional, that will probably be the end of it. We will not worry about spending infinite amounts of money trying to sequence things we know probably contain little information. We could define the end of it to be the identification of all the human genes—that is, we will be done when we have located the coding sequences and can declare that human beings on the average contain, say, 248,000 genes, with variations such that some individuals, for example, have a gene present in four copies and some in three, and that for some the gene is nonessential. It has recently been learned that only a third of yeast genes are essential. Knock out two-thirds of them and the yeast still multiply. Studying things that are not essential will keep the people in the yeast world going for a long time. I think we can safely say the project will be over when we can identify the genes. 14

We probably will be unable to identify the genes until we get most of the DNA sequenced, because we will not know where they are. It would be nice if the whole program could be done by copy DNA (cDNA)—that is, by purely functional DNA[2]—so that we would not have to sequence all the junk, but we will never know whether we have all the cDNAs. This is not to say we should not do cDNA; we will actually fund grants for people trying to find better techniques for getting rare cDNA in tissue-specific places. But I think that we have got to sequence the whole thing. 15

In the first five years, we will push to achieve three major objectives. First, we will try to get good genetic maps, so that each chromosome has enough genetic markers[3] on it actually to locate a gene if a pedigree is available. Currently, we have only about 150 markers that are sufficiently informative for assigning the location of genes. We have started a crash program to persuade people to make a lot of markers and to put them into a public repository made available to the whole world. We want to change the current practice among researchers of not sharing their markers because 16

---

[2]*DNA:* Watson considers "functional DNA" only that kind of DNA that copies the messenger RNA molecules that contain instructions for synthesizing proteins.

[3]*genetic marker:* genetic "signposts"—differences in a complementary pair of chromosomes—that help locate particular genes.

they want to be the first to find a gene and encourage everyone to make markers available to everyone.

The second objective is to make overlapping fragments of DNA available so that anyone looking for a gene in a particular piece of a certain chromosome will be able to get it by paying some nominal sum. The fragment will not be totally free, but it will certainly be there for anyone who seriously wants it. Techniques for doing this seem to be available now; it should not require more than $10 million to stockpile overlapping fragments of a given chromosome. To put this figure into perspective, Francis Collins has said that finding the cystic fibrosis gene was expensive—between $10 million and $50 million. If all the markers had been available, it would have cost only $5 million. I think we can establish an overlapping fragment library for the entire human genome for a couple of hundred million dollars, which will certainly reduce the costs of subsequent disease hunts. We will end up with a map of overlapping fragments, each one identified by three or four DNA sequences along it called sequence tag sites. With PCR,[4] researchers will be able to pull out all the human DNA that may be wanted. 17

The third major objective is to support scientists trying to do megabase[5] sequencing in one place in a reasonable period of time. An example of this type of project is a proposal from Walter Gilbert to sequence a mycoplasma, which is really a small (800 kilobases) bacterium. Gilbert's proposal, whether he lives up to it or not, is to do a million bases a year within two years. We want to encourage people to do sequencing of megabases with the aim of reducing the cost—so that within a couple of years it will fall to about a dollar a base pair, and then perhaps even to fifty cents. We will not accept a grant application from someone who proposes to sequence some DNA the old fashioned way, with graduate students or postdoctoral fellows, at the current cost—five to ten dollars a base pair—just out of curiosity about it. . . . 18

The NIH genome project will also try to get some real data on model organisms. I will be happy if we get ten quite different bacteria sequenced up through yeast. We are now supporting a joint program between the Medical Research Council, in England, and the Laboratory of Molecular Biology in Cambridge, and the group in St. Louis that has developed yeast artificial chromosomes to sequence the genome of a roundworm. The roundworm community is eager to do it because they've already got the overlapping DNA fragments. We hope to get the sequence out in ten years. It's about the equivalent of an average human chromosome—about a hundred megabases—but with less repetitive DNA, and so probably with fewer problems. There is also an effort to sequence a plant genome, arabadopsis, which we hope will be led by the National Science Founda- 19

[4]*PCR:* polymerase chain reaction: a powerful technique for amplifying a gene sequence, for obtaining a large amount of DNA from a small amount.
[5]*megabase:* one million base pairs.

tion with help from other agencies, including ourselves. This is roughly seventy megabases, and the project should be a real boon to botany. Except for perhaps one bacterium, none of this probably would ever have been funded in the absence of the human genome program.

Among the reasons for wanting to find bacterial genes is to help find the human ones. People ask, How are you going to identify a gene if it is interspersed with so much junk and you lack a cDNA? How are you going to know you have it? That is obviously going to be hard in some cases, but if you have obtained the corresponding bacterial gene without many repetitive sequences and if you are clever, you ought to be able to spot the differences. I can imagine that typical work for undergraduates will be to find the gene once all the sequences has been obtained. Professors could tell their students: If you can identify a gene, we will let you go on to graduate school and do real science. 20

The human genome project is sufficiently justifiable so that if no other country wants to help fund it, the United States should do the whole thing. We are rich enough to do it. But I doubt that we will be allowed to do it alone, because others are going to worry that it might actually be commercially interesting, and they will worry that we will be disinclined to distribute the data very fast if we have paid for it ourselves. It is my hope that we can spread out of the cost of sequencing and data distribution over many countries. As soon as a gene has been identified, it should be thrown into an international data base. 21

But there are problems that I don't see how to get around. If a stretch of DNA is sequenced in an academic laboratory, a university lawyer will say, "That looks like a serotonin receptor. Patent it!" Mutant forms of the cystic fibrosis gene have been patented by the universities of Toronto and Michigan. They will get some royalties and maybe build better student unions with the revenues. I am at a loss to know how to put valuable DNA sequences in the public domain fast when a lot of people want to keep them private. I just hope that other major nations come in. The Japanese will not let anyone who doesn't pay for it see their work. I figure that strategy might work. People might actually pay for sequence information if that is the only way to get to see it. So I have to seem a bad guy and say: I *will* withhold information that we generate if other countries refuse to join in an open sharing arrangement. But, in truth, it would be very distasteful to me to get into a situation where we were withholding the data for reasons of national advantage. 22

The acquisition of human DNA information has already begun to pose serious ethical problems. I think that somehow we have to get it into the laws that anyone's DNA—the message it gives—is confidential and that the only one who has a right to look at it is the person herself or himself. Still, the ethics get complicated if you can spot a gene in a newborn child that produces a disease for which no treatment exists. Sometimes these defects will be hard to spot, but sometimes, as in muscular dystrophy, they can be very easy to detect. As we begin to get data of this kind, people are 23 going to get nervous and some are going to be violent opponents of the project unless they can feel that they or their friends will not be discriminated against on the basis of their DNA. If someone can go look at your DNA and see that you have a deletion on one of your anti-oncogenes and that you will be more liable to die of cancer at an early age, then you might be discriminated against in, say, employment or insurance coverage.

Laws are needed to prevent genetic discrimination and to protect rights 24
that should not be signed away too easily. If you are poor, it will be highly tempting to say, "Yes, look at my DNA because I want the job in the asbestos factory." If you have no money, a job in an asbestos factory is better than no job. Issues like these demand a lot of discussion, at least so that DNA-related laws are not enacted prematurely. For that reason, we are putting more than 3 percent of the genome project money into an ethics program; and we will put more into it if we find that it needs more.

We have faced up to this challenge already with DNA fingerprints. The 25
National Center for Genome Research has given $50,000 to the National Research Council–National Academy of Sciences study on DNA fingerprinting, which has lawyers and judges advising it. The police want a DNA register of sex offenders; other people may want one of dishonest accountants. People will want DNA fingerprints to prove that a politician's children are really his. At a meeting in Leicester, England, Alec Jeffries showed a slide of a letter from a woman who runs a small hotel in Wales and who wrote that it would be a good idea to have a DNA fingerprint register of bedwetters. Different people will want different information—the possibilities are unlimited. I don't think *anyone* should have access to anyone else's DNA fingerprints.

We need to explore the social implications of human genome research 26
and figure out some protection for people's privacy so that these fears do not sabotage the entire project. Deep down, I think that the only thing that could stop our program is fear; if people are afraid of the information we will find, they will keep us from finding it. We have to convince our fellow citizens somehow that there will be more advantages to knowing the human genome than to not knowing it.

▲ ▲ ▲

Review Questions

1. Why do some scientific researchers oppose the Human Genome Project, according to Watson?
2. Why does Watson believe that DNA research, including the Human Genome Project, should be of the highest priority?
3. What are the immediate objectives of the Human Genome Project?
4. According to Watson, what are some of the ethical problems associated with DNA research?

Discussion and Writing Suggestions

1. Watson concludes, "We have to convince our fellow citizens somehow that there will be more advantages to knowing the human genome than to not knowing it." Has Watson convinced you that the Human Genome Project is both a good thing in itself and a useful expenditure of public funds? If so, which arguments made the greatest impression on you, and why? If not, what are your chief concerns? Should the project be canceled? Should restrictions be placed on genetic research? If so, what kind of restrictions?
2. To what extent, if any, does Watson's own personal stake in the success of the Human Genome Project (and in the success of biotechnology, in general) affect the way that you read this article and accept his arguments? Explain.
3. Watson is a scientist trying to persuade people (both his fellow scientists and others interested in scientific matters) that the project he heads is a vital one. Setting aside for the moment your own views of the genome project, to what extent do you think Watson has done a good job of explaining this scientific project? In particular, did you find this article difficult to follow because of the language in which Watson explained genetic concepts? If so, how might he have made his explanations easier to understand?
4. Watson argues that information gleaned from the Human Genome Project should be made available to all interested parties and that whatever has been discovered in one country should be made available to an international database. A genetic cure for a particular disease might be discovered more rapidly if more than one group of scientists were attacking the problem. But private companies might argue that they are entitled to the patents and financial profits from their own discoveries—that without such rights and rewards, they have no incentive to invest large amounts of money in research. What are your views on this subject? How can the fruits of genetic research be made widely available, while the rights of companies to earn reasonable profits from their research are protected?
5. Write either (a) an editorial or (b) a short story concerned with one of the ethical problems of DNA research discussed by Watson at the end of his article. Expand on or dramatize one or more of these potential problem areas.

The Politics of Genetics

ANNE FAUSTO-STERLING
DIANE PAUL
MARSHA SAXTON

In the following passage, three women discuss aspects of the Human Genome Project that seem to them problematic. (See description of this project in the preceding article.) In the first part of the selection, which appeared in The Women's Review of Books *(July 1994), an interviewer questions biologist Anne Fausto-Sterling of Brown University, a biologist, and Diane Paul of the University of Massachusetts/Boston, a political scientist and historian of science. In the second part, disability rights activist Marsha Saxton comments on aspects of the preceding discussion.*

Women's Review: First of all, what is the Human Genome Project? . . . 1

Diane Paul: The original idea for the project came from Robert Sinsheimer, the Chancellor of the University of California at Santa Cruz—who also, by the way, is the person who coined the phrase "new eugenics" in 1965. Back in 1985, he called a bunch of scientists together to consider the idea of sequencing the human genome, that is, determining the exact DNA sequence of the 3 billion base pairs of a complete set of chromosomes. . . . 2

WR: Can one of you explain simply what is meant by "human genome?" 3

Anne Fausto-Sterling: The human genome is considered to be, for the purposes of the Project, all of the DNA that is inside the nucleus of the cell. That DNA is subpackaged at several levels. The first set of subpackages for humans is the 23 pairs of chromosomes, or 46 total, each pair being roughly identical. Then within that—lengths and lengths of DNA wrapped up and packaged into each chromosome—the DNA itself is made up of subunits that are called bases. It's the order of the bases, or the sequence of the base, that contains the information for what the chromosomes or genes do. Not all of those chromosomes and bases are informational. Strictly speaking they are not all genes—they don't all carry information for making an RNA or a protein. Some are structural or junk. For some, no one knows what they do. 4

DP: So the longstanding project of geneticists has always been first to relate a particular chromosome to a particular trait—a disease or a non-disease trait, like hair color—and then ultimately to take that gene itself, once they know where it is on the chromosome, and analyze the sequence of the gene in order to figure out how it works. The other thing that often doesn't get discussed is that there are often other genomes in the cell that are not included in the Human Genome Project. Especially, there are sequences of DNA in the mitochondria, which are little organelles, sub-cellular structures that live inside cells. The DNA there is much smaller in quantity and has a different evolutionary origin. It does 5 carry information, and its malfunctions do sometimes lead to a disease state. But the Human Genome Project doesn't mean that, it means strictly the genetic information inside the nucleus of the cell, even though there are residual parts of that cell that do carry genetic information that can be of great consequence for human development.

WR: Diane, a few minutes ago you mentioned "mapping" and "sequencing"—can you explain the distinction? What kinds of things are these researchers looking for? 6

DP: The Project is usually conceptualized as having three elements. There are two kinds of mapping—there's genetic mapping and there's physical mapping—and then there's sequencing. In an attempt to build a wider constituency, the project shifted to the least controversial of these. Genetic mapping is nothing new, and even people who were very critical of the project would have loved to have the genetic map. A genetic map is a way to identify the relative location of genes or markers along a chromosome. It's a very old project and goes back to the 1910s, when people were trying to create genetic maps of Drosophila by making standard genetic crosses, which you can't do in humans. In humans, to make a genetic map, you have to track the inheritance of chromosome fragments through families, and that allows you to focus the search for a specific gene onto a specific fraction of the total genome. 7

Then there are physical maps of a chromosome, linear arrays of DNA fragments spanning the length of each chromosome. They provide the means to move from an approximate chromosomal location, which is provided by the linkage map, to an actual gene. 8

WR: So if we compare it to a regular map in an atlas, this genetic linkage map is like a much larger-scale map of the same area as the physical map? 9

DP: That's right. Almost everybody—at least everybody I know—who was extremely critical of the Genome Project loved the idea of the genetic linkage map. Many of the people who thought that, scientifically, it didn't make any sense to sequence the entire human genome, were very enthusiastic about the prospect of having a complete genetic and even a physical map. So, the project came to focus on these. The sequencing—that is, determining the sequence of the 3 billion base pairs—remained a part of the rhetoric, but was downplayed relative to the other elements. Most of even the most effective critics, the scientific critics, eventually climbed on board. 10

WR: What about the ethical and political implications of all this? Its been alleged that the project is going to lead to a "new eugenics." Do you think that's realistic? 11

DP: I think that depends on what you mean by eugenics, which is a highly contested word. People don't agree on what eugenics is. They all agree that it's bad, but that's very different from agreeing on what it is. And really, anytime you can reach complete agreement on what is bad, it ought to make you suspicious. I would go so far as to say that eugenics has be- 12 come a kind of approved anxiety about the Genome Project. Everybody worries about it, even James Watson. I think that's because it's harmless. Every discussion of the social implications of the Genome Project, whether in books or articles or TV programs, has some segment on eugenics. Eugenics conjures up negative images, and it's usually the worst, the most absurd and terrible that one sees—images of immigrants being turned away at Ellis Island. And playing these over and over is a way of saying, "My God, these were terrible people in the past and fortunately we're nothing like that." So denouncing eugenics is often a way of signaling that one is socially concerned and worthy of trust.

But in fact, you can hear people denounce eugenics who then pro- 13
mote policies that from many other people's perspectives would be what *they* mean by eugenics. Abby Lippman, a critic of genetic medicine, defines all prenatal diagnosis as eugenics. Most geneticists, on the other hand, would insist that eugenics has to involve coercion, usually on the part of the state for some purpose of its own. The effect of a broad definition is to associate genetic medicine with odious practices and to make us suspicious. The narrow definition dissociates us from the same practices and thus reassures us. So there's a political struggle as to how the word is to be applied.

But why do we care about eugenics? We care about it because it's had 14
a particular history. In my own work I came to the conclusion that it is misuse of energy to try to determine what is and what isn't eugenics. We can ask, perhaps more productively, what it is that people fear when they express anxiety about eugenics. Here I think there are basically three issues. One is fear of the state—fear of direct government—the classic programs of segregation and sterilization. Nazi breeding programs. Yet even though those are the images we tend to associate with eugenics, it's what people fear least, for very good reasons. It seems extremely unlikely, for political reasons, that the state would intervene in that kind of direct way. For one thing, you have an extremely strong Right to Life movement. Here the women's movement and the Right to Life movement converge. You would have to defeat extraordinarily broad and diverse social forces in order, say, to demand that a woman abort a fetus diagnosed with some condition, or force people to undergo gene therapy. What I think people worry about more is a second issue, coercion of a more subtle kind. Pressures that are generated through the health insurance system and HMO policies and, at this point, most markedly through doctor pressure.

WR: Could you give us a couple of examples of this? 15

DP: Sure. Fear of losing your health insurance benefits if an insurance 16
company discovers that you carry a gene, something the predictive test makes it possible to recognize, a gene that will manifest itself later in life. Or refusing to cover your children if you go ahead and have them when your partner is a carrier of a "bad" gene. Fear of being cut off from the insurance system, or fear of just being unable to pay the downstream costs of caring for a severely handicapped child.

WR: It sounds as though the onus of deciding whether to give birth to any 17
physically or mentally impaired child would then fall on the individual family and primarily the women in that family.

DP: Yes; and then there are increasing pressures from doctors worrying 18
about malpractice suits. It's very easy to demonstrate informed consent—all you have to do is take the prenatal diagnostic test. So how do you have informed refusal? When a woman says she doesn't want to have the test, it's strongly in the doctor's interest to get her to change her mind. The legal system—or the conjoined legal-medical system—is perhaps the strongest force in the routinization of tests. Women are not demanding them: testing is being driven by the providers.

AF: And this is something that's already under way, and it's being speeded 19
up and broadened in very alarming ways: one of the things the Project is doing is moving away from the clear-cut, single-locus gene to talk about things that it broadly views as genetic tendencies. It will talk about traits such as tendency to heart attack, and it will look for major and minor genes involved in increasing the probability that someone will have a heart attack or heart disease.

DP: Or various forms of cancer. 20

AF: Yes. So we are not talking about immediately giving birth to severely 21
disabled children or to children who will die at very young ages. We are expanding beyond that to children who stand a higher probability of dropping dead of a heart attack when they're forty.

WR: But then again the whole issue of risk assessment falls back on the 22
parents and particularly on the mother.

AF: Right. We are talking about both expanding the probabilities involved 23
in decisions into much murkier areas and about opening this whole other can of worms, which is: what will knowledge of particular genes tell us about human development? As long as we're focusing on a gene for Tay-Sachs, for instance, we can know close to certainly what the outcome for someone who is homozygous for that gene will be. When we start talking about genes for height, or baby fat, or cholesterol production, we start moving into an area where there are literally hundreds of factors that contribute.

DP: This brings me back to another of the anxieties I was talking about— 24
what some people call "eugenics by default." What happens when these technologies make it possible to choose desirable characteristics and consumers demand them? This is very complicated for a number of reasons. Although this is a source of substantial anxiety, but so far, at least in the US, there is little evidence that women are interested in perfect babies. The big story about these technologies right now is how little they are used—there are all these DNA tests that are available and going unused and all these companies that are going under.

AF: But there is another component to this, which I think will be part of 25
the future: active attempts to manipulate the human genome to change the genetic sequences in a baby. So that instead of aborting a Tay-Sachs baby, you would ultimately isolate the embryo the way you might for

fertilization, and inject it with good DNA. In other words, alter the gene in the embryo so that you would not give birth to a Tay-Sachs baby at all.

DP: I agree. I think there are various ways that this could come about and it's almost bound to come about—maybe not with the population at large, but with middle-class professionals, who already are demanding to do some of these things. I think that's the most interesting and potentially very troublesome aspect of all this, and it's one we will have a very hard time thinking through, because the people who are most worried about these developments are the ones most committed to the principle of reproductive autonomy. For them, reproductive autonomy trumps any other value. I am not one of them, but if you are, then you have no way of coping with this problem of values in conflict. To do anything to restrict genetic intervention requires constraints on individual decisions, and the people who would be most worried about the outcomes of a complete laissez-faire policy are the people who hold reproductive choice as an absolute. Then you're just caught in a dilemma, and the market will prevail. 26

WR: It seems that what is being injected here are consumer values of a not-very-disguised kind—that you can go shopping for a designer baby, in the way that you can go shopping for a car. 27

AF: Yes. There are people who defend the use of human growth hormone to make kids taller, when they have nothing wrong with them except that they might turn out to be five feet tall. They often use a human suffering argument, that kids will be mercilessly teased in school and that they, as parents, need to do everything possible to make their child's life as pain-free as possible. It's the idea that we or our children are entitled to a perfect world and life without pain, and that it can be bought. Or that at least in those places where it can be bought, that if we are good parents, we should buy it for them. I am not necessarily in favor of eliminating pain; I don't think the world owes us a living. I don't think that it's even good to raise a child to believe that there shouldn't be pain in the world. You shield children from certain kinds of things, but far more effective parenting, it seems to me, is to help children cope with far more complex futures. 28

The thing that disturbs me deeply about this business of eliminating short stature with hormones is that we're teaching kids that they don't have to cope with difference—either their own or someone else's. Instead, we ultimately look forward to a world where we will wipe out difference. I think you understand how profoundly disturbing a vision that is. Even within the borders of the US we are becoming a more diverse society. Now more than ever we need to be raising children to deal with the confusion and pain and also teach them some of the joy that difference brings. People in the disabilities movement see it as a not-very-distant assault on themselves. 29

The other thing that concerns me is raised by that quote from Watson. 30

WR: That this is our best weapon against disease? 31

AF: Yes. This is a deeply ethnocentric view of where disease problems lie. 32
What counts as disease? This requires attention. We're focusing on two things. We're focusing in on inherited genetic diseases, which are relatively rare—most people in the world don't die of those—and we are focusing in on a constellation of diseases that are typical of advanced capitalism. Those are the cancers. People in the Third World don't primarily die of those either. The truth is that the Human Genome Project will be very relevant to certain disease problems faced by citizens living under advanced capitalism. They are completely irrelevant to the disease patterns faced by the majority of the world who are dying of malnutrition, dehydration, infectious diseases. We already know a lot about these and we also know about how to make them stop, but we are not investing the resources to do that. For example, there's only one entomological research institute in all of Africa, though insects are a major source of food loss on the African continent. So, if we are talking about the best thing to do worldwide with available resources to save as many lives as possible, the Human Genome Project is pretty low on the list. Its very conceptualization is ethnocentric in a very deep way.

WR: So what do you think is the prognosis for the Human Genome Pro- 33
ject?

AF: I'm not sure. I think research will continue, and I also think it will con- 34
tinue to try to figure out ways to change the genetic structure—in particular, to affect what's called the germ line. That is, those cells in the body which end up becoming sperm and eggs. There are two kinds of gene therapy. One is already in the news. People are trying to change particular cells—like if your blood cells make a bad form of hemoglobin you change the cells that generate blood cells so that they'll make good hemoglobin instead. That form of therapy would be a new way of treating an individual with a genetic illness—it's performed on the individual and it's one generation long.

But the body is divided up into two lines of cells. Essentially, early in 35
development, one line of cells is cordoned off. It's called the germ line, and those cells do only one thing: they divide and they make new germ cells, which are either eggs or sperm. All the rest of the cells in the body become somatic cells. So the first form of therapy that I've talked about just affects somatic cells and therefore isn't transmitted from one generation to the next. The other form would target the germ cells themselves so that if, for example, you were a carrier for sickle cell anemia, the idea would be to change your germ cells so that you would no longer carry one gene for sickle cell anemia. That would be an inherited change, be passed on from generation to generation.

But there are always new mutations, and I think that nature will al- 36
ways foil our attempt at total control—and that's a reassuring thing.

WR: Is it practically possible to change the germ cells? 37

AF: It's starting to happen now. We already do it with mice, with farm ani- 38
mals.

WR: So in fact the time to move on to humans is not too distant? 39

AF: No, it's not. It will be within fifteen years, I think. 40

WR: Is that because humans are just more complex? 41

AF: No, it's really because we demand a higher frequency of accuracy. 42 We're not allowed to experiment at will with humans and discard the experiments that don't work. We have to get the technique with animals working with 100 percent accuracy, or close to it, and do all sorts of controls for safety, and that will certainly take time—but I don't think it's out of reach. The dangers of this would be very "science fictiony," in that it could lead to attempts that are much less crude at tailor-making people with desirable traits. I think Diane is right—an overcontrolling state may not be the main thing to fear in our culture. I think it's more likely to happen through cultural pressures here than economic pressures.

WR: Like the insurance industry? 43

AF: And a very complex consumer culture that sets up wants and desires 44 that take on a life of their own. So it is a much more insidious form of social control. What's interesting is that five years ago, when people were trying to sell the Human Genome Project, everybody was very clear: they said "No, no, no—we would never be talking about the germ line therapy. We would only be talking about somatic therapy. It would not alter the evolutionary course of the human species." No one is saying that any more. Commissions have been set up to study the implications of tinkering with the germ line. So there has been a real sea change in that particular area.

WR: It sounds as if the Project itself is going to go on? 45

AF: It will for some time. I think the question will be whether it turns out 46 that it also involves a lot of oversimplifications and misconceptions of how human development works. That's what I mean when I say that nature may confound it. Human development is going to turn out to be way too complex and way too unlinked to the genome for the sort of "holy grail" that Watson or Gilbert talk about to be reached. But if that ever becomes evident, it may not be for a while.

Marsha Saxton comments:

I come to the genome debate from a perspective that perplexes many 47 scientists and medical professionals. My colleagues and I have disabilities; we are purportedly the ones helped by genetic advances, yet we are critical of much of the research. I'm a member of the Ethical, Legal, Social Implications (ELSI) Program of the Human Genome Initiative. ELSI receives approximately five percent of the genome budget to fund social research on relevant ethical issues. This is the first program in the history of federally funded science to address the ethical impact of scientific innovation.

Anne and Diane identify some key concerns about genome research. I 48 think health care providers are trying, despite the profit-based health care system, to do good work. Scientists and clinicians have seen patients die, and some have watched their own family members struggle with genetic conditions. These professionals are committed to improving life for people they care about. My objection is to the narrow view the medical system takes of disease and the alleviation of suffering. What misses getting addressed in medical training is the social construction of disease, or the social factors that contribute to suffering.

As Diane says, the word "eugenics" has become a slur, its original 49
meaning obscured. While the notion of eugenics arose in the 1800s, what underlay eugenic ideology in its day still besets us: class oppression, racism, sexism and prejudice against "difference." Genetics became the scientific justification for these oppressions. Whether we call it eugenics or not, genetic science is still sometimes being used as a tool to perpetuate oppression.

The current round of improving the race has targeted people with dis- 50
eases and disabilities through prenatal screening and selective abortion. Just as selective abortion of female fetuses manifests sexism in India, these procedures expose this country's devaluation of people with disabilities, and belies the Americans with Disabilities Act, which legally protects them. We can pinpoint where particular disabling conditions are placed along the continuum of acceptability by how vigorously screening is pursued.

Tay-Sachs disease is often raised as justification for prenatal screening. 51
But as a rare disease, it's a poor basis for a paradigm. As epidemiologist Abby Lippman says, "Rare cases make bad policies." Conditions receiving priority attention for prenatal screening are Down's Syndrome, spina bifida, cystic fibrosis and Fragile X, whose clinical outcomes are usually mildly to moderately disabling. Individuals with these conditions can live good lives. There are severe cases, but the medical system tends to underestimate the functional abilities, and overestimate the "burden" of these disabled citizens. The structure of the social security and disability benefits system actually discourages disabled people from working and marrying, reinforcing the stereotypes of dependence.

Prenatal screening and genetic testing are supported by that corner- 52
stone of contemporary political rhetoric, cost benefit. But dollars per child's life don't factor out. In fact, families with disabled children who are familiar with the actual impact of the disabilities tend *not* to seek the tests for subsequent children. These children and their families are not "suffering" from diseased genes, but from oppressive attitudes and a lack of resources that would allow people with differences to be integrated into our communities.

This treatment of people with disabilities serves as a wedge into the 53
broader issue of "quality control" of all humans. If a disease condition (like Down's Syndrome) is clearly unacceptable, how long before the line moves toward other characteristics fraught with social charge: attractiveness, height, intelligence . . . ? Pre-implantation diagnosis, now used with in vitro fertilization, offers the prospect of "admission" standards for fetuses.

Selective abortion is promoted in doctors' offices as "reproductive op- 54
tion" and "personal choice." But as anthropologist Rayna Rapp notes, "private choices always have public consequences." Using selective abortion

to eliminate the "problem of disabled children" will not challenge the fundamental oppression of women who in a sexist family structure provide most of the care for children in general, for elderly parents and those disabled in accidents or from non-genetic diseases. Supporters of "cost benefit" analysis would argue for the benefits of eliminating disabled children as opposed to the costs of maintaining them. But the cost benefit argument disintegrates in the face of the enormous resources expended for a few rare genetic disorders. The diseases of poverty are unprofitable for the science industries, but bankrupting to our humanness.

Anne commented that marketing for prenatal tests is provider-driven, 55 not woman-driven. We are being sold the illusion that the problems of mothers are being addressed by medical science. The economy undervalues mothering as a job. Add this to the stereotyping of disabled people as worthless and burdensome, and it becomes difficult to value the life of a fetus with a "defect." Disabled children may not fit into the schemes of those who back prenatal testing, but no child fits into a scheme that oppresses mothers and therefore devalues all children. It's time to reform the medical market, make it responsive to the pervasive difficulties of procreation—harmful or unworkable birth control, inadequate prenatal resources.

Profit-based insurance companies reduce costs by eliminating cover- 56 age for "pre-existing conditions."Now these companies are refusing coverage in the cases of individuals who have family members with genetic conditions that imply a "family gene," or in cases where a genetic test reveals a possible "susceptibility" to conditions like hemophilia and Huntington's disease. Coverage is denied even when the people under company scrutiny have no symptoms of illness and may never develop any. But genetic status may soon determine employability, since employers are wary of expensive premiums. The fear of "genetic discrimination" has haunted the prospect of releasing new tests for colon and breast cancer. These technologies mostly offer diagnosis. Since treatments or cures are decades away, the benefits are dubious except to insurance companies.

Abby Lippman and others have coined the term "geneticization" for 57 ascribing genetic causes to socially undesirable behaviors such as alcoholism, homosexuality, homelessness, shyness. This enables society once again to blame the (genes of the) victim, setting social institutions and citizens free from responsibility for challenging oppression.

Such wrenching ethical nightmares arise out of these new technolo- 58 gies! The privacy and civil liberty issues of testing, data banking and genetic labeling make us agonize at our most intimate levels of self. The media's inclination is to dwell on the moral dilemmas, and reduce them to soap opera melodramas. Are these the only important concerns about the technologies? I think not. The underlying economic motives must be exposed and debated.

▲ ▲ ▲

Review Questions

1. What are the scientific—and political—differences between genetic mapping and genetic sequencing, according to Fausto-Sterling and Paul?
2. Diane Paul notes that "eugenics has become a kind of approved anxiety about the Genome Project." What does she mean? What does this "approved anxiety" have to do with what she later claims is a "political struggle" about how the word "eugenics" is applied?
3. Paul expresses concern that the Genome Project is "moving away from the clear-cut single-locus gene" toward a focus on "genetic tendencies." What is the difference between the two, and why does she perceive the latter as dangerous?
4. What is the essential difference between genetic work on somatic cells and genetic work on germ cells?
5. What is "geneticization," according to Marsha Saxton? Why does she view it as a dangerous tendency?

Discussion and Writing Suggestions

1. Based on this interview and on the response by Marsha Saxton, what is your understanding of how work on the Human Genome Project may lead to one type of eugenics or another? To what extent do you share these authors' concerns about the potential for abuse, or even oppression? Explain your reasons for believing as you do, providing examples.
2. Diane Paul discusses some unusual alliances associated with the Genome Project. For example, she notes that at one point the women's movement and the Right to Life movement (often at odds because of their differing stances on abortion) may share the same concerns about gene research. She also points out that those most concerned about the manipulation of the human genome to change the genetic sequence are likely to be the same people who are most insistent upon reproductive freedom. Assume the role of a leader of one of these groups who must write a letter requesting support to the leader of another group. Explain the need to temporarily resolve your differences or personal ideological dilemmas (identify what these are) to work on a common goal.
3. Why does Diane Paul believe that the Human Genome Project is "ethnocentric in a very deep way"? To what extent do you agree?
4. Marsha Saxton believes that genetic science is "sometimes being used as a tool to perpetuate oppression." She also believes that there are "underlying economic motives" for this oppression. What does she mean? Considering the evidence she adduces to support her view, to what extent do you agree?

5. One feminist writer, Linda Bullard, has argued that genetic research "is *inherently* eugenic in that it always requires someone to decide what is a good and a bad gene." Is this a fair statement? Why or why not?
6. Responding to a question about "designer babies," Anne Fausto-Sterling expresses concern that parents—demanding perfect babies and a pain-free social environment—will make use of genetic techniques to, say, make their kids taller or otherwise less "different" from an ideal norm. A a prospective parent, would you be inclined to take advantage of the kind of knowledge from biotechnology likely to be available in the near future and to select in the kind of characteristics you would desire in your offspring? To select *out* characteristics you or others view as undesirable? To what extent do you think that such parental choices should be legally restricted? You may wish to couch your response in the form of a letter to a friend or relative.
7. To what extent do you see parallels between the concerns expressed by the authors in this selection and the concerns expressed in the selection from Huxley's *Brave New World*? Discuss some of the key similarities and some of the key differences.
8. Write either (a) an editorial or (b) a short story or film treatment concerned with one of the ethical problems of genome research discussed by Fausto-Sterling, Paul, or Saxton. Expand upon or dramatize one or more of the potential problem areas.

Call for a Worldwide Survey of Human Genetic Diversity

LUIGI L. CAVALLI-SFORZA
ALLAN. C. WILSON
C. R. CANTOR
R. M. COOK-DEEGAN
MARY-CLAIRE KING

In late 1993, in an open letter in the journal Genomics, *a group of renowned scientists called for support for a Human Genetic Diversity Project—an enterprise related to, but different in kind from, the Human Genome Project. As the article that follows this one will reveal, the Diversity Project later ran into some unexpected—and non-technological—obstacles. But when first proposed, it garnered an overwhelmingly positive response. We reprint it here not only because it represents an important contemporary contribution to biotechnology, but also because it illustrates the kind of controversy over the ethical applications of sci-*

ence in which scientists are increasingly becoming embroiled. This article is designed to be read in conjunction with the one that follows by Jo Ann C. Gutin.

Luigi Luca Cavalli-Sforza, professor emeritus of genetics at Stanford Medical School, is the author of The History and Geography of Human Genes *(1994). Allan C. Wilson (who died in 1992) was an evolutionary biologist at the University of California at Berkeley. C. R. Cantor, R. M. Cook-Deegan, and Mary-Claire King (a geneticist and a political activist who has defended human rights in El Salvador and Argentina) also teach at Berkeley. Cook-Deegan conducts research at the National Institute of Medicine, National Academy of Sciences in Washington, D.C. This article first appeared in the November 1991 issue of* Genomics.

Note: *References have been deleted from this reprinting.*

The Human Genome Project can now grasp a vanishing opportunity to preserve the record of our genetic heritage. A major goal of the Human Genome Project is to create biological tools that will permit access to any region of a human genome. One of the more important reasons to do this is to understand human diversity, both normal variation and that responsible for inherited diseases. The genetic diversity of people now living harbors the clues to the evolution of our species, but the gate to preserve these clues is closing rapidly. We call upon geneticists and public and private agencies to collaborate now in collecting sufficient material to record human ethnic and geographic diversity before this possibility is irretrievably lost. 1

Human genomes that exist today have been determined by historical population structure and dynamics. Hence, information from nuclear and mitochondrial genes from present-day populations worldwide can document prehistoric migrations, natural selection, the social structure of populations, and the frequency and types of mutations our species has experienced. The novel perspective of genetics can supplement and strengthen findings from archeology, linguistics, and history. 2

The populations that can tell us the most about our evolutionary past are those that have been isolated for some time, are likely to be linguistically and culturally distinct, and are often surrounded by geographic barriers. Isolated human populations contain much more informative genetic records than more recent, urban ones. Such isolated human populations are being rapidly merged with their neighbors, however, destroying irrevocably the information needed to construct our evolutionary history. Population growth, famine, war, and improvements in transportation and communication are encroaching on once stable populations. It would be tragically ironic if, during the same decade that biological tools for understanding our species were created, major opportunities for applying them were squandered. 3

We must act now to preserve our common heritage. Preserving this historic record will entail a systematic, international effort to select populations of special interest throughout the world, to obtain samples, to analyze 4

DNA with current technologies, and to preserve samples for analysis in the future. Recent advances in techniques for establishing permanent cell lines and for obtaining DNA by amplification of very small samples of blood, hair, or other tissue make a collection program feasible. Cell lines have already been established for 20 to 80 individuals from each of 13 populations from all parts of the world.

Logistical obstacles to collecting representative samples from the 5
world are daunting, but could be surmounted with sufficient planning and financial commitment. The most expensive portion of the project will be sample collection, processing, and long-term storage. Because the populations of greatest interest are far from airports and modern laboratories, regional facilities to process samples will be necessary. This problem could be solved by providing equipment and training to centers in appropriate locales. The final collection of samples could be distributed among facilities such as the Cornell Institute in the United States, the UN-IDO-supported biotechnology research centers in New Delhi and Trieste, and designated facilities in Latin America and the Middle East. The need for dedicated storage facilities is already apparent.

Once collected, DNA from cell nuclei and from mitochondria can be 6
analyzed to illuminate variation, selection, population structure, migration, mutation frequency, mechanisms of mutation, and other genetic events of our past. These processes can be examined quite inexpensively by determining the genotype of each individual at perhaps 100 loci selected for different mutation rates.

A complete survey would be worldwide and geographically compre- 7
hensive. Among indigenous populations of great interest are peoples of the Sahara, of eastern, western, and southern Africa, the Etas of Japan, insular populations in Malaysia and southeastern Asia; ethnic minorities of China, Polynesians, aboriginal populations of Australia and Melanesia, the Kurds of eastern Turkey, peoples of the Caucasus, the Lapps, the Basques, other peoples in the Pyrenees, Appenines, Carpathians, and Alps, and the many indigenous American populations. Among these very informative groups have been many peoples historically vulnerable to exploitation by outsiders. Hence, asking for samples alone, without consideration of a population's needs for medical treatment and other benefits, will inevitably lead to the same sense of exploitation and abandonment experienced by the survivors of Hiroshima and Nagasaki. It will be essential to integrate the study of peoples with response to their related needs.

We call for a concerted effort to obtain and store samples from diverse 8
populations in order to understand human variation. We urge national funding agencies to gaze favorably on proposals to collect and preserve DNA samples from human populations worldwide. In the United States, the relevant agencies include the National Institute of General Medical Sciences, the National Center for Human Genome Research, the National Science Foundation, and the genome program at the Department of Energy. Medical and biological research funding agencies in other countries can also as-

sist in the effort. We urge that international organizations such as UNESCO, WHO, and UNIDO (UMDO) consider supporting such efforts and that the Human Genome Organization (HUGO) assist in promoting and coordinating a worldwide program. HUGO has asked us to prepare a proposal for a worldwide genetic survey. We hope colleagues interested in joining the effort will be in touch with us. The potential medical gains from the Human Genome Project are immense, and the benefits these will bring are enormous. The potential intellectual benefits of understanding human diversity and its origins are equally striking. By an intense scrutiny of human diversity, we will make enormous leaps in our grasp of human origins, evolution, prehistory, and potential.

▲ ▲ ▲

Review Questions

1. What is the main rationale of the Human Genome Diversity Project, according to its authors?
2. Why does the Human Genome Diversity Project need to focus on peoples who have been relatively isolated from modern life? Why is it essential to proceed with the project as soon as possible?
3. What kind of steps does the project involve?

Discussion and Writing Suggestions

1. To what extent does the authors' proposal seem to you worthwhile, worthy of support? To what extent do you detect possible ethical problems in the conception of the project?
2. This passage is short but was extremely effective in garnering support for the project it proposes. Examine the authors' argument closely, analyzing the way it has been designed to elicit a favorable response. How have the authors laid the foundation for their appeal? How has the appeal been presented? How have possible objections been answered in advance? How do the opening and closing work to enhance the appeal of the proposal?

End of the Rainbow

JO ANN C. GUTIN

As indicated in the headnote to the preceding selection, the open letter by Cavalli-Sforza and his colleagues calling for a Human Genome Diversity Project met with a favorable initial response from the scientific community but ran into problems later. The nature of those problems is discussed in the following article by Jo Ann C. Gutin, which originally appeared in the November 1994 issue of Discover, *a popular magazine covering science issues. As you read it you might consider how the kind of objections leveled at the Human Genome Diversity project correlates with the kind of concerns about the Human Genome Project expressed by Diane Paul, Anne Fausto-Sterling, and Marsha Saxton in "The Politics of Genetics."*

When Henry Greely is perplexed or troubled, his body English tells you as clearly as his words: the Stanford law professor and bioethicist leans back in his chair, stares into the middle distance, and slowly, absently tousles his own hair. 1

In his modest office this morning he's discussing the challenges of his two-year stint as one of the bioethicists on the organizing committee of the North American arm of the Human Genome Diversity Project. ("Has it only been since '92?" he wonders aloud. "It feels longer.") After two and a half hours spent grappling with variations on a single theme—"Why are some people so mad about the Human Genome Diversity Project?"—Greely's hair is decidedly the worse for wear. 2

That it should upset people seems curious. On paper, which is really the only place it exists so far, the project appears to be a singularly uncontroversial idea. It is merely a call for a coordinated effort by scientists on every continent to record the dwindling regional genetic diversity of *Homo sapiens* by taking DNA samples from several hundred distinct human populations and storing the samples in gene banks. Researchers could then examine the DNA for clues to the evolutionary histories of the populations and to their resistance or susceptibility to particular diseases. 3

Yet today the architects of the three-year-old program—a group of geneticists and anthropologists with irreproachable academic and political credentials—stand accused of being neocolonialists, gene pirates, and pawns in a conspiracy to develop race-specific biological weapons. The atmosphere surrounding the work is thick with suspicion: Greely recently heard one rumor about a medical researcher whose ongoing study in the Caribbean was abruptly shut down by charges that he would use his subjects' blood samples to clone a race of slaves. "Obviously *Jurassic Park* didn't help us," Greely says, managing a wan smile. 4

Clearly, though, reaction to the diversity project far exceeds mere blockbuster-induced paranoia about the perils of genetic engineering. University professors and indigenous peoples alike are voicing objections, and while the academic critique tends to be less vivid than what appears in the popular press, racism is the shared subtext. Is the Human Genome Diversity Project scientific colonialism, using the genes of Third World people to answer obscure academic questions or—worse—provide expensive medical cures for the privileged citizens of the developed world? Might it backfire and inadvertently supply more fodder for ethnic battles, as if any more fodder were needed? Or are its organizers merely victims of bad timing? Are the 1990s an impossible moment in human history to launch a project touching two of the rawest nerves in the culture: genes and race? 5

The Human Genome Diversity Project began innocently enough in 1991 with an impassioned open letter to the readers of the journal *Ge-* 6 *nomics* by a number of prominent researchers, among them the geneticist Luigi Luca Cavalli-Sforza of Stanford and Mary-Claire King and Allan Wilson of the University of California at Berkeley. The genus *Homo,* argued the letter's authors, has reached a critical juncture: indigenous peoples are being absorbed into the larger gene pool at an escalating rate, and if the information contained in their DNA is not collected quickly, it may be lost to humankind forever. "The genetic diversity of people now living harbors the clues to the evolution of our species," they wrote, "but the gate to preserve these clues is closing rapidly." They urged members of the Human Genome Organization—an international consortium of scientists who are interested in human genetics—to "grasp a vanishing opportunity to preserve a record of our genetic heritage."

Their plea was heard not only by the nonprofit Human Genome Organization but by funding agencies that included the National Institutes of Health, the Department of Energy, and the National Science Foundation; all gave the letter's authors seed money, charging them with devising a way to collect a wider range of DNA. 7

Backers of the project saw it as a necessry adjunct to the much larger and better-funded Human Genome Project. The Human Genome Project often gets billed as the effort to map and sequence *the* set of human genes, but as Diversity Project organizers gently point out, that isn't quite accurate. Molecular anthropologist Ken Weiss, head of the North American Diversity Project committee, notes that the literal human genome is "the whole ball of wax," the sum of 5 billion people's DNA. What Human Genome Project researchers are actually analyzing is a sort of composite genome: 23 chromosome pairs donated by a mere handful of U.S. and European scientists. (As one wag observed, when they're finally mapped, those chromosomes will tell researchers everything there is to know "about one French farmer and a lady from Philadelphia.") And even *that* will take about 15 years and cost some $3 billion. 8

That's where the Human Genome Diversity Project would come in—it would supplement, particularize, and colorize the chromosome maps drawn by the Human Genome Project. As Weiss observes, "If we don't go ahead with this, then in ten years when the Human Genome Project is done, a Navajo, say, will look at those results and ask, 'Why did they bother? How well does that represent *me?*'" 9

From the outset, all the scientists involved called for sensitivity toward the sampled populations. These groups would include "historically vulnerable" people, warned the original *Genomics* letter, and using them merely as research subjects would inevitably lead to a "sense of exploitation and abandonment." 10

Yet the critiques began almost immediately. "The Human Genome Diversity ('Vampire') Project," reads a communiqué from the Central Australian Aboriginal Congress, "is legalized theft." "Your process," says a letter to the National Science Foundation from Chief Leon Shenandoah of the 11

Onondaga Council of Chiefs, "is unethical, invasive, and may even be criminal. It violates the group rights and human rights of . . . indigenous peoples around the world."

The project's friends are perplexed by the commotion, believing that aside from its giant scale, the work doesn't constitute anything fundamentally new. Researchers have been collecting biological materials from indigenous groups for years; the Diversity Project is merely a way to organize that collection. Far from being a high-tech threat, say its backers, the project will do a better job of safeguarding subjects' rights and will generate better science than the scattershot data collection that preceded it. 12

As the guidelines stand today, anthropologists and geneticists around the world will be asked to gather blood samples from the groups they routinely study; the groups will participate in the Human Genome Diversity Project only if they want to. In addition, all the researchers will adhere to strict and uniform standards of informed consent; the property rights of donor populations to their DNA will be protected; and the material will be stored in a gene library accessible to all qualified researchers rather than disappearing into a refrigerator in one scientist's lab. The establishment of cell lines that will survive for 20 to 25 years—an expensive process—will guarantee that scientists into the next century will be able to ask questions of the genes that no one has yet thought of. 13

Why is the project necessary? After all, all humans, no matter what their ancestry, share most of their DNA. As Mary-Claire King is fond of saying, "We are all different, yet we are all the same." Every human carries about 6 billion base pairs—the chemical rungs of the DNA ladder—in the nuclei of his or her cells. Our personal DNA code differs from that of a random stranger by two rungs for every thousand, or .2 percent of the whole. The differences are smaller between family members and larger between people whose ancestors are unlikely to have intermingled in recent history. Still, a random sample of people in any small group from any location in the world—from rural Sweden to the Ituri Forest to Tierra del Fuego—will turn up 85 percent of all the genetic variation our species contain. 14

Nevertheless, the remaining 15 percent of human genetic variation isn't distributed randomly. It has a geographic pattern, which stems from past population movements and matings. Interestingly, the larger part of that 15 percent difference is not racial: almost 9 percent is reflected in differences among ethnic and linguistic groups within any given race. Only 6 percent represents genetic differences between races. 15

These kinds of patterns interest anthropologists and geneticists. The interest isn't merely historical: some of the variation finds expression in physical differences that intrigue medical researchers. The Navajo, for example, have very high rates of high blood pressure, some of which may be genetic in origin. Genetic research without Navajo samples won't illuminate that problem. African Americans, as another example, experience high failure rates in organ transplants, partly because donors and recipients, 16 even if both are of African origin, may have geographically different ancestries. If geneticists understood DNA variation on the African continent, tissue matching could be done more efficiently.

But—and this is the message that Diversity Project proponents repeat like a mantra—the patterns of variation that appear at the genetic level cut across visible racial divisions. Moving from the physical traits that scientists call phenotype—things like skin color and hair type—to the genetic level is like moving closer and closer to a pointillist painting. Twenty feet from Seurat's *La Grande Jatte,* for instance, you see Parisians and their dogs, but at two feet the image dissolves into dabs of pigment that might belong to a Parisian, a dog, or a tree. It's the same way with the human phenotype and the human genotype. "The closer in you go from what you see on the surface," notes Diversity Project planner Marc Feldman of Stanford, "the more unity there is." 17

This genetic unity means, for instance, that white Americans, though ostensibly far removed from black Americans in phenotype, can sometimes be better tissue matches for them than are *other* black Americans. "After the Diversity Project," predicts planning-committee member Georgia Dunston of Howard University, "we won't have the luxury of drawing distinctions between one another based on skin pigmentation anymore." 18

That day, however, may be a long time coming, judging from the initial criticism of the project. Perhaps what's most ironic about such criticism is that the scientists most involved in the project have established track records in human rights. As Feldman observes, "All of us have worked throughout our lives in an antiracist framework. Our political credentials are in order." 19

Charter member and 1960s activist Mary-Claire King, for instance, was putting her genetic expertise on the political line long before the Diversity Project was proposed: in Argentina she used DNA analysis to help reunite the kidnapped children of "disappeared" political prisoners with their grandmothers. In El Salvador she's been helping UN workers identify the remains of the 794 villagers of El Mozote, who were massacred by the American-trained military in 1981. 20

Throughout the 1970s, three-year project veteran Feldman publicly took on Nobel Prize–winning physicist William Shockley, who argued that whites are intellectually superior to blacks, debating him at the podium and in the press. Feldman currently heads the Morrison Institute for Population and Resource Studies at Stanford, which trains scientists and government officials from the developing world in ecology, population biology, and demographics. 21

And then there's Luca Cavalli-Sforza. It's Cavalli-Sforza, professor emeritus of genetics at the Stanford medical school, who remains both the project's biggest booster and the biggest target for the flak it takes. "Any sensible person can see this is important research," he says with characteristic aplomb. "But I must tell you, I was completely unprepared for the negative reactions we have encountered." 22

Straight-backed, silver-haired, and courtly—he registers somewhere between Marcello Mastroianni and David Niven on the charm meter—Cavalli-Sforza comes by his confidence honestly. A member of the Royal Society and the National Academy of Sciences, a recipient of the Huxley Medal for Biology and the Order of Merit of the Italian Republic, the 72-year-old Cavalli-Sforza is widely regarded as one of the world's leading geneticists. Though he has worked in the United States for most of his adult life, he remains an Italian in everything from his citizenship to his accent to his style of dress, which by American scientific standards is extraordinarily debonair. 23

Cavalli-Sforza has spent his entire career decoding the genetic clues to our hidden past, and he recently summed up his life's work in a 1,032-page magnum opus called *The History and Geography of Human Genes.* In the preface, he and coauthors Paolo Menozzi and Alberto Piazza note that written history, linguistics, and archeology are flawed tools for reconstructing the history of human evolution: "Only genes . . . have the degree of permanence necessary," they say, for discussing *Homo sapiens'* 100,000 years of "fissions, fusions, and migrations of populations." 24

Yet if Cavalli-Sforza is a man entranced by genes and the evolutionary patterns they reveal, he is acutely aware of how genetic information can be willfully misused, particularly when mixed with notions of race. "I get hate mail from neo-Nazi groups all the time," he says, gesturing at the pile in his office that awaited him on his return from a six-month sabbatical in Italy. 25

Cavalli-Sforza considers visible racial traits mere physiological frosting, functional adaptations of an organism to its environment, but his correspondents don't agree. "To say that race doesn't exist is a lie. And only an idiot would believe it," reads one laboriously handwritten example, which attributes Cavalli-Sforza's intellectual stance to a degenerative mental disease. Others are nastier, even frightening; all are anonymous. He shrugs dismissively, immune after years of attacks. "People like this never sign their names." 26

The criticism that's harder to shrug off, however, comes from more respectable quarters, including some members of the scientific community, for "crimes" ranging from colonialism to outright racism. Some anthropologists suggest that Cavalli-Sforza got off on the wrong foot in 1991 by referring to African "tribes" but European "ethnic groups" before a large audience of anthropologists whose support for the project he was trying to enlist. "That's when he lost us," says one critic, who implies that the choice of words revealed a disturbing glimpse of a colonial mentality at the highest level of the project. 27

Ken Weiss heatedly rejects this interpretation. As for raising awareness of indigenous peoples, "I would say categorically that Luca has done more than anyone in the history of the species." He has his own explanation for the negative reaction to the project among some of his colleagues. "Many anthropologists," he contends, "are lamentably ignorant about genetics." And that ignorance breeds unwarranted suspicion, he thinks. "Laypeople sometimes have this idea that there's a black gene or a white gene, or a 28 gene for criminal behavior. And there are a lot of anthropologists who don't know much more than that. If some anthropologists are worried that the project might be used for racist purposes, then maybe that's because deep down they really believe that there is a gene for race, and they are afraid to find it. But I'm not afraid of that, because I know a race gene doesn't exist. And that's what the project will show."

It seems clear that the high-profile Diversity Project has brought a long-simmering anthropological unease with genetics to a rolling boil. In particular, cultural anthropologists fear that the Human Genome Diversity Project gives intellectual legitimacy and—at a hoped-for $5 million a year for five years—a financial leg up to an approach they think shortchanges human complexity. Not surprisingly, they argue that it's more important to study and preserve the world's cultures than its genes. Greely, who has a long-standing amateur interest in anthropology, first became aware of this strain at a project-related meeting in Mount Kisco, New York, in 1993. "It was sort of like going out with somebody and being invited to Christmas dinner at her parents' house, with all of the family there," he recalls. "And suddenly they're reliving old arguments—what Uncle Joe said to so-and-so 20 years ago—and you don't have the foggiest idea what's going on. Fascinating, but I had the sense of being an outsider at a family fight." 29

Cavalli-Sforza attributes this family fight to a fundamental misunderstanding of how science itself works. "Some people say we should take a more *holistic* approach," he says, using quasi-audible italics to convey just how naive an idea this is. "What they don't see is that any science involves initial reductionism. You must simplify first, so you can get a handle on the problem." In an aside not calculated to win converts, he adds, "I don't think cultural anthropologists are scientists at all—more philosophers or social critics." 30

But cultural anthropologists are not the only ones taking serious issue with the Diversity Project. Biological anthropologist Jonathan Marks of Yale thinks its potential for answering evolutionary questions is being oversold. "You don't need molecular genetics to tell you that Danes are more closely related to Swedes than they are to Iroquois—just look at a map!" he says. "And it's not going to be able to tell you whether they're more closely related to Austrians than to Swiss, because at that level we're *all* mutts. This is 1990s genetics applied to questions anthropologists stopped asking in the 1940s." 31

Yet even the harshest scientific critics stop short of accusing project members of anything worse than naïveté ("a grand naïveté," Marks amends). "I think what you have here," says anthropologist Jason Clay, "is a bunch of honor roll scientists who are in way over their heads." 32

Clay, who founded and edited a journal focusing on the problems of indigenous peoples, supports the Diversity Project in theory. "You can't be afraid of information," he says. Yet as the head of Rights and Resources, an organization that brings together Third World agriculturists and "green" businesses like Ben & Jerry's and the Body Shop, he wonders about the details. Judging from his own experience with indigenous peoples, Clay says, 33 well-intentioned explanations of why researchers want individuals' DNA will be useless. "Some of these groups don't know about germs, much less about genes or property rights," he explains. "What could 'informed consent' possibly mean to them?"

He also worries about the uses to which the samples might be put. In 34
the past, botanicals taken from Third World countries have been used to develop new pharmaceuticals that are then sold back to their countries of origin at a profit. What if the Diversity Project were to uncover a gene that confers resistance to, say, an environmental toxin? "Indigenous peoples have been mined for their resources by big companies, and mined for their ideas by anthropologists," he says. "Now they are being mined for their molecules?"

Jon Marks concurs. "Just imagine how it seems to indigenes," he says. 35
"'We've taken your land, we've eradicated your life-ways, we've killed your people, but—guess what?—we're going to save your cells.'"

In response to these criticisms, Feldman simply sighs. "Look, if the 36
Malaysian government is going to allow the Negrito population to be eliminated by selling their land to the Japanese timber companies," he replies wearily, "there's not much the Genome Diversity Project can do about that. We're scientists, not politicians."

Still, however acrimonious it got, the debate about the Diversity Pro- 37
ject was confined mostly to the laboratory, the seminar room and the faculty lounge until 1992. That's when the Rural Advancement Foundation International got into the act. RAFI, an advocacy group concerned with issues of biodiversity and intellectual property, has for a decade been sounding the alarm over what it considers to be biopiracy: the theft of intellectual property rights of indigenous peoples. And it doesn't see the Diversity Project as an exception. "I think they're very naive with regard to the commercialization of cell lines," says Hope Shand, the research director of RAFI-USA. "If the cells are in repositories that are open to everyone, what's to prevent somebody from patenting them?"

According to RAFI's point of view, First World agribusiness has made a 38
fortune from plant strains developed by Third World agriculturists, without funneling any of the profits back to the original owners. The fledgling Diversity Project, RAFI believes, could easily become a vehicle for similar abuses—not so much by project scientists as by outside researchers who might well be less scrupulous in their use of the sampled DNA. "There is nothing in international law," notes RAFI member Jean Christie, "that assures us those abuses won't take place."

RAFI workers have told indigenous leaders of their suspicions, button- 39
holed delegates at conventions, and E-mailed activist groups worldwide. Partly as a result of this lobbying, the European Green party, joined by the World Council of Indigenous Peoples and the Guaymi General Congress, has called for suspension of the Human Genome Diversity Project.

All this troubles Hank Greely very deeply; he sees the intellectual 40
property issue as a misplaced concern. "There's no reason the project and RAFI should be enemies," he says. "There's no commercial money in the

project, no pharmaceutical-industry backing. This is pure science." He concedes that the patent question is a knotty one but insists "we're happy to do what's right. It's just not clear, yet, exactly what's the best way to do that."

While the patent question may eventually yield to time, legislation, and good intentions, it may take more heroic measures to counter the darkest charge leveled against the project: genocide. "Unscrupulous parties," warns a RAFI newsletter, could "devise cheap and targeted biological weapons," effective against specific races, by using data collected by the researchers. The Diversity Project, in RAFI's view, makes the specter of genocide a biotechnological reality. 41

This claim is the one that sends project scientists around the bend. "If people understood human genetics," snaps Feldman, "they'd know it can't be done." 42

"It's ludicrous," says University of Florida anthropologist and project committee member John Moore, "to suggest that we could be indifferent to the destruction of what most interests us." 43

"This is the most incredible rubbish, this DNA-poison idea," says Cavalli-Sforza. "It is part of a hate campaign waged against us." 44

But RAFI won't back down from its claims. "We're not scientists," says Christie, "but we've done research on biological warfare. People say our protests are naive, radical, or ill-conceived, but they're not." 45

Predictably, Hank Greely has a more measured response to even this dire accusation. "Governments *have* engaged in biological warfare," he says, recalling that in the nineteenth century the United States gave blankets impregnated with smallpox virus to Native Americans. "Indigenous people are right to be skeptical when people from the developed world come to them saying they want to help. It's a kind of survival trait—groups that didn't have it are probably gone now." 46

Greely doesn't for a moment think these fears are warranted vis-à-vis the Diversity Project, but in his view that's not the point. "If people are worried," he says, in what amounts to the ethicist's credo, "you have to deal with their fears, whether or not they have any basis." 47

It appears that his credo will guide the future progress of the Diversity Project. Feldman admits that they've made some mistakes—"You could call it arrogance," he says; "we sort of took it for granted that everyone would see this was a great project"—but he's certain they're on the right track at last. The McArthur Foundation has awarded the North American committee a grant to develop an ethics program, and project leaders will be holding international meetings for groups whose cooperation is being sought—meetings to explain the project as well as to answer questions about it. Feldman describes the first few such meetings, held in the spring of 1994, as "frank and good." Jon Marks applauds the trend. "Look, I think the project is a great idea; you can never have enough scientific data. The collection just has to be done right. It has to be done respectfully." 48

And Cavalli-Sforza, father of Diversity Project, is heartened by the progress he's been seeing. The Chinese have established a Diversity Project committee, he reports, and collection has started in the British Isles, 49 where the people of Cornwall have begun giving DNA samples. "We are still working on the ethics here," he says, "but that's very important. There cannot be any misunderstanding. We need to be—is the word *fireproof?* No—*bulletproof.* We need to be bulletproof."

Review Questions

1. What is the essential nature of the controversy over the Human Genome Diversity Project?
2. Summarize the difference between the Human Genome Project and the Human Genome Diversity Project.
3. How do defenders of the Human Genome Diversity Project respond to the main charges leveled against them?
4. Summarize the concerns of RAFI (Rural Foundation Advancement International) about the Human Genome Diversity Project.

Discussion and Writing Suggestions

1. What is the significance of the title of this article, "End of the Rainbow"? Do you think the title appropriate?
2. Having read both the open letter by Cavalli-Sforza and his colleagues (preceding selection) and the present article, what is your reaction to the charges made against the Human Genome Diversity Project—particularly charges that the project is "unethical" and "invasive" and that it "violates the group rights and human rights of . . . indigenous peoples around the world"? Base your reaction on more than just your own personal opinion; provide support from additional sources that you have read or from your own observations.
3. Why do you think that Cavalli-Sforza's use of the word "tribes" when addressing the audience of anthropologists (paragraph 27) met with such a hostile reception? Do you agree that the negative reaction was justified?
4. To what extent do you find a correlation between the kind of concerns about genetics expressed by Diane Paul and Marsha Saxton in "The Politics of Genetics" and the kind of charges made against the Human Genome Diversity Project? What are the common fears?
5. To what extent do you find evidence that the author of this article, Jo Ann Gutin, favors one side of the controversy over the other? Based on how she presents her article, what she chooses to emphasize, and her overall tone, do you see a bias on one side or the other? Explain.

When Science Takes the Witness Stand

PETER J. NEUFELD
NEVILLE COLMAN

Former football (and movie) star O.J. Simpson has done more than all the geneticists in the country to focus public attention on DNA. In 1994 Simpson was charged with murdering his ex-wife and a male companion. Prosecutors grounded their case largely on DNA evidence: They called upon numerous expert witnesses who testified that genetic matching of blood samples at the murder scene, in Simpson's car, and in his home conclusively proved his guilt. For weeks, both the jury and millions of Americans listened to detailed testimony about how the blood samples were gathered, transported, stored, tested, and retested. For their part, Simpson's defense attorneys argued that the collection and storage procedures were sloppy and that the labs' testing procedures were questionable. [Simpson was acquitted of the charges.] One of those defense attorneys was Peter Neufeld, co-author of the following article, which—we must emphasize—was written four years before *the Simpson case. But in their article, Neufeld and co-author Neville Colman lay out in general terms some of the more specific arguments that were made about the DNA procedures in the Simpson case.*

"When Science Takes the Witness Stand," then, is not about the Simpson case, but about the more general issues raised by the use of DNA testing in courts of law—that is, its use for forensic (as opposed to clinical or research) purposes. If each human being does have a unique DNA "fingerprint," then DNA could prove to be—indeed has proved to be—a powerful tool not only in helping to convict the guilty, but also to exonerate the innocent. But the supposed certainty of DNA evidence is here called into question by Neufeld and Colman. As you read it, withhold final judgment on their *case until you read the next article, "DNA in Court," by William Tucker. (For additional perspective on Neufeld's association with the Simpson case, see "On the Defensive," by T.J. English, in* New York, *January 2, 1995.)*

Neufeld and Colman collaborated for several years on the problem of admitting new scientific evidence into criminal cases and have lectured on the subject to both defense attorneys and prosecutors. Neufeld, an attorney specializing in criminal defense and civil-rights litigation, was co-counsel of People v. Castro, *in which DNA evidence was first successfully challenged. He is a member of the New York State Governor's panel on forensic analysis. Neufeld received his J.D. in 1975 from the New York University School of Law and is adjunct professor at the Fordham University School of Law. Colman is director of the Center for Clinical Laboratories at Mount Sinai Medical Center in New York City. He received his M.D. in 1969 and his Ph.D. in 1974 from the University of the Witwa-*

tersrand, Johannesburg. He has advised counsel and testified in legal proceedings involving the admissability of scientific evidence. This article first appeared in Scientific American, *May 1990.*

A reader advisory: *You may find parts of this article difficult because it assumes a level of scientific knowledge that many readers (and juries!) do not possess. Don't worry about passages you don't understand: as long as you keep focused on the main lines of Neufeld and Colman's argument, you'll get what the authors want you to get from their article. In fact, most sections of the piece should give you no problem at all; but you may wish to skim or just skip over the following groups of paragraphs, which are more technical: 19–23, 28–31, 38–46.*

In the early evening of November 21, 1974, powerful bombs ripped through two pubs in the industrial city of Birmingham, England, leaving 21 dead and 162 injured. The government immediately blamed the Irish Republican Army for the attacks and mounted a massive search for the perpetrators. After a railroad clerk reported that six Irishmen had boarded a train in Birmingham minutes before the first bomb blast, police intercepted the men as they disembarked at the port of Heysham. The six men were taken to the police station, and there, their hands were swabbed with chemicals that would reveal the presence of any nitrites, which would be consistent with the recent handling of explosives. The forensic scientist who performed this procedure, known as the Greiss test, reported positive findings on the right hands of two of the six suspects. That evidence became the linchpin of the government's successful prosecution of the "Birmingham Six." 1

Now, 16 years later, the six men may be released. The Greiss test, on which their convictions had been largely based, has proved unreliable. It turns out that a variety of common substances such as old playing cards, cigarette packages, lacquer and aerosol spray will, along with explosives, yield a positive result. As it happened, the six men had spent most of their train ride to Heysham playing cards and smoking cigarettes. 2

The Birmingham case raises troubling issues about the application of forensic technology to criminal investigations. Since the discovery of fingerprinting at the turn of the century, science has assumed an increasingly powerful role in the execution of justice. Indeed, scientific testimony is often the deciding factor for the judicial resolution of civil and criminal cases. The scientific analysis of fingerprints, blood, semen, shreds of clothing, hair, weapons, tire treads and other physical evidence left at the scene of a crime can seem more compelling to a jury than the testimony of eyewitnesses. As one juror put it after a recent trial in Queens, N.Y., "You can't argue with science." 3

Scientists generally welcome this trend. Because the scientific community polices scientific research, subjecting new theories and findings to peer review and independent verification, it is often assumed the same standards prevail when science is applied to the fact-finding process in a judicial trial. 4

But in reality such controls are absent in a court of law. Instead nonscientists—lawyers, judges and jurors—are called on to evaluate critically the competence of a scientific witness. Frequently lawyers are oblivious of potential flaws in a scientific method or argument and so fail to challenge it. At other times, the adversaries in a case will present opposing expert opinions, leaving it up to a jury of laypersons to decide the merits of the scientific arguments.

The disjunction between scientific and judicial standards of evidence 5
has allowed novel forensic methods to be used in criminal trials prematurely or without verification. The problem has become painfully apparent in the case of forensic DNA profiling, a recent technique that in theory can identify an individual from his or her DNA with a high degree of certainty. Although many aspects of forensic DNA identification have not been adequately examined by the scientific community, police and prosecutors have carried out DNA analysis in more than 1,000 criminal investigations in the U.S. since 1987. Few of these cases reached trial. In most instances defendants pleaded guilty on advice of counsel after a presumably infallible DNA test declared a match.

Several recent cases have raised serious reservations about the claims 6
made for DNA evidence. Last spring, during a pretrial hearing at *People v. Castro* in New York City, Michael L. Baird of Lifecodes Corporation of Valhalla, N.Y., one of the two major commercial forensic DNA laboratories in the U.S., reported the odds of a random match between a bloodstain and the suspect at one in 100 million. Eric S. Lander of Harvard University and the Massachusetts Institute of Technology examined the same data and arrived at odds of one in 24. Ultimately, several proponents of DNA testing denounced Lifecodes' data in the case as scientifically unreliable. Some of Lifecodes' key methods were repudiated, casting doubt on the integrity of hundreds of earlier criminal convictions. The ongoing debate over DNA testing underscores the need to deal more effectively with the difficulties that arise whenever complex scientific technology is introduced as evidence in a court of law.

A trial is ideally a search for truth. To help juries in their quest, the law 7
allows qualified experts to testify and express opinions on matters in which they are professionally trained. Yet the esoteric nature of an expert's opinions, together with the jargon and the expert's scholarly credentials, may cast an aura of infallibility over his or her testimony. Hence, to prevent juries from being influenced by questionable evidence or expert testimony, U.S. courts usually review the material in a pretrial hearing or outside the presence of the jury.

To be admitted as evidence, a forensic test should, as a matter of com- 8
mon sense, satisfy three criteria: the underlying scientific theory must be considered valid by the scientific community; the technique itself must be known to be reliable; and the technique must be shown to have been properly applied in the particular case.

The expression of common sense in a court of law, however, is at times elusive. A majority of U.S. courts decide on the admissibility of scientific evidence based on guidelines established in 1923 by *Frye v. U.S.,* in which the Court of Appeals for the District of Columbia affirmed a lower court's decision to exclude evidence derived from a precursor of the polygraph. "Just when a scientific principle or discovery crosses the line between the experimental and demonstrable stages is difficut to define," the court declared in *Frye.* "Somewhere in this twilight zone the evidential force of the principle must be recognized, and while courts will go a long way in admitting expert testimony deduced from a well-recognized scientific principle or discovery, the thing from which the deduction is made must be sufficiently established to have gained general acceptance in the particular field in which it belongs." 9

Judges, scientists, lawyers and legal scholars have all criticized the *Frye* standard. Some say it is too vague. Some argue that it is unduly restrictive. Still others complain that it is not restrictive enough. Should "general acceptance," for example, require a consensus or a simple majority of scientists? Also, what is it that must be generally accepted? In the case of DNA profiling, is it the theory that no two individuals, except for identical twins, have the same DNA? Is it the various techniques employed in the test, such as Southern blotting and gel electrophoresis? Or is it the specific application of DNA profiling to dried blood and semen samples recovered from the scene of a crime? 10

Furthermore, what is the appropriate "particular field" in which a technique must be accepted? Does a test for DNA profiling have to be accepted only by forensic serologists, or must it also be recognized by the broader community of human geneticists, hematologists and biochemists? In a recent California case, DNA evidence analyzed by means of the polymerase chain reaction (PCR) was excluded because that method was not generally accepted by forensic scientists. Yet several months earlier a Texas court that was evaluating the identical PCR method looked more broadly to the opinions of molecular biologists and human geneticists and reached the opposite conclusion. 11

For many applications of science to forensics, the underlying theory is well established, and legal debate rages mainly over whether one must prove only that a technique is generally accepted for scientific research or more strictly, that the technique is reliable when applied to forensics. 12

Why the distinction between nonforensic and forensic applications? Scientists commonly accept that when any technology is tried in a different application, such as forensics, it must be tested thoroughly to ensure an empirical understanding of the technique's usefulness and limitations. Indeed, many a technique that has proved reliable for research—polygraphy, for example—has turned out to be of questionable reliability when applied to forensic casework. 13

Clearly, in order for the courts to evaluate forensic evidence, judges and lawyers must be able to appreciate the scientific issues at hand. Regret- 14 tably, lawyers rarely do more than review the qualifications of the expert (typically based on perfunctory queries about institutional affiliation and publications) and verify the facts on which the expert's conclusions are based. The reason for this limited inquiry is simple: most lawyers and judges lack the adequate scientific background to argue or decide the admissibility of expert testimony. Often judges think—mistakenly, in our opinion—that justice is best served by admitting expert testimony into evidence and deferring to the jury for the determination of its weight.

The problem of scientific illiteracy is compounded by the tendency of 15
judges to refuse to reconsider the validity of a particular kind of scientific evidence once it has been accepted by another judge in an earlier case. This practice is founded on the well-recognized need to respect precedent in order to ensure the uniform administration of justice. But in the case of forensic tests, the frequent failure of courts to take a fresh look at the underlying science has been responsible for many a miscarriage of justice.

Perhaps the most notorious example of the problem is the so-called 16
paraffin test (a cousin of the Greiss test employed in the Birmingham Six investigation), which was used by crime laboratories throughout the U.S. to detect nitrite and nitrate residues, presumably from gunpowder, on suspects' hands to show that they had recently fired a gun. The test was first admitted as scientific evidence in a 1936 trial in Pennsylvania. Other states then simply adopted that decision without independently scrutinizing the research.

For the next 25 years innumerable people were convicted with the help 17
of this test. It was not until the mid 1960s that a comprehensive scientific study revealed damning flaws in the paraffin test. In particular, the test gave an unacceptably high number of false positives: substances other than gunpowder that gave a positive reading included urine, tobacco, tobacco ash, fertilizer and colored fingernail polish. In this instance the legal process failed, allowing people accused of crimes to be convicted on evidence that later proved to be worthless.

More recently the debate over scientific courtroom evidence has cen- 18
tered on two applications of biotechnology: protein-marker analysis and DNA identification. Both techniques employ gel electrophoresis to reveal genetic differences, called polymorphisms, in blood proteins and DNA. These two techniques can potentially match blood, semen or other such evidence found at a crime scene to a suspect or victim.

In the late 1960s crime laboratories became interested in protein poly- 19
morphisms in populations. The techniques for studying protein polymorphisms were originally developed as tools for population geneticists and were experimentally tested, published in refereed journals and independently verified. The techniques were then modified by and for law-enforcement personnel in order to cope with problems unique to forensic samples, such as their often limited quantity, their unknown age and the presence of unidentified contaminants. These modifications were rarely published in the scientific literature or validated by independent workers.

For example, molecular geneticists study polymorphic proteins in red 20
blood cells and serum by using fresh, liquid blood and analyzing it under controlled laboratory conditions, all subject to scientific peer review. These techniques were then adapted for use on forensic samples of dried blood by the introduction of various modifications, few of which were subjected to comparable scientific scrutiny. No one ever adequately explored the effects of environmental insults to samples, such as heat, humidity, temperature and light. Neither did anyone verify the claim that forensic samples would not be affected significantly by microbes and unknown substances typically found on streets or in carpets.

One of the major modifications made by forensic laboratories was the 21
"multisystem" test. In the original version of this test, three different polymorphic proteins were identified in a single procedure; the purpose was to derive as much information as possible from a small sample. The three-marker multisystem test was further modified by the addition of a fourth protein marker in 1980 by the New York City Medical Examiner's serology laboratory.

By 1987 evidence derived from the "four-in-one" multisystem had 22
been introduced in several hundred criminal prosecutions in New York State. In that year, however, during a pretrial hearing in *People v. Seda*, the director of the New York City laboratory admitted under cross-examination that only one article had been published about that system—and that the article had recommended the test be used only to screen out obvious mismatches because of a flaw that tended to obscure the results.

In *People v. Seda,* the judge ruled that the four-in-one multisystem did 23
not satisfy the *Frye* standard of general acceptance by the scientific community and so could not be introduced into evidence. Unfortunately, *Seda* was the first case involving the test in which the defense went to the effort of calling witnesses to challenge the technology. Consequently, the integrity of hundreds of earlier convictions stands in doubt.

In the past two years DNA profiling has all but eclipsed protein mark- 24
ers in forensic identification. The technique is based on a method originally developed to study the inheritance of diseases, both to identify the disease-causing genes in families known to harbor an inherited disease and to predict individual susceptibility when the gene is known.

Crime investigators have embraced the new technique because it offers 25
two significant advantages over conventional protein markers. First, DNA typing can be conducted on much smaller and older samples. And second, DNA typing was reported to offer from three to 10 orders of magnitude greater certainty of a match. Promotional literature distributed by Lifecodes asserts that its test "has the power to identify one individual in the world's population." Not to be outdone, Cellmark Diagnostics in Germantown, Md.—Lifecodes' main competitor—claims that with its method, "the chance that any two people will have the same DNA print is one in 30 billion." Yet, as testimony in the *Castro* case showed, such claims can be dubious.

The hype over DNA typing spreads the impression that a DNA profile identifies the "genetic code" unique to an individual and indeed is as unique as a fingerprint. Actually, because 99 percent of the three billion base pairs in human DNA are identical among all individuals, forensic scientists look for ways to isolate the relatively few variable regions. These regions can be cut out of DNA by restriction enzymes and are called restriction fragment length polymorphisms (RFLPs). 26

For DNA identification, one wants RFLPs that are highly polymorphic—that is, those that have the greatest number of variants, or alleles, in the population. It turns out that certain regions of human DNA contain "core" sequences that are repeated in tandem, like freight cars of a train. The number of these repeated sequences tends to vary considerably from person to person; one person might have 13 repeated units at that locus, whereas another might have 29. Special restriction enzymes cut DNA into millions of pieces, including fragments that contain the repeated segments. Because the number of repeated segments varies among individuals, so too does the overall length of these fragments vary. 27

How can these variable fragments be picked out of the haystack of irrelevant DNA segments? The answer lies in "probes" that bind only to fragments containing the core sequence. If the core sequence occurs at only one DNA locus, the probe is called a single-locus probe. If the core sequence occurs at many different loci, the probe is called a multilocus probe. Forensic laboratories currently make use of three different methods of DNA typing: single-locus RFLP, multilocus RFLP and the polymerase chain reaction. Because the single-locus system is the one most widely employed in forensic DNA identification, we will describe it in some detail. [See Figure 1, p. 628.] 28

For forensic DNA identification by single-locus RFLP analysis, DNA from various sources is digested with restriction enzymes, placed in separate lanes on an electrophoretic gel and subjected to an electric field. The field pulls fragments down the lane, with smaller fragments traveling faster than larger ones. The fragments, now sorted by size, are denatured into single strands and transferred from the gel onto a nitrocellulose or nylon membrane, which fixes the fragments in place. (Incidentally, anyone who handles nitrocellulose might test positive on the Greiss test!) 29

At this point, a radioactive probe is applied, which hybridizes, or binds, to the polymorphic fragments. The mesh is then laid on a sheet of X-ray film to produce an autoradiograph. The radioactively labeled fragments are thereby revealed as a series of bands resembling a railroad track with irregularly spaced ties; the position of the bands is a measure of the size of the polymorphic fragments. The probe can be rinsed away, and a new probe can be applied to identify a different set of alleles. 30

The autoradiograph resulting from a single-locus probe will ordinarily show alleles of two distinct sizes, one inherited from each parent; such a pattern indicates that the person is heterozygous for that locus. If the probe reveals only one distinct allele, it is assumed that the person inherited the 31

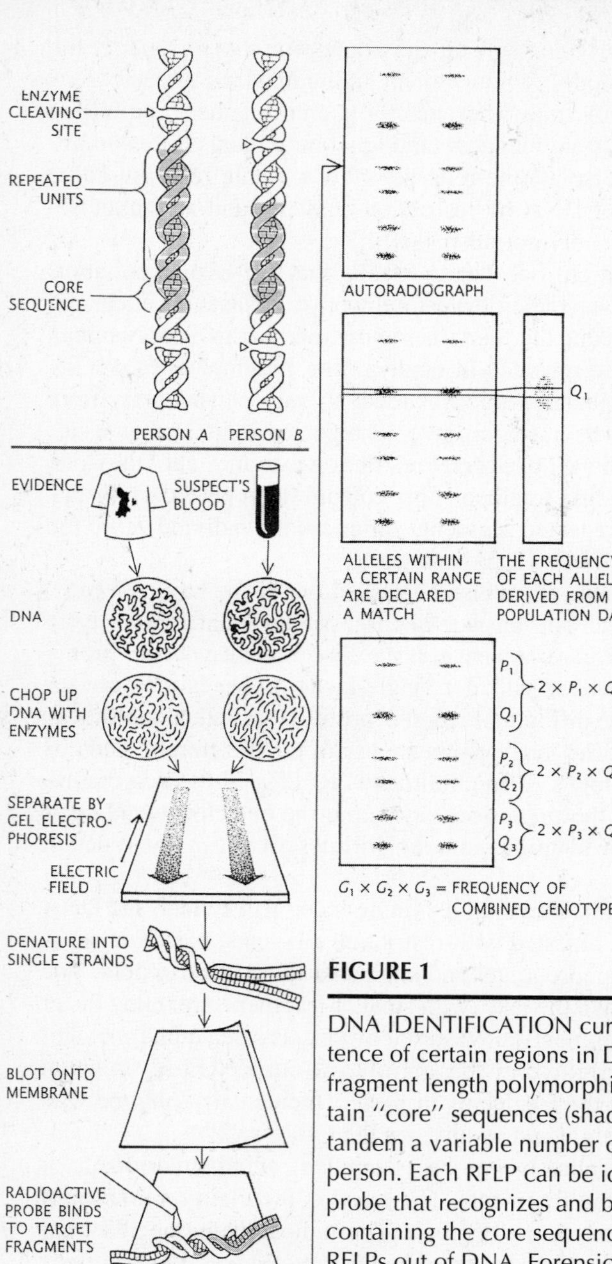

FIGURE 1

DNA IDENTIFICATION currently hinges on the existence of certain regions in DNA, called restriction fragment length polymorphisms (RFLPs), which contain "core" sequences (shading) that are repeated in tandem a variable number of times from person to person. Each RFLP can be identified by a special probe that recognizes and binds to any fragment containing the core sequence. Special enzymes snip RFLPs out of DNA. Forensic casework involves taking DNA extracted from evidence and from, for example, a suspect's blood, breaking it up into RFLPs and separating them by gel electrophoresis. A radioactive probe binds to the RFLPs, whose positions are then recorded as dark bands on X-ray film. If the striped patterns from the evidence and from the suspect appear to match, one then calculates the probability of such a match occurring by chance.

same-size allele from both parents and that the person is homozygous for the locus. Forensic DNA-testing laboratories typically employ several single-locus probes, each of which binds to a different site.

To determine whether two samples of DNA come from a single source, one examines the bands identified by a particular probe on the autoradiograph and decides whether they match. One then refers to data from population-genetics studies to find out how often that particular allele size occurs. A typical allele might be found in 10 percent of the population, making it not all that unlikely that two random people will carry the same allele. But if one looks at alleles at three or four different sites, it becomes increasingly unlikely that two individuals will have the same alleles for all the sites. It is this hypothesis that gives DNA profiling its persuasive power. 32

How well does forensic DNA profiling stand up under the *Frye* standard? Certainly the underlying theory—that no two people, except for identical twins, have the identical DNA—is unquestioned, and so DNA identification is possible in theory. But is that theory being applied to give a reliable forensic test? And if so, is that test being carried out properly? 33

In scientific and medical research, DNA typing is most often employed to trace the inheritance of disease-causing alleles within a family. In this diagnostic application, however, one can assume that one allele was inherited from the mother and the other from the father. Because each parent has only two alleles for that gene, barring a mutation, the pattern observed in the child is limited at most to four possible combinations. In addition, if the results are ambiguous, one can rerun the experiment with fresh blood samples or refer to the alleles of other family members. 34

In forensic DNA typing, however, it is much more difficult to determine whether an allele from one sample is identical to an allele from another. [See Figure 2, p. 630.] In the RFLP systems employed in forensics, the number of alleles can run into the hundreds—in contrast to the four from which one must choose when identifying the alleles of a child whose parents are known. Indeed, forensic RFLP systems produce so many different alleles that they virtually form a continuum. In some RFLPs the most common alleles can be crowded into a quarter-inch span on a 13-inch lane. Gel electrophoresis can resolve only a limited number of alleles, however—perhaps between 30 and 100 depending on the particular RFLP—and so alleles that are similar, but not the same, in size may be declared identical. Hence, it can become difficult indeed to declare with confidence that one band matches another. What is worse, forensic samples are often limited in amount and so cannot be retested if ambiguities arise. 35

These inherent difficulties are further complicated by a problem called band shifting. This phenomenon occurs when DNA fragments migrate at different speeds through separate lanes on a single gel. It has been attributed to a number of factors, involving variables such as the preparation of gels, the concentrations of sample DNA, the amount of salt in the DNA solution and contamination. Band shifting can occur even if the various lanes 36

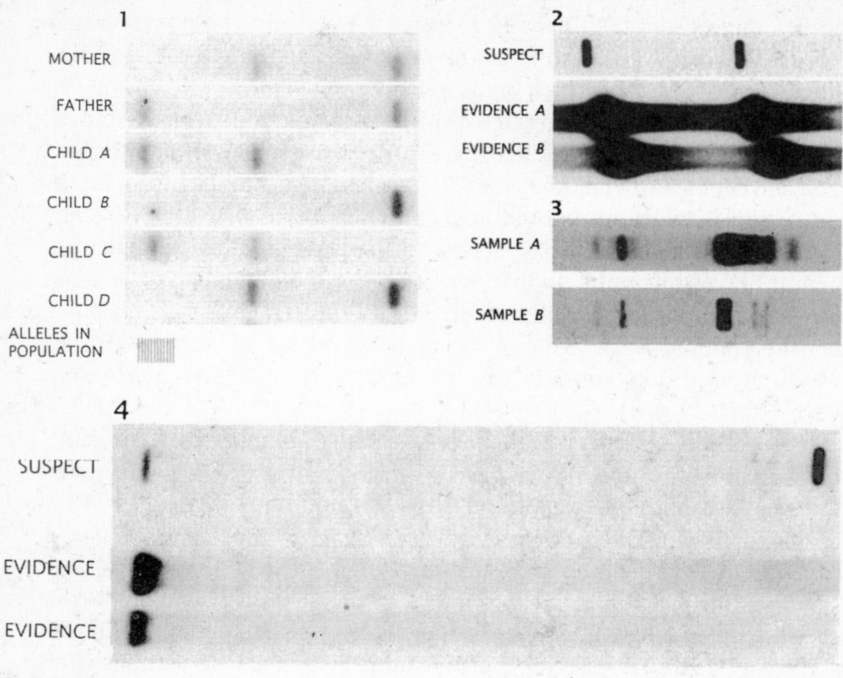

FIGURE 2

FORENSIC DNA TYPING is fraught with uncertainty. If the autoradiographs in group 1 are assumed to be from one family, then the alleles of the children must be derived from the parents, even though one of the bands for child *C* is visibly shifted. But if that same lane were of a person whose parentage is unknown, then the band could correspond to one of the other alleles (*shaded bands*) observed in the population. In group 2, the band patterns from the suspect and from evidence *A* and *B* appear to be displaced relative to one another, which may indicate a band shift. In group 3, sample *A* contains all of the bands from sample *B,* along with extra bands, possibly from contaminants. In group 4, a suspect has two bands, whereas the forensic evidence has only one; the "missing" band may have resulted because degradation of the DNA destroyed the larger fragments. On the other hand, all of these cases could also indicate a real genetic difference.

contain DNA from the same person. Because allele sizes in forensic RFLP systems are closely spaced, it is difficult to know whether the relative positions of bands arise purely from the size of allele fragments or whether band shifting might play a part.

The courts' handling of band shifting is an excellent illustration of the 37
problems that arise when courts, rather than the scientific peer-review process, take on the task of determining whether a method is reliable. Two years ago, when DNA evidence was first introduced in U.S. courtrooms, most forensic DNA scientists rejected the existence of band shifting. But now some experts think band shifting occurs in perhaps 30 percent of forensic DNA tests. There are now many theories about the cause, but as of this writing not one refereed article on the subject has been published.

Forensic DNA laboratories are rushing to develop special probes that bind to monomorphic loci—restriction-enzyme fragments that are the same size in every person—as a possible way to control for band shifting. In theory, if the monomorphic regions are displaced, one would know that band shifting had occurred and could then calculate a correction factor. The difficulty again is that neither this method, nor any other possible solution, has been peer reviewed. 38

Yet in a rape case tried last December in Maine, *State v. McLeod,* the laboratory director who had supervised the DNA tests for the prosecution testified that a correction factor derived from a monomorphic probe allowed him to declare a match between the suspect's blood and the semen recovered from the victim, even though the bands were visibly shifted. When evidence then came to light that a second monomorphic probe indicated a smaller correction factor, which did not account for the disparity between the bands, he acknowledged the monomorphic probes may yield inconsistent correction factors; nevertheless, he argued that the first correction was appropriate to the bands in question. The prosecutor, though, recognized the folly of defending this argument in the absence of published supporting data and withdrew the DNA evidence. In dozens of other cases, however, judges have been persuaded by the same types of arguments, even though there is no body of research to guide the court. As a matter of common sense, the proper place to first address such issues is in scientific journals, not the courtroom. 39

Another major problem that arises in forensic DNA typing is contamination. More often than not, crime-scene specimens are contaminated or degraded. The presence of bacteria, organic material or degradation raises the risk of both false positives and false negatives. For example, contamination can degrade DNA so that the larger fragments are destroyed. In such instances a probe that should yield two bands may yield only one (the smaller band). 40

Research laboratories employ internal controls to avoid the misinterpretation that can result from such artifacts. But such controls may not be suitable for forensic casework. For example, one suggested control for band shifting is to run a mixing experiment: sample *A* is run in lane one, sample *B* in lane two and *A* and *B* in lane three. If both samples are from the same person, then ideally lane three would produce one set of bands, whereas if they are from different people, it would show two sets of bands. Unfortunately, in forensic casework there is often not enough material to run a mixing experiment. What is more, recent unpublished studies indicate that certain contaminants, such as dyes, can bind to DNA and alter its mobility in a gel, so that a mixing experiment using samples from the same person can produce two sets of bands. 41

The power of forensic DNA typing arises from its ability not only to demonstrate that two samples exhibit the same pattern but also to suggest that the pattern is extremely rare. The validity of the data and assumptions on which forensic laboratories have been relying to estimate the rarity are currently being debated within the scientific community. 42

43 There are two particularly important criticisms. First, because it is difficult to discriminate accurately among the dozens of alleles at a particular locus, the task of calculating the frequency with which each allele appears in the population is inherently compromised. Second, the statistical equations for calculating the frequency of a particular pattern of alleles apply only to a population that has resulted from random mating—a condition that is called Hardy-Weinberg equilibrium.

44 If a population is in Hardy-Weinberg equilibrium, one can assume allele types are shuffled at random. The occurrence of one allele is then independent of the occurence of a second allele. One can therefore calculate the frequency of the "genotype," or a particular pair of alleles, for a specific locus by multiplying the frequency of each allele and doubling it (because one has the same probability of inheriting each allele from both parents). The frequency of a genotype for a combination of loci is then obtained simply by multiplying the frequency of the genotype for each individual locus. For example, if the genotypes at loci *A, B, C* and *D* each occur in 10 percent of the population, then the probability that a person would have these genotypes at all four loci is .1 multiplied by itself four times: .0001.

45 Forensic DNA laboratories carry out these calculations based on data they have assembled themselves. Most of the data have not been published in peer-review journals or independently validated. One problem is that none of the major laboratories employs the same RFLP system. And even if the laboratories decide to adopt uniform probes and enzymes, the results may still differ significantly unless they all also adopt identical protocols. Commercial DNA-testing laboratories are reluctant to do so, however, because each considers its RFLP system to be proprietary, and the probes and enzymes are sold or licensed to crime laboratories around the country.

46 Another serious issue is that some populations may not be in equilibrium, in which case neither the alleles nor the various loci may be independent. For such a population, there is as yet no consensus on how to calculate the frequency of a genotype (given the limited data bases of the forensic DNA laboratories). As matters stand, population geneticists are debating whether various racial and ethnic communities exhibit significant population substructures so as to preclude the use of current data bases for the highly polymorphic systems employed in forensic DNA identification. For example, do Hispanics in the U.S. constitute a single mixed population? Or is there nonrandom mating, with Cubans more likely to mate with other Cubans and Chicanos more likely to mate with other Chicanos? Should there be a separate data base on allele frequencies within each of these subpopulations? To find out, population geneticists will need to gather more data. [See Figure 3, p. 633.]

47 More than 1,000 criminal investigations in the U.S. have now involved DNA evidence, but in only a few dozen cases has DNA evidence been challenged in a pretrial hearing. According to our own study of these hearings, until the *Castro* case in New York, not one of these hearings addressed the problems of forensic DNA typing that distinguish it from diag-

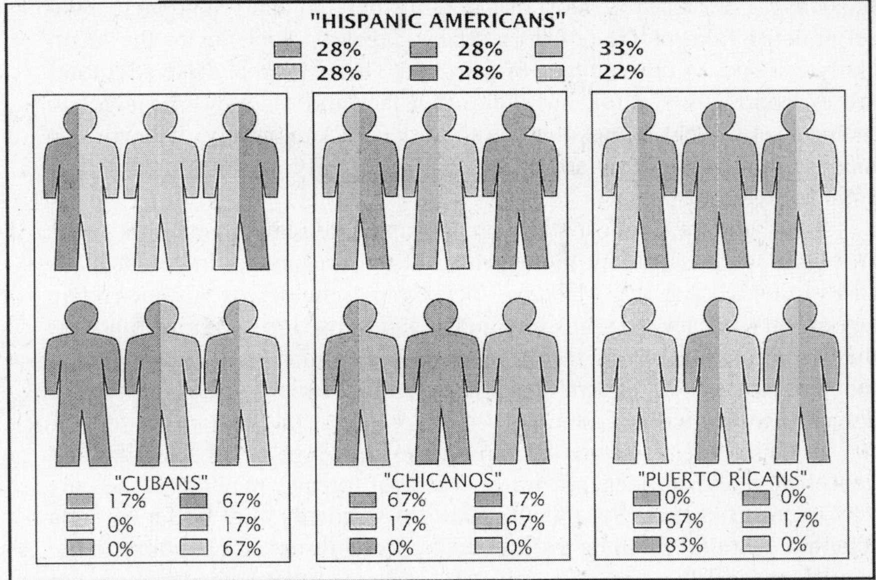

FIGURE 3

POPULATION DATA may not yet be reliable enough to calculate the frequency of a genotype accurately. In the hypothetical Hispanic-American population depicted here, a particular DNA site has six distinct alleles, each represented by its own shade. Heterozygous individuals are shaded to represent the two alleles inherited from the parents; homozygous individuals, who have inherited the same allele from both parents, are shaded in one tone. Allele frequencies for the entire population differ markedly from allele frequencies for the subgroups shown here.

nostic DNA typing. In all but two of the early hearings, defense attorneys failed to obtain the raw population data on which conclusions about allele frequencies were predicated. In the first four appeals-court decisions on DNA evidence, the defense failed to present any expert witnesses during trial, and cross-examination of the prosecution's expert witnesses was at best perfunctory.

Some of this was not for lack of trying. The defense counsel in one case explained that he had asked dozens of molecular biologists to testify but all had refused. Interviews with some of the scientists revealed that most of them, being familiar with scientific research involving DNA typing, assumed the forensic application of the technique would be equally reliable. Some who were aware of possible problems were reluctant to criticize the technology publicly for fear that this would be misconstrued as a general attack on the underlying science. 48

Another troubling fact is that defense attorneys are often not able to spend the time or funds required to deal with the complexities of the issues. Novel scientific evidence is most often used to solve violent crimes, and defendants in such cases come predominantly from the less affluent sectors 49 of society. Consequently, most of them must rely on court-appointed counsel selected from public-defender offices, legal-aid societies or the financially less successful members of the private bar. Many of these advocates are exceptionally skillful, but they often lack the time and resources to mount a serious challenge to scientific evidence. And frankly, there are also many less-than-adequate attorneys who are simply overwhelmed by the complexity of the subject.

What is more, in most states a court-appointed lawyer may not retain 50
an expert witness without the approval of the trial judge. In recent DNA cases in Oklahoma and Alabama, for example, the defense did not retain any experts, because the presiding judge had refused to authorize funds. In the *Castro* case, a critical factor in the defense's successful challenge was the participation of several leading scientific experts—most of whom agreed to testify without a fee.

Because defendants are seldom able to challenge novel scientific evi- 51
dence, we feel that independent overseeing of forensic methods is the only way to ensure justice. Specifically, national standards must be set before a scientific technique can be transferred from the research laboratory to the courtroom, and there must be laws to ensure that these standards are enforced.

The regulation of forensic laboratories has an excellent model: the 52
Clinical Laboratories Improvement Act of 1967 (which was amended in 1988). The act established a system of accreditation and proficiency testing for clinical laboratories that service the medical profession. The law was enacted to ensure that such service laboratories, which are not subject to the same peer scrutiny as research laboratories, would nonetheless provide reliable products and services.

In contrast, no private or public crime laboratory today is regulated by 53
any government agency. Nor is there any mandatory accreditation of forensic laboratories or requirement that they submit to independent proficiency testing. It is also troubling that there are no formally enforced, objective criteria for interpreting forensic data. Four fifths of the forensic laboratories in North America are within police or prosecutor agencies, and so there is an enormous potential for bias because technicians may be aware of the facts of the case. In short, there is more regulation of clinical laboratories that determine whether one has mononucleosis than there is of forensic laboratories able to produce DNA test results that can help send a person to the electric chair.

Accreditation and proficiency testing will work only if implemented 54
with care. National standards for forensic testing must serve the interests of justice, not of parties who have vested interests in the technology. This is not an imaginary danger: from 1988 to 1989 a committee of the American Association of Blood Banks set out to develop national standards for forensic DNA typing and brought in two scientists to provide expertise in molecular genetics; these two happened to be the senior scientists at Lifecodes and Cellmark, the two companies that perform virtually all commercial forensic DNA identification in the U.S.

Some observers suggest delegating the task of setting national standards for forensic DNA identification to the Federal Bureau of Investigation. But there is reason to be wary of this approach. Last year the FBI began to perform forensic DNA identification without first publishing its methodology in refereed journals. In the few pretrial hearings that have challenged DNA tests conducted by the FBI, the bureau has been reluctant to supply the raw data on which it based its criteria, citing its "privilege against self-criticism"—a concept that, incidentically, has little precedent in law. The FBI also opposes independent proficiency testing, arguing that no outsider is qualified to evaluate the bureau's performance. In addition, at a recent FBI-sponsored symposium on DNA typing that attracted 300 forensic scientists from around the country, FBI personnel were alone in opposing proposals requiring laboratories to explain in writing the basis for their conclusions and to have their reports signed by the scientists and technicians who conducted the test. 55

The FBI's stance on these issues flies against norms established elsewhere in the scientific community. For example, if the author of a scientific article refused to divulge his or her raw data to peer review, the article would be rejected. There is also a clear consensus in favor of independent proficiency tests. If a clinical laboratory refused to comply with any reasonable public request to examine the results of proficiency tests, it would risk losing its accreditation. And it would be unthinkable for a diagnostic laboratory to deliver to the obstetrician of a pregnant woman an unsigned report with only the word "abort" appearing on the page. 56

Independent scientists are finally beginning to awaken to the urgency of these issues. Last fall the New York State Forensic DNA Analysis Panel proposed detailed requirements for certifying, licensing and accrediting forensic DNA laboratories. The Congressional Office of Technology Assessment is expected to issue a report on the regulation of DNA typing by the time this article appears. The National Academy of Sciences has appointed a committee to study appropriate standards for DNA typing and is expected to issue a report early next year. 57

It is regrettable that these measures were set in motion only after flaws in current DNA typing came to light in the courtroom. We hope the anticipated reforms will enhance the interests of justice in the future, although this may be small solace to defendants who were wrongfully convicted or to crime victims who saw the true culprit set free. It is our hope that, with appropriate national standards and regulation of forensic laboratories, powerful new forensic techniques such as DNA typing will serve an important and beneficial role in criminal justice. When all is said and done, there should be no better test for identifying a criminal—or for exonerating an innocent suspect. 58

▲ ▲ ▲

Review Questions

1. What is the Greiss test? How is it relevant to the forensic use of DNA?
2. Identify the three criteria that must be satisfied for a forensic test to be admitted into evidence. What problems have been associated with these criteria?
3. Why is DNA evidence seldom challenged in court, according to Neufeld and Colman?
4. What concerns do the authors have about the kind of DNA tests performed in forensic (as opposed to clinical) laboratories?

Discussion and Writing Suggestions

1. You may have had some trouble following the authors' explanations of DNA testing procedures. If so, which parts presented the greatest difficulties? Try to write a summary of or paraphrase one or more of these parts, taking your cues not only from what the authors are saying, but also from the context of the discussion at that point.
2. Imagine that you are a prosecuting attorney arguing that DNA evidence conclusively places the accused at the scene of a brutal murder. Attorney (or expert witness) Neufeld or Colman has testified that due to ambiguous allele matching, band shifting, contamination by the police, sloppy handling by the lab (or some combination of these), the DNA evidence is not reliable and should be disregarded. There is no other physical evidence to link the accused to the crime (there may be circumstantial evidence). Write that part of your closing statement to the jury attempting to rebut Neufeld or Colman's contentions. You'll have to make up some details of the case, but don't stray too far from the scenario presented above.
3. This article originally appeared in *Scientific American,* a magazine for readers particularly interested in issues of science and technology. What assumptions do you infer the authors make about their readers' intellectual level and their degree of comprehension of scientific issues? For example, what kinds of things do they assume their readers already know—and so do not need to have explained? How might this article have been written differently had it appeared in *Time* or *Newsweek,* which are general interest periodicals? How might it have been different had it appeared in *Discover,* another magazine intended for people interested in science, but which assumes an audience with less specialized knowledge? (Jo Ann C. Gutin's article "End of the Rainbow" first appeared in *Discover.* To what extent is it written in a different style?)
4. One of the authors is an attorney, and both are practiced in making presentations in court; and so it is worth looking at this article as a legal *argument,* a systematic presentation of a case. What is the authors' central contention in this "case"? What is their strategy for pre-

senting evidence in a systematic way, for clinching their argument? Have they succeeded in persuading you (the "juror") that their argument is reasonable and valid? If so, why? If not (or not entirely), why not?

DNA in Court

WILLIAM TUCKER

Many scientists—and lawyers—would take issue with some of the conclusions drawn by Neufeld and Colman in the preceding article. For example, Paul Mones, a defense attorney and author of Stalking Justice, *points out that the forensic use of DNA is not a highly controversial issue in the scientific community: "There are close to 100 articles on DNA fingerprinting in the scientific literature and only about half a dozen are critical of the procedure" ("Perspective on DNA Testing,"* Los Angeles Times, *Oct. 7 1994, B7). Mones maintains that while most of the anti-DNA arguments focus on the possibility of wrongfully convicting the innocent, the actuality is that DNA evidence will help to exonerate, not convict an innocent person." In the following article, William Tucker, the New York correspondent of* The American Spectator, *expands upon this line of reasoning, arguing that the use of DNA in criminal cases should be expanded, not restricted. The article first appeared in the November 1994 issue of* The American Spectator. *(Some references to the O.J. Simpson case have been omitted.)*

. . . How did DNA profiling—almost a decade old and widely employed in other countries—end up having such a rough ride through the American justice system? The science itself is not at issue. There has never been a case where one laboratory declared a match in DNA samples and another laboratory declared the opposite. Believe it or not, the only major controversy now surrounding the technique is whether the chances of an innocent person being falsely implicated are 1-in–10,000 (a high estimate arbitrarily chosen by a maverick scientist) or 1-in–10 million (a widely accepted figure that has been verified by an examination of all the DNA records on file with the FBI). 1

Other forensic evidence long accepted in American courtrooms offers levels of certainty that are nowhere near that range. Blood-type identification, accepted in courts for decades, offers at best only a 90 percent verification (1-in–10 possibility of a chance match-up). Handwriting analysis and psychiatric testimony in insanity cases usually come down to a "battle of experts." Only with "dermatoglyphic" fingerprinting (the marks on the end of your finger) are the probabilities of the same general order of magnitude. Yet with DNA profiling, defense attorneys have successfully argued that, if scientists cannot agree whether the technology is 99.99999 percent certain or 99.99999999 percent certain, then *it shouldn't be used at all.* 2

DNA profiling begins with the established theory that no two people, except identical twins, have the same genetic makeup. Each cell in the body contains a complete set of genes. A clot of blood, a trace of skin underneath a victim's fingernails, a drop of semen, the follicle attached to a single strand of hair—all contain enough cells to provide the information for a positive or negative match with a criminal suspect. 3

DNA profiling is particularly useful in rapes and murders in which the victim struggles or the criminal leaves behind some trace of tissue or bodily fluid. A recent newspaper article noted that rapists are now wearing condoms in 20 percent of all attacks. Although the report attributed this to fear of AIDS, a more likely explanation is that word is circulating among rapists that leaving semen at the scene is the equivalent of leaving your calling card. 4

A complete reading of the human genome is beyond present capabilities. The Human Genome Project has undertaken a 15-year effort to map all forty-six human chromosomes, and several private firms are trying to short-circuit the process. One day we may be able to read the genome like a telephone directory. At this point, genetic profiling reads only one ten-thousandth of the information in the genome—just as a fingerprint reads only a tiny fraction of the body's physical profile. Because of peculiar characteristics of this portion of the genome, however, this tiny fraction has proved significant for making highly individual identifications. 5

In 1985, Alec Jeffreys, a geneticist at the University of Leicester, England, proposed making forensic identifications with "junk" DNA, the mysterious, non-functioning genetic material that makes up about 95 percent of the human genome. This material serves no known purpose. It may just be "hitchhiking" from generation to generation without contributing anything to the organism. Or it may serve as "packing material," protecting the working genes from harmful mutations, the way newspapers stuffed in a box will protect its fragile contents. 6

Junk DNA varies from one individual to the next. Different people have different DNA sequences at their junk sites. In addition, these characteristic sequences repeat themselves a different number of times in different people—a phenomenon called "variable number tandem repeats" (VNTRs). One person may have only one repetition at his junk site, while another may have two dozen. Most sites have more than a hundred known variations, which are called "alleles." 7

Other genetic markers such as hair color, height, and weight tend to vary by population. People living near the equator, for example, generally have darker skin, while people in cold climates generally grow bulkier to conserve heat. VNTRs, however—like fingerprints and blood types—appear to vary randomly across populations, with no ethnic or racial associations. 8

In 1986, Jeffreys proposed that VNTRs could be used for criminal identifications. He invented a "multi-locus" molecular probe that surveyed about fifteen to twenty VNTR sites, measuring their varying lengths. The chances that any two people would have the same variation at one site is 9 about 1-in–50. The chance that they would match up at *every* one of the fifteen to twenty sites is well beyond 1-in–1-trillion. (The whole earth's population is only 5–6 billion.)

The test is now used in paternity suits. In criminal cases, however, "multi-locus" probes did not always prove practical. "The difficulty is that we rarely have enough genetic material in the sample," says Mark Stolorow, director of operations at Cellmark Diagnostics, which is running the tests in the Simpson case. "With paternity suits, we can just take blood samples out of someone's arm. But in criminal cases, we're often dealing with a speck of blood found on the sidewalk." Thus, Jeffreys's multi-locus "genetic fingerprinting" (the name is trademarked) was supplanted by a "single-locus" probe, which, given about 8,000 cells (the amount in a drop of blood), can provide a "genetic profile" with somewhat lower degrees of certainty. 10

In 1987, Jeffreys licensed his technology to Imperial Chemical, a British firm, which set up Cellmark Diagnostics, in Bethesda, Maryland. Lifecodes, Inc., now in Stamford, Connecticut, also went into the business, using a slightly different technology. Eighty different state crime labs, plus the FBI, have also entered the field. About 4,000 samples of DNA were tested last year, at an average of $1,000 per test. The number of probes used depends on how much genetic material is available and how much a prosecutor wants to spend. At five probes, the theoretical chances of two individuals having the same profile are 1-in–50^5, or 1-in–312-million. 11

In actuality, the alleles do not occur with the same frequency. Some are common while others are rare. If you have common alleles, you may match with 2,500 other people in the country (1-in–100,000), while if your alleles are rare, the match may be only 1-in–1-billion. In 1992, Neil J. Risch and Bernard Devlin of Yale University, using the FBI's database, generated 7.6 million genetic fingerprints and found only one chance match at the *three*-probe level. At the four-probe level there were none. They estimated the chances of a match for five probes at 1-in–10-billion. 12

From its inception, DNA profiling has implicated the guilty and exonerated the innocent in a way that was previously unthinkable. In an early case in England, two adolescent girls in a small village had been raped and murdered over a three-year period. Police asked males in the village to give a DNA sample for comparison. No matches were found, but it was later reported that one Colin Pitchfork had bribed someone else to substitute a sample for him. Pitchfork was checked again and turned out to be a match. (This case was chronicled by Joseph Wambaugh in *The Blooding*.) 13

In an early incident in the United States, a young couple were murdered at an isolated campground in Colorado. The woman had been raped and a semen deposit was found. A random check against profiles of known sex criminals turned up a match with a paroled felon in Florida. Once he was under suspicion, eyewitnesses were able to place him near the scene of the crime. The man was tried and convicted. 14

In another instance, a man in Georgia allegedly killed his 10-year-old daughter after raping her. The defendant claimed the rape was actually 15 committed by his 12-year-old son and that he had accidentally killed the daughter in trying to break up the rape. Genetic profiling was done on both father and son. The semen on the little girl's clothes belonged to the father. (Even for close relatives, the chance of a coincidental match-up is only 1-in–1,000.) The man was sentenced to life in prison.

Finally, another 10-year-old girl in Tennessee was molested in her home by a "large black man." A local handyman with a record of child molestation had been seen near the crime by a neighbor, and immediately came under suspicion. A DNA comparison, however, showed the handyman could not have been the attacker. He was promptly dismissed as a suspect. 16

DNA profiling has proved just as important in clearing the innocent as it has in implicating the guilty. American laboratories report that 30 percent of tests yield negative matches, exonerating innocent suspects who would otherwise have gone to trial. Scotland Yard reports the same percentages. 17

So things stood until 1989, when a handful of lawyers mounted a counterattack. The principal players have been Peter Neufeld, a New York defense attorney, and Barry Scheck, a professor at the Benjamin Cardozo School of Law in New York. "The attitude up to that point had been that DNA fingerprinting was infallible," said Neufeld. "Juries were awed. As one juror put it, 'You can't argue with science.' We decided to show you could." Neufeld has not only carried through the battle in court, he has also succeeded in becoming the resident expert on the subject in the pages of *Scientific American* [See pp. 622–37.] Not surprisingly, Neufeld and Scheck have been hired by the Simpson defense team as its chief DNA experts. 18

The first important case involved Jose Castro, a South Bronx janitor accused of stabbing to death Vilma Ponce and her two-year-old daughter in 1987. When Castro came under suspicion, a speck of blood was found on his watch. The sample was sent to Lifecodes, which said it belonged to the victim. Neufeld and Scheck challenged the admissibility of the evidence on the grounds that the lab work was sloppy and there were too many uncertainties in the technology. 19

Genetic experts from both sides converged on the scene. Before testimony began, Eric S. Lander, of MIT's Whitehead Institute for Biomedical Research, testifying for the defense, and Richard J. Roberts, of Cold Spring Harbor Laboratories, testifying for the prosecution, decided to get together and issue a joint statement. Both were somewhat disenchanted with Lifecodes's performance. 20

In particular, they were concerned that Lifecodes was declaring matches in instances where the X-ray images that read the VNTRs were identical but shifted slightly out of place—a phenomenon called "band-shifting." The laboratories claim it is not a problem. "It's like having two pieces of identical wallpaper that are hung poorly," says Michael Baird, lab director at Lifecodes. "You can see the patterns are identical, but they're slightly displaced." 21

Lander and Roberts argued that band-shifting created too much uncertainty. They also pointed out that Lifecodes had declared one match when the bands were outside the 5 percent range of error. In a blind test submitted by the California Association of Criminal Laboratory Directors, Cellmark had also misread one sample in fifty as a match. In 1989, Judge Gerald Sheindlin threw out the evidence tying the blood of the victim to Castro's watch—although evidence showing Castro himself was not the source of the blood was admitted. Castro pleaded guilty anyway and was sentenced to a lengthy prison term. 22

Two years later, the battle was joined again in an Ohio case. Three members of the Hell's Angels had killed a young man they mistook for another gang member. Blood from one of the defendants was found in the victim's truck. Neufeld, Lander, and other critics squared off against the Department of Justice, which was supported by two prominent geneticists, Thomas Caskey of Baylor, and Kenneth Kidd of Yale. 23

This time the prosecution won, but not before a lot of expert blood had been spilled. Lander—who was embarrassed on the witness stand—turned out to have received a $28,000 fee for testifying. Neufeld and Scheck counterattacked by accusing Caskey of profiting from the technology because he held a patent in the field and received a $15,000 annual royalty. Neufeld and Scheck twice attempted to have the case reopened on the basis of Caskey's alleged conflict of interest, but the conviction has been allowed to stand. 24

In 1990, in *Scientific American,* Neufeld laid out the full case against DNA fingerprinting. Neufeld compared DNA profiling to the Greiss test, a chemical test for nitrates from explosives, which had been used to convict six Irishmen in an IRA bmbing. "It turns out that a variety of common substances such as old playing cards, cigarette packages, lacquer and aerosol spray will, along with explosives, yield a positive result [in the Greiss test]," wrote Neufeld. Neufeld then outlined similar potential flaws in DNA profiling: samples were small, DNA could be changed by the presence of impurities and bacteria, the sample might degenerate in a number of ways. The band-shifting problem distorted results. Samples could be accidentally switched or mislabeled—any number of things might happen. As a result of all this an innocent person might be convicted of a crime. 25

But Neufeld's opening analogy was misleading. The major problem with the Greiss test was that it produced false positives. Substances other than the target chemical could give the same results. With DNA analysis, however—and particularly with the problems mentioned by Neufeld—the only real problem is false *negatives.* The chances of an innocent person being implicated are next to nil, but the chances of a guilty person being falsely exonerated are reasonably high. 26

To simplify, suppose that a suspect has a five-allele code that reads: 26–13–12–27–11. The forensic sample, which also contains his genes, has the same code. Now suppose the forensic sample degenerates, as Neufeld suggested. It can only degenerate *away* from a positive match. (In practice, 27 the lab would probably call the results "inconclusive," which happens in 10 to 30 percent of all tests.)

Now suppose the suspect is innocent. What are the chances that a forensic sample will degenerate *into* his code of 26–13–12–27–11? They are, in fact, approximately the same as the likelihood that a chance mismatch will occur in the first place—about 1-in–10 million. 28

The great irony is that, while arguing that DNA profiling should not be used *against* criminal suspects, Neufeld and Scheck are simultaneously representing 600 condemned prisoners who claim that DNA analysis will prove they are innocent. Despite the much greater problem of false negatives, the attorneys argue that DNA evidence is valid when used on the side of the defense. 29

As a final argument against admissibility, Neufeld also raised what was soon to become the principal objection to DNA profiling: the idea that the genetic markers used in DNA analysis are not randomly distributed by racial groups, that they follow the pattern of hair and eye color, rather than blood types and fingerprints. Thus, when compared against people in a suspect's own racial or ethnic group, the chances of an accidental match-up might be higher. 30

The argument was later expanded by Richard Lewontin, a maverick population geneticist at Harvard and co-founder (with fellow Harvardian Stephen Jay Gould) of the left-wing academic group Science for the People. In 1991, Lewontin co-authored an article in *Science* that argued that patterns at separate VNTR sites might be inherited as a unit, creating similar genetic profiles among small, inbred populations. This "pose[s] a particularly difficult problem for the forensic use of VNTRs if the wrong ethnic group is used as the reference population." In order to avoid chance mistakes, it would be necessary to develop much more data about "subgroups that are likely to be relevant in forensic applications." The authors identified these groups as blacks, Hispanics, and Amerinds, and speculated that the chances of a false match-up within these populations might be as high as 1-in–10,000. 31

Now, 10,000-to–1 is still pretty long odds—certainly enough to erase any element of reasonable doubt where other incriminating evidence is present. But Neufeld wanted to go a step further. Instead of merely increasing the odds, he now argued that there was no "consensus" about DNA technology in the scientific community and therefore the technique should be excluded altogether from criminal trials. Appeals courts in California, Massachusetts, Arizona, Minnesota, and five other states bought the argument and previous convictions were overturned in each state. 32

The unsubtle point behind Lewontin's talk of forensic "relevance" is this: since blacks, Hispanics, and Indians commit a disproportionate share of all crimes, an individual *within* one of these groups may end up being implicated by the newfangled technology. (Actually, the black population has proved to be more genetically diversified than any other racial group.) As a later *Scientific American* article put it, "An innocent suspect racially 33 or ethnically similar to that of a criminal could have an inflated chance of matching a forensic sample—and thus be wrongly convicted."

All this assumes that suspects are implicated in crimes solely on the 34
basis of their race—which in some cases they are. Critics of forensic DNA like to point to a Texas case where a murderer was selected out of a small, inbred black population. But in other cases, the logic of "ethnic ceilings" is wholly irrelevant. In the case of the campground murder, for example, the suspect could have been anyone. When he was identified, it was not because of his race, but by a semen sample. Thus it made no sense to compute the odds *only* against his racial group. Wherever factors other than race have been the key to singling out a suspect, ethnic ceilings on DNA profiles are irrelevant.

In 1991, the National Academy of Sciences gave the technology a 35
ringing endorsement. In an effort to placate critics, however, the commission recommended that ethnic ceilings be adopted that would give race-adjusted odds for each positive identification. By purely arbitrary choice, the committee proposed that no allele should be assumed to occur with less than 10 percent frequency—a number that still produces odds of more than 6 million-to-1 at five probes. Protests arose, and this year the NAS convened a second panel to reconsider the ceilings hypothesis. In defending O.J. Simpson, Neufeld now argues that the appointment of this new committee proves that the technology is *still* too controversial to be admitted in court.

The Simpson case, of course, is a good example of the ceilings fallacy. 36
Why is O.J. Simpson a suspect in the killing of Nicole Brown and Ronald Goldman? Is it because he is black? Is it because somebody spotted a "dark-skinned intruder" and thought it might be O.J.?

No. Simpson is a suspect because of (1) his previous relationship to 37
one of the victims; (2) his documented record of threats and violence against her; and (3) his failure to give any convincing account of his whereabouts at the time of the murder. The other logical choice is that the murder was committed by an unknown intruder, but that intruder does not have to match Simpson's racial profile. The correct reference group for Simpson's positive DNA match is the entire population of the United States.

Using the figures compiled from the FBI files by Devlin and Kidd as a 38
conservative estimate, there is a *1-in-7-million* chance that the blood found at the scene belongs to someone other than O.J. This means that in the entire population of Los Angeles (3.5 million), there is less than a 50 percent chance that *any* other individual has Simpson's DNA profile.

Does this seem complicated? Then look at it this way. For the sake of 39
argument, assume there is a 1-in-10,000 chance that Simpson's DNA would match up with that of another black person, as Lewontin's "ceilings" hypothesis suggests. There is still nothing to prove that the intruder was black. The longer odds, according to Lewontin, that Simpson's profile matches with someone of another ethnic group must also be factored into the equation. The result, once again, is that in all of Southern California,

there is probably only one person who shares Simpson's genetic profile. The odds that Simpson himself, rather than this unknown person, was the source of the blood at the crime scene seem reasonably convincing.

So why has this kind of technological advance had such a rough time 40
being accepted in American courtrooms?

The answer can be found in the structure of the American legal profes- 41
sion. Among attorneys who practice criminal law, the overwhelming majority are working on the side of the defense. Of the approximately 200,000 lawyers engaged in criminal work, only an eighth are prosecutors, while the remainder are representing criminal clients. Career prosecutors are government functionaries who labor at modest salaries. Many defense attorneys toil in obscurity, but those that are successful are the high rollers of the trade. Moreover, most young prosecutors—however unwittingly—are *training* to become defense attorneys. After serving an apprenticeship with the state, they generally—if reluctantly—switch sides. The incentives are overwhelming. A good prosecutor can triple his salary by going into private (defense) practice.

On the civil side, on the other hand, plaintiff attorneys are the high 42
rollers, raking off contingency fees from the nation's escalating damage awards. Civil attorneys on the defense side are generally corporate functionaries. The American Association of Trial Lawyers is dominated by plaintiff attorneys—just as the criminal justice committees of the state legislatures and bar associations are dominated by defense lawyers.

All this has had an enormous impact on American justice. In *The Liti- 43
gation Explosion,* Walter Olson has documented how the rules of evidence in civil courtrooms have been widely expanded over the past four decades to favor plaintiffs. The process of "discovery," for example, is completely unique to the American courtroom. In other countries, you sue someone on the basis of evidence you already have at hand. In America, plaintiffs can make vague, unspecified charges and then force a defendant to hand over whole truckloads of corporate or personal information so that the plaintiff can wade through them in search of wrongdoing.

"Depositions," by the same token, were once out-of-court interviews 44
limited to people who were on their deathbed or otherwise unable to appear in court. Under pressure from the plaintiff bar, however, the courts turned depositions into a format where plaintiff attorneys can hold private interrogations. If your spouse sues you for divorce, his or her attorney can interrogate you about your sex life, your personal thoughts—anything he deems relevant. You have no "right to remain silent," but can only hire your own attorney. It is not surprising that plaintiff attorneys often refer to themselves as "private attorneys general," empowered by the state to ransack people's belongings and personal lives in search of evidence for civil litigation.

On the other hand, the rules of evidence in *criminal* courts have 45
changed radically in the opposite direction. Since the 1960s, the various "exclusionary rules" have limited the power of the police to investigate anything. Search warrants must specify exactly what the police expect to find *before* they start looking. If something turns up that wasn't listed in the

warrant, it may not be admissible as evidence, no matter how incriminating. Interrogations, under the *Miranda* rule, must be held in a formulaic setting, with suspects continually reminded of their right to remain silent or contact an attorney. Many defense attorneys profess that there is no such thing as an "uncoerced confession," since any suspect fully aware of his rights would contact his lawyer, who would tell him not to say anything.

Under these circumstances, it is not surprising to find that many lawyers and law professors now argue that it is useless to seek justice in the criminal courts and that the civil courts are the proper place for redressing criminal damages. . . . The same legal principles that have kept DNA fingerprinting from being used in criminal trials will be turned around to argue for its admissibility in civil courts. In fact, many of the same attorneys will probably end up making the argument. 46

Still, one can't come away from the issue without the impression that the attorneys opposing DNA evidence are trying to hold back a tidal wave of scientific research. Genetics is the most rapidly exploding field in the scientific world. Whatever objections can be raised today will probably be overcome tomorrow. The "polymerase chain reaction" (PCR), a technique that uses a microbe found in hot springs to "amplify" small amounts of DNA, is now being used to make identifications with as little as 20 cells. Experts in the field say the VNTR method may be outdated within three years. If critics do succeed in having the few private labs taken off the job, their work will be taken over by the FBI and the state crime labs—an outcome that is unlikely to make opponents any happier. At best, defense attorneys can only hope to continue muddying the waters, grasping at every letter-to-the-editor as proof that a "scientific consensus" has yet to be reached. . . . 47

▲ ▲ ▲

Review Questions

1. What are alleles?
2. Why is it generally easier to establish genetic identity in paternity than in criminal cases, according to Tucker?
3. Why does Tucker consider Neufeld and Colman's opening analogy of the Greiss test (to DNA testing) misleading?
4. Why does Tucker reject the idea that the chances of genetic matches need to be calculated differently for different ethnic and racial groups?
5. How does Tucker account for the difficulty that DNA evidence has had in being established in criminal cases?

Discussion and Writing Suggestions

1. On what points about the use of DNA as evidence would Neufeld and Colman be likely to agree with Tucker? On what points would they likely disagree? Explain.

2. After reading both Neufeld-Colman's and Tucker's articles, whose arguments about the reliability of DNA testing do you find more persuasive? Explain.
3. In discussing the use of DNA evidence to determine guilt or innocence, Tucker cites six specific cases. The final two of these, however—the Castro case and the Hell's Angels case—have also been cited by those who question the use and reliability of DNA evidence (Castro, in fact, was Neufeld's own case). For what purpose does Tucker employ these last two cases? To what extent do they contribute to the persuasiveness of his argument?
4. In a selection that appears in Chapter 7 of this text, "Left, Right, Center: The American Political Spectrum," Donald Lazere classifies *The American Spectator* (the magazine in which Tucker's article originally appeared) as a "center-to-left conservative" magazine. If you have read at least portions of Chapter 7, see if you can determine qualities and statements in Tucker's article that make it "conservative."
5. Write a critique of Tucker's article. Draw upon your responses to the Review Questions, and follow the procedures for critique covered in Chapter 3 of this text.

▼

SYNTHESIS ACTIVITIES

1. Suppose you are writing a survey article on biotechnology for a general audience magazine, such as *Time* or *Atlantic Monthly*. You want to introduce your readers to the subject, tell them what it is and what it may become, and you want to focus, in particular, on the advantages and disadvantages of biotechnology. Drawing on the sources you have read in this chapter, write such an article (i.e., an explanatory synthesis). For background information on the subject you can draw on sources like Starr and the introduction to this chapter. Other sources, like those by Brownlee et al., Nelkin, Watson, Fausto-Sterling et al., Cavalli-Sforza et al., Gutin, Neufeld and Colman, and Tucker, offer many case studies illustrating advantages and disadvantages. And, of course, Huxley serves as a dark example of the kind of thing that *could* happen if biotechnology is used for unethical purposes.
2. Write an editorial (i.e., an argument synthesis) arguing that additional regulations need to be placed on biotechnology. Specify the chief problem areas, as you see them, and indicate the regulations needed in order to deal with these problems.

   You may want to begin with a survey of biotechnology (in which you acknowledge its advantages) but then narrow your focus to the problem areas. Categorize the problem areas (e.g., problems for prospective parents, for the workplace, for the courtroom, for the commercial applications of biotechnology). The suggested regulations—and explanations of why they are necessary—might be discussed throughout the editorial or saved for the end.

3. *Brave New World* represents one artist's view of how scientific knowledge might be abused to ensure social stability and conformity. Huxley focused on the possibility of dividing fertilized human ova into identical parts and then conditioning the ova before "birth." Write a short story (or a play or screenplay) that represents your own nightmare vision. You may want to focus on other aspects of genetic engineering: the problem of forced genetic testing, of eugenics (creating "perfect" people or eliminating "imperfect" ones), of fostering uniformity among the population, of some fantastic commercial application of bioengineering, or even of some aspect of cloning (among the films dealing with cloning are Ira Levin's *The Boys from Brazil,* Woody Allen's *Sleeper,* and Steven Spielberg's *Jurassic Park*).

   Decide whether the story is to be essentially serious or comic (satirical)—or something in between. Create characters (try to avoid caricatures) who will enact the various aspects of the problem, as you see it. And create a social and physical setting appropriate to the story you want to tell.

4. Write an article for a magazine like *Newsweek* or *Time* or *U.S. News & World Report* on the current status of biotechnology—as of August 2050. Try to make the article generally upbeat (unlike the nightmare vision called for in the previous question), but be frank also about the problems that have been encountered, as well as the problems that remain. Refer, at some point in your article, to views of biotechnology from the late 1980s and the early 1990s to establish some basis for comparison between what they thought "then" and what they think "now." You might model your article on the piece by Brownlee, Cook, and Hardigg or on any contemporary news magazine article of comparable scope. The language should be lively and vivid, and you should include as many "facts" as you can think of. Study your model articles for ideas about how to organize your material.

5. Write a newsmagazine article on the Human Genome Project or the Human Genome Diversity project, focusing on what is being done and how, as well as on the expected benefits and potential problems arising from the project. Draw on Nelkin, Watson, Fausto-Sterling et al., Cavalli-Sforza et al., and Gutin.

6. Imagining that you are writing for a legal periodical, compose a two- to three-page editorial arguing either that the forensic use of DNA should be expanded or that it should be further restricted. Draw primarily on Neufeld-Colman and Tucker, though you will probably

want to supplement your sources by doing some additional research on the subject.

RESEARCH ACTIVITIES

1. The main focal points of the debate over genetic engineering and testing have been (1) whether or not the new biotechnologies are safe and ethical; (2) whether or not they will benefit agriculture and food processing; (3) whether or not they require stricter regulation (and if so, what kind); (4) whether or not genetic testing (or the use of genetic testing) by employers and insurance companies is ethical; (5) whether or not genetic testing of fetuses is ethical; (6) whether or not work should proceed on the Human Genome Project and/or the Human Genome Diversity Project; (7) whether or not geneticists should work on biologial weapons. Select *one* of these areas and research the current status of the debate.

   In addition to relevant articles, see Jeremy Rifkin, *Algeny* (1983) and *Declaration of a Heretic* (1985); Jack Doyle, *Altered Harvest* (1985); Brian Stableford, *Future Man* (1984); Steve Olson, *Biotechnology: An Industry Comes of Age* (1986); Richard Noel Re, *Bioburst* (1986); Edward J. Sylvester and Lynn C. Klotz, *The Gene Age* (1987); Joseph Fletcher, *Ethics of Genetic Control* (1988); Gerald R. Campbell, *Biotechnology: An Introduction* (1988); Charles Pilar and Keith R. Yamamoto, *Gene Wars* (1988); David Suzuki and Peter Knudtson, *Genethics* (1989); Andrew Linzey, *Slavery: Human and Animal* (1988); Monsanto Company, *Agriculture and the New Biology* (1989); and Daniel J. Kevles and Leroy Hood, *The Code of Codes: Scientific and Social Issues in the Human Genome Project* (1992).
2. Investigate the latest developments in DNA "fingerprint" technology. How has such technology been employed in recent criminal cases? What is the legal status of such technology at both the federal and the local levels? What ethical issues are at stake, according to proponents and opponents of DNA fingerprinting?
3. In August 1992, researchers announced that they had managed through genetic engineering to produce mice that developed cystic fibrosis. Scientists believed that by studying the course of this disease in mice, they would be able to devise new therapies for the treatment of this usually fatal disease in humans. Follow up on either this development or some other development involving the genetic engineering of laboratory animals to further medical research. Describe what is involved in the procedure, how it was developed, the results to date, and the ethical debate that may have ensued about its practice.
4. Research and discuss some aspect of the early history of genetic engineering as it developed in the 1970s. Begin with a survey of Wat-

son and Crick's work with DNA in the early 1950s, describe some of the early experiments in this area, discuss some of the concerns expressed both by scientists and laypersons, and cover in some detail the Asilomar (California) Conference of 1975 at which scientists worked out guidelines for future research.

5. Research some of the most significant recent advances in biotechnology, categorize them, and report on your findings. You may also wish to consider the Human Genome Project. Use some of the same categories suggested in Research Activity 1, but focus here less on the debate (which you need not ignore) than on what is currently being done, on who is doing it, on the obstacles yet to overcome, and on the anticipated benefits on the research and development.
6. In 1989 James D. Watson was appointed to head NIH's Human Genome Project. Watson's appointment and his subsequent work as director of the project generated some controversy. Research Watson's professional activities since his discovery with Francis Crick of the structure of DNA, focusing on his more recent activities. See especially, the article on Watson, "The Double Helix," which appeared in *The New Republic,* July 9 and 16, 1990. How do Watson's professional colleagues—and others—assess his more recent work?
7. Write a paper on biotechnology critic Jeremy Rifkin and the critical reaction to his activities and his books. Consult the *Reader's Guide to Periodical Literature* and locate important articles by and about Rifkin during the past decade or so. Locate Rifkin's books and survey them. Most important, look up reviews of Rifkin's books, starting with the listings in *Book Review Digest.* (This is an annual index that lists reviews during a given year and provides brief excerpts from the most important reviews.)

    Begin your paper by summarizing Rifkin's life and work thus far. (Your introductory paragraphs should probably focus on the controversy surrounding Rifkin.) Then focus on the reaction to his work. You may want to divide your paper into sections on positive and negative reactions; or you may want to organize by critical reviews of his various books and activities. At the conclusion, develop an overall assessment of the significance and value of Rifkin's work.
8. Research the current status of either the Human Genome Project or the Human Genome Diversity Project. To what extent have the kinds of objections and concerns described in Gutin's "End of the Rainbow" slowed down, derailed, or otherwise affected the latter project? To what extent has the project you selected made progress in achieving its goals?
9. Research one of the cases (including the Simpson case) mentioned in either Neufeld and Colman's article ("When Science Takes the Witness Stand") or Tucker's ("DNA in Court"), and explain how DNA matching was a significant factor in the presentation and outcome of the case, or in a subsequent appeal. *Or* review several cases in

which DNA was a factor, and focus on the relationships between them, in terms of the use of genetic testing and matching.

10. In asserting that both geneticists and journalists have been guilty of making grandiose claims about genetic research, Dorothy Nelkin cites the kind of metaphors ("genetic instructions," "program," "medical crystal ball," etc.) that geneticists use to characterize their work. Research several recent articles about genetic research or developments in newspapers and magazines and see if you can find enough evidence to support Nelkin's charges. Or do her concerns appear to be overblown? Your sources should include statements by geneticists.
11. Since the mid-1970s, genetic technology has been regulated not only by scientists themselves, working as a body, but also by federal agencies, such as the White House Office of Science and Technology Policy; the U.S. Department of Agriculture (USDA: overseeing genetically engineered plants); the NIH's Recombinant DNA Advisory Committee (RAC: overseeing laboratory research); the Environmental Protection Agency (EPA: approving field testing of commercial products affecting the environment); and the Food and Drug Administration (FDA: approving animal and human pharmaceuticals). Research and report on some of the most significant regulations imposed on the biotechnology industry, consider the views of critics and of scientists themselves, and indicate your own position (and possibly some of your own proposals) on existing and additional regulations.
12. If your college or university has scientists on its faculty who are working on DNA research, interview them to find out what they are doing. Ask them how they feel about some of the ethical issues covered in this chapter. Ask them to recommend references in the professional literature that will enable you to understand more fully the aims of their research; then consult some of these references and use them to provide context for your discussion of this research.
13. Conduct and write a summary report on student attitudes on biotechnology and write a report based on this survey. Devise questions that focus on the main areas of controversy (see Research Activity 1). Phrase your questions in a way that allows a range of responses (perhaps on a scale of 1 to 5, or using modifiers like "strongly agree," "agree somewhat," "disagree somewhat," "strongly disagree"); don't ask for responses that require a yes/no or approve/disapprove response. (See pages 169–70.) Attempt to correlate the responses to such variables as academic major, student status (lower division, upper division, graduate), gender, ethnic background, geographical area of origin (urban, suburban, rural). Determine whether respondents personally know someone with a disease for which a genetic cure is either possible or under consideration. Determine also how much prior knowledge of biotechnology your respondents have.

12

From Fiction to Film: Exploring the Film Adaptation

Devotees of the Academy Awards know that the "Best Screenplay" award comes in two categories: best original script and best script adapted from another medium. That other medium is generally fiction (sometimes drama), and casual viewers might be forgiven for thinking that a film based on an already-written story is less of an accomplishment than one based on an original story (though the "originality" of the umpteenth cop-buddy or *Die-Hard*–type movie is perhaps open to question). But as most high school students know, both Shakespeare and his audiences were perfectly happy with plays adapted from another medium—epics, histories, or earlier plays; and so the interesting question becomes not whether or not the story is original, but what has *this* particular artist done with this familiar story to make it fresh and interesting for a new set of audiences?

From the earliest years of the film era audiences have been thrilled, dissatisfied, or simply bewildered to see how best sellers and old favorites have been translated from fiction to film. In the late 1930s plans to make the film version of *Gone With the Wind* from Margaret Mitchell's best-selling novel worked the reading public into feverish anticipation; when it was released, almost everyone—including the author—proclaimed it a gratifyingly successful adaptation, faithful not only to the substance but also to the spirit of the novel. In the 1970s, *The Godfather* became one of those rare examples of a film adaptation that actually is better than the novel on which it is based. In other cases, adaptations have been crashing disappointments (*Catch-22, Bonfire of the Vanities)* or so different from their sources (*Apocalypse Now,* based on Conrad's *Heart of Darkness*; the 1964 version of *The Killers,* based on Hemingway's short story) as to raise questions about whether they should be considered adaptations at all.

Recent years have seen a reversal of the usual novel-into-film process, with many popular films being made into novels—a marketing device known as *novelization.* In some cases (e.g., Louisa May Alcott's *Little Women*) the process actually comes full circle, with novels turned into films and then turned back into novels. This generally occurs when a classic novel has been made into a film so compelling that viewers want to re-experience the story on the printed page, though without having to undergo the difficulties of reading "literature."

But what *is* involved in adapting fiction to film? Is it just a matter of transferring dialogue in fiction to dialogue in the screenplay (and making up dialogue that isn't actually supplied in the original), and finding visual equivalents for the descriptions of the fiction writer? In some cases, this approach works quite well. Consider the opening of William Golding's *Lord of the Flies* (1954), twice made into film (in 1963 and 1990):

> The boy with fair hair lowered himself down the last few feet of rock and began to pick his way toward the lagoon. Though he had taken off his school sweater and trailed it now from one hand, his grey shirt stuck to him and his hair was plastered to his forehead. All around him the long scar smashed into the jungle was a bath of heat. He was clambering heavily among the creepers and broken trunks when a bird, a vision of red and yellow, flashed upwards with a witch-like cry, and this cry was echoed by another.
>
> "Hi," it said, "Wait a minute!"

The phrase about the long scar being a "bath of heat" might present some difficulty, but otherwise a competent filmmaker should have little problem in translating Golding's vivid descriptions into visual equivalents and in portraying action on screen that matches the action in the narrative.

Now consider the first few sentences of Saul Bellow's *Seize the Day* (1956):

> When it came to concealing his troubles, Tommy Wilhelm was not less capable than the next fellow. So at least he thought, and there was a certain amount of evidence to back him up. He had once been an actor—no, not quite, an extra—and he knew what acting should be. Also, he was smoking a cigar, and when a man is smoking a cigar, wearing a hat, he has an advantage; it is harder to find out how he feels. He came from the twenty-third floor down to the lobby on the mezzanine to collect his mail before breakfast, and he believed—he hoped—that he looked passably well: doing all right. It was a matter of sheer hope, because there was not much that he could add to his present effort.

Adapting this passage presents problems of an entirely different order than adapting *Lord of the Flies.* (This narrative is written in "third-person limited point of view"; that is, the narrator can read the mind of the protagonist and only of the protagonist.) A filmmaker can show Tommy Wilhelm smoking a cigar, wearing a hat, and coming down to the lobby on the mezzanine. But how does the filmmaker communicate that Tommy thinks he is not less capable than the next fellow at concealing his troubles. Or what he is thinking—or hoping—about anything? Or that he had once been an actor—actually, not quite an actor, but an extra? The filmmaker could, of course, have Tommy run into an old friend, and they could have a conversation in which all this comes out; but most people who have read and liked Bellow's novel would find such a device unacceptably clumsy. (The novel was in fact made into a fine movie in 1986, with Robin Williams in an uncharacteristically subdued performance as Tommy Wilhelm.)

Finally, consider the opening sentences of Marilynne Robinson's lyrical novel *Housekeeping* (1981):

> My name is Ruth. I grew up with my younger sister, Lucille, under the care of my grandmothers, Mrs. Sylvia Foster, and when she died, of her sisters-in-law, Misses Lily and Nona Foster, and when they fled, of her daughter, Mrs. Sylvia Fisher. Through all these generations of elders we lived in one house, my grandmother's house, built for her by her husband, Edmund Foster, an employee of the railroad, who escaped this world years before I entered it. It was he who put us down in this unlikely place. He had grown up in the Middle West, in a house dug out of the ground, with windows just at earth level and just at eye level, so that from without, the house was a mere mound, no more a human stronghold than a grave, and from within, the perfect horizontality of the world in that place foreshortened the view so severely that the horizon seemed to circumscribe the sod house and nothing more. So my grandfather began to read what he could find of travel literature, journals of expeditions to the mountains of Africa, to the Alps, the Andes, the Himalayas, the Rockies. . . .

In this case, the filmmaker might well throw up her hands at the prospect of finding a cinematic equivalent for this first-person recounting of family history and the family house and how the view from the house was circumscribed to the point that the narrator's grandfather took to reading travel books to gain a wider perspective on the world. Even assuming that such details could emerge naturally from later dialogue, how would a screenwriter or director convey the particular force of the term "escaped this world" or "the perfect horizontality of the world in that place"? In fact, *Housekeeping* was made into a moving film by director Bill Forsyth (1987), but it was successful on its own filmic terms, not because it simply recorded the main events of the plot or because it was literally "faithful" to the novel.

The essential difference between fiction and film has been pinpointed by Fred H. Marcus, professor of film at California State University, Los Angeles:

> Most simply, film is visual; fiction is verbal. Short stories are created with words, films with images. As a result, fiction communicates indirectly with a reader through symbols which the reader transcribes into mental images and meanings. The viewer, on the other hand, receives screen images more directly. There is a danger that the filmgoer may experience these images more or less passively, whereas the reader must actively use his imagination to interpret the verbal symbols. (*Short Story/Short Film*, Prentice-Hall, 1987: 129)

Frequently, readers are disappointed with film adaptations because their imaginations are more creative than—or at least different from—the director's, and their mind's eye produces images that the filmmaker (or the actor or the set designer) is unable to match. But perhaps even more important to the successful adaptation than the visual image is the *tone*—or the emotional feeling, or perhaps the ironic stance, of the film. As George Linden has written:

> . . . a director can change the plot of a novel, he can eliminate certain characters and scenes, and he can include scenes not included in the novel without violating it. But he cannot seriously violate the theme of the novel, and the one thing he must be able to translate into his new medium is its tone. If the tone of a work is lost, the work is lost; but the tone of a novel must be rendered in an aural-visual patterning instead of by use of descriptive dialogue or other narrative device. (*Reflections on the Screen*, 49; qtd. in Marcus, 234)

In this light, consider one critic's judgment that the use of color in the 1990 version of *Lord of the Flies* "purges the original of its poetry." The implication here is that the decision to use black and white or color has consequences for the tone of the film (color suggests realism, which may have been inappropriate for Golding's fable).

This chapter will provide you with opportunities to think about the process of adapting fiction to film—and thus to ponder the essential differences between these two different but related art forms and to gain insight into the particular requirements and strengths of each. We will examine two adaptations in particular: films based on Daphne du Maurier's "The Birds" and Agatha Christie's "Witness for the Prosecution." Research Activities at the end of this chapter will direct you to numerous other feature films based on short stories and novels. We focus here on short stories, rather than novels, simply as a matter of convenience: to save time and to enable us to reprint the complete works on which the films are based.

The chapter begins with three articles that discuss the relationships between fiction and film and the unique properties of each: Timothy Corrigan's "Fiction and Film," Charles Eidsvik's "Why Adaptations Are Good for Literature—and for Movies," and Joseph M. Boggs's "The Problems of Adaptation." These pieces will provide you with a conceptual framework that will help you assess the two stories/films that form the larger part of this chapter (as well as other fictional works and film adaptations listed in the "Research Activities"). The two stories that follow—"The Birds" by Daphne du Maurier and "Witness for the Prosecution" by Agatha Christie—will be interesting to compare and contrast because they are such different types of narrative and because they are examples of varying degrees of adaptation. The action of "The Birds" is largely unexplained and so gives rise to a variety of interpretations, while "Witness for the Prosecution" is a tightly plotted mystery whose secret (different in the story and in the film) is revealed at the end. "The Birds" is an example of a relatively loose adaption, in that many important elements of character and story undergo significant alteration during the transformation from story to film. "Witness for the Prosecution" is more faithful as an adaptation, though important changes have been made. Remember, however, that faithfulness to the original story is not the sole (or perhaps even the main) criterion by which we judge the success of an adaptation.

The body of the chapter concludes with an appendix, "A Glossary of Film Terms," that provides definitions of essential film concepts and thus a vocabulary by which you can discuss the technicalities of film adaptation. Like other chapters in this book, this one concludes with Synthesis Activities and Research Activities, though they are somewhat expanded from their counterparts elsewhere. The Synthesis Activities are anchored by a chapter assignment that provides extensive guidance for the evaluation of a particular film adaptation that you will select. And the Research Activities begin with a long list of literary works that have been adapted into film.

▼

FOR INSTRUCTORS: FILM AVAILABILITY NOTE

Videos of *The Birds* and *Witness for the Prosecution,* one for every institution, are available through your Longman representative.

▼

A NOTE ON VARIANT ADAPTATIONS AND SCREENPLAY FORMAT

Some of the assignments in this chapter will ask you to develop your own screenplay segments based on either fiction or your own imagination. To give you an idea of screenplay format while at the same time illustrating how different screenwriters can come up with entirely different approaches to adapting a story, we reprint the following excerpts.

Toward the end of his short life, the American writer Stephen Crane (1871–1900) wrote "The Upturned Face," a powerful short story set near a Civil War battlefield. The action of the story consists simply of the burial of a soldier just killed by a sniper. As two officers shovel dirt on the dead man and react to the grim business at hand, we gain vivid insights into the nature of war and death. We reprint the first few paragraphs of Crane's story, followed by a "shot analysis" of the opening of a 10-minute film by Edward Folger based on the story, followed by a screenplay for another, unproduced version of the story by Jim Stinson. (A screenplay differs from a shot analysis in that the former is written before the film is made, whereas the latter is a shot-by-shot description of the actual film. Published screenplays do not always reflect the finished film, owing to changes during production and editing.) *Note:* In your own screenplays, you may omit the shot descriptions (close-up, medium shot, etc.) if you feel uncomfortable dealing with them, and simply write dialogue and descriptions of the setting, the characters, and their actions.

The Upturned Face

STEPHEN CRANE

"What will we do now?" said the adjutant, troubled and excited.

"Bury him," said Timothy Lean.

The two officers looked down close to their toes where lay the body of their comrade. The face was chalk-blue; gleaming eyes stared at the sky. Over the two upright figures was a windy sound of bullets, and on the top of the hill Lean's prostrate company of Spitzbergen infantry was firing measured volleys.

"Don't you think it would be better—" began the adjutant. "We might leave him until to-morrow."

"No," said Lean. "I can't hold that post an hour longer. I've got to fall back, and we've got to bury old Bill."

"Of course," said the adjutant, at once. "Your men got entrenching tools?"

Lean shouted back to his little line, and two men came slowly, one with a pick, one with a shovel. They stared in the direction of the Rostina sharpshooters. Bullets cracked near their ears. "Dig here," said Lean gruffly. The men, thus caused to lower their glances to the turf, became hurried and frightened, merely because they could not look to see whence the bullets came. The dull beat of the pick striking the earth sounded amid the swift snap of close bullets. Presently the other private began to shovel.

"I suppose," said the adjutant, slowly, "we'd better search his clothes for—things."

Lean nodded. Together in curious abstraction they looked at the body. Then Lean stirred his shoulders suddenly, arousing himself.

"Yes," he said, "we'd better see what he's got." He dropped to his knees, and his hands approached the body of the dead officer. But his hands wavered over the buttons of the tunic. The first button was brick-red with drying blood, and he did not seem to dare touch it. . . .

▲ ▲ ▲

shot analysis
THE UPTURNED FACE

SCREENPLAY BY *EDWARD FOLGER*

1. Pyramid Films on black.

2. Black. THE UPTURNED FACE.

FADE OUT:

3. CLOSE-UP: A man's hands opening a paper cylinder. He removes a pill from the cylinder and lifts it out of the frame.

CUT TO:

4. CLOSE-UP: The man, a soldier, sits against a tree. Another man flashes past. The man drinks from a canteen.

CUT TO:

5. MEDIUM SHOT: Two soldiers. The man with the canteen seated at left; the other (the adjutant) standing at right. He wears a sword. The adjutant speaks.

ADJ.

Come on!

The adjutant exits behind trees in upper center of frame. The seated man spits out a mouthful of water and closes his canteen. He rises, grabbing his hat and rifle, and trots after the adjutant, meanwhile putting on his hat. He exits from frame. Hold on green Southern landscape.

CUT TO:

6. LONG SHOT: Pan fast right through trees. A man running. He runs toward camera into a close-up. He is the man with the canteen. A shot sounds; the man falls out of frame. Hold on trees in background. The adjutant's voice, off-screen, calls out.

ADJ.

Bill!

CUT TO:

7. LONG SHOT: Green background. The adjutant, running left, slows down and comes into a two-shot with the fallen body. He pauses and looks down at the body; another officer, Lean, runs into frame from down left.

CUT TO:

8. CLOSE-UP: Two-shot. The adjutant and Lean looking down. Lean looks at the adjutant and back down. The adjutant removes his hat, wipes his face, and looks at Lean.

ADJ.

What do we do now?

Lean looks up, then down,

LEAN

Bury him.

ADJ.

Here? Now? I mean, couldn't we—

LEAN

Can't drag him back through the marsh.

ADJ.

Maybe if we come back tomorrow—

Lean pauses, shakes his head.

ADJ.

Your men got any trenching tools?

CUT TO:

9. LONG SHOT: Three men with their backs to the camera firing.

CUT TO:

10. CLOSE-UP: Lean, looking away from camera, calls two names. He turns to look at the body.

CUT TO:

11. LONG SHOT: Foliage. A man crosses right; another follows.

CUT TO:

12. TWO-SHOT: Lean and adjutant. Another man runs into frame. Sound of firing.

CUT TO:

13. Lean points.

LEAN

You men dig here.

CUT TO:

14. MEDIUM SHOT: Adjutant looks right. Two men cross in background. Sound of digging.

ADJ.

I suppose we ought to check his belongings.

CUT TO:

15. MEDIUM SHOT: Lean looks down left, nods, and bends to body. . . .

screenplay
The Upturned Face
JIM STINSON

FADE IN:

1. VERY WIDE SHOT, WALKING: A peaceful, rural scene very early on a glorious Spring morning. A fence-bordered dirt road divides rolling farm meadows dotted with small copses of trees. The sun, just risen, is driving off the last dew sparkles and fingers of mist. A breeze rustles translucent leaves. Birds sing and chatter loudly; occasional barks and a distant cock-crow suggest a farmyard not far away.

We are striding briskly across a field, parallel to the road. Heavy footfalls confirm that this is a point-of-view shot. A rough, energetic voice is humming the barracks tune "Beer, Beer, Beer."

The camera swings right, then left, surveying the scene, then returns to the line of travel.

BILL (Voice-Over)

(grumbling absent-mindedly)

. . . always get the bum details . . .

The shot continues, accompanied by the bird calls and Bill's own sounds, unnaturally clear and distinct.

BILL (Voice-Over)

(in the middle of his song)

. . . hm hm hm hm so queer,
In the Quar – ter – mas – ter's . . .

1a. CAMERA HALTS, centering a copse of trees about one hundred yards away.

BILL (Voice-Over)

(inspecting the copse)

Hmmm.

1b. WALKING RESUMES as he dismisses the copse of trees from his mind.

BILL (Voice-Over)

(finishing the verse)

. . . Corps!

(muttering)

Well, they gotta be *some*place.

(singing again)

My eyes – are dim,
I can – not see—ee-ee,

1c. CAMERA HALTS, centering another stand of trees on the far side of the road. The singing breaks off again, leaving the natural sounds loud on the track. Hold a moment, then

1d. WALKING RESUMES.

BILL (Voice-Over)

(singing)

There are – no – flies – on – meeeee!

2. JUMP CUT TO CLOSE ON TREES: a muzzle flash and smoke puff; sharp gunshot report.

3. WALKING SHOT: A sickening thud and the camera is knocked violently to a sitting position.

BILL (Voice-Over)

(breath only)

Uhhhh!!

The camera tilts very slowly forward to frame booted feet and khaki legs stretched out. The left leg pulls back out of the shot as Bill gets it under him and attempts to rise. He gets part-way up, then totters.

A Lee-Enfield type rifle drops into the shot, onto the foot. A trickle of bright blood splashes the boot briefly, then stops. The birds resume their cheerful gabble.

Very slowly, the camera tilts upward, continuing steadily past horizontal and into the air. It jars slightly and stops, framing empty blue sky.

4. CLOSE-UP: A feisty blue jay scolds his way along a branch.

SUPERIMPOSE FIRST MAIN TITLE

5. CLOSE-UP: An energetic ground squirrel searches, gobbles, chews.

SUPERIMPOSE SECOND MAIN TITLE

6. CLOSE-UP: Translucent tree leaves sparkle in the sunshine.

SUPERIMPOSE LAST MAIN TITLE

FADE TO BLACK. The sounds of nature continue a moment, unnaturally clear in the blackness. Then we hear

ADJUTANT

(still over black screen)

What'll we do now?

DIRECT CUT TO:

7. CLOSE-UP, HIGH ANGLE: Bill's blunt, seamed, dead face; a trickle of dried blood out of one corner of the mouth, through the dirty beard. Calm empty eyes staring sightlessly.

7a. ZOOM OUT, revealing the chunky head and shoulders of a grizzled veteran in his early fifties: longish hair, once blond; untidy olive uniform of officer rank. The widening shot shows the body lying on its back, feet nearest camera. Lean and the adjutant stand at the feet, backs to camera, framing the corpse. Bird and insect sounds continue. The hot light suggests mid-afternoon.

8. MEDIUM SHOT: Lean, a tall, rangy man of forty with a thatch of hair and beard. He replies as if giving the obvious answer to a self-evident question:

LEAN

Bury him.

. . .

▲ ▲ ▲

Some Questions for Consideration:

1. How do the openings of the screenplays differ from the opening of the short story?
2. How do they differ from each other?
3. What is the likely effect of these differences on our emotional reaction to what is happening?
4. Why do you think neither screenwriter chose to begin his film with the adjutant's question, "What will we do now?"
5. Without having seen a film version of this story, can you guess which version will be more visually interesting?
6. To what extent does each screenplay convey the *tone* of Crane's prose?

Fiction and Film

TIMOTHY CORRIGAN

Fiction is, of course, a much older art form than film. For that matter, epic poetry is an even older art form than fiction, going back to at least 700 b.c. But if there are significant differences between Homer's Iliad, *Cervantes'* Don Quixote, *and Stone's* Nixon, *there are also crucial similarities: all have themes, stories, characters, and points of view. How these age-old attributes account for the particular content of films and for their* particular *effects on us is the subject of this passage by Timothy Corrigan, a professor of film studies at Temple University. Corrigan's in-*

sights should be helpful to you throughout this chapter as you pursue your investigations into the relationships between films and the literary works on which they are based.

This passage has been slightly rearranged from the form in which it originally appeared in Corrigan's book A Short Guide to Writing About Film, *(2nd ed., 1994).* Note: *Since Corrigan's text (as the title indicates) concerns writing about film, his occasional references to the "writer" refer, unless otherwise indicated, to the person writing about films, rather than to the screenwriter.*

FILM AND THE OTHER ARTS

Although the movies are one of the youngest of the arts, they have absorbed the structures and forms of many older arts. Not surprisingly, therefore, writing about film requires some of the critical language of these other literary and visual arts: we speak of "plot" and "character" in both films and novels, and terms such as "point of view" are part of the critical vocabulary of painting, literature, and the movies. Borrowed terminology allows a critic to make important connections with other fields, but it also demands that a writer about film be sensitive to how terms and structures change when they are applied to film. Here we will look at four related terms that film studies share with the literary and visual arts: *theme, narrative, character,* and *point of view.* 1

Theme

Going over the notes that you have taken on the film, you may wish first to identify the *themes* of the movie, which often comes down to stepping back and asking what this film is "about": the triumph of good over evil in *Star Wars* (1977), for example, or the tragic confusions of war in *Platoon* (1986). Themes, in many case, become the foundation for an analysis, because they point to the main ideas that inform a movie. They are not, strictly speaking, the "moral" or message of the movie; they are the large and the small ideas that help explain the actions and events in it. Ask, for example: 2

- Who are the central characters?
- What do they represent in themselves and in relation to each other? the importance of individuality or society? human strength or human compassion?
- How do the characters' actions create a story with meaning or a constellation of meanings?
- Does the story emphasize the benefits of change or endurance?
- What kind of life or what actions does the film ask you to value or criticize, and why?
- If there is no coherent message or story, why not?

- How does the movie make you feel? happy? depressed? confused? and why?

Having stated a principal theme in a film (and perhaps one or two subsidiary themes), a writer needs to explain them in terms of the specific situation and aims of the movie. The more sensitive a writer's vocabulary, the more refined the perception and argument will be. Thus, "alienation" may very well describe the broadest thematic lines of Chaplin's *City Lights* (1931), Capra's *You Can't Take It with You* (1938), Woody Allen's *Shadows and Fog* (1992), and Bertolucci's *The Conformist* (1970). Although this may be a good start, however, a sharp analysis demands that the writer make finer distinctions about the historical, stylistic, and structural ways that theme is manifested in each movie. Does that alienation seem inevitable, perhaps even desirable? Does it lead to new knowledge or is it a disaster that could have been avoided? Is it presented as a tragic or comic problem in the movie? Writing about *The Conformist,* a student might develop the theme of alienation by observing that here it relates to the protagonist's sexuality and the fascist period in Italy and that, unlike the first two movies (and to some extent in the third), the movie never really resolves this alienation. The writer might extend that argument by describing how the main character regularly seems entrapped and isolated by the rigorous framing of the camera (Figure 1), and by the many frames within the image as a whole (door frames, window frames, etc.). Note, however, that this kind of consideration of alienation in *The Conformist* does not attempt to fashion a simplified and inappropriate moral. One cannot conclude that "in *The Conformist,* alienation is an evil which dooms the character to misery." 3

FIGURE 1.

The frames within the framing of *The Conformist.*

While identifying themes provides an important foundation for your analysis, writing about the movies involves a wide range of special terms that will help you organize and clarify your topic. . . . 4

Narrative

When most of us refer to the movies, we often have in mind narrative movies, not documentaries or experimental films. A *narrative* has two principal components: 5

- The *story* is all the events that are presented to us or that we can infer have happened.
- The *plot* is the arrangement or construction of those events in a certain order or structure.

All films that sketch the life of Napoleon would tell the same story, describing his birth, his rise to power, the French Revolution, its aftermath, and his exile to Elba. The plots in these different movies could, however, be structured and arranged in various ways: one might begin with Napoleon's last days at Elba and tell his story through a series of flashbacks, showing events that occurred earlier than ones already shown; another might start with his birth and move chronologically through his life. 6

Always ask yourself how the narrative of the film you are watching is constructed. Is it a movie with a story line? If not, why not? Is the story told chronologically, or does the plot rearrange events in an unusual temporal order? Is there a reason for the particular plot structure? What in the story is left out in the actual plot construction? Are there reasons for including some material and omitting other material? Does the way in which the story is told become a prominent feature of the film and thus a central factor in an analysis of it? How do you recognize the narrative structure: is there a voice-over in which a character's voice describes events, thereby making it clear that he or she is organizing the plot? Are there technical elements that give dramatic indications about the way the story is structured, such as the change from black and white to color in *The Wizard of Oz* or Abel Gance's use of three screens in his *Napoleon?* What propels the story: a mystery as in *The Big Sleep* (1946)? a desire to reach a goal, as in *The Wizard of Oz?* Is it difficult to determine this, as in some modern movies in which the plot seems to have no definite direction? 7

The various relationships between a story, its plot, and a narrative style are numerous. When most of us think of a narrative film, however, we probably have in mind what is often called the classical narrative. To discuss any kind of film narrative it is useful to have some sense of this important narrative form. A classical narrative usually has: 8

1. A plot development in which there is a logical relationship between one event and another

2. A sense of closure at the end (a happy or a tragic ending, for example)
3. Stories that are focused on characters
4. A narrative style that attempts to be more or less objective

Not all classical narratives are the same, of course, and many fine essays are about the variations and innovations within this model. For instance, they may discuss the role of class in these stories or the ambiguous endings in others. One student began his paper on Howard Hawks's *The Big Sleep* by observing:

> This classic mystery story does not make complete sense. It seems as if the complicated plot has lost track of the story, and frequently it is very difficult to follow the logic of who killed whom and why. Nonetheless, <u>The Big Sleep</u> remains a model of classical filmmaking in the way it concentrates all the action on the main characters, Bogart and Bacall. If the plot is confused, these characters make you forget that confusion and realize that the story is about them.
>
> Bill Evans

In the following paragraphs, Gerald Mast [in *Howard Hawks: Storyteller*] looks at narrative structure as it applies to many Hawks films, such as *To Have and Have Not* (1944) and *His Girl Friday* (1940). Note how Mast first places his analysis in the literary tradition of narrative, then moves to a discussion of plots constructed upon the notion of "surprising inevitability." 9

> What is a good story? First, there is the construction of an action—not just enumerating a string of events but organizing those events into a coherent and powerful shape. The construction of a narrative action relies on a very interesting paradox, of which Hawks was well aware. On the one hand, the events in a narrative must seem to flow spontaneously, naturally, surprisingly; nothing must be expected, nothing foreseen. On the other hand, the events in a narrative must be prepared for, motivated, foreshadowed; nothing is unexpected, everything foreseen. On the one hand, everything that happens to King Lear is a surprise; on the other, everything in the play proceeds from Kent's command in the beginning to "See better, Lear." It is surprising that Emma Woodhouse discovers that it is Mr. Knightley whom she really must marry; yet everything in *Emma* points the way to this inevitable and inescapable discovery. The paradox of narrative construction is that it synthesizes the accidents of nature—which seem random—and the patterns of logic—which are fixed; the outcome of events is simultaneously inevitable yet surprising to the reader or viewer when the inevitable occurs. The narrative that is insufficiently spontaneous and surprising is familiarly condemned

as contrived, overplotted, unnatural, and stilted; the narrative that is insufficiently patterned is familiarly condemned as random, wandering, arbitrary, and formless.

How does Hawks's story construction relate to this paradox of surprising inevitability? In over forty years of filmmaking, collaborating with over a dozen major writers, Howard Hawks builds every story in an identical four-part structure. The first part is a prologue that either (1) establishes the conflict in a past or present close relationship of the major characters (this is the usual pattern of Ben Hecht's scripts for Hawks) or (2) initiates a conflict by the collision of two apparently opposite characters upon their initial meeting (this is the usual Furthman-Faulkner pattern). The second and third parts develop the central conflict established in the first, either by letting one of the conflicting characters or life styles dominate in the second part, then the other in the third, or by letting one of the characters work alone in the second part, then both of them together in the third. And the fourth section resolves the central conflict, often by a return to the original physical setting of the prologue, but in which setting the warring characters now see themselves and one another in a new light. Occasionally Hawks adds a very brief epilogue or "tag" to return the narrative full circle to its beginning. Whatever else one can say about this narrative structure, it gives a Hawks story the firmness of shape, the elegance, economy, and symmetry that allow surprising events to transpire within the firm logic and structure of a controlled pattern. (30–31)

Not all movies are classical narratives or even narratives; some movies 10
are *nonnarrative,* meaning they do not tell stories. Experimental films, for example, may avoid stories and investigate questions unrelated to narrative, such as the abstract patterns of light and shadow on film. Documentary films may present real events, such as a typical day at a factory or the religious ritual of an Indian tribe, without organizing those events as a story. In addition, many movies create narratives that are outside the classical tradition or that may intentionally confront that tradition in order to tell their stories in a distinctive manner.

When you watch a movie that seems to avoid a traditional story line or 11
that appears to tell its story in an unusual or perhaps confusing way, ask yourself how the movie is organizing its plot and narration and what it is trying to achieve. Does the story seem illogical, as in some Buñuel films in which events follow the logic of a dream? Does the narrative seem to be telling two or more stories that are difficult to connect, such as in *Hiroshima Mon Amour* (1959), in which the story of a woman and her Nazi lover is told alongside the story of the bombing of Hiroshima? Does the movie have a confusing beginning or an unresolved conclusion? Why? How do these or other narrative strategies relate to the stories being told? With *Hiroshima Mon Amour,* a writer might, after some thought, begin by observing that both stories concern World War II and are told by two newly met lovers; the difficulty in the narrative structure might then be related to the woman's pain in organizing and communicating her memories to someone who comes from a different culture but with a similar historical crisis.

Once you have learned to recognize classical narrative forms, you should be more aware of how stories can be told in a variety of other ways.

Characters

Characters are a common topic for analysis in literature, drama, and film. They are the individuals who populate narrative and nonnarrative films. Whether they are main characters or minor characters, they normally focus the action and often the themes of a movie. Often a discussion of film concentrates on what happens to the characters or how they change. In a movie like *My Dinner with André* (1981), which films the dinner conversation between two men, the movie could more accurately be described as being about two characters telling stories rather than a story about two characters. Keep in mind that an analysis of characters in a movie can be boring or seem simpleminded when you approach them as though they are merely reflections of real people or when you blur the difference between the star and the character. Yet, if you remain attuned to the variety in character types, you will begin to see subtleties and complications in how characters function and what they can mean in different films. As an exercise, consider the characters portrayed by Lillian Gish in *Broken Blossoms* (1919), Lauren Bacall in *The Big Sleep,* and Diane Keaton in *Annie Hall* (1977) and describe how and why those characters are so different. 12

You can begin an analysis of characters by asking yourself whether those characters seem or are meant to seem realistic. What makes them realistic? Are they defined by their clothes, their conversation, or something else? If they do not appear to be realistic, why not, and why are they meant to seem strange or fantastic? Do the characters fit the setting of the story? Does the movie focus on one or two characters, as in *The Big Sleep,* or on many, as in *Nashville,* in which there doesn't seem to be a central character? Do the characters change? in what ways? What values do the characters seem to represent, that is, what do they say about such matters as independence, sexuality, and political belief? These are the kinds of questions you will want to consider in order to make more sense of characters and determine why they are important. 13

Point of View

Like narrative, *point of view* is a term that film shares with the literary and visual arts. In the broadest sense it refers to the position from which something is seen and, by implication, how that point of view determines what you see. In the simplest sense, the point of view is purely physical. My point of view regarding a house across the street will be very different when I look from the rooftop of my house than when I look from the basement window. In a more sophisticated sense, point of view can be psychological or cultural: a child's point of view regarding a dentist's office will probably not be the same as an adult's. 14

In the same way, we can talk about the point of view that a camera has in relationship to a person or an action and even the point of view that a narrative directs at its subject. Movies commonly use an *objective point of view,* whereby most of what is shown is not confined to any one person's perspective. In *Gone with the Wind* (1939) and *Lawrence of Arabia* (1962), the audience sees scenes and events (the battle of Atlanta, Lawrence's journeys) that are supposedly objective in their scope and accuracy, beyond the knowledge or perspective of any one person. In specific scenes, however, that audience may be aware that they are seeing another character only through Rhett's or Lawrence's eyes, and at these times, the camera is recreating that individual's *subjective point of view.* Some movies might experiment with the possibilities of point of view: in *Apocalypse Now* (1979), we seem to see the entire story from Captain Willard's (Martin Sheen's) point of view; he introduces the story as something that has already happened to him, but despite this indication of historical objectivity many of the scenes recreate his very personal, nightmarish perspective on the war in Vietnam. 15

Point of view is central to writing about films because films are basically about seeing the world in a certain way. Approach point of view by using two general guidelines: 16

1. Notice how and when the camera creates the point of view of an individual character.
2. Notice whether the story is told mostly from an objective point of view or from the subjective perspective of one single person.

Ask yourself in what ways the point of view determines what you see. Does it limit or prejudice your vision in any way? What can you tell about the characters through whose eyes you see? Are they aggressive? suspicious? clever? in love?

Because the movies incorporate the traditions of books, plays, and even sculpture and painting, such concepts as narrative, character, and point of view are not only useful but necessary in analyzing film. Often they are the basis for a comparative essay that examines a story and its adaptation as a film. Other essays might compare different film versions of one story or a group of films by one director. When you write a comparative essay of this kind, be sensitive to and careful about not only how these terms connect art forms, but how they highlight differences. Be aware of how the film medium might change the message of an original book or play: look at how a literary or artistic achievement is translated successfully into a movie, and consider what may have been lost. To compare the film *Apocalypse Now* and the short novel *Heart of Darkness* (1898), a writer may choose to discuss the subjective point of view that describes one Captain Willard's journey through Vietnam and the other Captain Willard's—Marlowe's—journey into Africa. That comparison will be much sharper and more revealing if the writer can show how certain literary techniques (long sentences full of repetitions, for example) create one 17 point of view and how certain film techniques (the use of light and shadow, for instance) create the other.

▲ ▲ ▲

Review Questions

1. According to Corrigan, a film's theme is more than simply its moral or message. What else does it entail?
2. What is the difference between story and plot?
3. What is a "classical narrative"?
4. What is the difference between *objective* and *subjective* point of view in film and fiction?

Discussion and Writing Suggestions

1. Select a film you have seen recently (or an older film that you are very familiar with) and discuss its thematic content, using several of the questions posed by Corrigan in the "Theme" section. Do not merely respond to the questions one after the other, but try to integrate your responses into a coherent, focused essay on the film.
2. Select a film whose plot structure represents a departure from the kind of "classical narrative" pattern described by Corrigan (paragraph 8). How do you account for the atypical pattern? What is the effect of this pattern on the viewer? How would the effect have been different had the story been told in a more conventional fashion?
3. Corrigan quotes at length Gerald Mast's analysis of the typical plot pattern of Howard Hawks's films. Select either (1) a group of films by a particular director (e.g., Oliver Stone, Martin Scorsese) or (2) a group of films belonging to a particular genre (e.g., cop-buddy films, female ensemble films) and analyze their plot structures in similar fashion, illustrating your explanations of each component of the action with plots or plot segments of the films under consideration.
4. Think of two or three of the most memorable characters you have seen in recent movies (or, again, in older movies, if they are fresh in your mind). What makes these characters so memorable? The fact that they are true to life? The fact that they are totally *unlike* real people you know? The fact that they are admirable? Or contemptible? Use the questions Corrigan poses at the end of his section on characters, and apply them to the characters you are considering. Shape your response into an essay.
5. Attempt to recall a film or a particular sequence in a film that is dramatically powerful because of its subjective point of view (e.g., the swimming pool sequence in *The Graduate* [1967], the final sequence of *Alien* [1979], the suicide scene in *Dead Poets Society* [1989]). Describe, as specifically as you can, how this subjectivity accounts for the impact of the film or the sequence. If you have easy access to a video of this film, examine one or two scenes closely to see just how the effects are

achieved. You may wish to consult the "Glossary of Film Terms" at the end of this chapter for terminology that will help you describe the cinematography and editing of the film.

Why Adaptations Are Good for Literature —And for Movies

CHARLES EIDSVIK

Charles Eidsvik's essay, "Why Adaptations are Good for Literature—And for Movies," appears in the text Film And/As Literature, *by John Harrington. Eidsvik, like Joseph Boggs in the selection following this one, is sensitive to the unfair expectations viewers bring to adaptations. If we approached adaptations a bit differently, he suggests, we would recognize that they "advance the art of film." Eidsvik's article is written somewhat tongue-in-cheek, and you may be unsure about whether or not to take him seriously. But in his own offbeat way, he attempts to explore the often symbiotic relationship between literature and film and to examine the relative strengths of each medium. Charles Eidsvik has written reviews for the journal* Film Quarterly *and is the author of* Cineliteracy: Film Among the Arts *(1978).*

1 Expectations have a lot to do with how we react to movies. The higher our expectations, the more frequent our disappointment. Usually we do not feel cheated if a film has only ten or twenty good minutes in it; a few really good moments are enough to make a film worthwhile and twenty good minutes is rather a treat. Moreover, if we do get twenty good minutes we are willing to put up with a lot during the other hour or two that the film runs. But such is not the case if the film is an adaptation of a book or a play, especially if that book or play is well known and highly regarded. Not only are our expectations higher for adaptations; what we are willing to put up with is radically less. If adaptations reached the level we expected—not wanted, but *expected*—they would all be masterpieces. Most adaptations are not, of course, masterpieces. Rather they are, on the average, average, which is to say that they have a few good moments, enough to justify our evening. Except that our sense of the work adapted makes us feel betrayed, and therefore blind to the good moments. If there *are* ten or twenty or even thirty good minutes, we are still unsatisfied and come out of the theatre feeling ambivalent or even cheated and utterly blind to the ways in which twenty good minutes *in an adaptation* can contain more originality than one is apt to find in whole masterpieces.

2 Masterpieces, as Picasso pointed out, are seldom very original; truly original works are seldom well enough done to be masterpieces. Masterpieces are (after our critical rhetoric is exhausted) no more or less than works so successful that they transcend or make us forgive their limitations. But originality and success are rare bedfellows; a whole platoon of

ambitious failures and lucky breakthroughs usually precedes and lays the groundwork for each recognizable masterpiece. The failures and breakthroughs attempt newness. When twenty minutes of originality occurs in film history—even when twenty minutes of innovative excellence happens—I am so startled I want to wake my friends to tell them. I have, over a dozen years as a film connoisseur, found that the urge to wake my friends occurs most frequently after I have seen an adaptation. I refuse to believe that is because I have a soft spot for adaptations. I habitually sneer at adaptations and quote Alain Resnais to the effect that they are "warmed-over meals." It's just that experience forces me to admit that adaptations frequently provide major advances in the art of film. The art of film, after all, does not proceed from masterpiece to masterpiece; art advances twenty minutes at a time and is only consolidated in its successes by works we consider masterful. There is no *single* good reason why adaptations should provide newness; each film has *its* reasons. But it seems that the attempt to adapt a work which is not "cinematically-conceived" into "cinematic terms" forces film-makers into attempting original solutions. Sometimes the attempted solutions expose "cinematic terms" for the cliched conventions they so frequently are; sometimes the solutions are successful because they show us new cinematic terms; and sometimes the solutions work for no known reason at all except that response to films is as perverse as human response itself.

• • •

There are four good reasons adaptations are good for literature, and five why they are good for film. First, the literary. 3

One. Movies work as introductions to books. Books sell better if they have been filmed, and read better, because the film aids the imagination. Books (and their authors) can use all the help they can get. A movie is a ninety-minute free "ad" circulated to millions of people. What's more, the movie people *pay* to advertise books. Advertisement tends to make a book into a temporary folk-myth, or undergraduate cult piece. That social importance is otherwise virtually unattainable because of the difficulties of advertising books by ordinary methods. Movies make books "stand out" as important and, secondarily, remind us that dramatic literature was meant to be acted. 4

Two. Movies help get books out of college classrooms and into the streets where they can do some good. There is a sense in which literature is defused by its respectability. Shakespeare's original popularity was attained in a theatre in London's red-light district; his audience had in it whores and pickpockets and vagabonds. Dickens circulated originally by means of newspaper serialization; his work was by no means designed as the subject of seminars. Literature loses its "presence," its virility, when given no other environment than library or classroom; movie adaptations help restore literature's significance. I have a great deal more faith in the potency of a book first encountered via a movie adaptation than in its power if it is first encountered in a college classroom. 5

Three. Movies help restore literature's links with its past. The modern novel and modern theatre have gone experimental and thereby rejected the easy-access melodramatic modes of popular Victorian drama and fiction, modes which connect literature to its roots in popular storytelling. Movies are, in an important sense, the extension of Victorian melodrama. The joycean-faulknerian modernist novel, left to its own devices, would leave us all brain, and with restricted carotid and jugular at that. Movies connect us with literature's gutty past, a past which, like it or not, is necessary to the nourishment even of the brainy present. Were I to be isolated on a desert island for a month, I would take along Joyce's *Ulysses,* but that book is a hell of a way to spend Saturday night. 6

Four. Movies help make writers self-conscious, nervous, and aggressively experimental. Movies are, after all, a co-opting medium, a great middle-class sponge of ideas, plots, and characters. Writers hate being coopted; they hate the fact that movies can reach audiences better than books; they hate taking money to see their creative offspring gang-raped in a screenwriters' conference room; they hate the formulaic-cliché side of Hollywood. I tend to think that hate helps reinforce the paranoiac love of romantic individuality necessary to literary genius. Except for Joyce and Dos Passos, who loved movies, just about everyone involved in inventing literary modernism hated film. Dislike of the movies has been useful to the advance of literature. The whole Lawrencean-Joycean-Millerian thrust of modern literature has been to explore the dangerous, to keep from being co-opted by the *kitsch* trade, to stay authentic. I believe film has kept modern literature pure by producing adaptations which serve as cautionary tales about what will happen to your work if you sell out, if you popularize. Reason four of course contradicts reason three, but that contradiction points to the fact that movies, by carrying on literature's popular traditions, free serious writers from having to carry on those traditions themselves. 7

The five reasons why adaptations are good for movies are less subtle than the reasons adaptations are good for books. The first reason is so unsubtle I blush to mention it. Books are almost the only source of intelligence to be found in Los Angeles County. They *are* the only source of new ideas. I am not trying to offend movie lovers. I am merely trying to describe the process of making a commercial film. Films are not written; they are produced. A book can start with a tantalizing image which slowly grows until it becomes a novel. But a Hollywood film starts with a producer wanting to make a movie, then deciding what sort of movie he wants to make, and then going out and getting the materials, "properties" and personnel to do the job. To get the money to make a film, a producer must convince his backers that the odds are good for making a profit. There are only two ways of doing that: dominoes and adaptations. In dominoes, the producer shows that his movie is just like other money-making movies and will therefore topple audience resistance. Lining up stars, genre, plotline, theme, and approach, the producer attempts to cash in on a proven formula. The only other way is adaptations, where the fact that a book sold well 8 proves that an audience exists for something outside the formula. It's a choice between Lumiere's train coming into the station one more time (but *this* time with *two headlights* to make it *really* exciting!!) and the adaptation. That choice being a little too much for financiers to make, producers frequently make a synthesis of formulaic elements with adapted story-material and, in the resulting films, create successes which then can be formulized and mixed with new adaptation-material in an ever-evolving way.

Two. Literature provides raw material for film. Even if filmmakers wanted to work purely from formulaic, non-literary sources, they couldn't. Film is an industrial institution with raw-material needs far beyond the native resources of Hollywood. Literature is a source of high-grade ore which can be cheaply turned into "product." 9

Three. Adaptations keep the middle class in shape. The middle class has always relied on being able to co-opt fringe fantasies; the ability to co-opt is necessary to its survival. Hollywood, as the mouthpiece of middle-classness, must be able to co-opt whatever artistic ideas are new and dangerous, if middle-class fantasies are to be kept safe. By turning dangerous books into Consumer Romance (the genre which subsumes most Hollywood genres) our institutions are protected. To someone like me with two cars and a banking habit, it is very reassuring to know Hollywood is protecting us. 10

• • •

Four. Adaptations present film with technical challenges. Film, more than any other medium, depends on technical flexibility. Film technology is, as a standardized system, only as good as it has to be; adaptations, by presenting technical problems, help keep the equipment from rigidifying. I don't think we would have the sound film if it were not for the desire to put adapted plays and dialogue-dependent novels onto film. The widely variegated conventions of the novel have dictated the use of adaptable equipment for novel adaptations. Technical advances allow the art to advance. 11

Five. Literature gives filmmakers an inferiority complex. Culturally and in terms of respectability, the novel and theatre are ranked above the cinema. Without the adaptation to keep literature's quality-standards clearly in view, Hollywood's anti-intellectual biases would be given freer reign. The social dimension is important in the production of art. The first wish of the producer or director is, of necessity, to make money; he has to do that to keep working. But the *nouveaux-riches* have a compulsion to legitimize themselves, to social-climb above the level of money-grubbers. Becoming artists or backing artistic projects is, for the filmmaker, the route to respectability. The process is no different than the way the bourgeoisie usually buys its way into the aristocracy, but when a filmmaker social-climbs, we benefit. 12

The five reasons for film lovers to be grateful for the adaptation are, like the reasons given for literature-lovers, both contradictory and overlapping. That is precisely because the marriage of literature and film has nothing to do with logic as philosophy departments teach it; rather, it has to do with the irrational logics of economics, art history, and the processes of 13 creation. The forces the adaptation sets in motion are by no means conducive to a happy marriage between book culture and the film world; the opposite is the case. But we benefit from the lousy marriage between literature and film, a marriage in which the battleground is, often as not, the process of adaptation. All good marriages more or less resemble one another. It is the bad ones which are interesting and from which grow offspring strong enough and violent enough to create new directions in evolution.

▲ ▲ ▲

Review Questions

1. Why are viewers often disappointed with adaptations, according to Eidsvik?
2. Why do adaptations often provide newness in cinema?
3. What are the four reasons adaptations are good for literature?
4. What are the five reasons adaptations are good for film?

Discussion and Writing Suggestions

1. Characterize and comment on the *tone* of this article. For instance, what is the effect of sentences like, "Adaptations keep the middle class in shape," or "Literature gives filmmakers an inferiority complex"? To what extent does such "smart-alec" language mask serious points about literature and film?
2. Based on Eidsvik's two sets of reasons, write a paragraph or two summarizing his views on how the two art forms interact and how the process of making film adaptations advances the techniques of film.
3. Eidsvik suggests that a film is redeemed, is worth watching, if it "has only ten or twenty good minutes." Do you agree?
4. "The art of film, after all, does not proceed from masterpiece to masterpiece; art advances twenty minutes at a time and is only consolidated in its successes by works we consider masterful." Read paragraph 2 and comment on this sentence.
5. In your experience, which is more satisfying: seeing an adaptation *before* or *after* you have read the original story? Try to explain your reactions, especially in light of what Eidsvik says about *expectations* in paragraph 1.
6. Of the four reasons Eidsvik claims that adaptations are good for literature, which seem most compelling? Why? What more general point does Eidsvik make about literature (particularly, modern literature) in relation to these four reasons?
7. Eidsvik writes that movies originate not with an idea but with a producer's "wanting to make a movie, then deciding what sort of movie he wants to make." Does this process surprise you at all? To what extent might such a process have a detrimental effect on the finished product?

8. Do you agree that films make dangerous fantasies safe for middle-class American viewers? In what sense does a movie that depicts casual (sexual) relations, for instance, or violence let viewers exercise their fantasies—safely? Eidsvik uses the word "co-opt"; what does he mean?

The Problems of Adaptation

JOSEPH M. BOGGS

Joseph M. Boggs, of Western Kentucky University, is author of The Art of Watching Films *(3rd ed., 1991), in which the following appears. Boggs is adamant in his belief that film adaptations stand as unique works of art that must be judged on their own terms. For Boggs, the standard of judgment should not be the literalness with which the director has translated scenes from a story onto the screen. Other considerations, which Boggs will alert you to, come into play, including the "cinematic potential" of the original story and the creative artistry of the director and actors. As the title of Boggs's book suggests, there is an art to watching films—and, in this particular case, adaptations.*

One of the most difficult problems of film analysis arises when we see 1
a film adaptation of a play we have seen or a novel we have read, for we generally approach such films with completely unreasonable expectations. Usually we expect the film to duplicate exactly the experience we had in seeing the play or in reading the novel. That is, of course, completely impossible. Since we have already experienced the story and are familiar with the characters and events, the adaptation is bound to lack some of the freshness of the original. But many factors other than familiarity should be considered if we are to approach an adaptation with the proper frame of mind. To know what we can reasonably expect from film adaptations of a play or a novel requires insight into the kinds of changes that will occur, as well as an understanding of the relative strengths and weaknesses of the media involved.

CHANGE IN MEDIUM

Some changes are to be expected because the medium in which a story is 2
told has a definite effect on the story itself. Each medium has its strengths and limitations, and any adaptation from one medium to another must take these factors into account and adapt the subject matter to take advantage of the strengths of the new medium. Thus, if we are to judge a film adaptation fairly, we should recognize that although a novel, a play, or a film can tell generally the same story, each medium is a work of art in its own right. And in spite of the fact that some properties are shared by all three, each medium has its own distinctive techniques, conventions, consciousness, and viewpoint. We do not expect an oil painting to have the same effect as

a statue or a woven tapestry depicting the same subject, and we should look on the film adaptation of a novel or a play in much the same manner.

CHANGE IN CREATIVE ARTISTS

The influence that any change in creative talents has on a work of art must 3
certainly be considered. No two creative minds are alike, and once the reins are passed from one creative hand to another the end product is different. Some kind of creative shift occurs in almost any kind of adaptation. Even when a novelist or playwright adapts his or her work for the screen, changes (sometimes rather drastic) are sure to be made. Some of those changes may be required by the new medium. For example, the average novel contains more material than a film could ever hope to include, so the screenwriter or director must choose what to leave in and what to take out. Because the novel cannot be translated intact, its emphasis may have to be changed, even if the novelist is writing the screenplay. Sometimes, problems arise that are totally beyond the screenwriter's or director's control. . . . The most significant changes, however, come about because the novelist or playwright must surrender some artistic control to the director and the actors.

• • •

CINEMATIC POTENTIAL OF THE ORIGINAL WORK

Renata Adler wrote, "Not every written thing aspires to be a movie." And, 4
indeed, some plays and novels are more adaptable to the film medium than others. The style in which a novel is written, for example, certainly affects its adaptability to film. Randall Stewart and Dorothy Bethurum point out important differences in the novelistic styles of Ernest Hemingway and Henry James:

> It is interesting to observe that two such influential prose writers as Hemingway and Henry James should be at the opposite poles of style: one (Hemingway) giving us the rhythms of speech, the other (James) literary convolutions found only on the printed page, one (Hemingway) elemental and sensuous, the other (James) complex and infinitely qualifying. Each style is admirably fitted for the purpose for which it is intended. James is concerned primarily with the intellectual analysis of experience. Hemingway's aim is the sensuous and emotional rendering of experience.[1]

Because of the differences in their style, a Hemingway novel would be more easily adapted to the screen than a novel by Henry James. The last point made by Stewart and Bethurum is especially important: Hemingway's sensuous and emotional rendering of experience is cinematic; James's intellectual analysis of experience is not. The difference in the two

[1]Randall Stewart and Dorothy Bethurum, *Modern American Narration* (Chicago, Scott, Foresman, 1954), pp. 66–67.

writers' styles and their adaptability to the screen can be observed in the following samples of their work:

> Mrs. Gereth had said she would go with the rest to church, but suddenly it seemed to her that she would not be able to wait till church-time for relief: breakfast, at Waterbath, was a punctual meal, and she had still nearly an hour on her hands. Knowing the church to be near, she prepared in her room for the little rural walk, and on her way down again, passing through corridors and observing imbecilities of decoration, the aesthetic misery of the big commodious house, she felt a return of the tide of last night's irritation, a renewal of everything she could secretly suffer from ugliness and stupidity. Why did she consent to such contacts, why did she so rashly expose herself? She had had, heaven knew, her reasons, but the whole experience was to be sharper than she had feared. To get away from it and out into the air, into the presence of sky and trees, flowers and birds was a necessity of every nerve. The flowers of Waterbath would probably go wrong in color and the nightingales sing out of tune; but she remembered to have heard the place described as possessing those advantages that are usually spoken of as natural. There were advantages enough it clearly didn't possess. It was hard for her to believe that a woman could look presentable who had been kept awake for hours by the wall-paper in her room; yet none the less, as in her fresh widow's weeds she rustled across the hall, she was, as usual, the only person in the house incapable of wearing in her preparation the horrible stamp of the exceptional smartness that would be conspicuous in a grocer's wife. She would rather have perished than to have looked *endimanchée*.
>
> —Opening paragraph from *The Spoils of Poynton* by Henry James

> Nick stood up. He was all right. He looked up the track at the lights of the caboose going out of sight around the curve. There was water on both sides of the track, then tamarack swamp.
>
> He felt of his knee. The pants were torn and skin was barked. His hands were scraped and there were sand and cinders driven up under his nails. He went over to the edge of the track down the little slope to the water and washed his hands. He washed them carefully in the cold water, getting the dirt out from the nails. He squatted down and bathed his knee.
>
> —First two paragraphs of "The Battler" by Ernest Hemingway[2]

Although the problems of adapting a play to the screen are not gener- 5
ally as great as those presented by the James novel, playwrights also have styles that affect the ease with which their plays can be adapted to film. Tennessee Williams, for example, is a more cinematic playwright than Edward Albee, basically because Williams's verbal imagery is more concrete and sensual and because his plays contain speeches—such as the one describing Sebastian's death in *Suddenly Last Summer*—that lend themselves to visual flashbacks.

NOVELISTIC VERSUS CINEMATIC POINT OF VIEW

Point of view is an important factor in any novel. The fictional point of 6
view controls and dictates the form and shape of the novel and determines

[2]Reprinted from "The Battler" by Ernest Hemingway with the permission of Charles Scribner's Sons.

its emphasis, tone, strengths, and limitations. A change in point of view is almost as important in a work of fiction as a change from one medium to another, for the point of view of a novel determines to a large degree what the novelist can and cannot do. To appreciate the difficulties the filmmaker faces in translating a novel into film requires some familiarity with five literary viewpoints.

1. **First-Person Point of View.** A character who has participated in or observed the action of the story gives us an eyewitness or first-hand account of what happened and his or her responses to it. 7

> Yes sir. Flem Snopes has filled the whole country full of spotted horses. You can hear folks running them all day and all night, whooping and hollering, and the horses running back and forth across them little wooden bridges ever now and then kind of like thunder. Here I was this morning pretty near halfway to town, with a team ambling along and me setting in the buckboard about half asleep, when all of a sudden something come swurging up outen the bushes and jumped the road clean, without touching hoof to it. It flew right over my team big as a billboard and flying through the air like a hawk. It taken me thirty minutes to stop my team and untangle the harness and the buckboard and hitch them up again.
>
> —Opening paragraph of "Spotted Horses," by William Faulkner[3]

2. **Omniscient-Narrator Point of View.** An all-seeing, all-knowing narrator, capable of reading the thoughts of all the characters and capable of being several places at once if need be, tells the story. 8

> There was a woman who was beautiful, who started with all the advantages, yet she had no luck. She married for love, and the love turned to dust. She had bonny children, yet she felt they had been thrust upon her, and she could not love them. They looked at her coldly, as if they were finding fault with her. And hurriedly she felt she must cover up some fault in herself. Yet what it was that she must cover up she never knew. Nevertheless, when her children were present, she always felt the center of her heart go hard. This troubled her, and in her manner she was all the more gentle and anxious for her children, as if she loved them very much. Only she could not feel love, no, not for anybody. Everybody else said of her: "She is such a good mother. She adores her children." Only she herself, and her children themselves, knew it was not so. They read it in each other's eyes.
>
> There was a boy and two little girls. They lived in a pleasant house, with a garden, and they had discreet servants, and felt themselves superior to anyone in the neighborhood.
>
> Although they lived in style, they felt always an anxiety in the house. There was never enough money.
>
> —Opening paragraphs of "The Rocking-Horse Winner," by D. H. Lawrence.[4]

---

[3]William Faulkner, "Spotted Horses," from *The Faulkner Reader* (New York: Random House, 1959).

[4]From "The Rocking-Horse Winner," *The Complete Short Stories of D. H. Lawrence,* vol. 3.

3. **Third-Person Limited Point of View.** The narrator is omniscient 9
except for the fact that his or her powers of mind reading are limited to or at least focused on a single character. This character's thoughts are extremely important to the novel, for he or she becomes the central intelligence through which we view the action.

Although Bertha Young was thirty she still had moments like this when she wanted to run instead of walk, to take dancing steps on and off the pavement, to bowl a hoop, to throw something up in the air and catch it again, or to stand still and laugh at nothing—at nothing, simply.

What can you do if you are thirty and, turning the corner of your own street, you are overcome, suddenly, by a feeling of bliss—absolute bliss!— as though you'd suddenly swallowed a bright piece of that late afternoon sun and it burned in your bosom, sending out a little shower of sparks into every particle, into every finger and toe? . . .

Oh, is there no way you can express it without being "drunk and disorderly"? How idiotic civilization is! Why be given a body if you have to keep it shut up in a case like a rare, rare fiddle?

Opening paragraphs of "Bliss" by Katherine Mansfield[5]

4. **Dramatic Point of View.** We are not conscious of a narrator, for 10
the author does not comment on the action but simply describes the scene, telling us what happens and what the characters say, so we get a feeling of being there, observing the scene as we would in a play. This is also known as the *concealed,* or *effaced, narrator point of view.*

The door of Henry's lunchroom opened and two men came in. They sat down at the counter.

"What's yours?" George asked them.

"I don't know," one of the men said. "What do you want to eat, Al?"

"I don't know," said Al. "I don't know what I want to eat."

Outside it was getting dark. The street light came on outside the window. The two men at the counter read the menu. From the other end of the counter Nick Adams watched them. He had been talking to George when they came in.

"I'll have a roast pork tenderloin with apple sauce and mashed potatoes," the first man said.

"It isn't ready yet."

"What the hell do you put it on the card for?"

"That's the dinner," George explained. "You can get that at six o'clock."

George looked at the clock on the wall behind the counter. "It's five o'clock."

"The clock says twenty minutes past five," the second man said.

"It's twenty minutes fast."

"Oh, to hell with the clock," the first man said. "What have you got to eat?"

—Opening paragraphs of "The Killers," by Ernest Hemingway[6]

5. **Stream of Consciousness or Interior Monologue.** This is a kind of first-person narrative, except the participant in the action is not consciously narrating the story. What we get instead is a unique kind of inner view, as though a microphone and a movie camera in the fictional character's mind were recording for us every thought, image, and impression that passes through the character's brain, without the conscious acts of organization, selectivity, or narration. 11

Stay mad. My shirt was getting wet and my hair. Across the roof hearing the roof loud now I could see Natalie going through the garden among the rain. Get wet I hope you catch pneumonia go on home Cowface. I jumped hard as I could into the hog-wallow the mud yellowed up to my waist stinking I kept on plunging until I fell down and rolled over in it. "Hear them in swimming, sister? I wouldn't mind doing that myself." If I had time. When I have time. I could hear my watch. *Mud was warmer than the rain it smelled awful. She had her back turned I went around in front of her. You know what I was doing? She turned her back I went around in front of her the rain creeping into the mud flatting her bodice through her dress it smelled horrible. I was hugging her that's what I was doing. She turned her back I went around in front of her. I was hugging her I tell you. I don't give a damn what you were doing . . .*

—From *The Sound and the Fury* by William Faulkner[7]

Of the five points of view possible in a novel, three require of the narrator an ability to look inside a character's mind to "see" what he or she is thinking. Omniscient, third-person limited, and stream of consciousness all stress the thoughts, concepts, or reflections of a character—elements that are difficult to depict cinematically. These three fictional points of view have no natural cinematic equivalents. George Bluestone discusses this problem in *Novels into Film:* 12

> The rendition of mental states—memory, dream, imagination—cannot be as adequately represented by film as by language. . . . The film, by arranging external signs for our visual perception, or by presenting us with dialogue, can lead us to *infer* thought. But it cannot show us thought directly. It can show us characters thinking, feeling, and speaking, but it cannot show us their thoughts and feelings. A film is not thought; it is perceived.[8]

---

[6]Reprinted from "The Killers" by Ernest Hemingway with the permission of Charles Scribner's Sons.

[7]Reprinted by permission of Random House, Inc., from William Faulkner, *The Sound and the Fury.* Copyright 1929 by William Faulkner. Copyright renewed 1956 by William Faulkner.

[8]George Bluestone. *Novels into Film* (Berkley: University of California Press, 1957), pp. 47–48.

Another problem arises from the fact that in three of the viewpoints—first person, omniscient, and third-person limited—we are aware of a narrator, of someone telling a story. The sense of a narrator, or a novelistic point of view, can be imposed (or superimposed) on a film through voice-over narration added to the soundtrack. But this is a not a natural cinematic quality, and it is rarely completely successful in duplicating or even suggesting the novelistic viewpoints. In film we usually simply see the story unfold. Thus the dramatic point of view is the only novelistic viewpoint that can be directly translated into cinema. But few if any novels are written from the strict dramatic point of view, because this viewpoint requires so much of the reader's concentration; he or she must read between the lines for significance or meaning. This viewpoint is usually restricted to short stories. 13

The usual "solution" to these problems of adaptation is to ignore the novel's point of view, omit the prose passages stressing thought or reflection, and simply duplicate the most dramatic scenes. The problem, of course, is that the prose passages and the point of view often constitute much of the novel's essence. This means that filmmakers cannot always capture a novel's essence cinematically. 14

• • •

PHILOSOPHICAL REFLECTIONS

Often, the most striking passages in a novel are those in which we sense an inner movement of the author's mind toward some truth of life and are aware that our own mind is being stretched by his or her contemplation and reflection. Such passages do not stress external action but rather lead to an internal questioning of the meaning and significance of events, taking the reader on a kind of cerebral excursion into a gray world where the camera cannot go. The following passage from *All the King's Men,* for example, could not really be effectively treated in film: 15

> Two hours later, I was in my car and Burden's Landing was behind me, and the bay, and windshield wipers were making their busy little gasp and click like something inside you which had better not stop. For it was raining again. The drops swung and swayed down out of the dark into my headlights like a bead portiere of bright metal beads which the car kept shouldering through.
>
> There is nothing more alone than being in a car at night in the rain. I was in the car. And I was glad of it. Between one point on the map and another point on the map, there was the being alone in the car in the rain. They say you are not you except in terms of relation to other people. If there weren't any other people there wouldn't be any you, and not being you or anything, you can really lie back and get some rest. It is a vacation from being you. There is only the flow of the motor under your foot spinning that frail thread of sound out of its metal gut like a spider, that filament, that nexus, which isn't really there, between the you which you have just left in one place and the you which you will be when you get to the other place.

> You ought to invite those two you's to the same party some time. Or you might have a family reunion for all the you's with barbecue under the trees. It would be amusing to know what they would say to each other.
>
> But meanwhile, there isn't either one of them, and I am in the car in the rain at night.[9]

Because *All the King's Men* is full of such passages, this one could not be singled out for treatment in voice-over narration. It is also highly improbable that the dramatic scene described here (the narrator, Jack Burden, driving alone in the rain at night) could suggest his thoughts even to a viewer who had read the novel.

When a visual image in a novel is more closely related to a philosophical passage and serves as a trigger to a reflection, there is a greater probability that the filmmaker will be able to suggest the significance of the image to those who have read the novel, but even this is by no means certain. The first of the following two passages from *All the King's Men* gives us a rather clear visual image and could be effectively treated on film. The second is primarily the narrator's reflection on the significance of the visual image and could at best be only suggested in a film: **16**

> In a settlement named Don Jon, New Mexico, I talked to a man propped against the shady side of the filling station, enjoying the only patch of shade in a hundred miles due east. He was an old fellow, seventy-five if a day, with a face like sun-brittled leather and pale-blue eyes under the brim of a felt hat which had once been black. The only thing remarkable about him was the fact that while you looked into the sun-brittled leather of the face, which seemed as stiff and devitalized as the hide on a mummy's jaw, you would suddenly see a twitch in the left cheek, up toward the pale-blue eye. You would think he was going to wink, but he wasn't going to wink. The twitch was simply an independent phenomenon, unrelated to the face or to what was behind the face or to anything in the whole tissue of phenomena which is the world we are lost in. It was remarkable, in that face, the twitch which lived that little life all its own. I squatted by his side, where he sat on a bundle of rags from which the handle of a tin skillet protruded, and listened to him talk. But the words were not alive. What was alive was the twitch, of which he was no longer aware. . . .
>
> We rode across Texas to Shreveport, Louisiana, where he left me to try for north Arkansas. I did not ask him if he had learned the truth in California. His face had learned it anyway, and wore the final wisdom under the left eye. The face knew that the twitch was the live thing. Was all. But, having left that otherwise unremarkable man, it occurred to me, as I reflected upon the thing which made him remarkable, that if the twitch was all, what was it that could know that twitch was all? Did the leg of the dead frog in the laboratory know that the twitch was all when you put the electric current through it? Did the

---

[9]Excerpted from *All the King's Men,* copyright 1946, 1974 by Robert Penn Warren. Reprinted by permission of Harcourt Brace Jovanovich, Inc. Excerpt appears on pp. 128–129 of the Bantam Books (1974) edition.

man's face know about the twitch, and how it was all? Ah, I decided, that is the mystery. That is the secret knowledge. That is what you have to go to California to have a mystic vision to find out. That the twitch can know that the twitch is all. Then, having found that out, in the mystic vision, you feel clean and free. You are at one with the Great Twitch.[10]

SUMMARIZING A CHARACTER'S PAST

In the novel, when a character first appears, the novelist often provides us 17
with a quick thumbnail sketch of his or her past, as illustrated by the summary of the origins and past history of Billy, the deaf mute boy from Larry McMurtry's novel, *The Last Picture Show:*

> While the boys worked Sam stood by the stove and warmed his aching feet. He wished Sonny weren't so reckless economically, but there was nothing he could do about it. Billy was less of a problem partly because he was so dumb. Billy's real father was an old railroad man who had worked in Thalia for a short time just before the war: his mother was a deaf and dumb girl who had no people except an aunt. The old man cornered the girl in the balcony of the picture show one night and begat Billy. The sheriff saw to it that the old man married the girl, but she died when Billy was born and he was raised by the family of Mexicans who helped the old man keep the railroad track repaired. After the war the hauling petered out and the track was taken up. The old man left and got a job bumping cars on a stockyards track in Oklahoma, leaving Billy with the Mexicans. They hung around for several more years, piling prickly pear and grubbing mesquite, but then a man from Plainview talked them into moving out there to pick cotton. They snuck off one morning and left Billy sitting on the curb in front of the picture show.
>
> From then on, Sam the Lion took care of him. Billy learned to sweep, and he kept all three of Sam's places swept out: in return he got his keep and also, every single night, he got to watch the picture show. He always sat in the balcony, his broom at his side: for years he saw every show that came to Thalia and so far as anyone knew, he liked them all. He was never known to leave while the screen was lit.[11]

McMurtry summarizes a character's whole background in two brief paragraphs. In the film version, no background on Billy is provided whatsoever. Such information could not be worked into the film's dialogue without bringing in an outsider, some character who didn't know Billy, to ask about his past. But having characters spend a great deal of time talking about the backgrounds of other characters does not make for good cinema—it becomes too static, too talky. The only alternative is to dramatize such paragraphs visually. But this type of material not only lacks the importance to

---

[10]Excerpted from *All the King's Men,* copyright 1946, 1974 by Robert Penn Warren. Reprinted by permission of Harcourt Brace Jovanovich, Inc. Excerpt appears on pp. 313–314 of the Bantam Books (1974) edition.

[11]Excerpted from *The Last Picture Show* by Larry McMurtry (New York: Dell, 1966), pp. 8–9.

justify such treatment, it would also have to be forced into the main plot structure in a very unnatural manner. Thus, the kind of background information given in the passages above is simply not suited to a natural cinematic style, and the background of many film characters therefore remains a mystery. Because novels can and do provide this kind of information, they possess a dimension of depth in characterization that films usually lack.

▲ ▲ ▲

Review Questions

1. Why do we usually bring unfair expectations to film adaptations, according to Boggs?
2. What are the qualities that make some original stories more cinematic than others?
3. In what ways can a story's point of view—particularly first person, omniscient, and third-person limited—present obstacles to adaptation?
4. What is the natural point of view of a movie?
5. Why do adaptations sometimes miss the "essence" of a story?
6. Why do written stories more easily capture depth of character than films?

Discussion and Writing Suggestions

1. Boggs claims that we're likely to have unfair expectations of films that have been adapted from stories. Reflect on a film you've seen that was based on a story you had read previously. Try to reconstruct your expectations before seeing the film—and then your reactions to the film. Were your expectations unreasonable? Explain.
2. Is it inevitable, in your view, that a "great" story that turns on a character's deeply felt emotion or idea must suffer when adapted for film? Boggs has enumerated the ways in which film cannot capture a character's "interior." Have you seen any adaptations in which this was not so?
3. Review Boggs's summary of the different points of view possible in written stories. As you read each passage that Boggs offers to illustrate a particular point of view, make notes about how you would convey that passage's content cinematically. What visual and auditory elements would you use to convey interior and exterior states?
4. What are your expectations on seeing a film versus reading a story? Is there any sense in which you feel that films should (or do) require less work on the part of the viewer than stories do on the part of the reader? Explain.
5. Do you resist at all the notion that films should be studied? In the context of this question, reflect on the title to the text from which the Boggs's selection was excerpted: *The Art of Watching Films.* What would make watching films an "art"?

The Birds

DAPHNE DU MAURIER

Daphne Du Maurier's "The Birds" is the first of two stories available for your study of film adaptation. "The Birds" is largely an exterior story of observable, physical action. But as you will see, observable events in "The Birds" trigger interior states—terror, for one—that a director needs to relate on-screen. We suggest that you first read and enjoy the story. Then, before viewing the adaptation by Alfred Hitchcock, reread—this time with a "filmic" eye: pay special attention to the moments in the story that you think offer particularly rich possibilities for film and the moments you think will pose difficulties. On a technical level, you might want to question how a director might arrange particular scenes (that is, how to logically present the stages of dramatic action) to make a convincing adaptation.

Daphne Du Maurier (1907–1989) was a British writer and author of several novels: Rebecca, Jamaica Inn, The King's General, The Parasites, My Cousin Rachel, *and* The Scapegoat. *Her short stories include "The Birds," "Kiss Me Again, Stranger," and "Frenchman's Creek."*

Alfred Hitchcock (1899–1980) was a widely acclaimed director of the thriller, who over a long career is credited with several masterpieces of the genre: Notorious *(1946),* Rear Window *(1954),* Vertigo *(1958), and* North by Northwest *(1959). At the age of 26, Hitchcock directed his first silent film,* The Pleasure Garden *(1925). His first "talkie" was* Blackmail *(1929). Over the next decade, he would make five feature-length films that established him as a master of suspense who could keep audiences transfixed in a what's-next guessing game. Hitchcock adapted three of Daphne Du Maurier's works: the novels* Jamaica Inn *(1939) and* Rebecca *(1940), and "The Birds" (1963).*

As you watch the film and as you read the story, you might note your level of suspense as a reader/viewer. Do the story and the adaptation keep you equally on the edge of your seat?

Two sets of "Discussion and Writing Suggestions" follow the story. The first set, under the heading "FICTION," assumes that you have read the story but have not yet seen the film (see end of paragraph 1 of this headnote). The second set, under "FILM," assumes that you have both read the story and seen the film.

On December the third the wind changed overnight and it was winter. 1
Until then the autumn had been mellow, soft. The leaves had lingered on the trees, golden red, and the hedgerows were still green. The earth was rich where the plough had turned it.

Nat Hocken, because of a wartime disability, had a pension and did not 2
work full-time at the farm. He worked three days a week, and they gave him the lighter jobs: hedging, thatching, repairs to the farm buildings.

Although he was married, with children, his was a solitary disposition; 3
he liked best to work alone. It pleased him when he was given a bank to

build up, or a gate to mend at the far end of the peninsula, where the sea surrounded the farm land on either side. Then, at midday, he would pause and eat the pastry that his wife had baked for him, and sitting on the cliff's edge would watch the birds. Autumn was best for this, better than spring. In spring the birds flew inland, purposeful, intent; they knew where they were bound, the rhythm and ritual of their life brooked no delay. In autumn those that had not migrated overseas but remained to pass the winter were caught up in the same driving urge, but because migration was denied them followed a pattern of their own. Great flocks of them came to the peninsula, restless, uneasy, spending themselves in motion; now wheeling, circling in the sky, now settling to feed on the rich new-turned soil, but even when they fed it was as though they did so without hunger, without desire. Restlessness drove them to the skies again.

Black and white, jackdaw and gull, mingled in strange partnership, seeking some sort of liberation, never satisfied, never still. Flocks of starlings, rustling like silk, flew to fresh pasture, driven by the same necessity of movement, and the smaller birds, the finches and the larks, scattered from tree to hedge as if compelled. 4

Nat watched them, and he watched the sea birds too. Down in the bay they waited for the tide. They had more patience. Oyster-catchers, redshank, sanderling and curlew watched by the water's edge; as the slow sea sucked at the shore and then withdrew, leaving the strip of seaweed bare and the shingle churned, the sea birds raced and ran upon the beaches. Then that same impulse to flight seized upon them too. Crying, whistling, calling, they skimmed the placid sea and left the shore. Make haste, make speed, hurry and begone; yet where, and to what purpose? The restless urge of autumn, unsatisfying, sad, had put a spell upon them and they must flock, and wheel, and cry; they must spill themselves of motion before winter came. 5

Perhaps, thought Nat, munching his pastry by the cliff's edge, a message comes to the birds in autumn, like a warning. Winter is coming. Many of them perish. And like people who, apprehensive of death before their time, drive themselves to work or folly, the birds do likewise. 6

The birds had been more restless than ever this fall of the year, the agitation more marked because the days were still. As the tractor traced its path up and down the western hills, the figure of the farmer silhouetted on the driving seat, the whole machine and the man upon it would be lost momentarily in the great cloud of wheeling, crying birds. There were many more than usual, Nat was sure of this. Always, in autumn, they followed the plough, but not in great flocks like these, nor with such clamour. 7

Nat remarked upon it, when hedging was finished for the day. "Yes," said the farmer, "there are more birds about than usual; I've noticed it too. And daring, some of them, taking no notice of the tractor. One or two gulls came so close to my head this afternoon I thought they'd knock my cap off! As it was, I could scarcely see what I was doing, when they were overhead and I had the sun in my eyes. I have a notion the weather will change. It will be a hard winter. That's why the birds are restless." 8

Nat, tramping home across the fields and down the lane to his cottage, saw the birds still flocking over the western hills, in the last glow of the sun. No wind, and the grey sea calm and full. Campion in bloom yet in the hedges, and the air mild. The farmer was right, though, and it was that night the weather turned. Nat's bedroom faced east. He woke just after two and heard the wind in the chimney. Not the storm and bluster of a sou'westerly gale, bringing the rain, but east wind, cold and dry. It sounded hollow in the chimney, and a loose slate rattled on the roof. Nat listened, and he could hear the sea roaring in the bay. Even the air in the small bedroom had turned chill: a draught came under the skirting of the door, blowing upon the bed. Nat drew the blanket around him, leant closer to the back of his sleeping wife, and stayed wakeful, watchful, aware of misgiving without cause. 9

Then he heard the tapping on the window. There was no creeper on the cottage walls to break loose and scratch upon the pane. He listened, and the tapping continued until, irritated by the sound, Nat got out of bed and went to the window. He opened it, and as he did so something brushed his hand, jabbing at his knuckles, grazing the skin. Then he saw the flutter of the wings and it was gone, over the roof, behind the cottage. 10

It was a bird, what kind of bird he could not tell. The wind must have driven it to shelter on the sill. 11

He shut the window and went back to bed, but feeling his knuckles wet put his mouth to the scratch. The bird had drawn blood. Frightened, he supposed, and bewildered, the bird, seeking shelter, had stabbed at him in the darkness. Once more he settled himself to sleep. 12

Presently the tapping came again, this time more forceful, more insistent, and now his wife woke at the sound, and turning in the bed said to him, "See to the window, Nat, it's rattling." 13

"I've already seen to it," he told her, "there's some bird there, trying to get in. Can't you hear the wind? It's blowing from the east, driving the birds to shelter." 14

"Send them away," she said. "I can't sleep with that noise." 15

He went to the window for the second time, and now when he opened it there was not one bird upon the sill but half a dozen; they flew straight into his face, attacking him. 16

He shouted, striking out at them with his arms, scattering them; like the first one, they flew over the roof and disappeared. Quickly he let the window fall and latched it. 17

"Did you hear that?" he said. "They went for me. Tried to peck my eyes." He stood by the window, peering into the darkness, and could see nothing. His wife, heavy with sleep, murmured from the bed. 18

"I'm not making it up," he said, angry at her suggestion. "I tell you the birds were on the sill, trying to get into the room." 19

Suddenly a frightened cry came from the room across the passage where the children slept. 20

"It's Jill," said his wife, roused at the sound, sitting up in bed. "Go to her, see what's the matter." 21

Nat lit the candle, but when he opened the bedroom door to cross the passage the draught blew out the flame. 22

There came a second cry of terror, this time from both children, and stumbling into their room he felt the beating of wings about him in the darkness. The window was wide open. Through it came the birds, hitting first the ceiling and the walls, then swerving in midflight, turning to the children in their beds. 23

"It's all right, I'm here," shouted Nat, and the children flung themselves, screaming, upon him, while in the darkness the birds rose and dived and came for him again. 24

"What is it, Nat, what's happened?" his wife called from the further bedroom, and swiftly he pushed the children through the door to the passage and shut it upon them, so that he was alone now, in their bedroom, with the birds. 25

He seized a blanket from the nearest bed, and using it as a weapon flung it to right and left about him in the air. He felt the thud of bodies, heard the fluttering of wings, but they were not yet defeated, for again and again they returned to the assault, jabbing his hands, his head, the little stabbing beaks sharp as a pointed fork. The blanket became a weapon of defence; he wound it about his head, and then in greater darkness beat at the birds with his bare hands. He dared not stumble to the door and open it, lest in doing so the birds should follow him. 26

How long he fought with them in the darkness he could not tell, but at last the beating of the wings about him lessened and then withdrew, and through the density of the blanket he was aware of light. He waited, listened; there was no sound except the fretful crying of one of the children from the bedroom beyond. The fluttering, the whirring of the wings had ceased. 27

He took the blanket from his head and stared about him. The cold grey morning light exposed the room. Dawn, and the open window, had called the living birds; the dead lay on the floor. Nat gazed at the little corpses, shocked and horrified. They were all small birds, none of any size; there must have been fifty of them lying there upon the floor. There were robins, finches, sparrows, blue tits, larks and bramblings, birds that by nature's law kept to their own flock and their own territory, and now, joining one with another in their urge for battle, had destroyed themselves against the bedroom walls, or in the strife had been destroyed by him. Some had lost feathers in the fight, others had blood, his blood, upon their beaks. 28

Sickened, Nat went to the window and stared out across his patch of garden to the fields. 29

It was bitter cold, and the ground had all the hard black look of frost. Not white frost, to shine in the morning sun, but the black frost that the east wind brings. The sea, fiercer now with the turning tide, whitecapped and steep, broke harshly in the bay. Of the birds there was no sign. Not a sparrow chattered in the hedge beyond the garden gate, no early missel-thrush or blackbird pecked on the grass for worms. There was no sound at all but the east wind and the sea. 30

Nat shut the window and the door of the small bedroom, and went 31
back across the passage to his own. His wife sat up in bed, one child asleep beside her, the smaller in her arms, his face bandaged. The curtains were tightly drawn across the window, the candles lit. Her face looked garish in the yellow light. She shook her head for silence.

"He's sleeping now," she whispered, "but only just. Something must 32
have cut him, there was blood at the corner of his eyes. Jill said it was the birds. She said she woke up, and the birds were in the room."

His wife looked up at Nat, searching his face for confirmation. She 33
looked terrified, bewildered, and he did not want her to know that he was also shaken, dazed almost, by the events of the past few hours.

"There are birds in there," he said, "dead birds, nearly fifty of them. 34
Robins, wrens, all the little birds from hereabouts. It's as though madness seized them, with the east wind." He sat down on the bed beside his wife, and held her hand. "It's the weather," he said, "it must be that, it's the hard weather. They aren't the birds, maybe, from here around. They've been driven down, from up country."

"But Nat," whispered his wife, "it's only this night that the weather 35
turned. There's been no snow to drive them. And they can't be hungry yet. There's food for them, out there, in the fields."

"It's the weather," repeated Nat. "I tell you, it's the weather." 36

His face too was drawn and tired, like hers. They stared at one another 37
for a while without speaking.

"I'll go downstairs and make a cup of tea," he said. 38

The sight of the kitchen reassured him. The cups and saucers, neatly 39
stacked upon the dresser, the table and chairs, his wife's roll of knitting on her basket chair, the children's toys in a corner cupboard.

He knelt down, raked out the old embers and relit the fire. The glowing 40
sticks brought normality, the steaming kettle and the brown teapot comfort and security. He drank his tea, carried a cup to his wife. Then he washed in the scullery, and putting on his boots, opened the back door.

The sky was hard and leaden, and the brown hills that had gleamed in 41
the sun the day before looked dark and bare. The east wind, like a razor, stripped the trees, and the leaves, crackling and dry, shivered and scattered with the wind's blast. Nat stubbed the earth with his boot. It was frozen hard. He had never known a change so swift and sudden. Black winter had descended in a single night.

The children were awake now. Jill was chattering upstairs and young 42
Johnny crying once again. Nat heard his wife's voice, soothing, comforting. Presently they came down. He had breakfast ready for them, and the routine of the day began.

"Did you drive away the birds?" asked Jill, restored to calm because of 43
the kitchen fire, because of day, because of breakfast.

"Yes, they've all gone now," said Nat. "It was the east wind brought 44
them in. They were frightened and lost. They wanted shelter."

"They tried to peck us," said Jill. "They went for Johnny's eyes." 45

"Fright made them do that," said Nat. "They didn't know where they 46
were, in the dark bedroom."

"I hope they won't come again," said Jill. "Perhaps if we put bread for 47
them outside the window they will eat that and fly away."

She finished her breakfast and then went for her coat and hood, her 48
school books and her satchel. Nat said nothing, but his wife looked at him across the table. A silent message passed between them.

"I'll walk with her to the bus," he said. "I don't go to the farm today." 49

And while the child was washing in the scullery he said to his wife, 50
"Keep all the windows closed, and the doors too, Just to be on the safe side. I'll go to the farm. Find out if they heard anything in the night." Then he walked with his small daughter up the lane. She seemed to have forgotten her experience of the night before. She danced ahead of him, chasing the leaves, her face whipped with the cold and rosy under the pixie hood.

"Is it going to snow, Dad?" she said. "It's cold enough." 51

He glanced up at the bleak sky, felt the wind tear at his shoulders. 52

"No," he said, "it's not going to snow. This is a black winter, not a 53
white one."

All the while he searched the hedgerows for the birds, glanced over the 54
top of them to the fields beyond, looked to the small wood above the farm where the rooks and jackdaws gathered. He saw none.

The other children waited by the bus stop, muffled, hooded like Jill, the 55
faces white and pinched with cold.

Jill ran to them, waving. "My Dad says it won't snow," she called, "it's 56
going to be a black winter."

She said nothing of the birds. She began to push and struggle with an- 57
other little girl. The bus came ambling up the hill. Nat saw her on it, then turned and walked back towards the farm. It was not his day for work, but he wanted to satisfy himself that all was well. Jim, the cowman, was clattering in the yard.

"Boss around?" asked Nat. 58

"Gone to market," said Jim. "It's Tuesday, isn't it?" 59

He clumped off round the corner of a shed. He had no time for Nat. 60
Nat was said to be superior. Read books, and the like. Nat had forgotten it was Tuesday. This showed how the events of the preceding night had shaken him. He went to the back door of the farmhouse and heard Mrs. Trigg singing in the kitchen, the wireless making a background to her song.

"Are you there, missus?" called out Nat. 61

She came to the door, breaming, broad, a good-tempered woman. 62

"Hullo, Mr. Hocken," she said. "Can you tell me where this cold is 63
coming from? Is it Russia? I've never seen such a change. And it's going on, the wireless says. Something to do with the Arctic Circle."

"We didn't turn on the wireless this morning," said Nat. "Fact is, we 64
had trouble in the night."

"Kiddies poorly?" 65

"No . . ." He hardly knew how to explain it. Now, in daylight, the bat- 66
tle of the birds would sound absurd.

He tried to tell Mrs. Trigg what had happened, but he could see from 67
her eyes that she thought his story was the result of a nightmare.

"Sure they were real birds," she said, smiling, "with proper feathers 68
and all? Not the funny-shaped kind, that the men see after closing hours on
a Saturday night?"

"Mrs. Trigg," he said, "there are fifty dead birds, robins, wrens, and 69
such, lying low on the floor of the children's bedroom. They went for me;
they tried to go for young Johnny's eyes."

Mrs. Trigg stared at him doubtfully. 70

"Well there, now," she answered, "I suppose the weather brought them. 71
Once in the bedroom, they wouldn't know where they were to. Foreign
birds maybe, from that Arctic Circle."

"No," said Nat, "they were the birds you see about here every day." 72

"Funny thing," said Mrs. Trigg, "no explaining it, really. You ought to 73
write up and ask the *Guardian.* They'd have some answer for it. Well, I
must be getting on."

She nodded, smiled, and went back into the kitchen. 74

Nat, dissatisfied, turned to the farm gate. Had it not been for those 75
corpses on the bedroom floor, which he must now collect and bury somewhere, he would have considered the tale exaggeration too.

Jim was standing by the gate. 76

"Had any trouble with the birds?" asked Nat. 77

"Birds? What birds?" 78

"We got them up our place last night. Scores of them, came in the chil- 79
dren's bedroom. Quite savage they were."

"Oh?" It took time for anything to penetrate Jim's head. "Never heard 80
of birds acting savage," he said at length. "They get tame, like, sometimes.
I've seen them come to the windows, for crumbs."

"These birds last night weren't tame." 81

"No? Cold maybe. Hungry. You put out some crumbs." 82

Jim was no more interested than Mrs. Trigg had been. It was, Nat 83
thought, like air raids in the war. No one down this end of the country knew
what the Plymouth folk had seen and suffered. You had to endure something yourself before it touched you. He walked back along the lane and
crossed the stile to his cottage. He found his wife in the kitchen with young
Johnny.

"See anyone?" she asked. 84

"Mrs. Trigg and Jim," he answered. "I don't think they believed me. 85
Anyway, nothing wrong up there."

"You might take the birds away," she said. "I daren't go into the room 86
to make the beds until you do. I'm scared."

"Nothing to scare you now," said Nat. "They're dead, aren't they?" 87

He went up with a sack and dropped the stiff bodies into it, one by one. 88
Yes, there were fifty of them, all told. Just the ordinary common birds of

the hedgerow, nothing as large even as a thrush. It must have been fright that made them act the way they did. Blue tits, wrens, it was incredible to think of the power of their small beaks, jabbing at his face and hands the night before. He took the sack out into the garden and was faced now with a fresh problem. The ground was too hard to dig. It was frozen solid, yet no snow had fallen, nothing had happened in the past hours but the coming of the east wind. It was unnatural, queer. The weather prophets must be right. The change was something connected with the Arctic Circle.

The wind seemed to cut him to the bone as he stood there, uncertainly, 89
holding the sack. He could see the whitecapped seas breaking down under in the bay. He decided to take the birds to the shore and bury them.

When he reached the beach below the headland he could scarcely 90
stand, the force of the east wind was so strong. It hurt to draw breath, and his bare hands were blue. Never had he known such cold, not in all the bad winters he could remember. It was low tide. He crunched his way over the shingle to the softer sand and then, his back to the wind, ground a pit in the sand with his heel. He meant to drop the birds into it, but as he opened up the sack the force of the wind carried them, lifted them, as though in flight again, and they were blown away from him along the beach, tossed like feathers, spread and scattered, the bodies of the fifty frozen birds. There was something ugly in the sight. He did not like it. The dead birds were swept away from him by the wind.

"The tide will take them when it turns," he said to himself. 91

He looked out to sea and watched the crested breakers, combing green. 92
They rose stiffly, curled, and broke again, and because it was ebb tide the roar was distant, more remote, lacking the sound and thunder of the flood.

Then he saw them. The gulls. Out there, riding the seas. 93

What he had thought at first to be the whitecaps of the waves were 94
gulls. Hundreds, thousands, tens of thousands . . . They rose and fell in the trough of the seas, heads to the wind, like a mighty fleet at anchor, waiting on the tide. To eastward, and to the west, the gulls were there. They stretched as far as his eye could reach, in close formation, line upon line. Had the sea been still they would have covered the bay like a white cloud, head to head, body packed to body. Only the east wind, whipping the sea to breakers, hid them from the shore.

Nat turned, and leaving the beach climbed the steep path home. Some- 95
one should know of this. Someone should be told. Something was happening, because of the east wind and the weather, that he did not understand. He wondered if he should go to the call box by the bus stop and ring up the police. Yet what could they do? What could anyone do? Tens and thousands of gulls riding the sea there, in the bay, because of storm, because of hunger. The police would think him mad, or drunk, or take the statement from him with great calm. "Thank you. Yes, the matter has already been reported. The hard weather is driving the birds inland in great numbers." Nat looked about him. Still no sign of any other bird. Perhaps the cold had sent them all from up country? As he drew near to the cottage his wife came to

meet him, at the door. She called to him, excited. "Nat," she said, "it's on the wireless. They've just read out a special news bulletin. I've written it down."

"What's on the wireless?" he said. 96

"About the birds," she said. "It's not only here, it's everywhere. In 97
London, all over the country. Something has happened to the birds."

Together they went into the kitchen. He read the piece of paper lying 98
on the table.

"Statement from the Home Office at 11 A.M. today. Reports from all 99
over the country are coming in hourly about the vast quantity of birds flocking above towns, villages and outlying districts, causing obstruction and damage and even attacking individuals. It is thought that the Arctic air stream, at present covering the British Isles, is causing birds to migrate south in immense numbers, and that intense hunger may drive these birds to attack human beings. Householders are warned to see to their windows, doors and chimneys, and to take reasonable precautions for the safety of their children. A further statement will be issued later."

A kind of excitement seized Nat; he looked at his wife in triumph. 100

"There you are," he said, "let's hope they'll hear that at the farm. Mrs. 101
Trigg will know it wasn't any story. It's true. All over the country. I've been telling myself all morning there's something wrong. And just now, down on the beach, I looked out to sea and there are gulls, thousands of them, tens of thousands, you couldn't put a pin between their heads, and they're all out there, riding on the sea, waiting."

"What are they waiting for, Nat?" she asked. 102

He stared at her, then looked down again at the piece of paper. 103

"I don't know," he said slowly. "It says here the birds are hungry." 104

He went over to the drawer where he kept his hammer and tools. 105

"What are you going to do, Nat?" 106

"See to the windows and the chimneys too, like they tell you." 107

"You think they would break in, with the windows shut? Those spar- 108
rows and robins and such? Why, how could they?"

He did not answer. He was not thinking of the robins and the sparrows. 109
He was thinking of the gulls . . .

He went upstairs and worked there the rest of the morning, boarding 110
the windows of the bedrooms, filling up the chimney bases. Good job it was his free day and he was not working at the farm. It reminded him of the old days, at the beginning of the war. He was not married then, and he had made all the blackout boards for his mother's house in Plymouth. Made the shelter too. Not that it had been of any use, when the moment came. He wondered if they would take these precautions up at the farm. He doubted it. Too easygoing, Harry Trigg and his missus. Maybe they'd laugh at the whole thing. Go off to a dance or a whist drive.

"Dinner's ready." she called him, from the kitchen. 111

"All right. Coming down." 112

He was pleased with his handiwork. The frames fitted nicely over the 113
little panes and at the base of the chimneys.

When dinner was over and his wife was washing up, Nat switched on the one o'clock news. The same announcement was repeated, the one which she had taken down during the morning, but the news bulletin enlarged upon it. "The flocks of birds have caused dislocation in all areas," read the announcer, "and in London the sky was so dense at ten o'clock this morning that it seemed as if the city was covered by a vast black cloud. 114

"The birds settled on rooftops, on window ledges and on chimneys. The species included blackbird, thrush, the common house sparrow, and, as might be expected in the metropolis, a vast quantity of pigeons and starlings, and that frequenter of the London river, the black-headed gull. The sight has been so unusual that traffic came to a standstill in many thoroughfares, work was abandoned in shops and offices, and the streets and pavements were crowded with people standing about to watch the birds." 115

Various incidents were recounted, the suspected reason of cold and hunger stated again, and warnings to householders repeated. The announcer's voice was smooth and suave. Nat had the impression that this man, in particular, treated the whole business as he would an elaborate joke. There would be others like him, hundreds of them, who did not know what it was to struggle in darkness with a flock of birds. There would be parties tonight in London, like the ones they gave on election nights. People standing about, shouting and laughing, getting drunk. "Come and watch the birds!" 116

Nat switched off the wireless. He got up and started work on the kitchen windows. His wife watched him, young Johnny at her heels. 117

"What boards for down here too?" she said. "Why, I'll have to light up before three o'clock. I see no call for boards down here." 118

"Better be sure than sorry," answered Nat. "I'm not going to take any chances." 119

"What they ought to do," she said, "is to call the army out and shoot the birds. That would soon scare them off." 120

"Let them try," said Nat. "How'd they set about it?" 121

"They have the army to the docks," she answered, "when the dockers strike. The soldiers go down and unload the ships." 122

"Yes," said Nat, "and the population of London is eight million or more. Think of all the buildings, all the flats, and houses. Do you think they've enough soldiers to go round shooting birds from every roof?" 123

"I don't know. But something should be done. They ought to do something." 124

Nat thought to himself that "they" were no doubt considering the problem at that very moment, but whatever "they" decided to do in London and the big cities would not help the people here, three hundred miles away. Each householder must look after his own. 125

"How are we off for food?" he said. 126

"Now, Nat, whatever next?" 127

"Never mind. What have you got in the larder?" 128

"It's shopping day tomorrow, you know that. I don't keep uncooked food hanging about, it goes off. Butcher doesn't call till the day after. But I can bring back something when I go in tomorrow." 129

Nat did not want to scare her. He thought it possible that she might not 130
go to town tomorrow. He looked in the larder for himself, and in the cupboard where she kept her tins. They would do, for a couple of days. Bread was low.

"What about the baker?" 131

"He comes tomorrow too." 132

He saw she had flour. If the baker did not call she had enough to bake 133
one loaf.

"We'd be better off in the old days," he said, "when the women baked 134
twice a week, and had pilchards salted, and there was food for a family to last a siege, if need be."

"I've tried the children with tinned fish, they don't like it," she said. 135

Nat went on hammering the boards across the kitchen windows. Can- 136
dles. They were low in candles too. That must be another thing she meant to buy tomorrow. Well, it could not be helped. They must go early to bed tonight. That was, if . . .

He got up and went out of the back door and stood in the garden, look- 137
ing down towards the sea. There had been no sun all day, and now, at barely three o'clock, a kind of darkness had already come, the sky sullen, heavy, colourless like salt. He could hear the vicious sea drumming on the rocks. He walked down the path, halfway to the beach, and then he stopped. He could see the tide had turned. The rock that had shown in midmorning was now covered, but it was not the sea that held his eyes. The gulls had risen. They were circling, hundreds of them, thousands of them, lifting their wings against the wind. It was the gulls that made the darkening of the sky. And they were silent. They made not a sound. They just went on soaring and circling, rising, falling, trying their strength against the wind.

Nat turned. He ran up the path, back to the cottage. 138

"I'm going for Jill," he said. "I'll wait for her, at the bus stop." 139

"What's the matter?" asked his wife. "You've gone quite white." 140

"Keep Johnny inside," he said. "Keep the door shut. Light up now, and 141
draw the curtains."

"It's only just gone three," she said. 142

"Never mind. Do what I tell you." 143

He looked inside the toolshed, outside the back door. Nothing there of 144
much use. A spade was too heavy, and a fork no good. He took the hoe. It was the only possible tool, and light enough to carry.

He started walking up the lane to the bus stop, and now and again 145
glanced back over his shoulder.

The gulls had risen higher now, their circles were broader, wider, they 146
were spreading out in huge formation across the sky.

He hurried on; although he knew the bus would not come to the top of 147
the hill before four o'clock he had to hurry. He passed no one on the way. He was glad of this. No time to stop and chatter.

At the top of the hill he waited. He was much too soon. There was half 148
an hour still to go. The east wind came whipping across the fields from the higher ground. He stamped his feet and blew upon his hands. In the dis-

tance he could see the clay hills, white and clean, against the heavy pallor of the sky. Something black rose from behind them, like a smudge at first, then widening, becoming deeper, and the smudge became a cloud, and the cloud divided again into five other clouds, spreading north, east, south and west, and they were not clouds at all; they were birds. He watched them travel across the sky, and as one section passed overhead, within two or three hundred feet of him, he knew, from their speed, they were bound inland, up country, they had no business with the people here on the peninsula. They were rooks, crows, jackdaws, magpies, jays, all birds that usually preyed upon the smaller species; but this afternoon they were bound on some other mission.

"They've been given the towns," thought Nat, "they know what they have to do. We don't matter so much here. The gulls will serve for us. The others go to the towns." 149

He went to the call box, stepped inside and lifted the receiver. The exchange would do. They would pass the message on. 150

"I'm speaking from Highway," he said, "by the bus stop. I want to report large formations of birds travelling up country. The gulls are also forming in the bay." 151

"All right," answered the voice, laconic, weary. 152

"You'll be sure and pass this message on to the proper quarter?" 153

"Yes . . . yes . . ." Impatient now, fed up. The buzzing note resumed. 154

"She's another," thought Nat, "she doesn't care. Maybe she's had to answer calls all day. She hopes to go to the pictures tonight. She'll squeeze some fellow's hand, and point up at the sky, and 'Look at all them birds!' She doesn't care." 155

The bus came lumbering up the hill. Jill climbed out and three or four other children. The bus went on towards the town. 156

"What's the hoe for, Dad?" 157

They crowded around him, laughing, pointing. 158

"I just brought it along," he said. "Come on now, let's get home. It's cold, no hanging about. Here, you. I'll watch you across the fields, see how fast you can run." 159

He was speaking to Jill's companions, who came from different families, living in the council houses. A short cut would take them to the cottages. 160

"We want to play a bit in the lane," said one of them. 161

"No, you don't. You go off home, or I'll tell your mammy." 162

They whispered to one another, round-eyed, then scuttled off across the fields. Jill stared at her father, her mouth sullen. 163

"We always play in the lane," she said. 164

"Not tonight, you don't," he said. "Come on now, no dawdling." 165

He could see the gulls now, circling the fields, coming in towards the land. Still silent. Still no sound. 166

"Look, Dad, look over there, look at all the gulls." 167

"Yes. Hurry, now." 168

"Where are they flying to? Where are they going?" 169

"Up country, I dare say. Where it's warmer." 170

He seized her hand and dragged her after him along the lane. 171

"Don't go so fast. I can't keep up." 172

The gulls were copying the rooks and crows. They were spreading out 173
in formation across the sky. They headed, in bands of thousands, to the four compass points.

"Dad, what is it? What are the gulls doing?" 174

They were not intent upon their flight, as the crows, as the jackdaws 175
had been. They still circled overhead. Nor did they fly so high. It was as though they waited upon some signal. As though some decision had yet to be given. The order was not clear.

"Do you want me to carry you, Jill? Here, come pickaback." 176

This way he might put on speed; but he was wrong. Jill was heavy. She 177
kept slipping. And she was crying, too. His sense of urgency, of fear, had communicated itself to the child.

"I wish the gulls would go away. I don't like them. They're coming 178
closer to the lane."

He put her down again. He started running, swinging Jill after him. As 179
they went past the farm turning he saw the farmer backing his car out of the garage. Nat called to him.

"Can you give us a lift?" he said. 180

"What's that?" 181

Mr. Trigg turned in the driving seat and stared at them. Then a smile 182
came to his cheerful, rubicund face.

"It looked as though we're in for some fun," he said. "Have you seen 183
the gulls? Jim and I are going to take a crack at them. Everyone's gone bird crazy, talking of nothing else. I hear you were troubled in the night. Want a gun?"

Nat shook his head. 184

The small car was packed. There was just room for Jill, if she crouched 185
on top of petrol tins on the back seat.

"I don't want a gun," said Nat, "but I'd be obliged if you'd run Jill 186
home. She's scared of the birds."

He spoke briefly. He did not want to talk in front of Jill. 187

"O.K.," said the farmer, "I'll take her home. Why don't you stop be- 188
hind and join the shooting match? We'll make the feathers fly."

Jill climbed in, and turning the car the driver sped up the lane. Nat fol- 189
lowed after. Trigg must be crazy. What use was a gun against a sky of birds?

Now Nat was not responsible for Jill he had time to look about him. 190
The birds were circling still, above the fields. Mostly herring gull, but the black-backed gull amongst them. Usually they kept apart. Now they were united. Some bond had brought them together. It was the black-backed gull that attacked the smaller birds, and even newborn lambs, so he'd heard. He'd never seen it done. He remembered this now, though, looking above him in the sky. They were coming in towards the farm. They were circling lower in the sky, and the black-backed gulls were to the front, the black-

backed gulls were leading. The farm, then, was their target. They were
making for the farm.

Nat increased his pace towards his own cottage. He saw the farmer's 191
car turn and come back along the lane. It drew up beside him with a jerk.

"The kid has run inside," said the farmer. "Your wife was watching for 192
her. Well, what do you make of it? They're saying in town the Russians
have done it. The Russians have poisoned the birds."

"How could they do that?" asked Nat. 193

"Don't ask me. You know how stories get around. Will you join my 194
shooting match?"

"No, I'll get along home. The wife will be worried else." 195

"My missus says if you could eat gull, there'd be some sense in it," 196
said Trigg, "we'd have roast gull, baked gull, and pickle 'em into the bargain. You wait until I let off a few barrels into the brutes. That'll scare
'em."

"Have you boarded your windows?" asked Nat. 197

"No. Lot of nonsense. They like to scare you on the wireless. I've had 198
more to do today than to go round boarding up my windows."

"I'd board them now, if I were you." 199

"Garn. You're windy. Like to come to our place to sleep?" 200

"No, thanks all the same." 201

"All right. See you in the morning. Give you a gull breakfast." 202

The farmer grinned and turned his car to the farm entrance. 203

Nat hurried on. Past the little wood, past the old barn, and then across 204
the stile to the remaining field.

As he jumped the stile he heard the whir of wings. A black-backed gull 205
dived down at him from the sky, missed, swerved in flight, and rose to dive
again. In a moment it was joined by others, six, seven, a dozen black-
backed and herring mixed. Nat dropped his hoe. The hoe was useless. Covering his head with his arms he ran towards the cottage. They kept coming
at him from the air, silent save for the beating wings. The terrible, fluttering
wings. He could feel the blood on his hands, his wrists, his neck. Each stab
of a swooping beak tore his flesh. If only he could keep them from his eyes.
Nothing else mattered. He must keep them from his eyes. They had not
learnt yet how to cling to a shoulder, how to rip clothing, how to dive in
mass upon the head, upon the body. But with each dive, with each attack,
they became bolder. And they had no thought for themselves. When they
dived low and missed, they crashed, bruised and broken, on the ground. As
Nat ran he stumbled, kicking their spent bodies in front of him.

He found the door, hammered upon it with his bleeding hands. Be- 206
cause of the boarded windows no light shone. Everything was dark.

"Let me in," he shouted, "it's Nat. Let me in." 207

He shouted loud to make himself heard above the whirr of the gull's 208
wings.

Then he saw the gannet, poised for the dive, above him in the sky. The 209
gulls circled, retired, soared, one with another, against the wind. Only the
gannet remained. One single gannet, above him in the sky. The wings

folded suddenly to its body. It dropped, like a stone. Nat screamed, and the door opened. He stumbled across the threshold, and his wife threw her weight against the door.

They heard the thud of the gannet as it fell. 210

His wife dressed his wounds. They were not deep. The backs of his 211
hands had suffered most, and his wrists. Had he not worn a cap they would have reached his head. As to the gannet . . . the gannet could have split his skull.

The children were crying, of course. They had seen the blood on their 212
father's hands.

"It's all right now," he told them. "I'm not hurt. Just a few scratches. 213
You play with Johnny, Jill. Mammy will wash these cuts."

He half-shut the door to the scullery, so that they could not see. His 214
wife as ashen. She began running water from the sink.

"I saw them overhead," she whispered. "They began collecting just as 215
Jill ran in with Mr. Trigg. I shut the door fast, and it jammed. That's why I couldn't open it at once, when you came."

"Thank God they waited for me," he said. "Jill would have fallen at 216
once. One bird alone would have done it."

Furtively, so as not to alarm the children, they whispered together, as 217
she bandaged his hands and the back of his neck.

"They're flying inland," he said, "thousands of them. Rooks, crows, all 218
the bigger birds. I saw them from the bus stop. They're making for the towns."

"But what can they do, Nat?" 219

"They'll attack. Go for everyone out in the streets. Then they'll try the 220
windows, the chimneys."

"Why don't the authorities do something? Why don't they get the 221
army, get machine guns, anything?"

"There's been no time. Nobody's prepared. We'll hear what they have 222
to say on the six o'clock news."

Nat went back into the kitchen, followed by his wife. Johnny was play- 223
ing quietly on the floor. Only Jill looked anxious.

"I can hear the birds," she said. "Listen, Dad." 224

Nat listened. Muffled sounds came from the windows, from the door. 225
Wings brushing the surface, sliding, scraping, seeking a way of entry. The sound of many bodies, pressed together, shuffling on the sills. Now and again came a thud, a crash, as some bird dived and fell. "Some of them will kill themselves that way," he thought, "but not enough. Never enough."

"All right," he said aloud. "I've got boards over the windows, Jill. The 226
birds can't get in."

He went and examined all the windows. His work had been thorough. 227
Every gap was closed. He would make extra certain, however. He found wedges, pieces of old tin, strips of wood and metal and fastened them at the sides to reinforce the boards. His hammering helped to deafen the sound of

the birds, the shuffling, the tapping, and more ominous—he did not want his wife or the children to hear it—the splinter of cracked glass.

"Turn on the wireless," he said, "let's have the wireless." 228

This would drown the sound also. He went upstairs to the bedrooms 229
and reinforced the windows there. Now he could hear the birds on the roof, the scraping of claws, a sliding, jostling sound.

He decided they must sleep in the kitchen, keep up the fire, bring down 230
the mattresses and lay them out on the floor. He was afraid of the bedroom chimneys. The boards he had placed at the chimney bases might give way. In the kitchen they would be safe, because of the fire. He would have to make a joke of it. Pretend to the children they were playing at camp. If the worst happened, and the birds forced an entry down the bedroom chimneys, it would be hours, days perhaps, before they could break down the doors. The birds would be imprisoned in the bedrooms. They could do no harm there. Crowded together, they would stifle and die.

He began to bring the mattresses downstairs. At sight of them his 231
wife's eyes widened in apprehension. She thought the birds had already broken in upstairs.

"All right," he said cheerfully, "we'll all sleep together in the kitchen 232
tonight. More cosy here by the fire. Then we shan't be worried by those silly old birds tapping at the windows."

He made the children help him rearrange the furniture, and he took the 233
precaution of moving the dresser, with his wife's help, across the window. It fitted well. It was an added safeguard. The mattresses could now be lain, one beside the other, against the wall where the dresser had stood.

"We're safe enough now," he thought, "we're snug and tight, like an 234
air-raid shelter. We can hold out. It's just the food that worries me. Food and coal for the fire. We've enough for two or three days, not more. By that time . . ."

No use thinking ahead as far as that. And they'd be giving directions 235
on the wireless. People would be told what to do. And now, in the midst of many problems, he realised that it was dance music only coming over the air. Not Children's Hour, as it should have been. He glanced at the dial. Yes, they were on the Home Service all right. Dance records. He switched to the Light programme. He knew the reason. The usual programmes had been abandoned. This only happened at exceptional times. Elections, and such. He tried to remember if it had happened in the war, during the heavy raids on London. But of course. The B.B.C. was not stationed in London during the war. The programmes were broadcast from other, temporary quarters. "We're better off here," he thought, "we're better off here in the kitchen, with the windows and the doors boarded, then they are up in the towns. Thank God we're not in the towns."

At six o'clock the records ceased. The time signal was given. No mat- 236
ter if it scared the children, he must hear the news. There was a pause after the pips. Then the announcer spoke. His voice was solemn, grave. Quite different from midday.

"This is London," he said. "A National Emergency was proclaimed at 237
four o'clock this afternoon. Measures are being taken to safeguard the lives and property of the population, but it must be understood that these are not easy to effect immediately, owing to the unforeseen and unparalleled nature of the present crisis. Every householder must take precautions to his own building, and where several people live together, as in flats and apartments, they must unite to do the utmost they can to prevent entry. It is absolutely imperative that every individual stays indoors tonight, and that no one at all remains on the streets, or roads, or anywhere without doors. The birds, in vast numbers, are attacking anyone on sight, and have already begun an assault upon buildings; but these, with due care, should be impenetrable. The population is asked to remain calm, and not to panic. Owing to the exceptional nature of the emergency, there will be no further transmission from any broadcasting station until 7 A.M. tomorrow."

They played the National Anthem. Nothing more happened. Nat 238
switched off the set. He looked at his wife. She stared back at him.

"What's it mean?" said Jill. "What did the news say?" 239

"There won't be any more programmes tonight," said Nat. "There's 240
been a breakdown at the B.B.C."

"Is it the birds?" asked Jill. "Have the birds done it?" 241

"No," said Nat, "it's just that everyone's very busy, and then of course 242
they have to get rid of the birds, messing everything up, in the towns. Well, we can manage without the wireless for one evening."

"I wish we had a gramophone," said Jill. "That would be better than 243
nothing."

She had her face turned to the dresser, backed against the windows. 244
Try as they did to ignore it, they were all aware of the shuffling, the stabbing, the persistent beating and sweeping of wings.

"We'll have supper early," suggested Nat, "something for a treat. Ask 245
Mammy. Toasted cheese, eh? Something we all like?"

He winked and nodded at his wife. He wanted the look of dread, of ap- 246
prehension to go from Jill's face.

He helped with the supper, whistling, singing, making as much clatter 247
as he could, and it seemed to him that the shuffling and the tapping were not so intense as they had been at first. Presently he went up to the bedrooms and listened, and he no longer heard the jostling for place upon the roof.

"They've got reasoning powers," he thought, "they know it's hard to 248
break in here. They'll try elsewhere. They won't waste their time with us."

Supper passed without incident, and then, when they were clearing 249
away, they heard a new sound, droning, familiar, a sound they all knew and understood.

His wife looked up at him, her face alight. "It's planes," she said, 250
"they're sending out planes after the birds. That's what I said they ought to do, all along. That will get them. Isn't that gunfire? Can't you hear guns?"

It might be gunfire, out at sea. Nat could not tell. Big naval guns might 251
have an effect upon the gulls out at sea, but the gulls were inland now. The guns couldn't shell the shore, because of the population.

"It's good, isn't it," said his wife, "to hear the planes?" And Jill, catch- 252
ing her enthusiasm, jumped up and down with Johnny. "The planes will get the birds. The planes will shoot them."

Just then they heard a crash two miles distant, followed by a second, 253
then a third. The droning became more distant, passed away out to sea.

"What was that?" asked his wife. "Were they dropping bombs on the 254
birds?"

"I don't know," answered Nat. "I don't think so." 255

He did not want to tell her that the sound they had heard was the crash- 256
ing of aircraft. It was, he had no doubt, a venture on the part of the authorities to send out reconnaissance forces, but they might have known the venture was suicidal. What could aircraft do against birds that flung themselves to death against propeller and fuselage but hurtle to the ground themselves? This was being tried now, he supposed, over the whole country. And at a cost. Someone high up has lost his head.

"Where have the planes gone, Dad?" asked Jill. 257

"Back to base," he said. "Come on, now, time to tuck down for bed." 258

It kept his wife occupied, undressing the children before the fire, see- 259
ing to the bedding, one thing and another, while he went round the cottage again, making sure that nothing had worked loose. There was no further drone of aircraft, and the naval guns had ceased. "Waste of life and effort," Nat said to himself. "We can't destroy enough of them that way. Cost too heavy. There's always gas. Maybe they'll try spraying with gas, mustard gas. We'll be warned first, of course, if they do. There's one thing, the best brains of the country will be on to it tonight."

Somehow the thought reassured him. He had a picture of scientists, 260
naturalists, technicians, and all those chaps they called the backroom boys, summoned to a council; they'd be working on the problem now. This was not a job for the government, for the chiefs of staff—they would merely carry out the orders of the scientists.

"They'll have to be ruthless," he thought. "Where the trouble's worst 261
they'll have to risk more lives, if they use gas. All the livestock, too, and the soil—all contaminated. As long as everyone doesn't panic. That's the trouble. People panicking, losing their heads. The B.B.C. was right to warn us of that."

Upstairs in the bedrooms all was quiet. No further scraping and stab- 262
bing at the windows. A lull in battle. Forces regrouping. Wasn't that what they called it, in the old wartime bulletins? The wind hadn't dropped, though. He could still hear it, roaring in the chimneys. And the sea breaking down on the shore. Then he remembered the tide. The tide would be on the turn. Maybe the lull in battle was because of the tide. There was some law the birds obeyed, and it was all to do with the east wind and the tide.

He glanced at his watch. Nearly eight o'clock. It must have gone high 263
water an hour ago. That explained the lull: the birds attacked with the flood tide. It might not work that way inland, up country, but it seemed as if it was so this way on the coast. He reckoned the time limit in his head. They had six hours to go, without attack. When the tide turned again, around one-twenty in the morning, the birds would come back . . .

There were two things he could do. The first to rest, with his wife and 264
children, and all of them snatch what sleep they could, until the small hours. The second to go out, see how they were faring at the farm, see if the telephone was still working there, so that they might get news from the exchange.

He called softly to his wife, who had just settled the children. She 265
came halfway up the stairs and he whispered to her.

"You're not to go," she said at once, "you're not to go and leave me 266
alone with the children. I can't stand it."

Her voice rose hysterically. He hushed her, calmed her. 267

"All right," he said, "all right. I'll wait till morning. And we'll get the 268
wireless bulletin then too, at seven. But in the morning, when the tide ebbs again, I'll try for the farm, and they may let us have bread and potatoes, and milk too."

His mind was busy again, planning against emergency. They would 269
not have milked, of course, this evening. The cows would be standing by the gate, waiting in the yard, with the household inside, battened behind boards, as they were here at the cottage. That is, if they had time to take precautions. He thought of the farmer, Trigg, smiling at him from the car. There would have been no shooting party, not tonight.

The children were asleep. His wife, still clothed, was sitting on her 270
mattress. She watched him, her eyes nervous.

"What are you going to do?" she whispered. 271

He shook his head for silence. Softly, stealthily, he opened the back 272
door and looked outside.

It was pitch dark. The wind was blowing harder than ever, coming in 273
steady gusts, icy, from the sea. He kicked at the step outside the door. It was heaped with birds. There were dead birds everywhere. Under the windows, against the walls. These were the suicides, the divers, the ones with broken necks. Wherever he looked he saw dead birds. No trace of the living. The living had flown seaward with the turn of the tide. The gulls would be riding the seas now, as they had done in the forenoon.

In the far distance, on the hill where the tractor had been two days be- 274
fore, something was burning. One of the aircraft that had crashed; the fire, fanned by the wind, had set light to a stack.

He looked at the bodies of the birds, and he had a notion that if he 275
heaped them, one upon the other, on the window sills they would make added protection for the next attack. Not much, perhaps, but something. The bodies would have to be clawed at, pecked, and dragged aside, before the living birds gained purchase on the sills and attacked the panes. He set

to work in the darkness. It was queer; he hated touching them. The bodies were still warm and bloody. The blood matted their feathers. He felt his stomach turn, but he went on with his work. He noticed, grimly, that every windowpane was shattered. Only the boards had kept the birds from breaking in. He stuffed the cracked panes with the bleeding bodies of the birds.

When he had finished he went back into the cottage. He barricaded the kitchen door, made it doubly secure. He took off his bandages, sticky with the birds' blood, not with his own cuts, and put on fresh plaster. 276

His wife had made him cocoa and he drank it thirstily. He was very tired. 277

"All right," he said, smiling, "don't worry. We'll get through." 278

He lay down on his mattress and closed his eyes. He slept at once. He dreamt uneasily, because through his dreams there ran a thread of something forgotten. Some piece of work, neglected, that he should have done. Some precaution that he had known well but had not taken, and he could not put a name to it in his dreams. It was connected in some way with the burning aircraft and the stack upon the hill. He went on sleeping, though; he did not awake. It was his wife shaking his shoulder that awoke him finally. 279

"They've begun," she sobbed, "they've started this last hour, I can't listen to it any longer, alone. There's something smelling bad too, something burning." 280

Then he remembered. He had forgotten to make up the fire. It was smouldering, nearly out. He got up swiftly and lit the lamp. The hammering had started at the windows and the doors, but it was not that he minded now. It was the smell of singed feathers. The smell filled the kitchen. He knew at once what it was. The birds were coming down the chimney, squeezing their way down to the kitchen range. 281

He got sticks and paper and put them on the embers, then reached for the can of paraffin. 282

"Stand back," he shouted to his wife, "we've got to risk this." 283

He threw the paraffin onto the fire. The flame roared up the pipe, and down upon the fire fell the scorched, blackened bodies of the birds. 284

The children woke, crying. "What is it?" said Jill. "What's happened?" 285

Nat had no time to answer. He was raking the bodies from the chimney, clawing them out onto the floor. The flames still roared, and the danger of the chimney catching fire was one he had to take. The flames would send away the living birds from the chimney top. The lower joint was the difficulty, though. This was choked with the smouldering helpless bodies of the birds caught by fire. He scarcely heeded the attack on the windows and the door: let them beat their wings, break their beaks, lose their lives, in the attempt to force an entry into his home. They would not break in. He thanked God he had one of the old cottages, with small windows, stout walls. Not like the new council houses. Heaven help them up the lane, in the new council houses. 286

"Stop crying," he called to the children. "There's nothing to be afraid 287
of, stop crying."

He went on raking at the burning, smouldering bodies as they fell into 288
the fire.

"This'll fetch them," he said to himself, "the draught and the flames to- 289
gether. We're all right, as long as the chimney doesn't catch. I ought to be
shot for this. It's all my fault. Last thing I should have made up the fire. I
knew there was something."

Amid the scratching and tearing at the window boards came the sud- 290
den homely striking of the kitchen clock. Three A.M. A little more than four
hours yet to go. He could not be sure of the exact time of high water. He
reckoned it would not turn much before half-past seven, twenty to eight.

"Light up the Primus," he said to his wife. "Make us some tea, and the 291
kids some cocoa. No use sitting around doing nothing."

That was the line. Keep her busy, and the children too. Move about, 292
eat, drink; always best to be on the go.

He waited by the range. The flames were dying. But no more black- 293
ened bodies fell from the chimney. He thrust his poker up as far as it could
go and found nothing. It was clear. The chimney was clear. He wiped the
sweat from his forehead.

"Come on now, Jill," he said, "bring me some more sticks. We'll have 294
a good fire going directly." She wouldn't come near him, though. She was
staring at the heaped singed bodies of the birds.

"Never mind them," he said, "we'll put those in the passage when I've 295
got the fire steady."

The danger of the chimney was over. It could not happen again, not if 296
the fire was kept burning day and night.

"I'll have to get more fuel from the farm tomorrow," he thought. "This 297
will never last. I'll manage, though. I can do all that with the ebb tide. It
can be worked, fetching what we need, when the tide's turned. We've just
got to adapt ourselves, that's all."

They drank tea and cocoa and ate slices of bread and Bovril. Only half 298
a loaf left, Nat noticed. Never mind, though, they'd get by.

"Stop it," said young Johnny, pointing to the windows with his spoon, 299
"stop it, you old birds."

"That's right," said Nat, smiling, "we don't want the old beggars, do 300
we? Had enough of 'em."

They began to cheer when they heard the thud of the suicide birds. 301

"There's another, Dad," cried Jill, "he's done for." 302

"He's had it," said Nat, "there he goes, the blighter." 303

This was the way to face up to it. This was the spirit. If they could keep 304
this up, hang on like this until seven, when the first news bulletin came
through, they would not have done too badly.

"Give us a fag," he said to his wife. "A bit of a smoke will clear away 305
the smell of the scorched feathers."

"There's only two left in the packet," she said. "I was going to buy you 306
some from the Co-op."

"I'll have one," he said. "T'other will keep for a rainy day." 307

No sense trying to make the children rest. There was no rest to be got 308
while the tapping and the scratching went on at the windows. He sat with one arm round his wife and the other round Jill, with Johnny on his mother's lap and the blankets heaped about them on the mattress.

"You can't help admiring the beggars," he said, "they've got persis- 309
tence. You'd think they'd tire of the game, but not a bit of it."

Admiration was hard to sustain. The tapping went on and on and a new 310
rasping note struck Nat's ear, as though a sharper beak than any hitherto had come to take over from its fellows. He tried to remember the names of birds, he tried to think which species would go for this particular job. It was not the tap of the woodpecker. That would be light and frequent. This was more serious, because if it continued long the wood would splinter as the glass had done. Then he remembered the hawks. Could the hawks have taken over from the gulls? Were there buzzards now upon the sills, using talons as well as beaks? Hawks, buzzards, kestrels, falcons—he had forgotten the birds of prey. He had forgotten the gripping power of the birds of prey. Three hours to go, and while they waited, the sound of the splintering wood, the talons tearing at the wood.

Nat looked about him, seeing what furniture he could destroy to fortify 311
the door. The windows were safe, because of the dresser. He was not certain of the door. He went upstairs, but when he reached the landing he paused and listened. There was a soft patter on the floor of the children's bedroom. The birds had broken through . . . He put his ear to the door. No mistake. He could hear the rustle of wings, and the light patter as they searched the floor. The other bedroom was still clear. He went into it and began bringing out the furniture, to pile at the head of the stairs should the door of the children's bedroom go. It was a preparation. It might never be needed. He could not stack the furniture against the door, because it opened inward. The only possible thing was to have it at the top of the stairs.

"Come down, Nat, what are you doing?" called his wife. 312

"I won't be long," he shouted. "Just making everything ship-shape up 313
here."

He did not want her to come; he did not want her to hear the pattering 314
of the feet in the children's bedroom, the brushing of those wings against the door.

At five-thirty he suggested breakfast, bacon and fried bread, if only to 315
stop the growing look of panic in his wife's eyes and to calm the fretful children. She did not know about the birds upstairs. The bedroom, luckily, was not over the kitchen. Had it been so she could not have failed to hear the sound of them, up there, tapping the boards. And the silly, senseless thud of the suicide birds, the death and glory boys, who flew into the bedroom, smashing their heads against the walls. He knew them of old, the herring gulls. They had no brains. The black-backs were different, they knew what they were doing. So did the buzzards, the hawks . . .

He found himself watching the clock, gazing at the hands that went so 316
slowly round the dial. If his theory was not correct, if the attack did not

cease with the turn of the tide, he knew they were beaten. They could not continue through the long day without air, without rest, without more fuel, without . . . his mind raced. He knew there were so many things they needed to withstand siege. They were not fully prepared. They were not ready. It might be that it would be safer in the towns after all. If he could get a message through, on the farm telephone, to his cousin, only a short journey by train up country, they might be able to hire a car. That would be quicker—hire a car between tides . . .

His wife's voice, calling his name, drove away the sudden, desperate desire for sleep. 317

"What is it? What now?" he said sharply. 318

"The wireless," said his wife. "I've been watching the clock. It's nearly seven." 319

"Don't twist the knob," he said, impatient for the first time, "it's on the Home where it is. They'll speak from the Home." 320

They waited. The kitchen clock struck seven. There was no sound. No chimes, no music. They waited until a quarter past, switching to the Light. The result was the same. No news bulletin came through. 321

"We've heard wrong," he said. "They won't be broadcasting until eight o'clock." 322

They left it switched on, and Nat thought of the battery, wondered how much power was left in it. It was generally recharged when his wife went shopping in the town. If the battery failed they would not hear the instructions. 323

"It's getting light," whispered his wife. "I can't see it, but I can feel it. And the birds aren't hammering so loud." 324

She was right. The rasping, tearing sound grew fainter every moment. So did the shuffling, the jostling for place upon the step, upon the sills. The tide was on the turn. By eight there was no sound at all. Only the wind. The children, lulled at last by the stillness, fell asleep. At half-past eight Nat switched the wireless off. 325

"What are you doing? We'll miss the news," said his wife. 326

"There isn't going to be any news," said Nat. "We've got to depend upon ourselves." 327

He went to the door and slowly pulled away the barricades. He drew the bolts, and kicking the bodies from the step outside the door breathed the cold air. He had six working hours before him, and he knew he must reserve his strength for the right things, not waste it in any way. Food, and light, and fuel; these were the necessary things. If he could get them in sufficiency, they could endure another night. 328

He stepped into the garden, and as he did so he saw the living birds. The gulls had done to ride the sea, as they had done before; they sought sea food, and the buoyancy of the tide, before they returned to the attack. Not so the land birds. They waited and watched. Nat saw them, on the hedgerows, on the sill, crowded in the trees, outside in the field, line upon line of birds, all still, doing nothing. 329

He went to the end of his small garden. The birds did not move. They 330
went on watching him.

"I've got to get food," said Nat to himself. "I've got to go to the farm 331
to find food."

He went back to the cottage. He saw to the windows and the doors. He 332
went upstairs and opened the children's bedroom. It was empty, except for the dead birds on the floor. The living were out there, in the garden, in the fields. He went downstairs.

"I'm going to the farm," he said. 333

His wife clung to him. She had seen the living birds from the open 334
door.

"Take us with you," she begged. "We can't stay here alone. I'd rather 335
die than stay here alone."

He considered the matter. He nodded. 336

"Come on, then," he said. "Bring baskets, and Johnny's pram. We can 337
load up the pram."

They dressed against the biting wind, wore gloves and scarves. His 338
wife put Johnny in the pram. Nat took Jill's hand.

"The birds," she whimpered, "they're all out there, in the fields." 339

"They won't hurt us," he said, "not in the light." 340

They started walking across the field towards the stile, and the birds 341
did not move. They waited, their heads turned to the wind.

When they reached the turning to the farm, Nat stopped and told his 342
wife to wait in the shelter of the hedge with the two children.

"But I want to see Mrs. Trigg," she protested. "There are lots of things 343
we can borrow, if they went to market yesterday; not only bread, and . . ."

"Wait here," Nat interrupted. "I'll be back in a moment." 344

The cows were lowing, moving restlessly in the yard, and he could see 345
a gap in the fence where the sheep had knocked their way through, to roam unchecked in the front garden before the farmhouse. No smoke came from the chimneys. He was filled with misgiving. He did not want his wife or the children to go down to the farm.

"Don't gib now," said Nat, harshly, "do what I say." 346

She withdrew with the pram into the hedge, screening herself and the 347
children from the wind.

He went down alone to the farm. He pushed his way through the herd 348
of bellowing cows, which turned this way and that, distressed, their udders full. He saw the car standing by the gate, not put away in the garage. The windows of the farmhouse were smashed. There were many dead gulls lying in the yard and around the house. The living birds perched on the group of trees behind the farm and on the roof of the house. They were quite still. They watched him.

Jim's body lay in the yard . . . what was left of it. When the birds had 349
finished, the cows had trampled him. His gun was beside him. The door of the house was shut and bolted, but as the windows were smashed it was

easy to lift them and climb through. Trigg's body was close to the telephone. He must have been trying to get through to the exchange when the birds came for him. The receiver was hanging loose, the instrument torn from the wall. No sign of Mrs. Trigg. She would be upstairs. Was it any use going up? Sickened, Nat knew what he would find.

"Thank God," he said to himself, "there were no children." 350

He forced himself to climb the stairs, but halfway he turned and de- 351
scended again. He could see her legs, protruding from the open bedroom door. Beside her were the bodies of the black-backed gulls, and an umbrella, broken.

"It's no use," thought Nat, "doing anything. I've only got five hours, 352
less than that. The Triggs would understand. I must load up with what I can find."

He tramped back to his wife and children. 353

"I'm going to fill up the car with stuff," he said. "I'll put coal in it, and 354
paraffin for the Primus. We'll take it home and return for a fresh load."

"What about the Triggs?" asked his wife. 355

"They must have gone to friends," he said. 356

"Shall I come and help you, then?" 357

"No; there's a mess down there. Cows and sheep all over the place. 358
Wait, I'll get the car. You can sit in it."

Clumsily he backed the car out of the yard and into the lane. His wife 359
and the children could not see Jim's body from there.

"Stay here," he said, "never mind the pram. The pram can be fetched 360
later. I'm going to load the car."

Her eyes watched his all the time. He believed she understood, other- 361
wise she would have suggested helping him to find the bread and groceries.

They made three journeys altogether, backwards and forwards be- 362
tween their cottage and the farm, before he was satisfied they had everything they needed. It was surprising, once he started thinking, how many things were necessary. Almost the most important of all was planking for the windows. He had to go round searching for timber. He wanted to renew the boards on all the windows at the cottage. Candles, paraffin, nails, tinned stuff; the list was endless. Besides all that, he milked three of the cows. The rest, poor brutes, would have to go on bellowing.

On the final journey he drove the car to the bus stop, got out, and went 363
to the telephone box. He waited a few minutes, jangling the receiver. No good, though. The line was dead. He climbed onto a bank and looked over the countryside, but there was no sign of life at all, nothing in the fields but the waiting, watching birds. Some of them slept—he could see the beaks tucked into the feathers.

"You'd think they'd be feeding," he said to himself, "not just standing 364
in that way."

Then he remembered. They were gorged with food. They had eaten 365
their fill during the night. That was why they did not move this morning . . .

No smoke came from the chimneys of the council houses. He thought 366
of the children who had run across the fields the night before.

"I should have known," he thought. "I ought to have taken them home with me." 367

He lifted his face to the sky. It was colourless and grey. The bare trees on the landscape looked bent and blackened by the east wind. The cold did not affect the living birds, waiting out there in the fields. 368

"This is the time they ought to get them," said Nat, "they're a sitting target now. They must be doing this all over the country. Why don't our aircraft take off now and spray them with mustard gas? What are all our chaps doing? They must know, they must see for themselves." 369

He went back to the car and got into the driver's seat. 370

"Go quickly past that second gate," whispered his wife. "The postman's lying there. I don't want Jill to see." 371

He accelerated. The little Morris bumped and rattled along the lane. The children shrieked with laughter. 372

"Up-a-down, up-a-down," shouted young Johnny. 373

It was a quarter to one by the time they reached the cottage. Only an hour to go. 374

"Better have cold dinner," said Nat. "Hot up something for yourself and the children, some of that soup. I've no time to eat now. I've got to unload all this stuff." 375

He got everything inside the cottage. It could be sorted later. Give them all something to do during the long hours ahead. First he must see to the windows and the doors. 376

He went round the cottage methodically, testing every window, every door. He climbed onto the roof, also, and fixed boards across every chimney, except the kitchen. The cold was so intense he could hardly bear it, but the job had to be done. Now and again he would look up, searching the sky for aircraft. None came. As he worked he cursed the inefficiency of the authorities. 377

"It's always the same," he muttered, "they always let us down. Muddle, muddle, from the start. No plan, no real organisation. And we don't matter, down here. That's what it is. The people up country have priority. They're using gas up there, no doubt, and all the aircraft. We've got to wait and take what comes." 378

He paused, his work on the bedroom finished, and looked out to sea. Something was moving out there. Something grey and white amongst the breakers. 379

"Good old Navy," he said, "they never let us down. They're coming down channel, they're turning in the bay." 380

He waited, straining his eyes, watering in the wind, towards the sea. He was wrong, though. It was not ships. The Navy was not there. The gulls were rising from the sea. The massed flocks in the fields, with ruffled feathers, rose in formation from the ground, and wing to wing soared upwards in the sky. 381

The tide had turned again. 382

Nat climbed down the ladder and went inside the kitchen. The family were at dinner. It was a little after two. He bolted the door, put up the barricade, and lit the lamp. 383

"It's nighttime," said young Johnny. 384

His wife had switched on the wireless once again, but no sound came from it. 385

"I've been all round the dial," she said, "foreign stations, and that lot. I can't get anything." 386

"Maybe they have the same trouble," he said, "Maybe it's the same right through Europe." 387

She poured out a plateful of the Triggs' soup, cut him a large slice of the Triggs' bread, and spread their dripping upon it. 388

They ate in silence. A piece of the dripping ran down young Johnny's chin and fell onto the table. 389

"Manners, Johnny," said Jill, "you should learn to wipe your mouth." 390

The tapping began at the windows, at the door. The rustling, the jostling, the pushing for position on the sills. The first thud of the suicide gulls upon the step. 391

"Won't America do something?" said his wife. "They've always been our allies, haven't they? Surely America will do something?" 392

Nat did not answer. The boards were strong against the windows, and on the chimneys too. The cottage was filled with stores, with fuel, with all they needed for the next few days. When he had finished dinner he would put the stuff away, stack it neatly, get everything shipshape, handy-like. His wife could help him, and the children too. They'd tire themselves out, between now and a quarter to nine, when the tide would ebb; then he'd tuck them down on their mattresses, see that they slept good and sound until three in the morning. 393

He had a new scheme for the windows, which was to fix barbed wire in front of the boards. He had brought a great roll of it from the farm. The nuisance was, he'd have to work at this in the dark, when the lull came between nine and three. Pity he had not thought of it before. Still, as long as the wife slept, and the kids, that was the main thing. 394

The smaller birds were at the window now. He recognised the light tap-tapping of their beaks, and the soft brush of their wings. The hawks ignored the windows. They concentrated their attack upon the door. Nat listened to the tearing sound of splintering wood, and wondered how many million years of memory were stored in those little brains, behind the stabbing beaks, the piercing eyes, now giving them this instinct to destroy mankind with all the deft precision of machines. 395

"I'll smoke that last fag," he said to his wife. "Stupid of me, it was the one thing I forgot to bring back from the farm." 396

He reached for it, switched on the silent wireless. He threw the empty packet on the fire, and watched it burn. 397

▲ ▲ ▲

Discussion and Writing Suggestions

FICTION

1. Should this story be considered as a kind of Stephen King-type horror story? Should it be viewed as something else—perhaps an allegory in which the events are symbolic of other events that have nothing to do with birds at all? If the latter, what is the allegory about? Does your interpretation provide a plausible explanation of what happens and of how the characters react to what happens? What does it and does it *not* account for? (For example, what is the significance of the sudden onset of winter and of the "unnatural" weather? What is the significance of the birds not being foreign, but rather just common English birds?)
2. How does du Maurier build up tension and suspense before the first actual bird attack?
3. How does the narrator attempt to account for the behavior of the birds? Why does she not provide an explanation at the end of the story?
4. Throughout the story Nat and his wife place their faith for salvation in the authorities, and especially the military. How do you interpret the response of the authorities to the bird attacks? How do you read the significance of the results of the military response?
5. In a paragraph or two, summarize what you think happens after the end of the story.

FILM

1. How was your experience of *The Birds* changed by the adaptation of the story from fiction to film? By the shift in locale from southern England to northern California? The new set of main and subordinate characters? The specifics of the story? For example, how does the imagination experience change by the fact that the main characters of Hitchcock's film are relatively young singles, just starting a romantic relationship, as opposed to a middle-aged, married, working-class couple with kids? What is the effect of adding the subplot about the main character's mother resenting his woman friends? About the kid sister? About the ex-girlfriend? To what extent do you think that any or all of these changes were necessary? (Why couldn't Hitchcock, for example, have made a film of the exact story told by du Maurier?) Overall, to what extent do you think that Hitchcock's film is a good adaptation of du Maurier's story?
2. What dramatic purpose do the lovebirds serve in Hitchcock's film? To what extent is there a corresponding dramatic purpose in du Maurier's story?
3. While du Maurier's story opens with a mood of foreboding, Hitchcock's film opens in a light-hearted mood, almost as if it were a conventional romantic comedy. Examine the mixture of comedy and suspense in the film as it progresses, assessing its effectiveness.

4. Compare and contrast the theories advanced for the birds' attacks in the story and in the film. Of the explanations offered by the various people in the restaurant (after the attack at the school), which, if any, seems the most plausible?
5. Recall that in the chapter introduction, George Linden is quoted as saying that "if the tone of a work is lost, the work is lost." To what extent do you think that Hitchcock's film preserves the tone of Ms. du Maurier's story?
6. If you have access to a VCR and a copy of the video, study how cinematography, editing, and sound contribute to the effectiveness of one of the following scenes: (a) the massing of the birds at the jungle gym and the subsequent attack on the children at the school; (b) the attack outside the restaurant; (c) the attack on the Brenner house toward the end; (d) the final sequence, starting as Mitch gets Melanie's car from the garage. (Consult the "Glossary of Film Terms" at the end of this chapter for terminology.)
7. If there is a section of the film that you think could be improved upon, write a new version. Describe both the action, the cinematography, editing, music, and so forth as specifically as possible. In a preface, explain why you think your version would work better than Hitchcock's.

Witness for the Prosecution

AGATHA CHRISTIE

BILLY WILDER

Agatha Christie's "Witness for the Prosecution" is particularly interesting as a case study of adaptation because it has been incarnated in at least four forms: Christie's original short story, published in 1953; her own adaptation and expansion of the story later that year into a successful three-act play (by 1954 it was being performed in both London and New York); a film version adapted by Billy Wilder and Harry Kurnitz and directed by Wilder, released in 1957; and a CBS Hallmark Hall of Fame version televised in 1982. While we will focus on the original short story and the first film version (the 1982 version is not available outside of TV archives), we will also provide the opening and closing scenes of Christie's play and the screenplay, so that you may examine the degree to which the special nature of the printed page, the stage, and the screen influence the form that a given story may take.

In whatever form, "Witness for the Prosecution" is a successful example of a genre *story—in this case the courtroom genre. When reading or viewing genre stories (other examples include the western, science fiction, and romantic comedy), readers or viewers bring a particular set of expectations about the main and supporting characters, the basic situation, how this situation will be developed, and how it will be resolved. The storyteller's or filmmaker's job is to see that those expectations are met while sufficiently varying the characters and the plot to maintain the readers'/audiences' interest and delight. In the case of the courtroom drama, the most common situation is that a person accused of a serious crime, on the basis of apparently damning evidence, hires a skillful defense attorney, who uses every trick in the book (and some that aren't in the book) to win an acquittal.*

Agatha Christie (1890–1976) was the twentieth century's foremost writer of detective fiction. Born Agatha Miller in Devon, England, she was educated at home by her mother and worked on her first book while serving as a volunteer nurse during World War I. Though her first manuscript, The Mysterious Affair at Styles, *was rejected by at least six publishers, its eventual publication in 1920—which introduced the detective Hercule Poirot to the world—began a string of some 75 successful novels, along with short stories and plays. Besides Poirot, who appeared in such novels as* The Murder of Roger Ackroyd *(1926) and* Murder on the Orient Express *(1934), Christie also created Miss Jane Marple, who first appeared in* Murder in the Vicarage *(1930). Among Christie's eight plays are* Witness for the Prosecution *(1953),* Ten Little Indians *(1944), and* The Mousetrap *(1954), which set a world record for a continuous run at a single theater. Christie was married twice, first to Colonel Archibald Christie (whom she divorced in 1928) and then to archaeologist Sir Max Mallowan.*

Born in Sucha, Austria, in 1906, Billy Wilder attended law school for a time, then worked as a tabloid journalist before turning to screenwriting for German films. According to one critic, in these early screenplays "he began to develop the tightly woven, intricate narrative structures, marked by incredible reversals, paradoxes and reversions, that would characterize his best American work." Moving to Hollywood in 1933, Wilder proved adept at writing and later directing in a variety of genres, from comedy to film noir, to social problems and satire. As a screenwriter, Wilder usually worked in collaboration: his best-known co-authors on films he also directed were Charles Brackett—with whom he wrote Ninotchka *(1939),* Double Indemnity *(1944), and* Sunset Boulevard *(1950), and I.A.L. Diamond, with whom he wrote* Some Like It Hot *(1959),* The Apartment *(1960), and* One, Two, Three *(1961). Among his other best-known films are* Lost Weekend *(1945),* Stalag 17 *(1953),* Sabrina *(1954),* The Big Carnival *(also known as* Ace in the Hole*) (1954),* The Seven Year Itch *(1955), and* The Front Page *(1974).*

As you did with "The Birds," read the story first for pure enjoyment, then once more with an eye to the filmic possibilities of the narrative. How would you conceive this story if you were assigned to write or direct it? Remember that unlike most adaptations of novels, which require compression, a short story adaptation will require expansion and development if it is to become a feature-length film.

Following the story we present a few pages of side-by-side comparison of the opening and closing of the play by Christie and the screenplay by Wilder/Kurnitz. Try to account for the differences among story, play, and screenplay in terms of the special quality of each medium.

Mr. Mayherne adjusted his pince-nez and cleared his throat with a little dry-as-dust cough that was wholly typical of him. Then he looked again at the man opposite him, the man charged with willful murder.[1] 1

Mr. Mayherne was a small man, precise in manner, neatly, not to say foppishly dressed, with a pair of very shrewd and piercing gray eyes. By no means a fool. Indeed, as a solicitor, Mr. Mayherne's reputation stood very high. His voice, when he spoke to his client, was dry but not unsympathetic. 2

"I must impress upon you again that you are in very grave danger, and that the utmost frankness is necessary." 3

Leonard Vole, who had been staring in a dazed fashion at the blank wall in front of him, transferred his glance to the solicitor. 4

"I know," he said hopelessly. "You keep telling me so. But I can't seem to realize yet that I'm charged with murder—*murder*. And such a dastardly crime, too." 5

Mr. Mayherne was practical, not emotional. He coughed again, took off his pince-nez, polished them carefully, and replaced them on his nose. Then he said, "Yes, yes, yes. Now, my dear Mr. Vole, we're going to make a determined effort to get you off—and we shall succeed—we shall succeed. But I must have all the facts. I must know just how damaging the case against you is likely to be. Then we can fix upon the best line of defense." 6

Still the young man looked at him in the same dazed, hopeless fashion. To Mr. Mayherne the case had seemed black enough, and the guilt of the prisoner assured. Now, for the first time, he felt a doubt. 7

"You think I'm guilty," said Leonard Vole, in a low voice. "But, by God, I swear I'm not! It looks pretty black against me, I know that. I'm like a man caught in a net—the meshes of it all round me, entangling me whichever way I turn. But I didn't do it, Mr. Mayherne, I didn't do it!" 8

In such a position a man was bound to protest his innocence. Mr. Mayherne knew that. Yet, in spite of himself, he was impressed. It might be, after all, that Leonard Vole was innocent. 9

"You are right, Mr. Vole," he said gravely. "The case does look very black against you. Nevertheless, I accept your assurance. Now, let us get to facts. I want you to tell me in your own words exactly how you came to make the acquaintance of Miss Emily French." 10

"It was one day in Oxford Street. I saw an elderly lady crossing the road. She was carrying a lot of parcels. In the middle of the street she dropped them, tried to recover them, found a bus was almost on top of her, and just managed to reach the curb safely, dazed and bewildered by people 11

---

[1]In the British legal system, depending on the case being tried, a defendant may have two types of lawyers: a *solicitor* (Mr. Mayherne, in Christie's story) and a *barrister* (Sir Charles). A solicitor provides legal advice and prepares cases but is not a member of the bar and does not serve as a legal advocate except in the lower courts. A barrister, known also as a K.C. (King's Counsel) or Q.C. (Queen's Counsel), is authorized to argue cases in all courts.

having shouted at her. I recovered her parcels, wiped the mud off them as best I could, retied the string of one, and returned them to her."

"There was no question of your having saved her life?" 12

"Oh, dear me, no! All I did was to perform a common act of courtesy. 13 She was extremely grateful, thanked me warmly, and said something about my manners not being those of most of the younger generation—I can't remember the exact words. Then I lifted my hat and went on. I never expected to see her again. But life is full of coincidences. That very evening I came across her at a party at a friend's house. She recognized me at once and asked that I should be introduced to her. I then found out that she was a Miss Emily French and that she lived at Cricklewood. I talked to her for some time. She was, I imagine, an old lady who took sudden and violent fancies to people. She took one to me on the strength of a perfectly simple action which anyone might have performed. On leaving, she shook me warmly by the hand and asked me to come and see her. I replied, of course, that I should be very pleased to do so, and she then urged me to name a day. I did not want particularly to go, but it would have seemed churlish to refuse, so I fixed on the following Saturday. After she had gone, I learned something about her from my friends. That she was rich, eccentric, lived alone with one maid, and owned no less than eight cats."

"I see," said Mr. Mayherne. "The question of her being well off came 14 up as early as that?"

"If you mean that I inquired—" began Leonard Vole hotly, but Mr. 15 Mayherne stilled him with a gesture.

"I have to look at the case as it will be presented by the other side. An 16 ordinary observer would not have supposed Miss French to be a lady of means. She lived poorly, almost humbly. Unless you had been told the contrary, you would in all probability have considered her to be in poor circumstances—at any rate to begin with. Who was it exactly who told you that she was well off?"

"My friend, George Harvey, at whose house the party took place." 17

"Is he likely to remember having done so?" 18

"I really don't know. Of course it is some time ago now." 19

"Quite so, Mr. Vole. You see, the first aim of the prosecution will be to 20 establish that you were in low water financially—that is true, is it not?"

Leonard Vole flushed. 21

"Yes," he said, in a low voice. "I'd been having a run of infernal bad 22 luck just then."

"Quite so," said Mr. Mayherne again. "That being, as I say, in low wa- 23 ter financially, you met this rich old lady and cultivated her acquaintance assiduously. Now if we are in a position to say that you had no idea she was well off, and that you visited her out of pure kindness of heart—"

"Which is the case." 24

"I dare say. I am not disputing the point. I am looking at it from the 25 outside point of view. A great deal depends on the memory of Mr. Harvey.

Is he likely to remember that conversation or is he not? Could he be confused by counsel into believing that it took place later?"

Leonard Vole reflected for some minutes. Then he said steadily enough, but with a rather pale face, "I do not think that that line would be successful, Mr. Mayherne. Several of those present heard his remark, and one or two of them chaffed me about my conquest of a rich old lady." 26

The solicitor endeavored to hide his disappointment with a wave of the hand. 27

"Unfortunate," he said. "But I congratulate you upon your plain speaking, Mr. Vole. It is to you I look to guide me. Your judgment is quite right. To persist in the line I spoke of would have been disastrous. We must leave that point. You made the acquaintance of Miss French, you called upon her, the acquaintanceship progressed. We want a clear reason for all this. Why did you, a young man of thirty-three, good-looking, fond of sport, popular with your friends, devote so much of your time to an elderly woman with whom you could hardly have anything in common?" 28

Leonard Vole flung out his hands in a nervous gesture. 29

"I can't tell you—I really can't tell you. After the first visit, she pressed me to come again, spoke of being lonely and unhappy. She made it difficult for me to refuse. She showed so plainly her fondness and affection for me that I was placed in an awkward position. You see, Mr. Mayherne, I've got a weak nature—I drift—I'm one of those people who can't say no. And believe me or not, as you like, after the third or fourth visit I paid her I found myself getting genuinely fond of the old thing. My mother died when I was young, an aunt brought me up, and she, too, died before I was fifteen. If I told you that I genuinely enjoyed being mothered and pampered, I dare say you'd only laugh." 30

Mr. Mayherne did not laugh. Instead he took off his pince-nez again and polished them, a sign with him that he was thinking deeply. 31

"I accept your explanation, Mr. Vole," he said at last. "I believe it to be psychologically probable. Whether a jury would take that view of it is another matter. Please continue your narrative. When was it that Miss French first asked you to look into her business affairs?" 32

"After my third or fourth visit to her. She understood very little of money matters, and was worried about some investments." 33

Mr. Mayherne looked up sharply. 34

"Be careful, Mr. Vole. The maid, Janet Mackenzie, declares that her mistress was a good woman of business and transacted all her own affairs, and this is borne out by the testimony of her bankers." 35

"I can't help that," said Vole earnestly. "That's what she said to me." 36

Mr. Mayherne looked at him for a moment or two in silence. Though he had no intention of saying so, his belief in Leonard Vole's innocence was at that moment strengthened. He knew something of the mentality of elderly ladies. He saw Miss French, infatuated with the good-looking young man, hunting about for pretexts that would bring him to the house. What more likely than that she should plead ignorance of business, and beg him to help her with her money affairs? She was enough of a woman of the 37 world to realize that any man is slightly flattered by such an admission of his superiority. Leonard Vole had been flattered. Perhaps, too, she had not been adverse to letting this young man know that she was wealthy. Emily French had been a strong-willed old woman, willing to pay her price for what she wanted. All this passed rapidly through Mr. Mayherne's mind, but he gave no indication of it, and asked instead a further question.

"And did you handle her affairs for her at her request?" 38

"I did." 39

"Mr. Vole," said the solicitor, "I am going to ask you a very serious 40
question, and one to which it is vital I should have a truthful answer. You were in low water financially. You had the handling of an old lady's affairs—an old lady who, according to her own statement, knew little or nothing of business. Did you at any time, or in any manner, convert to your own use the securities which you handled? Did you engage in any transaction for your own pecuniary advantage which will not bear the light of day?" He quelled the other's response. "Wait a minute before you answer. There are two courses open to us. Either we can make a feature of your probity and honesty in conducting her affairs while pointing out how unlikely it is that you would commit murder to obtain money which you might have obtained by such infinitely easier means. If, on the other hand, there is anything in your dealings which the prosecution will get hold of—if, to put it baldly, it can be proved that you swindled the old lady in any way, we must take the line that you had no motive for the murder, since she was already a profitable source of income to you. You perceive the distinction. Now, I beg of you, take your time before you reply."

But Leonard Vole took no time at all. 41

"My dealings with Miss French's affairs were all perfectly fair and 42
above board. I acted for her interests to the very best of my ability, as anyone will find who looks into the matter."

"Thank you," said Mr. Mayherne. "You relieve my mind very much. I 43
pay you the compliment of believing that you are far too clever to lie to me over such an important matter."

"Surely," said Vole eagerly, "the strongest point in my favor is the lack 44
of motive. Granted that I cultivated the acquaintanceship of a rich old lady in the hopes of getting money out of her—that, I gather, is the substance of what you have been saying—surely her death frustrates all my hopes?"

The solicitor looked at him steadily. Then, very deliberately, he re- 45
peated his unconscious trick with his pince-nez. It was not until they were firmly replaced on his nose that he spoke.

"Are you not aware, Mr. Vole, that Miss French left a will under which 46
you are the principal beneficiary?"

"What?" The prisoner sprang to his feet. His dismay was obvious and 47
unforced. "My God! What are you saying? She left her money to me?"

Mr. Mayherne nodded slowly. Vole sank down again, his head in his 48
hands.

"You pretend you know nothing of this will?" 49

"Pretend? There's no pretense about it. I knew nothing about it." 50

"What would you say if I told you that the maid, Janet Mackenzie, 51
swears that you *did* know? That her mistress told her distinctly that she had consulted you in the matter, and told you of her intentions?"

"Say? That she's lying! No, I go too fast. Janet is an elderly woman. 52
She was a faithful watchdog to her mistress, and she didn't like me. She was jealous and suspicious. I should say that Miss French confided her intentions to Janet, and that Janet either mistook something she said, or else was convinced in her own mind that I had persuaded the old lady into doing it. I dare say that she herself believes now that Miss French actually told her so."

"You don't think she dislikes you enough to lie deliberately about the 53
matter?"

Leonard Vole looked shocked and startled. 54

"No, indeed! Why should she?" 55

"I don't know," said Mr. Mayherne thoughtfully. "But she's very bitter 56
against you."

The wretched young man groaned again. 57

"I'm beginning to see," he muttered. "It's frightful. I made up to her, 58
that's what they'll say, I got her to make a will leaving her money to me, and then I go there that night, and there's nobody in the house—they find her the next day—oh, my God, it's awful!"

"You are wrong about there being nobody in the house," said Mr. May- 59
herne. "Janet, as you remember, was to go out for the evening. She went, but about half past nine she returned to fetch the pattern of a blouse sleeve which she had promised to a friend. She let herself in by the back door, went upstairs and fetched it, and went out again. She heard voices in the sitting-room, though she could not distinguish what they said, but she will swear that one of them was Miss French's and one was a man's."

"At half past nine," said Leonard Vole. "At half past nine—" He 60
sprang to his feet. "But then I'm saved—saved—"

"What do you mean, saved?" cried Mr. Mayherne, astonished. 61

"By half past nine I was at home again! My wife can prove that. I left 62
Miss French about five minutes to nine. I arrived home about twenty past nine. My wife was there waiting for me. Oh, thank God—thank God! And bless Janet Mackenzie's sleeve pattern."

In his exuberance, he hardly noticed that the grave expression on the 63
solicitor's face had not altered. But the latter's words brought him down to earth with a bump.

"Who, then, in your opinion, murdered Miss French?" 64

"Why, a burglar, of course, as was thought at first. The window was 65
forced, you remember. She was killed with a heavy blow from a crowbar, and the crowbar was found lying on the floor beside the body. And several articles were missing. But for Janet's absurd suspicions and dislike of me, the police would never have swerved from the right track."

"That will hardly do, Mr. Vole," said the solicitor. "The things that 66
were missing were mere trifles of no value, taken as a blind. And the marks

on the window were not at all conclusive. Besides, think for yourself. You say you were no longer in the house by half past nine. Who, then, was the man Janet heard talking to Miss French in the sitting-room? She would hardly be having an amicable conversation with a burglar."

"No," said Vole. "No—" He looked puzzled and discouraged. "But, 67
anyway," he added with reviving spirit, "it lets me out. I've got an alibi. You must see Romaine—my wife—at once."

"Certainly," acquiesced the lawyer. "I should already have seen Mrs. 68
Vole but for her being absent when you were arrested. I wired to Scotland at once, and I understand that she arrives back tonight. I am going to call upon her immediately I leave here."

Vole nodded, a great expression of satisfaction settling down over his 69
face.

"Yes, Romaine will tell you. My God! it's a lucky chance that." 70

"Excuse me, Mr. Vole, but you are very fond of your wife?" 71

"Of course." 72

"And she of you?" 73

"Romaine is devoted to me. She'd do anything in the world for me." 74

He spoke enthusiastically, but the solicitor's heart sank a little lower. 75
The testimony of a devoted wife—would it gain credence?

"Was there anyone else who saw you return at nine-twenty. A maid, for 76
instance?"

"We have no maid." 77

"Did you meet anyone in the street on the way back?" 78

"Nobody I knew. I rode part of the way in a bus. The conductor might 79
remember."

Mr. Mayherne shook his head doubtfully. 80

"There is no one, then, who can confirm your wife's testimony?" 81

"No. But it isn't necessary, surely?" 82

"I dare say not. I dare say not," said Mr. Mayherne hastily. "Now 83
there's just one thing more. Did Miss French know that you were a married man?"

"Oh, yes." 84

"Yet you never took your wife to see her. Why was that?" 85

For the first time, Leonard Vole's answer came halting and uncertain. 86

"Well—I don't know." 87

"Are you aware that Janet Mackenzie says her mistress believed you to 88
be single, and contemplated marrying you in the future?"

Vole laughed. "Absurd! There was forty years' difference in age be- 89
tween us."

"It has been done," said the solicitor dryly. "The fact remains. Your 90
wife never met Miss French?"

"No—" Again the constraint. 91

"You will permit me to say," said the lawyer, "that I hardly understand 92
your attitude in the matter."

Vole flushed, hesitated, and then spoke. 93

"I'll make a clean breast of it. I was hard up, as you know. I hoped that Miss French might lend me some money. She was fond of me, but she wasn't at all interested in the struggles of a young couple. Early on, I found that she had taken it for granted that my wife and I didn't get on—were living apart. Mr. Mayherne—I wanted the money—for Romaine's sake. I said nothing, and allowed the old lady to think what she chose. She spoke of my being an adopted son to her. There was never any question of marriage—that must be just Janet's imagination." 94

"And that is all?" 95

"Yes—that is all." 96

Was there just a shade of hesitation in the words? The lawyer fancied so. He rose and held out his hand. 97

"Good-by, Mr. Vole." He looked into the haggard young face and spoke with an unusual impulse. "I believe in your innocence in spite of the multitude of facts arrayed against you. I hope to prove it and vindicate you completely." 98

Vole smiled back at him. 99

"You'll find the alibi is all right," he said cheerfully. 100

Again he hardly noticed that the other did not respond. 101

"The whole thing hinges a good deal on the testimony of Janet Mackenzie," said Mr. Mayherne. "She hates you. That much is clear." 102

"She can hardly hate me," protested the young man. 103

The solicitor shook his head as he went out. *Now for Mrs. Vole,* he said to himself. He was seriously disturbed by the way the thing was shaping. 104

The Voles lived in a small shabby house near Paddington Green. It was to this house that Mr. Mayherne went. 105

In answer to his ring, a big slatternly woman, obviously a charwoman, answered the door. 106

"Mrs. Vole? Has she returned yet?" 107

"Got back an hour ago. But I dunno if you can see her." 108

"If you will take my card to her," said Mr. Mayherne quietly, "I am quite sure that she will do so." 109

The woman looked at him doubtfully, wiped her hand on her apron, and took the card. Then she closed the door in his face and left him on the step outside. 110

In a few minutes, however, she returned with a slightly altered manner. 111

"Come inside, please." 112

She ushered him into a tiny drawing-room. Mr. Mayherne, examining a drawing on the wall, started up suddenly to face a tall, pale woman who had entered so quietly that he had not heard her. 113

"Mr. Mayherne? You are my husband's solicitor, are you not? You have come from him? Will you please sit down?" 114

Until she spoke he had not realized that she was not English. Now, observing her more closely, he noticed the high cheekbones, the dense blue-black of the hair, and an occasional very slight movement of the hands that was distinctly foreign. A strange woman, very quiet. So quiet as to make 115 one uneasy. From the very first Mr. Mayherne was conscious that he was up against something that he did not understand.

"Now, my dear Mrs. Vole," he began, "you must not give way—" 116

He stopped. It was so very obvious that Romaine Vole had not the 117
slightest intention of giving way. She was perfectly calm and composed.

"Will you please tell me about it?" she said. "I must know everything. 118
Do not think to spare me. I want to know the worst." She hesitated, then repeated in a lower tone, with a curious emphasis which the lawyer did not understand, "I want to know the worst."

Mr. Mayherne went over his interview with Leonard Vole. She listened 119
attentively, nodding her head now and then.

"I see," she said, when he had finished. "He wants me to say that he 120
came in at twenty minutes past nine that night?"

"He did come in at that time?" said Mr. Mayherne sharply. 121

"That is not the point," she said coldly. "Will my saying so acquit him? 122
Will they believe me?"

Mr. Mayherne was taken aback. She had gone so quickly to the core of 123
the matter.

"That is what I want to know," she said. "Will it be enough? Is there 124
anyone else who can support my evidence?"

There was a suppressed eagerness in her manner that made him 125
vaguely uneasy.

"So far there is no one else," he said reluctantly. 126

"I see," said Romaine Vole. 127

She sat for a minute or two perfectly still. A little smile played over her 128
lips.

The lawyer's feeling of alarm grew stronger and stronger. 129

"Mrs. Vole—" he began. "I know what you must feel—" 130

"Do you?" she asked. "I wonder." 131

"In the circumstances—" 132

"In the circumstances—I intend to play a lone hand." 133

He looked at her in dismay. 134

"But, my dear Mrs. Vole—you are overwrought. Being so devoted to 135
your husband—"

"I beg your pardon?" 136

The sharpness of her voice made him start. He repeated in a hesitating 137
manner, "Being so devoted to your husband—"

Romaine Vole nodded slowly, the same strange smile on her lips. 138

"Did he tell you that I was devoted to him?" she asked softly. "Ah! yes, 139
I can see he did. How stupid men are! Stupid—stupid—stupid—"

She rose suddenly to her feet. All the intense emotion that the lawyer 140
had been conscious of in the atmosphere was now concentrated in her tone.

"I hate him, I tell you! I hate him. I hate him. I hate him! I would like 141
to see him hanged by the neck till he is dead."

The lawyer recoiled before her and the smoldering passion in her eyes. 142

She advanced a step nearer and continued vehemently. 143

"Perhaps I shall see it. Supposing I tell you that he did not come in that 144
night at twenty past nine, but at twenty past ten? You say that he tells you he knew nothing about the money coming to him. Supposing I tell you he knew all about it, and counted on it, and committed murder to get it? Supposing I tell you that he admitted to me that night when he came in what he had done? That there was blood on his coat? What then? Supposing that I stand up in court and say all these things?"

Her eyes seemed to challenge him. With an effort he concealed his 145
growing dismay, and endeavored to speak in a rational tone.

"You cannot be asked to give evidence against your husband—" 146

"He is not my husband!" 147

The words came out so quickly that he fancied he had misunderstood 148
her.

"I beg your pardon? I—" 149

"He is not my husband." 150

The silence was so intense that you could have heard a pin drop. 151

"I was an actress in Vienna. My husband is alive but in a madhouse. So 152
we could not marry. I am glad now." She nodded defiantly.

"I should like you to tell me one thing," said Mr. Mayherne. He con- 153
trived to appear as cool and unemotional as ever. "Why are you so bitter against Leonard Vole?"

She shook her head, smiling a little. 154

"Yes, you would like to know. But I shall not tell you. I will keep my 155
secret."

Mr. Mayherne gave his dry little cough and rose. 156

"There seems no point in prolonging this interview," he remarked. 157
"You will hear from me again after I have communicated with my client."

She came closer to him, looking into his eyes with her own wonderful 158
dark ones.

"Tell me," she said, "did you believe—honestly—that he was innocent 159
when you came here today?"

"I did," said Mr. Mayherne. 160

"You poor little man." She laughed. 161

"And I believe so still," finished the lawyer. "Good evening, madam." 162

He went out of the room, taking with him the memory of her startled 163
face. *This is going to be the devil of a business,* said Mr. Mayherne to himself as he strode along the street.

Extraordinary, the whole thing. An extraordinary woman. A very 164
dangerous woman. Women were the devil when they got their knife into you.

What was to be done? That wretched young man hadn't a leg to stand 165
upon. Of course, possibly he did commit the crime.

No, said Mr. Mayherne to himself. *No—there's almost too much evi-* 166
dence against him. I don't believe this woman. She was trumping up the whole story. But she'll never bring it into court.

He wished he felt more conviction on the point. 167

The police court proceedings were brief and dramatic. The principal witnesses for the prosecution were Janet Mackenzie, maid to the dead woman, and Romaine Heilger, Austrian subject, the mistress of the prisoner. 168

Mr. Mayherne sat in court and listened to the damning story that the latter told. It was on the lines she had indicated to him in their interview. 169

The prisoner reserved his defense and was committed for trial. 170

Mr. Mayherne was at his wits' end. The case against Leonard Vole was black beyond words. Even the famous K.C. who was engaged for the defense held out little hope. 171

"If we can shake that Austrian woman's testimony, we might do something," he said dubiously. "But it's a bad business." 172

Mr. Mayherne had concentrated his energies on one single point. Assuming Leonard Vole to be speaking the truth, and to have left the murdered woman's house at nine o'clock, who was the man Janet heard talking to Miss French at half past nine? 173

The only ray of light was in the shape of a scapegrace nephew who had in bygone days cajoled and threatened his aunt out of various sums of money. Janet Mackenzie, the solicitor learned, had always been attached to this young man, and had never ceased urging his claims upon her mistress. It certainly seemed possible that it was this nephew who had been with Miss French after Leonard Vole left, especially as he was not to be found in any of his old haunts. 174

In all other directions, the lawyer's researches had been negative in their result. No one had seen Leonard Vole entering his own house, or leaving that of Miss French. No one had seen any other man enter or leave the house in Cricklewood. All inquiries drew blank. 175

It was the eve of the trial when Mr. Mayherne received the letter which was to lead his thoughts in an entirely new direction. 176

It came by the six-o'clock post. An illiterate scrawl, written on common paper and enclosed in a dirty envelope with the stamp stuck on crooked. 177

Mr. Mayherne read it through once or twice before he grasped its meaning. 178

Dear Mister:

Youre the lawyer chap wot acts for the young feller. If you want that painted foreign hussy showd up for wot she is an her pack of lies you come to 16 Shaw's Rents Stepney to-night It ull cawst you 2 hundred quid Arsk for Missis Mogson.

The solicitor read and reread this strange epistle. It might, of course, be a hoax, but when he thought it over, he became increasingly convinced that it was genuine, and also convinced that it was the one hope for the prisoner. The evidence of Romaine Heilger damned him completely, and the line the defense meant to pursue, the line that the evidence of a woman who had ad- 179 mittedly lived and immoral life was not to be trusted, was at best a weak one.

Mr. Mayherne's mind was made up. It was his duty to save his client at 180
all costs. He must go to Shaw's Rents.

He had some difficulty in finding the place, a ramshackle building in 181
an evil-smelling slum, but at last he did so, and on inquiry for Mrs. Mogson was sent up to a room on the third floor. On this door he knocked, and getting no answer, knocked again.

At this second knock, he heard a shuffling sound inside, and presently 182
the door was opened cautiously half an inch and a bent figure peered out.

Suddenly the woman, for it was a woman, gave a chuckle and opened 183
the door wider.

"So it's you, dearie," she said, in a wheezy voice. "Nobody with you, is 184
there? No playing tricks? That's right. You can come in—you can come in."

With some reluctance the lawyer stepped across the threshold into the 185
small, dirty room, with its flickering gas jet. There was an untidy unmade bed in a corner, a plain deal table, and two rickety chairs. For the first time Mr. Mayherne had a full view of the tenant of this unsavory apartment. She was a woman of middle age, bent in figure, with a mass of untidy gray hair and a scarf wound tightly round her face. She saw him looking at this and laughed again, the same curious, toneless chuckle.

"Wondering why I hide my beauty, dear? He, he, he. Afraid it may 186
tempt you, eh? But you shall see—you shall see."

She drew aside the scarf, and the lawyer recoiled involuntarily before 187
the almost formless blur of scarlet. She replaced the scarf again.

"So you're not wanting to kiss me, dearie? He, he, I don't wonder. And 188
yet I was a pretty girl once—not so long ago as you'd think, either. Vitriol, dearie, vitriol—that's what did that. Ah! but I'll be even with 'em—"

She burst into a hideous torrent of profanity which Mr. Mayherne tried 189
vainly to quell. She fell silent at last, her hands clenching and unclenching themselves nervously.

"Enough of that," said the lawyer sternly. "I've come here because I 190
have reason to believe you can give me information which will clear my client, Leonard Vole. Is that the case?"

Her eyes leered at him cunningly. 191

"What about the money, dearie?" she wheezed. "Two hundred quid, 192
you remember."

"It is your duty to give evidence, and you can be called upon to do so." 193

"That won't do, dearie. I'm an old woman, and I know nothing. But 194
you give me two hundred quid, and perhaps I can give you a hint or two. See?"

"What kind of hint?" 195

"What should you say to a letter? A letter from *her.* Never mind how I 196
got hold of it. That's my business. It'll do the trick. But I want my two hundred quid."

Mr. Mayherne looked at her coldly, and made up his mind. 197

"I'll give you ten pounds, nothing more. And only that if this letter is 198
what you say it is."

"Ten pounds?" She screamed and raved at him. 199

"Twenty," said Mr. Mayherne, "and that's my last word." 200

He rose as if to go. Then, watching her closely, he drew out a pocket- 201
book, and counted out twenty one-pound notes.

"You see," he said. "That is all I have with me. You can take it or leave 202
it."

But already he knew that the sight of the money was too much for her. 203
She cursed and raved impotently, but at last she gave in. Going over to the bed, she drew something out from beneath the tattered mattress.

"Here you are, damn you!" she snarled. "It's the top one you want." 204

It was a bundle of letters that she threw to him, and Mr. Mayherne un- 205
tied them and scanned them in his usual cool, methodical manner. The woman, watching him eagerly, could gain no clue from his impassive face.

He read each letter through, then returned again to the top one and read 206
it a second time. Then he tied the whole bundle up again carefully.

They were love letters, written by Romaine Heilger, and the man they 207
were written to was not Leonard Vole. The top letter was dated the day of the latter's arrest.

"I spoke true, dearie, didn't I?" whined the woman. "It'll do for her, 208
that letter?"

Mr. Mayherne put the letters in his pocket, then he asked a question. 209

"How did you get hold of this correspondence?" 210

"That's telling," she said with a leer. "But I know something more. I 211
heard in court what that hussy said. Find out where she was at twenty past ten, the time she says she was at home. Ask at the Lion Road Cinema. They'll remember—a fine upstanding girl like that—curse her!"

"Who is the man?" asked Mr. Mayherne. "There's only a Christian 212
name here."

The other's voice grew thick and hoarse, her hands clenched and un- 213
clenched. Finally she lifted one to her face.

"He's the man that did this to me. Many years ago now. She took him 214
away from me—a chit of a girl she was then. And when I went after him—and went for him, too—he threw the cursed stuff at me! And she laughed—damn her! I've had it in for her for years. Followed her, I have, spied upon her. And now I've got her! She'll suffer for this, won't she, Mr. Lawyer? She'll suffer?"

"She will probably be sentenced to a term of imprisonment for per- 215
jury," said Mr. Mayherne quietly.

"Shut away—that's what I want. You're going, are you? Where's my 216
money? Where's that good money?"

Without a word, Mr. Mayherne put down the notes on the table. Then, 217
drawing a deep breath, he turned and left the squalid room. Looking back, he saw the old woman crooning over the money.

He wasted no time. He found the cinema in Lion Road easily enough, and, shown a photograph of Romaine Heilger, the commissionaire recognized her at once. She had arrived at the cinema with a man some time after ten o'clock on the evening in question. He had not noticed her escort particularly, but he remembered the lady who had spoken to him about the picture that was showing. They stayed until the end, about an hour later. 218

Mr. Mayherne was satisfied. Romaine Heilger's evidence was a tissue of lies from beginning to end. She had evolved it out of her passionate hatred. The lawyer wondered whether he would ever know what lay behind that hatred. What had Leonard Vole done to her? He had seemed dumfounded when the solicitor had reported her attitude to him. He had declared earnestly that such a thing was incredible—yet it had seemed to Mr. Mayherne that after the first astonishment his protests had lacked sincerity. 219

He did know. Mr. Mayherne was convinced of it. He knew, but he had no intention of revealing the fact. The secret between those two remained a secret. Mr. Mayherne wondered if some day he should come to learn what it was. 220

The solicitor glanced at his watch. It was late, but time was everything. He hailed a taxi and gave an address. 221

"Sir Charles must know of this at once," he murmured to himself as he got in. 222

The trial of Leonard Vole for the murder of Emily French aroused widespread interest. In the first place the prisoner was young and good-looking, then he was accused of a particularly dastardly crime, and there was the further interest of Romaine Heilger, the principal witness for the prosecution. There had been pictures of her in many papers, and several fictitious stories as to her origin and history. 223

The proceedings opened quietly enough. Various technical evidence came first. Then Janet Mackenzie was called. She told substantially the same story as before. In cross-examination counsel for the defense succeeded in getting her to contradict herself once or twice over her account of Vole's association with Miss French; he emphasized the fact that though she had heard a man's voice in the sitting-room that night, there was nothing to show that it was Vole who was there, and he managed to drive home a feeling that jealousy and dislike of the prisoner were at the bottom of a good deal of her evidence. 224

Then the next witness was called. 225

"Your name is Romaine Heilger?" 226

"Yes." 227

"You are an Austrian subject?" 228

"Yes." 229

"For the last three years you have lived with the prisoner and passed yourself off as his wife?" 230

Just for a moment Romaine Heilger's eyes met those of the man in the dock. Her expression held something curious and unfathomable. 231

"Yes." 232

The questions went on. Word by word the damning facts came out. On the night in question the prisoner had taken out a crowbar with him. He had returned at twenty minutes past ten, and had confessed to having killed the old lady. His cuffs had been stained with blood, and he had burned them in the kitchen stove. He had terrorized her into silence by means of threats. 233

As the story proceeded, the feeling of the court which had, to begin with, been slightly favorable to the prisoner, now set dead against him. He himself sat with downcast head and moody air, as though he knew he were doomed. 234

Yet it might have been noted that her own counsel sought to restrain Romaine's animosity. He would have preferred her to be more unbiased. 235

Formidable and ponderous, counsel for the defense arose. 236

He put it to her that her story was a malicious fabrication from start to finish, that she had not even been in her own house at the time in question, that she was in love with another man and was deliberately seeking to send Vole to his death for a crime he did not commit. 237

Romaine denied these allegations with superb insolence. 238

Then came the surprising denouement, the production of the letter. It was read aloud in court in the midst of a breathless stillness. 239

"Max, beloved, the Fates have delivered him into our hands! He has been arrested for murder—but, yes, the murder of an old lady! Leonard, who would not hurt a fly! At last I shall have my revenge. The poor chicken! I shall say that he came in that night with blood upon him—that he confessed to me. I shall hang him, Max—and when he hangs he will know and realize that it was Romaine who sent him to his death. And then—happiness, Beloved! Happiness at last!"

There were experts present ready to swear that the handwriting was that of Romaine Heilger, but they were not needed. Confronted with the letter, Romaine broke down utterly and confessed everything. Leonard Vole had returned to the house at the time he said, twenty past nine. She had invented the whole story to ruin him. 240

With the collapse of Romaine Heilger, the Case for the Crown collapsed also. Sir Charles called his few witnesses, the prisoner himself went into the box and told his story in a manly straightforward manner, unshaken by cross-examination. 241

The prosecution endeavored to rally, but without great success. The judge's summing up was not wholly favorable to the prisoner, but a reaction had set in and the jury needed little time to consider their verdict. 242

"We find the prisoner not guilty." 243

Leonard Vole was free! 244

Little Mr. Mayherne hurried from his seat. He must congratulate his client. 245

He found himself polishing his pince-nez vigorously, and checked himself. His wife had told him only the night before that he was getting a habit of it. Curious things, habits. People themselves never knew they had them. 246

247 An interesting case—a very interesting case. That woman, now, Romaine Heilger.

248 The case was dominated for him still by the exotic figure of Romaine Heilger. She had seemed a pale, quiet woman in the house at Paddington, but in court she had flamed out against the sober background, flaunting herself like a tropical flower.

249 If he closed his eyes he could see her now, tall and vehement, her exquisite body bent forward a little, her right hand clenching and unclenching itself unconsciously all the time.

250 Curious things, habits. That gesture of hers with the hand was her habit, he supposed. Yet he had seen someone else do it quite lately. Who was it now? Quite lately—

251 He drew in his breath with a gasp as it came back to him. The woman in Shaw's Rents—

252 He stood still, his head whirling. It was impossible—impossible—yet, Romaine Heilger was an actress.

253 The K.C. came up behind him and clapped him on the shoulder.

254 "Congratulated our man yet? He's had a narrow shave, you know. Come along and see him."

255 But the little lawyer shook off the other's hand.

256 He wanted one thing only—to see Romaine Heilger face to face.

257 He did not see her until some time later, and the place of their meeting is not relevant.

258 "So you guessed," she said, when he had told her all that was in his mind. "The face? Oh! that was easy enough, and the light of that gas jet was too bad for you to see the makeup."

259 "But why—why—"

260 "Why did I play a lone hand?" She smiled a little, remembering the last time she had used the words.

261 "Such an elaborate comedy!"

262 "My friend—I had to save him. The evidence of a woman devoted to him would not have been enough—you hinted as much yourself. But I know something of the psychology of crowds. Let my evidence be wrung from me, as an admission, damning me in the eyes of the law, and a reaction in favor of the prisoner would immediately set in."

263 "And the bundle of letters?"

264 "One alone, the vital one, might have seemed like a—what do you call it?—put-up job."

265 "Then the man called Max?"

266 "Never existed, my friend."

267 "I still think," said little Mr. Mayherne, in an aggrieved manner, "that we could have got him off by the—er—normal procedure."

268 "I dared not risk it. You see you thought he was innocent—"

269 "And you knew it? I see," said little Mr. Mayherne.

270 "My dear Mr. Mayherne," said Romaine, "you do not see at all. I knew—he was guilty!"

NOTE TO THE READER

Following are excerpts from the two adaptations of Agatha Christie's story "Witness for the Prosecution" described in the headnote (pp. 712–13). For ease of comparison, the excerpts are presented side-by-side. On the left-hand, even-numbered, pages are the opening and closing segments from Christie's dramatic adaptation of the story. On the right-hand, odd-numbered, pages (through p. 745 and then on both left- and right-hand pages through the end) are the opening and closing segments of Billy Wilder's film version. Note that the screenplay is printed in typescript style to differentiate it from the stage play.

Note on character names: In the stage play Romain's name remains the same as in the story; in the screenplay her name has been changed to Christine. In the stage play the name of the solicitor, Mr. Mayherne, has been changed to Mayhew. Sir Charles, the King's Counsel (K.C.) in the short story, has been changed to Sir Wilfred Robarts in both the stage play and the film, and he is now a Queen's Counsel (Q.C.), since Queen Elizabeth II was inaugurated in 1953.

Witness for the Prosecution: *A Play*

AGATHA CHRISTIE

Act One

SCENE: The chambers of Sir Wilfrid Robarts, Q.C.

The scene is Sir Wilfrid's private office. It is a narrow room with the door L. *and a window* R. *The window has a deep built-in window seat and overlooks a tall plain brick wall. There is a fireplace* C. *of the back wall, flanked by bookcases filled with heavy legal volumes. There is a desk* R.C. *with a swivel chair* R. *of it and a leather-covered upright chair* L. *of it. A second upright chair stands against the bookcases* L. *of the fireplace. In the corner up* R. *is a tall reading desk, and in the corner up* L. *are some coat-hooks attached to the wall. At night the room is lit by electric candle-lamp wall-brackets* R. *and* L. *of the fireplace and an angle-poise lamp on the desk. The light switch is below the door* L. *There is a bell push* L. *of the fireplace. The desk has a telephone on it and is littered with legal documents. There are the usual deed-boxes and there is a litter of documents on the window seat.*

When the Curtain rises it is afternoon and there is sunshine streaming in through the window R. *The office is empty.* GRETA, *Sir Wilfrid's typist, enters immediately. She is an adenoidal girl with a good opinion of herself. She crosses to the fireplace, doing a "square dance" step, and takes a paper from a box-file on the mantelpiece.* CARTER, *the Chief clerk, enters. He carries some letters.* GRETA *turns, sees* CARTER, *crosses and quietly exits.* CARTER *crosses to the desk and puts the letters on it. The TELEPHONE rings.* CARTER *lifts the receiver.*

CARTER: *(Into the telephone.)* Sir Wilfrid Robart's Chambers . . . Oh, it's you, Charles . . . No, Sir Wilfrid's in Court . . . Won't be back just yet . . . Yes, Shuttleworth Case . . . What—with Myers for the prosecution and Banter trying it? . . . He's been giving judgment for close on two hours already . . . No, not an earthly this evening. We're full up. Can give you an appointment tomorrow . . . No, couldn't possibly. I'm expecting Mayhew, of Mayhew and Brinskill you know, any minute now . . . Well, so long. *(He replaces the receiver and sorts the documents on the desk.)*

GRETA: *(Enters. She is painting her nails.)* Shall I make the tea, Mr. Carter?

CARTER: *(Looking at his watch.)* It's hardly time yet, Greta.

GRETA: It is by my watch.

CARTER: Then your watch is wrong.

GRETA: *(Crossing to* C.*)* I put it right by the radio.

CARTER: Then the radio must be wrong.

GRETA: *(Shocked.)* Oh, not the radio, Mr. Carter. That *couldn't* be wrong.

CARTER: This watch was my father's. It never gains nor loses. They don't make watches like that nowadays. *(He shakes his head, then suddenly changes his manner and picks up one of the typewritten papers.)* Really,

Witness for the Prosecution: A Screenplay

BILLY WILDER AND HARRY KURNITZ

1. COURTROOM NO. 1 — THE OLD BAILEY

A murder trial is about to begin. The venerable chamber of British justice is filled. The participants for the Prosecution and Defense are in their places. So is the jury. So are the spectators. Only the Prisoner's Dock and raised seats of the Judge and city dignitaries are still vacant. Three knocks from a wooden mallet are heard. An usher rises and calls out, "SILENCE!" Everyone stands. A door opens and the Judicial procession solemnly enters: the Sheriff, the City Marshal, the Mace-Bearer, the Sword-Bearer, the Lord Mayor, and finally, the Judge. All in full regalia.

The usher beneath the witness box delivers the opening proclamation:

USHER:

SILENCE! BE UPSTANDING IN COURT! ALL PERSONS WHO HAVE ANYTHING FURTHER TO DO BEFORE MY LORDS THE QUEEN'S JUSTICES OF OYER AND TERMINER AND GENERAL GAOL DELIVERY FOR THE JURISDICTION OF THE GENERAL CRIMINAL COURT DRAW NEAR AND GIVE YOUR ATTENTION. GOD SAVE THE QUEEN!

The CAMERA has begun to move in slowly on the bench. As the dignitaries take their places we superimpose the CREDIT TITLES. The Sword-Bearer affixes the Sword, point upmost, above the central chair. The Judge bows first to the Jury, then to the Bar, finally to those with him on the Bench. He sits. Everybody follows suit. The trial has begun.

Meanwhile, the CAMERA has moved in on the gleaming sword and holds there until the last of the Credits FADES OUT:

FADE OUT:

FADE IN:

2. LONDON SQUARE (DAY)

A bobby, framed very large in the foreground, is directing traffic. Among the moving cars, quite conspicuous, is a vintage high-bodied Rolls Royce.

3. INT. OF ROLLS-ROYCE (DAY)

A vintage chauffeur is driving. In the back seat are SIR WILFRID ROBARTS and his nurse, MISS PLIMSOLL. Sir Wilfrid is sixty, pale, ill-tempered. A lap robe is tucked around his legs. He has been quite ill. That accounts for the uniformed nurse, Miss Plimsoll: she is forty-five, brisk, unbearably chatty.

MISS PLIMSOLL:

(looking out the window)

What a beautiful day! I've been hoping that we'd have a bit of sun for our homecoming. I always say it's worth having all the fog just to appreciate the sunshine. Is there too much of a draught? Shall I roll up the window?

your typing. Always mistakes. *(He crosses to* R. *of* GRETA.*)* You've left out a word.

GRETA: Oh, well—just one word. Anyone might do that.

CARTER: The word you have left out is the word *not.* The omission of it entirely alters the sense.

GRETA: Oh, does it? That's rather funny when you come to think of it. *(She giggles.)*

CARTER: It is not in the least funny. *(He tears the letter in half and hands the piece to her.)* Do it again. You may remember I told you last week about the celebrated case of Bryant and Horsfall. Case of a will and a trust fund, and entirely owing to a piece of careless copying by a clerk . . .

GRETA: *(Interrupting.)* The wrong wife got the money, I remember.

CARTER: A woman divorced fifteen years previously. Absolutely contrary to the intention of the testator, as his lordship himself admitted. But the wording had to stand. They couldn't do anything about it. *(He crosses above the desk to* R. *of it.)*

GRETA: I think *that's* rather funny, too. *(She giggles.)*

CARTER: Counsel's Chambers are no place to be funny in. The Law, Greta, is a serious business and should be treated accordingly.

GRETA: You wouldn't think so—to hear some of the jokes Judges make.

CARTER: That kind of joke is the prerogative of the Bench.

GRETA: And I'm always reading in the paper about "laughter in Court."

CARTER: If that's not caused by one of the Judge's remarks you'll find he'll threaten to have the Court cleared.

GRETA: *(Crossing to the door.)* Mean old thing. *(She turns and crosses to* L. *of the desk.)* Do you know what I read the other day, Mr. Carter. *(Sententiously.)* "The Law's an Ass." I'm not being rude. It's a quotation.

CARTER: *(Coldly.)* A quotation of a facetious nature. Not meant to be taken seriously. *(He looks at his watch.)* You can make the tea—*(He pauses, waiting for the exact second.)*—now, Greta.

GRETA: *(Gladly.)* Oh, thank you, Mr. Carter. *(She crosses quickly to the door.)*

CARTER: Mr. Mayhew, of Mayhew and Brinskill, will be here shortly. A Mr. Leonard Vole is also expected. They may come together or separately.

GRETA: *(Excitedly.)* Leonard Vole? *(She crosses to the desk.)* Why, that's the name—it was in the paper . . .

CARTER: *(Repressively.)* The tea, Greta.

GRETA: Asked to communicate with the police as he might be able to give them useful information.

CARTER: *(Raising his voice.) Tea!*

GRETA: *(Crossing to the door and turning.)* It was only last . . .

*(*CARTER *glowers at* GRETA.*)*

The tea, Mr. Carter. *(*GRETA, *abashed but unsatisfied, exits.)*

CARTER: *(Continues his arrangement of the papers, muttering to himself.)* These girls. Sensational—inaccurate—I don't know what the Temple's

SIR WILFRID:

Just roll up your mouth. You talk too much. If I'd known how much you talked I would never have come out of my coma.

(pushing down the lap-robe)

This thing weighs a ton.

MISS PLIMSOLL:

Now, now – we've been flat on our back for two months – we'd better be careful!

She has pulled up the robe and tries to tuck him in again.

He slaps her hand.

4. THE GATE OF LINCOLN'S INN (DAY)

The Porter at the gate recognizes the Rolls, salutes Sir Wilfrid and waves the car through.

5. EXT. LINCOLN'S INN (DAY)

The Rolls proceeds through the Square. It is all very sedate: the old buildings wearing ivy and some barristers wearing robes and wigs.

6. INT. ROLLS-ROYCE (DAY)

MISS PLIMSOLL:

(peering out)

Lovely! It must be perfectly lovely to live and work in the Inns of Court. How lucky you lawyers are!

(a beat)

I almost married a lawyer once. I was in attendance when he had his appendectomy. We became engaged as soon as he could sit up. But then peritonitis set in. He went like that.

(snaps her fingers)

SIR WILFRID:

He certainly was a lucky lawyer!

7. EXT. SIR WILFRID'S BUILDING (DAY)

The Rolls pulls up before a dignified corner building occupied by many barristers. The chauffeur jumps out, opens the door. Miss Plimsoll emerges, holds out a helping hand to Sir Wilfrid.

MISS PLIMSOLL:

Teeny-weeny steps, now Sir Wilfrid. We must remember – we had a teeny-weeny heart attack.

SIR WILFRID:

(ignoring her hand)

Shut up!

(to the chauffeur)

Williams, my cane.

Williams hands him an invalid's cane, with rubber tip. He starts briskly for the stone steps leading to the entrance. In background, Williams is taking luggage from the boot.

8. THE ANTEROOM OF SIR WILFRID'S CHAMBERS (DAY)

coming to. *(He examines a typewritten document, makes an angry sound, picks up a pen and makes a correction.)*

GRETA: *(Enters. Announcing)* Mr. Mayhew.

*(*MR. MAYHEW *and* LEONARD VOLE *enter.* MAYHEW *is a typical middle-aged solicitor, shrewd and rather dry and precise in manner.* LEONARD *is a likeable, friendly young man, about twenty-seven. He is looking faintly worried.* MAYHEW *carries a brief-case.)*

MAYHEW: *(Giving his hat to* GRETA.*)* Sit down, Mr. Vole. *(He crosses and stands above the desk.)* Good afternoon, Carter. *(He puts his briefcase on the desk.)*

*(*GRETA *takes* LEONARD'S *hat and hangs both on the pegs above the door. She then exits, staring at* LEONARD *over her shoulder.)*

CARTER: Good afternoon, Mr. Mayhew. Sir Wilfrid shouldn't be long, sir, although you never can tell with Mr. Justice Banter. I'll go straight over to the Robing Room and tell him that you're here! *(He hesitates.)* with . . . *(He crosses below the desk to* R. *of* LEONARD.*)*

MAYHEW: With Mr. Leonard Vole. Thank you, Carter. I'm afraid our appointment was at rather short notice. But in this case time is—er—rather urgent.

*(*CARTER *crosses to the door.)*

How's the lumbago?

CARTER: *(Turning.)* I only feel it when the wind is in the East. Thank you for remembering, Mr. Mayhew. *(*CARTER *exits hurriedly.)*

*(*MAYHEW *sits* L. *of the desk.* LEONARD *prowls uneasily.)*

MAYHEW: Sit down, Mr. Vole.

LEONARD: Thanks—I'd rather walk about. I—this sort of thing makes you feel a bit jumpy. *(He crosses down* L.*)*

MAYHEW: Yes, yes, very probably . . .

GRETA: *(Enters. She speaks to* MAYHEW, *but stares with fascinated interest at* LEONARD.*)* Would you care for a cup of tea, Mr. Mayhew? I've just made it.

LEONARD: *(Appreciatively.)* Thanks, I don't mind if I . . .

MAYHEW: *(Interrupting; decisively.)* No, thank you.

*(*GRETA *turns to exit.)*

LEONARD: *(To* GRETA.*)* Sorry. *(He smiles at her.)*

*(*GRETA *smiles at* LEONARD *and exits. There is a pause.)*

(He crosses up R. *Abruptly and with a rather likeable air of bewilderment.)* What I mean is, I can't believe it's *me* this is happening to. I keep thinking—perhaps it's all a dream and I'll wake up presently.

MAYHEW: Yes, I suppose one might feel like that.

LEONARD: *(Moving to* R. *of the desk.)* What I mean is—well, it seems so silly.

MAYHEW: *(Sharply.)* Silly, Mr. Vole?

A serious room. The decor is old and oaky. So are the three female employees, Miss McHugh, Miss Johnson and Miss O'Brien. Doors lead to Sir Wilfrid's private office and to the offices of his clerk and juniors. A staircase rises to the floor above, where Sir Wilfrid's living quarters are situated.

Miss Johnson has been leaning out the window. She turns back into the room, excited.

MISS JOHNSON:

Here he comes!

There is instant activity. Miss O'Brien rings a handbell. CARTER, Sir Wilfrid's elderly clerk, rushes out from his own room. A charwoman comes running down the staircase. Miss McHugh has taken a bouquet of flowers from a file cabinet. They line up in a rehearsed formation, facing the door. Sir Wilfrid enters rapidly, followed by Miss Plimsoll and Williams.

SIR WILFRID:

Good afternoon.

He proceeds toward his office, ignoring the reception line-up. In passing he whisks the flowers from Miss McHugh's hand.

SIR WILFRID:

Thank you very much. Everybody back to work.

MISS MCHUGH:

Sir Wilfrid, please — if you don't mind — I would like to read a little poem which we have composed to welcome you —

She has whipped out a long sheet of legal-size paper, typewritten on both sides.

SIR WILFRID:

(interrupting)

Very touching, Miss McHugh. You can recite it after office hours, on your own time. Now back to work.

He starts for his room, sees Miss O'Brien sobbing, her cheeks streaked with tears.

SIR WILFRID:

What's the matter with <u>you</u>?

MISS O'BRIEN:

Nothing — I'm just happy that you're your old self again.

SIR WILFRID:

(a sweeping gesture with his cane)

One more manifestation of such sentimentality — whether in poetry or prose — and I shall instantly go back to the hospital.

MISS PLIMSOLL:

Not very likely. They won't take you back.

(to the staff)

He wasn't really discharged, you know — he was expelled. For conduct unbecoming a cardiac patient.

LEONARD: Well, yes. I mean I've always been a friendly sort of chap—get on with people and all that. I mean, I'm not the sort of fellow that does—well, anything violent. *(He pauses.)* But I suppose it will be—all right, won't it? I mean you don't get convicted for things you haven't done in this country, do you?

MAYHEW: Our English judicial system is, in my opinion, the finest in the world.

LEONARD: *(Is not much comforted. Crossing above the desk to* L.*)* Of course there was that case of—what was his name—Adolf Beck. I read about it only the other day. After he'd been in prison for years, they found out it was another chap called Smith. They gave him a free pardon then. That's a thing that seems odd to me—giving you a "pardon" for something you haven't done.

MAYHEW: It is the necessary legal term.

LEONARD: *(Bringing the chair from* L. *of the fireplace and setting it* C.*)* Well, it doesn't seem right to me.

MAYHEW: The important thing was that Beck was set at liberty.

LEONARD: Yes, it was all right for him. But if it had been murder now—*(He sits astride the chair* C.*)* if it had been murder it would have been too late. He would have been hanged.

MAYHEW: *(Dry but kindly.)* Now, Mr. Vole, there is really no need to take a—er—morbid point of view.

LEONARD: *(Rather pathetically.)* I'm sorry, sir. But you see, in a way, I'm rather getting the wind up.

MAYHEW: Well, try and keep calm. Sir Wilfrid Robarts will be here presently and I want you to tell your story to him exactly as you told it to me.

LEONARD: Yes, sir.

MAYHEW: But meantime perhaps we might fill out a little more of the detail—er—background. You are at present, I understand, out of a job?

LEONARD: *(Embarrassed.)* Yes, but I've got a few pounds put by. It's not much, but if you can see your way . . .

MAYHEW: *(Upset.)* Oh, I'm not thinking of—er—legal fees. It's just the—er—pictures I'm trying to get clear. Your surroundings and—er—circumstances. How long have you been unemployed?

LEONARD: *(Answers everything readily, with an engaging friendliness.)* About a couple of months.

MAYHEW: What were you doing before that?

LEONARD: I was in a motor servicing firm—kind of mechanic, that's what I was.

MAYHEW: How long had you worked there?

LEONARD: Oh, about three months.

MAYHEW: *(Sharply.)* Were you discharged?

LEONARD: No, I quit. Had words with the foreman. Proper old b— *(He breaks off.)* That is, he was a mean sort of chap, always picking on you.

MAYHEW: Hm! And before that?

SIR WILFRID:

Put these in water —

(shoving the flowers at her)

Blabbermouth!

(to his clerk)

Come on in, Carter.

He goes on into his office, followed by Carter.

9. INT. SIR WILFRID'S PRIVATE OFFICE (DAY)

A large, somber room of faded elegance. On one wall is a painting of Sir Wilfrid in wig and gown. Sir Wilfrid enters, puts a monocle suspended from a black ribbon in his eye, and looks about. Behind him, Carter closes the padded door.

SIR WILFRID:

Look at this room! It's really extraordinarily ugly! Very old and very musty, and I never knew I could miss anything so much!

(turning to Carter)

Missed you, too, you musty old buzzard.

CARTER:

Thank you Sir. I'm not a religious man, Sir Wilfrid, but when they carted you off in that ambulance, I went out and lit a candle.

• • •

[The following section is the conclusion of the screenplay.]

49. INT. COURTROOM (DAY)

The Jury is filing back into its seats. There is a hush of expectation.

Leonard Vole, nerves strained to the breaking point, is in the Dock. His eyes anxiously scan the Jurors, as if to try to guess their verdict. Then his gaze wanders toward Sir Wilfrid and Brogan-Moore, just seating themselves. Sir Wilfrid, leaning forward, does not meet his eyes. He looks past the Dock toward —

The glass-panelled door leading into the Courtroom. The Courtroom Officer stands on guard. The door, opening inward, is pushed just slightly open and through the aperature we see Christine tensely awaiting the verdict.

In the Gallery, the spectators are silent, motionless, in taut anticipation of the result. Among them is Miss Plimsoll and beside her, the dark girl.

In the Court, the Clerk rises.

CLERK:

The prisoner will stand up.

Vole and the Warders rise.

CLERK:

Members of the Jury, are you all agreed upon your verdict?

FOREMAN:

(rising)

LEONARD: I worked in a petrol station, but things got a bit awkward and I left.

• • •

[The following passage is from the final part of Act Three]

(LEONARD *rises.*)

Members of the Jury, are you all agreed upon your verdict?

FOREMAN: *(Standing.)* We are.

CLERK: Do you find the prisoner, Leonard Vole, guilty or not guilty?

FOREMAN: Not guilty, my lord.

(A buzz of approbation goes round the court.)

USHER: *(Rising and moving down* C.*)* Silence!

JUDGE: Leonard Vole, you have been found not guilty of the murder of Emily French on October fourteenth. You are hereby discharged and are free to leave the Court. *(He rises.)*

*(*ALL *rise. The* JUDGE *bows to the Court and exits up* R.*, followed by the* ALDERMAN *and the* JUDGE'S CLERK.*)*

USHER: All persons who have anything further to do before my lady the Queen's justices of Oyer and Terminer and general gaol delivery for the jurisdiction of the Central Criminal Court may depart hence and give your attendance here again tomorrow morning at ten-thirty o'clock. God Save The Queen.

(The USHER, *the* JURY *and the* STENOGRAPHER *exit down* R. *The* BARRISTERS, ASSISTANTS *and the* CLERK OF THE COURT *exit up* C. *The* WARDER *and the* POLICEMAN *exit up* L. LEONARD *leaves the dock and crosses to* MAYHEW.*)*

MAYHEW: Congratulations, my boy!

LEONARD: I can't thank you enough.

MAYHEW: *(Tactfully indicating* SIR WILFRID.*)* This is the man you've got to thank.

(LEONARD *crosses to* C. *to meet* SIR WILFRID, *but comes face to face with* MYERS, *who glares at him, and exits up* C. SIR WILFRID *crosses to* R. *of* LEONARD.*)*

LEONARD: *(Turning to* SIR WILFRID.*)* Thank you, sir *(His tone is less spontaneous than it was to* MAYHEW. *He dislikes* SIR WILFRID *it seems.)* You—you've got me out of a very nasty mess.

SIR WILFRID: Nasty mess! Do you hear that, John? Your troubles are over now, my boy.

MAYHEW: *(Moving to* L. *of* LEONARD.*)* But it was a near thing, you know.

LEONARD: *(Unwillingly.)* Yes, I suppose it was.

SIR WILFRID: If we hadn't been able to break that woman down . . .

LEONARD: Did you have to go for her the way you did? It was terrible the way she went to pieces. I can't believe . . .

SIR WILFRID: *(With all the force of his personality.)* Look here, Vole, you're not the first young man I've known who's been so crazy over a woman

We are.

CLERK:

Do you find the prisoner at the bar, Leonard Stephen Vole, guilty or not guilty?

Vole is trying to stand steady. The palms of his hands are moist and he automatically rubs them against his coat.

FOREMAN:

Not guilty, my lord.

Excitement breaks loose. There is a burst of applause and some cheers.

Vole sits down abruptly, exhausted. His eyes close tightly for a moment.

In the Gallery, where all the spectators, including Miss Plimsoll, are cheering and applauding, her brunette neighbor is weeping.

Myers turns toward Sir Wilfrid and makes a gallant gesture of salute in defeat. Sir Wilfrid, leaning forward, does not see Myers, but Brogan-Moore nudges him. He turns toward Myers, with a casual gesture of acknowledgment, then turns back toward the glass-panelled door.

In the slightly open doorway, Christine Vole is standing, her face completely immobile. She withdraws her hand and the door slowly closes, blocking her from view.

During this, the Usher is trying to re-establish order.

USHER:

Silence! Silence!

The courtroom calms down.

JUDGE:

Leonard Stephen Vole, you have been found not guilty of the murder of Emily Jane French on September 14th. You are hereby discharged and are free to leave the Court.

He rises, the Courtroom rises with him. He bows to the Court and the Court bows back. Then the Judge exits, followed by the Alderman and Judge's Clerk.

There is again an upsurge of excitement. Spectators are trying to reach Vole, but are pushed toward the exits by the police and warders. Vole shakes hands with his warders. The Jury is filing out, as do Myers and his associates. The Gallery, too, is emptying.

USHER:

(during this)

All persons who have anything further to do before the Queen's Justices of Oyer and Terminer and general gaol delivery for the jurisdiction of the Central Criminal Court may depart hence and give your attendance here again tomorrow morning at 10:30 o'clock. God Save The Queen.

Vole, jubilant, has come down from the Dock and is shaking hands with Carter, Mayhew, Brogan-Moore, and finally comes to Sir Wilfrid who is silently leaning forward in his chair.

that he's been blinded to what she's really like. That woman did her level best to put a rope round your neck.

MAYHEW: And don't you forget it.

LEONARD: Yes, but why? I can't see why. She's always seemed so devoted. I could have sworn she loved me—and yet all the time she was going with this other fellow. *(He shakes his head.)* It's unbelievable—there's something there I don't understand.

WARDER: *(Enters up* L. *and moves to* L. *of the table.)* Just two or three minutes more, sir. We'll slip you out to a car by the side entrance.

LEONARD: Is there still a crowd?

(ROMAINE, *escorted by the* POLICEMAN, *enters up* L.*)*

POLICEMAN: *(In the doorway.)* Better wait in here, ma'am. The crowd's in a nasty mood. I'd let them disperse before you try to leave.

ROMAINE: *(Moving down* L. *of the table.)* Thank you.

(The POLICEMAN *and the* WARDER *exit up* L. ROMAINE *crosses towards* LEONARD.*)*

SIR WILFRID: *(Intercepting* ROMAINE.*)* No, you don't.

ROMAINE: *(Amused.)* Are you protecting Leonard from me? Really, there's no need.

SIR WILFRID: You've done enough harm.

ROMAINE: Mayn't I even congratulate Leonard on being free?

SIR WILFRID: No thanks to you.

ROMAINE: And rich.

LEONARD: *(Uncertainly.)* Rich?

MAYHEW: Yes, I think, Mr. Vole, that you will certainly inherit a great deal of money.

LEONARD: *(Boyishly.)* Money doesn't seem to mean so much after what I've been through. Romaine, I can't understand . . .

ROMAINE: *(Smoothly.)* Leonard, I can explain.

SIR WILFRID: No!

(SIR WILFRID *and* ROMAINE *look at each other like antagonists.)*

ROMAINE: Tell me, do those words the Judge said mean that I shall—go to prison?

SIR WILFRID: You will quite certainly be charged with perjury and tried for it. You will probably go to prison.

LEONARD: *(Awkwardly.)* I'm sure that—that everything will come right. Romaine, don't worry.

MAYHEW: Will you never see sense, Vole? Now we must consider practicalities—this matter of probate.

(MAYHEW *draws* LEONARD *down* R., *where they murmur together.* SIR WILFRID *and* ROMAIN *remain, measuring each other.)*

SIR WILFRID: It may interest you to know that I took your measure the first time we met. I made up my mind then to beat you at your little game, and by God I've done it. I've got him off—in spite of you.

VOLE:

Thank you, Sir Wilfrid. Thank you for everything. You were wonderful.

SIR WILFRID:

Let's say we were lucky all around.

A Warder carrying a large envelope has come up.

WARDER:

I have your belongings – if you'll be kind enough to come with me, Mr. Vole, and sign the papers, we can release you.

VOLE:

Mister Vole! They didn't call me mister when they checked me in.

MAYHEW:

I'll go along with you. I've brought your coat and your hat.

VOLE:

Let's go quickly, before they change their mind.

They go into the Prisoner's Dock and down the steps leading below. A policeman and usher are gathering up the exhibits.

BROGAN-MOORE:

(looking after Vole, smiling)

Chipper, isn't he? An hour ago he had one foot on the gallows and the other on a banana peel.

(to Wilfrid)

You ought to be very proud, Wilfrid.

(Wilfrid's brow is lined with thought)

Are you?

SIR WILFRID:

Not yet. We've disposed of the gallows, but there is still that banana peel – somewhere – under somebody's foot.

There is the sound of angry commotion outside the Courtroom's Main Entrance. The Policeman and Usher, who have been collecting the exhibits, drop their work and go quickly to investigate. Sir Wilfrid, Brogan-Moore and Carter look OFF.

Through the glass-panelled door we can see a bit of a riot – the crowd in an ugly mood, shouting insults and waving fists. The Policeman and Usher try to break it up, and we see that the object of the crowd is Christine.

The Policeman and Usher help her into the Courtroom. She is dishevelled, a little roughed up, her hat in one hand, and she is rubbing her shin.

POLICEMAN:

Better wait here until we get rid of that crowd, Madam.

CHRISTINE:

Thank you.

ROMAINE: In *spite*—of me.

SIR WILFRID: You don't deny, do you, that you did your best to hang him?

ROMAINE: Would they have believed me if I had said that he was at home with me that night, and did not go out? Would they?

SIR WILFRID: *(Slightly uncomfortable.)* Why not?

ROMAINE: Because they would have said to themselves: this woman loves this man—she would say or do anything for him. They would have had sympathy with me, yes. But they would not have *believed* me.

SIR WILFRID: If you'd been speaking the truth they would.

ROMAINE: I wonder. *(She pauses.)* I did not want their sympathy—I wanted them to dislike me, to mistrust me, to be convinced that I was a liar. And then, when my lies were broken down—when the believed . . . *(In the Cockney accent of the* WOMAN *who visited* SIR WILFRID *at his office.)* So now you know the whole story, mister—like to kiss me?

SIR WILFRID: *(Thunderstruck.)* My God!

ROMAINE: *(As herself.)* Yes, the woman with the letters. I wrote those letters. I brought them to you. I was that woman. It wasn't *you* who won freedom for Leonard. It was *I.* And because of it I shall go to prison. *(Her eyes close.)* But at the end of it Leonard and I will be together again. Happy—loving each other.

SIR WILFRID: *(Moved.)* My dear . . . But couldn't you trust me? We believe, you know, that our British system of justice upholds the truth. We'd have got him off.

ROMAINE: I couldn't risk it. *(Slowly.)* You see, you *thought* he was innocent . . .

SIR WILFRID: *(With quick appreciation.)* And you *knew* he was innocent. I understand.

ROMAINE: But you do not understand at all. *I* knew he was *guilty.*

SIR WILFRID: *(Thunderstruck.)* But aren't you afraid?

ROMAINE: Afraid?

SIR WILFRID: Of linking your life with a murderer's.

ROMAINE: You don't understand—we love each other.

SIR WILFRID: The first time I met you I said you were a very remarkable woman—I see no reason to change my opinion. *(Crosses and exits up* C.*)*

WARDER: *(Off up* L.*)* It's no good going in there, miss. It's all over.

(There is a COMMOTION off up L. *and then a* GIRL *comes running on up* L. *She is a very young strawberry blonde with a crude, obvious appeal. She rushes to* LEONARD *through the* Q.C.'s *bench and meets him down* R.C.*)*

GIRL: Len, darling, you're free. *(She embraces him.)* Isn't it wonderful? They're trying to keep me out. Darling, it's been awful. I've been nearly crazy.

ROMAINE: *(With sudden violent harshness.)* Leonard—who—is—this girl!

GIRL: *(To* ROMAINE, *defiantly.)* I'm Len's girl. I know all about *you.* You're not his wife. Never have been. *(She crosses to* R. *of* ROMAINE.*)* You're years older than him, and you just got hold of him—and you've done

Policeman and Usher go out again to break up the disturbance.

Sir Wilfrid, Brogan-Moore and Carter look at her. Then Carter resumes gathering up the defense papers, also bringing up Sir Wilfrid's thermos from under his seat.

CARTER:

Ready, sir? Miss Plimsoll will be waiting.

SIR WILFRID:

Let me finish the last of the cocoa —

(uncapping the thermos)

While I am still beyond her jurisdiction.

He motions to Carter and to Brogan-Moore to get out. Now he is alone in the Courtroom with Christine.

He sips the brandy, studying her over the rim of the cup. She brushes her suit, straightens her stockings, looks around as if for something she had lost.

CHRISTINE:

I never thought you British could get so emotional — especially in a public place.

SIR WILFRID:

I apologize for my compatriots.

CHRISTINE:

It's all right. I don't mind being callled names or pushed around, or even kicked in the shin — but now I have a ladder in my last pair of nylons.

SIR WILFRID:

In case you're not familiar with our prison regulations — no silk stockings.

CHRISTINE:

Prison? Will I go to prison?

SIR WILFRID:

You heard the learned judge. You will quite certainly be charged with perjury, tried for it, and to prison you shall go.

CHRISTINE:

Well — it won't be for life, will it?

SIR WILFRID:

If I were retained for the prosecution, it would be.

CHRISTINE:

You loath me, don't you? Like the people outside. What a wicked woman I am, and how brilliantly you exposed me, and saved Leonard's life. The great Sir Wilfrid Robarts did it again!

(firmly)

Well, let me tell you something — you didn't do it alone! You had help!

your best to hang him. But that's all over now. *(She turns to* LEONARD.*)* We'll go abroad like you said on one of your cruises—to all those grand places. We'll have a wonderful time.

ROMAINE: Is—this—true? Is she your girl, Leonard?

LEONARD: *(Hesitates, then decides that the situation must be accepted.)* Yes, she is.

(The GIRL *crosses above* LEONARD *to* R. *of him.)*

ROMAINE: After all I've done for you . . . What can *she* do for you that can compare with that?

LEONARD: *(Flinging off all disguise of manner, and showing coarse brutality.)* She's fifteen years younger than you are. *(He laughs.)*

(ROMAINE *flinches as though struck.)*

(He crosses to R. *of* ROMAINE. *Menacingly.)* I've got the money. I've been acquitted, and I can't be tried again, so don't go shooting off your mouth, or you'll just get *yourself* hanged as an accessory after the fact. *(He turns to the* GIRL *and embraces her.)*

ROMAINE: *(Picks up the knife from the table. Throwing her head back in sudden dignity.)* No, that will not happen. I shall not be tried as an accessory after the fact. I shall not be tried for perjury. I shall be tried for murder— *(She stabs* LEONARD *in the back.)* the murder of the only man I ever loved.

(LEONARD *drops. The* GIRL *screams. Mayhew bends over* LEONARD, *feels his pulse and shakes his head.)*

(She looks up at the JUDGE's *seat.)* Guilty, my lord.

CURTAIN

SIR WILFRID:

What are you driving at?

CHRISTINE:

I am not driving at anything any more — Leonard is free, and we did it!

SIR WILFRID:

We?

CHRISTINE:

That's right. Remember when I came to see you, and you said that no jury would believe an alibi given by a loving wife, no matter how much she swore that her husband was innocent? That gave me the idea. —

SIR WILFRID:

What idea?

CHRISTINE:

The idea that I should be a witness, not for my husband, but for the prosecution — that I should swear that Leonard was guilty — and that you should expose me as a vicious liar — because only then, would they believe that Leonard was innocent!

He stares at her, fumbling for his monocle. She crosses slowly toward him.

CHRISTINE:

So now you know the whole story, Sir Wilfrid:

(lapsing into Cockney)

I'll give you somethin' to dream about, mister.

She leans over, and like the Cockney woman in the Euston Station, pulls the hair from one side of her face:

CHRISTINE:

Wanna kiss me, Ducky?

SIR WILFRID:

(shocked)

I suspected something — but not that — never that!

Christine re-adjusts her hair, speaks gently now to Sir Wilfrid, who is plainly stunned.

CHRISTINE:

Thank you for the compliment. It's been a long time since I was an actress, and I never before played such an important role —

SIR WILFRID:

And all those blue letters? —

CHRISTINE:

It took me hours to write them — to invent Max — there never was a Max, there never has been anyone but Leonard — only Leonard.

SIR WILFRID:

(with some difficulty)

My dear — could you not have trusted me? — worked with me truthfully and honorably? — we would have won.

CHRISTINE:

I could not run that risk. You see, you thought he was innocent —

SIR WILFRID:

And you knew he was innocent. I understand.

CHRISTINE:

No, Sir Wilfrid, you do not understand at all —

(after a beat)

I knew he was guilty!

SIR WILFRID:

What?

(stunned disbelief)

No! That can't be true. No!

CHRISTINE:

(a low, urgent voice)

Listen to me — once and for all — Leonard came home a few minutes past ten — he had blood on the sleeves of his jacket — he did tell me he had killed the woman. Only I could save him — he pleaded with me —

SIR WILFRID:

And you saved him — a murderer!

CHRISTINE:

Again, you don't understand — I love him.

She looks off. The camera pans to the Barristers' door, where Vole is standing in his trench coat, hat in hand. He is smiling complacently. He has been standing there for a little while, and has overheard.

VOLE:

(to Wilfrid)

I told you she was an actress — and a good one. —

(moving easily toward them)

I knew she would do something for me — I just didn't know what, or how. —

CHRISTINE:

Leonard . . . darling!

She starts to embrace him. He doesn't respond to her, instead looks over her shoulder at Sir Wilfrid.

VOLE:

Fooled you completely, didn't she?

SIR WILFRID:

It's you, Vole who really fooled me —

(violently)

— after thirty-five years — to be so stupid and so blind —

(tears the wig from his head)

– Wilfrid the Fox!

VOLE:

Easy – we both got out of it alive – let's stay this way –

(seeing Wilfrid gasping with fury)

– here, take a pill.

WILFRID:

There are still courts in England – they're not through with you yet.

VOLE:

Oh, yes they are - you've done too good a job. You got me off, and I can't be tried again – that's the law, and you know it.

CHRISTINE:

You can't touch him <u>now</u> – nobody can.

WILFRID:

(passionately)

You'll pay for this somehow – they'll hang you –

VOLE:

No they won't. As for paying for it – let's double your fee – there'll be plenty of money when the will goes through – I'm not cheap – I want everybody to get something out of it. There's Janet MacKenzie – let's get <u>her</u> that new hearing aid –

(looking at Wilfrid's thermos)

And a new one of those for you – 18 karat gold, if they make one.

(and to Christine)

And when they try you for perjury, there'll be 5,000 pounds to get you off easy.

CHRISTINE:

I don't care, Leonard – just so we'll be together again – you don't know what I went through standing in the witness box, having to face you in the dock and saying I never loved you –

(she kisses him, but he does not respond)

Leonard, what is it?

She looks at him anxiously, then tries to kiss him again. He draws away, looking past her. She turns in the same direction. Miss Plimsoll enters with the brunette girl.

MISS PLIMSOLL:

Sir Wilfrid – the luggage is in the car – we've only 20 minutes to make the boat train –

(then aware of the girl)

Oh – this is a nice young lady I met in the gallery during the trial –

(she stops astounded as the girl runs to Vole)

GIRL:

Len! Oh, Len! They've been trying to keep me away from you – it's had me nearly crazy –

They kiss, and in marked contrast to Christine's embrace, Vole returns it with some enthusiasm.

CHRISTINE:

(shocked)

Leonard – who is this girl?

GIRL:

I'm not this girl - I'm <u>his</u> girl – tell her, Len.

Vole doesn't reply, grins uneasily at Christine with a self-conscious shrug. It gradually dawns on Christine.

CHRISTINE:

Leonard, is this the girl who was with you in the travel bureau – the girl you said you hardly knew – didn't even know her name? –

GIRL:

That's right – <u>that's</u> who I am. And I know all about <u>you</u>. You're not his wife; never have been. You're years older than he is. We've been going together for months and we're going away on one of those cruises – just like they said in court – tell her yourself, Len.

CHRISTINE:

(calmly, controlled with difficulty)

Yes, Len, tell me yourself.

VOLE:

(very simply)

Sorry, Christine. That's how it is.

CHRISTINE:

No!

VOLE:

(to the girl)

Come on Diana, let's go.

Miss Plimsoll and Sir Wilfrid are watching the scene. Sir Wilfrid is spinning his monocle on the ribbon, the light flashing from it.

Vole and the girl have taken a few steps and are near the exhibit table when Christine steps forward quickly, holding Vole by the arm.

CHRISTINE:

(near hysteria)

Leonard, you can't! – not after what I've done. I won't let you –

VOLE:

(pushing her away)

You're being silly now. I saved your life getting you out of Germany – you saved mine getting me out of this mess. So we're even. It's all over.

CHRISTINE:

Don't, Leonard — don't leave me.

VOLE:

Now pull yourself together. They'll have you up here for perjury — don't make it worse or they'll try you as an accessory, and you know what that means.

CHRISTINE:

(holding on to him)

Let them. Let them try me for perjury, or an accessory —

(he shakes himself loose from her. Her eyes fall on the flickering light from Wilfrid's monocle, flashing on the blade of the knife on the exhibit table)

— or better yet, let them try me for murder!

She grabs the knife, lurches after him, and with one wild swoop plunges the knife into him. He looks at her as if almost in surprise, then crumples instantly. Diana shrieks piercingly.

Christine stands quietly erect, the knife no longer in her hand. Miss Plimsoll rushes forward, professional nurse that she is, and kneels beside Vole, her hand on his wrist.

Sir Wilfrid, still twirling his monocle, turns his eyes to the main door, thru which come running three court officers, drawn by the girl's scream. They swoop down on Christine, surrounding Vole's body.

Sir Wilfrid sits quietly, watching. From off we hear an officer crying "Get a doctor!" and the sobbing of Diana. Then Miss Plimsoll comes to Wilfrid. He looks up at her.

MISS PLIMSOLL:

She killed him.

SIR WILFRID:

(shaking his head)

She executed him.

Sir Wilfrid looks off toward Christine. A policeman is by the body and giving unheard instructions. Two policemen start to lead Christine out. Carter, distraught and puzzled, comes in, makes his way to Sir Wilfrid.

CARTER:

(not realizing)

I — I've sent the luggage on ahead, and I've got a car waiting outside.

Then Carter gasps as he sees. But Wilfrid's eyes are still on the big main doors through which the police are just taking out Christine. She stops in the open doors, looks back at Wilfrid. Miss Plimsoll looks at Wilfrid, then at the doors, then back to him.

SIR WILFRID:

(to himself)

. . . a remarkable woman!

CARTER:

You can just barely make the boat train, Sir Wilfrid.

MISS PLIMSOLL:

(softly)

Better bring the luggage back, and you can dismiss the car —

(to Sir Wilfrid)

— we're not going yet, are we?

There is a long exchange of looks between the two, then Miss Plimsoll reaches down for his wig, hands it to him.

SIR WILFRID:

(a declaration of love)

Thank you, Miss Plimsoll.

He gets up with some difficulty and straightens up.

SIR WILFRID:

(to Carter)

Get Brogan-Moore to my chambers, and have Mayhew there, too. We are appearing for the defense in the trial of Christine Vole.

He moves away from his seat and walks past the Bench to the barrister's exit, an erect and dignified figure.

Miss Plimsoll looks after him with great pride. She suddenly sees the thermos bottle.

MISS PLIMSOLL:

(calling after him)

Sir Wilfrid! — you forgot your brandy!

He stops, smiling. She grabs the thermos and takes it to him quickly. He puts his arm across her shoulder as they walk out of the courtroom.

THE END

▲ ▲ ▲

Discussion and Writing Suggestions

FICTION

1. What is the significance of the title of this story? Why do you think Christie chose this title?
2. In terms of the overall events of this story, Mr. Mayherne is a relatively minor character. Yet he is "onstage" almost all the time, with every major development seen from his point of view. In the first few paragraphs Christie takes great pains to establish his character. Why do you think the

author placed so much importance on the lawyer? What is his *narrative* function, and why is it important, dramatically, that he be presented as the kind of man he is?

3. Critique Christie's story by applying some of the questions posed by Corrigan in "Fiction and Film." In particular apply some of the questions under his sections on "Theme" (paragraph 2), "Narrative" (paragraph 7), "Character" (paragraph 13) and "Point of View" (paragraph 16). Based on your responses to these questions, to what extent do you consider "Witness for the Prosecution" a skillful work of narrative? In what areas do you think it falls short? In particular, why do you think it is not the kind of fiction generally studied in literature courses?
4. Imagine that Christie had told this story in chronological order. Thus, in such a version, the early scenes would have showed Vole meeting Emily French after picking up her dropped packages on the street, later finding out how wealthy she was, and then conspiring with Romaine Heilger to get the old woman's fortune in just the manner that they did. How would the effect of such a chronologically based version of "Witness for the Prosecution" have been different from Christie's actual story?
5. Suppose that a filmmaker, determined to be absolutely faithful to Christie's story, decided to film it exactly as written, creating no new dialogue and no new scenes. Thus, most of the first half of the film would have consisted of the conversation between Vole and Mayherne; the next section, the dialogue between Mayherne and Romaine Heilger; then, after some quick shots of the police court proceedings, the dialogue between Mayherne and "Mrs. Mogson," followed by more quick shots of the trial, including the verdict; and a final scene between Mayherne and Romaine Heilger. To what extent would such a film have been effective: dramatically interesting and involving? Explain your response.
6. Sketch out a treatment for a film version of Christie's story. Which of the present scenes would you retain, what scenes would you cut or further develop, what new scenes would you add? To what extent would you modify the existing plot? How would you change the characters (if at all)? What new characters would you create, which existing characters would you change or further develop? (If you like, cast actors and actresses for the film and explain your choices.)

FILM

1. Examining the opening sequences of short story, play, and film, what chief differences do you find? Why do you suppose that Christie began her story with the interview between Mayherne and Vole, and her play with Sir Wilfrid's clerk, Carter, answering the telephone before having a dialogue with the typist, Greta? Why did Wilder and Kurnitz begin their screenplay with a brief sequence in the courtroom, followed by Sir Wil-

frid returning from the hospital? To what extent is each action sequence suited to the medium in which it appears?

2. Consider the most obvious difference between the story and the film (and the play): the twist about Leonard Vole's girlfriend and the final piece of dramatic action: a twist that has the effect of changing Leonard's entire motivation for his actions. The ending is clearly effective theater and effective filmmaking (judging by the great popularity of both adaptations). Do you think this ending would have improved the original story? Why or why not?
3. Make a list of some of the other main differences between story and film. Consider plot, characters, setting. For example, while Mr. Mayherne in the story has been transformed to Mr. Mayhew in the film, his dramatic role has been largely usurped by Sir Wilfrid Robarts, a new character. What do you think is the reason for this change? In the story, Mr. Mayherne first meets Romaine when he goes to her "small shabby house"; in the film, her counterpart Christine visits Sir Wilfrid's office. In the story Mayherne goes to see "Mrs. Mogson" in an "evil-smelling slum"; in the film he meets her at Euston railway station (in the play she comes to his office). In the story, the trial is largely summarized; but it takes up more than half of the film. Try to account for these and other differences in terms of the different natures and the different requirements of the short story and of the film.
4. Assess the role of humor in the film: for example, Sir Wilfrid's cat-and-mouse games over cigars and drinks with Miss Plimsoll, Leonard Vole's eggbeater, Janet Mackenzie's testimony. Would such comic elements have been appropriate for the story? Why or why not?
5. Consider the following paragraph from the short story, during Mayherne's first interview with Leonard Vole, as he is trying to determine the veracity of his client:

> Mr. Mayherne looked at him for a moment or two in silence. Though he had no intention of saying so, his belief in Leonard Vole's innocence was at that moment strengthened. He knew something of the mentality of elderly ladies. He saw Miss French, infatuated with the good-looking young man, hunting about for pretexts that would bring him to the house. What more likely than that she should plead ignorance of business, and beg him to help her with her money affairs? . . .

How does Wilder attempt to find a cinematic equivalent for this piece of interior monologue? Locate other passages in the story that focus on thoughts (rather than actions or words) and examine how such moments are translated in the film. Assess the effectiveness of these cinematic transformations.

Suppose you were a young screenwriter assigned to modernize Christie's story so that it were now set in the present day in some large American city. (If you prefer, suppose yourself a television writer for some existing dramatic series, such as "Law and Order.") What changes would you make to give the story a more contemporary feel? To make it credible and cinematically effective for today's audiences? By the same token, what elements in the existing film might not work with today's audiences? Why?

APPENDIX

▼

A Glossary of Film Terms

DAVID BORDWELL
KRISTIN THOMPSON

The following glossary defines some of the key terms you will find useful in discussing film. Written by David Bordwell and Kristen Thompson, both of the University of Wisconsin, it is excerpted from their film text Film Art: An Introduction (4th ed.).

*We have rearranged the terms into the following categories: **CINEMATOGRAPHY**, which includes the **photographic** aspects of the shot (film stock, exposure, color of black and white, filters, focal length, special effects, etc.), the **framing** of the shot (angle, height, distance of framing, various types of camera movement, zooms), and the **duration** of the shot; **MISE-EN-SCENE** (literally, staging an action), which includes **setting, lighting, costume,** and the **behavior of the characters/actors; EDITING** (the joining of shot to shot, with various types of relationships possible: **graphic, rhythmic, spatial, temporal); SOUND;** and **NARRATIVE** aspects.*

CINEMATOGRAPHY

cinematography A general term for all the manipulations of the film strip by the camera in the shooting phase and by the laboratory in the developing phase.

angle of framing The position of the frame in relation to the subject it shows: above it, looking down (a high angle); horizontal, on the same level (a straight-on angle); looking up (a low angle). Also called "camera angle."

crane shot A shot with a change in framing accomplished by having the camera above the ground and moving through the air in any direction.

dolly A camera support with wheels, used in making *tracking shots.*

establishing shot A shot, usually involving a distant framing, that shows the spatial relations among the important figures, objects, and setting in a scene.

extreme close-up A framing in which the scale of the object shown is very large; most commonly, a small object or a part of the body.

extreme long shot A framing in which the scale of the object shown is very small; a building, landscape, or crowd of people would fill the screen.

following shot A shot with framing that shifts to keep a moving figure onscreen.

framing The use of the edges of the film frame to select and to compose what will be visible onscreen.

front projection Composite process whereby footage meant to appear as the background of a shot is projected from the front onto a screen: figures in the foreground are filmed in front of the screen as well. This is the opposite of *rear projection.*

long shot A framing in which the scale of the object shown is small; a standing human figure would appear nearly the height of the screen.

long take A shot that continues for an unusually lengthy time before the transition to the next shot.

matte shot A type of process shot in which different areas of the image (usually actors and setting) are photographed separately and combined in laboratory work.

mixing Combining two or more sound tracks by recording them onto a single one.

mobile frame The effect on the screen of the moving camera, a *zoom lens,* or certain *special effects;* the framing shifts in relation to the scene being photographed. See also *crane shot, pan, tilt, tracking shot.*

normal lens A lens that shows objects without severely exaggerating or reducing the depth of the scene's planes. In 35-mm filming, a normal lens is 35 to 50 mm. See also *telephoto lens, wide-angle lens.*

pan A camera movement with the camera body turning to the right or left on a stationary tripod. On the screen, it produces a mobile framing which scans the space horizontally.

point-of-view shot (POV shot) A shot taken with the camera placed approximately where the character's eyes would be, showing what the character would see; usually cut in before or after a shot of the character looking.

process shot Any shot involving rephotography to combine two or more images into one, or to create a special effect; also called "composite shot." See also *matte shot, rear projection, special effects.*

racking focus Shifting the area of sharp focus from one plane to another during a shot; the effect on the screen is called "rack focus."

rear projection A technique for combining a foreground action with a background action filmed earlier. The foreground is filmed in a studio, against a screen; the background imagery is projected from behind the screen. The opposite of *front projection.*

reestablishing shot A return to a view of an entire space after a series of closer shots following the *establishing shot.*

reframing Short panning or tilting movements to adjust for the figures' movements, keeping them onscreen or centered.

shot 1. In shooting, one uninterrupted run of the camera to expose a series of frames. Also called a *take.* 2. In the finished film, one uninterrupted image with a single static or mobile framing.

shot/reverse shot Two or more shots edited together that alternate characters, typically in a conversation situation. In *continuity editing,* characters in one framing usually look left, in the other framing, right. Over-the-shoulder framings are common in shot/reverse-shot editing.

special effects A general term for various photographic manipulations that create fictitious spatial relations in the shot, such as *superimposition, matte shots,* and *rear projection.*

superimposition The exposure of more than one image on the same film strip.

take In filmmaking, the shot produced by one uninterrupted run of the camera. One shot in the final film may be chosen from among several takes of the same action.

telephoto lens A lens of long focal length that affects a scene's perspective by enlarging distant planes and making them seem close to the foreground planes. In 35-mm filming, a lens of 75-mm length or more. See also *normal lens, wide-angle lens.*

tilt A camera movement with the camera body swiveling upward or downward on a stationary support. It produces a mobile framing that scans the space vertically.

tracking shot A mobile framing that travels through space forward, backward, or laterally. See also *crane shot, pan,* and *tilt.*

wide-angle lens A lens of short focal length that affects a scene's perspective by distorting straight lines near the edges of the frame and by exaggerating the distance between foreground and background planes. In 35-mm filming, a wide-angle lens is 30 mm or less. See also *normal lens, telephoto lens.*

zoom lens A lens with a focal length that can be changed during a shot. A shift toward the *telephoto* range enlarges the image and flattens its planes together, giving an impression of moving into the scene's space, while a shift toward the *wide-angle* range does the opposite.

MISE-EN-SCENE

mise-en-scene All the elements placed in front of the camera to be photographed: the settings and props, lighting, costumes and make-up, and figure behavior.

high-key lighting Illumination that creates comparatively little contrast between the light and dark areas of the shot. Shadows are fairly transparent and brightened by fill light.

key light In the three-point lighting system, the brightest illumination coming into the scene.

low-key lighting Illumination that creates strong contrast between light and dark areas of the shot, with deep shadows and little fill light.

three-point lighting A common arrangement using three directions of light on a scene: from behind the subjects (backlighting), from one bright source (key light), and from a less bright source balancing the key light (fill light).

screen direction The right-left relationships in a scene, set up in an establishing shot and determined by the position of characters and objects in the frame; by the directions of movement; and by the characters' eyelines. *Continuity editing* will attempt to keep screen direction consistent between shots.

EDITING

editing 1. In filmmaking, the task of selecting and joining camera takes. 2. In the finished film, the set of techniques that governs the relations among shots.

axis of action In the *continuity editing* system, the imaginary line that passes from side to side through the main actors, defining the spatial relations of all the elements of the scene as being to the right or left. The camera is not supposed to cross the axis at a cut and thus reverse those spatial relations. Also called the "180° line."

continuity editing A system of cutting to maintain continuous and clear narrative action. Continuity editing relies upon matching screen direction, position, and temporal relations from shot to shot.

crosscutting Editing that alternates shots of two or more lines of action occurring in different places, usually simultaneously.

cut 1. In filmmaking, the joining of two strips of film together with a splice. 2. In the finished film, an instantaneous change from one framing to another. See also *jump cut.*

cut-in An instantaneous shift from a distant framing to a closer view of some portion of the same space.

dialogue overlap In editing a scene, arranging the cut so that a bit of dialogue or noise coming from shot A is heard under a shot of character B or of another element in the scene.

dissolve A transition between two shots during which the first image gradually disappears while the second image gradually appears; for a moment the two images blend in *superimposition.*

eyeline match A cut obeying the *axis of action* principle, in which the first shot shows a person looking off in one direction and the second shows a nearby space containing what he or she sees. If the person looks left, the following shot should imply that the looker is offscreen right.

fade 1. *Fade-in:* A dark screen that gradually brightens as a shot appears. 2. *Fade-out:* A shot gradually darkens as the screen goes black. Occasionally fade-outs brighten to pure white or to a color.

graphic match Two successive shots joined so as to create a strong similarity of compositional elements (e.g., color, shape).

jump cut An elliptical cut that appears to be an interruption of a single shot. Either the figures seem to change instantly against a constant background, or the background changes instantly while the figures remain constant.

match on action A continuity cut that places two different framings of the same action together at the same moment in the gesture, making it seem to continue uninterrupted.

montage 1. A synonym for *editing.* 2. An approach to editing developed by the Soviet filmmakers of the 1920s; it emphasizes dynamic, often discontinuous, relationships between shots and the juxtaposition of images to create ideas not present in either one by itself.

montage sequence A segment of a film that summarizes a topic or compresses a passage of time into brief symbolic or typical images. Frequently dissolves, fades, superimpositions, and wipes are used to link the images in a montage sequence.

SOUND

diegetic sound Any voice, musical passage, or sound effect presented as originating from a source within the film's world. See also *nondiegetic sound.*

nondiegetic sound Sound, such as mood music or a narrator's commentary, represented as coming from a source outside the space of the narrative.

offscreen sound Simultaneous sound from a source assumed to be in the space of the scene but in an area outside what is visible onscreen.

sound bridge 1. At the beginning of one scene, the sound from the previous scene carries over briefly before the sound from the new scene begins. 2. At the end of one scene, the sound from the next scene is heard, leading into that scene.

synchronous sound Sound that is matched temporally with the movements occurring in the images, as when dialogue corresponds to lip movements.

NARRATIVE

ellipsis In a narrative film, the shortening of *plot* duration achieved by omitting intervals of *story* duration.

motif An element in a film that is repeated in a significant way.

narrative form A type of filmic organization in which the parts relate to each other through a series of causally related events taking place in a specific time and space.

plot In a narrative film, all the events that are directly presented to us, including their causal relations, chronological order, duration, frequency, and spatial locations. Opposed to *story,* which is the viewer's imaginary construction of all the events in the narrative.

scene A segment in a narrative film that takes place in one time and space or that uses crosscutting to show two or more simultaneous actions.

sequence Term commonly used for a moderately large segment of a film, involving one complete stretch of action. In a narrative film, often equivalent to a *scene.*

story In a narrative film, all the events that we see and hear, plus all those that we infer or assume to have occurred, arranged in their presumed causal relations, chronological order, duration, frequency, and spatial locations. Opposed to *plot,* which is the film's actual presentation of certain events in the narrative.

▲ ▲ ▲

▼

SYNTHESIS ACTIVITIES

1. This assignment will direct you in writing an essay based on your reading of a story and your viewing of a film adaptation. First, an assumption: We believe (and this assignment reflects the belief) that the change in medium from fiction to film brings about a change in artistic product. As films, "The Birds" and "Witness for the Prosecution" are distinct works of art that bear a relationship to their fictional counterparts but are not identical with them. As such, film adaptations must be judged *as films*: The measure of their success ought not to be the literalness with which a director translates scenes of the story onto the screen.[1] Some other measure that *you*—in consultation with this chapter's authors—will define must be applied to adaptations. Assume that film adaptations will differ from their fictional namesakes. It is precisely these differences, along with the artistic decisions they represent, that provide the focus of this assignment.

PREPARING TO WRITE

Select a work of fiction and a film adaptation with which to work. You'll find "The Birds" and "Witness for the Prosecution" in this chapter, along with (under "Research Activities") a list of other short stories, books, and plays that have been adapted into films. Read the story and view the film adaptation. Prepare for your essay by keeping detailed notes as you do each of the following:

(A) Read the story at least twice and attempt to understand its elements *as* a story. Be conscious of its plot structure, themes, tone, characters, and point of view.

(B) Reflect on the story as a candidate for adaptation. If you were adapting the story to film, what changes would you make—and why? Consider what story elements would be problematic for film, and what elements (given the different qualities of fiction

[1]Synthesis Activity 3 gives you a chance to argue against this assumption.

and film) might be more effective if changed. (Consult the introduction to this chapter, Boggs (pages 674–83) and the stories in this chapter for help in thinking about these changes. Some possibilities: point of view, characters, plot structure, setting, and time period.)

(C) View the film adaptation several times. Pay close attention to the film's essential elements: plot, structure, themes, tone, characters, and point of view. Study the film *as* a film. What visual and auditory strategies has the director employed to represent important elements of the film, such as character and setting? (As needed, draw on "A Glossary of Film Terms" to describe these strategies.)

(D) Think comparatively:

- What overall differences and differences in specific scenes do you observe between story and film?
- Speculate on the decisions (by writers, producers, and directors) that may have prompted these differences.

(E) Reflect on the overall success of the film as a unique work of art.

- How do the differences contribute to—or detract from—the film?
- To what extent does the film communicate the essential tone and mood of the original? Recall (from the introduction to this chapter) George Linden, who claims that "if the tone of a work is lost, the work is lost."
- Do you feel that the director's decisions to deviate from the story violate any important story elements—or, by contrast, heighten and improve upon any elements?
- How compatible is the director's "reading" of the story with your reading? What were your expectations before viewing the film? Were your expectations inflated (as Boggs and Eidsvik suggest they were likely to be)? Did the film meet your expectations? Why or why not?

YOUR ASSIGNMENT

Study your notes made in response to items A–E, above. In a well-developed essay in which you refer specifically to both story and film, argue that the film adaptation succeeds, succeeds partially, or fails. A successful essay will convince others that your judgment is well-reasoned and worth serious consideration. Either explicitly or implicitly, you'll need to establish standards by which you're evaluating the film. (Recall that literalness in translating scenes of the story to the screen is *not* an acceptable standard for this assignment.)

Write for your classmates. Because some may have worked with other materials, you should provide background—a story line—detailed enough for readers to follow your discussion.

You'll need to demonstrate that you know the story and film quite well. Given that you'll be discussing both, *comparison and contrast* will be an important strategy for development. Comparisons should do more than list the ways in which the film departs from the story. You and your readers should expect such differences. The challenge will be to make your comparisons support some larger point—your sense of the film's overall success, which you'll present in the context of a single, compelling idea: your thesis.

2. Write an essay in which you reflect on your experiences as a reader of stories and as a viewer of films. As the person to whom these works of art are directed, what are the various ways in which you respond to each art form? What are the demands each places on you? What are the differences in being an expert reader of a story and an expert "reader" of a film? This assignment calls on you to do something quite difficult: first, to watch yourself reading and viewing, and to report on what you observe; second, to present your reflections in an essay and then to draw some larger meaning, some conclusion, from them. As you prepare to write, your thinking will be inductive: You will gather data (your reflections); then you will examine the data for patterns, so that you can present a coherent overview to the readers of your essay. To keep your essay grounded in particulars, be sure to refer often to the stories in this chapter, and to the adaptations.
3. Write an argumentative essay in which you disagree with a key assumption of this chapter: that faithfulness to a story should *not* be the criterion we should use when judging the success of an adaptation. This premise is laid out explicitly in Synthesis Activity 1, paragraph 1. The thesis of your argument would be that faithfulness to the original is, in fact, an excellent criterion by which to judge an adaptation. The strategies by which you argue and the particular sources you use to illustrate key points will be yours to decide. For the purposes of this essay, focus on a single story and its adaptation.
4. Choose one of the stories in this chapter (though you may find it useful, for the sake of comparison/contrast, to refer to other film adaptations). Read it three times. Choose one of the adaptations. View it three times. In an explanatory essay, describe what happens in the course of your successive readings and viewings. To generate the raw materials from which you will write your essay, be sure to make extensive notes after each reading or viewing. Before you write a first draft, reread your notes. What patterns emerge?
5. In this explanatory essay, you will write an extensive analysis of a single scene from a story and its subsequent treatment in a film adaptation. Locate one scene of "The Birds" or "Witness for the Prosecution" (the stories) that particularly interests you. Turn, now, to the

adaptation. Questions to consider: How did the screenwriters and the director treat the scene? What decisions did they make concerning the scene? How do these decisions reflect an interpretation of the story? How do these decisions reflect an awareness of the limits and the strengths of film? Your essay should open with a summary of the scene in the context of the larger movie. (For help on summarizing a narrative, see Chapter 1.)

The goal of this essay is to follow closely, even intimately, the moves a director makes in adapting a single scene from a story. Depending on how technical you want to be, you can draw on "A Glossary of Film Terms" at the end of this chapter. These terms will give you a "filmic" vocabulary with which to discuss the director's work. Your essay will largely be explanatory—that is, unless you wish to critique the director's decisions and argue that a different filmic presentation of the scene would have been better.

▼

RESEARCH ACTIVITIES

The following is a selected list of films based on literary texts. Film title and author (and title of the literary source, if different from film title) are followed by year of release and the name of the director. Most of this list is an abbreviated version of listings that appeared in *The Reel List: A Categorical Companion to Over 2,000 Memorable Films* by Lynne Arany, Tom Dyja, and Gary Goldsmith (Delta, 1995).

English Lit: 18th and 19th Centuries

Adventures of Robinson Crusoe, **Daniel Defoe** (1954, Luis Buñuel)
Tom Jones, **Henry Fielding** (1963, Tony Richardson)
Pride and Prejudice, **Jane Austen** (1940, Robert Z. Leonard)
Becky Sharp, **William Makepeace Thackeray** ***(Vanity Fair)*** (1935, Rouben Mamoulian)
Jane Eyre, **Charlotte Brönte** (1944, Robert Stevenson; 1996, Franco Zeffirelli)
Wuthering Heights, **Emily Brönte** (1939, William Wyler; 1953, Luis Bruñuel; 1970, Robert Fuerst)
Tom Brown's School Days, **Thomas Hughes** (1951, Gordon Parry)
Great Expectations, **Charles Dickens** (1946, David Lean)
Oliver Twist, **Charles Dickens** (1948, David Lean)
The Picture of Dorian Gray, **Oscar Wilde** (1946, Albert Lewin)

English Lit: 20th Century

A Clockwork Orange, **Anthony Burgess** (1971, Stanley Kubrick)
The Horse's Mouth, **Joyce Cary** (1958, Ronald Neame)
Howard's End, **E.M. Forster** (1992, James Ivory)
Lord of the Flies, **William Golding** (1963, Peter Brook)

Sons and Lovers, **D.H. Lawrence** (1960, Jack Cardiff)
The Rocking Horse Winner, **D.H. Lawrence** (1949, Anthony Pelissier)
1984, **George Orwell** (1984, Michael Radford)
Saturday Night and Sunday Morning, **Alan Sillitoe** (1960, Karel Reisz)
The Loved One, **Evelyn Waugh** (1965, Tony Richardson)
Orlando, **Virginia Woolf** (1993, Sally Potter)

American Lit: 19th Century

The Red Badge of Courage, **Stephen Crane** (1951, John Huston)
Carrie, **Theodore Dreiser** ***(Sister Carrie)*** (1952, William Wyler)
Scarlett Letter, **Nathaniel Hawthorne** (1973, Wim Wenders)
Kwaidan, **Lafcadio Hearn** (1964, Masaki Kobayashi)
The Innocents, **Henry James** ***(The Turn of the Screw)*** (1961, Jack Clayton)
The Heiress, **Henry James** ***(Washington Square)*** (1949, William Wyler)
Moby Dick, **Herman Melville** (1956, John Huston)
House of Usher, **Edgar Allen Poe** ***(The Fall of the House of Usher)*** (1960, Roger Corman)
Huckleberry Finn, **Mark Twain** (1939, Richard Thorpe)
The Age of Innocence, **Edith Wharton** (1993, Martin Scorsese)

American Lit: 20th Century

Chilly Scenes of Winter (original film title, ***Head Over Heels),*** **Anne Beattie** (1982, Joan Micklin Silver)
Naked Lunch, **William Burroughs** (1991, David Cronenberg)
Breakfast at Tiffany's, **Truman Capote** (1961, Blake Edwards)
Short Cuts, **Raymond Carver** ***(short stories)*** (1993, Robert Altman)
Mr. and Mrs. Bridge, **Evan S. Connell, Jr.** ***(Mr. Bridge)*** (1990, James Ivory)
The Great Gatsby, **F. Scott Fitzgerald** (1974, Jack Clayton)
The Last Tycoon, **F. Scott Fitzgerald** (1976, Elia Kazan)
Fried Green Tomatoes, **Fanny Flagg** (1991, John Avnet)
Catch-22, **Joseph Heller** (1970, Mike Nichols)
The Sun Also Rises, **Ernest Hemingway** (1957, Henry King)
A Farewell to Arms, **Ernest Hemingway** (1932, Frank Borsage)
For Whom the Bell Tolls, **Ernest Hemingway** (1943, Sam Wood)
The Snows of Kilamanjaro, **Ernest Hemingway** (1952, Henry King)
To Have and Have Not, **Ernest Hemingway** (1944, Howard Hawks)
The Killers, **Ernest Hemingway** (1946, Robert Siodmak)
The Old Man and the Sea, **Ernest Hemingway** (1958, John Sturges)
To Kill a Mockingbird, **Harper Lee** (1962, Robert Mulligan)
A River Runs Through It, **Noman Maclean** (1992, Robert Redford)
The Group, **Mary McCarthy** (1966, Sidney Lumet)
The Heart Is a Lonely Hunter, **Carson McCullers** (1968, Robert Ellis Miller)

The Naked and the Dead, **Norman Mailer** (1958, Raoul Walsh)
Lolita, **Vladimir Nabokov** (1962, Stanley Kubrick)
Wise Blood, **Flannery O'Connor** (1979, John Huston)
The Fountainhead, **Ayn Rand** (1949, King Vidor)
The Accidental Tourist, **Anne Tyler** (1988, Lawrence Kasdan)
The Witches of Eastwick, **John Updike** (1987, George Miller)
Slaughterhouse-Five, **Kurt Vonnegut** (1972, George Roy Hill)
The Color Purple, **Alice Walker** (1985, Steven Spielberg)
All the King's Men, **Robert Penn Warren** (1949, Robert Rossen)
The Day of the Locust, **Nathaniel West** (1975, John Schlesinger)

Russian Lit: 19th and 20th Centuries

The Three Sisters, **Anton Chekhov** (1970, Laurence Olivier)
The Idiot, **Fyodor Dostoyevsky** (1951, Akira Kurosawa)
The Brothers Karamazov, Fyodor Dostoyevsky (1958, Richard Brooks)
Doctor Zhivago, **Boris Pasternak** (1965, David Lean)
The Queen of Spades, **Alexander Pushkin** (1948, Thorold Dickinson)
One Day in the Life of Ivan Denisovich, **Alexander Solzhenitsyn** (1971, Casper Wrede)
Anna Karenina, **Leo Tolstoy** (1935, Clarence Brown)
War and Peace, **Leo Tolstoy** (1956, King Vidor)

The Bard Adapted

Chimes at Midnight (also known as ***Falstaff) (Henry IV, Parts 1 and 2, Henry V)*** (1966, Orson Welles)
Hamlet (1948, Laurence Olivier; 1990, Franco Zeffirelli)
Henry V (1944, Laurence Olivier; 1989, Kenneth Branagh)
Julius Caesar (1953, Joseph L. Mankiewicz)
Macbeth (1948, Orson Welles)
A Midsummer Night's Dream (1935, Max Reinhardt)
Much Ado About Nothing (1993, Kenneth Branagh)
Othello (1951, Orson Welles)
Romeo and Juliet (1936, George Cukor; 1954, Renato Castellani; 1968, Franco Zeffirelli)

The Bard Loosley Adapted

My Own Private Idaho (Henry IV, Parts 1 and 2) (1991, Gus Van Sant)
Ran (King Lear) (1985, Akira Kurosawa)
Joe Macbeth (1955, Ken Hughes)
Throne of Blood (Macbeth) (1957, Akira Kurosawa)
Men of Respect (Macbeth) (1991, William Reilly)
Smiles of a Summer Night (A Midsummer Night's Dream) (1955, Ingmar Bergman)
Jubal (Othello) (1956, Delmer Daves)

West Side Story (Romeo and Juliet) (1961, Robert Wise)
Kiss Me, Kate (Taming of the Shrew) (1953, George Sidney)
Forbidden Planet (The Tempest) (1956, Fred Wilcox)
Tempest (1982, Paul Mazursky)

1. Select a film (or several related films) from the list above, read the work on which it was based, and assess the film as an adaptation. Draw upon the discussions in the chapter introduction and in Eidsvik and Boggs as a basis for formulating your analysis and evaluation; draw also upon the "A Glossary of Film Terms" to make your discussion as precise as possible. You may wish to draw upon reviews and other secondary sources about both the film and the literary work on which it was based. The single best source for critical articles on film (if available in your library) is the CD-ROM version of *Film Index International.* This reference tool will direct you to numerous sources about thousands of films since the beginning of the sound era (late 1920s). Other valuable reference sources on film include the *International Index to Film Periodicals, Film Literature Index, Film Review Annual,* the collected *New York Times Film Reviews,* and *Variety Film Reviews.* (You may also consult the *Readers' Guide to Periodical Literature* under "Motion Pictures" (or, more recently, "Movies"). Some of the major film reviewers, such as Pauline Kael, Stanley Kauffmann, and John Simon, have published book-length collections of their reviews. Your college library may have other online reference tools to access sources on film, and most of the commercial online services, such as Prodigy and AmericaOnline, provide access to film reviews—though these tend to be relatively recent. Commercial CD-ROMs about film, such as Microsoft's *Cinemania* and Infobusiness's *Mega Movie Guide,* are also available (the latter, however, is less useful as a source of reviews than as a powerful film database).
2. Select a literary work that has inspired more than one adaptation and write an evaluative analysis comparing and contrasting the multiple adaptations. For example, numerous films have been made of such nineteenth century horror tales as Mary Shelley's *Frankenstein* and Bram Stoker's *Dracula,* and three have been made of Robert Louis Stevenson's *Dr. Jekyll and Mr. Hyde.* Such Dickens novels as *Great Expectations* and *Oliver Twist* have also inspired multiple adaptations. More contemporary novels include *Lord of the Flies* and *1984.* Ernest Hemingway's *The Killers* has been adapted twice, and there have been at least five *Huckleberry Finn*s (the latest a 1993 Walt Disney version called *The Adventures of Huck Finn*). If you want to examine drama, there are numerous *Hamlets* and *Macbeths* and two brilliant *Henry V*s, one by Laurence Olivier, the other by Kenneth Branagh. For more contemporary drama, consider Arthur Miller's *Death of a Salesman* (the Fredric March and Dustin Hoffman versions), or John Osborne's *Look Back in Anger* (the Richard Burton

and Kenneth Branagh versions). Your college media services division may have copies of these on videotape. For secondary sources, use some of the reference tools mentioned in Research Activity 1.

3. Select either the film version of *The Birds* or *Witness for the Prosecution* and write a summary and an assessment of the critical response to the film. Use some of the reference tools mentioned in Research Activity 1.
4. Select a film that has been adapted from a work of fiction and research the problems involved in transferring this particular work from the page to the screen. One of the best-known accounts of such an adaptation is Lillian Ross's *Picture* (1952), which gives a detailed account of the making of John Huston's adaptation of Stephen Crane's Civil War novel *The Red Badge of Courage.* Use both print sources and electronic databases to discover other accounts of the process of making a film based on a literary work. There are innumerable sources on the making of *Gone With the Wind* and *The Wizard of Oz*—though much of this material is Hollywood press agentry or gossip journalism. [In some cases, "The Making of . . ." videos may be useful; see Eleanor Coppola's documentary footage in *Hearts of Darkness: A Filmmaker's Apocalypse* (1991), on the making of her husband's *Apocalypse Now.*] Don't neglect contemporary accounts in newspapers and magazines, particularly the trade papers (if you have access to them), such as *Variety* and *The Hollywood Reporter.*
5. Locate the script for a film based on a short story or a novel. Read the story or novel, and then read the script. Finally, watch the film adaptation. Write a three-way comparison-contrast in which you examine differences and similarities in *plot, characters,* and *tone* among the three. To save on your wear and tear, begin this assignment by consulting the list of literary works for which films have been made (the list begins these Research Activities). With list in hand, check the online catalog at your library for available film scripts. (You might call nearby college and university libraries, some of which may hold special film collections.) Locate the novel, play, or story; locate the film on videotape. When you have all three elements available, begin your work.
6. Research the role of the screenwriter in the production of films (which, for this assignment, need not be adaptations). When in the process of a film's creation does the screenwriter become involved? To what extent does the screenwriter stay involved through film production? What differences do screenwriters find between writing original scripts and writing adaptations? In the hierarchy of people involved in the creation of a film—producer, director, cinematographer, actors—what is the screenwriter's relative value? There are many ways of calculating value, the most pertinent one for Hollywood being money. What are screenwriters paid, relative to other talent?

7. Investigate and explain the process by which a work of fiction or drama becomes a candidate for adaptation and then an actual film. You will need to investigate the "movie-making machinery" of Hollywood and of independent studios to learn how literary properties are sold. What is the role of the original writer of the literary work in the sale of his or her work for possible adaptation? What is the role of the literary agent? The producer? Do directors acquire the rights to literary works? What is an "option"? What percentage of literary works put under agreement eventually become films?
8. Conduct research into the ways that we comprehend the world visually, as opposed to verbally. Apply whatever insights you gain in your research to "The Birds" or "Witness for the Prosecution." Reread one of the stories, and then view the adaptations several times. Given your background reading on visual comprehension, analyze the ways in which the director communicates essential elements of the story *visually.* One of the requirements of this assignment is that you be able to identify "essential" elements of the story, which you may want to do by identifying a theme, an underlying tone or mood to the story, or a specific moment. You would then turn to the ways that Hitchcock or Wilder communicates that element without having actors speak. Depending on the extent to which you're comfortable using filmic vocabulary, consult the glossary on pages 754–59 and draw on the terms there in your discussion.

13
Business Ethics

Business ethics—both as an academic discipline and as an evolving set of principles used to guide decision making in large and small companies—is a relatively new concept in American life. Before the 1960s and 1970s, the proper role of business was understood as providing goods and services to a consuming public, for profit. Most Americans might have agreed with the sentiment that "What's good for General Motors is good for the country" and trusted General Motors to define "good" on its own terms. No longer. Scandals in business saw corporations dumping toxic chemicals and withholding information about product defects from the public; with the increasing tendency of large companies to gobble up smaller ones came a general wariness of corporations. In response to this wariness, businesses began to consider their social responsibilities. More and more, confronted with the reality of government regulation, managers and executives felt compelled to provide the public with an account of hazards in the workplace or in the environment, of questionable labor or management practices, or of economic decisions that might disrupt entire communities. Business also began to take into consideration public concern over corporate policy *before* decisions were made.

By the 1970s, corporations around the country began accepting the view that they had responsibilities to stakeholders as well as to shareholders—to all who were affected by the conduct of business, be that effect monetary, physical, psychological, or environmental. Money was no longer the only concern. Writing in 1971, the Committee for Economic Development noted:

> Today it is clear that the terms of the contract between society and business are, in fact, changing in substantial and important ways. Business is being asked to assume broader responsibilities to society than ever before and to serve a wider range of human values. Business enterprises, in effect, are being asked to contribute more to the quality of American life than just supplying quantities of goods and services.[1]

[1]From pp. 29–30 in *Social Responsibilities of Business Corporations* by the Committee for Economic Development (New York: CED, 1971).

The acknowledgment of corporate America's social responsibilities came just in time, apparently, as Americans began showing their impatience with "business as usual." In a survey conducted in 1968, 70 percent of respondents felt that businesses were managing to earn profits while at the same time showing decent concern for the public's welfare. In 1978, only 15 percent of respondents felt the same way. By 1985, more than half of the respondents to selected surveys claimed that corporate executives are dishonest, that businesses show little regard for the society in which they operate, and that executives violate the public trust whenever money is to be made. For example, in 1992, a leading ethicist who consults with some of America's largest companies reported that, based on in-house surveys, "between 20 percent and 30 percent of middle managers have written deceptive internal reports." That is to say, one-fifth to one-third of the managers surveyed admit to lying.

The news is rife with examples of ethical misconduct. Recall the space shuttle *Challenger* disaster, in which the decision to launch was made over the protest of engineers who warned of potentially disastrous defects in the very parts that failed. Recall the Exxon *Valdez* fiasco that saw hundreds of miles of pristine Alaskan coastal waters despoiled by crude oil: The oil leaked from the ruptured hold of a tanker whose captain had left the bridge command to a subordinate unqualified to navigate the vessel in Prince William Sound; setting the causes of the accident aside, Exxon representatives argued with Alaskan and federal officials over the limits of corporate liability in cleaning up the mess. The corporate impulse was to limit corporate cost, whatever the larger environmental cost to the people of Alaska. And recall the spate of mergers in recent years that have left newly acquired companies too heavily in debt to deal flexibly with employees. Other examples of ethical misconduct or ethically questionable practices fill the nightly news and the morning headlines. In early 1992, Sears, one of America's largest retailers, was rocked by scandal when an investigation by a California consumer agency revealed that the company's auto service centers had been systematically overcharging customers and performing unnecessary repairs. Threatened with the shutdown of all its service centers in the state, Sears agreed to a costly settlement. More pervasive than these high-profile stories, and perhaps more damaging, are the "little" violations of ethical standards forced on managers or other employees who are asked, or forced, everyday to sacrifice personal values for company gain.

The study of ethics, of course, is not new. From the time of Aristotle (384–322 B.C.), philosophers have debated the standards by which we judge right or good behavior. The systematic study of ethics as applied to business, however, *is* new, and we see in it (according to a past president of the Society for Business Ethics) "an attempt . . . to revive the importance and legitimacy of making moral claims in the world of practical affairs."[2] Two associ-

[2]W. Michael Hoffman. "Business Ethics in the United States: Its Past Decade and Its Future," *Business Insights* 5, No. 1 (Spring/Summer, 1989): 8.

ated developments have accompanied the rise of business ethics. First, corporations have begun drafting codes of ethics for their employees. Second, courses in business ethics are being taught at the graduate and undergraduate levels in schools around the country. The thrust of these courses has been both to justify the need for ethics in business and to provide a model by which students, future business leaders, can make ethical judgments in the world of work.

It is likely that in your life as a person who conducts business of one sort or another you will face an ethical dilemma: You could act one way and maintain your principles—but, perhaps, lose a job or an important account; you could act another way and help to secure your fortune—but, perhaps, at the expense of your integrity. The pressures on people in business to make money, on the one hand, but to do the "right" thing, on the other, are real and often painfully difficult. It is these pressures—clearly defining them and responding to them—that form the subject matter of this chapter. First, writing on "The Case of the Collapsed Mine," Richard T. De George poses a series of questions that effectively surveys the field of business ethics. Next, in "The Study of Ethics: An Orientation," Phillip V. Lewis and Henry E. Speck, III ground our discussion of business ethics by introducing three questions that underlie the larger study of ethics. Economist Milton Friedman follows with a direct attack on the notion that businesses should be socially responsible. In "Pure Profit," journalist Peter Carlin explores the struggles of ice cream makers Ben Cohen and Jerry Greenfield, as they attempt to run a socially responsible business *and* be profitable. Then, in "Ethics in Business," philosopher Gerald F. Cavanagh presents a strategy for analyzing ethical dilemmas and defining courses of action. The second section of the chapter, Cases for Analysis and Discussion, begins with "A Note on the Case Method" by Denis Collins and Laura V. Page. The authors introduce the case method and offer a second strategy for analyzing ethical dilemmas. Given these selections, you will have the tools to read, analyze, and respond to several case studies that raise questions about ethical behavior in business: "The Layoff," "The Pricing Dilemma," "The Ticket Purchase," "Peter Green's First Day," "Matt Goldspan's Trilogy," and "Why Should My Conscience Bother Me?"

The Case of the Collapsed Mine

RICHARD T. DE GEORGE

Studying business ethics can make one sensitive to issues and questions that might otherwise have escaped notice, had no formal training been available. A business situation fraught with dilemmas for one person might for another simply be business as usual, and this is the problem: one person sees conflict; another person sees none. So we begin the chapter with a selection that demonstrates how someone who is sensitive to ethical dilemmas would approach a particular incident. In "The Case of the Collapsed Mine," Richard T. De George presents a case study and then raises a series of questions that, in effect, provides an overview of business ethics. For instance, De George takes up questions of the value of human life as measured against the cost of designing very safe, or relatively safe, products; and the need to restructure systems that reward loyalty at the expense of morality. These are questions you will read more about in the selections to follow. You may be surprised (as we were) by the number of questions De George can draw from the case.

Richard T. De George is University Distinguished Professor of Philosophy and Courtesy Professor of Management at the University of Kansas. He is the author or editor of over fifteen books and more than one hundred scholarly articles concerning business ethics. De George has traveled worldwide in discussing issues of applied ethics; he has served as president of the American Philosophical Association (Central Division) and at the University of Kansas has won awards for his teaching and scholarship. De George was educated at Fordham University (B.A.), University of Louvain, Belgium (Ph.B.), and Yale (M.A. and Ph.D.).

The following case illustrates the sorts of questions that might arise in business ethics and various ways to approach them. Consider the case of the collapsed mine shaft. In a coal mining town of West Virginia, some miners were digging coal in a tunnel thousands of feet below the surface. Some gas buildup had been detected during the two preceding days. This had been reported by the director of safety to the mine manager. The buildup was sufficiently serious to have closed down operations until it was cleared. The owner of the mine decided that the buildup was only marginally dangerous, that he had coal orders to fill, that he could not afford to close down the mine, and that he would take the chance that the gas would dissipate before it exploded. He told the director of safety not to say anything about the danger. On May 2nd, the gas exploded. One section of the tunnel collapsed, killing three miners and trapping eight others in a pocket. The rest managed to escape. 1

The explosion was one of great force and the extent of the tunnel's collapse was considerable. The cost of reaching the men in time to save their lives would amount to several million dollars. The problem facing the manager was whether the expenditure of such a large sum of money was worth it. What, after all, was a human life worth? Whose decision was it and how should it be made? Did the manager owe more to the stockholders of the corporation or to the trapped workers? Should he use the slower, safer, and cheaper way of reaching them and save a large sum of money or the faster, more dangerous, and more expensive way and possibly save their lives? 2

He decided on the latter and asked for volunteers. Two dozen men volunteered. After three days, the operation proved to be more difficult than anyone had anticipated. There had been two more explosions and three of those involved in the rescue operation had already been killed. In the meantime, telephone contact had been made with the trapped men who had been fortunate enough to find a telephone line that was still functioning. They 3 were starving. Having previously read about a similar case, they decided that the only way for any of them to survive long enough was to draw lots, and then kill and eat the one who drew the shortest straw. They felt that it was their duty that at least some of them should be found alive; otherwise, the three volunteers who had died rescuing them would have died in vain.

After twenty days the seven men were finally rescued alive; they had cannibalized their fellow miner. The director of safety who had detected the gas before the explosion informed the newspapers of his report. The manager was charged with criminal negligence; but before giving up his position, he fired the director of safety. The mine eventually resumed operation. 4

There are a large number of issues in the above account. . . . 5

The director of safety is in some sense the hero of the story. But did he fulfill his moral obligation before the accident in obeying the manager and in not making known either to the miners, the manager's superior, or to the public the fact that the mine was unsafe? Did he have a moral obligation after the explosion and rescue to make known the fact that the manager knew the mine was unsafe? Should he have gone to the board of directors of the company with the story or to someone else within the company rather than to the newspapers? All these questions are part of the phenomenon of worker responsibility. To whom is a worker responsible and for what? Does his moral obligation end when he does what he is told? Going public with inside information such as the director of safety had is commonly known as "blowing the whistle" on the company. Frequently those who blow the whistle are fired, just as the director of safety was. The whole phenomenon of whistle blowing raises serious questions about the structure of companies in which employees find it necessary to take such drastic action and possibly suffer the loss of their jobs. Was the manager justified in firing the director of safety? 6

The manager is, of course, the villain of the story. He sent the miners into a situation which he knew was dangerous. But, he might argue, he did it for the good of the company. He had contracts to fulfill and obligations to the owners of the company to show a profit. He had made a bad decision. Every manager has to take risks. It just turned out that he was unlucky. Does such a defense sound plausible? Does a manager have an obligation to his workers as well as to the owners of a company? Who should take precedence and under what conditions does one group or the other become more important? Who is to decide and how? 7

The manager decided to try to save the trapped miners even though it would cost the company more than taking the slower route. Did he have the right to spend more of the company's money in this way? How does one evaluate human life in comparison with expenditure of money? It sounds moral to say that human life is beyond all monetary value. In a sense it is. However, there are limits which society and people in it can place on the amount they will, can, and should spend to save lives. The way to decide, however, does not seem to be to equate the value of a person's life with the amount of income he would produce in his remaining years, if he lives to a 8 statistically average age, minus the resources he would use up in that period. How does one decide? How do and should people weigh human lives against monetary expenditure? In designing automobiles, in building roads, in making many products, there is a trade-off between the maximum safety that one can build into the product and the cost of the product. Extremely safe cars cost more to build than relatively safe cars. We can express the difference in terms of the number of people likely to die driving the relatively safe ones as opposed to the extremely safe ones. Should such decisions be made by manufacturers, consumers, government, or in some other way?

The manager asked for volunteers for the rescue work. Three of these 9
volunteers died. Was the manager responsible for their deaths in the same way that he was responsible for the deaths of the three miners who had died in the first mine explosion? Was the company responsible for the deaths in either case? Do companies have obligations to their employees and the employees' families in circumstances such as these, or are the obligations only those of the managers? If the manager had warned the miners that the level of gas was dangerous, and they had decided that they wanted their pay for that day and would work anyway, would the manager have been responsible for their deaths? Is it moral for people to take dangerous jobs simply to earn money? Is a system that impels people to take such jobs for money a moral system? To what extent is a company morally obliged to protect its workers and to prevent them from taking chances?

The manager was charged with criminal negligence under the law. Was 10
the company responsible for anything? Should the company have been sued by the family of the dead workers? If the company were sued and paid damages to the families, the money would come from company profits and hence from the profits of the shareholders. Is it fair that the shareholders be penalized for an incident they had nothing to do with? How is responsibility shared and/or distributed in a company, and can companies be morally responsible for what is done in their name? Are only human beings moral agents and is it a mistake to use moral language with respect to companies, corporations, and businesses?

The decision of the trapped miners to cast lots to determine who would 11
be killed and eaten also raises a number of moral issues. Our moral intuitions can provide in this case no ready answer as to whether their decision was morally justifiable, since the case is not an ordinary one. How to think about such an issue raises the question of how moral problems are to be resolved and underscores the need for some moral theory as guidelines by which we can decide unusual cases. A number of principles seem to conflict—the obligation not to kill, the consideration that it is better for one person to die rather than eight, the fact noted by the miners that three persons had already died trying to rescue them, and so on. The issue here is not one peculiar to business ethics, but it is rather a moral dilemma that requires some technique of moral argument to solve.

The case does not tell us what happened to either the manager or the 12
director of safety. Frequently the sequel to such cases is surprising. The

managers come off free and ultimately rewarded for their concern for the company's interest, while the whistle blower is black-balled throughout the industry. The morality of such an outcome seems obvious—justice does not always triumph. What can be done to see that it triumphs more often is a question that involves restructuring the system.

Business ethics is sometimes seen as conservative and is also used as a defense of the status quo. Sometimes it is seen as an attack on the status quo and hence viewed as radical. Ideally it should be neither. It should strive for objectivity. When there are immoral practices, structures, and actions occurring, business ethics should be able to show that these actions are immoral and why. But it should also be able to supply the techniques with which the practices and structures that are moral can be defended as such. The aim of business ethics is neither defense of the status quo nor its radical change. Rather it should serve to remedy those aspects or structures that need change and protect those that are moral. It is not a panacea. It can secure change only if those in power take the appropriate action. But unless some attention is paid to business ethics, the moral debate about practices and principles central to our society will be more poorly and probably more immorally handled than otherwise. 13

▲ ▲ ▲

Discussion and Writing Suggestions

1. Of the many questions that De George poses regarding "The Case of the Collapsed Mine," which question or set of questions seems most likely to get at the heart of the case? Explain your choice.
2. De George writes: "When there are immoral practices, structures, and actions occurring, business ethics should be able to show that these actions are immoral and why. But it should also be able to supply the techniques with which the practices and structures that are moral can be defended as such." Based on what you've read and seen on news reports, and based on your own experience, perhaps, to what extent are people in business amenable to discussing reasons that an action may or may not be ethical?
3. In paragraph 6, De George poses several questions and then writes: "All these questions are part of the phenomenon of worker responsibility." *Worker responsibility,* then, becomes a category of questions. Reread the selection and create categories for the other questions that De George asks. For instance, some questions concern corporate responsibility, some concern the prohibition against killing, and so on. Compare your categories with a classmate's. (These categories will provide something of an index to the issues addressed in this chapter and, more generally, an index to the concerns of business ethicists.)

4. Summarize the significant details of an event in your own work experience and draw out those elements that raised ethical dilemmas for you or someone you know. In the fashion of De George, write a brief essay in which you pose a series of questions about the event and the behaviors of the people involved.

The Study of Ethics: An Orientation

PHILLIP V. LEWIS
HENRY E. SPECK, III

"The Study of Ethics" appeared in somewhat longer form in a special issue of The Journal of Business Communication *(Summer 1990) devoted to business ethics. The authors, both professors at Abilene Christian University, believe that an overview of the history of ethics "provides the . . . framework in which both to discuss and to seek answers to the three necessary and sequential questions about business ethics: (1) What is ethics and what does it mean to be ethical; (2) why be ethical; and (3) how can one be ethical?"*

Our study of business ethics is divided into what we take to be *the* three necessary and sequential questions. One: *what* is ethics, and what does it mean to be ethical? Before one can decide whether he or she subscribes to the proposition that one ought to be ethical in one's business (as well as all other) practices, a working definition of the words *ethics* and *ethical* is required. Two: *why* be ethical? An adequate answer to this apparently simple question is not easy. Perhaps that is why an answer is so rarely attempted by texts on the subject. We hold that valid reasons for pursuing ethical conduct are required. Three: *how* can one be ethical? We suggest that an adequate answer to this question is to be found in an examination of history. For us, this means the roots of Western Civilization. 1

WHAT IS ETHICS?

First, *what* is business ethics and what does it mean to be ethical? Present and future managers need a clear, working definition of the words *ethics* and *ethical.* Acceptable definitions must include the following: Ethics is concerned with moral obligation, character, responsibility; social justice; the good life. Hence to be ethical means to pursue right conduct, to fulfill one's moral obligations and responsibilities, to seek social justice and the good life. 2

But there is an immediate and rather obvious difficulty here. What is meant by the words *right, moral, just, good*? Have they some objective, clearly definable meaning to which we all may subscribe? What seems right to one person often seems wrong to another. What the government decrees as just often strikes a particular citizen as unjust. For example, what 3 is the just price of a given product or commodity? Is it right for the government to make laws regulating business? Is it good or bad for labor to strike against management? An answer to this question will be suggested when considering the next question.

WHY BE ETHICAL?

Second, *why* be ethical (i.e., right, moral, just, good)? It obviously, so we 4
assume, is better to be right than wrong, moral than immoral, just than unjust, good than bad. In reality this is not a very satisfactory answer. It fails to explain *why* we think it is better to be so. For example: *why* is it wrong to steal? Is it always wrong to steal? Is it ever right to steal? (Consider the case of Robin Hood.) Most would agree that stealing is a form of unethical conduct. But why do we so agree? Is it because we have looked into the question and found it to be so, or because our personal experience tells us that it is so?

The answer, quite clearly, is: in all probability not. Rather, we hold it 5
wrong to steal because we have been told that it is wrong. That is to say, we hold stealing to be wrong on some authority other than our own (e.g., God, the state, our elders). It is a part of our social education, accepted by most of us without question much in the way that we accept without question that we know what is meant by the words stealing and wrong. We do not even stop to consider that the word stealing is not value-free.

Unfortunately, it does not help a great deal to see these terms defined. 6
The matter is complex, as indeed it is with all ethical questions. Experience teaches us that as often as not the wrong appears victorious, financially or otherwise. It is equally clear that the "just" do not appear to be either healthier or wealthier than the "unjust." Nor do they appear to live better or longer. Indeed, to judge by appearances, the opposite is as often the case as not. Nor is there anything new in all this. The biblical character Job, the hero of the Mesopotamian *Epic of Gilgamesh,* and the writer of the Book of Ecclesiastes, to cite but three examples, observed this apparent fact over two thousand years ago. It gave them pause, even as it should give us pause.

No, if present and future managers really wish to answer the "why" 7
question, they need to inquire for a reason beyond "so-and-so (the Bible, Congress, my parents and / or teachers) tells me so." They need to ask why it is that they believe (or should believe), despite their own experience and that of countless others down through the recorded annals of history, that it really is better to be ethical than unethical. They also need to know why the words *right, moral, just, good* possess values of approval and the opposites of these words values of disapproval. They certainly need to know why such acts as stealing are unethical even when one is not apprehended.

In reality there are only two possible answers to the question, "why be 8
ethical?" These answers are to be found in the separate approaches to human activity which underlie the Western Tradition. It will be simplest to call these two approaches: Judeo-Christian and Graeco-Roman. These sep-

arate traditions may be labeled as *theistic* and *humanistic,* respectively. Moses / Jesus and Socrates / Plato represent the two traditions.

For the Jew or Christian, the answer to the question "Why be ethical?" 9
is both clear and simple. God commands it. Do not steal because God has said, "Thou shalt not steal." Conversely do that which is good because God has commanded both Jews and Christians to do so (e.g., "Thou shalt love thy neighbor as thyself").

For many Jews and Christians, this is a sufficient answer. It is accepted 10
without question that God's commandments are good for His creation. But the nonbeliever will hardly be satisfied by an answer which simply states: The Bible tells me so. (Indeed, when it comes to such questions as hypocrisy, the Bible has not convinced many of the believers.) And to say that the state tells me so obviously has not convinced large segments of the populace to pursue ethical conduct. We therefore need to consider the answer supplied by humanism.

Socrates / Plato provide an alternative answer to the question, "*Why* be 11
ethical?" Socrates believed passionately in the ethical life as being what mattered most to human beings (more than pleasure, wealth, physical health, or anything else). The immediate question, then, is this: *Why* did Socrates so believe? The answer is complex, but an answer can be found in a later dialogue by Plato—*The Republic.* In Book X, a man by the name of Glaucon asks the question: Why should one be just rather than unjust, particularly if he is neither apprehended nor even observed in his unjust actions. In Book XI, Socrates replies: because injustice leads to harmful consequences for the individual who is unjust. Conversely, it is to be implied, justice leads to beneficial results for the individual who is just.

Clearly Socrates does not mean that the just cannot be physically 12
harmed. Rather, he means that it is better to seek what we should call psychic rewards rather than physical health, riches, power, or fame. Only in this way can a person achieve happiness and those things which constitute happiness (e.g., harmony of the material and non-material, balance, self-sufficiency, peace, fulfillment, and inner contentment). Only by pursuing the ethical life can someone hope to realize his or her full potentialities as a human being. In one sense, Socrates meant what modern psychiatrists mean when they speak of the integrated psyche; in another, he meant self-realization. In short, for Socrates, self-interest and the ethical life are one and the same thing. Hence the words *right, moral, just, good* (for Socrates) mean those things which are life-enhancing; *wrong, immoral, unjust, bad* mean those things which are detrimental to the human psyche in any way.

We see then that although there are two possible ways of approaching 13
an answer to the question "*Why be ethical?*" the answers suggested are, upon analysis, virtually identical. Both traditions define the ethical (i.e., the right, good, moral, just) life in terms of what is life-enhancing or beneficial to life, both for oneself and for others, both now and in the future. Conversely, the unethical (i.e., the wrong, bad, immoral, unjust) life is defined in terms of what is life-threatening or detrimental to life, both to oneself and to others, both in the present and in the future.

While this definition does not explain in every case precisely what is ethical or unethical behavior, it does explain *why* the individual should pursue the ethical life. It is in his or her best self-interest. This self-interest is, by definition, neither narrow nor cynical but a broad, "self-regarding" view of the individual who realizes that he or she lives in the context of other individuals who collectively go into making up "society." In both traditions, the emphasis is on creative self-realization, or the absence thereof, and not the fear of punishment. 14

There also is agreement that the ethical life involves clear knowledge of what is ethical and what is not. Such knowledge is not easily come by, nor is it to be achieved simply by knowing the values handed down *a priori* by tradition. Rather, it is part of a learning process focused on self-realization. We should willingly undertake this process because it is in our best self-interests to do so. As Socrates says in the *Apology,* "The unexamined life is not worth living." 15

HOW CAN ONE BE ETHICAL?

We thus come to the third question: "*How* can one be ethical?" A decision that it is in one's best self-interest to be ethical requires an answer to the question. How is one to know *precisely* what is in one's best self-interest? Current research and publications on business ethics (as well as on ethics in general) attempt to answer this question by presenting a variety of ethical systems from which to choose. We hold that it is more useful to observe that all such systems are part of an historical context (i.e., the origins of Western Civilization) and should be considered organically, nor piecemeal. 16

Historically, the Judeo-Christian tradition is characterized by an unquestioning faith in an eternal God who not only is creator of the universe and all things in it but who has revealed His will through chosen emissaries, first the prophets of the Jewish Bible and later, for Christians, through Jesus of Nazareth. The Graeco-Roman tradition is substantively different. It places its faith in man and the power of human reason. As the Greek Sophist Protagoras said, "Man is the measure of all things." The tradition rightly therefore is referred to as "humanistic." Hence, while both traditions are based on faith, the nature and object of that faith fundamentally differ. 17

Further, while for both Socrates and Plato, absolute Truth exists just as surely as God exists for Jews and Christians, there is another fundamental distinction to be made. For the Jew or Christian, Truth is *revealed.* In the Graeco-Roman tradition, it is there to be *discovered.* This distinction is made clear by contrasting Jesus and Socrates. Jesus said, "He that hath seen me hath seen the Father." Socrates is recorded by Plato in the *Apology* to have said: "I am wiser than . . . [other men] to this small extent, that I do not think that I know what I do not know." 18

While the Jew or Christian can accept on faith the moral principles of his or her religion as the absolute commandments of God, it remains to (a) discover which of the principles found in the Bible constitute absolutes 19 and (b) how those which the believer takes to be absolute are to be interpreted in specific cases. (There also is the difficulty surrounding the knotty question, "*Who* is to make the decisions?") Despite the quantity of ink spilt over the centuries by both Jews and Christians, there is no agreement on the answers to these questions. Hence the continuing sectarianism of both religious communities.

In turning to the Graeco-Roman tradition, it is important to observe 20
that the question "*How* can one be ethical?" has nothing to do with religion, much less with God or the gods. As there is no meaningful afterlife in Graeco-Roman thought, it follows that ethics must be concerned with this life. State religion was almost entirely concerned with ritual, not dogma. While it helped society to get on with the business of everyday life, it had little or nothing to do with ethical (or unethical) behavior.

When Greek thinkers first approached the question of how to be ethi- 21
cal, they produced a theory known as "ethical relativism." Such men were known as "Sophists." The Sophists taught, for a fee, that there were no absolutes, certainly not any which could be discovered. Truth was relative. Right and wrong, justice and injustice, good and bad, moral and immoral were simply names. Their meaning depended entirely on the individual. As Protagoras maintained, "With regard to the gods, I have no means of knowing either that they exist or that they do not. For many are the obstacles that impede knowledge, both the obscurity of the question and the shortness of human life."

Into this arena of skepticism stepped, first, Socrates, then Plato, to 22
combat the Sophistic view by attempting to establish the existence of absolutes. Plato argued that we know moral absolutes exist for the very simple reason that we possess innate knowledge of them. We say, for example, this thing is hot or cold. In so doing, we do not mean that it is absolutely hot or absolutely cold. Rather, we mean that it is hotter or colder than some other thing. The question therefore arises: Where do we get the knowledge which allows us to know that there is such a thing as *hot,* not simply *hotter*; how is it that we can always imagine something hotter than the thing in question? There is no time to give a developed answer to this question here. Suffice it to say that no less a thinker than the late Bertrand Russell considered Plato's "Theory of Knowledge" as good a solution to the problems of epistemology (i.e., how we know what we know) as any yet advanced.

But, even if we accept the Platonic argument for the existence of ab- 23
solutes, it remains to ask: how are they to be discovered? The answer is found in the Socratic Method (though there is some question as to whether Socrates invented or inherited this method).

First, says Socrates, in order to learn anything, we must admit that we 24
are ignorant. Once we have admitted our ignorance, we may turn to the question of defining the terms of the discussion. In the case of ethics, this meant attempting to define such words as *good, moral, just, right.*

The Socratic method began with a process of adduction. This is to say 25
that we first collect instances of what we agree to be good, right, moral, just actions. Then we search for a common quality, or qualities (i.e., we adduce

them) in these actions in order to construct a general definition of the particular term. Once we have our general definition, we can create a deductive syllogism which will enable us to determine whether a specific action is in accordance with our definition.

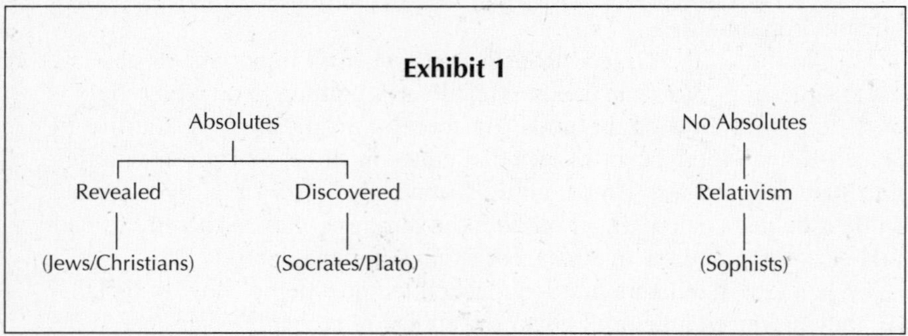

Thus *how* to behave ethically depends on one's choice of absolutes. 26
People differ, however, on whether these absolutes are *revealed by God* (Jews / Christians) or remain to be *discovered by man* (Socrates / Plato). Others (the Sophists) do not believe in absolutes. The schema in Exhibit 1 may be applied. This schema allows both students and managers to categorize ethical thinkers, and systems, in a simple and useful manner which is easily retained in the memory. . . .

Ethical theory discussions present a diversity of ethical options. They 27
do not, however, present an organic base for studying and understanding business ethics. The above discussion holds that a study of Western Civilization provides the framework for both discussing and seeking answers to ethical queries. Via a study of history a more focused position can be found for understanding the ethical orientations of business ethics.

Review Questions

1. Lewis and Speck organize their discussion of ethics around three questions: What is ethics? Why be ethical? How can one be ethical? Summarize their answer to each of these questions.
2. In response to which of the authors' three questions are systems of ethics designed? Why?
3. What is "humanism"? In what ways is it connected to the differences between the Judeo-Christian and the Greco-Roman traditions?
4. What is ethical relativism?
5. What is the Socratic Method?
6. How can a difference in the way people perceive absolutes lead to conflict?

Discussion and Writing Suggestions

1. The authors point out that, on the strength of our own experience and on the strength of what we know about history and literature, people who behave ethically live no longer and are no wealthier than people who are unjust. Based on your experience, is this so? Does this disturb you? Does this affect the way in which you regard questions of ethics?
2. To what extent do the two traditions that the authors discuss continue, in our own era, to define fundamental ways of seeing the world? Choose one conflict that divides our society. To what extent do you see the two traditions at work?
3. The Judeo-Christian and Greco-Roman traditions teach that fear of punishment (see paragraph 14) is not the proper inducement to ethical action. Do you agree? From what you can observe of the business world, what is the motivation for people to act ethically? Does fear play a role?
4. Socrates said, "The unexamined life is not worth living." In your view, is this assertion valid? To the extent you think so, how might it apply to dealings in business?
5. Having read this selection, can you now identify a time when, without realizing it, you understood or worked out a problem by using the Socratic Method?

The Social Responsibility of Business Is to Increase Its Profits

MILTON FRIEDMAN

By 1970, a growing number of business leaders were declaring that their practices ought to be more ethical and in tune with community needs. In a famous article appearing in the New York Times Magazine *on September 13, 1970, Milton Friedman argued that in a free-market system such as ours business has an obligation not to be socially responsible. The debate was launched—and is still not settled. If Friedman is right, business ethicists are out of a job and American businesses should be left to their own devices, within the constraints of law, to behave in whatever manner maximizes profits for shareholders. "The Social Responsibility of Business" has become a classic in the literature of business ethics.*

Milton Friedman (b. 1912) has had a long and distinguished career. He served as Professor of Economics at the University of Chicago from 1948 to 1982; he has been a Senior Research Fellow at the Hoover Institution at Stanford University since 1976. He has served on Presidential commisions, has been a President of the American Economic Association, and has won numerous awards for his work—including a Nobel

Prize for Economics in 1976, a National Medal of Science in 1988, and a Presidential Medal of Freedom, also in 1988. His many publications include A Program for Monetary Stability *(1960);* Capitalism and Freedom *(1962);* A Theoretical Framework for Monetary Analysis *(1971); and* Money Mischief *(1992).*

When I hear businessmen speak eloquently about the "social responsibilities of business in a free-enterprise system," I am reminded of the wonderful line about the Frenchman who discovered at the age of 70 that he had been speaking prose all his life. The businessmen believe that they are defending free enterprise when they declaim that business is not concerned "merely" with profit but also with promoting desirable "social" ends; that business has a "social conscience" and takes seriously its responsibilities for providing employment, eliminating discrimination, avoiding pollution and whatever else may be the catchwords of the contemporary crop of reformers. In fact they are—or would be if they or anyone else took them seriously—preaching pure and unadulterated socialism. Businessmen who talk this way are unwitting puppets of the intellectual forces that have been undermining the basis of a free society these past decades. 1

The discussions of the "social responsibilities of business" are notable for their analytical looseness and lack of rigor. What does it mean to say that "business" has responsibilities? Only people can have responsibilities. A corporation is an artificial person and in this sense may have artificial responsibilities, but "business" as a whole cannot be said to have responsibilities, even in this vague sense. The first step toward clarity in examining the doctrine of the social responsibility of business is to ask precisely what it implies for whom. 2

Presumably, the individuals who are to be responsible are businessmen, which means individual proprietors or corporate executives. Most of the discussion of social responsibility is directed at corporations, so in what follows I shall mostly neglect the individual proprietor and speak of corporate executives. 3

In a free-enterprise, private-property system, a corporate executive is an employee of the owners of the business. He has direct responsibility to his employers. That responsibility is to conduct the business in accordance with their desires, which generally will be to make as much money as possible while conforming to the basic rules of the society, both those embodied in law and those embodied in ethical custom. Of course, in some cases his employers may have a different objective. A group of persons might establish a corporation for an eleemosynary purpose—for example, a hospital or a school. The manager of such a corporation will not have money profit as his objective but the rendering of certain services. 4

In either case, the key point is that, in his capacity as a corporate executive, the manager is the agent of the individuals who own the corporation or establish the eleemosynary institution, and his primary responsibility is to them. 5

Needless to say, this does not mean that it is easy to judge how well he is performing his task. But at least the criterion of performance is straightforward, and the persons among whom a voluntary contractual arrangement exists are clearly defined. 6

Of course, the corporate executive is also a person in his own right. As a person, he may have many other responsibilities that he recognizes or assumes voluntarily—to his family, his conscience, his feelings of charity, his church, his clubs, his city, his country. He may feel impelled by these responsibilities to devote part of his income to causes he regarded as worthy, to refuse to work for particular corporations, even to leave his job, for example, to join his country's armed forces. If we wish, we may refer to some of these responsibilities as "social responsibilities." But in these respects he is acting as a principal, not an agent; he is spending his own money or time or energy, not the money of his employers or the time or energy he has contracted to devote to their purposes. If these are "social responsibilities," they are the social responsibilities of individuals, not of business. 7

What does it mean to say that the corporate executive has a "social responsibility" in his capacity as businessman? If this statement is not pure rhetoric, it must mean that he is to act in some way that is not in the interest of his employers. For example, that he is to refrain from increasing the price of the product in order to contribute to the social objective of preventing inflation, even though a price increase would be in the best interests of the corporation. Or that he is to make expenditures on reducing pollution beyond the amount that is in the best interests of the corporation or that is required by law in order to contribute to the social objective of improving the environment. Or that, at the expense of corporate profits, he is to hire "hard-core" unemployed instead of better-qualified available workmen to contribute to the social objective of reducing poverty. 8

In each of these cases, the corporate executive would be spending someone else's money for a general social interest. Insofar as his actions in accord with his "social responsibility" reduce returns to stockholders, he is spending their money. Insofar as his actions raise the price to customers, he is spending the customers' money. Insofar as his actions lower the wages of some employees, he is spending their money. 9

The stockholders or the customers or the employees could separately spend their own money on the particular action if they wished to do so. The executive is exercising a distinct "social responsibility," rather than serving as an agent of the stockholders or the customers or the employees, only if he spends the money in a different way than they would have spent it. 10

But if he does this, he is in effect imposing taxes, on the one hand, and deciding how the tax proceeds shall be spent, on the other. 11

This process raises political questions on two levels: principle and consequences. On the level of political principle, the imposition of taxes and the expenditure of tax proceeds are governmental functions. We have established elaborate constitutional, parliamentary and judicial provisions to con- 12 trol these functions, to assure that taxes are imposed so far as possible in accordance with the preferences and desires of the public—after all, "taxation without representation" was one of the battle cries of the American Revolution. We have a system of checks and balances to separate the legislative function of imposing taxes and enacting expenditures from the executive function of collecting taxes and administering expenditure programs and from the judicial function of mediating disputes and interpreting the law.

Here the businessman—self-selected or appointed directly or indirectly by stockholders—is to be simultaneously legislator, executive and jurist. He is to decide whom to tax by how much and for what purpose, and he is to spend the proceeds—all this guided only by general exhortations from on high to restrain inflation, improve the environment, fight poverty and so on and on. 13

The whole justification for permitting the corporate executive to be selected by the stockholders is that the executive is an agent serving the interests of his principal. This justification disappears when the corporate executive imposes taxes and spends the proceeds for "social" purposes. He becomes in effect a public employee, a civil servant, even though he remains in name an employee of a private enterprise. On grounds of political principle, it is intolerable that such civil servants—insofar as their actions in the name of social responsibility are real and not just window-dressing—should be selected as they are now. If they are to be civil servants, then they must be selected through a political process. If they are to impose taxes and make expenditures to foster "social" objectives, then political machinery must be set up to guide the assessment of taxes and to determine through a political process the objectives to be served. 14

This is the basic reason why the doctrine of "social responsibility" involves the acceptance of the socialist view that political mechanisms, not market mechanisms, are the appropriate way to determine the allocation of scarce resources to alternative uses. 15

On the grounds of consequences, can the corporate executive in fact discharge his alleged "social responsibilities"? On the one hand, suppose he could get away with spending the stockholders' or customers' or employees' money. How is he to know how to spend it? He is told that he must contribute to fighting inflation. How is he to know what action of his will contribute to that end? He is presumably an expert in running his company—in producing a product or selling it or financing it. But nothing about his selection makes him an expert on inflation. Will his holding down the price of his product reduce inflationary pressure? Or, by leaving more spending power in the hands of his customers, simply divert it elsewhere? Or, by forcing him to produce less because of the lower price, will it simply contribute to shortages? Even if he could answer these questions, how much cost is he justified in imposing on his stockholders, customers and employees for this social purpose? What is his appropriate share and what is the appropriate share of others? 16

17 And, whether he wants to or not, can he get away with spending his stockholders', customers' or employees' money? Will not the stockholders fire him? (Either the present ones or those who take over when his actions in the name of social responsibility have reduced the corporation's profits and the price of its stock.) His customers and his employees can desert him for other producers and employers less scrupulous in exercising their social responsibilities.

18 This facet of "social responsibility" doctrine is brought into sharp relief when the doctrine is used to justify wage restraint by trade unions. The conflict of interest is naked and clear when union officials are asked to subordinate the interest of their members to some more general social purpose. If the union officials try to enforce wage restraint, the consequence is likely to be wildcat strikes, rank-and-file revolts and the emergence of strong competitors for their jobs. We thus have the ironic phenomenon that union leaders—at least in the U.S.—have objected to Government interference with the market far more consistently and courageously than have business leaders.

19 The difficulty of exercising "social responsibility" illustrates, of course, the great virtue of private competitive enterprise—it forces people to be responsible for their own actions and makes it difficult for them to "exploit" other people for either selfish or unselfish purposes. They can do good—but only at their own expense.

20 Many a reader who has followed the argument this far may be tempted to remonstrate that it is all well and good to speak of government's having the responsibility to impose taxes and determine expenditures for such "social" purposes as controlling pollution or training the hard-core unemployed, but that the problems are too urgent to wait on the slow course of political processes, that the exercise of social responsibility by businessmen is a quicker and surer way to solve pressing current problems.

21 Aside from the question of fact—I share Adam Smith's skepticism about the benefits that can be expected from "those who affected to trade for the public good"—this argument must be rejected on grounds of principle. What it amounts to is an assertion that those who favor the taxes and expenditures in question have failed to persuade a majority of their fellow citizens to be of like mind and that they are seeking to attain by undemocratic procedures what they cannot attain by democratic procedures. In a free society, it is hard for "good" people to do "good," but that is a small price to pay for making it hard for "evil" people to do "evil," especially since one man's good is another's evil.

22 I have, for simplicity, concentrated on the special case of the corporate executive, except only for the brief digression on trade unions. But precisely the same argument applies to the newer phenomenon of calling upon stockholders to require corporations to exercise social responsibility (the recent G.M. crusade, for example). In most of these cases, what is in effect involved is some stockholders trying to get other stockholders (or cus-

tomers or employees) to contribute against their will to "social" causes favored by the activists. Insofar as they succeed, they are again imposing taxes and spending the proceeds.

The situation of the individual proprietor is somewhat different. If he acts to reduce the returns of his enterprise in order to exercise his "social responsibility," he is spending his own money, not someone else's. If he wishes to spend his money on such purposes, that is his right, and I cannot see that there is any objection to his doing so. In the process, he, too, may impose costs on employees and customers. However, because he is far less likely than a large corporation or union to have monopolistic power, any such side effects will tend to be minor. 23

Of course, in practice the doctrine of social responsibility is frequently a cloak for actions that are justified on other grounds rather than a reason for those actions. 24

To illustrate, it may well be in the long-run interest of a corporation that is a major employer in a small community to devote resources to providing amenities to that community or to improving its government. That may make it easier to attract desirable employees, it may reduce the wage bill or lessen losses from pilferage and sabotage or have other worthwhile effects. Or it may be that, given the laws about the deductibility of corporate charitable contributions, the stockholders can contribute more to charities they favor by having the corporation make the gift than by doing it themselves, since they can in that way contribute an amount that would otherwise have been paid as corporate taxes. 25

In each of these—and many similar—cases, there is a strong temptation to rationalize these actions as an exercise of "social responsibility." In the present climate of opinion, with its widespread aversion to "capitalism," "profits," the "soulless corporation" and so on, this is one way for a corporation to generate goodwill as a by-product of expenditures that are entirely justified in its own self-interest. 26

It would be inconsistent of me to call on corporate executives to refrain from this hypocritical window-dressing because it harms the foundations of a free society. That would be to call on them to exercise a "social responsibility"! If our institutions, and the attitudes of the public make it in their self-interest to cloak their actions in this way, I cannot summon much indignation to denounce them. At the same time, I can express admiration for those individual proprietors or owners of closely held corporations or stockholders of more broadly held corporations who disdain such tactics as approaching fraud. 27

Whether blameworthy or not, the use of the cloak of social responsibility, and the nonsense spoken in its name by influential and prestigious businessmen, does clearly harm the foundations of a free society. I have been impressed time and again by the schizophrenic character of many businessmen. They are capable of being extremely far-sighted and clear-headed in matters that are internal to their businesses. They are incredibly short-sighted and muddle-headed in matters that are outside their businesses but 28 affect the possible survival of business in general. This short-sightedness is strikingly exemplified in the calls from many businessmen for wage and price guidelines or controls or incomes policies. There is nothing that could do more in a brief period to destroy a market system and replace it by a centrally controlled system than effective governmental control of prices and wages.

The short-sightedness is also exemplified in speeches by businessmen 29
on social responsibility. This may gain them kudos in the short run. But it helps to strengthen the already too prevalent view that the pursuit of profits is wicked and immoral and must be curbed and controlled by external forces. Once this view is adopted, the external forces that curb the market will not be the social consciences, however highly developed, of the pontificating executives; it will be the iron fist of Government bureaucrats. Here, as with price and wage controls, businessmen seem to me to reveal a suicidal impulse.

The political principle that underlies the market mechanism is unanim- 30
ity. In an ideal free market resting on private property, no individual can coerce any other, all cooperation is voluntary, all parties to such cooperation benefit or they need not participate. There are no "social" values, no "social" responsibilities in any sense other than the shared values and responsibilities of individuals. Society is a collection of individuals and of the various groups they voluntarily form.

The political principle that underlies the political mechanism is confor- 31
mity. The individual must serve a more general social interest—whether that be determined by a church or a dictator or a majority. The individual may have a vote and a say in what is to be done, but if he is overruled, he must conform. It is appropriate for some to require others to contribute to a general social purpose whether they wish to or not.

Unfortunately, unanimity is not always feasible. There are some re- 32
spects in which conformity appears unavoidable, so I do not see how one can avoid the use of the political mechanism altogether.

But the doctrine of "social responsibility" taken seriously would ex- 33
tend the scope of the political mechanism to every human activity. It does not differ in philosophy from the most explicitly collectivist doctrine. It differs only by professing to believe that collectivist ends can be attained without collectivist means. That is why, in my book *Capitalism and Freedom,* I have called it a "fundamentally subversive doctrine" in a free society, and have said that in such a society, "there is one and only one social responsibility of business—to use its resources and engage in activities designed to increase its profits so long as it stays within the rules of the game, which is to say, engages in open and free competition without deception or fraud."

▲ ▲ ▲

Review Questions

1. According to Friedman, what's the difference between being an owner of a company and acting as an "agent" for the company's owners?
2. How does corporate social responsibility undermine the basis of a free society, according to Friedman?
3. What is Friedman's objection to corporate responsibility based on the "political principle"?
4. In terms of "consequences," why can't a corporate executive attempt to run a socially responsible business?
5. What is Friedman's answer to critics who suggest that the government's response to social problems is too slow and cumbersome—and that it is business's responsibility to affect quicker social change?
6. How is social responsibility used, sometimes, as a "cloak" for corporate self-interest?
7. What is the "ideal free market"? Why is some "political mechanism" necessary, according to Friedman? What is the danger of too much political involvement in the free market?

Discussion and Writing Suggestions

Friedman's article sets one pole in the debate over whether or not businesses should worry about social responsibilities. The argument has drawn many challenges. These Discussion and Writing Suggestions are based on one such critique by Colin Grant, professor of religious studies at Mount Allison University. You can find his article, "Friedman Fallacies," in the *Journal of Business Ethics* [(Vol. 10, 1991: 907–14).]

1. Grant claims that Friedman makes an "empirical error"; that is, Friedman incorrectly characterizes business as an activity that operates in total isolation from society. In fact, says Grant, businesses are intimately involved in society in the ways they attempt to influence the writing of laws. Since business *is* involved in the "political mechanism," an empirical fact that directly contradicts Friedman's claims, Friedman is wrong to argue that the political mechanism should have no, or minimal, say in how business is run. Your comment?
2. Grant claims that Friedman mistakenly equates ethics with the law. In fact, the two are not identical. There is legal behavior that is not ethical, and ethical behavior that is not legal. Again as a matter of descriptive fact, many businesses appreciate this distinction and do not act any way they wish until fined or otherwise corrected by laws. In your experience, is this true? Can you provide examples of business decisions that seemed guided by considerations of what was ethical as opposed to legal? or what was legal as opposed to ethical?

3. Grant claims that Friedman mistakenly describes shareholders as being interested in one thing only: ever-increasing profits. But clearly there are many shareholders in corporations who do not take such a view. Do you own any stock? Do you know anyone who does? What are your (their) views on the social responsibilities of business?
4. According to Grant, Friedman mistakenly believes in a free-market system that is completely isolated from the social world and the ecological world. Friedman argues that the free-market system, which is dedicated to one thing—profits, has to treat pollution or exhausted natural resources as unfortunate but necessary costs of doing business. If those costs become too high, the free market responds by changing its actions to lessen these now unacceptable costs. Following Friedman's logic, responsibility, per se, does not enter into the discussion—only relative degrees of profit and loss. Clearly, says Grant, businesses do not regulate their environmental mistakes in this way; and ecological disasters have occurred, worldwide, because of unfettered free-market business. According to Grant, the "market is free only because nature and the most vulnerable of our own species pay its real costs." Your comment?
5. At the end of his critique, Grant identifies (what for him is) the fundamental difficulty with Friedman's argument: "the assumption that the economic can be significant in itself and that concentration on its demands can, and even will, lead to fullness of life. The impact on the environment, east and west, suggests that this is not so. Reflection adds that it cannot be so. The more the focus is on short-term economic gain for its own sake the more detrimental the long-term effect can be expected to be." Do you agree that this is a fundamental difficulty with Friedman's argument?

Pure Profit

PETER CARLIN

Ben & Jerry's Homemade, Inc. exists partly as a direct challenge to Milton Friedman's argument that the business of business is to increase profits. Operating initially from a converted gas station in the college town of Burlington, Vermont, Ben Cohen and Jerry Greenfield launched what would become a $150 million business, based on a commitment to high-quality ice cream and to social responsibility. We "see ourselves," says one of the founders, "as somewhat of a social service agency and somewhat of an ice cream company." As you read, you might consider: Whose values in business do you find more compelling—Friedman's or those of a self-described "funky" corporation? This article first appeared in the Los Angeles Times Magazine *(February 5, 1995). Writer Peter Carlin co-authored the book* Beyond the Limits: A Woman's Triumph on Everest *(1993).*

One of the dividends of owning stock in Ben & Jerry's Homemade Inc. is being invited to the annual stockholders' meeting. This gives you an excuse to eat lots of ice cream, check out Ben & Jerry's 40-foot solarized stage bus and then spend two days listening to the Band, Bo Diddley, Michelle Shocked and the Kwanzaa Music Workshop Performance play at the Ben & Jerry's One World One Heart Festival. You also get to attend the financial meeting. Here, one company co-founder might lead the investors in a hymn while the other makes a point about product standards by splitting open a pint of ice cream with a samurai sword. 1

As the minutes of its official meeting would indicate, Ben & Jerry's still hews closely to a guiding principle co-founder Jerry Greenfield uttered in 1978, soon after he and Ben Cohen cranked their first gallon of ice cream in a converted Burlington, Vt., garage: "If it's not fun, why do it?" And that corporate philosophy, along with a social conscience and a line of wickedly good ice cream products, attracts a unique kind of investor to these meetings. Like Ben Cohen and Jerry Greenfield, Ben & Jerry's investors are prone to message T-shirts, beards and glasses. They are educated, middle- to upper-middle-class professionals who load the kids into the Volvo and drive to the Ben & Jerry's gathering at the Sugarbush Ski Resort in Warren, Vt., confident that the shouts of children will not be frowned upon during the chairman's big speech. 2

And when it's their turn to address questions to the board of directors, Ben & Jerry's investors are less likely to raise financial details than to suggest a new flavor their daughter thought up. Or wonder if the company might develop sugar-free ice cream for diabetics. Even in a year marked by stalled market growth, flattened profits and a dizzying 72% drop in share price, the only investor to mention the declining value of her Ben & Jerry's stock at the annual meeting last June was the New York City schoolteacher who haltingly expressed her gratitude for "the privilege of supporting this company." 3

As the stockholders made clear, their investment in this ice cream company has less to do with its profitability than how it goes about making its profits. What Ben & Jerry's offers its investors is the chance to buy into a company that reminds them of themselves. A company that is innovative and impassioned about its product, but also values-driven. A company with a freewheeling sense of humor, but also a serious commitment to its community. Business on a human scale, in other words. But how long can this go on? 4

Now a $150-million corporation that produces one of the two leading super-premium brands of ice cream in the country, Ben & Jerry's has long since edged into the realm of big business. So far, the company has maintained its human connection, thanks in large part to the warm, community-friendly vision of its co-founders. But now Cohen and Greenfield are stepping back from their company's daily operations, making room for a new chief executive whose background in traditional business will, they hope, help streamline the company's often troubled internal management and al- 5 low it to adjust to shrinking domestic demand by pursuing previously untapped markets in Europe and Asia.

Wall Street analysts applaud Ben & Jerry's willingness to professionalize their operation. What's less clear is how the new company will feel to its original and most loyal constituency—the customers who value its high-touch funkiness. Will the pressures wrought by success force the company to sacrifice the non-corporate values that made it so appealing? 6

Ben & Jerry's isn't the only formerly small, socially responsible company whose mainstream success threatens to hoist it upon its own ethical petard. The Patagonia outdoor equipment company defines itself by a rigid commitment to environmentalism, yet many of its most popular garments start life as heavily processed raw materials. Acknowledging this paradox in 1991, Patagonia founder Yvon Chouinard decided to put the brakes on his company's expansion. "Most of the evils in this world," he warns, "are caused by unlimited growth." This is not an opinion shared by Seattle coffee baron Howard Schultz, who believes his expanding chain of Starbucks coffee bars can push a vision of corporate responsibility and worker empowerment across the nation. 7

Schultz's worker-friendly notions would seem to make Starbucks among those who consider themselves patrons of ethics-driven industries. But on the wings of its success, Starbucks has taken on the features of a bird of prey. Humane businesses do not flourish at the expense of their competitors, some observers insist: When it comes to capitalist dogfighting, the higher you go, the lower you are. But if free-market competition is somehow unethical, does that mean success is socially irresponsible? Is it possible for any company built on small-business ideals to grow into a big business without sacrificing its integrity? 8

A few days before the stockholder meeting last year, Ben & Jerry's held a press conference at its Waterbury, Vt., headquarters to announce Ben Cohen's resignation as chief executive officer. As he acknowledged, the daily machinations of a $150-million company had grown too complex for any "multi-college dropout and failed pottery teacher" to run. But before the mood could become too dark, Cohen's partner, Jerry Greenfield, appeared, holding a poster that showed the two ice cream moguls scowling under top hats and pointing their fingers like chubby Uncle Sams. "Yo!" read the tag line. "We want *you* to be our CEO!" In order to find a new boss, Cohen explained, the company was holding an essay contest. Whoever wrote the best 100-word essay describing why he or she would make a good Ben & Jerry's CEO, he swore, would win the job. 9

Behind the frivolity lurked a much more traditional business story. Confronting internal management problems, a shrinking domestic market and aggressive plans for international expansion, the Ben & Jerry's board of directors (of which Cohen and Greenfield are, respectively, chair and vice-chair) hired a corporate headhunter to find an experienced chief executive. And when the time comes to extend a salary offer, the board intends to break B&J tradition by proffering a package worth more, maybe much 10 more, than the $150,000 salary of President and Chief Operating Officer Chuck Lacy, a sum that adheres to the company salary cap of seven times the $8 an hour paid to entry-level workers. To some members of Ben & Jerry's extended family, this shift toward traditional corporate behavior was nothing less than an outrage. And when the media finished chortling over the essay contest, some reporters cast a dark eye on the dismantled 7-to-1 ratio, asserting that the once-lovable ice cream kings had not only broken a promise to their own people but also betrayed a kind of public trust.

Which, on one level, seems ludicrous. As long as Ben & Jerry's continues pumping out New York Super Fudge Chunk and Wavy Gravy, why should an ice cream lover ponder the ethics of internal corporate machinations. Maybe because Cohen and Greenfield have spent the past 17 years pondering those ethics? And as they are discovering, it's not always easy to be the real-life subject of a folk tale. 11

The legend of Ben & Jerry is recorded in a promotional film shown on tours of the company's factory (the 250,000 annual visitors make Ben & Jerry's Waterbury plant the most popular destination in Vermont). Combining still photos, clumsy home videos and giggling dialogue by the founders, the film tells a story of alternative entrepreneurial triumph: In 1978, two boyhood chums from Long Island, N.Y., send away for a $5 course to learn how to make ice cream, then open shop in a converted gas station in collegiate Burlington, Vt. Success comes quickly, thanks to the boys' commitment to quality and their ability to mix wild flavors with wacky promotions and giveaways. By 1981, Ben & Jerry's is honored by Time magazine as "the best ice cream in the world," and Cohen and Greenfield expand their horizons, hand-packing pints for sale all around New England. Evil Big Business threatens when corporate behemoth Pillsbury, owners of the leading super-premium ice cream, Häagen-Dazs, tries to do in the aspiring hippies by forcing distributors to choose between the leading brand and the upstarts from Vermont. But the puckish Cohen and Greenfield take their case directly to the people with the war cry, "What's the Doughboy afraid of?" Pillsbury backs down, and the barrage of favorable publicity rockets Ben & Jerry's into every market in the nation. 12

Already successful beyond their wildest imaginings, Cohen and Greenfield become capitalist Robin Hoods, bestowing generous salaries and benefits on their lower-rung employees, buying blueberries from Native American tribes and brownies from a bakery that hires homeless workers. They set up a foundation to donate 7.5% of their pretax profits ($808,000 in 1993) to groups supporting AIDS patients, homeless people and environmental causes. Community spirit and a stubborn insistence on Doing the Right Thing add depth to the company's alternative-business persona, but as the movie makes clear, the real source of Ben & Jerry's triumph—and last May, Ben & Jerry's surpassed Häagen-Dazs to become the nation's top-selling super-premium ice cream—is the company's human scale. And it is this very thought that concludes the Ben & Jerry's movie, cast into a catchy jingle: 13

There ain't no Häagen, there ain't no Dazs,
There ain't no Frusen, there ain't no Glädjè,
There ain't no one named Steve at Steve's,
But there's two real guys at Ben & Jerry's!

When I shake hands with the two real guys, they look like they have just rolled out of bed. It is 8:30 on a Tuesday morning, and the founders of Ben & Jerry's are back from a weeklong business trip, their shirts untucked, hair standing at eccentric angles, eyelids heavy with sleep or the lack of it. But even as jet-lagged, middle-aged founders of a company that employs 600 workers, Cohen (the bearded, balding one) and Greenfield (the baby-faced one) project a laid-back boyishness. This morning they come wielding Native American ceremonial rattles, just-discovered gifts that will join the amiable clutter of toys, books and CDs crowding their small enclave. Joined by a sliding glass door, their walls papered with posters, the connected offices feel like a clubhouse. A small freezer packed with ice cream samples hums in the corner, and a sweet, milky aroma thickens the air. 14

This clubhouse, however, has been a busy place lately. Putting aside their rattles, Cohen and Greenfield talk about expanding their grasp on the American market, of ramping up new product lines and following Häagen-Dazs into overseas markets. Cohen once equated corporate growth with spiritual death, but he has a new perspective, "I think growth is exciting," he says. "It's, uh—" 15

"Exhilarating!" cries the more outgoing Greenfield. "Intoxicating." 16

And frequently hobbled by their social priorities. When increased demand forced the company to lease production space at a factory in Indiana, for instance, it shipped Vermont dairy products to the Midwest production line rather than violate the pledge to use only local milk and cream. And while Ben & Jerry's staff is proud of the fact that the brownies in their treats come from a New York bakery that employs homeless people, they rarely discuss the efforts taken to help the Greyston Bakery ship brownies that didn't have to be separated with a hammer and chisel. 17

The tangling of social and business goals is only one of the problems souring life within the ice cream empire. As those happy-go-lucky "Yo! We want *you* to be our CEO!" posters proclaim, none of the executives at Ben & Jerry's has ever worked in a company as large as Ben & Jerry's. That observation may be funny on a poster, but it seems much less amusing to the company's staff when materials don't arrive at factories on time, production lines get backed up, and no one can describe exactly why things keep turning out that way. "There's a lot of responsibility going head-to-head with Häagen-Dazs," says Fletcher Dean, who works in the public relations department. "You'll see people in the hallway ready to tear their hair out." 18

By the end of 1994, the internal mood had become so dark, says Elizabeth Bankowski, who directs the company's social mission, that the company asked author Milton Moskowitz to remove them from the most recent 19 edition of "The 100 Best Companies to Work for in America." Why? "Because we're not!" Bankowski grieves. "We're going through tough times, and people are not feeling happy about the way we've managed the company in the last year."

That includes Wall Street. As a plummeting stock price (as low as 9 1/2 from a high of 33 3/4) might indicate, the financial district is not pleased. It's time, says Jean-Michel Valette, a senior analyst for San Francisco's Hambrecht & Quist, for Ben & Jerry's to admit it's a mainstream business. "They've already built a strong brand image with real appeal to the consumer," Valette says. "That's magic. Now they have to fix the easy part. They need to embrace people who can help the company navigate the traditional issues: Distribution, production, management." 20

But whoever emerges from the field of 20 CEO finalists culled by the headhunt (which included two or three candidates from the "Yo!" essay contest), will still be running a company that weighs the bottom line of its social mission just as seriously as its economic bottom line. "At Ben & Jerry's," Cohen explains, "we see ourselves as somewhat of a social service agency and somewhat of an ice cream company. We seek to hire people who support the goals of the company—to produce the highest-possible quality ice cream, to make a reasonable profit and to institute a concern for the social benefit of the community." [Bob Holland is Ben & Jerry's new CEO.] 21

Cohen knows that Ben & Jerry's finely tuned sense of morality is crucial to its financial performance. When he talks about the company's commitment to the Greyston Bakery, for instance, a dreamy look passes over his ruddy features. He muses about how we're all part of the same spirit energy, so the positive energy that goes into supporting Greyston comes back to the company through increased ice cream sales. "You could never prove that," he acknowledges. "But just because it's intangible doesn't mean it's not true and not valid. And we're saying it is." 22

• • •

Not everyone in business accepts the notion that the community's best interests are served by companies that take pains to do good. As conservative economist Milton Friedman once asserted, a business's real social responsibility is to make lots of money for its shareholders, create jobs for the community and pay taxes to the government. Thus, opulent employee benefits, self-imposed Earth taxes and the like only compromise the business's actual purpose. Another risk of being so outwardly pious is in setting a standard, even a perceived standard, that you'll never be able to meet. . . . 23

[T]he fact that Ben & Jerry's takes such pains to maintain its products' purity only made it more delicious for the media to report last summer that the company had discovered artificial flavors in some of their mix-in products and that the cherries in Cherry Garcia were preserved with sulfur dioxide. So much for "all-natural," sniggered a chorus of wise-guy reporters, although most neglected to mention that the revelations about the artificial ingredients came straight from Ben & Jerry's 1993 annual report. 24

Ben Cohen accepts this criticism with a shrug. "The purpose of aspirations," he says, "is to have something to work toward. If you achieve all of your aspirations, well, you didn't set your aspirations high enough." 25

• • •

Cohen *is* looking tired as we wrap up our conversation in the cozy little clubhouse he shares with Jerry Greenfield. It's probably the jet lag weighing down his eyelids, but then again, things are rarely what they seem in the world of big business. The Two Real Guys of ice cream say they're committed to making business a less artificial experience. Still, industry spins its illusions, even at Ben & Jerry's. For instance, all of that childlike Ben & Jerry's script, once hand-lettered by their friend Lynn Severence, is now a computer-generated font. 26

"Well," Greenfield says, "there was a time when I answered every customer letter individually. That wasn't an image, that was reality, in the same way having one person do our hand-lettering was reality. But we can't do that anymore. It's too much for a single person to do." 27

Granted. But like all triumphant alternative entrepreneurs, Cohen and Greenfield must measure the distance between where they started and where they are now and pose a few unsettling questions. Does the pressure of the marketplace inevitably erode your soul? Will success render Ben & Jerry into corporate icons, as hollow and artificial as the Pillsbury Doughboy? Or can a bit of humanity filter through the vastness of a multinational corporation? Cohen thinks it can. "The gas station might have been funky in relation to other mom and pop shops," he says. "Ben & Jerry's today is funky in relation to other $150-million corporations." 28

▲ ▲ ▲

Review Questions

1. What are some of the policies distinguishing Ben & Jerry's from other corporations?
2. What is the fundamental challenge facing Ben & Jerry's?
3. How did the pressures of success take their toll on Ben & Jerry's?
4. Recount Ben & Jerry's run-in with Pillsbury.
5. The drive for higher profits was not the only pressure leading Ben & Jerry's to search for new management. What were the other pressures at work?

Discussion and Writing Suggestions

1. Ben Cohen and Jerry Greenfield do not fit Milton Friedman's definition of the profit-seeking manager "agent"; nor do shareholders of Ben & Jerry's fit Friedman's profile of investors who demand ever-higher profits. While the company is earning $150 million annually, there are indications that operations are not smooth (hence, the hir-

ing of a new CEO). To what degree do the successes and challenges of Ben & Jerry's undercut or confirm the foundations of Friedman's argument?

2. Reread paragraph 8. How do you suppose Milton Friedman would respond to the questions at the end of the paragraph?
3. Go eat several pints of Ben & Jerry's ice cream with your friends. Do a search in several electronic databases to locate articles on Ben & Jerry's growing business through 1994, and then write the 100-word essay explaining why you want to become the company's new CEO.
4. "As long as Ben & Jerry's continues pumping out New York Super Fudge Chunk and Wavy Gravy, why should an ice cream lover ponder the ethics of internal corporate machinations" (paragraph 11). Your answer—both with respect to Ben and Jerry's ice cream and, more generally, with respect to consumer products?
5. When searching for a new CEO, Ben Cohen said: "we see ourselves as somewhat of a social service agency and somewhat of an ice cream company. We seek to hire people who support the goals of the company—to produce the highest-possible quality ice cream, to make a reasonable profit and to institute a concern for the social benefit of the community" (paragraph 21). Based on your impressions of business life in America, how typical is this corporate self-portrait?
6. Respond in writing to any of the questions from the article's final paragraph.

Ethics in Business

GERALD F. CAVANAGH

The case method is used as an instructional strategy in schools of business and departments of business ethics in colleges and universities around the country. Students read varied accounts (real or hypothetical) of life in the world of business and then are asked to analyze a case and advise the principals what to do. For instance, students of business might read about specific business transactions (or the preliminaries leading up to such transactions); accounts of interpersonal behaviors within organizations that call for management to take action; or accounts of organizational structures and how these impede or promote productivity. One class of cases that students are increasingly being asked to read involves ethical dilemmas faced by corporate executives, managers, and individual contributors. In all these cases, students are expected to conduct a systematic analysis and make specific, defensible recommendations.

In cases concerning financial analysis, you would perhaps be asked to use spreadsheets in arriving at your recommendations. In cases concerning ethical analysis, you would be expected to use one or another model—a set of well-defined criteria—in arriving at your recommenda-

tions. Gerald Cavanagh offers such a model in his "Ethics in Business," which appeared originally in his American Business Values *(1984), a text written for college course work. You'll find Cavanagh's discussion clearly written and organized (divided into sections and subsections), but you may also find the discussion somewhat difficult, for Cavanagh must define three ethical theories in order to establish his model for decision making. Read slowly, take notes, and respond to all the review questions on page 811 as you read, and you will find the discussion in your grasp—which is important, because you'll be asked to apply Cavanagh's model to several cases.*

Gerald Cavanagh is professor of management, associate dean, and director of Graduate Programs in the University of Detroit's College of Business and Administration. Cavanagh holds a B.S. in engineering, has graduate degrees in philosophy, theology, and management (Ph.D., Michigan State University), and was ordained a Jesuit priest in 1964. He has served on boards of trustees of several universities, and he referees papers for several scholarly journals and for national meetings of the Academy of Management. He has also given ethics workshops at universities throughout the country.

> Freedom is expendable, stability is indispensable.
>
> —Arnold Toynbee

No human institution can long exist without some consensus on what is right and what is wrong. Managers recognize the need for ethical norms in their daily dealings. Decisions made at every level of the firm are influenced by ethics, whether these be decisions which affect quality of work, employment opportunity, safety of worker or product, truth in advertising, use of toxic materials, or operations in third world countries. An increasing sense of the importance of ethical norms among executives is demonstrated by the facts that 1

1. Almost three-quarters of U.S. firms now have a code of ethics.[1]
2. More than 100 boards of directors of large firms have established an ethics, social responsibility, or public policy committee of the board.[2]
3. Speeches of chief executive officers and annual reports more often allude to the importance of ethics in business decisions.[3]

---

[1]According to a survey by Opinion Research Corporation, 73 percent of the larger corporations in the United States now have a written code of ethics. See *Chronicle of Higher Education.* August 6, 1979, p. 2. [All footnotes by Cavanagh unless otherwise noted.]

[2]"Business Strategies for the 1980's," in *Business and Society: Strategies for the 1980's* (Washington, D.C.: U.S. Department of Commerce, 1980), pp. 33–34.

[3]For example, Reginald Jones of General Electric, who was selected by his fellow CEOs as the best CEO, has often made a strong case for ethics. See, for example, Reginald Jones, "Managing in the 1980's," address at Wharton School, February 4, 1980, p. 5. See also Richard J. Bennett, chairman of Schering-Plough, "A New Compact in the Age of Limits," address at Fordham University, November 5, 1981.

Managers understand that without ethics the only restraint is the law. Without ethics, any business transaction that was not witnessed and recorded could not be trusted. If government regulation and legislation are perceived to be unneeded and burdensome, then each manager must possess a set of internalized and operative ethical criteria for decision making. Or, as some have put it: "Shall we be honest and free, or dishonest and policed?" 2

NEED FOR ETHICS IN BUSINESS

A significant minority of large American firms have been involved not only in unethical activities but also in illegal activities. During the 1970s, 11 percent of the largest U.S. firms were convicted of bribery, criminal fraud, illegal campaign contributions, tax evasion, or some sort of price fixing. Firms with two or more convictions include Allied, American Airlines, Bethlehem Steel, Diamond International, Firestone, Goodyear, International Paper, J. Ray McDermott, National Distillers, Northrop, Occidental Petroleum, Pepsico, Phillips Petroleum, Rapid-American, R. J. Reynolds, Schlitz, Seagram, Tenneco, and United Brands. Those that lead the list with at least four convictions each are Braniff International, Gulf Oil, and Ashland Oil.[4] Perhaps Gulf and Ashland will suffer the same punishment meted out to [now bankrupt] Braniff! 3

Most of the major petroleum firms illegally contributed to Richard Nixon's reelection committee in the mid-1970s: Gulf, Getty, Standard of California, Phillips, Sun, Exxon, and Ashland. The chairman of Phillips personally handed Richard Nixon $50,000 in Nixon's own apartment. Many firms were also involved in multimillion-dollar foreign payments: Exxon, Lockheed, Gulf, Phillips, McDonnell Douglas, United Brands, and Mobil.[5] The presidents of Gulf, American Airlines, and Lockheed lost their jobs because of the unethical payments. Other presidents just as guilty—Northrop, Phillips, and Exxon—were excused by their boards. Firms based in the United States are, of course, not alone in engaging in unethical behavior. Sixteen executives of two large Japanese electronics firms, Hitachi and Mitsubishi, were indicted for stealing trade secrets from IBM.[6] 4

Corporate Pressure and Fraud

Embezzlement, fraud, and political backbiting are most often due to personal greed. Bribery, price fixing, and compromising product and worker safety generally stem from the pressure for bottom line results. In a study 5

[4]Irwin Ross, "How Lawless Are Big Companies?" *Fortune,* December 1, 1980, pp. 56–64. See also Robert K. Elliott and John J. Willingham, *Management Fraud: Detection and Deterrence* (New York: Petrocelli Books, 1980).

[5]Marshall B. Clinard and Peter C. Yeager, *Corporate Crime* (New York: Free Press, 1980); and "Drive to Curb Kickbacks and Bribes by Business," *U.S. News & World Report,* September 4, 1978, pp. 41–44.

[6]"IBM Data Plot Tied to Hitachi and Mitsubishi." *Wall Street Journal,* June 23, 1982, p. 4.

of managers at several firms, 59 to 70 percent "feel pressured to compromise personal ethics to achieve corporate goals."[7] This perception increases among lower level managers. A majority felt that most managers would not refuse to market off-standard and possibly dangerous products. On the more encouraging side, 90 percent supported a code of ethics for business and the teaching of ethics in business schools.

This pressure and organizational climate can influence the ethical 6
judgments of individual managers. What the manager finds unethical in another setting or before taking this job is more readily considered acceptable behavior once the job is taken. Two recent research studies question whether American executives have a sufficient sensitivity to ethical issues, and whether their work environment works against such a sensitivity. Public affairs officers in firms have the direct responsibility for dealing with a wide variety of stakeholders: customers, suppliers, local community, and shareholders. These officers are a principal conduit through which the firm is informed of new social concerns. Evidence shows that even though these public affairs officers spend more time with these various stakeholders, they tend to be poor listeners. In fact, according to this study, the more contact company officers have with external publics, the less sensitive they become to their concerns.[8]

Another study was in an ethically sensitive area: corporate political ac- 7
tivities. It was found that the more involvement a company officer had in these activities, the less likely he or she would be alert to ethical issues. The more involved the manager was, the more dulled became her or his conscience. There are many ethically debatable areas with regard to a firm's political activities, and this evidence shows that those who are most involved in these activities are precisely those who are less sensitive to the moral and ethical issues involved. The more involved manager is more likely to declare a debatable activity to be ethically acceptable and is also more likely to declare as gray an activity that fellow managers would declare ethically unacceptable.[9]

Laboratory research has shown that unethical behavior tends to rise as 8
the climate becomes more competitive, and it increases even more if such behavior is rewarded. However, a threat of punishment tends to deter unethical behavior. Whether a person acts ethically or unethically is also very strongly influenced by the individual's personal ethical values and by informal organizational policy.[10]

---

[7]Archie Carroll, "Managerial Ethics: A Post-Watergate View," *Business Horizons,* April 1975, pp. 75–80; and "The Pressure to Compromise Personal Ethics," *Business Week,* January 31, 1977, p. 107. See also "Some Middle Managers Cut Corners to Achieve High Corporate Goals," *Wall Street Journal,* November 8, 1979, pp. 1, 19.

[8]Jeffrey Sonnenfeld, "Executive Differences in Public Affairs Information Gathering," *Academy of Management Proceedings,* 1981, ed. Kae H. Chung, p. 353.

[9]Steven N. Brenner, "Corporate Political Actions and Attitudes," *Academy of Management Proceedings,* 1981, pp. 361–362.

[10]W. Harvey Hegarty and Henry P. Sims Jr., "Unethical Decision Behavior: An Overview of Three Experiments," *Academy of Management Proceedings,* 1979, p. 9.

These instances of unethical behavior of managers point to the need for (1) a sensitive and informed conscience, (2) the ability to make ethical judgments, and (3) a corporate climate that rewards ethical behavior and punishes unethical behavior. Technical education does not bring with it better ethics, as we have seen, for example in Nazi Germany. In fact, as society becomes more technical, complex, and interdependent, the need for ethics increases dramatically. When encounters are person to person, there exists the built-in sanction of having to live with the people one has lied to. In the large, complex organization, or when one deals with people over the telephone or via a computer, ethical sensitivities and decision-making abilities are far more important. 9

Ethical Theories

Ethical criteria and ethical models have been the subject of considerable thinking over the centuries. Of all the ethical systems, businesspeople feel most at home with utilitarian theory—and not surprisingly, as it traces its origins to Adam Smith, the father of both modern economics and utilitarian ethics. Jeremy Bentham[11] and John Stuart Mill[12] more precisely formulated utilitarianism a bit later. Utilitarianism evaluates behavior in terms of its consequences. That action which results in the greatest net gain for all parties is considered moral. 10

Rights theories focus on the entitlements of individual persons. Immanuel Kant[13] (personal rights) and John Locke[14] (property rights) were the first to present developed theories of rights. Justice theories have a longer tradition, going back to Plato and Aristotle in the fifth century B.C.[15] Theoretical work in each of these traditions has continued to the present.[16] For an overview of these three theories—history, strengths and weaknesses, and when most useful—see Table A. 11

Utilitarianism

Utilitarianism judges that an action is right if it produces the greatest utility, "the greatest good for the greatest number." It is very much like a cost-benefit analysis applied to all parties who would be touched by a particular decision: That action is right that produces the greatest net benefit, when all 12

---

[11]Jeremy Bentham, *An Introduction to the Principles of Morals and Legislation* (1789) (New York: Hafner, 1948).

[12]John Stuart Mill, *Utilitarianism* (1863) (Indianapolis, Ind.: Bobbs-Merrill, 1957).

[13]Immanuel Kant, *The Metaphysical Elements of Justice* (1797), tr. J. Ladd (New York: Library of Liberal Arts, 1965).

[14]John Locke, *The Second Treatise of Government* (1690) (New York: Liberal Arts Press, 1952).

[15]Aristotle, *Ethics,* tr. J. A. K. Thomson (London: Penguin, 1953).

[16]For example, John Rawls, *A Theory of Justice* (Cambridge, Mass.: Belknap, 1971). See two books of readings: Thomas Donaldson and Patricia Werhane, *Ethical Issues in Business* (Englewood Cliffs, N.J.: Prentice-Hall, 1979); and Tom Beauchamp and Norman Bowie, *Ethical Theory and Business* (Englewood Cliffs, N.J.: Prentice-Hall, 1979).

Table A. ***Ethical Models for Business Decisions***

DEFINITION AND ORIGIN	STRENGTHS	WEAKNESSES	WHEN USED
Utilitarianism			
"The greatest good for the greatest number: Bentham (1748–1832), Adam Smith (1723–1790), David Ricardo (1772–1823)	1. Concepts, terminology, methods are easiest for businesspersons to work with; justifies a profit maximization system. 2. Promotes view of entire system of exchange beyond "this firm." 3. Encourages entrepreneurship, innovation, productivity.	1. Impossible to measure or quantify all important elements. 2. "Greatest good" can degenerate into self-interest. 3. Can result in abridging person's rights. 4. Can result in neglecting less powerful segments of society.	1. Use in all business decisions, and will be dominant criteria in 90%. 2. Version of model is implicitly used already, although scope is generally limited to "this firm."
Theory of Justice			
Equitable distribution of society's benefits and burdens: Aristotle (384–322 B.C.), Rawls (1921-)	1. The "democratic" principle. 2. Does not allow a society to become status- or class-dominated. 3. Ensure that minorities, poor, handicapped receive opportunities and a fair share of output.	1. Can result in less risk, incentive, and innovation. 2. Encourages sense of "entitlement."	1. In product decisions usefulness to *all* in society. 2. In setting salaries for unskilled workers, executives. 3. In public policy decisions: to maintain a floor of living standards for all. 4. Use with, for example, performance appraisal, due process, distribution of rewards and punishments.
Theory of Rights			
Individual's freedom is not to be violated: Locke (1635–1701)—property; Kant (1724–1804)—personal rights	1. Ensures respect for individual's property and personal freedom. 2. Parallels political "Bill of Rights."	1. Can encourage individualistic, selfish behavior.	1. Where individual's property or personal rights are in question. 2. Use with, for example, employee privacy, job tenure, work dangerous to person's health.

the costs and benefits to all the affected parties are taken into consideration. Although it would be convenient if these costs and benefits could be measured in some comparable unit, this is not always possible. Many important values (for example, human life and liberty) cannot be quantified. So it is sufficient to state the number and the magnitude of the costs and benefits as clearly and accurately as possible.

The utilitarian principle says that the right action is that which produces the greatest net benefit over any other possible action. However, this does not mean that the best act is that which produces the greatest good for the person performing the action. Rather, it is the action that produces the greatest summed net good for all those who are affected by the action. Utilitarianism can handle some ethical cases quite well, especially those that are complex and affect many parties. Although the model and the methodology are clear, carrying out the calculations is often difficult. Taking into account so many affected parties, along with the extent to which the action touches them, can be a calculation nightmare. 13

Hence several shortcuts have been proposed that can reduce the complexity of utilitarian calculations. Each shortcut involves a sacrifice of accuracy for ease of calculation. Among these shortcuts are (1) adherence to a simplified rule (for example, the Golden Rule, "Do unto others as you would have them do unto you"); (2) for ease of comparison, calculate costs and benefits in dollar terms; and (3) take into account only those directly affected by the action, putting aside indirect effects. In using the above decision-making strategies, an individual should be aware that they are simplifications and that some interests may not be sufficiently taken into consideration. 14

A noteworthy weakness of utilitarianism as an ethical norm is that it can advocate, for example, abridging an individual's right to a job or even life, for the sake of the greater good of a larger number of people. This, and other difficulties, are discussed elsewhere.[17] One additional caution in using utilitarian rules is in order: It is considered unethical to opt for the benefit of narrower goals (for example, personal goals, career, or money) at the expense of the good of a larger number, such as a nation or a society. Utilitarian norms emphasize the good of the group; it is a large-scale ethical model. In this sort of calculation, an individual and what is due that individual may be underemphasized. Rights theory has been developed to give appropriate emphasis to the individual and the standing of that individual with peers and within society. 15

Rights of the Individual

A right is a person's entitlement to something.[18] Rights may flow from the legal system, such as the U.S. constitutional rights of freedom of conscience or freedom of speech. The U.S. Bill of Rights and the United Na- 16

[17]Gerald F. Cavanagh, Dennis J. Moberg, and Manuel Velasquez, "The Ethics of Organizational Politics," *Academy of Management Review,* 6 (July 1981), 363–374; and the more complete treatments in Manuel Velasquez, *Business Ethics: Concepts and Cases* (Englewood Cliffs, N.J.: Prentice-Hall, 1982), pp. 46–58; and Richard T. De George, *Business Ethics* (New York: Macmillan, 1982), pp. 47–54.

[18]Velasquez, *Business Ethics,* p. 29. See also Thomas Donaldson, *Corporations and Morality* (Englewood Cliffs, N.J.: Prentice-Hall, 1982).

tions Universal Declaration of Human Rights are classical examples of individual rights spelled out in some detail in documents. Legal rights, as well as others which may not be written into law, stem from the human dignity of the person. Moral rights have these characteristics: (1) They enable individuals to pursue their own interests, and (2) they impose correlative prohibitions and/or requirements on others. That is, every right has a corresponding duty. My right to freedom of conscience is supported by the prohibition of other individuals from unnecessarily limiting that freedom of conscience. From another perspective, my right to be paid for my work corresponds to a duty of mine to perform "a fair day's work for a fair day's pay." In the latter case, both the right and duty stem from the right to private property, which is a traditional pillar of American life and law. However, the right to private property is not absolute. A factory owner may be forced by law, as well as by morality, to spend money on pollution control or safety equipment. For a listing of selected rights and other ethical norms, see Table B.

Judging morality by reference to individual rights is quite different 17
from using utilitarian standards. Rights express the requirements of morality from the standpoint of the individual; rights protect the individual from the encroachment and demands of society or the state. Utilitarian standards promote society's benefit and are relatively insensitive to a single individual, except insofar as that individual's welfare affects the overall good of society.

A business contract establishes rights and duties that were not there be- 18
fore: The right of the purchaser to receive what was agreed upon, and the right of the seller to be paid what was agreed. Formal written contracts and informal verbal agreements are essential to business transactions.

Immanuel Kant recognized that an emphasis on rights can lead one to 19
focus largely on what is due oneself. So he formulated what he called his "categorical imperatives." As the first of these, Kant said, "I ought never to act except in such a way that I can also will that my maxim should become a universal law." Another way of putting this is: "An action is morally right for a person in a certain situation if and only if the person's reason for carrying out the action is a reason that he would be willing to have every person act on, in any similar situation."[19] As a measure of a difficult judgment, Kant asks if our reason for taking this action is the same reason that would allow others to do the same thing. Note that Kant is focusing on a person's motivation or intention, and not on the consequences of the action, as is true of utilitarianism.

Kant's second categorical imperative cautions us against using other 20
people as a means to our own ends: "Never treat humanity simply as a means, but always also as an end." An interpretation of the second imperative is: "An action is morally right for a person if and only if in performing

[19]Immanuel Kant, *Groundwork of the Metaphysics of Morals,* tr. H. J. Paton (New York: Harper & Row, 1964), pp. 62–90. See also Velasquez, *Business Ethics,* pp. 66–69.

TABLE B. ***Some Selected Ethical Norms***

Utilitarian

1. *Organizational goals* should aim at *maximizing the satisfactions* of the organization's constituencies.
2. The members of an organization should attempt to gain its goals as *efficiently* as possible by consuming as few inputs as possible and by minimizing the external costs which organizational activities impose on others.
3. The employee should use *every effective means* to achieve the goals of the organization, and should neither jeopardize those goals nor enter situations in which personal interests conflict significantly with the goals.

Rights

1. *Life and safety:* The individual has the right not to have her or his life or safety unknowingly and unnecessarily endangered.
2. *Truthfulness.* The individual has a right not to be intentionally deceived by another, especially on matters about which the individual has the right to know.
3. *Privacy:* The individual has the right to do whatever he or she chooses to do outside working hours and to control information about his or her private life.
4. *Freedom of conscience:* The individual has the right to refrain from carrying out any order that violates those commonly accepted moral or religious norms to which the person adheres.
5. *Free speech:* The individual has the right to criticize conscientiously and truthfully the ethics or legality of corporate actions so long as the criticism does not violate the rights of other individuals within the organization.
6. *Private property:* The individual has a right to hold private property, especially insofar as this right enables the individual and his or her family to be sheltered and to have the basic necessities of life.

Justice

1. *Fair treatment:* Persons who are similar to each other in the relevant respects should be treated similarly; persons who differ in some respect relevant to the job they perform should be treated differently in proportion to the difference between them.
2. *Fair administration of rules:* Rules should be administered consistently, fairly, and impartially.
3. *Fair compensation:* Individuals should be compensated for the cost of their injuries by the party that is responsible for those injuries.
4. *Fair blame:* Individuals should not be held responsible for matters over which they have no control.
5. *Due process:* The individual has a right to a fair and impartial hearing when he or she believes that personal rights are being violated.

Source: Reprinted by permission of American Management Association from *Organizational Dynamics,* Autumn 1983.

the action the person does not use others merely as a means for advancing his or her own interests, but also both respects and develops their capacity to choose for themselves."[20] Capital, plant, and machines are all to be used to serve men and women's purposes. On the other hand, individual persons are not to be used merely as instruments for achieving one's interests. This rules out deception, manipulation, and exploitation of other people.

[20]Kant, *Groundwork;* Velasquez, *Business Ethics,* p. 68.

Justice

Justice requires all persons, and thus managers too, to be guided by fairness, equity, and impartiality. Justice calls for evenhanded treatment of groups and individuals (1) in the distribution of the benefits and burdens of society, (2) in the administration of laws and regulations, and (3) in the imposition of sanctions and means of compensation for wrongs a person has suffered. An action or policy is just in comparison with the treatment accorded to others. 21

Standards of justice are generally considered to be more important than utilitarian consideration of consequences. If a society is unjust to some group of its members (for example, apartheid treatment of blacks in South Africa), we generally consider that society unjust and condemn it, even if the results of the injustices bring about greater productivity. On the other hand, we seem to be willing to trade off some equity, if the results will bring about greater benefits for all. 22

Standards of justice are not as often in conflict with individual rights as are utilitarian norms. This is not surprising, since justice is largely based on the moral rights of individuals. The moral right to be treated as a free and equal person, for example, undergirds the notion that benefits and burdens should be distributed equitably. Personal moral rights are so basic that they generally may not be traded off (for example, free consent, right to privacy, freedom of conscience, right to due process) to bring about a better distribution of benefits in a society. On the other hand, property rights may be abridged (for example, graduated income tax, tax on pollution) for the sake of a more fair distribution of benefits and burdens. 23

Distributive justice becomes important when there are not enough of society's goods to satisfy all needs or not enough people to bear the burdens. The question then becomes: What is a just distribution? The fundamental principle is that equals should be treated equally, and unequals treated in accord with their inequality. For example, few would argue that a new person who is hired for the same job as a senior worker with twenty years' experience should receive the same pay as the experienced worker. People performing work of greater responsibility or working more difficult hours would be eligible for greater pay. However, it is clear that pay differentials should be related to the work itself, not on some arbitrary bias of the employer. 24

Having said all of the above does not determine what is a fair distribution of society's benefits and burdens. In fact quite different notions of equity are generally proposed. A classic difference is the capitalist model (justice based on contribution) versus the socialist ("from each according to abilities, to each according to needs"). A more recent contribution to justice theory has been the work of John Rawls.[21] Rawls would have us construct the rules and laws of society as if we did not know what role we were to play in that society. We do not know if we would be rich or poor, male or 25

[21]Rawls, *A Theory of Justice.*

female, African or European, manager or slave, handicapped or physically and mentally fit. He calls this the "veil of ignorance." The exercise is intended to try to rid ourselves of our status, national, and sexist biases. Under such circumstances each of us would try to design the rules of society to be of the greatest benefits to all, and not to undermine the position of any group. Thus Rawls proposes that people generally develop two principles:

1. Each person is to have an equal right to the most extensive liberty compatible with similar liberty for others.
2. Social and economic inequalities are to be arranged so that they are both reasonably expected to be to everyone's advantage and attached to positions and offices open to all.

The first principle is consonant with the American sense of liberty and thus is not controversial in the United States. The second principle is more egalitarian, and also more controversial. However, Rawls maintains that if people are honest behind the "veil of ignorance" they will opt for a system of justice that is most fair to all members of that society.

SOLVING ETHICAL DILEMMAS

Any human judgment is preceded by two steps: gathering data and analyz- **26**
ing the data. Before any ethically sensitive situation can be assessed, it is essential that all the relevant data be at hand. As an aid to analysis, the three classical norms—utility, rights, and justice—have been offered. For a schematic diagram of how ethical decision making can proceed, see Figure A. The diagram is simplified, but nevertheless it can be an aid in our handling of ethical problems.

Let us apply our scheme to the case of an executive padding her ex- **27**
pense account.[22] For our purposes, we will accept the limited data as provided in the case. Applying the utility criteria, we would judge that although padding the expense account satisfies the interests of the executive doing it, it does not optimize the concerns of others: shareholders, customers, more honest executives, and people in other firms in similar situations. It also adds to the expense of doing business. Hence, it seems that utility would not allow for such padding. The rights of individuals are not so involved here: The executive has no right to the extra money, although we might make the case that the shareholders' and customers' right to private property is being violated. With regard to justice, salary and commissions are the ordinary compensation for individuals. Expense accounts have a quite different purpose.

[22]Cavanagh, here, is referring to a case in which "an executive earning $30,000 a year has been padding his/her expense account by about $1,500 a year." In a survey of 1,700 "business execu-e readers of *Harvard Business Review,"* 85 percent thought that the padding—or false report-; of expenses—was unethical. [Behrens and Rosen]

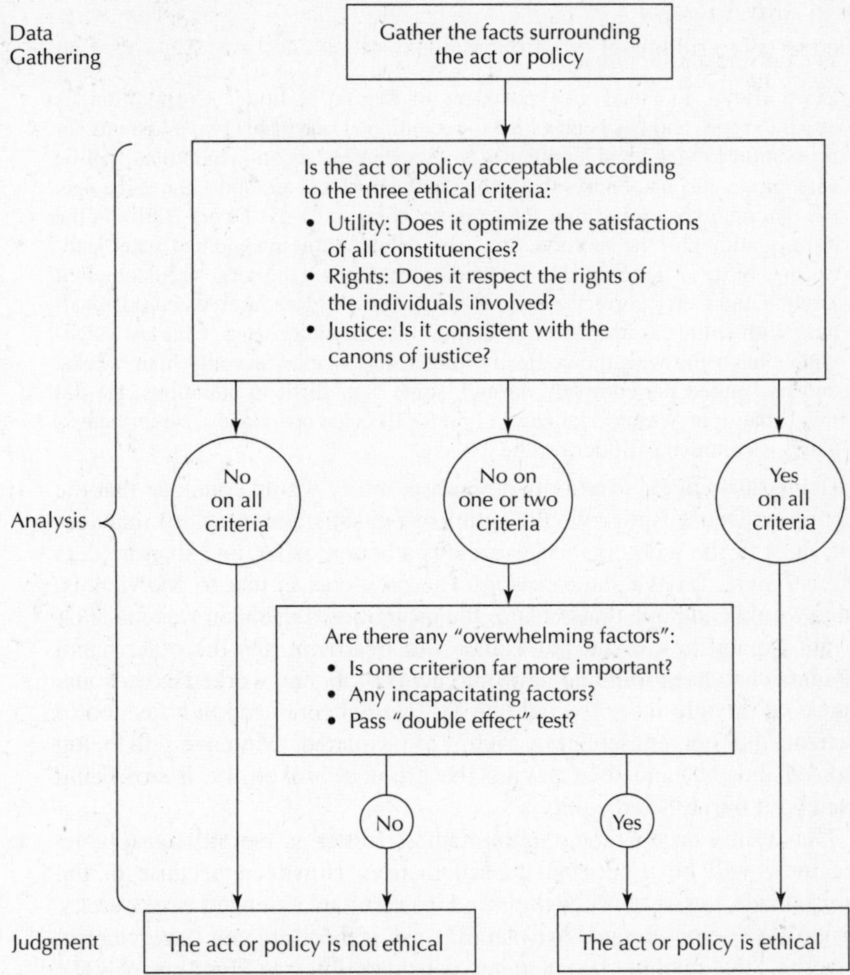

FIGURE A. ***Flow diagram of ethical decision making.***
Source: Reprinted by permission of American Management Association from *Organizational Dynamics.* Autumn 1983. © 1983. American Management Association, N. Y. All rights reserved.

In this instance, most managers responding to the case held that it was unethical for the executive to pad her expense account. John Rawls would maintain that any one of us would set the rules in this fashion, given the fact that we would not know what role we ourselves would have in the society. Hence, we conclude that padding one's expense account is judged unethical on all three ethical norms, so it is clearly wrong. Notice that this agrees with the judgment of 73 percent of the executives who were asked. **28**

On the other hand, the *Wall Street Journal* recently described an entrepreneur who sells blank official-looking receipts of fifty different plausible but fictitious restaurants. The individual can then fill out the receipts as he likes and can submit them to his firm for reimbursement. And he has the receipts to prove the purchase of the meal! What would we say of the ethics of selling such receipts? Of purchasing them and using them? **29**

Model Aids Solution

Let us examine another case: 30

> Brian Curry, financial vice president of Digital Robotics Corporation, is about to retire and has been asked to recommend one of his two assistants for promotion to vice president. Curry knows that his recommendations will be acted upon. He also knows that, since both assistants are about the same age, the one not chosen will find future promotions unlikely. Debra Butler is the most qualified for the position. She is bright and outgoing and has better leadership ability. Moreover, her father is president of the largest customer of Digital, and Curry correctly reasons that they will more likely keep this business with Butler as an officer of Digital. On the other hand, Charles McNicholas has been with the company longer, has worked seventy-hour weeks, and has pulled the company through some very difficult situations. He did this because he was told he was in line for the vice presidency. Nevertheless, Curry recommends Butler for the job.

Using our schema to examine this case, utility would conclude that the selection of Debra Butler would optimize the satisfaction of top management, most of the workers, because she is a better leader, and shareholders and customers, for the same reason. The only cost is that to McNichols. Justice would conclude that because the promotional decision was made on relevant capabilities, it did not violate fair treatment. On the other hand, McNichols had been told that he would get the job, and worked extra hours because he thought the job would be his. He is being used in a fashion to which he did not consent. His rights are violated. Moreover, in being promised the job, and then having the promise broken, he is not being treated with fairness and equity. 31

Thus utility accepts the appointment of Butler as morally acceptable, since there will be a net gain in satisfaction. However, because of the promise made earlier to McNichols and his resultant extended work weeks, his rights are being violated.We can then ask if there are any "overwhelming factors" that ought to be taken into consideration (see Figure A, p. 807). 32

Overwhelming Factors

"Overwhelming factors" are data from the situation which may, in a given case, justify overriding one of the three ethical criteria: utility, rights, or justice. Overwhelming factors can be examined when there is a conflict in the conclusions drawn from the ethical norms. The first of the overwhelming factors are *incapacitating factors.* That is, if there are any elements that coerce an individual into a certain posture, then that individual is not held to be fully responsible. Managers at an H. J. Heinz plant felt great pressure from top management to show a profit. They could not do as well as was expected, so they began to juggle the books. While this meant cumulative overstatement of profits of $8.5 million, the managers who did the falsification would probably be judged less unethical than the top management that brought the unrelenting pressure to bear. Even though the act of falsifying 33 the books was objectively unethical, the plant manager did not bear full responsibility because he was pressured by superiors.[23]

Second, the manager might not be able to utilize the criteria because she does not possess full information. She might think that another employee is embezzling from the bank. However, to report the employee to superiors might ruin the individual's reputation. So, even though stealing is a violation of justice, in this case there is not yet sufficient information to utilize the criteria. Finally, the manager may be sincerely uncertain of the criteria or their applicability in this particular case. 34

To return to the appointment of a financial vice president case: While utility would clearly call for recommending Debra Butler for the vice president's position, justice would call for considering McNichols' claim on the position more strongly. McNichols has worked harder, having considered this to be proportionate to the future promised reward. Moreover, since the position has been promised to him, fair treatment would call for some special consideration. Justice would probably say that, under these special circumstances, McNichols should get the position. 35

Because there is now a conflict between these two norms, it is necessary to see if any overwhelming factors should be taken into account. There seems to be little coercion involved, certainly no physical coercion. Curry made his decision freely. There might have been psychological coercion, however, if Debra Butler's father had mentioned the possible promotion to top management at Digital. Even without his mentioning it, the situation may still have caused psychological pressure for Curry. 36

The ultimate solution of this case would depend on a number of factors: How much better a manager would Butler be than McNichols, and how would this affect the firm's performance and the jobs of others at Digital? Exactly what sort of promise was made to McNichols? Was it clear and unequivocal? If the promise was more in McNichols' mind, and if Butler's performance would be judged to be significantly better than McNichols', then Curry could ethically recommend Butler. However, some sort of compensation should be made to McNichols. 37

Another kind of overwhelming factor occurs when criteria come to differing conclusions on the same case. The so-called *principle of double effect* can be useful here. When an act has both a good effect and a bad effect (for example, appointing Butler and not appointing McNichols), one may morally perform the act under three conditions: (1) One does not directly intend the bad effect (Curry is not trying to backstab or get back at McNichols); (2) the bad effect is not a means to the good end but is simply a side effect (the nonappointment of McNichols is not a means to Butler being appointed); and (3) the good effect sufficiently outweighs the bad (Butler's performance would be significantly superior to McNichols'). So this case 38

[23]"Some Middle Managers Cut Corners to Achieve High Corporate Goals," *Wall Street Journal* November 8, 1979, pp. 1, 19.

passes the test of the double effect. Hence, in sum, Curry may ethically recommend Butler for the vice presidency.

Case of the Flammable Crib

Let us examine another case, this one on the issue of product safety and quality: 39

> Assume you are president of a firm which manufactures baby cribs. You have the option of installing either of two pads: a less expensive one which meets what you feel to be too lenient federal safety requirements regarding flammability (a requirement which you are quite sure was established as a result of pressure from your industry) and one which is safe but somewhat more expensive. Assume that the safe pad will not bring a higher price for the crib.

Would using the flammable pad be unjust to purchasers? Initially, it 40
would seem that there is no injustice here—all purchasers of baby cribs are being treated the same. A possible source of injustice, however, would be to the consumer, who is presuming that he is purchasing a safe and not flammable baby crib. When examining rights, this becomes even clearer: The consumer presumes that his baby will be safe and that the product being sold has sufficient safeguards. The fact that the firm meets federal safety requirements does not settle the question, since the president is convinced that these are too lenient and were only set because of pressure from the industry. At stake are the lives of infants who might be burned. In fact, statistics tell us that some infants will be burned needlessly. As with sleepwear and toys, special precautions must be taken with infants and young children, since they cannot protect themselves. Although they don't smoke in bed, they nevertheless cannot put out a fire once it has begun from whatever source.

Applying the utilitarian norm demands weighing the costs and benefits 41
of the two pads to all parties. The cheaper pad would result in lower cost to the consumer and probably better enable the firm to meet the lower price of its competitors. The cost of the lower priced pad would be the cost of the infants who would be burned because the cheaper pad was used. On the other hand, the safer pad could be advertised as such, and it might establish the firm as a manufacturer of safe children's goods. Presuming that there is a significant difference in the flammability, and thus the number of children's lives saved, utility would probably call for installing the safer pad. Since there are no ethical criteria that would call for the installation of the cheaper pad, we can then judge that ethics would ask the president to call for the safer, even though more expensive, pad.

This judgment is also the judgment of corporate executives. In a sur- 42
vey of chief executive officers, 94 percent would use the safe pad, even though it is more expensive.[24] Perhaps these executives are using a shortcut

[24] "Business Executives and Moral Dilemmas," *Business and Society Review* (Spring 1975), p. 55.

ethical test of a possible action: Would I do it if I knew that the decision was to be featured on this evening's TV news? Can my decision bear the sharp scrutiny of a probing reporter?

• • •

Ethics is a system of moral principles and the methods for applying them; ethics thus provides the tools to make moral judgments. It encompasses the language, concepts, and models that enable an individual to effect moral decisions. 43

Mature ethical judgments are not always easy to make. The facts of the case are not always clear-cut; the ethical criteria or principles to be used are not always agreed upon even by the experts themselves. Hence, ethics seems to most businesspeople, indeed to most Americans, to be subjective, amorphous, and ill-defined and thus not very useful. Just as with politics and religion, there is often more heat than light in discussion. This lack of confidence in ethics is unfortunate, since without some commonly agreed-upon ethical principles, it is everyone for himself or herself, and trust, which is basic to all business dealings, is undermined. 44

▲ ▲ ▲

Review Questions

1. Why, in order to prevent the intrusion of government into business, must "each manager . . . possess a set of internalized and operative ethical criteria for decision making"?
2. Briefly decline the ethical theories of utility, justice, and rights.
3. What is an "overwhelming factor" in the context of making a decision about ethics?
4. What is the principle of "double effect," and how is it applied in the context of making a decision about ethics?

Discussion and Writing Suggestions

1. According to Cavanagh, between 59 and 70 percent of managers surveyed "feel pressured to compromise personal ethics to achieve corporate goals." Are you surprised? Why or why not? Develop your response into a brief essay.
2. Do you agree with Cavanagh's analysis of the Digital Robotics case, in which Debra Butler was recommended for vice president over Charles McNichols? Why? If you disagree, provide a rationale for your decision, as Cavanagh does for his.
3. How practical is it, in your view, to apply Cavanagh's flow diagram for making ethical decisions? How important is it for the conduct of ethical business that managers use *some* systematic model for making difficult decisions?

Cases for Analysis and Discussion

Following, you'll find cases for analysis and discussion, each of which will raise certain ethical dilemmas. In business schools around the country, the "case method" is an instructional technique of long standing. Whether the course be in finance, business law, management training, investment strategies, or business ethics, the rationale for presenting cases is the same. The "case," usually a narrative account, re-creates a problem or a particular challenge in a business context. The case amounts to raw data that the student reviews in light of principles learned in class. The student then is asked to define problems and to recommend or evaluate courses of action, based on a clear method of analysis.

The cases that follow present ethical dilemmas that resulted from business dealings. As we've suggested, your job will be to read the cases, to define the problems, and to evaluate or recommend courses of action. What would you do in similar circumstances or if you were asked to advise those involved? What business decisions would follow from your recommendations? What would be the consequences of those decisions? These among other questions are fundamental to case-method instruction.

A Note on the Case Method

DENIS COLLINS
LAURA V. PAGE

The following article introduces the second part of this chapter, "Cases for Analysis and Discussion." In this "Note on the Case Method," Denis Collins, professor of Business Ethics at the University of Wisconsin, Madison, and Laura Page, a management consultant, introduce the rationale behind case studies in business ethics; they also present a second method (in addition to the one offered by Cavanagh) for analyzing the cases that follow.

WHY TEACH ETHICS?

Let's get right down to it. Do you know what *you* would do if you owned a business and: 1

- You must cut back on labor and lay one person off, and you do not have a formal lay-off policy. All your employees are good workers. If you decide to let the person with the least seniority go, this turns out to be a newly hired and talented minority woman, a single mother, who desperately needs your better-than-minimum-wage job.
- You must secure new working capital and an interested investor wants to visit your store at a time when your customer count is typically at its lowest seasonal level. In order to impress the investor,

you consider asking friends to come in and pretend to be shopping at the time of the investor's visit.

- Circumstances have resulted in your having a local monopoly on a product that is in very high demand. You know you can set a price extremely high and sell them all. However, if you charge "whatever the market will bear" for the high-demand product, the price will be well above what your most loyal middle-class customers can afford.

These are not unusual cases for anyone who owns a small business. Ethical dilemmas occur every day. Most business owners and managers view finance, pricing and lay-off problems as business problems, not as ethical problems. But they are ethical problems. Any decision that affects the welfare of other people is an ethical issue. Every issue has the potential to become an ethical dilemma where every possible solution has positive and negative consequences. 2

Our job, and yours—if you accept it—is to help business owner/managers see the ethical nature of their decisions and to give them tools for resolving ethical dilemmas. 3

We have heard many objections from our colleagues, students and clients regarding discussing business ethics. Some argue that the discussion of ethics is a high-brow luxury, which is unnecessary, inconclusive and time-consuming. This is how we respond to objections to the discussion of ethics: 4

- *"Ethics is a 'cost' of doing business that I cannot afford, especially during start-up or hard economic times."* Acting ethically can indeed be costly. However, it can also be more costly to be unethical. Ethics is not an "operating cost" to be measured in dollars and cents. Rather, it is a personal values system that is activated or left dormant at each moment of decision-making. There is no escaping ethics. There is an ethic underlying every business transaction that involves human beings. Sometimes it is a good ethic and sometimes it is a bad ethic. For instance, treating employees with respect and dignity is a good business ethic. Treating employees like tools that can be manipulated, and then discarded, is a bad business ethic.
- *"All ethics are relative; there is no right answer."* Some may argue that ethics are relative and that there is no right answer. It is obvious, however, that some answers are better than others, even when we are unsure what is absolutely right or wrong. Most decisions have more than two alternatives—one right and one wrong. Our modern media have oversimplified our mind-set. Life is more complex than good or bad, true or false, guilty or innocent, yes or no, legal or illegal. Most decisions are a shade of gray. Skilled decision-makers look for the better answer among many alternatives. Generating the alternatives and weighing the consequences are skills to be learned.
- *"Business is business; and the business of business is making profits."* Business must indeed be profitable to survive. However, being

ethical and profitable is not only possible but probable with time and effort. Yes, it will not be easy. Life is not easy.

- *"I am ethical because everything I do is legal."* What is legal is not always ethical, and what is ethical is not always legal. The law is only a guide. It can never translate all our values into what we should and should not do in all circumstances. The law covers only a small part of human activity.
- *"Everyone else does it, including all my competitors, so I am at a competitive disadvantage if I don't do it, too."* Just because everyone else is doing something is not sufficient moral rationale for doing that thing. That may explain it, but it does not justify it. Moral values are not determined simply by majority vote.
- *"It's the government's fault."* Two wrongs do not make a right. Even a government, when wrong, cannot make a right.
- *"I don't have time to worry about ethics."* Time spent carefully considering ethical decisions is wasted only when the decision-maker learns nothing from the effort.
- *"I'm not a philosopher. And they all disagree on what's right and wrong anyway."* Philosophers do not have a monopoly on determining right and wrong behavior. We all judge intentions and behavior every day. Philosophers have simply studied these issues with greater regularity.
- *"Who do you think you are to impose your views on me?"* Based upon our conversations with small business owner/managers and our reading of the business press, it is clear that our society demands more ethical behavior from business today. Business is a social institution. Society is always imposing its views on all of us, and we either accept them or reject them. Our society does have strong positive values that it "imposes" on us, such as honesty, fairness, non-discrimination, loyalty, justice. Sometimes these values are in conflict, sometimes they come into conflict, with profit-making, and sometimes they conflict with the personal values of individuals. The business cases we have written are meant to provoke discussion of values, not to give final answers of right or wrong.

The purpose of facilitating ethical discussions is to give people in- 5
sights into their own ethical reasoning and to encourage them to reflect on their actions. Research on ethical behavior indicates that people generally act in more ethical ways when they are sensitized to the issues and when they discuss the dilemmas with other people. Case study discussions give seminar participants practice in doing exactly that.

• • •

[Analyze a case and decide on a course of action. Subject each course of action (or alternate courses of action) to these five questions before reaching a final decision. Later, you will be called on to use these questions as a guide to making decisions about cases involving business ethics.]

- Will the action clearly help more people than it will harm?
- How well can the people who are harmed recover from the type of harm produced?
- Is this a win-lose solution where the decision-maker wins and the other parties lose?
- What rights/values/principles are being honored?
- What rights/values/principles are being broken?

• • •

By exposing proposed solutions to these questions, the strengths and weaknesses of the answers will come to light. 6

This process will most likely *not* result in your finding one answer that all participants agree is the most ethical. Your goal is not to reach an ultimate consensus or agreement. Rather, your goal is to point out the consequences of behavior and promoting clearer and more subtle thinking on the subject of ethics. . . . 7

A "good" answer [to an ethical problem] is one that minimizes harm to others and does not violate rights, values and principles that are important to the individual and the broader society. Clearly this is a difficult undertaking. Everyone holds a different set of values and prioritizes them differently. Some people, for example, rank freedom above all other values. Others place loyalty to family at the top. Prioritizing values is a never-ending process for society and individuals. Our principles are a function of various factors, including experience, family background, cultural heritage, economic status and church affiliation. The commonalities in values, however, are much greater than the differences. The "relative" nature of ethics has been grossly exaggerated. 8

▲ ▲ ▲

Review Questions

1. How do Collins and Page define an ethical problem?
2. Summarize the often-heard objections to the teaching of business ethics—and summarize the authors' responses.
3. What is the purpose of analyzing cases in business ethics?
4. What is the goal of analyzing the ethical issues in a business decision?
5. What constitutes a "good" answer to an ethical dilemma?

Discussion and Writing Suggestions

1. To what extent do you think discussing fictionalized cases can help your decision-making process when you're confronted with an ethical dilemma in the future?
2. Choose one of the authors' objections to business ethics cited and refuted by the authors. Expand on this objection and argue vigorously for it. Does the response that Collins and Page offer seem adequate to you? Explain.

3. The authors assert that ethical dilemmas "occur every day." Describe a recent event that posed an ethical dilemma—even if this is an event unrelated to business. Explain the ethical dilemma embedded in the situation. To the extent appropriate, examine the event in light of the five questions for analysis that the authors provide. How did you respond? How did others respond? Was the resolution satisfactory?
4. The authors suggest that ethical discussions need not reach consensus. Is this end point satisfactory, in your view?

Case 1: The Layoff

DENIS COLLINS
LAURA V. PAGE

You are the owner of a small printing company. The firm has been in operation for 10 years and employs 40 people, nonunion, both full-time and part-time. Your firm is growing rapidly and, for the most part, relies upon overtime to meet current production demands. Thirty people work as print production workers. 1

In response to a need for increased productivity, the company purchases a new press. The new technology allows you not only to eliminate overtime, but also to lay off one production employee. The press also has the advantage of being able to better handle environmentally friendly recycled papers and natural-based inks. Because you have a small production shop, all of your workers are generalists; they rotate between a variety of printing tasks. The company has never developed a lay-off policy. 2

After doing much strategic planning, you conclude that it will take at least one year to gain enough new customers to avoid the lay-off. You feel this period is too long to carry an unneeded employee. You also conclude that no significantly new job skills will be needed in the near future, so you reject a skills-retraining strategy. 3

You have had a gainsharing plan in effect for two years that has encouraged your employees to identify cost savings opportunities and to share in them. As a result, you cannot pinpoint any other significant cost savings to avoid the layoff. You have concluded, therefore, that you must lay off one person. 4

You have never formally conducted performance appraisals. You firmly believe that all your employees are excellent workers. 5

You have decided not to use the least hours worked as a lay-off criteria. You need the flexibility of using the part-time person for fill-in work. The worker that you consider a troublemaker is actually a good team leader and liked by most of the other employees. Your highest-paid worker is also the most skilled, and you definitely do not want to lose this person. None of your employees really needs any significant amount of new training to do 6 their current jobs, so there is no way to maximize savings based on training needs criteria.

You asked the employees for a volunteer, but no one came forward. 7

You have come up with a list of three possible terminations. However 8
you feel stuck because each requires a difficult choice:

First, if you choose the least senior person, you would eliminate a sin- 9
gle mother, whom you hired as a result of your affirmative action plan. She is performing well.

Second, if you choose based upon cost savings, you would lay off a 10
full-time employee who has the highest medical bills due to a recently detected heart condition. The long term medical costs are likely to be very large and your insurance rates will go up.

Third, if you choose based upon safety record, you would have to lay 11
off an older worker who is two years from retirement.

Whatever is decided will need to be justified to all company employ- 12
ees. The decision has importance for symbolic reasons and as precedent-setting policy.

What would you do?

▲ ▲ ▲

Review Questions

1. What are the facts of the case? What is the central problem?
2. Why can the employer not find savings, aside from the layoff?
3. What factors make selecting the employee to be laid off particularly difficult?

Discussion and Writing Suggestions[1]

1. What is the value of loyalty, as expressed by seniority?
2. When looking for ways to save money, what other goals are important to you?
3. In a general layoff, how can you avoid discriminating against women and minorities who are most likely the most recently hired?
4. What are the symbolic implications of firing someone who is close to retirement? Should people close to retirement be given special consideration in this decision?
5. Should you consider the circumstances of a person's spouse and other dependents when making this decision?
6. Should your decision be made an official policy, or should any future layoffs be done on a case-by-case basis?

---

[1]These questions are taken directly from Collins and Page's discussion notes for this case. The questions assume that you are the employer and decision-maker.

7. Does the owner have the right to make this decision without employee input?

Case 2: The Pricing Dilemma

DENIS COLLINS
LAURA V. PAGE

You own a children's clothing store. Most of your profit is dependent upon Christmas sales, representing 60 percent of your income. Normally you do not sell children's toys. For the past few years you have been converting a portion of your store space to the selling of popular toys during the holiday season. You spend thousands of dollars on inventory. Your marketing strategy has been to stock known bestsellers and to sell at very low discounted prices. 1

You have always used the tag line, "The best toys at the lowest prices," in your media campaign. Toy sales have been a very successful strategy. Sales volume is high and, though the margins are small, the "extra" profit has been considerable. Due to a continued recession, however, you are not too optimistic about the survival of your business. Also, this year your sales are much lower than expected because there has been an increase in second-hand clothing stores in the neighborhood, at least two of which regularly carry children's clothing. Although you considered a number of other strategic options, you decided in September to go ahead again and order toys for the holiday season. 2

One day in early December, your store manager comes to you and strongly recommends a substantial price increase for the very hard-to-get Galactic Robot, which has been heavily advertised by the manufacturer. The manufacturer appears to be pursuing a strategy of over-advertising and under-producing a product to create a demand that will carry over after the holidays. 3

Your store manager has visited other stores and reports that they have very low inventory that will run out in a day or two. Demand clearly far exceeds supply. Every child in the community wants a Galactic Robot this year. You and your store manager made the right guess when you purchased your inventory. You are well-stocked with over 100 of these robots. 4

Your store is located in a working-class neighborhood that lies next to an upper-middle-class area. You have always relied upon the working class as your primary customer. The suggested retail price for the Galactic Robot is $30 and you have been selling them for a discounted $25. Your store manager suggests that you quadruple the retail price from $25 to $100. He is convinced that you would have no problem selling the inventory at that price, if not to the working-class customers, then at least to the upper-middle-class. Several people have called offering you $150 in cash, off-the-books and no questions asked, if you guarantee them immediate delivery. 5

You have thought about accepting this offer. You have also thought about raising the price higher, to over $200.

What would you do?

▲ ▲ ▲

Review Questions

1. What are the facts of the case? What is the central problem?
2. What are the class issues involved?
3. What "off-the-record" offers are made?

Discussion and Writing Suggestions[1]

1. Is it overpricing a product to charge a price that some people are willing and able to pay? Is there such a thing as a "fair" price?
2. Are you discriminating against your loyal working-class customers if you suddenly raise prices to a level they cannot afford?
3. Is a high price justifiable [if you are in danger of] . . . going out of business?
4. If you raised your prices, would your advertising campaign become "false" advertising, because you promised "the lowest price" in previous ads?
5. Would raising prices break an implied promise to suppliers, because of their "suggested" retail price?
6. How important is it to you that by accepting off-the-book payments of $150 you are committing tax evasion?
7. Would your decision differ if the product were a critical pharmaceutical drug, rather than a children's toy?
8. If you decide on the higher price, would sharing some of the windfall profits with the store manager be important?

Case 3: The Ticket Purchase

BARBARA A. SPENCER

CAROL M. LEHMAN

You are a junior partner in a small ticket brokerage firm in Omaha, Nebraska. The purpose of your company is to purchase tickets to popular concerts and sporting events, which will be in turn resold. Your typical market is upper-level executives and other professionals who do not have time to stand in long lines to purchase their own tickets. 1

[1]These questions are taken directly from Collins and Page's discussion notes for this case. The questions assume that you are the employer and decision-maker.

Record store regulations allow each individual to purchase only four tickets to any particular event. In the past, you have hired students to stand in line to purchase tickets. Even paying minimum wage, you are finding this practice to be far too expensive to maintain adequate profits. 2

You soon realized that some other less expensive method must be identified to secure the tickets. Several weeks ago you hired a homeless person to stand in line. While he was waiting in line, you gave him two meals (pizza for lunch and chicken for dinner). In return for the four tickets, you then paid him $50. Quite pleased with this experiment, you continually hired more homeless people to purchase tickets. They seemed to like the food and the money, and your profits rose steadily. 3

You thought everything was going great until yesterday when you received a phone call from one of the record stores where tickets are sold. The store manager is upset about two things. First, loyal customers are complaining that they have stood in line for hours only to be told that all tickets had been sold. Secondly, she feels that these individuals camping out in front of her store may damage the store's image. One particularly irate customer voiced displeasure in having to wait in line with "shabby-looking people with unwashed hair." 4

And, then, today the morning paper contained a very brash article questioning the ethics of your practice. With paper in hand and very disturbed, Julie Liddell, the senior partner, rushes into your office. Having already read the article, you quickly say, "Honestly, this negative publicity came as a real surprise to me. I believed that we were not only serving our customers but were also helping the homeless—giving them two meals and money they otherwise would not have had." 5

Regaining her usual calm disposition, your partner asks you to analyze this practice more thoroughly, and you agree to provide the partner a written report of your analysis by Friday. Starting your analysis, you ask yourself these questions: *Are you really helping the homeless or are you taking advantage of their predicament? Are you hurting anyone? Should you continue to hire the homeless to buy tickets? If so, should you change your procedures somehow?* 6

▲ ▲ ▲

Review Questions

1. What are the facts of the case? What is the central problem?
2. Who are the "stakeholders"—the ones affected by this dilemma?

Discussion and Writing Questions[1]

1. What costs and benefits would each alternative have for each stakeholder?
2. What are the brokerage firm's obligations to each stakeholder?

---

[1]These questions are taken directly from Spencer and Lehman's teaching notes for this case. The questions assume that you are the junior partner in the ticket brokerage firm.

3. Write an analytical memorandum report to your partner including these points: (a) State the problem as you see it. (b) Applying . . . ethics theories, decide whether it is ethical to hire the homeless. Your analysis should include the costs, benefits, and obligations imposed on each stakeholder. (c) Based on your assessment of the ethical dilemma, make a recommendation to your partner.

Case 4: Peter Green's First Day

LAURA L. NASH

Peter Green came home to his wife and new baby a dejected man. What a contrast to the morning, when he had left the apartment full of enthusiasm to tackle his first customer in his new job at Scott Carpets. And what a customer! Peabody Rug was the largest carpet retailer in the area and accounted for 15% of the entire volume of Peter's territory. When Peabody introduced a Scott product, other retailers were quick to follow with orders. So when Bob Franklin, the owner of Peabody Rug, had called District Manager John Murphy expressing interest in "Carpet Supreme," Scott's newest commercial-duty home carpet, Peter knew that a $15,000–$20,000 order was a real profitability, and no small show for his first sale. And it was important to do well at the start, for John Murphy had made no bones about his scorn for the new breed of salespeople at Scott Carpet. 1

Murphy was of the old school: in the business since his graduation from a local high school, he had fought his way through the stiffest retail competition in the nation to be District Manager of the area at age fifty-eight. Murphy knew his textiles, and he knew his competitors' textiles. He knew his customers, and he knew how well his competitors knew his customers. Formerly, when Scott Carpet had needed to fill sales positions, it had generally raided the competition for experienced personnel, put them on a straight commission, and thereby managed to increase sales and maintain its good reputation for service at the same time. When Murphy had been promoted eight years ago to the position of District Manager, he had passed on his sales territory to Harvey Katchorian, a sixty-year-old mill rep and son of an immigrant who had also spent his life in the carpet trade. Harvey had had no trouble keeping up his sales and had retired from the company the previous spring after forty-five years of successful service in the industry. Peter, in turn, was to take over Harvey's accounts, and Peter knew that John Murphy was not sure that his original legacy to Harvey was being passed on to the best salesperson. 2

Peter was one of the new force of salespeople from Scott's Sales Management Program. In 1976 top management had created a training program to compensate for the industry's dearth of younger salespeople with long-term management potential. Peter, a college graduate, had entered Scott's five-month training program immediately after college and was the first graduate of the program to be assigned to John Murphy's district. Murphy had made it known to top management from the start that he did not think 3 the training program could compensate for on-the-job experience, and he was clearly withholding optimism about Peter's prospects as a salesperson despite Peter's fine performance during the training program.

Peter had been surprised, therefore, when Murphy volunteered to accompany him on his first week of sales "to ease your transition into the territory." As they entered the office at Peabody Rug, Murphy had even seemed friendly and said reassuringly, "I think you'll get along with Bob. He's a great guy—knows the business and has been a good friend of mine for years." 4

Everything went smoothly. Bob liked the new line and appeared ready to place a large order with Peter the following week, but he indicated that he would require some "help on the freight costs" before committing himself definitely. Peter was puzzled and unfamiliar with the procedure, but Murphy quickly stepped in and assured Bob that Peter would be able to work something out. 5

After the meeting, on their way back to Scott Carpets' district office, Peter asked Murphy about freight costs. Murphy sarcastically explained the procedure: Because of its large volume, Peabody regularly "asked for a little help to cover shipping costs," and got it from all or most suppliers. Bob Franklin was simply issued a credit for defective merchandise. By claiming he had received second-quality goods, Bob was entitled to a 10%–25% discount. The discount on defective merchandise had been calculated by the company to equal roughly the cost of shipping the 500-lb. rolls back to the mill, and so it just about covered Bob's own freight costs. The practice had been going on so long that Bob demanded "freight assistance" as a matter of course before placing a large order. Obviously, the merchandise was not defective, but by making an official claim, the sales representative could set in gear the defective-merchandise compensation system. Murphy reiterated, as if to a two-year-old, the importance of a Peabody account to any sales rep, and shrugged off the freight assistance as part of doing business with such an influential firm. 6

Peter stared at Murphy. "Basically, what you're asking me to do, Mr. Murphy, is to lie to the front office." 7

Murphy angrily replied, "Look, do you want to make it here or not? If you do, you ought to know you need Peabody's business. I don't know what kind of fancy think they taught you at college, but where I come from you don't call your boss a liar." 8

From the time he was a child, Peter Green had been taught not to lie or steal. He believed these principles were absolute and that one should support one's beliefs at whatever personal cost. But during college the only even remote test of his principles was his strict adherence to the honor system in taking exams. 9

As he reviewed the conversation with Murphy, it seemed to Peter that there was no way to avoid losing the Peabody account, which would look bad on his own record as well as Murphy's—not to mention the loss in commissions for them both. He felt badly about getting into a tiff with 10

Murphy on his first day out in the territory, and knew Murphy would feel betrayed if one of his salespeople purposely lost a major account.

The only out he could see, aside from quitting, was to play down the whole episode. Murphy had not actually *ordered* Peter to submit a claim for damaged goods (was he covering himself legally?), so Peter could technically ignore the conversation and simply not authorize a discount. He knew very well, however, that such a course was only superficially passive, and that in Murphy's opinion he would have lost the account on purpose. As Peter sipped halfheartedly at a martini, he thought bitterly to himself, "Boy, they sure didn't prepare me for this in Management Training. And I don't even know if this kind of thing goes on in the rest of Murphy's district, let alone in Scott's eleven other districts." 11

▲ ▲ ▲

Review Questions

1. Why was John Murphy skeptical about Peter Green's abilities as a salesperson?
2. What are "freight costs," and how do they tie in to the general question of business ethics?

Discussion and Writing Suggestions

1. What would you do if you were Peter Green? Which considerations would take priority, and why?
2. If Green decides to "lie to the front office," who will be hurt? Is it in the best interest of Scott Carpets (as well as of Bob Franklin, John Murphy, and Peter himself) to go along with the lie that Peabody Rug had received defective merchandise and so was entitled to a credit?
3. Murphy is an experienced, successful salesman, and Scott Carpets is a successful company. Yet the way they do business is being questioned by a young man fresh out of college, with little or no practical experience—a young man who relies primarily on the "absolute" principles of honor and integrity that he had been taught as a child. To what extent do you think that there is an inherent conflict or incompatibility between basic ethical principles and business success?
4. Assume for the moment that a sales representative from a competing carpeting manufacturer was willing and eager to issue a defective merchandise credit to Peabody Rug. If you were Peter Green, would this knowledge make it easier for you to issue the credit?

Case 5: Matt Goldspan's Trilogy

JAY A. HALFOND

Matt Goldspan was a valued member of a thriving financial services company, where he had worked for the decade since completing college. To 1 recognize his performance, his company paid for his MBA program, provided ample financial rewards, and, within the last three years, elevated him to manager of one of the major branch offices. As a 32-year-old branch manager, Matt was now the supervisor of thirty-five employees.

Even though his enterprise was financial, he ultimately believed his skills and priorities were in how well he handled people. He particularly relished the interactions with both staff and clients. He felt he had the best of both worlds: autonomy as the manager of a small business, with the security and mentorship of a larger company. His staff respected his poise and dynamism, as well as his ability to encourage cooperation and finesse any interpersonal differences. He invested much of his time in motivating and overseeing the work of his employees. He was careful not to become too remote as he tried to develop several of his key staff into intermediate positions of authority. 2

The parent company played a hands-off role: because Matt had justified autonomy and trust, the executives in corporate headquarters have tried to support, without infringing upon, the activities of the branch office. 3

I: SALARY INEQUITIES

Denise Contra reported directly to Matt as his executive assistant. Among other responsibilities, Denise maintained the office's personnel records. She had worked in the office for fifteen years. Denise was somewhat of a fixture in the operation: even though she had received a few promotions, she had not been particularly ambitious or restive. She had always viewed her work as supplemental to her family responsibilities yet an important source of income. 4

Since her recent divorce, Denise had shared some of her anxieties about money with Matt. She was now the sole supporter of her three children, and had found the financial and emotional strains very difficult to bear. Denise had always been a steady, reliable employee, though not much beyond satisfactory in her performance. Matt's ability to help her was limited to expressions of his sympathy. 5

One afternoon, Denise timidly confronted Matt with the results of a study she had conducted: 6

> Matt, I know you didn't ask me to look into this, but I knew the company would find this information important. What I have discovered is that the women in our office are not being paid fairly compared to the men—based on their positions and years of service. 7
>
> Most of our employees are women, and, like me, many have been in their jobs for a long time. I've seen men brought in at higher salaries, and, in some cases, promoted more quickly than the women. So when I began to look at current salaries, I wasn't surprised to see a pattern emerge. 8
>
> I am not blaming you, since many of these inequities began long before you became a supervisor. But I would like you to do something, if you can, to fix the situation. If you're not able to, maybe it should be referred to corporate to resolve. Since merit review time is approaching, you could use the raise 9

pool to address this problem. Men wouldn't like it, but it's as if they've had access to our money for all these years. And it would straighten things out, quickly, once and for all.

Regardless, I would appreciate your reactions to my numbers. You'll see that *I,* in particular, deserve to be paid more. 10

II: AFFIRMATIVE ACTION

Within the past two years, Matt's corporation had centralized hiring procedures to promote more aggressive hiring of minorities in all ranks of the company. Matt himself was a firm believer in providing opportunities to those disadvantaged, and took pride in the success he had had, without corporate intervention, to create an integrated workplace. Since his clientele were heterogeneous, he believed that affirmative action was not only morally desirable, but contributed to the success of his business. Matt did, however, resent this one intrusion into his autonomy. He believed that corporate controls only added bureaucracy, not better hiring practices—at least within his operation. He prided himself on the outreach efforts he would normally make, the democratic and comprehensive means he used to screen applicants, and the open-mindedness he conveyed to his staff about increasing the diversity of the office personnel. 11

Celina Longstreet, Vice-President for Affirmative Action, mandated a procedure, endorsed by the Board of Directors, that required that she approve all letters of employment *before* the candidate is offered the position officially. Logistically, this added about a week to the process; under the rare instance when a question was raised, the delay could be longer. 12

Matt had a critical opening in the data processing section of his office. The previous employee had left abruptly, and, to the dismay of the office, had poorly documented the intricacies of her systems. It had become impossible to produce routine correspondence to customers on the status of their accounts. While Matt frantically attempted to recruit someone who would be a "quick start," he had a temporary programmer try to generate the reports. Subtle but embarrassing errors only led to further customer questions and complaints. 13

Fortunately, one candidate surfaced who seemed perfect. Alicia Verango was referred by a friend of one of Matt's staff. Matt was able to get honest and substantial references, as well as verify that the candidate had previously worked in a remarkably similar environment. Because she was returning to the workplace after a maternity absence, she was available immediately. Others who interviewed the candidates concurred enthusiastically that Alicia was also their first choice. 14

Once he had satisfied himself that Alicia was the ideal candidate for the position, Matt called her: 15

> Alicia, you'll be pleased to hear that we were all very impressed with you here, and would like you to start as soon as possible. I'm even confident we can pay the salary we had discussed. 16

If you can begin as soon as next Monday, you should come directly to my office and I'll introduce you and help get you situated. Our corporate headquarters requires some paperwork, but we'll try to get you on the payroll as soon as possible. They'll technically need to make the "offer" to you, and explain benefits, and so on. The important thing is that we need you a.s.a.p.! I'm certain you'll be a real asset to our operation. 17

Alicia was thrilled with this challenging opportunity and agreed to begin work that following week. Several days later, Matt received a call from Celina Longstreet: 18

Matt, I just received the paperwork on an Alicia Verango. She seems adequately qualified for the requirements of the position. But, before I approve an offer to her, I need to be assured that you did not overlook a qualified minority candidate. I see you had a black applicant from another branch office. He's clearly not as good as Verango, but he still seems to meet the minimal qualifications. And this would be an opportunity to promote a minority employee. I'd like to sit down with you next week to see if he can do the job. Maybe I'll invite his supervisor to attend. 19

I know you're anxious to fill this position. I also appreciate that you've been through an exhaustive process. But I'm responsible for seeing that our broader, more long term objectives are also met. I'll work hard to ensure that we reach a resolution within a few weeks. 20

III. EMPLOYEE THEFT

Harriet Wearington was a black employee who was a model for the efforts Matt had tried to make in promoting minority employees. Harriet was a single mother who had begun working part-time five years prior in the lowest clerical position in the office. When her son entered his teens and Harriet was able to work more hours, Matt promoted her steadily to where she was now office manager for customer services. She was an exemplary, hard-working employee, well-regarded by the five employes who reported to her. 21

Each summer, Harriet's son, Jason, would help out in the office. He would run errands, maintain office supplies and inventory, and file customer correspondence. Matt had indicated to Harriet that Jason should not work directly for his mother, but be available to help others throughout the branch office. But, in fact, Harriet tended to supervise Jason and ensure he was kept busy. Some staff resented that Harriet seemed to have a personal assistant in Jason, but most felt assured that Harriet, in particular, would be both fair and demanding in how she utilized her son. 22

Late one July, Denise Contra came in Matt's office and closed his door. 23

Matt, you're not going to believe the call I just received from the office supply place down the street. It seems Jason Wearington tried to use *our* charge account there to buy over a hundred dollars of video supplies for himself and his friends. 24

> The manager called us and I told Harriet. She's furious—and mortified! I told her I'd let you know. She probably knows you'll have to let Jason go. That store manager certainly won't want to see Jason again. When I told some of the others in the office they felt just terrible for Harriet—and bad for you that you'd have to fire her son. 25

Matt knew Denise was right, even though he was somewhat annoyed at her lack of discretion. He did not want to embarrass Harriet by summoning her into his office, so at lunch time he stopped by her desk to ask her if she wanted to go for a walk to the park across the street. Harriet was very grateful for the opportunity to vent her frustrations:

> Matt, I'm so ashamed. I can't believe he'd do such a stupid, dishonest thing. And can you believe he tried to deny it! Then when I told him how embarrassing this was for me, he broke down and cried. He cried, can you believe it? He said he didn't think about how it would hurt me, or that it was stealing. Some of his so-called friends, it seems, goaded him into doing it. 26
>
> We've agreed to a punishment. This was such an important lesson for him, Matt. It's hard raising a teenager alone, but in a strange way, I'm almost glad this happened here. I'm glad he was caught and that he was confronted by what he did wrong. He returned the merchandise and apologized to the store manager. I'm going to stop by the store also. It's so hard to face the others, though. 27
>
> I told him I'm going to watch him like a hawk! And I'll fire him if anything ever happens again. Even if he's my son, I can't tolerate dishonesty and theft. I think he'll be okay now. He's a good kid, really he is, but this is a tough period in a child's life. 28

▲ ▲ ▲

Review Questions[1]

SALARY INEQUITIES

1. What is Matt Goldspan's immediate dilemma?
2. Matt has an interpersonal problem and, perhaps, a problem with the system in which he works. Identify these problems.

AFFIRMATIVE ACTION

3. In what way did Matt act prematurely and precipitously?
4. What were Matt's motives in taking this action?

---

[1]The questions for this case are taken directly from Jay Halfond's "Teaching Notes" for the Matt Goldspan trilogy. Phrasings have been altered to fit the format of *Writing and Reading Across the Curriculum.*

EMPLOYMENT THEFT

5. Summarize the case.
6. What political and ethical dilemmas does Matt face?

Discussion and Writing Suggestions

SALARY INEQUITIES

1. How should Matt determine the validity of Denise's data?
2. Even if Matt determines that salary differences are inherently unfair, how should he respond?

AFFIRMATIVE ACTION

3. Do you believe that affirmative action is a justified approach to integrating the workplace, even when it results in a less qualified applicant being hired?
4. Is Matt's well-intended hiring approach more justified than the external control system that monitors affirmative action? Is Matt being constrained by excessive bureaucracy or by legitimate corporate concern?
5. Matt is clearly making a choice between the immediate needs of his office and the more long-term interests of his parent company. Is this Matt's decision to make?

EMPLOYMENT THEFT

6. What is nepotism, and is Jason's situation an example?
7. Was Harriet's response to Jason reasonable and fair?
8. How should Matt now respond? Whose expectations should now prevail—Denise's or Harriet's?

Case 6: Why Should My Conscience Bother Me?

KERMIT VANDIVIER[1]

The B. F. Goodrich Co. is what business magazines like to speak of as "a major American corporation." It has operations in a dozen states and as many foreign countries, and of these far-flung facilities, the Goodrich plant at Troy, Ohio, is not the most imposing. It is a small, one-story building, once used to manufacture airplanes. Set in the grassy flatlands of west-central Ohio, it employs only about six hundred people. Nevertheless, it is one of the three largest manufacturers of aircraft wheels and brakes, a leader in a most profitable industry. Goodrich wheels and brakes support such well- 1

[1]Reporter, *Daily News,* in Troy, Ohio.

known planes as the F111, the C5A, the Boeing 727, the XB70 and many others. Its customers include almost every aircraft manufacturer in the world.

Contracts for aircraft wheels and brakes often run into millions of dollars, and ordinarily a contract with a total value of less than $70,000, though welcome, would not create any special stir of joy in the hearts of Goodrich sales personnel. But purchase order P-23718, issued on June 18, 1967, by the LTV Aerospace Corporation, and ordering 202 brake assemblies for a new Air Force plane at a total price of $69,417, was received by Goodrich with considerable glee. And there was good reason. Some ten years previously, Goodrich had built a brake for LTV that was, to say the least, considerably less than a rousing success. The brake had not lived up to Goodrich's promises, and after experiencing considerable difficulty, LTV had written off Goodrich as a source of brakes. Since that time, Goodrich salesmen had been unable to sell so much as a shot of brake fluid to LTV. So in 1967, when LTV requested bids on wheels and brakes for the new A7D light attack aircraft it proposed to build for the Air Force, Goodrich submitted a bid that was absurdly low, so low that LTV could not, in all prudence, turn it down. 2

Goodrich had, in industry parlance, "bought into the business." Not only did the company not expect to make a profit on the deal; it was prepared, if necessary, to lose money. For aircraft brakes are not something that can be ordered off the shelf. They are designed for a particular aircraft, and once an aircraft manufacturer buys a brake, he is forced to purchase all replacement parts from the brake manufacturer. The $70,000 that Goodrich would get for making the brake would be a drop in the bucket when compared with the cost of the linings and other parts the Air Force would have to buy from Goodrich during the lifetime of the aircraft. Furthermore, the company which manufactures brakes for one particular model of an aircraft quite naturally has the inside track to supply other brakes when the planes are updated and improved. 3

Thus, that first contract, regardless of the money involved, is very important, and Goodrich, when it learned that it had been awarded the A7D contract, was determined that while it may have slammed the door on its own foot ten years before, this time, the second time around, things would be different. The word was soon circulated throughout the plant: "We can't bungle it this time. We've got to give them a good brake, regardless of the cost." 4

There was another factor which had undoubtedly influenced LTV. All aircraft brakes made today are of the disk type, and the bid submitted by Goodrich called for a relatively small brake, one containing four disks and weighing only 106 pounds. The weight of any aircraft part is extremely important. The lighter a part is, the heavier the plane's payload can be. The four-rotor, 106-pound brake promised by Goodrich was about as light as could be expected, and this undoubtedly had helped move LTV to award the contract to Goodrich. 5

The brake was designed by one of Goodrich's most capable engineers, John Warren. A tall, lanky blond and a graduate of Purdue, Warren had come from the Chrysler Corporation seven years before and had become adept at aircraft brake design. The happy-go-lucky manner he usually maintained belied a temper which exploded whenever anyone ventured to offer any criticism of his work, no matter how small. On these occasions, Warren would turn red in the face, often throwing or slamming something and then stalking from the scene. As his coworkers learned the consequences of criticizing him, they did so less and less readily, and when he submitted his preliminary design for the A7D brake, it was accepted without question. 6

Warren was named project engineer for the A7D, and he, in turn, assigned the task of producing the final production design to a newcomer to the Goodrich engineering stable, Searle Lawson. Just turned twenty-six, Lawson had been out of the Northrup Institute of Technology only one year when he came to Goodrich in January 1967. Like Warren, he had worked for a while in the automotive industry, but his engineering degree was in aeronautical and astronautical sciences, and when the opportunity came to enter his special field, via Goodrich, he took it. At the Troy plant, Lawson had been assigned to various "paper projects" to break him in, and after several months spent reviewing statistics and old brake designs, he was beginning to fret at the lack of challenge. When told he was being assigned to his first "real" project, he was elated and immediately plunged into his work. 7

The major portion of the design had already been completed by Warren, and major assemblies for the brake had already been ordered from Goodrich suppliers. Naturally, however, before Goodrich could start making the brakes on a production basis, much testing would have to be done. Lawson would have to determine the best materials to use for the linings and discover what minor adjustments in the design would have to be made. 8

Then, after the preliminary testing and after the brake was judged ready for production, one whole brake assembly would undergo a series of grueling, simulated braking stops and other severe trials called qualification tests. These tests are required by the military, which gives very detailed specifications on how they are to be conducted, the criteria for failure, and so on. They are performed in the Goodrich plant's test laboratory, where huge machines called dynamometers can simulate the weight and speed of almost any aircraft. After the brakes pass the laboratory tests, they are approved for production, but before the brakes are accepted for use in military service, they must undergo further extensive flight tests. 9

Searle Lawson was well aware that much work had to be done before the A7D brake could go into production, and he knew that LTV had set the last two weeks in June, 1968, as the starting dates for flight tests. So he decided to begin testing immediately. Goodrich's suppliers had not yet delivered the brake housing and other parts, but the brake disks had arrived, and using the housing from a brake similar in size and weight to the A7D 10 brake, Lawson built a prototype. The prototype was installed in a test wheel and placed on one of the big dynamometers in the plant's test laboratory. The dynamometer was adjusted to simulate the weight of the A7D and Lawson began a series of tests, "landing" the wheel and brake at the A7D's landing speed, and braking it to a stop. The main purpose of these preliminary tests was to learn what temperatures would develop within the brake during the simulated stops and to evaluate the lining materials tentatively selected for use.

During a normal aircraft landing the temperatures inside the brake may reach 1000 degrees, and occasionally a bit higher. During Lawson's first simulated landings, the temperature of his prototype brake reached 1500 degrees. The brake glowed a bright cherry-red and threw off incandescent particles of metal and lining material as the temperature reached its peak. After a few such stops, the brake was dismantled and the linings were found to be almost completely disintegrated. Lawson chalked this first failure up to chance and, ordering new lining materials, tried again. 11

The second attempt was a repeat of the first. The brake became extremely hot, causing the lining materials to crumble into dust. 12

After the third such failure, Lawson, inexperienced though he was, knew that the fault lay not in defective parts or unsuitable lining material but in the basic design of the brake itself. Ignoring Warren's original computations, Lawson made his own, and it didn't take him long to discover where the trouble lay—the brake was too small. There simply was not enough surface area on the disks to stop the aircraft without generating the excessive heat that caused the linings to fail. 13

The answer to the problem was obvious but far from simple—the four-disk brake would have to be scrapped, and a new design, using five disks, would have to be developed. The implications were not lost on Lawson. Such a step would require the junking of all the four-disk-brake subassemblies, many of which had now begun to arrive from the various suppliers. It would also mean several weeks of preliminary design and testing and many more weeks of waiting while the suppliers made and delivered the new subassemblies. 14

Yet, several weeks had already gone by since LTV's order had arrived, and the date for delivery of the first production brakes for flight testing was only a few months away. 15

Although project engineer John Warren had more or less turned the A7D over to Lawson, he knew of the difficulties Lawson had been experiencing. He had assured the young engineer that the problem revolved around getting the right kind of lining material. Once that was found, he said, the difficulties would end. 16

Despite the evidence of the abortive tests and Lawson's careful computations, Warren rejected the suggestion that the four-disk brake was too light for the job. Warren knew that his superior had already told LTV, in rather glowing terms, that the preliminary tests on the A7D brake were very successful. Indeed, Warren's superiors weren't aware at this time of 17 the troubles on the brake. It would have been difficult for Warren to admit not only that he had made a serious error in his calculations and original design but that his mistakes had been caught by a green kid, barely out of college.

Warren's reaction to a five-disk brake was not unexpected by Lawson, and, seeing that the four-disk brake was not to be abandoned so easily, he took his calculations and dismal test results one step up the corporate ladder. 18

At Goodrich, the man who supervises the engineers working on projects slated for production is called, predictably, the projects manager. The job was held by a short, chubby and bald man named Robert Sink. A man truly devoted to his work, Sink was as likely to be found at his desk at ten o'clock on Sunday night as ten o'clock on Monday morning. His outside interests consisted mainly of tinkering on a Model-A Ford and an occasional game of golf. Some fifteen years before, Sink had begun working at Goodrich as a lowly draftsman. Slowly, he worked his way up. Despite his geniality, Sink was neither respected nor liked by the majority of the engineers, and his appointment as their supervisor did not improve their feelings about him. They thought he had only gone to high school. It quite naturally rankled those who had gone through years of college and acquired impressive specialties such as thermodynamics and astronautics to be commanded by a man whom they considered their intellectual inferior. But, though Sink had no college training, he had something even more useful: a fine working knowledge of company politics. 19

Puffing upon a Meerschaum pipe, Sink listened gravely as young Lawson confided his fears about the four-disk brake. Then he examined Lawson's calculations and the results of the abortive tests. Despite the fact that he was not a qualified engineer, in the strictest sense of the word, it must certainly have been obvious to Sink that Lawson's calculations were correct and that a four-disk brake would never have worked on the A7D. 20

But other things of equal importance were also obvious. First, to concede that Lawson's calculations were correct would also mean conceding that Warren's calculations were incorrect. As projects manager, he not only was responsible for Warren's activities, but, in admitting that Warren had erred, he would have to admit that he had erred in trusting Warren's judgment. It also meant that, as projects manager, it would be he who would have to explain the whole messy situation to the Goodrich hierarchy, not only at Troy but possibly on the corporate level at Goodrich's Akron offices. And, having taken Warren's judgment of the four-disk brake at face value (he was forced to do this since, not being an engineer, he was unable to exercise any engineering judgment of his own), he had assured LTV, not once but several times, that about all there was left to do on the brake was pack it in a crate and ship it out the back door. 21

There's really no problem at all, he told Lawson. After all, Warren was an experienced engineer, and if he said the brake would work, it would work. Just keep on testing and probably, maybe even on the very next try, it'll work out just fine. 22

Lawson was far from convinced, but without the support of his superiors there was little he could do except keep on testing. By now, housings for the four-disk brake had begun to arrive at the plant, and Lawson was able to build up a production model of the brake and begin the formal qualification tests demanded by the military. 23

The first qualification attempts went exactly as the tests on the prototype had. Terrific heat developed within the brakes and, after a few, short, simulated stops, the linings crumbled. A new type of lining material was ordered and once again an attempt to qualify the brake was made. Again, failure. 24

On April 11, the day the thirteenth test was completed, I became personally involved in the A7D situation. 25

I had worked in the Goodrich test laboratory for five years, starting first as an instrumentation engineer, then later becoming a data analyst and technical writer. As part of my duties, I analyzed the reams and reams of instrumentation data that came from the many testing machines in the laboratory, then transcribed it to a more usable form for the engineering department. And when a new-type brake had successfully completed the required qualification tests, I would issue a formal qualification report. 26

Qualification reports were an accumulation of all the data and test logs compiled by the test technicians during the qualification tests, and were documentary proof that a brake had met all the requirements established by the military specifications and was therefore presumed safe for flight testing. Before actual flight tests were conducted on a brake, qualification reports had to be delivered to the customer and to various government officials. 27

On April 11, I was looking over the data from the latest A7D test, and I noticed that many irregularities in testing methods had been noted on the test logs. 28

Technically, of course, there was nothing wrong with conducting tests in any manner desired, so long as the test was for research purposes only. But qualification test methods are clearly delineated by the military, and I knew that this test had been a formal qualification attempt. One particular notation on the test logs caught my eye. For some of the stops, the instrument which recorded the brake pressure had been deliberately miscalibrated so that, while the brake pressure used during the stops was recorded as 1000 psi (the maximum pressure that would be available on the A7D aircraft), the pressure had actually been 1100 psi! 29

I showed the test logs to the test lab supervisor, Ralph Gretzinger, who said he had learned from the technician who had miscalibrated the instrument that he had been asked to do so by Lawson. Lawson, said Gretzinger, readily admitted asking for the miscalibration, saying he had been told to do so by Sink. 30

I asked Gretzinger why anyone would want to miscalibrate the data-recording instruments. 31

"Why? I'll tell you why," he snorted. "That brake is a failure. It's way too small for the job, and they're not ever going to get it to work. They're 32 getting desperate, and instead of scrapping the damned thing and starting over, they figure they can horse around down here in the lab and qualify it that way."

An expert engineer, Gretzinger had been responsible for several innovations in brake design. It was he who had invented the unique brake system used on the famous XB70. A graduate of Georgia Tech, he was a stickler for detail and he had some very firm ideas about honesty and ethics. "If you want to find out what's going on," said Gretzinger, "ask Lawson, he'll tell you." 33

Curious, I did ask Lawson the next time he came into the lab. He seemed eager to discuss the A7D and gave me the history of his months of frustrating efforts to get Warren and Sink to change the brake design. "I just can't believe this is really happening," said Lawson, shaking his head slowly. "This isn't engineering, at least not what I thought it would be. Back in school, I thought that when you were an engineer, you tried to do your best, no matter what it cost. But this is something else." 34

He sat across the desk from me, his chin propped in his hand. "Just wait," he warned. "You'll get a chance to see what I'm talking about. You're going to get in the act, too, because I've already had the word that we're going to make one more attempt to qualify the brake, and that's it. Win or lose, we're going to issue a qualification report!" 35

I reminded him that a qualification report could only be issued after a brake had successfully met all military requirements, and therefore, unless the next qualification attempt was a success, no report would be issued. 36

"You'll find out," retorted Lawson. "I was already told that regardless of what the brake does on test, it's going to be qualified." He said he had been told in those exact words at a conference with Sink and Russell Van Horn. 37

This was the first indication that Sink had brought his boss, Van Horn, into the mess. Although Van Horn, as manager of the design engineering section, was responsible for the entire department, he was not necessarily familiar with all phases of every project, and it was not uncommon for those under him to exercise the what-he-doesn't-know-won't-hurt-him philosophy. If he was aware of the full extent of the A7D situation, it meant that matters had truly reached a desperate stage—that Sink had decided not only to call for help but was looking toward that moment when blame must be borne and, if possible, shared. 38

Also, if Van Horn had said, "Regardless what the brake does on test, it's going to be qualified," then it could only mean that, if necessary, a false qualification report would be issued! I discussed this possibility with Gretzinger, and he assured me that under no circumstances would such a report ever be issued. 39

"If they want a qualification report, we'll write them one, but we'll tell it just like it is," he declared emphatically. "No false data or false reports are going to come out of this lab." 40

On May 2, 1968, the fourteenth and final attempt to qualify the brake was begun. Although the same improper methods used to nurse the brake 41 through the previous tests were employed, it soon became obvious that this too would end in failure.

When the tests were about half completed, Lawson asked if I would start preparing the various engineering curves and graphic displays which were normally incorporated in a qualification report. "It looks as though you'll be writing a qualification report shortly," he said. 42

I flatly refused to have anything to do with the matter and immediately told Gretzinger what I had been asked to do. He was furious and repeated his previous declaration that under no circumstances would any false data or other matter be issued from the lab. 43

"I'm going to get this settled right now, once and for all," he declared. "I'm going to see Line [Russell Line, manager of the Goodrich Technical Services Section, of which the test lab was a part] and find out just how far this thing is going to go!" He stormed out of the room. 44

In about an hour, he returned and called me to his desk. He sat silently for a few moments, then muttered, half to himself, "I wonder what the hell they'd do if I just quit?" I didn't answer and I didn't ask him what he meant. I knew. He had been beaten down. He had reached the point when the decision had to be made. Defy them now while there was still time—or knuckle under, sell out. 45

"You know," he went on uncertainly, looking down at his desk, "I've been an engineer for a long time, and I've always believed that ethics and integrity were every bit as important as theorems and formulas, and never once has anything happened to change my beliefs. Now this. . . . Hell, I've got two sons I've got to put through school and I just. . . . " His voice trailed off. 46

He sat for a few more minutes, then, looking over the top of his glasses, said hoarsely, "Well, it looks like we're licked. The way it stands now, we're to go ahead and prepare the data and other things for the graphic presentation in the report, and when we're finished, someone upstairs will actually write the report. 47

"After all," he continued, "we're just drawing some curves, and what happens to them after they leave here, well, we're not responsible for that." 48

He was trying to persuade himself that as long as we were concerned with only one part of the puzzle and didn't see the completed picture, we really weren't doing anything wrong. He didn't believe what he was saying, and he knew I didn't believe it either. It was an embarrassing and shameful moment for both of us. 49

I wasn't at all satisfied with the situation and decided that I too would discuss the matter with Russell Line, the senior executive in our section. 50

Tall, powerfully built, his teeth flashing white, his face tanned to a coffee-brown by a daily stint with a sun lamp, Line looked and acted every inch the executive. He was a crossword-puzzle enthusiast and an ardent golfer, and though he had lived in Troy only a short time, he had been accepted into the Troy Country Club and made an official of the golf committee. He commanded great respect and had come to be well liked by those of us who worked under him. 51

He listened sympathetically while I explained how I felt about the A7D situation, and when I had finished, he asked me what I wanted him to do about it. I said that as employees of the Goodrich Company we had a responsibility to protect the company and its reputation if at all possible. I said I was certain that officers on the corporate level would never knowingly allow such tactics as had been employed on the A7D. 52

"I agree with you," he remarked, "but I still want to know what you want me to do about it." 53

I suggested that in all probability the chief engineer at the Troy plant, H. C. "Bud" Sunderman, was unaware of the A7D problem and that he, Line, should tell him what was going on. 54

Line laughed, good-humoredly. "Sure, I could, but I'm not going to. Bud probably already knows about this thing anyway, and if he doesn't, I'm sure not going to be the one to tell him." 55

"But why?" 56

"Because it's none of my business, and it's none of yours. I learned a long time ago not to worry about things over which I had no control. I have no control over this." 57

I wasn't satisfied with this answer, and I asked him if his conscience wouldn't bother him if, say, during flight tests on the brake, something should happen resulting in death or injury to the test pilot. 58

"Look," he said, becoming somewhat exasperated, "I just told you I have no control over this thing. Why should my conscience bother me?" 59

His voice took on a quiet, soothing tone as he continued. "You're just getting all upset over this thing for nothing. I just do as I'm told, and I'd advise you to do the same." 60

He had made his decision, and now I had to make mine. 61

I made no attempt to rationalize what I had been asked to do. It made no difference who would falsify which part of the report or whether the actual falsification would be by misleading numbers or misleading words. Whether by acts of commission or omission, all of us who contributed to the fraud would be guilty. The only question left for me to decide was whether or not I would become a party to the fraud. 62

Before coming to Goodrich in 1963, I had held a variety of jobs, each a little more pleasant, a little more rewarding than the last. At forty-two, with seven children, I had decided that the Goodrich Company would probably be my "home" for the rest of my working life. The job paid well, it was pleasant and challenging, and the future looked reasonably bright. My wife and I had bought a home and we were ready to settle down into a comfortable, middle-age, middle-class rut. If I refused to take part in the A7D fraud, I would have to either resign or be fired. The report would be written by someone anyway, but I would have the satisfaction of knowing I had had no part in the matter. But bills aren't paid with personal satisfaction, nor house payments with ethical principles. I made my decision.[2] 63

▲ ▲ ▲

[2]Turn to page 840 for the author's concluding discussion on what happened in this case. Before reading that discussion, however, try to anticipate Vandivier's decision.

Review Questions

1. Why did Lawson conclude that Warren's design was flawed?
2. Why did Warren not consider redesigning the brakes? Why did Sink choose to support Warren, instead of Lawson, when he must have realized that Lawson was right about the brakes?
3. Both Ralph Gretzinger and Vandivier at first refused to go along with the demand that they falsify test data. Why did both men eventually cave in to their superiors?
4. At what point did Vandivier consult a lawyer? Why then—and not earlier?

Discussion and Writing Suggestions

1. If you were Vandivier, would you have acted as he did? (Consider especially the personal dilemma he describes in paragraphs 62–63.) Do you believe that he acted responsibly at all stages of this case? Explain.
2. In paragraph 71 on pages 840–41, Vandivier says that he and Lawson "discussed such things as the Nuremberg trials [the post World War II tribunals at which Nazi officials were found guilty of war crimes] and how they related to our guilt and complicity in the A7D situation." To what extent do you see parallels between these two situations?
3. Apply Cavanagh's ethical decision-making model, or the questions developed by Collins and Page, to this case. To what extent do the principles of utilitarianism, rights, and justice apply? Are there any "overwhelming factors" that could help determine which principles are more important in this case? To what extent do any of the "Five Questions" help you decide on an ethical course of action?
4. Assume that you are a member of a commission charged with investigating the Goodrich case. Assume also that you found Vandivier's account of the matter to be credible. Consider all of the things that went wrong, and try to devise safeguards—in the form of a series of recommendations—to prevent such mishaps in the future.
5. Ethically, what similarities do you find between this case and the Peter Green case? (Consider, for example, the similarities between Peter Green and Searle Lawson.) What differences do you find?

▼

SYNTHESIS ACTIVITIES

1. Analyze the ethical dilemma in any of the cases you've read in this chapter. Consider the case in two ways:
   - Analyze the dilemma based on Gerald Cavanagh's strategy for making ethical business decisions.

- Analyze the case following the questions set out in Collins and Pa.ge.

Having conducted your two analyses, choose one as the basis for writing a memo in which you review the dilemma and suggest a course of action. Assume you are a business consultant, writing to a company owner faced with the dilemma presented in the case. Your memo should review the pertinent facts, identify the dilemma, analyze the dilemma (according to materials provided by Cavanagh or Collins and Page), and present a course of action—which you justify based on your analysis.

2. Devise your own criteria for making ethical business decisions. As you devise these criteria, bear in mind (that is, if you reject Friedman's argument) that a decision maker in business must seek to balance financial needs with the rights of employees, consumers, owners (shareholders), and the community. Then, using your criteria, analyze one of the cases presented in this chapter. Write a memo, as described in the first Synthesis Activity.
3. Present one of the cases in this chapter to five or more college-age people. Present the same case to several older people you know who are in business. Try for an equal representation of women and men. Ask respondents in each group, "What would you do?" Study your notes or your tape-recorded transcripts. Do any gender or generational patterns emerge? Present your findings in a comparison-contrast synthesis.
4. How effective is studying and discussing hypothetical dilemmas (that is, studying cases) in preparing you for the pressures of actual dilemmas in the workplace? Develop an answer into an argument synthesis that draws on three or more cases in this chapter. If possible, refer to actual ethical dilemmas with which you've struggled in your own work.
5. Write an argument synthesis in which you present your views on the question: Does a business have an obligation to be socially responsible, if it is otherwise meeting all its legal obligations? Essentially, you will be siding with Friedman or with Ben Cohen and Jerry Greenfield in this debate. In an effort to keep the discussion from becoming too abstract, try to ground your discussion in a particular case, which you can invent or report on directly, provided you've heard of it through news accounts or know it through first-hand experience.
6. To what extent do you feel that dilemmas of business ethics originate in a confusion of two codes of ethics: what we might call "church" ethics and business ethics? That is, do you feel that people in business operate according to one code of conduct and that the same people, after business hours, operate according to a different code? (Lewis and Speck may help you to define this latter set.) In your view, should one code predominate both in and out of business? Develop an argument synthesis in which you take a stand on the question. In an effort to keep the discussion from becoming too abstract, try to ground your discussion in a particular case, which you can in-

vent or report on directly, provided you've heard of it through news accounts or know it through first-hand experience.

▼

RESEARCH ACTIVITIES

1. Research the practice of intelligence gathering in business. A business professional must pay close attention to competitors, but how close? Is espionage permissible? In looking for sources, consult the cumulative indexes of two journals: *Business Ethics* and *Business Horizons.* The following books should be of use: Ian Gordon, *Beat the Competition: How to Use Competitive Intelligence to Develop Winning Business Strategies* (1989); Howard Sutton, *Competitive Intelligence* (1988); William L. Sammon, ed., *Business Competitor Intelligence: Methods for Collecting, Organizing, and Using Information* (1984); Richard M. Greene, Jr., *Business Intelligence and Espionage* (1966).
2. Research the history of business ethics in America, and address this question: To what extent have Americans, over their history, been careful to observe standards of ethical behavior in their business dealings? The following study will be especially helpful: Peter Baida, *Poor Richard's Legacy: American Business Values from Benjamin Franklin to Donald Trump* (1990).
3. Locate as many books as you can on the topic of "climbing-the-ladder-to-corporate-success." Make a study of the advice in these books and report on the ethical values implicit in them. Can you classify varieties of advice? Do you find yourself agreeing with any particular strategies? What does your agreement reveal about *you*?
4. Investigate the topic of whistleblowing, the action a lone employee takes when he or she feels that a company's unethical behavior may harm the public. Under what conditions should an employee blow the whistle? What are the personal ramifications of blowing the whistle? How do companies and fellow employees respond to whistleblowers? What are the laws that protect whistleblowers? One possible source: Sissela Bok, *On the Ethics of Concealment and Revelation* (1982). Many books on the general topic of business ethics have chapters devoted to whistleblowing.
5. Choose some company that interests you, and to which you have at least limited access. Investigate the extent to which the topic of business ethics is on people's minds and on the company's agenda. Does the company have a formal code of ethics? Does the company have in place a procedure for employees who wish to raise questions about the ethics of particular practices? Has the company asked any of its employees to attend workshops on business ethics? Does the company feel the need to address any of these questions?

6. Investigate and report on any of the insider trading scandals of the 1980s. You might begin by doing a literature search on two names: Ivan Boesky and Michael Milken. In your paper, explain how insider trading works and why it is both ethically problematic and illegal.

▲ ▲ ▲

Following are the concluding paragraphs to the Vandivier case, presented earlier.

Conclusion to "Why Should My Conscience Bother Me?"

. . . The next morning, I telephoned Lawson and told him I was ready to begin on the qualification report. 64

In a few minutes, he was at my desk, ready to begin. Before we started, I asked him, "Do you realize what we are going to do?" 65

"Yeah," he replied bitterly, "we're going to screw LTV. And speaking of screwing," he continued, "I know now how a whore feels, because that's exactly what I've become, an engineering whore. I've sold myself. It's all I can do to look at myself in the mirror when I shave. I make me sick." 66

I was surprised at his vehemence. It was obvious that he too had done his share of soul-searching and didn't like what he had found. Somehow, though, the air seemed clearer after his outburst, and we began working on the report. 67

I had written dozens of qualification reports, and I knew what a "good" one looked like. Resorting to the actual test data only on occasion, Lawson and I proceeded to prepare page after page of elaborate, detailed engineering curves, charts, and test logs, which purported to show what had happened during the formal qualification tests. Where temperatures were too high, we deliberately chopped them down a few hundred degrees, and where they were too low, we raised them to a value that would appear reasonable to the LTV and military engineers. Brake pressure, torque values, distances, times—everything of consequence was tailored to fit the occasion. 68

Occasionally, we would find that some test either hadn't been performed at all or had been conducted improperly. On those occasions, we "conducted" the test—successfully, of course—on paper. 69

For nearly a month we worked on the graphic presentation that would be a part of the report. Meanwhile, the fourteenth and final qualification attempt had been completed, and the brake, not unexpectedly, had failed again. 70

During that month, Lawson and I talked of little else except the enormity of what we were doing. The more involved we became in our work, the more apparent became our own culpability. We discussed such things as the Nuremberg trials and how they related to our guilt and complicity in the A7D situation. Lawson often expressed his opinion that the brake was 71 downright dangerous and that, once on flight tests, "anything is liable to happen."

I saw his boss, John Warren, at least twice during that month and needled him about what we were doing. He didn't take the jibes too kindly but managed to laugh the situation off as "one of those things." One day I remarked that what we were doing amounted to fraud, and he pulled out an engineering handbook and turned to a section on laws as they related to the engineering profession. 72

He read the definition of fraud aloud, then said, "Well, technically I don't think what we're doing can be called fraud. I'll admit it's not right, but it's just one of those things. We're just kinda caught in the middle. About all I can tell you is, do like I'm doing. Make copies of everything and put them in your SYA file." 73

"What's an 'SYA' file?" I asked. 74

"That a 'save your ass' file." He laughed. 75

On June 5, 1968, the report was officially published and copies were delivered in person to the Air Force and LTV. Within a week, flight tests were begun at Edwards Air Force Base in California. Searle Lawson was sent to California as Goodrich's representative. Within approximately two weeks, he returned because some rather unusual incidents during the tests had caused them to be canceled. 76

His face was grim as he related stories of several near crashes during landings—caused by brake troubles. He told me about one incident in which, upon landing, one brake was literally welded together by the intense heat developed during the test stop. The wheel locked, and the plane skidded for nearly 1500 feet before coming to a halt. The plane was jacked up and the wheel removed. The fused parts within the brake had to be pried apart. 77

Lawson had returned to Troy from California that same day, and that evening, he and others of the Goodrich engineering department left for Dallas for a high-level conference with LTV. 78

That evening I left work early and went to see my attorney. After I told him the story, he advised that, while I was probably not actually guilty of fraud, I was certainly part of a conspiracy to defraud. He advised me to go to the Federal Bureau of Investigation and offered to arrange an appointment. The following week he took me to the Dayton office of the FBI, and after I had been warned that I would not be immune from prosecution, I disclosed the A7D matter to one of the agents. The agent told me to say nothing about the episode to anyone and to report any further incident to him. He said he would forward the story to his superiors in Washington. 79

A few days later, Lawson returned from the conference in Dallas and said that the Air Force, which had previously approved the qualification report, had suddenly rescinded that approval and was demanding to see some of the raw test data taken during the tests. I gathered that the FBI had passed the word. 80

Finally, early in October 1968, Lawson submitted his resignation, to take effect on October 25. On October 18, I submitted my own resignation, 81 to take effect on November 1. In my resignation, addressed to Russell Line, I cited the A7D report and stated: "As you are aware, this report contained numerous deliberate and willful misrepresentations which, according to legal counsel, constitute fraud and expose both myself and others to criminal charges of conspiracy to defraud. . . . The events of the past seven months have created an atmosphere of deceit and distrust in which it is impossible to work. . . . "

On October 25, I received a sharp summons to the office of Bud Sunderman. As chief engineer at the Troy plant, Sunderman was responsible for the entire engineering division. Tall and graying, impeccably dressed at all times, he was capable of producing a dazzling smile or a hearty chuckle or immobilizing his face into marble hardness, as the occasion required. 82

I faced the marble hardness when I reached his office. He motioned me to a chair. "I have your resignation here," he snapped, "and I must say you have made some rather shocking, I might even say irresponsible, charges. This is very serious." 83

Before I could reply, he was demanding an explanation. "I want to know exactly what the fraud is in connection with the A7D and how you can dare accuse this company of such a thing!" 84

I started to tell some of the things that had happened during the testing, but he shut me off saying, "There's nothing wrong with anything we've done here. You aren't aware of all the things that have been going on behind the scenes. If you had known the true situation, you would never have made these charges." He said that in view of my apparent "disloyalty" he had decided to accept my resignation "right now," and said it would be better for all concerned if I left the plant immediately. As I got up to leave he asked me if I intended to "carry this thing further." 85

I answered simply, "Yes," to which he replied, "Suit yourself." Within twenty minutes, I had cleaned out my desk and left. Forty-eight hours later, the B. F. Goodrich Company recalled the qualification report and the four-disk brake, announcing that it would replace the brake with a new, improved, five-disk brake at no cost to LTV. 86

Ten months later, on August 13, 1969, I was the chief government witness at a hearing conducted before Senator William Proxmire's Economy in Government Subcommittee of the Congress's Joint Economic Committee. I related the A7D story to the committee, and my testimony was supported by Searle Lawson, who followed me to the witness stand. Air Force officers also testified, as well as a four-man team from the General Accounting Office, which had conducted an investigation of the A7D brake at the request of Senator Proxmire. Both Air Force and GAO investigators declared that the brake was dangerous and had not been tested properly. 87

Testifying for Goodrich was R. G. Jeter, vice-president and general counsel of the company, from the Akron headquarters. Representing the Troy plant was Robert Sink. These two denied any wrongdoing on the part of the Goodrich Company, despite expert testimony to the contrary by Air Force and GAO officials. Sink was quick to deny any connection with the writing of the report or of directing any falsifications, claiming to be on the 88

West Coast at the time. John Warren was the man who supervised its writing, said Sink.

As for me, I was dismissed as a high-school graduate with no technical training, while Sink testified that Lawson was a young, inexperienced engineer. "We tried to give him guidance," Sink testified, "but he preferred to have his own convictions." 89

About changing the data and figures in the report, Sink said: "When you take data from several different sources, you have to rationalize among those data what is the true story. This is part of your engineering know-how." He admitted that changes had been made in the data, "but only to make them more consistent with the overall picture of the data that is available." 90

Jeter pooh-poohed the suggestion that anything improper occurred, saying: "We have thirty-odd engineers at this plant . . . and I say to you that it is incredible that these men would stand idly by and see reports changed or falsified. . . . I mean you just do not have to do that working for anybody. . . . Just nobody does that." 91

The four-hour hearing adjourned with no real conclusion reached by the committee. But, the following day the Department of Defense made sweeping changes in its inspection, testing and reporting procedures. A spokesman for the DOD said the changes were a result of the Goodrich episode. 92

The A7D is now in service, sporting a Goodrich-made five-disk brake, a brake that works very well, I'm told. Business at the Goodrich plant is good. Lawson is now an engineer for LTV and has been assigned to the A7D project. And I am now a newspaper reporter. 93

At this writing, those remaining at Goodrich are still secure in the same positions, all except Russell Line and Robert Sink. Line has been rewarded with a promotion to production superintendent, a large step upward on the corporate ladder. As for Sink, he moved up into Line's old job. 94

Credits

Richard Bernstein, *Bilingual Education: A War of Words.* Excerpt from "A War of Words," by Richard Bernstein from THE NEW YORK TIMES October 14, 1990. Copyright © 1990 by The New York Times Company. Reprinted by permission.

Rosalie Pedalino Porter, *Perils in the Demand for Biculturalism.* From: FORKED TONGUE, THE POLITICS OF BILINGUAL EDUCATION by ROSALIE PEDALINO PORTER. Copyright © 1990 by Basic Books, Inc. Reprinted by permission of BasicBooks, a division of HarperCollins Publishers, Inc.

From: "Eastman School Outcomes: Math," by James Crawford from BILINGUAL EDUCATION: HISTORY, POLITICS, THEORY, AND PRACTICE, 3/e. (Los Angeles: Bilingual Educational Services, 1995). Reprinted by permission.

From: Henry Treuba, "Linguisitic Minority Student Population with Limited English Proficiency," from RAISING SILENT VOICES Copyright © 1989 by Heinle & Heinle/Newbury House Publishers Boston, MA. Reprinted by permission.

Charles Ostman, *Total Surveillance.* From: Charles Ostman, "Total Surveillance," MONDO 2000, Issue 13, 1995, pp, 16–19. Reprinted by permission.

Irving J. Sloan, *Privacy and Technology.* From: Irving J. Sloan, "Privacy and Technology," in Sloan (ed) LAW OF PRIVACY RIGHTS IN A TECHNOLOGICAL SOCIETY, 2/e. Copyright © 1986. Reprinted by permission of Oceana Publications, Inc.

Bill Clinton, *Ending Welfare as We Know It.* From: Bill Clinton, "Remarks to the National Governors' Association," February 2, 1993. WEEKLY COMPILATION OF PRESIDENTIAL DOCUMENTS. February 5, 1993: 125–28.

Charles Murray, *The Coming White Underclass.* From: Charles Murray, "The Coming White Underclass," THE WALL STREET JOURNAL, October 29, 1993. Reprinted with permission of The Wall Street Journal © 1993 Dow Jones & Company. All rights reserved.

Charles Krauthammer, *Subsidized Illegitmacy.* From: Charles Krauthammer, "Subsidized Illegitmacy," WASHINGTON POST, November 19, 1993; A29. © 1993, Washington Post Writers Group. Reprinted with permission.

Teresa McCrary, *Getting Off the Welfare Carousel.* From NEWSWEEK, December 6, 1993. Copyright © 1993, Newsweek, Inc. All rights reserved. Reprinted by permission.

Virginia I. Postrel, *The Character Issue.* Reprinted with permission, from the 1994 issue of REASON Magazine. Copyright 1995 by the Reason Foundation, 3415 S. Sepulveda Blvd, Suite 400, Los Angeles, CA 90034.

Alexander Cockburn, *Eugenics Nuts Would Have Loved Norplant.* From: Alexander Cockburn, "Eugenics Nuts Would Have Loved Norplant," LOS ANGELES TIMES, June 30, 1994. Reprinted by permission.

Robert Scheer, *Newt's Welfare: Think of It as a Homeless Drill.* From: Robert Scheer, "Newt's Welfare: Think of It as a Homeless Drill," LOS ANGELES TIMES, February 12, 1995. Reprinted by permission.

Sumner M. Rosen, *The True End of Welfare Reform.* From: Sumner Rosen, "The True End of Welfare Reform," THE NATION, April 3, 1995; 456. Reprinted with permission from THE NATION magazine. © The Nation Company, L.P.

From: "What Good Is Government [Bill Clinton]. . . And Can We Make It Better," [Newt Gingrich] NEWSWEEK April 10, 1995. Reprinted by permission.

Bob Ortega, *Ban the Bargains.* Reprinted by permission of THE WALL STREET JOURNAL, © 1993 Dow Jones & Company, Inc. All Rights Reserved Worldwide.

Albert Norman, *Eight Ways to Stop the Store.* From: Albert Norman, "Eight Ways to Stop the Store," THE NATION, March 28, 1994. Reprinted with permission from THE NATION magazine. © The Nation Company, L.P.

Kenneth E. Stone, *Competing with the Discount Mass Merchandisers.* Reprinted by permission of Kenneth E. Stone.

Sarah Anderson, *Wal-Mart's War on Main Street.* From: Sarah Anderson, "Wal-Mart's War on Main Street," PROGRESSIVE, November 1994, pp 19–21. Reprinted by permission from THE PROGRESSIVE, 409 East Main Street, Madison, WI 53703.

Jo Ann Johnston, *Who's Really the Villian?* From: Jo Ann Johnston, "Who's Really the Villian?" BUSINESS ETHICS, May/June 1995, pp 16–18. This article reprinted with permission from: Business Ethics Magazine, 52 S. 10th Street, Suite 110, Minneapolis, MN 55403–2001. 612–962–4702.

James F. Moore, *Savvy Expansion and Leadership.* Reprinted by permission of HARVARD BUSINESS REVIEW. Excerpts and exhibits from "Predators and Prey: A New Ecology of Competition" by James F. Moore, May/June 1993. Copyright © 1993 by the President and Fellows of Harvard College; all rights reserved.

Garry Trudeau, *Doonesbury on Wal-Mart.* DOONESBURY © 1994 G.B. Trudeau. Reprinted with permission of UNIVERSAL PRESS SYNDICATE. All rights reserved.

Victor Kamber and Bradley O'Leary, *Political Quiz: Are You a Liberal or a Conservative?* From: Victor Kamber and Bradley O'Leary, "The Political Quiz Show," USA WEEKEND (Sunday Supplement) October 1994. Reprinted by permission of Victor Kamber and Bradley O'Leary.

Jeff Smith, *The L.A. Riots: A Case Study of Debate Across the Political Spectrum.* Reprinted by permission of Jeff Smith.

Donald P. Lazere, *Guides to the Political Conflicts.* From: Donald P. Lazere, "Teaching the Political Conflicts," COMPOSITION AND COMMUNICATION, May 1992. Copyright © 1992 by the National Council of Teachers of English. Reprinted with permission.

A Voter's Manual for the Political Parties and the Candidates. From: "1994 California Ballot Pamphlet and Party Platforms" (and WWW on-line). Retitled "A Voter's Manual for the Parties and the Candidates." California Secretary of State's Office.

James MacGregor Burns et al., *Liberalism, Conservatism, Socialism, Libertarianism.* From: Burns/Pelatson: GOVERNMENT BY THE PEOPLE, 16/E, © 1995, pp 169–182. Reprinted by permission of Prentice-Hall, Inc., Upper Saddle River, NJ 07458.

Donna Woolfolk Cross, *Politics: The Art of Bamboozling.* Excerpts from OUR GANG by Philip Roth. Copyright © 1971 by Philip Roth. Main text from Donna Woolfolk Cross, WORD ABUSE. Reprinted by permission.

A Debate on Welfare. From: THE CONGRESSIONAL RECORD, as reprinted in CONGRESSIONAL DIGEST and Thomas's Legislative Information on the Internet: (World Wide Web).

"The Education of a Torturer" by Janice T. Gibson and Mika Haritos-Fatouros. Reprinted with permission from PSYCHOLOGY TODAY Magazine. Copyright © 1986 (Sussex Publishers, Inc.).

Doris Lessing, *Groups Minds.* "GROUP MINDS" from PRISONS WE CHOOSE TO LIVE INSIDE by DORIS LESSING Copyright © 1988 by Doris Lessing. Reprinted by permission of HarperCollins Publishers, Inc.

Stanley Milgram, *The Perils of Obedience.* "THE PERILS OF ODEDIENCE'' from OBEDIENCE TO AUTHORITY by STANLEY MILGRAM. Copyright © 1974 by Stanley Milgram. Reprinted by permission of HarperCollins Publishers, Inc. Reprinted by permission of HarperCollins Publishers, Inc.

Diana Baumrind, *Review of Stanley Milgram's Experiments on Obedience.* Excerpt from "Some Thoughts on Ethics of Research: After Reading Milgram's BEHAVIORAL STUDY OF OBEDIENCE," by Diana Baumrind from AMERICAN PSYCHOLOGIST 19, 1964, pp 421–423. Copyright © 1964 by the American Psychological Association and Diana Baumrind. Reprinted by permission.

Moti Nissani, *Review of Stanley Milgram's Experiments on Obedience.* From: "A Reintepretation of Stanley Milgram's Observations on Obedience to Authority," AMERICAN PSYCHOLOGIST, December 1990, pp 1384–85. Copyright © 1990 by the American Psychological Association. Reprinted by permission.

Philip K. Zimbardo, *The Stanford Prison Experiment.* From: "The Mind is a Formidable Jailer," by Philip K. Zimbardo. THE NEW YORK TIMES Magazine April 8, 1973. Copyright © 1973 by The New York Times Company. Reprinted by permission.

Erich Fromm, *Disobedience as a Psychological and Moral Problem.* EXCERPT AS SUBMITTED from ON DISOBEDIENCE AND OTHER ESSAYS by ERICH FROMM. Copyright © 1981 by the Estate of Erich Fromm. Reprinted by permission of HarperCollins Publishers, Inc.

Susan Walton, *The Obedient, Unlived Life.* From: "The Cautious and Obedient Life Can Be a Life Unlived," by Susan Walton. THE NEW YORK TIMES June 4, 1987. Copyright © 1987 by

The New York Times Company. Reprinted by permission.

Shirley Jackson, *The Lottery.* "The Lottery" from THE LOTTERY AND OTHER STORIES by Shirley Jackson. Copyright © 1949 by Shirley Jackson. Copyright renewed © 1977 by Laurence Hyman, Barry Hyman, Mrs. Sarah Webster and Mrs. Joanne Schunrer. Reprinted by permission of Farrar, Straus & Giroux, Inc. "Biography of a Story," from COME ALONG WITH ME by Shirley Jackson. Copyright © 1948, 1952, © 1960 by Shirley Jackson. Used by permission of Viking Penguin, a division of Penguin Books, USA Inc.

Bryan Glastonbury and Walter LaMendola, *The Nature and Meaning of Data.* From: The Integrity of Intelligence: A Bill of Rights for the Information Age by Glastonbury and LaMendola. Copyright © 1992. Reprinted with permission of St. Martin's Press, Incorporated.

John Whalen, *You're Not Paranoid: They Really* Are *Watching You.* From: John Whalen, "You're Not Paranoid: They Really Are Watching You," WIRED, March 1995, pp 76–95. Reprinted by permission of John Whalen.

CQ Researcher, *Privacy in the Workplace.* From: "Privacy in the Workplace—The Issues," CONGRESSIONAL RESEARCHER, November 19, 1993 (Vol. 3, No. 43), p 101. Reprinted by permission.

Anne Wells Branscomb, *The Changing Nature of Information.* EXCERPT AS SUBMITTED from WHO OWNS INFORMATION by ANNE WELLS BRANSCOMB. Copyright © 1994 by Anne Wells Branscomb. Reprinted by permission of BasicBooks, a division of HarperCollins Publishers, Inc.

Alan F. Westin, *Computers in the Workplace: Elysium or Panopticon.* From: Alan F. Westin, Opening remarks in session on "Computers in the Workplace: Elysium or Panopticon?" in Proceedings of the Second Conference on Computers, Freedom, and Privacy, Washington, March 18–20, 1992. Reprinted by permission.

Kristin Bell DeTienne, *Big Brother or Friendly Coach: Computer Monitoring in the 21st Century.* From: Kristin Bell DeTienne, "Big Brother or Friendly Coach? Computer Monitoring in the 21st Century," THE FUTURIST, September/October 1993, Vol. 27, No. 5, pp 33–37. Reproduced with permission from THE FUTURIST, published by the World Future Society, 7910 Woodmont Avenue, Suite 450, Bethesda, Maryland 20814.

Stith Thompson, *Universality of the Folktale.* From: Stith Thompson, "Universality of the Folktale." Copyright © 1951 by Holt, Rinehart and Winston. Reprinted by permission of Holt, Rinhart, and Winston, Inc.

Charles Perrault, *Cinderella.* From: Charles Perrault, "Cinderella" in FAIRY TALES translated by Geoffrey Brereton. Reprinted by permission.

Jakob and Wilhelm Grimm, *Ashputtle.* From GRIMM's TALES FOR YOUNG AND OLD by Jakob and Wilhelm Grimm. Copyright © 1977 by Ralph Manheim. Used by permission of Doubleday, a division of Bantam Doubleday Dell Publishing Group, Inc.

Tanith Lee, *When the Clock Strikes.* Excerpt from "When the Clock Strikes" from RED AS BLOOD by Tanith Lee. Copyright © 1983 by Tanith Lee. Reprinted by permission of DAW Books, Inc.

Tuan Ch'êng-Shih, *A Chinese "Cinderella."* "The Chinese Cinderella Story," by Tuan Ch'eng-Shih, translated by Arthur Waley. FOLKLORE 58, March 1947, pp 226–238. Reprinted by permission of the Folklore Society.

The Maiden, the Frog, and the Chief's Son (An African "Cinderella"). Excerpt from "Cinderella in Africa," by William Bascom from CINDERELLA: A FOLKLORE CASEBOOK edited by Alan Dundes. Reprinted by permission of Garland Publishing, Inc.

Oochigeaskw—The Rough-Faced Girl (A Native American "Cinderella"). "The Algonquin Cinderella" from WORLD TALES: THE EXTRAORDINARY COINCIDENCE OF STORIES TOLD IN ALL TIMES, IN ALL PLACES by Indries Shah, copyright © 1979 by Technographia, S.A. and Harcourt Brace & Company, reprinted by permission of Harcourt Brace & Company.

Campbell Grant, *Walt Disney's "Cinderella."* "Walt Disney's 'Cinderella,'" adapted by Campbell Grant, © The Walt Disney Company.

Anne Sexton, *Cinderella.* "Cinderella" from TRANSFORMATIONS. Copyright © 1971 by Anne Sexton. Reprinted by permission of Houghton Mifflin Company. All rights reserved.

James Finn Garner, *The Politically Correct Cinderella.* Reprinted with permission of Macmillan General Reference, USA, a Division of Simon & Schuster, Inc., from POLITICALLY CORRECT BEDTIME STORIES by James Finn Garner. Copyright © 1994 by James Finn Garner.

Bruno Bettelheim, *"Cinderella": A Story of Sibling Rivalry and Oedipal Conflicts.* From: THE USES OF ENCHANTMENT by Bruno Bettelheim. Copyright © 1975, 1976 by Bruno Bettelheim. Reprinted by permission of Alfred A. Knopf, Inc.

Madonna Kolenschlag, *A Feminist View of "Cinderella."* EXCERPT AS SUBMITTED from KISS SLEEPING BEAUTY GOOD-BYE, REVISED EDITION by MADONNA KOLENSCHLAG. Copyright © 1979 by Madonna Kolbenschlag. Reprinted by permission of HarperCollins Publishers, Inc.

Jane Yolen, *America's "Cinderella."* From: Jane Yolen, "America's Cinderella," as published in CHILDREN's LITERATURE IN EDUCATION, Volume 8, pp 21–29. Reprinted by permission of Curtis Brown, Ltd. Copyright © 1977 by Jane Yolen.

Cecie Starr and Ralph Taggart, *Recombinant DNA and Genetic Engineering.* BIOLOGY: THE UNITY AND DIVERSITY OF LIFE, 7/E, pp 246–257. Copyright © 1995 Wadsworth Publishing Company. Reprinted with permission.

Shannon Brownlee, Gareth C. Cook, and Viva Hardigg, *Tinkering with Destiny.* From: Shannon Brownlee, Gareth C. Cook, and Viva Hardigg, "Tinkering With Destiny,'' Copyright, August 22, 1994, US News & World Report.

Aldous Huxley, *Brave New World.* EXCERPT AS SUBMITTED from BRAVE NEW WORLD by ALDOUS HUXLEY. Copyright © 1932, 1960 by Aldous Huxley. Reprinted by permission of HarperCollins Publishers, Inc., and Random House UK Limited.

Dorothy Nelkin, *The Grandiose Claims of Geneticists.* From: Dorothy Nelkin, "The Grandiose Claims of Geneticists," CHRONICLE OF HIGHER EDUCATION, March 3, 1993: B3–4. Copyright © 1993 by Dorothy Nelkin. Reprinted by permission of Dorothy Nelkin. This material is developed more fully in Dorothy Nelkin and M. Susan Lindee, THE DNA MYSTIQUE: THE GENE AS A CULTURAL ICON, New York: W.H. Freeman, 1995.

James D. Watson, *The Human Genome Project: A Personal View.* Reprinted by permission of the publisher from THE CODE OF CODES: SCIENTIFIC AND SOCIAL ISSUES IN THE HUMAN GENOME PROJECT by Daniel J. Kevles and Leroy Hood, Cambridge, Mass.: Harvard University Press, Copyright © 1992 by Daniel J. Kevles and Leroy Hood.

Anne Fausto-Sterling, Diane Paul, and Marsha Saxton, *The Politics of Genetics.* From: Anne Fausto-Sterling, Diane Paul, and Marsha Saxton, "The Politics of Genetics," THE WOMEN's

REVIEW OF BOOKS, July 1994: 17ff. Copyright © 1994 The Women's Review of Books.

Luigi L. Cavalli-Sforza, et. al., *Call for a Worldwide Survey of Human Genetic Diversity.* From: Cavalli-Sforza, et. al., "Call for a Worldwide Survey of Human Diversity," GENOMICS, November 1991: 490–491. Reprinted by permission of Academic Press.

Jo Ann C. Gutin, *End of the Rainbow.* From: Jo Ann C. Gutin, "End of the Rainbow," DISCOVER, November 1994: 71–75. Jo Ann C. Gutin/© 1994 The Walt Disney Co. Reprinted with permission of Discover Magazine.

Peter J. Neufeld and Neville Colman, *When Science Takes the Witness Stand.* "Illustrations from: "When Science Takes the Witness Stand," by Peter Neufeld and Neville Colman, SCIENTIFIC AMERICAN, May 1990. Reprinted with permission. Copyright © 1990 by Scientific American, Inc. All rights reserved. Article reprinted by permission of the authors.

William Tucker, *DNA in Court.* From: William Tucker, "OJ's DNA in Court," THE AMERICAN SPECTATOR, November 1994: 24–29. Copyright THE AMERICAN SPECTATOR. Reprinted by permission.

From: Fred H. Marcus, SHORT STORY/SHORT FILM. Reprinted by permission.

From: Fred H. Marcus, SHORT STORY/SHORT FILM. Reprinted by permission.

From: HOWARD HAWKS, STORYTELLER by Gerald Mast. Copyright © 1982 by Gerald Mast. Reprinted by permission of Oxford University Press, Inc.

From: Fred H. Marcus, SHORT STORY/SHORT FILM. Reprinted by permission.

Joseph Boggs, *The Problems of Adaptation.* From: Joseph Boggs, "The Problems of Adaptation," excerpted from THE ART OF WATCHING FILMS, 3/E. Copyright © 1991. Reprinted by permission of Mayfield Publishing Company. Excerpts from ALL THE KING's MEN, copyright 1946 and renewed 1974 by Robert Penn Warren, reprinted by permission of Harcourt Brace & Company.

Dauphne du Maurier, *"The Birds."* Reproduced with permission of Curtis Brown, Ltd., London on behalf of The Chichester Partnership. Copyright Daphne du Maurier 1952.

From: Agatha Christie, WITNESS FOR THE PROSECUTION. Reprinted by permission.

From: Agatha Christie, THE MOUSETRAP AND OTHER PLAYS. Reprinted by permission.

From: Agatha Christie, WITNESS FOR THE PROSECUTION. Screenplay by Billy Wilder and Harry Kurnitz. Reprinted by permission

David Bordwell and Kristin Thompson, *A Glossary of Film Terms.* From: David Bordwell and Kristin Thompson, FILM ART: AN INTRODUCTION 4/e. Copyright © 1993 The McGraw-Hill Companies. Reprinted by permission of The McGraw-Hill Companies.

From THE REEL LIST by Lynne Arany, Tom Dyja, and Gary Goldsmith. Copyright © 1995 by Lynne Arany, Tom Dyja, and Gary Goldsmith. Used by permission of Dell Books, a division of Bantam Doubleday Dell Publishing Group, Inc.

Richard T. De George, *The Case of the Collapsed Mine.* Reprinted with permission of Macmillan Publishing Company from BUSINESS ETHICS by Richard De George. Copyright © 1989 by Macmillan Publishing Co.

Phillip V. Lewis and Henry E. Speck III, *The Study of Ethics: An Orientation.* From: Phillip V. Lewis and Henry E. Speck III, "Ethical Orientations for Understanding Business Ethics," JOUR-

NAL OF BUSINESS COMMUNICATION, Summer 1990, Vol. 27, No. 3. Reprinted by permission.

Milton Friedman, *The Social Responsibility of Business Is to Increase Its Profits.* From: "The Social Responsibility of Business Is to Increase Its Profits," by Milton Friedman. THE NEW YORK TIMES Magazine September 13, 1970. Copyright © 1970 by The New York Times Company. Reprinted by permission.

Peter Carlin, *Pure Profit.* "Pure Profit," by Peter Carlin. Originally published in the Los Angeles Times Magazine, copyright 1995 by Peter Carlin.

Gerald F. Cavanagh, *Ethics in Business.* From: Gerald F. Cavanagh, AMERICAN BUSINESS VALUES, second edition. © 1984, pp 126–150. Reprinted by permission of Prentice-Hall, Inc., Upper Saddle River, New Jersey. The material in this chapter owes much to several years of work with Manuel Velasquez, S.J., and Dennis Moberg of the University of Santa Clara, Santa Clara, California.

Reprinted by permission of the publisher, from ORGANIZATIONAL DYNAMICS Autumn/1983. Copyright © 1983. American Management Association, New York. All rights reserved.

From: Denis Collins and Laura V. Page, "Teaching Business Ethics: A Practical Guide and Case Studies," SMALL BUSINESS FORUM, Vol. 10, No. 1, 63–80. Spring, 1992. Reprinted by permission from SMALL BUSINESS FORUM, 432 N. Lake Street, Madison, WI 53706–1498. Copyright 1992 by Board of Regents, University of Wisconsin System.

Laura L. Nash, *Peter Green's First Day.* Copyright © 1980 by the President and Fellows of Harvard College. Harvard Business School case #380–186. This case was prepared by Laura Nash under the direction of John B. Matthews as the basis for class discussion, rather than to illustrate either effective of ineffective handling of an administrative situation. Reprinted by permission of the Harvard Business School.

Jay A. Halfond, *Matt Goldspan's Trilogy.* "Matt Goldspan's Trilogy" by Jay A. Halfond from JOURNAL OF BUSINESS ETHICS. 10 (1991), pp. 317–321. Reprinted by permission of Kluwer Academic Publishers.

Kermit Vandivier, *Why Should My Conscience Bother Me?* "Why Should My Conscience Bother Me?" by Kermit Vandivier, from IN THE NAME OF PROFIT by Robert Heilbroner. Copyright © 1972 by Doubleday, a division of Bantam Doubleday Dell Publishing Group, Inc. Used by permission of Bantam Doubleday Dell Publishing Group, Inc.

From: Grant Collin, "Friedman Fallacies," JOURNAL OF BUSINESS ETHICS, Vol. 10:907–914, 1991. Reprinted by permission of Kluwer Academic Publishers.

From: Barbara A. Spencer and Carol M. Lehrian, "Analyzing Ethical Issues: Essential Ingredients in the Business Communication Course of the 1990's" BULLETIN OF THE ASSOCIATION FOR BUSINESS COMMUNICATION, Vol. 53, No. 3, September 1990. Reprinted by permission.